FUNDAMENTALS OF TRANSNATIONAL LITIGATION:
THE UNITED STATES, CANADA, JAPAN, AND THE EUROPEAN UNION
Second Edition

LexisNexis Law School Publishing Advisory Board

Paul Caron
Professor of Law
Pepperdine University School of Law
Herzog Summer Visiting Professor in Taxation
University of San Diego School of Law

Bridgette Carr
Clinical Professor of Law
University of Michigan Law School

Olympia Duhart
Professor of Law and Director of Lawyering Skills & Values Program
Nova Southeastern University, Shepard Broad Law School

Samuel Estreicher
Dwight D. Opperman Professor of Law
Director, Center for Labor and Employment Law
NYU School of Law

Steven I. Friedland
Professor of Law and Senior Scholar
Elon University School of Law

Carole Goldberg
Jonathan D. Varat Distinguished Professor of Law
UCLA School of Law

Oliver Goodenough
Professor of Law
Vermont Law School

Paul Marcus
Haynes Professor of Law
William and Mary Law School

John Sprankling
Distinguished Professor of Law
McGeorge School of Law

FUNDAMENTALS OF TRANSNATIONAL LITIGATION:
THE UNITED STATES, CANADA, JAPAN, AND THE EUROPEAN UNION

Second Edition

John O. Haley
William R. Orthwein Distinguished Professor of Law Emeritus
Washington University in St. Louis
Professor of Law
Vanderbilt University
Affiliate Professor of Law
University of Washington (Seattle)

Casebook ISBN: 978-1-6328-0237-8
Looseleaf ISBN: 978-1-6328-0236-1
eBook ISBN: 978-1-6328-0235-4

Library of Congress Cataloging-in-Publication Data

Haley, John Owen

Fundamentals of transnational litigation : the United States, Canada, Japan, and the European Union / John O. Haley, William R. Orthwein Professor of Law Emeritus, School of Law, Washington University in St. Louis; Professor of Law, School of Law, Vanderbilt University; Affiliate Professor of Law, School of Law, University of Washington. — Second Edition.

pages cm

Includes index.

ISBN 978-1-63280-237-8 (hardbound)

1. Conflict of laws--Civil procedure. 2. Civil procedure--United States . 3. Civil procedure--Canada. 4. Civil procedure--Japan. 5. Civil procedure--European Union countries. I. Title.

K7615.H35 2014

340.9--dc23

2014037486

This publication is designed to provide authoritative information in regard to the subject matter covered. It is sold with the understanding that the publisher is not engaged in rendering legal, accounting, or other professional services. If legal advice or other expert assistance is required, the services of a competent professional should be sought.

LexisNexis and the Knowledge Burst logo are registered trademarks of Reed Elsevier Properties Inc., used under license. Matthew Bender and the Matthew Bender Flame Design are registered trademarks of Matthew Bender Properties Inc.

Copyright © 2014 Matthew Bender & Company, Inc., a member of LexisNexis. All Rights Reserved.

No copyright is claimed by LexisNexis or Matthew Bender & Company, Inc., in the text of statutes, regulations, and excerpts from court opinions quoted within this work. Permission to copy material may be licensed for a fee from the Copyright Clearance Center, 222 Rosewood Drive, Danvers, Mass. 01923, telephone (978) 750-8400.

NOTE TO USERS

To ensure that you are using the latest materials available in this area, please be sure to periodically check the LexisNexis Law School web site for downloadable updates and supplements at www.lexisnexis.com/lawschool.

Editorial Offices
630 Central Ave., New Providence, NJ 07974 (908) 464-6800
201 Mission St., San Francisco, CA 94105-1831 (415) 908-3200
www.lexisnexis.com

MATTHEW◆BENDER

Dedication

Dedicated
to
Dan Fenno Henderson
(1921–2001)
&
Yasuhiro Fujita
(1935–2012)

Preface to Second Edition

Lawyers involved in litigation involving parties from two or more countries cannot be concerned solely with the relevant rules and standards that apply in only a single country. Parochial approaches do not suffice. By definition cross-border litigation requires lawyers to be cognizant of at least the basic differences in issues and approaches in other counties and legal systems. For lawyers involved — or may become involved — in such cross-border lawsuits in U.S. courts an awareness of the basic contrasts between U.S. law and the law in the most significant of the U.S. partners in trade — the European Union, Canada, China, Japan, Mexico, and Germany — has become increasingly imperative. These materials are designed first and foremost to meet that need. They thus focus primarily on three of the most significant in terms of volume of our trade partners — Canada, Japan, and the European Union — with references to Chinese, German, and Mexican law added as appropriate throughout.

The emphasis on Canadian law should require little explanation. Canada first provides an especially instructive comparative focus as our largest national trade partner thus potentially the most significant for cross-border civil and commercial litigation. Canadian approaches are also instructive in the contrast of Canada with the United States as a federal common law system. Study of Canadian law enables us to appreciate better the exceptional features of the United States law within the common law world.

The continued inclusion of Japan also remains amply justified. Japan's prominence among the industrial democracies with well-established legal systems remains unequalled as the world's third largest economy and, next to Canada, the United States' leading partner in terms of both trade and investment. These factors help to explain the prevalence of litigation between parties from both countries in both countries. For comparative purposes, Japan is also exemplary. As a unitary civil law system with basically similar if not identical approaches to other civil law jurisdictions for resolving common issues and problems of transnational litigation, Japan provides an ideal national comparative perspective.

Finally, no materials on the fundamental aspects of transnational litigation would be complete without at least a basic introduction to European law under the 1968 Brussels Convention, EU Regulation 44/2001, and, from 2015, Regulation (EU) No. 1215/2012. Those concerned with the harmonization of the rules for the recognition and enforcement of foreign country judgments in addition to the more mundane aspects of transnational litigation and international commercial arbitration must pay heed to developments in EU law.

The materials have a secondary but still equally important aim. As expressed in the Preface to the first edition, the initial, unpublished versions were developed between 1967 and 1971 by Dan Fenno Henderson and Yasuhiro Fujita for an advanced comparative law course in the University of Washington Asian Law Program. The course was designed to introduce law students from both the United States and Japan to fundamental issues that arise in transnational litigation between parties from each country. They were thus originally developed for a course in which students from across the Pacific — increasingly around the globe — would participate and share both their understandings of their own systems as well as their difficulty in comprehending the contrasting concepts

Preface to Second Edition

and underlying — often unstated — assumptions of their fellow students (and instructors) trained in others.

On an equally pedagogical note, the emphasis on judicial decisions and virtual exclusion of secondary sources is purposeful. Also as noted in the initial version, for purposes of case analysis and basic comprehension of potentially applicable legal rules and principles, lawyers today — especially those involved in transnational litigation — must become familiar with a variety of judicial decisions and their often idiosyncratic styles. Moreover, as these materials are intended to demonstrate, the legal rules and principles that apply today have been and will be continuously developed and articulated throughout the world in the context of adjudication and judicial decisions. These materials and the courses for which they have been prepared are premised on the proposition that detailed study of comparative case law has become globally essential to sound legal education.

Let me conclude with a special note of gratitude. The compilation of these materials would not have been possible without assistance of many individuals. Special thanks continue to be owed to Robert Britt and his colleagues at the University of Washington Gallagher Law Library for their on-going assistance. Appreciation must also be extended to Nancy C. Cummings and law librarians Wei Luo and Tove Kloving of the Washington University in St. Louis School of Law as well as Lindsey Ingham and Catherine Deane at the Vanderbilt Law School. Finally, these materials reflect the efforts and influence of literally hundreds of law students from across the United States and around the globe who studied from earlier versions. Needless to say, all of the errors and omission remain mine.

Table of Contents

Chapter 1 ADJUDICATORY JURISDICTION 1

I. INTRODUCTION 1
II. COMMON LAW APPROACHES — THE UNITED STATES 1
   A. Categories and Courts 1
   B. The Tradition 4
        Pennoyer v. Neff 4
        Questions 10
        International Shoe Co. v. State of Washington, Office of Unemployment Compensation and Placement 11
        Questions 15
   C. The Legacy 15
     1. *Quasi in Rem* Jurisdiction 16
        Shaffer v. Heitner 16
        Questions and Problems 24
        Amoco Overseas Oil Co. v. Compagnie Nationale Algerienne de Navigation 27
        Banco Ambrosiano, S.P.A. v. Artoc Bank & Trust Ltd. 30
        Questions 33
     2. *In Rem* Jurisdiction: Marriage as the *Res* 33
        In re the Marriage of Kimura 33
        Questions and Problem 39
     3. *In Personam* Jurisdiction 40
        Burnham v. Superior Court of California, County of Marin 40
        Questions and Problem 45
   D. State Long-Arm Statutes 46
       California Code of Civil Procedure Act, § 410.10 46
        § 410.10 Jurisdiction exercisable 46
        § 410.40 Action arising out of contract providing for application of California law 46
       New York Civil Practice Law and Rules §§ 301, 302 47
        § 301. Jurisdiction over persons, property or status. 47
        § 302. Person jurisdiction by acts of non-domiciliaries 47
       Louisiana Rev. Stat. § 13:3201 48
       Questions 49
       Problem 49
       Question 49
       Restatement (Third) Foreign Relations Law of the United States (1986) 50

Table of Contents

	§ 421. Jurisdiction to Adjudicate	50
	World-Wide Volkswagen Corp. v. Woodson	51
	Questions	58
	Gruca v. Alpha Therapeutic Corporation and the Green Cross Corporation	59
	Questions	67
	Helicopteros Nacionales de Colombia v. Hall	67
	Questions	71
	Asahi Metal Industry Co., Ltd. v. Superior Court of California, Solano County	72
	Questions	80
	Goodyear Dunlop Tires Operations S.A. v. Brown	81
	Questions	86
	J. McIntyre Machinery Ltd. v. Nicastro	87
	Questions	100
	Daimler AG v. Bauman et al.	100
	Questions and Problems	08
III.	COMMON LAW VARIATIONS — CANADA	109
	Morguard Investments Ltd. v. de Savoye	111
	Questions	124
	B.C. Court Jurisdiction and Proceedings Transfer Act	125
	Club Resorts Ltd. v. Van Breda	128
	1991 Civil Code of Quebec	130
	Book X Title Three International Jurisdiction of Quebec Authorities	130
	Chapter I General Provisions	130
	Spar Aerospace Ltd. v. American Mobile Satellite Corp.	131
	Questions and Problem	146
IV.	CIVIL LAW APPROACHES	146
V.	JAPAN	149
A.	General Forum: Domicile	149
	Code of Civil Procedure	149
	Gotō v. Malaysia Airlines	150
	Questions	152
	CGI K.K. v. Advanced Connectek Co., Ltd.	152
	Notes and Questions	154
	Kōno v. Kōno	154
	Questions	156
B.	Special Jurisdiction: Place of Performance	157
	Code of Civil Procedure	157
	Nihon System Wear K.K. v. Kensuke Koo	157

Table of Contents

	Questions and Note	159
	K.K. Bungei Shunjū v. Miyata	160
	Note and Questions	161
C.	Special Jurisdiction: Place of the Tort	161
	Code of Civil Procedure	161
	Ōkuma v. The Boeing Company	162
	Questions	165
	K.K. Bungei Shunjū v. Miyata	165
	Question	166
	K.K. Tsuburaya Productions v. Chaiyo Film Co., Ltd.	166
	Question	168
D.	Special Jurisdiction: Place of Property	168
	Code of Civil Procedure	168
	Loustalot v. Admiral Sales Co. Ltd.	169
	Note	172
	Yasutomi v. United Netherlands Nav. Co.	173
	Questions	175
	Tsuburaya Productions K.K. v. Chaiyo Film Co., Ltd.	175
	Questions	176
E.	Special Jurisdiction: Joint Defendants	176
	Code of Civil Procedure	176
	Inoue v. Aviaco Airlines	177
	Questions	180
VI.	EUROPEAN UNION	180
A.	Regulation (EU) No. 1215/2102 of the European Parliament and of the Council	180
	Group Josi Reinsurance Company SA v. Universal General Insurance Company (UGIC)	182
	Questions	185
B.	Joint Defendants	186
	Athanasios Kalfelis v. Bankhaus Schröder, Münchmeyer, Hengst and Co. and Others	187
	Questions	190
	Roche Nederland BV and Others v. Frederick Primus, Milton Goldenberg	190
C.	Excessive Jurisdiction	197
	Thinet International S.A. v. Saudi Basic Industries Corporation	198
	Review Problem	199

Table of Contents

Chapter 2		**FOREIGN SOVEREIGN IMMUNITY AND RELATED ABSTENTION DOCTRINES**	201

I.		COMMON LAW APPROACHES — UNITED STATES	201
	A.	Foreign Sovereign Immunity	201
		The Schooner Exchange v. McFaddon	201
		Questions	204
		The 1952 Tate Letter	204
		Question	207
		Foreign Sovereign Immunities Act of 1976	208
		Republic of Argentina and Banco Central de la Republica Argentina v. Weltover, Inc.	208
		Republic of Argentina, Petitioner v. NML Capital, Ltd.	213
		Problems and Notes	215
	B.	Act of State	217
		Banco Nacional de Cuba v. Sabbatino	217
		Alfred Dunhill of London, Inc. v. Republic of Cuba	235
		Problem and Questions	250
		International Association of Machinists and Aerospace Workers (IAM) v. The Organization of the Petroleum Exporting Countries (OPEC)	251
		Questions	258
		Questions and Problem	259
	C.	Foreign Sovereign Compulsion	260
		Interamerican Refining Corp. v. Texaco Maracaibo, Inc.	260
		Problems and Questions	267
II.		FOREIGN SOVEREIGN IMMUNITY IN CANADA	268
		Gouvernement de la République Démocratique du Congo v. Venne ..	268
		Questions and Note	277
III.		FOREIGN SOVEREIGN IMMUNITY IN JAPAN	278
		Tokyo Sanyō Bōeki K.K., et al. v. The Islamic Republic of Pakistan	278
		Note	280
IV.		DOMESTIC STATE LIABILITY IN EAST ASIA AND THE EUROPEAN UNION	281
		Nippon Hodo Company, Ltd. v. United States	281
		Extended Note	286
V.		EUROPEAN UNION	292
		Francovich and Bonifaci v. Italy	292
		Köbler v. Austria	299
		Questions and Review Problems	312

Table of Contents

Chapter 3	**PARALLEL LITIGATION**	**317**
I.	THE PROBLEM	317
	Marubeni America Co. v. Kansai Iron Works Ltd.	318
	Tōhō K.K. v. Hachitsuka	321
	Questions	323
	Dan F. Henderson, *Introduction — U.S. Japanese Trade: Its Scope and Legal Framework*	324
II.	COMMON LAW APPROACHES — UNITED STATES	326
A.	Forum Non Conveniens	326
	Piper Aircraft Company v. Reyno	326
	Questions	333
	Sinochem International Co. Ltd. v. Malaysia International Shipping Corp.	333
	Questions	338
	Nai-Chao v. The Boeing Company	338
	Questions	350
	Myers v. The Boeing Company	350
	Questions	359
	U.S.O. Corporation v. Mizuho Holding Company	360
	Questions	364
B.	The Role of Experts	365
	In re Union Carbide Corporation Gas Plant Disaster at Bhopal, India in December, 1984	365
	Bodum USA, Inc. v. La Cafetiere, Inc.	373
	Questions	383
C.	Stays and Anti-Suit Injunctions	384
	Turner Entertainment Co. v. Degeto Film GmbH	384
	Questions	395
	Seattle Totems Hockey Club, Inc. v. National Hockey League ...	395
	Questions	398
	Kaepa, Inc. v. Achilles Corporation	398
	Problem and Questions	405
III.	COMMON LAW APPROACHES — CANADA	406
A.	Forum Non Conveniens	406
	Amchem Products Inc. v. British Columbia (Workers' Compensation Board)	406
	Spar Aerospace Ltd. v. American Mobile Satellite Corp.	411
	Club Resorts Ltd. v. Van Breda	416
	Questions	419
B.	Anti-Suit Injunctions	420
	Amchem Products Inc. v. British Columbia (Workers'	

Table of Contents

	Compensation Board)	420
	Questions	425
IV.	CIVIL LAW APPROACHES	425
A.	Japan	426
	Mukoda v. The Boeing Co.	426
	Note and Questions	429
	Masaki Bussan K.K. v. Nanka Seimen Company	430
	Questions	433
	K.K. Family v. Miyahara	434
	Questions	435
	Note and Question	436
	K.K. Mizuho Bank v. U.S.O. Corporation and Matsuda	436
	Problem and Questions	440
B.	European Union	441
	Gubisch Maschinenfabrik KG v. Giulio Palumbo	441
	Question	444
	Mærsk Olie & Gas A/S v. Firma M. de Haan en W. de Boer	445
	Questions	452
	Owusu v. Jackson	452
	Questions and Note	460
	Review Questions and Problems	460

Chapter 4	**SERVICE OF PROCESS ABROAD**	**463**
I.	INTRODUCTION	463
	Convention on the Service Abroad of Judicial and Extrajudicial Documents in Civil or Commercial Matters	464
II.	UNITED STATES	466
A.	General	466
	Volkswagenwerk Aktiengesellschaft v. Schlunk	466
	Questions	472
B.	German Service in the United States Under the Service Convention	474
	Ackermann v. Levine	474
	Questions	480
C.	Service by Mail to Japanese Defendants	481
	Shoei Kako Co., Ltd. v. Superior Court of the State of California for the City and County of San Francisco	481
	Questions	489
	Suzuki Motor Co., Ltd. v. The Superior Court of San Bernardino County	489
	Questions	495
	Bankston v. Toyota Motor Corporation	495

Table of Contents

		Questions	497
		Nuovo Pignone, SpA v. Storman Asia M/V	500
		Brockmeyer v. May	503
		Question	509
III.		JAPAN	509
	A.	General	509
		Ueno v. Zavicha Blagojevic	509
		Hiroko Saeki Inc. v. Ozaki	511
		Questions	512
	B.	United States Consular Practice	512
		Consular Convention Between Japan and the United States of America	512
		Questions	514
		Review Problem	514

Chapter 5		**TAKING OF EVIDENCE ABROAD**	**517**
I.		INTRODUCTION	517
		Convention on the Taking of Evidence Abroad in Civil or Commercial Matters	518
		Note	520
II.		DISCOVERY ABROAD IN AID OF LITIGATION IN THE UNITED STATES	520
		Société Nationale Industrielle Aerospatiale v. U.S. Dist. Ct. for the Southern District of Iowa	520
		Questions	529
		In re Westinghouse Electric Corporation Uranium Contracts Litigation	530
		Questions and Note	537
		Insurance Corp. of Ireland, Ltd. v. Compagnie des Bauxites de Guinee	538
		Questions	546
		Tiffany v. Forbse	547
		Republic of Argentina, Petitioner v. NML Capital, Ltd.	559
		Questions	563
		Questions	564
		United States Department of State, Japan Judicial Assistance	566
		Questions	568
		In the Circuit Court of the Third Circuit State of Hawaii	569
III.		DISCOVERY IN THE UNITED STATES IN AID OF LITIGATION ABROAD	574
		28 U.S.C. § 1782	574
		Questions	575

Table of Contents

	Intel Corporation v. Advanced Micro Devices, Inc.	575
	Questions	585
	Restatement (Third) of Foreign Relations Law § 442	586
	Review Problem	587

Chapter 6   **RECOGNITION AND ENFORCEMENT OF FOREIGN-COUNTRY JUDGMENTS AND ARBITRAL AWARDS** **589**

I.		RECOGNITION AND ENFORCEMENT OF FOREIGN-COUNTRY JUDGMENTS	590
	A.	United States	590
		Hilton v. Guyot	590
		Questions	600
		Ackermann v. Levine	601
		Questions	605
		Uniform Foreign-Country Judgments Recognition Act (2005)	605
		Section 4. Standards for Recognition of Foreign-Country Judgment	607
		Section 5. Personal Jurisdiction	613
		American Law Institute (ALI), Proposed Federal Foreign Judgments Recognition and Enforcement Act	614
		§ 5 Nonrecognition of a Foreign Judgment	615
		§ 6 Recognition and Enforcement of Foreign Judgments	616
		§ 7 Reciprocal Recognition and Enforcement of Foreign Judgments	617
		Questions	617
		Somportex Limited v. Philadelphia Chewing Gum Corporation	618
		Questions	622
		Koster v. Automark Industries, Incorporated	623
		Questions	626
		The Royal Bank of Canada v. Trentham Corporation	626
		The Royal Bank of Canada v. Trentham Corporation	636
		Questions	639
		Southwest Livestock and Trucking Company, Inc. v. Ramon	640
		Questions	645
	B.	Canada	645
		Beals v. Saldanha	650
		Questions	674
	C.	Japan	675
		Sadhwani v. Sadhwani	675
		Questions and Note	681
		Northcon I v. Mansei Kōgyō K. K.	682

Table of Contents

		Note and Question	684
D.		European Union	685
		Section 328 Recognition of foreign judgments	686
		Questions and Note	687
II.		RECOGNITION AND ENFORCEMENT OF ARBITRAL AWARDS	687
		1958 Convention on the Recognition and Enforcement of Foreign Arbitral Awards	687
A.		United States	688
		Frontera Resources Azerbaijan Corporation v. State Oil Company of the Azerbaijan Republic	689
		Questions	696
		Diapulse Corporation of America v. Carba, Ltd.	697
		Questions	700
		Landegger v. Bayerische Hypotheken und Wechsel Bank	700
		Questions	704
		Ahmed Alghanim & Sons, W.L.L. v. Toys "R" Us, Inc.	704
		Questions	712
B.		Canada	712
		Yugraneft Corp. v. Rexx Management Corp.	712
		Questions	726
C.		Japan	727
		American President Lines, Ltd. v. Subra Kabushiki Kaisha	727
		Question	731
		Texaco Overseas Tankship Ltd. v. Okada Shipping Co., Ltd.	731
		Questions	735
D.		European Union	735
		Review Problems	736

Chapter 7		**CHOICE OF FORUM**	**737**
I.		CHOICE OF COURT (PROROGATION) AGREEMENTS	737
		Council Decision 2009/397/EC of 26 February 2009 on the Signing on Behalf of the European Community of the Convention on Choice of Court Agreements	738
A.		United States	740
		M/S Bremen and Unterweser Reederei, GmbH v. Zapata Off-Shore Company	740
		Note	744
		Professional Ins. Corp. v. Sutherland	744
		Questions and Problem	747
B.		Canada	749

Table of Contents

		Grecon Dimter Inc. v. J.R. Normand Inc.	749
		Questions and Note	756
	C.	Japan	757
		Tokyo Marine and Fire Insurance Company v. Royal Interocean Lines	757
		Questions	761
	D.	European Union	761
		EC Council Regulation No. 44/2001 — Jurisdiction and Enforcement of Judgments	761
		Note and Question	762
		Erich Gasser GmbH v. MISAT Srl	762
		Regulation (EU) No 1215/2012 of the European Parliament and of the Council	769
		Questions	772
II.		ARBITRATION AGREEMENTS	773
	A.	United States	774
		Scherk v. Alberto-Culver Co.	774
		Questions	783
		Mitsubishi Motors Corporation v. Soler Chrysler-Plymouth, Inc.	783
		Questions	794
		U.S. Titan, Inc. v. Guangzhou Zhen Hua Shipping Co., Ltd.	794
		Questions	804
	B.	Canada	804
		Dell Computer Corp. v. Union des Consommateurs	804
		Questions	837
		Rogers Wireless Inc. v. Muroff	837
		Questions	841
	C.	Japan	842
		Compania de Transportes der me Sociodato Anomia v. Mataichi K.K.	842
		Questions	843
		K.K. Amerido Nihon v. Drew Chemical Corp.	844
		Questions	848
	D.	European Union	848
		Allianz SpA Formerly Riunione Adriatica di Sicurtà SpA, Generali Assicurazioni Generali SpA v. West Tankers Inc.	848
		Question	854
		Review Problem	854

Table of Contents

Appendix A	CODE OF CIVIL PROCEDURE OF JAPAN	857
Appendix B	REGULATION (EU) No 1215/2012 OF THE EUROPEAN PARLIAMENT AND OF THE COUNCIL	869

Table of Cases TC-1

Index I-1

Chapter 1

ADJUDICATORY JURISDICTION

I. INTRODUCTION

Our exploration of fundamental aspects of transnational litigation begins with comparative perspectives on judicial jurisdiction. Indicative of the complexity of the problems in this area is the lack of a shared understanding of what is meant by the term "jurisdiction." Not only do the basic conceptions of jurisdiction differ in common and civil law systems but countries within each tradition also favor strikingly contrasting approaches. A common definition or approach may never be reached. To understand and, as lawyers, to deal effectively with these differences and contrasts is a primary aim of this chapter.

II. COMMON LAW APPROACHES — THE UNITED STATES

A. Categories and Courts

The notion of adjudicatory jurisdiction in legal systems influenced by the English Common Law Tradition comprises two separate categories — jurisdiction with respect to the subject matter of the case and jurisdiction either over the parties (i.e., *in personam* actions) or the "thing" (*res*) that is the object of the case (i.e., *in rem* actions). The authority of the court over the parties or the *res* in the latter two instances is understood to encompass the authority to issue enforceable orders directed to either. These conceptions have developed, it should be noted, in the context of the particular U.S. constitutional framework in which the rules and standards related to adjudicatory jurisdiction have evolved. The "constitutionalization" of the standards for jurisdiction is an exceptional feature of U.S. law, although, as we will examine below, Canada has recently adopted a somewhat analogous approach.

Subject-Matter Jurisdiction — General versus Limited: Whether a court has competence to adjudicate the petitioner's claim first raises a question of subject-matter jurisdiction. To the extent that the court has "general" jurisdiction, it is competent to adjudicate any legally cognizable claim. If, on the other hand, the court as established by law has jurisdiction to adjudicate only statutorily (or constitutionally) enumerated claims, it is a court of limited subject-matter jurisdiction. In the United States, state courts are ordinarily courts of "general" subject-matter jurisdiction. Thus, as explained below, to the extent that a state court has personal jurisdiction over the parties based on service of process within the state, it has authority or "competence" to adjudicate any legal claim arising between them. In some instances, however, the subject-matter jurisdiction of a state court may be restricted, as noted below, for example, in cases reserved by the U.S. Constitution and federal statute to the exclusive jurisdiction of the federal courts.

Personal Jurisdiction — General or Specific: In cases where the courts have general subject matter jurisdiction and general jurisdiction over the parties, they have the competence to adjudicate any legally cognizable claim with respect to the parties. However, in certain cases, the courts may have competence to exercise *in personam* jurisdiction over a party only in a restricted set of cases as determined by statute or case law. Typical examples of such "specific" jurisdiction are cases arising under state-long-arm statutes that allow extraterritorial service for certain categories of claims or actions.

Under article III of the U.S. Constitution, all federal courts in contrast have limited jurisdiction to adjudicate only—

> Cases, in Law and Equity, arising under this Constitution, the Laws of the United States, and Treaties made, or which shall be made, under their Authority; to all Cases affecting Ambassadors, other public Ministers and Consuls; to all Cases of admiralty and maritime Jurisdiction; to Controversies to which the United States shall be a Party; to Controversies between two or more States; between a State and Citizens of another State; between Citizens of different States; between Citizens of the same State claiming Lands under Grants of different States, and between a State, or the Citizens thereof, and foreign States, Citizens or Subjects.

The Eleventh Amendment further restricts the jurisdiction of federal courts to exclude "any suit in law or equity, commenced or prosecuted against one of the United States by Citizens of another State, or by Citizens or Subjects of any Foreign State." By statute in civil cases, the adjudicatory jurisdiction of federal courts extends in general to cases in which the United States government is a party or that arise under the United States Constitution or a federal law, or controversies between states or between the United States and foreign governments.

Concurrent State Court Jurisdiction: Since the first Judiciary Act of 1789, the concurrent jurisdiction of state courts has been recognized for all cases except those reserved by the Constitution or statute to the "exclusive jurisdiction" of federal courts. State courts, as noted, are generally courts of "general jurisdiction" and as such are competent otherwise to adjudicate all legally cognizable claims under federal as well as state law, including federal constitutional issues. The U.S federal system provides another example of U.S. exceptionalism, albeit not uniqueness, as noted below with respect to Mexico.

Diversity of Citizenship: A case also may be filed in federal court based on the "diversity of citizenship" of the litigants, such as between citizens of different states, or between United States citizens and those of another country, but such cases must involve an amount "in controversy" of currently more than $75,000. Needless to say, cases based on the "diversity jurisdiction" of federal courts may be brought in an appropriate state court irrespective of the amount of money involved. In such "diversity" actions, under the 1938 U.S. Supreme Court decision in *Erie Railroad*

Co. v. Tompkins, 304 U.S. 64 (1938), the federal courts are to apply state law for lack of a "federal general common law."

Removal: Under Section 1441 of Title 28 of the United States Code, actions brought in a state court over which federal adjudicatory jurisdiction also exists may be "removed" by defendants to an appropriate federal court. However, if diversity of citizenship or alienage is the basis for federal jurisdiction, such removal is not permitted if any defendant in the state action is a citizen of such state. Transfer of venue from a federal court in one state to another with jurisdiction over the parties is also possible. *See* 28 U.S.C. § 1404.

Jurisdiction Over the Parties or Object of the Suit: The second category of adjudicatory jurisdiction in the United States has, as described above, traditionally been further divided into two basic forms: jurisdiction based on the court's control over a defendant's person (*in personam* or personal jurisdiction) and jurisdiction based on the court's control of the *res* or "thing," usually but not necessarily some form of attachable, tangible property (*in rem* jurisdiction). Both involve the authority of a court to adjudicate a claim understood traditionally as a notional exercise of its "power" based on the court's conceptual "seizure" either of the person through service of process or of the object of the suit by attachment or similar procedure (e.g., garnishment, sequestration, libel). In that service, attachment, or their equivalent are required for the courts to establish jurisdiction over defendants, as either persons or "things," traditional conceptions have continued validity in both the language and practice of adjudicatory jurisdiction in most common law jurisdictions. In this sense, at least vestiges of the "power" theory of jurisdiction thus remain. Hence "service" (or attachment) in U.S. law has two quite separate functions. It is the means by which jurisdiction over a party (or the *res*) is perfected and also the requisite method for providing notice.

In *in personam* actions based on service within the territory of the state, as mentioned above, state courts ordinarily have "general" jurisdiction with respect to the parties. However, service by mail or other means outside of the state may be provided by statute for "specific" categories of claims, such as cases arising out of contract or torts committed within the state. Ordinarily, as described below, service within the state should be possible in virtually all cases in which the courts would have "general jurisdiction" under current constitutional standards.

In rem jurisdiction, as mentioned, refers to the authority of a court to adjudicate a claim based, again notionally, on its power over a conceptual "thing" or *res* by means of seizure effected by attachment, garnishment, libel (admiralty), and the like. The common examples of *in rem* actions are suits to resolve disputed — actual or potential — claims of rights or interests involving both real and personal property as in the case of an action to quiet title to land or pursuant to an admiralty action based on the "libel" of a vessel. However, as in the case of civil actions related to marital status, a decedent's estate or a trust, the *res* may be purely conceptual. It need not be a corporeal thing at all.

Although the claim being adjudicated in an *in rem* action would ordinarily concern rights in the *res*, the issues may relate a quite separate matter. In cases where attachment of property is used to support judicial jurisdiction for the adjudication of such unrelated claims, a third category, *quasi in rem* jurisdiction, is sometimes used. Because the court's authority extends solely to the property subject to its control, however, the extent to which the court can order payment of the claim in *quasi in rem* actions is limited by its value. Conceptually the court order is directed to the *res* rather than the person of the defendant. For purposes of jurisdiction, however, due process requirements for connection to the state in question of the claim or the adverse party.

Constitutional Dimensions: Within the American federal system, all state court judgments are constitutionally required to be given "full faith and credit" by all other states.[1] Very early in the legal life of the republic, however, lack of jurisdiction was recognized as a defect that justified refusal by the courts of one state to give "full faith and credit" to the judgment of another.[2] The result was the so-called constitutionalization of judicial jurisdiction in American law. The adoption of the Fourteenth Amendment Due Process Clause provided an even more comprehensive basis for constitutional limitations on state assertion of judicial jurisdiction independent of the issue of interstate recognition.

B. The Tradition

PENNOYER v. NEFF
95 U.S. 714 (1878)

Mr. Justice Field delivered the opinion of the court.

This is an action to recover the possession of a tract of land, of the alleged value of $15,000, situated in the State of Oregon. The plaintiff [Neff] asserts title to the premises by a patent of the United States issued to him in 1866, under the act of Congress of Sept. 27, 1850, usually known as the Donation Law of Oregon. The defendant [Pennoyer] claims to have acquired the premises under a sheriff's deed, made upon a sale of the property on execution issued upon a judgment recovered against the plaintiff in one of the circuit courts of the State. The case turns upon the validity of this judgment.

It appears from the record that the judgment was rendered in February, 1866, in favor of J. H. Mitchell, for less than $300, including costs, in an action brought by him upon a demand for services as an attorney; that, at the time the action was commenced and the judgment rendered, the defendant therein, the plaintiff here, was a non-resident of the State that he was not personally served with process, and did not appear therein; and that the judgment was entered upon his default in not answering the complaint, upon a constructive service of summons by publication.

The Code of Oregon provides for such service when an action is brought against a non-resident and absent defendant, who has property within the State. It also provides, where the action is for the recovery of money or damages, for the attachment of the property of the non-resident. And it also declares that no natural person is subject to the jurisdiction of a court of the State, "unless he appear in the

---

[1] U.S. Const. art. IV, § 1.

[2] D'Arcy v. Ketchum, 52 U.S. (11 How.) 165 (1851).

court, or be found within the State, or be a resident thereof, or have property therein; and, in the last case, only to the extent of such property at the time the jurisdiction attached." Construing this latter provision to mean, that, in an action for money or damages where a defendant does not appear in the court, and is not found within the State, and is not a resident thereof, but has property therein, the jurisdiction of the court extends only over such property, the declaration expresses a principle of general, if not universal, law. The authority of every tribunal is necessarily restricted by the territorial limits of the State in which it is established. Any attempt to exercise authority beyond those limits would be deemed in every other forum, as has been said by this court, in illegitimate assumption of power, and be resisted as mere abuse. *In the case against the plaintiff, the property here in controversy sold under the judgment rendered was not attached, nor in any way brought under the jurisdiction of the court. Its first connection with the case was caused by a levy of the execution. It was not, therefore, disposed of pursuant to any adjudication, but only in enforcement of a personal judgment, having no relation to the property, rendered against a non-resident without service of process upon him in the action, or his appearance therein.* [Emphasis added.] The court below did not consider that an attachment of the property was essential to its jurisdiction or to the validity of the sale, but held that the judgment was invalid from defects in the affidavit upon which the order of publication was obtained, and in the affidavit by which the publication was proved.

There is some difference of opinion among the members of this court as to the rulings upon these alleged defects. . . .

If, therefore, we were confined to the rulings of the court below upon the defects in the affidavits mentioned, we should be unable to uphold its decision. But it was also contended in that court, and is insisted upon here, that the judgment in the State court against the plaintiff was void for want of personal service of process on him, or of his appearance in the action in which it was rendered and that the premises in controversy could not be subjected to the payment of the demand of a resident creditor except by a proceeding in rem; that is, by a direct proceeding against the property for that purpose. If these positions are sound, the ruling of the Circuit Court as to the invalidity of that judgment must be sustained, notwithstanding our dissent from the Iberia upon which it was made. And that they are sound would seem to follow from two well-established principles of public law respecting the jurisdiction of an independent State over persons and property. The several States of the Union are not, it is true, in every respect independent, many of the right and powers which originally belonged to them being now vested in the government created by the Constitution. But, except as restrained and limited by that instrument, they possess and exercise the authority of independent States, and the principles of public law to which we have referred are applicable to them. One of these principles is that every State possesses exclusive jurisdiction and sovereignty over persons and property within its territory. As a consequence, every State has the power to determine for itself the civil status and capacities of its inhabitants; to prescribe the subjects upon which they may contract, the forms and solemnities with which their contracts shall be executed, the rights and obligations arising from them, and the mode in which their validity shall be determined and their obligations enforced; and also the regulate the manner and conditions upon which property situated within such territory, both personal and real, may be acquired, enjoyed, and transferred. The other principle of public law referred to follows from the one mentioned; that is, that no State can exercise direct jurisdiction and authority over persons or property without its territory. The several States are of equal dignity and authority, and the independence of one implies the exclusion of power from all others. And so it is laid down by jurists, as an elementary principle, that the laws of one State have no operation outside of its territory, except so far as is allowed by comity; and that no tribunal established by it can extend its process beyond that territory so as to subject either persons or property to its decisions. "Any exertion of authority of this sort beyond this limit," says Story, "is a mere nullity, and incapable of binding such persons or property in any other tribunals." Story, Confl. Laws, sect. 539.

But as contracts made in one State may be enforceable only in another State, and property may be held by non-residents, the exercise of the jurisdiction which every State is admitted to possess over persons and property within its own territory will often affect persons and property without it. To any influence exerted in this way by a State affecting persons resident or property situated elsewhere, no objection can be justly taken; whilst any direct exertion of authority upon them, in an attempt to give ex-territorial operation to its laws, or to enforce an ex-territorial jurisdiction by its tribunals, would be deemed an encroachment upon the independence of the State in which the persons are domiciled or the property is situated, and be resisted as usurpation.

Thus the State, through its tribunals, may compel persons domiciled within its limits to execute, in pursuance of their contracts respecting property elsewhere situated, instruments in such form and with such solemnities as to transfer the title, so far as such formalities can be complied with; and the exercise of this jurisdiction in no manner interferes with the supreme control over the property by the State within which it is situated.

So the State, through its tribunals, may subject property situated within its limits owned by non-residents to the payment of the demand of its own citizens against them; and the exercise of this jurisdiction in no respect infringes upon the sovereignty of the State where the owners are domiciled. Every State owes protection to its own citizens; and, when non-residents deal with them, it is a legitimate and just exercise of authority to hold and appropriate any property owned by such non-residents to satisfy the claims of its citizens. It is in virtue of the State's jurisdiction over the property of the non-resident situated within its limits that its tribunals can inquire into that non-resident's obligations to its own citizens, and the inquiry can then be carried only to the extent necessary to control the disposition of the property. If the non-resident [has] no property in the State, there is nothing upon which the tribunals can adjudicate.

The want of authority of the tribunals of a State to adjudicate upon the obligations of non-residents, where they have no property within its limits, is not denied by the court below: but the position is assumed, that, where they have property within the State, it is immaterial whether the property is in the first instance brought under the control of the court by attachment or some other equivalent act, and afterwards applied by its judgment to the satisfaction of demands against its owner; or such demands be first established in a personal action, and the property of the non-resident be afterwards seized and sold on execution. But the answer to this position has already been given in the statement, that the jurisdiction of the court to inquire into and determine his obligations at all is only incidental to its jurisdiction over the property. Its jurisdiction in that respect cannot be made to depend upon facts to be ascertained after it has tried the cause and rendered the judgment. If the judgment be previously void, it will not become valid by the subsequent discovery of property of the defendant, or by his subsequent acquisition of it. The judgment, if void when rendered, will always remain void: it cannot occupy the doubtful position of being valid if property be found, and void if there be none. [Emphasis added.] . . .

The force and effect of judgments rendered against non-residents without personal service of process upon them, or their voluntary appearance, have been the subject of frequent consideration in the courts of the United States and of the several States, as attempts have been made to enforce such judgments in States other than those in which they were rendered, under the provision of the Constitution requiring that "full faith and credit shall be given in each State to the public acts, records, and judicial proceedings of every other State;" and the act of Congress providing for the mode of authenticating such acts, records, and proceedings, and declaring that, when thus authenticated, "they shall have such faith and credit given to them in every court within the United States as they have by law or usage in the courts of the State from which they are or shall or taken."

. . . .

Since the adoption of the Fourteenth Amendment to the Federal Constitution, the validity of such judgments may be directly questioned, and their enforcement in the State resisted, on the ground that proceedings in a court of justice to determine the personal rights and obligations of parties over whom that court has no jurisdiction do not constitute due process of law. Whatever difficulty may be experienced in giving to those terms a definition which will embrace every permissible exertion of power affecting private rights, and exclude such as is forbidden, there can be no doubt of their meaning when applied to judicial proceedings. They then mean a course of legal proceedings according to those rules and principles which have been established in our systems of jurisprudence for the protection and enforcement of private rights. To give such proceedings any validity, there must be a tribunal competent by its constitution — that is, by the law of its creation — to pass upon the subject-matter of the suit; and, if that involves merely a determination of the personal liability of the defendant, he must be brought within its jurisdiction by service of process within the State, or his voluntary appearance.

Except in cases affecting the personal status of the plaintiff, and cases in which that mode of service may be considered to have been assented to in advance, as hereinafter mentioned, the substituted service of process by publication, allowed by the law of Oregon and by similar laws in other States, where actions are brought against non-residents, is effectual only where, in connection with process against the person for commencing the action, property in the State is brought under the control of the court, and subjected to its disposition by process adapted to that purpose, or where the judgment is sought as a means of reaching such property or affecting some interest therein; in other words, where the action is in the nature of a proceeding in rem. . . .

. . . .

It follows from the views expressed that the personal judgment recovered in the State court of Oregon against the plaintiff herein, then a non-resident of the State, was without any validity, and did not authorize a sale of the property in controversy.

To prevent any misapplication of the views expressed in this opinion, it is proper to observe that we do not mean to assert, by any thing we have said, that a State may not authorize proceedings to determine the status of one of its citizens towards a non-resident, which would be binding within the State, though made without service of process or personal notice to the non-resident. The jurisdiction which every State possesses to determine the civil status and capacities of all its inhabitants involves authority to prescribe the conditions on which proceedings affecting them may be commenced and carried on within its territory.

Neither do we mean to assert that a State may not require a non-resident entering into a partnership or association within its limits, or making contracts enforceable there, to appoint an agent or representative in the State to receive service of process and notice in legal proceedings instituted with respect to such partnership, association, or contracts, or to designate a place where such service may be made and notice given, and provide, upon their failure, to make such appointment or to designate such place that service may be made upon a public officer designated for that purpose, or in some other prescribed way, and that judgments rendered upon such service may not be binding upon the non-residents both within and without the State. . . . Nor do we doubt that a State, on creating corporations or other institutions for pecuniary or charitable purposes, may provide a mode in which their conduct may be investigated, their obligations enforced, or their charters revoked, which shall require other than personal service upon their officers or members. Parties becoming members of such corporations or institutions would hold their interest subject to the conditions prescribed by law.

In the present case, there is no feature of this kind, and, consequently, no consideration of what would be the effect of such legislation in enforcing the contract of a non-resident can arise. The question here respects only the validity of a money judgment rendered in one State, in an action upon a simple contract against the resident of another, without service of process upon him, or his appearance therein.

Judgment affirmed.

Mr. Justice Hunt dissenting.

I am compelled to dissent from the opinion and judgment of the court, and, deeming the question involved to be important, I take leave to record my views upon it.

. . . .

The precise case is this: A statute of Oregon authorizes suits to be commenced by the service of a summons. In the case of a non-resident of the State, it authorizes the service of the summons to be made by publication for not less than six weeks, in a newspaper published in the county where the action is commenced. A copy of the summons must also be sent by mail, directed to the defendant at his place of residence, unless it be shown that the residence is not known and cannot be ascertained. It authorizes a judgment and execution to be obtained in such proceeding. Judgment in a suit commenced by one Mitchell in the Circuit Court of Multnomah County, where the summons was thus served, was obtained against Neff, the present plaintiff; and the land in question, situate in Multnomah County, was bought by the defendant Pennoyer, at a sale upon the judgment in such suit. This court now holds, that, by reason of the absence of a personal service of the summons on the defendant, the Circuit Court of Oregon had no jurisdiction, its judgment could not authorize the sale of land in said county, and, as a necessary result, a purchaser of land under it obtained no title; that, as to the former owner, it is a case of depriving a person of his property without due process of law.

In my opinion, this decision is at variance with the long-established practice under the statutes of the States of this Union, is unsound in principle, and, I fear, may be disastrous in its effects. It tends to produce confusion in titles which have been obtained under similar statutes in existence for nearly a century; it invites litigation and strife, and over throws a well-settled rule of property.

The result of the authorities on the subject, and the sound conclusions to be drawn from the principles which should govern the decision, as I shall endeavor to show, are these:

1. A sovereign State must necessarily have such control over the real and personal property actually being within its limits, as that it may subject the same to the payment of debts justly due to its citizens.

2. This result is not altered by the circumstance that the owner of the property is non-resident, and so absent from the State that legal process cannot be served upon him personally.

3. Personal notice of a proceeding by which title to property is passed is not indispensable; it is competent to the State to authorize substituted service by publication or otherwise, as the commencement of a suit against non-residents, the judgment in which will authorize the sale of property in such State.

4. It belongs to the legislative power of the State to determine what shall be the modes and means proper to be adopted to give notice to an absent defendant of the commencement of a suit; and if they are such as are reasonably likely to communicate to him information of the proceeding against him, and are in good faith designed to give him such information, and an opportunity to defend is provided for him in the event of his appearance in the suit, it is not competent to the judiciary to declare that such proceeding is void as not being by due process of law.

5. Whether the property of such non-resident shall be seized upon attachment as the commencement of a suit which shall be carried into judgment and execution, upon which it shall then be sold, or whether it shall be sold upon an execution and judgment without such preliminary seizure, is a matter not of constitutional power, but of municipal regulation only.

To say that a sovereign State has the power to ordain that the property of non-residents within its territory may be subjected to the payment of debts due to its citizens, if the property is levied upon at the commencement of a suit, but that it has not such power if the property is levied upon at the end of the suit, is a refinement and a depreciation of a great general principle that, in my judgment, cannot be sustained.

A reference to the statutes of the different States, and to the statutes of the United States, and to the decided cases, and a consideration of the principles on which they stand, will more clearly exhibit my view of the question.

The statutes are of two classes: first, those which authorize the commencement of actions by publication, accompanied by an attachment which is levied upon property, more or less, of an absent debtor; second, those giving the like mode of commencing a suit without an attachment.

. . . .

That a State can subject land within its limits belonging to non-resident owners to debts due to its own citizens as it can legislate upon all other local matters; that it can prescribe the mode and process by which it is to be reached, seems to me very plain.

. . . [I]f reasonable notice be given, with an opportunity to defend when appearance is made, the question of power will be fully satisfied.

QUESTIONS

1. The Court distinguishes *in rem* actions from *in personam* actions, indicating that the Oregon courts would have had jurisdiction to adjudicate Mitchell's claim had Oregon's statute provided for prior attachment of Neff's land. What is the difference between the two actions? Would it have made any significant difference to the outcome had Neff defaulted in such an action? Assuming Neff consulted you after receiving notice of such *in rem* action, what would you have advised him to do?

2. Was there any way that Oregon could have achieved the apparent purpose of the statute, creating a basis for an *in personam* action based on the ownership of land rather than the presence of the defendant within the state?

3. Would it have made any difference to the outcome of the case had the land in Oregon had been used extensively over many years by Neff and his family for vacations and he planned to retire there?

The Supreme Court's decision in *Pennoyer v. Neff* enshrined the "power" theory of *in personam* jurisdiction in American law. As a result, the legitimacy of statutory extensions of jurisdiction over non-residents, especially business enterprises incorporated elsewhere but engaged in commercial transactions within the state asserting jurisdiction, remained in question for over a half century.

INTERNATIONAL SHOE CO. v. STATE OF WASHINGTON, OFFICE OF UNEMPLOYMENT COMPENSATION AND PLACEMENT
326 U.S. 310 (1945)

Mr. Chief Justice Stone delivered the opinion of the Court.

The questions for decision are (1) whether, within the limitations of the due process clause of the Fourteenth Amendment, appellant, a Delaware corporation, has by its activities in the State of Washington rendered itself amenable to proceedings in the courts of that state to recover unpaid contributions to the state unemployment compensation fund exacted by state statutes, Washington Unemployment Compensation Act, Washington Revised Statutes, § 9998-103a through § 9998-123a, 1941 Supp., and (2) whether the state can exact those contributions consistently with the due process clause of the Fourteenth Amendment.

. . . .

In this case notice of assessment for the years in question was personally served upon a sales solicitor employed by appellant in the State of Washington, and a copy of the notice was mailed by registered mail to appellant at its address in St. Louis, Missouri. Appellant appeared specially before the office of unemployment and moved to set aside the order and notice of assessment on the ground that the service upon appellant's salesman was not proper service upon appellant; that appellant was not a corporation of the State of Washington and was not doing business within the state; that it had no agent within the state upon whom service could be made; and that appellant is not an employer and does not furnish employment within the meaning of the statute.

. . . .

The facts as found by the appeal tribunal and accepted by the state Superior Court and Supreme Court, are not in dispute. Appellant is a Delaware corporation, having its principal place of business in St. Louis, Missouri, and is engaged in the manufacture and sale of shoes and other footwear. It maintains places of business in several states, other than Washington, at which its manufacturing is carried on and from which its merchandise is distributed interstate through several sales units or branches located outside the State of Washington.

Appellant has no office in Washington and makes no contracts either for sale or purchase of merchandise there. It maintains no stock of merchandise in that state and makes there no deliveries of goods in intrastate commerce. During the years from 1937 to 1940, now in question, appellant employed eleven to thirteen salesmen under direct supervision and control of sales managers located in St. Louis. These salesmen resided in Washington; their principal activities were confined to that state; and they were compensated by commissions based upon the amount of their sales. The commissions for each year totaled more than $31,000. Appellant supplies its salesmen with a line of samples, each consisting of one shoe of a pair, which they display to prospective purchasers. On occasion they rent permanent sample rooms, for exhibiting samples, in business buildings, or rent rooms in hotels or business buildings temporarily for that purpose. The cost of such rentals is reimbursed by appellant.

The authority of the salesmen is limited to exhibiting their samples and soliciting orders from prospective buyers, at prices and on terms fixed by appellant. The salesmen transmit the orders to appellant's office in St. Louis for acceptance or rejection, and when accepted the merchandise for filling the orders is shipped f.o.b. from points outside Washington to the purchasers within the state. All the merchandise shipped into Washington is invoiced at the place of shipment from which collections are made. No salesman has authority to enter into contracts or to make collections.

The Supreme Court of Washington was of opinion that the regular and systematic solicitation of orders in the state by appellant's salesmen, resulting in a continuous flow of appellant's product into the state, was sufficient to constitute doing business in the state so as to make appellant amenable to suit in its courts. But it was also of opinion that there were sufficient additional activities shown to bring the case within the rule frequently stated, that solicitation within a state by the agents of a foreign corporation plus some additional activities there are sufficient to render the corporation amenable to suit brought in the courts of the state to enforce an obligation arising out of its activities there. The court found such additional activities in the salesmen's display of samples sometimes in permanent display rooms, and the salesmen's residence within the state, continued over a period of years, all resulting in a substantial volume of merchandise regularly shipped by appellant to purchasers within the state. The court also held that the statute as applied did not invade the constitutional power of Congress to regulate interstate commerce and did not impose a prohibited burden on such commerce.

Appellant's argument, renewed here, that the statute imposes an unconstitutional burden on interstate commerce need not detain us. For 53 Stat. 1391, 26 U.S.C. § 1606(a), 26 U.S.C.A. Int. Rev. Code, § 1606(a), provides that "No person required under a State law to make payments to an unemployment fund shall be relieved from compliance therewith on the ground that he is engaged in interstate or foreign commerce, or that the State law does not distinguish between employees engaged in interstate or foreign commerce and those engaged in intrastate commerce." It is no longer debatable that Congress, in the exercise of the commerce power, may authorize the states, in specified ways, to regulate interstate commerce or impose burdens upon it.

Appellant also insists that its activities within the state were not sufficient to manifest its "presence" there and that in its absence the state courts were without jurisdiction, that consequently it was a denial of due process for the state to subject appellant to suit. It refers to those cases in which it was said that the mere solicitation of orders for the purchase of goods within a state, to be accepted without the state and filled by shipment of the purchased goods interstate, does not render the corporation seller amenable to suit within the state. And appellant further argues that since it was not present within the state, it is a denial of due process to subject it to taxation or other money exaction. It thus denies the power of the state to lay the tax or to subject appellant to a suit for its collection.

Historically the jurisdiction of courts to render judgment in personam is

II. COMMON LAW APPROACHES — THE UNITED STATES

grounded on their de facto power over the defendant's person. Hence his presence within the territorial jurisdiction of court was prerequisite to its rendition of a judgment personally binding him. Pennoyer v. Neff, 95 U.S. 714, 733. But now that the capias ad respondendum has given way to personal service of summons or other form of notice, due process requires only that in order to subject a defendant to a judgment in personam, if he be not present within the territory of the forum, he have certain minimum contacts with it such that the maintenance of the suit does not offend "traditional notions of fair play and substantial justice."

Since the corporate personality is a fiction, although a fiction intended to be acted upon as though it were a fact, it is clear that unlike an individual its "presence" without, as well as within, the state of its origin can be manifested only by activities carried on in its behalf by those who are authorized to act for it. To say that the corporation is so far "present" there as to satisfy due process requirements, for purposes of taxation or the maintenance of suits against it in the courts of the state, is to beg the question to be decided. For the terms "present" or "presence" are used merely to symbolize those activities of the corporation's agent within the state which courts will deem to be sufficient to satisfy the demands of due process. L. Hand, J., in Hutchinson v. Chase & Gilbert, 2 Cir., 45 F.2d 139, 141. Those demands may be met by such contacts of the corporation with the state of the forum as make it reasonable, in the context of our federal system of government, to require the corporation to defend the particular suit which is brought there. An "estimate of the inconveniences" which would result to the corporation from a trial away from its "home" or principal place of business is relevant in this connection.

"Presence" in the state in this sense has never been doubted when the activities of the corporation there have not only been continuous and systematic, but also give rise to the liabilities sued on, even though no consent to be sued or authorization to an agent to accept service of process has been given. Conversely it has been generally recognized that the casual presence of the corporate agent or even his conduct of single or isolated items of activities in a state in the corporation's behalf are not enough to subject it to suit on causes of action unconnected with the activities there. To require the corporation in such circumstances to defend the suit away from its home or other jurisdiction where it carries on more substantial activities has been thought to lay too great and unreasonable a burden on the corporation to comport with due process.

While it has been held in cases on which appellant relies that continuous activity of some sorts within a state is not enough to support the demand that the corporation be amenable to suits unrelated to that activity, there have been instances in which the continuous corporate operations within a state were thought so substantial and of such a nature as to justify suit against it on causes of action arising from dealings entirely distinct from those activities.

Finally, although the commission of some single or occasional acts of the corporate agent in a state sufficient to impose an obligation or liability on the corporation has not been thought to confer upon the state authority to enforce it, other such acts, because of their nature and quality and the circumstances of their commission, may be deemed sufficient to render the corporation liable to suit. True, some of the decisions holding the corporation amenable to suit have been supported by resort to the legal fiction that it has given its consent to service and suit, consent being implied from its presence in the state through the acts of its authorized agents. But more realistically it may be said that those authorized acts were of such a nature as to justify the fiction. [Emphasis added.]

It is evident that the criteria by which we mark the boundary line between those activities which justify the subjection of a corporation to suit, and those which do not, cannot be simply mechanical or quantitative. The test is not merely, as has sometimes been suggested, whether the activity, which the corporation has seen fit to procure through its agents in another state, is a little more or a little less. Whether due process is satisfied must depend rather upon the quality and nature of the activity in relation to the fair and orderly administration of the laws which it was the purpose of the due process clause to insure. That clause does not contemplate that a state may make binding a judgment in personam against an individual or corporate defendant with which the state has no contacts, ties, or relations.

But to the extent that a corporation exercises the privilege of conducting activities within a state, it enjoys the benefits and protection of the laws of that state. The exercise of that privilege may give rise to obligations; and, so far as those obligations arise out of or are connected with the activities within the state, a procedure which requires the corporation to respond to a suit brought to enforce them can, in most instances, hardly be said to be undue.

Applying these standards, the activities carried on in behalf of appellant in the State of Washington were neither irregular nor casual. They were systematic and continuous throughout the years in question. They resulted in a large volume of interstate business, in the course of which appellant received the benefits and protection of the laws of the state, including the right to resort to the courts for the enforcement of its rights. The obligation which is here sued upon arose out of those very activities. It is evident that these operations establish sufficient contacts or ties with the state of the forum to make it reasonable and just according to our traditional conception of fair play and substantial justice, to permit the state to enforce the obligations which appellant has incurred there. Hence we cannot say that the maintenance of the present suit in the State of Washington involves an unreasonable or undue procedure. [Emphasis added.]

We are likewise unable to conclude that the service of the process within the state upon an agent whose activities establish appellant's "presence" there was not sufficient notice of the suit, or that the suit was so unrelated to those activities as to make the agent an inappropriate vehicle for communicating the notice. It is enough that appellant has established such contacts with the state that the particular form of substituted service adopted there gives reasonable assurance that the notice will be actual. Nor can we say that the mailing of the notice of suit to appellant by registered mail at its home office was not reasonably calculated to apprise appellant of the suit.

Only a word need be said of appellant's liability for the demanded contributions of the state unemployment fund. The Supreme Court of Washington, construing and applying the statute, has held that it imposes a tax on the privilege of employing appellant's salesmen within the state measured by a percentage of the wages, here the commissions payable to the salesmen. This construction we accept for purposes of determining the constitutional validity of the statute. The right to employ labor has been deemed an appropriate subject of taxation in this country and England, both before and since the adoption of the Constitution. And such a tax imposed upon the employer for unemployment benefits is within the constitutional power of the states.

Affirmed.

QUESTIONS

1. Is *International Shoe* an example of "general" or "specific" personal jurisdiction? What did the Court deem to be the constitutional requirements for each?

2. What two functions does the Court consider "service of process" to serve? Do both necessarily have constitutional dimensions?

3. Would the State of Washington been able to subject to a state tax earnings from the sale of shoes in the state by the St. Louis company had the Court in *International Shoe* held that Washington State's attempt to levy a worker's compensation tax directly on International Shoe exceeded the constitutional limits of an extraterritorial extension of state legislative jurisdiction? If so, what were the possible advantages to the State of Washington of the approach used in *International Shoe?*

4. Could the Oregon statute in *Pennoyer v. Neff* have satisfied the *International Shoe* tests? Would an *in rem* action, as suggested by the Court in *Pennoyer*, have done so? Would your answer differ had the land in Oregon had been used extensively over many years by Neff and his family for vacations, and he planned to retire there?

5. Assume (counterfactually) that Louisiana had included in its 1834 Civil Code a provision similar to article 14 of the 1805 French Civil Code allowing suits in French courts by any French national to enforce private law claims against any noncitizen regardless of the lack of presence in France. Would such a suit be constitutionally permitted under *International Shoe?* What if the provision in question was similar to article 68(1) of Quebec's pre-1991 Code of Civil Procedure that provided for personal jurisdiction based on property located within the province?

C. The Legacy

The Supreme Court's decision in *International Shoe* left considerable tensions in its wake. The new due process requirements provided a basis to challenge the traditional approaches set out in *Pennoyer v. Neff.* Left to the Supreme Court to work out in future cases was the relationship between the traditional concern with the power of the courts over property and persons and the emphasis on "minimum contacts" and "our traditional conception of fair play and substantial justice" as applied to cases involving assertions of either *in rem* or *in personam* jurisdiction. The extent to which *International Shoe* overturned or at least altered the constitutional underpinnings of *Pennoyer v. Neff* was unclear. Both decisions dealt with domestic cases. Both involved defendants with U.S. nationality. Their broader application to transnational disputes and foreign defendants awaited future decisions. We will subsequently examine current U.S. approaches in both contexts. Before doing so, we examine *quasi in rem* and *in rem* jurisdiction.

1. *Quasi in Rem* Jurisdiction

SHAFFER v. HEITNER*
433 U.S. 186 (1977)

Mr. Justice Marshall delivered the opinion of the Court.

The controversy in this case concerns the constitutionality of a Delaware statute that allows a court of that State to take jurisdiction of a lawsuit by sequestering any property of the defendant that happens to be located in Delaware. Appellants contend that the sequestration statute as applied in this case violates the Due Process Clause of the Fourteenth Amendment both because it permits the state courts to exercise jurisdiction despite the absence of sufficient contacts among the defendants, the litigation, and the State of Delaware and because it authorizes the deprivation of defendants' property without providing adequate procedural safeguards. We find it necessary to consider only the first of these contentions.

I

Appellee Heitner, a nonresident of Delaware, is the owner of one share of stock in the Greyhound Corp., a business incorporated under the laws of Delaware with its principal place of business in Phoenix, Ariz. On May 22, 1974, he filed a shareholder's derivative suit in the Court of Chancery for New Castle County, Del., in which he named as defendants Greyhound, its wholly owned subsidiary Greyhound Lines, Inc. and 28 present or former officers or directors of one or both of the corporations. In essence, Heitner alleged that the individual defendants had violated their duties to Greyhound by causing it and its subsidiary to engage in actions that resulted in the corporations being held liable for substantial damages in a private antitrust suit and a large fine in a criminal contempt action. The activities which led to these penalties took place in Oregon.

Simultaneously with his complaint, Heitner filed a motion for an order of sequestration of the Delaware property of the individual defendants pursuant to Del. Code Ann., Tit. 10, § 366 (1975). This motion was accompanied by a supporting affidavit of counsel which stated that the individual defendants were nonresidents of Delaware. The affidavit identified the property to be sequestered as "common stock, 3% Second Cumulative Preferenced Stock and stock unit credits of the Defendant Greyhound Corporation, a Delaware corporation, as well as all options and all

---

* Footnotes omitted.

warrants to purchase said stock issued to said individual Defendants and all contractural (sic) obligations, all rights, debts or credits due or accrued to or for the benefit of any of the said Defendants under any type of written agreement, contract or other legal instrument of any kind whatever between any of the individual Defendants and said corporation."

The requested sequestration order was signed the day the motion was filed. Pursuant to that order, the sequestrator "seized" approximately 82,000 shares of Greyhound common stock belonging to 19 of the defendants, and options belonging to another 2 defendants. These seizures were accomplished by placing "stop transfer" orders or their equivalents on the books of the Greyhound Corp. So far as the record shows, none of the certificates representing the seized property was physically present in Delaware. The stock was considered to be in Delaware, and so subject to seizure, by virtue of Del. Code Ann., Tit. 8, § 169 (1975), which makes Delaware the situs of ownership of all stock in Delaware corporations.

All 28 defendants were notified of the initiation of the suit by certified mail directed to their last known addresses and by publication in a New Castle County newspaper. The 21 defendants whose property was seized (hereafter referred to as appellants) responded by entering a special appearance for the purpose of moving to quash service of process and to vacate the sequestration order. They contended that the ex parte sequestration procedure did not accord them due process of law and that the property seized was not capable of attachment in Delaware. In addition, appellants asserted that under the rule of *International Shoe Co. v. Washington*, 326 U.S. 310 (1945), they did not have sufficient contacts with Delaware to sustain the jurisdiction of that State's courts.

The Court of Chancery rejected these arguments in a letter opinion which emphasized the purpose of the Delaware sequestration procedure: "The primary purpose of 'sequestration' as authorized by 10 Del. C. § 366 is not to secure possession of property pending a trial between resident debtors and creditors on the issue of who has the right to retain it. On the contrary, as here employed, 'sequestration' is a process used to compel the personal appearance of a nonresident defendant to answer and defend a suit brought against him in a court of equity. It is accomplished by the appointment of a sequestrator by this Court to seize and hold property of the nonresident located in this State subject to further Court order. If the defendant enters a general appearance, the sequestered property is routinely released, unless the plaintiff makes special application to continue its seizure, in which event the plaintiff has the burden of proof and persuasion." App. 75–76.

. . . .

On appeal, the Delaware Supreme Court affirmed the judgment of the Court of Chancery. *Greyhound Corp. v. Heitner*, 361 A.2d 225 (1976). . . .

We noted probable jurisdiction. We reverse.

II

The Delaware courts rejected appellants' jurisdictional challenge by noting that this suit was brought as a quasi in rem proceeding. Since quasi in rem jurisdiction is traditionally based on attachment or seizure of property present in the jurisdiction, not on contacts between the defendant and the State, the courts considered appellants' claimed lack of contacts with Delaware to be unimportant. This categorical analysis assumes the continued soundness of the conceptual structure founded on the century-old case of *Pennoyer v. Neff*, 95 U.S. 714 (1878).

This analysis led to the conclusion that Mitchell's judgment against Neff could not be validly based on the State's power over persons within its borders, because Neff had not been personally served in Oregon, nor had he consensually appeared before the Oregon court. The Court reasoned that even if Neff had received personal notice of the action, service of process outside the State would have been ineffectual since the State's power was limited by its territorial boundaries. Moreover, the Court held, the action could not be sustained on the basis of the State's power over property within its borders because that property had not been brought before the court by attachment or any other procedure prior to judgment. Since the judgment which authorized the sheriff's sale was therefore invalid, the sale transferred no title. Neff regained his land.

From our perspective, the importance of Pennoyer is not its result, but the fact that its principles and corollaries derived from them became the basic elements of the constitutional doctrine governing state-court jurisdiction. As we have noted, under Pennoyer state authority to adjudicate was based on the jurisdiction's power over either persons or property. This fundamental concept is embodied in the very vocabulary which we use to describe judgments. If a court's jurisdiction is based on its authority over the defendant's person, the action and judgment are denominated "in personam" and can impose a personal obligation on the defendant in favor of the plaintiff. If jurisdiction is based on the court's power over property within its territory, the action is called "in rem" or "quasi in rem." The effect of a judgment in such a case is limited to the property that supports jurisdiction and does not impose a personal liability on the property owner, since he is not before the court. In Pennoyer's terms, the owner is affected only "indirectly" by an in rem judgment adverse to his interest in the property subject to the court's disposition. [Emphasis added.]

The *Pennoyer* rules generally favored nonresident defendants by making them harder to sue. This advantage was reduced, however, by the ability of a resident plaintiff to satisfy a claim against a nonresident defendant by bringing into court any property of the defendant located in the plaintiff's State. For example, in the well-known case of *Harris v. Balk*, 198 U.S. 215 (1905), Epstein, a resident of Maryland, had a claim against Balk, a resident of North Carolina. Harris, another North Carolina resident, owed money to Balk. When Harris happened to visit Maryland, Epstein garnished his debt to Balk. Harris did not contest the debt to Balk and paid it to Epstein's North Carolina attorney. When Balk later sued Harris in North Carolina, this Court held that the Full Faith and Credit Clause, U.S. Const., Art. IV, § 1, required that Harris' payment to Epstein be treated as a discharge of his debt to Balk. This Court reasoned that the debt Harris owed Balk was an intangible form of property belonging to Balk, and that the location of that property traveled with the debtor. By obtaining personal jurisdiction over Harris, Epstein had "arrested" his debt to Balk, 198 U.S., at 223, and brought it into the Maryland court. Under the structure established by *Pennoyer*, Epstein was then entitled to proceed against that debt to vindicate his claim against Balk, even though Balk himself was not subject to the jurisdiction of a Maryland tribunal. . . .

Pennoyer itself recognized that its rigid categories, even as blurred by the kind of action typified by Harris, could not accommodate some necessary litigation. Accordingly, Mr. Justice Field's opinion carefully noted that cases involving the personal status of the plaintiff, such as divorce actions, could be adjudicated in the plaintiff's home State even though the defendant could not be served within that State. 95 U.S., at 733–735. Similarly, the opinion approved the practice of considering a foreign corporation doing business in a State to have consented to being sued in that State. . . .

The advent of automobiles, with the concomitant increase in the incidence of individuals causing injury in States where they were not subject to in personam actions under *Pennoyer*, required further moderation of the territorial limits on jurisdictional power. This modification, like the accommodation to the realities of interstate corporate activities, was accomplished by use of a legal fiction that left the conceptual structure established in *Pennoyer* theoretically unaltered. The fiction used was that the out-of-state motorist, who it was assumed could be excluded altogether from the State's highways, had by using those highways appointed a designated state official as his agent to accept process. Since the motorist's "agent" could be personally served within the State, the state courts could obtain in personam jurisdiction over the nonresident driver.

The motorists' consent theory was easy to administer since it required only a finding that the out-of-state driver had used the State's roads. By contrast, both the fictions of implied consent to service on the part of a foreign corporation and of corporate presence required a finding that the corporation was "doing business" in the forum State. Defining the criteria for making that finding and deciding whether they were met absorbed much judicial energy. While the essentially quantitative tests which emerged from these cases purported simply to identify circumstances under which presence or consent could be attributed to the corporation, it became clear that they were in fact attempting to ascertain "what dealings make it just to subject a foreign corporation to local suit." *Hutchinson v. Chase & Gilbert*, 45 F.2d 139, 141 (CA2 1930) (L. Hand, J.). In *International Shoe*, we acknowledged that fact.

The question in International Shoe was whether the corporation was subject to the judicial and taxing jurisdiction of Washington. Mr. Chief Justice Stone's opinion for the Court began its analysis of that question by noting that the historical basis of in personam jurisdiction was a court's power over the defendant's person. That power, however, was no longer the central concern:

> "But now that the capias ad respondendum has given way to personal service of summons or other form of notice, due process requires only that in order to subject a defendant to a judgment in personam, if he be not present within the territory of the forum, he have certain minimum

contacts with it such that the maintenance of the suit does not offend 'traditional notions of fair play and substantial justice.'" 326 U.S., at 316.

Thus, the inquiry into the State's jurisdiction over a foreign corporation appropriately focused not on whether the corporation was "present" but on whether there have been "such contacts of the corporation with the state of the forum as make it reasonable, in the context of our federal system of government, to require the corporation to defend the particular suit which is brought there." Id., at 317.

Mechanical or quantitative evaluations of the defendant's activities in the forum could not resolve the question of reasonableness:

"Whether due process is satisfied must depend rather upon the quality and nature of the activity in relation to the fair and orderly administration of the laws which it was the purpose of the due process clause to insure. That clause does not contemplate that a state may make binding a judgment in personam against an individual or corporate defendant with which the state has no contacts, ties, or relations." Id., at 319.

Thus, the relationship among the defendant, the forum, and the litigation, rather than the mutually exclusive sovereignty of the States on which the rules of Pennoyer rest, became the central concern of the inquiry into personal jurisdiction. . . . [Emphasis added.]

It is clear, therefore, that the law of state-court jurisdiction no longer stands securely on the foundation established in Pennoyer. *We think that the time is ripe to consider whether the standard of fairness and substantial justice set forth in International Shoe should be held to govern actions in rem as well as in personam.* [Emphasis added.]

III

The case for applying to jurisdiction in rem the same test of "fair play and substantial justice" as governs assertions of jurisdiction in personam is simple and straightforward. It is premised on recognition that "(t)he phrase, 'judicial jurisdiction over a thing', is a customary elliptical way of referring to jurisdiction over the interests of persons in a thing." Restatement (Second) of Conflict of Laws § 56, Introductory Note (1971) (hereafter Restatement). This recognition leads to the conclusion that in order to justify an exercise of jurisdiction in rem, the basis for jurisdiction must be sufficient to justify exercising "jurisdiction over the interests of persons in a thing." The standard for determining whether an exercise of jurisdiction over the interests of persons is consistent with the Due Process Clause is the minimum-contacts standard elucidated in *International Shoe.*

This argument, of course, does not ignore the fact that the presence of property in a State may bear on the existence of jurisdiction by providing contacts among the forum State, the defendant, and the litigation. For example, when claims to the property itself are the source of the underlying controversy between the plaintiff and the defendant, it would be unusual for the State where the property is located not to have jurisdiction. In such cases, the defendant's claim to property located in the State would normally indicate that he expected to benefit from the State's protection of his interest. The State's strong interests in assuring the marketability of property within its borders and in providing a procedure for peaceful resolution of disputes about the possession of that property would also support jurisdiction, as would the likelihood that important records and witnesses will be found in the State. The presence of property may also favor jurisdiction in cases such as suits for injury suffered on the land of an absentee owner, where the defendant's ownership of the property is conceded but the cause of action is otherwise related to rights and duties growing out of that ownership.

It appears, therefore, *that jurisdiction over many types of actions which now are or might be brought in rem would not be affected by a holding that any assertion of state-court jurisdiction must satisfy the International Shoe standard.* [Emphasis added.] For the type of quasi in rem action typified by *Harris v. Balk* and the present case, however, accepting the proposed analysis would result in significant change. These are cases where the property which now serves as the basis for state-court jurisdiction is completely unrelated to the plaintiff's cause of action. *Thus, although the presence of the defendant's property in a State might suggest the existence of other ties among the defendant, the State, and the litigation, the presence of the property alone would not support the State's jurisdiction. If those other ties did not exist, cases over which the State is now thought to have jurisdiction could not be brought in that forum.*

Since acceptance of the International Shoe test would most affect this class of cases, we examine the arguments against adopting that standard as they relate to this category of litigation. . . .

The primary rationale for treating the presence of property as a sufficient basis for jurisdiction to adjudicate claims over which the State would not have jurisdiction if International Shoe applied is that a wrongdoer "should not be able to avoid payment of his obligations by the expedient of removing his assets to a place where he is not subject to an in personam suit." Restatement § 66, Comment a. Accord, Developments 955.

This justification, however, does not explain why jurisdiction should be recognized without regard to whether the property is present in the State because of an effort to avoid the owner's obligations. Nor does it support jurisdiction to adjudicate the underlying claim. At most, it suggests that a State in which property is located should have jurisdiction to attach that property, by use of proper procedures, as security for a judgment being sought in a forum where the litigation can be maintained consistently with International Shoe. Moreover, we know of nothing to justify the assumption that a debtor can avoid paying his obligations by removing his property to a State in which his creditor cannot obtain personal jurisdiction over him. The Full Faith and Credit Clause, after all, makes the valid in personam judgment of one State enforceable in all other States. [Emphasis added.]

It might also be suggested that allowing in rem jurisdiction avoids the uncertainty inherent in the *International Shoe* standard and assures a plaintiff of a forum. We believe, however, that the fairness standard of *International Shoe* can be easily applied in the vast majority of cases. Moreover, when the existence of jurisdiction in a particular forum under International Shoe is unclear, the cost of simplifying the litigation by avoiding the jurisdictional question may be the sacrifice of "fair play and substantial justice." That cost is too high.

We are left, then, to consider the significance of the long history of jurisdiction based solely on the presence of property in a State. Although the theory that territorial power is both essential to and sufficient for jurisdiction has been undermined, we have never held that the presence of property in a State does not automatically confer jurisdiction over the owner's interest in that property. This history must be considered as supporting the proposition that jurisdiction based solely on the presence of property satisfies the demands of due process, but it is not decisive. "[T]raditional notions of fair play and substantial justice" can be as readily offended by the perpetuation of ancient forms that are no longer justified as by the adoption of new procedures that are inconsistent with the basic values of our constitutional heritage. The fiction that an assertion of jurisdiction over property is anything but an assertion of jurisdiction over the owner of the property supports an ancient form without substantial modern justification. Its continued acceptance would serve only to allow state-court jurisdiction that is fundamentally unfair to the defendant.

We therefore conclude that all assertions of state-court jurisdiction must be evaluated according to the standards set forth in International Shoe and its progeny. [Emphasis added.]

IV

The Delaware courts based their assertion of jurisdiction in this case solely on the statutory presence of appellants' property in Delaware. Yet that property is not the subject matter of this litigation, nor is the underlying cause of action related to the property. Appellants' holdings in Greyhound do not, therefore, provide contacts with Delaware sufficient to support the jurisdiction of that State's courts over appellants. If it exists, that jurisdiction must have some other foundation. [Emphasis added.]

Appellee Heitner did not allege and does not now claim that appellants have ever set foot in Delaware. Nor does he identify any act related to his cause of action as having taken place in Delaware. Nevertheless, he contends that appellants' positions as directors and officers of a corporation chartered in Delaware provide sufficient "contacts, ties, or relations," *International Shoe Co. v. Washington*, 326 U.S., at 319, with that State to give its courts jurisdiction over appellants in this stockholder's derivative action. This argument is based primarily on what Heitner asserts to be the strong interest of Delaware in supervising the management of a Delaware corporation. That interest is said to derive from the role of Delaware law in establishing the corporation and defining the obligations owed to it by its officers and directors. In order to protect this interest, appellee concludes, Delaware's courts must have jurisdiction over corporate fiduciaries such as appellants.

This argument is undercut by the failure of the Delaware Legislature to assert the state interest appellee finds so compelling. Delaware law bases jurisdiction, not on appellants' status as corporate fiduciaries, but rather on the presence of their property in the State. *Although the sequestration procedure used here may be most frequently used in derivative suits against officers and directors, the authorizing statute evinces no specific concern with such actions. Sequestration can be used in any suit against a nonresident. . . . If Delaware perceived its interest in securing jurisdiction over corporate fiduciaries to be as great as Heitner suggests, we would expect it to have enacted a statute more clearly designed to protect that interest.* [Emphasis added.]

The Due Process Clause "does not contemplate that a state may make binding a judgment . . . against an individual or corporate defendant with which the state has no contacts, ties, or relations." *International Shoe Co. v. Washington*, 326 U.S., at 319. Delaware's assertion of jurisdiction over appellants in this case is inconsistent with that constitutional limitation on state power. The judgment of the Delaware Supreme Court must, therefore, be reversed.

It is so ordered.

MR. JUSTICE REHNQUIST took no part in the consideration or decision of this case.

MR. JUSTICE POWELL, concurring. [Opinion omitted.]

MR. JUSTICE STEVENS, concurring in the judgment. [Opinion omitted.]

MR. JUSTICE BRENNAN, concurring in part and dissenting in part.

I join Parts I–III of the Court's opinion. I fully agree that the minimum-contacts analysis developed in *International Shoe Co. v. Washington*, 326 U.S. 310 (1945), represents a far more sensible construct for the exercise of state-court jurisdiction than the patchwork of legal and factual fictions that has been generated from the decision in *Pennoyer v. Neff*, 95 U.S. 714 (1878). It is precisely because the inquiry into minimum contacts is now of such overriding importance, however, that I must respectfully dissent from Part IV of the Court's opinion.

I

The primary teaching of Parts I–III of today's decision is that a State, in seeking to assert jurisdiction over a person located outside its borders, may only do so on the basis of minimum contacts among the parties, the contested transaction, and the forum State. The Delaware Supreme Court could not have made plainer, however, that its sequestration statute, Del. Code Ann., Tit. 10, § 366 (1975), does not operate on this basis, but instead is strictly an embodiment of quasi in rem jurisdiction, a jurisdictional predicate no longer constitutionally viable . . . .

. . . .

My concern with the inappropriateness of the Court's action is highlighted by two other considerations. First, an inquiry into minimum contacts inevitably is highly dependent on creating a proper factual foundation detailing the contacts between the forum State and the controversy in question. Because neither the plaintiff-appellee nor the state courts viewed such an inquiry as germane in this instance, the Court today is unable to draw upon a proper factual record in reaching its conclusion; moreover, its disposition denies appellee the normal opportunity to seek discovery on the contacts issue. Second, it must be remembered that the Court's ruling is a constitutional one and necessarily will affect the reach of the jurisdictional laws of all 50 States. Ordinarily this would counsel restraint in constitutional pronouncements. Certainly it should have cautioned the Court against reaching out to decide a question that, as here, has yet to emerge from the state courts ripened for review on the federal issue.

II

Nonetheless, because the Court rules on the minimum-contacts question, I feel impelled to express my view. . . . Unlike the Court, I . . . would not foreclose Delaware from asserting jurisdiction over appellants were it persuaded to do so on the basis of minimum contacts.

It is well settled that a derivative lawsuit as presented here does not inure primarily to the benefit of the named plaintiff. Rather, the primary beneficiaries are the corporation and its owners, the shareholders. . . .

Viewed in this light, the chartering State has an unusually powerful interest in insuring the availability of a convenient forum for litigating claims involving a possible multiplicity of defendant fiduciaries and for vindicating the State's substantive policies regarding the management of its domestic corporations. . . .

In this instance, Delaware can point to at least three interrelated public policies that are furthered by its assertion of jurisdiction. First, the State has a substantial interest in providing restitution for its local corporations that allegedly have been victimized by fiduciary misconduct, even if the managerial decisions occurred outside the State. The importance of this general state interest in assuring restitution for its own residents previously found expression in cases that went outside the then-prevailing due process framework to authorize state-court jurisdiction over nonresident motorists who injure others within the State. . . .

. . . .

I thus do not believe that it is unfair to insist that appellants make themselves available to suit in a competent forum that Delaware might create for vindication of its important public policies directly pertaining to appellants' fiduciary associations with the State.

QUESTIONS AND PROBLEMS

1. Restate the holding in *Shaffer v. Heitner* and its application. Would an amendment of the Delaware statute providing that the directors of all companies incorporated in Delaware thereby "consent" to be sued and authorize the Secretary of States to act as their agent for service in any civil

suit for violation of their legal duties to the corporation satisfy the requirements of *Shaffer v. Heitner?*

2. What do you think that Justice Brennan meant by "the patchwork of legal and factual fictions" of *Pennoyer v. Neff* and its aftermath?

3. In which, if any, of the following instances would the attachment of property owned by a nonresident be permitted to establish *quasi in rem* jurisdiction:

A. A Dutch corporation contracts with a German company to tow an ocean-going, self-elevating drilling rig from the Gulf of Mexico to a point off of the coast of Colombia to drill for oil. The German company's deep sea tug departs from Texas with the rig in tow bound for Colombia. While the flotilla is in international waters in the Gulf of Mexico, a severe storm arises, causing serious damage to the rig. The Dutch company instructs the German vessel to tow the damaged rig to Mobile, the nearest port of refuge. Thereafter the Dutch company commences a suit in admiralty in the United States District Court at Mobile, seeking damages against the German company in *personam* and the vessel *in rem*, alleging negligent towage and breach of contract. Assume that the German company has no office in the United States and does no business in either Alabama or the United States. Would *International Shoe* and *Shaffer v. Heitner* preclude both or either bases of the suit?

B. A Chinese company based in Shanghai engages in the manufacture of luxury leather goods for a major European company that are resold and exported to retailers around the world. The company independently purchases its raw materials from various sources, including a major Argentine leather dealer. The payments are all made in New York to a bank where both the Chinese and Argentine companies maintain accounts. Upon receipt of documents of title and subsequent inspection of the leather, the Chinese company is to authorize transfers of funds to the Argentine company's account — one-half of the contract amount upon receipt of the shipping documents and one-half after inspection of goods. The Chinese company has no other business relationship in or with the State of New York. A few months ago, the Chinese Company received both documents and the goods without authorizing any transfer of funds, alleging that the Argentine company had shipped inferior leather that did not conform to the sales contract. The Argentine company denies the claim and petitions a New York court for attachment of the entire balance of the Chinese company's account in the New York bank, seeking to have their claim against the Chinese company for breach of contract adjudicated in New York. May the New York court grant the petition? What if the Argentine company sought to secure the Chinese firm's assets pending a suit or arbitration abroad?

C. A German company seeks to enforce a German judgment (or in the alternative, an arbitral award by a Swiss arbitration panel) against a

> Chinese firm pursuant to a choice of forum clause in a sales contract between the two enterprises first initiated by seizure of an incidental deposit of funds in a Seattle branch of a Chinese bank for the account of the Chinese firm by a Seattle purchaser of similar Chinese goods. Assume further that the transaction between the Seattle and Chinese firms occurred in Shanghai and had no other connection with Seattle save for the deposit. Would the King County (Seattle) Superior Court have jurisdiction for the attachment and subsequent recognition and enforcement of the judgment (or arbitral award)? Would denial of jurisdiction justify, contrary to Justice Marshall's view, *"the assumption that a debtor can avoid paying his obligations by removing his property to a State in which his creditor cannot obtain personal jurisdiction over him"* in cases involving *quasi in rem* jurisdiction in actions to enforce foreign country judgments or foreign arbitral awards? *See* Chapter 6.

The impact of *Shaffer v. Heitner* on Delaware law was actually short-lived. Almost immediately the Delaware legislature responded to the Court's explicit invitation and enacted the following provision to provide for service on non-resident directors of companies incorporated in Delaware:

§ 3114. Service of process on nonresident directors, trustees, members of the governing body or officers of Delaware corporations.

(a) Every nonresident of this State who after September 1, 1977, accepts election or appointment as a director, trustee or member of the governing body of a corporation organized under the laws of this State or who after June 30, 1978, serves in such capacity, and every resident of this State who so accepts election or appointment or serves in such capacity and thereafter removes residence from this State shall, by such acceptance or by such service, be deemed thereby to have consented to the appointment of the registered agent of such corporation (or, if there is none, the Secretary of State) as an agent upon whom service of process may be made in all civil actions or proceedings brought in this State, by or on behalf of, or against such corporation, in which such director, trustee or member is a necessary or proper party, or in any action or proceeding against such director, trustee or member for violation of a duty in such capacity, whether or not the person continues to serve as such director, trustee or member at the time suit is commenced. Such acceptance or service as such director, trustee or member shall be a signification of the consent of such director, trustee or member that any process when so served shall be of the same legal force and validity as if served upon such director, trustee or member within this State and such appointment of the registered agent (or, if there is none, the Secretary of State) shall be irrevocable.

Nor has the decision in *Shaffer v. Heitner* been deemed to apply to other *quasi in rem* actions so long as *International Shoe* standards are satisfied.

AMOCO OVERSEAS OIL CO. v. COMPAGNIE NATIONALE ALGERIENNE DE NAVIGATION*
605 F.2d 648 (2d Cir. 1979)

GURFEIN, CIRCUIT JUDGE:

This is an appeal from an order of the District Court for the Southern District of New York (Hon. Charles H. Tenney, Judge) refusing appellant's motion under F.R.Civ.P. 60(b) to reopen a previous default judgment entered on behalf of appellees. *Amoco Overseas Oil Co. v. Compagnie Nationale Algerienne*, 459 F. Supp. 1242 (S.D.N.Y. 1978). Appellant broadly argues that there was no jurisdiction to enter the original default judgment and that in any event the District Judge should have set the judgment aside.

This case is a procedural "comedy of errors." In the summer of 1976 appellant Compagnie Nationale Algerienne de Navigation ("C.N.A.N.") entered into a contract of Tanker Voyage Charter Party with appellee Amoco Transport Company ("Transport") for the carriage of a large quantity of crude oil from Egypt to a port outside the United States. The contract was negotiated between C.N.A.N.'s broker in France and Transport's broker, Poten & Partners, Inc. ("Poten"), in New York. The oil was shipped by Amoco Egypt Oil Company and was to be delivered to appellee Amoco Overseas Oil Company ("Overseas").

Delivery was ultimately made in Curacao, Netherlands Antilles. [Sometime] after the oil was discharged, and after the freight payments had been deposited with Poten in New York for remittance to C.N.A.N., appellees discovered that the full quantity of oil due had not actually been delivered. They commenced this action quasi in rem on August 20, 1976 by obtaining an order of attachment against funds credited to C.N.A.N. in Poten's account at the First National City Bank in New York City.

The attachment was effected under state law, N.Y.C.P.L.R. §§ 6201 Et seq., pursuant to F.R.Civ.P. Supplemental Rule B (for certain admiralty and maritime claims). By inadvertence, appellees did not also utilize the federal procedure which may be employed "in addition" under Rule B(1). Accordingly, it was incumbent upon them to perfect their state quasi in rem jurisdictional base by complying with New York statutory requirements. § 6214. Among these is the requirement that within 90 days after the order of attachment is levied upon the property it must actually be taken into custody by the sheriff (if tangible) or the plaintiff must commence a special proceeding against the garnishee. § 6214(c), (d) & (e). Otherwise, the levy becomes void. § 6214(e). The 90-day period here started to run on August 20.

Appellees failed to have the funds taken into custody or to commence a special proceeding during the 90-day period. On October 21, 1976, before the 90-day period had expired, however, the District Court entered a default judgment for inquest, finding that appellant was in default and assigning assessment of damages to a magistrate. On March 21, 1977, unaware that the levy upon the funds had lapsed, the District Court adopted the magistrate's findings and two days later entered final

---

* Footnotes omitted.

judgment for $378,977.33 against appellant.

When appellees sought to execute this judgment, the Bank refused to surrender the funds because the levy had become void. Appellees hastened back to court to reattach the funds both under Admiralty Rule B and by seeking Ex parte an "extension nunc pro tunc" of the time period during which to perfect the original attachment. The extension nunc pro tunc was granted on March 31, 1977, and on April 1, 1977, an amended default judgment was entered. Though it is quite clear that C.N.A.N. had actual notice of the action before Judge Tenney, it did not respond or appear in any way. Having ignored the United States court during the proceedings and for approximately a year after final judgment, appellant finally made its first appearance.

On April 1, 1978, appellant made a motion in the District Court seeking relief from the default judgment under F.R.Civ.P. 60(b); inasmuch as April 1 was a Saturday, the motion was not actually docketed until April 3, more than a year after final judgment.

Appellant attacked the jurisdiction of the court to enter the judgment on several grounds, asserting that (1) under state law jurisdiction under the void attachment could not be restored by an order nunc pro tunc; (2) restoration of the levy was in any event barred after January 1977 when the Foreign Sovereign Immunities Act of 1976, 28 U.S.C. § 1602 Et seq., came into effect; and (3) quasi in rem jurisdiction in this case was a violation of due process. . . .

Judge Tenney rejected the jurisdictional challenges, ruling that (1) state law permitted a nunc pro tunc restoration of the levy; (2) the Immunities Act did not apply because jurisdiction over appellant was originally asserted before the Act came into effect; and (3) the jurisdiction quasi in rem was governed by traditional admiralty principles and was not, in any event, within the scope of the Supreme Court's recent decision in *Shaffer v. Heitner*, 433 U.S. 186 (1977), concerning due process limitations on quasi in rem jurisdiction. . . . From this decision, C.N.A.N. appeals.

. . . .

III

Appellant's final challenge to the jurisdiction of the court below is based upon the due process clause as it restricts the assertion of personal jurisdiction through proceedings by attachment. Because jurisdiction over appellant here is quasi in rem, appellant argues that it is invalid under the Supreme Court's recent decision in *Shaffer v. Heitner*, 433 U.S. 186 (1977).

Shaffer completed the process of supplanting the old doctrine of personal jurisdiction based upon state sovereignty with a newer theory of personal jurisdiction stemming from notions of due process. . . . Under the regime of *Shaffer*, the test of " 'fair play and substantial justice' " that governs in personam jurisdiction controls in rem jurisdiction as well. *Shaffer, supra,* 433 U.S. at 207. But this extension of the "fair play" test to the ostensible exercise of jurisdiction over property is not necessarily incompatible with the principle of jurisdiction quasi in rem because "the presence of property in a State may bear on the existence of jurisdiction by providing contacts among the forum State, the defendant, and the litigation." . . .

Analyzing *Shaffer* from that standpoint several distinguishing aspects of the instant case become evident. First, and most notable, is the fact that here, unlike *Shaffer*, the property attached is related to the matter in controversy. See *Shaffer*, *supra*, 433 U.S. at 207–09. Far from being present in New York adventitiously . . . the freights that were attached were in Poten's accounts in New York pursuant to the Charter Party. Had there been some default in the payment of the freights therefore, C.N.A.N. might well have availed itself of the opportunity to sue Poten, whom it designated to receive the freights, in New York, and possibly also Poten's principal, Amoco Transport. . . .

Second, *Shaffer* involved an attempt by one domestic state to assert jurisdiction over defendants who, it appears, could have been sued in at least one other state in the United States. 433 U.S. at 190, 211 n.37. Here, on the other hand, the jurisdictional issue is whether appellant may be sued in the United States at all. We have no way of knowing whether appellant would be amenable to suit elsewhere in the world. Thus, there are elements of "jurisdiction by necessity" in this case. . . .

Third, *Shaffer* did not consider assertion of jurisdiction over property in the admiralty context. Because the perpetrators of maritime injury are likely to be peripatetic, *Ex Parte Louisville Underwriters*, 134 U.S. 488, 493 (1890), and since the constitutional power of the federal courts is separately derived in admiralty, U.S. Constitution Art. III § 2, suits under admiralty jurisdiction involve separate policies to some extent. This tradition suggests not only that jurisdiction by attachment of property should be accorded special deference in the admiralty context, but also that maritime actors must reasonably expect to be sued where their property may be found.

Bearing these considerations in mind, we believe that the presence of the freights in New York, sent to New York with the agreement of appellant, is a sufficient basis for personal jurisdiction under the due process standard of *Shaffer v. Heitner*. Our conviction that it is fair to assert jurisdiction here is strengthened by the fact that the parties to the Charter also specified that arbitration was to take place in New York. The existence of such an agreement carries considerable weight in demonstrating that it is not unfair to require the parties to litigate in the forum in which arbitration was designated to take place.

. . . .

The judgment appealed from is affirmed.

BANCO AMBROSIANO, S.P.A. v. ARTOC BANK & TRUST LTD.
62 N.Y.2d 65, 476 N.Y.S.2d 64, 464 N.E.2d 432 (1984)

WACHTLER, J.

(1) Plaintiff commenced this action by the attachment of approximately $8 million, representing the balance of defendant's account with its New York correspondent bank. Defendant's appeal, taken pursuant to leave granted by the Appellate Division, focuses primarily on the question of whether this attempted assertion of quasi in rem jurisdiction over defendant's property is consistent with due process. We agree with the lower courts that the contacts among defendant, the forum and the litigation are sufficient to render this limited exercise of jurisdiction inoffensive to principles of due process.

Plaintiff Banco Ambrosiano (Ambrosiano) is an Italian banking corporation, the principal office of which is in Milan. Prior to being placed in liquidation, Ambrosiano was involved in the international banking business and, in this connection, maintained a representative office in New York City. Defendant Artoc Bank and Trust Limited (Artoc), also a banking corporation, is organized under the laws of Nassau, Bahamas, and regularly engages in international transactions. Many of these transactions involve the borrowing and lending of United States dollars, which requires that the transfers be handled through a United States bank. For this purpose, Artoc utilizes an account with its New York correspondent bank, Brown Brothers Harriman and Co. (Brown Brothers). Neither Ambrosiano nor Artoc is authorized to engage in the banking business in this State.

Ambrosiano brought this action to recover $15 million which it allegedly loaned to Artoc, and which has not been repaid. Three transactions, each involving $5 million, were entered into by the parties. The memoranda drawn by Artoc indicate that Ambrosiano was to deposit these sums in Artoc's account with Brown Brothers, and that repayment was to be made to Ambrosiano's account with its New York correspondent bank. Artoc contends, in its defense, that the purpose of the transaction was to reloan the funds to Ambrosiano's controlled subsidiary in Peru and that it was understood that Artoc was to repay these sums only if and when the ultimate recipient repaid them.

With respect to the jurisdictional issue, it appears that all negotiations concerning this agreement were made outside of New York and all communications took place among the Bahamas, Italy, and Peru. The only connection with New York is that the funds were deposited to a New York bank account, were to be repaid to another New York bank account, and apparently were transferred to a New York account on behalf of the ultimate recipient. Artoc argues that the sole reason New York banks were utilized is that the transaction was to be in United States dollars and therefore had to be handled through such clearing accounts. In any event, it is clear that Artoc's sole contact with this State was its maintenance of the correspondent bank account with Brown Brothers.

Ambrosiano commenced this action by obtaining an ex parte restraining order enjoining Brown Brothers from transferring the funds in Artoc's account. Ambrosiano's motion to confirm the attachment was granted over Artoc's challenge to the exercise of jurisdiction over its property. Special Term, noting that Ambrosiano conceded the lack of in personam jurisdiction, found that the property bore a reasonable relationship to the cause of action and that this relationship was sufficient to form the basis for quasi in rem jurisdiction. The Appellate Division unanimously affirmed.

Prior to the Supreme Court's expansion of the recognized bases for extraterritorial jurisdiction over a nondomiciliary, those who wished to sue in this State often resorted to the doctrine of quasi in rem jurisdiction to force a nondomiciliary defendant to litigate a claim in a forum where the defendant happened to own property. The conceptual basis for the State's power to adjudicate the claim was defendant's property, which was brought before the court by virtue of its seizure or attachment. Any resulting judgment was viewed as a judgment against the property only.

With the holding in *International Shoe Co. v Washington* (326 U.S. 310) the approach to jurisdictional analysis was greatly altered. While jurisdictional power had been a function of the defendant's presence, actual or constructive, in the forum State, *International Shoe* shifts the focus of the inquiry to the nature and quality of the defendant's contacts with the State. Those contacts must be such as to "make it reasonable and just, according to our traditional conception of fair play and substantial justice" to require the defendant to litigate the claim in the particular forum (*id.*, at p 320). Where the cause of action arises out of the defendant's activities in or contacts with the State, the extraterritorial exercise of jurisdiction is deemed reasonable.

The long-arm jurisdiction legitimized by the *International Shoe* court was implemented in this State by statute. When the CPLR [Civil Practice Law and Rules] took effect in 1963, it contained two relevant sections. CPLR 301 preserves all previously existing jurisdictional bases, providing that the courts "may exercise such jurisdiction over persons, property, or status as might have been exercised heretofore." The long-arm statute, CPLR 302, provides that when a cause of action arises out of certain activities either occurring within the State or having an impact within the State, jurisdiction may be exercised over a nondomiciliary. Importantly, in setting forth certain categories of bases for long-arm jurisdiction, CPLR 302 does not go as far as is constitutionally permissible. Thus, a situation can occur in which the necessary contacts to satisfy due process are present, but in personam jurisdiction will not be obtained in this State because the statute does not authorize it [citations omitted].

Even with the adoption of the long-arm statute, quasi in rem jurisdiction, which had been carried forward by virtue of CPLR 301, remained a viable method for subjecting a nondomiciliary to suit in this State. The use of this doctrine was drastically limited, however, by the Supreme Court's decision in *Shaffer v Heitner* (433 U.S. 186). There, the court held that the minimum contacts analysis set forth in International Shoe is applicable to actions involving quasi in rem as well as in personam jurisdiction (*id.*, at p 207). Thus, when the property serving as the jurisdictional basis has no relationship to the cause of action and there are no other ties among the defendant, the forum and the litigation, quasi-in-rem jurisdiction will be lacking (*id.*, at pp 208–209).

Although it may appear, at first blush, that the usefulness of quasi-in-rem jurisdiction has been eliminated by *Shaffer*, inasmuch as the minimum contacts necessary to support it will also generally provide in personam jurisdiction, that is not the case, at least in New York. As noted above CPLR 302 does not provide for in personam jurisdiction in every case in which due process would permit it. Thus, a "gap" exists in which the necessary minimum contacts, including the presence of defendant's property within the State, are present, but personal jurisdiction is not authorized by CPLR 302. It is appropriate, in such a case, to fill that gap utilizing quasi in rem principles [citations omitted]. Whether quasi in rem jurisdiction exists in a given case involves an inquiry into the presence or absence of the constitutionally mandated minimum contacts [citations omitted]. Given this limited inquiry, cases in which we have determined that a given set of facts is insufficient for the exercise of personal jurisdiction, will not necessarily be dispositive [citations omitted].

Turning to the facts of the present case, we hold that the relationship between the defendant Artoc, the litigation and this State is sufficient to make it fair that Artoc be compelled to defend here. Artoc stresses that its only contact with New York is the maintenance of its correspondent bank account and urges that the mere presence of this property is insufficient to sustain jurisdiction. What Artoc appears to overlook is the quality of this contact and its significance in the context of this litigation. This is not a case in which property is coincidentally located within the State's borders and forms the only relevant link to defendant; rather, Artoc's account with Brown Brothers is closely related to plaintiff's claim. It is the very account through which Artoc effectuated the transaction at issue, directing Ambrosiano to pay funds to the account and presumably directing Brown Brothers to transfer the funds out of this account to their ultimate recipient. Nor is this transaction an isolated one, for it appears that Artoc utilizes this account regularly to accomplish its international banking business, communicating with Brown Brothers for disbursements of funds on its behalf and directing others to deposit funds there. Finally, with respect to performance of the agreement which forms the basis for Ambrosiano's claim, Artoc not only directed that the funds be deposited in its New York account, but it also agreed to repay these amounts (according to Artoc, only if Ambrosiano's Peruvian subsidiary repaid them) to Ambrosiano's New York account. These factors — the relationship between the cause of action and the property, the activities to be performed in New York under the parties' agreement, and Artoc's other ties with New York — combine to render the exercise of quasi in rem jurisdiction appropriate in this case. The dictates of due process are not offended by requiring Artoc to defend this claim in New York, as it has maintained a significant connection with the State and undertaken purposeful activity here [citations omitted]. . . .

Accordingly, the order of the Appellate Division should be affirmed, with costs.

II. COMMON LAW APPROACHES — THE UNITED STATES 33

CHIEF JUDGE COOKE and JUDGES JASEN, JONES, MEYER and SIMONS concur; JUDGE KAYE taking no part.

QUESTIONS

What difference did or should it make that unlike *Shaffer v. Heitner* both *Amoco Overseas Oil Co. v. Compagnie Nationale Algerienne de Navigation* and *Banco Ambrosiano, S.p.A. v. Artoc Bank & Trust Ltd.* were transnational cases? *Should* this have made a difference in the following decision by the Iowa Supreme Court? Note that all of the decisions of the U.S. Supreme Court cited by the Iowa court were domestic cases involving the Good Faith and Credit Clause.

---

2. *In Rem* Jurisdiction: Marriage as the *Res*

We have previously examined examples of *in rem* actions based on attachment of real, personal, or intangible property within a jurisdiction. We turn now to an example of *in rem* jurisdiction in a case where the *res* or "thing" is totally fictional, not property at all. As indicated by the facts, the transnational aspects of this and like family law cases are considerable. Such cases pose significant problems for lawyers not well-versed in comparative family law in providing adequate advice to the parties on both sides. Moreover, as noted in the cases discussed previously, the Supreme Court explicitly exempted family law from the due process requirements applicable in other civil actions. An overriding question remains as to whether such exemption from due process protections applies or should apply in cases affecting fundamental legal relationships of persons — albeit not as defendants — who are not citizens, domiciliaries, residents, or even casual visitors of the United States.

IN RE THE MARRIAGE OF KIMURA
471 N.W.2d 869 (Iowa 1991)

LAVORATO, JUSTICE.

In this dissolution of marriage proceeding the district court dissolved the marriage of two Japanese citizens. The husband lives here, on a permanent residency status. The wife lives in Japan, has never been here, and has never had any contact with this state. The wife unsuccessfully challenged the district court's jurisdiction to dissolve the marriage. The wife also unsuccessfully challenged the husband's compliance with the residency requirements for a dissolution found in Iowa Code section 598.6 (1987). Finally, the wife was not able to convince the district court to decline jurisdiction on the ground that Japan was the more convenient forum to dissolve the marriage. Because we agree with the district court on all three issues, we affirm.

I. Background Facts and Proceedings.

Ken and Fumi Kimura were married in Japan in 1965. Both are Japanese citizens. They have a daughter and a son. The daughter, Izumi, was twenty-three at the time of the dissolution hearing. The son, Naoki, was twenty-one. Ken and Fumi have lived apart since September 1973.

Ken graduated from Kobe University Medical School in Japan. Currently, he is a pediatric surgeon at the University of Iowa Hospitals and Clinics in Iowa City.

In July 1986 Ken was invited to come to the United States where he took a position at the Long Island Jewish Medical Center in New Hyde Park, New York. When he came to the States, Ken had an H-1 visa. Such a visa is a temporary one, issued to persons with special talents or abilities that may be useful to the United States. The prospective employer or other individual inviting the person must apply to the United States government for the visa.

In October 1986 the center filed an application on Ken's behalf for permanent residency status. Permanent residency status confers several privileges. First, the individual having such a status may live in the United States for as long as the person desires. Second, such a person is entitled to a "green card" that permits the person to obtain employment in the United States on a permanent basis. Last, four years after receiving permanent status, the person may apply for United States citizenship. Ken received permanent residency status in October 1987. He received his green card the following month.

In February 1987 Ken had been invited to the University of Iowa as a guest lecturer. While at the university, Ken met with Dr. Richard Soper, Director of Pediatric Surgery at the University of Iowa Hospitals and Clinics. They discussed possible faculty positions for Ken at the university.

Ken was interviewed at the university in July. In October he was hired as an Associate Professor of Medicine. This is a tenure-track position, but there is no guarantee of tenure. A tenure-track position calls for at least a permanent residency status. In November, after receiving his green card, Ken moved to Iowa City where he began working at the university.

In March 1988 Ken filed a divorce mediation proceeding with the family court in Japan. In July he withdrew from the proceeding. Apparently he could not attend that court's reconciliation proceeding between himself and Fumi because of his work.

In December Ken filed a petition for dissolution of marriage in Johnson County District Court. He alleged that he had resided in Iowa for more than one year. He further alleged that his residency was not just for the purpose of obtaining a dissolution. Finally, he alleged a breakdown of the marital relationship.

Because personal service was not possible on Fumi in Iowa, a copy of the petition was mailed to her in Japan. In addition, notice of the petition was published in the Iowa City Press Citizen on December 14, December 21, and December 28.

In February 1989 Fumi filed a preanswer motion in which she contested the district court's subject matter and personal jurisdiction. She asked that the Iowa proceedings be dismissed or abated.

On April 7 Fumi amended her preanswer motion. She alleged that on March 16, 1988, she herself had filed a divorce mediation proceeding in Japan and that the Japanese court had personal and subject matter jurisdiction. She asked the district court in the alternative to stay the Iowa proceedings so that the Japanese court could hear all the issues related to the marriage.

On April 18 the district court denied Fumi's motion. *The court concluded it had subject matter jurisdiction. But it also concluded it had no personal jurisdiction over Fumi. The court carefully noted that its relief had to be confined to a "determination of the marital status" of the parties. The court acknowledged it could not decide any issues requiring personal jurisdiction. Finally, the court refused to defer to the Japanese court. The court gave two Iberia for its refusal. First, Ken had fulfilled all legal requirements under Iowa law to pursue the dissolution action here. Second, Fumi made no compelling showing why the district court should defer.* [Emphasis added.]

The following month Fumi unsuccessfully sought an interlocutory ruling in this court on these issues. Following this she filed an answer to Ken's petition.

In her answer Fumi denied Ken was a resident of Johnson County, Iowa; denied the petition was filed in good faith; denied that Ken had resided in Iowa for more than one year; and denied his residence in Iowa was in good faith. She also alleged that the Iowa proceedings should be stayed, dismissed, or abated in favor of the pending proceeding in Japan. Finally, she asked that a conciliator in Japan be appointed pursuant to Iowa Code section 598.16. The record fails to show whether a conciliator was appointed. Such appointment is mandatory when a request for it is made in a responsive pleading. *In re Marriage of Schroeder*, 393 N.W.2d 808, 809 (Iowa 1986). However, no issue is raised here on that point.

On July 18, 1989, the parties' attorneys prepared and signed a pretrial conference report in which they stated that Fumi "continues to challenge the court's jurisdiction to determine even the marital status."

On October 10, 1989, Fumi again challenged the subject matter jurisdiction of the district court. She did so in a motion to decline subject matter jurisdiction. She urged two grounds: (1) Japan does not recognize a separation of the issues of marital status from property division; and (2) Japan is the nation that has the most significant contacts to the marital status of the parties.

Fumi supported the motion with an extensive affidavit. In it she points out that *under Japanese law the "person whose improper conduct caused the marital problems is not entitled to a divorce." She suggests Ken is that person. So under Japanese law he would not be entitled to a divorce. She further suggests that if Ken prevails here he would achieve something he could not achieve in Japan. She concludes she would therefore be "effectively . . . denied the protection of the laws of [her] country, and [Ken would] achieve a result which his country would deny him."* [Emphasis added.]

Two days later, the matter proceeded to final hearing. Fumi did not personally appear but her attorney did. Fumi's attorney asked the court to consider her affidavit in support of her motion to decline subject matter jurisdiction.

At the hearing Ken appeared and testified as did Dr. Soper. The court heard testimony about the circumstances surrounding Ken's coming to Iowa, his residence status, the breakdown of the marriage, and his green card, which was introduced into evidence.

On the same day of the hearing the court filed its decree. The court found that there had been a breakdown of the marital relationship. The court concluded that Ken had satisfied the residency requirements of Iowa Code section 598.6. It then dissolved the marriage and assigned costs to Ken.

Fumi appealed.

II. The Due Process Challenge.

Fumi poses the issue this way: "Iowa's assertion of jurisdiction over respondent (who has no contacts with Iowa) or her marriage based solely on petitioner's alleged residence in Iowa violates the due process clauses of the United States and Iowa Constitutions."

The federal fourteenth amendment prohibits a state from "depriv[ing] any person of life, liberty, or property, without due process of law. . . ." U.S. Const. amend. XIV, § 1. Its counterpart is found in article I, section 9 of the Iowa Constitution and is virtually the same: "[N]o person shall be deprived of life, liberty, or property, without due process of law." When state and federal constitutional provisions contain a similar guarantee, we usually deem them to be identical in scope, import, and purpose. *State v. Scott*, 409 N.W.2d 465, 467 (Iowa 1987).

Early on, due process required the personal presence of the defendant in the forum state as a condition for rendering a binding personal or in personam judgment against the defendant. *Pennoyer v. Neff*, 95 U.S. 714, 733 (1878). The rule was expanded in *International Shoe Co. v. Washington*, 326 U.S. 310 (1945). Now due process does not require such personal presence. Due process only requires that the defendant have certain minimum contacts with the forum state. However, those contacts must be such "that the maintenance of the suit does not offend traditional notions of fair play and substantial justice." *International Shoe*, 326 U.S. at 316. Simply put, there must be a connection among the forum, the litigation, and the defendant.

The rule was otherwise with respect to actions in rem and quasi in rem. An in rem judgment affects the interests of all persons in designated property. A quasi in rem judgment affects the interests of particular persons in designated property. *Hanson v. Denckla*, 357 U.S. 235, 246 n. 13 (1958). In these two classes of cases, the physical presence of the defendant's property in the forum was enough to allow state courts to assert jurisdiction. *Pennoyer*, 95 U.S. at 730–31.

This last rule was swept away in *Shaffer v. Heitner*, 433 U.S. 186 (1977). In Shaffer, the Supreme Court rejected "Pennoyer's premise that a proceeding 'against' the property is not a proceeding against the owner of the property." *Shaffer*, 433 U.S. at 205. In effect, the Court equated in personam jurisdiction with

II. COMMON LAW APPROACHES — THE UNITED STATES

in rem and quasi in rem jurisdiction. *Id.* at 212. And the Court concluded that "all assertions of state court jurisdiction must be evaluated according to the standards set forth in International Shoe and its progeny." *Id.*; accord *Burnham v. Superior Court of Cal.*, 495 U.S. 604 (1990) ("quasi in rem jurisdiction . . . and in personam jurisdiction are really one and the same and must be treated alike"); *Percival v. Bankers Trust Co.*, 450 N.W.2d 860, 863 (Iowa 1990). So in those states — like Iowa — hat extend judicial jurisdiction as far as the Constitution permits, a plaintiff who is unable to obtain personal jurisdiction over a defendant will be unable to obtain quasi in rem jurisdiction by virtue of the presence of defendant's property in the state. Vernon, *State Court Jurisdiction: A Preliminary Inquiry Into the Impact of Shaffer v. Heitner*, 63 Iowa L. Rev. 997, 1000–01 (1978) [hereinafter *State-Court Jurisdiction*].

Fumi relies on *Shaffer* in support of her contention that jurisdiction to grant the dissolution must be tested by the minimum contacts standard of *International Shoe*. A footnote in *Shaffer* suggests her reliance is misplaced.

Although the *Shaffer* Court concluded that all assertions of state-court jurisdiction must conform to the standards of *International Shoe* and, thus, be based upon a nexus among the forum, the litigation, and the defendant, the nexus requirement is unlikely to apply to cases in which status provides the basis of the asserted jurisdiction. The power to dissolve the marriage status in an ex parte proceeding normally is thought to stem, at least in part, from the perception of the marriage status as a res, and thus, as a "thing" to which the court's jurisdiction can attach. *Despite the obvious analogy between in rem and quasi in rem jurisdiction based on the presence of property and ex parte-divorce jurisdiction based on the presence of a res (marriage status), the Court specifically noted in a footnote [n. 30] that it was not suggesting "that jurisdictional doctrines other than those discussed in text, such as the particularized rules governing adjudications of status, are inconsistent with the standard of fairness." The all-inclusive language of the Shaffer conclusion, therefore, may not include cases in which status is the basis of the asserted jurisdiction. As far as the Shaffer holding is concerned, the forum — litigation — plaintiff nexus recognized as sufficient by the Court in Williams v. North Carolina [, 317 U.S. 287 (1942)] seems to remain a valid basis of jurisdiction for ex parte divorces.* [Emphasis added.] . . .

In *Williams v. North Carolina*, 317 U.S. 287 (1942) [hereinafter *Williams I*], the question was whether full faith and credit had to be given to a foreign divorce decree where only one spouse was domiciled in the foreign state and the other spouse had never been there. *Williams I*, 317 U.S. at 298–99. The Supreme Court held that the foreign state's high interest in the marital status of its domiciliaries required that full faith and credit be given such a decree. Id. The Court did require, however, that substituted service on the absent spouse meet due process standards, that is, reasonably calculated to give the absent spouse actual notice and an opportunity to be heard. *Id.*

In Williams I the Court had difficulty classifying dissolution proceedings. Though it did not view such proceedings as in rem actions neither did it view them as mere in personam actions. *Id.* at 297, 63 S. Ct. at 212–13. According to the Court, domicile of one spouse within the forum state gave that state the power to dissolve the marriage regardless of where the marriage occurred. *Id.* at 298, 63 S. Ct. at 213. This court too has deemed domicile as essential to dissolution of marriage jurisdiction. See *Cooper v. Cooper,* 217 N.W.2d 584, 586 (Iowa 1974).

The cases generally adopt the following explanation of the components for a dissolution of marriage proceeding: *It is commonly held that an essential element of the judicial power to grant a divorce, or jurisdiction, is domicil. A court must have jurisdiction of the res, or the marriage status, in order that it may grant a divorce. The res or status follows the domicils of the spouses; and therefore, in order that the res may be found within the state so that the courts of the state may have jurisdiction of it, one of the spouses must have a domicil within the state.* [Emphasis added; citation omitted.]

Williams v. North Carolina reached the Supreme Court a second time. The Court held that while the finding of domicile by the state that granted the decree is entitled to prima facie weight, it is not conclusive in a sister state but might be relitigated there. *Williams v. North Carolina,* 325 U.S. 226, 238–39 (1945) [*Williams II*].

The divisible divorce doctrine emerged in *Estin v. Estin,* 334 U.S. 541, 549 (1948). In *Estin* the Court held that Nevada in an ex parte divorce proceeding could change the marital status of those domiciled within its boundaries. The power to do so stems from Nevada's "considerable interest in preventing bigamous marriages and in protecting the offspring of marriages from being [illegitimate]." *Estin,* 334 U.S. at 546. But Nevada could not wipe out the absent spouse's claim for alimony under a New York judgment in a prior separation proceeding because Nevada had no personal jurisdiction over the absent spouse. *Id.* at 548–49. So New York did not have to give full faith and credit to that part of the Nevada decree which purported to eliminate the support obligation of its domiciliary. *Id.* at 549.

The divisible divorce doctrine simply recognizes the court's limited power where the court has no personal jurisdiction over the absent spouse. In these circumstances the court has jurisdiction to grant a divorce to one domiciled in the state but no jurisdiction to adjudicate the incidents of the marriage, for example, alimony and property division. In short, the divisible divorce doctrine recognizes both the in rem and in personam nature of claims usually raised in dissolution of marriage proceedings.

We conclude that the all-inclusive language of the Shaffer conclusion does not include dissolution of marriage proceedings. In other words, jurisdiction to grant such a dissolution is not to be tested by the minimum contacts standard of International Shoe.

We further conclude that domicile continues to be the basis for a court's jurisdiction to grant a dissolution of marriage decree. So the courts of this state have the power to grant dissolution of marriage decrees provided the petitioner is domiciled in this state. Such power exists even though the petitioner's spouse is absent from this state, has never been here, and was constructively rather than personally served. [Emphasis added.]

. . . .

II. COMMON LAW APPROACHES — THE UNITED STATES

The district court adjudicated only the marital status. And that was done based on Ken being domiciled in this state. None of the incidents of the marriage — for example, alimony and property division — were adjudicated because the court did not have personal jurisdiction over Fumi.

. . . .

We affirm the district court's ruling on the preanswer motion challenging jurisdiction and the judgment dissolving the marriage.

Affirmed.

QUESTIONS AND PROBLEM

1. What are the relevant differences in granting an *ex parte* divorce in cases in which both spouses are domiciled or resident in the United States — albeit in different states — in contrast to cases like *In re the Marriage of Kimura* in which one spouse resides outside of the United States? What would be the effect were Japan not to recognize the Iowa judgment? What would have been the result in *Williams v. North Carolina* (*Williams I*) had the U.S. Supreme Court ruled that North Carolina did not have to extend full faith and credit to the Nevada divorce? (The *Williams* case involved a couple who were married in Nevada after their respective previous marriages were dissolved by a Nevada court in ex parte proceedings. Upon return to North Carolina they were prosecuted and convicted for bigamous cohabitation.)

2. What information would an attorney representing Fumi Kimura need to know about Japanese marriage and divorce law in order to provide her with adequate representation and counsel?

3. Assume the following: Cho Lin Park, a 38-year-old Korean woman, married Min Suk Lee, 43, in Pusan, Korea, 18 years ago. They have two daughters, one 16 and the other 13 years old. Neither Cho Lin nor her two children have ever traveled outside of Korea. Min Suk, however, left Korea in 1995 to study in the United States. A graduate of Seoul National University College of Medicine, Min Suk had practiced pediatrics in his father's clinic in Pusan for nine years. Min Suk spent two years in Seattle for research at the University of Washington. In 1997, he received a prestigious Arlin Hankor Fellowship for advanced research at the Washington University in St. Louis on gene-based immunities to certain common childhood diseases. In 2000, Min Suk moved to Nashville, accepting a research and clinical teaching post at the Vanderbilt University Medical School. He currently lives in Belle Meade, Tennessee.

Two weeks ago, Cho Lin received by mail notice of a lawsuit filed by Min Suk in a Tennessee trial court for the dissolution of the marriage. Upon receipt she immediately contacted her brother, a lawyer in Seoul, who in turn has contacted you. He asks for an explanation of the proceeding and your advice as to what steps his sister should take. How would you reply?

3. *In Personam* Jurisdiction

We conclude our examination of the legacy of *Pennoyer* and *International Shoe* with federal due process and state statutory parameters for *in personam* jurisdiction, commencing with the leading case on "tag" jurisdiction — that is, jurisdiction based solely on service of process on a natural person who is physically present within the territory of the state. It too involved divorce.

BURNHAM v. SUPERIOR COURT OF CALIFORNIA, COUNTY OF MARIN*
495 U.S. 604 (1990)

JUSTICE SCALIA announced the judgment of the Court and delivered an opinion in which THE CHIEF JUSTICE and JUSTICE KENNEDY join, and in which JUSTICE WHITE joins with respect to Parts I, II-A, II-B, and II-C.

The question presented is whether the Due Process Clause of the Fourteenth Amendment denies California courts jurisdiction over a nonresident, who was personally served with process while temporarily in that State, in a suit unrelated to his activities in the State.

I

Petitioner Dennis Burnham married Francie Burnham in 1976 in West Virginia. In 1977 the couple moved to New Jersey, where their two children were born. In July 1987 the Burnhams decided to separate. They agreed that Mrs. Burnham, who intended to move to California, would take custody of the children. Shortly before Mrs. Burnham departed for California that same month, she and petitioner agreed that she would file for divorce on grounds of "irreconcilable differences."

In October 1987, petitioner filed for divorce in New Jersey state court on grounds of "desertion." Petitioner did not, however, obtain an issuance of summons against his wife and did not attempt to serve her with process. Mrs. Burnham, after unsuccessfully demanding that petitioner adhere to their prior agreement to submit to an "irreconcilable differences" divorce, brought suit for divorce in California state court in early January 1988.

In late January, petitioner visited southern California on business, after which he went north to visit his children in the San Francisco Bay area, where his wife resided. He took the older child to San Francisco for the weekend. Upon returning the child to Mrs. Burnham's home on January 24, 1988, petitioner was served with a California court summons and a copy of Mrs. Burnham's divorce petition. He then returned to New Jersey.

Later that year, petitioner made a special appearance in the California Superior

---

* Footnotes omitted.

Court, moving to quash the service of process on the ground that the court lacked personal jurisdiction over him because his only contacts with California were a few short visits to the State for the purposes of conducting business and visiting his children. The Superior Court denied the motion, and the California Court of Appeal denied mandamus relief, rejecting petitioner's contention that the Due Process Clause prohibited California courts from asserting jurisdiction over him because he lacked "minimum contacts" with the State. The court held it to be "a valid jurisdictional predicate for in personam jurisdiction" that the "defendant [was] present in the forum state and personally served with process." We granted certiorari.

II

A

The proposition that the judgment of a court lacking jurisdiction is void traces back to the English Year Books, and was made settled law by Lord Coke in *Case of the Marshalsea*, 10 Coke Rep. 68b, 77a, 77 Eng. Rep. 1027, 1041 (K.B. 1612). Traditionally that proposition was embodied in the phrase coram non judice, "before a person not a judge"— meaning, in effect, that the proceeding in question was not a judicial proceeding because lawful judicial authority was not present, and could therefore not yield a judgment. American courts invalidated, or denied recognition to, judgments that violated this common-law principle long before the Fourteenth Amendment was adopted. In *Pennoyer v. Neff*, 95 U.S. 714 (1878), we announced that the judgment of a court lacking personal jurisdiction violated the Due Process Clause of the Fourteenth Amendment as well.

To determine whether the assertion of personal jurisdiction is consistent with due process, we have long relied on the principles traditionally followed by American courts in marking out the territorial limits of each State's authority. That criterion was first announced in *Pennoyer v. Neff, supra*, in which we stated that due process "mean[s] a course of legal proceedings according to those rules and principles which have been established in our systems of jurisprudence for the protection and enforcement of private rights," *id*., at 733, including the "well-established principles of public law respecting the jurisdiction of an independent State over persons and property," *id.*, at 722. In what has become the classic expression of the criterion, we said in *International Shoe Co. v. Washington*, 326 U.S. 310 (1945), that a state court's assertion of personal jurisdiction satisfies the Due Process Clause if it does not violate "'traditional notions of fair play and substantial justice.'" . . .

B

Among the most firmly established principles of personal jurisdiction in American tradition is that the courts of a State have jurisdiction over nonresidents who are physically present in the State. The view developed early that each State had the power to hale before its courts any individual who could be found within its borders, and that once having acquired jurisdiction over such a person by properly serving him with process, the State could retain jurisdiction to enter judgment against him, no matter how fleeting his visit. That view had antecedents in English common-law practice, which sometimes allowed "transitory" actions, arising out of events outside the country, to be maintained against seemingly nonresident defendants who were present in England. Justice Story believed the principle, which he traced to Roman origins, to be firmly grounded in English tradition: "[B]y the common law[,] personal actions, being transitory, may be brought in any place, where the party defendant may be found," for "every nation may . . . rightfully exercise jurisdiction over all persons within its domains." J. Story, Commentaries on the Conflict of Laws §§ 554, 543 (1846). . . . [Emphasis added.]

Recent scholarship has suggested that English tradition was not as clear as Story thought, [references omitted] Accurate or not, however, judging by the evidence of contemporaneous or near-contemporaneous decisions, one must conclude that Story's understanding was shared by American courts at the crucial time for present purposes: 1868, when the Fourteenth Amendment was adopted. . . .

Decisions in the courts of many States in the 19th and early 20th centuries held that personal service upon a physically present defendant sufficed to confer jurisdiction, without regard to whether the defendant was only briefly in the State or whether the cause of action was related to his activities there. . . . States, moreover, had statutes or common-law rules that exempted from service of process individuals who were brought into the forum by force or fraud, or who were there as a party or witness in unrelated judicial proceedings. These exceptions obviously rested upon the premise that service of process conferred jurisdiction. Particularly striking is the fact that, as far as we have been able to determine, not one American case from the period (or, for that matter, not one American case until 1978) held, or even suggested, that in-state personal service on an individual was insufficient to confer personal jurisdiction. Commentators were also seemingly unanimous on the rule.

This American jurisdictional practice is, moreover, not merely old; it is continuing. It remains the practice of, not only a substantial number of the States, but as far as we are aware all the States and the Federal Government — if one disregards (as one must for this purpose) the few opinions since 1978 that have erroneously said, on grounds similar to those that petitioner presses here, that this Court's due process decisions render the practice unconstitutional. [Emphasis added.]

C

Despite this formidable body of precedent, petitioner contends, in reliance on our decisions applying the *International Shoe* standard, that in the absence of "continuous and systematic" contacts with the forum, see n. 1, *supra*, a nonresident defendant can be subjected to judgment only as to matters that arise out of or relate to his contacts with the forum. This argument rests on a thorough misunderstanding of our cases.

Nothing in International Shoe or the cases that have followed it, however, offers support for the very different proposition petitioner seeks to establish today: that a defendant's presence in the forum is not only unnecessary to validate novel, nontraditional assertions of jurisdiction, but is itself no longer sufficient to establish jurisdiction. That proposition is unfaithful to both elementary logic and the foundations of our due process jurisprudence. . . .

The short of the matter is that jurisdiction based on physical presence alone constitutes due process because it is one of the continuing traditions of our legal system that define the due process standard of "traditional notions of fair play and substantial justice." That standard was developed by analogy to "physical presence," and it would be perverse to say it could now be turned against that touchstone of jurisdiction. [Emphasis added.]

D

Petitioner's strongest argument, though we ultimately reject it, relies upon our decision in *Shaffer v. Heitner*, 433 U.S. 186 (1977). . . .

It goes too far to say, as petitioner contends, that *Shaffer* compels the conclusion that a State lacks jurisdiction over an individual unless the litigation arises out of his activities in the State. *Shaffer*, like *International Shoe*, involved jurisdiction over an absent defendant, and it stands for nothing more than the proposition that when the "minimum contact" that is a substitute for physical presence consists of property ownership it must, like other minimum contacts, be related to the litigation. Petitioner wrenches out of its context our statement in *Shaffer* that "all assertions of state-court jurisdiction must be evaluated according to the standards set forth in *International Shoe* and its progeny," 433 U.S., at 212. . . .

The logic of *Shaffer*'s holding — which places all suits against absent nonresidents on the same constitutional footing, regardless of whether a separate Latin label is attached to one particular basis of contact — does not compel the conclusion that physically present defendants must be treated identically to absent ones. As we have demonstrated at length, our tradition has treated the two classes of defendants quite differently, and it is unreasonable to read *Shaffer* as casually obliterating that distinction. *International Shoe* confined its "minimum contacts" requirement to situations in which the defendant "be not present within the territory of the forum," 326 U.S., at 316, and nothing in *Shaffer* expands that requirement beyond that.

It is fair to say, however, that while our holding today does not contradict *Shaffer*, our basic approach to the due process question is different. *We have conducted no independent inquiry into the desirability or fairness of the prevailing in-state service rule, leaving that judgment to the legislatures that are free to amend it; for our purposes, its validation is its pedigree, as the phrase "traditional notions of fair play and substantial justice" makes clear.* Shaffer did conduct such an independent inquiry, asserting that " 'traditional notions of fair play and substantial justice' can be as readily offended by the perpetuation of ancient forms that are no longer justified as by the adoption of new procedures that are inconsistent with the basic values of our constitutional heritage." 433 U.S., at 212. Perhaps that assertion can be sustained when the "perpetuation of ancient forms" is engaged in by only a very small minority of the States. Where, however, as in the present case,* *a jurisdictional principle is both firmly approved by tradition and still favored, it is impossible to imagine what standard we could appeal to for the judgment that it is "no longer justified." While in no way receding from or casting doubt upon the holding of Shaffer or any other case, we reaffirm today our time-honored approach . . . . For new procedures, hitherto unknown, the Due Process Clause requires analysis to determine whether "traditional notions of fair play and substantial justice" have been offended. International Shoe, 326 U.S., at 316. But a doctrine of personal jurisdiction that dates back to the adoption of the Fourteenth Amendment and is still generally observed unquestionably meets that standard.* [Emphasis added.]

Because the Due Process Clause does not prohibit the California courts from exercising jurisdiction over petitioner based on the fact of in-state service of process, the judgment is

Affirmed.

JUSTICE WHITE, concurring in part and concurring in the judgment.

I join Parts I, II-A, II-B, and II-C of Justice Scalia's opinion and concur in the judgment of affirmance. The rule allowing jurisdiction to be obtained over a nonresident by personal service in the forum State, without more, has been and is so widely accepted throughout this country that I could not possibly strike it down, either on its face or as applied in this case, on the ground that it denies due process of law guaranteed by the Fourteenth Amendment. Although the Court has the authority under the Amendment to examine even traditionally accepted procedures and declare them invalid, e.g., Shaffer v. Heitner, 433 U.S. 186, (1977), there has been no showing here or elsewhere that as a general proposition the rule is so arbitrary and lacking in common sense in so many instances that it should be held violative of due process in every case. Furthermore, until such a showing is made, which would be difficult indeed, claims in individual cases that the rule would operate unfairly as applied to the particular nonresident involved need not be entertained. At least this would be the case where presence in the forum State is intentional, which would almost always be the fact. Otherwise, there would be endless, fact-specific litigation in the trial and appellate courts, including this one. *Here, personal service in California, without more, is enough* [emphasis added], and I agree that the judgment should be affirmed.

JUSTICE BRENNAN, with whom JUSTICE MARSHALL, JUSTICE BLACKMUN, and JUSTICE O'CONNOR join, concurring in the judgment.

I agree with Justice Scalia that the Due Process Clause of the Fourteenth Amendment generally permits a state court to exercise jurisdiction over a defendant if he is served with process while voluntarily present in the forum State I do not perceive the need, however, to decide that a jurisdictional rule that " 'has been immemorially the actual law of the land,' " *ante,* at 2115, quoting *Hurtado v. California,* 110 U.S. 516, 528 (1884), automatically comports with due process simply by virtue of its "pedigree." Although I agree that history is an important factor in establishing whether a jurisdictional rule satisfies due process requirements, I cannot agree that it is the only factor such that all traditional rules of jurisdiction are, ipso facto, forever constitutional. Unlike Justice Scalia, I would undertake an "independent inquiry into the . . . fairness of the prevailing in-state service rule." *Ante*, at 2116. I therefore concur only in the judgment.

. . . .

In this case, it is undisputed that petitioner was served with process while voluntarily and knowingly in the State of California. I therefore concur in the judgment.

JUSTICE STEVENS, concurring in the judgment.

As I explained in my separate writing, I did not join the Court's opinion in *Shaffer v. Heitner*, 433 U.S. 186 (1977), because I was concerned by its unnecessarily broad reach. *Id.*, at 217–219 (opinion concurring in judgment). The same concern prevents me from joining either Justice Scalia's or Justice Brennan's opinion in this case. *For me, it is sufficient to note that the historical evidence and consensus identified by Justice Scalia, the considerations of fairness identified by Justice Brennan, and the common sense displayed by Justice White, all combine to demonstrate that this is, indeed, a very easy case.* [Emphasis added.] Accordingly, I agree that the judgment should be affirmed.

QUESTIONS AND PROBLEM

1. What is the primary function of service as articulated by Justice Scalia? Does service merely involve "notice" as described in *International Shoe*? Under *Burnham* could a state provide by statute that its courts have general jurisdiction in all cases over parties "domiciled" or "present" in the state upon the filing of an action with separate provision for notification by official delivery of the complaint and subpoena either by mail within the state or directly in cases where a natural person who is not domiciled or resident but who is physically present in the state? Assume the statute further provides that corporations either incorporated or with their principal place of business in the state are deemed to be "domiciled" in the state for purposes of jurisdiction.

2. Assume that various Japanese companies engaged in the manufacture of products exported to the United States were mutually to agree to a minimum sales price for all exports. A U.S. competitor files a treble damage action in a U.S. district court in California, where a major portion of the exports are shipped or sold. Would the court have jurisdiction over any one of the companies were a director or officer with comprehensive legal authority under Japanese law to represent the company in all matters personally served in connection with such suit while he happened to be in California on a holiday trip, say visiting Disney Land with a granddaughter on her 12th birthday? Assume the court issued a discovery order. Would it

> have personal jurisdiction over the director or officer to compel testimony?

D. State Long-Arm Statutes

Once the Supreme Court had approved state legislative extension of personal jurisdiction over non-resident corporations in *International Shoe*, state "long-arm" statutes became a staple of United States law. Prior to *International Shoe* state judicial *in personam* jurisdiction over non-residents had been recognized in only three basic situations — cases where the defendants were "doing business" within the state, where motorists were defending against claims from accidents arising within the state, and in actions for divorce or annulment (based on the notion that the courts have *in personam* jurisdiction if *both* parties to the marriage resided within the state for the legislative prerequisite period of time or, for in an *in rem* action, as indicated in the *Kimura* case, that the marital *"res"* could be located where *either* spouse resided and the corresponding legislative determinations of the requirements for residency). Only in the case of corporations "doing business" within the state was judicial jurisdiction considered appropriate for the adjudication of any claims — including those unrelated to the activities of the corporation in the state — in other words, a basis for "general" *in personam* jurisdiction. In each of the other cases, including claims against individuals, partnerships, and unincorporated associations "doing business" in the state — even when "systematic and continuous" — for purposes of *in personam* jurisdiction, the claim was required to relate to the defendant's "specific" nexus with the state. Two basic patterns emerged. The broadest approach is exemplified by the California statute. A narrower approach, initially adopted in Illinois, is illustrated by the New York legislation.

CALIFORNIA CODE OF CIVIL PROCEDURE ACT, § 410.10

§ 410.10 *Jurisdiction exercisable*

A court of this state may exercise jurisdiction on any basis not inconsistent with the Constitution of this state or of the United States. *(Added by Stats. 1969.c. 1610. § 3.)*

§ 410.40 Action arising out of contract providing for application of California law

Any person may maintain an action or proceeding in a court of this state against a foreign corporation or nonresident person where the action or proceeding arises out of or relates to any contract, agreement, or undertaking for which a choice of California law has been made in whole or in part by the parties thereto and which (a) is a contract, agreement, or undertaking, contingent or otherwise, relating to a transaction involving in the aggregate not less than one million dollars ($1,000,000), and (b) contains a provision or provisions under which the foreign corporation or nonresident agrees to submit to the jurisdiction of the courts of this state.

This section applies to contract, agreements, and undertakings entered into before, on, or after its effective date; it shall be fully retroactive.

Contracts, agreements, and undertakings selecting California law entered into before the effective date of this section shall be valid, enforceable, and effective as if this section had been in effect on the date they were entered into; and actions and proceedings commencing in a court of this state before the effective date of this section may be maintained as if this section were in effect on the date they were commenced. *(Added by Stats. 1992. c. 615 (S.B. 1804), § 5.)*

NEW YORK CIVIL PRACTICE LAW AND RULES §§ 301, 302
(as amended through September 1, 1982)

§ 301. *Jurisdiction over persons, property or status.*

A court may exercise such jurisdiction over persons, property, or status as might have been exercised heretofore.

§ 302. Person jurisdiction by acts of non-domicillaries

(a) Acts which are the basis of jurisdiction. As to a cause of action arising from any of the acts enumerated in this section, a court may exercise personal jurisdiction over any non-domiciliary, or his executor or administrator, who in person or through an agent:

1. transacts any business within the state or contracts anywhere to supply goods or services in the state; or

2. commits a tortuous act within the state, except as to a cause of action for defamation of character arising from the act; or

3. commits a tortuous act without the state causing injury to person or property within the state, except as to a cause of action for defamation of character arising from the act, if he

(i) regularly does or solicits business, or engages in any other persistent course of conduct, or derives substantial revenue from goods used or consumed or services rendered, in the state, or

(ii) expects or should reasonably expect the act to have consequences in the state and derives substantial revenue from interstate or international commerce; or

(iii) owns, uses or possesses any real property situated within the state.

(b) Personal jurisdiction over non-resident defendant in matrimonial actions or family court proceedings. A court in any matrimonial action or family court proceeding involving a demand for support, alimony, maintenance, distributive awards or special relief in matrimonial actions may exercise personal jurisdiction over the respondent or defendant notwithstanding the fact that he or she no longer is a resident or domiciliary of this state, or over his or her executor or administrator, if the party seeking support is a resident of or domiciled in this state at the time such demand is made, provided, that this state was the matrimonial domicile of the parties before their separation, or the defendant abandoned the plaintiff in this state, or the claim for support, alimony, maintenance, distributive awards or special relief in matrimonial actions accrued under the laws of this state or under an agreement executed in this state.

(c) Effect of appearance. Where personal jurisdiction is based solely on, an appearance does not confer such jurisdiction with respect to causes of action not arising from an act enumerated in this section.

LOUISIANA REV. STAT. § 13:3201
Personal jurisdiction over nonresidents

A. A court may exercise personal jurisdiction over a nonresident, who acts directly or by an agent, as to a cause of action arising from any one of the following activities performed by the nonresident:

(1) Transacting any business in this state.

(2) Contracting to supply services or things in this state.

(3) Causing injury or damage by an offense or quasi offense committed through an act or omission in this state.

(4) Causing injury or damage in this state by an offense or quasi offense committed through an act or omission outside of this state if he regularly does or solicits business, or engages in any other persistent course of conduct, or derives revenue from goods used or consumed or services rendered in this state.

(5) Having an interest in, using or possessing a real right on immovable property in this state.

(6) Non-support of a child, parent, or spouse or a former spouse domiciled in this state to whom an obligation of support is owed and with whom the nonresident formerly resided in this state.

(7) Parentage and support of a child who was conceived by the nonresident while he resided in or was in this state.

(8) Manufacturing of a product or component thereof which caused damage or injury in this state, if at the time of placing the product into the stream of commerce, the manufacturer could have foreseen, realized, expected, or anticipated that the product may eventually be found in this state by reason of its nature and the manufacturer's marketing practices.

B. In addition to the provisions of Subsection A, a court of this state may exercise personal jurisdiction over a nonresident on any basis consistent with the constitution of this state and of the Constitution of the United States.

II. COMMON LAW APPROACHES — THE UNITED STATES

QUESTIONS

1. Which of the state statutes quoted above provide the broadest bases for personal jurisdiction? Under which, if any, is the distinction between "general" and "specific" jurisdiction relevant?

2. In what ways does the Louisiana statute differ from the New York statute?

PROBLEM

Assume the following: Tōyō Sangyō (TS) is the world's largest manufacturer of passenger cars. It exports millions of vehicles around the world each year. Over the past two years, as a result of a defective part in the accelerator, thousands of vehicles have had "sticky" gas pedals, preventing deceleration even upon application of brakes. As a result of numerous accidents, suits against TS and TS USA, TS's wholly owned U.S. subsidiary, have been filed in California, New York, and Louisiana, as well as against Aichi Kōgyō (AK), a small independent subcontractor that produces and supplies various auto parts for TS. AK is allegedly responsible for the defective accelerators. What actions would be necessary for all three firms be subject to the personal jurisdiction of the courts in each of these states? What if AK was not named a defendant in the principal action but was named a defendant by TS?

As indicated previously with respect to *Shaffer v. Heitner* and *In re the Marriage of Kimura*, the distinction between domestic cases involving defendants who are residents of other states as opposed to transnational cases with defendants who reside outside of the U.S. has been rather elusive. Although courts do acknowledge the difference, no significant jurisprudence has yet developed.

QUESTION

How helpful in providing useful guidance is the Restatement (Third) Foreign Relations Law of the United States, excerpted below? To what extent do the bases of permitted adjudicatory jurisdiction correspond to those allowed under the Due Process Clause as construed in the previous cases? What justifications might be made for a more narrow scope?

RESTATEMENT (THIRD) FOREIGN RELATIONS LAW OF THE UNITED STATES (1986)

§ 421. Jurisdiction to Adjudicate

(1) A state may exercise jurisdiction through its courts to adjudicate with respect to a person or thing if the relationship of the state to the person or thing is such as to make the exercise of jurisdiction reasonable.

(2) In general, a state's exercise of jurisdiction to adjudicate with respect to a person or thing is reasonable if, at the time jurisdiction is asserted:

(a) the person or thing is present in the territory of the state, other than transitorily;

(b) the person, if a natural person, is domiciled in the state;

(c) the person, if a natural person, is resident in the state;

(d) the person, if a natural person, is a national of the state;

(e) the person, if a corporation or comparable juridical person, is organized pursuant to the law of the state;

(f) a ship, aircraft or other vehicle to which the adjudication relates is registered under the laws of the state;

(g) the person, whether natural or juridical, has consented to the exercise of jurisdiction;

(h) the person, whether natural or juridical, regularly carries on business in the state;

(i) the person, whether natural or juridical, had carried on activity in the state, but only in respect of such activity;

(j) the person, whether natural or juridical, had carried on outside the state an activity having a substantial, direct, and foreseeable effect within the state, but only in respect of such activity; or

(k) the thing that is the subject of adjudication is owned, possessed, or used in the state, but only in respect of a claim reasonably connected with that that thing.

(3) A defense of lack of jurisdiction is generally waived by any appearance by or on behalf of a person or thing (whether as plaintiff, defendant, or third party), if the appearance is for a purpose that does not include a challenge to the exercise of jurisdiction.

WORLD-WIDE VOLKSWAGEN CORP. v. WOODSON*
444 U.S. 286 (1980)

MR. JUSTICE WHITE delivered the opinion of the Court.

The issue before us is whether, consistently with the Due Process Clause of the Fourteenth Amendment, an Oklahoma court may exercise *in personam* jurisdiction over a nonresident automobile retailer and its wholesale distributor in a products-liability action, when the defendants' only connection with Oklahoma is the fact that an automobile sold in New York to New York residents became involved in an accident in Oklahoma. Respondents Harry and Kay Robinson purchased a new Audi automobile from petitioner Seaway Volkswagen, Inc. (Seaway), in Massena, N.Y., in 1976. The following year the Robinson family, who resided in New York, left that State for a new home in Arizona. As they passed through the State of Oklahoma, another car struck their Audi in the rear, causing a fire which severely burned Kay Robinson and her two children.

I

The Robinsons subsequently brought a products-liability action in the District Court for Creek County, Okla., claiming that their injuries resulted from defective design and placement of the Audi's gas tank and fuel system. They joined as defendants the automobile's manufacturer, Audi NSU Auto Union Aktiengesellschaft (Audi); its importer Volkswagen of America, Inc. (Volkswagen); its regional distributor, petitioner World-Wide Volkswagen Corp. (World-Wide); and its retail dealer, petitioner Seaway. Seaway and World-Wide entered special appearances, claiming that Oklahoma's exercise of jurisdiction over them would offend the limitations on the State's jurisdiction imposed by the Due Process Clause of the Fourteenth Amendment.

The facts presented to the District Court showed that World-Wide is incorporated and has its business office in New York. It distributes vehicles, parts, and accessories, under contract with Volkswagen, to retail dealers in New York, New Jersey, and Connecticut. Seaway, one of these retail dealers, is incorporated and has its place of business in New York. Insofar as the record reveals, Seaway and World-Wide are fully independent corporations whose relations with each other and with Volkswagen and Audi are contractual only. Respondents adduced no evidence that either World-Wide or Seaway does any business in Oklahoma, ships or sells any products to or in that State, has an agent to receive process there, or purchases advertisements in any media calculated to reach Oklahoma. In fact, as respondents' counsel conceded at oral argument, Tr. of Oral Arg. 32, there was no showing that any automobile sold by World-Wide or Seaway has ever entered Oklahoma with the single exception of the vehicle involved in the present case.

Despite the apparent paucity of contacts between petitioners and Oklahoma, the District Court rejected their constitutional claim and reaffirmed that ruling in denying petitioners' motion for reconsideration. Petitioners then sought a writ of

---

* Footnotes omitted.

prohibition in the Supreme Court of Oklahoma to restrain the District Judge, respondent Charles S. Woodson, from exercising *in personam* jurisdiction over them. They renewed their contention that, because they had no "minimal contacts," App. 32, with the State of Oklahoma, the actions of the District Judge were in violation of their rights under the Due Process Clause.

The Supreme Court of Oklahoma denied the writ, 585 P.2d 351 (1978), holding that personal jurisdiction over petitioners was authorized by Oklahoma's "long-arm" statute Okla. Stat., Tit. 12, § 1701.03(a)(4) (1971). Although the court noted that the proper approach was to test jurisdiction against both statutory and constitutional standards, its analysis did not distinguish these questions, probably because § 1701.03(a)(4) has been interpreted as conferring jurisdiction to the limits permitted by the United States Constitution. The court's rationale was contained in the following paragraph, 585 P.2d, at 354:

The State Supreme Court rejected jurisdiction based on § 1701.03(a)(3), which authorizes jurisdiction over any person "causing tortious injury in this state by an act or omission in this state." Something in addition to the infliction of tortious injury was required.

"In the case before us, the product being sold and distributed by the petitioners is by its very design and purpose so mobile that petitioners can foresee its possible use in Oklahoma. This is especially true of the distributor, who has the exclusive right to distribute such automobile in New York, New Jersey and Connecticut. The evidence presented below demonstrated that goods sold and distributed by the petitioners were used in the State of Oklahoma, and under the facts we believe it reasonable to infer, given the retail value of the automobile, that the petitioners derive substantial income from automobiles which from time to time are used in the State of Oklahoma. This being the case, we hold that under the facts presented, the trial court was justified in concluding that the petitioners derive substantial revenue from goods used or consumed in this State."

We granted certiorari, 440 U.S. 907 (1979), to consider an important constitutional question with respect to state-court jurisdiction and to resolve a conflict between the Supreme Court of Oklahoma and the highest courts of at least four other States. We reverse.

II

The Due Process Clause of the Fourteenth Amendment limits the power of a state court to render a valid personal judgment against a nonresident defendant. [Citation omitted.] A judgment rendered in violation of due process is void in the rendering State and is not entitled to full faith and credit elsewhere. [Citation omitted.] Due process requires that the defendant be given adequate notice of the suit, [citation omitted] and be subject to the personal jurisdiction of the court, [citation omitted]. In the present case, it is not contended that notice was inadequate; the only question is whether these particular petitioners were subject to the jurisdiction of the Oklahoma courts.

As has long been settled, and as we reaffirm today, a state court may exercise personal jurisdiction over a nonresident defendant only so long as there exist "minimum contacts" between the defendant and the forum State. *International Shoe Co. v. Washington, supra,* at 316. The concept of minimum contacts, in turn, can be seen to perform two related, but distinguishable, functions. It protects the defendant against the burdens of litigating in a distant or inconvenient forum. And it acts to ensure that the States through their courts, do not reach out beyond the limits imposed on them by their status as coequal sovereigns in a federal system.

The protection against inconvenient litigation is typically described in terms of "reasonableness" or "fairness." We have said that the defendant's contacts with the forum State must be such that maintenance of the suit "does not offend 'traditional notions of fair play and substantial justice.'" *International Shoe Co. v. Washington, supra,* at 316, quoting *Milliken v. Meyer,* 311 U.S. 457, 463 (1940). The relationship between the defendant and the forum must be such that it is "reasonable . . . to require the corporation to defend the particular suit which is brought there." 326 U.S., at 317. Implicit in this emphasis on reasonableness is the understanding that the burden on the defendant, while always a primary concern, will in an appropriate case be considered in light of other relevant factors, including the forum State's interest in adjudicating the dispute, [citation omitted]; the plaintiff's interest in obtaining convenient and effective relief, [citation omitted], at least when that interest is not adequately protected by the plaintiff's power to choose the forum, [citation omitted]; the interstate judicial system's interest in obtaining the most efficient resolution of controversies; and the shared interest of the several States in furthering fundamental substantive social policies, [citation omitted]. The limits imposed on state jurisdiction by the Due Process Clause, in its role as a guarantor against inconvenient litigation, have been substantially relaxed over the years. As we noted in *McGee v. International Life Ins. Co., supra,* 355 U.S., at 222–223, this trend is largely attributable to a fundamental transformation in the American economy:

> "Today many commercial transactions touch two or more States and may involve parties separated by the full continent. With this increasing nationalization of commerce has come a great increase in the amount of business conducted by mail across state lines. At the same time modern transportation and communication have made it much less burdensome for a party sued to defend himself in a State where he engages in economic activity."

The historical developments noted in *McGee,* of course, have only accelerated in the generation since that case was decided. Nevertheless, we have never accepted the proposition that state lines are irrelevant for jurisdictional purposes, nor could we, and remain faithful to the principles of interstate federalism embodied in the Constitution. The economic interdependence of the States was foreseen and desired by the Framers. In the Commerce Clause, they provided that the Nation was to be a common market, a "free trade unit" in which the States are debarred from acting as separable economic entities. *H. P. Hood & Sons, Inc. v. Du Mond,* 336 U.S. 525, 538 (1949). But the Framers also intended that the States retain many essential attributes of sovereignty, including, in particular, the sovereign power to try causes in their courts. The sovereignty of each State, in turn, implied a limitation on the sovereignty of all of its sister States — a limitation express or implicit in both the original scheme of the Constitution and the Fourteenth Amendment. Hence, even while abandoning the shibboleth that "[t]he authority of every tribunal is necessarily restricted by the territorial limits of the State in which it is established," *Pennoyer v. Neff, supra,* 95 U.S., at 720, we emphasized that the reasonableness of asserting jurisdiction over the defendant must be assessed "in the context of our federal system of government," *International Shoe Co. v. Washington,* 326 U.S., at 317, and stressed that the Due Process Clause ensures not only fairness, but also the "orderly administration of the laws," *id.,* at 319. As we noted in *Hanson v. Denckla,* 357 U.S. 235, 250–251 (1958):

> "As technological progress has increased the flow of commerce between the States, the need for jurisdiction over nonresidents has undergone a similar increase. At the same time, progress in communications and transportation has made the defense of a suit in a foreign tribunal less burdensome. In response to these changes, the requirements for personal jurisdiction over nonresidents have evolved from the rigid rule of *Pennoyer v. Neff,* 95 U.S. 714, to the flexible standard of *International Shoe Co. v. Washington,* 326 U.S. 310. But it is a mistake to assume that this trend heralds the eventual demise of all restrictions on the personal jurisdiction of state courts. Those restrictions are more than a guarantee of immunity from inconvenient or distant litigation. They are a consequence of territorial limitations on the power of the respective States."

Thus, the Due Process Clause "does not contemplate that a state may make binding a judgment *in personam* against an individual or corporate defendant with which the state has no contacts, ties, or relations." *International Shoe Co. v. Washington,* 326 U.S., at 319. Even if the defendant would suffer minimal or no inconvenience from being forced to litigate before the tribunals of another State; even if the forum State has a strong interest in applying its law to the controversy; even if the forum State is the most convenient location for litigation, the Due Process Clause, acting as an instrument of interstate federalism, may sometimes act to divest the State of its power to render a valid judgment. [Citation omitted.]

III

Applying these principles to the case at hand, we find in the record before us a total absence of those affiliating circumstances that are a necessary predicate to any exercise of state-court jurisdiction. Petitioners carry on no activity whatsoever in Oklahoma. They close no sales and perform no services there. They avail themselves of none of the privileges and benefits of Oklahoma law. They solicit no business there either through salespersons or through advertising reasonably calculated to reach the State. Nor does the record show that they regularly sell cars at wholesale or retail to Oklahoma customers or residents or that they indirectly, through others, serve or seek to serve the Oklahoma market. In short, respondents seek to base jurisdiction on one, isolated occurrence and whatever inferences can be drawn therefrom: the fortuitous circumstance that a single Audi automobile, sold in New York to New York residents, happened to suffer an accident while passing through Oklahoma. [Emphasis added.]

It is argued, however, that because an automobile is mobile by its very design and purpose it was "foreseeable" that the Robinsons' Audi would cause injury in

Oklahoma. Yet "foreseeability" alone has never been a sufficient benchmark for personal jurisdiction under the Due Process Clause. . . .

If foreseeability were the criterion, a local California tire retailer could be forced to defend in Pennsylvania when a blowout occurs there, see *Erlanger Mills, Inc. v. Cohoes Fibre Mills, Inc.*, 239 F.2d 502, 507 (CA4 1956); a Wisconsin seller of a defective automobile jack could be haled before a distant court for damage caused in New Jersey, *Reilly v. Phil Tolkan Pontiac, Inc.*, 372 F.Supp. 1205 (N.J. 1974); or a Florida soft-drink concessionaire could be summoned to Alaska to account for injuries happening there, see *Uppgren v. Executive Aviation Services, Inc.*, 304 F. Supp. 165, 170–171 (Minn. 1969). Every seller of chattels would in effect appoint the chattel his agent for service of process. His amenability to suit would travel with the chattel. We recently abandoned the outworn rule of *Harris v. Balk*, 198 U.S. 215 (1905), that the interest of a creditor in a debt could be extinguished or otherwise affected by any State having transitory jurisdiction over the debtor. *Shaffer v. Heitner*, 433 U.S. 186 (1977). Having inferred the mechanical rule that a creditor's amenability to a *quasi in rem* action travels with his debtor, we are unwilling to endorse an analogous principle in the present case.

This is not to say, of course, that foreseeability is wholly irrelevant. But the foreseeability that is critical to due process analysis is not the mere likelihood that a product will find its way into the forum State. Rather, it is that the defendant's conduct and connection with the forum State are such that he should reasonably anticipate being haled into court there. [Citations omitted.] The Due Process Clause, by ensuring the "orderly administration of the laws," *International Shoe Co. v. Washington*, 326 U.S., at 319, 66 S. Ct., at 159, gives a degree of predictability to the legal system that allows potential defendants to structure their primary conduct with some minimum assurance as to where that conduct will and will not render them liable to suit.

When a corporation "purposefully avails itself of the privilege of conducting activities within the forum State," *Hanson v. Denckla*, 357 U.S., at 253, it has clear notice that it is subject to suit there, and can act to alleviate the risk of burdensome litigation by procuring insurance, passing the expected costs on to customers, or, if the risks are too great, severing its connection with the State. Hence if the sale of a product of a manufacturer or distributor such as Audi or Volkswagen is not simply an isolated occurrence, but arises from the efforts of the manufacturer or distributor to serve directly or indirectly, the market for its product in other States, it is not unreasonable to subject it to suit in one of those States if its allegedly defective merchandise has there been the source of injury to its owner or to others. The forum State does not exceed its powers under the Due Process Clause if it asserts personal jurisdiction over a corporation that delivers its products into the stream of commerce with the expectation that they will be purchased by consumers in the forum State. [Citation omitted.] But there is no such or similar basis for Oklahoma jurisdiction over World-Wide or Seaway in this case. Seaway's sales are made in Massena, N. Y. World-Wide's market, although substantially larger, is limited to dealers in New York, New Jersey, and Connecticut. There is no evidence of record that any automobiles distributed by World-Wide are sold to retail customers outside this tristate area. It is foreseeable that the purchasers of automobiles sold by World-Wide and Seaway may take them to Oklahoma. But the mere "unilateral activity of those who claim some relationship with a nonresident defendant cannot satisfy the requirement of contact with the forum State." Hanson v. Denckla, supra, at 253. In a variant on the previous argument, it is contended that jurisdiction can be supported by the fact that petitioners earn substantial revenue from goods used in Oklahoma. The Oklahoma Supreme Court so found, 585 P.2d, at 354–355, drawing the inference that because one automobile sold by petitioners had been used in Oklahoma, others might have been used there also. While this inference seems less than compelling on the facts of the instant case, we need not question the court's factual findings in order to reject its reasoning.

This argument seems to make the point that the purchase of automobiles in New York, from which the petitioners earn substantial revenue, would not occur *but for* the fact that the automobiles are capable of use in distant States like Oklahoma. Respondents observe that the very purpose of an automobile is to travel, and that travel of automobiles sold by petitioners is facilitated by an extensive chain of Volkswagen service centers throughout the country, including some in Oklahoma. However, financial benefits accruing to the defendant from a collateral relation to the forum State will not support jurisdiction if they do not stem from a constitutionally cognizable contact with that State. [Citation omitted.] In our view, whatever marginal revenues petitioners may receive by virtue of the fact that their products are capable of use in Oklahoma is far too attenuated a contact to justify that State's exercise of *in personam* jurisdiction over them.

Because we find that petitioners have no "contacts, ties, or relations" with the State of Oklahoma, *International Shoe Co. v. Washington, supra*, 326 U.S., at 319, the judgment of the Supreme Court of Oklahoma is

Reversed.

Mr. Justice Marshall, with whom Mr. Justice Blackmun joins, dissenting.

For over 30 years the standard by which to measure the constitutionally permissible reach of state-court jurisdiction has been well established:

"[D]ue process requires only that in order to subject a defendant to a judgment *in personam*, if he be not present within the territory of the forum, he have certain minimum contacts with it such that the maintenance of the suit does not offend 'traditional notions of fair play and substantial justice.'" *International Shoe, Co. v. Washington*, 326 U.S. 310, 316, 66 S. Ct. 154, 158, 90 L. Ed. 95 (1945), quoting *Milliken v. Meyer*, 311 U.S. 457, 463 (1940).

The corollary, that the Due Process Clause forbids the assertion of jurisdiction over a defendant "with which the state has no contacts, ties, or relations," 326 U.S., at 319, is equally clear. The concepts of fairness and substantial justice as applied to an evaluation of "the quality and nature of the [defendant's] activity," *ibid.*, are not readily susceptible of further definition, however, and it is not surprising that the constitutional standard is easier to state than to apply.

This is a difficult case, and reasonable minds may differ as to whether respondents have alleged a sufficient "relationship among the defendant[s], the forum, and the litigation," *Shaffer v. Heitner*, 433 U.S. 186, 204 (1977), to satisfy the requirements of *International Shoe*. I am concerned, however, that the majority has reached its result by taking an unnecessarily narrow view of petitioners' forum-related conduct. The majority asserts that "respondents seek to base jurisdiction on one, isolated occurrence and whatever inferences can be drawn therefrom: the fortuitous circumstance that a single Audi automobile, sold in New York to New York residents, happened to suffer an accident while passing through Oklahoma." *Ante*, at 566. If that were the case, I would readily agree that the minimum contacts necessary to sustain jurisdiction are not present. But the basis for the assertion of jurisdiction is not the happenstance that an individual over whom petitioner had no control made a unilateral decision to take a chattel with him to a distant State. Rather, jurisdiction is premised on the deliberate and purposeful actions of the defendants themselves in choosing to become part of a nationwide, indeed a global, network for marketing and servicing automobiles.

. . . .

To be sure, petitioners could not know in advance that this particular automobile would be driven to Oklahoma. They must have anticipated, however, that a substantial portion of the cars they sold would travel out of New York. Seaway, a local dealer in the second most populous State, and World-Wide, one of only seven regional Audi distributors in the entire country . . . would scarcely have been surprised to learn that a car sold by them had been driven in Oklahoma on Interstate 44, a heavily traveled transcontinental highway. In the case of the distributor, in particular, the probability that some of the cars it sells will be driven in every one of the contiguous States must amount to a virtual certainty. This knowledge should alert a reasonable businessman to the likelihood that a defect in the product might manifest itself in the forum State — not because of some unpredictable, aberrant, unilateral action by a single buyer, but in the normal course of the operation of the vehicles for their intended purpose.

. . . .

Manifestly, the "quality and nature" of commercial activity is different, for purposes of the *International Shoe* test, from actions from which a defendant obtains no economic advantage. Commercial activity is more likely to cause effects in a larger sphere, and the actor derives an economic benefit from the activity that makes it fair to require him to answer for his conduct where its effects are felt. The profits may be used to pay the costs of suit, and knowing that the activity is likely to have effects in other States the defendant can readily insure against the costs of those effects, thereby sparing himself much of the inconvenience of defending in a distant forum.

Of course, the Constitution forbids the exercise of jurisdiction if the defendant had no judicially cognizable contacts with the forum. But as the majority acknowledges, if such contacts are present the jurisdictional inquiry requires a balancing of various interests and policies. [Citation omitted.] I believe such contacts are to be found here and that, considering all of the interests and policies at stake, requiring petitioners to defend this action in Oklahoma is not beyond the bounds of the Constitution.

Accordingly, I dissent.

MR. JUSTICE BLACKMUN, dissenting.

I confess that I am somewhat puzzled why the plaintiffs in this litigation are so insistent that the regional distributor and the retail dealer, the petitioners here, who handled the ill-fated Audi automobile involved in this litigation, be named defendants. It would appear that the manufacturer and the importer, whose subjectability to Oklahoma jurisdiction is not challenged before this Court, ought not to be judgment-proof. It may, of course, ultimately amount to a contest between insurance companies that, once begun, is not easily brought to a termination. Having made this much of an observation, I pursue it no further.

For me, a critical factor in the disposition of the litigation is the nature of the instrumentality under consideration. It has been said that we are a nation on wheels. What we are concerned with here is the automobile and its peripatetic character. One need only examine our national network of interstate highways, or make an appearance on one of them, or observe the variety of license plates present not only on those highways but in any metropolitan area, to realize that any automobile is likely to wander far from its place of licensure or from its place of distribution and retail sale. Miles per gallon on the highway (as well as in the city) and mileage per tankful are familiar allegations in manufacturers' advertisements today. To expect that any new automobile will remain in the vicinity of its retail sale — like the 1914 electric driven car by the proverbial "little old lady"— is to blink at reality. The automobile is intended for distance as well as for transportation within a limited area. It therefore seems to me not unreasonable — and certainly not unconstitutional and beyond the reach of the principles laid down in *International Shoe Co. v. Washington*, 326 U.S. 310 (1945), and its progeny — to uphold Oklahoma jurisdiction over this New York distributor and this New York dealer when the accident happened in Oklahoma. . . . I would affirm the judgment of the Supreme Court of Oklahoma. Because the Court reverses that judgment, it will now be about parsing every variant in the myriad of motor vehicles fact situations that present themselves. Some will justify jurisdiction and others will not. All will depend on the "contact" that the Court sees fit to perceive in the individual case.

QUESTIONS

1. Audi NSU Auto Union Aktiengesellschaft (Audi) and Volkswagen of America, Inc. (Volkswagen) did not contest jurisdiction. Assuming that the Oklahoma long-arm statute is similar or the same as that of New York, what do you think was the basis for adjudicatory jurisdiction over each?

2. Did the Oklahoma courts have general or specific subject-matter jurisdiction in this case? Would either have had an arguable due process defense under *International Shoe?* Is there additional information about the companies would you need to know to answer these questions?

GRUCA v. ALPHA THERAPEUTIC CORPORATION AND THE GREEN CROSS CORPORATION*
19 F. Supp. 2d 862 (N.D. Ill. 1998)

MEMORANDUM OPINION AND ORDER

GOTTSCHALL, DISTRICT JUDGE.

In her Fifth Amended Complaint, plaintiff Peggy Gruca seeks to add a new defendant, The Green Cross Corporation ("Green Cross"). Green Cross has made a limited appearance to move to dismiss the Fifth Amended Complaint for lack of personal jurisdiction. For the Iberia set forth below, the motion is granted.

BACKGROUND

Gruca filed this action on behalf of herself, her two minor children, and the estate of her late husband, Stephen Poole against four defendants. Poole was a hemophiliac with a severe deficiency of Factor VIII in his plasma. Factor VIII is a protein necessary for clotting. Poole used a commercially prepared product called Factor VIII concentrate, which was prescribed by his doctor, to treat bleeding episodes. The defendants allegedly manufactured the Factor VIII concentrate used by Poole.

In 1986, Poole was diagnosed with AIDS, and he died in 1987. Plaintiff brought this action asserting a variety of negligence claims against the defendants for their failure to minimize the risks of transmitting viruses, including the virus that causes AIDS, through the Factor VIII concentrate. At the close of a seven-week trial in 1993, a jury returned a verdict in favor of the defendants and the district court entered judgment for defendants. On appeal, plaintiff's motion for a new trial was granted. The case was eventually transferred to this court.

Three of the four defendants in the 1993 trial settled with plaintiff. Alpha Therapeutic Corporation ("Alpha") was the only one of the four defendants that did not reach a settlement. Plaintiff filed a Fifth Amended Complaint ("the Complaint") against Alpha. The Complaint also named Green Cross as a defendant for the first time. Green Cross is a foreign corporation organized under the laws of Japan and is the parent corporation of Alpha.

Alpha was established by Green Cross in 1978. Green Cross acquired the Abbott Scientific Products Division (ASPD) from Abbott Laboratories, Inc. in 1978 and transferred the assets of ASPD directly to Alpha. Alpha collects plasma from donors and manufactures and sells products made from human plasma.

In the Complaint, plaintiff alleges that Green Cross and Alpha were negligent in collecting plasma and manufacturing Factor VIII concentrate. Although the Complaint alleges that both Green Cross and Alpha committed the various negligent acts, it is clear from her briefs on the motion to dismiss that plaintiff is not contending that the actions of Green Cross alone are sufficient to provide this court

---

* Footnotes omitted.

with personal jurisdiction. From the Complaint and the briefs, it appears that Alpha collected plasma from donors and manufactured and sold Factor VIII concentrate in Illinois and that Alpha allegedly sold the Factor VIII that infected Poole with HIV. Plaintiff claims that Green Cross' involvement with Alpha is sufficient to establish personal jurisdiction over Green Cross. In particular, plaintiff argues that Alpha is the alter ego of or was substantially controlled by Green Cross, or alternatively, that Alpha and Green Cross were joint venturers.

DISCUSSION

A federal district court in Illinois has personal jurisdiction over a nonresident party only if an Illinois state court would have jurisdiction. On a motion to dismiss for lack of personal jurisdiction, the plaintiff bears the burden of establishing a prima facie case of personal jurisdiction. Id. In deciding a motion to dismiss for lack of personal jurisdiction, a court may receive and consider affidavits from the parties. Factual disputes must be resolved in favor of the plaintiff. The plaintiff must show that Illinois law permits jurisdiction and that the exercise of jurisdiction will not offend due process. The Illinois long-arm statute permits the exercise of jurisdiction over claims arising out of the defendant's transaction business or commission of a tort. The statute also permits jurisdiction over a "corporation doing business" in Illinois.

Here, plaintiff does not contend that Green Cross itself engaged in the transactions or committed the torts giving rise to the claims. Likewise, plaintiff does not assert that Green Cross itself is doing business in Illinois. It is undisputed that Green Cross itself has not marketed or sold blood products in Illinois and has not collected or processed plasma in Illinois. Green Cross itself does not conduct any business in Illinois, manufacture or sell any products in Illinois, or have any employees in Illinois. Instead, plaintiff argues that Green Cross' involvement with Alpha is sufficient to permit this court to exercise personal jurisdiction over Green Cross. In particular, plaintiff argues that jurisdiction over Green Cross is proper (1) because Alpha is the alter ego of Green Cross or is at least substantially controlled by Green Cross; or, alternatively, (2) because Alpha and Green Cross are joint venturers. There is no dispute that this court has jurisdiction over Alpha. Therefore, to determine if Green Cross is within this court's jurisdiction, it is necessary to examine the relationship between Green Cross and Alpha.

I. Alpha as Alter Ego of or Substantially Controlled by Green Cross

Jurisdiction over a subsidiary is not sufficient to confer jurisdiction over an out-of-state parent. *IDS*, 958 F. Supp. at 1265–66. When a subsidiary is doing business in Illinois, the mere existence of a parent-subsidiary relationship does not enable a court to exercise jurisdiction over a foreign parent. Id. Instead, the party arguing for jurisdiction must allege something more than the existence of the parent-subsidiary relationship and that the subsidiary is doing business in Illinois.

Courts have not developed a bright-line test for determining when it is appropriate to exercise jurisdiction over a parent corporation based upon the activities of its subsidiary. In *Cannon Mfg. Co. v. Cudahy Packing Co.*, 267 U.S. 333

(1925), the Supreme Court considered whether a subsidiary's activities in North Carolina could establish that the parent corporation was doing business in North Carolina. The Court framed the issue as "whether the corporate separation carefully maintained must be ignored in determining the existence of jurisdiction." *Id.* at 336. In holding that the parent was not subject to jurisdiction in North Carolina, the Court noted that "[t]he corporate separation, though perhaps merely formal, was real. It was not pure fiction." *Id.* at 337.

The continuing validity of *Cannon* is in doubt. Since *Cannon* was decided, the constitutional standards for exercising jurisdiction have been drastically revised. Most importantly, the "physical presence" test has been replaced by the "minimum contacts" standard. *International Shoe Co. v. Washington*, 326 U.S. 310, 316 (1945). Thus, in more recent years, courts deciding personal jurisdiction issues have looked at the "real" rather than the "formal" relationship between the parent and the subsidiary. The Supreme Court explicitly stated that "[n]o question of the constitutional powers of the state, or of the federal government, is directly presented." *Cannon*, 267 U.S. at 336. Thus, *Cannon* never purported to set out the constitutional limits for when jurisdiction may be exercised over a parent corporation based on the activities of its subsidiary. Instead, the decision seemed to rest on principles of the law of corporations.

Illinois courts appear to use two approaches in examining whether the activities of the subsidiary give rise to jurisdiction over the parent. Under one approach, Illinois courts examine whether the parent and subsidiary have maintained formal separation and observed corporate formalities. If not, then the corporate veil of the subsidiary may be pierced, the activities of the subsidiary may be attributed to the parent, and the court may exercise jurisdiction over the parent. This approach is consistent with *Cannon*'s emphasis on the formal relationship between parent and subsidiary. However, Illinois courts have also shown a willingness to employ a more flexible approach that examines the nature of the activities by the subsidiary and the degree of control exercised by the parent over the subsidiary. These approaches are examined in more detail below.

A. Tests for Piercing the Corporate Veil and Substantial Control

As noted above Illinois courts seem to recognize two methods by which a plaintiff can establish jurisdiction over a foreign parent corporation based on the activities of its subsidiary. First, the party alleging jurisdiction can provide evidence that justifies piercing the corporate veil of the subsidiary. [Citation omitted.] In Illinois, a corporation's veil may be pierced only if (1) there is such "unity of interest and ownership that the separate personalities of the corporation" and the subsidiary no longer exist; and (2) "adherence to the fiction of separate corporate existence would sanction a fraud or promote injustice." *Hystro Prods., Inc. v. MNP Corp.*, 18 F.3d 1384, 1388–89 (7th Cir. 1994) (quoting *Van Dorn Co. v. Future Chem. and Oil Corp.*, 753 F.2d 565, 569–70 (7th Cir. 1985)). To determine if there is a sufficient "unity of interest and ownership" between two corporations to justify piercing the veil, Illinois courts look to four factors: "(1) the failure to maintain adequate corporate records or to comply with corporate formalities, (2) the commingling of funds or assets, (3) undercapitalization, and (4) one corporation treating the assets of another as its own." *Van Dorn*, 753 F.2d at 570.

Second, a plaintiff can establish jurisdiction over a parent corporation by showing that the parent substantially controls the activities of a subsidiary doing business in Illinois. . . . [T]he opinion in *Graco, Inc. v. Kremlin, Inc.*, 558 F. Supp. 188 (N.D. Ill. 1982) identifies several factors to consider in determining if a parent is so closely linked to its subsidiary that jurisdiction over the subsidiary creates jurisdiction over the parent:

> [W]hether the parent arranges financing for and capitalization of the subsidiary; whether separate books, tax returns and financial statements are kept; whether officers or directors are the same; whether the parent holds its subsidiary out as an agent; the method of payment made to the parent by the subsidiary; and how much control is exerted by the parent over the daily affairs of its subsidiary. *Id.* at 191.

Plaintiff contends that she has provided sufficient evidence to establish jurisdiction under either method. After examining plaintiff's allegations and evidence in support of jurisdiction, the court will return to the factors set out in *Van Dorn* and *Graco*.

B. The Relationship Between Green Cross and Alpha

Plaintiff argues that numerous factors indicate substantial control by Green Cross over Alpha. Plaintiff contends that Green Cross acquired the assets of ASPD (and transferred the assets to Alpha) in order to ensure that Green Cross would have an adequate supply of plasma and blood products. A substantial portion of Alpha's sales are to Green Cross. As of 1980, 79.7 percent of Alpha's income from net sales was derived from sales to Green Cross. (Compl. ¶ 14.) However, plaintiff offers no evidence that these sales were anything other than ordinary, market-rate contractual sales.

Plaintiff maintains that Green Cross used Alpha as an instrument to expand Green Cross' international operations. Plaintiff cites to "The Green Cross Corporation Annual Report 1982," which stated in part:

> Our key overseas operation is Alpha Therapeutic Corporation (ATC), a wholly owned subsidiary in the United States. Until 1978, when we established ATC, our prospects for sustaining growth were hampered by a shortage in the domestic supply of plasma. Since then, ATC has steadily provided various blood products and semiprocessed materials, meeting approximately 80 percent of our needs for these products. Last year, ATC's sales rose 16 percent and profits have continued to climb.
>
> ATC is also being used to expand our international marketing efforts. In August 1978 ATC established Alpha GmbH in Germany. In addition, ATC acquired in October 1982 a 50 percent interest in Laboratorios Grifols S.A. of Spain, and supplied manufacturing technology for the production of plasma products. This arrangement has further strengthened our marketing position for plasma products in Europe. (Pl's Resp., Ex. D at 2.)

However, as Green Cross points out, the report clearly identifies Alpha as a separate entity from Green Cross, refers to sales and profits by Alpha, and describes Alpha's expansion in Europe. The ambiguous references to "[o]ur key overseas operation," "our international marketing efforts" and "our marketing position" are consistent with Alpha's existence as a separate entity. They do not show that Alpha exists merely as an instrument for marketing and selling Green Cross' products. . . .

Plaintiff contends that "Green Cross dictated the markets into which Alpha could sell." (Pl's Supp. Resp. at 8.) However, at best, the deposition testimony cited offers limited support for this assertion. Plaintiff refers to the deposition testimony of Alpha's former president and CEO, Samuel Dale Anderson, Sr., who stated that "[w]hen I got to Alpha we had a very small percentage of the business in Europe. We wanted to be-we didn't want the Green Cross to take that responsibility away from us so we put a lot of effort into Europe and dramatically increased our market share." (Pl's Resp., Ex. B at 51.) At most, this testimony indicates a fear that Green Cross would act to reduce Alpha's presence in the European market. It does not establish that Green Cross ever exercised control over Alpha's marketing in Europe or elsewhere.

Plaintiff also claims that Green Cross exercised control over Alpha's budget. The testimony cited by plaintiff indicates that Green Cross engaged in some oversight of the budget.

. . . .

Thus, it appears that Alpha's president submitted a proposed budget and discussed it with Green Cross. However, this is rather slight evidence of Green Cross' purported "substantial control" over Alpha. Green Cross required its wholly owned subsidiary to present a budget plan. There is no evidence that Green Cross played any role in creating the initial budget proposal or that Green Cross ever vetoed any of the proposed budget. At most this suggests oversight by Green Cross over its investment in Alpha.

Plaintiff asserts that Green Cross' 1982 Annual Report also indicates that Green Cross failed to maintain separate financial statements for Green Cross and Alpha. The 1982 report specifies that it contains "consolidated financial statements [that] include the accounts of Green Cross, Alpha Therapeutic Corporation ("Alpha" a wholly-owned U.S. Corporation) and Alpha's subsidiary in Germany." (Pl's Resp., Ex. D at 11.) However, this indicates only that the separate financial statements of Green Cross and Alpha were consolidated for the purposes of the annual report. The annual report itself makes clear that Alpha maintains its own separate financial statements. (See Pl's Resp., Ex. D at 20.) Green Cross and Alpha have provided affidavits stating that they do not commingle finances or share assets. (Def's Mem., Ex. B ¶ 13; Def's Mem., Ex. C ¶ 9.)

Plaintiff also argues that substantial overlap between the officers and directors of Alpha and Green Cross provides further evidence of Green Cross' control over Alpha. Plaintiff notes that a majority of Alpha's Board of Directors were also members of Green Cross' Board of Directors. Plaintiff also argues that Green Cross "monitored Alpha's internal affairs through liaisons, who monitored both Alpha's finances and research and development." (Pl's Supp. Resp. at 8.) However, plaintiff does not assert that these liaisons controlled the operations of Alpha — indeed, plaintiff claims only that the liaisons "monitored" Alpha's operations.

Finally, plaintiff notes that Alpha and Green Cross collaborated on research and development programs. For one product, Green Cross developed the product and conducted animal studies. Alpha performed quality control testing, found people for preclinical studies, and, later, conducted the clinical studies on the product. The product was eventually licensed by the Food and Drug Administration (FDA), and Alpha's former Vice-President of Regulatory Affairs did much of the work in connection with obtaining the FDA license. In addition, some Green Cross employees came to the United States to work with Alpha's research and development department.

C. Examining the Relationship in Light of the Factors in *Van Dorn* and *Graco*

Looking first at the factors set out in *Van Dorn*, it is clear that plaintiff has failed to establish that Alpha and Green Cross have sufficient "unity of interest and ownership" to justify piercing the corporate veil. The four factors are (1) the failure to maintain adequate corporate records or to comply with corporate formalities; (2) the commingling of funds or assets; (3) undercapitalization; and (4) one corporation treating the assets of another as its own. [Citation omitted.]

The only evidence of factors (1) and (2) is Green Cross' 1982 Annual Report, which contained a consolidated financial statement. However, as noted above, the report itself made clear that Alpha does maintain its own financial statements, and there is no evidence that Alpha failed to maintain adequate records or comply with corporate formalities. Plaintiff claims that Alpha is undercapitalized based upon the statement by the former president of Alpha, Thomas Drees, that after Green Cross bought Alpha it put a lot of money into Alpha. (Pl's Resp., Ex. C at 2748.) In response, Green Cross offers affidavits stating that "Green Cross has not funded, and does not fund, Alpha." (Def's Mem., Ex. C ¶ 9.) Even if this court were to find that the vague statement by Drees is sufficient to create a factual conflict (which must be resolved in favor of plaintiff) as to whether Green Cross funded Alpha, Drees' statement is insufficient to establish undercapitalization. There is no evidence that the assets of Alpha are insubstantial or that funds are transferred to and from Alpha when necessary to meet current obligations. [Citation omitted.] Indeed, the only evidence provided by plaintiff indicates that Green Cross transferred funds to improve the capitalization of Alpha, intending to assist Alpha's transition to self-sufficiency. Finally, there is little, if any, evidence of Green Cross treating the assets of Alpha as its own assets. A high proportion of Alpha's sales may have been to Green Cross, but there is no evidence that these sales were anything other than market-rate transactions. There is no evidence that Green Cross transferred assets to and from Alpha without regard to the corporate forms. The only evidence suggesting that Green Cross may have used its control over Alpha to impose some obligations on Alpha is the allegation that Green Cross required Alpha to perform some research and development on products created by Green Cross. However, the nature of this research and development cooperation is ill-defined, and, in the absence of some evidence on the other factors set out in *Van Dorn*, it is inadequate to justify piercing the corporate veil.

Turning now to the question of whether Green Cross exercised sufficient control over Alpha to create jurisdiction over Green Cross, the court will examine the evidence in light of the factors set out in *Graco*. As noted above, *Graco* set out several factors to consider when determining if the parent should be viewed as doing business through the subsidiary:

(1) Whether the parent arranges financing for and capitalization of the subsidiary;

(2) Whether separate books, tax returns and financial statements are kept;

(3) Whether officers or directors are the same;

(4) Whether the parent holds its subsidiary out as an agent;

(5) The method of payment made to the parent by the subsidiary; and

(6) How much control is exerted by the parent over the daily affairs of its subsidiary.

Other than the vague statement that Green Cross put a lot of money into Alpha, there is no evidence that Green Cross arranges financing or capitalization for Alpha. Plaintiff cited to the consolidated financial statements in the 1982 annual report, but even that report indicated that Alpha maintains its own financial records. There is no other evidence that Green Cross does not keep its own books, tax returns and financial statements. Plaintiff has provided no evidence that Green Cross holds Alpha out as its agent. Finally, plaintiff has not shown that the method of payments between Alpha and Green Cross suggests that Alpha is merely an instrument of Green Cross.

To support her contention that Green Cross dominates Alpha, plaintiff relies primarily on the third and the sixth factors. A majority of Alpha's directors were also directors of Green Cross. While such overlap provides some evidence of control (or at least the potential for control), on its own it is not sufficient. As noted in *IDS*, "the 'overlap of executives and directors' between the parent and subsidiary . . . 'does not approach the level of control' required to vest the court with jurisdiction." 958 F. Supp. at 1266 (quoting *Integrated Bus.*, 714 F. Supp. at 300). Plaintiff notes that the until his death in 1983, the president of Green Cross often came to the United States for Alpha's board meetings. However there is little evidence that officers at Green Cross exerted substantial control over Alpha, and in particular, over the "daily affairs" of Alpha. Though plaintiff makes numerous allegations that Green Cross controlled Alpha, she has provided insufficient evidence of such control. Plaintiff notes that Green Cross kept liaisons at Alpha, but there is no evidence that the liaisons exerted any control over the operations at Alpha. Indeed, plaintiff alleges only that the liaisons "monitored" Alpha's operations. Plaintiff's assertion that Green Cross controlled Alpha's marketing is not supported by the evidence. Plaintiff has provided evidence that Alpha had to present a budget to Green Cross, but this appears to be little more than oversight. There is no evidence that Green Cross was involved in the preparation of the budget or that Green Cross exercised a veto over the budget.

Plaintiff has failed to establish that Green Cross exerted substantial control over Alpha. Green Cross created Alpha to ensure that Green Cross would have an adequate supply of plasma, and a large percentage of Alpha's sales have been to

Green Cross. There is substantial overlap between the boards of directors. Green Cross and Alpha have cooperated on some research and development. Nevertheless, Alpha has maintained a separate corporate existence. Alpha appears to maintain control over its daily operations and has not operated as a mere instrument of Green Cross. Green Cross is not doing business in Illinois through Alpha.

This conclusion is consistent with other cases that have examined when the activities of the subsidiary may give rise to jurisdiction over the parent. . . .

II. Alpha and Green Cross as Joint Venturers

Plaintiff argues that even if the evidence does not establish that Alpha was substantially controlled by Green Cross, it does show that Alpha and Green Cross were joint venturers. Plaintiff contends that jurisdiction over one co-venturer, Alpha, is sufficient to establish jurisdiction over the other co-venturer, Green Cross.

Plaintiff devoted little space to this argument in her briefs, discussing the issue for the first time in her supplemental response to the motion to dismiss. This court concludes that the argument is without merit.

"A joint venture is an association of two or more persons to carry out a single enterprise for profit. Whether a joint venture exists is a question of the intent of the parties." *Fitchie v. Yurko*, 212 Ill. App. 3d 216, 570 N.E.2d 892, 899–900, 156 Ill. Dec. 416 (1992). In examining the parties' intent, a court should look to the following elements: (1) an agreement, express or implied, to carry on an enterprise; (2) a demonstration of intent by the parties to be joint venturers; (3) a joint interest, as reflected in the contribution of property, finances, effort, skill or knowledge by each party to the joint venture; (4) a measure of proprietorship or joint control over the enterprise; and (5) a provision for sharing of profits or losses. Id. at 900.

Plaintiff asserts that "Green Cross were co-venturers in the collection of plasma for use in plasma-derived products, and the sale of those products." (Pl's Supp.Resp. at 12.) However, the evidence does not support the finding of an intent to carry out a joint venture. Green Cross created Alpha to ensure that Green Cross would have an adequate supply of plasma, but there is no evidence that the parties intended that Alpha's plasma collection would be part of a joint venture. There is some, though not much, evidence that Green Cross may have contributed some funds to Alpha. In addition, there is evidence that Green Cross and Alpha collaborated on some research and development. However, there is no evidence that they collaborated on any work related to plasma collection. There is some, but again not much, evidence that Green Cross exercises limited control over Alpha, but there is no evidence that Green Cross exerted any control over Alpha's plasma collection activities. There is no evidence of any provision for sharing of profits or losses from the purported joint venture. Indeed, there is no evidence that Green Cross was involved in the collection of plasma by Alpha, and there is no evidence that the sales of plasma from Alpha to Green Cross were anything other than market sales. Plaintiff has not established the existence of a joint venture between Alpha and Green Cross.

Conclusion

The analysis under the various tests outlined above is consistent with notions of due process. Under federal due process standards, a court may exercise personal jurisdiction over a nonresident party if the party has purposely established minimum contacts with the forum state. *Here, Green Cross itself has not established minimum contacts with Illinois, the activities of Alpha cannot be attributed to Green Cross, and there is insufficient evidence that Green Cross participated in a joint venture with Alpha in Illinois. Moreover, requiring Green Cross to submit to the jurisdiction of this court would impose a considerable burden on Green Cross. Green Cross is a Japanese company with no office or employees in Illinois. Green Cross does not have sufficient contacts with the State of Illinois to permit this court to exercise jurisdiction over Green Cross. Green Cross is not doing business in Illinois, and the claims do not arise out of a tortious act or a business transaction by Green Cross in Illinois. Alpha has not been shown to be the alter ego of Green Cross, and Green Cross does not substantially control Alpha. Therefore jurisdiction over Alpha is insufficient to establish jurisdiction over Green Cross. Finally, Green Cross and Alpha were not joint venturers.* [Emphasis added.] Green Cross' motion to dismiss for lack of personal jurisdiction is granted. The complaint is dismissed as to the defendant Green Cross.

QUESTIONS

What must a plaintiff show under Illinois law to allow a court to "pierce the corporate veil" and exercise personal jurisdiction over a parent company by virtue of the activities within the state of a subsidiary? What if by contract the parent firm has "appointed" the subsidiary as its agent for all sales and distribution in North America? How would jurisdiction over the parent ordinarily be established?

HELICOPTEROS NACIONALES DE COLOMBIA v. HALL[*]
466 U.S. 408 (1984)

JUSTICE BLACKMUN delivered the opinion of the Court.

We granted certiorari in this case to decide whether the Supreme Court of Texas correctly ruled that the contacts of a foreign corporation with the State of Texas were sufficient to allow a Texas state court to assert jurisdiction over the corporation in a cause of action not arising out of or related to the corporation's activities within the State.

---

[*] Footnotes omitted.

I

Petitioner Helicopteros Nacionales de Colombia, S.A. (Helicol), is a Colombian corporation with its principal place of business in the city of Bogota in that country. It is engaged in the business of providing helicopter transportation for oil and construction companies in South America. On January 26, 1976, a helicopter owned by Helicol crashed in Peru. Four United States citizens were among those who lost their lives in the accident. Respondents are the survivors and representatives of the four decedents.

At the time of the crash, respondents' decedents were employed by Consorcio, a Peruvian consortium, and were working on a pipeline in Peru. Consorcio is the alter ego of a joint venture named Williams-Sedco-Horn (WSH). The venture had its headquarters in Houston, Tex. Consorcio had been formed to enable the venturers to enter into a contract with Petro Peru, the Peruvian state-owned oil company. Consorcio was to construct a pipeline for Petro Peru running from the interior of Peru westward to the Pacific Ocean. Peruvian law forbade construction of the pipeline by any non-Peruvian entity.

Consorcio/WSH needed helicopters to move personnel, materials, and equipment into and out of the construction area. In 1974, upon request of Consorcio/WSH, the chief executive officer of Helicol, Francisco Restrepo, flew to the United States and conferred in Houston with representatives of the three joint venturers. At that meeting, there was a discussion of prices, availability, working conditions, fuel, supplies, and housing. Restrepo represented that Helicol could have the first helicopter on the job in 15 days. The Consorcio/WSH representatives decided to accept the contract proposed by Restrepo. Helicol began performing before the agreement was formally signed in Peru on November 11, 1974. The contract was written in Spanish on official government stationery and provided that the residence of all the parties would be Lima, Peru. It further stated that controversies arising out of the contract would be submitted to the jurisdiction of Peruvian courts. In addition, it provided that Consorcio/WSH would make payments to Helicol's account with the Bank of America in New York City.

Aside from the negotiation session in Houston between Restrepo and the representatives of Consorcio/WSH, Helicol had other contacts with Texas. During the years 1970–1977, it purchased helicopters (approximately 80% of its fleet), spare parts, and accessories for more than $4 million from Bell Helicopter Company in Fort Worth. In that period, Helicol sent prospective pilots to Fort Worth for training and to ferry the aircraft to South America. It also sent management and maintenance personnel to visit Bell Helicopter in Fort Worth during the same period in order to receive "plant familiarization" and for technical consultation. Helicol received into its New York City and Panama City, Fla., bank accounts over $5 million in payments from Consorcio/WSH drawn upon First City National Bank of Houston.

Beyond the foregoing, there have been no other business contacts between Helicol and the State of Texas. Helicol never has been authorized to do business in Texas and never has had an agent for the service of process within the State. It never has performed helicopter operations in Texas or sold any product that reached Texas, never solicited business in Texas, never signed any contract in Texas, never had any employee based there, and never recruited an employee in Texas. In addition, Helicol never has owned real or personal property in Texas and never has maintained an office or establishment there. Helicol has maintained no records in Texas and has no shareholders in that State. None of the respondents or their decedents were domiciled in Texas, but all of the decedents were hired in Houston by Consorcio/WSH to work on the Petro Peru pipeline project.

Respondents instituted wrongful-death actions in the District Court of Harris County, Tex., against Consorcio/WSH, Bell Helicopter Company, and Helicol. Helicol filed special appearances and moved to dismiss the actions for lack of in personam jurisdiction over it. The motion was denied. After a consolidated jury trial, judgment was entered against Helicol on a jury verdict of $1,141,200 in favor of respondents.

The Texas Court of Civil Appeals, Houston, First District, reversed the judgment of the District Court, holding that in personam jurisdiction over Helicol was lacking. The Supreme Court of Texas, with three justices dissenting, initially affirmed the judgment of the Court of Civil Appeals. App. to Pet. for Cert. 46a–62a. Seven months later, however, on motion for rehearing, the court withdrew its prior opinions and, again with three justices dissenting, reversed the judgment of the intermediate court. In ruling that the Texas courts had in personam jurisdiction, the Texas Supreme Court first held that the State's long-arm statute reaches as far as the Due Process Clause of the Fourteenth Amendment permits. Thus, the only question remaining for the court to decide was whether it was consistent with the Due Process Clause for Texas courts to assert in personam jurisdiction over Helicol.

II

The Due Process Clause of the Fourteenth Amendment operates to limit the power of a State to assert in personam jurisdiction over a nonresident defendant. *Pennoyer v. Neff*, 95 U.S. 714 (1878). Due process requirements are satisfied when in personam jurisdiction is asserted over a nonresident corporate defendant that has "certain minimum contacts with [the forum] such that the maintenance of the suit does not offend 'traditional notions of fair play and substantial justice.'" *International Shoe Co. v. Washington*, 326 U.S. 310, 316 (1945), quoting *Milliken v. Meyer*, 311 U.S. 457, 463 (1940). When a controversy is related to or "arises out of" a defendant's contacts with the forum, the Court has said that a "relationship among the defendant, the forum, and the litigation" is the essential foundation of in personam jurisdiction. *Shaffer v. Heitner*, 433 U.S. 186, 204 (1977).

Even when the cause of action does not arise out of or relate to the foreign corporation's activities in the forum State, due process is not offended by a State's subjecting the corporation to its in personam jurisdiction when there are sufficient contacts between the State and the foreign corporation. [Emphasis added.] In *Perkins* [*v. Benguet Consolidated Mining Co.*, 342 U.S. 437 (1952)], the Court addressed a situation in which state courts had asserted general jurisdiction over a defendant foreign corporation. During the Japanese occupation of the Philippine Islands, the president and general manager of a Philippine mining corporation maintained an office in Ohio from which he conducted activities on behalf of the company. He kept company files and held directors' meetings in the office, carried on correspondence relating to the business, distributed salary checks drawn on two active Ohio bank accounts, engaged an Ohio bank to act as transfer agent, and supervised policies dealing with the rehabilitation of the corporation's properties in the Philippines. In short, the foreign corporation, through its president, "ha[d] been carrying on in Ohio a continuous and systematic, but limited, part of its general business," and the exercise of general jurisdiction over the Philippine corporation by an Ohio court was "reasonable and just." 342 U.S., at 438, 445.

All parties to the present case concede that respondents' claims against Helicol did not "arise out of," and are not related to, Helicol's activities within Texas. We thus must explore the nature of Helicol's contacts with the State of Texas to determine whether they constitute the kind of continuous and systematic general business contacts the Court found to exist in Perkins. We hold that they do not. [Emphasis added.]

It is undisputed that Helicol does not have a place of business in Texas and never has been licensed to do business in the State. *Basically, Helicol's contacts with Texas consisted of sending its chief executive officer to Houston for a contract-negotiation session; accepting into its New York bank account checks drawn on a Houston bank; purchasing helicopters, equipment, and training services from Bell Helicopter for substantial sums; and sending personnel to Bell's facilities in Fort Worth for training.* [Emphasis added.]

The one trip to Houston by Helicol's chief executive officer for the purpose of negotiating the transportation-services contract with Consorcio/WSH cannot be described or regarded as a contact of a "continuous and systematic" nature, as Perkins described it, see also *International Shoe Co. v. Washington*, 326 U.S., at 320, and thus cannot support an assertion of in personam jurisdiction over Helicol by a Texas court. Similarly, Helicol's acceptance from Consorcio/WSH of checks drawn on a Texas bank is of negligible significance for purposes of determining whether Helicol had sufficient contacts in Texas. There is no indication that Helicol ever requested that the checks be drawn on a Texas bank or that there was any negotiation between Helicol and Consorcio/WSH with respect to the location or identity of the bank on which checks would be drawn. Common sense and everyday experience suggest that, absent unusual circumstances, the bank on which a check is drawn is generally of little consequence to the payee and is a matter left to the discretion of the drawer. Such unilateral activity of another party or a third person is not an appropriate consideration when determining whether a defendant has sufficient contacts with a forum State to justify an assertion of jurisdiction.

The Texas Supreme Court focused on the purchases and the related training trips in finding contacts sufficient to support an assertion of jurisdiction. We do not agree with that assessment, for the Court's opinion in *Rosenberg Bros. & Co. v. Curtis Brown Co.*, 260 U.S. 516 (1923) (Brandeis, J., for a unanimous tribunal), makes clear that purchases and related trips, standing alone, are not a sufficient basis for a State's assertion of jurisdiction.

The defendant in *Rosenberg* was a small retailer in Tulsa, Okla., who dealt in men's clothing and furnishings. It never had applied for a license to do business in New York, nor had it at any time authorized suit to be brought against it there. It never had an established place of business in New York and never regularly carried on business in that State. Its only connection with New York was that it purchased from New York wholesalers a large portion of the merchandise sold in its Tulsa store. The purchases sometimes were made by correspondence and sometimes through visits to New York by an officer of the defendant. The Court concluded: "Visits on such business, even if occurring at regular intervals, would not warrant the inference that the corporation was present within the jurisdiction of [New York]." *Id.*, at 518.

This Court in *International Shoe* acknowledged and did not repudiate its holding in *Rosenberg*. See 326 U.S., at 318. *In accordance with Rosenberg, we hold that mere purchases, even if occurring at regular intervals, are not enough to warrant a State's assertion of in personam jurisdiction over a nonresident corporation in a cause of action not related to those purchase transactions. Nor can we conclude that the fact that Helicol sent personnel into Texas for training in connection with the purchase of helicopters and equipment in that State in any way enhanced the nature of Helicol's contacts with Texas.* [Emphasis added.] The training was a part of the package of goods and services purchased by Helicol from Bell Helicopter. The brief presence of Helicol employees in Texas for the purpose of attending the training sessions is no more a significant contact than were the trips to New York made by the buyer for the retail store in Rosenberg.

III

We hold that Helicol's contacts with the State of Texas were insufficient to satisfy the requirements of the Due Process Clause of the Fourteenth Amendment. Accordingly, we reverse the judgment of the Supreme Court of Texas.

It is so ordered.

JUSTICE BRENNAN, dissenting. [Omitted.]

QUESTIONS

1. Assume that Helicopteros insisted that the helicopters purchased from Bell in Texas be equipped with seats purchased from a Colombian manufacturer that subsequently sold them to Bell in Texas and that the plaintiffs in the action alleged that a contributing cause of the accident was the negligent design of the seats. Would Texas courts have adjudicatory jurisdiction over the seat manufacturer?

2. Would your answer differ had Bell purchased the allegedly defective seats in China from a small manufacturer that mainly produces and sells seats for automobiles to a Korean automaker that exports automobiles throughout the Pacific region, including the United States?

ASAHI METAL INDUSTRY CO., LTD. v. SUPERIOR COURT OF CALIFORNIA, SOLANO COUNTY (CHENG SHIN RUBBER INDUSTRIAL CO., LTD., REAL PARTY IN INTEREST)
480 U.S. 102 (1987)

JUSTICE O'CONNOR announced the judgment of the Court and delivered the unanimous opinion of the Court with respect to Part I, the opinion of the Court with respect to Part II-B, in which THE CHIEF JUSTICE, JUSTICE BRENNAN, JUSTICE WHITE, JUSTICE MARSHALL, JUSTICE BLACKMUN, JUSTICE POWELL, and JUSTICE STEVENS join, and an opinion with respect to Parts II-A and III, in which THE CHIEF JUSTICE, JUSTICE POWELL, and JUSTICE SCALIA join.

This case presents the question whether the mere awareness on the part of a foreign defendant that the components it manufactured, sold, and delivered outside the United States would reach the forum State in the stream of commerce constitutes "minimum contacts" between the defendant and the forum State such that the exercise of jurisdiction "does not offend 'traditional notions of fair play and substantial justice.'" *International Shoe Co. v. Washington*, 326 U.S. 310, 316 (1945), quoting *Milliken v. Meyer*, 311 U.S. 457, 463 (1940).

I

On September 23, 1978, on Interstate Highway 80 in Solano County, California, Gary Zurcher lost control of his Honda motorcycle and collided with a tractor. Zurcher was severely injured, and his passenger and wife, Ruth Ann Moreno, was killed. In September 1979, Zurcher filed a product liability action in the Superior Court of the State of California in and for the County of Solano. Zurcher alleged that the 1978 accident was caused by a sudden loss of air and an explosion in the rear tire of the motorcycle, and alleged that the motorcycle tire, tube, and sealant were defective. Zurcher's complaint named, inter alia, Cheng Shin Rubber Industrial Co., Ltd. (Cheng Shin), the Taiwanese manufacturer of the tube. Cheng Shin in turn filed a cross-complaint seeking indemnification from its codefendants and from petitioner, Asahi Metal Industry Co., Ltd. (Asahi), the manufacturer of the tube's valve assembly. Zurcher's claims against Cheng Shin and the other defendants were eventually settled and dismissed, leaving only Cheng Shin's indemnity action against Asahi.

California's long-arm statute authorizes the exercise of jurisdiction "on any basis not inconsistent with the Constitution of this state or of the United States." Cal.Civ.Proc.Code Ann. § 410.10 (West 1973). Asahi moved to quash Cheng Shin's service of summons, arguing the State could not exert jurisdiction over it consistent with the Due Process Clause of the Fourteenth Amendment.

In relation to the motion, the following information was submitted by Asahi and Cheng Shin. Asahi is a Japanese corporation. It manufactures tire valve assemblies in Japan and sells the assemblies to Cheng Shin, and to several other tire manufacturers, for use as components in finished tire tubes. Asahi's sales to Cheng Shin took place in Taiwan. The shipments from Asahi to Cheng Shin were sent from

II. COMMON LAW APPROACHES — THE UNITED STATES

Japan to Taiwan. Cheng Shin bought and incorporated into its tire tubes 150,000 Asahi valve assemblies in 1978; 500,000 in 1979; 500,000 in 1980; 100,000 in 1981; and 100,000 in 1982. Sales to Cheng Shin accounted for 1.24 percent of Asahi's income in 1981 and 0.44 percent in 1982. Cheng Shin alleged that approximately 20 percent of its sales in the United States are in California. Cheng Shin purchases valve assemblies from other suppliers as well, and sells finished tubes throughout the world.

In 1983 an attorney for Cheng Shin conducted an informal examination of the valve stems of the tire tubes sold in one cycle store in Solano County. The attorney declared that of the approximately 115 tire tubes in the store, 97 were purportedly manufactured in Japan or Taiwan, and of those 97, 21 valve stems were marked with the circled letter "A", apparently Asahi's trademark. Of the 21 Asahi valve stems, 12 were incorporated into Cheng Shin tire tubes. The store contained 41 other Cheng Shin tubes that incorporated the valve assemblies of other manufacturers. Declaration of Kenneth B. Shepard in Opposition to Motion to Quash Subpoena, App. to Brief for Respondent 5-6. An affidavit of a manager of Cheng Shin whose duties included the purchasing of component parts stated: " 'In discussions with Asahi regarding the purchase of valve stem assemblies the fact that my Company sells tubes throughout the world and specifically the United States has been discussed. I am informed and believe that Asahi was fully aware that valve stem assemblies sold to my Company and to others would end up throughout the United States and in California.' " 39 Cal. 3d 35, 48, n. 4, 216 Cal. Rptr. 385, 392, n. 4, 702 P.2d 543, 549–550, n. 4 (1985). An affidavit of the president of Asahi, on the other hand, declared that Asahi " 'has never contemplated that its limited sales of tire valves to Cheng Shin in Taiwan would subject it to lawsuits in California.' " *Ibid.* The record does not include any contract between Cheng Shin and Asahi. Tr. of Oral Arg. 24.

Primarily on the basis of the above information, the Superior Court denied the motion to quash summons, stating: "Asahi obviously does business on an international scale. It is not unreasonable that they defend claims of defect in their product on an international scale." Order Denying Motion to Quash Summons, *Zurcher v. Dunlop Tire & Rubber Co.*, No. 76180 (Super. Ct., Solano County, Cal., Apr. 20, 1983).

The Court of Appeal of the State of California issued a peremptory writ of mandate commanding the Superior Court to quash service of summons. The court concluded that "it would be unreasonable to require Asahi to respond in California solely on the basis of ultimately realized foreseeability that the product into which its component was embodied would be sold all over the world including California." App. to Pet. for Cert. B5–B6.

The Supreme Court of the State of California reversed and discharged the writ issued by the Court of Appeal. 39 Cal. 3d 35, 216 Cal. Rptr. 385, 702 P.2d 543 (1985). The court observed: "Asahi has no offices, property or agents in California. It solicits no business in California and has made no direct sales [in California]." *Id.*, at 48, 216 Cal. Rptr., at 392, n. 4, 702 P.2d, at 549. Moreover, "Asahi did not design or control the system of distribution that carried its valve assemblies into California." *Id.*, at 49, 216 Cal. Rptr., at 392, 702 P.2d, at 549. Nevertheless, the court found the exercise of jurisdiction over Asahi to be consistent with the Due Process

Clause. It concluded that Asahi knew that some of the valve assemblies sold to Cheng Shin would be incorporated into tire tubes sold in California, and that Asahi benefited indirectly from the sale in California of products incorporating its components. The court considered Asahi's intentional act of placing its components into the stream of commerce — that is, by delivering the components to Cheng Shin in Taiwan — coupled with Asahi's awareness that some of the components would eventually find their way into California, sufficient to form the basis for state court jurisdiction under the Due Process Clause.

We granted certiorari, 475 U.S. 1044 (1986), and now reverse.

II

A

[O'CONNER, REHNQUIST, POWELL, SCALIA]

The Due Process Clause of the Fourteenth Amendment limits the power of a state court to exert personal jurisdiction over a nonresident defendant. "[T]he constitutional touchstone" of the determination whether an exercise of personal jurisdiction comports with due process "remains whether the defendant purposefully established 'minimum contacts' in the forum State." *Burger King Corp. v. Rudzewicz*, 471 U.S. 462, 474 (1985), quoting *International Shoe Co. v. Washington*, 326 U.S., at 316. Most recently we have reaffirmed the oft-quoted reasoning of *Hanson v. Denckla*, 357 U.S. 235, 253 (1958), that minimum contacts must have a basis in "some act by which the defendant purposefully avails itself of the privilege of conducting activities within the forum State, thus invoking the benefits and protections of its laws." *Burger King*, 471 U.S., at 475. "Jurisdiction is proper . . . where the contacts proximately result from actions by the defendant himself that create a 'substantial connection' with the forum State." *Ibid.*, quoting *McGee v. International Life Insurance Co.*, 355 U.S. 220, 223, (1957) (emphasis in original).

Applying the principle that minimum contacts must be based on an act of the defendant, the Court in *World-Wide Volkswagen Corp. v. Woodson*, 444 U.S. 286 (1980), rejected the assertion that a consumer's unilateral act of bringing the defendant's product into the forum State was a sufficient constitutional basis for personal jurisdiction over the defendant. It had been argued in *World-Wide Volkswagen* that because an automobile retailer and its wholesale distributor sold a product mobile by design and purpose, they could foresee being haled into court in the distant States into which their customers might drive. The Court rejected this concept of foreseeability as an insufficient basis for jurisdiction under the Due Process Clause. *Id.*, at 295–296. The Court disclaimed, however, the idea that "foreseeability is wholly irrelevant" to personal jurisdiction, concluding that "[t]he forum State does not exceed its powers under the Due Process Clause if it asserts personal jurisdiction over a corporation that delivers its products into the stream of commerce with the expectation that they will be purchased by consumers in the forum State." *Id.*, at 297–298. The Court reasoned:

"When a corporation 'purposefully avails itself of the privilege of conducting activities within the forum State,' *Hanson v. Denckla*, 357 U.S. [235,] 253, it has clear notice that it is subject to suit there, and can act to alleviate the risk of burdensome litigation by procuring insurance, passing the expected costs on to customers, or, if the risks are too great, severing its connection with the State. Hence if the sale of a product of a manufacturer or distributor . . . is not simply an isolated occurrence, but arises from the efforts of the manufacturer or distributor to serve, directly or indirectly, the market for its product in other States, it is not unreasonable to subject it to suit in one of those States if its allegedly defective merchandise has there been the source of injury to its owners or to others." *Id.*, at 297.

In *World-Wide Volkswagen* itself, the state court sought to base jurisdiction not on any act of the defendant, but on the foreseeable unilateral actions of the consumer. Since *World-Wide Volkswagen*, lower courts have been confronted with cases in which the defendant acted by placing a product in the stream of commerce, and the stream eventually swept defendant's product into the forum State, but the defendant did nothing else to purposefully avail itself of the market in the forum State. Some courts have understood the Due Process Clause, as interpreted in *World-Wide Volkswagen*, to allow an exercise of personal jurisdiction to be based on no more than the defendant's act of placing the product in the stream of commerce. Other courts have understood the Due Process Clause and the above-quoted language in *World-Wide Volkswagen* to require the action of the defendant to be more purposefully directed at the forum State than the mere act of placing a product in the stream of commerce.

The reasoning of the Supreme Court of California in the present case illustrates the former interpretation of *World-Wide Volkswagen*. The Supreme Court of California held that, because the stream of commerce eventually brought some valves Asahi sold Cheng Shin into California, Asahi's awareness that its valves would be sold in California was sufficient to permit California to exercise jurisdiction over Asahi consistent with the requirements of the Due Process Clause. The Supreme Court of California's position was consistent with those courts that have held that mere foreseeability or awareness was a constitutionally sufficient basis for personal jurisdiction if the defendant's product made its way into the forum State while still in the stream of commerce.

Other courts, however, have understood the Due Process Clause to require something more than that the defendant was aware of its product's entry into the forum State through the stream of commerce in order for the State to exert jurisdiction over the defendant. In the present case, for example, the State Court of Appeal did not read the Due Process Clause, as interpreted by *World-Wide Volkswagen*, to allow "mere foreseeability that the product will enter the forum state [to] be enough by itself to establish jurisdiction over the distributor and retailer." App. to Pet. for Cert. B5. In *Humble v. Toyota Motor Co.*, 727 F.2d 709 (CA8 1984), an injured car passenger brought suit against Arakawa Auto Body Company, a Japanese corporation that manufactured car seats for Toyota. Arakawa did no business in the United States; it had no office, affiliate, subsidiary, or agent in the United States; it manufactured its component parts outside the United States and delivered them to Toyota Motor Company in Japan. The Court of Appeals, adopting the reasoning of the District Court in that case, noted that although it "does not doubt that Arakawa could have foreseen that its product would find its way into the United States," it would be "manifestly unjust" to require Arakawa to defend itself in the United States.

We now find this latter position to be consonant with the requirements of due process. The "substantial connection," between the defendant and the forum State necessary for a finding of minimum contacts must come about by an action of the defendant purposefully directed toward the forum State. *The placement of a product into the stream of commerce, without more, is not an act of the defendant purposefully directed toward the forum State. Additional conduct of the defendant may indicate an intent or purpose to serve the market in the forum State, for example, designing the product for the market in the forum State, advertising in the forum State, establishing channels for providing regular advice to customers in the forum State, or marketing the product through a distributor who has agreed to serve as the sales agent in the forum State. But a defendant's awareness that the stream of commerce may or will sweep the product into the forum State does not convert the mere act of placing the product into the stream into an act purposefully directed toward the forum State.* [Emphasis added.]

Assuming, arguendo, that respondents have established Asahi's awareness that some of the valves sold to Cheng Shin would be incorporated into tire tubes sold in California, respondents have not demonstrated any action by Asahi to purposefully avail itself of the California market. Asahi does not do business in California. It has no office, agents, employees, or property in California. It does not advertise or otherwise solicit business in California. It did not create, control, or employ the distribution system that brought its valves to California. There is no evidence that Asahi designed its product in anticipation of sales in California. On the basis of these facts, the exertion of personal jurisdiction over Asahi by the Superior Court of California exceeds the limits of due process.

B

[All JUSTICES except SCALIA]

The strictures of the Due Process Clause forbid a state court to exercise personal jurisdiction over Asahi under circumstances that would offend " 'traditional notions of fair play and substantial justice.' " *International Shoe Co. v. Washington*, 326 U.S., at 316; quoting *Milliken v. Meyer*, 311 U.S., at 463.

We have previously explained that the determination of the reasonableness of the exercise of jurisdiction in each case will depend on an evaluation of several factors. A court must consider the burden on the defendant, the interests of the forum State, and the plaintiff's interest in obtaining relief. It must also weigh in its determination "the interstate judicial system's interest in obtaining the most efficient resolution of controversies; and the shared interest of the several States in furthering fundamental substantive social policies." World-Wide Volkswagen, 444 U.S., at 292 (citations omitted).

A consideration of these factors in the present case clearly reveals the unrea-

II. COMMON LAW APPROACHES — THE UNITED STATES 77

sonableness of the assertion of jurisdiction over Asahi, even apart from the question of the placement of goods in the stream of commerce. [Emphasis added.]

Certainly the burden on the defendant in this case is severe. Asahi has been commanded by the Supreme Court of California not only to traverse the distance between Asahi's headquarters in Japan and the Superior Court of California in and for the County of Solano, but also to submit its dispute with Cheng Shin to a foreign nation's judicial system. The unique burdens placed upon one who must defend oneself in a foreign legal system should have significant weight in assessing the reasonableness of stretching the long arm of personal jurisdiction over national borders.

When minimum contacts have been established, often the interests of the plaintiff and the forum in the exercise of jurisdiction will justify even the serious burdens placed on the alien defendant. In the present case, however, the interests of the plaintiff and the forum in California's assertion of jurisdiction over Asahi are slight. All that remains is a claim for indemnification asserted by Cheng Shin, a Taiwanese corporation, against Asahi. The transaction on which the indemnification claim is based took place in Taiwan; Asahi's components were shipped from Japan to Taiwan. Cheng Shin has not demonstrated that it is more convenient for it to litigate its indemnification claim against Asahi in California rather than in Taiwan or Japan.

Because the plaintiff is not a California resident, California's legitimate interests in the dispute have considerably diminished. The Supreme Court of California argued that the State had an interest in "protecting its consumers by ensuring that foreign manufacturers comply with the state's safety standards." 39 Cal. 3d, at 49, 216 Cal. Rptr., at 392, 702 P.2d, at 550. The State Supreme Court's definition of California's interest, however, was overly broad. The dispute between Cheng Shin and Asahi is primarily about indemnification rather than safety standards. Moreover, it is not at all clear at this point that California law should govern the question whether a Japanese corporation should indemnify a Taiwanese corporation on the basis of a sale made in Taiwan and a shipment of goods from Japan to Taiwan. The possibility of being haled into a California court as a result of an accident involving Asahi's components undoubtedly creates an additional deterrent to the manufacture of unsafe components; however, similar pressures will be placed on Asahi by the purchasers of its components as long as those who use Asahi components in their final products, and sell those products in California, are subject to the application of California tort law.

World-Wide Volkswagen also admonished courts to take into consideration the interests of the "several States," in addition to the forum State, in the efficient judicial resolution of the dispute and the advancement of substantive policies. In the present case, this advice calls for a court to consider the procedural and substantive policies of other nations whose interests are affected by the assertion of jurisdiction by the California court. The procedural and substantive interests of other nations in a state court's assertion of jurisdiction over an alien defendant will differ from case to case. In every case, however, those interests, as well as the Federal interest in Government's foreign relations policies, will be best served by a careful inquiry into the reasonableness of the assertion of jurisdiction in the particular case, and an unwillingness to find the serious burdens on an alien defendant outweighed by minimal interests on the part of the plaintiff or the forum State. "Great care and reserve should be exercised when extending our notions of personal jurisdiction into the international field." *United States v. First National City Bank*, 379 U.S. 378, 404 (1965) (Harlan, J., dissenting).

Considering the international context, the heavy burden on the alien defendant, and the slight interests of the plaintiff and the forum State, the exercise of personal jurisdiction by a California court over Asahi in this instance would be unreasonable and unfair. [Emphasis added.]

III

[O'CONNER, REHNQUIST, POWELL, and SCALIA]

Because the facts of this case do not establish minimum contacts such that the exercise of personal jurisdiction is consistent with fair play and substantial justice, the judgment of the Supreme Court of California is reversed, and the case is remanded for further proceedings not inconsistent with this opinion.

It is so ordered.

JUSTICE BRENNAN, with whom JUSTICE WHITE, JUSTICE MARSHALL, and JUSTICE BLACKMUN join, concurring in part and concurring in the judgment.

I do not agree with the interpretation in Part II-A of the stream-of-commerce theory, nor with the conclusion that Asahi did not "purposely avail itself of the California market." Ante, at 1034. I do agree, however, with the Court's conclusion in Part II-B that the exercise of personal jurisdiction over Asahi in this case would not comport with "fair play and substantial justice," International Shoe Co. v. Washington, 326 U.S. 310, 320 (1945). [Emphasis added.] This is one of those rare cases in which "minimum requirements inherent in the concept of 'fair play and substantial justice'... defeat the reasonableness of jurisdiction even [though] the defendant has purposefully engaged in forum activities." *Burger King Corp. v. Rudzewicz*, 471 U.S. 462, 477–478 (1985). I therefore join Parts I and II-B of the Court's opinion, and write separately to explain my disagreement with Part II-A.

Part II-A states that "a defendant's awareness that the stream of commerce may or will sweep the product into the forum State does not convert the mere act of placing the product into the stream into an act purposefully directed toward the forum State." *Ante*, at 1033. Under this view, a plaintiff would be required to show "[a]dditional conduct" directed toward the forum before finding the exercise of jurisdiction over the defendant to be consistent with the Due Process Clause. *Ibid*. I see no need for such a showing, however. The stream of commerce refers not to unpredictable currents or eddies, but to the regular and anticipated flow of products from manufacture to distribution to retail sale. As long as a participant in this process is aware that the final product is being marketed in the forum State, the possibility of a lawsuit there cannot come as a surprise. Nor will the litigation present a burden for which there is no corresponding benefit. A defendant who has placed goods in the stream of commerce benefits economically from the retail sale of the final product in the forum State, and indirectly benefits from the State's laws that regulate and facilitate commercial activity. These benefits accrue regardless of whether that participant directly conducts business in the forum State, or engages in additional conduct directed toward that State. Accordingly, most courts and commentators have found that jurisdiction premised on the placement of a product into the stream of commerce is consistent with the Due Process Clause, and have not required a showing of additional conduct.

The endorsement in Part II-A of what appears to be the minority view among Federal Courts of Appeals represents a marked retreat from the analysis in *World-Wide Volkswagen v. Woodson*, 444 U.S. 286, (1980).

The Court reasoned that when a corporation may reasonably anticipate litigation in a particular forum, it cannot claim that such litigation is unjust or unfair, because it "can act to alleviate the risk of burdensome litigation by procuring insurance, passing the expected costs on to consumers, or, if the risks are too great, severing its connection with the State." *Ibid*.

The Court in *World-Wide Volkswagen* thus took great care to distinguish "between a case involving goods which reach a distant State through a chain of distribution and a case involving goods which reach the same State because a consumer . . . took them there." *Id.*, at 306–307 (Brennan, J., dissenting). The California Supreme Court took note of this distinction, and correctly concluded that our holding in World-Wide Volkswagen preserved the stream-of-commerce theory.

In this case, the facts found by the California Supreme Court support its finding of minimum contacts. The court found that "[a]lthough Asahi did not design or control the system of distribution that carried its valve assemblies into California, Asahi was aware of the distribution system's operation, and it knew that it would benefit economically from the sale in California of products incorporating its components." App. to Pet. for Cert. C-11. Accordingly, I cannot join the determination in Part II-A that Asahi's regular and extensive sales of component parts to a manufacturer it knew was making regular sales of the final product in California is insufficient to establish minimum contacts with California.

JUSTICE STEVENS, with whom JUSTICE WHITE and JUSTICE BLACKMUN join, concurring in part and concurring in the judgment.

The judgment of the Supreme Court of California should be reversed for the Iberia stated in Part II-B of the Court's opinion. While I join Parts I and II-B, I do not join Part II-A for two Iberia. First, it is not necessary to the Court's decision. An examination of minimum contacts is not always necessary to determine whether a state court's assertion of personal jurisdiction is constitutional. *Part II-B establishes, after considering the factors set forth in World-Wide Volkswagen Corp. v. Woodson, that California's exercise of jurisdiction over Asahi in this case would be "unreasonable and unfair." This finding alone requires reversal* [emphasis added]; this case fits within the rule that "minimum requirements inherent in the concept of 'fair play and substantial justice' may defeat the reasonableness of jurisdiction even if the defendant has purposefully engaged in forum activities."

Burger King, 471 U.S., at 477–478, (quoting *International Shoe Co. v. Washington*). Accordingly, I see no reason in this case for the plurality to articulate "purposeful direction" or any other test as the nexus between an act of a defendant and the forum State that is necessary to establish minimum contacts.

Second, even assuming that the test ought to be formulated here, Part II-A misapplies it to the facts of this case. The plurality seems to assume that an unwavering line can be drawn between "mere awareness" that a component will find its way into the forum State and "purposeful availment" of the forum's market. *Ante*, at 1033. Over the course of its dealings with Cheng Shin, Asahi has arguably engaged in a higher quantum of conduct than "[t]he placement of a product into the stream of commerce, without more. . . ." *Ibid.* Whether or not this conduct rises to the level of purposeful availment requires a constitutional determination that is affected by the volume, the value, and the hazardous character of the components. In most circumstances I would be inclined to conclude that a regular course of dealing that results in deliveries of over 100,000 units annually over a period of several years would constitute "purposeful availment" even though the item delivered to the forum State was a standard product marketed throughout the world.

QUESTIONS

1. The decision that California courts did not have personal jurisdiction over Asahi in this case was unanimous. The nine justices differed, however, in their Iberia. Identify each of the tests articulated in the opinion and the subscribing justices. Which test do you consider to be the most appropriate? Why?

2. In Part II-B of the opinion all of the justices except for Scalia emphasize the "international context" of the case, why do you think Justice Scalia did not join the others in agreement?

3. Given the "international context" of the case, can you think of any argument that it would be reasonable for California courts to have competence to assert personal jurisdiction over Asahi in this and similar cases? Subsequent to the decision, what options might have been available to Cheng Shin to recover from Asahi? Assuming that Asahi was at fault as alleged, what, if any, are the economic consequences in not permitting Cheng Shin to recover in this action? Could an argument be made that adjudication of Cheng Shin's claim against Asahi is reasonable in light of international judicial efficiency? Could a similar argument be made in *Helicopteros* or in the following case — *Goodyear Dunlop Tires Operations S.A. v. Brown?*

GOODYEAR DUNLOP TIRES OPERATIONS S.A. v. BROWN*
564 U.S. ___, 131 S. Ct. 2846 (2011)

JUSTICE GINSBURG delivered the opinion of the Court.

This case concerns the jurisdiction of state courts over corporations organized and operating abroad. We address, in particular, this question: Are foreign subsidiaries of a United States parent corporation amenable to suit in state court on claims unrelated to any activity of the subsidiaries in the forum State?

A bus accident outside Paris that took the lives of two 13-year-old boys from North Carolina gave rise to the litigation we here consider. Attributing the accident to a defective tire manufactured in Turkey at the plant of a foreign subsidiary of The Goodyear Tire and Rubber Company (Goodyear USA), the boys' parents commenced an action for damages in a North Carolina state court; they named as defendants Goodyear USA, an Ohio corporation, and three of its subsidiaries, organized and operating, respectively, in Turkey, France, and Luxembourg. Goodyear USA, which had plants in North Carolina and regularly engaged in commercial activity there, did not contest the North Carolina court's jurisdiction over it; Goodyear USA's foreign subsidiaries, however, maintained that North Carolina lacked adjudicatory authority over them.

A state court's assertion of jurisdiction exposes defendants to the State's coercive power, and is therefore subject to review for compatibility with the Fourteenth Amendment's Due Process Clause. *International Shoe Co. v. Washington*, 326 U.S. 310, 316 (1945) (assertion of jurisdiction over out-of-state corporation must comply with " 'traditional notions of fair play and substantial justice' " (quoting *Milliken v. Meyer*, 311 U.S. 457, 463 (1940))). Opinions in the wake of the pathmarking *International Shoe* decision have differentiated between general or all purpose jurisdiction, and specific or case-linked jurisdiction. *Helicopteros Nacionales de Colombia, S. A. v. Hall*, 466 U.S. 408, 414, nn. 8, 9 (1984).

A court may assert general jurisdiction over foreign (sister-state or foreign-country) corporations to hear any and all claims against them when their affiliations with the State are so "continuous and systematic" as to render them essentially at home in the forum State. See International Shoe, 326 U.S., at 317. Specific jurisdiction, on the other hand, depends on an "affiliatio[n] between the forum and the underlying controversy," principally, activity or an occurrence that takes place in the forum State and is therefore subject to the State's regulation. [Emphasis added.] In contrast to general, all purpose jurisdiction, specific jurisdiction is confined to adjudication of "issues deriving from, or connected with, the very controversy that establishes jurisdiction." von Mehren & Trautman, [Jurisdiction to Adjudicate: A Suggested Analysis, 79 Harv. L. Rev. 1121, 1136 (1966)].

Because the episode-in-suit, the bus accident, occurred in France, and the tire alleged to have caused the accident was manufactured and sold abroad, North Carolina courts lacked specific jurisdiction to adjudicate the controversy. The North Carolina Court of Appeals so acknowledged. *Brown v. Meter*, 199 N. C. App. 50,

---

* Footnotes omitted.

57–58, 681 S. E. 2d 382, 388 (2009). Were the foreign subsidiaries nonetheless amenable to general jurisdiction in North Carolina courts? Confusing or blending general and specific jurisdictional inquiries, the North Carolina courts answered yes. Some of the tires made abroad by Goodyear's foreign subsidiaries, the North Carolina Court of Appeals stressed, had reached North Carolina through "the stream of commerce"; that connection, the Court of Appeals believed, gave North Carolina courts the handle needed for the exercise of general jurisdiction over the foreign corporations. *Id.*, at 67–68, 681 S. E. 2d, at 394–395.

A connection so limited between the forum and the foreign corporation, we hold, is an inadequate basis for the exercise of general jurisdiction. Such a connection does not establish the "continuous and systematic" affiliation necessary to empower North Carolina courts to entertain claims unrelated to the foreign corporation's contacts with the State.

I

On April 18, 2004, a bus destined for Charles de Gaulle Airport overturned on a road outside Paris, France. Passengers on the bus were young soccer players from North Carolina beginning their journey home. Two 13-year-olds, Julian Brown and Matthew Helms, sustained fatal injuries. The boys' parents, respondents in this Court, filed a suit for wrongful-death damages in the Superior Court of Onslow County, North Carolina, in their capacity as administrators of the boys' estates. Attributing the accident to a tire that failed when its plies separated, the parents alleged negligence in the "design, construction, testing, and inspection" of the tire. 199 N. C. App., at 51, 681 S. E.2d, at 384 (internal quotation marks omitted).

Goodyear Luxembourg Tires, SA (Goodyear Luxembourg), Goodyear Lastikleri T. A. S. (Goodyear Turkey), and Goodyear Dunlop Tires France, SA (Goodyear France), petitioners here, were named as defendants. Incorporated in Luxembourg, Turkey, and France, respectively, petitioners are indirect subsidiaries of Goodyear USA, an Ohio corporation also named as a defendant in the suit. Petitioners manufacture tires primarily for sale in European and Asian markets. Their tires differ in size and construction from tires ordinarily sold in the United States. They are designed to carry significantly heavier loads, and to serve under road conditions and speed limits in the manufacturers' primary markets.

In contrast to the parent company, Goodyear USA, which does not contest the North Carolina courts' personal jurisdiction over it, petitioners are not registered to do business in North Carolina. They have no place of business, employees, or bank accounts in North Carolina. They do not design, manufacture, or advertise their products in North Carolina. And they do not solicit business in North Carolina or themselves sell or ship tires to North Carolina customers. Even so, a small percentage of petitioners' tires (tens of thousands out of tens of millions manufactured between 2004 and 2007) were distributed within North Carolina by other Goodyear USA affiliates. These tires were typically custom ordered to equip specialized vehicles such as cement mixers, waste haulers, and boat and horse trailers. Petitioners state, and respondents do not here deny, that the type of tire involved in the accident, a Goodyear Regional RHS tire manufactured by Goodyear Turkey, was never distributed in North Carolina.

Petitioners moved to dismiss the claims against them for want of personal jurisdiction. The trial court denied the motion, and the North Carolina Court of Appeals affirmed. Acknowledging that the claims neither "related to, nor . . . ar[o]se from, [petitioners'] contacts with North Carolina," the Court of Appeals confined its analysis to "general rather than specific jurisdiction," which the court recognized required a "higher threshold" showing: A defendant must have "continuous and systematic contacts" with the forum. *Id.*, at 58, 681 S. E. 2d, at 388 (internal quotation marks omitted). That threshold was crossed, the court determined, when petitioners placed their tires "in the stream of interstate commerce without any limitation on the extent to which those tires could be sold in North Carolina." *Id.*, at 67, 681 S. E. 2d, at 394.

Nothing in the record, the court observed, indicated that petitioners "took any affirmative action to cause tires which they had manufactured to be shipped into North Carolina." *Id.*, at 64, 681 S. E. 2d, at 392. The court found, however, that tires made by petitioners reached North Carolina as a consequence of a "highly-organized distribution process" involving other Goodyear USA subsidiaries. *Id.*, at 67, 681 S. E. 2d, at 394. Petitioners, the court noted, made "no attempt to keep these tires from reaching the North Carolina market." *Id.*, at 66, 681 S. E. 2d, at 393. Indeed, the very tire involved in the accident, the court observed, conformed to tire standards established by the U.S. Department of Transportation and bore markings required for sale in the United States. *Ibid.* As further support, the court invoked North Carolina's "interest in providing a forum in which its citizens are able to seek redress for [their] injuries," and noted the hardship North Carolina plaintiffs would experience "[were they] required to litigate their claims in France," a country to which they have no ties. *Id.*, at 68, 681 S. E. 2d, at 394. The North Carolina Supreme Court denied discretionary review. *Brown v. Meter*, 364 N. C. 128, 695 S. E. 2d 756 (2010).

We granted certiorari to decide whether the general jurisdiction the North Carolina courts asserted over petitioners is consistent with the Due Process Clause of the Fourteenth Amendment.

II

A

The Due Process Clause of the Fourteenth Amendment sets the outer boundaries of a state tribunal's authority to proceed against a defendant. *Shaffer v. Heitner*, 433 U.S. 186, 207 (1977). The canonical opinion in this area remains *International Shoe*, 326 U.S. 310, in which we held that a State may authorize its courts to exercise personal jurisdiction over an out-of-state defendant if the defendant has "certain minimum contacts with [the State] such that the maintenance of the suit does not offend 'traditional notions of fair play and substantial justice.'" *Id.*, at 316 (quoting *Meyer*, 311 U.S., at 463).

Endeavoring to give specific content to the "fair play and substantial justice" concept, the Court in *International Shoe* classified cases involving out-of-state corporate defendants. First, as in *International Shoe* itself, jurisdiction unquestionably could be asserted where the corporation's in-state activity is "continuous and systematic" and *that activity gave rise to the episode-in-suit* [emphasis in opinion]. 326 U.S., at 317. Further, the Court observed, the commission of certain "single or occasional acts" in a State may be sufficient to render a corporation answerable in that State with respect to those acts, though not with respect to matters unrelated to the forum connections. *Id.*, at 318. The heading courts today use to encompass these two *International Shoe* categories is "specific jurisdiction." [Reference and citation omitted.]

International Shoe distinguished from cases that fit within the "specific jurisdiction" categories, "instances in which the continuous corporate operations within a state [are] so substantial and of such a nature as to justify suit against it on causes of action arising from dealings entirely distinct from those activities." 326 U.S., at 318. Adjudicatory authority so grounded is today called "general jurisdiction." Helicopteros, 466 U.S., at 414, n. 9. For an individual, the paradigm forum for the exercise of general jurisdiction is the individual's domicile; for a corporation, it is an equivalent place, one in which the corporation is fairly regarded as at home. [Reference omitted; emphasis added.]

Since *International Shoe*, this Court's decisions have elaborated primarily on circumstances that warrant the exercise of specific jurisdiction, particularly in cases involving "single or occasional acts" occurring or having their impact within the forum State. As a rule in these cases, this Court has inquired whether there was "some act by which the defendant purposefully avail[ed] itself of the privilege of conducting activities within the forum State, thus invoking the benefits and protections of its laws." *Hanson v. Denckla*, 357 U.S. 235, 253 (1958). [Emphasis added.] See, *e.g., World-Wide Volkswagen Corp. v. Woodson*, 444 U.S. 286, 287, 297 (1980) (Oklahoma court may not exercise personal jurisdiction "over a nonresident automobile retailer and its wholesale distributor in a products-liability action, when the defendants' only connection with Oklahoma is the fact that an automobile sold in New York to New York residents became involved in an accident in Oklahoma"); *Burger King Corp. v. Rudzewicz*, 471 U.S. 462, 474–475 (1985) (franchisor headquartered in Florida may maintain breach-of-contract action in Florida against Michigan franchisees, where agreement contemplated ongoing interactions between franchisees and franchisor's headquarters); *Asahi Metal Industry Co. v. Superior Court of Cal., Solano Cty.*, 480 U.S. 102, 105 (1987) (Taiwanese tire manufacturer settled product liability action brought in California and sought indemnification there from Japanese valve assembly manufacturer; Japanese company's "mere awareness . . . that the components it manufactured, sold, and delivered outside the United States would reach the forum State in the stream of commerce" held insufficient to permit California court's adjudication of Taiwanese company's cross-complaint); *id.*, at 109 (opinion of O'Connor, J.); *id.*, at 116–117 (Brennan, J., concurring in part and concurring in judgment). [Reference omitted.]

In only two decisions postdating *International Shoe*, discussed *infra*, at 11–13, has this Court considered whether an out-of-state corporate defendant's in-state contacts were sufficiently "continuous and systematic" to justify the exercise of general jurisdiction over claims unrelated to those contacts: *Perkins v. Benguet Consol. Mining Co.*, 342 U.S. 437 (1952) (general jurisdiction appropriately exercised over Philippine corporation sued in Ohio, where the company's affairs were overseen during World War II); and *Helicopteros*, 466 U.S. 408 (helicopter owned by Colombian corporation crashed in Peru; survivors of U.S. citizens who died in the crash, the Court held, could not maintain wrongful-death actions against the Colombian corporation in Texas, for the corporation's helicopter purchases and purchase-linked activity in Texas were insufficient to subject it to Texas court's general jurisdiction).

B

Many States have enacted long-arm statutes authorizing courts to exercise specific jurisdiction over manufacturers when the events in suit, or some of them, occurred within the forum state . . . . Typically, in such cases, a nonresident defendant, acting *outside* the forum, places in the stream of commerce a product that ultimately causes harm *inside* the forum [emphasis in opinion]. [Reference omitted.]

As the North Carolina Court of Appeals recognized, this provision of the State's long-arm statute "does not apply to this case," for both the act alleged to have caused injury (the fabrication of the allegedly defective tire) and its impact (the accident) occurred outside the forum. . . .

To justify the exercise of general jurisdiction over petitioners, the North Carolina courts relied on the petitioners' placement of their tires in the "stream of commerce." See *supra*, at 5 . . . . The North Carolina court's stream-of-commerce analysis elided the essential difference between case-specific and all-purpose (general) jurisdiction. Flow of a manufacturer's products into the forum, we have explained, may bolster an affiliation germane to *specific* jurisdiction . . . . But ties serving to bolster the exercise of specific jurisdiction do not warrant a determination that, based on those ties, the forum has *general* jurisdiction over a defendant. [Citation omitted.]

A corporation's "continuous activity of some sorts within a state," *International Shoe* instructed, "is not enough to support the demand that the corporation be amenable to suits unrelated to that activity." 326 U.S., at 318. Our 1952 decision in *Perkins v. Benguet Consol. Mining Co.* remains "[t]he textbook case of general jurisdiction appropriately exercised over a foreign corporation that has not consented to suit in the forum." *Donahue v. Far Eastern Air Transport Corp.*, 652 F. 2d 1032, 1037 ((CADC 1981).

. . . .

We next addressed the exercise of general jurisdiction over an out-of-state corporation over three decades later, in *Helicopteros*. In that case, survivors of United States citizens who died in a helicopter crash in Peru instituted wrongful-death actions in a Texas state court against the owner and operator of the helicopter, a Colombian corporation. The Colombian corporation had no place of business in Texas and was not licensed to do business there. "Basically, [the company's] contacts with Texas consisted of sending its chief executive officer to Houston for a contract-negotiation session; accepting into its New York bank account checks drawn on a Houston bank; purchasing helicopters, equipment, and training services from [a Texas enterprise] for substantial sums; and sending personnel to [Texas] for training." 466 U.S., at 416. These links to Texas, we determined, did not "constitute the kind of continuous and systematic general business contacts . . . found to exist in *Perkins*," and were insufficient to support the exercise of jurisdiction over a claim that neither "ar[o]se out of . . . no[r] related to" the defendant's activities in Texas. *Id.*, at 415–416 (internal quotation marks omitted).

Helicopteros concluded that "mere purchases [made in the forum State], even if occurring at regular intervals, are not enough to warrant a State's assertion of [general] jurisdiction over a nonresident corporation in a cause of action not related to those purchase transactions." *Id.*, at 418. We see no reason to differentiate from the ties to Texas held insufficient in *Helicopteros*, the sales of petitioners' tires sporadically made in North Carolina through intermediaries. Under the sprawling view of general jurisdiction urged by respondents and embraced by the North Carolina Court of Appeals, any substantial manufacturer or seller of goods would be amenable to suit, on any claim for relief, wherever its products are distributed. But cf. *World-Wide Volkswagen*, 444 U.S., at 296 (every seller of chattels does not, by virtue of the sale, "appoint the chattel his agent for service of process").

Measured against *Helicopteros* and *Perkins*, North Carolina is not a forum in which it would be permissible to subject petitioners to general jurisdiction. Unlike the defendant in *Perkins*, whose sole wartime business activity was conducted in Ohio, petitioners are in no sense at home in North Carolina. Their attenuated connections to the State, see *supra*, at 4–5, fall far short of the "the continuous and systematic general business contacts" necessary to empower North Carolina to entertain suit against them on claims unrelated to anything that connects them to the State. [Citation omitted.]

C

Respondents belatedly assert a "single enterprise" theory, asking us to consolidate petitioners' ties to North Carolina with those of Goodyear USA and other Goodyear entities. In effect, respondents would have us pierce Goodyear corporate veils, at least for jurisdictional purposes . . . . Neither below nor in their brief in opposition to the petition for certiorari did respondent surge disregard of petitioners' discrete status as subsidiaries and treatment of all Goodyear entities as a "unitary business," so that jurisdiction over the parent would draw in the subsidiaries as well. . . . Respondents have therefore forfeited this contention, and we do not address it. . . .

For the Iberia stated, the judgment of the North Carolina Court of Appeals is

Reversed.

QUESTIONS

1. Assume that the two North Carolina boys had died in a plane accident in France caused by the collision of an Air France jet manufactured by Airbus

in Germany and a private jet owned and operated by a wealthy Swiss businessman. Under what circumstances, if any, would a North Carolina court have adjudicatory jurisdiction over Société Air France SA; its parent company, Air France-KLM; Airbus: its parent company, EADS; or the Swiss businessman?

2. What if the plaintiffs in *Goodyear Dunlop Tires Operations S.A. v. Brown* had been able to show that the Turkish manufacturer was wholly owned and closely managed and effectively controlled by Goodyear USA?

3. Would, in your view, the outcome in *Goodyear Dunlop Tires Operations S.A. v. Brown* have differed had the fatal accident occurred in North Carolina, assuming that the bus involved in the accident had been manufactured in the U.K. by the Wright Group, a small U.K. bus manufacturer, but sold with the tires manufactured in Turkey in the U.S. in a sales promotion event in North Carolina?

J. McINTYRE MACHINERY LTD. v. NICASTRO
564 U.S. ___, 131 S. Ct. 2780 (2011)

JUSTICE KENNEDY announced the judgment of the Court and delivered an opinion, in which THE CHIEF JUSTICE, JUSTICE SCALIA, and JUSTICE THOMAS join.

Whether a person or entity is subject to the jurisdiction of a state court despite not having been present in the State either at the time of suit or at the time of the alleged injury, and despite not having consented to the exercise of jurisdiction, is a question that arises with great frequency in the routine course of litigation. The rules and standards for determining when a State does or does not have jurisdiction over an absent party have been unclear because of decades-old questions left open in *Asahi Metal Industry Co. v. Superior Court of Cal., Solano Cty.*, 480 U.S. 102 (1987).

Here, the Supreme Court of New Jersey, relying in part on *Asahi*, held that New Jersey's courts can exercise jurisdiction over a foreign manufacturer of a product so long as the manufacturer "knows or reasonably should know that its products are distributed through a nationwide distribution system that might lead to those products being sold in any of the fifty states." *Nicastro v. McIntyre Machinery America, Ltd.*, 201 N. J. 48, 76, 77, 987 A. 2d 575, 591, 592 (2010). Applying that test, the court concluded that a British manufacturer of scrap metal machines was subject to jurisdiction in New Jersey, even though at no time had it advertised in, sent goods to, or in any relevant sense targeted the State.

That decision cannot be sustained. Although the New Jersey Supreme Court issued an extensive opinion with careful attention to this Court's cases and to its own precedent, the "stream of commerce" metaphor carried the decision far afield. Due process protects the defendant's right not to be coerced except by lawful judicial power. As a general rule, the exercise of judicial power is not lawful unless the defendant "purposefully avails itself of the privilege of conducting activities within the forum State, thus invoking the benefits and protections of its laws." *Hanson v.*

Denckla, 357 U.S. 235, 253 (1958). There may be exceptions, say, for instance, in cases involving an intentional tort. But the general rule is applicable in this products-liability case, and the so-called "stream-of-commerce" doctrine cannot displace it.

I

This case arises from a products-liability suit filed in New Jersey state court. Robert Nicastro seriously injured his hand while using a metal-shearing machine manufactured by J. McIntyre Machinery, Ltd. (J. McIntyre). The accident occurred in New Jersey, but the machine was manufactured in England, where J. McIntyre is incorporated and operates. The question here is whether the New Jersey courts have jurisdiction over J. McIntyre, notwithstanding the fact that the company at no time either marketed goods in the State or shipped them there. Nicastro was a plaintiff in the New Jersey trial court and is the respondent here; J. McIntyre was a defendant and is now the petitioner.

At oral argument in this Court, Nicastro's counsel stressed three primary facts in defense of New Jersey's assertion of jurisdiction over J. McIntyre. See Tr. of Oral Arg. 29–30.

First, an independent company agreed to sell J. McIntyre's machines in the United States. J. McIntyre itself did not sell its machines to buyers in this country beyond the U.S. distributor, and there is no allegation that the distributor was under J. McIntyre's control.

Second, J. McIntyre officials attended annual conventions for the scrap recycling industry to advertise J. McIntyre's machines alongside the distributor. The conventions took place in various States, but never in New Jersey.

Third, no more than four machines (the record suggests only one, see App. to Pet. for Cert. 130a), including the machine that caused the injuries that are the basis for this suit, ended up in New Jersey.

In addition to these facts emphasized by respondent, the New Jersey Supreme Court noted that J. McIntyre held both United States and European patents on its recycling technology. 201 N. J., at 55, 987 A. 2d, at 579. It also noted that the U.S. distributor "structured [its] advertising and sales efforts in accordance with" J. McIntyre's "direction and guidance whenever possible," and that "at least some of the machines were sold on consignment to" the distributor. *Id.*, at 55, 56, 987 A. 2d, at 579 (internal quotation marks omitted).

In light of these facts, the New Jersey Supreme Court concluded that New Jersey courts could exercise jurisdiction over petitioner without contravention of the Due Process Clause. Jurisdiction was proper, in that court's view, because the injury occurred in New Jersey; because petitioner knew or reasonably should have known "that its products are distributed through a nationwide distribution system that might lead to those products being sold in any of the fifty states"; and because petitioner failed to "take some reasonable step to prevent the distribution of its products in this State." *Id.*, at 77, 987 A. 2d, at 592.

Both the New Jersey Supreme Court's holding and its account of what it called "[t]he stream-of-commerce doctrine of jurisdiction," *id.*, at 80, 987 A. 2d, at 594, were incorrect, however. This Court's *Asahi* decision may be responsible in part for that court's error regarding the stream of commerce, and this case presents an opportunity to provide greater clarity.

II

The Due Process Clause protects an individual's right to be deprived of life, liberty, or property only by the exercise of lawful power. [Citation omitted.] This is no less true with respect to the power of a sovereign to resolve disputes through judicial process than with respect to the power of a sovereign to prescribe rules of conduct for those within its sphere. [Citations omitted.] A court may subject a defendant to judgment only when the defendant has sufficient contacts with the sovereign "such that the maintenance of the suit does not offend 'traditional notions of fair play and substantial justice.'" *International Shoe Co. v. Washington*, 326 U.S. 310, 316 (1945) (quoting *Milliken v. Meyer*, 311 U.S. 457, 463 (1940)). Freeform notions of fundamental fairness divorced from traditional practice cannot transform a judgment rendered in the absence of authority into law. As a general rule, the sovereign's exercise of power requires some act by which the defendant "purposefully avails itself of the privilege of conducting activities within the forum State, thus invoking the benefits and protections of its laws," *Hanson*, 357 U.S., at 253, though in some cases, as with an intentional tort, the defendant might well fall within the State's authority by reason of his attempt to obstruct its laws. In products-liability cases like this one, it is the defendant's purposeful availment that makes jurisdiction consistent with "traditional notions of fair play and substantial justice."

A person may submit to a State's authority in a number of ways. There is, of course, explicit consent. [Citation omitted.] Presence within a State at the time suit commences through service of process is another example. [Citation omitted.] Citizenship or domicile — or, by analogy, incorporation or principal place of business for corporations — also indicates general submission to a State's powers. [Citation omitted.] Each of these examples reveals circumstances, or a course of conduct, from which it is proper to infer an intention to benefit from and thus an intention to submit to the laws of the forum State. [Citation omitted.] These examples support exercise of the general jurisdiction of the State's courts and allow the State to resolve both matters that originate within the State and those based on activities and events elsewhere. [Citation omitted.] By contrast, those who live or operate primarily outside a State have a due process right not to be subjected to judgment in its courts as a general matter.

There is also a more limited form of submission to a State's authority for disputes that "arise out of or are connected with the activities within the state." *International Shoe Co., supra*, at 319. Where a defendant "purposefully avails itself of the privilege of conducting activities within the forum State, thus invoking the benefits and protections of its laws," *Hanson, supra*, at 253, it submits to the judicial power of an otherwise foreign sovereign to the extent that power is exercised in connection with the defendant's activities touching on the State. In other words, submission through contact with and activity directed at a sovereign may justify specific jurisdiction "in a suit arising out of or related to the defendant's contacts with the forum." *Helicopteros, supra*, at 414, n. 8; see also *Goodyear, post*, at 2.

The imprecision arising from *Asahi*, for the most part, results from its statement of the relation between jurisdiction and the "stream of commerce." The stream of commerce, like other metaphors, has its deficiencies as well as its utility. It refers to the movement of goods from manufacturers through distributors to consumers, yet beyond that descriptive purpose its meaning is far from exact. This Court has stated that a defendant's placing goods into the stream of commerce "with the expectation that they will be purchased by consumers within the forum State" may indicate purposeful availment. *World-Wide Volkswagen Corp. v. Woodson*, 444 U.S. 286, 298 (1980) (finding that expectation lacking). But that statement does not amend the general rule of personal jurisdiction. It merely observes that a defendant may in an appropriate case be subject to jurisdiction without entering the forum — itself an unexceptional proposition — as where manufacturers or distributors "seek to serve" a given State's market. *Id.*, at 295. The principal inquiry in cases of this sort is whether the defendant's activities manifest an intention to submit to the power of a sovereign. In other words, the defendant must "purposefully avai[l] itself of the privilege of conducting activities within the forum State, thus invoking the benefits and protections of its laws." *Hanson, supra*, at 253; *Insurance Corp., supra*, at 704–705 ("[A]ctions of the defendant may amount to a legal submission to the jurisdiction of the court"). Sometimes a defendant does so by sending its goods rather than its agents. The defendant's transmission of goods permits the exercise of jurisdiction only where the defendant can be said to have targeted the forum; as a general rule, it is not enough that the defendant might have predicted that its goods will reach the forum State.

In *Asahi*, an opinion by Justice Brennan for four Justices outlined a different approach. It discarded the central concept of sovereign authority in favor of considerations of fairness and foreseeability. As that concurrence contended, "jurisdiction premised on the placement of a product into the stream of commerce [without more] is consistent with the Due Process Clause," for "[a]s long as a participant in this process is aware that the final product is being marketed in the forum State, the possibility of a lawsuit there cannot come as a surprise." 480 U.S., at 117 (opinion concurring in part and concurring in judgment). It was the premise of the concurring opinion that the defendant's ability to anticipate suit renders the assertion of jurisdiction fair. In this way, the opinion made foreseeability the touchstone of jurisdiction.

The standard set forth in Justice Brennan's concurrence was rejected in an opinion written by Justice O'Connor; but the relevant part of that opinion, too, commanded the assent of only four Justices, not a majority of the Court.

That opinion stated: "The 'substantial connection' between the defendant and the forum State necessary for a finding of minimum contacts must come about by an action of the defendant purposefully directed toward the forum State. The placement of a product into the stream of commerce, without more, is not an act of the defendant purposefully directed toward the forum State." *Id.*, at 112 (emphasis deleted; citations omitted).

Since *Asahi* was decided, the courts have sought to reconcile the competing opinions. But Justice Brennan's concurrence, advocating a rule based on general notions of fairness and foreseeability, is inconsistent with the premises of lawful judicial power. This Court's precedents make clear that it is the defendant's actions, not his expectations, that empower a State's courts to subject him to judgment.

The conclusion that jurisdiction is in the first instance a question of authority rather than fairness explains, for example, why the principal opinion in *Burnham* "conducted no independent inquiry into the desirability or fairness" of the rule that service of process within a State suffices to establish jurisdiction over an otherwise foreign defendant. 495 U.S., at 621. As that opinion explained, "[t]he view developed early that each State had the power to hale before its courts any individual who could be found within its borders." *Id.*, at 610. Furthermore, were general fairness considerations the touchstone of jurisdiction, a lack of purposeful availment might be excused where carefully crafted judicial procedures could otherwise protect the defendant's interests, or where the plaintiff would suffer substantial hardship if forced to litigate in a foreign forum. That such considerations have not been deemed controlling is instructive. See, *e.g., World-Wide Volkswagen, supra*, at 294.

Two principles are implicit in the foregoing. First, personal jurisdiction requires a forum-by-forum, or sovereign-by-sovereign, analysis. The question is whether a defendant has followed a course of conduct directed at the society or economy existing within the jurisdiction of a given sovereign, so that the sovereign has the power to subject the defendant to judgment concerning that conduct. Personal jurisdiction, of course, restricts "judicial power not as a matter of sovereignty, but as a matter of individual liberty," for due process protects the individual's right to be subject only to lawful power. *Insurance Corp.*, 456 U.S. 694 (1982). But whether a judicial judgment is lawful depends on whether the sovereign has authority to render it.

The second principle is a corollary of the first. Because the United States is a distinct sovereign, a defendant may in principle be subject to the jurisdiction of the courts of the United States but not of any particular State. This is consistent with the premises and unique genius of our Constitution. Ours is "a legal system unprecedented in form and design, establishing two orders of government, each with its own direct relationship, its own privity, its own set of mutual rights and obligations to the people who sustain it and are governed by it." *U.S. Term Limits, Inc. v. Thornton*, 514 U.S. 779, 838 (1995) (Kennedy, J., concurring). For jurisdiction, a litigant may have the requisite relationship with the United States Government but not with the government of any individual State. That would be an exceptional case, however. If the defendant is a domestic domiciliary, the courts of its home State are available and can exercise general jurisdiction. And if another State were to assert jurisdiction in an inappropriate case, it would upset the federal balance, which posits that each State has a sovereignty that is not subject to unlawful intrusion by other States. Furthermore, foreign corporations will often target or concentrate on particular States, subjecting them to specific jurisdiction in those forums.

It must be remembered, however, that although this case and *Asahi* both involve foreign manufacturers, the undesirable consequences of Justice Brennan's approach are no less significant for domestic producers. The owner of a small Florida farm might sell crops to a large nearby distributor, for example, who might then distribute them to grocers across the country. If foreseeability were the controlling criterion, the farmer could be sued in Alaska or any number of other States' courts without ever leaving town. And the issue of foreseeability may itself be contested so that significant expenses are incurred just on the preliminary issue of jurisdiction. Jurisdictional rules should avoid these costs whenever possible.

The conclusion that the authority to subject a defendant to judgment depends on purposeful availment, consistent with Justice O'Connor's opinion in Asahi, does not by itself resolve many difficult questions of jurisdiction that will arise in particular cases. The defendant's conduct and the economic realities of the market the defendant seeks to serve will differ across cases, and judicial exposition will, in common-law fashion, clarify the contours of that principle. [Emphasis added.]

III

In this case, petitioner directed marketing and sales efforts at the United States. [Emphasis added.] It may be that, assuming it were otherwise empowered to legislate on the subject, the Congress could authorize the exercise of jurisdiction in appropriate courts. That circumstance is not presented in this case, however, and it is neither necessary nor appropriate to address here any constitutional concerns that might be attendant to that exercise of power. [Citation omitted.] Nor is it necessary to determine what substantive law might apply were Congress to authorize jurisdiction in a federal court in New Jersey. [Citation omitted.] A sovereign's legislative authority to regulate conduct may present considerations different from those presented by its authority to subject a defendant to judgment in its courts. *Here the question concerns the authority of a New Jersey state court to exercise jurisdiction, so it is petitioner's purposeful contacts with New Jersey, not with the United States, that alone are relevant.* [Emphasis added]

Respondent has not established that J. McIntyre engaged in conduct purposefully directed at New Jersey. Recall that respondent's claim of jurisdiction centers on three facts: The distributor agreed to sell J. McIntyre's machines in the United States; J. McIntyre officials attended trade shows in several States but not in New Jersey; and up to four machines ended up in New Jersey. The British manufacturer had no office in New Jersey; it neither paid taxes nor owned property there; and it neither advertised in, nor sent any employees to, the State. Indeed, after discovery the trial court found that the "defendant does not have a single contact with New Jersey short of the machine in question ending up in this state." App. to Pet. for Cert. 130a. These facts may reveal an intent to serve the U.S. market, but they do not show that J. McIntyre purposefully availed itself of the New Jersey market.

It is notable that the New Jersey Supreme Court appears to agree, for it could "not find that J. McIntyre had a presence or minimum contacts in this State — in any jurisprudential sense — that would justify a New Jersey court to exercise jurisdiction in this case." 201 N. J., at 61, 987 A. 2d, at 582. The court nonetheless held that petitioner could be sued in New Jersey based on a "stream-of-commerce theory of jurisdiction." *Ibid.* As discussed, however, the stream-of-commerce metaphor cannot supersede either the mandate of the Due Process Clause or the limits on judicial authority that Clause ensures. The New Jersey Supreme Court also cited "significant policy Iberia" to justify its holding, including the State's "strong interest in protecting its citizens from defective products." *Id.*, at 75, 987 A. 2d, at 590. That interest is doubtless strong, but the Constitution commands restraint before discarding liberty in the name of expediency.

Due process protects petitioner's right to be subject only to lawful authority. At no time did petitioner engage in any activities in New Jersey that reveal an intent to invoke or benefit from the protection of its laws. New Jersey is without power to adjudge the rights and liabilities of J. McIntyre, and its exercise of jurisdiction would violate due process. The contrary judgment of the New Jersey Supreme Court is

Reversed.

JUSTICE BREYER, with whom JUSTICE ALITO joins, concurring in the judgment.

The Supreme Court of New Jersey adopted a broad understanding of the scope of personal jurisdiction based on its view that "[t]he increasingly fast-paced globalization of the world economy has removed national borders as barriers to trade." *Nicastro v. McIntyre Machinery America, Ltd.*, 201 N. J. 48, 52, 987 A. 2d 575, 577 (2010). I do not doubt that there have been many recent changes in commerce and communication, many of which are not anticipated by our precedents. But this case does not present any of those issues. So I think it unwise to announce a rule of broad applicability without full consideration of the modern-day consequences.

In my view, the outcome of this case is determined by our precedents. *Based on the facts found by the New Jersey courts, respondent Robert Nicastro failed to meet his burden to demonstrate that it was constitutionally proper to exercise jurisdiction over petitioner J. McIntyre Machinery, Ltd. (British Manufacturer), a British firm that manufactures scrap-metal machines in Great Britain and sells them through an independent distributor in the United States (American Distributor). On that basis, I agree with the plurality that the contrary judgment of the Supreme Court of New Jersey should be reversed.* [Emphasis added.]

I

In asserting jurisdiction over the British Manufacturer, the Supreme Court of New Jersey relied most heavily on three primary facts as providing constitutionally sufficient "contacts" with New Jersey, thereby making it fundamentally fair to hale the British Manufacturer before its courts: (1) The American Distributor on one occasion sold and shipped one machine to a New Jersey customer, namely, Mr. Nicastro's employer, Mr. Curcio; (2) the British Manufacturer permitted, indeed wanted, its independent American Distributor to sell its machines to anyone in America willing to buy them; and (3) representatives of the British Manufacturer attended trade shows in "such cities as Chicago, Las Vegas, New Orleans, Orlando, San Diego, and San Francisco." *Id.*, at 54–55, 987 A. 2d, at 578–579. In my view, these facts do not provide contacts between the British firm and the State of New Jersey constitutionally sufficient to support New Jersey's assertion of jurisdiction in this case. None of our precedents finds that a single isolated sale, even if accompanied by the kind of sales effort indicated here, is sufficient. Rather, this

Court's previous holdings suggest the contrary. The Court has held that a single sale to a customer who takes an accident-causing product to a different State (where the accident takes place) is not a sufficient basis for asserting jurisdiction. [Citation omitted.] And the Court, in separate opinions, has strongly suggested that a single sale of a product in a State does not constitute an adequate basis for asserting jurisdiction over an out-of-state defendant, even if that defendant places his goods in the stream of commerce, fully aware (and hoping) that such a sale will take place. See *Asahi Metal Industry Co. v. Superior Court of Cal., Solano Cty.*, 480 U.S. 102, 111, 112 (1987) (opinion of O'Connor, J.) (requiring "something more" than simply placing "a product into the stream of commerce," even if defendant is "awar[e]" that the stream "may or will sweep the product into the forum State"); *id.*, at 117 (Brennan, J., concurring in part and concurring in judgment) (jurisdiction should lie where a sale in a State is part of "the regular and anticipated flow" of commerce into the State, but not where that sale is only an "edd[y]," *i.e.*, an isolated occurrence); *id.*, at 122 (Stevens, J., concurring in part and concurring in judgment) (indicating that "the volume, the value, and the hazardous character" of a good may affect the jurisdictional inquiry and emphasizing Asahi's "regular course of dealing").

Here, the relevant facts found by the New Jersey Supreme Court show no "regular . . . flow" or "regular course" of sales in New Jersey; and there is no "something more," such as special state-related design, advertising, advice, marketing, or anything else. Mr. Nicastro, who here bears the burden of proving jurisdiction, has shown no specific effort by the British Manufacturer to sell in New Jersey. He has introduced no list of potential New Jersey customers who might, for example, have regularly attended tradeshows. And he has not otherwise shown that the British Manufacturer "purposefully avail[ed] itself of the privilege of conducting activities" within New Jersey, or that it delivered its goods in the stream of commerce "with the expectation that they will be purchased" by New Jersey users. *World-Wide Volkswagen, supra*, at 297–298 (internal quotation marks omitted).

There may well have been other facts that Mr. Nicastro could have demonstrated in support of jurisdiction. And the dissent considers some of those facts. See post, at 3 (opinion of GINSBURG, J.) (describing the size and scope of New Jersey's scrap-metal business). But the plaintiff bears the burden of establishing jurisdiction, and here I would take the facts precisely as the New Jersey Supreme Court stated them. [Emphasis added.]

Accordingly, on the record present here, resolving this case requires no more than adhering to our precedents. . . .

. . . I again reiterate that I would adhere strictly to our precedents and the limited facts found by the New Jersey Supreme Court. And on those grounds, I do not think we can find jurisdiction in this case. Accordingly, though I agree with the plurality as to the outcome of this case, I concur only in the judgment of that opinion and not its reasoning.

JUSTICE GINSBURG, with whom JUSTICE SOTOMAYOR and JUSTICE KAGAN join, dissenting.

A foreign industrialist seeks to develop a market in the United States for machines it manufactures. It hopes to derive substantial revenue from sales it makes to United States purchasers. Where in the United States buyers reside does not matter to this manufacturer. Its goal is imply to sell as much as it can, wherever it can. It excludes no region or State from the market it wishes to reach. But, all things considered, it prefers to avoid products liability litigation in the United States. To that end, it engages a U.S. distributor to ship its machines stateside. Has it succeeded in escaping personal jurisdiction in a State where one of its products is sold and causes injury or even death to a local user?

Under this Court's pathmarking precedent in *International Shoe Co. v. Washington*, 326 U.S. 310 (1945), and subsequent decisions, one would expect the answer to be unequivocally, "No." But instead, six Justices of this Court, in divergent opinions, tell us that the manufacturer has avoided the jurisdiction of our state courts, except perhaps in States where its products are sold in sizeable quantities. . . .

I

. . . .

In sum, McIntyre UK's regular attendance and exhibitions at ISRI conventions was surely a purposeful step to reach customers for its products "anywhere in the United States." At least as purposeful was McIntyre UK's engagement of McIntyre America as the conduit for sales of McIntyre UK's machines to buyers "throughout the United States." *Given McIntyre UK's endeavors to reach and profit from the United States market as a whole, Nicastro's suit, I would hold, has been brought in a forum entirely appropriate for the adjudication of his claim.* [Emphasis added.] He alleges that McIntyre UK's shear machine was defectively designed or manufactured and, as a result, caused injury to him at his workplace. The machine arrived in Nicastro's New Jersey workplace not randomly or fortuitously, but as a result of the U.S. connections and distribution system that McIntyre UK deliberately arranged. On what sensible view of the allocation of adjudicatory authority could the place of Nicastro's injury within the United States be deemed off limits for his products liability claim against a foreign manufacturer who targeted the United States (including all the States that constitute the Nation) as the territory it sought to develop?

II

A few points on which there should be no genuine debate bear statement at the outset. First, all agree, Mc-Intyre UK surely is not subject to general (all-purpose) jurisdiction in New Jersey courts, for that foreign-country corporation is hardly "at home" in New Jersey. See *Goodyear Dunlop Tires Operations, S. A. v. Brown*, post, at 2–3, 9–13. The question, rather, is one of specific jurisdiction, which turns on an "affiliatio[n] between the forum and the underlying controversy." *Goodyear Dunlop*, post, at 2 [reference omitted]. Second, no issue of the fair and reasonable allocation of adjudicatory authority among States of the United States is present in this case. New Jersey's exercise of personal jurisdiction over a foreign manufacturer whose dangerous product caused a workplace injury in New Jersey does not tread on the domain, or diminish the sovereignty, of any sister State. Indeed, among States of the United States, the State in which the injury occurred would seem most suitable for litigation of a products liability tort claim. [Citation omitted.]

Third, the constitutional limits on a state court's adjudicatory authority derive from considerations of due process, not state sovereignty. As the Court clarified in *Insurance Corp. of Ireland v. Compagnie des Bauxites de Guinee*, 456 U.S. 694 (1982): "The restriction on state sovereign power described in *World-Wide Volkswagen Corp.* . . . must be seen as ultimately a function of the individual liberty interest preserved by the Due Process Clause. That Clause is the only source of the personal jurisdiction requirement and the Clause itself makes no mention of federalism concerns. Furthermore, if the federalism concept operated as an independent restriction on the sovereign power of the court, it would not be possible to waive the personal jurisdiction requirement: Individual actions cannot change the powers of sovereignty, although the individual can subject himself to powers from which he may otherwise be protected." *Id.*, at 703, n. 10. . . .

Finally, in *International Shoe* itself, and decisions thereafter, the Court has made plain that legal fictions, notably "presence" and "implied consent," should be discarded, for they conceal the actual bases on which jurisdiction rests. . . .

Whatever the state of academic debate over the role of consent in modern jurisdictional doctrines, the plurality's notion that consent is the animating concept draws no support from controlling decisions of this Court. Quite the contrary, the Court has explained, a forum can exercise jurisdiction when its contacts with the controversy are sufficient; invocation of a fictitious consent, the Court has repeatedly said, is unnecessary and unhelpful. . . .

III

This case is illustrative of marketing arrangements for sales in the United States common in today's commercial world. A foreign-country manufacturer engages a U.S. company to promote and distribute the manufacturer's products, not in any particular State, but anywhere and everywhere in the United States the distributor can attract purchasers. The product proves defective and injures a user in the State where the user lives or works. Often, as here, the manufacturer will have liability insurance covering personal injuries caused by its products. . . .

When industrial accidents happen, a long-arm statute in the State where the injury occurs generally permits assertion of jurisdiction, upon giving proper notice, over the foreign manufacturer. For example, the State's statute might provide, as does New York's long-arm statute, for the "exercise [of] personal jurisdiction over any non domiciliary . . . who . . . "commits a tortious act without the state causing injury to person or property within the state, . . . if he . . . expects or should reasonably expect the act to have consequences in the state and derives substantial revenue from interstate or international commerce." N. Y. Civ. Prac. Law Ann. § 302(a)(3)(ii) (West 2008). Or, the State might simply provide, as New Jersey does, for the exercise of jurisdiction "consistent with due process of law." N. J. Ct. Rule 4:4-4(b)(1) (2011).

The modern approach to jurisdiction over corporations and other legal entities, ushered in by *International Shoe*, gave prime place to reason and fairness. Is it not fair and reasonable, given the mode of trading of which this case is an example, to require the international seller to defend at the place its products cause injury Do not litigational convenience and choice-of-law considerations point in that direction? On what measure of reason and fairness can it be considered undue to require McIntyre UK to defend in New Jersey as an incident of its efforts to develop a market for its industrial machines anywhere and everywhere in the United States? Is not the burden on McIntyre UK to defend in New Jersey fair, *i.e.*, a reasonable cost of transacting business internationally, in comparison to the burden on Nicastro to go to Nottingham, England to gain recompense for an injury he sustained using McIntyre's product at his workplace in Saddle Brook, New Jersey?

McIntyre UK dealt with the United States as a single market. Like most foreign manufacturers, it was concerned not with the prospect of suit in State X as opposed to State Y, but rather with its subjection to suit anywhere in the United States. . . .

In sum, McIntyre UK, by engaging McIntyre America to promote and sell its machines in the United States, "purposefully availed itself" of the United States market nationwide, not a market in a single State or a discrete collection of States. McIntyre UK thereby availed itself of the market of all States in which its products were sold by its exclusive distributor. "Th[e] 'purposeful availment' requirement," this Court has explained, simply "ensures that a defendant will not be haled into a jurisdiction solely as a result of 'random,' 'fortuitous,' or 'attenuated' contacts." *Burger King, 471 U.S., at 475.* [Emphasis added.] Adjudicatory authority is appropriately exercised where "actions by the defendant *himself*" give rise to the affiliation with the forum. *Ibid.* How could McIntyre UK not have intended, by its actions targeting a national market, to sell products n the fourth largest destination for imports among all States of the United States and the largest scrap metal market? See *supra*, at 3, 10, n. 6. But see *ante*, at 11 (plurality opinion) (manufacturer's purposeful efforts to sell its products nationwide are "not . . . relevant" to the personal jurisdiction inquiry).

Courts, both state and federal, confronting facts similar to those here, have rightly rejected the conclusion that a manufacturer selling its products across the USA may evade jurisdiction in any and all States, including the State where its defective product is distributed and causes injury. They have held, instead, that it would undermine principles of fundamental fairness to insulate the foreign manufacturer from accountability in court at the place within the United States where the manufacturer's products caused injury. . . .

IV

A

While this Court has not considered in any prior case the now-prevalent pattern presented here — a foreign country manufacturer enlisting a U.S. distributor to develop a market in the United States for the manufacturer's products — none of the Court's decisions tug against the judgment made by the New Jersey Supreme Court. McIntyre contends otherwise, citing *World-Wide Volkswagen*, and *Asahi Metal Industry Co. v. Superior Court of Cal., Solano Cty.*, 480 U.S. 102 (1987).

World-Wide Volkswagen concerned a New York car dealership that sold solely in the New York market, and a New York distributor who supplied retailers in three States only: New York, Connecticut, and New Jersey. 444 U.S., at 289. New York residents had purchased an Audi from the New York dealer and were driving the new vehicle through Oklahoma en route to Arizona. On the road in Oklahoma, another car struck the Audi in the rear, causing a fire which severely burned the Audi's occupants. *Id.*, at 288. Rejecting the Oklahoma courts' assertion of jurisdiction over the New York dealer and distributor, this Court observed that the defendants had done nothing to serve the market for cars in Oklahoma. *Id.*, at 295–298. Jurisdiction, the Court held, could not be based on the *customer's* unilateral act of driving the vehicle to Oklahoma. *Id.*, at 298; see *Asahi*, 480 U.S., at 109 (opinion of O'Connor, J.) (*World-Wide Volkswagen* "rejected the assertion that a *consumer's* unilateral act of bringing the defendant's product into the forum State was a sufficient constitutional basis for personal jurisdiction over the defendant").

Notably, the foreign manufacturer of the Audi in *World-Wide Volkswagen* did not object to the jurisdiction of the Oklahoma courts and the U.S. importer abandoned its initially stated objection. 444 U.S., at 288, and n. 3. And most relevant here, the Court's opinion indicates that an objection to jurisdiction by the manufacturer or national distributor would have been unavailing. To reiterate, the Court said in *World-Wide Volkswagen* that, when a manufacturer or distributor aims to sell its product to customers in several States, it is reasonable "to subject it to suit in [any] one of those States if its allegedly defective [product] has there been the source of injury." *Id.*, at 297.

Asahi arose out of a motorcycle accident in California. Plaintiff, a California resident injured in the accident, sued the Taiwanese manufacturer of the motorcycle's tire tubes, claiming that defects in its product caused the accident. The tube manufacturer cross-claimed against Asahi, the Japanese maker of the valve assembly, and Asahi contested the California courts' jurisdiction. By the time the case reached this Court, the injured plaintiff had settled his case and only the indemnity claim by the Taiwanese company against the Japanese valve-assembly manufacturer remained.

The decision was not a close call. The Court had before it a foreign plaintiff, the Taiwanese manufacturer, and a foreign defendant, the Japanese valve-assembly maker, and the indemnification dispute concerned a transaction between those parties that occurred abroad. All agreed on the bottom line: The Japanese valve-assembly manufacturer was not reasonably brought into the California courts to litigate a dispute with another foreign party over a transaction that took place outside the United States.

Given the confines of the controversy, the dueling opinions of Justice Brennan and Justice O'Connor were hardly necessary. How the Court would have "estimate[d] . . . the inconveniences," see *International Shoe*, 326 U.S., at 317 (internal quotation marks omitted), had the injured Californian originally sued Asahi is a debatable question. Would this Court have given the same weight to the burdens on the foreign defendant had those been counterbalanced by the burdens litigating in Japan imposed on the local California plaintiff? Cf. *Calder v. Jones*, 465 U.S. 783, 788 (1984) (a plaintiff's contacts with the forum "may be so manifold as to permit jurisdiction when it would not exist in their absence").

In any event, Asahi, unlike McIntyre UK, did not itself seek out customers in the United States, it engaged no distributor to promote its wares here, it appeared at no trade shows in the United States, and, of course, it had no Web site advertising its products to the world. Moreover, Asahi was a component-part manufacturer with "little control over the final destination of its products once they were delivered into the stream of commerce." *A. Uberti*, 181 Ariz., at 572, 892 P. 2d, at 1361. It was important to the Court in *Asahi* that "those who use Asahi components in their final products, and sell those products in California, [would be] subject to the application of California tort law." 480 U.S., at 115 (majority opinion). To hold that *Asahi* controls this case would, to put it bluntly, be dead wrong.

B

The Court's judgment also puts United States plaintiffs at a disadvantage in comparison to similarly situated complainants elsewhere in the world. Of particular note, within the European Union, in which the United Kingdom is a participant, the jurisdiction New Jersey would have exercised is not at all exceptional. The European Regulation on Jurisdiction and the Recognition and Enforcement of Judgments provides for the exercise of specific jurisdiction "in matters relating to tort . . . in the courts for the place where the harmful event occurred." Council Reg. 44/2001, Art. 5, 2001 O. J. (L. 12) 4. The European Court of Justice has interpreted this prescription to authorize jurisdiction either where the harmful act occurred or at the place of injury. [Citation omitted.]

V

The commentators who gave names to what we now call "general jurisdiction" and "specific jurisdiction" anticipated that when the latter achieves its full growth, considerations of litigational convenience and the respective situations of the parties would determine when it is appropriate to subject a defendant to trial in the plaintiff's community. [Reference omitted.] *As to the parties, courts would differently appraise two situations: (1) cases involving a substantially local plaintiff, like Nicastro, injured by the activity of a defendant engaged in interstate or international trade; and (2) cases in which the defendant is a natural or legal person whose economic activities and legal involvements are largely home-based, i.e., entities without designs to gain substantial revenue from sales in distant markets.* [Emphasis added.] . . .

For the Iberia stated, I would hold McIntyre UK answerable in New Jersey for the harm Nicastro suffered at his workplace in that State using McIntyre UK's shearing machine. While I dissent from the Court's judgment, I take heart that the plurality opinion does not speak for the Court, for that opinion would take a giant step away from the "notions of fair play and substantial justice" underlying

International Shoe. 326 U.S., at 316 (internal quotation marks omitted).

QUESTIONS

1. To what extent does *J. McIntyre Machinery Ltd. v. Nicastro* resolve issues left undecided in *Asahi?* Conversely, what issues are left unresolved?

2. What additional facts would a plaintiff's lawyer need to establish in a case otherwise factually similar to *J. McIntyre Machinery Ltd. v. Nicastro* to satisfy Justices Breyer and Alito?

3. Would, in your view, Justices Ginsburg, Sotomayor, and Kagan have agreed with the California Supreme Court in *Asahi?*

4. Assume that a commercial aircraft manufacturer in the U.S. provides specifications for specialized metal cutting equipment to one of Japan's major general trading companies that in turn places an order for the machinery with a small manufacturer in Japan that has not before sold any product or otherwise engaged in business in the United States. Assume further that subsequently a worker at the U.S. manufacturing plant loses an arm while using the equipment and seeks damages. In your view would any of the justices in *J. McIntyre Machinery Ltd. v. Nicastro* agree that a state court could exercise *in personam* jurisdiction over the Japanese manufacturer under a state long-arm statute that provides for adjudicatory jurisdiction to the extent constitutionally allowed under the Due Process Clause of the Fourteenth Amendment?

DAIMLER AG v. BAUMAN ET AL.*
560 U.S. ___, 134 S. Ct. 746 (2014)

JUSTICE GINSBURG delivered the opinion of the Court.

This case concerns the authority of a court in the United States to entertain a claim brought by foreign plaintiffs against a foreign defendant based on events occurring entirely outside the United States. The litigation commenced in 2004, when twenty-two Argentinian residents1 filed a complaint in the United States District Court for the Northern District of California against Daimler Chrysler Aktiengesellschaft (Daimler), a German public stock company, headquartered in Stuttgart, that manufactures Mercedes-Benz vehicles in Germany. The complaint alleged that during Argentina's 1976–1983 "Dirty War," Daimler's Argentinian subsidiary, Mercedes-Benz Argentina (MB Argentina), collaborated with state security forces to kidnap, detain, torture, and kill certain Argentina workers, among them, plaintiffs or persons closely related to plaintiffs. Damages for the alleged human-rights violations were sought from Daimler under the laws of the United States, California, and Argentina. Jurisdiction over the lawsuit was predicated on

---

* Footnotes omitted.

II. COMMON LAW APPROACHES — THE UNITED STATES

the California contacts of Mercedes-Benz USA, LLC (MBUSA), a subsidiary of Daimler incorporated in Delaware with its principal place of business in New Jersey. MBUSA distributes Daimler-manufactured vehicles to independent dealerships throughout the United States, including California.

The question presented is whether the Due Process Clause of the Fourteenth Amendment precludes the District Court from exercising jurisdiction over Daimler in this case, given the absence of any California connection to the atrocities, perpetrators, or victims described in the complaint. Plaintiffs invoked the court's general or all purpose jurisdiction. California, they urge, is a place where Daimler may be sued on any and all claims against it, wherever in the world the claims may arise. . . . Exercises of personal jurisdiction so exorbitant, we hold, are barred by due process constraints on the assertion of adjudicatory authority.

In *Goodyear Dunlop Tires Operations, S. A.* v. *Brown*, 564 U. S. ___ (2011), we addressed the distinction between general or all-purpose jurisdiction, and specific or conduct linked jurisdiction. As to the former, we held that a court may assert jurisdiction over a foreign corporation "to hear any and all claims against [it]" only when the corporation's affiliations with the State in which suit is brought are so constant and pervasive "as to render [it] essentially at home in the forum State." *Id.*, at ___ (slip op., at 2). Instructed by *Goodyear*, we conclude Daimler is not "at home" in California, and cannot be sued there for injuries plaintiffs attribute to MB Argentina's conduct in Argentina.

I

In 2004, plaintiffs (respondents here) filed suit in the United States District Court for the Northern District of California, alleging that MB Argentina collaborated with Argentinian state security forces to kidnap, detain, torture, and kill plaintiffs and their relatives during the military dictatorship in place there from 1976 through 1983, a period known as Argentina's "Dirty War." Based on those allegations, plaintiffs asserted claims under the Alien Tort Statute, 28 U. S. C. § 1350, and the Torture Victim Protection Act of 1991, 106 Stat. 73, note following 28 U. S. C. § 1350, as well as claims for wrongful death and intentional infliction of emotional distress under the laws of California and Argentina. The incidents recounted in the complaint center on MB Argentina's plant in Gonzalez Catan, Argentina; no part of MB Argentina's alleged collaboration with Argentinian authorities took place in California or anywhere else in the United States. Plaintiffs' operative complaint names only one corporate defendant: Daimler, the petitioner here. Plaintiffs seek to hold Daimler vicariously liable for MB Argentina's alleged malfeasance. Daimler is a German *Aktiengesellschaft* (public stock company) that manufactures Mercedes-Benz vehicles in Germany and has its headquarters in Stuttgart. At times relevant to this case, MB Argentina was a subsidiary wholly owned by Daimler's predecessor in interest. Daimler moved to dismiss the action for want of personal jurisdiction. Opposing the motion, plaintiffs submitted declarations and exhibits purporting to demonstrate the presence of Daimler itself in California. Alternatively, plaintiffs maintained that jurisdiction over Daimler could be founded on the California contacts of MBUSA, a distinct corporate entity that, according to plaintiffs, should be treated as Daimler's agent for jurisdictional purposes.

MBUSA, an indirect subsidiary of Daimler, is a Delaware limited liability corporation. MBUSA serves as Daimler's exclusive importer and distributor in the United States, purchasing Mercedes-Benz automobiles from Daimler in Germany, then importing those vehicles, and ultimately distributing them to independent dealerships located throughout the Nation. Although MBUSA's principal place of business is in New Jersey, MBUSA has multiple California-based facilities, including a regional office in Costa Mesa, a Vehicle Preparation Center in Carson, and a Classic Center in Irvine. According to the record developed below, MBUSA is the largest supplier of luxury vehicles to the California market. In particular, over 10% of all sales of new vehicles in the United States take place in California, and MBUSA's California sales account for 2.4% of Daimler's worldwide sales.

The relationship between Daimler and MBUSA is delineated in a General Distributor Agreement, which sets forth requirements for MBUSA's distribution of Mercedes-Benz vehicles in the United States. That agreement established MBUSA as an "independent contracto[r]" that "buy[s] and sell[s] [vehicles] . . . as an independent business for [its] own account." App. 179a. The agreement "does not make [MBUSA] . . . a general or special agent, partner, joint venturer or employee of DAIMLERCHRYSLER or any Daimler Chrysler Group Company"; MBUSA "ha[s] no authority to make binding obligations for or act on behalf of DAIMLER-CHRYSLER or any DaimlerChrysler Group Company." The Ninth Circuit at first affirmed the District Court's judgment. Addressing solely the question of agency, the Court of Appeals held that plaintiffs had not shown the existence of an agency relationship of the kind that might warrant attribution of MBUSA's contacts to Daimler. *Bauman* v. *DaimlerChrysler Corp.*, 579 F. 3d 1088, 1096–1097 (2009). Judge Reinhardt dissented. In his view, the agency test was satisfied and considerations of "reasonableness" did not bar the exercise of jurisdiction. *Id.*, at 1098–1106. Granting plaintiffs' petition for rehearing, the panel withdrew its initial opinion and replaced it with one authored by Judge Reinhardt, which elaborated on reasoning he initially expressed in dissent. *Bauman v. Daimler-Chrysler Corp.*, 644 F. 3d 909 (CA9 2011).

Daimler petitioned for rehearing and rehearing en banc, urging that the exercise of personal jurisdiction over Daimler could not be reconciled with this Court's decision in *Goodyear Dunlop Tires Operations, S. A. v. Brown*, 564 U. S. ___ (2011). Over the dissent of eight judges, the Ninth Circuit denied Daimler's petition. See *Bauman* v. *DaimlerChrysler Corp.*, 676 F. 3d 774 (2011) (O'Scannlain, J., dissenting from denial of rehearing en banc).

We granted certiorari to decide whether, consistent with the Due Process Clause of the Fourteenth Amendment, Daimler is amenable to suit in California courts for claims involving only foreign plaintiffs and conduct occurring entirely abroad. [Citation omitted.]

II

Federal courts ordinarily follow state law in determining the bounds of their jurisdiction over persons. See Fed. Rule Civ. Proc. 4(k)(1)(A) (service of process is effective to establish personal jurisdiction over a defendant "who is subject to the jurisdiction of a court of general jurisdiction in the state where the district court is located"). Under California's long-arm statute, California state courts may exercise personal jurisdiction "on any basis not inconsistent with the Constitution of this state or of the United States." Cal. Civ. Proc. Code Ann. § 410.10 (West 2004).California's long-arm statute allows the exercise of personal jurisdiction to the full extent permissible under the U.S. Constitution. We therefore inquire whether the Ninth Circuit's holding comports with the limits imposed by federal due process. [Citation omitted.]

III

. . . . "The canonical opinion in this area remains *International Shoe [Co.* v. *Washington]*, 326 U. S. 310 [(1945)], in which we held that a State may authorize its courts to exercise personal jurisdiction over an out-of-state defendant if the defendant has 'certain minimum contacts with [the State] such that the maintenance of the suit does not offend "traditional notions of fair play and substantial justice." ' " *Goodyear*, 564 U. S., at ___ (slip op., at 6) (quoting *International Shoe*, 326 U. S., at 316). Following *International Shoe*, "the relationship among the defendant, the forum, and the litigation, rather than the mutually exclusive sovereignty of the States on which the rules of *Pennoyer* rest, became the central concern of the inquiry into personal jurisdiction." *Shaffer*, 433 U. S., at 204.

International Shoe's conception of "fair play and substantial justice" presaged the development of two categories of personal jurisdiction. The first category is represented by *International Shoe* itself, a case in which the instate activities of the corporate defendant "ha[d] not only been continuous and systematic, but also g[a]ve rise to the liabilities sued on." 326 U. S., at 317. *International Shoe* recognized, as well, that "the commission of some single or occasional acts of the corporate agent in a state" may sometimes be enough to subject the corporation to jurisdiction in that State's tribunals with respect to suits relating to that in-state activity. *Id.*, at 318. Adjudicatory authority of this order, in which the suit "aris[es] out of orrelate[s] to the defendant's contacts with the forum," *Helicopteros Nacionales de Colombia, S. A.* v. *Hall*, 466 U. S. 408, 414, n. 8 (1984), is today called "specific jurisdiction." See *Goodyear*, 564 U. S., at ___ (slip op., at 7) [citation omitted].

International Shoe distinguished between, on the one hand, exercises of specific jurisdiction, as just described, and on the other, situations where a foreign corporation's "continuous corporate operations within a state [are] so substantial and of such a nature as to justify suit against it on causes of action arising from dealings entirely distinct from those activities." 326 U. S., at 318. As we have since explained, "[a] court may assert general jurisdiction over foreign (sister-state or foreign-country) corporations to hear any and all claims against them when their affiliations with the State are so 'continuous and systematic' as to render them essentially at home in the forum State." *Goodyear*, 564 U. S., at ___ (slip op., at 2); see *id.*, at ___ (slip op., at 7); *Helicopteros*, 466 U. S., at 414, n. 9. Since *International Shoe*, "specific jurisdiction has become the centerpiece of modern jurisdiction theory, while general jurisdiction [has played] a reduced role." *Goodyear*, 564 U. S., at ___ (slip op., at 8) [citation omitted]. *International Shoe*'s momentous departure from *Pennoyer*'s rigidly territorial focus, we have noted, unleashed a rapid expansion of tribunals' ability to hear claims against out-of-state defendants when the episode in-suit occurred in the forum or the defendant purposefully availed itself of the forum. . . . Our post-*International Shoe* opinions on general jurisdiction, by comparison, are few. "[The Court's] 1952 decision in *Perkins* v. *Benguet Consol. Mining Co.* remains the textbook case of general jurisdiction appropriately exercised over a foreign corporation that has not consented to suit in the forum." *Goodyear*, 564 U. S., at ___ (slip op., at 11) (internal quotation marks and brackets omitted). The defendant in *Perkins*, Benguet, was a company incorporated under the laws of the Philippines, where it operatedgold and silver mines. Benguet ceased its mining operations during the Japanese occupation of the Philippines inWorld War II; its president moved to Ohio, where he kept an office, maintained the company's files, and oversaw the company's activities. *Perkins* v. *Benguet Consol. Mining Co.*, 342 U. S. 437, 448 (1952). The plaintiff, an Ohio resident, sued Benguet on a claim that neither arose in Ohio nor related to the corporation's activities in that State. We held that the Ohio courts could exercise general jurisdiction over Benguet without offending due process. *Ibid.* That was so, we later noted, because "Ohio was the corporation's principal, if temporary, place of business." *Keeton* v. *Hustler Magazine, Inc.*, 465 U. S. 770, 780, n. 11 (1984).

The next case on point, *Helicopteros*, 466 U. S. 408, arose from a helicopter crash in Peru. Four U. S. citizens perished in that accident; their survivors and representatives brought suit in Texas state court against the helicopter's owner and operator, a Colombian corporation. That company's contacts with Texas were confined to "sending its chief executive officer to Houston for a contract negotiation session; accepting into its New York bank account checks drawn on a Houston bank; purchasing helicopters, equipment, and training services from [a Texas-based helicopter company] for substantial sums; and sending personnel to [Texas] for training." *Id.*, at 416. Notably, those contacts bore no apparent relationship to the accident that gave rise to the suit. We held that the company's Texas connections did not resemble the "continuous and systematic general business contacts . . . found to exist in *Perkins*." *Ibid.* "[M]ere purchases, even if occurring at regular intervals," we clarified, "are not enough to warrant a State's assertion of *in personam* jurisdiction over a nonresident corporation in a cause of action not related to those purchase transactions." *Id.*, at 418.

Most recently, in *Goodyear*, we answered the question: "Are foreign subsidiaries of a United States parent corporation amenable to suit in state court on claims unrelated to any activity of the subsidiaries in the forum State?" 564 U. S., at ___ (slip op., at 1). That case arose from a bus accident outside Paris that killed two boys from North Carolina. The boys' parents brought a wrongful-death suit in North Carolina state court alleging that the bus's tire was defectively manufactured. The complaint named as defendants not only The Goodyear Tire and Rubber Company (Goodyear), an Ohio corporation, but also Goodyear's Turkish, French, and Luxembourgian subsidiaries. Those foreign subsidiaries, which manufactured tires for sale in Europe and Asia, lacked any affiliation with North Carolina. A small percentage of tires manufactured by the foreign subsidiaries were distributed in North Carolina, however, and on that ground, the North Carolina Court of Appeals held the subsidiaries amenable to the general jurisdiction of North Carolina courts.

We reversed, observing that the North Carolina court's analysis "elided the essential difference between case specific and all-purpose (general) jurisdiction."

Id., at ___ (slip op., at 10). Although the placement of a product into the stream of commerce "may bolster an affiliation germane to *specific* jurisdiction," we explained, such contacts "do not warrant a determination that, based on those ties, the forum has *general* jurisdiction over a defendant." *Id.*, at ___ (slip op., at 10–11). As *International Shoe* itself teaches, a corporation's "continuous activity of some sorts within a state is not enough to support the demand that the corporation be amenable to suits unrelated to that activity." 326 U. S., at 318. Because Goodyear's foreign subsidiaries were "in no sense at home in North Carolina," we held, those subsidiaries could not be required to submit to the general jurisdiction of that State's courts. 564 U. S., at ___ (slip op., at 13). See also *J. McIntyre Machinery, Ltd.* v. *Nicastro*, 564 U. S. ___, ___ (2011) (GINSBURG, J., dissenting) (slip op., at 7) (noting unanimous agreement that a foreign manufacturer, which engaged an independent U.S.-based distributor to sell its machines throughout the United States, could not be exposed to all-purpose jurisdiction in New Jersey courts based on those contacts).

As is evident from Perkins, Helicopteros, and Goodyear, general and specific jurisdiction have followed markedly different trajectories post-International Shoe. Specific jurisdiction has been cut loose from Pennoyer's sway, but we have declined to stretch general jurisdiction beyond limits traditionally recognized. As this Court has increasingly trained on the "relationship among the defendant, the forum, and the litigation," Shaffer, 433 U. S., at 204, i.e., specific jurisdiction, general jurisdiction has come to occupy a less dominant place in the contemporary scheme. [Emphasis added.]

IV

With this background, we turn directly to the question whether Daimler's affiliations with California are sufficient to subject it to the general (all-purpose) personal jurisdiction of that State's courts. In the proceedings below, the parties agreed on, or failed to contest, certain points we now take as given. Plaintiffs have never attempted to fit this case into the *specific* jurisdiction category. Nor did plaintiffs challenge on appeal the District Court's holding that Daimler's own contacts with California were, by themselves, too sporadic to justify the exercise of general jurisdiction. While plaintiffs ultimately persuaded the Ninth Circuit to impute MBUSA's California contacts to Daimler on an agency theory, at no point have they maintained that MBUSA is an alter ego of Daimler.

Daimler, on the other hand, failed to object below to plaintiffs' assertion that the California courts could exercise all-purpose jurisdiction over MBUSA. . . . We will assume then, for purposes of this decision only, that MBUSA qualifies as at home in California. [Emphasis added.]

A

In sustaining the exercise of general jurisdiction over Daimler, the Ninth Circuit relied on an agency theory, determining that MBUSA acted as Daimler's agent for jurisdictional purposes and then attributing MBUSA's California contacts to Daimler. The Ninth Circuit's agency analysis derived from Circuit precedent considering principally whether the subsidiary "performs services that are sufficiently important to the foreign corporation that if it did not have a representative to perform them, the corporation's own officials would undertake to perform substantially similar services." 644 F. 3d, at 920 (quoting *Doe* v. *Unocal Corp.*, 248 F. 3d 915, 928 (CA9 2001); emphasis deleted).

This Court has not yet addressed whether a foreign corporation may be subjected to a court's general jurisdiction based on the contacts of its in-state subsidiary. Daimler argues, and several Courts of Appeals have held, that a subsidiary's jurisdictional contacts can be imputed to its parent only when the former is so dominated by the latter as to be its alter ego. The Ninth Circuit adopted a less rigorous test based on what it described as an "agency" relationship. Agencies, we note, come in many sizes and shapes: "One may be an agent for some business purposes and not others so that the fact that one may be an agent for one purpose does not make him or her an agent for every purpose." 2 A C. J. S., Agency § 43, p. 367 (2013) (footnote omitted). A subsidiary, for example, might be its parent's agent for claims arising in the place where the subsidiary operates, yet not its agent regarding claims arising elsewhere. The Court of Appeals did not advert to that prospect. But we need not pass judgment on invocation of an agency theory in the context of general jurisdiction, for in no event can the appeals court's analysis be sustained. [Emphasis added.]

The Ninth Circuit's agency finding rested primarily on its observation that MBUSA's services were "important" to Daimler, as gauged by Daimler's hypothetical readiness to perform those services itself if MBUSA did not exist. Formulated this way, the inquiry into importance stacks the deck, for it will always yield a pro-jurisdiction answer: "Anything a corporation does through an independent contractor, subsidiary, or distributor is presumably something that the corporation would do 'by other means' if the independent contractor, subsidiary, or distributor did not exist." 676 F. 3d, at 777 (O'Scannlain, J., dissenting from denial of rehearing en banc). The Ninth Circuit's agency theory thus appears to subject foreign corporations to general jurisdiction whenever they have an in-state subsidiary or affiliate, an outcome that would sweep beyond even the "sprawling view of general jurisdiction" we rejected in *Goodyear*. 564 U. S., at ___ (slip op., at 12).

B

Even if we were to assume that MBUSA is at home in California, and further to assume MBUSA's contacts are imputable to Daimler, there would still be no basis to subject Daimler to general jurisdiction in California, for Daimler's slim contacts with the State hardly render it at home there. *Goodyear* made clear that only a limited set of affiliations with a forum will render a defendant amenable to all-purpose jurisdiction there. "For an individual, the paradigm forum for the exercise of general jurisdiction is the individual's domicile; for a corporation, it is an equivalent place, one in which the corporation is fairly regarded as at home." 564 U. S., at ___ (slip op., at 7) [citation omitted.] With respect to a corporation, the place of incorporation and principal place of business are "paradig[m] . . . bases for general jurisdiction." *Id.*, at 735. [Citation omitted.] Those affiliations have the virtue of being unique — that is, each ordinarily indicates only one place — as well as easily ascertainable. [Citation omitted.] These bases afford plaintiffs recourse to at least one clear and certain forum in which a corporate defendant may be sued on any and all claims.

Goodyear did not hold that a corporation may be subject to general jurisdiction only in a forum where it is incorporated or has its principal place of business; it simply typed those places paradigm all-purpose forums. *Plaintiffs would have us look beyond the exemplar bases Goodyear identified, and approve the exercise of general jurisdiction in every State in which a corporation "engages in a substantial, continuous, and systematic course of business." Brief for Respondents 16–17, and nn. 7–8. That formulation, we hold, is unacceptably grasping.* [Emphasis added.]

As noted, see *supra*, at 7–8, the words "continuous and systematic" were used in *International Shoe* to describe instances in which the exercise of *specific* jurisdiction would be appropriate. See 326 U. S., at 317 (jurisdiction can be asserted where a corporation's in-state activities are not only "continuous and systematic, but also give rise to the liabilities sued on"). Turning to all-purpose jurisdiction, in contrast, *International Shoe* speaks of "instances in which the continuous corporate operations within a state [are] so substantial and of such a nature as to justify suit . . . *on causes of action arising from dealings entirely distinct from those activities.*" *Id.*, at 318 (emphasis added [in opinion]). [Citation omitted.] Accordingly, the inquiry under *Goodyear* is not whether a foreign corpora-tion's in-forum contacts can be said to be in some sense "continuous and systematic," *it is whether that corpora-tion's "affiliations with the State are so 'continuous and systematic' as to render [it] essentially at home in the forum State." 564 U. S., at ___ (slip op., at 2).* [Emphasis added.]

Here, neither Daimler nor MBUSA is incorporated in California, nor does either entity have its principal place of business there. If Daimler's California activities sufficed to allow adjudication of this Argentina-rooted case in California, the same global reach would presumably be available in every other State in which MBUSA's sales are sizable. Such exorbitant exercises of all-purpose jurisdiction would scarcely permit out-of-state defendants "to structure their primary conduct with some minimum assurance as to where that conduct will and will not render them liable to suit." *Burger King Corp.*, 471 U. S., at 472 (internal quotation marks omitted). (slip op., at 1) (only natural persons are subject to liability under the TVPA).

The Ninth Circuit, moreover, paid little heed to the risks to international comity its expansive view of general jurisdiction posed. Other nations do not share the uninhibited approach to personal jurisdiction advanced by the Court of Appeals in this case. In the European Union, for example, a corporation may generally be sued in the nation in which it is "domiciled," a term defined to refer only to the location of the corporation's "statutory seat," "central admin-istration," or "principal place of business." European Parliament and Council Reg. 1215/2012, Arts. 4(1), and 63(1), 2012 O. J. (L. 351) 7, 18 [supreceding EC Regulation 44/2001, which in turn superceded the 1968 Brussels Convention, as detailed below]. See also *id.*, Art. 7(5), 2012 O. J. 7 (as to "a dispute *arising out of the operations of a branch, agency or other establishment*," a corporation may be sued "in the courts for the place where the branch, agency or other establishment is situated" (emphasis added [in opinion])). The Solicitor General informs us, in this regard, that "foreign governments' objections to some domestic courts' expansive views of general jurisdiction have in the past impeded negotiations of international agreements on the reciprocal recognition and enforcement of judgments." U. S. Brief 2 . . . . Considerations of international rapport thus reinforce our determination that subjecting Daimler to the general jurisdiction of courts in California would not accord with the "fair play and substantial justice" due process demands. *International Shoe*, 326 U. S., at 316 (quoting *Milliken* v. *Meyer*, 311 U. S. 457, 463 (1940)).

It was therefore error for the Ninth Circuit to conclude that Daimler, even with MBUSA's contacts attributed to it, was at home in California, and hence subject to suit there on claims by foreign plaintiffs having nothing to do with anything that occurred or had its principal impact in California.

C

Finally, the transnational context of this dispute bears attention. The Court of Appeals emphasized, as supportive of the exercise of general jurisdiction, plaintiffs' assertion of claims under the Alien Tort Statute (ATS), 28 U. S. C. § 1350, and the Torture Victim Protection Act of 1991 (TVPA), 106 Stat. 73, note following 28 U. S. C. § 1350. See 644 F. 3d, at 927 ("American federal courts, be they in California or any other state, have a strong interest in adjudicating and redressing international human rights abuses."). Recent decisions of this Court, however, have rendered plaintiffs' ATS and TVPA claims infirm. See *Kiobel* v. *Royal Dutch Petroleum Co.*, 569 U. S. ___, ___ (2013) (slip op., at 14) (presumption against extra-territorial application controls claims under the ATS); *Mohamad* v. *Palestinian Authority*, 566 U. S. ___, ___ (2012).

* * *

For the Iberia stated, the judgment of the United States Court of Appeals for the Ninth Circuit is

Reversed.

[Dissenting opinion by JUSTICE SOTOMAYOR omitted.]

QUESTIONS AND PROBLEMS

1. What standard is set out in *Daimler AG v. Bauman*, for determining whether a foreign corporation could be subject to the "general" jurisdiction of U.S. courts? Does the decision develop further the standards for personal jurisdiction articulated and applied in prior cases involving foreign corporate defendants?

2. Under what circumstances would you envision that extraterritorial service would be constitutionally necessary to establish general personal jurisdiction over a corporation or other juridical person or over a natural

> person as defendant?
>
> 3. To what extent does "international comity" have bearing on the issue of adjudicatory jurisdiction under the Due Process Clause? Was EU law — as evidenced by European Parliament and Council Reg. 1215/2012 — relevant to the decision?
>
> 4. Would a Chinese airline with an office in Los Angeles necessarily be subject to suit by the heirs of a Chinese passenger arising out of an accident involving a domestic flight that occurred in China in a Los Angeles court? Would your answer differ were the deceased passenger to have dual U.S.-Chinese nationality or the flight was booked in Los Angeles?
>
> 5. Assuming official notice of the lawsuit is provided, could a state subject to the general adjudicatory jurisdiction of its courts without either service of process or attachment of assets any party that consents to such jurisdiction or is a citizen or domiciliary of the state or is otherwise present within the state or conducts business or other activities on a systematic and continuous basis within the state? If not, why not?

III. COMMON LAW VARIATIONS — CANADA

Canada (but for Quebec) like the United States (but for Louisiana) is a common law jurisdiction with a federal system of government. Canada differs from the United States, however, in several fundamental respects. Among the most significant for our purposes here is the lack of a constitutional due process standard that serves to define both the minimum and maximum permissible statutory extensions of jurisdiction over parties outside of the territory of the province or state. Without the due process limitations of *Pennoyer v. Neff*, extensions of personal jurisdiction over parties outside of the geographical territory of a province are not necessarily *ultra vires*. For purposes of determining the jurisdictional validity of extraterritorial service (service *ex juris*), however, the activities of defendants within the province do currently constitute a primary focus of concern.

Canadian common law provinces within boundaries established by judicial decisions since the 1990 decision in *Morguard Investments Ltd. v. De Savoye*, extracted below, may enact statutes for expansive adjudicatory jurisdiction and extraterritorial service over parties to the extent that "a real and substantial connection" exists between defendant and the province with respect to the "subject matter" of the case. See the Uniform Court Jurisdiction and Proceedings Transfer Act (Uniform Law Conference of Canada). The text of the Act as enacted in British Colombia is extracted below. See also http://www.ulcc.ca/en/uniform-acts-new-order/current-uniform-acts/739-jurisdiction/civil-jurisdiction/1730-court-jurisdiction-proceedings-transfer-act. At least the "availability" of service no longer establishes jurisdiction. On the other hand, traditional notions of territoriality continue to constrain the authority of provincial legislatures with respect to real property and private law rights within the province. Thus, unlike Washington State after *International Shoe*, the Province of British Columbia would arguably at least not have the legislative competence to tax a company without offices or employees within the province.

A second difference is the role of the highest federal court — the Supreme Court of Canada. Unlike the U.S. Supreme Court, the Canadian Supreme Court (as well as its Australian counterpart) serves as the court of last resort for all jurisdictions adjudicating appeals from provincial, territorial, as well as federal judicial decisions. It thus functions as "national" rather than merely the highest "federal" court. Article 101 of the Canadian Constitution — combining the Constitution Acts of 1867 and 1982 — simply provides:

> The Parliament of Canada may, notwithstanding anything in this Act, from Time to Time provide for the Constitution, Maintenance, and Organization of a General Court of Appeal for Canada.

Pursuant to this provision, the Supreme Court Act of Canada (R.S., 1985, c. S-26) established the Supreme Court is "a general court of appeal for Canada" (Section 3) with "an appellate, civil and criminal jurisdiction within and throughout Canada" (Section 35). With respect to common law rules and standards, the Canadian Supreme Court is thus able to develop uniform common law rules and standards for the English-speaking provinces of Canada.

Quebec is, of course, the civil law exception, but the Canadian Supreme Court can create a degree of national uniformity by judicial construction of Quebec's codes and statutes, on-going work by the Uniform Law Conference of Canada to establish common statutory rules and standards, as well as "constitutional" decisions.

Supplementing this capacity for uniformity is another feature of the Canadian system. Judges for all but "provincial courts" (local trial courts of limited jurisdiction), the Tax Court, and the Supreme Court — that is, all judges for first instance superior courts and courts of appeal in each province as well as federal courts — are recruited and selected at the national level. They are formally appointed by the Governor General on the advice of the federal cabinet. Candidates are first reviewed by judicial advisory committees for each of Canada's 10 provinces and three territories (with three for Ontario and two for Quebec). The committees comprise representatives of the federal and provincial (or territorial) governments, the provincial (or territorial) law society, the Canadian Bar Association, the judiciary, and the general public. A representative of the police was added in 2006. The committees send the names of all candidates with a bifurcated favorable or unfavorable recommendation along with comments to the federal minister of Justice who makes the ultimate individual selections to send to the cabinet. The Canadian Judicial Council provides general oversight of the judiciary. Chaired by the Chief Justice, the Council comprises the chief justices and associate chief justices of Canada's superior courts, the senior judges of the territorial courts, and the Chief Justice of the Court Martial Appeal Court of Canada.

Finally, in contrast to the United States (as well as Australia), Canada does not have a constitutional Good Faith and Credit requirement. In contrast, for example, Article 118 of the Commonwealth of Australia Constitution Act provides:

> Recognition of laws etc. of States
>
> Full faith and credit shall be given, throughout the Commonwealth to the laws, the public Acts and records, and the judicial proceedings of every State.

The Canadian Constitution has no comparable provision. However, the appellate jurisdiction of the Supreme Court of Canada, like that of the Australian High Court, enables the Court to avoid some of the intrinsic problems of recognition and enforcement of the judgments by courts in other provinces through its ability to unify the common law of the nine English-speaking provinces and three territories with nationwide constitutional implications as exemplified in the following landmark decision.

MORGUARD INVESTMENTS LTD. v. DE SAVOYE
[1990] 3 S.C.R. 1077

[Official Court Summary]

The respondents were mortgagees of lands in Alberta. The appellant was the mortgagor and then resided in Alberta. He moved to British Columbia and has not resided or carried on business in Alberta since then. The mortgages fell into default and the respondents brought action in Alberta. Service was effected in accordance with the rules for service *ex juris* of the Alberta Court. The appellant took no steps to appear or to defend the actions. There was no clause in the mortgages by which he agreed to submit to the jurisdiction of the Alberta court and he did not attorn to its jurisdiction.

The respondents obtained judgments *nisi* in the foreclosure actions. At the expiry of the redemption period, they obtained orders for a judicial sale of the mortgaged properties to themselves and judgments were entered against the appellant for the deficiencies between the value of the property and the amount owing on the mortgages. The respondents then each commenced a separate action in the British Columbia Supreme Court to enforce the Alberta judgments for the deficiencies. Judgment was granted to the respondents by the Supreme Court in a decision which was upheld on appeal to the Court of Appeal. At issue here was the recognition to be given by the courts in one province to a judgment of the courts in another province in a personal action brought in the latter province at a time when the defendant did not live there.

Held: The appeal should be dismissed.

The common law regarding the recognition and enforcement of foreign judgments is anchored in the principle of territoriality as interpreted and applied by the English courts in the 19th century. This principle reflects one of the basic tenets of international law, that sovereign states have exclusive jurisdiction in their own territory. As a concomitant to this, states are hesitant to exercise jurisdiction over matters that may take place in the territory of other states. Because jurisdiction is territorial, a state's law has no binding effect outside its jurisdiction.

Modern states cannot live in splendid isolation and do give effect to judgments given in other countries in certain circumstances, such as judgments *in rem* and personal judgments. This was thought to be in conformity with the requirements of comity, which has been stated to be the deference and respect due by other states to the actions of a state legitimately taken within its territory. But comity is based not simply on respect for a foreign sovereign, but on convenience and even necessity. Modern times require that the flow of wealth, skills and people across boundaries be facilitated in a fair and orderly manner. Principles of order and fairness which ensure security of transactions with justice must underlie a modern system of private international law. The content of comity therefore must be adjusted in the light of a changing world order.

No real comparison exists between the interprovincial relationships of today and those obtaining between foreign countries in the 19th century. The courts made a serious error in transposing the rules developed for the enforcement of foreign judgments to the enforcement of judgments from sister-provinces. The considerations underlying the rules of comity apply with much greater force between the units of a federal state.

The 19th century English rules fly in the face of the obvious intention of the Constitution to create a single country with a common market and a common citizenship. The constitutional arrangements made to effect this goal, such as the removal of barriers to interprovincial trade and mobility guarantees, speak to the strong need for the enforcement throughout the country of judgments given in one province.

The Canadian judicial structure is so arranged that any concerns about differential quality of justice among the provinces can have no real foundation. All superior court judges — who also have superintending control over other provincial courts and tribunals — are appointed and paid by the federal authorities. All are subject to final review by the Supreme Court of Canada, which can determine when the courts of one province have appropriately exercised jurisdiction in an action and the circumstances under which the courts of another province should recognize such judgments. Further, Canadian counsels are all subject to the same code of ethics.

The courts in one province should give "full faith and credit" to the judgments given by a court in another province or a territory, so long as that court has properly, or appropriately, exercised jurisdiction in the action. Both order and justice militate in favour of the security of transactions. It is anarchic and unfair that a person should be able to avoid legal obligations arising in one province simply by moving to another province.

These concerns, however, must be weighed against fairness to the defendant. The taking of jurisdiction by a court in one province and its recognition in another must be viewed as correlatives and recognition in other provinces should be dependent on the fact that the court giving judgment "properly" or "appropriately" exercised jurisdiction. It may meet the demands of order and fairness to recognize a judgment given in a jurisdiction that had the greatest or at least significant contacts with the subject matter of the action. But it hardly accords with principles of order and fairness to permit a person to sue another in any jurisdiction, without regard to the contacts that jurisdiction may have to the defendant or the subject matter of the suit. If the courts of one province are to be expected to give effect to judgments given in another province, there must be some limit to the exercise of jurisdiction against persons outside the province. If it is reasonable to support the exercise of jurisdiction in one province, it is reasonable that the judgment be recognized in other provinces.

The approach of permitting suit where there is a real and substantial connection with the action provides a reasonable balance between the rights of the parties. It affords some protection against being pursued in jurisdictions having little or no connection with the transaction or the parties.

Here, the actions for the deficiencies properly took place in Alberta. The properties are situate there, and the contracts were entered into there by parties then resident in the province. Moreover, deficiency actions follow upon foreclosure proceedings, which should obviously take place in Alberta, and the action for the deficiencies cries out for consolidation with the foreclosure proceedings. There was a real and substantial connection between the damages suffered and the jurisdiction. Thus, the Alberta court properly had jurisdiction, and its judgment should be recognized and be enforceable in British Columbia.

The *Reciprocal Enforcement of Judgments Acts* in the various provinces were never intended to alter the rules of private international law. They simply provided for the registration of judgments as a more convenient procedure than by bringing an action to enforce a judgment given in another province. There is nothing to prevent a plaintiff from bringing such an action and thereby taking advantage of the rules of private international law as they may evolve over time.

[Decision]

Present: DICKSON C.J. and LA FOREST, L'HEUREUX-DUBÉ, SOPINKA, GONTHIER, CORY and MCLACHLIN JJ.

The judgment of the Court was delivered by

LA FOREST J.—

This appeal concerns the recognition to be given by the courts in one province to a judgment of the courts in another province in a personal action brought in the latter province at a time when the defendant did not live there. Specifically, the appeal deals with judgments granted in foreclosure proceedings for deficiencies on sale of mortgaged property.

FACTS

The respondents, Morguard Investments Limited and Credit Foncier Trust Company, became mortgagees of lands in Alberta in 1978. The appellant, Douglas De Savoye, who then resided in Alberta, was originally guarantor but later took title to the lands and assumed the obligations of mortgagor. Shortly afterwards, he moved to British Columbia and has not resided or carried on business in Alberta since. The mortgages fell into default and the respondents brought action in Alberta. The appellant was served with process in the actions by double registered mail addressed to his home in British Columbia pursuant to orders for service by the Alberta court in accordance with its rules for service outside its jurisdiction [service *ex juris*] There are rules to the same effect in British Columbia.

The appellant took no steps to appear or to defend the action. There was no clause in the mortgages by which he agreed to submit to the jurisdiction of the Alberta court, and he did not attorn to its jurisdiction.

The respondents obtained judgments *nisi* in the foreclosure actions. At the expiry of the redemption period, they obtained "Rice Orders" against the appellant. Under these orders, a judicial sale of the mortgaged properties to the respondents took place and judgments were entered against the appellant for the deficiencies between the value of the property and the amount owing on the mortgages. The respondents then each commenced a separate action in the British Columbia Supreme Court to enforce the Alberta judgments for the deficiencies. Judgment was granted to the respondents by the Supreme Court in a decision which was upheld on appeal to the British Columbia Court of Appeal. The appellant then sought and was granted leave to appeal to this Court, [1989] 1 S.C.R. viii.

THE JUDGMENTS BELOW

Supreme Court of British Columbia

The appellant argued that the respondents were not entitled to enforce the Alberta judgments because he had never attorned to the jurisdiction of the Alberta court. The chambers judge, Boyd L.J.S.C., noted that the Alberta court clearly had jurisdiction over the subject properties and the foreclosure proceedings. Nothing in the material, she noted, indicated that in granting orders for substitutional service upon the appellant, the Alberta court improperly exercised its discretion to assume jurisdiction, or that any other court would have been a more convenient forum in which to adjudicate the matter. She, therefore, concluded that the Alberta court had jurisdiction to make the orders in question. The judge then reviewed the substance of the orders and ordered that the respondents were entitled to judgment for the deficiencies: (1987), 18 B.C.L.R. (2d) 262, [1988] 1 W.W.R. 87.

Court of Appeal

The Court of Appeal, in Iberia given by Seaton J.A., dismissed the appeal: (1988), 27 B.C.L.R. (2d) 155, [1988] 5 W.W.R. 650, 29 C.P.C. (2d) 52. In its view, the Alberta default judgments could be enforced on the basis of reciprocity, more specifically reciprocity of jurisdictional practice in the two provinces. A British Columbia court, it held, should recognize an Alberta judgment if the Alberta court took jurisdiction in circumstances in which, if the facts were transposed to British Columbia, the courts of British Columbia would have taken jurisdiction as well.

In reviewing the question of the jurisdiction of the Alberta court, Seaton J.A. concluded that the Alberta judgments for the deficiency on the mortgage loans were enforceable by action in British Columbia because British Columbia's own courts, faced with a similar case, would have exercised jurisdiction under the British Columbia Rules of Court authorizing service *ex juris* without leave. He noted that such grounds for exercising jurisdiction over a defendant resident outside the province were long established in English and Canadian law. He referred to *Comber v. Leyland*, [1898] A.C. 524 (H.L.), which held, at p. 527, that:

... where the parties have agreed that something is to be done in this country, some part of the subject-matter of the contract is to be executed within this country, it is a sort of consent of the parties that wherever they may be living, or wherever the contract may have been made, that question may be litigated in this country.

In Seaton J.A.'s view, this reasoning led logically to the assumption of jurisdiction, and reciprocally to the recognition by other courts. In this context, he cited *Travers v. Holley*, [1953] 2 All E.R. 794, where the English Court of Appeal had recognized a divorce decree granted in New South Wales [Australia] on the ground that the English courts would in similar circumstances have exercised jurisdiction in the same way. If that reasoning were to be applied to courts of other provinces, judgments of other provinces should be enforced if the British Columbia courts exercise similar jurisdiction.

Seaton J.A. acknowledged, however, that this view has not prevailed in judgments *in personam* in which class the judgments concerned here fell. However, he noted that the leading case on the point, *Emanuel v. Symon*, [1908] 1 K.B. 302 (C.A.), had been decided at the beginning of the century when travel from one country to another was impractical (in that case between Western Australia and England). As well, he observed, there was then an unstated assumption that the administration of justice in other countries was inferior.

Considerations such as these, Seaton J.A. stated, had no application to the situation here. He favoured acknowledging a difference between foreign judgments and judgments in other provinces, and he observed that such a difference had been accepted for certain purposes, such as in determining the factors to be taken into account in deciding whether to grant a *Mareva* injunction prohibiting the transfer of goods to a place outside the court's jurisdiction; see *Aetna Financial Services Ltd. v. Feigelman*, [1985] 1 S.C.R. 2, at p. 35. He also drew support from the fact that all superior court judges are appointed, paid and removed by the same government, and that the *Canadian Charter of Rights and Freedoms* applies throughout Canada. He further referred to the Australian Constitution which provides for recognition by each state of judgments of other states in the Commonwealth.

He then reviewed the British Columbia decisions which had followed the English position, but found none that was binding and preferred the view of "reciprocal" recognition of judgments proposed in certain periodical writings. . . . He then referred to and followed the judgment of Gow Co. Ct. J. (as he then was) in *Marcotte v. Megson* (1987), 19 B.C.L.R. (2d) 300, which had accepted the jurisdictional reciprocity approach for judgments *in personam*.

THE ISSUE

No one denies the Alberta court's jurisdiction to entertain the actions and enforce them there if it can. It would be surprising if they did. They concern transactions entered into in Alberta by individuals who were resident in Alberta at the time of the transactions and involve land situate in that province. Though the defendant appellant was outside Alberta at the time the actions were brought and judgment given, the Alberta rules for service outside the jurisdiction permitted him to be served in British Columbia. These rules are similar to those in other provinces, and specifically British Columbia. The validity of such rules does not appear to have been subjected to much questioning, a matter to which I shall, however, return.

The issue, then, as already mentioned, is simply whether a personal judgment validly given in Alberta against an absent defendant may be enforced in British Columbia where he now resides. [Emphasis added.]

The English Background

The law on the matter has remained remarkably constant for many years. It originated in England during the 19th century and, while it has been subjected to considerable refinement, its general structure has not substantially changed. The two cases most commonly relied on, *Singh v. Rajah of Faridkote*, [1894] A.C. 670 (P.C.), and *Emanuel v. Symon, supra*, date from the turn of the century.

Before concluding this review of the English background, I should make reference to *Indyka v. Indyka*, [1969] 1 A.C. 33, in which the House of Lords found another technique for going beyond the strict categories in *Symon*. In that case, their Lordships held that the English courts would recognize a divorce decree granted in a foreign country to a wife resident there though her husband was then domiciled in England.

It should be observed, however, that this case, too, involved matrimonial status and did not extend to an action *in personam*; see *New York v. Fitzgerald*, [1983] 5 W.W.R. 458 (B.C.S.C.), *per* Sheppard L.J.S.C.

The Canadian Background

In Canada, the courts have until recent years unanimously accepted the authority of *Emanuel v. Symon, supra*, in dealing with the recognition of foreign judgments; [citation omitted]. This was, of course, inevitable so far as foreign judgments were concerned until 1949 when appeals to the Privy Council were abolished. But, the approach was not confined to foreign judgments. It was extended to judgments of other provinces, which for the purposes of the rules of private international law are considered "foreign" countries; see, for example, *Lung v. Lee* (1928), 63 O.L.R. 194 (C.A.). There is thus a plethora of cases throughout Canada where two persons have entered into a contract in one province, frequently when both were resident there at the time, but the plaintiff has found it impossible to enforce a judgment given in that province because the defendant had moved to another province when the action was brought. . . . *Essentially, then, recognition by the courts of one province of a personal judgment against a defendant given in another province is dependant on the defendant's presence at the time of the action in the province where the judgment was given, unless the defendant in some way submits to the jurisdiction of the court giving the judgment.* [Emphasis added.]

. . . .

Held — Judgment for plaintiff.

Reason would suggest that inside the Confederation of Canada the principle of reciprocity of jurisdiction should apply. The action was concerned, and only concerned, with a judgment of a next-door province, not a foreign state but a partner in Confederation, which could not be registered as a domestic judgment because the defendant never submitted to the jurisdiction of the Alberta court. Because the judgment was a default judgment, it could have been opened up on the merits had the defendant chosen to do so, but he deliberately chose not to do so, preferring to rest his defence on the grounds of "no presence" and "no submission". In those circumstances, there being as between Alberta and British Columbia reciprocity of jurisdiction, it was appropriate to apply the principle that our courts should recognize a jurisdiction which they themselves claim.

The British Columbia Court of Appeal in the present case has now added its support to the call that reason dictates the evolution of the common law to permit the enforcement of *in personam* judgments given in sister-provinces.

The appellant in this case, of course, relies on the law as stated in *Symon, supra*. The respondents naturally rely on the Court of Appeal's judgment and particularly the "reciprocity" approach.

I should also note that the *Indyka* case, *supra*, has been followed in Canada; [citation omitted].

ANALYSIS

The common law regarding the recognition and enforcement of foreign judgments is firmly anchored in the principle of territoriality as interpreted and applied by the English courts in the 19th century; see *Rajah of Faridkote, supra*. This principle reflects the fact, one of the basic tenets of international law, that sovereign states have exclusive jurisdiction in their own territory. As a concomitant to this, states are hesitant to exercise jurisdiction over matters that may take place in the territory of other states. Jurisdiction being territorial, it follows that a state's law has no binding effect outside its jurisdiction. Great Britain, and specifically its courts, applied that doctrine more rigourously than other states; [citation omitted]. The English approach, we saw, was unthinkingly adopted by the courts of this country, even in relation to judgments given in sister-provinces.

Modern states, however, cannot live in splendid isolation and do give effect to judgments given in other countries in certain circumstances. Thus a judgment *in rem*, such as a decree of divorce granted by the courts of one state to persons domiciled there, will be recognized by the courts of other states. In certain circumstances, as well, our courts will enforce personal judgments given in other states. Thus, we saw, our courts will enforce an action for breach of contract given by the courts of another country if the defendant was present there at the time of the action or has agreed to the foreign court's exercise of jurisdiction. *This, it was thought, was in conformity with the requirements of comity, the informing principle of private international law, which has been stated to be the deference and respect due by other states to the actions of a state legitimately taken within its territory. Since the state where the judgment was given had power over the litigants, the judgments of its courts should be respected.* [Emphasis added.]

But a state was under no obligation to enforce judgments it deemed to fall outside the jurisdiction of the foreign court. In particular, the English courts refused to enforce judgments on contracts, wherever made, unless the defendant was within the jurisdiction of the foreign court at the time of the action or had submitted to its jurisdiction. And this was so, we saw, even of actions that could most appropriately be tried in the foreign jurisdiction, such as a case like the present where the personal obligation undertaken in the foreign country was in respect of property located there. Even in the 19th century, this approach gave difficulty, a difficulty in my view resulting from a misapprehension of the real nature of the idea of comity, an idea based not simply on respect for the dictates of a foreign sovereign, but on the convenience, nay necessity, in a world where legal authority is divided among sovereign states of adopting a doctrine of this kind. [Emphasis added.]

. . . .

The world has changed since the above rules were developed in 19th century England. Modern means of travel and communications have made many of these 19th century concerns appear parochial. The business community operates in a world economy and we correctly speak of a world community even in the face of decentralized political and legal power. Accommodating the flow of wealth, skills and people across state lines has now become imperative. Under these circumstances, our approach to the recognition and enforcement of foreign judgments would appear ripe for reappraisal. Certainly, other countries, notably the United States and members of the European Economic Community, have adopted more generous rules for the recognition and enforcement of foreign judgments to the general advantage of litigants.

However that may be, there is really no comparison between the interprovincial relationships of today and those obtaining between foreign countries in the 19th century. Indeed, in my view, there never was and the courts made a serious error in transposing the rules developed for the enforcement of foreign judgments to the enforcement of judgments from sister-provinces. The considerations underlying the rules of comity apply with much greater force between the units of a federal state, and I do not think it much matters whether one calls these rules of comity or simply relies directly on the Iberia of justice, necessity and convenience to which I have already adverted. Whatever nomenclature is used, our courts have not hesitated to cooperate with courts of other provinces where necessary to meet the ends of justice.

In any event, the English rules seem to me to fly in the face of the obvious intention of the Constitution to create a single country. This presupposes a basic goal of stability and unity where many aspects of life are not confined to one jurisdiction. A common citizenship ensured the mobility of Canadians across provincial lines, a position reinforced today by s. 6 of the *Charter*; [citation omitted]. In particular, significant steps were taken to foster economic integration. One of the central features of the constitutional arrangements incorporated in the *Constitution Act, 1867* was the creation of a common market. Barriers to interprovincial trade were removed by s. 121. Generally trade and commerce between the provinces was seen to be a matter of concern to the country as a whole; see

Constitution Act, 1867, s. 91(2). The Peace, Order and Good Government clause gives the federal Parliament powers to deal with interprovincial activities [citations omitted]. And the combined effect of s. 91(29) and s. 92(10) does the same for interprovincial works and undertakings.

These arrangements themselves speak to the strong need for the enforcement throughout the country of judgments given in one province. But that is not all. *The Canadian judicial structure is so arranged that any concerns about differential quality of justice among the provinces can have no real foundation. All superior court judges — who also have superintending control over other provincial courts and tribunals — are appointed and paid by the federal authorities. And all are subject to final review by the Supreme Court of Canada, which can determine when the courts of one province have appropriately exercised jurisdiction in an action and the circumstances under which the courts of another province should recognize such judgments. Any danger resulting from unfair procedure is further avoided by sub-constitutional factors, such as for example the fact that Canadian lawyers adhere to the same code of ethics throughout Canada.* [Emphasis added.] . . .

These various constitutional and sub-constitutional arrangements and practices make unnecessary a "full faith and credit" clause such as exists in other federations, such as the United States and Australia. The existence of these clauses, however, does indicate that a regime of mutual recognition of judgments across the country is inherent in a federation. Indeed, the European Economic Community has determined that such a feature flows naturally from a common market, even without political integration. To that end its members have entered into the 1968 [Brussels] Convention on Jurisdiction and Enforcement of Judgments in Civil and Commercial Matters [superceded by EC Regulation 44/2001 and as of 2015 European Parliament and Council Reg. 1215/2012 — covered *infra*].

The integrating character of our constitutional arrangements as they apply to interprovincial mobility is such that some writers have suggested that a "full faith and credit" clause must be read into the Constitution and that the federal Parliament is, under the "Peace, Order and Good Government" clause, empowered to legislate respecting the recognition and enforcement of judgments throughout Canada. The present case was not, however, argued on that basis, and I need not go that far. For present purposes, it is sufficient to say that, in my view, *the application of the underlying principles of comity and private international law must be adapted to the situations where they are applied, and that in a federation this implies a fuller and more generous acceptance of the judgments of the courts of other constituent units of the federation. In short, the rules of comity or private international law as they apply between the provinces must be shaped to conform to the federal structure of the Constitution.* [Emphasis added.]

. . . As I see it, the courts in one province should give full faith and credit, to use the language of the United States Constitution, to the judgments given by a court in another province or a territory, so long as that court has properly, or appropriately, exercised jurisdiction in the action. I referred earlier to the principles of order and fairness that should obtain in this area of the law. Both order and justice militate in favour of the security of transactions. It seems anarchic and unfair that a person should be able to avoid legal obligations arising in one province simply by moving to another province. Why should a plaintiff be compelled to begin an action in the province where the defendant now resides, whatever the inconvenience and costs this may bring, and whatever degree of connection the relevant transaction may have with another province? And why should the availability of local enforcement be the decisive element in the plaintiff's choice of forum?

These concerns, however, must be weighed against fairness to the defendant. I noted earlier that the taking of jurisdiction by a court in one province and its recognition in another must be viewed as correlatives, and I added that recognition in other provinces should be dependent on the fact that the court giving judgment "properly" or "appropriately" exercised jurisdiction. It may meet the demands of order and fairness to recognize a judgment given in a jurisdiction that had the greatest or at least significant contacts with the subject-matter of the action. *But it hardly accords with principles of order and fairness to permit a person to sue another in any jurisdiction, without regard to the contacts that jurisdiction may have to the defendant or the subject-matter of the suit. Thus, fairness to the defendant requires that the judgment be issued by a court acting through fair process and with properly restrained jurisdiction.* [Emphasis added.]

As discussed, fair process is not an issue within the Canadian federation. The question that remains, then, is when has a court exercised its jurisdiction appropriately for the purposes of recognition by a court in another province? This poses no difficulty where the court has acted on the basis of some ground traditionally accepted by courts as permitting the recognition and enforcement of foreign judgments — in the case of judgments *in personam* where the defendant was within the jurisdiction at the time of the action or when he submitted to its judgment whether by agreement or attornment. In the first case, the court had jurisdiction over the person, and in the second case by virtue of the agreement. No injustice results.

The difficulty, of course, arises where, as here, the defendant was outside the jurisdiction of that court and he was served *ex juris*. To what extent may a court of a province properly exercise jurisdiction over a defendant in another province? The rules for service *ex juris* in all the provinces are broad, in some provinces, Nova Scotia and Prince Edward Island, very broad indeed. It is clear, however, that if the courts of one province are to be expected to give effect to judgments given in another province, there must be some limits to the exercise of jurisdiction against persons outside the province.

It will be obvious from the manner in which I approach the problem that I do not see the "reciprocity approach" as providing an answer to the difficulty regarding *in personam* judgments given in other provinces, whatever utility it may have on the international plane. Even there, I am more comfortable with the approach taken by the House of Lords in *Indyka v. Indyka, supra*, where the question posed in a matrimonial case was whether there was a real and substantial connection between the petitioner and the country or territory exercising jurisdiction. I should observe, however, that in a case involving matrimonial status, the subject-matter of the action and the petitioner are obviously at the same place. That is not necessarily so of a personal action where a nexus may have to be sought between the subject-matter of the action and the territory where the action is brought.

III. COMMON LAW VARIATIONS — CANADA

Turning to the present case, it is difficult to imagine a more reasonable place for the action for the deficiencies to take place than Alberta. As noted earlier, the properties were situate in Alberta, and the contracts were entered into there by parties then both resident in the province. Moreover, deficiency actions follow upon foreclosure proceedings, which should obviously take place in Alberta, and the action for the deficiencies cries out for consolidation with the foreclosure proceedings in some manner similar to a Rice Order. A more "real and substantial" connection between the damages suffered and the jurisdiction can scarcely be imagined. In my view, the Alberta court had jurisdiction, and its judgment should be recognized and be enforceable in British Columbia. [Emphasis added.]

DISPOSITION

I would dismiss the appeal with costs.

Appeal dismissed with costs.

In 1993 the Supreme Court extended *Morguard* in the case of *Hunt v. T&N plc*, [1993] 4 S.C.R. 289. *Hunt* involved a discovery order issued by a British Columbia provincial court during the course of an action for damages resulting from the inhalation of asbestos fibers. The order required the production of documents by the defendants, all companies engaged in the production of asbestos and manufacture of asbestos products. They were organized and headquartered in Quebec. In response to the court's order, the defendants obtained a judgment by the Quebec Provincial Court forbidding the defendants from sending documents out of the province pursuant to Quebec statute prohibiting discovery of documents held by enterprises in Quebec. Hunt, the plaintiff, then sought an enforcement order by the Supreme Court of British Columbia (the court of first instance) to compel production of the documents. The court dismissed his petition. On appeal, the British Columbia Court of Appeal upheld the dismissal. Both courts ruled that the British Columbia courts did not have jurisdiction over the constitutional validity of a Quebec statute. The Supreme Court of Canada reversed, holding that the Quebec statute, in the words of Justice La Forest, "should be read as not applying to the provinces since such application would be *ultra vires* under the constitutional principle set forth in the *Morguard* case." Justice La Forest continued:

> The basic thrust of *Morguard* was that in our federation a greater degree of recognition and enforcement of judgments given in other provinces was called for. *Morguard* was careful to indicate, however, that a court must have reasonable grounds for assuming jurisdiction. One must emphasize that the ideas of "comity" are not an end in themselves, but are grounded in notions of order and fairness to participants in litigation with connections to multiple jurisdictions.
>
> In *Morguard*, a more accommodating approach to recognition and enforcement was premised on there being a "real and substantial connection" to the forum that assumed jurisdiction and gave judgment. Contrary to the comments of some commentators and lower court judges, this was not meant to be a rigid test, but was simply intended to capture the idea

that there must be some limits on the claims to jurisdiction. Indeed I observed (at p. 1104) that the "real and substantial connection" test was developed in *Indyka v. Indyka*, [1969] 1 A.C. 33, in a case involving matrimonial status (where sound policy demands generosity in recognition), and that in a personal action a nexus may need to be sought between the subject-matter and the territory where the action is brought. I then considered the test developed in *Moran v. Pyle National (Canada) Ltd.*, *supra*, for products liability cases as an example of where jurisdiction would be properly assumed. The exact limits of what constitutes a reasonable assumption of jurisdiction were not defined, and I add that no test can perhaps ever be rigidly applied; no court has ever been able to anticipate all of these. However, though some of these may well require reconsideration in light of *Morguard*, the connections relied on under the traditional rules are a good place to start. More than this was left to depend on the gradual accumulation of connections defined in accordance with the broad principles of order and fairness; [reference omitted]. But I think that the general approach was solidly based.

Since the matter has been the subject of considerable commentary, I should note parenthetically that I need not, for the purposes of this case, consider the relative merits of adopting a broad or narrow basis for assuming jurisdiction and the consequences of this decision for the use of the doctrine of *forum non conveniens*. Whatever approach is used, the assumption of and the discretion not to exercise jurisdiction must ultimately be guided by the requirements of order and fairness, not a mechanical counting of contacts or connections. Here, the courts below found that there was, on the authorities, jurisdiction, and that there was no reason to apply the doctrine of *forum non conveniens*. In light of commentaries on *Morguard*, I should perhaps also add that I need not consider the implications, if any, of *Morguard* on choice of law and other aspects of conflicts law.

Finally, I noted in *Morguard* . . . that a number of commentators had suggested that the federal Parliament had power to legislate respecting the recognition and enforcement of judgments, and in my view that suggestion is well founded. This issue is ultimately related to the rights of the citizen, trade and commerce and other federal legislative powers, including that encompassed in the peace, order and good government clause. But subject to these overriding powers, I see no reason why the provinces should not be able to legislate in the area, subject, however, to the principles in *Morguard* and to the demands of territoriality as expounded in the cases, [citation omitted].

APPLICATION OF *MORGUARD* PRINCIPLES TO THE IMPUGNED STATUTE

I now turn to the issue whether the impugned statute is consistent with the principles I have just set forth. I say at the outset that I do not think it is. A province undoubtedly has an interest in protecting the property of its residents within the province, but it cannot do so by unconstitutional means. Here the means chosen are intended to unconditionally refuse recognition to orders and thereby impede litigation, not only in foreign countries but in other provinces. At least when a court order is sought, if not before, a judicial order in another province will be denied effect. There are no qualifications. No discretion is given so it can scarcely be said that the Act respects the principles of order and fairness which must, under the *Morguard* principle, inform the procedures required for litigation having extraprovincial effects. Apart from the legislative aspect, the situation in *Morguard* differed in that the appellant there sought refusal of recognition after the judgment was rendered. But the constitutional mandate cannot be avoided by a preemptive strike. The whole purpose of a blocking statute is to impede successful litigation or prosecution in other jurisdictions by refusing recognition and compliance with orders issued there. Everybody realizes that the whole point of blocking statutes is not to keep documents in the province, but rather to prevent compliance, and so the success of litigation outside the province that that province finds objectionable. This is no doubt part of sovereign right, but it certainly runs counter to comity. In the political realm it leads to strict retaliatory laws and power struggles. And it discourages international commerce and efficient allocation and conduct of litigation. It has similar effects on the interprovincial level, effects that offend against the basic structure of the Canadian federation.

As a matter of legislative history, we were told, the Ontario and Quebec statutes were precipitated by the aggressively extraterritorial, "long arm" antitrust statutes of the United States. Unfortunately, these blocking statutes are a blunt response, and themselves have become like long arm statutes that haphazardly end up harming individuals who were not in the jurisdiction and are not pursuing the actions against which the blocking statutes were allegedly originally aimed.

This could, no doubt, be defended on the basis of sovereignty. Indeed the federal Parliament is expressly permitted by our Constitution to legislate with internationally extraterritorial effect. But this appeal is concerned with the provinces within Confederation. *Morguard* requires that the rules of private international law must be adapted to the structure of our federation. In a federation, we assume that there is more commonality as to what is acceptable action; we have many common procedures. We even have similar conflicts rules, related, for example, to jurisdiction and deference, and to procedures regarding the *lex fori*. And courts are required, by constitutional restraints, to assume jurisdiction only where there are real and substantial connections to that place. [Emphasis added.] In terms of policy, the presence of such blocking statutes is an anachronism, not even, so we were told, aimed at interprovincial litigation at its inception in the 1940s, but definitely inimical to such litigation if applied on the interprovincial level.

If blocking statutes of the type now in effect in both Ontario and Quebec were possible under the Constitution, they would have the potential of affecting the rights of litigants in all the other provinces, whenever the defendant was a Quebec or Ontario business. Discovery is a very important tool of civil litigation. It is especially important in cases of this type, where there are allegations of some sort of product liability. The ultimate plaintiff must have a tool to access the otherwise internal documents, especially of large corporate monoliths. And given that there are allegations of civil conspiracy in this case, it is all the more necessary. That British Columbia, despite what was stated in the courts below, considers discovery central is evident in that refusal to comply with a demand is one of the few procedural violations that will result in a default judgment in the province. Most other instances of non-compliance with *Rules of Court* are treated as irregularities that can be remedied; see Rule 2. Moreover, the trend of the case law on Rule 26 is to emphasize the importance of the right to discovery, even at the cost of considerable loss of confidentiality.

. . . The essential effect then, and indeed the barely shielded intent, is to impede the substantive rights of litigants elsewhere. It would force parties to conduct litigation in multiple fora and compel more plaintiffs to choose to litigate in the courts of Ontario and Quebec. Other provinces could, of course, follow suit. It is inconceivable that in devising a scheme of union comprising a common market stretching from sea to sea, the Fathers of Confederation would have contemplated a situation where citizens would be effectively deprived of access to the ordinary courts in their jurisdiction in respect of transactions flowing from the existence of that common market. The resultant higher transactional costs for interprovincial transactions constitute an infringement on the unity and efficiency of the Canadian marketplace, as well as unfairness to the citizen.

The lack of order and fairness in the present situation is evident in a further incongruity. It is that full rights of discovery are available to parties in the civil procedure of Ontario and Quebec. It is not as if these jurisdictions have a totally different tradition of civil procedure. If the litigation was proceeding in either of those provinces there would be full discovery. And if both parties to the action had been from British Columbia there would be discovery. But somehow, because of the fortuitous combination of litigation in British Columbia involving a defendant from Quebec or Ontario, the discovery process is barred.

In light of the foregoing, I conclude that the Quebec Business Concerns Records Act is constitutionally inapplicable to other provinces, and consequently in the present case. [Emphasis added.]

QUESTIONS

1. Could under Canadian Law before or after *Morguard* a provincial parliament validly enact a statute extending general personal jurisdiction with service *ex juris* to non-residents owning property in the province?

2. What is meant by a "real and substantial connection" with the case? Is this test similar to or substantially different from the International Shoe "minimum contacts" test?

3. Could under Canadian law before or after *Morguard* a provincial parliament validly enact a statute subjecting a non-resident company without an office or employees in the province but which advertises and sells goods or services within the province through independent contractors who for a commission take orders, received and filled outside of the province?

4. What was the distinction before and after *Morguard* between private international law and inter-provincial or national law?

5. How would *Shaffer v. Heitner* and the *Burnham* cases have been decided under Canadian law before and after *Morguard*?

6. Would *In re Kimura* have been decided differently by the Supreme Court of Canada?

7. In what ways does the reasoning in *Morguard* differ from the U.S. Supreme Court cases examined above? What explains the differences?

8. How does the appellate role of the Canadian Supreme Court differ from that of the U.S. Supreme Court? How would you characterize the *Morguard* decision both before and after *Hunt*?

9. Contrast the treatment of English cases by the Canadian Supreme Court as authority with the virtual neglect of English cases by the U.S. Supreme Court. Can you offer any explanation for this difference?

10. In what ways have U.S. Supreme Court decisions on judicial jurisdiction influenced Canadian law?

Subsequent to the *Morguard* and *Hunt* decisions, various provinces, including Quebec, have made statutory changes to the rules on jurisdiction and service *ex juris*. For the English-speaking provinces, a principal vehicle has been adoption, as noted, of the Uniform Court Jurisdiction and Proceedings Transfer Act proposed by the Uniform Law Conference of Canada. The result is greater uniformity at least within the English-speaking provinces and territories and, as in the case of Quebec, harmonized rules for intra-provincial and transnational adjudicatory jurisdiction.

B.C. COURT JURISDICTION AND PROCEEDINGS TRANSFER ACT
[SBC 2003] CHAPTER 28 (2003)

Proceedings against a person

   3 A court has territorial competence in a proceeding that is brought against a person only if

      (a) that person is the plaintiff in another proceeding in the court to which the proceeding in question is a counterclaim,

      (b) during the course of the proceeding that person submits to the court's jurisdiction,

      (c) there is an agreement between the plaintiff and that person to the effect that the court has jurisdiction in the proceeding,

(d) that person is ordinarily resident in British Columbia at the time of the commencement of the proceeding, or

(e) there is a real and substantial connection between British Columbia and the facts on which the proceeding against that person is based.

. . . .

Real and substantial connection

10 Without limiting the right of the plaintiff to prove other circumstances that constitute a real and substantial connection between British Columbia and the facts on which a proceeding is based, a real and substantial connection between British Columbia and those facts is presumed to exist if the proceeding

(a) is brought to enforce, assert, declare or determine proprietary or possessory rights or a security interest in property in British Columbia that is immovable or movable property,

(b) concerns the administration of the estate of a deceased person in relation to

(i) immovable property in British Columbia of the deceased person, or

(ii) movable property anywhere of the deceased person if at the time of death he or she was ordinarily resident in British Columbia,

(c) is brought to interpret, rectify, set aside or enforce any deed, will, contract or other instrument in relation to

(i) property in British Columbia that is immovable or movable property, or

(ii) movable property anywhere of a deceased person who at the time of death was ordinarily resident in British Columbia,

(d) is brought against a trustee in relation to the carrying out of a trust in any of the following circumstances:

(i) the trust assets include property in British Columbia that is immovable or movable property and the relief claimed is only as to that property;

(ii) that trustee is ordinarily resident in British Columbia;

(iii) the administration of the trust is principally carried on in British Columbia;

(iv) by the express terms of a trust document, the trust is governed by the law of British Columbia,

(e) concerns contractual obligations, and

(i) the contractual obligations, to a substantial extent, were to be performed in British Columbia,

(ii) by its express terms, the contract is governed by the law of British Columbia, or

(iii) the contract

(A) is for the purchase of property, services or both, for use other than in the course of the purchaser's trade or profession, and

(B) resulted from a solicitation of business in British Columbia by or on behalf of the seller,

(f) concerns restitutionary obligations that, to a substantial extent, arose in British Columbia,

(g) concerns a tort committed in British Columbia,

(h) concerns a business carried on in British Columbia,

(i) is a claim for an injunction ordering a party to do or refrain from doing anything

(i) in British Columbia, or

(ii) in relation to property in British Columbia that is immovable or movable property,

(j) is for a determination of the personal status or capacity of a person who is ordinarily resident in British Columbia,

(k) is for enforcement of a judgment of a court made in or outside British Columbia or an arbitral award made in or outside British Columbia, or

(l) is for the recovery of taxes or other indebtedness and is brought by the government of British Columbia or by a local authority in British Columbia.

The Canadian common law approach to adjudicatory jurisdiction was further articulated in the Supreme Court judgment of April 18, 2012 in *Club Resorts Ltd. v. Van Breda*. The decision, summarized below, articulates the applicable standards for determining the adjudicatory jurisdiction of the courts in the English-speaking provinces and territories as well as for abstention under the *forum non conveniens* doctrine, as examined in Chapter 3 on Parallel Litigation.

CLUB RESORTS LTD. v. VAN BREDA
2012 SCC 17, [2012] 1 S.C.R. 572

Coram: McLachlin C.J. and Binnie,* LeBel, Deschamps, Fish, Abella, Charron,* Rothstein and Cromwell JJ. (*Binnie and Charron JJ. took no part in the judgment.)

[Official Court Summary]

In separate cases, two individuals were injured while on vacation outside of Canada. Morgan Van Breda suffered catastrophic injuries on a beach in Cuba. Claude Charron died while scuba diving, also in Cuba. Actions were brought in Ontario against a number of parties, including the appellant, Club Resorts Ltd., a company incorporated in the Cayman Islands that managed the two hotels where the accidents occurred. Club Resorts sought to block those proceedings, arguing that the Ontario courts lacked jurisdiction and, in the alternative, that a Cuban court would be a more appropriate forum on the basis of the doctrine of *forum non conveniens*. In both cases, the motion judges found that the Ontario courts had jurisdiction with respect to the actions against Club Resorts. In considering *forum non conveniens*, it was also held that the Ontario court was clearly a more appropriate forum. The two cases were heard together in the Court of Appeal. The appeals were both dismissed.

Held: The appeals should be dismissed.

This case concerns the elaboration of the "real and substantial connection" test as an appropriate common law conflicts rule for the assumption of jurisdiction. In determining whether a court can assume jurisdiction over a certain claim, the preferred approach in Canada has been to rely on a set of specific factors which are given presumptive effect, as opposed to a regime based on an exercise of almost pure and individualized judicial discretion. Given the nature of the relationships governed by private international law, the framework for the assumption of jurisdiction cannot be an unstable, *ad hoc* system made up on the fly on a case-by-case basis — however laudable the objective of individual fairness may be. There must be order in the system, and it must permit the development of a just and fair approach to resolving conflicts. Justice and fairness are undoubtedly essential purposes of a sound system of private international law. But they cannot be attained without a system of principles and rules that ensure security and predictability in the law governing the assumption of jurisdiction by a court. The identification of a set of relevant presumptive connecting factors and the determination of their legal nature and effect will bring greater clarity and predictability to the analysis of the problems of assumption of jurisdiction, while at the same time ensuring consistency with the objectives of fairness and efficiency that underlie this branch of the law. From this perspective, a clear distinction must be maintained between, on the one hand, the factors or factual situations that link the subject matter of the litigation and the defendant to the forum and, on the other hand, the principles and analytical tools, such as the values of fairness and efficiency or the principle of comity.

To meet the common law real and substantial connection test, the party arguing that the court should assume jurisdiction has the burden of identifying a presumptive connecting factor that links the subject matter of the litigation to the forum. Jurisdiction must be established primarily on the basis of objective factors that connect the legal situation or the subject matter of the litigation with the forum. Abstract concerns for order, efficiency or fairness in the system are no substitute for connecting factors that give rise to a "real and substantial" connection for the purposes of the law of conflicts. In a case concerning a tort, the following factors are presumptive connecting factors that, *prima facie*, entitle a court to assume jurisdiction over a dispute:

(a) the defendant is domiciled or resident in the province;

(b) the defendant carries on business in the province;

(c) the tort was committed in the province; and

(d) a contract connected with the dispute was made in the province.

Although the factors set out in the list are considered presumptive, this does not mean that the list of recognized factors is complete, as it may be reviewed over time and updated by adding new presumptive connecting factors. When a court considers whether a new connecting factor should be given presumptive effect, the values of order, fairness and comity can serve as useful analytical tools for assessing the strength of the relationship with a forum to which the factor in question points. These values underlie all presumptive connecting factors, whether listed or new. In identifying new presumptive factors, a court should look to connections that give rise to a relationship with the forum that is similar in nature to the ones which result from the listed factors. Relevant considerations include:

(a) Similarity of the connecting factor with the recognized presumptive connecting factors;

(b) Treatment of the connecting factor in the case law;

(c) Treatment of the connecting factor in statute law; and

(d) Treatment of the connecting factor in the private international law of other legal systems with a shared commitment to order, fairness and comity.

The presumption of jurisdiction that arises where a recognized connecting factor — whether listed or new — applies is not irrebuttable. The burden of rebutting the presumption of jurisdiction rests, of course, on the party challenging the assumption of jurisdiction. That party must negate the presumptive effect of the listed or new factor and convince the court that the proposed assumption of jurisdiction would be inappropriate. This could be accomplished by establishing facts which demonstrate that the presumptive connecting factor does not point to any real relationship between the subject matter of the litigation and the forum or points only to a weak relationship between them.

. . . .

In *Van Breda*, a contract was entered into in Ontario. The existence of a contract made in Ontario that is connected with the litigation is a presumptive connecting factor that, on its face, entitles the courts of Ontario to assume jurisdiction in this case. Club Resorts has failed to rebut the presumption of jurisdiction that arises where this factor applies. Therefore, there was a sufficient connection between the Ontario court and the subject matter of the litigation. Club Resorts has not discharged its burden of showing that a Cuban court would clearly be a more appropriate forum. While a sufficient connection exists between Cuba and the subject matter of the litigation to support an action there, issues related to the fairness to the parties and to the efficient disposition of the claim must be considered. A trial held in Cuba would present serious challenges to the parties. All things considered, the burden on the plaintiffs clearly would be far heavier if they were required to bring their action in Cuba.

In *Charron*, the facts supported the conclusion that Club Resorts was carrying on a business in Ontario, which is a presumptive connecting factor. Club Resorts' commercial activities in Ontario went well beyond promoting a brand and advertising. Its representatives were in the province on a regular basis and it benefitted from the physical presence of an office in Ontario. It therefore follows that it has been established that a presumptive connecting factor applies and that the Ontario court is *prima facie* entitled to assume jurisdiction. Club Resorts has not rebutted the presumption of jurisdiction that arises from this connecting factor and therefore the Ontario court has jurisdiction on the basis of the real and substantial connection test. Furthermore, Club Resorts failed to discharge its burden of showing that a Cuban court would clearly be a more appropriate forum in the circumstances of this case. Considerations of fairness to the parties weigh heavily in favour of the plaintiff.

Contrast the applicable provisions of the Uniform Court Jurisdiction and Proceedings Transfer Act as enacted in British Columbia and the decision in *Club Resorts Ltd. v. Van Breda* with those of the 1991 Civil Code of Quebec for international jurisdiction and the Canadian Supreme Court decision in *Spar Areospace Ltd. v. American Mobile Satellite Corporation* below. In *Spar*, the application of the provisions of the international private law provisions of the Civil Code of Quebec under the standards established in *Morguard* and *Hunt* is the central concern:

1991 CIVIL CODE OF QUEBEC
[Code Civil de Quebec]

BOOK X
TITLE THREE INTERNATIONAL JURISDICTION OF QUEBEC AUTHORITIES

CHAPTER I GENERAL PROVISIONS

3134. In the absence of any special provision, the Quebec authorities have jurisdiction when the defendant is domiciled in Quebec.

. . . .

3136. Even though a Quebec authority has no jurisdiction to hear a dispute, it may hear it, if the dispute has a sufficient connection with Quebec, where proceedings cannot possibly be instituted outside Quebec or where the institution of such proceedings outside Quebec cannot reasonably be required.

. . . .

3138. A Quebec authority may order provisional or conservatory measures even if it has no jurisdiction over the merits of the dispute.

[The Special Provisions (Chapter II) cover "Personal Actions of an Extrapatrimonial and Family Nature," (Division I) "Personal Actions of a Patrimonial Nature," (Division II) and "Real and Mixed Actions" (Division III)]

SPAR AEROSPACE LTD. v. AMERICAN MOBILE SATELLITE CORP.
[2002] 4 S.C.R. 205, 2002 SCC 78

The judgment of the Court was delivered by LEEBEL J.

I. Introduction

[1] This appeal examines the private international law issues that arise when a business venture between multi-jurisdictional parties meets with a calamitous end, leading to the filing of an extra-contractual action claiming damages in the province of Quebec. Specifically, this case engages a number of preliminary issues to be determined before the merits of the action are considered, including: whether Quebec courts can assert jurisdiction in the matter pursuant to art. 3148 of the *Civil Code of Quebec*, S.Q. 1991, c. 64 ("*C.C.Q*"); whether there must be a real and substantial connection between the action and the province of Quebec; and whether jurisdiction should be declined on the basis of the doctrine of *forum non conveniens*, pursuant to art. 3148 *C.C.Q.*

[2] On October 4, 1999, Duval Hesler J. of the Quebec Superior Court dismissed the appellants' motions, confirming the jurisdiction of the Quebec courts. The appellants' appeals to the Quebec Court of Appeal were dismissed on May 24, 2000. On June 11, 2002, the appellants' further appeal to this Court was dismissed. These are the Iberia following that decision.

II. Facts

[3] The appellant and respondent companies are involved in various aspects of the manufacture and operation of satellites. In November 1990, one of the four appellants, Motient Corporation ("Motient", previously conducting business under the name "American Mobile Satellite Corporation"), entered into a contract with Hughes Aircraft Company ("Hughes Aircraft", which is not a party to this litigation) for the construction of a satellite by the latter. On September 3, 1991 (with amendments agreed to on January 8, 1993), Hughes Aircraft entered into a

subcontract with the respondent, Spar Aerospace Limited ("Spar"), for the manufacture of the communication payload of the satellite at its Ste-Anne-de-Bellevue establishment in the province of Quebec ("Quebec").

[4] The satellite was launched into orbit on April 7, 1995. The in-orbit testing that followed was successful and Motient accepted the spacecraft. Motient then engaged the second appellant, Viacom Inc. ("Viacom", formerly Westinghouse Electric Corporation), to conduct ground station testing with the third appellant, Satellite Transmissions Systems ("STS"). Motient contracted with the fourth appellant, Hughes Communications Inc. ("Hughes Communications"), to monitor and control the satellite's performance. Unfortunately, during the testing, serious damage was caused to the satellite and Hughes Aircraft refused to pay the respondent performance-incentive payments provided for in the subcontract agreement, beyond the initial payment of $148,113.58 made around November 2, 1995.

[5] The respondent commenced an action in Quebec alleging that signals from the ground station to the satellite pushed the latter into overdrive, causing severe damage. The respondent holds the appellants responsible for a number of problems, including: the improper calibration of the transmitting equipment, insufficient wiring, inadequate surveillance, and the lack of a communication system between the ground station in Virginia and Hughes Communications in California. In its lawsuit, the respondent claims $819,657 for loss of performance incentives, $50,000 for loss of future profits caused by loss of reputation and $50,000 for expenses incurred in investigating the damages to the satellite.

[6] The appellants all brought declinatory motions challenging the jurisdiction of the Quebec courts to hear this matter, pursuant to art. 163 of the *Code of Civil Procedure*, R.S.Q., c. C-25 ("*C.C.P.*"), and art. 3148 *C.C.Q.* In addition, two of the appellants (Motient and Viacom) sought to have the action dismissed on the basis of the doctrine of *forum non conveniens* pursuant to art. 3135 *C.C.Q.*

[7] The challenge to jurisdiction was based on a number of facts. First, the respondent's head office was located in Toronto in the province of Ontario, and none of the appellants have their place of business in Quebec. Motient was located in Virginia, Hughes Communications in California, Viacom in Pennsylvania and STS in New York. Secondly, although none of the appellants are party to the "Fixed Price Subcontract" to manufacture the payload between "Hughes Aircraft Company, El Segundo, California U.S.A. and Spar Aerospace Limited, Ste-Anne-de-Bellevue, Quebec, Canada", this contract is significant as it indicates that it governed by the laws of California (art. 23). Thirdly, the respondent was sued by a number of insurers in relation with the same event before a California court and unsuccessfully challenged its jurisdiction. However, that lawsuit was settled out of court.

III. Statutory Provisions

[8] *Civil Code of Quebec*, S.Q. 1991, c. 64

> 3135. Even though a Quebec authority has jurisdiction to hear a dispute, it may exceptionally and on an application by a party, decline jurisdiction if it considers that the authorities of another country are in a better position to decide.

3148. In personal actions of a patrimonial nature, a Quebec authority has jurisdiction where

(1) the defendant has his domicile or his residence in Quebec;

(2) the defendant is a legal person, is not domiciled in Quebec but has an establishment in Quebec, and the dispute relates to its activities in Quebec;

(3) a fault was committed in Quebec, damage was suffered in Quebec, an injurious act occurred in Quebec or one of the obligations arising from a contract was to be performed in Quebec;

(4) the parties have by agreement submitted to it all existing or future disputes between themselves arising out of a specified legal relationship;

(5) the defendant submits to its jurisdiction.

However, a Quebec authority has no jurisdiction where the parties, by agreement, have chosen to submit all existing or future disputes between themselves relating to a specified legal relationship to a foreign authority or to an arbitrator, unless the defendant submits to the jurisdiction of the Quebec authority.

IV. Judgments Below

[Omitted]

V. Issues

[13] 1. Do the Quebec courts have competence in the present matter pursuant to the factors set out in art. 3148(3) *C.C.Q.*?

2. Should the criterion of a "real and substantial connection" be used when determining whether or not a Quebec authority has international jurisdiction under art. 3148 *C.C.Q.*?

3. [Discussion and decision as to Issue 3 — whether jurisdiction be declined on the basis of the doctrine of *forum non conveniens*, pursuant to art. 3135 *C.C.Q.*— included Chapter 3 on Parallel Litigation.]

VI. Analysis

A. *Overview of General Principles of Private International Law*

[14] The private international law rules engaged in the case at bar are derived largely from a web of interrelated principles that underlie the private international legal order. The following is a brief overview of these fundamental principles and discusses how they are manifested in modern private international law rules.

[15] One of the key principles underpinning the various private international law rules is international comity. One of the earliest and most influential works on the topic was Dutch jurist U. Huber's 1689 essay, *De conflictu legum diversarum in diversis imperiis* (for translation and elaboration, see D. J. L. Davies, "The Influence of Huber's *De Conflictu Legum* on English Private International Law", in *The British Year Book of International Law* (1937), vol. 18, p. 49). Huber opined that, based on the customs of mutual deference and respect between nations, comity attenuates the principle of territoriality by allowing states to apply foreign laws so that rights acquired under them can retain their force, provided that they do not prejudice the states' powers or rights. (See C. Emanuelli, *Droit international privé québécois* (2001), at pp. 20–21; G. Goldstein and E. Groffier, *Droit international privé*, t. I, *Théorie générale* (1998), at p. 20; H. E. Yntema, "The Comity Doctrine" (1966–67), 65 *Mich. L. Rev.* 1; and E. F. Scoles et al., eds., *Conflict of Laws* (3rd ed. 2000), at pp. 14–15.) This approach was enthusiastically supported by American J. Story's influential 1834 text, *Commentaries on the Conflict of Laws, Foreign and Domestic*, ch. 11, at para. 35 (quoted in J.-G. Castel, *Droit international privé québécois* (1980), at p. 15; see also: Scoles et al., *supra*, at pp. 18–19; and Emanuelli, *supra*, at p. 22.)

[16] Despite its importance, comity has proven a difficult concept to define in legal terms (see: J.-G. Castel and J. Walker, *Canadian Conflict of Laws* (5th ed. (loose leaf)), at pp. 1.13–1.14). Some authors have questioned its utility in the determination of private international law issues, especially in matters concerning the applicability of foreign law. See, for example, *Cheshire and North's Private International Law* (13th ed. 1999), at p. 5, where the authors state that "The word itself is incompatible with the judicial function, for comity is a matter for sovereigns, not for judges required to decide a case according to the rights of the parties." And in *Dicey and Morris on the Conflict of Laws* (13th ed. 2000), vol. 1, at p. 5, it is observed that:

> Story used it to mean more than mere courtesy, but something rather less than equivalent to international law. Dicey was highly critical of the use of comity to explain the conflict of laws ("a singular specimen of confusion of thought produced by laxity of language") . . . . [Footnotes omitted.]

[17] Notwithstanding these limitations, comity is still considered a useful guiding principle when applying the rules of private international law. For example, the notion of comity is invoked today as a guiding principle in the context of anti-suit injunctions, as noted by the editors of *Dicey and Morris, supra*, at p. 6:

> More recently, comity has been invoked to justify the caution which is required in the exercise of the power to grant injunctions to restrain proceedings in foreign courts. Comity requires that the English forum should have a sufficient interest in, or connection with, the matter in question to justify the indirect interference with the foreign court which such an injunction entails. [Footnote omitted.]

[18] On a more practical level, it has been remarked that "the theory has performed a useful function in freeing our subject from parochialism, and making our judges more internationalist in outlook and more tolerant of foreign law than they might otherwise have been". (See J. H. C. Morris, *The Conflict of Laws* (5th ed. 2000), at p. 535.)

[19] The notion of comity has retained its vitality in the jurisprudence of Canadian courts. This Court has adopted the following definition of the concept:

> . . . the recognition which one nation allows within its territory to the legislative, executive or judicial acts of another nation, having due regard both to international duty and convenience, and to the rights of its own citizens or of other persons who are under the protection of its laws. (*Hilton v. Guyot*, 159 U.S. 113 (1895), at p. 164) [Citations omitted.]

[20] This Court has indicated that "the twin objectives sought by private international law in general and the doctrine of international comity in particular [are] order and fairness". (See *Holt Cargo, supra*, at para. 71, *per* Binnie J.; *Morguard, supra*, at p. 1097; and *Hunt v. T&N PLC*, [1993] 4 S.C.R. 289, at p. 325, *per* La Forest J.) When giving effect to these two objectives, Binnie J. observed that "the Court gave pre-eminence to the objective of order" (*Holt Cargo, supra*, at para. 71). As noted by La Forest J. in *Tolofson v. Jensen*, [1994] 3 S.C.R. 1022, at p. 1058: "Order is a precondition to justice."

[21] The three principles of comity, order and fairness serve to guide the determination of the principal private international law issues: jurisdiction *simpliciter, forum non conveniens*, choice of law, and recognition of foreign judgments. Given that these three principles are at the heart of the private international legal order, it is not surprising that the various issues are interrelated. For example, W. Tetley points out that the "*'forum non conveniens*' doctrine (founded on the 'real and substantial connection' test), is now also an essential feature of Canadian conflicts theory and practice". (See W. Tetley, "Current Developments in Canadian Private International Law" (1999), 78 *Can. Bar Rev.* 152, at p. 155.) Also, in *Amchem Products Inc. v. British Columbia (Workers' Compensation Board)*, [1993] 1 S.C.R. 897, Sopinka J. observed, at p. 933, that the criterion of "juridical advantage" is a factor to be considered both in deciding whether to decline jurisdiction on the basis of the doctrine of *forum non conveniens* and in determining whether or not an injustice would result if a plaintiff is allowed to proceed in a foreign jurisdiction, in the context of an anti-suit injunction.

[22] The various rules governing the private international law order of Quebec are found primarily in Book Ten of the *C.C.Q.*, subsuming or complementing the rules of civil procedure found in the *Code of Civil Procedure*. See J. A. Talpis and J.-G. Castel, "Interpreting the rules of private international law" in *Reform of the Civil Code*, vol. 5B, *Private International Law* (1993). These rules cover a broad range of interrelated topics, including: the jurisdiction of the court (art. 3136, 3139 and 3148 *C.C.Q.*); the discretionary powers of the court to eliminate inappropriate fora (under the doctrine of *forum non conveniens* codified in art. 3135 *C.C.Q.*, through the recourse to the *lis pendens* power in art. 3137, or by issuance of an anti-suit injunction pursuant to art. 3135 *C.C.Q.* and art. 46 *C.C.P.*); and they allow Quebec courts to recognize and enforce foreign decisions (art. 3155 *C.C.Q.*).

[23] As the basic rules of private international law are codified in Quebec, courts must interpret those rules by first examining the specific wording of the provisions of the *C.C.Q.* and then inquiring whether or not their interpretation is consistent with the principles which underlie the rules. Given that the provisions of the *C.C.Q.* and of the *C.C.P.* do not refer directly to the principles of comity, order and fairness,

and that the principles are at best, vaguely defined, it is important to emphasize that these principles are not binding rules in themselves. Instead, they inspire the interpretation of the various private international law rules and reinforce the interconnected nature of the issues. (For a discussion on the relationships between the various private international law rules, see: J. A. Talpis, *"If I am from Grand-Mère, Why Am I Being Sued in Texas?" Responding to Inappropriate Foreign Jurisdiction in Quebec-United States Crossborder Litigation* (2001), at pp. 22 and 43–69). With these background principles in mind, I now turn to the issues at bar.

B. *Application of Private International Law Rules*

1. Do the Quebec courts have competence in the present matter pursuant to the factors set out in art. 3148(3) *C.C.Q.*?

[24] Although three of the four appellants made independent arguments on this issue (Viacom adopted the written arguments of Motient), their basic position is that both the Quebec Superior Court and the Quebec Court of Appeal erred in their respective interpretations of art. 3148(3) *C.C.Q.* Those provisions read as follows:

> 3148. In personal actions of a patrimonial nature, a Quebec authority has jurisdiction where
>
> . . . .
>
> (3) a fault was committed in Quebec, *damage was suffered in Quebec, an injurious act occurred in Quebec* or one of the obligations arising from a contract was to be performed in Quebec; [Emphasis added.]

[25] Although there are four possible grounds for asserting jurisdiction under art. 3148(3), only two remain relevant to this appeal and are examined in turn. The first is the "damage" ground, which was accepted by Duval Hesler J. of the Quebec Superior Court, leading her to confirm the jurisdiction of the Quebec courts. The second is the "injurious act" ground, which was accepted by the Quebec Court of Appeal, also resulting in the confirmation of the Quebec courts' jurisdiction.

(i) *The "damage" ground under art. 3148(3)*

[26] The appellants Motient and Viacom submit that "none of the damages claimed by Respondent can be said to have been 'suffered in Quebec' ", but rather, they were suffered at the respondent's domicile or head office in Toronto, Ontario. Under the civil law of Quebec, legal persons have a patrimony; although a corporation may have several places of business, it can have but one patrimony. While no clear rule exists in Quebec for the localization of damage, or for the localization of the corporate patrimony, one approach suggests the localization of economic loss with the respondent's patrimony and the localization of damage to reputation at the place of the respondent's domicile. In addition, the appellants note that the respondent is no longer manufacturing satellites at the Ste-Anne-de-Bellevue establishment because it has sold the division along with the establishment itself.

[27] The appellant Hughes Communications argues that, in this case, jurisdiction

would have been denied by the Quebec Court of Appeal had it not been for the presence of the claim for a nominal sum for loss of reputation. It submits that it is inconsistent with order and fairness that the addition of so minor a claim to an action can confer jurisdiction where otherwise none would exist.

[28] According to the appellant STS, it is possible to situate the damage in a particular location when it is tangible, but it is more difficult to situate the damage when tangible goods have been damaged in a particular location and financial interests are damaged somewhere else as an indirect result of the material damage. STS argues that the respondent is an indirect victim. The direct victim is Motient, whose satellite was damaged. STS submits that the loss of incentive payments is not sufficient to establish a solid link with the Quebec courts.

[29] The respondent submits that it has suffered damage to its reputation in Quebec, which has resulted in a loss of profits, loss of clientele and loss of future profits. It emphasizes that the Quebec legislature did not indicate the nature or the amount of the damage that must be suffered in order for Quebec courts to assert jurisdiction under art. 3148(3).

[30] Despite the interesting arguments raised by the appellants, I agree with the respondent that the motions judge did not err when she found that the Quebec courts can assert jurisdiction on the basis of "damage" having been suffered in Quebec. There is ample support for the motions judge's decision given the procedural context of the jurisdictional rules of Quebec, as well as in the evidence presented by the respondent.

[31] First, it appears that the procedural context for challenging jurisdiction at a preliminary stage supports the idea that art. 3148 establishes a broad basis for finding jurisdiction. In order to challenge jurisdiction in a preliminary motion, one must bring a declinatory motion to dismiss under art. 163 *C.C.P.* Case law has established that a judge hearing such a motion is not to consider the merits of the case, but rather, is to take as averred the facts that are alleged by the plaintiff to bring it within the jurisdictional competence of the Quebec courts [citations omitted].

[32] The declinatory motion allows the defendants to challenge the facts alleged by the plaintiff. Indeed, in the case at bar, the appellants adduced evidence to demonstrate that the incentive payments were made to the respondent's head office in Toronto and not to the respondent's establishment in Ste-Anne-de-Bellevue. Nevertheless, the fact remains that the role of the motions judge is to refrain from evaluating the evidence of parties unless the facts are specifically contested by the parties. In my opinion, reading in limitations with respect to the amount and nature of the damage that must be suffered in the jurisdiction before the court can assert its competence may improperly require the motions judge to prematurely decide the merits of the case.

[33] In the case at bar, I agree with the motions judge that the respondent made a *prima facie* case that it suffered damage in Quebec. Although the respondent's head office is in Ontario, the evidence provided by Gerald Bush (Vice-President and General Manager of Spar) demonstrates that the operation in Ste-Anne-de-Bellevue had established its own reputation independently of the national reputa-

tion the respondent enjoyed (A.R., at pp. 99–100). In particular, Bush testified that more than half of the company's Canadian space operations and between 80 to 85 percent of its spacecraft work was located at the Ste-Anne-de-Bellevue facility (A.R., at pp. 86–90).

[34] More support for the respondent's position is found in its evidence that the Quebec facility suffered injuries as a result of the withholding of the incentive payments, even though these were to be made to the corporate headquarters in Toronto (see Mr. Bush's testimony, A.R., at p. 114). The appellants did not successfully rebut this evidence.

[35] In addition, the subcontract between the respondent and Hughes Aircraft for the manufacture of the payload identifies the respondent as being located at Ste-Anne-de-Bellevue, a fact that tends to strengthen its argument that its reputation was in fact associated with its Quebec operation. Therefore, taking the facts as alleged, it seems that any damage to reputation suffered by the respondent was suffered by its establishment in the Province of Quebec, and not at its corporate offices in Ontario.

[36] The appellant STS relies on European case law to assert that only direct damage and not indirect damage can be used to link the action to the jurisdiction. In my view, there is nothing in the wording of art. 3148(3) to suggest that such a limitation was intended. Therefore, I do not agree with the appellant's submission that the damages are either too indirect or too nominal in this case to meet the requirements for asserting jurisdiction. Such a finding would require a premature assessment of the evidence, as outlined above.

[37] In their arguments, the appellants seem to conflate the issue of the "damage" suffered in Quebec with the issue of the amount of damages claimed in Quebec. In this case, we are only concerned with the former as art. 3148 requires that "damage" be suffered in Quebec in order to ground jurisdiction. The amount of damages that the respondent is claiming is not a concern for the jurisdiction question but may be one of many factors to be considered in a *forum non conveniens* application, as set out below. Based on the analysis set out above, I agree with the Superior Court that the damage to the respondent's reputation sufficiently meets the "damage" requirement of art. 3148.

(ii) *The "injurious act" ground under art. 3148(3)*

[38] Motient and Viacom argue that the Quebec Court of Appeal erred in both its interpretation of the term "injurious act" and its application of this criterion to the alleged attack on the respondent's reputation. The appellants submit that "injurious act" refers to the "physical acts of the defendant or the person or thing under his care, supervision or ownership, the material elements of the fault in question, or the specific events causing Respondent's damage" (Motient's factum, at para. 26). Turning to the application of art. 3148, Motient and Viacom claim that no "injurious act", as they define it, occurred in Quebec. Although the Court of Appeal characterized the damage to reputation as an "attack on" or "interference" with the respondent's reputation in Quebec, they say that the respondent is not claiming an attack on its reputation but rather damage to its reputation as a consequence of

events which occurred in the United States.

[39] Hughes Communications put forward the argument that if there was a loss of reputation, it was a loss incurred by the respondent and not by one of its operations. In addition, the Court of Appeal failed to distinguish between the "injurious act" and its consequences. Hughes Communications argues that "[h]ere, the alleged loss of reputation would be the consequence of injurious acts committed in the United States" (Hughes Communications' factum, at para. 29).

[40] STS argues that the Court of Appeal erred because the attack on reputation is not the source of the damage, rather, it is the damage that the respondent alleges to have resulted from the damage to the satellite. Such an indirect damage is insufficient to establish the jurisdiction of the court in a place where the respondent merely has an establishment which is not even the location of its corporate head office.

[41] The respondent does not directly address this question of whether or not the Court of Appeal erred in confirming jurisdiction on the "injurious act" ground. Instead, it seems to place more emphasis on the ground of "damage" to confirm the jurisdiction of the Quebec courts, as accepted by the motions judge above.

[42] Given the legislative history and context of art. 3148(3) *C.C.Q.*, I prefer the reasoning of the motions judge to that of the Court of Appeal. Prior to the adoption of the *C.C.Q.* in 1994, the international jurisdiction of Quebec courts was governed by art. 68 *C.C.P.*, which granted jurisdiction if: (1) the defendant was domiciled in Quebec; (2) if the whole cause of action arose in Quebec; (3) for actions in contract, if the contract was made in Quebec. Though art. 68 still applies to govern jurisdiction for disputes in the province, the *C.C.Q.* now sets out a code governing private international law. Unlike art. 68 *C.C.P.*, which requires that the whole cause of action arise in Quebec, art. 3148(3) *C.C.Q.* sets out four different grounds for the Quebec courts to assume jurisdiction: (1) a fault was committed in Quebec; (2) damage was suffered in Quebec; (3) an injurious act occurred in Quebec; or (4) one of the obligations arising from a contract was to be performed in Quebec. In order to interpret "injurious act" in a manner that reflects the development of the rule and that will not render redundant the three other grounds set out in art. 3148(3), it must refer to a damage-causing event that attracts no-fault liability; see H. P. Glenn, "Droit international privé", in *La réforme du Code civil* (1993), vol. 3, 669, at p. 754.

[43] As no such claim is advanced in this case, it is my opinion that the Court of Appeal erred in finding that the damage to reputation allegedly suffered by the respondent at its Quebec operation constituted an "injurious act". As noted above, I agree with the finding of the motions judge that the respondent made a *prima facie* case that it suffered damage in Quebec, so as to allow a Quebec court to assert jurisdiction over this matter.

2. *Should the criterion of a "real and substantial connection" be used when determining whether or not a Quebec authority has international jurisdiction under art. 3148 C.C.Q.?*

[44] Prior to examining the substantive aspects of this issue, I note that the appellants face an important limitation to the scope of their argument. As the Chief Justice dismissed the appellants' application to state a constitutional question (*Hughes Communications Inc. v. Spar Aerospace Ltd.*, S.C.C., No. 28070, October 9, 2001), the appellants are precluded from arguing whether or not "there is a constitutional limit on the jurisdiction of provincial courts over non-resident defendants corresponding to the rule of private international law requiring a real and substantial connection between the subject matter of an action and the jurisdiction in which it is prosecuted" (Notice of Motion to State a Constitutional Question, Schedule "A"). As this Court's jurisprudence establishes, if the Court is not faced with a direct constitutional question, it generally limits the scope of its inquiry to the interpretation of a statutory provision in accordance with the sovereign intent of the legislature. (See: *Moysa v. Alberta (Labour Relations Board)*, [1989] 1 S.C.R. 1572, at p. 1580, where Sopinka J. remarked that "If the facts of the case do not require that constitutional questions be answered, the Court will ordinarily not do so. This policy of the Court not to deal with abstract questions is of particular importance in constitutional matters". See also: *Bell ExpressVu Limited Partnership v. Rex*, [2002] 2 S.C.R. 559, 2002 SCC 42, at para. 62, where Iacobucci J. stated that "when a statute comes into play during judicial proceedings, the courts (absent any challenge on constitutional grounds) are charged with interpreting and applying it in accordance with the sovereign intent of the legislator".)

[45] The alternative argument advanced by Motient and Viacom is that jurisdiction cannot be assumed by Quebec courts on the basis of either an "injurious act" or "damage" in Quebec under art. 3148 because this Court has enunciated a further constitutional requirement in *Morguard* and *Hunt*, that there must be a "real and substantial connection" between the forum and the action in order for jurisdiction to be assumed. The appellants argue that no such connection exists on the facts of this case. The Quebec Court of Appeal, at para. 20, seemed to recognize this requirement by referring to art. 3164 and the requirement therein that the [TRANSLATION] "dispute is substantially connected with the country whose authority is seised of the case".

[46] Motient and Viacom contend that the Quebec Court of Appeal erred in finding that the alleged damage to reputation was substantial. This is a case where the most tenuous of connections between the dispute and the Quebec forum exist. In addition, a claim for a "nominal amount" of $50,000 does not constitute a substantial link between the dispute and Quebec. The appellants further submit that the respondent's decision to bring its claim commenced in the province of Quebec is motivated by the fact that in contrast to common law jurisdictions, there is no principle prohibiting the recovery of pure economic loss in Quebec. This advantage would make the forum more attractive to corporations who have branch offices in Quebec, even though the losses will ultimately be suffered by the head office in another jurisdiction.

[47] Hughes Communications adds that it is manifest from the respondent's pleadings that there is no real connection, much less a "real and substantial connection", between this claim and Quebec. The respondent is domiciled in Ontario; all the appellants are domiciled in the United States; and the alleged negligence occurred in the United States. Hughes Communications notes that in *Hunt*, the doctrine of full faith and credit was described as being a constitutional imperative, therefore, the requirement of a "real and substantial connection" as a condition for assuming jurisdiction must also be a constitutional imperative. Moreover, even if no constitutional restrictions were involved, comity requires that jurisdiction be appropriately assumed.

[48] STS observes that the new *C.C.Q.* provides not only rules for the jurisdictional competence of the Quebec courts, but also for the competence of foreign authorities for the purpose of recognition and enforcement of foreign judgments (art. 3164). In the case of foreign courts, the Quebec legislature imposed an additional criterion: that the dispute be substantially connected with the country whose authority is seised of the case. The Quebec Court of Appeal recognized that this requirement applies equally to the jurisdiction of Quebec courts but refused to apply the concept to narrow the scope of art. 3148. In addition, all of the appellants argue that the decision of the Court of Appeal is at odds with another case decided recently by a majority of the same court: *Quebecor Printing Memphis Inc. v. Regenair Inc.*, [2001] R.J.Q. 966.

[49] For its part, the respondent submits that *Morguard* and *Hunt* have no relevance since the issue in those cases concerned the recognition of judgments from a sister province and not the jurisdictional competence of a Canadian court. At any rate, if the appellants wish to challenge the constitutionality of art. 3148 then they must address the question to the Attorney General, pursuant to art. 95 *C.P.C.* This was not done in the case at bar as the Chief Justice dismissed the appellants' application to state a constitutional question. In any event, the criterion of a "real and substantial" link is a common law principle that should not be imported into the civil law. Similarly, it would be contrary to principles of interpretation to add this criterion into art. 3148 where it is also not specifically mentioned.

[50] Turning to the substantive arguments, I cannot accept the appellants' arguments that the "real and substantial connection" requirement set out in *Morguard* and *Hunt* is an additional criterion that must be satisfied in determining the jurisdiction of the Quebec courts in this case. My conclusion with respect to this issue is based on two considerations: (i) the context of the "real and substantial connection" and its relationship with the principles of comity, order and fairness; and (ii) the nature of the private international law scheme set out in Book Ten of the *C.C.Q.*

(i) *The context of the "real and substantial connection" and its relationship with the principle of comity*

[51] I agree with the appellants that *Morguard* and *Hunt* establish that it is a constitutional imperative that Canadian courts can assume jurisdiction only where a "real and substantial connection" exists: see La Forest J. in *Hunt, supra*, at p. 328: "courts are required, *by constitutional restraints*, to assume jurisdiction only

where there are real and substantial connections to that place" (emphasis added). However, it is important to emphasize that *Morguard* and *Hunt* were decided in the context of interprovincial jurisdictional disputes. In my opinion, the specific findings of these decisions cannot easily be extended beyond this context. In particular, the two cases resulted in the enhancing or even broadening of the principles of reciprocity and speak directly to the context of interprovincial comity within the structure of the Canadian federation; see *Morguard, supra*, at p. 1109, and *Hunt, supra*, at p. 328.

[52] In *Morguard*, La Forest J. agreed with the flexible approach taken by Dickson J. (as he then was) with respect to the application of the "real and substantial connection" criterion in *Moran v. Pyle National (Canada) Ltd.*, [1975] 1 S.C.R. 393, and wrote at p. 1106:

> At the end of the day, he rejected any rigid or mechanical theory for determining the situs of the tort. Rather, he adopted "a more flexible, qualitative and quantitative test", posing the question, as had some English cases there cited, in terms of whether it was "inherently reasonable" for the action to be brought in a particular jurisdiction, or whether, to adopt another expression, there was a "real and substantial connection" between the jurisdiction and the wrongdoing.

> He also delimited the decision to only address the modern interprovincial context (at p. 1098):

> . . . there is really no comparison between the interprovincial relationships of today and those obtaining between foreign countries in the 19th century. *Indeed, in my view, there never was and the courts made a serious error in transposing the rules developed for the enforcement of foreign judgments to the enforcement of judgments from sister-provinces. The considerations underlying the rules of comity apply with much greater force between the units of a federal state,* and I do not think it much matters whether one calls these rules of comity or simply relies directly on the reasons of justice, necessity and convenience to which I have already adverted. (Emphasis added [in judgment].)

[53] In *Hunt, supra*, at p. 321, La Forest J. stated that a central idea in *Morguard* was comity. It is apparent from his reasons in both cases, however, that federalism was the central concern underlying both decisions. At p. 1099 of *Morguard*, La Forest J. commented that adopting the traditional English rules in the Canadian context seemed to "fly in the face of the obvious intention of the Constitution to create a single country". In *Hunt*, at p. 322, he listed four factors that supported "a more cooperative spirit in recognition and enforcement . . . (1) common citizenship, (2) interprovincial mobility of citizens, (3) the common market created by the union as reflected in ss. 91(2), 91(10), 121 and the peace, order and good government clause, and (4) the essentially unitary structure of our judicial system with the Supreme Court of Canada at its apex". At p. 323 of *Hunt*, La Forest J. drew a clear distinction between the rules pertaining to an international situation and the rules applicable to interprovincial disputes:

> ... I do not think litigation engendered against a corporate citizen located in one province by its trading and commercial activities in another province should necessarily be subject to the same rules as those applicable to international commerce.

[54] *Morguard* and *Hunt* have been cited by this Court in a number of cases which seem to confirm that the "real and substantial connection" was specially crafted to address the challenges posed by multiple jurisdictions within a federation. See *Tolofson, supra*, where La Forest J. observed, at p. 1064:

> The nature of our constitutional arrangements — a single country with different provinces exercising territorial legislative jurisdiction — would seem to me to support a rule that is certain and that ensures that an act committed in one part of this country will be given the same legal effect throughout the country. This militates strongly in favour of the *lex loci delicti* rule. In this respect, given the mobility of Canadians and the many common features in the law of the various provinces as well as the essentially unitary nature of Canada's court system, I do not see the necessity of an invariable rule that the matter also be actionable in the province of the forum. That seems to me to be a factor to be considered in determining whether there is a real and substantial connection to the forum to warrant its exercise of jurisdiction. Any problems that might arise could, I should think, be resolved by a sensitive application of the doctrine of *forum non conveniens*.

See also *Antwerp Bulkcarriers, N.V. (Re)*, [2001] 3 S.C.R. 951, 2001 SCC 91, at para. 51, where Binnie J. for the Court remarked: "The Trustees rely on the principles of international comity but, as pointed out by this Court in *Morguard, supra*, the considerations underlying rules of comity apply with even greater force between the units of a federal state than they do internationally". In my view, there is nothing in these cases that supports the appellants' contention that the constitutional "real and substantial connection" criterion is required in addition to the jurisdiction provisions found in Book Ten of the *C.C.Q.*

(ii) *The private international law scheme of Book Ten of the C.C.Q.*

[55] As mentioned above, Book Ten of the *C.C.Q.* sets out the private international law rules for the Province of Quebec and must be read as a coherent whole and in light of the principles of comity, order and fairness. In my view, it is apparent from the explicit wording of art. 3148, as well as the other provisions of Book Ten, that the system of private international law is designed to ensure that there is a "real and substantial connection" between the action and the province of Quebec and to guard against the improper assertion of jurisdiction.

[56] Looking at the wording of art. 3148 itself, it is arguable that the notion of a "real and substantial connection" is already subsumed under the provisions of art. 3148(3), given that each of the grounds listed (fault, injurious act, damage, contract) seems to be an example of a "real and substantial connection" between the province of Quebec and the action. Indeed, I am doubtful that a plaintiff who succeeds in proving one of the four grounds for jurisdiction would not be considered to have

satisfied the "real and substantial connection" criterion, at least for the purposes of jurisdiction *simpliciter*.

[57] Next, from my examination of the system of rules found in Book Ten, it seems that the "real and substantial connection" criterion is captured in other provisions, to safeguard against the improper assumption of jurisdiction. In particular, it is my opinion that the doctrine of *forum non conveniens*, as codified at art. 3135, serves as an important counterweight to the broad basis for jurisdiction set out in art. 3148. In this way, it is open to the appellants to demonstrate, pursuant to art. 3135, that although there is a link to the Quebec authorities, another forum is, in the interests of justice, better suited to take jurisdiction.

[58] There is abundant support for the proposition that art. 3148 sets out a broad basis for jurisdiction. As Emanuelli, *supra*, remarks at p. 91:

> [TRANSLATION] In practice, a number of recent judicial decisions have based the jurisdiction of Quebec courts on the fact that damage had been suffered in Quebec. This criterion, which has been broadly interpreted in the case law, thus enables the international jurisdiction of these courts to be expanded. *In fact, in the majority of cases, it enables the plaintiff's courts to assume jurisdiction.* (Emphasis added [in judgment].) [Citations omitted.]

[59] This approach was confirmed in the minority reasons of Philippon J. (*ad hoc*) in *Quebecor Printing, supra*. Philippon J. would have dismissed the appeal, based on the interconnected scheme of the various provisions of Book Ten and, in particular, the interplay between the jurisdictional and *forum non conveniens* questions. Philippon J.'s approach allows for a broad basis for jurisdiction, and tests the "real and substantial connection" requirement more stringently when examining the *forum non conveniens* argument. As he explained, in para. 32:

> [TRANSLATION] Such an application of the concept of damage can result in the recognition of a jurisdiction that proves to be disproportionate. If that happens, it is at the stage of applying the doctrine of *forum non conveniens* that the problem must be dealt with, as in the case where, by analogy, according to the authors Goldstein and Groffier, a collateral obligation of minimal value could be a basis to assume jurisdiction. (Footnote omitted [in judgment].) [Citation omitted.]

[60] In Glenn, "Droit international privé", *supra*, at p. 754, the author also remarks on the interplay between the jurisdictional criteria under art. 3148 and the *forum non conveniens* doctrine under art. 3135:

> [TRANSLATION] The complexity of modern-day civil liability disputes raises the possibility that the application of article 3148, and in particular para. 3, can be moderated by the concepts of *forum non conveniens* and forum of necessity (arts. 3135 and 3136).

[61] I note that STS argues that the criterion of damage in art. 3148(3) should be read narrowly and refers to cases decided by the European Court of Justice under the *Convention on jurisdiction and the enforcement of judgments in civil and commercial matters*, September 27, 1968 ("*Brussels Convention*"). In my view, it is

important to note that, unlike the *C.C.Q.*, the *Brussels Convention* does not provide the same safeguard against the inappropriate exercise of jurisdiction, namely, the power to stay actions on the basis of *forum non conveniens* or otherwise (see *Cheshire and North's Private International Law, supra*, at pp. 330–31). It is perhaps understandable, then, that the European Court of Justice would seek to interpret the jurisdictional ground of the *Brussels Convention* in a narrower fashion than would a court who enjoys a further discretionary power to decline jurisdiction.

[62] In addition, it is important to bear in mind that other private international law rules set out under Book Ten of the *C.C.Q.* also appear to ensure that the "real and substantial connection" criterion is respected. For example, a substantial connection requirement is also a prerequisite for the recognition of the jurisdiction of foreign courts under art. 3164 *C.C.Q.* Also, in matters of choice of law, art. 3126 *C.C.Q.* calls for an application of the principle of *lex loci delicti*, the law of the jurisdiction where the tort or wrong is considered to have occurred; [citation omitted]. Article 3082 *C.C.Q.* serves as an exception to this rule in circumstances where it is clear that the matter is only remotely connected with the legal system prescribed by art. 3126 and is much more closely connected with the law of another country. Therefore, by giving effect to the proximity principle, it seems that art. 3082 operates in the context of choice of law in a manner similar to which art. 3135 (*forum non conveniens*) functions in the context of choice of jurisdiction.

[63] In the case at bar, it seems reasonable to conclude that the requirement for a "real and substantial connection" between the action and the authority asserting jurisdiction is reflected in the overall scheme established by Book Ten. In my view, the appellants have not provided, nor does there seem to be, given the context of this case, any basis for the courts to apply the *Morguard* constitutional principle in order to safeguard against this action being heard in a forum with which it has no real and substantial connection.

[64] At this point, assuming for the sake of argument that this appeal would fall to be decided under a pure "real and substantial connection test", without any reference to the provisions of the code, it is interesting to note that the result would not change. For example, the connecting factors listed below in the review of the application of the doctrine of *forum non conveniens* point to a sufficient connection with the Quebec forum, which would support the decision of the trial judge to retain jurisdiction over the claim. As this case concerns the initial assumption of jurisdiction by a court, it would be premature to enter into any discussion of the application of the "real and substantial connection test" in respect of the recognition and enforcement of interprovincial judgments. The question may have to be addressed when it comes up, in a proper case, where issues arising out of the drafting of arts. 3164 and 3168 *C.C.Q.* could be reviewed in light of the constitutional principle of comity which governs the recognition and enforcement of interprovincial judgments.

. . . .

> **QUESTIONS AND PROBLEM**
>
> 1. Contrast the Quebec Civil Code provisions with the provisions of the Louisiana statute quoted previously, as well as the provisions of the B.C. (Uniform) statute on court jurisdiction. How do they differ in substance and language? Were a case similar to *Club Resorts* subject to the Quebec Civil Code provisions quoted above to reach the Supreme Court of Canada, would the outcome differ in your opinion?
>
> 2. Which rules and principles of judicial jurisdiction are most similar — those of Louisiana and Quebec? Those of the English-speaking provinces of Canada and the United States (except Louisiana)? Those of the Canadian provinces, including Quebec? Those of the United States, including Louisiana? Are any identifiable differences more semantic than substantial? Can you identify any circumstances or factual contexts in which their application might lead to different outcomes?
>
> 3. Assume a Mexican tourist agency has entered a contract with a Quebec travel firm for an exclusive right to lease rooms in a Mexican resort for three years. Subsequently in apparent violation of the agreement, the Quebec firm contracts with several Mexican hotels in the resort to reserve for itself blocks of rooms during the three year period. Under the standards set out in *Spar Areospace*, in an action for breach of contract brought by the Mexican tourist agency against the Quebec travel firm, could the Quebec court assert jurisdiction over the three Mexican hotels, assuming that they were not parties to the contract? Would your answer differ if the contract between the Mexican tourist agency and the Quebec travel firm included a forum selection clause in favor of the Quebec courts? See *Impulsora Turistica de Occidente, S.A. de C.V. v. Transat Tours Canada Inc.*, [2007] 1 S.C.R. 867, 2007 SCC 20.

IV. CIVIL LAW APPROACHES

Civil law systems, as illustrated by Quebec, generally define adjudicatory jurisdiction in terms of the territorial allocation of judicial authority within the overall judicial structure. The civilian conception of judicial jurisdiction focuses on territorial location or *situs* of the domicile of the defendant as well as the plaintiff's claim and is thus akin to notions of "venue" in common law jurisdictions. Civil law systems do not conceive of adjudicatory jurisdiction in terms of either *in personam* or *in rem* actions — in other words, the courts' authority *over* the parties or the *res*. Hence service (or more accurately, official delivery of the complaint and summons — in French, *la signification et la notification* — provides the required notice but is not a jurisdictional prerequisite. (As we will examine in detail in Chapter 4, the common law term "service" has no full counterpart in the legal language of civil law jurisdictions — in other words, nearly all languages but English.)

The two fundamental, territorial grounds for allocating personal adjudicatory jurisdiction in virtually all civil law systems are: (1) for all claims the "domicile" (*domicile* in French, *domicilio* in Spanish, *jūsho* in Japanese, *Wohnsitz* in German, and *zhùsuǒ* in Chinese) of the defendant as the defendant's "general forum" and (2) the *situs* of some aspect of the transaction or dispute from which the plaintiff's claim arises, such as the place of performance of an "obligation," a concept that includes most if not all *in personam* rights and it thus not limited to contract unless expressly stated. A second common *situs* for purposes of jurisdiction (venue) is the place of the act or injury in the case of an action for damages in tort (delict).

The rules for adjudicatory jurisdiction in some counties may not make the categorical distinction between "general forum" and "special forum" rules explicit, but in effect they pertain nevertheless. For example, as amended through 2012, the Code of Civil Procedure for the Federal District of Mexico (which tends to be replicated in separate codes of the each of the 31 Mexican states[a]) provides for the territorial jurisdiction of its courts in Article 24, which in pertinent part reads in English translation as follows:

By virtue of territory the tribunals with competence are:

1. [the court] of the place that the defendant was legally required to be for the performance of its obligations [which include contracts, unjust enrichment, as well as delicts];

2. [the court] of the place designated for performance of the obligation;

3. [the court] of the location of the thing, in the case of real actions [actions involving *in rem* or property rights, such as ownership, servitudes, and usufructs] involving disputes related to immovable property or arising from leases . . . ;

4. [the court] of the domicile of the defendant, the case of real actions related to movable property or personal actions or marital status;

5. [the court] of the domicile of the debtor, in the event of insolvency.

Under German and Japanese law, if the domicile of a natural person is unknown, the general forum is determined by residence (*Aufenthaltsort* in German, *kyosho* in Japanese). The "domicile" for corporations and other juridical persons is ordinarily the location of their managerial headquarters or principal office within the national territory. Chinese law is exemplary. Article 241 of the 2007 Civil Procedure Law of the People's Republic of China provides in English translation:

A lawsuit brought against a defendant who has no domicile in the People's Republic of China concerning a contract dispute or other disputes over property rights and interests, if the contract is signed or performed within

---

[a] Mexico is unusual even among other countries in Latin America in its replication of not only the federal presidential political structure of the U.S. but also the allocation of private law and civil procedure to the states. Thus unlike most countries in Latin America — even those with a federal system — Argentina, Brazil and Venezuela — Mexico does not have either a national civil code or code of civil procedure. All are state codes. However, both in most Mexican states essentially duplicate those of the Federal District (Mexico City). Moreover, in cases involving recognition and enforcement of foreign judgments and other instances of international cooperation, the provisions of the Federal Code must be followed. See *infra*, Chapter 6.

the territory of the People's Republic of China, or the object of the action is within the territory of the People's Republic of China, or the defendant has detainable property within the territory of the People's Republic of China, or the defendant has its representative agency, branch, or business agent within the territory of the People's Republic of China, may be under the jurisdiction of the people's court located in the place where the contract is signed or performed, the subject of the action is located, the defendant's detainable property is located, the infringing act takes place, or the representative agency, branch or business agent is located.

Most if not all civil law jurisdictions also provide for the territorial competence of their courts to adjudicate claims to attachable property within the judicial district, as noted in the case of both China and Mexico above. However, civil law systems do not recognize the distinction between *in personam* and *in rem* jurisdiction or judgments based, as noted, in common law systems on the courts' authority over the parties or the *res*. This should not be confused with the dichotomy between *in personam* (obligation) and *in rem* (real) rights, which is a fundamental conceptual feature of all civil law systems. Thus in civil law systems an *in rem* or real action is a lawsuit in which real or personal property rights are at issue.

In a number of jurisdictions, especially those influenced by German law, like China and Japan, the location of "detainable" or "attachable" property owned by the defendant has been a basis for jurisdiction over *in personam* monetary claims unrelated to the property. Article 23 of the 2002 German Code of Civil Procedure continues to recognize such judicial jurisdiction in cases involving monetary claims against a defendant without domicile in districts in which property (both real and personal) of the defendant is located. Recent judicial decisions have added the requirement that there must also be some other "sufficient connection" with Germany.[b]

French law adds the nationality of the plaintiff. Article 14 of the 1805 Civil Code provides:

> An alien, even if not residing in France, may be cited before French Courts for the performance of obligations contracted by him in France with a French person; he may be called before the Courts of France for obligations contracted by him in a foreign country towards French persons.

As examined in greater detail below, European Union law has for over four decades by treaty or regulation disallowed recognition by courts within the EU of judgments handed down by courts within the EU in cases brought against persons domiciled within the EU based solely on attachable assets — that is, with unrelated claims — within the territory (the German rule) as well as the French "nationality" principle. The same is true for transient jurisdiction based solely on personal service within the territory (the Common Law rule). The EU regulations do not apply, however, to suits brought in courts outside of the EU. Thus judgments grounded on such otherwise impermissible jurisdictional grounds are not only

---

[b] [*Muduroglu Ltd. v. TC Ziraat Bankasi,*] German Bundesgerichtshof (XI Senate for Civil Matters), Judgment of 2 July 1991, BGH 2.7.1991.

permitted but also, if recognized by the court of a member state under its national rules, such judgments must also be recognized and enforced — in other words, given "full faith and credit"— by all member states.

V. JAPAN

The Japanese rules on adjudicatory jurisdiction exemplify the approach of civil law systems generally, but especially those influenced by German law. Until 2012 Japan had no special rules of adjudicatory jurisdiction for transnational litigation. As illustrated in the cases extracted below, until 2012, the allocations of adjudicatory competence of its courts were like Germany based on generally applicable rules located in the 1890 and 1996 codes of civil procedure for the allocation of territorial jurisdiction within the national system. These rules remain in effect, but amendments (Sections 3-2 through 3-12, enacted and promulgated in 2011, effective in 2012) to the 1996 Code of Civil Procedure, which replaced the 1890 Code without any change to the provisions on adjudicatory jurisdiction, explicitly provide the bases for adjudicatory jurisdiction in civil and commercial suits involving one or more foreign parties. (The relevant provisions of the Code including the 2011 amendments are set out in English translation in Appendix A.) However, the legislation notably made little if any change to the rules and standards developed by the courts over a half century. In effect they confirmed legislatively existing judicial approaches and precedents including, as we shall examine below as well as in Chapter 3 on Parallel Litigation, those related to dismissal of actions on the basis of the principles of *jōri* (reason), articulated by the Supreme Court in two early cases included in these materials in both the 1982 *Gotō v. Malaysia Airlines* decision extracted below as well as the 1975 decision in *Tokyo Marine and Fire Insurance Co. v. Royal Interocean Lines* (Sup. Ct., 3rd P.B., 1975) in Chapter 7.

In Japan, as in other civil law jurisdictions, the primary basis for adjudicatory jurisdiction remains the domicile (*jūsho*) of the defendant as its "general forum." Similarly, "special forum" rules based on the "*situs*" of the claim additionally provide potentially broad bases for extraterritorial jurisdiction in some instances over parties or claims having little if any direct nexus with the forum, comparable to many Canadian provinces prior to the *Morguard* decision.

A. General Forum: Domicile

Code of Civil Procedure
Article 4 [*General forum*]

[Applicable to transnational cases through 2011]

Article 4 [*General forum*]

    1. A civil action is within the jurisdiction of the court with jurisdiction over the general forum of the defendant.

2. The general forum of a person is determined by his domicile [*jūsho*]⁴, in case his does domicile is not in Japan or his domicile is unknown, by his residence [*kyosho*], and in case he does not have residence in Japan or his residence is unknown, by his last domicile.

. . . .

4. The general forum of a juristic person or other association or foundation is determined by its principal office or place of business, and, in the event, it has no office or place of business, by the domicile of its representative or person in charge of its business [in Japan].

[Applicable rule for transnational cases after 2012]

Article 3-2 [*Jurisdiction Based on Domicile*]

1. In civil actions brought against a natural persons, the courts shall have jurisdiction [*kankatsu*] if his domicile is in Japan or, in case his domicile is not in Japan or is unknown, his residence in Japan; or, if he has no residence in Japan or if his residence is unknown, he has ever had their domicile in Japan prior to the filing of the action (except in cases where he has established his domicile abroad after having been domiciled in Japan).

. . . .

3. In civil actions against a juridical person, or other association or foundation, the courts shall have jurisdiction if its principal office or place of business is in Japan or if the domicile of its representative or principal person in charge of their business is in Japan in the event [such defendant] does not have an office or principal place of business in Japan or the location [of such office or place of business] is unknown.

GOTŌ v. MALAYSIA AIRLINES
Supreme Court, 2d P.B., Judgment of 16 October 1981
35 Minshū (No. 7) 1224 (1981)
[English translation in 26 *Japanese Annual of International Law* (JAIL) 122 (1983)]

The judgment in *Gotō v. Malaysia Airlines* was the first postwar Supreme Court statement on the issue of whether and on what grounds the adjudicatory jurisdiction of Japanese courts extends to actions against non-Japanese defendants arising out of events that occur outside of Japan. The decision confirmed that the existing rules and principles of the Code of Civil Procedure as construed and applied by the courts define the procedures for transnational litigation. The case involved a claim for damages brought by the surviving spouse and two children of Tomio Gotō, who had died in a Malaysia Airlines crash in Johore Bahrn, Malaysia, on December 4, 1977. The action was misfiled in the Nagoya District Court, which dismissed the

---

⁴ Domicile (*jūsho*) is defined in article 21 of the Civil Code as the "principal place where a person lives." In other words the place where a person's life is centered. See also article 102 of the French Civil Code.

action on the grounds that Japanese courts lacked adjudicatory jurisdiction over the airline company in this case. On appeal the Nagoya High Court reversed and remanded the case to the Nagoya District Court for trial on the merits (despite the Nagoya court's lack of jurisdiction on other grounds). The defendant airline appealed to the Supreme Court. The Court affirmed the Nagoya High Court's judgment, allowing the plaintiffs to sue the airline company for compensatory damages in Japan.

DISPOSITION
(*shūbun*)

1. The *jōkoku*[c] appeal in this case is dismissed.
2. The *jōkoku* appellant shall bear the costs of appeal.

REASONS
(*riyū*)

This case involves a claim for compensatory damages by Japanese citizens against a foreign corporation. The appellees allege that on December 4, 1977, pursuant to an air transport contract concluded in the Federation of Malaysia, Tomio Gotō boarded a plane operated by the appellant from Penang to Kuala Lumpur. The plane crashed in Johore Bahrn in Malaysia on the same day. Tomio Gotō died in the crash. Inasmuch as this constituted a breach of the air transport contract, the appellant is liable for payment of 40,454,442 yen in compensatory damages for the injury caused by the crash of the plane to the successors, the appellees Michiko Gotō (wife), Yukiko Gotō and Takayuki Gotō (children) in proportion to their shares in succession, which are one-third each. Accordingly, each appellee demands the appellant pay 13,330,000 yen for the above damages.

Adjudicatory jurisdiction (*saiban kankatsu*) is generally deemed an effect of national sovereignty. The scope of adjudicatory jurisdiction is in principle co-extensive with the [territorial] scope of national sovereignty. Consequently, if a defendant is a foreign corporation with a main office abroad, it is ordinarily beyond the adjudicatory jurisdiction of Japan unless it is willing to subject itself to Japanese jurisdiction. *Nevertheless, a defendant can be exceptionally subjected to the adjudicatory jurisdiction of Japan whatever its nationality or wherever located if the case relates to Japan or if the defendant has some legal nexus with Japan.* With respect to the limits of such exceptions, we have no statutes expressly prescribing international adjudicatory jurisdiction, no applicable treaties, nor any well-defined, generally recognized rules of international law. Under these circumstances, it is reasonable to determine international adjudicatory jurisdiction in accordance with the principles of jōri, which require fairness between the parties and just and prompt administration of justice. Under these principles, a defendant may be appropriately subjected to the jurisdiction of Japan when the requirements of the provisions for domestic territorial jurisdiction (tochi kankatsuken) set out in the [1890] Code of Civil Procedure are satisfied [emphasis

---

[c] The term *jōkoku* designates the second appeal limited to questions of law. Virtually all appeals to the Supreme Court of Japan are *jōkoku* appeals.

added], for example, when the defendant's domicile (article 2 [1996 Code, art.4 (i)]), if a juridical person or other association, office or place of business (article 4 [1996 Code, art. 4 (4)]), the place performance (article 5 [1996 Code, art. 5 (i)]), the location the defendant's property (article 8 [1996 Code, art. 5(iv)]), the place of tort (article 5 [1996 Code, art. 5 (ix)]) or any other place for trial (*saiban-seki*) set forth in the Code of Civil Procedure is located in Japan. [See Appendix A for the comparable provisions of 1996 Code.]

According to the findings of the court below, the appellant is a Malaysian corporation established under the Company Law of the Federation of Malaysia and has its head office in that country. The appellant has appointed Gyokushō Chō as its representative in Japan and has established a place of business in Tokyo. On these premises, the appellant may be reasonably subjected to the jurisdiction of Japan, even though it is a foreign corporation that has its head office abroad. Therefore, we affirm the decision of the court below, which held that a Japanese court has jurisdiction over this case. The judgment of the court below is not erroneous as the appellant argues. We cannot accept the appellant's argument which criticizes the judgment below from a point of view different from our above-stated view.

Thus, in accordance with Articles 401, 95 and 89 of the [1890] Code of Civil Procedure, this Court unanimously renders the judgment as stated in the Decree.

JUSTICE TADAYOSHI KINOSHITA
JUSTICE KAZUO KURIMOTO
JUSTICE YASUYOSHI SHIONO
JUSTICE GOICHI MIYAZAKI

QUESTIONS

1. In *Gotō v. Malaysia Airlines*, what was the source of the rule for international jurisdiction applied by the Japanese Supreme Court?

2. Although the Court found that the general forum of Malaysia Airlines was in Tokyo where it maintained its primary Japanese office, the Court affirmed the decision by the Nagoya High Court allowing the lawsuit to proceed in Nagoya, holding that the issue could not be addressed on second (*jōkoku*) appeal. How would a U.S. court have dealt with the issue?

CGI K.K. v. ADVANCED CONNECTEK CO., LTD.
Yokohama District Court Judgment of 16 June 2007
Hanrei jihō (No. 1941) 124 (2007)
[English translation in 550 JAIL 244 (2007)]

The plaintiff in this case, CGI K.K., was a Japanese corporation engaged in the manufacture and sale of electronic parts. The defendant, Advanced Connectek (ACON), was a Taiwanese company engaged in the manufacture and sale of peripheral equipment used for electrical devices, including personal computers.

CGI brought the action in the Yokohama District Court for payment of the purchase price and delay damages from the alleged non-performance of a contract for the sale of a machine used to manufacture devices for connecting the ends of optical fibers. The contract expressly provided for Japanese law as the governing law but did not designate any forum. ACON sought dismissal on the grounds that the court lacked jurisdiction. ACON had no office or representative in Japan but its president (principal shareholder) was also the president (and principal shareholder) of Renten-Kagi K.K. (Renten), a company incorporated in Japan that promoted the sale of ACON's products and provided after-sale services. The plaintiff argued the defendant was engaged in "substantial and continuous commercial activity" in Japan with Renten functioning as its Japanese office. In the following judgment, the court of first instance, the Yokohama District Court, rejected the argument and dismissed the suit for lack of adjudicatory jurisdiction.

Disposition
(*shūbun*)

1. This lawsuit is dismissed.
2. The plaintiff shall bear the litigation costs.

Facts and Reasons
(*jijitsu oyobi riyū*)

No internationally recognized treaty or customary international law rule exists to determine the circumstances under which our country may exercise international adjudicatory jurisdiction for civil lawsuits where a defendant is a foreign company. It is therefore appropriate to decide this case in accordance with the principles of *jōri*, which require fairness between the parties and just and prompt administration of justice. In the absence of exceptional circumstances, it is reasonable to hold that defendants are subject to the adjudicatory jurisdiction of our courts to the extent that any of the bases for territorial jurisdiction provided in our the Code of Civil Procedure apply. In this case the plaintiff argues that the defendant engages in substantial and continuous commercial activities in Japan, and therefore that jurisdiction should be affirmed. However, the concept of 'substantial and continuous commercial activities' does not constitute a necessarily clear criterion. Hence, we cannot accept the plaintiff's argument.

Renten is not a subsidiary of ACON. It has an independent legal status separate from the defendant. Moreover, although, admittedly, the same person is president of both Renten, and the defendant and Renten is listed as a 'branch' or 'subsidiary' of the defendant company on the defendant's website, there is insufficient evidence to demonstrate that the latter was under such complete control of the former to conclude that it functioned as an office or place of business of the defendant [in Japan]. Since Renten did not constitute an 'office or place of business' of the defendant [in Japan], we find no jurisdictional basis as set out in Articles 5(v) and 4(4) of the [1996] Code of Civil Procedure.

Having thoroughly examined all the other materials relevant to this case, no circumstances can be found for the court to establish jurisdiction as provided by the

Code of Civil Procedure, and no circumstances can be found to establish international adjudicatory jurisdiction in Japan.

JUDGE FUMIAKI TSUCHIYA
JUDGE FUMITOMO ICHIKI
JUDGE AYUMI YOSHIOKA

NOTES AND QUESTIONS

1. Article 5(v) replicates the "general forum" provision of Article 4(4) with respect to the appropriate court in cases involving "civil actions for monetary and other claims against property [*zaisanken*]." Under article 4(4), for suits "against persons who have an office or place of business and involving business at such an office or place of business" in Japan, the appropriate forum is the court in the district where "such office or place of business" is located.

2. The Court rejected the plaintiff's argument that jurisdiction should have been affirmed inasmuch as the defendant was engaged in "substantial and continuous commercial activities in Japan." Moreover, the defendant had a wholly owned and apparently fully controlled subsidiary in Japan. What then was lacking? To what extent was *jōri* relevant to the Court's decision?

KŌNO v. KŌNO
Supreme Court, 2nd P.B., Judgment of 21 June 1996
50 Minshū (No. 7) 1451 (1996)
[Adapted from Prominent Judgments of the Supreme Court; also translated in 40 JAIL 333 (1997)][7]

This case involved a second appeal from a divorce action brought in Japan by a Japanese national who had been living for several years in Germany. He had married a German national in the former Democratic Republic of Germany in 1982. A daughter was born in 1984, and in 1988 the family moved to West Berlin. A year later the couple separated. The daughter remained with her father, who brought her to Japan in April 1989. Three months later, the wife filed for divorce in West Berlin. The husband did not appear, and the German court entered a default judgment that became final in February 1990. The German judgment affirmed the divorce and awarded parental authority to the wife. Meanwhile in a parallel action, a few days after the wife had filed for divorce in Germany, the husband filed for divorce in Japan. In the contested divorce action brought by the husband in the Urawa District Court, the wife apparently challenged jurisdiction and sought recognition and enforcement of the German divorce decree. The Urawa District Court initially dismissed the husband's divorce action for lack of jurisdiction

---

[7] Adapted from translation by Sir Ernest Satow Chair of Japanese Law, University College, University of London.

inasmuch as the wife had never resided in Japan. On first appeal, however, the Tokyo High Court reversed and upheld the jurisdiction of the Urawa court. The wife appealed to the Supreme Court.

Disposition
(*shūbun*)

1. The *jōkoku* appeal in this case is dismissed.
2. The *jōkoku* appellant shall bear the litigation costs.

Reasons
(*riyū*)

The representative of the appellant argues that the judgment of the high court, which acknowledged the jurisdiction of the Japanese court of first instance in an action by the appellee, a Japanese national claiming divorce in the present case against the appellant, a German citizen, is contrary to the law. The summary of the facts ascertained by the record is as follows:

The appellee and the appellant married in the then German Democratic Republic (hereinafter, 'GDR') in the manner valid in the country on May 15, 1982 and the eldest daughter was born on May 23, 1985. The appellee and the family had been living in Berlin (GDR) from 1988. The appellant has refused to live with the appellee since January 1989. The appellee returned to Japan under the pretext of a trip in April 1989, informed the appellant that he had no intention to return to the GDR, and continues living in Japan. On July 8, 1989, the appellant initiated action for divorce at the Family Court of Charlottenburg, West Berlin where she resides. The service of writ, summons of this litigation to the appellee was by public notice. The proceedings continued without response [or appearance] by the appellee. The judgment affirming the claim of the appellant and granting the appellant parental rights over the eldest daughter became effective on May 2, 1990. The appellee initiated the present action on July 26, 1989. (The writ was served on the appellant on September 20, 1990.)

The place of residence of the defendant is an important factor which should be taken into consideration in determining the international jurisdiction of courts also in divorce cases. It is a matter of course that if the defendant resides in Japan, jurisdiction of the Japanese court should be acknowledged. However, it cannot be denied that even in cases where the defendant does not reside in Japan, if the nexus between the divorce claim and Japan can be acknowledged from the place of residence of the plaintiff and other factors, there are instances where the jurisdiction of the Japanese court should be acknowledged. In the absence of statutory provisions on transnational jurisdiction and insufficient development of international customary law, it is reasonable to conclude that the problem of under what circumstances the jurisdiction of Japan should be acknowledged must be determined in accordance with the principles of *jōri*, which require fairness to the parties and just and prompt administration of justice. In determining the existence of jurisdiction, the inconvenience of the defendant who is forced to respond to the claim should naturally be considered, but on the other hand, whether there is any legal or factual impediment to the plaintiff in initiating a divorce action in the defendant's country of residence and if there is such impediment, its extent should be considered and the care should be taken to ensure that the interest of the plaintiff who claims divorce should not be left unprotected.

In the present case, according to the facts established above, by the taking of effect of the judgment . . . , the divorce has taken effect and the marriage between the appellee and the appellant has already been terminated in the GDR (according to the record, it is ascertained that the appellant has returned to her maiden name). However, in Japan, since the above judgment cannot be recognized as valid since it failed to fulfill the [notice] requirement of Article 200(2) of the [1890] Code of Civil Procedure [Article 118 (2) of the 1996 Code], the marriage has not been terminated. Under such circumstances, even if the appellee initiates an action claiming divorce in the GDR, it is highly possible that the claim would be found unlawful because the marriage has already been terminated. Therefore, for the appellee, there is no way but to initiate action claiming divorce in Japan. Taking this into consideration, it is in accordance with *jōri* [reason] to acknowledge international jurisdiction of the court of Japan in the present action claiming divorce. The judgment of the original instance can be upheld in conclusion. [Citations omitted.] . . .

JUSTICE SHIGEHARU NEGISHI
JUSTICE KATSUYA ŌNISHI
JUSTICE SHINICHI KAWAI
JUSTICE HIROSHI FUKUDA

QUESTIONS

1. To what extent can the decision in this case be reasonably explained by the application of *jōri*, or more simply by the application of relevant provisions of the Code of Civil Procedure? What other explicit or implicit rationales seem to determine the outcome?

2. Given the outcome in this case, would in your opinion a Japanese court recognize the divorce decree in *In re the Marriage of Kimura?*

3. Comparing *Kōno v. Kōno* with *In re the Marriage of Kimura*, what are the apparent differences in jurisdiction and notice in transnational divorce actions under German and U.S. law? Would a U.S. court have jurisdiction in a case similar to the German court enabling it to order dissolution of the marriage and award custody? Compare *In re the Marriage of Kimura* with the apparent jurisdiction of the New Jersey and California courts in *Burnham*.

B. Special Jurisdiction: Place of Performance

Code of Civil Procedure

[Applicable to transnational cases through 2011]

Article 5 [*Forum for civil actions for monetary and other claims against property (zaisanken)*]

The following civil actions may be brought before the court having jurisdiction over the following locations:

(i) actions involving monetary and other claims against assets [*zaisanken*]: place of performance;

(ii) actions for payment of promissory notes or checks: place of payment indicated on the promissory note or check;

[Applicable rule for transnational cases after 2012]

Article 3-3 (*Jurisdiction over Actions related to Duties under Contracts and other Obligations*)Personal Injury Action Defenses Damages

The actions described in each of the following provisions may be brought in a Japanese court.

(i) Actions to enforce contract duties as well as actions for management of affairs without mandate (*jimu kanri*) or unjust enrichment (*futō rieki*) arising out of contractual undertakings, actions for damages for non-performance of contractual duties, and other actions arising under contract if the place of performance under the contract in Japan or the place of performance of the contract under the law selected by the parties to the contract is in Japan;

(ii) Actions for payment of money under a promissory note (*tegata*) or check (*kogite*) if the place of payment is in Japan; . . . .

NIHON SYSTEM WEAR K.K. v. KENSUKE KOO
Tokyo High Court Judgment of 24 March 1999
Hanrei jihō (No. 1700) 41 (2000)
[English translation in 44 JAIL 184 (2001)]

In 1988 and again in 1989, Shūjin Tada, a classic car buff and representative director of the plaintiff company, contracted with Kensuke Koo, a Japanese national living in California, who had been introduced to Tada by a mutual friend named Suzuki, for the purchase and restoration of an antique car. For each transaction, Tada (apparently acting through his company) paid Koo $78,000. Delays ensued in the restoration work and, nearly ten years later, neither car had been shipped to Japan. In 1996 Tada, again through his company, filed suit in Japan for delivery of the cars or, in the alternative, return of the amounts paid under the contracts. During the course of the hearings in the case, Tada decided to cancel the contracts and only seek only return of the amounts paid. Koo responded with a motion to dismiss for lack of adjudicatory jurisdiction inasmuch as he did not have domicile or residence in Japan, nor was the place of performance of the contract in Japan. The Tokyo District Court agreed. In a judgment of March 19, 1988, the court dismissed the action for lack of adjudicatory jurisdiction.[8] The High Court reversed in the following judgment:

DISPOSITION
(shūbun)

1. [We] quash the judgment below.

2. [We] order the *kōso*[e] appellee to pay the *kōso* appellant 20, 603,700 yen plus as interest 6 percent of 9, 855,300 yen of the total for each year from March 25, 1988 and of the remaining 10,748,400 yen from May 15, 1989.

3. Litigation costs for the first and second trials are to be borne by the *kōso* appellee.

REASONS
(riyū)

II. Even though the defendant does not have a domicile in Japan, we cannot deny the international adjudicatory jurisdiction of our country in a case with legal nexus with our country. In such a case, lacking applicable internationally recognized standards and sufficiently developed international customary law, it is appropriate to recognize the international adjudicatory jurisdiction of our courts in accordance with principles of *jōri*, which require fairness between the parties and the just and prompt administration of justice. Accordingly, the defendants may be subject in principle to the jurisdiction of our courts in actions brought in our country when any one of the grounds for adjudicatory jurisdiction in the Code of Civil Procedure is satisfied. However, international adjudicatory jurisdiction should be denied in exceptional circumstances under which adjudication in our country would be contrary to the sense of fairness between the parties and the just and prompt administration of justice [citing *K.K. Family v. Miyahara* (Sup. Ct., 3nd P.B., Nov. 11, 1997) 51 Minshū (No. 10) 4055 (1997), exerpted in Chapter 3].

In the case before us, we find that each the sales contracts (1) and (2) in question, was an ordinary sales contract for an automobile concluded between the *kōso* appellant domiciled in Tokyo and the *kōso* appellee who resides in California. . . . *The kōso appellee has listed his domicile as Japan on his Family Registration. He has returned to Japan on occasion over the years. He is able to receive mail addressed to him through his parents who reside at the aforementioned domicile.* [Emphasis added.] In addition, *both contracts were concluded through the introduction of Suzuki who resides [in Japan]. . . . Suzuki's testimony . . . is therefore essential in order to confirm what was intended with respect to the importation of the automobiles and the processes of the contracts. Judging from the formation process of the contracts in question, the kōso appellant (through Suzuki) made the*

---

[8] Hanrei Times (No. 997) 286 (1999), translated in 44 JAIL 186 (2001).

[e] *Kōso* appeals are first appeals on questions of law with *de novo* findings of fact, which are binding on second, *jōkoku*, appeals.

"*offer*" . . . . *Therefore regardless of whether Suzuki acted as an agent or a messenger, under the Law on the Application of Law (Hōrei), articles 7(2) and 9(2), the applicable law of this case is understood to be Japanese law.* [Emphasis added.] If so, since this action was brought by against the defendant for return of the contract money resulting from cancellation of the contracts, it was by no means beyond his expectation of that he would be sued in Japan as the place of performance of the above duty to return the payments. *From the facts stated above, we conclude that it is not contrary to fairness between the parties and the just and prompt administration of justice to require the defendant to appear before a Japanese court.* [Emphasis added.] Therefore, lacking exceptional factors that might lead us not to recognize adjudicatory jurisdiction over this case, as stated above, we are of the opinion that the Japanese court has jurisdiction over this action. . . .

JUDGE FUMIO ARAI
JUDGE TAKASHI OHSHIMA
JUDGE TATEO TOYOTA

QUESTIONS AND NOTE

1. How are the "domicile" of expatriate Japanese nationals and "place of performance" defined in *Nihon System Wear K.K. v. Kensuke Koo?*

2. Why do you suppose the district court rejected the argument that the defendant — Kensuke Koo — was not a Japanese domiciliary for purposes of adjudicatory jurisdiction? Does the Tokyo High Court at least suggest that this finding may have been in error? We return to the problem of the "domicile" of Japanese nationals residing abroad in connection with our consideration of the Supreme Court's decision on *K.K. Family v. Miyahara*, excerpted, as noted, in Chapter 3].

Today for domestic litigation, article 5(iv) of the Code of Civil Procedure provides as a special basis for adjudicatory jurisdiction the "place of performance" of "obligations," a technical term that is understood in virtually all civil law codes to include all *in personam* rights including contracts, quasi-contracts as well as delicts and quasi-delicts. This provision was applied in all cases decided prior to 2012. The newly added article 3-3(i) for jurisdiction in international cases clarifies the scope of "obligations" specifically *to include* unjust enrichment, management of affairs without a mandate (*negotiorium gestio*), as well as contract, but thereby *eliminating* delicts. As described below, Regulation (EU) No. 1215/2012 (which replaced EC Regulation 44/2001 and, with exceptions, the 1968 Brussels Convention) similarly provides for the "place of performance" of contracts as a special basis for adjudicatory jurisdiction. Regulation (EU) No. 1215/2012 (and EC Regulation 44/2001) amended the 1968 Brussels Convention but only substituted two separate categories — in the event the "obligation in question" is a contract for the sale of goods the place of performance is the

> place of delivery. If it is a contract for services, the place of performance is the place where the services were to be provided. As noted above, article 24 (1) of the Federal Code of Civil Procedure of Mexico covers the place of performance of an obligation, but article 241 of the Chinese Civil Procedure Law Chinese law restricts the place of performance to contracts.

K.K. BUNGEI SHUNJŪ v. MIYATA

Tokyo District Court Judgment of 28 August 1989 *Hanrei jihō* (No. 1338) 121 (1989)

[English translation in 33 JAIL 206 (1990)]

K.K. Bungei Shunjū publishes a popular Japanese magazine. In one of its issues an article alleged that Nozomi Miyata, the defendant in this case, had murdered his wife in California. Miyata answered by filing a libel suit against Bungei Shunjū in California. Miyata argued that the libel occurred in California in that the magazines were sold in California and read by people living there who can read Japanese. Bungei Shunjū responded in turn by filing this action for "confirmation" (declaration) that it was not liable to Miyata for any damages. Miyata, as defendant, moved to dismiss the lawsuit for lack of jurisdiction. Lack of jurisdiction based on the "place of performance" was the first of two grounds for jurisdiction. The court entered an interlocutory judgment in favor of the defendant Miyata with its reasons for denying jurisdiction as the place of performance as follows: (We return to the decision and the second ground for jurisdiction *infra*.)

DISPOSITION
(*shūbun*)

1. This suit is dismissed.
2. The plaintiff bears the costs of litigation.

REASONS
(*riyū*)

. . . .

2. Our country has no pertinent statures or treaties with respect to international adjudicatory jurisdiction related to civil suits against Japanese nationals living abroad as defendants, Nor have any well-defined principles of international law been established to deal with such cases. Under these circumstances, it is reasonable to decide such cases in accordance with the principles of *jōri*, which require fairness between the parties and the just and prompt administration of justice. In concrete terms, indeed it is true that the provisions on territorial venue in the Code of Civil Procedure do not provide for international jurisdiction by themselves, but they do reflect the principle of reasonable consideration in allocating jurisdiction. Therefore, it is appropriate to recognize the international jurisdiction of the Japanese courts when one of the bases for territorial venue is found in Japan under the provisions in the Code, provided that recognition of adjudicatory jurisdiction would not be contrary to the above principles of *jōri*

because exceptional circumstances arising out of the special nature of the international litigation in this instance.

3.(1) Inasmuch as the domicile of the defendant is in California, the United States of America, the jurisdiction of the Japanese cannot be admitted based upon Article 2 of the Code of Civil Procedure.

(2) Under article 484 of the Civil Code, the place of performance of the obligation to pay damages is the domicile of the claimant. Consequently the place of the performance of the obligation as prescribed in article 5 of the Code of Civil Procedure is in this case the United States, where the claimant lives. *Therefore, international jurisdiction of Japan cannot be recognized [by virtue of the place of performance of an obligation, including an obligation arising under a delict or tort]*. [Emphasis added.]

NOTE AND QUESTIONS

1. Unless limited by code or statutory provisions for adjudicatory jurisdiction, as indicated in *Bungei Shunjū v. Miyata*, the "place of performance" may also include the place for payment of damages for breach or violation of any *in personam* right, such as unjust enrichment (restitution) as well as delicts (torts).

2. What would be the place of performance of an employment contract concluded in the United States between a U.S. national and U.S. law firm to work for two years in Tokyo in the legal department of one of the firm's Japanese clients? Would it matter whether the firm paid the lawyer's salary and expenses in U.S. dollars in the U.S. or in Japanese yen in Japan (in either instance by direct deposit in a bank account)? We return to this question below in connection of the rules for special jurisdiction under Regulation (EU) No. 1215/2012.

C. Special Jurisdiction: Place of the Tort

Code of Civil Procedure

[Applicable to transnational cases through 2011]

Article 5 [*Forum for civil actions for monetary and other claims against property (zaisanken)*]

The following civil actions may be brought before the court having jurisdiction over the following locations:

. . . .

(ix) actions for damages in tort: place where the tort occurred;

[Applicable rule for transnational cases after 2012]

Article 3-3 [*Jurisdiction over Actions Related to Duties Under Contracts and Other Obligations*]

The actions described in each of the following provisions may be brought in a Japanese court.

. . . .

(viii) Actions relating to delicts [torts] if the delict occurred in Japan (except where the effects of a delict committed abroad has occurred in Japan but normally such effect in Japan would have been unforeseeable.

ŌKUMA v. THE BOEING COMPANY
Tokyo District Court Judgment of 27 March 1984
Hanrei jihō (No. 1113) 26 (1984)
[English translation in 28 JAIL 248 (1985)]

On September 10, 1964, a helicopter owned by the Air Self-Defense Forces of Japan crashed into a farm in Fukuoka prefecture. Fourteen crewmen died. The accident was allegedly caused by a breakdown of a socket by which a shaft of the rear rotor was secured. The successors of the deceased crewmen brought an action for damages against The Boeing Company, claiming from approximately ¥13,120,000 to ¥38,140,000 per decedent.

The helicopter in this case had been manufactured in the United States by the Vertol Aircraft Company, an American corporation. It was sold to the U.S. Air Force in 1955. Five years later, in July 1960, the U.S. Air Force supplied it to Japan's Air Self-Defense Forces. As the result of an acquisition, also in 1960, The Boeing Company, in turn, had substantially assumed all assets and debts of the Vertol Aircraft Company, which was then dissolved.

The Boeing Company as defendant moved to dismiss the action for lack of adjudicatory jurisdiction on the following grounds:

(1) The essential evidence as to whether or not Vertol had been at fault in the manufacture of the helicopter in question and whether or not the defendant succeeded the liability of Vertol is located in the United States not in Japan. At the time of manufacture, Vertol could not have possibly foreseen that an accident would occur in Japan. Therefore, from the viewpoint of the expeditious examination of the evidence in a trial as well as the protection of a defendant who is suddenly sued in an unexpected place, it is not appropriate for a Japanese court to have jurisdiction over this action.

(2) Furthermore, even if the above grounds were deemed to be insufficient to preclude jurisdiction by a Japanese court, the plaintiffs must prove *prima facie* that Vertol was responsible for the accident and that the defendant has assumed Vertol's liability. The burden of proof in such an international case should be heavier than that in a purely domestic case,

inasmuch as foreign defendants in particular should not have to contest the merits of groundless actions.

The Tokyo District Court rejected these arguments.

DISPOSITION
(*shūbun*)

This suit is subject to the adjudicatory jurisdiction of Japanese courts.

REASONS
(*riyū*)

1. The defendant contends that Japanese courts do not have adjudicatory jurisdiction over the action in this case. We examine this point below.

2. As indicated in the proceedings in this case, we recognize that the defendant is a foreign company established under the laws of the State of Delaware in the United States of America, and has its head office in the State of Washington in the same country.

With regard to the international adjudicatory jurisdiction in a civil proceeding involving transnational commercial factors and a foreign corporation as a party, under the present situation without any directly applicable rules of domestic law nor any treaties or clear, established principles of international law, it is reasonable to decide on the issue in accordance with principles of *jōri*, which require fairness between the parties and just and prompt administration of justice. It is consistent with these principles for a Japanese court to have jurisdiction over the case when the requirements for at least one of the provisions for domestic territorial jurisdiction set out in the Code of Civil Procedure of Japan are satisfied.

3. The gist of the plaintiffs' claim in this case according to their complaint, is that, they seek damages from the defendant as successor of Vertol Company because the crewmen of the helicopter of whom they are the successors, died in the crash of the helicopter produced by Vertol Company. According to them, this accident was caused by a defect of one of the parts of the helicopter — that is, a breakdown of a socket by which a shaft of the rotor was secured.

It is apparent that the plaintiffs' claim in this case based upon the above cause comes under "a suit relating to a tort" prescribed in article 15, paragraph 1 [current article 5, paragraph 9] of the Code of Civil Procedure. Also, it is reasonable to construe that "the place where the act occurred" in the same clause, as called the place of tort, includes not only the place where the tortious act was committed but also the place where the injury took place.

4. [The Court then proceeded to summarize the facts of the case, concluding that "the plaintiffs' injury occurred in Japan as a result of the tortious act of the Vertol Aircraft Company" and thereby the defendant, which has assumed Vertol's liabilities. The Court therefore held that, inasmuch as Japan was the place of the tort, Japanese courts had adjudicatory jurisdiction based on the provisions of the Code of Civil Procedure.]

The defendant argues that the plaintiffs must prove prima facie the following two facts: the accident was caused by a defect of the helicopter produced by the Vertol Aircraft Company and the defendant succeeded the liability of the Vertol Aircraft Company relating to this accident. With regard to these two points, the defendant contends that Vertol Company has nothing to do with the accident because the socket which the plaintiffs claims to be the cause of the accident was produced by the Lycoming Company, as a subcontractor of the Parsons Company, and was supplied to the U.S. Air Force by the Parsons Company. Vertol Aircraft Company had no part in its production, supply, or maintenance. Also, the acquisition of the Vertol Aircraft Company by the defendant was a transfer of business. There was no agreement to the effect that the defendant assumed liability for any future debts of the Vertol Aircraft Company including any liability resulting from the accident in this case.

Even in cases, as here, where the facts upon which the adjudicatory jurisdiction is based coincide with the facts upon which the merits of the claim are based, this Court considers it inappropriate to make the defendant bear the burden of contesting the merits of the case by admitting the jurisdiction merely based upon the assertion of the plaintiff. It should be appropriate, however, for the court to determine the issue of jurisdiction after tentative examination of the evidence concerned. The questions to be determined are not only whether or not "the place of tort" as a basis of jurisdiction is in Japan but also whether or not a "tort" as the basis of the claim in this case was committed in Japan. . . .

5. Even though one of the requirements prescribed in the Code of Civil Procedure exists in Japan as mentioned above, if, because of the peculiar circumstances in the case, a trial in Japan would violate basic principles of civil procedure, such as realization of impartiality between the parties and of a just and speedy adjudication, it would, however, be reasonable to deny the jurisdiction of the Japanese court. Subsequently, the Court will examine whether or not there were peculiar circumstances as stated above in this case.

Judging from the recognized facts that the helicopter and the socket in this case were both produced in the United States and supplied to the U.S. Air Force; the defendant and the Vertol Aircraft Company are corporations both established under American law and have or had their head offices in the United States, it can be expected that adjudication of this case in a Japanese court would cause some inconvenience for the defendant and for the court in examining the evidence. However, inasmuch as the defendant is a corporation with large capital that manufactures aircraft that fly worldwide; that The Boeing Company provided all of the capital for its affiliated company; that the defendant has an office in Japan; that the plaintiffs reside in Japan, where the tort was committed; and that the Investigation Committee of the Air Self-Defense Forces of Japanese investigated the cause of the crash in this case. In the light of these facts, it cannot be that the trial of this case [in Japan] would cause such disadvantage for the defendant as to deprive it of the opportunity to defend itself; and it would not result in such inconvenience as to infringe upon the fair and speedy trial concerning the examination of the evidence.

There are no other facts sufficient to recognize the peculiar circumstances as mentioned above. Consequently, it should be said that the peculiar circumstances to deny the jurisdiction do not exist in this case.

JUDGE KEIICHI MURASHIGE
JUDGE HIDETOSHI SOMIYA
JUDGE KEN FUJISHITA

QUESTIONS

1. How does this case differ from *Gotō v. Malaysia Airlines?* Why were the special forum rules for tort actions at issue in this case? Does the judgment provide the answer?

2. What can one at least infer concerning the corporate structure of The Boeing Company and its operations in Japan? Through which form of business organization would you surmise that the company operates in Japan — a branch office or a wholly-owned sales subsidiary?

3. The district court judges in this case deemed the jurisdictional provisions of the 1890 Code of Civil Procedure to be applicable" Does this mean that *jōri* was irrelevant to the outcome? Under what circumstances, if any, according to the court, might the place where the accident and injury occurred *not* qualify as the place of the tort?

K.K. BUNGEI SHUNJŪ v. MIYATA
Tokyo District Court Judgment of 28 August 1989, *supra*

Recall that Bungei Shunjū, the publisher of a popular Japanese magazine, included an article in one of its issues alleging that the defendant, Nozomi Miyata, murdered his wife. Miyata responded with a libel suit in California. Bungei Shunjū in turn filed this action in Japan. As we have seen previously, the court dismissed the suit for lack of adjudicatory jurisdiction first on the grounds that Japan was not the place for performance in terms of the payment of damages for a delict committed in California. In this excerpt, the court explains why Japan also cannot be deemed the place where the tort occurred.

REASONS
(*riyū*)

. . . .

(3) Next, we consider the international jurisdiction in cases involving torts. The defendant in this action filed a suit for damages with the Supreme Court of Los Angeles County of California on September 7, 1984 against the plaintiff and the author of the article in question, claiming libel and violation of privacy. This suit is still pending. In that lawsuit, the defendant alleges that his fame was infringed by the fact that the magazines [containing the allegedly libelous article] were sold in

the United States, particularly in California, and the article identifying him as the murderer of his wife was read within the Japanese community there. The defendant does not claim in the California suit that publication of the magazine in Japan was a tort; moreover, his claim in this case is the same as the above. Indeed, as maintained by the plaintiff, "the place where the act was committed" *(locus delicti commissi)* as prescribed in [current article 5(ix)] of the Code of Civil Procedure includes not only the place where the damage occurs but also the place where the tortious act was done. However, Japan is not that place in both meanings. The tort alleged by the defendant in this case is not the editing and publication of the magazines in Japan but rather the sales of the magazines in California that infringed his reputation there. Consequently, as the place of tort in this case is the United States, the international jurisdiction of Japanese courts cannot be admitted based upon [article 5(ix)] of the Code.

(4) There are no other facts which make it possible for Japanese courts to admit the jurisdiction.

JUDGE KEIKO OKITA
JUDGE ICHIRŌ OZAWA
JUDGE MAKI AIZAWA

QUESTION

How would you characterize the alleged tort (delict) in this case? Would you agree with the court that it was "committed" in California?

K.K. TSUBURAYA PRODUCTIONS v. CHAIYO FILM CO., LTD.

Supreme Court, 2nd P.B., Judgment of 8 June 2001
55 Minshū (No. 4) 727 (2001)
[Adapted from Judgments of the Supreme Court of Japan, also translated in 45 JAIL 151 (2002)]

In a contract dated March 4, 1976 the appellant Tsuburaya Production Company granted Chaiyo Film Company, a Thai company with no office or representative in Japan, the exclusive rights outside of Japan to the copyrighted telefilm "Ultraman" for an unlimited period of time. In July 1996 Tsuburaya sent Chaiyo a letter confirming the exclusive rights to the film outside of Japan. Tsuburaya, however, also granted to a Japanese firm, Bandai, the rights to the film in Japan and Southeast Asia. Upon learning of the Bandai license, in July 1996 Chaiyo sent letters to various Bandai subsidiaries in Hong Kong, Singapore, and Thailand warning them that any use of the work would constitute an infringement of Chaiyo's exclusive rights to the work in Thailand and the region. In response, Tsuburaya filed both a criminal complaint and civil suit in Thailand, claiming that the purported contract licensing the film was a forgery and seeking an injunction to prevent

Chaiyo from infringing Tsuburaya's copyright under the Berne Convention as well as compensation for tortuous conduct. Tsuburaya also brought a similar civil action against Chaiyo in the Tokyo District Court seeking confirmation that the purported contract was not authentic, that Tsuburaya held the copyright to the work in Thailand, and that Chaiyo had no right to use the work. Tsuburaya also sought injunctive relief and compensation for tortuous conduct by Chaiyo.

The Tokyo District Court and, on first (*kōso*) appeal, the Tokyo High Court both dismissed the action. The Tokyo High Court determined that the use of the registered seals of the company as well as Tsuburaya's representative director was sufficient to establish the prima facie validity of the contract. Thus the court denied jurisdiction on the basis of tort. As discussed below, the court also denied jurisdiction based on the location of the subject matter of the claim, finding that the claim related to the property (the copyright) in this case was located in Thailand.

The Supreme Court (2nd Petty Bench) quashed the judgment, reversing the decision and remanded the case to the Tokyo District Court for trial. On the issue of jurisdiction based on the *situs* of the tort, the Court held:

> In an action for compensation against the defendant who does not have a domicile in Japan, in order to acknowledge the international jurisdiction of the Japanese court based upon the provision on the venue of court in tort in the Code of Civil Procedure, as a rule, it is sufficient if the objective facts that the legally protected interest of the plaintiff has been harmed in Japan by the act of the defendant which took place in Japan are proved.

The Court reasoned:

> In order to acknowledge the international jurisdiction of the Japanese court based upon the provision on the jurisdiction for tort in the Code of Civil Procedure, as a rule, it is sufficient if the objective facts that the legally protected interest of the plaintiff has been damaged in Japan by the act of the defendant which took place in Japan are proved. This is because if such facts exist, normally, there is a reasonable ground for compelling the defendant to respond to the action, and from the viewpoint of allocation of the judicial function among the countries, there is sufficient legal nexus to justify the exercise of judicial power by Japan.

> In relation to claim (i), the objective circumstance is clear that by the appellee causing delivery of the Warning to the recipient companies in Japan, the business of the appellant has been disturbed, and therefore, the international jurisdiction of the Japanese court should be acknowledged in claim (i).

> The original instance court, based upon the presupposition that in order to acknowledge international court jurisdiction of the Japanese court in relation to a claim for compensation based upon tort, the existence of a tort needs to be proved by prima facie examination of evidence above a certain level (hereinafter, 'Prima Facie proof'), ruled that prima facie proof exists for the existence of grounds for exemption from unlawfulness, and denied international court jurisdiction of Japanese court in claim (i). This ruling (a) presupposes that in order to acknowledge international court jurisdiction

based upon the provisions on court jurisdiction in the Code of Civil Procedure, it is required to establish the existence of a tort, including the absence of the grounds for the exemption of unlawfulness in one way or another; (b) if the existence of a tort is acknowledged solely on the assertion of the plaintiff, it may lead to cases where the defendant is forced to respond to an action even in cases where there is no legal nexus with Japan, and is unjustifiable; (c) conversely, if the level of proof required to the existence of a tort is set at the same level as in the consideration of the case on its merit, it will be against the basic structure of the procedure that the determination of the jurisdiction is a logical prerequisite to the consideration of the case on its merit; and (d) is understood to have adopted the solution of acknowledging the existence of a tort by prima facie proof. Although (b) and (c) of the above ruling are justifiable, as mentioned above, the prerequisite (a) is wrong, and therefore, there is no reason to adopt a solution such as (d). Furthermore, if one is to determine the existence or absence of a tort by prima facie proof, the criteria for the standard of proof is unclear, and as compared to the normal standard of proof, the standard may differ from court to court. This will make the prediction of the result by the parties, namely foreign parties, more difficult, and thus, is inappropriate. Therefore, the above ruling of the original instance court has erred in the interpretation and application of the law.

QUESTION

What evidence do you suppose the plaintiff would have had to tender to provide "prima facie" proof that the place of the tort was in Japan?

D. Special Jurisdiction: Place of Property

Code of Civil Procedure

[Applicable to transnational cases through 2011]

Article 5 [*Forum for civil actions for monetary and other claims against property (zaisanken)*]

The following civil actions may be brought before the court having jurisdiction over the following locations:

. . . .

(iv) actions involving monetary and other claims against the assets of persons who do not have domicile (in case of a legal person, office or place of business; hereinafter the same) in Japan or whose domicile is unknown: the place where *the subject of the claim or its security or an attachable asset of defendant is located;* [Emphasis added.]

[Applicable rule for transnational cases after 2012]

Article 3-3 [*Jurisdiction over Actions related to Duties under Contracts and other Obligations*]

The actions described in each of the following provisions may be brought in a Japanese court.

. . . .

(iii) Actions related to rights in assets (*zaidanken jō no uttae*), if the action is for the payment of money, if the defendant's *attachable assets are located in Japan (unless value of such assets is extremely low).* [Emphasis added.]

LOUSTALOT v. ADMIRAL SALES CO. LTD.
Tokyo District Court Judgment of 11 June 1959
10 Kakyū minshū 1204 (1959)

This early international jurisdiction case involved a claim for wrongful discharge under Japanese law by a U.S. citizen living in Japan against his employer, a U.S. corporation without an office or other establishment in Japan. However, the plaintiff did have in his possession a suitcase full of samples of the defendant's products (owned by the defendant) that were used to promote sales in Asia. Again the initial issue was the adjudicatory jurisdiction of the Japanese courts.

DISPOSITION
(*shūbun*)

This lawsuit is dismissed and the costs of litigation are borne by the plaintiff.

REASONS
(*riyū*)

First, we decide whether or not a Japanese court has adjudicatory jurisdiction over this case.

Inasmuch as a country's adjudicatory jurisdiction is considered an aspect of sovereign authority, the scope of adjudicatory jurisdiction is the same as that of sovereignty. In this sense, in principle a country may exercise jurisdiction over any person who is present in that country and also over any citizen even though outside of the country. In light of this general rule, Japanese jurisdiction does not usually extend to a defendant if he is a foreigner living outside Japan unless he voluntarily submits to Japanese jurisdiction. This view accords with the international application of the [civil law] principle that the 'plaintiff must bring suit at the general forum of the defendant.' However, as generally known, most modern countries have taken the view that a country has jurisdiction over a case, regardless of where the parties live, if the case has a certain connection with the particular country, for example, a case concerning land located in that country. The jurisdiction based on the parties' choice of forum is another example. However, what contacts with the suit are sufficient for the recognition of adjudicatory jurisdiction is left to each country to determine. As a matter of fact, no common national approach exists. Nonetheless, broad recognition [of adjudicatory jurisdiction] risks conflict with adjudicatory jurisdiction as a function of the sovereignty of other countries on the one hand, and, on the other, may easily have extremely unjust consequences for the parties, especially defendants. For these reasons, certain restrictions are necessary.

We have at present no statutory provisions, no relevant treaties and no established rules of international law as to what kind of suit should come under our adjudicatory jurisdiction. However, the Code of Civil Procedure, in its provisions on jurisdiction (*kankatsuken*), especially territorial jurisdiction (*tochi-kankatsu*), provides that certain types of cases come under the adjudicatory jurisdiction of a particular court because of certain connections with the subject matter or with land. We may appropriately ascertain from these provisions what connections with our country are necessary. Even so, however, under the general principle of territorial jurisdiction based on the general forum of the defendant or, additionally, certain other factors, all cases ultimately come under the jurisdiction of one of our country's courts under the allocation of territorial jurisdiction in the Code of Civil Procedure. Even when special territorial jurisdiction is recognized out of fairness to the parties because of competing jurisdiction based on the general forum rules or the convenience of adjudication, conflict between the parties is relatively rare. If there is notable damage or delay in the treatment of the case in the designated court, the case may be transferred to another court in order to avoid such harm (Code of Civil Procedure [former] article 31). However, because of difficulty in access to the court, differences in language and law, and so forth, serious conflict can arise with respect to international jurisdiction as to which country has jurisdiction over the case. Moreover, no system exists for transferring cases to another country's court in order to avoid unjust results. Therefore, it is inappropriate simply to apply the Code of Civil Procedure, which is internal law, as the standard for determining jurisdiction. We must think of its scope based on consideration of the factors described above.

The present suit is contact action brought by a U.S. citizen who at present resides in Japan, against a juridical person established under the law of the State of California, U.S.A., which has the principal office in California but no branch or office in Japan.

This country may exercise jurisdiction over the plaintiff, in that since he resides in here, thereby coming under our sovereign power, and because, by bringing the suit, he has voluntarily submitted to our jurisdiction. However, the defendant is a foreign juridical person in a foreign country. Therefore, the jurisdiction of this country does not, as a rule, extend to the defendant. However, as explained above, there are certain cases may come under jurisdiction of this country because of certain contacts with Japan, regardless of the location of the defendant. Therefore, we have to examine further cases with this problem of contacts.

Article 8 [current article 5, paragraph (iv)] of the Code of Civil Procedure may have some relevance for a test to determine whether Japan can exercise jurisdiction over this suit. As alleged by the plaintiff, article 8 provided a special forum for those who have no domicile (*jūsho*) (see Civil Code art. 21) in Japan, in order to protect their rights and to make easy practice of their rights. Thus, the article allows bringing a suit against people whose personal relation with Japan is slight. Since these are the purposes of the article 8, it may appear that the nationality or the residence of the defendant does not matter at all, and that if the requirements of the article are fulfilled, then jurisdiction of our country should extend even to a foreign juridical person that does not have an office in Japan. *In this suit, however, the location of the subject-matter of claim or security is not in question. Only the location of "any attachable property of the defendant" is relevant.* [Emphasis added.]

However, if we construe article 8 Code of Civil Procedure as indicated above and decide that our country has jurisdiction over the defendant insofar as he has attachable property in Japan, regardless of its nature, quantity, number or value, it may be convenient and effective for the plaintiff who is at present in Japan and who has chosen this court, but it will inevitably cause significant disadvantage to the defendant who is not in this country. If the defendant's property in this country were land, and if the suit involved a claim directly connected with such land, then, we may find a close relationship between the property and our country. *But when [the attachable asset] is a movable, the relationship between the property and the territory of Japan is slight. Especially, here where the property involved is, as alleged in the plaintiff's complaint, some sample commodities and the like. Considering the fact that the plaintiff has been acting as a salesman in various East Asian countries including Japan, only mere chance is the property located in this country. Accordingly it seems to be fair and reasonable to rule that such contact is not sufficient to make this case an exception to the principle that the jurisdiction of this country does not extend to a foreigner (or a foreign juristic person) located outside this country.* [Emphasis added.] It is just for us to conclude that there is no sufficient reason, in this case, for violating the basic right of defendant that he be sued where he is domiciled or resides.

Some countries entertain jurisdiction merely because defendant's property exists in the territory or merely by way of attachment of the property. However, as the defendant pointed out, many countries do not assume jurisdiction merely because defendant's property exists inside their territory. Thus, our interpretation given above is not against the general practice of various countries. The plaintiff argues that such interpretation is against the principle of justice as it would make a Japanese citizen unable to bring a suit or collect judgment in a Japanese court on obligation rights against a foreigner or a foreign juristic person who used to be in Japan, even when he wants to get a debt from the property left in Japan by the foreigner or the foreign juristic person. However, in such a situation, there would always be other contacts that can provide a basis for jurisdiction of our country over the case (e.g., place of performance, place of contract, place of tort, etc.). Also, the Code of Civil Procedure article 8 would directly apply to such a case (as the relevant "venue" provision). Therefore, the plaintiff's argument is groundless.

* * *

The court continued by rejecting three other grounds for jurisdiction argued by the plaintiff: that the contract of this case was to be performed in Japan, that the contract was subject to Japanese substantive law, and that by having an attorney making an appearance on its behalf, the defendant voluntarily submitted to the court's jurisdiction. With respect to the second point, the court found that the contract was made in California and that there was no evidence to support the claim that the parties mutually intended Japanese law to govern the contract. Similarly, the court found no evidence to support the claim that the obligation (contract) was to be performed in Japan:

> The Civil Code of this country provides that when there is no declaration of intention concerning the place of payment, payment should be made at the present address of the creditor, unless the obligation right is delivery of specific things (Civil Code article 484). However, as explained above, the contract in this case is not governed by the Japanese law. It would be different if the Law of California, the law of the place of contract, provides that the present address of the creditor should be the place of performance. But, insofar as such a California rule was not found in the proceedings, we cannot say that the place of performance is Japan.

With respect to the third claim, the court responded:

> Even in the event the defendant appears before a Japanese court to answer in the examination of the case on the merits, if he has previously declared his intention to dispute the existence of Japanese jurisdiction, the Japanese court cannot necessarily acquire jurisdiction merely because of his appearance. As noted above, the defendant in this case has disputed Japanese jurisdiction from the beginning, and he is answering on the merits because the court has not decided that issue but allowed, or forced, the parties to advance the cause. Although he has not made a specific reservation, it can be well understood that he intends to answer on the merits only in case his contention of the non-existence of Japanese jurisdiction is rejected. . . . Similarly, we cannot assume jurisdiction over this case merely because the representative of the defendant has appeared before a Japanese court in the procedure for perpetuating testimony.

NOTE

The name of the plaintiff in this case is uncertain. Foreign words are transcribed in Japanese in a syllabary (*katagana*) that does not distinguish between "r's" and "l's" nor certain other sounds in English. Thus the plaintiff's name could be "Rostarot" or "Lostarot" or "Lostalot" or something similar. The choice of Loustalot is entirely arbitrary — although he may have lost a lot.

YASUTOMI v. UNITED NETHERLANDS NAV. CO.
Yokohama District Court Judgment of 1966 17 Kakyū minshū (Nos. 9–10) 874 (1966)
[Adapted from translation in 13 JAIL 159 (1969)]

In July 1963 the Sinoutakerk, a ship owned and operated by the United Netherlands Navigation Co., collided with a yacht in the Uraga Channel of Tokyo Bay. The collision caused the death of Shigeo Yasutomi. His wife and children sought a provisional attachment of the Servaaskert, also owned by the defendant, which had called at the Port of Yokohama, pursuant to a suit for damages as his successors, alleging that the collision was caused by the gross negligence of the captain of the Sinoutakerk. United Netherlands Navigation Co., a Dutch company, without an office or other assets in Japan, challenged the adjudicatory jurisdiction of the court. The Yokohama District Court affirmed the attachment of the vessel and upheld its jurisdiction under Code of Civil Procedure, article 8, currently article 5(iv). The court gave the following reasons for its decision:

Reasons
(riyū)

1. (Whether or not the court has adjudicatory jurisdiction and the applicable law)

Neither party contests that the defendant has its principal office in the Netherlands, and that it has no branch office or assets other than the attached vessel in Japan. This Court is to review the decision allowing the provisional attachment of the defendant's vessel Servaaskert, which called at the Port of Yokohama. The attachment was issued to protect the right to claim compensation for damages [as detailed previously]. This case involves an ordinary lawsuit based on a claim instituted against the respondent, the defendant [in the principal action], by the claimants, the obligees in this case, who are Japanese residing in Japan, for damages caused by the Sinouttkert, which is owned by the defendant and which collided with a yacht sailed by the late Shigeo Yagutomi. Because the jurisdiction to adjudicate the claim for a provisional attachment must be considered prior to examination of the merits of the case, this Court will first review this point.

The matter of designating the court qualified to handle a case of compensation for damages arising from a collision of vessels has long been argued in terms of the question whether the court should be a court of (1) the country of the defendant tortfeasor, (2) the country of the injured plaintiff, (3) the country where the collision occurred, (4) the country where the assailant vessel or the victimized vessel is located, or (5) the country where one of the vessels is registered. In order to arrive at a mutually agreeable international standard, the "Treaty for Integration of Some Provisions relating to Civil Jurisdiction over Collision Cases" was concluded in 1962. According to this Treaty, a plaintiff can bring a case either before the court of the place where an attachment has been effected (or the court of the place where the guaranty money for the attachment has been deposited), or before the court of the place where the collision occurred when the collision occurred in a harbor or inland waters. *As Japan has not as yet ratified or entered into this Treaty, [the issue of jurisdiction in] this case cannot be decided under said Treaty. Consequently, a court's jurisdiction over such a case can only be determined theoretically at the present time, as a case concerning general civil jurisdiction in ordinary international private law suits, in view of the fact that there is neither a treaty nor a generally recognized principle of the international law.* [Emphasis added.]

Fundamentally speaking, the exercise of a nation's adjudicatory jurisdiction is a sovereign act of the nation and therefore jurisdiction should, in principle, cover the same sphere as that covered by the sovereign right. From such a viewpoint, when a defendant is a foreign corporation having its main office in a foreign country, the jurisdiction of Japanese courts would not extend to such a defendant unless the defendant voluntarily submits itself to jurisdiction. There is an exceptional case, however, in which a nation's jurisdiction extends to the parties irrespective of the location of the parties concerned insofar as sovereignty covers a case that has a connection with the country. The sphere subject to such sovereignty is left to each nation's discretion. As far as Japan is concerned, no law directly determines such sphere, and because of the absence of such law, there is no alternative but to deduce that sphere theoretically from the special jurisdictional provisions of civil procedure concerning real property, i.e., it shall be conjectured that those who have land subject to the special jurisdiction of Japan should in principle submit themselves to the jurisdiction of the Japanese courts.

Article 8 of the Code of Civil Procedure provides for the local jurisdiction of Japanese court at the place where the defendant's attachable assets are located, even though the defendant is a nonresident foreigner. It goes without saying that such local jurisdiction depends on the existence of the jurisdiction of the Japanese courts. Thus, jurisdiction over such cases is, in the opinion of this Court, granted because the effective prosecution of judicial decisions is perfectly secured. This opinion holds true regardless of whether the assets are movables having little connection with the place or things located there accidentally. [Emphasis added.]

Returning to our specific case, [the evidence] indicates that the defendant's vessel Servaaskerk was calling at the Port of Yokohama on June 26, 1965, and had not completed her preparations for sailing. Accordingly, the claimants are entitled to demand compensation of damages against the Defendant. This court has jurisdiction over the place where the attachable asset (attachment over the asset is permitted as described hereunder) is located whether or not the defendant has a main office or a branch office in Japan. This Court is, therefore, of the opinion that it has jurisdiction over the instant case. [Emphasis added.] (This Court will not elaborate on its opinion concerning the existence of the possibility of Japanese jurisdiction based on Japan as the place of performance of an obligation or the place of commission of tortious act.)

As discussed above, it is needless to argue that this Court had jurisdiction over the instant suit concerning provisional attachment to secure the execution of the final judgment in the ordinary law suit, since this Court has jurisdiction over the proceeding for final judgment in the ordinary lawsuit. This Court trusts that the foregoing opinion coincides with and does not contradict the spirit of the aforementioned Treaty.

Further, as the place of the collision of the instant case was within Japanese waters, the law applicable to the suit concerning the right of indemnification for damages caused by such tortious act should be determined by Article 11 of the *Hōrei* (Law concerning the Application of Laws) of Japan, where the tortious act occurred.

II. (Existence of Rights Protected by Provisional Attachment.)

As concluded above, the captain [of the Servaaskerk] in the course of duty caused the defendant's vessel to collide with Shigeo Yasutomi's yacht, thereby causing Yasutomi's death. And according to Evidence *Ko* No. 2, the authenticity of which is agreed to by both parties, the captain is deemed to have been negligent as to the collision, as asserted by the claimants, and therefore the defendant is liable for damages pursuant to article 690 of the Commercial Code.

JUDGE KUNIO TAGUCHI

QUESTIONS

1. In both *Loustalot v. Admiral Sales* and *Yasutomi v. United Netherlands Nav. Co.*, the defendants' having attachable assets in the district was the claimed basis for adjudicatory jurisdiction under former article 8 and current article 5(iv) of the Code of Civil Procedure. What other special forum rules could, at least arguably, have been applicable?

2. The court in *Yasutomi* stated that article 8, current article 5(iv), applied "regardless of whether the assets are movables having little connection with the place or things located there accidentally." Would, in your view Judge Taguchi, the judge in *Yasutomi*, have decided *Loustalot v. Admiral Sales* differently? Note that the 2011 amendment, article 3-3(iii), codifies *Yasutomi* and *Loustalot* in confirming that the assets need have no relation to the claim in the suit. However, the value of the assets cannot be insignificant.

TSUBURAYA PRODUCTIONS K.K. v. CHAIYO FILM CO., LTD.
Supreme Court, 2nd P.B., Judgment of 8 June 2001
55 Minshū (No. 4) 727 (2001)

As described above, this case involved an alleged infringement of a copyright held by a Japanese firm, which rights the defendant claimed to have been licensed to it by the plaintiff. The lower court had held that Japanese court lacked adjudicatory jurisdiction by virtue of inadequate proof of a tort and that the location of "object of the claim" at issue was Thailand, not Japan. The Supreme Court reversed on both grounds, holding that the location of the copyright was Japan and thus that Japanese courts have jurisdiction under article 5(iv):

In relation to claim (ii) [for the recognition of the fact that the appellee does not have a copyright over the telfilm at issue], the *object of the claim* [emphasis added] is located in Japan, and therefore, it is evident that the venue of court by the location of the property as provided by the Code of Civil Procedure of Japan exists (Art. 5(iv), the [1996] Code of Civil Procedure, Art.8 of the previous [1890] Code of Civil Procedure).

Copyright is protected by the Berne Convention in the member countries in a mutual way. If the appellee jointly holds the copyright of the Present Works in the Kingdom of Thailand with the appellant, the joint copyright of the appellee will be protected in Japan as well. The fact that the appellee asserts that he jointly holds the copyright of the Present Works under the Procedure in Thailand is sufficient to justify the maturity of the dispute involving claim (ii) and the interest for recognition, and the judgment of the original instance court which denied the interest for recognition has erred in the interpretation and application of the law.

QUESTIONS

1. Compare the language of articles 5(iv) and 3-2(iv) of the Code of Civil Procedure as amended in 2011, quoted above. Under the Supreme Court decision in *Tsuburaya Productions v. Chaiyo Film Co.*, could all Japanese copyright holders have been able to sue in Japan any infringers worldwide before 2012 under articles 5(iv)? Does current law — article 3-2(iii) — allow such suits against defendants with no other connection with Japan?

2. Would your answer be the same were the suit to involve patent or trademark infringement of a foreign patent or trademark held by a Japanese firm and licensed to a foreign party — as in the case of the copyright license in *Tsuburaya Productions v. Chaiyo Film Co.*? Is there any other basis for such a suit under the provisions of the Code of Civil Procedure included here?

E. Special Jurisdiction: Joint Defendants

Code of Civil Procedure

[Applicable to transnational cases through 2011]

Article 7 [*Joinder of Claims*]

Where two or more claims are to be made by a single action, such action may be filed with the court which shall have jurisdiction over one of those claims pursuant to the provisions of Article 4 to the preceding Article (excluding Article 6(iii)); provided, however, that with regard to an action brought by two or more persons or an action brought against two or more persons, this shall apply only in the case specified in the first sentence of Article 38.

Article 38 [*Conditions for Joinder of Claims*]

> 1. If the rights or liabilities for a suit are common to more than one person or are based on the same ground of facts or laws, such more than one person may sue or be sued as co-litigants. The same will be applied if the rights or liabilities for the suit are the same and based on the same kind of facts and laws.

[Applicable rule for transnational cases after 2012]

Article 3-6 [*Joinder of Claims*]

> Where two or more claims are joined in a single action and courts of Japan have jurisdiction only over one of them, such action may be filed with the courts of Japan only if the particular claim over which the jurisdiction exists has a close connection with the other claims. However, with respect to actions brought by or against two or more persons, the foregoing applies only in the cases described in the first paragraph of Article 38.

INOUE v. AVIACO AIRLINES
Tokyo District Court Judgment of 8 May 1987
Hanrei jihō (No. 1232) 40 (1987)
[English translation in 31 JAIL 220 (1988)]

On December 7, 1983, at Madrid-Barajas Airport, Spain, an Aviaco Airlines plane accidently entered the runway as Iberia Airlines Flight 350 was taking off. In the resulting collision 135 people died. Of the passengers killed, 93 were on the Iberia flight and 42 on Aviaco aircraft. Subsequently heirs of Japanese passengers aboard the Iberia aircraft brought damage claims against both airlines in the Tokyo District Court. Aviaco Airlines is based and incorporated in Spain and does no business in Japan.

DISPOSITION
(*shūbun*)

Japanese courts have jurisdiction to adjudicate this lawsuit.

REASONS
(*riyū*)

A. . . . The issue in this case is whether our courts have jurisdiction to adjudicate this lawsuit.

1. . . . Lacking any relevant statutory rules on international adjudicatory jurisdiction over such a civil action against foreign corporations as the present one as well as any relevant treaties or established and generally recognized principles of international law, it is reasonable to decide the question in accordance with the principles of *jōri*, which require fairness between the parties and just and prompt administration of justice. To find venue in Japan for the local territorial competence provided in the Code of Civil Procedure . . . should satisfy these principles of

justice and reason to sustain the jurisdiction of Japanese court.

Moreover, if the jurisdiction of Japanese courts based on the provisions for joinder of claims provided by article 21 [of the 1890 Code, restated in articles 7 and 38 of the 1996 Code and applicable in transnational cases under article 3-6 of the Code as amended in 2011] of the accords with the ideas of promoting fairness between the parties and fair and prompt administration of justice, the above principles of *jōri* are satisfied.

2. In this case, plaintiffs initially brought an action against defendant and Iberia as codefendants. According to the purport of the parties' oral arguments, we find that Iberia has one of its offices of business in Tokyo . . . and, therefore, for that reason under article 4 [and current article 3-2] of Code of Civil Procedure, its general forum is located in Japan. We also find, by the purport of the parties' oral argument that the deceased passengers entered into the international air transport contract in Japan. (Japan was the place of departure and destination. Zurich, Paris, Madrid were stopping places). Japan therefore has jurisdiction over Iberia Airlines under article 28 of the Convention for the Unification of Certain Rules Relating to International Carriage by Air ("Warsaw Convention"). . . . Consequently, inasmuch as the plaintiffs' claims against Iberia Airlines and the defendant are both for damages based on the same cause of action, i.e., the accident in question, we find that Japanese courts have jurisdiction over the present action against the defendant under article 21 of the [1890] Code of Civil Procedure for joinder of claims.

3. We now turn to the question whether or not to sustain jurisdiction of the Japanese court over the present action on the ground that we find venue for the joinder of claims accords with the principles of *jōri*, which require fairness between the parties and just and prompt administration of justice.

(1) Fairness between the parties

Both the claim against Iberia and the claim against the defendant arise from the same fact, namely the accident at bar. If the Japanese court denies its jurisdiction over the action against the defendant, plaintiffs would be compelled to bring an action against the defendant in Spain, in addition to the action in Japan against Iberia. However it would be extremely burdensome for plaintiffs to be compelled to bring another action against the defendant with respect to the case arisen from the same accident. On the other hand, although the defendant would no doubt incur a considerable disadvantage by being obliged to defend in Japan, that disadvantage is outweighed by the plaintiffs' burden and should be tolerated by the defendant. Therefore we think it appropriate, in light of the fairness between the parties, to sustain the jurisdiction of the Japanese court over this action.

(2) Just administration of justice

In response to the action by plaintiffs, Iberia seeks for dismissal of the plaintiffs' claim, and contends that it accepts no liability in this case since the accident was caused by Aviaco aircraft's entering the runway while the Iberia aircraft was proceeding on the same runway in accordance with the instructions of the air-traffic controller, and that it took all possible necessary measures to avoid the occurrence of the accident. . . . Thus, if the claim against Iberia and the claim against the defendant are to be tried and judged by different courts, there is a risk of having inconsistent or conflicting decisions made as to how this accident happened (. . .) and the existence or nonexistence or degree of negligence on the part of Iberia and the defendant. This would obviously be unsound in light of the fair administration of justice, and we must conclude that the uniform finding and judgment must be made on the above-mentioned points.

It is easily seen that the evidence as to the cause or circumstances of the accident are mainly located in Spain where the accident occurred. However, we could hardly believe that of the evidence likely to be needed for determining the circumstances of the occurrence of the accident, and the existence or nonexistence or degree of the defendant's liability, there is one that can only be examined in Spain or cannot be presented to this Court by plaintiffs, or the defendant and Iberia. Besides, there is a way through judicial assistance to entrust the authority of Spain to examine the evidence there. Furthermore, plaintiffs had presented the technical report prepared by the Spanish government's . . . Accident Research Board, which we believe would show the circumstances of the occurrence of the accident and the cause and effect of the accident. Hence, the existence of evidence in Spain does not create such serious difficulty for the Japanese court to find facts in the case at bar.

If the Japanese court tries this case, it may apply the law of Spain as the governing law for ton. In such a case, the Japanese court would not have much difficulty in the proper application of the Spanish law.

Thus, even in the eyes of the fair administration of justice, it is not necessarily improper for the Japanese court to assert jurisdiction over the present case, and it would rather be reasonable for the Japanese court to do so in order to make uniform findings and judgments in accordance with the claim as to Iberia Air Lines.

(3) Prompt administration of justice

As to the cause of the accident, we admit that a more prompt trial would be forthcoming if the evidence is examined in Spain. However, as to the calculation of damages, considering that a large number of Plaintiffs are involved in this case, far more speedy administration of justice will be expected if the examination of evidence takes place in Japan, where plaintiffs are domiciled.

As we considered the above, it well conforms to the ideas of promoting fairness between the parties and fair and prompt administration of justice to sustain the jurisdiction of the court of this country in the case at bar.

4. Thus we conclude that it is proper and in accordance with the principles of justice and reason to sustain the jurisdiction of our court for the instant case on the ground that venue for joinder of claims under Article 21 of the [1890] CCP is located in Japan."

5. Accordingly, the Japanese court has jurisdiction to adjudicate the case at bar, and we render the judgment as stated above.

Judge Shuichi Yazaki
Judge Koichi Kigasawa
Judge Masanori Tsukiji

QUESTIONS

1. Are the provisions for joint defendants under the Japanese Code of Civil Procedure and the outcome of *Inoue v. Aviaco Airlines* reasonable? Do they make sense? Do you agree with the court that they are fair?

2. Assume that a California resident had been among the deceased passengers of the ill-fated Iberia Airlines flight. Would a California court have adjudicatory jurisdiction over Aviaco Airlines in a suit brought by the administrator of the estate? What if the passenger had been a resident of Quebec or of British Columbia? Would either a Quebec or British Columbia court have jurisdiction over Aviaco in a suit brought by the deceased passenger's successors?

VI. EUROPEAN UNION

A. Regulation (EU) No. 1215/2102 of the European Parliament and of the Council

On December 20, 2012, the European Union issued Regulation (EU) No. 1215/2012 of the European Parliament and of the Council on jurisdiction and the recognition and enforcement of judgments in civil and commercial matters to become fully effective on January 10, 2015. The new Regulation recast and repealed Council Regulation 44/2001. (For a complete copy of Regulation No. 1215/2012, see Appendix B.) With several notably significant revisions (detailed below in chapters 6 and 7), Regulation (EU) No. 1215/2012 restates EC Regulation 44/2001and the 1968 Brussels Convention (which has remained in effect in a few overseas territories of EU member states pursuant to Article 355 of the Treaty on the Functioning of the European Union [TFEU]). The Regulation is binding on the courts of all EU member states.

In general, as in Japan and virtually all civil law jurisdictions, the domicile of the defendant determines the general forum or jurisdiction. The principal provisions of the 2012 Regulation that relate to jurisdiction thus apply as before when the defendant in a civil action is domiciled within a member state. Article 4(1) of the 2012 Regulation provides:

> Subject to this Regulation, persons domiciled in a Member State shall, whatever their nationality, be sued in the courts of that Member State.

Under article 62 the municipal law of the forum determines the domicile of natural persons as defendants. Article 63, however, provides that:

1. For the purposes of this Regulation, a company or other legal person or association of natural or legal persons is domiciled at the place where it has its:

(a) statutory seat, or

(b) central administration, or

(c) principal place of business.

2. For the purposes of Ireland, Cyprus and the United Kingdom "statutory seat" means the registered office or, where there is no such office anywhere, the place of incorporation or, where there is no such place anywhere, the place under the law of which the formation took place.

3. In order to determine whether a trust is domiciled in the Member State whose courts are seised of the matter, the court shall apply its rules of private international law.

Under article 3 a person — natural or juridical — domiciled in a member state may be sued in the courts of another member state solely under the special jurisdiction rules that continue to be set out in sections 2 through 6 (arts. 7 through 24). Under article 7 these include place of performance in matters related to contracts (¶ 1), the place where the "harmful event occurred" or "may occur" in cases of tort, delict or quasi-delict (¶ 2), as well as cases damages, or restitution for criminal acts (¶ 3), cases arising out of operations of a branch, agency, or other "establishment" (¶ 5), trusts (¶ 6), and salvage (¶ 7). Section 3 (arts. 10 through 16) provide special jurisdiction rules for cases involving insurance. Special jurisdiction rules are also provided for consumer contracts in section 4 (arts. 17–19) and employment in section 5 (arts. 20–23). Section 6 (art. 24.) identifies cases of exclusive jurisdiction and, finally, section 7 (arts. 25 and 26) deals with prorogation or choice of forum agreements.

As detailed below, the 2012 Regulation continues in effect the prohibition of "excessive" or "exorbitant" jurisdiction in cases brought in a court of a member state against a defendant domiciled in a member state. However, as we shall see, the 2012 Regulation continues to defer to national rules with respect to cases brought in member states against defendants not domiciled in a member state.

Articles 18(1), 21(2), 24, and 25 are special provisions permitting consumers and employees to sue the "other party to the contract" or employers regardless of their domicile in courts where the consumer is domiciled (art. 18[1]) or "the employee habitually carries out his work or in the courts for the last place where he did so" or "if the employee does not or did not habitually carry out his work in any one country, in the courts for the place where the business which engaged the employee is or was situated (art. 21[2]).

Articles 24 covers instances of exclusive jurisdiction (e.g., cases involving rights *in rem* in immovable property, issues related to formalities of company law, registries, and intellectual property). Finally, article 25 deals with choice of court clauses (a topic to which we return in Chapter 7).

The following case illustrates the European Court's interpretation of similar provisions under the 1968 the Brussels Convention:

GROUP JOSI REINSURANCE COMPANY SA v. UNIVERSAL GENERAL INSURANCE COMPANY (UGIC)
Judgment of the Court (Sixth Chamber) of 13 July 2000 [Case C-412/98]
European Court Reports 2000 I-05925

JUDGMENT

GROUNDS

1 By judgment of 5 November 1998, received at the Court on 19 November 1998, the Cour d'Appel (Court of Appeal), Versailles, referred to the Court for a preliminary ruling under the Protocol of 3 June 1971 on the interpretation by the Court of Justice of the [1968 Brussels] Convention . . . .

2 Those questions were raised in proceedings between Universal General Insurance Company (UGIC), in liquidation, an insurance company incorporated under Canadian law, having its registered office in Vancouver, Canada, and Group Josi Reinsurance Company SA (Group Josi, a reinsurance company incorporated under Belgian law, having its registered office in Brussels, concerning a sum of money claimed by UGIC from Group Josi in its capacity as party to a reinsurance contract.

The Convention

3 The rules of jurisdiction laid down by the Convention are to be found in Title II thereof, which contains Articles 2 to 24.

[Provisions of the 1968 Brussels Convention set out in paragraphs 4–18 of the judgment omitted.]

The main proceedings

18 It is apparent from the documents in the case in the main proceedings that UGIC instructed its broker, Euromepa, a company incorporated under French law, having its registered office in France, to procure a reinsurance contract with effect from 1 April 1990 in relation to a portfolio of comprehensive home-occupiers' insurance polices based in Canada.

19 By fax dated 27 March 1990, Euromepa offered Group Josi a share in that reinsurance contract, stating that the main reinsurers are Union Ruck with 24% and Agrippina Ruck with 20%.

20 By fax of 6 April 1990, Group Josi agreed to acquire a 7.5% share.

21 On 28 March 1990, Union Ruck had told Euromepa that it did not intend to retain its share after 31 May 1990 and, by letter of 30 March 1990, Agrippina Ruck had informed the same broker that it would reduce its share to 10% with effect from 1 June 1990, the reason for those withdrawals being changes in economic policy imposed by the American-based parent companies of those insurance undertakings.

22 On 25 February 1991, Euromepa sent Group Josi first a statement of account showing a debit balance and then a final calculation showing that Group Josi owed CAD 54 679.34 in respect of its share in the reinsurance transaction.

23 By letter of 5 March 1991, Group Josi refused to pay that amount, essentially on the ground that it had been induced to enter into the reinsurance contract by the provision of information which subsequently turned out to be false.

24 In those circumstances, on 6 July 1994, UGIC brought proceedings against Group Josi before the Tribunal de Commerce (Commercial Court), Nanterre, France.

25 Group Josi argued that that court lacked jurisdiction since the Tribunal de Commerce, Brussels, within whose territorial jurisdiction it has its registered office, had jurisdiction, and it relied, first, on the Convention and, second, in the event of the general law being found to apply, on Article 1247 of the French Code Civil (Civil Code).

26 By judgment of 27 July 1995, the Tribunal de Commerce, Nanterre, held that it had jurisdiction on the ground that UGIC is a company incorporated under Canadian law without a place of business in the Community and that the objection of lack of jurisdiction raised on the basis of the Convention cannot be applied to it. On the substance, the court ordered Group Josi to pay the sum claimed by UGIC, plus statutory interest as from 6 July 1994.

27 Group Josi subsequently appealed against that judgment before the Cour d'Appel, Versailles.

28 In support of its appeal, Group Josi submitted that the Convention applies to any dispute in which a connecting factor with the Convention is apparent. In the present case, the Convention should apply. The main connecting factor is that specified in the first paragraph of Article 2 of the Convention, namely the defendant's domicile. Since Group Josi has its registered office in Brussels and no subsidiary place of business in France, it can, in accordance with that provision, be sued only in a Belgian court. In addition, Group Josi relied on Article 5(1) of the Convention, arguing in this respect that the obligation in question, being payment of a contractual debt, was, in the absence of any stipulation to the contrary in the reinsurance contract, to be performed in the debtor's place of domicile, namely Brussels.

29 UGIC, on the other hand, contended that the rules of jurisdiction established by the Convention can apply only if the plaintiff is also domiciled in a Contracting State. Since UGIC is a company incorporated under Canadian law with no subsidiary place of business in a Contracting State, the Convention is not applicable in the present case.

30 The Cour d'Appel observed, first, that, although a dispute may be regarded as sufficiently integrated into the European Community to justify jurisdiction being vested in the courts of a Contracting State where, as in the present case, the defendant is domiciled in a Contracting State, it is a different question whether the specific rules of that convention can be used against a plaintiff domiciled in a

non-Contracting State, which would necessarily entail extending Community law to non-member countries.

31 Second, the Cour d'Appel noted that Article 7 of the Convention simply refers to matters relating to insurance without specifying further, so that the question arises whether reinsurance falls within the scope of the autonomous system of jurisdiction established by Articles 7 to 12a of the Convention. In this respect, it might be considered that the purpose of those articles is to protect the insured as the weak party to the insurance contract and that there is no such characteristic in matters of reinsurance, but, on the other hand, the text of the Convention does not contain any exclusion on that point.

The questions referred for preliminary ruling

32 Taking the view that, in those circumstances, the resolution of the dispute required an interpretation of the Convention, the Cour d'Appel, Versailles, decided to stay proceedings and to refer the following two questions to the Court for a preliminary ruling:

1. *Does the Brussels Convention of 27 September 1968 on Jurisdiction and the Enforcement of Judgments in Civil and Commercial Matters apply not only to 'intra-Community' disputes but also to disputes which are 'integrated into the Community'? More particularly, can a defendant established in a Contracting State rely on the specific rules on jurisdiction set out in that convention against a plaintiff domiciled in Canada?*

2. *Do the rules on jurisdiction specific to matters relating to insurance set out in Article 7 et seq. of the Brussels Convention apply to matters relating to reinsurance?* [Emphasis added.]

The first question

33 By its first question, the national court essentially seeks to ascertain whether the rules of jurisdiction laid down by the Convention apply where the defendant has its domicile or seat in a Contracting State, even if the plaintiff is domiciled in a non-member country.

59 . . . [T]he Convention does not, in principle, preclude the rules of jurisdiction which it sets out from applying to a dispute between a defendant domiciled in a Contracting State and a plaintiff domiciled in a non-member country.

60 As the Advocate General observed in paragraph 21 of his Opinion, it is thus fully in accordance with that finding that the Court has interpreted the rules of jurisdiction laid down by the Convention in cases where the plaintiff had his domicile or seat in a non-member country, although the provisions of the Convention in question did not establish any exception to the general principle that the courts of the Contracting State in which the defendant is domiciled are to have jurisdiction [citations omitted].

61 *In those circumstances, the answer to the first question must be that Title II of the Convention is in principle applicable where the defendant has its domicile or seat in a Contracting State, even if the plaintiff is domiciled in a non-member country. It would be otherwise only in exceptional cases where an express provision*

of the Convention provides that the application of the rule of jurisdiction which it sets out is dependent on the plaintiff's domicile being in a Contracting State. [Emphasis added.]

The second question

62 In this respect, it must be observed, first, that the rules of jurisdiction in matters relating to insurance, laid down in Section 3 of Title II of the Convention, apply expressly to certain specific types of insurance contracts, such as compulsory insurance, liability insurance, insurance of immovable property and marine and aviation insurance. Furthermore, point 3 of the first paragraph of Article 8 of the Convention expressly refers to co-insurance.

63 On the other hand, reinsurance is not mentioned in any of the provisions of that section.

. . . .

76 *In the light of all the foregoing, the answer to the second question must be that the rules of special jurisdiction in matters relating to insurance set out in Articles 7 to 12a of the Convention do not cover disputes between a reinsurer and a reinsured in connection with a reinsurance contract.* [Emphasis added.]

On those grounds,

THE COURT (Sixth Chamber),

in answer to the questions referred to it by the Cour d'Appel, Versailles, by judgment of 5 November 1998, hereby rules:

1. Title II of the [1968 Brussels] Convention . . . is in principle applicable where the defendant has its domicile or seat in a Contracting State, even if the plaintiff is domiciled in a non-member country. It would be otherwise only in exceptional cases where an express provision of that convention provides that the application of the rule of jurisdiction which it sets out is dependent on the plaintiff's domicile being in a Contracting State.

2. The rules of special jurisdiction in matters relating to insurance set out in Articles 7 to 12a of that convention do not cover disputes between a reinsurer and a reinsured in connection with a reinsurance contract. [Emphasis added.]

QUESTIONS

1. What was the principal consequence for UGIC as a result of the ECJ's decision that the rules of special jurisdiction of the 1968 Brussels Convention relating to insurance did not apply to disputes pertaining to a reinsurance contract between a reinsurer and a reinsured? Did the Tribunal de Commerce, Nanterre have jurisdiction as UGIC argued or could UGIC only sue Group Josi in a Belgian court as argued by Group Josi? What if UGIC had sued in Canada?

2. In which of the following cases would the provisions of Regulation (EU) No. 1215/2012, assuming they are the same as the 1968 Brussels Convention, apply:

   a. A suit brought in France by a German citizen residing (domiciled) in the U.S. against a French corporation.

   b. A suit brought in Germany by the German subsidiary of a U.S. corporation against a German company wholly owned by a Japanese enterprise.

   c. A suit brought in France by a French national, domiciled in France, against Saudi Arabian firm.

   d. An unjust enrichment action brought by a Turkish national domiciled in Germany against an Israeli firm with no office or business establishment in German but which has stock in a Germany company, the certificates for which are held by a German bank as security for a loan.

3. In what significant ways, if any, do the bases for adjudicatory jurisdiction recognized under Regulation (EU) No. 1215/2012 differ from those under Japanese law? Under article 21[2]) of the 2012 Regulation, for example, would a court in the EU unlike Japan have had jurisdiction under similar circumstances to adjudicate Loustalot's claim against his California employer?

B. Joint Defendants

Another particularly noteworthy basis for jurisdiction within the European Union is article 8 which provides:

A person domiciled in a Member State may also be sued:

1. where he is one of a number of defendants, in the courts for the place where any one of them is domiciled, provided the claims are so closely connected that it is expedient to hear and determine them together to avoid the risk of irreconcilable judgments resulting from separate proceedings;

2. as a third party in an action on a warranty or guarantee or in any other third party proceedings, in the court seised of the original proceedings, unless these were instituted solely with the object of removing him from the jurisdiction of the court which would be competent in his case;

3. on a counter-claim arising from the same contract or facts on which the original claim was based, in the court in which the original claim is pending;

4. in matters relating to a contract, if the action may be combined with an action against the same defendant in matters relating to rights in rem in immovable property, in the court of the Member State in which the property is situated.

ATHANASIOS KALFELIS v. BANKHAUS SCHRÖDER, MÜNCHMEYER, HENGST AND CO. AND OTHERS
Judgment of the Court (Fifth Chamber) of 27 September 1988,
Case 189/87 [1988] ECR 5565

JUDGMENT

GROUNDS

1 By order of 27 April 1987, which was received at the Court Registry on 16 June 1987, the Bundesgerichtshof referred to the Court for a preliminary ruling . . . two questions on the interpretation of Articles 5(3) and 6(1) of the [1968 Brussels] Convention.

2 The questions were raised in proceedings brought by Athanasios Kalfelis against Bankhaus Schroeder, Muenchmeyer, Hengst und Co., Frankfurt am Main, and Bankhaus Schroeder, Muenchmeyer, Hengst International SA, Luxembourg, and Ernst Markgraf, a procuration holder for the first-named bank.

3 Between March 1980 and July 1981 Mr Kalfelis concluded with the bank established in Luxembourg, through the intermediary of the bank established in Frankfurt am Main and with the participation of the latter's joint procuration-holder, a number of spot and futures stock-exchange transactions in silver bullion and for that purpose paid DM 344 868.52 to the bank in Luxembourg. The futures transactions resulted in a total loss. The object of Mr Kalfelis's action is to obtain an order that the defendants, as jointly and severally liable for the debt, should pay him DM 463 019.08 together with interest. His claim is based on contractual liability for breach of the obligation to provide information, on tort, pursuant to Paragraph 823(2) of the Buergerliches Gesetzbuch (Civil Code) in conjunction with Paragraph 263 of the Strafgesetzbuch (Criminal Code) and Paragraph 826 of the Buergerliches Gesetzbuch, since the defendants caused him to suffer loss as a result of their conduct contra bonos mores. He also alleges unjust enrichment, on the ground that futures stock-exchange contracts, such as futures transactions in silver bullion, are not binding on the parties by virtue of mandatory provisions of German law and therefore reclaims the sums which he paid over.

4 Bankhaus Schroeder, Muenchmeyer, Hengst International SA challenged the jurisdiction of the German courts at every stage of the procedure and therefore the Bundesgerichtshof stayed the proceedings and referred the following questions to the Court for a preliminary ruling:

"(1) (a) Must Article 6(1) of the EEC Convention be interpreted as meaning that there must be a connection between the actions against the various defendants?

(b) If Question (a) must be answered in the affirmative, does the necessary connection between the actions against the various defendants exist if the actions are essentially the same in fact and law (einfache Streitgenossenschaft), or must a connection be assumed to exist only if it is expedient to hear and determine them together to avoid the risk of irreconcilable judgments resulting from separate proceedings (for example, in cases of 'notwendige Streitgennossenschaft' (compulsory joinder))?

(2) (a) Must the term 'tort' in Article 5(3) of the EEC Convention be construed independently of the Convention or must it be construed according to the law applicable in the individual case (lex causae), which is determined by the private international law of the court applied to?

(b) Does Article 5(3) of the EEC Convention confer, in respect of an action based on claims in tort and contract and for unjust enrichment, accessory jurisdiction on account of factual connection even in respect of the claims not based on tort?"

. . . .

The first question

6 The first question submitted by the Bundesgerichtshof is intended essentially to ascertain whether, for Article 6(1) of the Convention to apply, a connection must exist between the claims made by the same plaintiff against several defendants and, if so, what the nature of that connection is.

7 Pursuant to Article 2 of the Convention, persons domiciled in a Contracting State are, subject to the provisions of the Convention, "whatever their nationality, to be sued in the courts of that State". Section 2 of Title II of the Convention, however, provides for "special jurisdictions", by virtue of which a defendant domiciled in a Contracting State may be sued in another Contracting State. One of the special jurisdictions is that provided for in Article 6(1) according to which a defendant may be sued "where he is one of a number of defendants, in the courts for the place where any one of them is domiciled".

8 The principle laid down in the Convention is that jurisdiction is vested in the courts of the State of the defendant's domicile and that the jurisdiction provided for in Article 6(1) is an exception to that principle. It follows that an exception of that kind must be treated in such a manner that there is no possibility of the very existence of that principle being called in question.

9 That possibility might arise if a plaintiff were at liberty to make a claim against a number of defendants with the sole object of ousting the jurisdiction of the courts of the State where one of the defendants is domiciled. As is stated in the report prepared by the committee of experts which drafted the Convention (Official Journal C 59, 5.3.1979, p. 1), such a possibility must be excluded. For that purpose, there must be a connection between the claims made against each of the defendants.

10 In order to ensure, as far as possible, the equality and uniformity of the rights and obligations under the Convention of the Contracting States and of the persons concerned, the nature of that connection must be determined independently.

11 In that regard, it must be noted that the abovementioned report prepared by the committee of experts referred expressly, in its explanation of Article 6(1), to the concern to avoid the risk in the Contracting States of judgments which are incompatible with each other. Furthermore, account was taken of that preoccupation in the Convention itself, Article 22 of which governs cases of related actions brought before courts in different Contracting States.

12 The rule laid down in Article 6(1) therefore applies where the actions brought against the various defendants are related when the proceedings are instituted, that is to say where it is expedient to hear and determine them together in order to avoid the risk of irreconcilable judgments resulting from separate proceedings. It is for the national court to verify in each individual case whether that condition is satisfied.

13 *It must therefore be stated in reply to the first question that for Article 6(1) of the Convention to apply there must exist between various actions brought by the same plaintiff against different defendants a connection of such a kind that it is expedient to determine those actions together in order to avoid the risk of irreconcilable judgments resulting from separate proceedings.* [Emphasis added.]

The second question

14 The second question submitted by the Bundesgerichtshof is intended essentially to ascertain, first, whether the phrase "matters relating to tort, delict or quasi delict" used in Article 5(3) of the Convention must be given an independent meaning or be defined in accordance with the applicable national law and, secondly, in the case of an action based concurrently on tortious or delictual liability, breach of contract and unjust enrichment, whether the court having jurisdiction by virtue of Article 5(3) may adjudicate on the action in so far as it is not based on tort or delict.

15 With respect to the first part of the question, it must be observed that the concept of "matters relating to tort, delict or quasi-delict" serves as a criterion for defining the scope of one of the rules concerning the special jurisdictions available to the plaintiff. . . .

16 Accordingly, the concept of matters relating to tort, delict or quasi-delict must be regarded as an autonomous concept which is to be interpreted, for the application of the Convention, principally by reference to the scheme and objectives of the Convention in order to ensure that the latter is given full effect.

17 In order to ensure uniformity in all the Member States, it must be recognized that the concept of "matters relating to tort, delict and quasi-delict" covers all actions which seek to establish the liability of a defendant and which are not related to a "contract" within the meaning of Article 5(1).

. . . .

21 In those circumstances, the reply to the second part of the second question must be that a court which has jurisdiction under Article 5(3) over an action in so far as it is based on tort or delict does not have jurisdiction over that action in so far as it is not so based.

On those grounds,

THE COURT (Fifth Chamber),

in reply to the questions submitted to it by the Bundesgerichtshof by order of 27 April 1987, hereby rules:

(1) For Article 6(1) of the Convention to apply there must exist between the various actions brought by the same plaintiff against different defendants a

connection of such a kind that it is expedient to determine the actions together in order to avoid the risk of irreconcilable judgments resulting from separate proceedings;

(2)(a) The term "matters relating to tort, delict or quasi-delict" used in Article 5(3) of the Convention must be regarded as an independent concept covering all actions which seek to establish the liability of a defendant and which are not related to a "contract" within the meaning of Article 5(1);

(b) A court which has jurisdiction under Article 5(3) over an action in so far as it is based on tort or delict does not have jurisdiction over that action in so far as it is not so based. [Emphasis added.]

QUESTIONS

1. How would *Asahi Metal* and *Inoue v. Aviaco Airlines* have been decided under the relevant provisions of Regulation (EU) No. 1215/2012, assuming that they have remained the same as those of the EEC Convention cited in the *Kalfelis* case?

2. Assume a well-known U.S. author seeks your advice regarding an alleged infringement of her copyright by a German publisher — the Jaeger Group — with separately incorporated, wholly owned subsidiaries in Belgium, the U.K., and Italy. Would Regulation (EU) No. 1215/2012 or EC Regulation 44/2001 or the 1968 Brussels Convention, permit a single infringement suit against all four companies as joint defendants?

ROCHE NEDERLAND BV AND OTHERS v. FREDERICK PRIMUS, MILTON GOLDENBERG

Judgment of the Court (First Chamber) of 13 July 2006 [Case C-539/03]

JUDGMENT

1. This reference for a preliminary ruling concerns the interpretation of Article 6(1) of the [Brussels] Convention . . . . ('the Brussels Convention').

2. The reference was made in the course of proceedings between Roche Nederland BV and eight other companies in the Roche group, on the one hand, and Drs Primus and Goldenberg, on the other, in respect of an alleged infringement of the latter's rights in a European patent of which they are the proprietors.

LEGAL BACKGROUND

The Brussels Convention

3. . . . . [T]he first paragraph of Article 2 of the [1968] Brussels Convention states:

'Subject to the provisions of this convention, persons domiciled in a Contracting State shall, whatever their nationality, be sued in the courts of that State.'

4. According to the first paragraph of Article 3 of the [1968] Brussels Convention:

'Persons domiciled in a Contracting State may be sued in the courts of another Contracting State only by virtue of the rules set out in Sections 2 to 6 of this Title.'

5. Article 6 of the [1968] Brussels Convention, which appears in Section 2 of Title II, entitled 'Special jurisdiction', states:

'[A defendant domiciled in a Contracting State] may also be sued:

(1) where he is one of a number of defendants, in the courts for the place where any one of them is domiciled;

. . . .

6. Article 16 of the Brussels Convention . . . entitled 'Exclusive jurisdiction', states:

'The following courts shall have exclusive jurisdiction, regardless of domicile:

. . . .

(4) in proceedings concerned with the registration or validity of patents, trade marks, designs, or other similar rights required to be deposited or registered, the courts of the Contracting State in which the deposit or registration has been applied for, has taken place or is under the terms of an international convention deemed to have taken place;

. . . .

7. Article Vd of the Protocol annexed to the Brussels Convention, which, pursuant to Article 65 of the latter, forms an integral part of the Convention, states:

'Without prejudice to the jurisdiction of the European Patent Office under the Convention on the Grant of European Patents, signed at Munich on 5 October 1973, the courts of each Contracting State shall have exclusive jurisdiction, regardless of domicile, in proceedings concerned with the registration or validity of any European patent granted for that State which is not a Community patent by virtue of the provisions of Article 86 of the Convention for the European Patent for the Common Market, signed at Luxembourg on 15 December 1975.'

8. Article 22 of the Brussels Convention, which appears in Section 8, entitled 'Lis pendens — related actions' of Title II thereof, provides that where related actions are brought in the courts of different Contracting States, any court other than the court first seised may, while the actions are pending at first instance, stay its proceedings or, under certain conditions, decline jurisdiction. According to the third paragraph of that provision:

'For the purposes of this article, actions are deemed to be related where they are so closely connected that it is expedient to hear and determine them together to avoid the risk of irreconcilable judgments resulting from separate proceedings.'

9. Under Article 27(3) of the Brussels Convention, which appears in Title III, concerning the rules on recognition and enforcement, and in Section I, entitled 'Recognition', a judgment is not to be recognised 'if the judgment is irreconcilable with a judgment given in a dispute between the same parties in the State in which recognition is sought'.

The Munich Convention

10. The Convention on the Grant of European Patents, signed in Munich on 5 October 1973 ('the Munich Convention'), establishes, according to Article 1 thereof, 'a system of law, common to the Contracting States, for the grant of patents for invention'.

11. Outside the scope of the common rules on granting patents, a European patent continues to be governed by the national law of each of the Contracting States for which it has been granted. In that regard, Article 2(2) of the Munich Convention states:

'The European patent shall, in each of the Contracting States for which it is granted, have the effect of and be subject to the same conditions as a national patent granted by that State . . . .

12. As regards the rights conferred on the proprietor of a European patent, Article 64(1) and (3) of that convention provides:

'(1) A European patent shall . . . confer on its proprietor from the date of publication of the mention of its grant, in each Contracting State in respect of which it is granted, the same rights as would be conferred by a national patent granted in that State.

. . . .

(3) Any infringement of a European patent shall be dealt with by national law.'

The main proceedings and the questions referred for a preliminary ruling

13. Drs Primus and Goldenberg, who are domiciled in the United States of America, are the proprietors of European patent No 131 627.

14. On 24 March 1997, they brought an action before the Rechtbank te s'-Gravenhage against Roche Nederland BV, a company established in the Netherlands, and eight other companies in the Roche group established in the United States of America, Belgium, Germany, France, the United Kingdom, Switzerland, Austria and Sweden ('Roche and Others'). The applicants claimed that those companies had all infringed the rights conferred on them by the patent of which they are the proprietors. That alleged infringement consisted in the placing on the market of immuno-assay kits in countries where the defendants are established.

15. The companies in the Roche group not established in the Netherlands contested the jurisdiction of the Netherlands' courts. As regards the substance, they based their arguments on the absence of infringement and the invalidity of the patent in question.

16. By judgment of 1 October 1997, the Rechtbank te s'-Gravenhage declared that it had jurisdiction and dismissed the applications of Drs Primus and Goldenberg. On appeal, the Gerechtshof te s'-Gravenhage (Regional Court of Appeal) set aside the judgment and, inter alia, prohibited Roche and Others from infringing the rights attached to the patent in question in all the countries designated in it.

17. The Hoge Raad (Supreme Court), hearing an appeal on a point of law, decided to stay the proceedings and refer the following questions to the Court for a preliminary ruling:

(1) 'Is there a connection, as required for the application of Article 6(1) of the Brussels Convention, between a patent infringement action brought by a holder of a European patent against a defendant having its registered office in the State of the court in which the proceedings are brought, on the one hand, and against various defendants having their registered offices in Contracting States other than that of the State of the court in which the proceedings are brought, on the other hand, who, according to the patent holder, are infringing that patent in one or more other Contracting States?

(2) If the answer to Question 1 is not or not unreservedly in the affirmative, in what circumstances is such a connection deemed to exist, and is it relevant in this context whether, for example,

– the defendants form part of one and the same group of companies?

– the defendants are acting together on the basis of a common policy, and if so is the place from which that policy originates relevant?

– the alleged infringing acts of the various defendants are the same or virtually the same?'

The questions referred for a preliminary ruling

18. By those questions, which it is appropriate to consider together, the national court asks essentially whether Article 6(1) of the Brussels Convention must be interpreted as meaning that it is to apply to European patent infringement proceedings involving a number of companies established in various Contracting States in respect of acts committed in one or more of those States and, in particular, where those companies, which belong to the same group, have acted in an identical or similar manner in accordance with a common policy elaborated by one of them.

19. By way of derogation from the principle laid down in Article 2 of the Brussels Convention, that a defendant domiciled in a Contracting State is to be sued in the courts of that State, in a case where there is more than one defendant, Article 6(1) of the Convention allows a defendant domiciled in one Contracting State to be sued in another Contracting State where one of the defendants is domiciled.

20. In the judgment in Case 189/87 *Kalfelis* [1988] ECR 5565, paragraph 12, the

Court held that for Article 6(1) of the Brussels Convention to apply there must exist, between the various actions brought by the same plaintiff against different defendants, a connection of such a kind that it is expedient to determine the actions together in order to avoid the risk of irreconcilable judgments resulting from separate proceedings.

21. The requirement of a connection does not derive from the wording of Article 6(1) of the Brussels Convention. It has been inferred from that provision by the Court in order to prevent the exception to the principle that jurisdiction is vested in the courts of the State of the defendant's domicile laid down in Article 6(1) from calling into question the very existence of that principle (*Kalfelis*, paragraph 8). That requirement was subsequently confirmed by the judgment in Case C-51/97 *Réunion Européenne and Others* [1998] ECR I-6511, paragraph 48, and was expressly enshrined in the drafting of Article 6(1) of Council Regulation (EC) No 44/2001 of 22 December 2000 on jurisdiction and the recognition and enforcement of judgments in civil and commercial matters (OJ 2001 L 12, p. 1), which succeeded the Brussels Convention.

22. The formulation used by the Court in *Kalfelis* repeats the wording of Article 22 of the Brussels Convention, according to which actions are deemed to be related where they are so closely connected that it is expedient to hear and determine them together to avoid the risk of irreconcilable judgments resulting from separate proceedings. Article 22 was interpreted in Case C-406/92 *Tatry* [1994] ECR I-5439, paragraph 58, to the effect that, in order to establish the necessary relationship between the cases, it is sufficient that separate trial and judgment would involve the risk of conflicting decisions, without necessarily involving the risk of giving rise to mutually exclusive legal consequences.

23. The scope given to the concept of 'irreconcilable' judgments by the judgment in *Tatry* in the context of Article 22 of the Brussels Convention is therefore wider than that given to the same concept in Case 145/86 *Hoffman* [1988] ECR 645, paragraph 22, in the context of Article 27(3) of the Convention, which provides that a judgment given in a Contracting State will not be recognised if it is irreconcilable with a judgment given in a dispute between the same parties in the State in which recognition is sought. In *Hoffmann*, the Court had held that, in order to ascertain whether two judgments are irreconcilable within the meaning of Article 27(3), it must be determined whether they entail legal consequences which are mutually exclusive.

24. Drs Primus and Goldenberg and the Netherlands Government argue that the broad interpretation of the adjective 'irreconcilable', in the sense of contradictory, which was given in *Tatry* in the context of Article 22 of the Brussels Convention, must be extended to the context of Article 6(1) of the Convention. Roche and Others and the United Kingdom Government, with whose arguments the Advocate General agreed in point 79 *et seq* of his Opinion, submit, by contrast, that such a transposition is not permissible given the differences between the purpose and the position of the two provisions in question in the scheme of the Brussels Convention, and that a narrower interpretation must be preferred.

25. However, it does not appear necessary in this case to decide that issue. It is sufficient to observe that, even assuming that the concept of 'irreconcilable'

judgments for the purposes of the application of Article 6(1) of the Brussels Convention must be understood in the broad sense of contradictory decisions, there is no risk of such decisions being given in European patent infringement proceedings brought in different Contracting States involving a number of defendants domiciled in those States in respect of acts committed in their territory.

26. As the Advocate General observed, in point 113 of his Opinion, in order that decisions may be regarded as contradictory it is not sufficient that there be a divergence in the outcome of the dispute, but that divergence must also arise in the context of the same situation of law and fact.

27. However, in the situation referred to by the national court in its first question referred for a preliminary ruling, that is in the case of European patent infringement proceedings involving a number of companies established in various Contracting States in respect of acts committed in one or more of those States, the existence of the same situation of fact cannot be inferred, since the defendants are different and the infringements they are accused of, committed in different Contracting States, are not the same.

28. Possible divergences between decisions given by the courts concerned would not arise in the context of the same factual situation.

29. Furthermore, although the Munich Convention lays down common rules on the grant of European patents, it is clear from Articles 2(2) and 64(1) of that convention that such a patent continues to be governed by the national law of each of the Contracting States for which it has been granted.

30. In particular, it is apparent from Article 64(3) of the Munich Convention that any action for infringement of a European patent must be examined in the light of the relevant national law in force in each of the States for which it has been granted.

31. It follows that, where infringement proceedings are brought before a number of courts in different Contracting States in respect of a European patent granted in each of those States, against defendants domiciled in those States in respect of acts allegedly committed in their territory, any divergences between the decisions given by the courts concerned would not arise in the context of the same legal situation.

32. Any diverging decisions could not, therefore, be treated as contradictory.

33. In those circumstances, even if the broadest interpretation of 'irreconcilable' judgments, in the sense of contradictory, were accepted as the criterion for the existence of the connection required for the application of Article 6(1) of the Brussels Convention, it is clear that such a connection could not be established between actions for infringement of the same European patent where each action was brought against a company established in a different Contracting State in respect of acts which it had committed in that State.

34. That finding is not called into question even in the situation referred to by the national court in its second question, that is where defendant companies, which belong to the same group, have acted in an identical or similar manner in accordance with a common policy elaborated by one of them, so that the factual situation would be the same.

35. The fact remains that the legal situation would not be the same (see paragraphs 29 and 30 of this judgment) and therefore there would be no risk, even in such a situation, of contradictory decisions.

36. Furthermore, although at first sight considerations of procedural economy may appear to militate in favour of consolidating such actions before one court, it is clear that the advantages for the sound administration of justice represented by such consolidation would be limited and would constitute a source of further risks.

37. Jurisdiction based solely on the factual criteria set out by the national court would lead to a multiplication of the potential heads of jurisdiction and would therefore be liable to undermine the predictability of the rules of jurisdiction laid down by the Convention, and consequently to undermine the principle of legal certainty, which is the basis of the Convention [citations omitted].

38. The damage would be even more serious if the application of the criteria in question gave the defendant a wide choice, thereby encouraging the practice of forum shopping which the Convention seeks to avoid and which the Court, in its judgment in *Kalfelis*, specifically sought to prevent (see *Kalfelis*, paragraph 9).

39. It must be observed that the determination as to whether the criteria concerned are satisfied, which is for the applicant to prove, would require the court seised to adjudicate on the substance of the case before it could establish its jurisdiction. Such a preliminary examination could give rise to additional costs and could prolong procedural time-limits where that court, being unable to establish the existence of the same factual situation and, therefore, a sufficient connection between the actions, would have to decline jurisdiction and where a fresh action would have to be brought before a court of another State.

40. Finally, even assuming that the court seised by the defendant were able to accept jurisdiction on the basis of the criteria laid down by the national court, the consolidation of the patent infringement actions before that court could not prevent at least a partial fragmentation of the patent proceedings, since, as is frequently the case in practice and as is the case in the main proceedings, the validity of the patent would be raised indirectly. That issue, whether it is raised by way of an action or a plea in objection, is a matter of exclusive jurisdiction laid down in Article 16(4) of the Brussels Convention in favour of the courts of the Contracting State in which the deposit or registration has taken place or is deemed to have taken place (*GAT*, paragraph 31). That exclusive jurisdiction of the courts of the granting State has been confirmed, as regards European patents, by Article Vd of the Protocol annexed to the Brussels Convention.

41. Having regard to all of the foregoing considerations, the answer to the questions referred must be that Article 6(1) of the Brussels Convention must be interpreted as meaning that it does not apply in European patent infringement proceedings involving a number of companies established in various Contracting States in respect of acts committed in one or more of those States even where those companies, which belong to the same group, may have acted in an identical or similar manner in accordance with a common policy elaborated by one of them.

. . . .

On those grounds, the Court (First Chamber) hereby rules:

Article 6(1) of the [1968 Brussels] Convention must be interpreted as meaning that it does **not** *apply in European patent infringement proceedings involving a number of companies established in various Contracting States in respect of acts committed in one or more of those States even where those companies, which belong to the same group, may have acted in an identical or similar manner in accordance with a common policy elaborated by one of them.* [Emphasis added.]

C. Excessive Jurisdiction

Among the most significant features of the 1968 Brussels Convention carried forward from the 1968 Brussels Convention in EC Regulation 44/2001 and, with modification, in Regulation (EU) No. 1215/2012 are the provisions that, first, prohibited recognition of adjudicatory jurisdiction in listed instances of "excessive" or "exorbitant" jurisdiction in cases involving defendants domiciled within a member state (see EC Regulation 44/2001, art. 3[2] and Annex 1) but permitting such extension of personal jurisdiction in cases where the defendant is domiciled in a nonmember state yet also, as discussed *infra*, requiring recognition and enforcement of such judgments by member states.

The 1968 Brussels Convention provided:

Article 3

. . . .

(2) In particular the rules of national jurisdiction set out in Annex I shall not be applicable as against [persons domiciled in a member state].

The rules of national jurisdiction listed in Annex I fell under three categories: (1) personal jurisdiction based solely on attachable assets or property (e.g., German Code of Civil Procedure, art. 23), (2) the nationality of the plaintiff (French Civil Code, arts. 14 and 15), and (3) in the case of the United Kingdom:

(a) the documents instituting the proceedings having been served on the defendant during his temporary presence in the United Kingdom; or

(b) the presence within the United Kingdom of property belonging to the defendant; or

(c) the seizure by the plaintiff of property situated in the United Kingdom.

With respect to defendants domiciled outside of the EU, existing national rules — including those prohibited as "excessive" controlled to the benefit of any plaintiff domiciled in the EU. Article 4 provided:

1. If the defendant is not domiciled in a Member State, the jurisdiction of the courts of each Member State shall, subject to Articles 22 and 23, be determined by the law of that Member State.

2. As against such a defendant, any person domiciled in a Member State may, whatever his nationality, avail himself in that State of the rules of

jurisdiction there in force, and in particular those specified in Annex I, in the same way as the nationals of that State.

Regulation (EU) No. 1215/2012 reaches the same result albeit less directly and without the prohibitory language. Article 5 provides:

> 1. Persons domiciled in a Member State may be sued in the courts of another Member State only by virtue of the rules set out in Sections 2 to 7 of this Chapter.
>
> 2. In particular, the rules of national jurisdiction of which the Member States are to notify the Commission pursuant to point (a) of Article 76(1) shall not be applicable as against the persons referred to in paragraph 1.

In lieu of outright prohibition, article 76(1)(a) provides:

> 1. The Member States shall notify the Commission of:
>
> (a) the rules of jurisdiction referred to in Articles 5(2) and 6(2).

The new regulations continue to allow national rules heretofore prohibited as excessive and thus inapplicable with respect defendants domiciled in the EU to remain applicable in cases in which the defendants are not domiciled in the EU. Article 6 reads:

> 1. If the defendant is not domiciled in a Member State, the jurisdiction of the courts of each Member State shall, subject to Article 18(1), Article 21(2) and Articles 24 and 25, be determined by the law of that Member State.
>
> 2. As against such a defendant, any person domiciled in a Member State may, whatever his nationality, avail himself in that Member State of the rules of jurisdiction there in force, and in particular those of which the Member States are to notify the Commission pursuant to point (a) of Article 76(1), in the same way as nationals of that Member State.

THINET INTERNATIONAL S.A. v. SAUDI BASIC INDUSTRIES CORPORATION

Court of Cassation (Civil Chamber 1), Judgment of September 30, 2009,
(No. 08-17587)
Bulletin 06/03/2010

In June 1998 the plaintiff, a French construction company with offices in Riyadh, Saudi Arabia, contracted with the defendant Saudi Basic Industries Corporation (SIBIC), a Saudi Arabian company for a project in Riyadh. The contract, written in Arabic, contained a prorogation clause designating a Saudi court (the Grievance Bureau). As a result of dispute over the performance of the contract, Thinet International brought an action against SIBIC under the contract with the Saudi court, which entered a judgment for Thinet. On appeal, the Saudi appellate court annulled the judgment on the grounds that the Grievance lacked jurisdiction over the suit as a "civil;" rather than commercial action. Thinet subsequently brought the action before the French Commercial Tribunal of Paris, arguing successfully that the Tribunal had jurisdiction under article 14 of the French Civil Code. SIBIC appealed first to the Paris Court of Appeal and finally to the Court of Cassation, challenging the competence of the Tribunal to adjudicate the case. The question presented to the Court of Cassation was whether French courts have adjudicatory jurisdiction over a dispute under article 14 where a court is held to lack competence to adjudicate the dispute despite its designation in a choice of forum clause.

The Court of Cassation (First Civil Chamber) found that a company incorporated under French law satisfies the French nationality requirement of article 14 and that French courts could properly exercise jurisdiction under the provision. The Court reasoned that article 14, although not mandatory, applied where, as in this case, the court designated by the parties as the forum of choice was held to lack competence to adjudicate the dispute and the petitioner had not waived or renounced its claim to jurisdiction under article 14 by bringing the dispute for adjudication by another foreign court.

REVIEW PROBLEM

In Paris in 1908, Ivan Morozov (1871–1921), a wealthy Russian textile manufacturer and collector of Impressionist art, purchased the Vincent van Gogh painting *The Night Café*. Nationalized and seized by the Bolshevik government in 1918, the painting, along with Morozov's entire collection, was among the principal works of the modernist collection in the Hermitage and Pushkin museums (with Morozov, an assistant curator). In the 1930s, the painting, along with others, was sold by the Soviet government. It was purchased in New York in 1933 by Stephen Carlton Clark (1882–1960), an avid collector who bequeathed it to Yale in 1961.

Assume you are an associate in a New Haven, Connecticut, law firm that represents Yale University. The curator of Yale's art museum comes to you with a letter from a French avocat representing Morozov's great-grandson Pierre Konowaloff, demanding return of *The Night Café* to his client. He threatens suit in Paris, where his client currently resides. You are asked your advice with respect to the possible jurisdiction of the French courts and the possibility of the enforcement of a French judgment against Yale in Europe. How would you advise Yale to respond? Note that under U.S. federal law the statute of limitations begins to run from the time the claimant makes the demand.

What if (counterfactually), the painting is on loan for display at the Van Gogh Museum in Amsterdam? Would your answer differ were the painting on loan in Vancouver, B.C., Montreal, Tokyo, Beijing, Mexico City, or Munich?

Chapter 2

FOREIGN SOVEREIGN IMMUNITY AND RELATED ABSTENTION DOCTRINES

In this chapter we begin an examination of doctrines that either require or allow courts to abstain from exercising jurisdiction over defendants or claims. Explored here are the first cluster of these doctrines based on principles and practices of public international law. In Chapter 3, we continue with doctrines of abstention (and anti-suit injunctions) in the context of parallel litigation.

Most if not all national states today recognize the immunity of foreign states and officials from suit in their courts as a fundamental principle of international law and comity. Closely related abstention doctrines in common law jurisdictions include "acts of state" and, at least in the United States, a "foreign sovereign compulsion" defense. For common law jurisdictions, foreign sovereign immunity represents in effect the extension to foreign governments, their organs and personnel of governmental immunity from lawsuits without consent recognized domestically within the municipal legal systems. With respect to *foreign* sovereign immunity, as detailed below, the traditional approach in effect granted analogous "absolute" immunity to states and state agencies and actors from suit without consent. This approach has been gradually modified, first within the civil law systems of continental Europe and then more broadly to include, as we shall see, the United States and more recently Canada and Japan. China and Mexico appear to continue to adhere to the absolute foreign sovereign immunity doctrine but both countries have signed the 2004 United Nations Convention on Jurisdictional Immunities of States and Their Property (not in force), which adopts a "restrictive" approach. (*See* https://treaties.un.org/Pages/ViewDetails.aspx?src=IND&mtdsg_no=III-13&chaptcr=3&lang=cn.)

I. COMMON LAW APPROACHES — UNITED STATES

A. Foreign Sovereign Immunity

THE SCHOONER EXCHANGE v. McFADDON
11 U.S. 116 (1812)

Present. All the judges.

THIS being a cause in which the sovereign right claimed by NAPOLEON, the reigning emperor of the French, and the political relations between the United States and France, were involved, it was, upon the suggestion of the Attorney

General, ordered to a hearing in preference to other causes which stood before it on the docket. It was an appeal from the sentence of the Circuit Court of the United States, for the district of Pennsylvania, which reversed the sentence of the District Court, and ordered the vessel to be restored to the libellants.

The case was this — on the 24th of August, 1811, John McFaddon & William Greetham, of the State of Maryland, filed their libel in the District Court of the United States, for the District of Pennsylvania, against the Schooner Exchange, setting forth that they were her sole owners, on the 27th of October, 1809, when she sailed from Baltimore, bound to St. Sebastians, in Spain. That while lawfully and peaceably pursuing her voyage, she was on the 30th of December, 1810, violently and forcibly taken by certain persons, acting under the decrees and orders of NAPOLEON, Emperor of the French, out of the custody of the libellants, and of their captain and agent, and was disposed of by those persons, or some of them, in violation of the rights of the libellants, and of the law of nations in that behalf. That she had been brought into the port of Philadelphia, and was then in the jurisdiction of that court, in possession of a certain Dennis M. Begon, her reputed captain or master. That no sentence or decree of condemnation had been pronounced against her, by any court of competent jurisdiction; but that the property of the libellants in her, remained unchanged and in full force. They therefore prayed the usual process of the court, to attach the vessel, and that she might be restored to them.

MARSHALL, CH. J. Delivered the opinion of the Court as follows:

This case involves the very delicate and important inquiry, whether an American citizen can assert, in an American court, a title to an armed national vessel, found within the waters of the United States.

The question has been considered with an earnest solicitude, that the decision may conform to those principles of national and municipal law by which it ought to be regulated.

. . . .

The jurisdiction of the nation within its own territory is necessarily exclusive and absolute. It is susceptible of no limitation not imposed by itself. Any restriction upon it, deriving validity from an external source, would imply a diminution of its sovereignty to the extent of the restriction, and an investment of that sovereignty to the same extent in that power which could impose such restriction.

All exceptions, therefore, to the full and complete power of a nation within its own territories, must be traced up to the consent of the nation itself. They can flow from no other legitimate source.

This consent may be either express or implied. In the latter case, it is less determinate, exposed more to the uncertainties of construction; but, if understood, not less obligatory.

This full and absolute territorial jurisdiction being alike the attribute of every sovereign, and being incapable of conferring extra-territorial power, would not seem to contemplate foreign sovereigns nor their sovereign rights as its objects.

. . .

This perfect equality and absolute independence of sovereigns, and this common interest impelling them to mutual intercourse, and an interchange of good offices with each other, have given rise to a class of cases in which every sovereign is understood to wave the exercise of a part of that complete exclusive territorial jurisdiction, which has been stated to be the attribute of every nation.

1st. One of these is admitted to be the exemption of the person of the sovereign from arrest or detention within a foreign territory.

If he enters that territory with the knowledge and license of its sovereign, that license, although containing no stipulation exempting his person from arrest, is universally understood to imply such stipulation.

2d. A second case, standing on the same principles with the first, is the immunity which all civilized nations allow to foreign ministers.

The assent of the sovereign to the very important and extensive exemptions from territorial jurisdiction which are admitted to attach to foreign ministers, is implied from the considerations that, without such exemption, every sovereign would hazard his own dignity by employing a public minister abroad. His minister would owe temporary and local allegiance to a foreign prince, and would be less competent to the objects of his mission. A sovereign committing the interests of his nation with a foreign power, to the care of a person whom he has selected for that purpose, cannot intend to subject his minister in any degree to that power; and, therefore, a consent to receive him, implies a consent that he shall possess those privileges which his principal intended he should retain-privileges which are essential to the dignity of his sovereign, and to the duties he is bound to perform.

3d. A third case in which a sovereign is understood to cede a portion of his territorial jurisdiction is where he allows the troops of a foreign prince to pass through his dominions.

. . . .

The preceding reasoning, has maintained the propositions that all exemptions from territorial jurisdiction, must be derived from the consent of the sovereign of the territory; that this consent may be implied or expressed; and that when implied, its extent must be regulated by the nature of the case, and the views under which the parties requiring and conceding it must be supposed to act.

. . . .

But in all respects different is the situation of a public armed ship. She constitutes a part of the military force of her nation; acts under the immediate and direct command of the sovereign; is employed by him in national objects. He has many and powerful motives for preventing those objects from being defeated by the interference of a foreign state. Such interference cannot take place without affecting his power and his dignity. The implied license therefore under which such vessel enters a friendly port, may reasonably be construed, and it seems to the Court, ought to be construed, as containing an exemption from the jurisdiction of the sovereign, within whose territory she claims the rites of hospitality.

Upon these principles, by the unanimous consent of nations, a foreigner is amenable to the laws of the place; but certainly in practice, nations have not yet asserted their jurisdiction over the public armed ships of a foreign sovereign entering a port open for their reception.

. . . .

It seems then to the Court, to be a principle of public law, that national ships of war, entering the port of a friendly power open for their reception, are to be considered as exempted by the consent of that power from its jurisdiction.

. . . .

The principles which have been stated, will now be applied to the case at bar.

In the present state of the evidence and proceedings, the Exchange must be considered as a vessel, which was the property of the Libellants, whose claim is repelled by the fact, that she is now a national armed vessel, commissioned by, and in the service of the emperor of France. The evidence of this fact is not controverted. But it is contended, that it constitutes no bar to an enquiry into the validity of the title, by which the emperor holds this vessel. Every person, it is alleged, who is entitled to property brought within the jurisdiction of our Courts, has a right to assert his title in those Courts, unless there be some law taking his case out of the general rule. It is therefore said to be the right, and if it be the right, it is the duty of the Court, to enquire whether this title has been extinguished by an act, the validity of which is recognized by national or municipal law.

If the preceding reasoning be correct, the Exchange, being a public armed ship, in the service of a foreign sovereign, with whom the government of the United States is at peace, and having entered an American port open for her reception, on the terms on which ships of war are generally permitted to enter the ports of a friendly power, must be considered as having come into the American territory, under an implied promise, that while necessarily within it, and demeaning herself in a friendly manner, she should be exempt from the jurisdiction of the country.

If this opinion be correct, there seems to be a necessity for admitting that the fact might be disclosed to the Court by the suggestion of the Attorney for the United States.

I am directed to deliver it, as the opinion of the Court, that the sentence of the Circuit Court, reversing the sentence of the District Court, in the case of the Exchange be reversed, and that of the District Court, dismissing the libel, be affirmed.

QUESTIONS

Writing for a unanimous court in *Verlinden B. V. v. Central Bank of Nigeria*, 461 U.S. 480 (1983), Chief Justice Burger described Chief Justice Marshall's opinion in *The Schooner Exchange* as follows:

> For more than a century and a half, the United States generally granted foreign sovereigns complete immunity from suit in the courts

> of this country. In *The Schooner Exchange v. M'Faddon*, 7 Cranch 116 (1812), Chief Justice Marshall concluded that, while the jurisdiction of a nation within its own territory "is susceptible of no limitation not imposed by itself," *id.*, at 136, the United States had impliedly waived jurisdiction over certain activities of foreign sovereigns. Although the narrow holding of *The Schooner Exchange* was only that the courts of the United States lack jurisdiction over an armed ship of a foreign state found in our port, that opinion came to be regarded as extending virtually absolute immunity to foreign sovereigns. [Citations omitted.]
>
> As *The Schooner Exchange* made clear, however, foreign sovereign immunity is a matter of grace and comity on the part of the United States, and not a restriction imposed by the Constitution. Accordingly, this Court consistently has deferred to the decisions of the political branches — in particular, those of the Executive Branch — on whether to take jurisdiction over actions against foreign sovereigns and their instrumentalities. [Citations omitted.]
>
> Do you agree that "*The Schooner Exchange* made clear" that "foreign sovereign immunity is a matter of grace and comity on the part of the United States"? If not, how would you characterize Chief Justice Marshall's view?

THE 1952 TATE LETTER

May 19, 1952.

MY DEAR MR. ATTORNEY GENERAL:

The Department of State has for some time had under consideration the question whether the practice of the Government in granting immunity from suit to foreign governments made parties defendant in the courts of the United States without their consent should not be changed. The Department has now reached the conclusion that such immunity should no longer be granted in certain types of cases. In view of the obvious interest of your Department in this matter I should like to point out briefly some of the facts which influenced the Department's decision.

A study of the law of sovereign immunity reveals the existence of two conflicting concepts of sovereign immunity, each widely held and firmly established. According to the classical or absolute theory of sovereign immunity, a sovereign cannot, without his consent, be made a respondent in the courts of another sovereign. According to the newer or restrictive theory of sovereign immunity, the immunity of the sovereign is recognized with regard to sovereign or public acts (*jure imperii*) of a state, but not with respect to private acts (*jure gestionis*). There is agreement by proponents of both theories, supported by practice, that sovereign immunity should not be claimed or granted in actions with respect to real property (diplomatic and perhaps consular property excepted) or with respect to the disposition of the property of a deceased person even though a foreign sovereign is the beneficiary.

The classical or virtually absolute theory of sovereign immunity has generally been followed by the courts of the United States, the British Commonwealth, Czechoslovakia, Estonia, and probably Poland.

The decisions of the courts of Brazil, Chile, China, Hungary, Japan, Luxembourg, Norway, and Portugal may be deemed to support the classical theory of immunity if one or at most two old decisions anterior to the development of the restrictive theory may be considered sufficient on which to base a conclusion.

The position of the Netherlands, Sweden, and Argentina is less clear since although immunity has been granted in recent cases coming before the courts of those countries, the facts were such that immunity would have been granted under either the absolute or restrictive theory. However, constant references by the courts of these three countries to the distinction between public and private acts of the state, even though the distinction was not involved in the result of the case, may indicate an intention to leave the way open for a possible application of the restrictive theory of immunity if and when the occasion presents itself.

A trend to the restrictive theory is already evident in the Netherlands where the lower courts have started to apply that theory following a Supreme Court decision to the effect that immunity would have been applicable in the case under consideration under either theory.

The German courts, after a period of hesitation at the end of the nineteenth century have held to the classical theory, but it should be noted that the refusal of the Supreme Court in 1921 to yield to pressure by the lower courts for the newer theory was based on the view that that theory had not yet developed sufficiently to justify a change. In view of the growth of the restrictive theory since that time the German courts might take a different view today.

The newer or restrictive theory of sovereign immunity has always been supported by the courts of Belgium and Italy. It was adopted in turn by the courts of Egypt and of Switzerland. In addition, the courts of France, Austria, and Greece, which were traditionally supporters of the classical theory, reversed their position in the 20's to embrace the restrictive theory. Rumania, Peru, and possibly Denmark also appear to follow this theory.

Furthermore, it should be observed that in most of the countries still following the classical theory there is a school of influential writers favoring the restrictive theory and the views of writers, at least in civil law countries, are a major factor in the development of the law. Moreover, the leanings of the lower courts in civil law countries are more significant in shaping the law than they are in common law countries where the rule of precedent prevails and the trend in these lower courts is to the restrictive theory.

Of related interest to this question is the fact that ten of the thirteen countries which have been classified above as supporters of the classical theory have ratified the Brussels Convention of 1926 under which immunity for government owned merchant vessels is waived. In addition the United States, which is not a party to the Convention, some years ago announced and has since followed, a policy of not claiming immunity for its public owned or operated merchant vessels. Keeping in mind the importance played by cases involving public vessels in the field of sovereign immunity, it is thus noteworthy that these ten countries (Brazil, Chile, Estonia, Germany, Hungary, Netherlands, Norway, Poland, Portugal, Sweden) and the United States have already relinquished by treaty or in practice an important part of the immunity which they claim under the classical theory.

It is thus evident that with the possible exception of the United Kingdom little support has been found except on the part of the Soviet Union and its satellites for continued full acceptance of the absolute theory of sovereign immunity. There are evidences that British authorities are aware of its deficiencies and ready for a change. The reasons which obviously motivate state trading countries in adhering to the theory with perhaps increasing rigidity are most persuasive that the United States should change its policy. Furthermore, the granting of sovereign immunity to foreign governments in the courts of the United States is most inconsistent with the action of the Government of the United States in subjecting itself to suit in these same courts in both contract and tort and with its long established policy of not claiming immunity in foreign jurisdictions for its merchant vessels. Finally, the Department feels that the widespread and increasing practice on the part of governments of engaging in commercial activities makes necessary a practice which will enable persons doing business with them to have their rights determined in the courts. For these reasons it will hereafter be the Department's policy to follow the restrictive theory of sovereign immunity in the consideration of requests of foreign governments for a grant of sovereign immunity.

It is realized that a shift in policy by the executive cannot control the courts but it is felt that the courts are less likely to allow a plea of sovereign immunity where the executive has declined to do so. There have been indications that at least some Justices of the Supreme Court feel that in this matter courts should follow the branch of the Government charged with responsibility for the conduct of foreign relations.

In order that your Department, which is charged with representing the interests of the Government before the courts, may be adequately informed it will be the Department's practice to advise you of all requests by foreign governments for the grant of immunity from suit and of the Department's action thereon.

Sincerely yours,

For the Secretary of State:

JACK B. TATE

Acting Legal Adviser

QUESTION

To what extent and for what purpose under domestic, municipal law would governmental acts (*jure imperii*) of a state be distinguished from the state's commercial acts (*jure gestionis*)?

FOREIGN SOVEREIGN IMMUNITIES ACT OF 1976
28 U.S.C. § 1602 et seq.

§ 1605: General exceptions to the jurisdictional immunity of a foreign state

(a) A foreign state shall not be immune from the jurisdiction of courts of the United States or of the States in any case—

. . . .

(2) in which the action is based upon a commercial activity carried on in the United States by the foreign state; or upon an act performed in the United States in connection with a commercial activity of the foreign state elsewhere; or upon an act outside the territory of the United States in connection with a commercial activity of the foreign state elsewhere and that act causes a direct effect in the United States;

REPUBLIC OF ARGENTINA AND BANCO CENTRAL DE LA REPUBLICA ARGENTINA v. WELTOVER, INC.
504 U.S. 607 (1992)

JUSTICE SCALIA delivered the opinion for a unanimous Court.

This case requires us to decide whether the Republic of Argentina's default on certain bonds issued as part of a plan to stabilize its currency was an act taken "in connection with a commercial activity" that had a "direct effect in the United States" so as to subject Argentina to suit in an American court under the Foreign Sovereign Immunities Act of 1976, 28 U.S.C. § 1602 et seq.

I

Since Argentina's currency is not one of the mediums of exchange accepted on the international market, Argentine businesses engaging in foreign transactions must pay in United States dollars or some other internationally accepted currency. In the recent past, it was difficult for Argentine borrowers to obtain such funds, principally because of the instability of the Argentine currency. To address these problems, petitioners, the Republic of Argentina and its central bank, Banco Central (collectively Argentina), in 1981 instituted a foreign exchange insurance contract program (FEIC), under which Argentina effectively agreed to assume the risk of currency depreciation in cross-border transactions involving Argentine borrowers. This was accomplished by Argentina's agreeing to sell to domestic borrowers, in exchange for a contractually predetermined amount of local currency, the necessary United States dollars to repay their foreign debts when they matured, irrespective of intervening devaluations.

Unfortunately, Argentina did not possess sufficient reserves of United States dollars to cover the FEIC contracts as they became due in 1982. The Argentine Government thereupon adopted certain emergency measures, including refinancing of the FEIC-backed debts by issuing to the creditors government bonds. These bonds, called "Bonods," provide for payment of interest and principal in United

States dollars; payment may be made through transfer on the London, Frankfurt, Zurich, or New York market, at the election of the creditor. Under this refinancing program, the foreign creditor had the option of either accepting the Bonods in satisfaction of the initial debt, thereby substituting the Argentine Government for the private debtor, or maintaining the debtor/creditor relationship with the private borrower and accepting the Argentine Government as guarantor.

When the Bonods began to mature in May 1986, Argentina concluded that it lacked sufficient foreign exchange to retire them. Pursuant to a Presidential Decree, Argentina unilaterally extended the time for payment and offered bondholders substitute instruments as a means of rescheduling the debts. Respondents, two Panamanian corporations and a Swiss bank who hold, collectively, $1.3 million of Bonods, refused to accept the rescheduling and insisted on full payment, specifying New York as the place where payment should be made. Argentina did not pay, and respondents then brought this breach-of-contract action in the United States District Court for the Southern District of New York, relying on the Foreign Sovereign Immunities Act of 1976 as the basis for jurisdiction. Petitioners moved to dismiss for lack of subject-matter jurisdiction, lack of personal jurisdiction, and forum non conveniens. The District Court denied these motions, 753 F.Supp. 1201 (S.D.N.Y. 1991), *and the Court of Appeals affirmed,* 941 F.2d 145 (CA2 1991). We granted Argentina's petition for certiorari, which challenged the Court of Appeals' determination that, under the Act, Argentina was not immune from the jurisdiction of the federal courts in this case. 502 U.S. 1024 (1992).

II

The Foreign Sovereign Immunities Act of 1976 (FSIA), 28 U.S.C. § 1602 et seq., establishes a comprehensive framework for determining whether a court in this country, state or federal, may exercise jurisdiction over a foreign state. Under the Act, a "foreign state shall be immune from the jurisdiction of the courts of the United States and of the States" unless one of several statutorily defined exceptions applies. § 1604 (emphasis added). The FSIA thus provides the "sole basis" for obtaining jurisdiction over a foreign sovereign in the United States. [Citation omitted.] The most significant of the FSIA's exceptions-and the one at issue in this case-is the "commercial" exception of § 1605(a)(2), which provides that a foreign state is not immune from suit in any case "in which the action is based upon a commercial activity carried on in the United States by the foreign state; or upon an act performed in the United States in connection with a commercial activity of the foreign state elsewhere; or upon an act outside the territory of the United States in connection with a commercial activity of the foreign state elsewhere and that act causes a direct effect in the United States." § 1605(a)(2).

In the proceedings below, respondents relied only on the third clause of § 1605(a)(2) to establish jurisdiction, 941 F.2d, at 149, and our analysis is therefore limited to considering whether this lawsuit is (1) "based . . . upon an act outside the territory of the United States"; (2) that was taken "in connection with a commercial activity" of Argentina outside this country; and (3) that "cause[d] a direct effect in the United States." The complaint in this case alleges only one cause of action on behalf of each of the respondents, viz., a breach-of-contract claim based on

Argentina's attempt to refinance the Bonods rather than to pay them according to their terms. The fact that the cause of action is in compliance with the first of the three requirements — that it is "based upon an act outside the territory of the United States" (presumably Argentina's unilateral extension) — is uncontested. The dispute pertains to whether the unilateral refinancing of the Bonods was taken "in connection with a commercial activity" of Argentina, and whether it had a "direct effect in the United States." We address these issues in turn.

A

Respondents and their amicus, the United States, contend that Argentina's issuance of, and continued liability under, the Bonods constitute a "commercial activity" and that the extension of the payment schedules was taken "in connection with" that activity. The latter point is obvious enough, and Argentina does not contest it; the key question is whether the activity is "commercial" under the FSIA.

The FSIA defines "commercial activity" to mean:

"[E]ither a regular course of commercial conduct or a particular commercial transaction or act. The commercial character of an activity shall be determined by reference to the nature of the course of conduct or particular transaction or act, rather than by reference to its purpose." 28 U.S.C. § 1603(d).

This definition, however, leaves the critical term "commercial" largely undefined: The first sentence simply establishes that the commercial nature of an activity does not depend upon whether it is a single act or a regular course of conduct; and the second sentence merely specifies what element of the conduct determines commerciality (i.e., nature rather than purpose), but still without saying what "commercial" means. Fortunately, however, the FSIA was not written on a clean slate. As we have noted, see *Verlinden B.V. v. Central Bank of Nigeria*, 461 U.S. 480, 486–489 (1983), the Act (and the commercial exception in particular) largely codifies the so-called "restrictive" theory of foreign sovereign immunity first endorsed by the State Department in 1952. The meaning of "commercial" is the meaning generally attached to that term under the restrictive theory at the time the statute was enacted. [Citations omitted.]

This Court did not have occasion to discuss the scope or validity of the restrictive theory of sovereign immunity until our 1976 decision in *Alfred Dunhill of London, Inc. v. Republic of Cuba*, 425 U.S. 682 [citations omitted]. Although the Court there was evenly divided on the question whether the "commercial" exception that applied in the foreign-sovereign-immunity context also limited the availability of an act-of-state defense, compare (plurality opinion), with *id.*, at 725–730 (Marshall, J., dissenting), there was little disagreement over the general scope of the exception. The plurality noted that, after the State Department endorsed the restrictive theory of foreign sovereign immunity in 1952, the lower courts consistently held that foreign sovereigns were not immune from the jurisdiction of American courts in cases "arising out of purely commercial transactions" [citations omitted]. The plurality further recognized that the distinction between state sovereign acts, on the one hand, and state commercial and private acts, on the other, was not entirely novel to American law. [Citations omitted.] The plurality stated that the restrictive theory of foreign sovereign immunity would not bar a suit based upon a foreign state's participation in the marketplace in the manner of a private citizen or corporation. 425 U.S., at 698–705. A foreign state engaging in "commercial" activities "do[es] not exercise powers peculiar to sovereigns"; rather, it "exercise[s] only those powers that can also be exercised by private citizens." *Id.*, at 704. The dissenters did not disagree with this general description. See *id.*, at 725. Given that the FSIA was enacted less than six months after our decision in *Alfred Dunhill* was announced, we think the plurality's contemporaneous description of the then-prevailing restrictive theory of sovereign immunity is of significant assistance in construing the scope of the Act.

In accord with that description, we conclude that when a foreign government acts, not as regulator of a market, but in the manner of a private player within it, the foreign sovereign's actions are "commercial" within the meaning of the FSIA. Moreover, because the Act provides that the commercial character of an act is to be determined by reference to its "nature" rather than its "purpose," 28 U.S.C. § 1603(d), the question is not whether the foreign government is acting with a profit motive or instead with the aim of fulfilling uniquely sovereign objectives. Rather, the issue is whether the particular actions that the foreign state performs (whatever the motive behind them) are the type of actions by which a private party engages in "trade and traffic or commerce," Black's Law Dictionary 270 (6th ed. 1990). [Citations omitted.] Thus, a foreign government's issuance of regulations limiting foreign currency exchange is a sovereign activity, because such authoritative control of commerce cannot be exercised by a private party; whereas a contract to buy army boots or even bullets is a "commercial" activity, because private companies can similarly use sales contracts to acquire goods [citations omitted].

The commercial character of the Bonods is confirmed by the fact that they are in almost all respects garden-variety debt instruments: They may be held by private parties; they are negotiable and may be traded on the international market (except in Argentina); and they promise a future stream of cash income. We recognize that, prior to the enactment of the FSIA, there was authority suggesting that the issuance of public debt instruments did not constitute a commercial activity. [Citation omitted.] There is, however, nothing distinctive about the state's assumption of debt (other than perhaps its purpose) that would cause it always to be classified as jure imperii, and in this regard it is significant that *Victory Transport* expressed confusion as to whether the "nature" or the "purpose" of a transaction was controlling in determining commerciality, *id.*, at 359–360. Because the FSIA has now clearly established that the "nature" governs, we perceive no basis for concluding that the issuance of debt should be treated as categorically different from other activities of foreign states.

Argentina contends that, although the FSIA bars consideration of "purpose," a court must nonetheless fully consider the context of a transaction in order to determine whether it is "commercial." Accordingly, Argentina claims that the Court of Appeals erred by defining the relevant conduct in what Argentina considers an overly generalized, a contextual manner and by essentially adopting a per se rule that all "issuance of debt instruments" is "commercial." See 941 F.2d, at 151 (" 'It is self-evident that issuing public debt is a commercial activity within the meaning of [the FSIA]' "), quoting *Shapiro v. Republic of Bolivia*, 930 F.2d 1013, 1018 (CA2

1991). We have no occasion to consider such a per se rule, because it seems to us that even in full context, there is nothing about the issuance of these Bonods (except perhaps its purpose) that is not analogous to a private commercial transaction.

Argentina points to the fact that the transactions in which the Bonods were issued did not have the ordinary commercial consequence of raising capital or financing acquisitions. Assuming for the sake of argument that this is not an example of judging the commerciality of a transaction by its purpose, the ready answer is that private parties regularly issue bonds, not just to raise capital or to finance purchases, but also to refinance debt. That is what Argentina did here: By virtue of the earlier FEIC contracts, Argentina was already obligated to supply the United States dollars needed to retire the FEIC-insured debts; the Bonods simply allowed Argentina to restructure its existing obligations. . . .

Argentina argues that the Bonods differ from ordinary debt instruments in that they "were created by the Argentine Government to fulfill its obligations under a foreign exchange program designed to address a domestic credit crisis, and as a component of a program designed to control that nation's critical shortage of foreign exchange." . . . We agree with the Court of Appeals [citation omitted] that it is irrelevant why Argentina participated in the bond market in the manner of a private actor; it matters only that it did so. We conclude that Argentina's issuance of the Bonods was a "commercial activity" under the FSIA.

B

The remaining question is whether Argentina's unilateral rescheduling of the Bonods had a "direct effect" in the United States, 28 U.S.C. § 1605(a)(2). . . . [W]e reject the suggestion that § 1605(a)(2) contains any unexpressed requirement of "substantiality" or "foreseeability." As the Court of Appeals recognized, an effect is "direct" if it follows "as an immediate consequence of the defendant's . . . activity." 941 F.2d, at 152.

. . . .

We . . . have little difficulty concluding that Argentina's unilateral rescheduling of the maturity dates on the Bonods had a "direct effect" in the United States. Respondents had designated their accounts in New York as the place of payment, and Argentina made some interest payments into those accounts before announcing that it was rescheduling the payments. Because New York was thus the place of performance for Argentina's ultimate contractual obligations, the rescheduling of those obligations necessarily had a "direct effect" in the United States: Money that was supposed to have been delivered to a New York bank for deposit was not forthcoming. We reject Argentina's suggestion that the "direct effect" requirement cannot be satisfied where the plaintiffs are all foreign corporations with no other connections to the United States. We expressly stated in *Verlinden* that the FSIA permits "a foreign plaintiff to sue a foreign sovereign in the courts of the United States, provided the substantive requirements of the Act are satisfied," 461 U.S., at 489.

Finally, Argentina argues that a finding of jurisdiction in this case would violate the Due Process Clause of the Fifth Amendment, and that, in order to avoid this difficulty, we must construe the "direct effect" requirement as embodying the "minimum contacts" test of *International Shoe Co. v. Washington*, 326 U.S. 310, 316 (1945). Assuming, without deciding, that a foreign state is a "person" for purposes of the Due Process Clause, cf. *South Carolina v. Katzenbach*, 383 U.S. 301, 323–324 (1966) (States of the Union are not "persons" for purposes of the Due Process Clause), we find that Argentina possessed "minimum contacts" that would satisfy the constitutional test. By issuing negotiable debt instruments denominated in United States dollars and payable in New York and by appointing a financial agent in that city, Argentina " 'purposefully avail[ed] itself of the privilege of conducting activities within the [United States].' " *Burger King Corp. v. Rudzewicz*, 471 U.S. 462, 475, quoting *Hanson v. Denckla*, 357 U.S. 235, 253 (1958).

We conclude that Argentina's issuance of the Bonods was a "commercial activity" under the FSIA; that its rescheduling of the maturity dates on those instruments was taken in connection with that commercial activity and had a "direct effect" in the United States; and that the District Court therefore properly asserted jurisdiction, under the FSIA, over the breach-of-contract claim based on that rescheduling. Accordingly, the judgment of the Court of Appeals is *Affirmed*.

REPUBLIC OF ARGENTINA, PETITIONER v. NML CAPITAL, LTD.
573 U.S. ___ (2014)

JUSTICE SCALIA delivered the opinion of the Court., in which ROBERTS, C. J., and KENNEDY, THOMAS, BREYER, ALITO, and KAGAN, JJ., joined. GINSBURG, J., filed a dissenting opinion. SOTOMAYOR, J., took no part in the decision of the case.

We must decide whether the Foreign Sovereign Immunities Act of 1976 (FSIA or Act), 28 U.S.C. §§ 1330, 1602 *et seq.*, limits the scope of discovery available to a judgment creditor in a federal postjudgment execution proceeding against a foreign sovereign. [Held the Act does not apply. We return to this decision and the permissible scope of discovery *infra* Chapter 5.]

. . . .

Foreign sovereign immunity is, and always has been, "a matter of grace and comity on the part of the United States, and not a restriction imposed by the Constitution." *Verlinden B. V. v. Central Bank of Nigeria*, 461 U.S. 480, 486 (1983). Accordingly, this Court's practice has been to "defe[r] to the decisions of the political branches" about whether and when to exercise judicial power over foreign states. *Ibid.* For the better part of the last two centuries, the political branch making the determination was the Executive, which typically requested immunity in all suits against friendly foreign states. *Id.*, at 486–487. But then, in 1952, the State Department embraced (in the so-called Tate Letter) the "restrictive" theory of sovereign immunity, which holds that immunity shields only a foreign sovereign's public, noncommercial acts. *Id.*, at 487, and n. 9. The Tate Letter "thr[ew] immunity determinations into some disarray," since "political considerations sometimes led the Department to file suggestions of immunity in cases where immunity would not have been available under the restrictive theory." *Republic of Austria v. Altmann*,

541 U.S. 677, 690 (2004) (internal quotation marks omitted). Further muddling matters, when in particular cases the State Department did *not* suggest immunity, courts made immunity determinations "generally by reference to prior State Department decisions." *Verlinden*, 461 U.S., at 487. Hence it was that "sovereign immunity decisions were [being] made in two different branches, subject to a variety of factors, sometimes including diplomatic considerations. Not surprisingly, the governing standards were neither clear nor uniformly applied." *Id.*, at 488.

Congress abated the bedlam in 1976, replacing the old executive-driven, factor-intensive, loosely common-law based immunity regime with the Foreign Sovereign Immunities Act's "comprehensive set of legal standards governing claims of immunity in every civil action against a foreign state." *Ibid.* The key word there — which goes a long way toward deciding this case — is *comprehensive*. We have used that term often and advisedly to describe the Act's sweep: "Congress established [in the FSIA] a comprehensive framework for resolving any claim of sovereign immunity." *Altmann*, 541 U.S., at 699. The Act "comprehensively regulat[es] the amenability of foreign nations to suit in the United States." *Verlinden, supra*, at 493. This means that "[a]fter the enactment of the FSIA, the Act — and not the pre-existing common law — indisputably governs the determination of whether a foreign state is entitled to sovereign immunity." *Samantar v. Yousuf*, 560 U.S. 305, 313 (2010). As the Act itself instructs, "[c]laims of foreign states to immunity should henceforth be decided by courts . . . in conformity with the principles *set forth in this [Act]*." 28 U.S.C. § 1602 (emphasis added). Thus, any sort of immunity defense made by a foreign sovereign in an American court must stand on the Act's text. Or it must fall.

The text of the Act confers on foreign states two kinds of immunity. First and most significant, "a foreign state shall be immune from the jurisdiction of the courts of the United States . . . except as provided in sections 1605 to 1607." § 1604. That provision is of no help to Argentina here: A foreign state may waive jurisdictional immunity, § 1605(a)(1), and in this case Argentina did so, see 695 F.3d, at 203. Consequently, the Act makes Argentina "liable in the same manner and to the same extent as a private individual under like circumstances." § 1606.

The Act's second immunity-conferring provision states that "the property in the United States of a foreign state shall be immune from attachment[,] arrest[,] and execution except as provided in sections 1610 and 1611 of this chapter." § 1609. The exceptions to this immunity defense (we will call it "execution immunity") are narrower. "The property in the United States of a foreign state" is subject to attachment, arrest, or execution if (1) it is "used for a commercial activity in the United States," § 1610(a), *and* (2) some other enumerated exception to immunity applies, such as the one allowing for waiver, see § 1610(a)(1)–(7). The Act goes on to confer a more robust execution immunity on designated international-organization property, § 1611(a), property of a foreign central bank, § 1611(b)(1),and "property of a foreign state . . . [that] is, or is intended to be, used in connection with a military activity" and is either "of a military character" or "under the control of a military authority or defense agency," § 1611(b)(2).

That is the last of the Act's immunity-granting sections. There is no third provision forbidding or limiting discovery in aid of execution of a foreign-sovereign judgment debtor's assets. Argentina concedes that no part of the Act "expressly address[es] [postjudgment] discovery." Brief for Petitioner 22. Quite right. The Act speaks of discovery only once, in a subsection requiring courts to stay discovery requests directed to the United States that would interfere with criminal or national-security matters, § 1605(g)(1). And that section explicitly suspends certain Federal Rules of Civil Procedure when such a stay is entered, see § 1605(g)(4). Elsewhere, it is clear when the Act's provisions specifically applicable to suits against sovereigns displace their general federal-rule counterparts. *See, e.g.*, § 1608(d). Far from containing the "plain statement" necessary to preclude application of federal discovery rules, *Société Nationale Industrielle Aérospatiale v. United States Dist. Court for Southern Dist. of Iowa*, 482 U.S. 522, 539 (1987), the Act says not a word on the subject.

PROBLEMS AND NOTES

1. Assume that a bank wholly owned by The Republic of Boliviana issued non-coupon bearer promissory notes, each in the amount of 50 million dollars, payable to the holder in 10 years and one day after issue. The notes stated that the Bolivianan Ministry of Finance guaranteed payment of the notes and that they were backed by the government. A Tennessee corporation acquired two of the notes but only after the Bolivianan Attorney General affirmed their validity. Two years later the corporation demanded payment at its principal office in Nashville. Boliviana refused payment, declaring that the notes were forgeries. The corporation then sued to collect. In response Boliviana moved to dismiss for lack of jurisdiction because of sovereign immunity. How would you advise the judge to rule? See *DRFP L.L.C. v. Republica Bolivariana de Venezuela*, 622 F.3d 513 (6th Cir. 2010).

2. In celebration of the 50th anniversary of as an independent, post-colonial state, the Government of Bogatvia has decided to issue a commemorative stamp. Pursuant to this plan the Bogatvian Ministry of Posts and Telecommunications entered a contract with the American Philatelic Society for a special event to be held in New York on the day of first issue and an advance purchase of 10,000 sheets that would be made available to Society members at a discounted price. Two months before the date of issue, the Government lost its parliamentary majority in a general election. The principal issue was the Bogatvia debt crisis. Upon taking office the new Government promptly disavowed all of its predecessors discretionary spending plans, including the celebration and the commemorative stamp. Having spent considerable amounts in advertising the availability of the stamps to members, the Society has filed suit against the Ministry in the U.S. District Court for the Southern District of New York. Counsel representing the Ministry have moved to dismiss the suit on the grounds of sovereign immunity. How would you advise the judge to rule? Is the decision in *OSS Nokalva, Inc. v. European Space Agency*, 617 F.3d 756 (3d Cir. 2010), helpful?

3. Assume that you were asked to advise lawyers for the Estate of Jacob Schwartz, a prominent Jewish art collector, whose collection of 19th century paintings was seized and sold by German government authorities in 1934 allegedly to satisfy payment of a fine imposed pursuant to a finding by an administrative tribunal that Schwartz had violated various currency regulations. Schwartz later died in prison. Soon afterwards Nazi officials discovered an additional cache of his paintings, which they also confiscated and sold. After the war, a court in Hamburg invalidated the 1933 proceedings, declaring that Schwartz's sentence and fine were null and void. Letters sent by Jacob to his brother living in Seattle between 1932 and 1934 showed Jacob's fears about the possibility of a Nazi regime taking power and, once these fears were realized, led him to begin plans to send his collection to his brother and to follow as soon as he was able. In one letter, he wrote:

> The paintings are yours to keep, donate, or sell. If you decide to donate any make certain that they go to a Jewish organization. The proceeds from any sales should be divided between members of the family and Jewish relief efforts in the United States. I fear the worst. Any funds provided to European organizations may soon disappear into a dark and evil hole.

The collection included the "Portrait of a Mona and a Woman in an Interior" by the 17th century Dutch master, Eglon van der Neer. With respect to the threshold issue of the adjudicatory jurisdiction of a U.S. court, would members of Jacob Schwartz's brother or surviving heirs have a justiciable claim against the Federal Republic of Germany for recovery of the value of the collection? *See Westfield v. Federal Republic of Germany*, 633 F.3d 409 (6th Cir. 2011).

What if the paintings were subsequently transferred to a public museum in Hamburg where some remain on display? *See Republic of Austria v. Altmann*, 541 U.S. 677 (2004). Would it make any difference whether instead the paintings had been subsequently sold to a series of dealers and private collectors, but Jacob Schwartz's surviving heirs have located at least one of the paintings in a public museum in Madrid on loan from a foundation established by a Swiss industrial magnate and avid art collector who had purchased the painting a few years ago from the estate of a prominent art collector in St. Louis? *See Cassirer v. Kingdom of Spain*, 616 F.3d 1019 (9th Cir. 2010), *cert. denied*, 131 S. Ct. 3057 (2011).

4. Assume that General Abioye Adebanje was the head of the armed forces in Obaji, a small, breakaway state adjacent to Nigeria. Obaji's independent status was promptly recognized by most countries including the United States. Within the year, however, the new president declared martial law and began to rule by decree. During the political protests that ensued, troops under the command of General Adebanje allegedly arrested over a hundred dissidents in the city of Obajomo. Most of those detained simply disappeared. Only a handful survived. A decade later, after retiring, General Adebanje moved to Southern California. One of the survivors of the alleged Obajomo "massacre" was Bayo Obyomi, an orphaned teenage girl who was taken in and later adopted by a missionary family. While a student at the University of California, Santa Barbara, Bayo discovered Adebanje's whereabouts. She promptly filed suit for damages under the Torture Victim Protection Act of 1991, 106 Stat. 73, and the Alien Tort Statute, 28 U.S.C. § 1350. In response, Adebanje's lawyers moved to dismiss the action, claiming immunity under the Foreign Sovereign Immunities Act, 28 U.S.C. §§ 1330, 1602 *et seq.* Were you the judge, how would you rule? *See Samantar v. Yousuf*, 560 U.S. 305, 130 S. Ct. 2278 (2010).

B. Act of State

BANCO NACIONAL DE CUBA v. SABBATINO*
376 U.S. 398 (1964)

MR. JUSTICE HARLAN delivered the opinion of the Court.

The question which brought this case here, and is now found to be the dispositive issue, is whether the so-called act of state doctrine serves to sustain petitioner's

---

* Footnotes omitted.

claims in this litigation. Such claims are ultimately founded on a decree of the Government of Cuba expropriating certain property, the right to the proceeds of which is here in controversy. The act of state doctrine in its traditional formulation precludes the courts of this country from inquiring into the validity of the public acts a recognized foreign sovereign power committed within its own territory.

I.

In February and July of 1960, respondent Farr, Whitlock & Co., an American commodity broker, contracted to purchase Cuban sugar, free alongside the steamer, from a wholly owned subsidiary of Compania Azucarera Vertientes-Camaguey de Cuba (C. A. V.), a corporation organized under Cuban law whose capital stock was owned principally by United States residents. Farr, Whitlock agreed to pay for the sugar in New York upon presentation of the shipping documents and a sight draft.

On July 6, 1960, the Congress of the United States amended the Sugar Act of 1948 to permit a presidentially directed reduction of the sugar quota for Cuba. On the same day President Eisenhower exercised the granted power. The day of the congressional enactment, the Cuban Council of Ministers adopted "Law No. 851," which characterized this reduction in the Cuban sugar quota as an act of "aggression, for political purposes" on the part of the United States, justifying the taking of countermeasures by Cuba. The law gave the Cuban President and Prime Minister discretionary power to nationalize by forced expropriation property or enterprises in which American nationals had an interest. Although a system of compensation was formally provided, the possibility of payment under it may well be deemed illusory. Our State Department has described the Cuban law as "manifestly in violation of those principles of international law which have long been accepted by the free countries of the West. It is in its essence discriminatory, arbitrary and confiscatory."

Between August 6 and August 9, 1960, the sugar covered by the contract between Farr, Whitlock and C. A. V. was loaded, destined for Morocco, onto the S. S. *Hornfels*, which was standing offshore at the Cuban port of Jucaro (Santa Maria). On the day loading commenced, the Cuban President and Prime Minister, acting pursuant to Law No. 851, issued Executive Power Resolution No. 1. It provided for the compulsory expropriation of all property and enterprises, and of rights and interests arising therefrom, of certain listed companies, including C. A. V., wholly or principally owned by American nationals. The preamble reiterated the alleged injustice of the American reduction of the Cuban sugar quota and emphasized the importance of Cuba's serving as an example for other countries to follow "in their struggle to free themselves from the brutal claws of Imperialism." In consequence of the resolution, the consent of the Cuban Government was necessary before a ship carrying sugar of a named company could leave Cuban waters. In order to obtain this consent, Farr, Whitlock, on August 11, entered into contracts, identical to those it had made with C. A. V., with the Banco Para el Comercio Exterior de Cuba, an instrumentality of the Cuban Government. The S. S. Hornfels sailed for Morocco on August 12.

Banco Exterior assigned the bills of lading to petitioner, also an instrumentality of the Cuban Government, which instructed its agent in New York, Société

Generale, to deliver the bills and a sight draft in the sum of $175,250.69 to Farr, Whitlock in return for payment. Société Generale's initial tender of the documents was refused by Farr, Whitlock, which on the same day was notified of C. A. V.'s claim that as rightful owner of the sugar it was entitled to the proceeds. In return for a promise not to turn the funds over to petitioner or its agent, C. A. V. agreed to indemnify Farr, Whitlock for any loss. Farr, Whitlock subsequently accepted the shipping documents, negotiated the bills of lading to its customer, and received payment for the sugar. It refused, however, to hand over the proceeds to Société Generale. Shortly thereafter, Farr, Whitlock was served with an order of the New York Supreme Court, which had appointed Sabbatino as Temporary Receiver of C. A. V.'s New York assets, enjoining it from taking any action in regard to the money claimed by C. A. V. that might result in its removal from the State. Following this, Farr, Whitlock, pursuant to court order, transferred the funds to Sabbatino, to abide the event of a judicial determination as to their ownership.

Petitioner then instituted this action in the Federal District Court for the Southern District of New York. Alleging conversion of the bills of lading, it sought to recover the proceeds thereof from Farr, Whitlock and to enjoin the receiver from exercising any dominion over such proceeds. Upon motions to dismiss and for summary judgment, the District Court, 193 F. Supp. 375, sustained federal in personam jurisdiction despite state control of the funds. It found that the sugar was located within Cuban territory at the time of expropriation and determined that under merchant law common to civilized countries Farr, Whitlock could not have asserted ownership of the sugar against C. A. V. before making payment. It concluded that C. A. V. had a property interest in the sugar subject to the territorial jurisdiction of Cuba. The court then dealt with the question of Cuba's title to the sugar, on which rested petitioner's claim of conversion. While acknowledging the continuing vitality of the act of state doctrine, the court believed it inapplicable when the questioned foreign act is in violation of international law. Proceeding on the basis that a taking invalid under international law does not convey good title, the District Court found the Cuban expropriation decree to violate such law in three separate respects: it was motivated by a retaliatory and not a public purpose; it discriminated against American nationals; and it failed to provide adequate compensation. Summary judgment against petitioner was accordingly granted.

The Court of Appeals, 307 F.2d 845, affirming the decision on similar grounds, relied on two letters (not before the District Court) written by State Department officers which it took as evidence that the Executive Branch had no objection to a judicial testing of the Cuban decree's validity. The court was unwilling to declare that any one of the infirmities found by the District Court rendered the taking invalid under international law, but was satisfied that in combination they had that effect. We granted certiorari because the issues involved bear importantly on the conduct of the country's foreign relations and more particularly on the proper role of the Judicial Branch in this sensitive area. 372 U.S. 905. For reasons to follow we decide that the judgment below must be reversed.

Subsequent to the decision of the Court of Appeals, the C. A. V. receivership was terminated by the State Supreme Court; the funds in question were placed in escrow, pending the outcome of this suit. C. A. V. has moved in this Court to be substituted as a party in the place of Sabbatino. Although it is true that Sabbatino's defensive interest in this litigation has largely, if not entirely, reflected that of C. A. V., this is true also of Farr, Whitlock's position. There is no indication that Farr, Whitlock has not adequately represented C. A. V.'s interest or that it will not continue to do so. Moreover, insofar as disposition of the case here is concerned, C. A. V. has been permitted as amicus to brief and argue its position before this Court. In these circumstances we are not persuaded that the admission of C. A. V. as a party is necessary at this stage to safeguard any claim either that it has already presented or that it may present in the future course of this litigation. Accordingly, we are constrained to deny C. A. V.'s motion to be admitted as a party, without prejudice however to the renewal of such a motion in the lower courts if it appears that C. A. V.'s interests are not adequately represented by Farr, Whitlock and that the granting of such a motion will not disturb federal jurisdiction. [Citations omitted.]

Before considering the holding below with respect to the act of state doctrine, we must deal with narrower grounds urged for dismissal of the action or for a judgment on the merits in favor of respondents.

II.

It is first contended that this petitioner, an instrumentality of the Cuban Government, should be denied access to American courts because Cuba is an unfriendly power and does not permit nationals of this country to obtain relief in its courts. Even though the respondents did not raise this point in the lower courts we think it should be considered here. If the courts of this country should be closed to the government of a foreign state, the underlying reason is one of national policy transcending the interests of the parties to the action, and this Court should give effect to that policy sua sponte even at this stage of the litigation.

. . . .

We hold that this petitioner is not barred from access to the federal courts.

. . . .

In these circumstances the question whether the rights acquired by Cuba are enforceable in our courts depends not upon the doctrine here invoked but upon the act of state doctrine discussed in the succeeding sections of this opinion.

. . . .

IV.

The classic American statement of the act of state doctrine, which appears to have taken root in England as early as 1674 [citation omitted], and began to emerge in the jurisprudence of this country in the late eighteenth and early nineteenth centuries, [citations omitted] is found in *Underhill v. Hernandez*, 168 U.S. 250, where Chief Justice Fuller said for a unanimous Court:

> "Every sovereign State is bound to respect the independence of every other sovereign State, and the courts of one country will not sit in judgment on the acts of the government of another done within its own territory.

Redress of grievances by reason of such acts must be obtained through the means open to be availed of by sovereign powers as between themselves."

Following this precept the Court in that case refused to inquire into acts of Hernandez, a revolutionary Venezuelan military commander whose government had been later recognized by the United States, which were made the basis of a damage action in this country by Underhill, an American citizen, who claimed that he had been unlawfully assaulted, coerced, and detained in Venezuela by Hernandez.

None of this Court's subsequent cases in which the act of state doctrine was directly or peripherally involved manifest any retreat from Underhill. See *American Banana Co. v. United Fruit Co.*, 213 U.S. 347; *Oetjen v. Central Leather Co.*, 246 U.S. 297; *Ricaud v. American Metal Co.*, 246 U.S. 304; *Shapleigh v. Mier*, 299 U.S. 468; *United States v. Belmont*, 301 U.S. 324; *United States v. Pink*, 315 U.S. 203. On the contrary in two of these cases, *Oetjen* and *Ricaud*, the doctrine as announced in *Underhill* was reaffirmed in unequivocal terms.

Oetjen involved a seizure of hides from a Mexican citizen as a military levy by General Villa, acting for the forces of General Carranza, whose government was recognized by this country subsequent to the trial but prior to decision by this Court. The hides were sold to a Texas corporation which shipped them to the United States and assigned them to defendant. As assignee of the original owner, plaintiff replevied the hides, claiming that they had been seized in violation of the Hague Conventions. In affirming a judgment for defendant, the Court suggested that the rules of the Conventions did not apply to civil war and that, even if they did, the relevant seizure was not in violation of them. 246 U.S., at 301–302. Nevertheless, it chose to rest its decision on other grounds. It described the designation of the sovereign as a political question to be determined by the legislative and executive departments rather than the judicial department, invoked the established rule that such recognition operates retroactively to validate past acts, and found the basic tenet of *Underhill* to be applicable to the case before it.

> "The principle that the conduct of one independent government cannot be successfully questioned in the courts of another is as applicable to a case involving the title to property brought within the custody of a court, such as we have here, as it was held to be to the cases cited, in which claims for damages were based upon acts done in a foreign country, for it rests at last upon the highest considerations of international comity and expediency. To permit the validity of the acts of one sovereign State to be reexamined and perhaps condemned by the courts of another would very certainly 'imperil the amicable relations between governments and vex the peace of nations.'" *Id.*, at 303–304.

In *Ricaud* the facts were similar — another general of the Carranza forces seized lead bullion as a military levy — except that the property taken belonged to an American citizen. The Court found *Underhill, American Banana,* and *Oetjen* controlling. Commenting on the nature of the principle established by those cases, the opinion stated that the rule

> "does not deprive the courts of jurisdiction once acquired over a case. It requires only that, when it is made to appear that the foreign government

has acted in a given way on the subject-matter of the litigation, the details of such action or the merit of the result cannot be questioned but must be accepted by our courts as a rule for their decision. To accept a ruling authority and to decide accordingly is not a surrender or abandonment of jurisdiction but is an exercise of it. It results that the title to the property in this case must be determined by the result of the action taken by the military authorities of Mexico . . . ." 246 U.S., at 309.

To the same effect is the language of Mr. Justice Cardozo in the *Shapleigh* case, supra, where, in commenting on the validity of a Mexican land expropriation, he said (299 U.S., at 471): "The question is not here whether the proceeding was so conducted as to be a wrong to our nationals under the doctrines of international law, though valid under the law of the situs of the land. For wrongs of that order the remedy to be followed is along the channels of diplomacy."

In deciding the present case the Court of Appeals relied in part upon an exception to the unqualified teachings of *Underhill*, *Oetjen*, and *Ricaud* which that court had earlier indicated. In *Bernstein v. Van Heyghen Freres Société Anonyme*, 163 F.2d 246, suit was brought to recover from an assignee property allegedly taken, in effect, by the Nazi Government because plaintiff was Jewish. Recognizing the odious nature of this act of state, the court, through Judge Learned Hand, nonetheless refused to consider it invalid on that ground. Rather, it looked to see if the Executive had acted in any manner that would indicate that United States Courts should refuse to give effect to such a foreign decree. Finding no such evidence, the court sustained dismissal of the complaint. In a later case involving similar facts the same court again assumed examination of the German acts improper, *Bernstein v. N. V. Nederlandsche-Amerikaansche Stoomvaart-Maatschappij*, 173 F.2d 71, but, quite evidently following the implications of Judge Hand's opinion in the earlier case, amended its mandate to permit evidence of alleged invalidity, 210 F.2d 375, subsequent to receipt by plaintiff's attorney of a letter from the Acting Legal Adviser to the State Department written for the purpose of relieving the court from any constraint upon the exercise of its jurisdiction to pass on that question.

This Court has never had occasion to pass upon the so-called *Bernstein* exception, nor need it do so now. For whatever ambiguity may be thought to exist in the two letters from State Department officials on which the Court of Appeals relied, 307 F.2d, at 858, is now removed by the position which the Executive has taken in this Court on the act of state claim; respondents do not indeed contest the view that these letters were intended to reflect no more than the Department's then wish not to make any statement bearing on this litigation.

The outcome of this case, therefore, turns upon whether any of the contentions urged by respondents against the application of the act of state doctrine in the premises is acceptable: (1) that the doctrine does not apply to acts of state which violate international law, as is claimed to be the case here; (2) that the doctrine is inapplicable unless the Executive specifically interposes it in a particular case; and (3) that, in any event, the doctrine may not be invoked by a foreign government plaintiff in our courts.

V.

Preliminarily, we discuss the foundations on which we deem the act of state doctrine to rest, and more particularly the question of whether state or federal law governs its application in a federal diversity case.

We do not believe that this doctrine is compelled either by the inherent nature of sovereign authority, as some of the earlier decisions seem to imply, see *Underhill, supra; American Banana, supra; Oetjen, supra*, at 303, or by some principle of international law. If a transaction takes place in one jurisdiction and the forum is in another, the forum does not by dismissing an action or by applying its own law purport to divest the first jurisdiction of its territorial sovereignty; it merely declines to adjudicate or makes applicable its own law to parties or property before it. The refusal of one country to enforce the penal laws of another (*supra*, pp. 413–414) is a typical example of an instance when a court will not entertain a cause of action arising in another jurisdiction. While historic notions of sovereign authority do bear upon the wisdom of employing the act of state doctrine, they do not dictate its existence.

That international law does not require application of the doctrine is evidenced by the practice of nations. Most of the countries rendering decisions on the subject fail to follow the rule rigidly. No international arbitral or judicial decision discovered suggests that international law prescribes recognition of sovereign acts of foreign governments [reference omitted], and apparently no claim has ever been raised before an international tribunal that failure to apply the act of state doctrine constitutes a breach of international obligation. If international law does not prescribe use of the doctrine, neither does it forbid application of the rule even if it is claimed that the act of state in question violated international law. The traditional view of international law is that it establishes substantive principles for determining whether one country has wronged another. Because of its peculiar nation-to-nation character the usual method for an individual to seek relief is to exhaust local remedies and then repair to the executive authorities of his own state to persuade them to champion his claim in diplomacy or before an international tribunal. [Citation omitted.] Although it is, of course, true that United States courts apply international law as a part of our own in appropriate circumstances [citations omitted], the public law of nations can hardly dictate to a country which is in theory wronged how to treat that wrong within its domestic borders.

Despite the broad statement in *Oetjen* that "The conduct of the foreign relations of our Government is committed by the Constitution to the Executive and Legislative . . . Departments," 246 U.S., at 302, it cannot of course be thought that "every case or controversy which touches foreign relations lies beyond judicial cognizance." *Baker v. Carr*, 369 U.S. 186, 211. The text of the Constitution does not require the act of state doctrine; it does not irrevocably remove from the judiciary the capacity to review the validity of foreign acts of state.

The act of state doctrine does, however, have "constitutional" underpinnings. It arises out of the basic relationships between branches of government in a system of separation of powers. It concerns the competency of dissimilar institutions to make and implement particular kinds of decisions in the area of international relations. The doctrine as formulated in past decisions expresses the strong sense of the

Judicial Branch that its engagement in the task of passing on the validity of foreign acts of state may hinder rather than further this country's pursuit of goals both for itself and for the community of nations as a whole in the international sphere. Many commentators disagree with this view; they have striven by means of distinguishing and limiting past decisions and by advancing various considerations of policy to stimulate a narrowing of the apparent scope of the rule. Whatever considerations are thought to predominate, it is plain that the problems involved are uniquely federal in nature. If federal authority, in this instance this Court, orders the field of judicial competence in this area for the federal courts, and the state courts are left free to formulate their own rules, the purposes behind the doctrine could be as effectively undermined as if there had been no federal pronouncement on the subject.

We could perhaps in this diversity action avoid the question of deciding whether federal or state law is applicable to this aspect of the litigation. New York has enunciated the act of state doctrine in terms that echo those of federal decisions decided during the reign of *Swift v. Tyson*, 16 Pet. 1. In *Hatch v. Baez*, 7 Hun 596, 599 (N. Y. Sup. Ct.), Underhill was foreshadowed by the words, "the courts of one country are bound to abstain from sitting in judgment on the acts of another government done within its own territory." More recently, the Court of Appeals in *Salimoff & Co. v. Standard Oil Co.*, 262 N. Y. 220, 224, 186 N. E. 679, 681, has declared, "The courts of one independent government will not sit in judgment upon the validity of the acts of another done within its own territory, even when such government seizes and sells the property of an American citizen within its boundaries." [Citations omitted.] Thus our conclusions might well be the same whether we dealt with this problem as one of state law [citations omitted], or federal law.

However, we are constrained to make it clear that an issue concerned with a basic choice regarding the competence and function of the Judiciary and the National Executive in ordering our relationships with other members of the international community must be treated exclusively as an aspect of federal law. It seems fair to assume that the Court did not have rules like the act of state doctrine in mind when it decided *Erie R. Co. v. Tompkins*. Soon thereafter, Professor Philip C. Jessup, now a judge of the International Court of Justice, recognized the potential dangers were *Erie* extended to legal problems affecting international relations. He cautioned that rules of international law should not be left to divergent and perhaps parochial state interpretations. His basic rationale is equally applicable to the act of state doctrine.

. . . .

. . . We conclude that the scope of the act of state doctrine must be determined according to federal law.

VI.

If the act of state doctrine is a principle of decision binding on federal and state courts alike but compelled by neither international law nor the Constitution, its continuing vitality depends on its capacity to reflect the proper distribution of functions between the judicial and political branches of the Government on matters bearing upon foreign affairs. It should be apparent that the greater the degree of codification or consensus concerning a particular area of international law, the more appropriate it is for the judiciary to render decisions regarding it, since the courts can then focus on the application of an agreed principle to circumstances of fact rather than on the sensitive task of establishing a principle not inconsistent with the national interest or with international justice. It is also evident that some aspects of international law touch much more sharply on national nerves than do others; the less important the implications of an issue are for our foreign relations, the weaker the justification for exclusivity in the political branches. The balance of relevant considerations may also be shifted if the government which perpetrated the challenged act of state is no longer in existence, as in the *Bernstein* case, for the political interest of this country may, as a result, be measurably altered. Therefore, rather than laying down or reaffirming an inflexible and all-encompassing rule in this case, we decide only that the Judicial Branch will not examine the validity of a taking of property within its own territory by a foreign sovereign government, extant and recognized by this country at the time of suit, in the absence of a treaty or other unambiguous agreement regarding controlling legal principles, even if the complaint alleges that the taking violates customary international law.

There are few if any issues in international law today on which opinion seems to be so divided as the limitations on a state's power to expropriate the property of aliens. There is, of course, authority, in international judicial and arbitral decisions, in the expressions of national governments, and among commentators for the view that a taking is improper under international law if it is not for a public purpose, is discriminatory, or is without provision for prompt, adequate, and effective compensation. However, Communist countries, although they have in fact provided a degree of compensation after diplomatic efforts, commonly recognize no obligation on the part of the taking country. Certain representatives of the newly independent and underdeveloped countries have questioned whether rules of state responsibility toward aliens can bind nations that have not consented to them and it is argued that the traditionally articulated standards governing expropriation of property reflect "imperialist" interests and are inappropriate to the circumstances of emergent states.

The disagreement as to relevant international law standards reflects an even more basic divergence between the national interests of capital importing and capital exporting nations and between the social ideologies of those countries that favor state control of a considerable portion of the means of production and those that adhere to a free enterprise system. It is difficult to imagine the courts of this country embarking on adjudication in an area which touches more sensitively the practical and ideological goals of the various members of the community of nations.

When we consider the prospect of the courts characterizing foreign expropriations, however justifiably, as invalid under international law and ineffective to pass title, the wisdom of the precedents is confirmed. While each of the leading cases in this Court may be argued to be distinguishable on its facts from this one — *Underhill* because sovereign immunity provided an independent ground and *Oetjen*, *Ricaud*, and *Shapleigh* because there was actually no violation of international law — the plain implication of all these opinions, and the import of express statements in *Oetjen*, 246 U.S., at 304, and *Shapleigh*, 299 U.S., at 471, is that the act of state doctrine is applicable even if international law has been violated. In *Ricaud*, the one case of the three most plausibly involving an international law violation, the possibility of an exception to the act of state doctrine was not discussed. Some commentators have concluded that it was not brought to the Court's attention, but Justice Clarke delivered both the *Oetjen* and *Ricaud* opinions, on the same day, so we can assume that principles stated in the former were applicable to the latter case.

The possible adverse consequences of a conclusion to the contrary of that implicit in these cases is highlighted by contrasting the practices of the political branch with the limitations of the judicial process in matters of this kind. Following an expropriation of any significance, the Executive engages in diplomacy aimed to assure that United States citizens who are harmed are compensated fairly. Representing all claimants of this country, it will often be able, either by bilateral or multilateral talks, by submission to the United Nations, or by the employment of economic and political sanctions, to achieve some degree of general redress. Judicial determinations of invalidity of title can, on the other hand, have only an occasional impact, since they depend on the fortuitous circumstance of the property in question being brought into this country. Such decisions would, if the acts involved were declared invalid, often be likely to give offense to the expropriating country; since the concept of territorial sovereignty is so deep seated, any state may resent the refusal of the courts of another sovereign to accord validity to acts within its territorial borders. Piecemeal dispositions of this sort involving the probability of affront to another state could seriously interfere with negotiations being carried on by the Executive Branch and might prevent or render less favorable the terms of an agreement that could otherwise be reached. Relations with third countries which have engaged in similar expropriations would not be immune from effect.

The dangers of such adjudication are present regardless of whether the State Department has, as it did in this case, asserted that the relevant act violated international law. If the Executive Branch has undertaken negotiations with an expropriating country, but has refrained from claims of violation of the law of nations, a determination to that effect by a court might be regarded as a serious insult, while a finding of compliance with international law, would greatly strengthen the bargaining hand of the other state with consequent detriment to American interests.

Even if the State Department has proclaimed the impropriety of the expropriation, the stamp of approval of its view by a judicial tribunal, however impartial, might increase any affront and the judicial decision might occur at a time, almost always well after the taking, when such an impact would be contrary to our national interest. Considerably more serious and far-reaching consequences would flow from a judicial finding that international law standards had been met if that determination flew in the face of a State Department proclamation to the contrary. When articulating principles of international law in its relations with other states, the Executive Branch speaks not only as an interpreter of generally accepted and traditional rules, as would the courts, but also as an advocate of standards it believes desirable for the community of nations and protective of national concerns. In short, whatever way the matter is cut, the possibility of conflict between the Judicial and Executive Branches could hardly be avoided.

Respondents contend that, even if there is not agreement regarding general standards for determining the validity of expropriations, the alleged combination of retaliation, discrimination, and inadequate compensation makes it patently clear that this particular expropriation was in violation of international law. If this view is accurate, it would still be unwise for the courts so to determine. Such a decision now would require the drawing of more difficult lines in subsequent cases and these would involve the possibility of conflict with the Executive view. Even if the courts avoided this course, either by presuming the validity of an act of state whenever the international law standard was thought unclear or by following the State Department declaration in such a situation, the very expression of judicial uncertainty might provide embarrassment to the Executive Branch.

Another serious consequence of the exception pressed by respondents would be to render uncertain titles in foreign commerce, with the possible consequence of altering the flow of international trade. If the attitude of the United States courts were unclear, one buying expropriated goods would not know if he could safely import them into this country. Even were takings known to be invalid, one would have difficulty determining after goods had changed hands several times whether the particular articles in question were the product of an ineffective state act.

Were respondents' position adopted, the courts might be engaged in the difficult tasks of ascertaining the origin of fungible goods, of considering the effect of improvements made in a third country on expropriated raw materials, and of determining the title to commodities subsequently grown on expropriated land or produced with expropriated machinery.

By discouraging import to this country by traders certain or apprehensive of nonrecognition of ownership, judicial findings of invalidity of title might limit competition among sellers; if the excluded goods constituted a significant portion of the market, prices for United States purchasers might rise with a consequent economic burden on United States consumers. Balancing the undesirability of such a result against the likelihood of furthering other national concerns is plainly a function best left in the hands of the political branches.

Against the force of such considerations, we find respondents' countervailing arguments quite unpersuasive. Their basic contention is that United States courts could make a significant contribution to the growth of international law, a contribution whose importance, it is said, would be magnified by the relative paucity of decisional law by international bodies. But given the fluidity of present world conditions, the effectiveness of such a patchwork approach toward the formulation of an acceptable body of law concerning state responsibility for expropriations is, to say the least, highly conjectural. Moreover, it rests upon the sanguine presupposition that the decisions of the courts of the world's major capital exporting country and principal exponent of the free enterprise system would be accepted as disinterested expressions of sound legal principle by those adhering to widely different ideologies.

It is contended that regardless of the fortuitous circumstances necessary for United States jurisdiction over a case involving a foreign act of state and the resultant isolated application to any expropriation program taken as a whole, it is the function of the courts to justly decide individual disputes before them. Perhaps the most typical act of state case involves the original owner or his assignee suing one not in association with the expropriating state who has had "title" transferred to him. But it is difficult to regard the claim of the original owner, who otherwise may be recompensed through diplomatic channels, as more demanding of judicial cognizance than the claim of title by the innocent third party purchaser, who, if the property is taken from him, is without any remedy.

Respondents claim that the economic pressure resulting from the proposed exception to the act of state doctrine will materially add to the protection of United States investors. We are not convinced, even assuming the relevance of this contention. Expropriations take place for a variety of reasons, political and ideological as well as economic. When one considers the variety of means possessed by this country to make secure foreign investment, the persuasive or coercive effect of judicial invalidation of acts of expropriation dwindles in comparison. The newly independent states are in need of continuing foreign investment; the creation of a climate unfavorable to such investment by wholesale confiscations may well work to their long-run economic disadvantage. Foreign aid given to many of these countries provides a powerful lever in the hands of the political branches to ensure fair treatment of United States nationals. Ultimately the sanctions of economic embargo and the freezing of assets in this country may be employed. Any country willing to brave any or all of these consequences is unlikely to be deterred by sporadic judicial decisions directly affecting only property brought to our shores. If the political branches are unwilling to exercise their ample powers to effect compensation, this reflects a judgment of the national interest which the judiciary would be ill-advised to undermine indirectly.

It is suggested that if the act of state doctrine is applicable to violations of international law, it should only be so when the Executive Branch expressly stipulates that it does not wish the courts to pass on the question of validity. [Citation omitted.] We should be slow to reject the representations of the Government that such a reversal of the *Bernstein* principle would work serious inroads on the maximum effectiveness of United States diplomacy. Often the State Department will wish to refrain from taking an official position, particularly at a moment that would be dictated by the development of private litigation but might be inopportune diplomatically. Adverse domestic consequences might flow from an official stand which could be assuaged, if at all, only by revealing matters best kept secret. Of course, a relevant consideration for the State Department would be the position contemplated in the court to hear the case. It is highly questionable whether the examination of validity by the judiciary should depend on an educated guess by the Executive as to probable result and, at any rate, should a prediction be wrong, the Executive might be embarrassed in its dealings with other countries. We do not now pass on the *Bernstein* exception, but even if it were deemed valid, its suggested extension is unwarranted.

However offensive to the public policy of this country and its constituent States an expropriation of this kind may be, we conclude that both the national interest and progress toward the goal of establishing the rule of law among nations are best served by maintaining intact the act of state doctrine in this realm of its application.

VII.

Finally, we must determine whether Cuba's status as a plaintiff in this case dictates a result at variance with the conclusions reached above. If the Court were to distinguish between suits brought by sovereign states and those of assignees, the rule would have little effect unless a careful examination were made in each case to determine if the private party suing had taken property in good faith. Such an inquiry would be exceptionally difficult, since the relevant transaction would almost invariably have occurred outside our borders. If such an investigation were deemed irrelevant, a state could always assign its claim.

. . . .

The judgment of the Court of Appeals is reversed and the case is remanded to the District Court for proceedings consistent with this opinion.

It is so ordered.

MR. JUSTICE WHITE, dissenting.

I am dismayed that the Court has, with one broad stroke, declared the ascertainment and application of international law beyond the competence of the courts of the United States in a large and important category of cases. I am also disappointed in the Court's declaration that the acts of a sovereign state with regard to the property of aliens within its borders are beyond the reach of international law in the courts of this country. However clearly established that law may be, a sovereign may violate it with impunity, except insofar as the political branches of the government may provide a remedy. This backward-looking doctrine, never before declared in this Court, is carried a disconcerting step further: not only are the courts powerless to question acts of state proscribed by international law but they are likewise powerless to refuse to adjudicate the claim founded upon a foreign law; they must render judgment and thereby validate the lawless act. Since the Court expressly extends its ruling to all acts of state expropriating property, however clearly inconsistent with the international community, all discriminatory expropriations of the property of aliens, as for example the taking of properties of persons belonging to certain races, religions or nationalities, are entitled to automatic validation in the courts of the United States. No other civilized country has found such a rigid rule necessary for the survival of the executive branch of its government; the executive of no other government seems to require such insulation from international law adjudications in its courts; and no other judiciary is apparently so incompetent to ascertain and apply international law.

The Court does not refer to any country which has applied the act of state doctrine in a case where a substantial international law issue is sought to be raised by an alien whose property has been expropriated. This country and this Court stand alone among the civilized nations of the world in ruling that such an issue is not cognizable in a court of law.

The Court notes that the courts of both New York and Great Britain have articulated the act of state doctrine in broad language similar to that used by this Court in *Underhill v. Hernandez*, 168 U.S. 250, and from this it infers that these courts recognize no international law exception to the act of state doctrine. The cases relied on by the Court involved no international law issue. For in these cases the party objecting to the validity of the foreign act was a citizen of the foreign state. It is significant that courts of both New York and Great Britain, in apparently the first cases in which an international law issue was squarely posed, ruled that the act of state doctrine was no bar to examination of the validity of the foreign act. *Anglo-Iranian Oil Co. v. Jaffrate*, [1953] Int'l L. Rep. 316 (Aden Sup. Ct.): "The Iranian Laws of 1951 were invalid by international law, for, by them, the property of the company was expropriated without any compensation." *Sulyok v. Penzintezeti Kozpont Budapest*, 279 App. Div. 528, 111 N. Y. S. 2d 75, *aff'd*, 304 N. Y. 704, 107 N. E. 2d 604 (foreign expropriation of intangible property denied effect as contrary to New York public policy).

I do not believe that the act of state doctrine, as judicially fashioned in this Court, and the reasons underlying it, require American courts to decide cases in disregard of international law and of the rights of litigants to a full determination on the merits.

I.

Prior decisions of this Court in which the act of state doctrine was deemed controlling do not support the 'assertion that foreign acts of state must be enforced or recognized or applied in American courts when they violate the law of nations . . . . These cases do not strongly imply or even suggest that the Court would woodenly apply the act of state doctrine and grant enforcement to a foreign act where the act was a clear and flagrant violation of international law as the District Court and the Court of Appeals have found in respect to the Cuban law challenged herein. [Citation omitted.]

II.

Though not a principle of international law, the doctrine of restraint, as formulated by this Court, has its roots in sound policy reasons, and it is to these we must turn to decide whether the act of state doctrine should be extended to cover wrongs cognizable under international law.

Whatever may be said to constitute an act of state, our decisions make clear that the doctrine of nonreview ordinarily applies to foreign laws affecting tangible property located within the territory of a government which is recognized by the United States. *Oetjen v. Central Leather Co.*, 246 U.S. 297; *Ricaud v. American Metal Co.*, 246 U.S. 304. This judicially fashioned doctrine of nonreview is a corollary of the principle that ordinarily a state has jurisdiction to prescribe the rules governing the title to property within its territorial sovereignty [citations omitted], a principle reflected in the conflict of laws rule, adopted in virtually all nations, that the lex loci is the law governing title to property. . . . That the act of state doctrine is rooted in a well-established concept of international law is evidenced by the practice of other countries. These countries, without employing any act of state doctrine, afford substantial respect to acts of foreign states occurring within their territorial confines. Our act of state doctrine, as formulated in past decisions of the Court, carries the territorial concept one step further. It precludes a challenge to the validity of foreign law on the ordinary conflict of laws ground of repugnancy to the public policy of the forum. Against the objection that the foreign act violates domestic public policy, it has been said that the foreign law provides the rule of decision, where the lex loci rule would so indicate, in American courts. [Citations omitted.]

The reasons that underlie the deference afforded to foreign acts affecting property in the acting country are several; such deference reflects an effort to maintain a certain stability and predictability in transnational transactions, to avoid friction between nations, to encourage settlement of these disputes through diplomatic means and to avoid interference with the executive control of foreign relations. To adduce sound reasons for a policy of nonreview is not to resolve the problem at hand, but to delineate some of the considerations that are pertinent to its resolution.

Contrary to the assumption underlying the Court's opinion, these considerations are relative, their strength varies from case to case, and they are by no means controlling in all litigation involving the public acts of a foreign government. . . .

. . . .

III.

I start with what I thought to be unassailable propositions: that our courts are obliged to determine controversies on their merits, in accordance with the applicable law; and that part of the law American courts are bound to administer is international law.

Article III, § 2, of the Constitution states that "the judicial Power shall extend to all Cases . . . affecting Ambassadors, other public Ministers and Consuls; — to all Cases of admiralty and maritime Jurisdiction;— to Controversies . . . between a State, or the Citizens thereof, and foreign States, Citizens or Subjects." And § 1332 of the Judicial Code gives the courts jurisdiction over all civil actions between citizens of a State and foreign states or citizens or subjects thereof. The doctrine that the law of nations is a part of the law of the land, originally formulated in England and brought to America as part of our legal heritage, is reflected in the debates during the Constitutional Convention and in the Constitution itself. This Court has time and again effectuated the clear understanding of the Framers, as embodied in the Constitution, by applying the law of nations to resolve cases and controversies. . . .

The Court accepts the application of rules of international law to other aspects of this litigation, accepts the relevance of international law in other cases and announces that when there is an appropriate degree of "consensus concerning a particular area of international law, the more appropriate it is for the judiciary to render decisions regarding it, since the courts can then focus on the application of an agreed principle to circumstances of fact rather than on the sensitive task of establishing a principle not inconsistent with the national interest or with international justice." *Ante*, p. 428. The Court then, rather lightly in my view, dispenses with its obligation to resolve controversies in accordance with "international justice" and the "national interest" by assuming and declaring that there are no areas of agreement between nations in respect to expropriations. . . .

IV.

The reasons for nonreview, based as they are on traditional concepts of territorial sovereignty, lose much of their force when the foreign act of state is shown to be a violation of international law. All legitimate exercises of sovereign power, whether territorial or otherwise, should be exercised consistently with rules of international law, including those rules which mark the bounds of lawful state action against aliens or their property located within the territorial confines of the foreign state. Although a state may reasonably expect that the validity of its laws operating on property within its jurisdiction will not be defined by local notions of public policy of numerous other states (although a different situation may well be presented when courts of another state are asked to lend their enforcement machinery to effectuate the foreign act), it cannot with impunity ignore the rules governing the conduct of all nations and expect that other nations and tribunals will view its acts as within the permissible scope of territorial sovereignty. Contrariwise, to refuse inquiry into the question of whether norms of the international community have been contravened by the act of state under review would seem to deny the existence or purport of such norms, a view that seems inconsistent with the role of international law in ordering the relations between nations. Finally, the impartial application of international law would not only be an affirmation of the existence and binding effect of international rules of order, but also a refutation of the notion that this body of law consists of no more than the divergent and parochial views of the capital importing and exporting nations, the socialist and free-enterprise nations.

. . . .

V.

There remains for consideration the relationship between the act of state doctrine and the power of the executive over matters touching upon the foreign affairs of the Nation. It is urged that the act of state doctrine is a necessary corollary of the executive's authority to direct the foreign relations of the United States and accordingly any exception in the doctrine, even if limited to clear violations of international law, would impede or embarrass the executive in discharging his constitutional responsibilities. Thus, according to the Court, even if principles of comity do not preclude inquiry into the validity of a foreign act under international law, due regard for the executive function forbids such examination in the courts.

Without doubt political matters in the realm of foreign affairs are within the exclusive domain of the Executive Branch, as, for example, issues for which there are no available standards or which are textually committed by the Constitution to the executive. But this is far from saying that the Constitution vests in the executive exclusive absolute control of foreign affairs or that the validity of a foreign act of state is necessarily a political question. International law, as well as a treaty or executive agreement, see *United States v. Pink*, 315 U.S. 203, provides an ascertainable standard for adjudicating the validity of some foreign acts, and courts are competent to apply this body of law, notwithstanding that there may be some cases where comity dictates giving effect to the foreign act because it is not clearly condemned under generally accepted principles of international law. And it cannot be contended that the Constitution allocates this area to the exclusive jurisdiction of the executive, for the judicial power is expressly extended by that document to controversies between aliens and citizens or States, aliens and aliens, and foreign states and American citizens or States.

. . . .

. . . The act of state doctrine formulated by the Court bars review in this case and will do so in all others involving expropriation of alien property precisely because of the lack of a consensus in the international community on rules of law governing foreign expropriations Contrariwise, it would seem that the act of state doctrine will not apply to a foreign act if it concerns an area in which there is unusual agreement among nations . . . , which is not the case with the broad area of expropriations. I fail to see how greater embarrassment flows from saying that the foreign act does not violate clear and widely accepted principles of international law than from saying, as the Court does, that nonexamination and validation are required because there are no widely accepted principles to which to subject the foreign act. As to potential embarrassment, the difference is semantic, but as to determining the issue on its merits and as to upholding a regime of law, the difference is vast.

. . . .

VI.

Obviously there are cases where an examination of the foreign act and declaration of invalidity or validity might undermine the foreign policy of the Executive Branch and its attempts at negotiating a settlement for a nationalization of the property of Americans. The respect ordinarily due to a foreign state, as reflected in the decisions of this Court, rests upon a desire not to disturb the relations between countries and on a view that other means, more effective than piecemeal adjudications of claims arising out of a large-scale nationalization program of settling the dispute, may be available. Precisely because these considerations are more or less present, or absent, in any given situation and because the Department of our Government primarily responsible for the formulation of foreign policy and settling these matters on a state-to-state basis is more competent than courts to determine the extent to which they are involved, a blanket presumption of nonreview in each case is inappropriate and a requirement that the State Department render a determination after reasonable notice, in each case, is necessary. Such an examination would permit the Department to evaluate whether adjudication would "vex the peace of nations," whether a friendly foreign sovereign is involved, and whether settlement through diplomacy or through an international tribunal or arbitration is impending. Based upon such an evaluation, the Department may recommend to the court that adjudication should not proceed at the present time. Such a request I would accord considerable deference and I would not require a full statement of reasons underlying it. But I reject the contention that the recommendation itself would somehow impede the foreign relations of the United States or unduly burden the Department. . . . The United States in its brief has disclaimed any such interest in the result in these cases, either in the ultimate outcome or the determination of validity, and I would take the Government at its word in this matter, without second-guessing the wisdom of its view.

This is precisely the procedure that the Department of State adopted voluntarily in the situation where a foreign government seeks to invoke the defense of immunity in our courts. If it is not unduly disruptive for the Department to determine whether to issue a certificate of immunity to a foreign government itself when it seeks one, a recommendation by the Department in cases where generally the sovereign is not a party can hardly be deemed embarrassing to our foreign relations. Moreover, such a procedure would be consonant with the obligation of courts to adjudicate cases on the merits except for reasons wholly sufficient in the particular case. As I understand it, the executive has not yet said that adjudication in this case would impede his functions in the premises; rather he has asked us to adopt a rule of law foreclosing inquiry into the subject unless the executive affirmatively allows the courts to adjudicate on the merits.

. . . .

VII.

The position of the Executive Branch of the Government charged with foreign affairs with respect to this case is not entirely clear. As I see it no specific objection by the Secretary of State to examination of the validity of Cuba's law has been interposed at any stage in these proceedings, which would ordinarily lead to an adjudication on the merits. Disclaiming, rightfully, I think, any interest in the outcome of the case, the United States has simply argued for a rule of nonexamination in every case, which literally, I suppose, includes this one. If my view had prevailed I would have stayed further resolution of the issues in this Court to afford the Department of State reasonable time to clarify its views in light of the opinion. In the absence of a specific objection to an examination of the validity of Cuba's law under international law, I would have proceeded to determine the issue and resolve this litigation on the merits.

ALFRED DUNHILL OF LONDON, INC. v. REPUBLIC OF CUBA*
425 U.S. 682 (1976)

MR. JUSTICE WHITE delivered the opinion of the Court.

Part III of this opinion is joined only by THE CHIEF JUSTICE, MR. JUSTICE POWELL, and MR. JUSTICE REHNQUIST.

The issue in this case is whether the failure of respondents to return to petitioner Alfred Dunhill of London, Inc. (Dunhill), funds mistakenly paid by Dunhill for cigars that had been sold to Dunhill by certain expropriated Cuban cigar businesses was an "act of state" by Cuba precluding an affirmative judgment against respondents.

I.

The rather involved factual and legal context in which this litigation arises is fully set out in the District Court's opinion in this case, *Menendez v. Faber, Coe & Gregg, Inc.*, 345 F. Supp. 527 (SDNY 1972), and in closely related litigation, *F. Palicio y Compania, S.A. v. Brush*, 256 F. Supp. 481 (SDNY 1966), aff'd, 375 F.2d 1011 (CA2), cert. denied, 389 U.S. 830, 88 S. Ct. 95, 19 L. Ed. 2d 88 (1967). For present purposes, the following recitation will suffice. In 1960, the Cuban Government confiscated the business and assets of the five leading manufacturers of Havana cigars. These companies, three corporations and two partnerships, were organized under Cuban law. Virtually all of their owners were Cuban nationals. None were American. These companies sold large quantities of cigars to customers in other countries, including the United States, where the three principal importers were Dunhill, Saks & Co. (Saks), and Faber, Coe & Gregg, Inc. (Faber). The Cuban Government named "interventors" to take possession of and operate the business of the seized Cuban concerns. Interventors continued to ship cigars to foreign purchasers, including the United States importers.

This litigation began when the former owners of the Cuban companies, most of whom had fled to the United States, brought various actions against the three American importers for trademark infringement and for the purchase price of any cigars that had been shipped to importers from the seized Cuban plants and that bore United States trademarks claimed by the former owners to be their property. Following the conclusion of the related litigation in *F. Palicio y Compania, S.A. v. Brush*, supra, the Cuban interventors and the Republic of Cuba were allowed to intervene in these actions, which were consolidated for trial. Both the former owners and the interventors had asserted their right to some $700,000 due from the three importers for postintervention shipments: Faber, $582,588.86; Dunhill, $92,949.70; and Saks, $24,250. It also developed that as of the date of intervention, the three importers owed sums totaling $477,200 for cigars shipped prior to intervention: Faber, $322,000; Dunhill, $148,600; and Saks, $6,600. These latter

---

* Footnotes omitted.

sums the importers had paid to interventors subsequent to intervention on the assumption that interventors were entitled to collect the accounts receivable of the intervened businesses. The former owners claimed title to and demanded payment of these accounts.

Based on the "act of state" doctrine which had been reaffirmed in *Banco Nacional de Cuba v. Sabbatino*, 376 U.S. 398, 84 S. Ct. 923, 11 L. Ed. 2d 804 (1964), the District Court held in *F. Palicio y Compania, S.A. v. Brush, supra*, and here, that it was required to give full legal effect to the 1960 confiscation of the five cigar companies insofar as it purported to take the property of Cuban nationals located within Cuba. Interventors were accordingly entitled to collect from the importers all amounts due and unpaid with respect to shipments made after the date of intervention. The contrary conclusion was reached as to the accounts owing at the time of intervention: Because the United States courts will not give effect to foreign government confiscations without compensation of property located in the United States and because under *Republic of Iraq v. First Nat. City Bank*, 353 F.2d 47 (CA2 1965), *cert. denied*, 382 U.S. 1027, 86 S. Ct. 648, 15 L. Ed. 2d 540 (1966), the situs of the accounts receivable was with the importer-debtors, the 1960 seizures did not reach the preintervention accounts, and the former owners, rather than the interventors, were entitled to collect them from the importers even though the latter had already paid them to interventors in the mistaken belief that they were fully discharging trade debts in the ordinary course of their business.

This conclusion brought to the fore the importers' claim that their payment of the preintervention accounts had been made in error and that they were entitled to recover these payments from interventors by way of set-off and counterclaim. Although their position that the 1960 confiscation entitled them to the sums due for preintervention sales had been rejected and the District Court had ruled that they "had no right to receive or retain such payments," interventors claimed those payments on the additional ground that the obligation, if any, to repay was a quasi-contractual debt having a situs in Cuba and that their refusal to honor the obligation was an act of state not subject to question in our courts. The District Court rejected this position for two reasons. First, the repayment obligated was more properly deemed situated in the United States and hence remained unaffected by any purported confiscatory act of the Cuban Government. Second, in the District Court's view, nothing had occurred which qualified for recognition as an act of state:

> "[T]here was no formal repudiation of these obligations by Cuban Government decree of general application or otherwise. . . . Here, all that occurred was a statement by counsel for the interventors, during trial, that the Cuban Government and the interventors denied liability and had refused to make repayment. This statement was made after the interventors had invoked the jurisdiction of this Court in order to pursue their claims against the importers for post-intervention shipments. It is hard to conceive how, if such a statement can be elevated to the status of an act of state, Any refusal by Any state to honor Any obligation at Any time could be considered anything else." 345 F. Supp., at 545.

The importers were accordingly held entitled to set off their mistaken payments to interventors for preintervention shipments against the amounts due from them for their post-intervention purchases. Faber and Saks, because they owed more than interventors were obligated to return to them, were satisfied completely by the right to set-off. But Dunhill and at last we arrive at the issue in this case was entitled to more from interventors $148,000 than it owed for postintervention shipments $93,000 and to be made whole, asked for and was granted judgment against interventors for the full amount of its claim, from which would be deducted the smaller judgment entered against it.

The Court of Appeals, *Menendez v. Saks & Co.*, 485 F.2d 1355 (CA2 1973), agreed that the former owners were entitled to recover from the importers the full amount of preintervention accounts receivable. It also held that the mistaken payments by importers to interventors gave rise to a quasi-contractual obligation to repay these sums. But, contrary to the District Court, the Court of Appeals was of the view that the obligation to repay had a situs in Cuba and had been repudiate in the course of litigation by conduct that was sufficiently official to be deemed an act of state: "(I)n the absence of evidence that the interventors were not acting within the scope of their authority as agents of the Cuban government, their repudiation was an act of state even though not embodied in a formal decree." *Id.*, at 1371. Although the repudiation of the interventors' obligation was considered an act of state, the Court of Appeals went on to hold that *First Nat. City Bank v. Banco Nacional de Cuba*, 406 U.S. 759 (1972), entitled importers to recover the sums due them from interventors by way of set-off against the amounts due from them for postintervention shipments. The act of state doctrine was said to bar the affirmative judgment awarded Dunhill to the extent that its claim exceeded its debt. The judgment of the District Court was reversed in this respect, and it is this action which was the subject of the petition for certiorari filed by Dunhill. In granting the petition [citation omitted], we requested the parties to address certain questions, the first being whether the statement by counsel for the Republic of Cuba that Dunhill's unjust-enrichment claim would not be honored constituted an act of state. The case was argued twice in this Court. We have now concluded that nothing in the record reveals an act of state with respect to interventors' obligation to return monies mistakenly paid to them. Accordingly we reverse the judgment of the Court of Appeals.

II.

The District Court and the Court of Appeals held that for purposes of this litigation interventors were not entitled to the preintervention accounts receivable by virtue of the 1960 confiscation and that, despite other arguments to the contrary, nothing based on their claim to those accounts entitled interventors to retain monies mistakenly paid on those accounts by importers. We do not disturb these conclusions. The Court of Appeals nevertheless observed that interventors had "ignored" demands for the return of the monies and had "fail(ed) to honor the importers' demand (which was confirmed by the Cuban government's counsel at trial)." This conduct was considered to be "the Cuban government's repudiation of its obligation to return the funds" and to constitute an act of state not subject to question in our courts. *Menendez v. Saks & Co.*, 485 F.2d, at 1369, 1371. We cannot agree.

In addition to the present petition the Court has before it the petition of the interventors, *Republic of Cuba v. Saks & Co.*, No. 73-1287, challenging, on the ground that the intervention successfully seized the accounts receivable and that the $477,000 properly belonged to them, the propriety of permitting even a set-off, and the conditional cross-petition of the importers, *Saks & Co. v. Republic of Cuba*, No. 73-1289, challenging the propriety of the judgment against them and in favor of the owners for the $477,000 due on preintervention shipments. Today we deny these petitions, 425 U.S. 991.

If interventors, having had their liability adjudicated and various defenses rejected, including the claimed act of state, with respect to preintervention accounts, represented by the Cuban confiscation in 1960, were nevertheless to escape repayment by claiming a second and later act of state involving the funds mistakenly paid them, it was their burden to prove that act. Concededly, they declined to pay over the funds; but refusal to repay does not necessarily assert anything more than what interventors had claimed from the outset and what they have continued to claim in this Court that the preintervention accounts receivable were theirs and that they had no obligation to return payments on those accounts. Neither does it demonstrate that in addition to authority to operate commercial businesses, to pay their bills and to collect their accounts receivable, interventors had been invested with sovereign authority to repudiate all or any part of the debts incurred by those businesses. Indeed, it is difficult to believe that they had the power selectively to refuse payment of legitimate debts arising from the operation of those commercial enterprises.

In the *"Gul Djemal,"* 264 U.S. 90, a supplier libeled and caused the arrest of the Gul Djemal, a steamship owned and operated for commercial purposes by the Turkish Government, in an effort to recover for supplies and services sold to and performed for the ship. The ship's master, "a duly commissioned officer of the Turkish Navy," *Id.*, at 94–95, appeared in court and asserted sovereign immunity, claiming that such an assertion defeated the court's jurisdiction. A direct appeal was taken to this Court, where it was held that the master's assertion of sovereign immunity was insufficient because his mere representation of his government as master of a commercial ship furnished no basis for assuming he was entitled to represent the sovereign in other capacities. Here there is no more reason to suppose that the interventors possess governmental as opposed to commercial, authority than there was to suppose that the master of the Gul Djemal possessed such authority. The master of the Gul Djemal claimed the authority to assert sovereign immunity while the interventors claim that they had the authority to commit an act of state, but the difference is unimportant. In both cases, a party claimed to have had the authority to exercise sovereign power. In both, the only authority shown is commercial authority.

We thus disagree with the Court of Appeals that the mere refusal of the interventors to repay funds followed by a failure to prove that interventors "were not acting within the scope of their authority as agents of the Cuban government" satisfied respondents' burden of establishing their act of state defense. [Citation omitted.] Nor do we consider *Underhill v. Hernandez*, 168 U.S. 250 (1897), heavily relied upon by the Court of Appeals, to require a contrary conclusion In that case and in (1918), and *Ricaud v. American Metal Co.*, 246 U.S. 304 (1918), it was apparently concluded that the facts were sufficient to demonstrate that the conduct in question was the public act of those with authority to exercise sovereign powers and was entitled to respect in our courts. We draw no such conclusion from the facts of the case before us now. As the District Court found, the only evidence of an act of state other than the act of nonpayment by interventors was "a statement by counsel for the interventors, during trial, that the Cuban Government and the interventors denied liability and had refused to make repayment." *Menendez v. Faber, Coe & Gregg, Inc.*, 345 F. Supp., at 545. But this merely restated respondents' original legal position and adds little if anything, to the proof of an act of state. No statute, decree, order, or resolution of the Cuban Government itself was offered in evidence indicating that Cuba had repudiated its obligations in general or any class thereof or that it had as a sovereign matter determined to confiscate the amounts due three foreign importers.

III.

If we assume with the Court of Appeals that the Cuban Government itself had purported to exercise sovereign power to confiscate the mistaken payments belonging to three foreign creditors and to repudiate interventors' adjudicated obligation to return those funds, we are nevertheless persuaded by the arguments of petitioner and by those of the United States that the concept of an act of state should not be extended to include the repudiation of a purely commercial obligation owed by a foreign sovereign or by one of its commercial instrumentalities. Our cases have not yet gone so far, and we decline to expand their reach to the extent necessary to affirm the Court of Appeals.

Distinguishing between the public and governmental acts of sovereign states on the one hand and their private and commercial acts on the other is not a novel approach. As the Court stated through Mr. Chief Justice Marshall long ago in *Bank of the United States v. Planters' Bank of Georgia*, 9 Wheat. 904, 907 (1824):

> "It is, we think, a sound principle, that when a government becomes a partner in any trading company, it divests itself, so far as concerns the transactions of that company, of its sovereign character, and takes that of a private citizen. Instead of communicating to the company its privileges and its prerogatives, it descends to a level with those with whom it associates itself, and takes the character which belongs to its associates, and to the business which is to be transacted." [Citations omitted.]

In this same tradition, *South Carolina v. United States*, 199 U.S. (1905), drew a line for purposes of tax immunity between the historically recognized governmental functions of a State and businesses engaged in by a State of the kind which theretofore had been pursued by private enterprise. Similarly, in *Ohio v. Helvering*, 292 U.S. 360, 369 (1934), the Court said: "If a state chooses to go into the business of buying and selling commodities, its right to do so may be conceded so far as the Federal Constitution is concerned; but the exercise of the right is not the performance of a governmental function . . . . When a state enters the market place seeking customers it divests itself of its [Q]uasi sovereignty [P]ro tanto, and takes on the character of a trader . . . ." It is thus a familiar concept that "there is a constitutional line between the State as government and the State as trader." [Citations omitted.]

It is the position of the United States, stated in an *Amicus* brief filed by the Solicitor General, that such a line should be drawn in defining the outer limits of the act of state concept and that repudiations by a foreign sovereign of its commercial debts should not be considered to be acts of state beyond legal question in our courts. Attached to the brief of the United States and to this opinion as Appendix 1 [omitted] is the letter of November 26, 1975, in which the Department of State, speaking through its Legal Adviser agrees with the brief filed by the Solicitor General and, more specifically, declares "we do not believe that the Dunhill case raises an act of state question because the case involves an act which is commercial and not public, in nature."

The major underpinning of the act of state doctrine is the policy of foreclosing court adjudications involving the legality of acts of foreign states on their own soil that might embarrass the Executive Branch of our Government in the conduct of our foreign relations. [Citation omitted.] But based on the presently expressed views of those who conduct our relations with foreign countries, we are in no sense compelled to recognize as an act of state the purely commercial conduct of foreign governments in order to avoid embarrassing conflicts with the Executive Branch. On the contrary, for the reasons to which we now turn, we fear that embarrassment and conflict would me likely ensue if we were to require that the repudiation of a foreign government's debts arising from its operation of a purely commercial business be recognized as an act of state and immunized from question in our courts.

Although it had other views in years gone by, in 1952, as evidenced by Appendix 2 (the Tate letter) attached to this opinion [omitted], the United States abandoned the absolute theory of sovereign immunity and embraced the restrictive view under which immunity in our courts should be granted only with respect to causes of action arising out of a foreign state's public or governmental actions and not with respect to those arising out of its commercial or proprietary actions. This has been the official policy of our Government since that time as the . . . letter of November 26, 1975 [from Monroe Leigh, The Legal Advisor, Department of State to the Solicitor General], confirms:

> "Moreover, since 1952, the Department of State has adhered to the position that the commercial and private activities of foreign states do not give rise to sovereign immunity. Implicit in this position is a determination that adjudications of commercial liability against foreign states do not impede the conduct of foreign relations, and that such adjudications are consistent with international law on sovereign immunity."

Repudiation of a commercial debt cannot, consistent with this restrictive approach to sovereign immunity, be treated as an act of state; for if it were, foreign governments, by merely repudiating the debt before or after its adjudication, would enjoy an immunity which our Government would not extend them under prevailing sovereign immunity principles in this country. This would undermine the policy supporting the restrictive view of immunity, which is to assure those engaging in commercial transactions with foreign sovereignties that their rights will be determined in the courts whenever possible.

Although at one time this Court ordered sovereign immunity extended to a commercial vessel of a foreign country absent a suggestion of immunity from the Executive Branch and although the policy of the United States with respect to its own merchant ships was then otherwise, *Berizzi Bros. Co. v. S.S. Pesaro*, 271 U.S. 562 (1926), the authority of that case has been severely diminished by later cases such as *Ex parte Peru*, 318 U.S. 578 (1943), and *Mexico v. Hoffman*, 324 U.S. 30 (1945). In the latter case the Court unanimously denied immunity to a commercial ship owned but not possessed by the Mexican Government. The decision rested on the fact that the Mexican Government was not in possession . . . .

. . . .

It is enough that we find no persuasive ground for allowing the immunity in this case, an important reason being that the State Department has declined to recognize it." 324 U.S. at 35, n.1.

Since that time, as we have said, the United States has adopted and adhered to the policy declining to extend sovereign immunity to the commercial dealings of foreign governments. It has based that policy in part on the fact that this approach has been accepted by a large and increasing number of foreign states in the international community; in part on the fact that the United States had already adopted a policy of consenting to be sued in foreign courts in connection with suits against its merchant vessels; and in part because the enormous increase in the extent to which foreign sovereigns had become involved in international trade made essential "a practice which will enable persons doing business with them to have their rights determined in the courts." Appendix 2 to this opinion [omitted], *Infra*, at 1870.

In the last 20 years, lower courts have concluded, in light of this Court's decisions in *Ex parte Peru, supra*, and *Mexico v. Hoffman, supra*, and from the Tate letter and the changed international environment, that *Berizzi Bros. Co. v. S.S. Pesaro, supra*, no longer correctly states the law; and they have declined to extend sovereign immunity to foreign sovereigns in cases arising out of purely commercial transactions. [Citations omitted.] Indeed, it is fair to say that the "restrictive theory" of sovereign immunity appears to be generally accepted as the prevailing law in this country. ALI, Restatement (Second), Foreign Relations Law of the United States, § 69 (1965).

Participation by foreign sovereigns in the international commercial market has increased substantially in recent years. [Citation omitted.] The potential injury to private businessmen and ultimately to international trade itself from a system in which some of the participants in the international market are not subject to the rule of law has therefore increased correspondingly. As noted above, courts of other countries have also recently adopted the restrictive theory of sovereign immunity. Of equal importance is the fact that subjecting foreign governments to the rule of law in their commercial dealings presents a much smaller risk of affronting their sovereignty than would an attempt to pass on the legality of their governmental acts In their commercial capacities, foreign governments do not exercise powers peculiar to sovereigns. Instead, they exercise only those powers that can also be exercised by private citizens. . . .

There may be little codification or consensus as to the rules of international law concerning exercises of Governmental powers, including military powers and expropriations, within a sovereign state's borders affecting the property or persons of aliens. However, more discernible rules of international law have emerged with regard to the commercial dealings of private parties in the international market. The restrictive approach to sovereign immunity suggests that these established rules should be applied to the commercial transactions of sovereign states.

Of course, sovereign immunity has not been pleaded in this case; but it is beyond cavil that part of the foreign relations law recognized by the United States is that the commercial obligations of a foreign government may be adjudicated in those courts otherwise having jurisdiction to enter such judgments. Nothing in our national policy calls on us to recognize as an act of state a repudiation by Cuba of an obligation adjudicated in our courts and arising out of the operation of a commercial business by one of its instrumentalities. For all the reasons which led the Executive Branch to adopt the restrictive theory of sovereign immunity, we hold that the mere assertion of sovereignty as a defense to a claim arising out of purely commercial acts by a foreign sovereign is no more effective if given the label "Act of State" than if it is given the label "sovereign immunity." Describing the act of state doctrine in the past we have said that it "precludes the courts of this country from inquiring into the validity of the Public acts a recognized foreign sovereign power committed within its own territory." *Banco Nacional de Cuba v. Sabbatino, supra*, 376 U.S., at 401 (emphasis added), and that it applies to "acts done within their own States, in the exercise of Governmental authority." *Underhill v. Hernandez*, 168 U.S., at 252 (emphasis added). We decline to extend the act of state doctrine to acts committed by foreign sovereigns in the course of their purely commercial operations. Because the act relied on by respondents in this case was an act arising out of the conduct by Cuba's agents in the operation of cigar businesses for profit, the act was not an act of state.

Reversed.

Mr. Justice Stevens, concurring.

For reasons stated in Parts I and II of the Court's opinion, I agree that the act of state doctrine does not bar the entry of the judgment in favor of Dunhill.

Mr. Justice Powell, concurring.

I join the opinion of the Court. Since the line between commercial and political acts of a foreign state often will be difficult to delineate, I write to reaffirm my view that even in cases deemed to involve purely political acts, it is the duty of the judiciary to decide for itself whether deference to the political branches of Government requires abstention. As I stated in *First Nat. City Bank v. Banco Nacional de Cuba*, 406 U.S. 759, 775–776 (1972) (concurring in judgment):

"Unless it appears that an exercise of jurisdiction would interfere with delicate foreign relations conducted by the political branches, I conclude that federal courts have an obligation to hear cases such as this."

Just as I saw no circumstances requiring judicial abstention in that case, I see none here. Nor can I foresee any in cases involving only the commercial acts of a foreign state.

MR. JUSTICE MARSHALL, with whom MR. JUSTICE BRENNAN, MR. JUSTICE STEWART, and MR. JUSTICE BLACKMUN join, dissenting.

The act of state doctrine commits the courts of this country not to sit in judgment on the acts of a foreign government performed within its own territory. Under any realistic view of the facts of this case, the interventors' retention of and refusal to return funds paid to them by Dunhill constitute an act of state, and no affirmative recovery by Dunhill can rest on the invalidity of that conduct. The Court of Appeals so concluded, and I would affirm its judgment.

I.

As of September 15, 1960, when the Cuban Government "intervened," or nationalized, five Cuban-owned cigar manufacturers, petitioner Dunhill had received some $148,600 worth of cigars for which it had not yet paid. In the period between intervention and February 1961, Dunhill took delivery of an additional $93,000 worth of shipments. Both the District Court and the Court of Appeals concluded that the intervention was to be given full legal effect with respect to the property of Cuban nationals located in Cuba, and that the interventors were therefore entitled to payment for postintervention shipments. [Citations omitted.] It is quite clear that that result was correct, and that it would have been no different had the intervened firms been owned by United States citizens. [Citation omitted.]

Since the date of intervention, the interventors have taken the position that they were also entitled to receive the amounts due to the intervened firms for preintervention shipments in the case of Dunhill, $148,600. And throughout this litigation, respondents, the interventors and the Republic of Cuba, have insisted that the act of state doctrine requires our courts to give full legal effect to the intervention decree insofar as it purported to nationalize the accounts receivable of the intervened firms. Both the District Court and the Court of Appeals held, however, that the accounts receivable involved here had their situs in New York, that the act of state doctrine did not apply, and that the attempted confiscation was ineffective. [Citations omitted.] In a separate petition for certiorari, which the Court today denies, and in the course of its presentation in this case, respondents have pursued their contention that the initial intervention should be recognized as having reached the preintervention accounts receivable. But that is not the respondents' sole contention, and it is not necessary for us to consider it here. For, as the Court of Appeals recognized, the act of state question took on a wholly different light when Dunhill paid the amount due for preintervention shipments to the interventors in Cuba.

The court of Appeals held that Dunhill's claim for return of the monies paid to the interventors for preintervention shipments sounds in quasi-contract; it arises, the court observed, not from Dunhill's contractual obligation to the owners, which is situated in New York, but from the interventors' receipt, appropriation, and refusal to return the funds, all of which have occurred apart from the contract and in Cuba. If the interventors' course of conduct is itself an act of state, therefore, there can be no doubt that the act of state doctrine applies.

The interventors have not taken any discrete, overt action for which to claim the status of an act of state. Rather, they have received and long retained the money paid to them for preintervention shipments, and they have ignored Dunhill's demands for its return. The Court declines to view this course of conduct as reflecting an exercise of sovereign power to retain the funds at issue after they arrived in Cuba, ...

I do not understand the Court to suggest, however, that the act of state doctrine can be triggered only by a "statute, decree, order, or resolution" of a foreign government, or that the presence of an act of state can only be demonstrated by some affirmative action by the foreign sovereign. While it is true that an act of state generally takes the form of an executive or legislative step formalized in a decree or measure [citations omitted], that is only because duly constituted governments generally act through formal means. When they do not, their acts are no less the acts of a state, and the doctrine, being a practical one, is no less applicable. Thus, in *Underhill v. Hernandez*, 168 U.S. 250 (1897), where the plaintiff sought recovery for his detention in Venezuela by reason of the then revolutionary forces' refusal to grant him a passport out of Ciudad Bolivar, the Court held that the act of state doctrine "must necessarily extend to the agents of governments ruling by paramount force as [a] matter of fact." *Id.*, at 252. The cases of *Oetjen v. Central Leather Co.*, 246 U.S. 297 (1918), and *Ricaud v. American Metal Co.*, 246 U.S. 304 (1918), are further illustrations of the practical approach the Court has always taken in determining whether an act of state is present. In each case the plaintiff claimed title to goods purchased from Mexican sellers but confiscated by generals of the Constitutionalist Carranza forces before delivery to the plaintiffs. The Generals, Villa and Pereyra respectively, had sold the goods to intermediate purchasers for the furtherance of the revolution, and the goods thereafter came into the United States in the possession of the defendant-assignees. The Court held that the seizures in question must be viewed as the action, in time of civil war, of a duly commissioned agent of the prevailing Mexican Government, and could not be subjected to the scrutiny of another sovereign's courts.

These cases demonstrate not only that an act of state need not be formalized in any particular manner, but also that it need not take the form of active, rather than passive, conduct. . . .

That a foreign sovereign has issued no formal decree and performed no "affirmative" act is not fatal, then, to an act of state claim. If the foreign state has exercised a sovereign power either to act or to refrain from acting there is an act of state. In a case very similar to this one, the New York Court of Appeals held that the Cuban bank's dishonoring of tax exemption certificates, the redemption of which had been suspended by a decision of the Cuban Currency Stablization Fund, was an act of state. *French v. Banco Nacional de Cuba*, 23 N.Y.2d 46, 295 N.Y.S.2d 433, 452,

242 N.E.2d 704, 717, (1968). The act of state, the court wrote, "was the defendant's refusal to perform; the currency regulations, though equally the product of an act of state, were simply the justification for the refusal."

. . . .

. . . [I]n the present case it is settled that the interventors received the payments for preintervention shipments on behalf of the *Cuban Government, Menendez v. Faber, Coe & Gregg, Inc.*, 345 F.Supp., at 532, and any lingering doubt that their retention was by virtue of a claim of right was dispelled by counsel for Cuba and the interventors at trial. Had possession been established in *The Navemar*, and the decree of appropriation been in doubt, the case would be in point, but in fact the contrary was true and the case is inapposite. It was in response to the suggestion that *The Navemar* case controlled this one that counsel for respondents made the statement, relied upon by the Court, *Ante*, at 1860 n. 8: "The statement of an ambassador, like the statement of a lawyer, is not proof of anything. It is merely an assertion made by the representative of a sovereign as to the position taken by that sovereign in litigation." Brief for Respondents 17 n. 8. In this case, unlike in *The Navemar* case, it is precisely the position of the foreign sovereign with respect to property in its possession that is significant.

II.

Mr. Justice White advances a contention, not adopted by the Court, that even if the Cuban Government "had purported to exercise sovereign power to confiscate" the monies at issue, . . . the act of state doctrine is inapplicable because of the "purely commercial" nature of the confiscation. While I am prompted to make several observations on the suggested rationale for a broad "commercial act" exception to the act of state doctrine, ultimately there is no need to consider whether, and under what circumstances, an exception for commercial acts might be appropriate. It will suffice to say that no such exception is appropriate in this case.

A

I note at the outset that the commercial act exception to the act of state doctrine is supported by the Department of State. In its most recent *Bernstein* letter, the Department has expressed the opinion that the conduct of foreign policy would suffer no embarrassment if the Court declined to apply the act of state doctrine to this case, if it declined to apply the doctrine to commercial cases in general, or, indeed, if it overruled *Banco Nacional de Cuba v. Sabbatino*, 376 U.S. 398 (1964). Mr. Justice White quite properly does not rely specifically upon the views of the Department; six Members of the Court in *First Nat. City Bank v. Banco Nacional de Cuba*, 406 U.S. 759 (1972) (hereinafter *Citibank*), disapproved finally the so-called Bernstein exception to the act of state doctrine, thus minimizing the significance of any letter from the Department of State (Douglas, J., concurring in result); *Ibid.* (Powell, J., concurring in judgment); *Id.*, at 776–777 (Brennan, J., dissenting). Whether the act of state question in this case is viewed as being confined to a single dispute or as extending to a broad class of disputes, the task of defining the role of the Judiciary is for this Court, not the Executive Branch.

B

In concluding that the act of state doctrine should not apply to the purely commercial acts of sovereign nations, Mr. Justice White relies heavily upon the widespread acceptance of the "restrictive theory" of sovereign immunity, which declines to extend immunity to foreign governments acting in a "private," or commercial, capacity. The restrictive theory of sovereign immunity has not been adopted by this Court, but even if we assume that it is the law in this country, it does not follow that there should be a commercial act exception to the act of state doctrine.

It is true, of course, that a particular litigant's claim may be as effectively defeated by application of the act of state doctrine as by a foreign government's invocation of sovereign immunity. But the doctrines of sovereign immunity and act of state, while related, differ fundamentally in their focus and in their operation. Sovereign immunity accords a defendant exemption from suit by virtue of its status. By contrast, the act of state doctrine exempts no one from the process of the court. Equally applicable whether a sovereign nation is a party or not, the act of state doctrine merely tells a court what law to apply to a case; it "concerns the limits for determining the validity of an otherwise applicable rule of law." In the absence of "unambiguous agreement regarding controlling . . . principles" of international law, Id., at 428, the act of state doctrine commands that the acts of a sovereign nation committed in its own territory be accorded presumptive validity.

The act of state doctrine, " 'although it shares with the immunity doctrine a respect for sovereign states,' serves important policies entirely independent of that rule." *Citibank, supra,* 406 U.S., at 795. (Brennan, J., dissenting), quoting *Sabbatino, supra,* 376 U.S., at 438. The act of state doctrine is not mandated by the text of the Constitution, but it does have " 'constitutional' underpinnings." *Sabbatino, supra,* 376 U.S., at 423.

> "It arises out of the basic relationships between branches of government in a system of separation of powers. It concerns the competency of dissimilar institutions to make and implement particular kinds of decisions in the area of international relations. The doctrine as formulated in past decisions expresses the strong sense of the Judicial Branch that its engagement in the task of passing on the validity of foreign acts of state may hinder rather than further this country's pursuit of goals both for itself and for the community of nations as a whole in the international sphere." *Ibid.*

As Mr. Justice Brennan has observed, the act of state doctrine reflects the notion that the validity of an act of a foreign sovereign is, under some circumstances, a "political question" not cognizable in our courts. The circumstances indicating the existence of a "political question" in Sabbatino included, as Mr. Justice Brennan summarized, "the absence of consensus on the applicable international rules, the unavailability of standards from a treaty or other agreement, the existence and recognition of the Cuban Government, the sensitivity of the issues to national concerns, and the power of the Executive alone to effect a fair remedy for all United States citizens who have been harmed." *Citibank, supra,* 406 U.S., at 788, 92 S. Ct., at 1823, 32 L. Ed. 2d, at 494; see *Sabbatino, supra,* 376 U.S., at 427–437.

The doctrine of sovereign immunity, concerned only with the status of a party to a lawsuit, does not focus on the other circumstances just mentioned; it is simply not designed to be responsive to the particular considerations underlying the act of state doctrine. Whatever exceptions there may be to sovereign immunity ought not be transferred automatically, therefore, to the act of state doctrine.

C

I question the wisdom of attempting the articulation of any broad exception to the act of state doctrine within the confines of a single case. The Court in *Sabbatino*, aware of the variety of situations presenting act of state questions and the complexity of the relevant considerations, eschewed any inflexible rule in favor of a case-by-case approach. [Citation omitted.] The carving out of broad exceptions to the doctrine is fundamentally at odds with the careful case-by-case approach adopted in *Sabbatino*.

Indeed, it is difficult to discern the precise scope of the "commercial act" exception contemplated by Mr. Justice WHITE. In the final analysis, however, it is unnecessary to consider whether the exception would be responsive to the concerns underlying the act of state doctrine in every case to which it might apply. If the exception covers this case, it is unresponsive.

Cuba's retention of and refusal to repay the funds at issue in this case took place against the background of the intervention, or nationalization, of the businesses and assets of five cigar manufacturers. As I have already indicated, the seizure and retention of the Dunhill funds were pursuant to the initial intervention decree. For all practical purposes, the seizure of the funds once they arrived in Cuba is indistinguishable from the seizure of the remainder of the cigar manufacturers' businesses. The seizure of the funds, like the initial seizures on September 15, reflected a purpose to exert sovereign power to its territorial limits in order to effectuate the intervention of ongoing cigar manufacturing businesses. It matters not that the funds have been determined by a United States court in this case to have belonged to Dunhill rather than the cigar manufacturers. What does matter is that Cuba retained the money in the course of its program of expropriating what it viewed as part and parcel of the businesses.

The applicability of the act of state doctrine in these circumstances is controlled by *Sabbatino* itself. As the Court there noted: "There are few if any issues in international law today on which opinion seems to be so divided as the limitation on a state's power to expropriate the property of aliens." 376 U.S., at 428. Indeed, the absence of any suggestion that Cuba's intervention program was discriminatory against United States citizens renders the lack of consensus as to applicable principles of law even more apparent here than in *Sabbatino*. See *Citibank*, 406 U.S., at 785 (Brennan, J., dissenting). And unless one takes the position that the amount of money or the value of property seized materially affects the sensitivity of the issues, we are guided in this case by the following observation in *Sabbatino*:

> "It is difficult to imagine the courts of this country embarking on adjudication in an area which touches more sensitively the practical and

ideological goals of the various members of the community of nations." 376 U.S., at 430, 84 S.Ct., at 941, 11 L.Ed.2d, at 825. (footnote omitted [in opinion]).

Regardless, then, of whether the presence of consensus as to controlling legal principles, or any other circumstances, would render the act of state doctrine inapplicable to some, or even most, acts that could be characterized as "purely commercial," the doctrine is fully applicable in this case.

III.

Since in my view the retention of and refusal to repay the funds at issue constitute an act of state that would ordinarily preclude an affirmative judgment against Cuba and the interventors, it is necessary for me to proceed to the second question on which we granted certiorari whether Dunhill may nonetheless secure an affirmative judgment in the peculiar circumstances of this case.

A

A brief recapitulation of the facts is necessary to understand Dunhill's contention that it is entitled to an affirmative recovery in spite of the presence of an act of state. Dunhill was one of three importers that had at the time of the intervention received cigars for which it had not yet paid. During the three months following intervention, each of the importers paid the interventors the amounts due for preintervention shipments. And in the period between intervention and February 1961, each of the importers took delivery of additional shipments, for which payment was not made.

This suit stems from nine suits brought against the importers by the former owners of the five intervened firms, Inter alia, to restrain payment to anyone else for goods manufactured by their firms or bearing their mark, and to recover for all such goods that the importers had already received. The interventors brought suit in the names of the intervened firms to enjoin the former owners' counsel from pursuing the nine actions in the firms' names, and to substitute their own attorneys for those of the former owners in the same nine suits. The District Court ruled as a preliminary matter that the interventors and not the former owners were entitled to sue for payment for the post-intervention shipments. [Citations omitted.] The original nine actions were then consolidated for trial, with the interventors pursuing their claim for payments for postintervention shipments, and both the former owners and the interventors pursuing their claims to the payments for preintervention shipments.

The district Court concluded that the former owners, not the interventors, were entitled to payment for preintervention shipments. Under its view that the interventors' refusal to return the monies paid for preintervention shipments did not involve an act of state, the District Court set off that amount ($477,000) against the amount owed by the importers to the interventors for postintervention shipments ($700,000). [Citation omitted.] Alone among the importers, Dunhill had paid the interventors more for preintervention shipments ($148,000) than it owed for postintervention shipments ($93,000). Accordingly the District Court directed that an "affirmative judgment" be entered in Dunhill's favor.

The Court of Appeals found an act of state in Cuba's retention of the monies paid for preintervention shipments. It interpreted the various views expressed in Citibank as indicating that this Court would nevertheless uphold the importers' counterclaims up to the limits of the respective claims asserted against them by the interventors. But the court reversed the judgment of the District Court insofar as it granted Dunhill affirmative recovery. [Citation omitted.] The second question on which we granted certiorari is whether, if Cuba's conduct constitutes an act of state, Dunhill may nonetheless assert its full counterclaim in the circumstances of this case, where the counterclaim exceeds Cuba's claim against it but is less than the amount owed to Cuba by the importers as a group.

B

The Court in *Citibankc* held that the act of state doctrine does not necessarily bar defendant from litigating the merits of a limited counterclaim against a foreign state suing in the courts of this country. Petitioner there was an American bank whose branches in Cuba had been nationalized. The bank responded by selling the collateral securing its loan of $10 million to the respondent Banco Nacional de Cuba, an instrumentality of the state. Banco Nacional then sued for the excess proceeds realized from the sale, and First National counterclaimed for an equal amount in damages resulting from the expropriation of its property. For various reasons asserted in three separate opinions, a bare majority of the Court allowed prosecution of the counterclaim, limited as it was to the amount recoverable against First National.

Because we are concerned here only with the status of a counterclaim in excess of a foreign state's principal claim, the precise question the Court addressed in *Citibank* whether a counterclaim limited by the amount of the foreign state's claim may be barred by the act of state doctrine does not cover the present situation. The approach adopted in Mr. Justice Brennan's dissent in *Citibank*, which would have barred a counterclaim limited by the amount of a foreign state's claim, would be sufficient, A fortiori, to bar Dunhill's excessive counterclaim. But even putting that approach aside, the judgment of the Court of Appeals denying affirmative relief to Dunhill should be affirmed.

An affirmative judgment for the excess of a counterclaim over a foreign state's principal claim is indistinguishable in any important respect from an ordinary affirmative judgment. In this case, the situation is precisely as it would be if Cuba had voluntarily recognized the validity of Dunhill's claim in an amount equal to its own, the parties had agreed extrajudicially to consider the claims as canceling each other out pro tanto, and Dunhill had then sued Cuba for the unsettled remainder of its claim. The courts would then be presented with an unadorned suit against a foreign sovereign, barred by the act of state doctrine. But an affirmative judgment offends the policy of judicial abstention from interference in international relations to an equal degree, whether it is founded upon a naked suit against a foreign state or an excessive counterclaim.

Dunhill contends, however, that the nature of the act of state question is affected by the fortuity that its counterclaim, while exceeding Cuba's principal claim against it, is for a lesser amount than the sum of the judgments entered in favor of Cuba against the three importers whose cases were consolidated for trial. This contention suffers from two fatal flaws.

First, the actions against Dunhill and the other importers were not merged; they were simply consolidated for trial in the interest of economy. The interventors, as substituted plaintiffs in the actions originally filed by the owners, asserted separate causes of action against each importer; no single transaction involved or gave rise to a claim against more than one importer. The actions thus did not lose their separate identities because of the consolidation. In these circumstances, a ruling allowing for a counterclaim on the theory that it does not exceed the foreign state's total judgments against those parties that happen to be before the District Court would be capricious indeed. The limitation on counterclaims would then be determined by the presence or absence of actions suitable for consolidation at a particular time in a particular court, and upon their outcomes.

. . . .

IV.

In conclusion, I would hold that the course of conduct undertaken by the interventors with respect to payments made for preintervention shipments constitutes an act of state, and that Dunhill is not entitled to an affirmative judgment on its counterclaim relating to those payments. I would affirm the judgment of the Court of Appeals.

PROBLEM AND QUESTIONS

Malidi Moherdi, the widow of Mohan Moherdi, the textile magnate and one of the wealthiest citizens of Kaldik, inherited from her husband a world-renowned collection of modern western art that he had acquired over the course of his very successful career. Several months ago, the Revolutionary Government of Kaldik, which came into power just before Mohan died, issued a decree confiscating the entire collection and transferring ownership to Kaldik's National Museum. At the time the decree went into effect, several of the paintings were on temporary loan for a special exhibition at the Art Institute of Chicago. Malidi has attached the paintings and brought an *in rem* action in the federal district court in Chicago for a declaratory judgment to affirm her ownership. The Kaldik National Museum almost immediately filed a counter petition in each suit for return of the paintings.

1. In your view, would the federal court in Chicago have and exercise adjudicatory jurisdiction? What arguments would you anticipate each petitioner making?

2. Would your answer differ in any of the following cases:

(a) Instead of confiscation, the legal action taken by the Kaldik Government had been a revision of the country's succession

> (inheritance) law (of Book Four of the Kaldik Civil Code) disqualifying women as successors. As a result Mohan's brother has inherited the collection, and he has brought the counterclaim asserting his ownership and seeking return of the paintings. (Would you answer differ if you learned that Mohan's brother's wife is the sister of the Revolutionary Republic of Kaldik's new Supreme Leader?)
>
> (b) The collection was indeed confiscated, as described above, but the seizure was justified under a statute outlawing and allowing seizure and destruction of "decadent" art. All paintings seized were destroyed in a public bonfire. The only ones that remain are those on loan to the Chicago Art Institute. Malidi Moherdi has also combined with the *in rem* action an *in personam* claim against Kaldik of monetary damages.

INTERNATIONAL ASSOCIATION OF MACHINISTS AND AEROSPACE WORKERS (IAM) v. THE ORGANIZATION OF THE PETROLEUM EXPORTING COUNTRIES (OPEC)[*]
649 F.2d 1354 (9th Cir. 1981), *cert. denied*, 454 U.S. 1163 (1982)

CHOY, CIRCUIT JUDGE:

I. Introduction

The members of the International Association of Machinists and Aerospace Workers (IAM) were disturbed by the high price of oil and petroleum-derived products in the United States. They believed the actions of the Organization of the Petroleum Exporting Countries, popularly known as OPEC, were the cause of this burden on the American public. Accordingly, IAM sued OPEC and its member nations in December of 1978, alleging that their price-setting activities violated United States anti-trust laws. IAM sought injunctive relief and damages. The district court entered a final judgment in favor of the defendants, holding that it lacked jurisdiction and that IAM had no valid anti-trust claim. We affirm the judgment of the district court on the alternate ground that, under the act of state doctrine, exercise of federal court jurisdiction in this case would be improper.

II. Factual Background

IAM is a non-profit labor association. Its members work in petroleum-using industries, and like most Americans, they are consumers of gasoline and other petroleum-derived products. They object to the high and rising cost of such products.

OPEC is an organization of the petroleum-producing and exporting nations of what is sometimes referred to as the Third World. The OPEC nations have organized to obtain the greatest possible economic returns for a special resource

---

[*] Footnotes omitted.

which they hope will remove them from the ranks of the underdeveloped and the poverty-plagued. OPEC was formed in 1960 by the defendants Iran, Iraq, Kuwait, Saudi Arabia, and Venezuela. The other defendants, Algeria, Ecuador, Gabon, Indonesia, Libya, Nigeria, Qatar, and the United Arab Emirates, joined thereafter.

The OPEC nations produce and export oil either through government-owned companies or through government participation in private companies. Prior to the formation of OPEC, these diverse and sometimes antagonistic countries were plagued with fluctuating oil prices. Without coordination among them, oil was often in oversupply on the world market resulting in low prices. The OPEC nations realized that self-interest dictated that they "formulate a system to ensure the stabilisation (sic) of prices by, among other means, the regulation of production, with due regard to the interests of the producing and of the consuming nations, and to the necessity of securing a steady income to the producing countries, an efficient economic and regular supply of this source of energy to consuming nations" OPEC Resolution of the First Conference, Resolution 1.1(3), September 1960.

OPEC achieves its goals by a system of production limits and royalties which its members unanimously adopt. There is no enforcement arm of OPEC. The force behind OPEC decrees is the collective self-interest of the 13 nations.

After formation of OPEC, it is alleged, the price of crude oil increased tenfold and more. Whether or not a causal relation exists, there is no doubt that the price of oil has risen dramatically in recent years, and that this has become of international concern.

Supporters of OPEC argue that its actions result in fair world prices for oil, and allow OPEC members to achieve a measure of economic and political independence. Without OPEC, they say, in the rush to the marketplace these nations would rapidly deplete their only valuable resource for ridiculously low prices.

Detractors accuse OPEC of price-fixing and worse in its deliberate manipulation of the world market and withholding of a resource which many world citizens have not learned to do without.

In December 1978, IAM brought suit against OPEC and its member nations. IAM's complaint alleged price fixing in violation of the Sherman Act, 15 U.S.C. § 1, and requested treble damages and injunctive relief under the Clayton Act, 15 U.S.C. §§ 15, 16. IAM claimed a deliberate targeting and victimization of the United States market, directly resulting in higher prices for Americans.

The defendants refused to recognize the jurisdiction of the district court, and they did not appear in the proceedings below. Their cause was argued by various amici, with additional information provided by court-appointed experts. The district court ordered a full hearing, noting that the Foreign Sovereign Immunities Act (FSIA) prohibits the entry of a default judgment against a foreign sovereignty "unless the claimant establishes his claim or right to relief by evidence satisfactory to the court." 28 U.S.C. § 1608(e).

The district court initially dismissed OPEC, the organization, since it had not been properly served. It also determined at an early stage in the proceedings that monetary damages were foreclosed by the indirect-purchaser rule of *Illinois Brick*

Co. v. Illinois, 431 U.S. 720 (1977). Thus the testimony at trial was directed to what remained of the complaint a suit for injunctive relief against the 13 OPEC nations individually.

The testimony was extensive. Experts in economics and international relations were examined and cross-examined. Exhibits, including masses of statistical and technical data, were received. A full day of legal argument concluded the proceedings below.

The record reflects an outstanding effort on the part of the district judge to amass the information necessary to understand the international politics and economy of oil and to marshal the legal arguments for and against IAM's requested relief.

At the close of the trial, the district judge granted judgment in favor of the defendants. The court held, first, that it lacked jurisdiction over the defendant nations under the Foreign Sovereign Immunities Act. The court further held that even if jurisdiction existed in the first instance, the anti-trust action failed because foreign sovereigns are not persons within the meaning of the Sherman Act and because there was no proximate causal connection between OPEC activities and domestic price increases. The court also decided that default judgment could not properly lie against the non-appearing defendants, and that the defendants had not waived their immunity.

III. Discussion

A. Sovereign Immunity

In the international sphere each state is viewed as an independent sovereign, equal in sovereignty to all other states. It is said that an equal holds no power of sovereignty over an equal. Thus the doctrine of sovereign immunity: the courts of one state generally have no jurisdiction to entertain suits against another state. This rule of international law developed by custom among nations. Also by custom, an exception developed for the commercial activities of a state. The former concept of absolute sovereign immunity gave way to a restrictive view. Under the restrictive theory of sovereign immunity, immunity did not exist for commercial activities since they were seen as non sovereign.

In 1976, Congress enacted the FSIA and declared that the federal courts will apply an objective nature-of-the-act test in determining whether activity is commercial and thus not immune: "The commercial character of an activity shall be determined by reference to the nature of the course of conduct or particular transaction or act, rather than by reference to its purpose." 28 U.S.C. § 1603(d).

A critical step in characterizing the nature of a given activity is defining exactly what that activity is. The immunity question may be determined by how broadly or narrowly that activity is defined. In this case, IAM insists on a very narrow focus on the specific activity of "price fixing." IAM argues that the FSIA does not give immunity to this activity. Under the FSIA a commercial activity is one which an individual might "customarily carr(y) on for profit." H.R.Rep.No.94-1487, 94th

Cong., 2d Sess. 16, reprinted in (1976) U.S.Code Cong. & Ad.News 6604, 6615. OPEC's activity, characterized by IAM as making agreements to fix prices, is one which is presumably done for profit; it is thus commercial and immunity does not apply.

The court below defined OPEC's activity in a different way: "[I]t is clear that the nature of the activity engaged in by each of these OPEC member countries is the establishment by a sovereign state of the terms and conditions for the removal of a prime natural resource to wit, crude oil from its territory." 477 F.Supp. at 567. The trial judge reasoned that, according to international law, the development and control of natural resources is a prime governmental function. Id. at 567–78. The opinion cites several resolutions of the United Nations' General Assembly, which the United States supported, and the United States Constitution, Art. 4, § 3, cl. 2, which treat the control of natural resources as governmental acts.

IAM argues that the district court's analysis strays from the path set forth in the FSIA. The control of natural resources is the purpose behind OPEC's actions, but the act complained of here is a conspiracy to fix prices. The FSIA instructs us to look upon the act itself rather than underlying sovereign motivations.

The district court was understandably troubled by the broader implications of an anti-trust action against the OPEC nations. The importance of the alleged price-fixing activity to the OPEC nations cannot be ignored. Oil reforums represent their only significant source of income. Consideration of their sovereignty cannot be separated from their near total dependence upon oil. We find that these concerns are appropriately addressed by application of the act of state doctrine. While we do not apply the doctrine of sovereign immunity, its elements remain relevant to our discussion of the act of state doctrine.

B. The Act of State Doctrine

The act of state doctrine declares that a United States court will not adjudicate a politically sensitive dispute which would require the court to judge the legality of the sovereign act of a foreign state. This doctrine was expressed by the Supreme Court in *Underhill v. Hernandez*, 168 U.S. 250, 252 (1897):

> "Every sovereign State is bound to respect the independence of every other sovereign State, and the courts of one country will not sit in judgment on the acts of the government of another done within its own territory."

The doctrine recognizes the institutional limitations of the courts and the peculiar requirements of successful foreign relations. To participate adeptly in the global community, the United States must speak with one voice and pursue a careful and deliberate foreign policy. The political branches of our government are able to consider the competing economic and political considerations and respond to the public will in order to carry on foreign relations in accordance with the best interests of the country as a whole. The courts, in contrast, focus on single disputes and make decisions on the basis of legal principles. The timing of our decisions is largely a result of our caseload and of the random tactical considerations which motivate parties to bring lawsuits and to seek delay or expedition. When the courts engage in piecemeal adjudication of the legality of the sovereign acts of states, they risk disruption of our country's international diplomacy. The executive may utilize protocol, economic sanction, compromise, delay, and persuasion to achieve international objectives. Ill-timed judicial decisions challenging the acts of foreign states could nullify these tools and embarrass the United States in the eyes of the world.

The act of state doctrine is similar to the political question doctrine in domestic law. It requires that the courts defer to the legislative and executive branches when those branches are better equipped to resolve a politically sensitive question. Like the political question doctrine, its applicability is not subject to clear definition. The courts balance various factors to determine whether the doctrine should apply.

While the act of state doctrine has no explicit source in our Constitution or statutes, it does have "constitutional underpinnings." *Banco Nacional de Cuba v. Sabbatino*, 376 U.S. 398, 423 (1964). The Supreme Court has stated that the act of state doctrine arises out of the basic relationships between branches of government in a system of separation of powers The doctrine as formulated in past decisions expresses the strong sense of the Judicial Branch that its engagement in the task of passing on the validity of foreign acts of state may hinder rather than further this country's pursuit of goals both for itself and for the community of nations as a whole in the international sphere. Id.

The principle of separation of powers is central to our form of democratic government. Just as the courts have carefully guarded their primary role as interpreters of the Constitution and the laws of the United States, so have they recognized the primary role of the President and Congress in resolution of political conflict and the adoption of foreign policy. [Citations omitted.]

The doctrine of sovereign immunity is similar to the act of state doctrine in that it also represents the need to respect the sovereignty of foreign states. The two doctrines differ, however, in significant respects. The law of sovereign immunity goes to the jurisdiction of the court. The act of state doctrine is not jurisdictional. *Ricaud v. American Metal Co.*, 246 U.S. 304, 309 (1918). Rather, it is a prudential doctrine designed to avoid judicial action in sensitive areas. Sovereign immunity is a principle of international law, recognized in the United States by statute. It is the states themselves, as defendants, who may claim sovereign immunity. The act of state doctrine is a domestic legal principle, arising from the peculiar role of American courts. It recognizes not only the sovereignty of foreign states, but also the spheres of power of the co equal branches of our government. Thus a private litigant may raise the act of state doctrine, even when no sovereign state is a party to the action. See, e. g., *Timberlane Lumber Co. v. Bank of America*, 549 F.2d 597, 606 (9th Cir. 1976). The act of state doctrine is apposite whenever the federal courts must question the legality of the sovereign acts of foreign states.

It has been suggested that the FSIA supersedes the act of state doctrine, or that the amorphous doctrine is limited by modern jurisprudence. We disagree.

Congress in enacting the FSIA recognized the distinction between sovereign immunity and the act of state doctrine. See, e. g., H.R.Rep.No.94-1487, 94th Cong., 2d Sess. 20 n.1, reprinted in (1976) U.S. Code Cong. & Ad. News 6619 n.1 ("The Committee has found it unnecessary to address the act of state doctrine in this legislation"); see generally Jurisdiction of U.S. Courts in Suits Against Foreign

States: Hearings on H.R.11315 Before the Subcomm. on Admin. Law and Governmental Relations of the House Comm. on the Judiciary, 94th Cong., 2d Sess.29-57 (1976); Immunities of Foreign States: Hearings on H.R.3493 Before the Subcomm. on Claims & Governmental Relations of the Committee on the Judiciary, 93d Cong., first Sess. 20 (1973) (the FSIA "in no way affects existing law concerning the extent to which the 'act of state' doctrine may be applicable in similar circumstances"). Indeed, because the act of state doctrine addresses concerns central to our system of government, the doctrine must necessarily remain a part of our jurisprudence unless and until such time as a radical change in the role of the courts occurs.

The act of state doctrine is not diluted by the commercial activity exception which limits the doctrine of sovereign immunity. While purely commercial activity may not rise to the level of an act of state, certain seemingly commercial activity will trigger act of state considerations. As the district court noted, OPEC's "price-fixing" activity has a significant sovereign component. While the FSIA ignores the underlying purpose of a state's action, the act of state doctrine does not. This court has stated that the motivations of the sovereign must be examined for a public interest basis. *Timberlane*, 549 F.2d at 607. When the state qua state acts in the public interest, its sovereignty is asserted. The courts must proceed cautiously to avoid an affront to that sovereignty. Because the act of state doctrine and the doctrine of sovereign immunity address different concerns and apply in different circumstances, we find that the act of state doctrine remains available when such caution is appropriate, regardless of any commercial component of the activity involved.

In addition to the public interest factor, a federal court must heed other indications which call for act of state deference. The doctrine does not suggest a rigid rule of application. In the *Sabbatino* case, the Supreme Court suggested a balancing approach:

> "some aspects of international law touch much more sharply on national nerves than do others; the less important the implications of an issue are for our foreign relations, the weaker the justification for exclusivity in the political branches." 376 U.S. at 428, 84 S.Ct. at 940.

The decision to deny access to judicial relief is not one we make lightly. In *Timberlane Lumber Co. v. Bank of America*, 549 F.2d 597, 606 (9th Cir. 1976), this court noted that "not every case is identical in its potential impact on our relations with other nations." The "touchstone" or "crucial element" is the potential for interference with our foreign relations. *Timberlane*, 549 F.2d at 607. This court has stated:

> "We do not wish to challenge the sovereignty of another nation, the wisdom of its policy, or the integrity and motivation of its action. On the other hand, repeating the terms of Sabbatino, "the less important the implications of an issue are for our foreign relations, the weaker the justification for exclusivity in the political branches." *Id.* (Citations omitted [in opinion].)

There is no question that the availability of oil has become a significant factor in international relations. The growing world energy crisis has been judicially recognized in other cases. See, e.g., *Occidental of UMM al Qaywayn, Inc. v. A*

Certain Cargo of Petroleum, 577 F.2d 1196 (5th Cir. 1978), *cert. denied*, 442 U.S. 928 (1979) (dismissing an action to determine rights to oil in the Persian Gulf as raising a nonjusticiable political question); *Hunt v. Mobil Oil Corp.*, 550 F.2d 68, 78 (2d Cir.) *cert. denied*, 434 U.S. 984 (1977) (affirming, on the basis of the act of state doctrine, dismissal of anti-trust claim where the act complained of was part of "a continuing and broadened confrontation between the East and West in an oil crisis which has implications and complications far transcending those suggested by appellants"). The record in this case contains extensive documentation of the involvement of our executive and legislative branches with the oil question. IAM does not dispute that the United States has a grave interest in the petro-politics of the Middle East, or that the foreign policy arms of the executive and legislative branches are intimately involved in this sensitive area. It is clear that OPEC and its activities are carefully considered in the formulation of American foreign policy.

The remedy IAM seeks is an injunction against the OPEC nations. The possibility of insult to the OPEC states and of interference with the efforts of the political branches to seek favorable relations with them is apparent from the very nature of this action and the remedy sought. While the case is formulated as an anti-trust action, the granting of any relief would in effect amount to an order from a domestic court instructing a foreign sovereign to alter its chosen means of allocating and profiting from its own valuable natural resources. On the other hand, should the court hold that OPEC's actions are legal, this "would greatly strengthen the bargaining hand" of the OPEC nations in the event that Congress or the executive chooses to condemn OPEC's actions. *Sabbatino*, 376 U.S. at 432.

A further consideration is the availability of internationally-accepted legal principles which would render the issues appropriate for judicial disposition. As the Supreme Court stated in *Sabbatino*, "It should be apparent that the greater the degree of codification or consensus concerning a particular area of international law, the more appropriate it is for the judiciary to render decisions regarding it, since the courts can then focus on the application of an agreed principle to circumstances of fact rather than on the sensitive task of establishing a principle not inconsistent with the national interest or with international justice." 376 U.S. at 428.

While conspiracies in restraint of trade are clearly illegal under domestic law, the record reveals no international consensus condemning cartels, royalties, and production agreements. The United States and other nations have supported the principle of supreme state sovereignty over natural resources. The OPEC nations themselves obviously will not agree that their actions are illegal. We are reluctant to allow judicial interference in an area so void of international consensus. An injunction against OPEC's alleged price-fixing activity would require condemnation of a cartel system which the community of nations has thus far been unwilling to denounce. The admonition in *Sabbatino* that the courts should consider the degree of codification and consensus in the area of law is another indication that judicial action is inappropriate here.

The district court was understandably reluctant to proceed on the complaint below and the act of state doctrine provides sound jurisprudential support for such reluctance. While the act of state doctrine does not compel dismissal as a matter of course, in a case such as this where the controlling issue is the legality of a sovereign act and where the only remedy sought is barred by act of state considerations dismissal is appropriate.

IV. Conclusion

The act of state doctrine is applicable in this case. The courts should not enter at the will of litigants into a delicate area of foreign policy which the executive and legislative branches have chosen to approach with restraint. The issue of whether the FSIA allows jurisdiction in this case need not be decided, since a judicial remedy is inappropriate regardless of whether jurisdiction exists. Similarly, we need not reach the issues regarding the indirect-purchaser rule, the extra-territorial application of the Sherman Act, the definition of "person" under the Sherman Act, and the propriety of injunctive relief.

The decision of the district court dismissing this action is AFFIRMED.

QUESTIONS

Is the *Dunhill* case, which Judge Choy does not cite, at all relevant to the case? In what respects did the Ninth Circuit determine that OPEC's activities were not "commercial" for purposes of foreign sovereign immunity? How relevant is the economic importance of the production and sale of petroleum to OPEC's member states in contrast to the production of sugar and tobacco to Cuba?

In 1990 in *W.S. Kirkpatrick & Co., Inc. v. Environmental Tectonics Corp., International*, 493 U.S. 400 (1990), the Supreme Court revisited the question of the applicability of the act of state doctrine in the context of a damage action brought by an unsuccessful bidder for a government construction contract in Nigeria. The complainant alleged that the defendant had obtained the contract by bribing Nigerian officials in violation of federal and state laws. The District Court granted summary judgment for the defendants on the grounds that the act of state doctrine barred judicial examination of the motivation for the government contract — an official act — and such inquiry could embarrass the executive branch and interfere with the conduct of foreign affairs. Finding that no such embarrassment would be likely to occur, the Court of Appeals for the Third Circuit reversed. The Supreme Court affirmed. Writing for a unanimous court, Justice Scalia further elaborated on the act of state doctrine and its application:

> This Court's description of the jurisprudential foundation for the act of state doctrine has undergone some evolution over the years. We once viewed the doctrine as an expression of international law, resting upon "he highest considerations of international comity and expediency," *Oetjen v. Central Leather Co.*, 246 U.S. 297, 303–304 (1918). We have more recently described it, however, as a consequence of domestic separation of powers, reflecting "the strong sense of the Judicial Branch that its engagement in the task of passing on the validity of foreign acts of state may hinder" the

conduct of foreign affairs, *Banco Nacional de Cuba v. Sabbatino*, 376 U.S. 398, 423 (1964). Some Justices have suggested possible exceptions to application of the doctrine, where one or both of the foregoing policies would seemingly not be served: an exception, for example, for acts of state that consist of commercial transactions, since neither modern international comity nor the current position of our Executive Branch accorded sovereign immunity to such acts, see *Alfred Dunhill of London, Inc. v. Republic of Cuba*, 425 U.S. 682, 695–706 (1976) (opinion of WHITE, J.); or an exception for cases in which the Executive Branch has represented that it has no objection to denying validity to the foreign sovereign act, since then the courts would be impeding no foreign policy goals, see *First National City Bank v. Banco Nacional de Cuba*, 406 U.S. 759, 768–770 (1972) (opinion of REHNQUIST, J.).

. . . .

In every case in which we have held the act of state doctrine applicable, the relief sought or the defense interposed would have required a court in the United States to declare invalid the official act of a foreign sovereign performed within its own territory.

. . . .

The short of the matter is this: Courts in the United States have the power, and ordinarily the obligation, to decide cases and controversies properly presented to them. The act of state doctrine does not establish an exception for cases and controversies that may embarrass foreign governments, but merely requires that, in the process of deciding, the acts of foreign sovereigns taken within their own jurisdictions shall be deemed valid. That doctrine has no application to the present case because the validity of no foreign sovereign act is at issue.

QUESTIONS AND PROBLEM

1. An open question remains as to whether, as with the restrictive approach to foreign sovereign immunity the act of state doctrine exempts "commercial activity". Both federal and state courts are split on the issue. *See, e.g., U.S. v. Giffen*, 326 F. Supp. 2d 497 (S.D.N.Y. 2004) and *Glen v. Club Mediterranee, S.A.*, 450 F.3d 1251, 1254 n.2 (11th Cir. 2006). To what extent might the act of state doctrine apply and the exception of "commercial activity" affect the outcome in an action by Pierre Konowaloff against Yale for recovery of the Vincent van Gogh painting *The Night Café* (Review Problem *supra*, Chapter 1)? *See Konowaloff v. Metropolitan Museum of Art*, 702 F.3d 140 (2d Cir. 2012).

2. The platinum group of metals (PGM), which includes rhodium, ruthenium, palladium, osmium, and iridium, are both essential for the automobile, chemical, petroleum refining, pharmaceutical, and electronics industries and rare. Two countries, South Africa and Russia, supply more than 90

> percent of the world's demand. Canada produces most of the remaining 10 percent. The United States consumes nearly 40 percent of the total annual supply.
>
> Assume that during a recent worldwide economic recession, the demand for PGM began to decline precipitously. A consequential fall in prices prompted authorities in the Ministry of Natural Resources of the Russian Federation and their counterparts from the South African Ministry of Mines in the Department of Minerals and Energy to meet secretly to discuss mutual cuts in production to bolster prices. They agreed to "advise" both public and private mining companies to negotiate and agree to output restrictions within parameters "suggested" by the respective ministries. Upon learning about the restrictions, the principal producers of PGM in Canada have in a series of secret meetings agree to make corresponding voluntary reductions of output with the knowledge and presumably approval of Canadian mining authorities.
>
> A few weeks ago, Nashua Metals, Inc., a San Francisco-based PGM dealer, learned of the agreements and is considering filing an antitrust suit. You are an associate in the law firm retained by Nashua Metals to represent them in such a suit. You have been asked by one of the senior partners for your opinion as to the applicability of *International Association of Machinists and Aerospace Workers (IAM) v. The Organization of the Petroleum Exporting Countries (OPEC)* to such an action in light of *Kirkpatrick Company v. Environmental Tectonics Corp.*

C. Foreign Sovereign Compulsion

INTERAMERICAN REFINING CORP. v. TEXACO MARACAIBO, INC.
307 F. Supp. 1291 (D. Del. 1970)

CALEB M. WRIGHT, CHIEF JUDGE.

This is an action arising under the United States antitrust laws, 15 U.S.C. §§ 1, 2, 15, commonly known as the Sherman and Clayton Acts. Plaintiff Interamerican Refining Corporation (Interamerican) alleges that defendants Texaco Maracaibo Inc., formerly the Superior Oil Company of Venezuela (Supven), Monsanto Company (Monsanto), Monsanto Venezuela, Inc. (Monven), wholly owned subsidiary of Monsanto, and Amoco Trading Corporation (Amoco), now survived by American International Oil Company, engaged in a concerted boycott designed to deny Interamerican Venezuelan crude oil required for its operations. Plaintiff seeks a judgment in treble the amount of damages suffered. Defendants have moved for summary judgment.

Interamerican was incorporated in October, 1959. The principal stockholders were Mr. Yervant Maxudian, Dr. Miguel Moreno, General Felix Roman Moreno, and later Mr. Jose Marcano. Mr. Maxudian was the principal executive officer. Interamerican planned to process low-cost Venezuelan crude oil in a bonded refinery in Bayonne, New Jersey, and to export the products or sell them as ship's bunker in New York harbor, thus avoiding United States import quota and tariff restrictions. Interamerican rented the Bayonne refinery from its owner, Petroleum Separating Company (Separating). One of the principal terms of the rental contract was a force majeure clause, designed to protect Interamerican, in the words of Mr. Maxudian, "if there was any interference, a change of administration in Venezuela where we couldn't get oil." The refinery was modified, at considerable cost to Interamerican, to meet its expected needs.

Defendants Supven and Monven held concessions from the Venezuelan government to explore for and produce crude oil. They were suppliers of crude oil, potential sellers to Amoco, a finding and trading company, and through Amoco to Interamerican. Defendant Monsanto neither produced nor traded crude oil and played no part in the events giving rise to this litigation. Plaintiff considers it responsible for the conduct of its subsidiary Monven.

Interamerican completed modification of the Bayonne refinery on January 18, 1960. It received its first shipment of crude oil from Amoco on January 26, pursuant to a contract executed the preceding day. Amoco had obtained that shipment from Monven and diverted it from its intended destination. Amoco delivered two additional shipments, pursuant to contracts dated February 4, 1960, and February 16, 1960, the oil for which was supplied by Supven. Contrary to earlier assurances of a willingness to supply Interamerican's long-term needs, Amoco informed Interamerican on March 15, 1960, that it could make no further shipments of Venezuelan crude oil. Amoco was unable to obtain oil from its suppliers, it said, because the Venezuelan government had forbidden further sales which, directly or indirectly, reached Interamerican. Operations at Bayonne were temporarily suspended on March 19, when processing of the last shipment was completed. Amoco tried without success to secure other supplies of suitable crude oil, and Interamerican attempted itself to obtain Venezuelan crude oil from other sources, both directly and with the aid of a shell corporation as purchasing agent. All suppliers refused to sell without the explicit permission of the Venezuelan government. Interamerican finally obtained one more cargo of Supven oil, but on August 15, 1960, it terminated operations.

Interamerican had notified Separating in April, 1960, of its difficulties and of its intent to invoke the force majeure clause in the rental contract. Arbitration on the contract commenced before a panel of the American Arbitration Association in September, 1960, and an award was made to Separating in December of that year. The award was confirmed by the Court of Appeals for the Second Circuit in November, 1961. 296 F.2d 124.

Plaintiff commenced this action against Supven and Monsanto by complaint dated March 6, 1964. The complaint was amended on July 22, 1964, to add Monven and Amoco.

The preceding are the basic facts on which plaintiff grounds its claim for treble damages. Suppliers Supven and Monven, trader Amoco, and unknown others are alleged to have conspired to destroy Interamerican's potentially profitable business. Plaintiff relies on the refusals to deal to establish a violation of the antitrust laws and on the undeniable damages sustained as a result of inability to obtain oil.

Defendants do not deny the refusals to deal nor the fact of damage. They base their defense on the statute of limitations and on the fact that the Venezuelan government forbade that compulsion by a foreign sovereign is a complete defense to a claim under the antitrust laws, and that the uncontroverted facts establish that defense as a matter of law.

The events on which defendants rely must be understood against the background of several conditions. Dr. Moreno and Mr. Maxudian both had histories of political activity in Venezuela. Neither considered himself friendly to or befriended by the Betancourt regime which had come to power in 1959. Dr. Moreno testified that Betancourt represented a continuation of the Larrazabal regime under whose auspices he had spent some unhappy moments in jail. It is not clear that Moreno was a persona non grata in the official sense, but the Venezuelan press remembered him unfavorably as "a chief conspirator in the 1948 coup."

Mr. Maxudian had served as oil consultant to two presidents between 1937 and 1945, and had refused to continue in that capacity under Betancourt. He admits having refused to work for Betancourt and having referred to him as "the Lenin of Latin America." According to the then president of Interamerican, both Mr. Maxudian and Dr. Moreno anticipated a change in the administration in Venezuela, that change being the reinstatement of Dr. Moreno.

The second condition is the relationship of the Venezuelan government to foreign oil concerns doing business there. These concerns hold their concessions subject to regulation by the government through the Ministry of Mines and Hydrocarbons. In April, 1959, that ministry established the Coordinating Commission for the Conservation of Commerce and Hydrocarbons (Coordinating Commission). The Coordinating Commission supervised concessionaires rigorously and conducted regular reviews of their sales policies. It also promulgated rules regarding the sale of oil extracted there. Those rules constituted "conditions for any shipment of Venezuelan petroleum to be made abroad." Sanctions for violation of the rules included suspension of the right to ship oil out of the country.

The third condition is the peculiar situation of Interamerican in the oil industry. Interamerican could buy, process, and sell without regard to import quotas or tariffs as long as it sold only for export or in New York harbor. It would therefore sell at prices lower than other companies subject to the tariff and import quotas and would sell entirely to foreign markets, two factors of concern to the Venezuelan government.

Soon after Interamerican received and began to process the first shipment of oil, Venezuelan authorities indicated their disapproval of sales to it by the concessionaires. The press reacted with considerable clamor both to the prices at which oil was sold to Interamerican and to the role of Dr. Moreno in the scheme. Articles of the day refer caustically to Dr. Moreno's new role as oilman and report official concern with the effect of sales to Interamerican on the stability of world oil prices. The Minister of Mines and Hydrocarbons is quoted announcing that "an end will be put to it" Carta Semanal, weekly publication of the Ministry of Mines and Hydrocarbons, described as "a medium of information of some of the activities of the Ministry

* * * and likewise containing data and information taken from technical manuals from abroad or locally," refers to investigations by the Coordinating Commission in the February 13, 1960, issue as follows:

> "The third and more recent of the cases concerns a negotiation effected by and between the Amoco Trading and, a Venezuelan unidentified petroleum producer, to import petroleum into the United States outside the quota of the restriction program, and reexport it in the form of products to European and Canadian markets. There is involved in the negotiation petroleum from Maracaibo Lake, Venezuela; the petroleum was sold at prices below the quotation prices; the new firm Inter-American Refining Corporation, whose Venezuelan representative is Dr. Miguel Moreno, Secretary of the Government Junta that rose into power following the Coup d'Etat of 1948, appears to be the intermediary."

The Coordinating Commission called officials of both Supven and Monven before it on March 2 and March 4, respectively. The two companies were then instructed that no further Venezuelan oil was to reach Interamerican.

The parties have much to say about the reasons for Venezuelan antipathy to Interamerican. Interamerican maintains that none of the reasons given by the government stand up under scrutiny, that their fragility is persuasive that no order was given. Certainly abnormal discounts cannot account for all the excitement. Interamerican was not the only company getting oil from Supven at below posted prices and Interamerican's offer to pay higher prices had no effect on the ban.

According to Monven's representative, the Commission was concerned that Interamerican might violate U.S. import laws and that certainly it would violate Venezuela's policy against sales to unnatural markets, e.g., Canada and Europe. In addition, it appears that the government opposed any sales to a bonded refinery in New York harbor, because of the low prices at which such a refinery could sell. The March 5, 1960, issue of Carta Semanal discussed the results of the hearing with the companies as follows: "The companies showed good acceptance of these plans and agreed to suspend the shipments of petroleum that might unbalance the natural markets of Canada, or determine the price structure through transactions like the structure of the Inter-American."

Whether or not such concerns were valid, it appears that they were indeed held. Both Dr. Acosta and Dr. Perez refer to them. Given Interamerican's stated purpose to produce only for export, its sales would inevitably find their way to "unnatural markets."

The presence of Dr. Moreno also had an effect on the fate of Interamerican. As indicated, both the regular press and Carta Semanal identified him with the Junta replaced by Betancourt. The following colloquy between Mr. Frank Leiva, Interamerican's emissary, and Dr. Perez, is instructive:

Perez: Dr. Moreno is interested in that company. You know our feelings about Dr. Moreno.

Leiva: Suppose Dr. Moreno were to get out of the company, would that help?

Perez: That would be of great material help if he were to get out of the company.

After receiving their orders from the Coordinating Commission, Monven and Supven notified Amoco that no further oil from them was to reach Interamerican. Amoco then notified Interamerican.

Interamerican's further efforts to procure oil through use of Hydrocarbons Ltd., Mr. Leiva's Bahamian shell, failed, as each producer who learned of the ultimate purchaser insisted on protective clauses in the sale contract. Mr. Leiva made two trips to Venezuela to attempt to intervene on behalf of Interamerican, the first of which succeeded in having one cargo released. But Supven, the supplier of that cargo, refused to ship further without the permission of Dr. Perez. Mr. Leiva was unable to secure further permission.

At the arbitration proceedings, plaintiff vigorously maintained that the Venezuelan compulsion had deprived it of the ability to obtain oil, and that such compulsion was within the force majeure clause of the contract. It introduced substantial evidence to prove the compulsion, but, as previously noted, the arbitrators made an award against it.

Interamerican admits that it has now reversed its position with regard to the good faith of its suppliers. It maintains that the arbitration award against it and the introduction at those proceedings of a certain letter written by Dr. Perez, Minister of Mines and Hydrocarbons, convinced it that defendants had not told it the truth.

The Court concludes . . . for reasons hereinafter stated, that the undisputed facts demonstrate that defendants were compelled by regulatory authorities in Venezuela to boycott plaintiff. It also holds that such compulsion is a complete defense to an action under the antitrust laws based on that boycott.

Because summary judgment is granted to all defendants on the ground stated, it is not necessary to decide the applicability of the statute of limitations.

The Law of Compulsion

No party presents dispositive authority that such acts as occurred here do or do not immunize trade restraints otherwise illegal. The statement in *Sabre Shipping Corp. v. American President Lines, Ltd.*, 285 F. Supp. 949 (S.D.N.Y. 1968), at 954, relied on by plaintiff, is not controlling. Judge Ryan's opinion, on a motion to dismiss, properly held that allegations that the unlawful activities were engaged in at the direction of the Japanese government were a matter for defense. His additional comment that if established such allegations might not immunize defendants, even if read literally, only reserves judgment on the conditions under which such direction might not be a defense.

Such conditions were present in *Continental Ore Co. v. Union Carbide and Carbon Corp.*, 370 U.S. 690 (1962) and *United States v. Sisal Sales Corp.*, 274 U.S. 268 (1927). In *Continental Ore*, Union Carbide's subsidiary, Electro Met of Canada, had been appointed by the Canadian government to be exclusive wartime purchasing agent for vanadium. That appointment did not immunize a conspiracy with the parent to monopolize vanadium production and sale. "Respondents are afforded no defense from the fact that Electro Met of Canada, in carrying out the bare act of purchasing vanadium from respondents rather than Continental, was acting in a manner permitted by Canadian law." 370 U.S. at 706–707.

In Sisal Sales defendants secured a monopoly through discriminatory legislation in Mexico and Yucatan. The Court held that inasmuch as the conspiracy was entered into an overt acts performed in this country, jurisdiction existed, and the legislation procured by the conspiracy was beside the point. "True, the conspirators were aided by discriminating legislation, but by their own deliberate acts, here and elsewhere, they brought about forbidden results within the United States." 274 U.S. at 276.

Nothing in the materials before the Court indicates that defendants either procured the Venezuelan order or that they acted voluntarily pursuant to a delegation of authority to control the oil industry. The narrow question for decision is the availability of genuine compulsion by a foreign sovereign as a defense.

Defendants rely on dicta in *Continental Ore, supra,* and in *United States v. The Watchmakers of Switzerland Information Center, Inc.*, 1963 Trade Cas. P70, 600 (S.D.N.Y.) and on language in some consent decrees to establish the defense. Without more, these would be scant authority. It requires no precedent, however, to acknowledge that sovereignty includes the right to regulate commerce within the nation. When a nation compels a trade practice, firms there have no choice but to obey. Acts of business become effectively acts of the sovereign. The Sherman Act does not confer jurisdiction on United States courts over acts of foreign sovereigns. By its terms, it forbids only anticompetitive practices of persons and corporations.

See also Brewster, *Antitrust and American Business Abroad* 94 (1958) and Fugate, *Antitrust Jurisdiction and Foreign Sovereignty*, 49 Va. L. Rev. 925 (1962), at 932, where it is said:

> "The real question is whose acts are the subject of inquiry. If the acts are those of a foreign government within its own jurisdiction, then the antitrust exception applies. The situation is the same if the foreign government through its laws, regulations, or orders, requires private parties to perform the anticompetitive acts. If, on the other hand, the acts complained of are in reality those of private parties who seek to hide behind the cloak of foreign law, the courts will attach antitrust liability." Also Fugate, Foreign Commerce and the Antitrust Laws (1958) §§ 2.16, 2.17.

In his book, Antitrust and American Business Abroad, Professor (now President) Kingman Brewster states a proposition which should be self-evident. Anticompetitive practices compelled by foreign nations are not restraints of commerce, as commerce is understood in the Sherman Act, because refusal to comply would put an end to commerce. Brewster 94. American business abroad does not carry with it the freedom and protection of competition it enjoys here, and our courts cannot impose them. Commerce may exist at the will of the government, and to impose liability for obedience to that will would eliminate for many companies the ability to transact business in foreign lands. Were compulsion not a defense, American firms abroad faced with a government order would have to choose one country or the other in which to do business. The Sherman Act does not go so far.

Plaintiff maintains that even if compulsion is a good defense, the acts of compulsion must be valid under Venezuelan laws. It urges the Court to consider the affidavit of a Venezuelan attorney to the effect that the Minister of Mines and Hydrocarbons had no authority to bar sales of crude oil to anyone and that no officer had authority to issue binding orders without putting them in writing and publishing them in the Gazeta Oficial. Since not legal, says plaintiff, the orders were not "compulsive."

This Court may not undertake such an inquiry. In *Banco Nacional de Cuba v. Sabbatino*, 376 U.S. 398 (1964), the Supreme Court held that it could not explore the validity under Cuban law of acts of expropriation by the Castro government. The act of state doctrine, based upon proper concepts of sovereignty and separation of powers, commands that conduct of foreign policy reside exclusively in the executive. For our courts to look behind the acts of a foreign government would impinge upon and perhaps impede the executive in that function. Whether or not Venezuelan officials acted within their authority and by legitimate procedures is therefore not relevant to the instant case.

Plaintiff's attempt to limit *Sabbatino* to expropriation decrees finds no support either in the holding or the rationale of that case. The principal decision relied on in Sabbatino dealt with a tort claim for refusal to grant a passport, unjustified confinement, assault, and abuse. [Citations omitted.] The reasons of policy which support the doctrine would hardly be served by limiting it to acts of expropriation.

The Propriety of Summary Judgment

Rule 56 of the Federal Rules of Civil Procedure provides that summary judgment may be rendered if the pleadings, depositions, answers to interrogatories and admissions of file, together with affidavits, if any, show that there is no genuine issue as to any material fact and that the moving party is entitled to judgment as a matter of law. Fed.R.Civ.P. 56(c). When either party moves for summary judgment the opposing party must respond with specific facts showing there is a genuine issue for trial. Fed.R.Civ.P. 56(e).

If the proper showing is made, summary judgment is as appropriate for a defense as for a claim. [Reference omitted.]

Plaintiff asserts that the evidence of compulsion is indirect, circumstantial, and oral, therefore insufficient. Consequently, according to plaintiff, issues of fact arise as to defendants' asserted defense. Neither law nor the record support such a position.

Both Mr. Walter Mengden, then president of Supven, and Mr. Frank Richardson, a Monven vice president, state that Venezuelan officials told them that sales to Interamerican must cease. Their testimony is neither circumstantial nor indirect; rather it is persuasive proof that such events occurred. Plaintiff offers no reason to doubt their credibility and no facts to contradict them.

. . . There is no evidence of conspiracy or of motive to boycott Interamerican. The relationship among supplier, trader, and refiner was essentially symbiotic, profitable to all, and nothing supports any other theory. What the uncontradicted evidence does show is that defendants were eager to sell to plaintiff, that they acted in good faith before and after the ban, and that all refusals to deal were based on compliance with authority which was in the words of Professor Brewster, "in fact, a sine qua non of doing business." Brewster, 92.

To permit this litigation to go beyond summary judgment would be improper as well as futile. The ends of justice and proper judicial administration require that it be terminated now.

Submit order in accordance herewith.

PROBLEMS AND QUESTIONS

1. Assume that Nashua Metals has filed a treble-damage antitrust action against the Russian, South African, and Canadian mining companies that have mutually agreed to restrict their PGM out in accordance with the suggested guidelines secretly issued by the relevant Russian and South African mining authorities, would any or all have a valid "foreign sovereign compulsion" defense?

2. What arguments might be reasonably made in favor or against a "foreign sovereign compulsion defense" in the following circumstances?

(a) China has a special Export Cartel Law that allows firms to enter into such agreements subject to governmental oversight and approval to ensure inter alia "that such agreements do not impede fair completion" and do not "interfere with China's relationships with other nations." The law does not provide that governmental officials may order or direct firms to enter into such an agreement.

Assume in addition that three significant automobile manufacturers have emerged in China. They generally sell small, economy vehicles at the lowest end of the market. In order to avoid competing with each other, they have agreed to an export cartel directed at the U.S. market. Their agreement sets a floor price for each model and provides that each firm shall inform the others once it has entered negotiations with a volume buyer, such as a car rental firm, the other two firms shall, under the agreement, make no offers or other solicitations to such buyer until informed that the negotiations have ended. All three firms are sued in an antitrust action.

(b) Would it make any difference if the defendant firms produced a letter signed by a Chinese government official that the relevant ministry had informally "directed" the firms to enter the agreement and that if any one firm had failed to do so, a formal action denying it an export license would have been issued?

(c) Would your answer to either (a) or (b) differ had, in response to U.S. auto manufacturer and labor demands for action against the "flood of cheap cars from China that threaten our jobs," U.S. trade officials had

> pressured the Chinese to force its auto exporters to curtail their exports and establish floor prices?
>
> See Mitsuo Matsushita & Lawrence Repeta, *Restricting the Supply of Japanese Automobiles: Sovereign Compulsion or Sovereign Collusion?*, 14 CASE W. RES. J. INT'L L. 47, 53–72 (1982).

II. FOREIGN SOVEREIGN IMMUNITY IN CANADA

GOUVERNEMENT DE LA RÉPUBLIQUE DÉMOCRATIQUE DU CONGO v. VENNE*
[1971] S.C.R. 997

[Official Court Summary]

The respondent, an architect, claimed to have been retained on behalf of the appellant government for the purpose of making preliminary studies and preparing sketches in relation to the national pavilion which the appellant proposed to build at Expo 67. The Congo decided not to proceed with the pavilion. The appellant filed a declinatory exception whereby it claimed that, by reason of its status as a sovereign state, it could not be impleaded in the Quebec Courts. The material before the Courts consisted of the declaration or claim, the declinatory exception and two formal admissions: that the appellant had accredited its chargé d'affaires as its commissioner general to the exhibition and also that the Democratic Republic of Congo is a sovereign State. The exception was dismissed by the trial judge, and his judgment was upheld by the Court of Appeal. The government of the Congo appealed to this Court.

Held (HALL and LASKIN JJ. dissenting): The appeal should be allowed.

Per FAUTEUX C.J. and ABBOTT, MARTLAND, JUDSON, RITCHIE, SPENCE and PIGEON JJ.:

The record as a whole discloses that the appellant's employment of the respondent was an act done in the performance of a sovereign act of state. It follows that the appellant could not be impleaded in the Courts of this country even if the so-called doctrine of restrictive sovereign immunity had been adopted in our Courts. Cases concerning sovereign immunity decided in the Courts of the United States in recent years are of little or no authority in Canada.

The proposition that a defendant can be taken to have submitted to the jurisdiction by entering a plea to the effect that it is not subject thereto, cannot be accepted. In any event, a sovereign state is not to be held to have submitted to a sovereign jurisdiction unless the submission be made in the face of the Court, coupled with a request that such jurisdiction be exercised.

---

* Footnotes omitted.

Per HALL and LASKIN JJ., *dissenting:* Resort to applicable rules of procedure for the purpose of asserting immunity and contesting jurisdiction cannot be converted into a submission to the Court's authority to deal with the merits. To be effective, waiver must be made in the face of the Court and at the time the Court is asked to exercise its jurisdiction.

The Court is faced with an unqualified contention that a sovereign state cannot as such be impleaded regardless of the activity in which it is engaged and out of which a suit against it is brought in a foreign domestic Court. To allow the declinatory exception would thus be to reaffirm the doctrine of absolute immunity. That doctrine is spent. It would be wrong to revive it on any view of a deficiency of evidence to overcome any suggested presumption that when a sovereign state acts through an accredited diplomatic representative any ensuing transaction with a private person is for a so-called public purpose. Since jurisdiction which is invoked as here cannot be effectively repudiated *ab initio* on the basis of unqualified immunity, the action should proceed. Even if the immunity claimed herein is to be tested on a restrictive basis, as it should be, there is not enough in the record before this Court upon which a ready affirmation of immunity can be founded. The claim cannot be allowed at this stage of the action.

RITCHIE J.— This is an appeal from a judgment of the Court of Appeal of the Province of Quebec dismissing an appeal from a judgment of the Superior Court of Montreal which disallowed the appellant's declinatory exception whereby it had claimed that, by reason of its status as a sovereign state, it could not be impleaded in the Quebec courts.

The respondent is an architect who claims to have been retained between February 1965 and March 1966 on behalf of the appellant for the purpose of making preliminary studies and preparing sketches in relation to the national pavilion which La République Démocratique du Congo (hereinafter called "The Congo") proposed to build at "Expo 67". The respondent's declaration incorporated by reference an unsigned copy of a contract, pursuant to which he claims to have been employed, and also certain sketches of the proposed pavilion which he claims to have furnished to the appellant. The respondent prepared a bill of $20,000 for services rendered which he subsequently reduced to $12,000 and which was not paid because the Congo decided not to proceed with the pavilion.

. . . .

Mr. Justice Leduc in the Superior Court and the three judges who sat on the Court of Appeal, were all of opinion that the contract in question was entered into by the Congo as a private commercial transaction and that it did not bear the character of an act of state or an act done for the public purpose of a foreign sovereign state.

. . . .

Accepting the finding that the contractual relations between the parties were of a purely private nature, Mr. Justice Owen proceeded to pose the problem as he understood it in the following terms:

The problem raised by this appeal is whether under conditions existing today our courts will continue to apply the doctrine or theory of absolute sovereign immunity or whether the time has come to apply a doctrine or theory of qualified or restrictive sovereign immunity.

In my opinion we should abandon the doctrine of absolute sovereign immunity and adopt a theory of restrictive sovereign immunity.

Stated briefly, the theory of sovereign immunity recognizes the classical doctrine that a foreign sovereign cannot, without his consent, be impleaded in the courts of another sovereign state, whereas according to the theory of restrictive sovereign immunity, which has been accepted by the United States State Department and consequently by the courts of that country, the immunity of the foreign sovereign is recognized only with regard to sovereign or public acts *(jure imperii)* but not with respect to private acts *(jure gestionis)*.

It accordingly appears to me, with all respect for the views of others, that the problem so dramatically posed by Mr. Justice Owen can only arise in this case if the judges of the Court of Appeal were right in adopting, without discussion, the finding of the learned trial judge that when the appellant employed the respondent to prepare sketches of the national pavilion which it proposed to build at a duly authorized international exhibition, it was not performing a public act of a sovereign state but rather one of a purely private nature.

. . . .

Mr. Justice Leduc, and consequently the Court of Appeal, adopted the view that the nature of the transaction here at issue was to be determined entirely on the basis that the respondent was a Montreal architect claiming against his employer and that the matter was therefore a purely private one. Considered from the point of view of the architect, it may well be that the contract was a purely commercial one, but, even if the theory of restrictive sovereign immunity were applicable, the question to be determined would not be whether the contractor was engaged in a private act of commerce, but whether or not the Government of the Congo, acting as a visiting sovereign state through its duly accredited diplomatic representatives, was engaged in the performance of a public sovereign act of state.

I think that it is of particular significance that the request for the respondent's services was made not only by the duly accredited diplomatic representatives of the Congo who were Commissioners General of the Exhibition, but also by the representative of the Department of Foreign Affairs of that country. (See declaration, para. 1). This makes it plain to me that in preparing for the construction of its national pavilion, a department of the Government of a foreign state, together with its duly accredited diplomatic representatives, were engaged in the performance of a public sovereign act of state on behalf of their country and that the employment of the respondent was a step taken in the performance of that sovereign act. It therefore follows in my view that the appellant could not be impleaded in the courts of this country even if the so-called doctrine of restrictive sovereign immunity had been adopted in our courts, and it is therefore unnecessary for the determination of this appeal to answer the question posed by Mr. Justice Owen and so fully considered by the Court of Appeal. In an area of the law which has been so widely canvassed by legal commentators and which has been the subject of varying judicial opinions in different countries, I think it would be undesirable to add further *obiter dicta* to those which have already been pronounced and I am accordingly content to rest my opinion on the ground that the appellant's employment of the respondent was in the performance of a sovereign act of state.

. . . .

Although, as I have indicated, I am content to base my decision on the premise that the appellant's employment of the respondent was an act done in the performance of a sovereign act of state, I think some consideration should be given to the careful and extensive arguments contained in the reasons for judgment in the Court of Appeal.

In this regard I think it should be pointed out that, as I have indicated, the decisions in the United States, upon which the reasons for judgment of Taschereau and Owen JJ. are clearly based, stem from opinions furnished by the State Department in that country which come to the courts by way of "letters of suggestion" and which are generally regarded as authoritative statements of the foreign policy of that country. In one of these letters, i.e., the Tate Letter, written in 1952 by Professor J.B. Tate who was then the acting legal adviser to the State Department, it was categorically stated that " . . . it will hereafter be the Department's policy to follow the restrictive theory of sovereign immunity in the consideration of requests of foreign governments for a grant of sovereign immunity." This position appears to have been generally accepted in the United States courts although they have some leeway in cases where the State Department refuses to make a suggestion of immunity, and the *Victory Transport* case, 336 F. 2d 354 (1964) is cited by Mr. Justice Owen as an example of an independent judicial acceptance of the theory of restrictive sovereign immunity. . . . It is thus clear that in such cases the question to be determined in the United States courts is whether it is the established policy of the State Department to recognize the immunity claimed in any particular case. As no such question arises in this country, I take the view that cases concerning sovereign immunity decided in the courts of the United States in recent years are of little or no authority in Canada.

. . . .

. . . What is substituted is the conception of an invitation by the host state to the visiting state. That is the core of what was laid down by Marshall C.J. in *The Schooner Exchange v. M'Faddon et al.*, (1812) 11 U.S. (7 Cranch) 116, which Duff C.J. adopts. The fundamental attitude which states adopt towards each other is the recognition and observance of individual sovereignty, that is, the acknowledgment of the absolute independence of each; and on this basic footing their intercourse is conducted. . . .

In the absence of something special or unusual, when a visiting sovereign steps upon the foreign soil he does so free from any submission to its immanent law; from that he remains insulated; and the recourse against what may be considered to be an infringement of the privileges of the invitation becomes a matter for diplomatic and not legal adjustment. . . .

Similarly in the present case, with the greatest respect for those who hold a different view, I am of opinion that the contract here sought to be enforced to which the appellant's diplomatic representative and one of its departments of government were parties, was a contract made by a foreign sovereign in the performance of a public act of state and that whatever view be taken of the doctrine of sovereign immunity, it was a matter in respect of which the Republic of the Congo cannot be impleaded in our courts. I would allow this appeal on that ground.

. . . .

The judgment of HALL and LASKIN JJ. was delivered by

LASKIN J. *(dissenting)* — This appeal arises out of a suit by an architect to recover from the Government of The Democratic Republic of Congo fees for his services. The services were those provided in the planning of a national pavilion which that country proposed to erect on an allotted site as a participant in the Universal and International Exhibition held in Montreal in 1967. Having been impleaded in the Superior Court of Quebec, Montreal District, the Government challenged the suit by a declinatory exception which was dismissed by Leduc J., and the dismissal was affirmed unanimously by the Quebec Court of Appeal. The interlocutory proceedings thus became the vehicle for the determination of the basic issues in the litigation, namely, the immunity of the foreign Government from suit and from the jurisdiction of the Quebec Superior Court.

The reasons upon which Leduc J. and the Quebec Court of Appeal proceeded were not fully concordant. The former purported to find, in a formal admission by the foreign Government that it had accredited its Chargé d'Affaires as its Commissioner General to the Montreal Exhibition, that the transaction with the architect amounted to a private law transaction cognizable before the Quebec Superior Court. In taking this view, Leduc J. accepted what he regarded as an evolved distinction in the law of sovereign immunity between public acts of a State and acts of a private character. He also found that invocation by the foreign Government of the processes of the Quebec Code of Civil Procedure amounted to a submission to the jurisdiction of the Superior Court. I take this as meaning that there was a waiver of immunity, assuming it existed, through an attributed consent to be impleaded.

The Quebec Court of Appeal flatly rejected the doctrine of absolute sovereign immunity, applied by this court in *Dessaulles v. Republic of Poland*, [1944] S.C.R. 275, [1944] 4 D.L.R. 1, and declared for a principle of restrictive sovereign immunity in accordance with developments in the domestic courts of some European countries and consonant with the executive policy of the United States reflected in the Tate Letter of 1952 (26 U.S. Department of State Bulletin 984). It found leeway to depart from this court's judgment in *Dessaulles* by referring to allegedly contrary indications in the later judgment in *Flota Maritima Browning de Cuba S.A. v. Republic of Cuba*, [1962] S.C.R. 598, 34 D.L.R. (2d) 628, 83 C.R.T.C. 219. It also went on to hold that it was incumbent on the foreign Government in this case to establish the circumstances in support of its claim of immunity. On the view of Owen J., this followed from the fact that immunity was a derogation from the general rule of domestic jurisdiction; and it also followed, in the view of the court as a whole, from the denial of a rule of absolute immunity. Since the court was of the opinion that no proof had been offered by the foreign Government to establish its claim of immunity, it held that the declinatory exception had been properly dismissed. The court's position on the burden of proof arising under a doctrine of restrictive immunity relieved it of any need to consider the situations in which immunity would be recognized. Its bare references to public and private acts, and to acts *jure imperii* and acts *jure gestionis*, left those situations at large.

. . . .

I begin my consideration of the central point in this case by noting that we are not concerned here with any claims to property, tangible or intangible, by any foreign State or agency thereof. Nor are we concerned with the status of any corporate or other body alleged to be an organ of a foreign State. There is in the present case a formal admission by the respondent that the Democratic Republic of Congo is a sovereign State. This determines its status for the purposes of this case without the necessity of seeking a certificate from the executive. No question is raised as to service of process, and hence only amenability to jurisdiction remains.

There is no doubt that there has been a shift in the positions of the domestic courts of various countries from the doctrine of absolute immunity, which prevailed through the nineteenth century and into the twentieth, to a restrictive doctrine. The Tate Letter enumerates the countries which have departed from the absolute view of immunity, and a recent text-book, *O'Connell*, International Law (2nd ed. 1970), p. 844 states that "the absolute view is not sanctioned by international law" and that "at the present time only English and perhaps Russian law reflects to any extent the traditional doctrine." This text-writer's assessment does not appear to embrace Canadian law (or even that of Australia, which is his base) unless he considers the two countries to be governed by the English rule. For Canada at any rate, the question is one for this court, subject to any binding Canadian treaty on the subject.

The restrictive view adopted in the Tate Letter is, it must be remembered, not a rule of law but a policy guide for the United States State Department. It has legal effect, however, through the conclusive force which the courts of the United States give to a suggestion made to the court by the State Department through the Justice Department that a claim of immunity be "recognized and allowed. [Citations omitted.] The practice of a "suggestion" by the executive to the courts goes back to the judgment of Marshall C.J. in *The Schooner Exchange v. M'Faddon*, (1812), 7 Cranch 116 at 147. I am not aware of any such "suggestion" practice in Canada. The executive here has gone no farther than to certify sovereign status, but, of course, under an absolute doctrine of immunity that would, in a case like the present one, be sufficient.

In the United States, the courts have leeway only where the State Department refuses to make a suggestion of immunity, and they have both granted and refused immunity in such a situation. [Citations omitted.] The *Victory Transport* case is apparently the first in which a United States federal court has unequivocally adopted the restrictive view of immunity, which had been a State Department policy even before being formalized in the Tate Letter. [Citation omitted.] There were indications before the *Victory Transport* case that the courts of the United States would accept the restrictive view as the governing one [citation omitted], and this now seems to be so.

The position in Great Britain is not, or not yet, clearly in the direction of a restrictive view. The flat assertion of the absolute view in *The Cristina*, [1938] A.C. 485 at 490, [1938] 1 All E.R. 719, by Lord Atkin became a much quoted paragraph in later English and Canadian cases. However, in *Sultan of Johore v. Abubakar, Tunku Aris Bendahara*, [1952] 1 All E.R. 1261, [1952] A.C. 318, Viscount Simon said, for the Privy Council, that "Their Lordships do not consider that there has been finally established in England . . . any absolute rule that a foreign independent sovereign cannot be impleaded in our courts in any circumstances" (at p. 1268). This could well refer, for example, to a probable qualification in respect of the use of property, or to competing claims to some chose in action rather than to a case like the present one where a foreign State is directly impleaded in a contract type of action. It does, however, leave the general question of immunity open to reconsideration.

The House of Lords returned to the issue of immunity in *Rahimtoola v. Nizam of Hyderabad*, [1958] A.C. 379, [1957] 3 All E.R. 441, which involved a contest between two claimants, one a former personal sovereign and the other a foreign State, in respect of a bank account in England. Viscount Simonds, who delivered the leading judgment, accepted the statement of the absolute view made by Lord Atkin in *The Cristina*. Lord Denning apart, the other Law Lords in the case proceeded on the same view so far as the issue of immunity concerned the direct impleading of a foreign sovereign or arose out of a claim to property or a chose in action clearly in the control of the foreign government, albeit not beneficially owned by it.

Before considering the views of Lord Denning (to which his colleagues in the case expressly withheld their assent) I wish to examine the decisions of this court on the question. The absolute immunity of a foreign sovereign State itself was recognized by Duff C.J. and by Hudson J. in the course of their reasons in *Reference as to Powers to Levy Rates on Foreign Legations and High Commissioners' Residences*, [1943] S.C.R. 208 [1943] 2 D.L.R. 481. That doctrine was not, however, in issue, and none of the other judges in the case dealt with it in any explicit sense. Similarly, passing references to absolute immunity were made in *Reference as to Exemption of United States Forces from Canadian Criminal Proceedings*, [1943] S.C.R. 483, 80 C.C.C. 161, [1943] 4 D.L.R. 11, as, for example, in the reasons of Rand J. The first direct consideration of the matter was in *Dessaulles v. Republic of Poland*, already referred to.

That case, like the present one, involved a declinatory exception by the respondent State when it was sued for fees for legal services and for an accounting. An official of the State had instituted disciplinary proceedings against the plaintiff before the Bar Council which was joined as mis-en-cause in his action against Poland. The Quebec Superior Court dismissed the declinatory exception on the ground that the institution of the disciplinary proceedings constituted a submission to the jurisdiction. This view was rejected unanimously by the Quebec Court of Appeal, [1943] Que. K.B. 224, which sustained the declinatory exception. On further appeal to this Court, the judgment of the Court of Appeal was affirmed. In addition to rejecting the contention that there had been a submission to jurisdiction, the Supreme Court was unanimous on the following statement of principle:

[TRANSLATION] There is no doubt that a sovereign state cannot be sued before foreign courts. This principle is founded upon the independence and dignity of states, and international comity has always respected it. The Courts have also adopted it as being the domestic law of all civilized countries.

I make two observations on this statement. First, it is clear that the absolute doctrine is not today part of the domestic law "de tous les pays civilisés". Second, neither the independence nor the dignity of States, nor international comity require vindication through a doctrine of absolute immunity. Independence as a support for absolute immunity is inconsistent with the absolute territorial jurisdiction of the host State; and dignity, which is a projection of independence or sovereignty, does not impress when regard is had to the submission of States to suit in their own courts. The Supreme Court of the United States has exposed the frailty of these considerations by allowing a counterclaim to be pursued against a sovereign State which invoked the jurisdiction of a domestic court: see *National City Bank of New York v. Republic of China, supra,* at p. 364. Nor is comity any more realistic a foundation for absolute immunity, unless it be through treaty. It is not correct to say, as did Lord Wright in *The Cristina, supra* at p. 502, that international comity or courtesy has ripened into a general principle of international law that supports absolute immunity. The former rule of practice and reciprocity in this respect has been abandoned. I should observe that another former prop of absolute immunity, that of extraterritoriality, which was in the main used to exclude domestic jurisdiction over foreign public ships, has long been recognized as a spent fiction, ruled out in this Court by Duff C.J. in the *Foreign Legations* Reference, *supra,* at p. 230, following the lead of Lord Atkin in *Chung Chi Cheung v. The King,* [1939] A.C. 160 at 174, [1938] 4 All E.R. 786. Rand J. took the same view in *St. John v. Fraser-Brace Overseas Corp.,* [1958] S.C.R. 263 at 267, 13 D.L.R. (2d) 177.

. . . .

I refer now to Lord Denning's canvass of general principle in the *Rahimtoola* case. It will suffice to quote one passage, a summarizing one, which, to put it briefly, would substitute function for status as the determinant of immunity; it is in these words:

> . . . it seems to me that at the present time sovereign immunity should not depend on whether a foreign government is impleaded, directly or indirectly, but rather on the nature of the dispute. Not on whether "conflicting rights have to be decided," but on the nature of the conflict. Is it properly cognizable by our courts or not? If the dispute brings into question, for instance, the legislative or international transactions of a foreign government, or the policy of its executive, the court should grant immunity if asked to do so, because it does offend the dignity of a foreign sovereign to have the merits of such a dispute canvassed in the domestic courts of another country: but if the dispute concerns, for instance, the commercial transactions of a foreign government (whether carried on by its own departments or agencies or by setting up separate legal entities), and it arises properly within the territorial jurisdiction of our courts, there is no ground for granting immunity.

The considerations which, in my view, make it preferable to consider immunity from the standpoint of function rather than status do not rest simply on a rejection of the factors which had formerly been said to underlie it. Affirmatively, there is the simple matter of justice to a plaintiff; there is the reasonableness of recognizing equal accessibility to domestic courts by those engaged in transnational activities, although one of the parties to a transaction may be a foreign State or an agency thereof; there is the promotion of international legal order by making certain disputes which involve a foreign State amenable to judicial processes, even though they be domestic; and, of course, the expansion of the range of activities and services in which the various States today are engaged has blurred the distinction between governmental and non-governmental functions or acts (or between so-called public and private domains of activity), so as to make it unjust to rely on status alone to determine immunity from the consequences of State action.

A shift from status to function means, of course, the substitution of a loose formula for a precise one, but it is dictated by factors and conditions which have impressive support from scholars as well as judges, and also in the practice of States as reflected in the restrictive doctrine adopted by their domestic courts and as reflected as well in the negotiation of treaties providing for waiver of immunity, as, for example, in commercial matters [citations omitted].

I note the general terms in which Lord Denning illustrated those classes of functions to which immunity should continue to attach. Another classification was proposed by the United States Court of Appeals for the Second Circuit in its reasons for judgment in the *Victory Transport* case, *supra*; it is as follows (at p. 360 of 336 F.2d):

> . . . we are disposed to deny a claim of sovereign immunity that has not been "recognized and allowed" by the State Department unless it is plain that the activity in question falls within one of the categories of strictly political or public acts about which sovereigns have traditionally been quite sensitive. Such acts are generally limited to the following categories:
>
> (1) internal administrative acts, such as expulsion of an alien.
>
> (2) legislative acts, such as nationalization.
>
> (3) acts concerning the armed forces.
>
> (4) acts concerning diplomatic activity.
>
> (5) public loans.
>
> We do not think that the restrictive theory adopted by the State Department requires sacrificing the interests of private litigants to international comity in other than these limited categories. Should diplomacy require enlargement of these categories, the State Department can file a suggestion of immunity with the court. Should diplomacy require contraction of these categories, the State Department can issue a new or clarifying policy pronouncement.
>
> . . . .

To allow the declinatory exception is thus to reaffirm the doctrine of absolute immunity. I have made plain my opinion that the doctrine is spent. If so, it would be wrong to revive it on any view of a deficiency of evidence to overcome any suggested presumption that when a sovereign State acts through an accredited diplomatic representative any ensuing transaction with a private person is for a so-called public purpose. At this stage of the action there is no question of requiring evidence from the plaintiff or from Congo to negate or establish immunity on a restrictive basis. That comes later. Hence, I need not now be concerned with fixing any burden of proof. The only question is whether the action should be throttled at its inception or whether it should be allowed to proceed. Since, in my view, jurisdiction which is invoked as here cannot be effectively repudiated *ab initio* on the basis of unqualified immunity, I am of opinion that the action should proceed.

I am fortified in this opinion on my view that even if the declinatory exception is read to claim immunity on a restrictive basis (as the appellant urged alternatively in its Factum and in argument), there is no factual basis on which it can be allowed at this stage of the action.

I would dismiss the appeal with costs.

Appeal *allowed with costs*, HALL and LASKIN J.J. *dissenting.*

QUESTIONS AND NOTE

1. In what respects does the decision by the Canadian Supreme Court in *Gouvernement de la République Démocratique du Congo v. Venne* differ from the U.S. Supreme Court decision in *Republic of Argentina and Banco Central De La Republica Argentina v. Weltover, Inc.?*

2. Would each Court have reached the same or a similar conclusion in the two cases?

3. Would your answers to the various questions and problems posed above differ under applicable Canadian rather than U.S. law?

In 1985, 14 years after the Canadian Supreme Court decision in *Gouvernement de la République Démocratique du Congo v. Venne*, the Canadian parliament enacted the State Immunity Act, R.S. 1985, C-S-18, which excludes immunity from adjudicatory jurisdiction for foreign states in a variety of proceedings, including those related to a commercial activity of the state (§ 5) or for personal injury or property damage occurring in Canada (§ 6).

III. FOREIGN SOVEREIGN IMMUNITY IN JAPAN

TOKYO SANYŌ BŌEKI K.K., ET AL. v. THE ISLAMIC REPUBLIC OF PAKISTAN
Supreme Court, 2nd P.B., Judgment of 21 July 2006
60(6) Minshū 2542 (2006)

Two Japanese trading companies sued The Islamic Republic of Pakistan for payments due under a series of quasi loan-for-consumption [quasi-*mutuum*] computer sales contracts with the Ministry of Defense in the late 1980s and early 1990s. In a default judgment, the Tokyo District Court awarded the plaintiff trading companies the unpaid balances plus interest and delinquency charges amounting to over two billion yen (approximately 20 million U.S. dollars). On *kōso* appeal by Pakistan, the Tokyo High Court reversed the first instance decision and dismissed the claims, holding that Pakistan was immune from suit in Japanese courts under principles of international law. In response, the plaintiffs filed a second appeal (*jōkoku*) with the Supreme Court. The Supreme Court (2nd Petty Bench) in turn reversed the High Court and remanded the case to the Tokyo District Court.

REASONS
(*riyū*)

(1) With respect to immunity of foreign states from civil jurisdiction, it seems that, in the past, it was generally accepted that a state should be immune from the civil jurisdiction of another state of the forum unless there were special reasons such as the suit being related to real estate situated in the forum state or its willingness to subject itself to the civil jurisdiction of the forum state (the absolute immunity doctrine), and there was an international customary law based on such a doctrine. However, along with the expansion of the range of states' activities, another idea has gradually gained ground, that a state's acts should be divided into acts of sovereignty [*jure imperii*] and other acts [*jure privatorum* or *gestionis*], that is acts under private law or for business management (*gyōmu kanri*), and that it is inappropriate to hold the state immune from the civil jurisdiction of the forum state for not only its acts of sovereignty but also those under private law or for business management. At present, in accordance with such restrictive immunity doctrine, many states restrict the immunity of foreign states from the civil jurisdiction of their courts. Besides, the United Nations Convention on Jurisdictional Immunities of States and Their Property adopted at the 59th General Assembly of the United Nations as of December 2, 2004, also adopted this doctrine. In light of these circumstances, today, although the existence of the international customary law whereby a foreign state shall be immune from the civil jurisdiction of the forum state for its acts by sovereignty remains affirmable [citing *Yamaguchi, et al. v. The United States*, 56(4) Minshū 729 (2002)], it should be regarded that the international customary law whereby a foreign state shall also be immune from the civil jurisdiction of the forum state for its acts under private law or acts for commercial activities does not exist any

longer.

Next, we make examination on whether it is appropriate for Japanese courts to exercise their civil jurisdiction over a foreign state's acts under private law or commercial acts. Immunity of a state from the civil jurisdiction of the courts of another state is recognized based on the idea that individual states have their own sovereignty and they are on equal footing, and therefore they should mutually respect their sovereignty. However, it can be construed that even if Japanese courts exercise civil jurisdiction over a foreign state's acts under private law or acts for business management, such exercise of jurisdiction is not likely to infringe the state's sovereignty, and therefore, it should be concluded that there is no reasonable ground to hold the foreign state immune from the civil jurisdiction of Japanese courts for such acts. If a foreign state were granted immunity from the civil jurisdiction of Japanese courts even in cases where the exercise of civil jurisdiction is not likely to infringe the state's sovereignty, it would bring about an unfair consequence in that the private person involved in the state's acts under private law or acts for business management is unilaterally denied access to judicial remedy without reasonable grounds. Therefore, it is appropriate to construe that a foreign state shall not be immune from the civil jurisdiction of Japanese courts for its acts under private law or acts for business administration unless there are special circumstance where the exercise of civil jurisdiction by Japanese courts is likely to infringe the state's sovereignty.

(2) Needless to say, a foreign state shall not be immune from the civil jurisdiction of Japanese courts, irrespective of whether or not the act in question can be regarded as an act under private law or acts for business management, in cases where it has agreed to subject itself to the civil jurisdiction of Japanese courts under a treaty with Japan or other international agreements or where it filed a suit with a Japanese court, thereby manifesting the intention to willingly subject itself to the civil jurisdiction of Japanese courts in a particular litigation. In addition, it is appropriate to construe that, in cases where a foreign state has clearly manifested the intention to subject itself to the civil jurisdiction of Japanese courts by promising, under an explicit provision contained in a written contract entered into with a private person, that it would subject itself to the civil jurisdiction of Japanese courts for disputes that may arise from the contract, the state shall in principle not be immune from the civil jurisdiction of Japanese courts regarding such dispute. This is because, in such cases, the exercise of civil jurisdiction by Japanese courts over the foreign state is generally not likely to infringe the state's sovereignty, and furthermore, if the foreign state can claim immunity from the civil jurisdiction of Japanese courts, it would bring injustice between the parties to contracts and therefore contravene the doctrine of good faith.

(3) The decision of the Great Court of Cassation [*Daishin'in*] December 28, 1928 [*Matsuyama, et al. v. The Republic of China*, 7(12) Daishin minshū 1128 (1928)], cited by the court of the second instance, should be changed to the extent that it no longer conflicts with this reasoning.

(4) In this case, if, as argued by the appellants, the appellee concluded the sales contracts with the appellants to purchase high-performance computers, and after receiving delivery of the objects of sale, it concluded the quasi-loan contracts with the appellants to obtain loans to cover the sales price, these acts conducted by the appellee are, in nature, commercial transactions that can be conducted by a private person, and therefore it should be deemed that these acts fall within the category of acts under private law or acts for business administration, irrespective of the purpose of the acts. Assuming so, the appellee should not be immune from the civil jurisdiction of Japanese courts in this suit unless there are special circumstances as explained above.

According to the records, it is also obvious that the order forms prepared in the name of Corporation A, representing the appellee, contain a clause stating that the appellee agreed to conducts the judicial proceedings at Japanese courts in the event of any dispute over the Sales Contracts, and furthermore, it seems that under the written contracts for the quasi-loan contracts prepared in the name of Corporation A representing the appellee and provided for the appellants, this clause is applied mutatis mutandis to the quasi-loan contracts. Therefore, if Corporation A represented the appellee as argued by the appellants, this clause, which is an explicit provision contained in written contracts, can be regarded as the appellee's promise to subject itself to the civil jurisdiction of Japanese courts regarding a dispute arising from the contracts, and by reason of this clause, there is room to find the appellee to have clearly manifested the intention to subject itself to the civil jurisdiction of Japanese courts.

The court of the second instance, based on the reasoning given by the decision of the former Supreme Court mentioned above, and without examining the facts alleged by the appellants, upheld the appellee's claim for immunity from the civil jurisdiction of Japanese courts and dismissed this suit without prejudice. Such determination of the court of the second instance contains a violation of laws and regulations that apparently affected the judgment. The appellants' argument is well-grounded.

4. For the reasons stated above, the original judgment shall be quashed, and for further examination, this case shall be remanded to the court of the second instance.

JUSTICE ISAO IMAI JUSTICE SHIGEO TAKII
JUSTICE OSAMU TSUNO
JUSTICE RYŌJI NAKAGAWA
JUSTICE YUKI FURUTA

NOTE

For an analysis of this decision in English in the context of prior Japanese precedents and recent lower court decisions, see Dai Yokomizo,

> *State Immunity from Civil Jurisdiction*, 51 JAPANESE YEARBOOK OF INT'L L. 485 (2008).
>
> In 2009, the Japanese Diet enacted a special statute on foreign sovereign immunity that, in effect, codified the decision in *Tokyo Sanyō Bōeki K.K., et al. v. The Islamic Republic of Pakistan*. *See* Law concerning the Civil Jurisdiction of Japan with respect to Foreign States (*Gaikoku tō ni taisuru wagakuni no minji saibanken ni kansuru hōritsu*) Law No. 24, 2009.

IV. DOMESTIC STATE LIABILITY IN EAST ASIA AND THE EUROPEAN UNION

Our primary focus in this chapter thus far has been the adjudicatory jurisdiction of domestic courts in suits against *foreign* governments as well as the agencies and officials of *foreign* states and abstention from exercising such jurisdiction in suits that challenge or relate to the legality of the acts of *foreign* sovereigns. We now turn to a topic that has been almost completely neglected in discussion of state liability in the context of either international law and transnational litigation — the extent to which the any person — natural or juridical, citizen or alien, domiciliary or nondomiciliary — may bring a private action against a state, its agencies, or its officials in its own courts based on claims that would otherwise be justiciable against a nongovernmental, private party. In other words, we turn now to the question of domestic sovereign immunity in transnational litigation. We begin with a rather mundane case in which the issue of domestic sovereign immunity in Japan was raised as a potential bar to otherwise justiciable contract claims by Japanese firms against the United States.

NIPPON HODO COMPANY, LTD. v. UNITED STATES[*]
285 F.2d 766 (Ct. Cl. 1961)

JONES, CHIEF JUDGE.

Plaintiffs are Japanese corporations suing the United States on contract claims. In both cases, the defendant sought and was granted a separate trial on the issue of jurisdiction of this court; namely, whether such jurisdiction extends to suits against the United States by citizens of Japan. These cases were consolidated for trial of this mutual jurisdictional issue.

The plaintiffs proved that American citizens, in suits against the Government of Japan, are treated before the courts of Japan no less favorably than Japanese nationals. It is the defendant's major contention, however, that the plaintiffs have failed to prove that an American citizen in Japan could maintain against the Japanese Government the precise suit which plaintiffs bring here against the United States, and absent such proof this court is without jurisdiction under section 2502 of Title 28 United States Code.

---

[*] Footnotes deleted.

Section 2502 is as follows:

> "Citizens or subjects of any foreign government which accords to citizens of the United States the right to prosecute claims against their government in its courts may sue the United States in the Court of Claims if the subject matter is otherwise within such court's jurisdiction."

This section was codified in 1948, 62 Stat. 869, 976, but with minor changes it was simply a reenactment of the Act of March 3, 1911, 36 Stat. 1087, 1139, which in turn derived from the Act of July 27, 1868, 15 Stat. 243. The latter provided that no suit was to be maintained by or for an alien against the United States for any action taken under the Acts of 1863 and 1864 relating to the seizure of abandoned property in insurrectionary districts. A proviso added:

> "That this section shall not be construed so as to deprive aliens who are citizens or subjects of any government which accords to citizens of the United States the right to prosecute claims against such government in its courts, of the privilege of prosecuting claims against the United States in the court of claims, as now provided by law."

It appears that prior to this Act of 1868 aliens could bring suit in the Court of Claims without reference to reciprocal rights of United States citizens to sue in courts of foreign countries. [Citation omitted.]

It is apparent from a reading of the original act as well as the jurisdictional statute currently in force that access to this court by aliens is conditioned upon proof of reciprocity proof that a right is accorded citizens of the United States to prosecute claims against the alien government in the courts of that nation. It is the character of this required return in kind that is here in issue. The defendant contends that the return must be in specie.

This question has been before this court on previous occasions. In *Brodie v. United States*, 62 Ct. Cl. 29, it was contended that a British subject could not sue the United States in this court for patent infringement because an American (and similarly a British subject) could not prosecute such an action against the Crown. In answer to this we stated at page 46:

> "The true test is not whether a citizen of the United States may prosecute an action of a particular nature in a British court but whether the doors of British courts are open to American citizens for the prosecution of 'claims' against the Crown, but necessarily only such claims as might be prosecuted by British subjects, for there as here there are classes of action as to which the sovereign has not consented to be sued."

This was our announced construction of the statute in 1948 when the Congress reenacted the provisions without substantial change. Thereafter, in *Marcos v. United States*, 102 F.Supp. 547, 551, 122 Ct. Cl. 641, 648, a case involving a Philippine national, we restated the same position we had taken in *Brodie*, as follows:

> "The admission of American citizens to the Philippine courts with all of the rights of Philippine citizens as against the Philippine Government satisfies the requirements of Section 2502, and the fact that the consent of

the Philippine Government to be sued is more restricted than the consent of the United States Government to be sued, is not controlling. [Citation omitted.]"

The defendant continues to urge upon us its concept of reciprocity, a concept which demands that we do unto others precisely as they do unto us — and no more. Such a position, if accepted, would add no luster to the golden rule of conduct that long has guided our country in its international affairs. Furthermore, we doubt that it is in harmony with the attitude of Americans everywhere that their country is strong, generous, and willing to lead and act first. The Congress has provided that this court shall be open to any aliens whose government "accords to citizens of the United States the right to prosecute claims against their government in its courts." (Emphasis supplied.) We do not read "claims" to mean "claims of the precise nature brought before this court." The section contemplates on that American citizens enjoy an equal standing with foreigners in actions against the foreign State and does not require that the scope of actions for which the respective countries render themselves liable to suit shall be coextensively identical and in *pari materia*.

Perhaps there is some minimum amount of sovereign-liability in his own country which must be proved by an alien wishing to sue our Government in this court. We would carefully measure the scope of our jurisdiction in a situation where a rule in a foreign law book permits Americans free access to the courts but where it appears in practice that Americans are barred from the courts. The case before us does not present these difficulties. The plaintiffs have adequately proved that the Japanese open their courts to Americans in a multitude of causes against the Japanese Government, including, according to most authorities, suits for breach of contract.

The plaintiffs produced a deposition from a Japanese attorney, an experienced member of the Tokyo Bar Association, stating in unequivocal language that an American shared equally with a Japanese citizen "the right to sue the Japanese State for breach of Contract." This statement was affirmed by the Director of Litigation of the Japanese Ministry of Justice. Furthermore, in three separate inquiries our State Department sought to ascertain the status of American citizens before the courts of Japan. The replies from the Japanese Ministers of Foreign Affairs were as follows:

> "Citizens of the United States are given the right equally with the Japanese subjects to institute actions in Japanese courts against the Japanese Government in regard to claims arising from such legal relations between the citizens of the United States and the Japanese Government as belong to the domain of private law.

> "(T)he separateness of the courts of administrative law results in fact in few and unimportant suits against the Japanese Government whatever may be the statements in the codes with regard to the liability of the government to suits.

> "In civil cases the Japanese Government occupies a co-ordinate position before legal courts with Japanese subjects . . . . However, except in special instances which belong to the jurisdiction of the ordinary courts, legal

matters concerning public law become questions for administrative litigation.

"Contractual actions against the Japanese Government may be brought by both alien and Japanese nationals pursuant to general provisions of the Japanese civil and commercial codes."

The plaintiffs did fail to submit translations of any Japanese cases in which the State was sued for breach of contract. Little weight can be given to this omission when it is considered that we are dealing here not only with a different legal system but a different culture as well. Formal legal standards play a far less pervasive role in Japan in the creation and adjusting of principles regulating conduct than they play in the West. American scholars have repeatedly noted the amazing lack of litigation in Japan and the striking persistence in Japanese society of forms of dispute-resolution other than law. Those disputes involving public law which do arise are usually settled in administrative tribunals other than courts. The few court decisions available have only in recent years included a full statement of the facts in the published accounts.

The defendant has further emphasized that while the Japanese codes and statutes provide in some ways for suits against the Government, they fail to provide specifically for suits for breach of contract. We think the defendant has assumed too much, and has again overlooked the fact that the Japanese have accepted a system of jurisprudence whose tenets and history are different from those of our own. English common law started with the historic maxim that the "King can do no wrong," and the further proposition that the sovereign was immune from suit. "The King," reads a famous passage from Blackstone, "is not only incapable of doing wrong, but even of thinking wrong; he can never mean to do an improper thing; in him is no folly or weakness." This theory of state infallibility and immunity was incorporated into the jurisprudence of American democracy even though we had no King; the Chief of State was never sovereign. From the beginning sovereign power resided in the people, and the rights of individuals against the State were fundamental among our earliest legal principles.

While no one would question that for many years our law restrained suits against the Government, the responsibility of this position never went without challenge. "It is not too much to say," wrote an English observer, "that the whole Constitution has been erected upon the assumption that the King not only is capable of doing wrong, but is more likely to do wrong than other men if he is given a chance." Mr. Justice Frankfurter has asserted that whatever the ancient bases for the rule of immunity, "it undoubtedly runs counter to modern democratic notions to the moral responsibility of the State." *Great Northern Life Ins. Co. v. Read*, 322 U.S 47, 59 (dissenting opinion).

Today we know that our Government may be sued on a multitude of causes. Nevertheless, the doctrine of sovereign immunity has never been expressly repudiated by an American court. In our country the creation of State responsibility has been solely the result of legislation.

Civil law countries, on the other hand, particularly France, early in the development of their law, rejected both the concept that the King can do no wrong and the accompanying doctrine of sovereign immunity. These countries took the position instead that "the State is an honest man" and as such it will seek to repair damages caused by its wrongful acts. History shows that from this basic civil law premise the full development of state liability in these countries has been the handiwork of the judges and the courts.

Japanese law today is not the product of centuries of slow, organic growth; it did not develop along with, and as a part of, the whole society and culture. Less than a century ago the Japanese took their law bodily from the systems of continental Europe. The Japanese Civil Code is truthfully called the "fruit of comparative jurisprudence." The drafters surveyed the French, Swiss, and particularly the German civil codes and adopted from them broad teachings but no specific rules as to state responsibility. The multitude of European cases was examined but discarded. The result is a paradox: state liability in Japan is a commonly accepted fact but its proof by statutes and cases is difficult.

With this brief background, it is easier to understand and accept the statement of plaintiffs' deponent — "I have never known of any question being raised whether the citizen can sue the State. . . . Since it is the general opinion of the Japanese Bar that a citizen may bring an action against the State, equally for breach of contract, for payment of salary or damages of other kinds".

Both parties have briefed and argued the application and effect of the 1953 Treaty of Friendship, Commerce and Navigation between the United States of America and Japan, 4 U.S. Treaties 2063. We believe the proper disposition of this case does not require us to reach the issues thereby presented.

The court concludes as a matter of law that the plaintiffs are entitled to maintain their suits in this court pursuant to 28 U.S.C. § 2502, and the cases are returned to the trial commissioner with instructions to proceed with the remaining issues of law and fact, as previously directed.

It is so ordered.

DURFEE, MADDEN and WHITAKER, JUDGES, concur.

LARAMORE, JUDGE (dissenting).

I cannot agree with the majority for these reasons: The Treaty of Friendship entered into between the United States and Japan puts access to the courts on a reciprocal basis. Section 1 of Article IV of the Treaty provides that "nationals . . . of either party shall be accorded national treatment . . . with respect to access to the courts . . . ."

National treatment is defined in section 1 of Article XXII of the Treaty as follows:

> "The term 'national treatment' means treatment accorded within the territories of a party upon terms no less favorable than the treatment accorded therein, in like situations, to nationals, companies, . . . , as the case may be, of such party."

This, it seems to me, must mean that each government shall give equal treatment to the other with respect to access to the respective courts. As a matter of fact, this would appear to be in complete harmony with the primary purpose of the statute which permits a foreign citizen or corporation to sue the United States in cases wherein a foreign government accords to citizens of the United States the right to prosecute claims against their government in its courts. In other words, "equal treatment" would seem to be the controlling factor in both the Treaty and the statute.

Under these circumstances, the burden would be on the plaintiffs to prove that a citizen of the United States could prosecute a claim for breach of contract against the Japanese Government. This, in my opinion, the plaintiffs have failed to do. No statute or article of the constitution of Japan has been put in evidence from which this court could conclusively find a provision for suits in breach of contract. On the contrary, the constitution of Japan quite clearly shows that only suits in tort are cognizable by the courts of Japan.

Consequently, I would hold that section 2502 requires that United States citizens have the right to sue the Japanese Government in contract in its courts as a condition to maintenance of plaintiffs' suits in contract in this court. Otherwise, a Japanese citizen would have greater rights in the United States courts than those accorded them in their own country.

I would overrule the Brodie and Marcos cases cited in the majority opinion to the extent that they are in conflict with my views.

EXTENDED NOTE

Nippon Hodo Company, Ltd. v. United States reflects the problems of understanding and accommodating the contrasting approaches in common law and civil law systems to the problem of domestic state liability. In common law jurisdictions, such as the United States and Canada, the principles of foreign sovereign immunity reflect the generally applicable notion of governmental immunity from suit without consent, as expressed by Chief Justice Marshall in *The Schooner Exchange v. McFaddon*. For a more recent expression of this principle, case, see *Hui v. Castaneda*, 559 U.S. 799, 130 S. Ct. 1845 (2010). Based on the medieval dictum that "*le Roi ne peut mal faire*" (or, in English, "the King can do no wrong"), such restrictive approaches to state liability in domestic, municipal law have been abandoned or modified — with a few significant exceptions[a] — in nearly all contemporary national legal systems. In common law jurisdictions, this result has been achieved by legislation providing the requisite "consent to be sued" and judicial decisions that define the limits of immunity. Within most if not all civil law systems, the approach taken is quite different. The principles of foreign sovereign immunity do not apply to national and local governments, their agencies and personnel. Neither domestic government agencies nor governmental personnel — including judges — are deemed generally to be immune from suit.

---

[a] *See, e.g.*, Stump v. Sparkman, 435 U.S. 349 (1978) on the absolute immunity of judges acting in a "judicial capacity" regardless of the consequences and lack of any other legal redress.

Nonetheless, similar results — that is, to preclude state liability — are in some instances achieved by means of conceptual legal categories and institutional structures based at least since the early 19th century (and the French Revolution) on a dichotomy between public and private law and a dual structure of regular courts and administrative tribunals with separate and exclusive competences for adjudication of either private or public law claims. (The regular courts also adjudicate criminal cases.) Civil law systems, as noted below, differ in their approaches to these basic divisions of competence, but they generally share a common core in which the activities of the government organ and personnel have to be characterized and distinguished for each category. Thus embedded within the structures for state liability of most civil law jurisdictions is the distinction between the "commercial" (*jure gestionis*) and "governmental" (*jure imperii*) activities of the state and its actors. This dichotomy is particularly significant in Germany and Japan as well as other legal systems influenced by German law and legal science. To the extent that the activities of the state (and government actors generally) are deemed to be in the state's "capacity as a private individual" as in the case of commercial contracts, the state is subject to suit in the regular courts under private law rules. If, on the other hand, the state has acted in its governmental capacity, its liability becomes a matter of public or administrative law.

Civil law systems differ in the characterization of particular activities with, for example, a wider scope of private law versus public law liability in Germany in contrast to France. As Duncan Fairgrieve points out in his seminal comparison of state liability under English and French law,[b] the foundational case in France was the 1873 judgment of the *Tribunal des Conflicts* in the *l'arrêt Blanco* case[c] in which the tribunal held that the administrative courts had jurisdiction in actions against the state for injuries resulting from the acts of persons employed by the state. The complainant in the case, Agnès Blanco, sought damages for injuries caused by a vehicle owned and operated by the state Tobacco Administration.

The potential extent of state liability in France is illustrated by a recent Conseil d'État decision affirmed the liability of the state for damages claimed by a housemaid hired in Jakarta by a diplomat from the sultanate of Oman who was serving at UNESCO in Paris. Her wages and working conditions violated French labor law. She filed a claim with the French labor court, which ordered the diplomat to pay her €33,000 in unpaid salaries. Inasmuch as the diplomat enjoyed immunity from execution under the 1961 Vienna Convention on Diplomatic relations, the labor court judgment could not be enforced. The employee then sought direct relief from the French state. Rejected by the Ministry of Foreign Affairs, she petitioned the French administrative courts. In a 2011 decision the Conseil d'État held that the French state was strictly liable. Conseil d'État N 325253, judgment of Friday February 11, 2011 (http://arianeinternet.conseil-etat.fr/arianeinternet/ViewRoot.asp?View=Html&DMode=Html&PushDirectUrl
=1&Item=1&fond=DCE&texte=Conseil+d%92%C9tat+N+325253&Page=1&querytype=simple&NbEltPerPages=4&Pluriels=True).

---

[b] Duncan Fairgrieve, *State Liability in Tort: A Comparative Study* (2003).

[c] *See id.* at 287–288 for the decision in the case with English translation.

Even within the domain of *jure imperii*, the liability of the state has significantly expanded by a combination of constitutional, statutory, and judicial (and administrative) decisions. Bridging jurisdictional issues are provisions in the German Constitution (article 131 of the 1919 Weimar Constitution and article 34 of the Bonn Basic Law) as well as the German Civil Code (article 839) that provide for state liability for intentional or negligent violations of official duty:

Bonn Basic Law article 34:

If any person, in the exercise of a public office entrusted to him, violates his official obligations to a third party, liability rests in principle on the state or the public authority which employs him. In the case of willful intent or gross carelessness the right of recourse is reserved. With respect to the claim for compensation or the right of recourse, the jurisdiction of the ordinary courts must not be excluded.

BGH article 839:

(1) If an official intentionally or negligently breaches the official duty incumbent upon him in relation to a third party, then he must compensate the third party for damage arising from this. If the official is only responsible because of negligence, then he may only be held liable if the injured person is not able to obtain compensation in another way.

(2) If an official breaches his official duties in a judgment in a legal matter, then he is only responsible for any damage arising from this if the breach of duty consists in a criminal offence. This provision is not applicable to refusal or delay that is in breach of duty in exercising a public function.

(3) Liability for damage does not arise if the injured person has intentionally or negligently failed to avert the damage by having recourse to appeal.

The Italian and Spanish approaches differ from both Germany and France. As in most civil law countries today, state liability in Italy has long had constitutional underpinnings, but until recently the availability of redress for losses resulting from official omission or error or misconduct though either administrative or private law was quite limited. Statutory changes as well as a 1999 Supreme Court of Cassation decision[d] have expanded the liability of the state for misconduct by officials including judges. The 1948 Constitution is explicit:

Article 28

State officials and employees of other public bodies are directly responsible under criminal, civil, and administrative law for acts committed in violation of rights. Civil liability extends to the state and public bodies.

Italian law case law traditionally recognized claims against the state for damages only in cases in which state officials violated provisions of law that included a "subjective right" (*diritto soggettivo*). The language of Article 103(1) was considered to limit the competence of the regular courts to review the legality of official actions except those that involved subjective rights while, despite the language of Article

---

[d] *Cassazione Sezioni Unite*, no. 500 from 22nd July 1999.

113(1), the Italian Council of State (*Consiglio d'Stato*) was not considered to have the authority to award damages.[e]

Article 103(1)

The Council of State and the other bodies of judicial administration have jurisdiction over the protection of legitimate rights before the public administration and, in particular matters laid out by law, also of subjective rights (*diritto soggettivo*).

Article 113(1)

The judicial safeguarding of rights and legitimate interests (*interessi legitimi*) before the bodies *of ordinary or administrative justice* is always permitted against acts of the public administration. [Emphasis added.]

Matters first changed with the 1999 Supreme Court of Cassation decision allowing the regular courts to hold the state accountable for compensation to persons sustaining losses to legitimate interests (*interessi legitimi*) caused by the negligent actions. A year later the 1999 Supreme Court of Cassation decision was revered by a statute granting the administrative courts the exclusive authority to award damages against the state and state officials.[f]

Spain not only ensures a constitutional right to reparations from the state and public officials for injuries caused by state actors but establishes what may be the most comprehensive regime of state liability in Europe if not the world. Article 106 of the 1978 constitution, in English translation, reads:

Article 106

(1) The Courts control the regulatory power and the legality of administrative acts as well as its compliance with the objectives which justify it.

(2) Private individuals, under the terms established by the law, shall have the right to be indemnified for any harm they suffer in any of their property and rights, except in the cases of *force majeure*, whenever such harm is the result of the functioning of the public services.

Article 39 through 149 of Spain's 1992 statute on Public Administration and Administrative Procedure[g] provide for a unitary system of liability that applies to all administrative authorities. Any omission or conduct that is apt to cause harm irrespective of the nature or character of the conduct is made subject to liability. All persons, natural and legal, are covered. The identity of the individual officials who have caused the harm need not be identified.[h] Spain is one of the few countries to impose a regime of strict liability.[i]

---

[e] *See* Thomas Glyn Watkin, *The Italian Legal System* 149–150 (1997).

[f] Law No. 205, 21 January 2000.

[g] Ley No. 30/1992, de 26 de noviembre, de Régimen Jurídico de las Administraciones Públicas y del Procedimiento Administrativo Común.

[h] *See* Teresa Rodríguez de las Heras Ballell, *Introduction to Spanish Private Law* 290–291 (2010).

[i] Dari-Mattiacci et al, *supra* note 7, at 11.

The constitutions of Brazil, Colombia, Ecuador, Uruguay, and Mexico all guarantee state liability. The paths taken in Brazil and Colombia illustrate the European origins and diversity of approach. Colombia, for instance, follows the French approach with such suits adjudicated by its administrative courts under the Consejo de Estado. In May 2011, for example, the Colombian Council of State ruled that the military command had not acted sufficiently to prevent the August 1996 FSARC rebel attack on the Las Delicias base in Putumayo, in southern Colombia.[j] The court ordered the Ministry of Defense to pay $933,000 to three of the injured soldiers and the family of one of those killed. In the 2007 Filo Gringo Paramilitary Attack Case,[k] the court similarly awarded damages for omission — a failure to act to prevent a paramilitary attack of the village of Filo Gringo, in Northeastern Colombia. The suit for damages was brought by residents of the village, alleging they had been forced to abandon their homes and suffer significant losses as a result of a paramilitary attack in February 2000. The Government had failed to act to prevent the attack or to protect the villagers despite multiple threats by the paramilitary forces between 1999 and 2000. The court held the state liable.

Brazil, on the other hand, like Germany, treats state liability as a matter of private law. The current 1988 Constitution of Brazil provides:

Article 37(21)(6)

Public entities and private entities rendering public services are liable for the damages caused to third parties, by their agents, in such capacity, ensuring the right of recourse against the liable agent in cases of intent or fault.

Article 43 of the 2002 Civil Code supplements the constitutional guarantee as follows:

Article 43.

The legal entities of public law are civilly liable for acts of its agents that cause damage in that capacity to third parties, except that those agents causing damages through negligence or willful misconduct shall remain liable to the legal entities of public law for damages.

Consequently under Brazilian law and practice, vicarious liability of the state to compensate persons who have sustained for losses caused by official conduct is a matter of private law with an apparent right of the state to seek indemnification for any negligent or willful misconduct by the officials concerned.

In Japan the civil liability of the state and public entities has a long history. In the 1916 landmark *Tokushima Playground* case,[l] for example, the regular courts were held to have jurisdiction to adjudicate a claim for damages against the municipality for negligently maintaining playground equipment at a public school found to have caused the death of a child.

---

[j] Reported by the BBC at http://www.bbc.co.uk/news/world-latin-america-13611215.

[k] Council of State of Colombia, Judgment of August 15, 2007.

[l] Tokushima City v. Ose, 22 Minroku 1088 (Gr. Ct. Cass., June 1, 1916).

In 1946 a constitutional provision added during deliberations in the Diet.

Constitution article 17:

Every person may sue for compensation for damages (*songai baishō*) as provided by law from the State or a public entity, in case he has suffered injury through the tortious act (*fuhōkōi*) of any public official.

The State Compensation Law (*Kokka baishō hō*), Law No. 125, 1947), enacted a year later pursuant to the constitutional provision, provides an even more extensive basis for state liability:

State Compensation Law, article 1(1):

When a governmental official who is in a position to exercise the public authority of the State or of a public body has, in the course of performing his duties, illegally (*ihō ni*) caused damage to another person either intentionally or negligently, the State or the public body concerned shall be liable to compensate such damage.

In Japan the Supreme Court has held the state liable in several instances of regulatory failure as well as unconstitutional denial of voting rights to non-resident nationals. For example, in an April 2004 decision the third petty bench of the Japanese Supreme Court held the state liable for failure to require the use of mining equipment that could have reduced the incidence of black lung and similar diseases caused by inhalation of coal dust. *Japan v. Yamamoto*, 58 Minshū 1032 (Sup. Ct., 3rd P.B. Apr. 27, 2004). The case was followed in November 2004 by a Second Petty Bench decision similarly affirming the liability of the state for failure to have issued regulations to prevent disposal of methyl mercury in Minamata Bay once the determination had been made that the "Minamata Disease" was a form of mercury poisoning caused by eating fish that had ingested the dumped mercury compound waste. *Japan v. X*, 58 Minshū 1802 (Sup. Ct., 2nd P.B., Nov. 15, 2004). In 2005 the Supreme Court in an en banc decision held that the denial of voting rights to Japanese nationals residing abroad violated the constitution and that the state had thereby acted "illegally" (*ihō ni*) under article 1(1) of the State Compensation Law, thus subjecting the state to valid claims for civil damages. *Takase v. Japan*, 59 Minshū 2087 (Sup. Ct., G.B., Sept. 14, 2005). In other cases decided that year the Supreme Court held the state liable to lawyers for the failure of prosecutors to allow access to clients while under interrogation.[m] In another, a municipality was held to be liable in damages to an author as a result of the random removal of his works from the town library.[n]

The Japanese State Compensation Law has been replicated in Korea,[o] Taiwan,[p] as well as China[q] and Thailand.[r] Also noteworthy is the longstanding and extensive

---

[m] *See, e.g.*, Japan v. Jōsha. 59 Minshū 563 (Sup. Ct., 3rd P.B., April 19, 2005).

[n] Izawa v. Funabashi City, 59 Minshū 1569 (Sup. Ct., 1st P.B., July 14, 2005).

[o] *Kukka baesang pŏp* (State Compensation Law, Law No. 1899, 1967).

[p] *Kuochia peichang fa* (State Compensation Law, Law of 2 July 1980).

[q] *Zhonghua renmin gongheguo guojia peichang fa* (State Compensation Law of the People's Republic of China, May 12, 1994).

liability of the state to persons wrongfully convicted in the criminal process.[s] The standard compensation is the amount of their annual earnings times the number of years they were wrongfully imprisoned. China has a similar statute.

By common law standards state liability is extraordinarily extensive not only in most if not all other civil law jurisdictions worldwide but also, as the following cases indicate, under European Union regulations.

V. EUROPEAN UNION

FRANCOVICH AND BONIFACI v. ITALY
Joined Cases C-6/90 and C-9/90, E.C.J., Nov. 19, 1991
[1991] E.C.R. I-5357

GROUNDS OF THE JUDGMENT:

1 By orders of 9 July and 30 December 1989, which were received at the Court on 8 January and 15 January 1990 respectively, the Pretura di Vicenza (in Case C-6/90) and the Pretura di Bassano del Grappa (in Case C-9/90) referred to the Court for a preliminary ruling under Article 177 of the EEC Treaty a number of questions on the interpretation of the third paragraph of Article 189 of the EEC Treaty and Council Directive 80/987/EEC of 20 October 1980 on the approximation of the laws of the Member States relating to the protection of employees in the event of the insolvency of their employer (Official Journal 1980 L 283, p. 23).

2 Those questions were raised in the course of proceedings brought by Andrea Francovich and by Danila Bonifaci and Others (hereinafter referred to as "the plaintiffs") against the Italian Republic.

3 Directive 80/987 is intended to guarantee employees a minimum level of protection under Community law in the event of the insolvency of their employer, without prejudice to more favourable provisions existing in the Member States. In particular it provides for specific guarantees of payment of unpaid wage claims.

4 Under Article 11 the Member States were required to bring into force the laws, regulations and administrative provisions necessary to comply with the directive within a period which expired on 23 October 1983. The Italian Republic failed to fulfil that obligation, and its default was recorded by the Court in its judgment in Case 22/87 Commission v. Italy ([1989] ECR 143).

5 Mr Francovich, a party to the main proceedings in Case C-6/90, had worked for CDN Elettronica SnC in Vicenza but had received only sporadic payments on account of his wages. He therefore brought proceedings before the Pretura di Vicenza, which ordered the defendant to pay approximately LIT 6 million. In attempting to enforce that judgment the bailiff attached to the Tribunale di Vicenza

---

[r] *Praratchabanyat kwamrubpid khong chaonaatee nai tang lamerd* (Act on State Officials Liability for Tort, Law of 14 November 1996, B.E. 2539).

[s] *Keiji Hoshō Hō* (Criminal Compensation Law), Law No. 60, April 1, 1931 (effective January 1, 1932) and *Keiji Hoshō Hō* (Criminal Compensation Law), Law No. 1, 1950).

was obliged to submit a negative return. Mr Francovich then claimed to be entitled to obtain from the Italian State the guarantees provided for in Directive 80/987 or, in the alternative, compensation.

6 In Case C-9/90 Danila Bonifaci and 33 other employees brought proceedings before the Pretura di Bassano del Grappa, stating that they had been employed by Gaia Confezioni Srl, which was declared insolvent on 5 April 1985. When the employment relationships were discontinued, the plaintiffs were owed more than LIT 253 million, which was proved as a debt in the company's insolvency. More than five years after the insolvency they had been paid nothing, and the receiver had told them that even a partial distribution in their favour was entirely improbable. Consequently, the plaintiffs brought proceedings against the Italian Republic in which they claimed that, in view of its obligation to implement Directive 80/987 with effect from 23 October 1983, it should be ordered to pay them their arrears of wages, at least for the last three months, or in the alternative to pay compensation.

7 It was in those circumstances that the national courts referred the following questions, which are identical in both Cases, to the Court for a preliminary ruling:

"(1) Under the system of Community law in force, is a private individual who has been adversely affected by the failure of a Member State to implement Directive 80/897 — a failure confirmed by a judgment of the Court of Justice — entitled to require the State itself to give effect to those provisions of that directive which are sufficiently precise and unconditional, by directly invoking the Community legislation against the Member State in default so as to obtain the guarantees which that State itself should have provided and in any event to claim reparation of the loss and damage sustained in relation to provisions to which that right does not apply?"

"(2) Are the combined provisions of Articles 3 and 4 of Council Directive 80/987 to be interpreted as meaning that where the State has not availed itself of the option of laying down limits under Article 4, the State itself is obliged to pay the claims of employees in accordance with Article 3?"

"(3) If the answer to Question 2 is in the negative, the Court is asked to state what the minimum guarantee is that the State must provide pursuant to Directive 80/987 to an entitled employee so as to ensure that the share of pay payable to that employee may be regarded as giving effect to the directive."

8 Reference is made to the Report for the Hearing for a fuller account of the facts of the main proceedings, the procedure and the written observations submitted to the Court, which are mentioned or discussed hereinafter only in so far as is necessary for the reasoning of the Court.

9 The first question submitted by the national courts raises two issues, which should be considered separately. It concerns, first, the direct effect of the provisions of the directive which determine the rights of employees and, secondly, the existence and scope of State liability for damage resulting from breach of its obligations under Community law.

The direct effect of the provisions of the directive which determine the rights of employees

10 The first part of the first question submitted by the national courts seeks to determine whether the provisions of the directive which determine the rights of employees must be interpreted as meaning that the persons concerned can enforce those rights against the State in the national courts in the absence of implementing measures adopted within the prescribed period.

11 As the Court has consistently held, a Member State which has not adopted the implementing measures required by a directive within the prescribed period may not, against individuals, plead its own failure to perform the obligations which the directive entails. Thus wherever the provisions of a directive appear, as far as their subject-matter is concerned, to be unconditional and sufficiently precise, those provisions may, in the absence of implementing measures adopted within the prescribed period, be relied upon as against any national provision which is incompatible with the directive or in so far as the provisions of the directive define rights which individuals are able to assert against the State [citation omitted].

12 It is therefore necessary to see whether the provisions of Directive 80/987 which determine the rights of employees are unconditional and sufficiently precise. There are three points to be considered: the identity of the persons entitled to the guarantee provided, the content of that guarantee and the identity of the person liable to provide the guarantee. In that regard, the question arises in particular whether a State can be held liable to provide the guarantee on the ground that it did not take the necessary implementing measures within the prescribed period.

13 With regard first of all to the identity of the persons entitled to the guarantee, it is to be noted that, according to Article 1(1), the directive applies to employees' claims arising from contracts of employment or employment relationships and existing against employers who are in a state of insolvency within the meaning of Article 2(1), the latter provision defining the circumstances in which an employer must be deemed to be in a state of insolvency. Article 2(2) refers to national law for the definition of the concepts of "employee" and "employer". Finally, Article 1(2) provides that the Member States may, by way of exception and under certain conditions, exclude claims by certain categories of employees listed in the Annex to the directive.

14 Those provisions are sufficiently precise and unconditional to enable the national court to determine whether or not a person should be regarded as a person intended to benefit under the directive. A national court need only verify whether the person concerned is an employed person under national law and whether he is excluded from the scope of the directive in accordance with Article 1(2) and Annex 1 (as to the necessary conditions for such exclusion [citations omitted], and then ascertain whether one of the situations of insolvency provided for in Article 2 of the directive exists.

15 With regard to the content of the guarantee, Article 3 of the directive provides that measures must be taken to ensure the payment of outstanding claims resulting from contracts of employment or employment relationships and relating to pay for the period prior to a date determined by the Member State, which may choose one

of three possibilities: (a) the date of the onset of the employer's insolvency; (b) that of the notice of dismissal issued to the employee concerned on account of the employer's insolvency; (c) that of the onset of the employer's insolvency or that on which the contract of employment or the employment relationship with the employee concerned was discontinued on account of the employer's insolvency.

16 Depending on the choice it makes, the Member State has the option, under Article 4(1) and (2), to restrict liability to periods of three months or eight weeks respectively, calculated in accordance with detailed rules laid down in that Article. Finally, Article 4(3) provides that the Member States may set a ceiling on liability, in order to avoid the payment of sums going beyond the social objective of the directive. Where the exercise that option, the Member States must inform the Commission of the methods used to set the ceiling. In addition, Article 10 provides that the directive does not affect the option of Member States to take the measures necessary to avoid abuses and in particular to refuse or reduce liability in certain circumstances.

17 Article 3 of the directive thus leaves the Member State a discretion in determining the date from which payment of claims must be ensured. However, as is already implicit in the Court's case-law [citations omitted], the right of a State to choose among several possible means of achieving the result required by a directive does not preclude the possibility for individuals of enforcing before the national courts rights whose content can be determined sufficiently precisely on the basis of the provisions of the directive alone.

18 In this case, the result required by the directive in question is a guarantee that the outstanding claims of employees will be paid in the event of the insolvency of their employer. The fact that Articles 3 and 4(1) and (2) give the Member States some discretion as regards the means of establishing that guarantee and the restriction of its amount do not affect the precise and unconditional nature of the result required.

19 As the Commission and the plaintiffs have pointed out, it is possible to determine the minimum guarantee provided for by the directive by taking the date whose choice entails the least liability for the guarantee institution. That date is that of the onset of the employer's insolvency, since the two other dates, that of the notice of dismissal issued to the employee and that on which the contract of employment or the employment relationship was discontinued, are, according to the conditions laid down in Article 3, necessarily subsequent to the onset of the insolvency and thus define a longer period in respect of which the payment of claims must be ensured.

20 The possibility under Article 4(2) of limiting the guarantee does not make it impossible to determine the minimum guarantee. It follows from the wording of that Article that the Member States have the option of limiting the guarantees granted to employees to certain periods prior to the date referred to in Article 3. Those periods are fixed in relation to each of the three dates provided for in Article 3, so that it is always possible to determine to what extent the Member State could have reduced the guarantee provided for by the directive depending on the date which it would have chosen if it had transposed the directive.

21 As regards Article 4(3), according to which the Member States may set a

ceiling on liability in order to avoid the payment of sums going beyond the social objective of the directive, and Article 10, which states that the directive does not affect the option of Member States to take the measures necessary to avoid abuses, it should be observed that a Member State which has failed to fulfil its obligations to transpose a directive cannot defeat the rights which the directive creates for the benefit of individuals by relying on the option of limiting the amount of the guarantee which it could have exercised if it had taken the measures necessary to implement the directive (see, in relation to an analogous option concerning the prevention of abuse in fiscal matters, the judgment in Case 8/81 Becker v. Finanzamt Muenster-Innenstadt [1982] ECR 53, paragraph 34).

22 It must therefore be held that the provisions in question are unconditional and sufficiently precise as regards the content of the guarantee.

23 Finally, as regards the identity of the person liable to provide the guarantee, Article 5 of the directive provides that: "Member States shall lay down detailed rules for the organization, financing and operation of the guarantee institutions, complying with the following principles in particular: (a) the assets of the institutions shall be independent of the employers' operating capital and be inaccessible to proceedings for insolvency; (b) employers shall contribute to financing, unless it is fully covered by the public authorities; (c) the institutions' liabilities shall not depend on whether or not obligations to contribute to financing have been fulfilled."

24 It has been submitted that since the directive provides for the possibility that the guarantee institutions may be financed entirely by the public authorities, it is unacceptable that a Member State may thwart the effects of the directive by asserting that it could have required other persons to bear part or all of the financial burden resting upon it.

25 That argument cannot be upheld. It follows from the terms of the directive that the Member State is required to organize an appropriate institutional guarantee system. Under Article 5, the Member State has a broad discretion with regard to the organization, operation and financing of the guarantee institutions. The fact, referred to by the Commission, that the directive envisages as one possibility among others that such a system may be financed entirely by the public authorities cannot mean that the State can be identified as the person liable for unpaid claims. The payment obligation lies with the guarantee institutions, and it is only in exercising its power to organize the guarantee system that the State may provide that the guarantee institutions are to be financed entirely by the public authorities. In those circumstances the State takes on an obligation which in principle is not its own.

26 Accordingly, even though the provisions of the directive in question are sufficiently precise and unconditional as regards the determination of the persons entitled to the guarantee and as regards the content of that guarantee, those elements are not sufficient to enable individuals to rely on those provisions before the national courts. Those provisions do not identify the person liable to provide the guarantee, and the State cannot be considered liable on the sole ground that it has failed to take transposition measures within the prescribed period.

27 The answer to the first part of the first question must therefore be that the provisions of Directive 80/987 which determine the rights of employees must be interpreted as meaning that the persons concerned cannot enforce those rights against the State before the national courts where no implementing measures are adopted within the prescribed period.

Liability of the State for loss and damage resulting from breach of its obligations under Community law

28 In the second part of the first question the national court seeks to determine whether a Member State is obliged to make good loss and damage suffered by individuals as a result of the failure to transpose Directive 80/987.

29 The national court thus raises the issue of the existence and scope of a State' liability for loss and damage resulting from breach of its obligations under Community law.

30 That issue must be considered in the light of the general system of the Treaty and its fundamental principles.

(a) The existence of State liability as a matter of principle

31 It should be borne in mind at the outset that the EEC Treaty has created its own legal system, which is integrated into the legal systems of the Member States and which their Courts are bound to apply. The subjects of that legal system are not only the Member States but also their nationals. Just as it imposes burdens on individuals, Community law is also intended to give rise to rights which become part of their legal patrimony. Those rights arise not only where they are expressly granted by the Treaty but also by virtue of obligations which the Treaty imposes in a clearly defined manner both on individuals and on the Member States and the Community institutions [citations omitted].

32 Furthermore, it has been consistently held that the national courts whose task it is to apply the provisions of Community law in areas within their jurisdiction must ensure that those rules take full effect and must protect the rights which they confer on individuals [citations omitted].

33 The full effectiveness of Community rules would be impaired and the protection of the rights which they grant would be weakened if individuals were unable to obtain redress when their rights are infringed by a breach of Community law for which a Member State can be held responsible.

34 The possibility of obtaining redress from the Member State is particularly indispensable where, as in this case, the full effectiveness of Community rules is subject to prior action on the part of the State and where, consequently, in the absence of such action, individuals cannot enforce before the national courts the rights conferred upon them by Community law.

35 It follows that the principle whereby a State must be liable for loss and damage caused to individuals as a result of breaches of Community law for which the State can be held responsible is inherent in the system of the Treaty.

36 A further basis for the obligation of Member States to make good such loss and damage is to be found in Article 5 of the Treaty, under which the Member States are required to take all appropriate measures, whether general or particular, to ensure fulfilment of their obligations under Community law. Among these is the obligation to nullify the unlawful consequences of a breach of Community law [citation omitted].

37 It follows from all the foregoing that it is a principle of Community law that the Member States are obliged to make good loss and damage caused to individuals by breaches of Community law for which they can be held responsible.

(b) The conditions for State liability

38 Although State liability is thus required by Community law, the conditions under which that liability gives rise to a right to reparation depend on the nature of the breach of Community law giving rise to the loss and damage.

39 Where, as in this case, a Member State fails to fulfil its obligation under the third paragraph of Article 189 of the Treaty to take all the measures necessary to achieve the result prescribed by a directive, the full effectiveness of that rule of Community law requires that there should be a right to reparation provided that three conditions are fulfiled.

40 The first of those conditions is that the result prescribed by the directive should entail the grant of rights to individuals. The second condition is that it should be possible to identify the content of those rights on the basis of the provisions of the directive. Finally, the third condition is the existence of a causal link between the breach of the State's obligation and the loss and damage suffered by the injured parties.

41 Those conditions are sufficient to give rise to a right on the part of individuals to obtain reparation, a right founded directly on Community law.

42 Subject to that reservation, it is on the basis of the rules of national law on liability that the State must make reparation for the consequences of the loss and damage caused. In the absence of Community legislation, it is for the internal legal order of each Member State to designate the competent Courts and lay down the detailed procedural rules for legal proceedings intended fully to safeguard the rights which individuals derive from Community law [citations omitted].

43 Further, the substantive and procedural conditions for reparation of loss and damage laid down by the national law of the Member States must not be less favourable than those relating to similar domestic claims and must not be so framed as to make it virtually impossible or excessively difficult to obtain reparation [citation omitted].

44 In this case, the breach of Community law by a Member State by virtue of its failure to transpose Directive 80/987 within the prescribed period has been confirmed by a judgment of the Court. The result required by that directive entails the grant to employees of a right to a guarantee of payment of their unpaid wage claims. As is clear from the examination of the first part of the first question, the content of that right can be identified on the basis of the provisions of the directive.

45 Consequently, the national court must, in accordance with the national rules on liability, uphold the right of employees to obtain reparation of loss and damage caused to them as a result of failure to transpose the directive.

46 The answer to be given to the national court must therefore be that a Member State is required to make good loss and damage caused to individuals by failure to transpose Directive 80/987.

The second and third questions

47 In view of the reply to the first question referred by the national court, there is no need to rule on the second and third questions.

KÖBLER v. AUSTRIA
(Case C-224/01) — [2003] All ER (D) 73 (Sept. 30, 2003)

JUDGMENT

1 By an order of 7 May 2001, received at the Court on 6 June 2001, the Landesgericht für Zivilrechtssachen Wien (Regional Civil Court, Vienna) referred to the Court for a preliminary ruling under Article 234 EC a question on the interpretation of, first, Article 48 of the EC Treaty (now, after amendment, Article 39 EC) and, secondly, the judgments of the Court in Joined Cases C-46/93 and C-48/93 *Brasserie du Pêcheur and Factortame* [1996] ECR I-1029 and Case C-54/96 *Dorsch Consult* [1997] ECR I-4961.

2 Those questions were raised in the course of an action for a declaration of liability brought by Mr Köbler against the Republic of Austria for breach of a provision of Community law by a judgment of the Verwaltungsgerichtshof (Supreme Administrative Court), Austria.

Legal framework

3 Article 48(3) of the Gehaltsgesetz 1956 (law on salaries of 1956, BGBl. 1956/54), as amended in 1997 (BGBl. I, 1997/109) (hereinafter the GG), provides: In so far as may be necessary in order to secure the services of a scientific expert or an artist from the country or from abroad, the Federal President may grant a basic salary higher than that provided for in Article 48(2) on appointment to a post as a university professor (Article 21 of the Bundesgesetz über die Organisation der Universitäten (Federal law on the organisation of universities), BGBl. 1993/805, hereinafter the UOG 1993) or as an ordinary professor of universities or of an institution of higher education.

4 Article 50a(1) of the GG is worded as follows: A university professor (Article 21 of the UOG 1993) or an ordinary professor at a university or an institution of higher education who has completed 15 years service in that capacity in Austrian universities or institutions of higher education and who for four years has been in receipt of the length-of-service increment provided for in Article 50(4) shall be eligible, with effect from the date on which those two conditions are fulfilled, for a

special length-of-service increment to be taken into account in the calculation of his retirement pension the amount of which shall correspond to that of the length-of-service increment provided for in Article 50(4).

Dispute in the main proceedings

5 Mr Köbler has been employed since 1 March 1986 under a public-law contract with the Austrian State in the capacity of ordinary university professor in Innsbruck (Austria). On his appointment he was awarded the salary of an ordinary university professor, tenth step, increased by the normal length-of-service increment.

6 By letter of 28 February 1996, Mr Köbler applied under Article 50a of the GG for the special length-of-service increment for university professors. He claimed that, although he had not completed 15 years' service as a professor at Austrian universities, he had completed the requisite length of service if the duration of his service in universities of other Member States of the European Community were taken into consideration. He claimed that the condition of completion of 15 years service solely in Austrian universities — with no account being taken of periods of service in universities in other Member States — amounted to indirect discrimination unjustified under Community law.

7 In the dispute to which Mr Köbler's claim gave rise, the Verwaltungsgerichtshof, Austria, referred to the Court, by order of 22 October 1997, a request for a preliminary ruling which was registered at the Registry of the Court under Case number C-382/97.

8 By letter of 11 March 1998, the Registrar of the Court asked the Verwaltungsgerichtshof whether, in the light of the judgment of 15 January 1998 in Case C-15/96 *Schöning-Kougebetopoulou* [1998] ECR I-47, it deemed it necessary to maintain its request for a preliminary ruling.

9 By order of 25 March 1998 the Verwaltungsgerichtshof asked the parties for their views on the request by the Registrar of the Court, since on a provisional view the legal issue which was the subject-matter of the question submitted for a preliminary ruling had been resolved in favour of Mr Köbler.

10 By order of 24 June 1998, the Verwaltungsgerichtshof withdrew its request for a preliminary ruling and, by a judgment of the same date, dismissed Mr Köbler's application on the ground that the special length-of-service increment was a loyalty bonus which objectively justified a derogation from the Community law provisions on freedom of movement for workers.

11 That judgment of 24 June 1998 states in particular: . . . In its order for reference of 22 October 1997 [in Case C-382/97] the Verwaltungsgerichtshof took the view that the special length-of-service increment for ordinary university professors is in the nature of neither a loyalty bonus nor a reward, but is rather a component of salary under the system of career advancement. That interpretation of the law, which is not binding on the parties to proceedings before the Verwaltungsgerichtshof, cannot be upheld . . . . It is thus clear that the special length-of-service increment under Paragraph 50a of the 1956 salary law is unrelated

to the market value assessment to be undertaken in the course of the appointment procedure, but, rather, its purpose must be seen as the provision of a positive incentive to academics in a very mobile labour market to spend their career in Austrian universities. It cannot therefore be a component of salary as such and, because of its function as a loyalty bonus, requires a certain length of service as an ordinary university professor at Austrian universities as a precondition for eligibility. The treatment of the special length-of-service increment as a component of monthly earnings and the consequent permanent character of the loyalty bonus do not essentially preclude the above interpretation. Since, in Austria, — in so far as this is of relevance in the present case — the legal personality of the universities is vested in the Federal State alone, the rules in Paragraph 50a of the 1956 salary law apply to only one employer — in contrast to the situation in Germany contemplated in the judgment of the Court of Justice in Case C-15/96 *Kalliope Schöning-Kougebetopoulou* [1998] ECR I-47. Previous periods of service are taken into account in reckoning length of service, as the plaintiff demands, in the course of the assessment of market value in the appointment procedure. There is no provision for any further account to be taken of such previous periods of service in the special length-of-service increment even for Austrian academics who resume teaching in Austria after spending time working abroad and such provision would not be consistent with the notion of rewarding many years' loyalty to an employer deemed by the Court of Justice to justify a rule which in itself breaches the prohibition on discrimination. As the claim which the complainant seeks to assert here is for a special length of service increment under Paragraph 50a of the 1956 salary law which is a statutory loyalty bonus and as such is recognised by the Court of Justice as justification for legislation conflicting with the prohibition on discrimination, the complaint based on breach of that prohibition on discrimination is unfounded; it should be dismissed . . . .

12 Mr Köbler brought an action for damages before the referring court against the Republic of Austria for reparation of the loss which he allegedly suffered as a result of the non-payment to him of a special length-of-service increment. He maintains that the judgment of the Verwaltungsgerichtshof of 24 June 1998 infringed directly applicable provisions of Community law, as interpreted by the Court in the judgments in which it held that a special length-of-service increment does not constitute a loyalty bonus.

13 The Republic of Austria contends that the judgment of the Verwaltungsgerichtshof of 24 June 1998 does not infringe the directly applicable Community law. Moreover, in its view, the decision of a court adjudicating at last instance such as the Verwaltungsgerichtshof cannot found an obligation to afford reparation as against the State.

The questions referred

14 Taking the view that in the case before it the interpretation of Community law was not free from doubt and that such interpretation was necessary in order for it to give its decision, the Landesgericht für Zivilrechtssachen Wien decided to stay proceedings and to refer the following questions to the Court for a preliminary ruling:

(1) *Is the case-law of the Court of Justice to the effect that it is immaterial as regards State liability for a breach of Community law which institution of a Member State is responsible for that breach [citation omitted] also applicable when the conduct of an institution purportedly contrary to Community law is a decision of a supreme court of a Member State, such as, as in this case, the Verwaltungsgerichtshof?* [Emphasis added.]

(2) *If the answer to Question 1 is yes: Is the case-law of the Court of Justice according to which it is for the legal system of each Member State to determine which court or tribunal has jurisdiction to hear disputes involving individual rights derived from Community law [citation omitted] also applicable when the conduct of an institution purportedly contrary to Community law is a judgment of a supreme court of a Member State, such as, in this case, the Verwaltungsgerichtshof?* [Emphasis added.]

(3) *If the answer to Question 2 is yes: Does the legal interpretation given in the abovementioned judgment of the Verwaltungsgerichtshof, according to which the special length-of-service increment is a form of loyalty bonus, breach a rule of directly applicable Community law, in particular the prohibition on indirect discrimination in Article 48 [of the Treaty] and the relevant settled case-law of the Court of Justice?* [Emphasis added.]

(4) *If the answer to Question 3 is yes: Is this rule of directly applicable Community law such as to create a subjective right for the applicant in the main proceedings?* [Emphasis added.]

(5) *If the answer to Question 4 is yes: Does the Court . . . have sufficient information in the content of the order for reference to enable it to rule itself as to whether the Verwaltungsgerichtshof in the circumstances of the main proceedings described has clearly and significantly exceeded the discretion available to it, or is it for the referring Austrian court to answer that question?* [Emphasis added.]

First and second questions

15 By its first and second questions, which must be examined together, the referring court is essentially asking whether the principle according to which Member States are obliged to make good damage caused to individuals by infringements of Community law for which they are responsible is also applicable where the alleged infringement stems from a decision of a court adjudicating at last instance and whether, if so, it is for the legal system of each Member State to designate the court competent to adjudicate on disputes relating to such reparation.

Observations submitted to the Court [omitted]

Principle of State liability

30 First, as the Court has repeatedly held, the principle of liability on the part of a Member State for damage caused to individuals as a result of breaches of Community law for which the State is responsible is inherent in the system of the Treaty [citations omitted].

31 The Court has also held that that principle applies to any case in which a Member State breaches Community law, whichever is the authority of the Member State whose act or omission was responsible for the breach [citations omitted].

32 In international law a State which incurs liability for breach of an international commitment is viewed as a single entity, irrespective of whether the breach which gave rise to the damage is attributable to the legislature, the judiciary or the executive. That principle must apply *a fortiori* in the Community legal order since all State authorities, including the legislature, are bound in performing their tasks to comply with the rules laid down by Community law which directly govern the situation of individuals [citation omitted].

33 In the light of the essential role played by the judiciary in the protection of the rights derived by individuals from Community rules, the full effectiveness of those rules would be called in question and the protection of those rights would be weakened if individuals were precluded from being able, under certain conditions, to obtain reparation when their rights are affected by an infringement of Community law attributable to a decision of a court of a Member State adjudicating at last instance.

34 It must be stressed, in that context, that a court adjudicating at last instance is by definition the last judicial body before which individuals may assert the rights conferred on them by Community law. Since an infringement of those rights by a final decision of such a court cannot thereafter normally be corrected, individuals cannot be deprived of the possibility of rendering the State liable in order in that way to obtain legal protection of their rights.

35 Moreover, it is, in particular, in order to prevent rights conferred on individuals by Community law from being infringed that under the third paragraph of Article 234 EC a court against whose decisions there is no judicial remedy under national law is required to make a reference to the Court of Justice.

36 Consequently, it follows from the requirements inherent in the protection of the rights of individuals relying on Community law that they must have the possibility of obtaining redress in the national courts for the damage caused by the infringement of those rights owing to a decision of a court adjudicating at last instance [citation omitted].

37 Certain of the governments which submitted observations in these proceedings claimed that the principle of State liability for damage caused to individuals by infringements of Community law could not be applied to decisions of a national court adjudicating at last instance. In that connection arguments were put forward based, in particular, on the principle of legal certainty and, more specifically, the principle of *res judicata*, the independence and authority of the judiciary and the absence of a court competent to determine disputes relating to State liability for such decisions.

38 In that regard the importance of the principle of *res judicata* cannot be disputed [citation omitted]. In order to ensure both stability of the law and legal relations and the sound administration of justice, it is important that judicial decisions which have become definitive after all rights of appeal have been

exhausted or after expiry of the time-limits provided for in that connection can no longer be called in question.

39 However, it should be borne in mind that recognition of the principle of State liability for a decision of a court adjudicating at last instance does not in itself have the consequence of calling in question that decision as *res judicata*. Proceedings seeking to render the State liable do not have the same purpose and do not necessarily involve the same parties as the proceedings resulting in the decision which has acquired the status of *res judicata*. The applicant in an action to establish the liability of the State will, if successful, secure an order against it for reparation of the damage incurred but not necessarily a declaration invalidating the status of *res judicata* of the judicial decision which was responsible for the damage. In any event, the principle of State liability inherent in the Community legal order requires such reparation, but not revision of the judicial decision which was responsible for the damage.

40 It follows that the principle of *res judicata* does not preclude recognition of the principle of State liability for the decision of a court adjudicating at last instance.

41 Nor can the arguments based on the independence and authority of the judiciary be upheld.

42 As to the independence of the judiciary, the principle of liability in question concerns not the personal liability of the judge but that of the State. The possibility that under certain conditions the State may be rendered liable for judicial decisions contrary to Community law does not appear to entail any particular risk that the independence of a court adjudicating at last instance will be called in question.

43 As to the argument based on the risk of a diminution of the authority of a court adjudicating at last instance owing to the fact that its final decisions could by implication be called in question in proceedings in which the State may be rendered liable for such decisions, the existence of a right of action that affords, under certain conditions, reparation of the injurious effects of an erroneous judicial decision could also be regarded as enhancing the quality of a legal system and thus in the long run the authority of the judiciary.

44 Several governments also argued that application of the principle of State liability to decisions of a national court adjudicating at last instance was precluded by the difficulty of designating a court competent to determine disputes concerning the reparation of damage resulting from such decisions.

45 In that connection, given that, for reasons essentially connected with the need to secure for individuals protection of the rights conferred on them by Community rules, the principle of State liability inherent in the Community legal order must apply in regard to decisions of a national court adjudicating at last instance, it is for the Member States to enable those affected to rely on that principle by affording them an appropriate right of action. Application of that principle cannot be compromised by the absence of a competent court.

46 According to settled case-law, in the absence of Community legislation, it is for the internal legal order of each Member State to designate the competent courts

and lay down the detailed procedural rules for legal proceedings intended fully to safeguard the rights which individuals derive from Community law [citations omitted].

47 Subject to the reservation that it is for the Member States to ensure in each case that those rights are effectively protected, it is not for the Court to become involved in resolving questions of jurisdiction to which the classification of certain legal situations based on Community law may give rise in the national judicial system [citations omitted].

48 It should be added that, although considerations to do with observance of the principle of *res judicata* or the independence of the judiciary have caused national legal systems to impose restrictions, which may sometimes be stringent, on the possibility of rendering the State liable for damage caused by mistaken judicial decisions, such considerations have not been such as absolutely to exclude that possibility. Indeed, application of the principle of State liability to judicial decisions has been accepted in one form or another by most of the Member States, as the Advocate General pointed out at paragraphs 77 to 82 of his Opinion, even if subject only to restrictive and varying conditions.

49 It may also be noted that, in the same connection, the ECHR and, more particularly, Article 41 thereof enables the European Court of Human Rights to order a State which has infringed a fundamental right to provide reparation of the damage resulting from that conduct for the injured party. The case-law of that court shows that such reparation may also be granted when the infringement stems from a decision of a national court adjudicating at last instance (see ECt.HR, *Dulaurans v. France*, 21 March 2000, not yet published).

50 It follows from the foregoing that the principle according to which the Member States are liable to afford reparation of damage caused to individuals as a result of infringements of Community law for which they are responsible is also applicable where the alleged infringement stems from a decision of a court adjudicating at last instance. It is for the legal system of each Member State to designate the court competent to adjudicate on disputes relating to such reparation.

Conditions governing State liability

51 As to the conditions to be satisfied for a Member State to be required to make reparation for loss and damage caused to individuals as a result of breaches of Community law for which the State is responsible, the Court has held that these are threefold: the rule of law infringed must be intended to confer rights on individuals; the breach must be sufficiently serious; and there must be a direct causal link between the breach of the obligation incumbent on the State and the loss or damage sustained by the injured parties [citation omitted].

52 State liability for loss or damage caused by a decision of a national court adjudicating at last instance which infringes a rule of Community law is governed by the same conditions.

53 With regard more particularly to the second of those conditions and its application with a view to establishing possible State liability owing to a decision of

a national court adjudicating at last instance, regard must be had to the specific nature of the judicial function and to the legitimate requirements of legal certainty, as the Member States which submitted observations in this case have also contended. State liability for an infringement of Community law by a decision of a national court adjudicating at last instance can be incurred only in the exceptional case where the court has manifestly infringed the applicable law.

54 In order to determine whether that condition is satisfied, the national court hearing a claim for reparation must take account of all the factors which characterise the situation put before it.

55 Those factors include, in particular, the degree of clarity and precision of the rule infringed, whether the infringement was intentional, whether the error of law was excusable or inexcusable, the position taken, where applicable, by a Community institution and non-compliance by the court in question with its obligation to make a reference for a preliminary ruling under the third paragraph of Article 234 EC.

56 In any event, an infringement of Community law will be sufficiently serious where the decision concerned was made in manifest breach of the case-law of the Court in the matter [citation omitted].

57 The three conditions mentioned at paragraph 51 hereof are necessary and sufficient to found a right in favour of individuals to obtain redress, although this does not mean that the State cannot incur liability under less strict conditions on the basis of national law [citation omitted].

58 Subject to the existence of a right to obtain reparation which is founded directly on Community law where the conditions mentioned above are met, it is on the basis of rules of national law on liability that the State must make reparation for the consequences of the loss and damage caused, with the proviso that the conditions for reparation of loss and damage laid down by the national legislation must not be less favourable than those relating to similar domestic claims and must not be so framed as to make it in practice impossible or excessively difficult to obtain reparation

59 *In the light of all the foregoing, the reply to the first and second questions must be that the principle that Member States are obliged to make good damage caused to individuals by infringements of Community law for which they are responsible is also applicable where the alleged infringement stems from a decision of a court adjudicating at last instance where the rule of Community law infringed is intended to confer rights on individuals, the breach is sufficiently serious and there is a direct causal link between that breach and the loss or damage sustained by the injured parties. In order to determine whether the infringement is sufficiently serious when the infringement at issue stems from such a decision, the competent national court, taking into account the specific nature of the judicial function, must determine whether that infringement is manifest. It is for the legal system of each Member State to designate the court competent to determine disputes relating to that reparation.* [Emphasis added.]

Third question

60 At the outset it must be recalled that the Court has consistently held that, in the context of the application of Article 234 EC, it has no jurisdiction to decide whether a national provision is compatible with Community law. The Court may, however, extract from the wording of the questions formulated by the national court, and having regard to the facts stated by the latter, those elements which concern the interpretation of Community law, for the purpose of enabling that court to resolve the legal problems before it [citations omitted].

61 In its third question the national court essentially seeks to ascertain whether Article 48 of the Treaty and Article 7(1) of Regulation (EEC) No 1612/68 of the Council of 15 October 1968 on freedom of movement for workers within the Community (OJ, English Special Edition 1968 (II), p. 475) are to be interpreted as meaning that they preclude the grant, under conditions such as those laid down in Article 50a of the GG, of a special length-of-service increment which, according to the interpretation of the Verwaltungsgerichtshof in its judgment of 24 June 1998, constitutes a loyalty bonus.

Observations submitted to the Court [omitted]

70 The special length-of-service increment granted by the Austrian State *qua* employer to university professors under Article 50a of the GG secures a financial benefit in addition to basic salary the amount of which is already dependent on length of service. A university professor receives that increment if he has carried on that profession for at least 15 years with an Austrian university and if, furthermore, he has been in receipt for at least four years of the normal length-of-service increment.

71 Accordingly, Article 50a of the GG precludes, for the purpose of the grant of the special length-of-service increment for which it provides, any possibility of taking into account periods of activity completed by a university professor in a Member State other than the Republic of Austria.

72 Such a regime is clearly likely to impede freedom of movement for workers in two respects.

73 First, that regime operates to the detriment of migrant workers who are nationals of Member States other than the Republic of Austria where those workers are refused recognition of periods of service completed by them in those States in the capacity of university professor on the sole ground that those periods were not completed in an Austrian university (see, in that connection, with regard to a comparable Greek provision, Case C-187/96 *Commission* v. *Greece* [1998] ECR I-1095, paragraphs 20 and 21).

74 Secondly, that absolute refusal to recognise periods served as a university professor in a Member State other than the Republic of Austria impedes freedom of movement for workers established in Austria inasmuch as it is such as to deter the latter from leaving the country to exercise that freedom. In fact, on their return to Austria, their years of experience in the capacity of university professor in another Member State, that is to say in the pursuit of comparable activities, are not

taken into account for the purposes of the special length-of-service increment provided for in Article 50a of the GG.

75 Those considerations are not altered by the fact relied on by the Republic of Austria that, owing to the possibility afforded by Article 48(3) of the GG to grant migrant university professors a higher basic salary in order to promote the recruitment of foreign university professors, their remuneration is often more than that received by professors of Austrian universities, even after account is taken of the special length-of-service increment.

76 In fact, on the one hand, Article 48(3) of the GG offers merely a possibility and does not guarantee that a professor from a foreign university will receive as from his appointment as a professor of an Austrian university a higher remuneration than that received by professors of Austrian universities with the same experience. Secondly, the additional remuneration available under Article 48(3) of the GG upon appointment is quite different from the special length-of-service increment. Thus, that provision does not prevent Article 50a of the GG from having the effect of occasioning unequal treatment in regard to migrant university professors as opposed to professors of Austrian universities and thus creates an impediment to the freedom of movement of workers secured by Article 48 of the Treaty.

77 Consequently, a measure such as the grant of a special length-of-service increment provided for in Article 50a of the GG is likely to constitute an obstacle to freedom of movement for workers prohibited in principle by Article 48 of the Treaty and Article 7(1) of Regulation No 1612/68. Such a measure could be accepted only if it pursued a legitimate aim compatible with the Treaty and were justified by pressing reasons of public interest. But even if that were so, application of that measure would still have to be such as to ensure achievement of the aim in question and not go beyond what is necessary for that purpose (see, inter alia, Case C-19/92 *Kraus* [1993] ECR I-1663, paragraph 32, Case C-55/94 *Gebhard* [1995] ECR I-4165, paragraph 37 and Case C-415/93 *Bosman* [1995] ECR I-4921, paragraph 104).

78 In its judgment of 24 June 1998 the Verwaltungsgerichtshof held that the special length-of-service increment provided for in Article 50a of the GG constituted under national law a bonus seeking to reward the loyalty of professors of Austrian universities to their sole employer, namely the Austrian State.

79 Accordingly, it is necessary to examine whether the fact that under national law that benefit constitutes a loyalty bonus may be deemed under Community law to indicate that it is dictated by a pressing public-interest reason capable of justifying the obstacle to freedom of movement that the bonus involves.

80 The Court has not yet had the opportunity of deciding whether a loyalty bonus can justify an obstacle to freedom of movement for workers.

82 In the present case the Verwaltungsgerichtshof held in its judgment of 24 June 1998 that the special length-of-service increment provided for in Article 50a of the GG rewards an employee's loyalty to a single employer.

. . . .

83 Although it cannot be excluded that an objective of rewarding workers' loyalty to their employers in the context of policy concerning research or university

education constitutes a pressing public-interest reason, given the particular characteristics of the measure at issue in the main proceedings, the obstacle which it entails clearly cannot be justified in the light of such an objective.

84 First, although all the professors of Austrian public universities are the employees of a single employer, namely the Austrian State, they are assigned to different universities. However, on the employment market for university professors, the various Austrian universities are in competition not only with the universities of other Member States and those of non-Member States but also amongst themselves. As to that second kind of competition the measure at issue in the main proceedings does nothing to promote the loyalty of a professor to the Austrian university where he performs his duties.

85 Second, although the special length-of-service increment seeks to reward workers' loyalty to their employer, it also has the effect of rewarding the professors of Austrian universities who continue to exercise their profession on Austrian territory. The benefit in question is therefore likely to have consequences in regard to the choice made by those professors between a post in an Austrian university and a post in the university of another Member State.

86 Accordingly, the special length-of-service increment at issue in the main proceedings does not solely have the effect of rewarding the employee's loyalty to his employer. It also leads to a partitioning of the market for the employment of university professors in Austria and runs counter to the very principle of freedom of movement for workers.

87 It follows from the foregoing that a measure such as the special length-of-service increment provided for in Article 50a of the GG results in an obstacle to freedom of movement for workers which cannot be justified by a pressing public-interest reason.

88 *Accordingly, the reply to the third question referred for a preliminary ruling must be that Articles 48 of the Treaty and 7(1) of Regulation No 1612/68 are to be interpreted as meaning that they preclude the grant, under conditions such as those laid down in Article 50a of the GG, of a special length-of-service increment which, according to the interpretation of the Verwaltungsgerichtshof in its judgment of 24 June 1998, constitutes a loyalty bonus.* [Emphasis added].

Fourth and fifth questions

89 By its fourth and fifth questions, which must be dealt with together, the national court is essentially seeking to ascertain whether, in the main proceedings, the liability of the Member State is incurred owing to an infringement of Community law by the judgment of the Verwaltungsgerichtshof of 24 June 1998.

Observations submitted to the Court [omitted]

100 It is clear from the case-law of the Court that it is, in principle, for the national courts to apply the criteria for establishing the liability of Member States for damage caused to individuals by breaches of Community law [citation omitted],

in accordance with the guidelines laid down by the Court for the application of those criteria [citations omitted].

101 None the less, in the present case the Court has available to it all the materials enabling it to establish whether the conditions necessary for liability of the Member State to be incurred are fulfilled.

The rule of law infringed, which must confer rights on individuals

102 The rules of Community law whose infringement is at issue in the main proceedings are, as is apparent from the reply to the third question, Articles 48 of the Treaty and 7(1) of Regulation No 1612/68. Those provisions specify the consequences resulting from the fundamental principle of freedom of movement for workers within the Community by way of the prohibition of any discrimination based on nationality as between the workers of the Member States, in particular as to remuneration.

103 It cannot be disputed that those provisions are intended to confer rights on individuals.

The sufficiently serious nature of the breach

. . . .

119 Moreover, as is clear from the reply to the third question, a measure such as the special length-of-service increment provided for in Article 50a of the GG, even if it may be classified as a loyalty bonus, entails an obstacle to freedom of movement for workers contrary to Community law. Accordingly, the Verwaltungsgerichtshof infringed Community law by its judgment of 24 June 1998.

120 It must therefore be examined whether that infringement of Community law is manifest in character having regard in particular to the factors to be taken into consideration for that purpose as indicated in paragraphs 55 and 56 above.

121 In the first place, the infringement of Community rules at issue in the reply to the third question cannot in itself be so characterised.

122 Community law does not expressly cover the point whether a measure for rewarding an employee's loyalty to his employer, such as a loyalty bonus, which entails an obstacle to freedom of movement for workers, can be justified and thus be in conformity with Community law. No reply was to be found to that question in the Court's case-law. Nor, moreover, was that reply obvious.

123 In the second place, the fact that the national court in question ought to have maintained its request for a preliminary ruling, as has been established at paragraph 118 hereof, is not of such a nature as to invalidate that conclusion. In the present case the Verwaltungsgerichtshof had decided to withdraw the request for a preliminary ruling, on the view that the reply to the question of Community law to be resolved had already been given in the judgment in *Schöning-Kougebetopoulou*, cited above. Thus, it was owing to its incorrect reading of that judgment that the Verwaltungsgerichtshof no longer considered it necessary to refer that question of interpretation to the Court.

124 In those circumstances and in the light of the circumstances of the case, the infringement found at paragraph 119 hereof cannot be regarded as being manifest in nature and thus as sufficiently serious.

125 It should be added that that reply is without prejudice to the obligations arising for the Member State concerned from the Court's reply to the third question referred.

126 *The reply to the fourth and fifth questions must therefore be that an infringement of Community law, such as that stemming in the circumstances of the main proceedings from the judgment of the Verwaltungsgerichtshof of 24 June 1998, does not have the requisite manifest character for liability under Community law to be incurred by a Member State for a decision of one of its courts adjudicating at last instance.* [Emphasis added.]

. . . .

On those grounds,

THE COURT, in answer to the questions referred to it by the Landesgericht für Zivilrechtssachen Wien by order of 7 May 2001, hereby rules:

1. *The principle that Member States are obliged to make good damage caused to individuals by infringements of Community law for which they are responsible is also applicable where the alleged infringement stems from a decision of a court adjudicating at last instance where the rule of Community law infringed is intended to confer rights on individuals, the breach is sufficiently serious and there is a direct causal link between that breach and the loss or damage sustained by the injured parties. In order to determine whether the infringement is sufficiently serious when the infringement at issue stems from such a decision, the competent national court, taking into account the specific nature of the judicial function, must determine whether that infringement is manifest. It is for the legal system of each Member State to designate the court competent to determine disputes relating to that reparation.* [Emphasis added.]

2. Article 48 of the EC Treaty (now, after amendment, Article 39 EC) and Article 7(1) of Regulation (EEC) No 1612/68 of the Council of 15 October 1968 on freedom of movement for workers within the Community are to be interpreted as meaning that they preclude the grant, under conditions such as those laid down in Article 50a of the Gehaltsgesetz 1956 (law on salaries of 1956), as amended in 1997, of a special length-of-service increment which, according to the interpretation of the Verwaltungsgerichtshof (Austria) in its judgment of 24 June 1998, constitutes a loyalty bonus.

3. *An infringement of Community law, such as that stemming in the circumstances of the main proceedings from the judgment of the Verwaltungsgerichtshof of 24 June 1998, does not have the requisite manifest character for liability under Community law to be incurred by a Member State for a decision of one of its courts adjudicating at last instance.* [Emphasis added.]

In a subsequent case, *Traghetti del Mediterraneo SpA in Liquidation v. Italian Republic*[u] the ECJ went beyond *Köbler* to opine that Community law precluded national legal rules that would lead to the exclusion of state liability in cases where, as set forth in *Köbler*, a "manifest infringement" of the applicable Community law was committed. The 2006 decision the concerned the failure of a court — in this case, the Italian Supreme Court of Cassation — to comply with EU law. The rules of Italian law at issue[v] required malice or gross negligence on the part of a court as a prerequisite for state liability.

QUESTIONS AND REVIEW PROBLEMS

1. To what extent might courts in East Asia or the European Union — or the United States and Canada — reasonably abstain from adjudicating a tort claim against a foreign government entity or actor that would be justiciable in a national court of the relevant country? Would it be appropriate, for example, for a United States or Canadian court to deny sovereign immunity of a Japanese or Italian judge in an action for misconduct in a criminal case in which the Japanese or Italian courts would arguably hold the judge personally liable? Or, conversely, would it be appropriate for a Japanese or Italian court to adjudicate a damage action against a North American judge who would enjoy immunity under U.S. or Canadian law?

2. Consider again *Cassirer v. Kingdom of Spain and Thyssen-Bornemisza Collection Foundation*, 616 F.3d 1019 (9th Cir. 2010), *cert. denied*, 131 S. Ct. 3057 (2011). The case involves a suit brought in the United States against the Kingdom of Spain and a foundation deemed to be an agency of the Spanish state for the recovery of the painting, *Rue Saint Honoré — Afternoon, Rain Effect*, by the French Impressionist, Camille Pissarro (1830–1903). The painting was allegedly owned by the plaintiff's grandmother, Lilly Cassirer Neubauer, who in 1939 was forced to turn it over to a Nazi official in return for an exit visa to leave Germany. The painting is currently in the Thyssen-Bornemisza Museum in Madrid. In 2010 the Ninth Circuit held that, under the commercial activity and "international takings" exceptions in 28 U.S.C. § 1605(a)(2) and (3), "foreign sovereign immunity" did not bar the Federal District Court for the Central District of California from exercising personal jurisdiction over the defendants.

---

[u] Case C-173/03, Judgment of the Court (Great Chamber) of 13 June 2006, published in Recueil 2006 p. I-5177.

[v] Law No. 117 of 1988, limited the liability of judges, and thus the vicarious liability of the state, to unfair damage resulting from the conduct, decision or judicial order issued by a judge/prosecutor either with "intention" or "serious negligence" while exercising his or her functions, or resulting from a "denial of justice" (art. 2).

What questions would lawyers representing the National Gallery of Art need to ask regarding Spanish law were hypothetically a suit filed jointly in Madrid by Romanov heirs and claimants to the Russian throne against the United States and the National Gallery for similar paintings that were allegedly part of the private collection of the Russian czars confiscated in 1917 and then sold by the Soviet Union in private sales to Andrew Mellon in 1930 and 1931 and subsequently donated to the National Gallery of Art in 1937?

Assume the plaintiffs include Maria Vladimirovna, Grand Duchess of Russia, the great-great-granddaughter in the male-line of Tsar Alexander II of Russia and claimant to the headship of the Imperial Family of Russia, who is domiciled in Spain, and Prince Nicholas Romanov, claimant to the headship of the House of Romanov and President of the Romanov Family Association, who is domiciled in Italy. The paintings include *The Alba Madonna* by Raphael (1483–1520), which was purchased in 1931 for $1,166,400, at the time the largest sum ever paid for a painting, as well as *The Annunciation* (1434) by the Flemish painter, Jan Van Eyck (1395–1441).

Chapter 3

PARALLEL LITIGATION

Plaintiffs commonly confront a choice of courts with jurisdiction to adjudicate their claims. Their decisions with respect to the preferred forum include a variety of factors related to both outcome and convenience, not the least of which are the applicable legal rules, including those relating to damages, and the costs they will incur. Plaintiffs do not, however, necessarily determine the ultimate forum. Defendants too may have options. One common choice particularly prevalent in transnational litigation in which a party is subject even potentially to suit as defendant in a foreign jurisdiction is to file as plaintiff a defensive parallel action in the home country. We have already encountered several examples of such lawsuits. As these as well as following cases illustrate, parallel lawsuits have seemingly become an endemic feature of transnational litigation involving U.S. and Japanese parties.

I. THE PROBLEM

We begin discussion of parallel litigation with two introductory examples. Our first set of cases begins with a claim for indemnification by the wholly owned U.S. subsidiary of one of Japan's major trading companies, Marubeni-Iida, against Kansai Iron Works K.K. (Kansai), a relatively small manufacturer of heavy machinery in Osaka, Japan. The claim arose out of litigation in Seattle, Washington, initially brought by a Boeing employee, who had been injured while working with a metal press manufactured by Kansai. As described by the Washington State Supreme Court in *Deutsch v. West Coast Machinery Company*, 497 P.2d 1311 (Wash. 1972):

> [T]he initial action was initiated by the plaintiff, Jerry Deutsch, against the defendants, West Coast Machinery Company (a Washington corporation hereafter referred to as West Coast), Marubeni America and Kansai. . . .
>
> The plaintiff, an employee of the Boeing Company on June 28, 1968, seriously injured his hand at work while operating a large mechanical metal press. The press was sold to the Boeing Company by West Coast. West Coast purchased the press from Marubeni America, which in turn purchased the press from Marubeni-Iida Co., Ltd. (a Japanese corporation hereafter referred to as Marubeni Japan). Marubeni Japan purchased the press from Kansai, the manufacturer and petitioner herein.
>
> Kansai is an Osaka, Japan company engaged in the manufacture of heavy machinery. In May of 1966, upon receipt of a purchase order from Marubeni Japan, Kansai manufactured a 110 ton openback non-inclinable power press. The record indicates that the press was manufactured according to extensive specification furnished by the Boeing Company. The

press was delivered to Marubeni Japan, a large Japanese trading company, which in turn shipped it to its subsidiary, Marubeni America, at its Los Angeles headquarters. The press was then sent to West Coast who delivered it to the Boeing Company. In January of 1967, Kansai sent its engineers to the Boeing Company in Washington to test the operation of the press.

Subsequently, a selector switch failed. At the request of Marubeni Japan, Kansai sent a replacement switch to West Coast for installation on the press. In June of 1967, Kansai sent its engineers to the Boeing Company with parts for the machine. Pursuant to Boeing Company policies, however, Boeing personnel made the actual repairs in replacement of the parts. In July of 1967, Kansai sent an engineer, Mr. Obatake, to the United States with respect to machinery in other states and to that located at the Boeing Company. Mr. Obatake, however, was not allowed to make any adjustments or repairs to the press.

The plaintiff Deutsch claims that the press was defective and malfunctioned, severing most of his left hand, for which he is asking $275,000. On April 10, 1970 Marubeni America filed a cross-claim for indemnification against Kansai.

Kansai contested jurisdiction. In September 1971 the trial court denied its motion to dismiss, and then in October 1971 Kansai successfully sought interlocutory review by the Washington Supreme Court. In June 1972, the Court affirmed the lower court in the cited decision. Thereupon the lawyer for Kansai sought a writ of certiorari for review by the U.S. Supreme Court.[a] The Supreme Court denied certiorari in the case on November 13, 1972. (409 U.S. 1009.) The case then went to trial with a final judgment in favor of Marubeni America against Kansai entered on October 17, 1974.

Meanwhile Kansai had filed an action with the Osaka District Court for confirmation that Marubeni America, Marubeni-Iida's U.S. subsidiary, had no right to indemnification in addition to a counter-claim. On October 14, 1974, the Osaka District Court entered the requested confirmation judgment. The decision was not appealed. A few months later, in early 1975, Marubeni America filed an action in the Osaka District Court to enforce the Washington State judgment.

MARUBENI AMERICA CO. v. KANSAI IRON WORKS LTD.
Osaka District Court Judgment of 22 December 1977
Hanrei Times (No. 361) 127 (1977)

DISPOSITION
(*shūbun*)

Both the claim [by Marubeni America for recognition of Washington State judgment] and the counterclaim [by Kansai Iron Works] are dismissed.

---

[a] *See* L. William Houger, *Kansai Iron Works Ltd. v. Marubeni-Iida, Inc. U.S. Supreme Court Transcript of Record with Supporting Pleadings* (2011).

REASONS
(*riyū*)

I. Regarding the Claim of the Plaintiff

A. There is no dispute between the parties that in the case between the parties . . . the Superior Court of King County in the State of Washington held on September 17, 1974, that the defendant shall pay $86,000 to the Defendant and that this decision became final on October 17, 1974.

B. According to the evidence [omitted], which is not in dispute, the Osaka District Court held on October 14, 1974, in the case between the parties . . . regarding the claim for a judgment confirming non-liability for damages that despite the decision of the Superior Court of King County in Washington . . . the Defendant is not liable to pay the Plaintiff ¥97,000,000 in indemnification as ordered by the Washington court. It is evident by the entire tenor of the oral proceedings that this decision had become final before the beginning of the suit before us.

C. According to the facts . . . and the court's findings, at the time the Plaintiff brought the present suit for enforcement of the Washington judgment there already existed a Japanese final judgment based on the same set of facts, which judgment conflicted with the Washington judgment.

Now we come to examine whether each of the requirements of article 200 [current article 118] of the Code of Civil Procedure is satisfied. It should be evident that to recognize a foreign judgment contrary to a Japanese judgment in a case between the same parties and based on the same set of facts is contrary to the order of the judicial system and against Article 200 (iii) of the Code, which requires "that the judgment of a foreign court must not be contrary to the public policy in Japan." Whether the former suit was brought, held or finalized earlier than the latter is not relevant since to recognize a foreign judgment that is inconsistent with a domestic judgment disturbs the order of our entire legal system.

Therefore, the U.S. judgment before us cannot be recognized for it does not satisfy Article 200 (iii) of the Code of Civil Procedure. Thus the claim of the Plaintiff is without merit, and we need not examine the rest of the points at issue.

. . . .

II. Concerning the Counterclaim of the Defendant [omitted]

III. Conclusion

Therefore, both the claim and the counterclaim are dismissed. Applying the Code of Civil Procedure Article 89 on the cost of the litigation, we render the judgment stated in the Disposition.

Judge Tōru Michishita
Judge Toshiyuki Suzuki
Judge Yasuo Shimoyama

As evidenced by the Kansai Iron Works cases, parallel litigation often becomes a game of speed for the plaintiffs and delay by the defendants in both actions as both parties seek to ensure that their respective suits will prevail either for recognition and enforcement in the other jurisdiction or as a final judgment that will preclude such recognition as *res judicata*. Thus the success by Kansai in these suits can be attributed first to the tactics of its lawyers in delaying the U.S. judgment — especially the appeal to the Washington State Supreme Court and thereafter the petition to the United States Supreme Court for writ of certiorari for review of the Washington Court's decision — and second the corresponding failure of the lawyers for Marubeni America to pursue similar delaying tactics by simply appealing the decision of the Osaka District Court to the Osaka High Court. This failure is perhaps best explained by the fact that the party with the real interest at stake in this case was not Marubeni America but its insurer. Indeed Marubeni America probably had little interest in pursuing a claim against Kansai Iron Works inasmuch as, evidenced by the initial sales transaction, it and its parent company. Marubeni-Iida Japan, appear to have had a fruitful business relationship with Kansai Iron Works.

Our second set of parallel cases commenced nearly two decades earlier with a transaction illustrative of Japan-U.S. deal-making in the early postwar period. The story begins in March 1954 when Tōhō K.K., a leading Japanese film company, sent one of its managerial employees (Yonemoto) to attend a film festival in Brazil to research the South American film market. Yonemoto was instructed to stop over in Los Angeles on his return to Tokyo to examine the financial affairs of Toho International, a California company organized by Tōhō K.K. to distribute Tōhō's films in South and North America. Yonemoto arrived in Los Angeles to discover that Toho International was in very poor financial condition. Upon receiving Yonemoto's report, Tōhō K.K. decided to terminate its prior distribution arrangements and to reassign Yonemoto. In June 1954 Yonemoto opened an office as Toho Film Distributor.

Learning that Yonemoto was reassigned to Los Angeles, his father asked Chieko Hachitsuka, a Los Angeles resident who had lived in the United States for many years and spoke very good English, to assist his son. Hachitsuka responded by introducing Yonemoto to a Japanese interpreter and helping him to translate letters and to find an apartment. She also arranged for a preview of Tōhō films and on one occasion even helped Yonemoto borrow money for travel expenses for a business trip to Hawaii.

During this time, Robert Fleming, who had been in Japan during the Allied Occupation, also became acquainted with Hachitsuka. Fleming was very interested in the production of movies. He had even had a role in the movie "Oath in the Sky" produced by the Shin-Tōhō K.K.. Learning from Hachitsuka about Yonemoto, Fleming began to make plans to produce films jointly with Tōhō K.K.. He made contact with John Beg, an independent film producer, and arranged to have Hachitsuka introduce him to Yonemoto.

In the course of the ensuing discussions, Fleming, Beg, and Yonemoto with Hachitsuka as interpreter dropped the idea of a film production venture in favor of importing American films into Japan. Yonemoto's having suggested that that quick-action films would be preferable, the group chose a war film, "Victory at Sea," as their initial selection. In August all four attended a preview of the film, after which Yonemoto purportedly said: "This film is splendid. To put the film on the screen in Japan must prove successful. We can obtain the license to import the film in Japan." Immediately thereafter, John Beg began negotiating with NBC for the purchase of distribution and screen rights to the film in Japan. In early August NBC agreed to sell the rights.

At another meeting Yonemoto, Hachitsuka, her father, Haruyuki Nagamine, and others agreed that the Farmland and Development Company, which was owned or at least controlled by Nagamine, would provide the necessary initial capital. Farmland then borrowed $18,000 from the California Tokyo Bank and on or about November, purchased the distribution and screen rights for the film in Japan, paying NBC out of the loan. In the meantime, Yonemoto inquired with Tōhō K.K. about the status of its foreign exchange import allocation, a legal pre-requisite at the time for an import license. Tōhō replied that its allocation of foreign reserve currency was already exhausted. Yonemoto then contacted Shin-Tōhō K. K., but was similarly informed that Shin-Tōhō too lacked the needed import exchange currency allocation. Yonemoto then attempted to obtain the import license on his own, telling Hachitsuka and the others that he would undertake to obtain it on his own responsibility. In the end, however, he was unsuccessful. Thus the effort to import the film "Victory at Sea" into Japan came to naught leaving Farmland with rights to the film but also its debt to the California Tokyo Bank.

A decade later, Hachitsuka along with Farmland, filed a suit for damages alleging breach of contract and fraud against Tōhō K.K., Yonemoto, and Tōhō's California subsidiary in California. As a defensive action in response, Tōhō K.K. and the two other defendants in the California suit filed a lawsuit in Tokyo seeking a declaratory (confirmation) judgment denying their liability, The case is thus one of the early examples of postwar U.S.-Japan parallel litigation,

The Japanese judgment was handed down first.

TŌHŌ K.K. v. HACHITSUKA
Tokyo District Court Judgment of 27 May 1965
16 Kakyū minshū (No. 5) 923 (1965)
[Above summary of facts and translation of decision adapted from the English translation in 11 JAIL 197 (1967)]

Disposition
(shūbun)

We confirm that the plaintiffs are not liable to the each defendant for compensatory damages in the amount of 93,000 U.S. dollars based on the tort [delict] detailed in the attached writing.

REASONS
(*riyū*)

1. Jurisdiction

First, we must consider whether or not this Court has adjudicartory jurisdiction over this case.

This is a suit for confirmation of the non-existence of an obligation to compensate for damages in tort [*fuhōkōi*]. This type of lawsuit suit is brought by a party who claims the non-existence of such obligation (as an alleged tortfeasor). The object of such action is the same regardless of whether it is a suit for damages or an action for confirmation of such claim brought by a party insisting on the existence of such an obligation (the party who alleges injury). Therefore, [article 5, paragraph 9] of the Code of Civil Procedure applies to this case. The claim made by the defendant (who asserts the existence of an obligation to pay damages in tort) should determine the *situs* of the alleged tort, which includes not only the place where a tortious act is committed but also the place where the consequent injury has occurred. [The Court continues with a summary of the evidence and concludes:] Tokyo is said to be one of the places where the loss resulting from the torts alleged by the defendant occurred. This Court therefore has jurisdiction over this case under [article 5, paragraph 9] of the Code of Civil Procedure. Accordingly, the defendant's argument with respect to the jurisdiction is groundless.

2. Applicable law

Second, the Court must decide the law of which country to apply. The Court considers the so-called "place where the facts forming the cause of such obligation have occurred" of article 11, paragraph 1, of the Law concerning the Application of Laws [*Hōrei*] (Law No. 11, June 21, 1898) to include at least the place where the injury caused by the tort claimed by the defendant occurs. As set forth above, the *situs* of at least a portion of such injury is Japan,. The *situs* of the remaining portion is the State of California, U.S.A. According to article 11, paragraphs 2 and 3 of said Law, even in case the governing law is the law of a foreign country as determined by application of paragraph 1 of article 11, the limitations according to Japanese law shall apply with respect to the elements and effects of tortious acts. In the light of the foregoing, this Court is of the opinion that the laws of the State of California shall not apply and that only Japanese law applies to this case.

3. Whether or not the acts of the plaintiff Yonemoto constitute torts

(1) [The facts found by the court are summarized above.]

(2) [Based on the facts set out above, we find the allegation to be without factual basis that] the plaintiff Yonemoto, shortly after August 3, 1954, without intention to repay the fund for the purchase price of the screen right in. Japan of the dim "Victory at Sea," and fully aware of the impossibility of importing said film into Japan, said to the defendant: "The plaintiff Toho is short of U.S. dollars necessary for the purchase of the screen right of said film. However, if the defendant will pay

the price for the plaintiff Tōhō, the advances will be repaid within six months. The plaintiff Tōhō will offer in Japan the license for the import into Japan of said film." To the contrary, the plan of importing into Japan the film "Victory at Sea" was made jointly by the plaintiff Yonemoto, the defendant, Robert Fleming, and John Beg for the purpose of gaining profit, and its accomplishment was intended. That is to say, the plan was a joint business venture of the above four persons that failed after it was begun. Therefore, among the alleged torts set forth . . . by the defendant, the portion based alleged facts that do not exist as aforesaid is groundless.

[The defendant also alleges that] even if the plan to import of the film into Japan was a joint business venture as set forth above, the fact of intentionally deceiving the defendant as set forth above would constitute a tort by the plaintiff Yonemoto against the defendant and others. . . . [Given the findings set for above] this Court is unable, however, to find that the plaintiff Yonemoto did in fact intend to deceive the defendant.

4. Conclusion

In the light of the foregoing, the plaintiff Yonemoto is not deemed to have committed the torts that the defendant alleges . . . . Therefore, it is unnecessary to decide the other issues. This Court is thus of the opinion that neither of the plaintiffs is liable for the damages . . . inflicted on the defendant by the alleged torts.

Therefore, this Court accepts the petition of the plaintiffs, which is deemed to be well grounded, and renders judgment as stated in the Disposition by applying article 89 of the Code of Civil Procedure with respect to the expenses of the suit.

JUDGE KANAME NISHIYAMA
JUDGE TOYONAGA NISHIKAWA
JUDGE TOYOZŌ UEDA.

QUESTIONS

1. The plaintiffs in California — Hachitsuka and Farmland — claimed damages for both tortious conduct and breach of contract. Why do you suppose the lawyers for Tōhō K.K. construed the cause of action in the Tokyo lawsuit as a tort action (in civil law terminology, a delict) but not a contract claim? From the facts found by the Tokyo District Court (stated above), which claim under California law (or U.S. law generally) would appear to be stronger?

2. What was Tōhō K.K. primary aim in bringing the suit? In your view did it achieve that purpose? As a matter of policy, should such suits be allowed under private international law principles? Could the defendants have successfully argued that such suits should be disallowed under the principles of *jōri*?

The judgment by the Tokyo District Court was handed down prior to the decision in the California litigation. Unfortunately the California decision was not reported, but we do have a comment on the problems that arose when Tōhō K.K. sought to have the Tokyo judgment recognized as a bar to the California case, thereby illustrating again the primary aim of parallel suits as well as the issues and problems — including the role of expert witnesses — that arise in their penultimate phase.

Dan F. Henderson, *Introduction — U.S. Japanese Trade: Its Scope and Legal Framework*
16 VAND. J. TRANSNAT'L L. 601, 616–620 (1983)*

Several years ago, some rather technical rules concerning res judicata were nearly misapplied in a California court case. . . . The summary below briefly discusses the typical lawyer-related problems in the case presented by the differences between the civil law and common law doctrines of res judicata (claim preclusion) and collateral estoppel (issue preclusion).

The California suit was *Farmland & Development Co. v. Toho Co. Ltd.* Hachitsuka (Farmland) and Yonemoto (Toho) had planned to export a United States film for showing in Japan. Hachitsuka, believing that Yonemoto had promised to obtain the necessary license for importing the film into Japan, bought through Farmland the rights to show the film in Japan for $14,000. Yonemoto, however, was unable to acquire the import license in Japan and the whole venture failed. Hachitsuka, having allegedly lost $93,000, sued Toho Corporation and Yonemoto in California on two separate legal theories: (1) breach of contract; and (2) tort (deceit). Yonemoto filed suit in Tokyo to obtain a declaratory judgment absolving him of tort liability and damages. Although he pleaded to negate the tort claim, Yonemoto failed to seek negation of the contract liability. Two independent suits, based on the same grounds and seeking opposite results, were pending on each side of the Pacific. The Tokyo court found no tort liability and duly rendered a judgment that Toho was not liable to Hachitsuka in tort. The California action, however, sought damages on two theories, contract and tort, a key difference that determined whether the Japanese judgment for Toho precluded Hachitsuka's later California recovery. Because the Tokyo judgment was handed down before the trial in California, Toho lawyers asserted the Tokyo judgment as a res judicata defense to the California suit. The question was whether judicially determined facts underlying the Japanese tort judgment estoppel Farmland from making contrary assertions in the contract claim in California.

Pursuant to California law, a foreign (Japanese) judgment bars the tort claim by res judicata and a previously litigated "fact" (here, no promise by Toho) necessary to such a judgment bars the contract claim by collateral estoppel. The California court, applying its choice of law rule, found that it must apply Japanese law and give the Japanese judgment the effect it would have had as a Japanese judgment under Japanese law. The critical question for the contract claim became: is there a doctrine of collateral estoppel (*sotenko*) in Japanese law?

---

* Reprinted with permission by *Vanderbilt Journal of Transnational Law.* Footnotes omitted.

I. THE PROBLEM

To determine the scope of a declaratory judgment and the existence of collateral estoppel in Japanese law, the California court heard conflicting expert testimony on provisions of the Japanese Code of Civil Procedure. The English translation (EHS) of the pertinent provision of the Code, although clear, is a bit awkward: "As far as the matters contained in the text [disposition] of a judgment which has become final and conclusive are concerned, they have *res judicata.*" Because the findings of fact are included in the published [disposition] of the court's opinion, res judicata (*kihanryoku*) seemingly would result under the pertinent Code section. This, however, is not the law in Japan. The word "text" [disposition] in the English translation is the EHS "English equivalent" for the Japanese word *shubun*. The *shubun*, which makes no findings of fact, is only a short order as opposed to the full text of the court's opinion. In this case the shubun read: "[I]t shall be confirmed that the plaintiffs [Toho and Yonemoto] are under no obligation to compensate for damages amounting to $93,000 due to the torts set forth in the annexed list . . . . The expense of the suit shall be borne by the defendant."

Under California law, Japanese law may be proven by expert witnesses. To ascertain the meaning of the applicable Code of Civil Procedure section, Toho, the California defendant, offered the English translation of the section quoted above through his expert witness. The expert stated that the Code provision should be interpreted to give effect to the facts underlying a Japanese judgment. Although this is a view held by some professors in Japan, it is not Japanese law. The Supreme Court of Japan consistently has refused to yield to the criticisms of several excellent young scholars and, following the opinion of Kaneko Hajime and other older scholars, has declined to make "collateral estoppel" a part of Japanese law.

This author was the plaintiffs' expert on Japanese law at the California trial and had great difficulty opposing the defendant's expert. The California judge naturally tended to favor the expert interpretation which was similar to California's own collateral estoppel practice. By finding that the EHS translation of *shubun* was misleading and reviewing the supporting court cases and the writings of Professor Kaneko, the judge properly limited the effect of the Japanese judgment and held that the judgment barred only the tort claim by *res judicata*. The plaintiff was then given the opportunity to submit evidence of the contract. This complex case illustrates the emphasis placed on legal language in litigation and the problems encountered when a language foreign to the law must be used to bridge two different legal systems. In bilateral lawsuits between Japanese and United States persons, genuine ambiguity frequently persists until the court actually speaks.

Whether the defendant even has the choice to seek an alternative forum — thus whether parallel litigation is possible — depends first and foremost on the particular rules of the jurisdiction in which a second suit is contemplated. In common law systems, judges have several discretionary tools at their disposal that allow them to dismiss or stay proceedings when another forum may be available or threatened, or when the adjudicatory process has already commenced elsewhere. Judges in common law systems generally also have the authority to enjoin a party from either filing or proceeding with a parallel lawsuit. In stark contrast, judges in most civil law jurisdictions lack such discretionary authority and may instead, as we shall see in our examination of European Union law, be compelled under *lis pendens* rules to deny or delay adjudication in any case that has been previously brought in another court.

Our discussion thus continues as in previous chapters with the common law doctrines of both the United States and Canada, which include *forum non conveniens*, the broadest and most significant in practice, as well as discretionary stays of the proceedings and anti-suit injunctions. We continue with the mixed approaches to parallel litigation in Japan and end with the mandatory *lis pendens* rules of the European Union.

II. COMMON LAW APPROACHES — UNITED STATES

A. *Forum Non Conveniens*

PIPER AIRCRAFT COMPANY v. REYNO*
454 U.S. 235 (1981)

JUSTICE MARSHALL delivered the opinion of the Court.

These cases arise out of an air crash that took place in Scotland. Respondent, acting as representative of the estates of several Scottish citizens killed in the accident, brought wrongful-death actions against petitioners that were ultimately transferred to the United States District Court for the Middle District of Pennsylvania. Petitioners moved to dismiss on the ground of *forum non conveniens*. After noting that an alternative forum existed in Scotland, the District Court granted their motions. 479 F. Supp. 727 (1979). The United States Court of Appeals for the Third Circuit reversed. 630 F.2d 149 (1980). The Court of Appeals based its decision, at least in part, on the ground that dismissal is automatically barred where the law of the alternative forum is less favorable to the plaintiff than the law of the forum chosen by the plaintiff. Because we conclude that the possibility of an unfavorable change in law should not, by itself, bar dismissal, and because we conclude that the District Court did not otherwise abuse its discretion, we reverse.

I

A

In July 1976, a small commercial aircraft crashed in the Scottish highlands during the course of a charter flight from Blackpool to Perth. The pilot and five passengers were killed instantly. The decedents were all Scottish subjects and residents, as are their heirs and next of kin. There were no eyewitnesses to the accident. At the time of the crash the plane was subject to Scottish air traffic control.

---

* Footnotes omitted.

The aircraft, a twin-engine Piper Aztec, was manufactured in Pennsylvania by petitioner Piper Aircraft Co. (Piper). The propellers were manufactured in Ohio by petitioner Hartzell Propeller, Inc. (Hartzell). At the time of the crash the aircraft was registered in Great Britain and was owned and maintained by Air Navigation and Trading Co., Ltd. (Air Navigation). It was operated by McDonald Aviation, Ltd. (McDonald), a Scottish air taxi service. Both Air Navigation and McDonald were organized in the United Kingdom. The wreckage of the plane is now in a hangar in Farnsborough, England.

The British Department of Trade investigated the accident shortly after it occurred. A preliminary report found that the plane crashed after developing a spin, and suggested that mechanical failure in the plane or the propeller was responsible. At Hartzell's request, this report was reviewed by a three-member Review Board, which held a 9-day adversary hearing attended by all interested parties. The Review Board found no evidence of defective equipment and indicated that pilot error may have contributed to the accident. The pilot, who had obtained his commercial pilot's license only three months earlier, was flying over high ground at an altitude considerably lower than the minimum height required by his company's operations manual.

In July 1977, a California probate court appointed respondent Gaynell Reyno administratrix of the estates of the five passengers. Reyno is not related to and does not know any of the decedents or their survivors; she was a legal secretary to the attorney who filed this lawsuit. [Emphasis added.] Several days after her appointment, Reyno commenced separate wrongful-death actions against Piper and Hartzell in the Superior Court of California, claiming negligence and strict liability. Air Navigation, McDonald, and the estate of the pilot are not parties to this litigation. The survivors of the five passengers whose estates are represented by Reyno filed a separate action in the United Kingdom against Air Navigation, McDonald, and the pilot's estate. Reyno candidly admits that the action against Piper and Hartzell was filed in the United States because its laws regarding liability, capacity to sue, and damages are more favorable to her position than are those of Scotland. Scottish law does not recognize strict liability in tort. Moreover, it permits wrongful-death actions only when brought by a decedent's relatives. The relatives may sue only for "loss of support and society."

On petitioners' motion, the suit was removed to the United States District Court for the Central District of California. Piper then moved for transfer to the United States District Court for the Middle District of Pennsylvania, pursuant to 28 U.S.C. § 1404(a). Hartzell moved to dismiss for lack of personal jurisdiction, or in the alternative, to transfer. In December 1977, the District Court quashed service on Hartzell and transferred the case to the Middle District of Pennsylvania. Respondent then properly served process on Hartzell.

B

In May 1978, after the suit had been transferred, both Hartzell and Piper moved to dismiss the action on the ground of *forum non conveniens*. The District Court granted these motions in October 1979. It relied on the balancing test set forth by this Court in *Gulf Oil Corp. v. Gilbert*, 330 U.S. 501 (1947), and its companion case,

Koster v. Lumbermens Mut. Cas. Co., 330 U.S. 518 (1947). In those decisions, the Court stated that a plaintiff's choice of forum should rarely be disturbed. However, when an alternative forum has jurisdiction to hear the case, and when trial in the chosen forum would "establish . . . oppressiveness and vexation to a defendant . . . out of all proportion to plaintiff's convenience," or when the "chosen forum [is] inappropriate because of considerations affecting the court's own administrative and legal problems," the court may, in the exercise of its sound discretion, dismiss the case. *Koster, supra,* at 524. To guide trial court discretion, the Court provided a list of "private interest factors" affecting the convenience of the litigants, and a list of "public interest factors" affecting the convenience of the forum. *Gilbert, supra,* 330 U.S. at 508–509.

. . . .

In opposing the motions to dismiss, respondent contended that dismissal would be unfair because Scottish law was less favorable. The District Court explicitly rejected this claim. It reasoned that the possibility that dismissal might lead to an unfavorable change in the law did not deserve significant weight; any deficiency in the foreign law was a "matter to be dealt with in the foreign forum." *Id.,* at 738.

C

On appeal, the United States Court of Appeals for the Third Circuit reversed and remanded for trial. The decision to reverse appears to be based on two alternative grounds. First, the Court held that the District Court abused its discretion in conducting the *Gilbert* analysis. Second, the Court held that dismissal is never appropriate where the law of the alternative forum is less favorable to the plaintiff.

The Court of Appeals began its review of the District Court's *Gilbert* analysis by noting that the plaintiff's choice of forum deserved substantial weight, even though the real parties in interest are nonresidents. It then rejected the District Court's balancing of the private interests. . . .

The Court of Appeals also rejected the District Court's analysis of the public interest factors. . . .

In any event, it appears that the Court of Appeals would have reversed even if the District Court had properly balanced the public and private interests. The court stated:

> "[I]t is apparent that the dismissal would work a change in the applicable law so that the plaintiff's strict liability claim would be eliminated from the case. But . . . a dismissal for *forum non conveniens,* like a statutory transfer, 'should not, despite its convenience, result in a change in the applicable law.' Only when American law is not applicable, or when the foreign jurisdiction would, as a matter of its own choice of law, give the plaintiff the benefit of the claim to which she is entitled here, would dismissal be justified." 630 F.2d, at 163–164 (footnote omitted) (quoting *DeMateos v. Texaco, Inc.,* 562 F.2d 895, 899 (CA3 1977), cert. denied, 435 U.S. 904 (1978)).

In other words, the court decided that dismissal is automatically barred if it would lead to a change in the applicable law unfavorable to the plaintiff.

We granted certiorari in these cases to consider the questions they raise concerning the proper application of the doctrine of *forum non conveniens*.

II

The Court of Appeals erred in holding that plaintiffs may defeat a motion to dismiss on the ground of *forum non conveniens* merely by showing that the substantive law that would be applied in the alternative forum is less favorable to the plaintiffs than that of the present forum. The possibility of a change in substantive law should ordinarily not be given conclusive or even substantial weight in the *forum non conveniens* inquiry.

We expressly rejected the position adopted by the Court of Appeals in our decision in *Canada Malting Co. v. Paterson Steamships, Ltd.*, 285 U.S. 413 (1932).
. . .

. . . .

In fact, if conclusive or substantial weight were given to the possibility of a change in law, the *forum non conveniens* doctrine would become virtually useless. Jurisdiction and forum requirements are often easily satisfied. As a result, many plaintiffs are able to choose from among several forums. Ordinarily, these plaintiffs will select that forum whose choice-of-law rules are most advantageous. Thus, if the possibility of an unfavorable change in substantive law is given substantial weight in the *forum non conveniens* inquiry, dismissal would rarely be proper.

Except for the court below, every Federal Court of Appeals that has considered this question after *Gilbert* has held that dismissal on grounds of *forum non conveniens* may be granted even though the law applicable in the alternative forum is less favorable to the plaintiff's chance of recovery. [Citations omitted.] Several courts have relied expressly on *Canada Malting* to hold that the possibility of an unfavorable change of law should not, by itself, bar dismissal. [Citations omitted.]

The Court of Appeals' approach is not only inconsistent with the purpose of the *forum non conveniens* doctrine, but also poses substantial practical problems. If the possibility of a change in law were given substantial weight, deciding motions to dismiss on the ground of *forum non conveniens* would become quite difficult. Choice-of-law analysis would become extremely important, and the courts would frequently be required to interpret the law of foreign jurisdictions. First, the trial court would have to determine what law would apply if the case were tried in the chosen forum, and what law would apply if the case were tried in the alternative forum. It would then have to compare the rights, remedies, and procedures available under the law that would be applied in each forum. Dismissal would be appropriate only if the court concluded that the law applied by the alternative forum is as favorable to the plaintiff as that of the chosen forum. The doctrine of *forum non conveniens*, however, is designed in part to help courts avoid conducting complex exercises in comparative law. As we stated in *Gilbert*, the public interest factors point towards dismissal where the court would be required to "untangle problems in conflict of laws, and in law foreign to itself." 330 U.S., at 509.

Upholding the decision of the Court of Appeals would result in other practical problems. At least where the foreign plaintiff named an American manufacturer as defendant, a court could not dismiss the case on grounds of *forum non conveniens* where dismissal might lead to an unfavorable change in law. The American courts, which are already extremely attractive to foreign plaintiffs, would become even more attractive. The flow of litigation into the United States would increase and further congest already crowded courts.

. . . .

We do not hold that the possibility of an unfavorable change in law should never be a relevant consideration in a *forum non conveniens* inquiry. Of course, *if the remedy provided by the alternative forum is so clearly inadequate or unsatisfactory that it is no remedy at all, the unfavorable change in law may be given substantial weight; the district court may conclude that dismissal would not be in the interests of justice.* [Emphasis added.] In these cases, however, the remedies that would be provided by the Scottish courts do not fall within this category. Although the relatives of the decedents may not be able to rely on a strict liability theory, and although their potential damages award may be smaller, there is no danger that they will be deprived of any remedy or treated unfairly.

III

The Court of Appeals also erred in rejecting the District Court's *Gilbert* analysis. The Court of Appeals stated that more weight should have been given to the plaintiff's choice of forum, and criticized the District Court's analysis of the private and public interests. However, the District Court's decision regarding the deference due plaintiff's choice of forum was appropriate. Furthermore, we do not believe that the District Court abused its discretion in weighing the private and public interests.

A

The District Court acknowledged that there is ordinarily a strong presumption in favor of the plaintiff's choice of forum, which may be overcome only when the private and public interest factors clearly point towards trial in the alternative forum. It held, however, that the presumption applies with less force when the plaintiff or real parties in interest are foreign.

The District Court's distinction between resident or citizen plaintiffs and foreign plaintiffs is fully justified. In Koster, the Court indicated that a plaintiff's choice of forum is entitled to greater deference when the plaintiff has chosen the home forum. 330 U.S., at 524. When the home forum has been chosen, it is reasonable to assume that this choice is convenient. When the plaintiff is foreign, however, this assumption is much less reasonable. Because the central purpose of any forum non conveniens inquiry is to ensure that the trial is convenient, a foreign plaintiff's choice deserves less deference. [Emphasis added.]

B

The *forum non conveniens* determination is committed to the sound discretion of the trial court. It may be reversed only when there has been a clear abuse of discretion; where the court has considered all relevant public and private interest factors, and where its balancing of these factors is reasonable, its decision deserves substantial deference. [Citations omitted.] Here, the Court of Appeals expressly acknowledged that the standard of review was one of abuse of discretion. In examining the District Court's analysis of the public and private interests, however, the Court of Appeals seems to have lost sight of this rule, and substituted its own judgment for that of the District Court.

(1)

In analyzing the private interest factors, the District Court stated that the connections with Scotland are "overwhelming." 479 F. Supp., at 732. This characterization may be somewhat exaggerated. Particularly with respect to the question of relative ease of access to sources of proof, the private interests point in both directions. *As respondent emphasizes, records concerning the design, manufacture, and testing of the propeller and plane are located in the United States. She would have greater access to sources of proof relevant to her strict liability and negligence theories if trial were held here.* [Emphasis added.] However, the District Court did not act unreasonably in concluding that fewer evidentiary problems would be posed if the trial were held in Scotland. A large proportion of the relevant evidence is located in Great Britain.

The Court of Appeals found that the problems of proof could not be given any weight because Piper and Hartzell failed to describe with specificity the evidence they would not be able to obtain if trial were held in the United States. It suggested that defendants seeking *forum non conveniens* dismissal must submit affidavits identifying the witnesses they would call and the testimony these witnesses would provide if the trial were held in the alternative forum. Such detail is not necessary. Piper and Hartzell have moved for dismissal precisely because many crucial witnesses are located beyond the reach of compulsory process, and thus are difficult to identify or interview. Requiring extensive investigation would defeat the purpose of their motion. Of course, defendants must provide enough information to enable the District Court to balance the parties' interests. Our examination of the record convinces us that sufficient information was provided here. Both Piper and Hartzell submitted affidavits describing the evidentiary problems they would face if the trial were held in the United States.

The District Court correctly concluded that the problems posed by the inability to implead potential third-party defendants clearly supported holding the trial in Scotland. Joinder of the pilot's estate, Air Navigation, and McDonald is crucial to the presentation of petitioners' defense. If Piper and Hartzell can show that the accident was caused not by a design defect, but rather by the negligence of the pilot, the plane's owners, or the charter company, they will be relieved of all liability. It is true, of course, that if Hartzell and Piper were found liable after a trial in the United States, they could institute an action for indemnity or contribution against these parties in Scotland. It would be far more convenient, however, to resolve all claims in one trial. The Court of Appeals rejected this argument. Forcing petitioners to rely on actions for indemnity or contributions would be "burdensome" but not "unfair." 630 F.2d, at 162. Finding that trial in the plaintiff's chosen forum would be burdensome, however, is sufficient to support dismissal on grounds of *forum non conveniens*.

(2)

The District Court's review of the factors relating to the public interest was also reasonable. On the basis of its choice-of-law analysis, it concluded that if the case were tried in the Middle District of Pennsylvania, Pennsylvania law would apply to Piper and Scottish law to Hartzell. It stated that a trial involving two sets of laws would be confusing to the jury. It also noted its own lack of familiarity with Scottish law. Consideration of these problems was clearly appropriate under Gilbert; in that case we explicitly held that the need to apply foreign law pointed towards dismissal. The Court of Appeals found that the District Court's choice-of-law analysis was incorrect, and that American law would apply to both Hartzell and Piper. Thus, lack of familiarity with foreign law would not be a problem. Even if the Court of Appeals' conclusion is correct, however, all other public interest factors favored trial in Scotland. [Emphasis added.]

Scotland has a very strong interest in this litigation. The accident occurred in its airspace. *All of the decedents were Scottish. Apart from Piper and Hartzell, all potential plaintiffs and defendants are either Scottish or English.* [Emphasis added.] As we stated in Gilbert, there is "a local interest in having localized controversies decided at home." 330 U.S., at 509. Respondent argues that American citizens have an interest in ensuring that American manufacturers are deterred from producing defective products, and that additional deterrence might be obtained if Piper and Hartzell were tried in the United States, where they could be sued on the basis of both negligence and strict liability. However, the incremental deterrence that would be gained if this trial were held in an American court is likely to be insignificant. *The American interest in this accident is simply not sufficient to justify the enormous commitment of judicial time and resources that would inevitably be required if the case were to be tried here.* [Emphasis added.]

IV

The Court of Appeals erred in holding that the possibility of an unfavorable change in law bars dismissal on the ground of *forum non conveniens*. It also erred in rejecting the District Court's *Gilbert* analysis. The District Court properly decided that the presumption in favor of the respondent's forum choice applied with less than maximum force because the real parties in interest are foreign. It did not act unreasonably in deciding that the private interests pointed towards trial in Scotland. Nor did it act unreasonably in deciding that the public interests favored trial in Scotland. Thus, the judgment of the Court of Appeals is

Reversed.

Justice Powell took no part in the decision of these cases.

Justice O'Connor took no part in the consideration or decision of these cases.

[Dissenting opinions omitted.]

QUESTIONS

1. What factors must a court consider in determining whether to dismiss an action as a *forum non conveniens*? Which appear from the decision in *Piper Aircraft Company v. Reyno* to be the most significant? Under what circumstances might an appellate court find "a clear abuse of discretion" in either granting or denying a motion to dismiss an action based on the *forum non conveniens* doctrine? How significant are "oppressiveness and vexation" to a defendant of the plaintiff's choice of forum? How significant was the fact that no U.S. citizens were parties to the action as plaintiffs?

2. Assume the foreign court does not have jurisdiction over a defendant under its generally applicable rules, must the court in the United States reject the motion for dismissal on the basis of the *forum non conveniens* doctrine? How could the defendant seeking dismissal respond?

3. What if any "choice of law" benefits to the plaintiff's choice of forum that would preclude dismissal on *forum non conveniens* grounds?

4. To what extent would a pending action in a foreign court alone justify dismissal on *forum non conveniens* grounds?

5. To what extent would or should the availability of class actions or the ability of U.S. courts to consolidate multiple individual actions in contrast to at least some civil law jurisdictions preclude dismissal on grounds of *forum non conveniens?* In your opinion, should the availability of joinder of defendants as in Canada, Japan, and the EU who would not be subject to jurisdiction in an action in the U.S. (*see Asahi Metals*) be considered? Should it be a positive or negative factor?

SINOCHEM INTERNATIONAL CO. LTD. v. MALAYSIA INTERNATIONAL SHIPPING CORP.
549 U.S. 422 (2007)

Justice Ginsburg delivered the opinion of the Court.

This case concerns the doctrine of *forum non conveniens*, under which a federal district court may dismiss an action on the ground that a court abroad is the more appropriate and convenient forum for adjudicating the controversy. We granted review to decide a question that has divided the Courts of Appeals: "Whether a district court must first conclusively establish [its own] jurisdiction before dismissing a suit on the ground of *forum non conveniens*?" Pet. for Cert. i. *We hold that a district court has discretion to respond at once to a defendant's forum non conveniens plea, and need not take up first any other threshold objection. In particular, a court need not resolve whether it has authority to adjudicate the cause (subject-matter jurisdiction) or personal jurisdiction over the defendant if it determines that, in any event, a foreign tribunal is plainly the more suitable arbiter of the merits of the case.* [Emphasis added.]

I

The underlying controversy concerns alleged misrepresentations by a Chinese corporation to a Chinese admiralty court resulting in the arrest of a Malaysian vessel in China. In 2003, petitioner Sinochem International Company Ltd. (Sinochem), a Chinese state-owned importer, contracted with Triorient Trading, Inc. (Triorient), a domestic corporation that is not a party to this suit, to purchase steel coils. Pursuant to the agreement, Triorient would receive payment under a letter of credit by producing a valid bill of lading certifying that the coils had been loaded for shipment to China on or before April 30, 2003. Memorandum and Order of Feb. 27, 2004, No. Civ. A. 03-3771 (ED Pa.), App. to Pet. for Cert. 48a–49a (hereinafter Feb. 27 Memo & Order).

Triorient subchartered a vessel owned by respondent Malaysia International Shipping Corporation (Malaysia International), a Malaysian company, to transport the coils to China. Triorient then hired a stevedoring company to load the steel coils at the Port of Philadelphia. A bill of lading, dated April 30, 2003, triggered payment under the letter of credit. *Id.*, at 49a.

On June 8, 2003, Sinochem petitioned the Guangzhou Admiralty Court in China for interim relief, i.e., preservation of a maritime claim against Malaysia International and arrest of the vessel that carried the steel coils to China. In support of its petition, Sinochem alleged that the Malaysian company had falsely backdated the bill of lading. The Chinese tribunal ordered the ship arrested the same day. *Id.*, at 50a; App. in No. 04-1816 (CA3), pp. 56a–57a (Civil Ruling of the Guangzhou Admiralty Court).

Thereafter, on July 2, 2003, Sinochem timely filed a complaint against Malaysia International and others in the Guangzhou Admiralty Court. Sinochem's complaint repeated the allegation that the bill of lading had been falsified resulting in unwarranted payment. Malaysia International contested the jurisdiction of the Chinese tribunal. Feb. 27 Memo & Order, at 50a; App. in No. 04-1816 (CA3), pp. 52a–53a (Civil Complaint in Guangzhou Admiralty Court). The admiralty court rejected Malaysia International's jurisdictional objection, and that ruling was affirmed on appeal by the Guangdong Higher People's Court. App. 16–23.

On June 23, 2003, shortly after the Chinese court ordered the vessel's arrest, Malaysia International filed the instant action against Sinochem in the United States District Court for the Eastern District of Pennsylvania. Malaysia International asserted in its federal court pleading that Sinochem's preservation petition to the Guangzhou court negligently misrepresented the "vessel's fitness and suitability to load its cargo." Feb. 27 Memo & Order, at 50a (internal quotation marks omitted).

As relief, Malaysia International sought compensation for the loss it sustained due to the delay caused by the ship's arrest. Sinochem moved to dismiss the suit on several grounds, including lack of subject-matter jurisdiction, lack of personal jurisdiction, *forum non conveniens*, and international comity. App. in No. 04-1816 (CA3), pp. 14a–20a, 39a–40a.

The District Court first determined that it had subject-matter jurisdiction under 28 U.S.C. § 1333(1) (admiralty or maritime jurisdiction). Feb. 27 Memo & Order, at 51a–54a. The court next concluded that it lacked personal jurisdiction over Sinochem under Pennsylvania's long-arm statute, 42 Pa. Cons. Stat. § 5301 *et seq.* (2002). Nevertheless, the court conjectured, limited discovery might reveal that Sinochem's national contacts sufficed to establish personal jurisdiction under Federal Rule of Civil Procedure 4(k)(2). Feb. 27 Memo & Order, at 55a–63a. The court did not permit such discovery, however, because it determined that the case could be adjudicated adequately and more conveniently in the Chinese courts. *Id.*, at 63a–69a; Memorandum and Order of Apr. 13, 2004, No. Civ. A. 03-3771 (ED Pa.), App. to Pet. for Cert. 40a–47a (hereinafter Apr. 13 Memo & Order) (denial of Rule 59(e) motion).

No significant interests of the United States were involved, the court observed, Feb. 27 Memo & Order, at 65a–67a; Apr. 13 Memo & Order, at 44a–47a, and while the cargo had been loaded in Philadelphia, the nub of the controversy was entirely foreign: The dispute centered on the arrest of a foreign ship in foreign waters pursuant to the order of a foreign court. Feb. 27 Memo & Order, at 67a. Given the proceedings ongoing in China, and the absence of cause "to second-guess the authority of Chinese law or the competence of [Chinese] courts," the District Court granted the motion to dismiss under the doctrine of *forum non conveniens. Id.*, at 68a.

A panel of the Court of Appeals for the Third Circuit agreed there was subject-matter jurisdiction under § 1333(1), and that the question of personal jurisdiction could not be resolved sans discovery. Although the court determined that *forum non conveniens* is a non merits ground for dismissal, the majority nevertheless held that the District Court could not dismiss the case under the *forum non conveniens* doctrine unless and until it determined definitively that it had both subject matter jurisdiction over the cause and personal jurisdiction over the defendant. 436 F.3d 349 (CA3 2006).

Judge Stapleton dissented. Requiring a district court to conduct discovery on a jurisdictional question when it "rightly regards [the forum] as inappropriate," he maintained, "subverts a primary purpose of" the *forum non conveniens* doctrine: "protect[ing] a defendant from . . . substantial and unnecessary effort and expense." *Id.*, at 368. The "court makes no assumption of law declaring power," Judge Stapleton observed, "when it decides not to exercise whatever jurisdiction it may have." *Id.*, at 370 (quoting *Ruhrgas AG v. Marathon Oil Co.*, 526 U.S. 574, 584 (1999), in turn quoting *In re Papandreou*, 139 F.3d 247, 255 (CADC 1998)).

We granted certiorari, 548 U.S. 942 (2006), to resolve a conflict among the Circuits on whether *forum non conveniens* can be decided prior to matters of jurisdiction. Compare 436 F.3d, at 361–364 (case below); *Dominguez-Cota v. Cooper Tire & Rubber Co.*, 396 F.3d 650, 652–654 (CA5 2005) (per curiam) (jurisdictional issues must be resolved in advance of a *forum non conveniens* ruling), with *Intec USA, LLC v. Engle*, 467 F.3d 1038, 1041 (CA7 2006); *In re Arbitration Between Monegasque de Reassurances S. A. M. (Monde Re) v. NAK Naftogaz of Ukraine*, 311 F.3d 488, 497–498 (CA2 2002); *In re Papandreou*, 139 F.3d, at 255–256 (*forum non conveniens* may be resolved ahead of jurisdictional issues). Satisfied that *forum non conveniens* may justify dismissal of an action though jurisdictional issues remain unresolved, we reverse the Third Circuit's judgment.

II

A federal court has discretion to dismiss a case on the ground of *forum non conveniens* "when an alternative forum has jurisdiction to hear [the] case, and . . . trial in the chosen forum would establish . . . oppressiveness and vexation to a defendant . . . out of all proportion to plaintiff's convenience, or . . . the chosen forum [is] inappropriate because of considerations affecting the court's own administrative and legal problems." *American Dredging Co. v. Miller*, 510 U.S. 443, 447–448 (1994) (quoting *Piper Aircraft Co. v. Reyno*, 454 U.S. 235, 241 (1981), in turn quoting *Koster v. (American Lumbermens Mut. Casualty Co.*, 330 U.S. 518, 524 (1947)). Dismissal for *forum non conveniens* reflects a court's assessment of a "range of considerations, most notably the convenience to the parties and the practical difficulties that can attend the adjudication of a dispute in a certain locality." *Quackenbush v. Allstate Ins. Co.*, 517 U.S. 706, 723 (1996) [citations omitted]. We have characterized *forum non conveniens* as, essentially, "a supervening venue provision, permitting displacement of the ordinary rules of venue when, in light of certain conditions, the trial court thinks that jurisdiction ought to be declined." *American Dredging*, 510 U.S., at 453; cf. *In re Papandreou*, 139 F.3d, at 255 (*forum non conveniens* "involves a deliberate abstention from the exercise of jurisdiction").

The common-law doctrine of *forum non conveniens* "has continuing application [in federal courts] only in cases where the alternative forum is abroad," *American Dredging*, 510 U.S., at 449, n. 2, and perhaps in rare instances where a state or territorial court serves litigational convenience best. [References omitted.] For the federal-court system, Congress has codified the doctrine and has provided for transfer, rather than dismissal, when a sister federal court is the more convenient place for trial of the action. See 28 U.S.C. § 1404(a) ("For the convenience of parties and witnesses, in the interest of justice, a district court may transfer any civil action to any other district or division where it might have been brought."); cf. § 1406(a) ("The district court of a district in which is filed a case laying venue in the wrong division or district shall dismiss, or if it be in the interest of justice, transfer such case to any district or division in which it could have been brought."); *Goldlawr, Inc. v. Heiman*, 369 U.S. 463, 466 (1962) (Section 1406(a) "authorize[s] the transfer of [a] cas[e] . . . whether the court in which it was filed had personal jurisdiction over the defendants or not.").

A defendant invoking *forum non conveniens* ordinarily bears a heavy burden in opposing the plaintiff's chosen forum. *When the plaintiff's choice is not its home forum, however, the presumption in the plaintiff's favor "applies with less force," for the assumption that the chosen forum is appropriate is in such cases "less reasonable.*" [Emphasis added.] *Piper Aircraft Co.*, 454 U.S., at 255–256.

III

Steel Co. v. Citizens for Better Environment, 523 U.S. 83 (1998), clarified that a federal court generally may not rule on the merits of a case without first determining that it has jurisdiction over the category of claim in suit (subject-matter jurisdiction) and the parties (personal jurisdiction). . . . Dismissal short of reaching the merits means that the court will not "proceed at all" to an adjudication of the cause. Thus, a district court declining to adjudicate state-law claims on discretionary grounds need not first determine whether those claims fall within its pendent jurisdiction. [Citation omitted.] Nor must a federal court decide whether the parties present an Article III case or controversy before abstaining under *Younger v. Harris*, 401 U.S. 37 (1971). [Citation omitted.] A dismissal under *Totten v. United States*, 92 U.S. 105 (1876) (prohibiting suits against the Government based on covert espionage agreements), we recently observed, also "represents the sort of 'threshold question' [that] . . . may be resolved before addressing jurisdiction." *Tenet v. Doe*, 544 U.S. 1, 7, n. 4 (2005). The principle underlying these decisions was well stated by the Seventh Circuit: "[J]urisdiction is vital only if the court proposes to issue a judgment on the merits." *Intec USA*, 467 F.3d, at 1041.

IV

A *forum non conveniens* dismissal "den[ies] audience to a case on the merits," *Ruhrgas*, 526 U.S., at 585; it is a determination that the merits should be adjudicated elsewhere. [Citation omitted.] The Third Circuit recognized that *forum non conveniens* "is a non-merits ground for dismissal." 436 F.3d, at 359. [Citation omitted.] *A district court therefore may dispose of an action by a forum non conveniens dismissal, bypassing questions of subject-matter and personal jurisdiction, when considerations of convenience, fairness, and judicial economy so warrant.* [Emphasis added.]

. . . .

. . . Proceedings to resolve the parties' dispute are underway in China, with Sinochem as the plaintiff. Jurisdiction of the Guangzhou Admiralty Court has been raised, determined, and affirmed on appeal. We therefore need not decide whether a court conditioning a *forum non conveniens* dismissal on the waiver of jurisdictional or limitations defenses in the foreign forum must first determine its own authority to adjudicate the case.

V

This is a textbook case for immediate forum non conveniens dismissal. The District Court's subject-matter jurisdiction presented an issue of first impression in the Third Circuit, see 436 F.3d, at 355, and was considered at some length by the courts below. Discovery concerning personal jurisdiction would have burdened Sinochem with expense and delay. And all to scant purpose: The District Court inevitably would dismiss the case without reaching the merits, given its well-

considered forum non conveniens appraisal. Judicial economy is disserved by continuing litigation in the Eastern District of Pennsylvania given the proceedings long launched in China. And the gravamen of Malaysia International's complaint — misrepresentations to the Guangzhou Admiralty Court in the course of securing arrest of the vessel in China — is an issue best left for determination by the Chinese courts. [Emphasis added.]

If, however, a court can readily determine that it lacks jurisdiction over the cause or the defendant, the proper course would be to dismiss on that ground. In the mine run of cases, jurisdiction "will involve no arduous inquiry" and both judicial economy and the consideration ordinarily accorded the plaintiff's choice of forum "should impel the federal court to dispose of [those] issue[s] first." *Ruhrgas*, 526 U.S., at 587–588. But where subject-matter or personal jurisdiction is difficult to determine, and *forum non conveniens* considerations weigh heavily in favor of dismissal, the court properly takes the less burdensome course.

For the reasons stated, the judgment of the Court of Appeals is reversed, and the case is remanded for proceedings consistent with this opinion.

QUESTIONS

What factors led Justice Ginsburg to conclude that this was *"a textbook case for immediate forum non conveniens dismissal?"* What is the likely consequence of the decision? In cases where the "reasonableness" of personal jurisdiction is at issue, are judges less or more likely to grant discretionary motions for dismissal on grounds of *forum non conveniens* or engage in the otherwise mandatory consideration of their competence to adjudicate the dispute under due process standards?

We turn now to two cases in which courts applied or rejected (as a matter of state law) the *Reyno* (as opposed to the *Gulf Oil*) test in the now familiar context of aircraft accidents involving multiple defendants of multiple nationalities. The Boeing Company was a defendant in both. An overarching question to consider is whether the *forum non conveniens* doctrine as applied served to advance appropriate purposes of policy.

NAI-CHAO v. THE BOEING COMPANY*
555 F. Supp. 9 (N.D. Cal. 1982)

ORRICK, DISTRICT JUDGE.

The complaints that comprise these consolidated or related actions arise from the crash of a Far Eastern Air Transport ("FEAT") Boeing 737 aircraft in Taiwan,

---

* Footnotes omitted.

Republic of China, on August 22, 1981. *Of the one hundred ten passengers and crew killed in the crash, eighty-seven were citizens and residents of Taiwan, eighteen were citizens of Japan, four were citizens of Canada, and one was a citizen of the United States. To date, five hundred sixty-four plaintiffs, seven of whom are United States citizens and four of whom are Taiwanese citizens presently residing in the United States, have filed suit in this Court* [emphasis added] asserting wrongful death claims based on theories of strict liability and negligence against The Boeing Company ("Boeing"), the manufacturer of the aircraft, and United Airlines, Inc. ("United"), which sold the aircraft to FEAT in 1976.

Defendant Boeing, acting also for defendant United, has moved to dismiss these actions on the ground of *forum non conveniens* or, alternatively, to transfer the actions pursuant to 28 U.S.C. § 1404(a) to the United States District Court for the Western District of Washington. *For the reasons set forth below, this Court finds that Taiwan is the appropriate forum for this litigation* and that the recent Supreme Court decision in *Piper Aircraft Co. v. Reyno*, 454 U.S. 235, 102 S. Ct. 252, 70 L. Ed. 2d 419 (1981), mandates the dismissal of these actions. Accordingly, defendants' motion to dismiss is granted, and will become effective *when the Court receives undertakings satisfactory to the Court from defendants Boeing and United that the following conditions have been or will be met, namely, that (1) the courts of Taiwan have, and will assert, jurisdiction to adjudicate the claims alleged in these actions; (2) defendants consent to submit themselves to personal jurisdiction in the appropriate Taiwanese court and to make their employees available to testify in Taiwan; (3) defendants agree to waive any statute of limitations defenses arising during the pendency of these actions; and (4) defendants consent to satisfy any judgment rendered against them in Taiwan.* [Emphasis added.]

I

On August 22, 1981, a Boeing 737 owned and operated by FEAT crashed on a flight between the Taiwanese cities of Taipei and Kaohsiung. Radar contact with the aircraft was lost about twelve minutes after takeoff from Taipei, after the aircraft reached its assigned cruise altitude of 22,000 feet. A number of Taiwanese reportedly observed the aircraft break up in the air. The wreckage was scattered over a seven-mile area in rugged terrain approximately sixty miles southwest of Taipei. All one hundred four passengers and six crew members aboard the aircraft were killed.

The Chinese Civil Aeronautics Administration ("CCAA") initiated an accident investigation, in which Boeing, United, and other American officials participated. The CCAA issued a preliminary report, but has made no final report and no finding of the probable cause of the accident. The United States National Transportation and Safety Board ("NTSB") performed an analysis of critical parts of the wreckage, and the CCAA is currently in the process of building a mock-up of the aircraft with the wreckage pieces to aid in its investigation.

FEAT purchased the aircraft from United in 1976, and owned, operated, and maintained the aircraft in the five-and-a-half years prior to the accident. All major maintenance of the aircraft was performed by FEAT personnel at Shungshan Airport in Taipei, pursuant to a maintenance program developed by Boeing in the

United States, and licensed and approved by the CCAA.

The complaints charge defendants with negligence and strict liability based on the allegedly defective design, manufacture, and/or assembly of the aircraft, and on the allegedly improper inspection and maintenance of the aircraft prior to the sale to FEAT in 1976. Plaintiffs assert that of the possible causes of the crash — defective design or manufacture, pilot error, bad weather, or sabotage — the most likely cause was a crack in the forward cargo compartment frame and skin which led to a loss of pressurization. Plaintiffs have submitted documentary evidence indicating that such cracks were discovered in several 737's operated in the United States, and that an investigation conducted by the NTSB revealed massive corrosion and metal fatigue of the lower forward cargo hold frame which appears consistent with plaintiffs' theory of the accident.

II

A

Under the principle of *forum non conveniens*, a court may resist the imposition of jurisdiction, even if jurisdiction is authorized by a general forum statute. *Gulf Oil Corp. v. Gilbert*, 330 U.S. 501, 67 S. Ct. 839, 91 L. Ed. 1055 (1947). The common law doctrine of *forum non conveniens* was partly displaced by the provisions of 28 U.S.C. § 1404(a), which require transfer rather than dismissal if the case can be heard in a more convenient district or division within the United States; the common law doctrine remains applicable, however, when the action should have been brought abroad. *Yerostathis v. A. Luisi, Ltd.*, 380 F.2d 377, 379 (9th Cir. 1967); *Paper Operations Consultants International, Ltd. v. SS Hong Kong Amber*, 513 F.2d 667, 670 (9th Cir. 1975).

The factors which the Court must consider in determining whether to grant a motion to dismiss on grounds of *forum non conveniens* were set forth by the Supreme Court in *Gilbert, supra*, 330 U.S. at 508–09, 67 S. Ct. at 843. The Court enumerated both the "private interest factors" affecting the convenience of the litigants and the "public interest factors" affecting the convenience of the forum. The private interest factors include "the relative ease of access to sources of proof; availability of compulsory process for attendance of unwilling, and the cost of obtaining attendance of willing, witnesses; possibility of view of premises, if view would be appropriate to the action; and all other practical problems that make trial of a case easy, expeditious and inexpensive." *Id.* at 508, 67 S. Ct. at 843. The public interest factors include the administrative difficulties flowing from court congestion; the local interest in having localized controversies at home; the interest in having the trial of a diversity case in a forum that is at home with the law that must govern the action; the avoidance of unnecessary problems in conflicts of law, or in application of foreign law; and the unfairness of burdening citizens in an unrelated forum with jury duty. *Id.* at 509, 67 S. Ct. at 843.

The Court in *Gilbert* noted that the plaintiff's choice of forum should not be disturbed "unless the balance is strongly in favor of the defendant." *Id.* at 508. The Court of Appeals for the Ninth Circuit has recently indicated that the standard to be applied is whether, in light of the factors, defendants have made a "clear showing" so as to establish either "(1) such oppression and vexation of a defendant as to be out of all proportion to the plaintiff's convenience, which may be shown to be slight or nonexistent, or (2) make trial in the chosen forum inappropriate because of considerations affecting the court's own administrative and legal problems." *Miskow v. Boeing Co.*, No. 79-3904 (9th Cir. Oct. 28, 1981), quoting *Paper Operations, supra*, 513 F.2d at 670. Where the issue is whether to dismiss the action or whether to transfer it to another district or division within the United States, the Ninth Circuit indicated in *Miskow* that dismissal is appropriate where the district court weighs the *Gilbert* factors and determines that transfer to another district or division will not significantly alleviate the burden that retention of jurisdiction would impose on private and public interests. *Id.*

On December 8, 1981, after the filing of Boeing's motion to dismiss, the Supreme Court issued its first decision addressing the doctrine of *forum non conveniens* in over thirty years, and applied the doctrine in a factual context strikingly similar to that now before this Court. In *Reyno, supra*, the Court elaborated further on the considerations set forth in *Gilbert* and applied the doctrine of *forum non conveniens* to dismiss a products liability action arising out of an airplane crash in Scotland on the grounds that Scotland was the proper forum. Because this Court finds that *Reyno* is dispositive of Boeing's motion to dismiss these actions, a detailed examination of the *Reyno* decision is appropriate.

In *Reyno*, the respondent, acting as representative of the estates of several Scottish citizens killed in an air crash in Scotland during a charter flight, instituted wrongful death actions in California state court against Piper Aircraft, which had designed and manufactured the plane in Pennsylvania, and Hartzell Corporation, which had manufactured the propellers in Ohio. At the time of the crash the plane was registered in Great Britain and was owned and operated by companies organized in the United Kingdom. The pilot and all of the decedents' heirs and next of kin were Scottish subjects and citizens, and the investigation of the accident was conducted by British authorities. Respondent sought to recover from petitioners on the basis of negligence or strict liability, the latter not recognized by Scottish law, and admitted that the action was filed in the United States because its laws regarding liability, capacity to sue, and damages are more favorable to respondent's position than those of Scotland.

On petitioners' motion, the action was removed to the United States District Court for the Central District of California, and was then transferred to the United States District Court for the Middle District of Pennsylvania, pursuant to 28 U.S.C. § 1404(a). The district court granted petitioners' motion to dismiss the action on the ground of *forum non conveniens*. Relying on the test set forth in *Gilbert*, and analyzing the private interest factors affecting the forum's convenience, the district court concluded that Scotland was the appropriate forum. The Court of Appeals for the Third Circuit reversed, holding that the district court had abused its discretion in conducting the *Gilbert* analysis and that, in any event, dismissal is automatically barred where the law of the alternative forum is less favorable to the plaintiff than the law of the forum chosen by the plaintiff.

The Supreme Court granted a petition for a *writ of certiorari* and reversed the court of appeals. The Court held first that the fact that the substantive law that would be applied in the alternative forum is less favorable to plaintiffs than that of the chosen forum does not preclude dismissal and should ordinarily not be given even substantial weight in the *forum non conveniens* inquiry. *Reyno, supra*, 454 U.S. at 244–253, 102 S. Ct. at 260–264. Second, the Court held that plaintiff's choice of forum deserves less deference when the plaintiff or the real parties in interest are foreign, because, where the plaintiff is not suing in the home forum, the assumption that the plaintiff's choice of forum is convenient is much less reasonable. Third, the Court held that the district court did not abuse its discretion in weighing the private and public interests under the *Gilbert* analysis and determining that the trial should be held in Scotland.

With regard to the district court's analysis of the private interest factors, the Court found that the district court reasonably concluded that fewer evidentiary problems would be posed if the trial were held in Scotland, because a large proportion of the relevant evidence was located there, and that the problems posed by the plaintiff's inability to implead potential Scottish third-party defendants (the pilot's estate, the plane's owners, and the charter company) supported holding the trial in Scotland. The Court also found the district court's analysis of the public interest factors to be reasonable, noting that, even apart from the question whether Scottish law might be applicable in part to the action, all other public interest factors favored trial in Scotland. The Court found that Scotland had a very strong interest in the litigation, because the accident occurred there, and all potential parties were either Scottish or English. The Court rejected respondent's argument that the United States' interest in deterring the production of defective products in this country justified retention of the litigation, noting that any additional deterrence that might be obtained from trial in an American court, where the manufacturer could be sued on strict liability as well as negligence theories, was not sufficient to justify the enormous commitment of judicial time and resources that would be required. *Id.* 454 U.S. at 258, 102 S. Ct. at 267.

B

We turn now to the application of the several factors which must be considered in determining whether the applicable law mandates a dismissal or transfer of the case pursuant to the doctrine of *forum non conveniens* as set forth above.

1. The Availability of an Alternative Forum

The Supreme Court held in *Reyno* that, "[a]t the outset of any *forum non conveniens* inquiry, the court must determine whether there exists an alternative forum." *Reyno, supra*, 454 U.S. at 254–255 n. 22, 102 S. Ct. at 265 n. 22. An alternative forum is ordinarily considered "adequate" if the defendant is amenable to process there. *Gilbert, supra*, 330 U.S. at 507, 67 S. Ct. at 842. This Court's consideration of defendants' motion to dismiss for *forum non conveniens* is premised on the condition that defendants submit to the jurisdiction of the Taiwanese court.

The Court recognized in *Reyno*, however, that where the remedy afforded by the alternative forum is so clearly unsatisfactory as to be no remedy at all, the district court may conclude that dismissal would not be in the interest of justice:

"In rare circumstances, however, where the remedy offered by the other forum is clearly unsatisfactory, the other forum may not be an adequate alternative, and the initial requirement may not be satisfied. Thus, for example, dismissal would not be appropriate where the alternative forum does not permit litigation of the subject matter of the dispute." *Reyno, supra,* 454 U.S. at 254–255 n. 22, 102 S. Ct. at 265 n. 22.

Plaintiffs suggest that, under the reasoning in Reyno, Taiwan is not an adequate forum on the grounds that (1) a Taiwanese court would not have jurisdiction over these actions; (2) the plaintiffs here would not have easy access to a Taiwanese court, because Chinese law requires that plaintiffs pay a filing fee amounting to one percent of the claim; and (3) United States law would govern these actions, and the application of foreign law would pose serious difficulties for a Taiwanese Court. [Emphasis added.]

Plaintiffs rely heavily on the affidavit of Judge Yu Ching Wang, a former district court judge in Taiwan, who is currently an appellate judge and a member of the Judicial Yuan, the highest judicial body of the Republic of China. [Emphasis added.] After careful consideration of plaintiffs' arguments, however, the Court finds that Taiwan is an adequate forum and, indeed, is the most appropriate forum for these plaintiffs.

Plaintiffs first argument is that Taiwan is an inadequate forum because the Chinese courts cannot at this point assume jurisdiction over these cases. According to Judge Wang, a Chinese court would have jurisdiction if these actions were originally filed in Taiwan, but can no longer assert such jurisdiction because the case has already been brought in the United States: "[S]hould the United States District Court send the case to the Republic of China with only the defendants' agreement, the Chinese court would not be competent to hear the case." Affidavit of Judge Yu Ching Wang attached to plaintiffs' motion filing affidavit filed January 22, 1982, at 2.

Judge Wang's conclusion is based on a misapprehension as to the nature of a dismissal for *forum non conveniens*. This Court clearly is not empowered to "send the case to the Republic of China with only the defendants' agreement"; this Court would simply dismiss the case, leaving the plaintiffs free to file these actions in Taiwan if they choose to do so. *The affidavit of defendants' expert, Dr. Charng-Ven Chen, a practicing attorney and law professor in Taipei, who has received Masters and Doctorate degrees from Harvard Law School, states that a forum non conveniens dismissal would not foreclose these plaintiffs from initiating actions in Taiwan, and that there is no law or case authority to the contrary. Dr. Chen's affidavit further states that the Taiwan court would have jurisdiction over these cases pursuant to the Civil Code of Procedure of the Republic of China, because the damage resulting from the allegedly tortious conduct occurred in China.* [Emphasis added.] Affidavit of Charng-Ven Chen in support of Boeing's motion to dismiss filed February 2, 1982, at 2.

The next argument advanced by plaintiffs is that Taiwan is not an adequate forum because the Chinese courts require payment of a filing fee amounting to one percent of the claim, and an additional fee of one-half percent is required for each appeal. The Court does not find this argument persuasive. Judge Wang himself notes that a party may obtain procedural relief from payment of the fee if the party is "devoid of the means to pay the cost." Judge Wang suggests that such relief is granted only in those cases where the plaintiff is completely destitute, but the Court notes that the plaintiffs here have not asserted that the filing fee requirement would make it impossible for them to prosecute this action in China, or even that the fee would be a serious hardship to them. Moreover, as Dr. Chen points out in his affidavit, under Chinese law the prevailing party may by court judgment recover the court costs from the losing party. Finally, the Court notes that the utilization of a filing fee is simply the method chosen by the Taiwanese government to finance its court system, and it seems fundamentally unfair to compel United States' citizens to "subsidize" an action which should have been brought in another forum, at least, where as here, the plaintiffs have not even attempted to argue that the requirements of the foreign judicial system constitute a serious obstacle. This Court rejects plaintiffs' contention that, should foreign laws require advancement of funds by a litigant not necessary in the United States, the foreign court must be deemed an inadequate forum, finding such a position without support in the case law or in common sense.

Finally, plaintiffs contend that Taiwan is not an adequate forum because, under Chinese choice of law rules, a Chinese court would be required to apply United States law to these actions, and the application of foreign law would be extremely difficult. Judge Wang asserts that:

> As all of the wrongful acts allegedly occurred in the United States and only the result occurred in the Republic of China, our jurisprudential interpretations of 'lex loci delicti' mandates that the law of the United States be applied in this case. * * * From my experience as a District Judge and High Court Judge, I personally feel it would be nearly impossible for our court system to adequately adjudicate this massive case against American defendants according to American law." Wang affidavit, *supra*, at 2.

Under *Gilbert*, the choice of law issue is properly considered in the context of the Court's analysis of the "public interest factors," *infra*. For purposes of plaintiffs' contention that the choice of law problem renders Taiwan an inadequate forum, it is sufficient to note that no case known to this Court has held an alternative forum to be inadequate simply because of the potential difficulties in applying foreign law, and this Court is unwilling to accept the proposition that a Chinese court is less competent than an American court in application of foreign law. The Court agrees with the reasoning of Dr. Chen that:

> "Assuming for the sake of argument that the court of the R.O.C. would apply the law of the place of commission, i.e. U.S. laws etc., the court of the R.O.C. will apply such laws without difficulty, otherwise the very existence of the Law of 6 June 1953 ["Law Governing the Application of Laws in Civil Matters Involving Foreign Elements"] loses its meaning. Any suggestion that the court of the ROC is not competent to analyse any foreign law is subject to criticism of prejudice. Chen affidavit, *supra*, at 2–3.

Thus, this Court finds that the threshold requirement of an adequate alternative forum is satisfied in this case, and proceeds to an analysis of the private and public interest factors set forth in *Gilbert*, and reaffirmed in *Reyno*.

2. The Private Interest Factors

Perhaps the most important private interest factor is the relative availability of evidence and witnesses. [Emphasis added.] Although relevant evidence and witnesses in this case are located both in the United States and Taiwan, it appears to the Court that discovery and trial on the issues of liability and damages will be greatly facilitated if this action proceeds in Taiwan.

Plaintiffs maintain that all of the documentary and physical evidence necessary to establish that the aircraft was defective is located in the United States. It appears that the evidence relating to the design and manufacture of the aircraft, maintenance records for the period that the aircraft was operated by United, documentation pertaining to 737 certification, and Boeing Airworthiness Directives and Service Bulletins, are all located in this country. Evidence pertaining to FEAT's maintenance, under the supervision of the CCAA, of the aircraft during the five-and-a-half-year period preceding the crash, however, is located in Taiwan. Evidence pertaining to the investigation of the accident by the CCAA, as well as the critical parts of the wreckage itself, appear to be in Taiwan. A view of the premises is obviously available only in Taiwan, and might assist defendants in establishing that the accident was caused wholly or in part by something other than a defective airframe. Moreover, virtually all of the evidence relating to proof of damages is in Taiwan, where the overwhelming majority of claimants reside, and the difficulties of adjudicating these foreign damage claims would be compounded by the presence of language barriers and the necessity for translation.

As to the availability of witnesses, the Court must consider both the availability of compulsory process for attendance of unwilling witnesses, and the cost of obtaining willing witnesses. Plaintiffs assert that all of the witnesses who can testify as to the design and manufacture of the aircraft, and the maintenance of the craft prior to the sale, are located in the United States. All these witnesses are clearly subject to process in this Court, and it is clearly more convenient for such witnesses to attend trial in this country than in Taiwan. On the other hand, all witnesses to the air crash, all witnesses who could testify as to the inspection and maintenance of the aircraft by FEAT and to supervision by the CCAA, and all witnesses who could testify regarding the investigation of the accident by Taiwanese authorities, as well as witnesses who knew the decedents and whose testimony would be necessary to ascertain damages, are located in Taiwan. It is doubtful whether this Court could enforce process compelling the attendance of persons with relevant knowledge who are not parties to this litigation, and compelling the litigants to try their case without the benefit of live testimony from important witnesses would impose a serious hardship upon them and upon this Court. The Supreme Court in *Gilbert* emphasized the importance of this factor, and said that:

> "[t]o fix the place of trial at a point where litigants cannot compel personal attendance and may be forced to try their cases on deposition, is to create

a condition not satisfactory to court, jury or most litigants." *Gilbert, supra,* 330 U.S. at 511, 67 S. Ct. at 844.

Although mechanisms for obtaining necessary documents and testimony from abroad exist, various procedural obstacles would no doubt limit the availability and scope of foreign discovery to the parties if trial were conducted in the United States.

Another critical private interest factor, in addition to the availability of evidence and witnesses, is the Court's ability to assert jurisdiction over all parties to the litigation, including potential third-party defendants. [Emphasis added.] The Court said in *Reyno* that the aircraft manufacturer should not be compelled to go to trial in a forum where the owner and operator of the aircraft cannot be joined:

> "Joinder of the pilot's estate, Air Navigation, and McDonald is crucial to the presentation of petitioners' defense. If Piper and Hartzell can show that the accident was caused not by a design defect, but rather by the negligence of the pilot, the plane's owners, or the charter company, they will be relieved of all liability. It is true, of course, that if Hartzell and Piper were found liable after a trial in the United States, they could institute an action for indemnity or contribution against these parties in Scotland. It would be far more convenient, however, to resolve all claims in one trial." *Reyno, supra,* 454 U.S. at 259, 102 S. Ct. at 267.

In the case at bar, the presence at trial of FEAT, the owner and operator of the aircraft for the five-and-one-half years preceding the accident, and of the CCAA, the Chinese regulatory authority, is critical to the defense. It is highly unlikely that the CCAA, as a foreign governmental agency, could be joined as a party in this action, and it is uncertain whether FEAT would be subject to general jurisdiction or specific tort jurisdiction based on its transaction of business in California. Plaintiffs' offer to indemnify the defendants for any liability apportioned by this Court to FEAT and the CCAA does not, in the opinion of this Court, eliminate the prejudice to defendants arising from their potential inability to implead third-party defendants, because, as a practical matter, the trier of fact cannot be expected to evaluate fairly the relative liability of parties not present at the trial.

3. The Public Interest Factors

A consideration of the public interest factors enumerated by the Supreme Court in *Gilbert* place beyond all doubt any question that this Court might have had regarding the proper forum for the trial of this lawsuit. Clearly the balance tips decidedly against the plaintiffs' choice of forum.

The three principles underlying the public interest factors have been aptly summarized by the D.C. Circuit in *Pain v. United Technologies Corp.*, 637 F.2d 775 (1980), a decision which the Supreme Court cited with approval in *Reyno*:

> *"[F]irst, that courts may validly protect their dockets from cases which arise within their jurisdiction, but which lack significant connection to it; second, that courts may legitimately encourage trial of controversies in the localities in which they arise; and third, that a court may validly consider its familiarity with governing law when deciding whether or not to retain*

jurisdiction over a case. [Emphasis added.] Thus, even when the private conveniences of the litigants are nearly in balance, a trial court has discretion to grant *forum non conveniens* upon finding that retention of jurisdiction would be unduly burdensome to the community, that there is little or no public interest in the dispute, or that foreign law will predominate if jurisdiction is retained." [Footnotes omitted; emphasis added]. *Id.* at 791–92.

It is beyond dispute that the docket of this Court is heavily congested, and that the Court can ill afford the time and expense of adjudicating a controversy which does not have significant connections to this forum, particularly where, as here, the case will require a massive expenditure of judicial resources. The Supreme Court in *Reyno* emphasized the principle that "there is a local interest in having localized controversies decided at home," *Reyno, supra,* 454 U.S. at 260, 102 S. Ct. 268; and found that Scotland had a "very strong interest" in the case because "the accident occurred in its airspace, the decedents were Scottish and, apart from Piper and Hartzell, all potential plaintiffs and defendants were either Scottish or English." *Id.* at 454 U.S. at 260, 102 S. Ct. at 268. Applying this reasoning to the case at bar, which involves an accident in Taiwan airspace, a Taiwan-registered aircraft operated by a Taiwan airline, and predominantly (87 of 110) Taiwanese decedents, it would appear that Taiwan has a strong local interest in this litigation.

Plaintiffs seek to establish a nexus with the United States by characterizing these actions as American products liability actions, stressing that the aircraft was designed and manufactured in this country and that the aircraft was inspected and maintained in accordance with the United States regulatory scheme. Plaintiffs suggest that, because Boeing aircraft are utilized extensively in the United States, this country has a predominant interest in retaining this litigation in order to deter the production of defective aircraft in the future.

The Supreme Court in *Reyno* expressly rejected the position urged by plaintiffs here, indicating that the interest of the United States in deterring the production of defective products was not sufficient to justify retention of the litigation:

> "Respondent argues that American citizens have an interest in ensuring that American manufacturers are deterred from producing defective products, and that additional deterrence might be obtained if Piper and Hartzell were tried in the United States, where they could be sued on the basis of both negligence and strict liability. However, the incremental deterrence that would be gained if this trial were held in an American court is likely to be insignificant. The American interest in this accident is simply not sufficient to justify the enormous commitment of judicial time and resources that would inevitably be required if the case were to be tried here." *Id.* at 454 U.S. at 260–261, 102 S. Ct. at 268.

The case at bar would require a much greater "commitment of judicial time and resources" than *Reyno*; and plaintiffs cannot, by characterizing their causes of action as product liability claims against American defendants, escape the fact that these claims arise in the context of a Taiwanese accident and that Taiwan has the predominant interest in this litigation.

The Supreme Court indicated in *Gilbert* and *Reyno* that another public interest factor supporting dismissal for *forum non conveniens*, in addition to the administrative burden on a forum which has only minimal contact with the controversy, and the local interest which another forum may have in the controversy, is the necessity of applying foreign law or of grappling with difficult choice of law questions. This Court must apply the choice of law rules of the California state courts, *Klaxon Co. v. Stentor Electric Manufacturing Co.*, 313 U.S. 487, 61 S. Ct. 1020, 85 L. Ed. 1477 (1941), and follow the "governmental interest" approach to determine whether the law of Taiwan or that of the United States would govern this action. *Reich v. Purcell*, 67 Cal. 2d 551, 63 Cal. Rptr. 31, 432 P.2d 727 (1967).

In *Hurtado v. Superior Court*, 11 Cal. 3d 574, 114 Cal. Rptr. 106, 522 P.2d 666 (1974), the California Supreme Court enumerated the three distinct governmental interests which may be implicated in wrongful death actions: (1) compensation for resident survivors; (2) deterrence of wrongful conduct within the jurisdiction; and (3) limitations upon the amount of damages recoverable. The parties have not suggested that the third factor, limitations upon damages, is of concern in the instant case. With regard to the most important governmental interest, the interest in compensating resident survivors, it is clear that Taiwan has the much greater interest since the vast majority of the beneficiaries are Taiwanese and the burden of supporting those survivors would fall upon the government of Taiwan. With regard to the governmental interest in deterring wrongful conduct, plaintiffs correctly note that the United States has an interest in deterring the production of defective aircraft which are heavily used in this country. In view of the relatively limited weight which the Supreme Court accorded to this interest in *Reyno*, however, and the fact that Taiwan has by far the predominant interest in assuring that its residents receive compensation, this Court finds it quite possible that Chinese law would be applied to this action, and thus that the action is more appropriately tried by a court familiar with Chinese law.

Finally, plaintiffs contend that the presence of United States plaintiffs in this action precludes the granting of defendants' motion to dismiss under the circumstances presented here. Plaintiffs attempt to distinguish *Reyno* on the grounds that all the plaintiffs in that case were foreign, and that an American plaintiff's choice of forum must be accorded greater deference.

The Supreme Court noted in *Reyno* that there is ordinarily a strong presumption in favor of the plaintiff's choice of forum, which may be overcome only when the private and public interest factors clearly point towards trial in the alternative forum, and indicated that a plaintiff's choice of forum is entitled to greater deference when the plaintiff has chosen the home forum. *Reyno, supra*, 454 U.S. at 257–259, 102 S. Ct. at 264–266. The Supreme Court went on to stress, however, that a plaintiff's right to sue in his home forum is by no means absolute, but rather must be evaluated in the context of the many other factors relevant to the convenience of the parties and of the Court:

> "A citizen's forum choice should not be given disposition weight, however. * * * Citizens or residents deserve somewhat more deference than foreign plaintiffs, but dismissal should not be automatically barred when a plaintiff has filed suit in his home forum. As always, if the balance of conveniences

suggests that trial in the chosen forum would be unnecessarily burdensome for the defendant or the court, dismissal is proper." *Id.* at 255–256 n. 23, 102 S. Ct. at 266 n. 23 (emphasis added [in opinion]).

The federal courts have not felt constrained to retain jurisdiction over predominantly foreign cases involving American plaintiffs where an examination of the *Gilbert* factors demonstrated that the action is more appropriately brought in a foreign forum.

Although recognizing the deference properly accorded to a plaintiff's choice of forum, particularly in regard to the American plaintiffs in this action, the Court finds that the plaintiffs' choice of an American forum is here outweighed by the private and public interest factors pointing towards dismissal of this action, and *that the presence of a handful of American plaintiffs does not preclude such dismissal.* [Emphasis added.] The Court finds that defendants have satisfied the standard set forth by the Ninth Circuit in *Paper Operations, supra,* 513 F.2d at 670, by making a "clear showing" that "trial in the chosen forum [is] inappropriate because of considerations affecting the court's own administrative and legal problems," and thus it is not necessary for defendants to establish "such oppression and vexation * * * as to be out of proportion to the plaintiff's convenience."

The Court also finds that the Western District of Washington is not a significantly more convenient forum, on the grounds that transfer would not significantly alleviate the burden that retention of jurisdiction would impose on private and public interests. While it is true that the principal place of business of defendant Boeing is in the Seattle area, the Court's analysis of the pertinent private and public interest factors compels the conclusion that Taiwan is the appropriate forum for these actions.

Accordingly, IT IS HEREBY ORDERED that defendant Boeing's motion to dismiss on the ground of *forum non conveniens* is granted and will become effective when this Court receives undertakings satisfactory to this Court from defendants Boeing and United that the following conditions have been or will be met, namely, that:

1. The courts of Taiwan have, and will assert, jurisdiction over these actions.

2. Defendants will submit themselves to the jurisdiction of the Taiwanese court, and will make their employees available to testify in Taiwan.

3. Defendants agree to waive any statute of limitations claims arising from the date that these actions were filed to the date that this Order dismissing the complaints becomes effective.

4. Defendants consent to satisfy any judgment that may be rendered against them in Taiwan.

> **QUESTIONS**
>
> 1. Why do you suppose attorneys for The Boeing Company sought a trial in this case in Taiwan rather than Washington State? Compare The Boeing Company's response to litigation in Japan in *Ōkuma v. The Boeing Company, infra*, Chapter 1?
>
> 2. In your view, was fact that only one U.S. national was killed in the accident and only seven U.S. citizens and four Taiwan citizens residing in the U.S. were among the 564 plaintiffs significant?
>
> 3. What role did the experts on Taiwan law play? Were the opinions of either or both critical to the decision?

MYERS v. THE BOEING COMPANY*
115 Wn.2d 123 (1990)

DURHAM, J.

After the trial court bifurcated plaintiffs' cause of action, defendant admitted liability and moved for a dismissal of the damages claims on *forum non conveniens* grounds. The trial court found that, as to damages, Japan was the more convenient forum and granted the motion. The Court of Appeals affirmed the trial court in an unpublished opinion. Plaintiffs appeal, contending that the trial court abused its discretion in bifurcating the action and in dismissing the damages claims. Plaintiffs also argue that the dismissal violated their treaty rights. Finding no error, we affirm.

On August 12, 1985, a Boeing 747 aircraft owned by Japan Air Lines (JAL) crashed while en route from Tokyo to Osaka, Japan. *Five hundred twenty people died in the crash, most of them Japanese nationals. Myers and Judkins, personal representatives, brought eight actions against Boeing and JAL on behalf of the estates of 71 Japanese nationals and 8 non-Japanese nationals.* [Emphasis added.] Upon motion by Boeing, to which plaintiffs did not object, the trial court consolidated the eight actions for "pretrial purposes." The consolidated actions were preassigned to the King County Track One system, Judge Gary M. Little presiding. Boeing then moved to dismiss all eight complaints on *forum non conveniens* grounds. In its motion papers, *Boeing stated that if the cases were dismissed and refiled in the decedents' countries, Boeing would agree not to contest liability.* [Emphasis added.]

In response to that motion, the trial court entered an order dated May 7, 1987, ruling as follows:

---

* Footnotes omitted.

1. The liability issue and the damage issue in these actions should be, and hereby are, bifurcated;

2. The issue of liability in these actions will be resolved in this jurisdiction;

3. Resolution of the question of what forum in which to determine damages is hereby reserved pending resolution of the liability question[.]

Based on admissions made by Boeing in a pretrial conference, the trial court entered a judgment dated July 24, 1987. The court found that Boeing admitted the following:

a. In 1978 Boeing repaired the aft pressure bulkhead of the accident airplane in Japan;

b. Boeing performed a portion of the bulkhead repair incorrectly;

c. The incorrect repair performed by Boeing was a proximate cause of the crash of the accident airplane on August 12, 1985; and

d. Boeing is liable to plaintiffs for compensatory damages resulting from the crash.

The trial court also found that Boeing admitted that a section of the final report of the Japanese Aircraft Accident Investigation Committee, which attributed the crash to fatigue cracks resulting from improper repairs made in 1978, accurately described the cause of the crash. Based on those findings, the court entered judgment that "Boeing [was] liable to plaintiffs for compensatory damages caused by the crash" and that "[the judgment was] a conclusive determination of Boeing's liability."

After the judgment was entered, JAL was dismissed from the suit on plaintiffs' motion. Boeing then renewed its motion to dismiss on forum non conveniens grounds as to the issue of damages, limited to the Japanese nationals. [Emphasis added.]

On September 10, 1987, the trial court granted Boeing's motion to dismiss. Conditions of the dismissal were that Boeing submits to jurisdiction in Japan, waive any statute of limitation defenses, admit liability for compensatory damages, and not oppose recognition in Japan of the judgment on liability entered on July 24, 1987. The trial court expressly granted plaintiffs the right to return to King County Superior Court for trial on damages if "the actions cannot be handled expeditiously in Japan." The court retained jurisdiction over the non-Japanese nationals "which were not the subject of Boeing's present *forum non conveniens* motion."

The Court of Appeals affirmed the trial court in an unpublished opinion. *Myers v. Boeing Co.*, noted at 53 Wn. App. 1043 (1989). This court granted plaintiffs' petition for review.

I Forum Non Conveniens

This court first recognized the doctrine of *forum non conveniens* in *Werner v. Werner*, 84 Wn.2d 360, 371, 526 P.2d 370 (1974). Under the doctrine, courts have discretionary power to "[decline] jurisdiction where, in the court's view, the difficulties of litigation militate for the dismissal of the action subject to a stipulation that the defendant submit to jurisdiction in a more convenient forum." *Werner*, at 370. The standard of review applicable to a decision to dismiss on *forum non conveniens* grounds is abuse of discretion. Such a dismissal may only be reversed if it is "manifestly unfair, unreasonable or untenable." *General Tel. Co. v. Utilities & Transp. Comm'n*, 104 Wn.2d 460, 474, 706 P.2d 625 (1985).

The doctrine presupposes that there are at least two forums in which the defendant is amenable to process. *Werner*, at 370. In *Gulf Oil Corp. v. Gilbert*, 330 U.S. 501, 508, 67 S. Ct. 839, 91 L. Ed. 1055 (1947), the United States Supreme Court set out the criteria for choosing the appropriate forum. This court adopted the Gulf Oil factors in *Johnson v. Spider Staging Corp.*, 87 Wn.2d 577, 555 P.2d 997 (1976).

. . . .

The trial court was "guided by" *Piper Aircraft Co. v. Reyno*, 454 U.S. 235, 102 S. Ct. 252, 70 L. Ed. 2d 419 (1981), *reh'g denied*, 455 U.S. 928 (1982). In that case, the United States Supreme Court, applying the *Gulf Oil* factors, affirmed the dismissal of a wrongful death action brought in Pennsylvania on behalf of the estates of six Scottish nationals killed in an airplane crash in Scotland. The airplane was manufactured in Pennsylvania. The trial court found, and the Supreme Court agreed, that Scotland was the more convenient forum. In upholding the forum decision, the Court held that under the *Gulf Oil* balancing test, "a foreign plaintiff's choice [of forum] deserves less deference" than that of a United States resident or citizen. *Reyno*, at 256.

On appeal, plaintiffs make a number of arguments. These arguments can be grouped around three main issues. First, plaintiffs argue that the trial court erred in its balancing of the *Gulf Oil/Spider Staging* factors. Second, plaintiffs argue that the trial court erroneously relied on the "lesser deference" standard of *Reyno*, thus adopting a standard that directly conflicts with *Spider Staging*. Third, plaintiffs argue that dismissal in this case is fundamentally unfair.

Gulf Oil Factors

We first consider plaintiffs' argument that the trial court erred in its balancing of the *Gulf Oil/Spider Staging* factors.

On appeal, plaintiffs do not assign error to any of the above findings of fact. Rather, plaintiffs contend that while the findings are "factually correct," the trial court erred when it balanced those findings using the *Gulf Oil/Spider Staging* factors.

Plaintiffs assert that the present case is "identical" to *Spider Staging*, mandating the same result. Plaintiffs argue that the fact that dismissal was reversed in *Spider Staging* and upheld in the present case necessarily leads to the conclusion that, in the present case, the trial court did not apply the *Spider Staging* standard properly. This argument is without merit.

Relying on the result to prove the conclusion ignores the nature of the test applied. In *Gulf Oil*, the Supreme Court expressly declined to set out categories of fact patterns mandating a specific result. Instead, the Court listed a number of factors to be considered, leaving the ultimate decision to the discretion of the trial court. *Gulf Oil*, at 508–09. While the factors to be considered remain constant, the balance and result are fact specific.

More importantly, there are a number of important differences between the facts of the present case and the facts of *Johnson v. Spider Staging Corp.*, 87 Wn.2d 577, 555 P.2d 997 (1976). In *Spider Staging*, a wrongful death action was brought in Washington by a Kansas resident who, while working in Kansas, fell to his death from a scaffold built in Washington. The trial court granted defendant *Spider Staging*'s motion to dismiss on the grounds of *forum non conveniens*. This court reversed the trial court, finding that the balance of factors did not "strongly favor the [defendants]." *Spider Staging*, at 580. Reviewing the factors, this court found the following:

> [A]ll of the evidence which pertains to the manufacturing and marketing of the scaffold is in Washington State. [Defendants] are Washington corporations, and all of their principal officers reside in King County. Both of the engineers who designed the scaffold live in King County. The two principal witnesses from Kansas [are willing to] appear in Washington. Also, [plaintiff] will bring the scaffold to Washington and give [defendants] an opportunity to examine it. *Spider Staging*, at 580.

Plaintiffs would have this court equate the practical problems in trying the case brought by the estate of one decedent from Kansas against a Washington manufacturer where liability is still at issue, with trying a case brought by the estates of 71 Japanese nationals where the only remaining issue is damages. Plaintiffs assert that the cases are "identical" despite the number of significant differences: the nature of issues to be resolved, the number of plaintiffs, the foreign citizenship of plaintiffs, the distances involved, and a language barrier.

. . . .

Plaintiffs argue that the result in *Spider Staging* necessarily leads to the conclusion that Washington's deterrent policy is the overriding interest in the present case and, therefore, Washington law must apply. However, plaintiffs fail to consider the balancing nature of the test. As already noted, there are significant differences between *Spider Staging* and the present case. The fact that liability is not at issue certainly must be taken into account. Also, Japan has a significant interest in the determination of the damages issue. The accident occurred in Japan, over 500 Japanese nationals died, and a large number of Japanese plaintiffs are involved in the present action. Most importantly, unlike the Kansas plaintiff in *Spider Staging*, plaintiffs here concede that Japanese law provides for full compensation.

. . . .

In addition to arguing that the trial court erred in its balancing of the *Gulf Oil/Spider Staging* factors, plaintiffs also rely on *Spider Staging* to urge this court to adopt a rule that would limit the trial court's discretion in *forum non conveniens* motions when the defendant is a Washington manufacturer and the plaintiff is a nonresident. According to plaintiffs, such a rule is needed to hold defendant accountable for its actions and to further the State's interest in deterring wrongful conduct. Plaintiffs' goal is a valid one. However, their reliance on *Spider Staging* to attempt to limit the trial court's discretion is misplaced for three reasons.

First, while the State's interest in deterring wrongful conduct by Washington manufacturers weighed heavily in the court's resolution of *Spider Staging*, the State's interest in deterrence was factored into the court's Choice of Law Analysis, not the *forum non conveniens* motion, and then only after the court found the contacts of the parties with Kansas and Washington to be evenly balanced. *Spider Staging*, at 582–83.

Second, and more importantly, *Spider Staging* did not reach the choice of law issue until the *forum non conveniens* issue was resolved because if the court found that Kansas was the proper forum, Kansas would determine the applicable law. *Spider Staging*, at 579. In resolving the *forum non conveniens* issue, the court expressly adopted the *Gulf Oil* factors. *Spider Staging*, at 579. There was no mention of deterrence as an overriding State's interest in the *forum non conveniens* analysis.

Finally, the State's interest in deterrence and holding manufacturers accountable for wrongful conduct is served when plaintiffs are fully compensated for their injuries, regardless of the forum. Plaintiffs have conceded that Japanese law provides full compensation.

Lesser Deference Standard

The next issue we consider is plaintiffs' contention that the trial court relied on the "lesser deference" standard of *Piper Aircraft Co. v. Reyno*, 454 U.S. 235, 102 S. Ct. 252, 70 L. Ed. 2d 419 (1981), *reh'g denied*, 455 U.S. 928 (1982), thus adopting a standard that directly conflicts with the standard of *Spider Staging*. In *Spider Staging*, the trial court's dismissal was reversed because "[t]he factors [did not] strongly favor the [defendants]." *Spider Staging*, at 580. Plaintiffs argue that this standard was ignored by the trial court in favor of the "lesser deference" standard of *Reyno*. Plaintiffs further argue that this reliance on the *Reyno* standard amounted to an abuse of discretion requiring reversal of the trial court's dismissal of plaintiffs' case in favor of a Japanese forum. This argument is without merit.

Although the trial court looked to *Reyno* for guidance, the court specifically found that "[r]egardless of the degree of deference shown plaintiffs' choice of forum, the Court is persuaded that the balance of private and public interest factors weighs heavily in favor of trial of damages in Japan." Finding of fact 6. Because of this finding, the resolution of the present case does not turn on the lesser deference standard of *Reyno*. However, we take this opportunity to expressly decline to adopt *Reyno*. We do so for three reasons.

First, as federal common law, Reyno is not binding on this court. Normally, however, we would certainly consider it as persuasive authority. That persuasiveness is undermined, however, by the fact that the lesser deference standard holding was concurred in by only a 4-person majority. [Emphasis added.]

Second, the relevant portion of the majority opinion consists solely of a few conclusory sentences with no supportive analysis or reasoning. This cursory treatment is especially distressing because the Court appears to be motivated by the need to respond to a maverick Court of Appeals decision, rather than the need to reach a well-reasoned decision.

The Court of Appeals held that "dismissal is never appropriate where the law of the alternative forum is less favorable to the plaintiff." *Reyno*, at 244. In doing so, it was the only circuit court that has considered the issue to take that position. The Supreme Court reversed, stating that the Court of Appeals' holding directly conflicts with the Court's express refusal to set out bright-line rules and the Court's repeated emphasis on the need to retain flexibility in deciding *forum non conveniens* motions. *Reyno*, at 261.

The Court also expressed concern that if a court could not dismiss the case on grounds of *forum non conveniens* where dismissal might lead to an unfavorable change in law, "[t]he American courts, which are already extremely attractive to foreign plaintiffs, would become even more attractive. The flow of litigation into the United States would increase and further congest already crowded courts." [Footnote omitted.] *Reyno*, at 252.

The seven sitting Justices joined in that portion of the opinion. A 4-person majority went on to hold that the "District Court properly decided that the presumption in favor of the [plaintiff's] forum choice applied with less than maximum force because the real parties in interest [were] foreign." *Reyno*, at 261. The Court stated that this distinction is "fully justified." *Reyno*, at 255. . . .

The Court's logic does not withstand scrutiny. The Court is comparing apples and oranges. *Foreigners, by definition, can never choose the United States as their home forum. The Court purports to be giving lesser deference to the foreign plaintiffs' choice of forum when, in reality, it is giving lesser deference to Foreign Plaintiffs, based solely on their status as foreigners. More importantly, it is not necessarily less reasonable to assume that a foreign plaintiff's choice of forum is convenient. Why is it less reasonable to assume that a plaintiff from British Columbia, who brings suit in Washington, has chosen a less convenient forum than a plaintiff from Florida bringing the same suit? To take it one step further, why is it less reasonable to assume that a plaintiff, who is a Japanese citizen residing in Wenatchee, who brings suit in Washington, has chosen a less convenient forum than a plaintiff from Florida bringing the same suit?* [Emphasis added.]

The Court's reference to the attractiveness of United States courts to foreigners, combined with a holding that, in application, gives less deference to foreign plaintiffs based on their status as foreigners, raises concerns about xenophobia. This alone should put us on guard.

Finally, we decline to adopt *Reyno* because it simply is not necessary. *Proper application of the Gulf Oil factors alone will lead to fair and equitable results. Under Gulf Oil, the decision whether or not to dismiss is, and will continue to be, based on the balancing of the factors as they relate to the plaintiff's choice of forum, not the plaintiff's status.* [Emphasis added.] This is as it should be. Furthermore, application of the *Gulf Oil* factors adequately protects against any perceived threat of foreign plaintiffs flooding United States courts. *Granting foreign plaintiffs equal deference will not result in more foreign cases being heard here if the balance of private and public interest factors in those cases does not otherwise favor a United States forum.* [Emphasis added.] For example, the *Reyno* Court held that the District Court did not abuse its discretion in deciding that the private and public interest factors favored trial in Scotland. *Reyno*, at 261. Thus, the result would have been the same without the application of the lesser deference standard.

Fundamental Fairness

Plaintiffs also argue that requiring them to bring their damages case in Japan is fundamentally unfair for two reasons. First, plaintiffs contend that the Japanese legal system is cumbersome. In that regard, the trial court found:

> There has been a great deal of material provided to the Court about the Japanese legal system and its judicial process. Everything the Court has read and heard leads the Court to believe that the Japanese court system can and will respond effectively to the challenges of assessing the claims of its citizens for damages to compensate them for their grievous losses. Finding of fact 10.

Plaintiffs' did not challenge this finding of fact. Furthermore, the trial court expressly reserved the plaintiffs' right to return to King County "if the actions cannot be handled expeditiously in Japan."

Plaintiffs second argument goes to the issue of "solatium", the Japanese term for general damages available to plaintiffs who prove that the defendant was guilty of gross negligence. According to plaintiffs, solatium will be awarded only if they prove design defect. Thus, they contend, the defendant's liability is still at issue. The trial court found as follows:

> The courts of Japan are an adequate and available alternative forum. . . . Japanese law provides an adequate remedy for plaintiffs' injuries. Substantial damages may be recovered for wrongful death under the laws of Japan. Finding of fact 8. Again, plaintiffs did not challenge this finding. More importantly, plaintiffs concede that Japanese law provides full compensation. At oral argument, plaintiffs also conceded that proceeding in the Japanese courts will not deprive them of their right to prove issues supporting a solatium award.

In sum, fundamental fairness does not require reversal in this case. Whenever a balancing test is used, as it is here, the result is necessarily fact specific. Under the facts of this case, dismissal was proper. This does not, however, mean that dismissal will be proper whenever foreign plaintiffs seek access to our courts. In each case, the factors must be weighed and balanced.

Based on the trial court's findings and the balancing of the private and public interest factors, the dismissal was not "manifestly unfair, untenable or unreasonable." *General Tel. Co. v. Utilities & Transp. Comm'n*, 104 Wn.2d 460, 474, 706 P.2d 625 (1985). Accordingly, we hold that the trial court did not abuse its discretion in granting Boeing's *forum non conveniens* motion.

II Bifurcation

Under the civil rules, a trial court may order a separate trial of liability and damages "in furtherance of convenience or to avoid prejudice, or when separate trials will be conducive to expedition and economy . . . always preserving inviolate the right of trial by jury." CR 42(b). While it is not a procedure to be liberally applied, the decision to bifurcate is within the discretion of the trial court. *Maki v. Aluminum Bldg. Prods.*, 73 Wn.2d 23, 25, 436 P.2d 186 (1968); *Brown v. General Motors Corp.*, 67 Wn.2d 278, 282, 407 P.2d 461 (1965).

Plaintiffs contend that the bifurcation resulted in the court conducting a partial review of the case, which focused only on damages. Plaintiffs equate applying the *forum non conveniens* analysis to only the damages case with failing to apply all the factors as required by *Gulf Oil* and *Spider Staging*. This argument is without merit.

When Boeing renewed its motion to dismiss as to the Japanese plaintiffs, liability was no longer at issue. The trial court applied the Gulf Oil factors to the only remaining issue — damages. If the trial court did not abuse its discretion in applying the *Gulf Oil* factors, any abuse of discretion requiring reversal must necessarily arise from the order bifurcating the action.

Other courts have conditioned *forum non conveniens* dismissals on defendant's willingness to stipulate to liability in the alternative forum. [Citations omitted.]

There is only one reported case where a trial court bifurcated the issues of liability and damages in the context of a *forum non conveniens* motion. In *Radigan v. Innisbrook Resort & Golf Club*, 150 N.J. Super. 427, 375 A.2d 1229 (1977), the trial court found that New Jersey, plaintiff's home forum, was an inconvenient forum for trying the liability issue in the personal injuries action, but not for trying the damages issue. The court bifurcated the two issues and directed that the liability issue be tried in Florida, defendant's home forum, followed by a trial on damages in New Jersey. *Radigan*, at 429. The appellate court stated that "[w]hile such a bifurcation, in an appropriate case, seems like a sensible idea, we entertain some doubt whether it would be permissible." *Radigan*, at 430. However, the court declined to resolve the issue, finding that the bifurcation itself was an abuse of discretion supporting reversal because the circumstances did not support a finding that Florida was the more convenient forum as to liability. *Radigan*, at 430.

Radigan is of little use in the current analysis, both because the court declined to rule whether bifurcation was "permissible" and because the trial court in *Radigan* contemplated two separate trials, with the Florida court deciding the liability issue and the parties then returning to New Jersey for a damages trial. In the present case, as in cases cited above, the liability issue was resolved without a trial and dismissal was granted to resolve the only remaining issue, damages.

III Treaty

Plaintiffs contend that the trial court violated the treaty rights of the Japanese nationals by dismissing their claims, while retaining jurisdiction over the claims brought by the non-Japanese nationals. In doing so, plaintiffs argue, the trial court denied plaintiffs "most-favored-nation treatment" guaranteed to the Japanese plaintiffs by treaty. Treaty of Friendship, Commerce, and Navigation, Apr. 2, 1953, United States-Japan, 4 U.S.T. 2063, 2077, T.I.A.S. No. 2863. This argument is without merit.

The treaty defines "national treatment" and "most-favored nation treatment" as meaning treatment "upon terms no less favorable" than citizens "in like situations". 4 U.S.T. at 2079. The situation of the Japanese citizens is comparable to a United States citizen who resides in one state bringing an action in a sister state. In fact, while arguing that the treaty bars the application of the "lesser deference" standard of *Reyno*, plaintiffs assert that the treaty entitles the Japanese plaintiffs to the same benefits enjoyed by the Kansas resident in *Spider*.

While, as plaintiffs note, the issue of treaty rights was not raised in *Reyno*, a number of federal courts have found that the treaty does not serve to bar dismissal of foreign plaintiffs on *forum non conveniens* grounds. . . .

. . . .

In summary, we hold that the trial court did not abuse its discretion in either the bifurcation or the *forum non conveniens* dismissal. We further hold that the dismissal did not violate the treaty rights of the Japanese nationals. We also take this opportunity to expressly decline to adopt the lesser deference standard of *Reyno*. Finding no error, we affirm.

CALLOW, C.J., BRACHTENBACH, DOLLIVER, DORE, ANDERSEN, and SMITH, JJ., and MCINTURFF, J. PRO TEM., concur.

UTTER, J. (concurring)

I write separately to emphasize that the civil rules do not sanction international bifurcation of cases. Because of this, the trial court's decision to bifurcate this case was an abuse of discretion. Because the parties did not complete pretrial discovery or try the case, this error cannot justify overruling the trial court's decision to dismiss the action. I agree that *forum non conveniens* principles justify the trial court's dismissal of the Japanese plaintiffs' case, in spite of the bifurcation error, and would affirm the trial court on that basis only.

Bifurcation under CR 42(b) applies to cases within a jurisdiction. . . . .

No statute or court rule authorizes transfer of single issues between jurisdictions. [Citations omitted.] Generally, complex litigation requires that the matter be handled by one judge, not by multiple jurisdictions. [Reference omitted.]

An examination of the record here shows why bifurcation between jurisdictions should be disfavored. The affidavits submitted to the trial court by experts on Japanese law disagreed about whether a Japanese court would consider the judgment made as to liability a final one to be given *res judicata* effect in Japan. Accordingly, the trial court made no finding of fact as to the res judicata issue. Moreover, because solatium depends in some measure on the degree of culpability, the liability judgment may not be sufficient to allow the Japanese court to determine damages. Although the record establishes that the Japanese judiciary can fairly try the case and award full compensation, it does not establish that it will avoid duplication of the effort already expended here.

Piecemeal international litigation raises the possibility not just of separate trials, but of two sets of appeals and international judicial conflict in the resolution of one case. . . .

I would hold, therefore, that bifurcation is an abuse of discretion absent a determination that the trials will be held in one jurisdiction. . . .

The majority correctly reaffirms our holding that the trial court may only disturb the plaintiffs choice of forum if the balance of factors strongly favors the defendant. . . . Given the findings of the trial court, we cannot conclude that it abused its discretion in deciding to disturb the plaintiffs' choice in this case. The trial court's bifurcation decision, however, was an abuse of discretion and we should so hold.

QUESTIONS

1. How do the standards for granting a *forum non conveniens* motion under Washington State law differ from U.S. federal law? Under *Erie v. Tompkins*, would the Washington State standards apply in a diversity suit filed in a U.S. District Court in Washington State? If not, why not?

2. In light of the cases excerpted above, how would you explain Boeing's litigation strategies? How successful were they?

3. Can either or both of the decisions in these cases be justified in terms of international judicial efficiency or fairness or some other rationale?

4. Justice Utter argues that his decision to bifurcate the issues for adjudication in *Myers* was an abuse of discretion. Do you agree?

We turn now to the first of two cases involving a Japanese bank and a holding company formed in the United States by members of a corporate group. The plaintiff, U.S.O. Corporation, was incorporated in Delaware as jointly owned enterprise of five firms in the Asahi corporate group — Asahi Industrial K.K., Asahi Homes Ltd., Asahi Corporation Ltd., Sunfoods Ltd., and Asahi Management K.K. Their purpose was to enable the principal member, Asahi Industrial, to invest in real estate in Illinois through a rather complex arrangement with a limited partnership that owned a share of a larger partnership that in turn owned real estate in Illinois. The defendant, the Mizuho Bank, was established on April 1, 2002, as the result of the merger of the Industrial Bank of Japan, the Dai-Ichi Kangyo Bank, and the retail operations of Fuji Bank. Its principal office is in Tokyo. Matsuda, the second defendant, had been appointed the administrator in bankruptcy proceedings with respect to the Asahi group and its constituent companies that had commenced in the Tokyo District Court on May 12, 2005, the decision in which is extracted *infra*.

Prior to the formation of Mizuho Bank, the Industrial Bank of Japan had been the main bank for the Asahi group. Upon its merger and the formation of Mizuho Bank, U.S.O. Corporation had deposited funds with Mizuho Bank as security for an outstanding loan to Asahi Industrial, its principal shareholder. In March 2003 Mizuho withdrew the funds to satisfy Asahi Industrial's debts. A month later U.S.O. Corporation and its director/owner filed suit in Illinois against Mizuho, claiming damages for unjust enrichment (restitution) and breach of contract for losses suffered as a result of its appropriation of funds in the security deposit. The Judge Joan Humphrey Lefkow of the U.S. District Court for the Northern District of Illinois, Eastern Division, dismissed the action on the grounds of *forum non conveniens*. The plaintiff appealed.

U.S.O. CORPORATION v. MIZUHO HOLDING COMPANY
547 F.3d 749 (7th Cir. 2008)

Before POSNER, RIPPLE, and EVANS, CIRCUIT JUDGES.

POSNER, CIRCUIT JUDGE. This diversity suit, in federal court under 28 U.S.C. § 1332(d)(2)(C), charges conversion by affiliated Japanese entities that we'll refer to collectively as "the bank." The district judge dismissed the suit on the basis of the doctrine of *forum non conveniens*. That venerable judge-made doctrine, securely a part of federal common law, authorizes a court to dismiss a suit if making the defendant defend in that court rather than in an alternative forum would burden the defendant unreasonably. . . .

The plaintiff, although incorporated in Delaware, is the wholly owned subsidiary of a Japanese company, and its headquarters are in Japan. It invested in a limited partnership also created under Delaware law; and as with the plaintiff the partnership's principal place of business was in Japan, and all its partners had Japanese addresses. The partnership invested in another limited partnership, which bought a building in Chicago. The suit charges the bank with having misappropriated $6.95 million from the plaintiff's bank account in Japan after the building was sold, that being the plaintiff's share of the proceeds from the sale. The suit also charges the bank with having skimmed an unspecified percentage of the annual return to which the plaintiff's investment entitled it before the bank was sold, and by doing so of having reduced that return to $500,000 in each of the ten years of the plaintiff's indirect investment in the building.

Most of the alleged bad acts were committed in Japan by Japanese persons and almost all the witnesses and documents are there; and eight months after this suit was filed the bank brought a mirror-image declaratory judgment suit in a Japanese court. That litigation is proceeding, the Japanese court having denied the plaintiff's motion to dismiss the suit because of the pendency of the present suit. [Emphasis added.]

There is no reason for identical suits to be proceeding in different courts in different countries thousands of miles apart. Such parallel proceedings incite a race to judgment in the hope that the judgment in the home forum will favor the home litigant and be usable to block the other suit by interposing a defense of res judicata in it. Oddly, none of the lawyers in this case seems to know much about Japanese law; they have been unable to tell us what if any weight the Japanese court would give a final judgment in the present suit should it end first. But Japan does have a doctrine of res judicata, and though narrower than ours it would bar an identical suit provided the judgment pleaded in bar was a judgment on the merits [emphasis added]. . . . One device for avoiding duplicate lawsuits is the doctrine of abstention articulated in *Colorado River Water Conservation District v. United States*, 424 U.S. 800, 818 (1976). It has sometimes been applied when identical concurrent litigation is, as in this case, pending abroad. . . . But as far as we know abstention has not been urged in either suit by any party to the present suit.

The bank has made a compelling case for the dismissal of this suit on the ground of *forum non conveniens. Dragging all those witnesses and documents from Japan to Chicago, supplying interpreters for the witnesses and translators for the documents, and conducting a trial largely on the basis of testimony given through interpreters and of documents translated from their original language, would impose unreasonable burdens not only on the defendants but also on the district court. Moreover, the law applicable to the issues in the case is almost certainly Japanese law, with which American judges have little familiarity. In fact, as we said, even the lawyers in this case, though their clients are Japanese firms, have little familiarity with Japanese law.* [Emphasis added.] And besides, the litigation in Japan is well advanced and the Japanese court has declined to abate it in favor of the U.S. litigation.

The plaintiff argues that there is a strong presumption in favor of a plaintiff's choice of forum, especially if the plaintiff is an American and the forum is an American court. In a veritable paroxysm of formalism the plaintiff's lawyers refuse to acknowledge that their client is "American" in only the most artificial sense, since it has no American presence except a Delaware certificate of incorporation. It had an indirect investment in an American building, but foreigners own a large chunk of the American economy without being thought Americans; by the end of 2006 foreign direct investment in the United States had reached $1.8 trillion. [Reference omitted.]

The plaintiff says that to look through the corporate form to the nationality of the plaintiff's managers and shareholders is to pierce the corporate veil without an adequate showing of undercapitalization, misrepresentation, neglect of corporate formalities, etc. That is nonsense. The purpose of the veil is to shield shareholders from personal liability for the corporation's debts in order to encourage investment; no one is trying to reach the personal assets of the plaintiff's shareholders.

Insisting (and with a straight face) on the Americanness of their foreign client, the plaintiff's lawyers argue that the presumption in favor of the plaintiff's choice of forum is nationalistic; it is about the right not of plaintiffs in general but of American plaintiffs to sue foreigners in American courts. Putting to one side for the moment that the plaintiff is not really "American," one can find language supportive of the nationalistic interpretation in some court of appeals decisions. In *SME Racks, Inc. v. Sistemas Mecanicos Para Electronica, S.A.*, 382 F.3d 1097, 1101 (11th Cir. 2004), for example, we read that courts "should require positive evidence of unusually extreme circumstances, and should be thoroughly convinced that material injustice is manifest before exercising any such discretion to deny a citizen access to the courts of this country." . . . But *SME Racks* was merely repeating language found in a 1955 case called *Burt v. Isthmus Development Co.*, 218 F.2d 353, 357 (5th Cir. 1955), and such language does not sort well with the Supreme Court's statement (made long after *Burt*) that "citizens or residents deserve somewhat more deference than foreign plaintiffs, but dismissal should not be automatically barred when a plaintiff has filed suit in his home forum. As always, if the balance of conveniences suggests that trial in the chosen forum would be unnecessarily burdensome for the defendant or the court, dismissal is proper." *Piper Aircraft Co. v. Reyno, supra*, 454 U.S. at 255 n. 23.

A foreign company that chooses to sue in the United States rather than in its own country is unlikely to experience inconvenience if the court invokes forum non conveniens against it. Realistically a Japanese company, our plaintiff should not be disconcerted to have to litigate against its Japanese adversaries in a Japanese court. [Emphasis added.] "[I]f the plaintiff is suing far from home, it is less reasonable to assume that the forum is a convenient one. [T]he risk that the chosen forum really has little connection to the litigation is greater." *In re Factor VIII or IX Concentrate Blood Products Litigation, supra*, 484 F.3d at 956. The plaintiff's home is Tokyo, which is quite a distance from Chicago.

Explaining why "citizens or residents deserve somewhat more deference than foreign plaintiffs" the Court in Piper pointed out that "when the home forum has been chosen, it is reasonable to assume that this choice is convenient." 454 U.S. at 235 n. 23. Convenience — the "central purpose" of *forum non conveniens, id.* at 256 — is not a euphemism for nationalism or protectionism. The demands of a global economy require that American courts be amenable to permitting litigation that can be handled much more efficiently in foreign forums to be sent to those forums. "International business transactions depend on evenhanded application of legal rules; hometown favoritism is the enemy of commerce." *Intec USA, LLC v. Engle*, 467 F.3d 1038, 1040 (7th Cir. 2006); . . . And so American plaintiffs may find themselves told to litigate in a foreign forum under an even-handed and pragmatic application of *forum non conveniens*.

Courts need to look behind an assertion that the plaintiff is "American," moreover, to determine whether the party has the sort of ties with the United States that make the American judicial forum convenient. The plaintiff's lawyers contend that the Japanese character of the nominally American plaintiff cannot be a consideration in deciding whether the presumption has been overcome; only the respective litigation burdens of the parties in one forum versus the other may be considered. This contradicts the plaintiff's "Americanism" argument, and is anyway wrong. The more tenuous a party's relation to the forum, the weaker its case for litigating there. The fact that a Japanese company has a Delaware corporate certificate but no offices or personnel in Chicago or for that matter anywhere else in the United States should not make it feel more at home litigating in Chicago than in Tokyo. The plaintiff keeps calling itself an "Illinois company," but it is not. It is an out-of-state corporation that had an indirect investment in a building located in Illinois. The Supreme Court has said that the presumption in favor of the plaintiff's choice of forum is diminished when it is not its home forum. *Sinochem Int'l Co. v. Malaysia Int'l Shipping Corp., supra*, 549 U.S. at 430, 127 S. Ct. 1184.

We do not question the presumption in favor of a plaintiff's choice of forum. Rules governing subject-matter jurisdiction, personal jurisdiction, venue, and removal (the defendants removed the plaintiff's suit, originally filed in an Illinois state court, to the federal district court in Chicago) limit a plaintiff's choice of forum, as do provisions for change of venue and for consolidating multidistrict litigation for pretrial proceedings. 28 U.S.C. §§ 1404, 1407. And the rules for allocating burdens of proof usually make the plaintiff's case harder to prove than the defendant's. The limits on personal jurisdiction are particularly important, as they often force a plaintiff to litigate on the defendant's home turf. And dismissal may have more serious consequences for a plaintiff, even if he can refile his suit elsewhere, than merely being transferred to another district court within the federal system-for the elsewhere is almost always a court in a foreign country. *Sinochem Int'l Co. v. Malaysia Int'l Shipping Corp.*, *supra*, 549 U.S. at 430. That is why the showing required to prove that the forum is indeed non conveniens is greater than that required for obtaining a change of venue from one district court to another. . . . Finally, it would complicate and prolong litigation if the plaintiff's choice of forum were just the starting point for the selection of the forum in which the case would actually be litigated. So the presumption is fine, but it is not to be treated, as the plaintiff would have us do, as a nigh-insurmountable obstacle to dismissal.

The plaintiff argues that its principal evidence, at least of its profit-skimming claim, is in the United States, consisting on the documentary side of the partnership agreements and on the witness side of accountants who will try to reconstruct the profits from the investment in the building. But the plaintiff is trying to make the tail wag the dog. The amount of money at stake in the profit-skimming claim appears to be tiny. . . .

. . . .

If the plaintiff really has no idea what its loss was, we cannot understand why it expects to be presenting at considerable expense a parade of witnesses and slew of documents in the district court should the case be tried here and why that uncertain expectation should be a reason for conducting the entire litigation in Chicago.

An argument made by the plaintiff that is related to the preceding one is that the limited scope of discovery allowed by Japanese courts will make it impossible to obtain justice in the Japanese litigation. The relation lies in the plaintiff's contention that the limitations of discovery will be felt most acutely with respect to the profit-skimming claim.

The argument reflects a misunderstanding of the difference between a common law system, such as that of the United States, and a civil law system, such as that of Japan. In the former, the burden of investigation falls on the parties' lawyers, and discovery procedures are designed to facilitate party investigation. In the latter, the burden of investigation falls on the judges, and the role of the lawyers is correspondingly diminished. *United States v. Filani*, 74 F.3d 378, 383 (2d Cir. 1996)

. . . .

. . . .

The plaintiff has given us no reason to suppose that Japanese procedures are inadequate to enable it to prove its profit-skimming claim. It tells us, moreover, that it does not intend to file that claim as a counterclaim in the Japanese litigation; this strengthens the inference that the claim is a makeweight, injected into the present suit for strategic reasons.

Thus far we have considered, with the partial exception of choice of law, considerations relating to the balance of convenience to the parties. The Supreme Court has told us also to consider how the public interest might be affected by the choice of forum:

> Factors of public interest also have place in applying the doctrine [of *forum non conveniens*]. Administrative difficulties follow for courts when litigation is piled up in congested centers instead of being handled at its origin. Jury duty is a burden that ought not to be imposed upon the people of a community which has no relation to the litigation. In cases which touch the affairs of many persons, there is reason for holding the trial in their view and reach rather than in remote parts of the country where they can learn of it by report only. There is a local interest in having localized controversies decided at home. There is an appropriateness, too, in having the trial of a diversity case in a forum that is at home with the state law that must govern the case, rather than having a court in some other forum untangle problems in conflict of laws, and in law foreign to itself.

. . . These considerations point as strongly to Japan as the proper forum for resolving the parties' dispute as the private-interest considerations do, except that we have no information about congestion in the Japanese court in Tokyo where the mirror-image litigation is pending. That uncertainty to one side, the local interest is that of Japan; to burden Americans with jury duty to resolve an intramural Japanese dispute would be gratuitous; and a Japanese court is more at home with Japanese law and Japanese firms than an American court would be. This last point bears on the public interest as well as the private interest in the choice of forum because "judges have an interest independent of party preference for not being asked to decide an issue that they cannot resolve intelligently." *Tomic v. Catholic Diocese of Peoria*, 442 F.3d 1036, 1042 (7th Cir. 2006).

The "public interest" is open-ended. There may be cases in which it will weigh heavily in favor of conducting international litigation in a U.S. rather than a foreign court . . . . This is not such a case.

Affirmed.

QUESTIONS

We revisit this case in connection with the ensuing litigation in Japan as well as discovery in the U.S. in aid of proceedings abroad in Chapter 5. Given the facts as described by Judge Posner, why, in your view, did the U.S.O. Corporation sue in the United States? How does Judge Posner define the nationality of a corporation? Under his view, would the Chrysler Group LLC, either while a subsidiary of Daimler Benz or today, with over 50 percent ownership, of Fiat, have been deemed a U.S. "national" for

> purposes of *forum non conveniens?* Or is ownership beside the point?

B. The Role of Experts

Issues of foreign law and, above all, assessments of the availability and "adequacy" of foreign judicial tribunals are paramount in the application of the *forum non conveniens* doctrine. The determination of these issues by judges without any prior experience or knowledge of the foreign law or legal system in question creates significant problems. Ultimately, as we have observed in the *Nai-Chao v. Boeing* case, *infra*, and other decisions examined thus far, generally judges generally rely on experts to provide the required information and data on which the necessary determinations are based. These experts are either retained by the parties or, more rarely, the trial judge. The following case exemplifies the role of experts and at least some of the cogent issues raised by their participation. We will subsequently consider whether judges should rely on outside experts under Federal Rule of Civil Procedure 44.1, which provides:

> A party who intends to raise an issue about a foreign country's law must give notice by a pleading or other writing. In determining foreign law, the court may consider any relevant material or source, including testimony, whether or not submitted by a party or admissible under the Federal Rules of Evidence. The court's determination must be treated as a ruling on a question of law.

IN RE UNION CARBIDE CORPORATION GAS PLANT DISASTER AT BHOPAL, INDIA IN DECEMBER, 1984[*]
634 F. Supp. 842 (S.D.N.Y. 1986)

KEENAN, DISTRICT JUDGE.

FACTUAL BACKGROUND

On the night of December 2-3, 1984 the most tragic industrial disaster in history occurred in the city of Bhopal, state of Madhya Pradesh, Union of India. Located there was a chemical plant owned and operated by Union Carbide India Limited ("UCIL"). The plant, situated in the northern sector of the city, had numerous hutments adjacent to it on its southern side which were occupied by impoverished squatters. UCIL manufactured the pesticides Sevin and Temik at the Bhopal plant at the request of, and with the approval of, the Government of India. (Affidavit of John MacDonald ("MacDonald Aff.") at 2). UCIL was incorporated under Indian law in 1934. 50.9% of its stock is owned by the defendant, Union Carbide Corporation, a New York corporation. (MacDonald Aff. at 1). Methyl isocyanate (MIC), a highly toxic gas, is an ingredient in the production of both Sevin and

---

[*] Footnotes omitted.

Temik. On the night of the tragedy MIC leaked from the plant in substantial quantities for reasons not yet determined.

The prevailing winds on the early morning of December 3, 1984 were from Northwest to Southeast. They blew the deadly gas into the overpopulated hutments adjacent to the plant and into the most densely occupied parts of the city. The results were horrendous. Estimates of deaths directly attributable to the leak range as high as 2,100. No one is sure exactly how many perished. Over 200,000 people suffered injuries — some serious and permanent — some mild and temporary. Livestock were killed and crops damaged. Businesses were interrupted.

On December 7, 1984 the first lawsuit was filed by American lawyers in the United States on behalf of thousands of Indians. *Dawani et al. v. Union Carbide Corp.*, S.D.W.Va. (84-2479). Since then 144 additional actions have been commenced in federal courts in the United States. The actions have all been joined and assigned by the Judicial Panel on Multidistrict Litigation to the Southern District of New York by order of February 6, 1985, 601 F. Supp. 1035.

The individual federal court complaints have been superseded by a consolidated complaint filed on June 28, 1985.

The Indian Government on March 29, 1985 enacted legislation, the Bhopal Gas Leak Disaster (Processing of Claims) Act (21 of 1985) ("Bhopal Act"), providing that the Government of India has the exclusive right to represent Indian plaintiffs in India and elsewhere in connection with the tragedy. Pursuant to the Bhopal Act, the Union of India, on April 8, 1985, filed a complaint with this Court setting forth claims for relief similar to those in the consolidated complaint of June 28, 1985.

By order of April 25, 1985 this Court established a Plaintiffs' Executive Committee, comprised of F. Lee Bailey and Stanley M. Chesley, Esqs., who represented individual plaintiffs and Michael V. Ciresi, Esq., whose firm represents the Union of India. Jack S. Hoffinger, Esq., who represents individual plaintiffs, was appointed liaison counsel for the Plaintiffs' Executive Committee.

On September 24, 1985, pursuant to the Bhopal Act, the Central Government of India framed a "scheme" for the Registration and Processing of Claims arising out of the disaster. According to the Union of India's counsel, over 487,000 claims have been filed in India pursuant to the "scheme."

There presently are 145 actions filed in the United States District Court for the Southern District of New York under the Judicial Panel for Multidistrict Litigation's order of February 6, 1985, involving approximately 200,000 plaintiffs.

Before this Court is a motion by the defendant Union Carbide Corporation ("Union Carbide") to dismiss the consolidated action on the grounds of *forum non conveniens*.

DISCUSSION

The doctrine of *forum non conveniens* allows a court to decline jurisdiction, even when jurisdiction is authorized by a general forum statute. In support of its position that the consolidated action before the Court should be transferred to a more convenient forum within the Union of India pursuant to this doctrine, Union Carbide relies on the United States Supreme Court's decisions in *Gulf Oil Corp. v. Gilbert*, 330 U.S. 501, 67 S. Ct. 839, 91 L. Ed. 1055 (1947) and *Piper Aircraft Co. v. Reyno*, 454 U.S. 235, 102 S. Ct. 252, 70 L. Ed. 2d 419 (1981). The plaintiffs cite numerous other lower United States federal court cases in their briefs and seek to distinguish the Supreme Court's decisions from this case. Of course, *Gilbert* and *Piper* are the touchstones in sorting out and examining the contentions of both sides to this motion on the various factors bearing on convenience.

Piper teaches a straightforward formulation of the doctrine of *forum non conveniens*. A district court is advised to determine first whether the proposed alternative forum is "adequate." This inquiry should proceed in the order followed below. Then, as a matter within its "sound discretion," *Piper* at 257, 102 S. Ct. at 266, the district court should consider relevant public and private interest factors, and reasonably balance those factors, in order to determine whether dismissal is favored. This Court will approach the various concerns in the same direct manner in which *Piper* and *Gilbert* set them out.

. . . .

1. Preliminary Considerations.

"At the outset of any *forum non conveniens* inquiry, the court must determine whether there exists an alternative forum." *Piper* at 254, n. 22. . . .

[P]laintiffs and amicus curiae argue that the Indian legal system is inadequate to handle the Bhopal litigation. In support of this position, plaintiffs have submitted the affidavit of Professor Marc S. Galanter of the University of Wisconsin Law School. Professor Galanter's credentials are impressive; he was a Fulbright Scholar at the Faculty of Law of Delhi University and specializes in South Asian Studies at the University of Wisconsin Law School. He is not, however, admitted to practice in India and the Court views his opinions concerning the Indian legal system, its judiciary and bar as far less persuasive than those of N.A. Palkhivala and J.B. Dadachanji, each of whom has been admitted to practice in India for over 40 years. Both are Senior Advocates before the Supreme Court of India. Mr. Palkhivala served as Indian Ambassador to the United States from 1977 to 1979, and has represented the Indian government on three occasions before international tribunals.

Although the outcome of this analysis, given the rule of Piper regarding change in law, seems self-evident, the Court will review plaintiffs' argument on the inadequacy of the Indian forum out of deference to the plaintiffs.

A. Innovation in the Indian Judicial System.

Professor Galanter describes the Indian common law legal system, inherited from the British, in terms of its similarity to that of other common law systems. He compares the system favorably to that of the United States or Great Britain in terms of the appellate structure, the rule of stare decisis, the role of the judiciary as "guardian of [India's] democratic structure and protector of citizens' rights."

(Galanter Aff., at 6–12) before pointing to its ostensible deficiencies. According to Professor Galanter, India's legal system "was imposed on it" during the period of colonial rule. (Galanter Aff. at 11). Galanter argues that "Indian legal institutions still reflect their colonial origins," (Galanter Aff. at 12), in terms of the lack of broad-based legislative activity, inaccessibility of legal information and legal services, burdensome court filing fees and limited innovativeness with reference to legal practice and education. (Galanter Aff. at 12).

On the question of innovativeness, Mr. Palkhivala responds with numerous examples of novel treatment of complex legal issues by the Indian Judiciary. In the words of the former ambassador of India to the United States, "a legal system is not a structure of fossils but is a living organism which grows through the judicial process and statutory enactments." (Palkhavala Aff. at 3). The examples cited by defendant's experts suggest a developed and independent judiciary. Plaintiffs present no evidence to bolster their contention that the Indian legal system has not sufficiently emerged from its colonial heritage to display the innovativeness which the Bhopal litigation would demand. Their claim in this regard is not compelling.

B. Endemic Delays in the Indian Legal System.

Galanter discusses the problems of delay and backlog in Indian courts. Indeed, it appears that India has approximately one-tenth the number of judges, per citizen, as the United States, and that postponements and high caseloads are widespread. Galanter urges that the backlog is a result of Indian procedural law, which allows for adjournments in mid-hearing, and for multiple interlocutory and final appeals. Numerous appeals and "[c]onsiderable delay [are] caused by the tendency of courts to avoid the decision of all the matters in issue in a suit, on the ground that the suit could be disposed of on a preliminary point." (Galanter Aff. at 17; 18–20, 21, quoting Indian Law Commission, 54th Report (1973) pp. 12–13).

This Court acknowledges that delays and backlog exist in Indian courts, but United States courts are subject to delays and backlog, too. *See* Remarks of Honorable Warren E. Burger, Chief Justice, Supreme Court of the United States, 100 F.R.D. 499, 534 (1983).

However, as Mr. Palkhivala states, while delays in the Indian legal system are a fact of judicial life in the proposed alternative forum, there is no reason to assume that the Bhopal litigation will be treated in ordinary fashion.

The Bhopal tragedy has already been approached with imagination in India. Demonstrating the creativity and flexibility of the Indian system, the Parliament of India has passed the Bhopal Act in order to deal with the cases arising from the sad events of December 3, 1984. The Bhopal Act permits the cases to be treated "speedily, effectively, equitably and to the best advantage of the claimants." (Palkhivala Aff. at 11).

Mr. Dadachanji refers to another Indian case which arose from a gas leak in New Delhi. The Chief Justice and another Justice of the Supreme Court of India ordered the presiding court to expedite adjudication of claims. *MC Mehta v. Union of India.* (Dadachanji Aff. at 11 and Annexure A thereto). In another instance, the Indian Supreme Court directed the High Court to hear a given matter on a daily basis, and set a deadline for delivering judgment (Dadachanji Aff. at 11 and Annexure B thereto). Other means of coping with delay are appointment of special tribunals by the Government of India (Dadachanji Aff. at 12 and Annexure C thereto), and assignment of daily hearing duties to a single special judge, otherwise unburdened, to hear a special matter. (Dadachanji Aff. at 11). This Court is persuaded, by the example of the Bhopal Act itself and other cases where special measures to expedite were taken by the Indian judiciary, that the most significant, urgent and extensive litigation ever to arise from a single event could be handled through special judicial accommodation in India, if required.

C. Procedural and Practical Capacity of Indian Courts.

Plaintiffs contend that the Indian legal system lacks the wherewithal to allow it "to deal effectively and expeditiously" with the issues raised in this lawsuit. (Memo in Opp. p. 53).

Plaintiffs urge that Indian practitioners emphasize oral skills rather than written briefs. They allegedly lack specialization, practical investigative techniques and coordination into partnerships. These factors, it is argued, limit the Indian bar's ability to handle the Bhopal litigation. As Mr. Dadachanji indicates, Indian lawyers have competently dealt with complex technology transfers, suggesting capability within the technological and scientific areas of legal practice, if not "specialization." (Dadachanji Aff. at 8). Moreover, Indian attorneys use experts, when necessary. As to investigative ability, Mr. Dadachanji persuasively points out that the Central Bureau of Investigation ("CBI") of the Union of India is well equipped to handle factual inquiry, as is the Commission of Enquiry constituted by the state of Madhya Pradesh. (Dadachanji Aff. at 8). While Indian attorneys may not customarily join into large law firms, and as Mr. Palkhivala states, are limited by present Indian law to partnerships of no more than twenty, this alone or even in concert with other factors does not establish the inadequacy of the Indian legal system. (Palkhivala Aff. at 8). There is no reason the Indian legislature could not provide for the expansion of law-firms, if such a choice is required. In any event, this Court is not convinced that the size of a law firm has that much to do with the quality of legal service provided. Many small firms in this country perform work at least on a par with the largest firms. Bigger is not necessarily better.

Moreover, since the Union of India purports to represent all the claimants, it is likely that if the case were transferred to India, the Attorney General or Solicitor General of India and the Advocate General of Madhya Pradesh, with attendant staffs, would represent the claimants. The Indian bar appears more than capable of shouldering the litigation if it should be transferred to India. (Palkhivala Aff. at 9).

Next, plaintiffs and Professor Galanter argue that the substantive tort law of India is not sufficiently developed to accommodate the Bhopal claims. Plaintiffs trace the lack of sophistication in Indian tort law to the presence of court fees for litigants as inhibiting the filing of civil suits. Though the filing fees may have had historical significance, they are irrelevant here. Professor Galanter acknowledges that court fees may be waived for "poor parties or for specific classes of litigants." (Galanter Aff. at 28). In fact, filing fees have been waived for claimants in India in the Bhopal litigation already begun there.

Professor Galanter asserts that India lacks codified tort law, has little reported case law in the tort field to serve as precedent, and has no tort law relating to disputes arising out of complex product or design liability. (Galanter Aff. at 30–36). As an illustration of the paucity of Indian tort law, Professor Galanter states that a search through the All-India Reports for the span from 1914 to 1965 revealed only 613 tort cases reported. (Galanter Aff. at 32). Mr. Dadachanji responds that tort law is sparsely reported in India due to frequent settlement of such cases, lack of appeal to higher courts, and the publication of tort cases in specialized journals other than the All-India Reports. (Dadachanji Aff. at 16–17; Palkhivala Aff. at 10). In addition, tort law has been codified in numerous Indian statutes. (Dadachanji Aff. at 16–17).

As Professor Galanter himself states, "the major categories of tort, their elements, the [theories] of liability, defenses, respondeat superior, the theories of damages — are all familiar." (Galanter Aff. at 37). What is different, Galanter asserts, is the complete absence of tort law relating to high technology or complex manufacturing processes. This is of no moment with respect to the adequacy of the Indian courts. With the groundwork of tort doctrine adopted from the common law and the precedential weight awarded British cases, as well as Indian ones, it is obvious that a well-developed base of tort doctrine exists to provide a guide to Indian courts presiding over the Bhopal litigation. In any event, much tort law applied in American cases involving complex technology has its source in legal principles first enunciated in Victorian England. *See, e.g., Rylands v. Fletcher*, 1868, L.R. 3 H.L. 330. As Mr. Palkhivala stated in his affidavit:

> The plant itself was the product of highly complex technology, but complexity of the technology cannot be equated with complexity of legal issues. The principles of liability and damages involved in the Bhopal cases are all well established in India. The complexity is not in the nature or determination of legal issues but in the application of the law to the events which took place in Bhopal. Well settled law is to be applied to an unusual occurrence. (Palkhivala Aff. at 7).

Plaintiffs next assert that India lacks certain procedural devices which are essential to the adjudication of complex cases, the absence of which prevent India from providing an adequate alternative forum. They urge that Indian pre-trial discovery is inadequate and that therefore India is an inadequate alternative forum. Professor Galanter states that the only forms of discovery available in India are written interrogatories, inspection of documents, and requests for admissions. Parties alone are subject to discovery. Third-party witnesses need not submit to discovery. Discovery may be directed to admissible evidence only, not material likely to lead to relevant or admissible material, as in the courts of the United States. Parties are not compelled to provide what will be actual proof at trial as part of discovery.

These limits on discovery are adopted from the British system. Similar discovery tools are used in Great Britain today. This Court finds that their application would perhaps, however, limit the victims' access to sources of proof. Therefore, pursuant to its equitable powers, the Court directs that the defendant consent to submit to the broad discovery afforded by the United States Federal Rules of Civil Procedure if or when an Indian court sits in judgment or presides over pretrial proceedings in the Bhopal litigation. Any dismissal of the action now before this Court is thus conditioned on defendant's consent to submit to discovery on the American model, even after transfer to another jurisdiction.

The ostensible lack of devices for third-party impleader or for organizing complex cases under the law of the state of Madhya Pradesh are two other procedural deficiencies which plaintiffs assert preclude a finding that India offers an adequate alternative forum. Assuming for the moment that, upon appropriate transfer, the Bhopal litigation would be adjudicated by the local district court in Bhopal, and that the law of Madhya Pradesh would be applied, this Court is still not moved by plaintiffs' argument regarding impleader or complex litigation.

Although no specific provision in the Indian Code of Civil Procedure permits the impleading of third-parties from whom contribution is sought, other provisions in the Code do provide for impleader. As both parties to this motion state, Order 1, Rule 10(2) of the Indian Code of Civil Procedure "allows the court to add additional parties if the presence of those parties is 'necessary in order to enable the Court effectively and completely to adjudicate upon and settle all questions involved in the suit.'" (Galanter Aff. at 60; Dadachanji Aff. at 18). Professor Galanter posits that a joint tortfeasor would not be considered a necessary party, and would not be joined. Defendant's expert, conversely, asserts that a party can be added to prevent multiplicity of suits and conflicts of decisions. Thus, Mr. Dadachanji argues, defendants would be able to seek contribution from third-parties if joinder would prevent repetitive litigation or inconsistency. Moreover, the broad provision of inherent powers to aid the ends of justice, as codified at Section 151 of the Indian Code of Civil Procedure would prevent an ultimate miscarriage of justice in the area of impleader. (Dadachanji Aff. at 19). The Court observes that the alleged problem would appear to act to the detriment of defendant, not plaintiffs. It is Union Carbide which urges that third-party defendants are necessary. (Memo in Support at 27–28). Defendant discounts the supposed unavailability of third-party impleader, while the plaintiffs find its lack objectionable. These postures lead the Court to the conclusion that this argument is not compelling in either direction. The lack of specific third-party practice will not concern the Court if it does not concern Union Carbide.

The absence of procedures or mechanisms within the Indian judiciary to handle complex litigation is presented as support for plaintiffs' position regarding the non-existence of an adequate alternative forum. Professor Galanter asserts, for example, that Indian judges do not promote settlements. The point is wholly irrelevant to the question of whether an adequate alternative forum exists. In any event, this Court has labored hard and long to promote settlement between the parties for over a year, to no avail. It would appear that settlement, although desirable for many reasons, including conservation of attorneys' fees and costs of litigation, preservation of judicial resources, and speed of resolution, is unlikely regardless of the level of activism of the presiding judge.

Plaintiffs' next contention is that since no class action procedure exists in India expeditious litigation of the Bhopal suits would be impossible. As with all of plaintiffs' other arguments, this purported deficiency does not constitute "no remedy" at all. Professor Galanter himself acknowledges that Order 1, Rule 8 of the Indian Code of Civil Procedure provides a mechanism for "representative" suits, "where there are numerous persons having the same interest in one suit." (Galanter Aff. at 54). Even if the current state of Indian law regarding "representative" suits involves application of the mechanism to pre-existing groups such as religious sects or associations, there is no reason to conclude that the Indian legislature, capable of enacting the Bhopal Act, would not see its way to enacting a specific law for class actions. In addition, it does not appear on the face of Order 1, Rule 8 that the "representative" suit is expressly limited to pre-existing groups. The Indian district court could adopt the rule for use in a newly created class of injured, whose members all have "the same interest" in establishing the liability of the defendant. An Indian court has law available to create a representative class, or perhaps a few different representative classes. The "scheme" for registration and processing of claims, see *supra*, at 4, could perform the task of evaluating the specific amounts of claims. Moreover, Mr. Dadachanji gives at least three examples where Indian courts have consolidated suits pursuant to their inherent power under Section 151 of the Indian Code of Civil Procedure. In at least one case, such consolidation allegedly occurred without consent of the parties. (Dadachanji Aff. at 9). The absence of a rule for class actions which is identical to the American rule does not lead to the conclusion that India is not an adequate alternative forum.

Final points regarding the asserted inadequacies of Indian procedure involve unavailability of juries or contingent fee arrangements in India. Plaintiffs do not press these arguments, but Mr. Palkhivala touches upon them. They are easily disposed of. The absence of juries in civil cases is a feature of many civil law jurisdictions, and of the United Kingdom. *Piper* at 252, n. 18, 102 S. Ct. at 264, n. 18 and citations therein. Furthermore, contingency fees are not found in most foreign jurisdictions. *Piper* at 252, n. 18, 102 S. Ct. at 264, n. 18. In any event, the lack of contingency fees is not an insurmountable barrier to filing claims in India, as demonstrated by the fact that more than 4,000 suits have been filed by victims of the Bhopal gas leak in India, already. According to Mr. Palkhivala, moreover, well-known lawyers have been known to serve clients without charging any fees. (Palkhivala Aff. at 8).

Plaintiffs' final contention as to the inadequacy of the Indian forum is that a judgment rendered by an Indian court cannot be enforced in the United States without resort to further extensive litigation. Conversely, plaintiffs assert, Indian law provides *res judicata* effect to foreign judgments, and precludes plaintiffs from bringing a suit on the same cause of action in India. (Galanter Aff. at 63–65). Mr. Dadachanji disputes this description of the Indian law of res judicata. He asserts that the pendency, or even final disposition, of an action in a foreign court does not prevent plaintiffs from suing in India upon the original cause of action. Plaintiffs would not be limited, Mr. Dadanchanji argues, to an Indian action to enforce the foreign judgment. (Dadachanji Aff. at 19–20). In addition, he states that an Indian court, before ordering that a foreign judgment be given effect, would seek to establish whether the foreign court had failed to apply Indian law, or misapplied Indian law. (Dadachanji Aff. at 20).

. . . .

CONCLUSION

It is difficult to imagine how a greater tragedy could occur to a peacetime population than the deadly gas leak in Bhopal on the night of December 2–3, 1984. The survivors of the dead victims, the injured and others who suffered, or may in the future suffer due to the disaster, are entitled to compensation. This Court is firmly convinced that the Indian legal system is in a far better position than the American courts to determine the cause of the tragic event and thereby fix liability. Further, the Indian courts have greater access to all the information needed to arrive at the amount of the compensation to be awarded the victims.

Therefore, the consolidated case is dismissed on the grounds of *forum non conveniens* under the following conditions:

1. Union Carbide shall consent to submit to the jurisdiction of the courts of India, and shall continue to waive defenses based upon the statute of limitations;

2. Union Carbide shall agree to satisfy any judgment rendered against it by an Indian court, and if applicable, upheld by an appellate court in that country, where such judgment and affirmance comport with the minimal requirements of due process;

3. Union Carbide shall be subject to discovery under the model of the United States Federal Rules of Civil Procedure after appropriate demand by plaintiffs.

SO ORDERED.

BODUM USA, INC. v. LA CAFETIERE, INC.
621 F.3d 624 (7th Cir. 2010)

EASTERBROOK, CHIEF JUDGE.

From the mid-1950s through 1991, Société des Anciens Etablissements Martin S.A. ("Martin") distributed a successful French-press coffee maker known as the Chambord. A French-press coffee maker (called a cafetière à piston in France) is a carafe in which hot water is mixed with coffee grounds. When the brewing is complete, a mesh screen attached to a rod drives the grounds to the bottom of the carafe. Clear coffee then can be poured from the top. In 1991 Bodum Holding purchased all of Martin's stock. Today subsidiaries of Bodum Holding sell throughout the world coffee makers that use the Chambord design and name.

Martin's principal investor and manager was Louis-James de Viel Castel, who had other businesses. One of these, the British firm Household Articles Ltd., sold a French-press coffee maker that it called La Cafetière, which closely resembles the Chambord design. Viel Castel wanted to continue Household's business after Bodum bought Martin. So Viel Castel and Jørgen Jepsen Bodum, the main investor in Bodum Holding, negotiated. An early draft agreement provided that Household could sell the Chambord design in the United Kingdom, but nowhere else. After several rounds of revisions, however, the agreement provided that Household would never sell a French-press coffee maker in France, that it would not use the trade names Chambord or Melior, and that for four years it would not distribute through the importers, distributors, or agents that Martin employed during 1990–91. The agreement was signed, and Bodum Holding acquired Martin.

La Cafetière, Inc., was incorporated in Illinois in 2006 to serve as the distributor of Household's products in the United States. One of these is the La Cafetière model, which carries the name "Classic" in this country. To avoid confusion between the corporation (which since 2008 has been one of Household's subsidiaries) and the product, we refer to the distributor as "Household." Household has itself been renamed The Greenfield Group, but we stick with the original name for simplicity. Bodum Holding's U.S. distributor (Bodum USA, Inc.) filed this suit under federal and state law, contending that the sale of any coffee maker similar to the Chambord design violates Bodum's common-law trade dress. Trade dress, a distinctive appearance that enables consumers to identify a product's maker, is a form of trademark. *See Two Pesos, Inc. v. Taco Cabana, Inc.*, 505 U.S. 763, 112 S. Ct. 2753, 120 L. Ed. 2d 615 (1992). The Chambord design is not registered as Bodum's trademark, but common-law marks may be enforced under both 15 U.S.C. § 1125(a), a part of the Lanham Act, and 815 ILCS 510/2(a). Household contends that the 1991 agreement permits it to sell the La Cafetière design anywhere in the world, except France, provided that it does not use the words Chambord or Melior — and Household has never used either of those marks. The district court agreed with this contention and granted summary judgment in Household's favor. 2009 U.S. Dist. *Lexis* 25555 (N.D. Ill. Mar. 24, 2009).

The Chambord design and the La Cafetière design are indeed similar, and although they are not identical a casual coffee drinker (or purchaser) would have trouble telling them apart. . . .

The right-hand version of the La Cafetière design looks closer to the Chambord design because of the domed lid and the ball on the piston. Household calls one design the Classic and the other the Optima; the parties do not make anything of the difference.

Bodum assumes that the proprietor of any distinctive design has an intellectual-property right in this design, which it alone can sell. That assumption is unwarranted. The Chambord design is distinctive — so much so that Martin received a design patent for it — but the patent expired many years ago. After a patent expires, other firms are free to copy the design to the last detail in order to increase competition and drive down the price that consumers pay. [Citations omitted.] A distinctive design may be protected as a trademark only if it has acquired secondary meaning — that is, if consumers associate the design with a particular manufacturer — and the design's identifying aspects are not functional. [Citation omitted.] Bodum has not produced evidence that the Chambord design has secondary meaning, so that purchasers of a La Cafetière coffee maker think that they are getting one of Bodum's products. But because Household has not asked us to affirm the district court on this ground, we move on to the contract.

Here is the critical language, from Article 4 of the contract:

In consideration of the compensation paid to Stockholder [Viel Castel] for the stocks of [Martin,] Stockholder guarantees, limited to the agreed compensation, see Article 2, that he shall not — for a period of four (4) years — be engaged directly or indirectly in any commercial business related to manufacturing or distributing [Martin's] products . . . . Notwithstanding Article 4 [Bodum Holding] agrees that Stockholder through Household . . . can manufacture and distribute any products similar to [Martin's] products outside of France. It is expressly understood that Household [] is not entitled, directly or indirectly, to any such activity in France, and that Household [] furthermore is not entitled, directly or indirectly, globally to manufacture and/or distribute coffee-pots under the trade marks and/or brand names of "Melior" and "Chambord," held by [Martin]. Stockholder agrees that Household [] is not entitled to use for a period of four (4) years the importers, distributors, and agents which [Martin] uses and/or has used the last year. Any violation of these obligations will constitute a breach of Stockholder's obligation according to Article 4.

The parties agree that this is an accurate translation of the French original, and that French substantive law governs its interpretation. The district judge thought that the contract is clear and that Household can sell its La Cafetière outside of France, if it does not use the Chambord or Melior names. Even if the La Cafetière or Classic model is identical to the Chambord model (which it is not, as a glance at the illustrations shows), a thing identical to something else also is "similar" to it.

Bodum contends that, under French law, the parties' intent prevails over the written word. Article 1156 of the French Civil Code provides: "One must in agreements seek what the common intention of the contracting parties was, rather than pay attention to the literal meaning of the terms." (Again this is an agreed translation, as are all other translations in this opinion.) Jørgen Bodum has submitted an affidavit declaring that he understood the contract to limit Household's sales of the La Cafetière model to the United Kingdom and Australia. This means, Bodum Holding insists, that there must be a trial to determine the parties' intent. It supports this position with the declaration of Pierre-Yves Gautier, a Professor of Law at Université Panthéon-Assas Paris II, who Bodum tenders as an expert on French law. Household has replied with declarations from two experts of its own.

Although Fed.R.Civ.P. 44.1 provides that courts may consider expert testimony when deciding questions of foreign law, it does not compel them to do so — for the Rule says that judges "may" rather than "must" receive expert testimony and adds that courts may consider "any relevant material or source". Judges should use the best of the available sources. The Committee Note in 1966, when Rule 44.1 was adopted, explains that a court "may engage in its own research and consider any relevant material thus found. The court may have at its disposal better foreign law materials than counsel have presented, or may wish to reexamine and amplify material that has been presented by counsel in partisan fashion or in insufficient detail."

Sometimes federal courts must interpret foreign statutes or decisions that have not been translated into English or glossed in treatises or other sources. Then experts' declarations and testimony may be essential. But French law, and the law of most other nations that engage in extensive international commerce, is widely available in English. Judges can use not only accepted (sometimes official) translations of statutes and decisions but also ample secondary literature, such as treatises and scholarly commentary. It is no more necessary to resort to expert declarations about the law of France than about the law of Louisiana, which had its origins in the French civil code, or the law of Puerto Rico, whose origins are in the Spanish civil code. No federal judge would admit "expert" declarations about the meaning of Louisiana law in a commercial case. [Emphasis added.]

Trying to establish foreign law through experts' declarations not only is expensive (experts must be located and paid) but also adds an adversary's spin, which the court then must discount. Published sources such as treatises do not have the slant that characterizes the warring declarations presented in this case. Because objective, English-language descriptions of French law are readily available, we prefer them to the parties' declarations. [Emphasis added.]

[Court's discussion of French law and sources on which it relied omitted] . . . .

POSNER, CIRCUIT JUDGE, concurring.

I join the majority opinion, and write separately merely to express emphatic support for, and modestly to amplify, the court's criticism of a common and authorized but unsound judicial practice. That is the practice of trying to establish the meaning of a law of a foreign country by testimony or affidavits of expert witnesses, usually lawyers or law professors, often from the country in question. [Citation omitted.]

The contract in this case is in writing and unambiguously entitles the defendant to continue to sell its "Classic" coffee maker in the United States, because, although it is a product "similar" to the plaintiff's coffee maker, only in France is the defendant forbidden to sell products "similar" to the plaintiff's products. The plaintiff argues that nevertheless it is entitled to a trial at which Jørgen Bodum, its principal, would testify that part of the deal the parties *thought* they were making, although it is not reflected in the written contract, was that the defendant would be barred from selling its "Classic" coffee maker in the United States because it is identical rather than merely "similar" to the plaintiff's "Chambord" coffee maker. (Yet the plaintiff concedes in its reply brief that "it may certainly be true that all identical products are similar.") The issue of contractual interpretation is governed by French law.

Rule 44.1 of the Federal Rules of Civil Procedure provides that a federal court, "in determining foreign law, . . . may consider any relevant material or source, including testimony, whether or not submitted by a party or admissible under the Federal Rules of Evidence." The committee note explains that the court "may engage in its own research and consider any relevant material thus found. The court may have at its disposal better foreign law materials than counsel have presented, or may wish to reexamine and amplify material that has been presented by counsel in partisan fashion or in insufficient detail." Thus the court doesn't *have* to rely on testimony; and in only a few cases, I believe, is it justified in doing so. This case is not one of them.

The only evidence of the meaning of French law that was presented to the district court or is found in the appellate record is an English translation of brief excerpts from the French Civil Code and affidavits by three French law professors (Pierre-Yves Gautier for the plaintiff and Christophe Caron and Jérôme Huet for the defendant, with Huet's affidavit adding little to Caron's). The district court did no research of its own, but relied on the parties' submissions.

When a court in one state applies the law of another, or when a federal court applies state law (or a state court federal law), the court does not permit expert testimony on the meaning of the "foreign" law that it has to apply. [Citations omitted.] This is true even when it's the law of Louisiana, [citations omitted] which is based to a significant degree on the *Code Napoléon* (curiously, adopted by Louisiana after the United States acquired Louisiana from France). [Citation and references omitted.]

Yet if the law to be applied is the law of a foreign country, even a country such as the United Kingdom, Canada, or Australia in which the official language is English and the legal system derives from the same source as ours, namely the English common law, our courts routinely rely on lawyers' testimony about the meaning of the foreign law. [Citations omitted.] Not only rely but sometimes suggest, incorrectly in light of Rule 44.1, that testimony is *required* for establishing foreign law. [Citation omitted.]

Lawyers who testify to the meaning of foreign law, whether they are practitioners or professors, are paid for their testimony and selected on the basis of the convergence of their views with the litigating position of the client, or their willingness to fall in with the views urged upon them by the client. These are the banes of expert testimony. When the testimony concerns a scientific or other technical issue, it may be unreasonable to expect a judge to resolve the issue without the aid of such testimony. But judges are experts on law, and there is an abundance of published materials, in the form of treatises, law review articles, statutes, and cases, all in English (if English is the foreign country's official language), to provide neutral illumination of issues of foreign law. I cannot fathom why in dealing with the meaning of laws of English-speaking countries that share our legal origins judges should prefer paid affidavits and testimony to published materials. [Emphasis added.]

It is only a little less perverse for judges to rely on testimony to ascertain the law of a country whose official language is not English, at least if is a major country and has a modern legal system. Although most Americans are monolingual, including most judges, there are both official translations of French statutes into English, [references omitted] *and abundant secondary material on French law, including French contract and procedural law, published in English.* [References omitted.] *Neither party cited any such material, except translations of statutory provisions; beyond that they relied on the affidavits of their expert witnesses.*

Because English has become the international *lingua franca*, it is unsurprising that most Americans, even when otherwise educated, make little investment in acquiring even a reading knowledge of a foreign language. But our linguistic provincialism does not excuse intellectual provincialism. It does not justify our judges in relying on paid witnesses to spoon feed them foreign law that can be found well explained in English-language treatises and articles. I do not criticize the district judge in this case, because he was following the common practice. But it is a bad practice, followed like so many legal practices out of habit rather than reflection. It is excusable only when the foreign law is the law of a country with such an obscure or poorly developed legal system that there are no secondary materials to which the judge could turn. The French legal system is obviously not of that character. The district court could — as this court did in *Abad v. Bayer Corp.*, 563 F.3d 663, 670–71 (7th Cir. 2009), with respect to the law of Argentina — have based his interpretation of French contract law on published writings as distinct from paid testimony.

Of course often the most authoritative literature will be in the language of the foreign country. But often too there will be official, or reputable unofficial, translations and when there are not the parties can have the relevant portions translated into English. Translations figure prominently in a variety of cases tried in American courts, such as drug-trafficking and immigration cases; why not in cases involving foreign law?

Article 1156 of the French Civil Code — the provision that the briefs principally discuss — states in its entirety: "*On doit dans les conventions rechercher quelle a été la commune intention des parties contractantes, plutôt que de s'arrêter au sens littéral des termes.*" In idiomatic English (the official English version is stilted), this means that in interpreting a contract one should search for what the parties' joint intention was, rather than stopping with the literal meaning of the contract's terms. The plaintiff argues that this means that no matter how clear the contract appears to be, a party is entitled to present evidence at trial that the parties intended something else. "French law," according to the plaintiff's opening brief, "clearly provides that an assessment of the parties' rights and obligations under the [contract] must be evaluated in light of the parties' mutual intent, regardless of whether the contract is deemed unambiguous."

What is true and worth noting is that the civil law — the law of Continental Europe, as distinct from Anglo-American law — of contracts places an emphasis on fault that is not found in the common law. As Holmes remarked, the common law conceives of contracts as options — when you sign a contract in which you promise a specified performance you buy an option to either perform as promised or pay damages, Oliver Wendell Holmes, "The Path of the Law," 10 *Harv. L.Rev.* 457, 462 (1897), unless damages are not an adequate remedy in the particular case. Whether you were at fault in deciding not to perform — you could have done so but preferred to pay damages because someone offered you a higher price for the goods that you'd promised to the other party to your contract — is therefore irrelevant.

In the civil law, in contrast, a party is in breach of his contract and therefore subject to a legal sanction only if he "could reasonably have been expected to behave in a different way," that is, only if he was at fault in failing to perform. Jürgen Basedow, "Towards a Universal Doctrine of Breach of Contract: The Impact of the CISG," 25 *Int'l Rev. L. & Econ.* 487, 496 (2005) ("the fault principle is often considered to be an indispensable part of the law of obligations in civil law countries"); [references omitted]. The civil law embraces the slogan *pacta sunt servanda* — promises are to be obeyed, not commuted to a price believed to approximate their value. That is why in the civil law the default remedy for breach of contract is (though more in principle than in practice) specific performance rather than damages. [References omitted.] You *should* have performed your promise, so the court will *order* you to do so.

The common law of contracts evolved from the law merchant, the civil law of contracts from canon law. [Reference omitted.] Priests do not take promise breaking quite as lightly as businessmen, but on the other hand are not attuned to commercial usages, such as options. Yet despite the difference in origins, differences in outcome under the two legal regimes are small and shrinking. [References omitted.] A difference at least in tone remains, however, and enables one to see why French law might, as the plaintiff contends, be more concerned to determine the parties' intentions than American law would be. For if an intention is innocent — a party never intended the promise that he is now accused of having broken — ascribing fault to him, viewed as a precondition to finding him guilty of a breach of contract, is a graver step. Conversely, if the party did intend the promise but somehow it failed to get written down intelligibly, he should not be permitted to break it by pointing to a writing. Hence the greater "readiness [of French courts] to have recourse to previous negotiations and subsequent conduct of the parties" in interpreting a contract, [Stefan Vogenauer, "Interpretation of Contracts: Concluding Comparative Observations," in Contract Terms 123 (Andrew Burrows & Edwin Peel eds. 2007)], at 150 — to conduct a deeper search into subjective understandings.

The civil-law culture is the basis for the plaintiff's claim to be entitled to a trial at which to present evidence that its contract with the defendant was intended to mean something different from what it says. This claim cannot be derived from Article 1156, which, as the majority opinion in this case points out, just tells the court to search for what the parties' joint intention was rather than stopping with the literal meaning of the contract's terms. That is no different from warnings in American contract law to be wary of literal interpretations of contracts because such interpretations often are mistaken. [Citations omitted.] It is based rather on the greater willingness (in principle — which will turn out to be an essential qualification) of a French court than of an American one to dig deeply for reassurance that it is not distorting the parties' intentions by blinding itself to everything that is not text.

The argument may seem to be supported by the fact that French law does not have a parol evidence rule applicable to commercial cases. [References omitted.] An approximation to that rule, and to the related "four corners" rule [citation and reference omitted], which forbids using extrinsic evidence to contradict an unambiguous written contract, is found in Article 1341 of the French Civil Code for ordinary contracts unless very small. (Neither rule is limited to oral evidence, despite the word "parol," which is derived from the French word for "word"; the parol evidence rule merely excludes extrinsic evidence concerning precontractual negotiations if the written contract was intended to be the parties' complete agreement [citations and reference omitted]. Article 1341 bars "proof by witnesses" that is inconsistent with the written contract unless there is a "commencement of proof in writing"— a writing originating with the defendant that makes it probable that an alleged fact about the parties' deal is true. [References omitted.]

But the limitations on extrinsic evidence in Article 1341 do not apply to commercial contracts, a possible characterization of the contract at issue in this case, though not an inevitable characterization for reasons explained in the majority opinion. Article 110-3 of the French Commercial Code provides that "with regard to traders, commercial instruments may be proven by any means unless the law specifies otherwise" (footnote omitted). And CISGAC Opinion No. 3, *supra*, states that "though the French Civil Code . . . incorporates a version of the Parol Evidence Rule for ordinary contracts, all forms of proof are generally available against merchants." [References omitted.]

This gap in French commercial law has little practical significance, however, because it mainly reflects the fact that civil law systems do not use juries in civil cases. As a result, their rules on admissibility of evidence are notably looser than in common law jurisdictions. [References omitted.] Although technically the parol evidence and four-corners rules are rules of contract law rather of evidence [citation and refereneces omitted], they are strongly influenced by concern lest trial by jury upset the expectations of contracting parties as embodied in written contracts. [Citation and references omitted.]

Unburdened by juries and tight rules of evidence, French courts could range further afield than American courts in search of subjective contractual intentions. Could — but don't. As explained in Vogenauer, *supra*, at 135–36, while "as a general rule, French and German law do not limit the admissibility of relevant external materials in the process of interpretation . . . this does not mean that it is easy for a party to induce a court to rely on extrinsic evidence in order to 'add to, vary or contradict a deed or other written instrument.' On the contrary, civilian systems are acutely aware of the need to strike a balance between the desire to achieve a materially 'right' outcome on the one hand, and the struggle for legal certainty on the other. As a consequence, *they are extremely reluctant to admit that the wording of a contract concluded in writing might be overridden by other factors* . . . . Extrinsic evidence can, however, be used for the purposes of interpreting a written document that contains internal contradictions or is otherwise unclear" (emphasis added, footnote omitted [in opinion]) — which is also true of American law, but irrelevant to this case.

Unlike American courts, moreover, "French commercial courts are staffed by members of the business community, who serve part-time as judges. There is no requirement that they have legal training. Hearings before French commercial courts typically last less than an hour. Witnesses are virtually never heard by the court. In any case, a French rule of evidence makes evidence originating from any of the parties inadmissible, which means that no employee of any of the two companies may validly testify." Gilles Cuniberti, "Beyond Contract — The Case for Default Arbitration in International Commercial Disputes," 32 *Fordham Int'l L.J.* 417, 431–32 (2009) (footnote omitted[, in opinion]). "The past continues to shape the present. This is especially true with respect to one particularity of the French judicial system which is rarely evoked — the absence of a jury in civil court proceedings, and the consequences this has on procedure, which remains 98% written, with no witnesses, no investigations ordered by the judge, and no cross-examination. The hearing is a sort of ritual, a rigid, immutable show in which the silent judge, flanked — for the moment at least — by two colleagues, listens to the 'pleadings': an exercise in solitary eloquence, a lengthy monologue by a lawyer who blindly and desperately attempts to breathe life into documents, or even affidavits, which are inert, consigned to paper, embedded in ritual phraseology, and accompanied by a document proving identity. It is the absence of any jury which has dictated the entire concept of what a civil court hearing should be." [Daniel Soulez Larivière, "Overview of the Problems of French Civil Procedure," 45 Am. J. Comp. L. 737, 743–44 (1997)], at 743–44. "[T]he tendency [in French civil litigation is] to prefer written proof of ultimate fact — evidence that can be analyzed on the basis of a writing even though its origins may be in oral testimony or other more difficult-to-appreciate forms of proof." [James Beardsley, "Proof of Fact in French Civil Procedure," 34 Am. J. Comp. L. 459 (1986)], at 470.

The plaintiff in our case wants to marry French substantive doctrine that might appear to permit a more far-ranging evidentiary exploration in a contract case to American trial procedure, which permits a far-ranging evidentiary exploration in many types of case but not in cases charging a breach of a clear written contract. The marriage has produced an ungainly hybrid that corresponds neither to French law nor to American law. It is true that some foreign legal systems heavily influenced by the civil codes do use common law procedure — as does Louisiana. [Reference omitted.] These typically are former code jurisdictions that were conquered, or in the case of Louisiana bought, by a common law nation such as Britain or the United States. But they do not do it on an ad hoc basis, as proposed by our plaintiff; and, so far as I can discover, they do not, by doing so, deny contracting parties the protection of a clearly written contract.

It is at least as difficult to persuade a French court (because of its composition and usages) to admit extrinsic evidence in a contract case as it is to persuade an American court to do so. [References omitted.] The happenstance that this case has been brought in an American court must not be allowed to produce a misfit between substantive and procedural law.

Curiously, one of the defendant's experts, Professor Caron, not only cites Article 1156 but asserts that in interpreting the "common intention of the parties . . . reference to the negotiations that may have taken place between the parties should be required." I don't think he means that there *is* a legal requirement; there isn't. I think he means it would be helpful to refer to the previous negotiations in this case because they support the defendant's position. Yet in its brief the defendant goes further and says that "Article 1156 simply *requires* that a court look beyond the literal meaning of the terms of an agreement, even where — as here — the terms of the agreement are plain and unambiguous" (emphasis added). This is not a correct interpretation of French law, or even one helpful to the defendant, since the contract unambiguously supports its position. The defendant acknowledges, on the basis of what appears to be its expert's misunderstanding or misstatement of French law, that it is not enough that the contract be unambiguous; the evidence of subjective intention must also be. Among other things this ignores the following exception, which is not inapplicable to commercial contracts, to the principle that "judicial interpretation of contracts is considered to entail questions of fact and therefore be subject to the discretion of the lower courts": in "cases in which there has been a distortion *(une dénaturation)* of the clear and precise terms of the contract . . . , the court is deemed to be faced not merely with a question of the interpretation of a contract, but rather a refusal to apply it." [Denis Tallon, "Contract Law," in Introduction to French Law 205 (George A. Bermann & Etienne Picard eds. 2008)] at 225 [additional reference omitted]. It must not refuse to apply it.

The parties' reliance on affidavits to establish the standard for interpreting their contract has produced only confusion. They should have relied on published analyses of French commercial law.

WOOD, CIRCUIT JUDGE, concurring.

While I endorse without reservation the majority's reading of the 1991 contract that is at the heart of this case, I write separately to note my disagreement with the discussion of FED.R.CIV.P. 44.1 in both the majority opinion, *ante* at 627–28, and in Judge Posner's concurring opinion. Rule 44.1 itself establishes no hierarchy for sources of foreign law, and I am unpersuaded by my colleagues' assertion that expert testimony is categorically inferior to published, English-language materials. Exercises in comparative law are notoriously difficult, because the U.S. reader is likely to miss nuances in the foreign law, to fail to appreciate the way in which one branch of the other country's law interacts with another, or to assume erroneously that the foreign law mirrors U.S. law when it does not. As the French might put it more generally, apparently similar phrases might be *faux amis*. A simple example illustrates why two words might be "false friends." A speaker of American English will be familiar with the word "actual," which is defined in Webster's Third New International Dictionary as "existing in act, . . . existing in fact or reality: really acted or acting or carried out — contrasted with *ideal* and *hypothetical* . . . ." WEBSTER'S THIRD NEW INTERNATIONAL DICTIONARY 22 (1993). So, one might say, "This is the actual chair used by George Washington." But the word "actuel" in French means "present" or right now. LE ROBERT & COLLINS COMPACT PLUS DICTIONNAIRE 7 (5th ed. 2003). A French person would thus use the term "les événements actuels" or "actualité" to refer to current events, not to describe something that really happened either now or in the past.

There will be many times when testimony from an acknowledged expert in foreign law will be helpful, or even necessary, to ensure that the U.S. judge is not confronted with a "false friend" or that the U.S. judge understands the full context of the foreign provision. Some published articles or treatises, written particularly for a U.S. audience, might perform the same service, but many will not, even if they are written in English, and especially if they are translated into English from another language. It will often be most efficient and useful for the judge to have before her an expert who can provide the needed precision on the spot, rather than have the judge wade through a number of secondary sources. In practice, the experts produced by the parties are often the authors of the leading treatises and scholarly articles in the foreign country anyway. In those cases, it is hard to see why the person's views cannot be tested in court, to guard against the possibility that he or she is just a mouthpiece for one party. Prominent lawyers from the country in question also sometimes serve as experts. That too is perfectly acceptable in principle, especially if the question requires an understanding of court procedure in the foreign country. In many places, the academic branch of the legal profession is entirely separate from the bar. Academic writings in such places tend to be highly theoretical and removed from the day-to-day realities of the practice of law. [Emphasis added.]

To be clear, I have no objection to the use of written sources of foreign law. Rule 44.1 permits the court to consider "any relevant material or source, including testimony, whether or not submitted by a party or admissible under the Federal Rules of Evidence." The written sources cited by both of my colleagues throw useful light on the problem before us in this case, and both were well within their rights to conduct independent research and to rely on those sources. There is no need, however, to disparage oral testimony from experts in the foreign law. That kind of testimony has been used by responsible lawyers for years, and there will be many instances in which it is adequate by itself or it provides a helpful gloss on the literature. The tried and true methods set forth in FED.R.EVID. 702 for testing the depth of the witness's expertise, the facts and other relevant information on which the witness has relied, and the quality of the witness's application of those principles to the problem at hand, suffice to protect the court against self-serving experts in foreign law, just as they suffice to protect the process for any other kind of expert.

Finally, my colleagues see no material difference between a judge's ability to research the laws of Louisiana or Puerto Rico and her ability to research the laws of France, Australia, or Indonesia. With respect, I cannot agree with them. Like the laws of the other 49 states, the law of Louisiana is based on many sources. One important such source is the Code Napoléon, but it is not the only source. Louisiana has legislation on the usual topics, it is part of the federal system, and its courts function much like the courts of other states. [References omitted.] Puerto Rico's system is somewhat less accessible for non-Spanish-speaking Americans. Interestingly, one finds Puerto Rican materials under the "International/Worldwide Materials" database in Westlaw®, not under the U.S. States database. This is so even though Congress has expressly defined Puerto Rico as a "state" for purposes of the diversity jurisdiction statute. See 28 U.S.C. § 1332(e) (2010). There is no denying the fact, however, that Puerto Rico is far more integrated into the U.S. legal system than any foreign country is. Since Puerto Rico falls within the jurisdiction of the First Circuit, see 28 U.S.C. § 41 (2010), the judges of that court regularly hear cases implicating Puerto Rican law. Furthermore, American law has greatly influenced the Puerto Rican legal system. [References omitted.] As a practical matter, therefore, the Supreme Court was on firm ground when it assumed, in the text of Rule 44.1, that only the law of a "foreign country" would be subject to the rule's procedures, not the law of a U.S. state, territory, or commonwealth.

For these reasons, although I join the majority's reasoning in all other respects, I do not share their views about the use of expert testimony to prove foreign law. I therefore concur in the judgment to that extent.

QUESTIONS

1. From the *Bhopal Plant Disaster* and *Bodum USA v. La Cafetiere* cases, what considerations would you suggest that the lawyers selecting experts

should keep in mind? What factors appear to be the most important in the selection of experts? And who should select them — the parties or the judge or all three? Indeed, are outside experts really necessary? Do you agree with the views expressed by Judges Easterbrook and Posner or those by Judge Wood?

2. In what respects, if any, is there a greater need for outside experts in cases involving the choice of a court in a civil law jurisdiction, such as Japan or Mexico, than in cases in which the choice involves a court in another common law jurisdiction, such as Canada or India? Are there unstated assumptions within all legal systems and cultures that even "experts" may have difficulty ferreting out?

3. In the context of a motion to dismiss on the basis of *forum non conveniens*, what issues should the experts (or the judge) address? Which are the most significant and why? Are issues of "law" paramount?

4. To what extent should the experts or judges (or their clerks) have both knowledge of the law and legal systems as well the *legal languages* of each country involved in the litigation? Even then issues remain — note the difference between Dan Fenno Henderson's translation of the term *shūbun* as "order" or "text," in his discussion of the *Hachitsuka* case *supra*, versus "disposition" used by the author throughout this casebook. Is there a difference in meaning or nuance?

C. Stays and Anti-Suit Injunctions

Dismissal of a case on the basis of *forum non conveniens* standards leaves the plaintiff with no feasible options but to appeal, settle, or litigate in the alternative forum. Denial of the defendant's motion for *forum non conveniens* dismissal, however, leaves the defendant with the option of bringing the suit in the alternative forum — assuming the defendant has not done so already. If, in any event, the defendant files a parallel suit in the United States or, as we shall see, another common law jurisdiction, the plaintiff has recourse in response to seek as defendant a stay of that proceeding or, as plaintiff before the court that denied the *forum non conveniens* motion to dismiss, a court order enjoining the defendant from either filing or proceeding with the parallel suit. These options are at issue in the following cases:

TURNER ENTERTAINMENT CO. v. DEGETO FILM GMBH
25 F.3d 1512 (11th Cir. 1994)

The U.S. licensor of television programming brought an action in the United States District Court for the Northern District of Georgia against a German distributor and broadcasters to enjoin use of certain technology to broadcast licensed works. Having previously filed suit in Germany, the defendants' moved to dismiss or stay the action. The District court denied the motion and granted a preliminary injunction. The defendants appealed. The German court had handed down its judgment in the meantime.

ANDERSON, CIRCUIT JUDGE:

This is an appeal of (1) the district court's grant of a preliminary injunction to plaintiff-appellee Turner Entertainment Co. ("Turner"), preventing defendants-appellants from broadcasting certain licensed works over the ASTRA satellites, and (2) the district court's denial of appellants' motion to dismiss or stay the American litigation in light of parallel proceedings under way in Germany. In the intervening period between the grant of the preliminary injunction and argument on this appeal, a judgment on the merits was rendered in the action in Germany. The German court found that the appellants should be able to broadcast via ASTRA for an increased fee to be determined at a later date. In light of this foreign judgment, we must decide whether to defer to the German court's judgment and dismiss or stay this action, or to ignore the German decision and continue essentially parallel proceedings. We hold that the preliminary injunction should be vacated, and that a stay of the American litigation is warranted.

I. FACTS AND PROCEEDINGS BELOW

This case involves a dispute over the interpretation of a License Agreement (the "Agreement") between the parties. The Agreement licensed certain entertainment properties to the appellants for television broadcast to the German population. Rapid changes in geopolitics and television technology since the inception of the Agreement led to the instant dispute over the limits of the contract.

A. The Parties

Defendant Degeto Film GmbH ("Degeto") is the exclusive agent for the other defendants. The remaining defendants are German public broadcasters; each serves one of the German political states (the "Lander"). Together the broadcasters, along with three other companies not a party to the American litigation, form a cooperative known as the Arbeitsgemeinschaft der offentlich rechtlichen Rundfunkanstalten der Bundesrepublik Deutschland ("ARD"). The defendants-appellants are collectively referred to in this opinion as ARD. ARD is supported by mandatory royalty fees and is obligated by German law to provide programming to the entire German population.

Although Degeto signed the Agreement with MGM/UA in 1984, Turner acquired the rights, through a series of transactions in the 1980's, to a substantial majority of the MGM/UA licensed properties covered by the Agreement. Thus, Turner purchased the rights and obligations under the Agreement as it pertains to those properties, and now stands in the shoes originally filled by MGM/UA.

B. The Agreement

ARD paid at least $60 million for an exclusive license to telecast the licensed works, under German copyright, to the German-speaking public, only in the German language. The licensed works include many old MGM movies, television series and cartoons. The Agreement expressly allows ARD to telecast the licensed works for reception within the licensed territory "by all means and methods now or hereafter known including but not limited to . . . DBS [direct broadcasting satellite] and/or communication satellite for purposes of so-called home television reception," so long as the works are broadcast in German. The licensed territory comprises virtually all of German-speaking Europe — the German Democratic Republic, the Federal Republic of Germany, German-speaking Switzerland, Austria, South Tyrol (a region in Italy), Liechtenstein and Luxembourg.

The Agreement states that the telecasts can originate in any place in the universe, but only for reception within the territory. Because the reception area, or "footprint," of satellite broadcasts does not easily conform to the political and cultural boundaries that comprise the licensed territory, the parties included an exception to the strict definition in the contract of the licensed territory. Thus, the contract states that "[t]he telecast can originate any place in the universe for reception only in the Territory as defined . . . below (inclusive of legitimate overspill as set forth in Paragraph 2(f) below)." The meaning of the term "overspill" generally, its applicability to ARD and/or ASTRA broadcasts, and the result that should obtain based on such determinations, has been a hotly contested issue in the litigation. Despite the importance of the term to the contract, no clear explanation of the meaning and scope of overspill exists in the contract. Paragraph 2(f) contains only a contextual definition of overspill and states in relevant part:

> Licensees acknowledge that broadcasts by satellite or otherwise in any language originating outside of the Territory might be received by television sets inside the Territory and that such reception shall not be deemed a breach hereof by MGM/UA. Further, notwithstanding the foregoing, if the overspill into the Territory is a result of compliance by MGM/UA's licensees with international conventions or treaties, including but not limited to the 1977 Geneva Convention, binding upon that licensee's territory, the licensee shall not be deemed to be in breach of its agreement with MGM/UA. In the event of illegitimate overspill into the Territory, Degeto shall notify MGM/UA and MGM/UA shall notify the entity whose signal is encroaching into the Territory to cease and desist from such encroaching activity. . . . MGM/UA shall provide in its own future standard license agreements that MGM/UA's licensees are prohibited from directing their signal into the Territory and from allowing their signal unintentionally to encroach into the Territory (except as to legitimate overspill as set forth above). . . .

Nothing more exists in the Agreement to define overspill.

In 1986 Degeto and MGM/UA amended the Agreement. The 1986 amendment, among other things, gave ARD the right to telecast certain licensed properties in English. English telecasts could not be broadcast, however, by DBS satellite, which at that time was the standard method for satellite broadcasting. The 1986 amendment also provided that "[t]he place of jurisdiction and applicable law with respect to disputes arising out of this Agreement shall only be (a) Frankfurt, Germany and/or (b) Los Angeles, California or such other city in the USA in which MGM/UA's parent company maintains its primary place of business." Thus, the seeds of the instant parallel litigation were planted in the Agreement, which provided for concurrent jurisdiction in Frankfurt, and, as a result of Turner's acquisition of the contract rights, Atlanta.

C. Technological and Geopolitical Changes Since the Agreement's Inception

ARD began broadcasting licensed works from Germany, in German, via the ASTRA 1B satellite in April of 1991. ARD maintains that it chose the ASTRA 1B satellite as a means of telecasting programming because (1) a substantial part of the former East German households, absorbed into the Federal Republic of Germany since the Agreement was drafted, can only receive television programming via satellite, apparently because of its poor communications infrastructure; and (2) there were no other satellites that Defendants could effectively use to reach the German-speaking television audience, which ARD is obligated to do by German law, because satellite dishes designed to receive the ASTRA signal are more common in Germany.

The ASTRA 1B is an FSS satellite, which means that it operates in the "fixed satellite service." Although the footprint of a DBS satellite could be as large as that of the ASTRA 1B, there are significant differences between the two satellites such that television reception of ASTRA 1B covers a much larger area. Relatively new technological developments have increased the sensitivity of common home satellite dish antennae and receivers, enabling FSS satellite signals to be received by anyone with a satellite dish in the satellite's service area. In contrast, DBS satellites require expensive decoding equipment that prohibit the common viewer from receiving its signals. Thus, the FSS satellite has revolutionized European television by allowing broadcasters to easily send their signal directly to viewers who own relatively inexpensive satellite reception dishes. Apparently, the home satellite dish is a more popular mode of television reception in Europe, compared to cable television, than in the U.S. The ASTRA 1B has a footprint over five times the size of the licensed territory; the footprint encompasses most of Europe. ASTRA 1B, therefore, is a prime vehicle for reaching a large European television audience. The Agreement's drafters failed to anticipate that such an easy method of reaching a pan-European audience would become a standard mode of broadcasting during the life of the Agreement.

D. The Dispute — Proceedings in Germany and Atlanta

In March 1993, Turner learned that ARD intended to broadcast its major program, "Das Erste," a program which apparently incorporates the use of licensed works, over ASTRA 1B in August 1993. Turner stated its opinion that transmitting licensed works via ASTRA violates the Agreement. After a flurry of communication between the parties, in which Turner attempted to prevent broadcasts via ASTRA and ARD refused Turner's requests, actions were filed by the parties within a week of each other in Germany and the United States. The German and American lawsuits proceeded concurrently.

1. The German proceedings.

The appellants filed a declaratory judgment action against Turner in Germany, on April 29, 1993, seeking judicial support for their interpretation that the

Agreement permitted the use of ASTRA 1B. The German action was filed in a German court of first consideration, the Landgericht Frankfurt am Main.

One of the key issues in the litigation concerned the term "overspill," namely, whether (1) overspill applied to the reception of ARD broadcasts outside the licensed territory, (2) whether overspill applied to FSS satellites so that the ASTRA footprint created overspill, and (3) if overspill did apply to the use of ASTRA, whether the overspill of ASTRA's signal was legitimate. The appellants maintained that the oversized footprint of ASTRA 1B comports with the Agreement because overspill as defined in the Agreement applies reciprocally to licensee and licensor, and that the overspill of ASTRA 1B is legitimate because (1) the broadcasts are in German and the licensed territory encompasses all viable markets for German television, rendering the overspill of German-language programming harmless, and (2) ARD receives no profit from the broadcasts.

The appellants made an alternative argument in the German court that the term overspill as used in the Agreement contemplated neither the new technology of FSS satellites nor the necessity of using them in order to obey the legal mandate that ARD reach the entire German population, and therefore that a gap exists in the contract. Appellants invited the German court to fill the gap in the contract, using the German doctrine of supplemental interpretation, by allowing ARD to broadcast Turner-licensed works via ASTRA, or alternatively to allow the broadcasts on ASTRA subject to the payment of an increased fee.

Turner argued that the Agreement's proviso allowing overspill did not apply reciprocally to licensee and licensor. Therefore, according to Turner's interpretation of the Agreement, Turner and its licensees outside Germany can overspill into the licensed territory, but ARD is strictly limited to broadcasting within the territory, and cannot overspill outside the licensed territory. Turner also made an alternative argument to the German court that a gap in the contract existed concerning the present state of affairs in European television; however, contrary to the appellants' proposal, Turner invited the German court to fill the gap by disallowing the use of ASTRA 1B.

The German court heard argument on the merits of the declaratory judgment action in Germany, and rendered a judgment on the merits on November 25, 1993. The German court held that because of its extensive range, ARD had no absolute right under the Agreement to broadcast via ASTRA. App. to Supp. Brief of Appellants, Tab 4, 23–24. However, the court found that the parties had not contemplated the current circumstances involving the new technology and the fact that ARD was compelled as a practical matter to broadcast outside the licensed territory in order to fulfill its legal obligation to bring its telecasts to the German public. *Id.* at 24–27. Given this gap in the operation of the contract, the German court determined that it was bound to apply the doctrine of good faith dealing to the situation. *Id.* at 25. The court attempted a supplemental interpretation of the contract to determine a result that parties bargaining in good faith would have negotiated.

The German court determined that Turner should permit ARD to use the satellite in order to properly fulfill its legal obligations. *Id.* at 29. However, the court determined that ARD would have to pay an increased fee for the privilege, to be determined by that court at a later date. *Id.* at 30. The German court relied on several factors in making this decision. The court noted that Turner had not envisioned concretely any additional licensing of German-language programming outside the licensed territory. *Id.* at 29. Also, the court noted that the licensed territory covers such a large proportion of the German-speaking public that, in its opinion, no significant economic interest of Turner was obliterated by ASTRA. *Id.* More importantly, the court emphasized (1) the wide distribution of ASTRA reception equipment in the license territory, making ASTRA the best method for reaching a wide audience, and (2) the statutory mandate for ARD to reach the German public; and determined that the just result was the payment of increased fees in exchange for the privilege of broadcasting via ASTRA. *Id.* Both parties have appealed the German decision, and Turner obtained a delay in the fee hearings pending the German appeal.

2. The Atlanta Proceedings.

Turner filed the instant breach of contract action approximately one week after the German action was filed, on May 6, 1993, in Fulton County Superior Court. Appellants removed, based on diversity, to the United States District Court for the Northern District of Georgia. Turner sought a preliminary and permanent injunction and damages caused by Defendants' alleged breach. The appellants countered with a motion to dismiss or stay the American proceedings in deference to the parallel proceedings in Germany. [Emphasis added.]

At the time of the June 29, 1993, hearing on the motion for preliminary injunction and the motion to dismiss or stay, no discovery had taken place in the American litigation; the parties filed affidavits supporting their arguments. The district court denied from the bench the motion to dismiss or stay the proceedings. On September 10, 1993, the district court, finding that Turner had a substantial likelihood of success on the merits of its case, granted Turner's motion for a preliminary injunction restraining ARD from telecasting Turner-owned licensed works from the ASTRA satellites. On September 29, 1993, however, the district court granted a stay of the preliminary injunction until October 28, 1993, conditioned on the posting of bond in the amount of $2 million by the appellants. Appellants filed an emergency motion to expedite this appeal and an emergency motion to stay the injunction pending appeal. On October 19, 1993, this court stayed the injunction pending appeal. Appellants challenge the preliminary injunction and the denial of their motion to dismiss or stay the domestic litigation. The stay of the preliminary injunction remains in effect by order of this court.

II. DISCUSSION

A. Whether to Dismiss or Stay the Domestic Litigation: International Abstention

ARD appeals the district court's denial of its Motion to Dismiss or Stay the American Litigation in deference to the parallel German proceedings. In the period since the district court denied the appellants' Motion to Dismiss or Stay the American Litigation, the German court has rendered a decision on the merits of the dispute, although it has not determined the fee to be paid by ARD to Turner. The existence of the German judgment adds new considerations to the decision whether to continue the American litigation. The issue is whether a federal court, which properly has jurisdiction over an action, should exercise its jurisdiction where parallel proceedings are ongoing in a foreign nation and a judgment has been reached on the merits in the litigation abroad.

Federal courts have a "virtually unflagging obligation" to exercise the jurisdiction conferred upon them. *Colorado River Water Conser. Dist. v. United States*, 424 U.S. 800, 817 (1976). Nevertheless, in some private international disputes the prudent and just action for a federal court is to abstain from the exercise of jurisdiction. Therefore, federal courts have begun to fashion principles that guide courts' actions in cases of concurrent jurisdiction in a federal court and the court of a foreign nation. This circuit has never considered the question of "international abstention." In other federal courts, at least two distinct but very similar approaches to international abstention have developed. Both have lifted criteria for analysis from case law concerning concurrent jurisdiction between federal and state courts.

One approach has taken the criteria enunciated in *Colorado River* and applied them to the international context. See *Ingersoll*, 833 F.2d at 685; *Laker Airways Ltd. v. Sabena, Belgian World Airlines*, 731 F.2d 909, 926–27 (D.C. Cir. 1984). These cases have at times injected the special concerns of "international comity" into the abstention analysis. [Citation omitted.] Another line of international abstention cases, developed in the Southern District of New York, applies a similar set of principles, with a clearer emphasis on the concerns of international comity implicated by the exercise of jurisdiction. See *Continental Time Corp. v. Swiss Credit Bank*, 543 F. Supp. 408, 410 (S.D.N.Y. 1982); *Ronar, Inc. v. Wallace*, 649 F. Supp. 310, 318 (S.D.N.Y. 1986); *Caspian Investments, Ltd. v. Vicom Holdings, Ltd.*, 770 F. Supp. 880, 883–84 (S.D.N.Y. 1991). These two sets of principles overlap to a large extent, and we find both lines of cases helpful to our analysis. Taking the two approaches together, courts have sought to fashion principles that will promote three readily identifiable goals in the area of concurrent international jurisdiction: (1) a proper level of respect for the acts of our fellow sovereign nations — a rather vague concept referred to in American jurisprudence as international comity; (2) fairness to litigants; and (3) efficient use of scarce judicial resources.

1. International Comity

The ramifications of international comity, in the abstention context, are suggested in the leading Supreme Court case, *Hilton v. Guyot*, 159 U.S. 113 (1895):

> "Comity," in the legal sense, is neither a matter of absolute obligation, on the one hand, nor of mere courtesy and good will, upon the other. But it is the recognition which one nation allows within its territory to the legislative, executive, or judicial acts of another nation, having due regard both to international duty and convenience, and to the rights of its own citizens, or of other persons who are under the protection of its laws.

"The comity thus extended to other nations . . . is the voluntary act of the nation by which it is offered, and is inadmissible when contrary to its policy, or prejudicial to its interests. But it contributes so largely to promote justice between individuals, and to produce a friendly intercourse between the sovereignties to which they belong, that courts of justice have continually acted upon it as part of the voluntary law of nations." 159 U.S. at 163–64, 165 (quoting *Bank v. Earle*, 38 U.S. (13 Pet.) 519, 589 (1839).

The Supreme Court continued:

When an action is brought in a court of this country, by a citizen of a foreign country against one of our own citizens, . . . and the foreign judgment appears to have been rendered by a competent court, having jurisdiction of the cause and of the parties, and upon due allegations and proofs, and opportunity to defend against them, and its proceedings are according to the course of a civilized jurisprudence, and are stated in a clear and formal record, the judgment is prima facie evidence, at least, of the truth of the matter adjudged; and it should be held conclusive upon the merits tried in the foreign court, unless some special ground is shown for impeaching the judgment, as by showing that it was affected by fraud or prejudice, or that by the principles of international law, and by the comity of our own country, it should not be given full credit and effect. 159 U.S. at 205–06.

In the context of international abstention case law, the meaning of international comity is derived from the above-quoted Supreme Court case on the recognition of judgments rendered in a foreign nation. General comity concerns include: (1) whether the judgment was rendered via fraud, see *Hilton*, 159 U.S. at 206, 16 S. Ct. at 159; (2) whether the judgment was rendered by a competent court utilizing proceedings consistent with civilized jurisprudence, *see id.*; and (3) whether the foreign judgment is prejudicial, in the sense of violating American public policy because it is repugnant to fundamental principles of what is decent and just. [Citation and reference omitted.]

Turner does not argue that the decision was rendered by fraud, or that the German court is not a competent court which follows civilized procedures. Germany's legal system clearly follows procedures that ensure that litigants will receive treatment that satisfies American notions of due process. Turner's sole argument is that the German court's decision is contrary to federal or Georgia public policy because it abrogates Turner's freedom of contract.

Turner has proffered a strained interpretation of the German court opinion in an attempt to portray the decision as something akin to a "forced judicial sale" of Turner's property. Turner argues that the Agreement clearly limited ARD's right to telecast to the licensed territory, defined in Paragraph 4 of the Agreement, and that the German court decision would force an unwilling Turner to enter into additional contractual provisions widening the defined territory at a royalty fee to be fixed by the court, all of which Turner argues is directly inconsistent with Paragraph 4 of the Agreement which defines the licensed territory. For the reasons that follow, we reject Turner's characterization of the German opinion, and we reject Turner's argument that the German decision violates American or Georgian public policy.

Turner's argument is along the following lines. Although conceding that Georgia law and the general common law of contracts provide for "gap filling" similar to the "supplemental interpretation" employed by the German court, Turner insists that such "gap filling" is impermissible when the result is a provision inconsistent with the provisions of the contract as written. Turner relies upon *Higginbottom v. Thiele Kaolin Co.*, 304 S.E.2d at 365, for this proposition.

We conclude, however, that the result of the German court decision is not inconsistent with the Agreement. The Agreement expressly gives ARD a right to telecast "by all means and methods now or hereafter known including but not limited to . . . DBS and/or communication satellite for purposes of so-called home television reception." Significantly, the grant also expressly provides that the "telecast can originate any place in the universe for reception only in the Territory as defined in paragraph 4 below (inclusive of legitimate overspill as set forth in ¶ 2(f) below)." Thus, to deny ARD the right to utilize the ASTRA satellite would conflict with the provisions of the Agreement. On the other hand, the German court reasonably concluded that the parties did not contemplate an overspill of the magnitude which results from recent technology, including the ASTRA satellites. Thus, the German court employed its "supplemental interpretation" and filled the gap in the contract in accordance with its determination of good faith dealings by the parties as to unforeseen eventualities. Because we conclude that the utilization of this "gap filling" methodology under these circumstances is consistent with the contract law of both Georgia and the general common law, we reject Turner's argument that the German court decision is in violation of Georgia public policy or in violation of fundamental notions of decency and fairness.

Also relevant to considerations of international comity are the relative strengths of the American and German interests. [Citations omitted.] In the instant case, the contract was written in English, with an American as one party to the contract, and includes a choice of law and forum selection provision designating this federal court and the applicable law (although the choice of law and forum is concurrent with Germany's). However, the central question in the case — whether the Agreement does or should permit ARD to broadcast via ASTRA — requires a thorough knowledge of European broadcasting technology and markets, and requires reference to European law. Most of the witnesses and experts in the litigation would be European. Furthermore, although an American entity is a party to the contract, there also are German parties and the choice of law and forum provisions also designate the German court and law. More importantly, the Agreement calls for performance of the contract, for the most part, in Germany, and the German interest and connection to the case is much more significant than the American.

Although Turner attempts to present the case as a garden variety contract action, there are complicated issues surrounding the case that require extensive knowledge of the European television market. Given exclusive jurisdiction over the matter, the federal forum would without doubt be capable of rendering a just result. However, the German court would seem to be the most sensible venue to determine a just result in this case. There appears to be no clear federal interest in trying this case. Certainly much is at stake in this litigation for both parties. However, the public interest in the litigation is more conspicuous in Germany, because the German parties include the German state broadcasters, and the salient issues in the case are of great moment to the state of television in Germany and the rest of Europe. There is no comparable federal interest in maintaining jurisdiction over the litigation.

While courts regularly permit parallel proceedings in an American court and a foreign court [citations omitted], once a judgment on the merits is reached in one of the cases, as in the German forum in this case, failure to defer to the judgment would have serious implications for the concerns of international comity. For example, the prospect of "dueling courts," conflicting judgments, and attempts to enforce conflicting judgments raise major concerns of international comity.

In sum, international comity concerns favor deference to the German proceedings in the instant case.

2. Fairness

With respect to the goal of fairness, relevant considerations include: (1) the order in which the suits were filed [citation omitted]; (2) the more convenient forum [citations omitted]; and (3) the possibility of prejudice to parties resulting from abstention. [Citation omitted.]

The instant lawsuits were filed almost simultaneously. The record reflects that the German action was filed one week prior to the American litigation, and the record does not show that the American suit was a reaction to the German suit. We note that none of the cases regarding concurrent international jurisdiction give priority solely on the basis of first-filing in a case where the suits were filed so closely together. [Citations omitted.] Whatever weight is to be accorded this one-week priority, of course, points toward the German forum. The other factors point even more strongly in that direction.

With respect to convenience of the forum, the weightier German interest, discussed above, indicates that the German court provides a more convenient forum for the litigation, as does the fact that most of the witnesses and experts in the litigation would be European, and the fact that the Agreement calls for performance of the contract, for the most part, in Germany. The significantly greater German interest in the litigation, discussed above, also supports the more general notion that concerns of fairness favor the German forum.

Before accepting or relinquishing jurisdiction a federal court must be satisfied that its decision will not result in prejudice to the party opposing the stay. [Citation omitted.] Ensuring the ability of the parties to fully and fairly litigate their claims in some tribunal surely is a paramount goal of international abstention principles. [Citation and quote omitted.] In the instant case, we see nothing that has occurred in the German proceedings to indicate that staying the litigation will foreclose any chance for Turner to obtain a fair and just result. For example, nothing has occurred in the German proceedings to date to dispel the expectation that Turner will have ample opportunity to fairly present to the German trial court at the next stage of the proceedings its evidence regarding the value of the ASTRA broadcasts in the areas outside the licensed territory defined in Paragraph 4 of the Agreement.

In sum, we conclude that fairness in this case indicates deference to the German proceedings.

3. Judicial Resources

Finally, courts have considered the efficient use of scarce judicial resources. Criteria relevant to efficiency include (1) the inconvenience of the federal forum [citation omitted]; (2) the desirability of avoiding piecemeal litigation [citations omitted]; (3) whether the actions have parties and issues in common [citation omitted]; and (4) whether the alternative forum is likely to render a prompt disposition [citation omitted]. We have already discussed the convenience of the federal forum. The desire to avoid piecemeal litigation is also relevant to the convenience of the forum. If both proceedings continued, the courts' calendars would have to be synchronized and the litigation would have to move back and forth across the Atlantic. We have already noted that the actions involve substantially the same parties and issues. Finally, the German court would seem as likely as the American forum to render a prompt disposition. Although the appeal of the German decision will not be heard until 1995, the German litigation has moved much farther along than the American action. There has been no discovery in the American litigation, while a trial on the merits has already occurred in Germany. Overall, we readily conclude that concerns regarding judicial efficiency militate strongly in favor of staying or dismissing the instant action in favor of the German litigation.

4. Conclusion on International Abstention

In summary, we conclude that the relevant concerns of international comity, fairness and efficiency point overwhelmingly, at this stage of the litigation, to deference to the German forum which has already rendered a judgment on the merits.

We also conclude that at this stage of the litigation, the appropriate resolution is a stay rather than a dismissal of the American action. The German court has yet to rule on appeal or to determine the manner or amount of the fee that the appellants shall pay to Turner. After the German litigation is complete, Turner may seek a hearing to determine whether the final results have altered any issues addressed herein. If not, the action should be dismissed. Either party also may add an action for enforcement of the foreign judgment at an appropriate time.

B. The Preliminary Injunction

The same concerns of international comity, fairness and efficiency, discussed fully above, indicate that it would be inappropriate to enjoin defendants-appellants from telecasting the licensed works or interfere with the ongoing legal proceedings in Germany. Thus, for the same reasons that we have decided to stay the instant suit, we conclude that the preliminary injunction entered by the district court must be vacated.

III. Conclusion

For the foregoing reasons, we vacate the judgment of the district court and remand the case to the district court with instructions to vacate its preliminary injunction and stay the litigation.

VACATED and REMANDED.

QUESTIONS

1. Which action was filed first in this case? Did this factor affect the outcome? Should it have? The court quotes from the opinion in *Hilton v. Guyot* (extracted in Chapter 6) on international comity. How was this relevant to the decision?

2. What factual and legal questions were at issue? Would, objectively, either a German or U.S. court be the more appropriate forum to determine these questions? Explain.

3. Would, in your view, Judge Posner agree with Judge Anderson that "[f]ederal courts have a 'virtually unflagging obligation' to exercise the jurisdiction conferred upon them"?

SEATTLE TOTEMS HOCKEY CLUB, INC. v. NATIONAL HOCKEY LEAGUE*
652 F.2d 852 (9th Cir. 1981)

Norris, Circuit Judge:

This appeal arises out of a private antitrust action brought in federal district court by appellees Vincent Abbey and Eldred Barnes, owners of the Seattle Totems, an ice hockey team in the now-defunct Western Hockey League. Named as defendants were the National Hockey League (NHL), Northwest Sports, owners of the Vancouver Canucks of the NHL, and various League officers and club owners. The suit charges defendants with unlawful monopolization of the ice hockey industry in North America and seeks, among other relief, to have certain agreements between Abbey and Barnes and Northwest Sports relating to the sale and management of the Seattle Totems declared void and unenforceable.

Approximately twenty-seven months after the filing of the antitrust action, Northwest Sports sued Abbey and Barnes in British Columbia Supreme Court for damages for breach of the same agreements that are being challenged as illegal and unenforceable in the appellees' antitrust action in federal district court. Abbey and Barnes then moved in the federal court action to enjoin Northwest Sports from

---

* Footnotes omitted.

prosecuting its contract claim in British Columbia on the ground that the claim constitutes a compulsory counterclaim to plaintiffs' antitrust complaint and must be pleaded in the pending federal antitrust action in Washington. The district court granted plaintiffs' motion and issued the injunction against prosecution of the Canadian suit. Northwest Sports appeals pursuant to 28 U.S.C. § 1292(a)(1).

I.

Northwest Sports does not deny that under Federal Rule of Civil Procedure 13(a) its contract claim would constitute a compulsory counterclaim in the pending antitrust action. Rather, it contends that Canadian law, and not Rule 13(a), governs the determination whether the contract claim is compulsory and that Canadian law would not require Northwest Sports to plead its claim as a compulsory counterclaim in the pending antitrust suit. In concluding that Rule 13(a) governs, the district court below relied on the general choice of law principle, restated in § 122 of the Restatement (Second) of Conflict of Laws (1971), that a court will apply its own rules of procedure to regulate the conduct of litigation before it. [Citation omitted.] Northwest Sports argues, however, that this general rule is inapplicable because the issue in question is "one whose resolution would be likely to affect the ultimate result of the case." Restatement (Second) of Conflict of Laws § 122, Comment a (1971). We find this argument without merit.

The issue before this court is not whether Canadian law governs the interpretation or the validity of the agreements between Northwest Sports and appellees, but rather whether all claims arising out of these agreements should be heard in a single forum. A determination that appellant's claim is a compulsory counterclaim which must be pleaded in the district court of Washington cannot reasonably be expected to affect the merits of appellant's contract claim. Moreover, the Supreme Court has emphasized the federal courts' overriding interest in applying their own rules of procedure and has indicated that in federal court the Federal Rules of Civil Procedure will almost invariably be applied if there is a Federal Rule governing the point in dispute. [Citations omitted.] Northwest Sports nevertheless argues that Canadian law is controlling because (1) the parties designated Canadian law as the law to be applied to the contract, and (2) Canada is the jurisdiction with the most significant relationship to the transaction. However, as noted above, the controlling choice of law principle is that a court's own local rules will be applied to determine how litigation shall be conducted. Appellants have failed to demonstrate why this principle is inapplicable in this case. Accordingly, we conclude that the district court properly looked to Fed.R.Civ.P. 13, and not Canadian law, to determine whether a defendant's contract claim must be pleaded as a compulsory counterclaim in the federal antitrust action pending before it.

II.

Federal Rule of Civil Procedure 13(a) requires a defendant in federal court to state as a counterclaim any claim he may have against the plaintiff that "arises out of the transaction or occurrence that is the subject matter" of the plaintiff's claim. The purpose of requiring a defendant to assert his claim as a counterclaim in a pending action is "to prevent multiplicity of actions and to achieve resolution in a single lawsuit of all disputes arising out of common matters." *Southern Construction Co. v. Pickard*, 371 U.S. 57, 60 (1962). The Rule bars a party who failed to assert a compulsory counterclaim in one action from instituting a second action in which that counterclaim is the basis of the complaint. [Citations omitted.] It is well-settled that in order to enforce this bar, a federal court may enjoin a party from bringing its compulsory counterclaim in a subsequent federal court action. [Citations omitted.] Northwest Sports maintains, however, that the district court abused its discretion by restraining Northwest Sports from proceeding in the courts of a foreign country in order to enforce the dictates of Rule 13(a) and avoid duplicative litigation. We disagree.

A federal district court with jurisdiction over the parties has the power to enjoin them from proceeding with an action in the courts of a foreign country, although the power should be "used sparingly." *Philp v. Macri*, 261 F.2d 945, 947 (9th Cir. 1958). "The issue is not one of jurisdiction, but one . . . of comity." *Canadian Filters Ltd. v. Lear Siegler, Inc.*, 412 F.2d 577, 578 (1st Cir. 1969). [Citation omitted.]

In re Unterweser Reederei Gmbh, 428 F.2d 888 (5th Cir. 1970), *aff'd on rehearing en banc*, 446 F.2d 907 (1971), *rev'd on other grounds sub nom. Bremen v. Zapata Off-Shore Co.*, 407 U.S. 1, 92 S. Ct. 1907, 32 L. Ed. 2d 513 (1972), is instructive. In that case, a federal district judge enjoined Unterweser Reederei from proceeding in the High Court of Justice in London, England on a claim that had been pleaded as a counterclaim in an action already pending in federal district court. In affirming the district court's issuance of the injunction, the Fifth Circuit noted that foreign litigation may be enjoined when it would (1) frustrate a policy of the forum issuing the injunction; (2) be vexatious or oppressive; (3) threaten the issuing courts in rem or quasi in rem jurisdiction; or (4) where the proceedings prejudice other equitable considerations. It then went on to hold that "allowing simultaneous prosecution of the same action in a foreign forum thousands of miles away would result in 'inequitable hardship' and 'tend to frustrate and delay the speedy and efficient determination of the cause.'" *Id.* at 896, quoting *In re Unterweser Reederei, Gmbh*, 296 F. Supp. 733, 735–36 (M.D. Fla. 1969).

Similarly, in *Bethell v. Peace*, 441 F.2d 495 (5th Cir. 1971), a federal district court held that a land-sale contract executed in Florida between Florida residents involving land in the Bahamas was invalid, and issued an injunction restraining the defendant from prosecuting an action in the Bahamas to quiet title. The Fifth Circuit affirmed, holding that it was within the district court's discretion to enjoin the foreign suit where the action would relieve the moving party "of the expense and vexation of having to litigate in a foreign court." *Id.* at 498. [Citations omitted.]

In the case before us, the validity of the 1972–74 agreements will be a central issue in both the Canadian and American litigations. Adjudicating this issue in two separate actions is likely to result in unnecessary delay and substantial inconvenience and expense to the parties and witnesses. Moreover, separate adjudications could result in inconsistent rulings or even a race to judgment.

In granting the injunction against Northwest Sports, the district court noted that it had considered the relevant factors, including "the convenience to the parties and witnesses, the interest of the courts in promoting the efficient administration of justice, and the potential prejudice to one party or the other," and concluded that the equitable balance weighs heavily in favor of plaintiffs, Abbey and Barnes. It also concluded that the policies animating Rule 13(a) and the rationale of the cases upholding injunctions against subsequently-filed federal court actions applied with equal force to this case where the compulsory counterclaim was brought in the courts of Canada. In view of these policies and cases, we cannot say that the district court abused its discretion by enjoining Northwest Sports from prosecuting its contract claim in Canadian court.

AFFIRMED.

QUESTIONS

1. Which action was filed first in this case? Did this factor affect the outcome? Should it have? In what respect was "international comity" relevant?

2. Did the nature of the claims in the two cases matter? Would, in your view, the outcome in the U.S. case differed had the Canadian suit involved an antitrust claim but the U.S. suit was an action for breach of contract?

3. How would you answer these questions in the context of the following case?

KAEPA, INC. v. ACHILLES CORPORATION*
76 F.3d 624 (5th Cir. 1996)

WIENER, CIRCUIT JUDGE:

The primary issue presented by this appeal is whether the district court erred by enjoining Defendant-Appellant Achilles Corporation from prosecuting an action that it filed in Japan as plaintiff, which essentially mirrored a lawsuit previously filed by Plaintiff-Appellee Kaepa, Inc. in state court and then being prosecuted in federal district court by Kaepa. Given the private nature of the dispute, the clear indications by both parties that claims arising from their contract should be adjudicated in this country, and the duplicative and vexatious nature of the Japanese action, we conclude that the district court did not abuse its discretion by barring the prosecution of the foreign litigation. Accordingly, we affirm the grant of the antisuit injunction.

---

* Footnotes omitted.

I.

FACTS AND PROCEEDINGS

This case arises out of a contractual dispute between two sophisticated, private corporations: Kaepa, an American company which manufactures athletic shoes; and Achilles, a Japanese business enterprise with annual sales that approximate one billion dollars. In April 1993, the two companies entered into a distributorship agreement whereby Achilles obtained exclusive rights to market Kaepa's footwear in Japan. The distributorship agreement expressly provided that Texas law and the English language would govern its interpretation, that it would be enforceable in San Antonio, Texas, and that Achilles consented to the jurisdiction of the Texas courts.

Kaepa grew increasingly dissatisfied with Achilles's performance under the contract. Accordingly, in July of 1994, Kaepa filed suit in Texas state court, alleging (1) fraud and negligent misrepresentation by Achilles to induce Kaepa to enter into the distributorship agreement, and (2) breach of contract by Achilles. Thereafter, Achilles removed the action to federal district court, and the parties began a laborious discovery process which to date has resulted in the production of tens of thousands of documents. In February 1995, after appearing in the Texas action, removing the case to federal court, and engaging in comprehensive discovery, Achilles brought its own action in Japan, alleging mirror-image claims: (1) fraud by Kaepa to induce Achilles to enter into the distributorship agreement, and (2) breach of contract by Kaepa.

Back in Texas, Kaepa promptly filed a motion asking the district court to enjoin Achilles from prosecuting its suit in Japan (motion for an antisuit injunction). Achilles in turn moved to dismiss the federal court action on the ground of *forum non conveniens*. The district court denied Achilles's motion to dismiss and granted Kaepa's motion to enjoin, ordering Achilles to refrain from litigating the Japanese action and to file all of its counterclaims with the district court. Achilles timely appealed the grant of the antisuit injunction.

II.

ANALYSIS

A. Propriety of the Antisuit Injunction

Achilles's primary argument is that the district court failed to give proper deference to principles of international comity when it granted Kaepa's motion for an antisuit injunction. We review the decision to grant injunctive relief for abuse of discretion Under this deferential standard, findings of fact are upheld unless clearly erroneous, whereas legal conclusions " 'are subject to broad review and will be reversed if incorrect.' "

It is well settled among the circuit courts — including this one — which have reviewed the grant of an antisuit injunction that the federal courts have the power to enjoin persons subject to their jurisdiction from prosecuting foreign suits. The circuits differ, however, on the proper legal standard to employ when determining whether that injunctive power should be exercised. We have addressed the propriety of an antisuit injunction on two prior occasions, in *In re Unterweser Reederei Gmbh* [428 F.2d 888] and *Bethell v. Peace* [441 F.2d 495]. Emphasizing in both cases the need to prevent vexatious or oppressive litigation, we concluded that a district court does not abuse its discretion by issuing an antisuit injunction when it has determined "that allowing simultaneous prosecution of the same action in a foreign forum thousands of miles away would result in 'inequitable hardship' and 'tend to frustrate and delay the speedy and efficient determination of the cause.' " [*Unterweser*, 428 F.2d at 890, 896]. The Seventh and the Ninth Circuits have either adopted or "incline[d] toward" this approach, but other circuits have employed a standard that elevates principles of international comity to the virtual exclusion of essentially all other considerations.

Achilles urges us to give greater deference to comity and apply the latter, more restrictive standard. We note preliminarily that, even though the standard espoused in *Unterweser* and *Bethell* focuses on the potentially vexatious nature of foreign litigation, it by no means excludes the consideration of principles of comity. We decline, however, to require a district court to genuflect before a vague and omnipotent notion of comity every time that it must decide whether to enjoin a foreign action.

In the instant case, for example, it simply cannot be said that the grant of the antisuit injunction actually threatens relations between the United States and Japan. First, no public international issue is implicated by the case: Achilles is a private party engaged in a contractual dispute with another private party. Second, the dispute has been long and firmly ensconced within the confines of the United States judicial system: Achilles consented to jurisdiction in Texas; stipulated that Texas law and the English language would govern any dispute; appeared in an action brought in Texas; removed that action to a federal court in Texas; engaged in extensive discovery pursuant to the directives of the federal court; and only then, with the federal action moving steadily toward trial, brought identical claims in Japan. Under these circumstances, we cannot conclude that the district court's grant of an antisuit injunction in any way trampled on notions of comity.

On the contrary, the facts detailed above strongly support the conclusion that the prosecution of the Japanese action would entail "an absurd duplication of effort" [*Allendale Mut. Ins. Co. v. Bull Data Systems, Inc.*, 10 F.3d 425, 430–431 (7th Cir. 1993)]. and would result in unwarranted inconvenience, expense, and vexation. Achilles's belated ploy of filing as putative plaintiff in Japan the very same claims against Kaepa that Kaepa had filed as plaintiff against Achilles smacks of cynicism, harassment, and delay. Accordingly, we hold that the district court did not abuse its discretion by granting Kaepa's motion for an antisuit injunction.

B. Rule 65 Requirements

Achilles also argues that the district court erred by failing to meet several requirements of Federal Rule of Civil Procedure 65 before issuing the antisuit injunction. Rule 65(a)(1) provides that "[n]o preliminary injunction shall be issued without notice to the adverse party." We have interpreted the notice requirement of Rule 65(a)(1) to mean that "where factual disputes are presented, the parties must be given a fair opportunity and a meaningful hearing to present their differing versions of those facts before a preliminary injunction may be granted" [*Commerce Park at DFW Freeport v. Mardian Construction Co.*, 729 F.2d 334, 342 (5th Cir. 1984)]. If no factual dispute is involved, however, no oral hearing is required; under such circumstances the parties need only be given "ample opportunity to present their respective views of the legal issues involved" [*Commerce Park*, 729 F.2d at 341]. In the instant case, the district court did not rely on any disputed facts in determining whether it could properly grant an antisuit injunction. Moreover, both parties presented comprehensive memoranda in support of their positions on the issue. Accordingly, the district court did not violate Rule 65(a)(1) by failing to conduct an oral hearing before granting the antisuit injunction.

Achilles also argues that the district court violated Rule 65(c) by not requiring Kaepa to post a bond. Rule 65(c) provides that "[n]o . . . preliminary injunction shall issue except upon the giving of security by the applicant, in such sum as the court deems proper . . . ." In holding that the amount of security required pursuant to Rule 65(c) "is a matter for the discretion of the trial court," we have ruled that the court "may elect to require no security at all" [*Corrigan Dispatch Company v. Casa Guzman*, 569 F.2d 300, 303 (5th Cir. 1978)]. Thus, the district court did not violate Rule 65(c) by failing to compel Kaepa to post a bond.

III.

Conclusion

For the foregoing reasons, the district court's grant of Kaepa's motion to enjoin the litigation of Achilles's action in Japan is *Affirmed*.

Emilio M. Garza, Circuit Judge, dissenting:

International comity represents a principle of paramount importance in our world of ever increasing economic interdependence. Admitting that "comity" may be a somewhat elusive concept does not mean that we can blithely ignore its cautionary dictate. Unless we proceed in each instance with respect for the independent jurisdiction of a sovereign nation's courts, we risk provoking retaliation in turn, with detrimental consequences that may reverberate far beyond the particular dispute and its private litigants. Amicable relations among sovereign nations and their judicial systems depend on our recognition, as federal courts, that we share the international arena with co-equal judicial bodies, and that we therefore act to deprive a foreign court of jurisdiction only in the most extreme circumstances. Because I feel that the majority's opinion does not grant the principle of international comity the weight it deserves, I must respectfully dissent.

I

A

I do not quarrel with the well established principle, relied on by the majority, that our courts have the power to control the conduct of persons subject to their jurisdiction, even to the extent of enjoining them from prosecuting in a foreign jurisdiction. I write to emphasize, however, that under concurrent jurisdiction, "parallel proceedings on the same in personam claim should ordinarily be allowed to proceed simultaneously, at least until a judgment is reached in one which can be pled as res judicata in the other." *Laker Airways Ltd. v. Sabena, Belgian World Airlines*, 731 F.2d 909, 926–27 (D.C. Cir. 1984). The filing of a second parallel action in another jurisdiction does not necessarily conflict with or prevent the first court from exercising its legitimate concurrent jurisdiction. *Id.* at 926. In the ordinary case, both forums should be free to proceed to a judgment, unhindered by the concurrent exercise of jurisdiction in another court.

The issuance of an antisuit injunction runs directly counter to this principle of tolerating parallel proceedings. An antisuit injunction "conveys the message . . . that the issuing court has so little confidence in the foreign court's ability to adjudicate a given dispute fairly and efficiently that it is unwilling even to allow the possibility." *Gau Shan Co. v. Bankers Trust Co.*, 956 F.2d 1349, 1355 (6th Cir. 1992). It makes no difference that in formal terms the injunction is only addressed to the parties. The antisuit injunction operates to restrict the foreign court's ability to exercise its jurisdiction as effectively as if it were addressed to the foreign court itself. [Citations omitted.] Enjoining the parties from litigating in a foreign court will necessarily compromise the principles of comity, and may lead to undesirable consequences. For example, the foreign court may react by issuing a similar injunction, thereby preventing any party from obtaining a remedy. [Citation omitted.] The foreign court may also be less inclined to enforce a judgment by our courts. The refusal to enforce a foreign judgment, however, is less offensive than acting to prevent the foreign court from hearing the matter in the first place. [Citation omitted.]

Antisuit injunctions intended to carve out exclusive jurisdiction may also have unintended, widespread effects on international commerce. Without "an atmosphere of cooperation and reciprocity between nations," the ability to predict future consequences of international transactions will inevitably suffer. *Id.* To operate effectively and efficiently, international markets require a degree of predictability which can only be harmed by antisuit injunctions and the resulting breakdown of cooperation and reciprocity between courts of different nations. *Id.* The attempt to exercise exclusive jurisdiction over international economic affairs is essentially an intrusion into the realm of international economic policy that should appropriately be left to our legislature and the treaty making process. As the court in *Laker Airways* stated, "Absent an explicit directive from Congress, this court has neither the authority nor the institutional resources to weigh the policy and political factors that must be evaluated when resolving competing claims of jurisdiction. In contrast, diplomatic and executive channels are, by definition, designed to exchange, negotiate, and reconcile the problems which accompany the realization of national interests within the sphere of international association." *Laker Airways*, 731 F.2d at 955.

The majority appears to require an affirmative showing that the granting of an antisuit injunction in this case would immediately and concretely affect adversely the relations between the United States and Japan. Unless there is evidence that this antisuit injunction would "actually threaten" the relations between the two countries, the majority is comfortable to assume otherwise. [Citation omitted.] Some courts have gone so far as to suggest that we might expect, for example, a representative of the foreign nation to convey their country's concern regarding the issuance of an antisuit injunction in that case. [Citation omitted.] Insisting on evidence of immediate and concrete harm, in the form of a diplomatic protest or otherwise, is both unrealistic and shortsighted. As with most transnational relations, the potential harm to international comity caused by the issuance of a specific antisuit injunction will be as difficult to predict, as it will be to remedy. It is precisely this troubling uncertainty, and the recognition that our courts are ill equipped to weigh these types of international policy considerations, that cautions us to make the respectful deference underlying international comity the rule rather than the exception.

B

In holding that the district court in this case did not abuse its discretion by enjoining Achilles, a Japanese corporation, from proceeding with its lawsuit filed in the sovereign nation of Japan, the majority appears to rely primarily on the duplicative nature of the Japanese suit and the resulting "unwarranted inconvenience, expense, and vexation." The inconvenience, expense and vexation, however, are factors likely to be present whenever there is an exercise of concurrent jurisdiction by a foreign court. [Citation omitted.] The majority's standard can be understood to hold, therefore, that "a duplication of the parties and issues, alone, is sufficient to justify a foreign antisuit injunction." *Gau Shan Co.*, 956 F.2d at 1353 [additional citation with quote omitted]. Under this standard, concurrent jurisdiction involving a foreign tribunal will rarely, if ever, withstand the request for an antisuit injunction.

By focusing on the potential hardship to Kaepa of having to litigate in two forums, the majority applies an analysis that is more appropriately brought to bear in the context of a motion to dismiss for forum non conveniens. [Citation omitted.] Considerations that are appropriate in deciding whether to decline jurisdiction are not as persuasive when deciding whether to deprive another court of jurisdiction. "The policies of avoiding hardships to the parties and promoting the economies of consolidation litigation 'do not outweigh the important principles of comity that compel deference and mutual respect for concurrent foreign proceedings. Thus, the better rule is that duplication of parties and issues alone is not sufficient to justify issuance of an antisuit injunction.'" *Gau Shan Co.*, 956 F.2d at 1355 (quoting *Laker Airways*, 731 F.2d at 928) [other citations omitted]. A dismissal on grounds of *forum non conveniens* by either court in this case would satisfy the majority's concern with avoiding hardship to the parties, without harming the interests of international comity. The district court is not in a position, however, to make the *forum non conveniens* determination on behalf of the Japanese court. In light of the important interests of international comity, the decision by a United States court to deprive a foreign court of jurisdiction must be supported by far weightier factors than would otherwise justify that court's decision to decline its own jurisdiction on *forum non conveniens* grounds.

C

Accordingly, I believe that the standard followed by the Second, Sixth, and D.C. Circuits more satisfactorily respects the principle of concurrent jurisdiction and safeguards the important interests of international comity. Under this stricter standard, a district court should look to only two factors in determining whether to issue an antisuit injunction: (1) whether the foreign action threatens the jurisdiction of the district court; and (2) whether the foreign action was an attempt to evade important public policies of the district court. [Citations omitted.]. Neither of these factors are present in this case.

"Courts have a duty to protect their legitimately conferred jurisdiction to the extent necessary to provide full justice to litigants." *Laker Airways*, 731 F.2d at 927. Where the concurrent proceeding effectively threatens to paralyze the jurisdiction of the court, or where the foreign court is attempting to carve out exclusive jurisdiction over the action, an antisuit injunction may legitimately be necessary to protect the court's jurisdiction. In those rare cases where the foreign action is interdictory rather than parallel, the issuance of an antisuit injunction is primarily a defensive action not inconsistent with the principles of international comity. The court in *Laker Airways* affirmed the issuance of an antisuit injunction where the foreign action "was instituted by the foreign defendants for the sole purpose of terminating the United States claim." *Id.* at 915. In fact, the British Court of Appeals had enjoined the plaintiff from pursuing its claims against British defendants in a United States court under United States law. *Id.* Significantly, the United States district court in *Laker Airways* also made clear that its injunction was intended solely to protect its jurisdiction by preventing the defendants from taking any action before a foreign court or governmental authority that would interfere with the litigation pending before the district court. *Id.* at 919. The injunction was not intended to prevent all concurrent proceedings in foreign courts, only those which directly threatened the district court's jurisdiction. There is no evidence in this case that Achilles' action in Japan in any way threatens the district court's exercise of its concurrent jurisdiction. While the Japanese action may eventually proceed to a judgment which can be pled as res judicata in the district court, no attempt has been made to carve out exclusive jurisdiction on behalf of the foreign tribunal.

As an example of where a court may need to act in order to protect its jurisdiction, a long-standing exception to the rule tolerating concurrent jurisdiction has been recognized for proceedings in rem or quasi in rem. [Citation omitted.] Because the second action may pose an inherent threat to the court's basis for jurisdiction, an antisuit injunction may be appropriate in an in rem or quasi in rem proceeding. *Id.* "Where jurisdiction is based on the presence of property within the court's jurisdictional boundaries, a concurrent proceeding in a foreign jurisdiction poses the danger that the foreign court will order the transfer of the property out of the jurisdictional boundaries of the first court, thus depriving it of jurisdiction over the matter. This concern of course is not present in this in personam proceeding." *Gau Shan Co.*, 956 F.2d at 1358. Likewise, this concern is not present in the current in personam proceeding, the focus of which is a distribution agreement. I note that *In re Unterweser Reederei, Gmbh*, relied on by the majority, was an in rem proceeding, justifying the more permissive standard applied to the issuance of an antisuit injunction in that case.

Under the second factor of the stricter standard, an antisuit injunction may also be appropriate where a party seeks to evade important policies of the forum by bringing suit in a foreign court. [Citation omitted.] "While an injunction may be appropriate when a party attempts to evade compliance with a statute of the forum that effectuates important public policies, an injunction is not appropriate merely to prevent a party from seeking 'slight advantages in the substantive or procedural law to be applied in a foreign court.'" *China Trade*, 837 F.2d at 37 (quoting *Laker Airways*, 731 F.2d at 931, n. 73). The policy favoring the resolution in a single lawsuit of all disputes arising out of a common matter does not, as noted earlier, outweigh the important interests of international comity. Rather, the principle enunciated under the second factor is "similar to the rule that a foreign judgment not entitled to full faith and credit under the Constitution will not be enforced within the United States when contrary to the crucial public policies of the forum in which enforcement is requested." *Laker Airways*, 731 F.2d at 931. Under this principle, a court is not required to give effect to a judgment that does violence to the forum's own fundamental interests. *Id.* Since the issuance of an antisuit injunction is a much greater and more direct interference with a foreign country's judicial process than is the refusal to enforce a judgment, it follows that an antisuit injunction should only be issued in the most extreme circumstances. Although the majority questions the purity of Achilles' motives in filing suit in Japan, there is no evidence that Achilles is attempting to evade any important policy of the United States forum.

II

Because neither factor supports the issuance of an antisuit injunction in this case, I believe the district court abused its discretion by enjoining Achilles from prosecuting an action filed in Japan. Accordingly, I respectfully dissent.

PROBLEM AND QUESTIONS

1. Assume that an employee of a U.S. company seriously injured his hand while operating a metal press manufactured in Japan. He has brought a personal injury action in a federal district court in Texas against his employer as well as the Japanese manufacturer. Anticipating the possibility that the Japanese company might bring a parallel suit in Japan for a judgment to confirm the company's non-liability, the plaintiff's lawyers seek an anti-suit injunction. What arguments would you anticipate would be made in support as well as in opposition to their motion? Which as a matter

> of policy would be the most persuasive?
>
> 2. Would your answer be the same were a parallel action already filed in Japan?
>
> 3. Recall the review problem in Chapter 1 involving the French action for recovery of van Gogh's *The Night Café* by Pierre Konowaloff. What arguments might Konowaloff's lawyers make in response to a parallel action brought by Yale University in a federal district court in New Haven? For a recent French judgment recognizing an anti-suit injunction against a French firm issued by a Georgia court pursuant to forum selection clause, see *In Zone Brands*, Civ. 1ère, 14 October 2009, pourvoin 08-16.369.

III. COMMON LAW APPROACHES — CANADA

A. *Forum Non Conveniens*

AMCHEM PRODUCTS INC. v. BRITISH COLUMBIA (WORKERS' COMPENSATION BOARD)
[1993] 1 S.C.R. 897

This case originated in an action filed by number of British Columbia residents against several U.S. manufacturers of asbestos in Texas. The Texas court accepted jurisdiction over the matter and heard the case. The manufacturers applied to the B.C. Supreme Court (the first instance trial court) to issue an anti-suit injunction, arguing that the proper forum for the plaintiffs would be in B.C. and not Texas. The B.C. Supreme Court issued the injunction. In response, Texas issued an "anti-anti-suit injunction." The B.C. Supreme Court judgment was upheld on appeal to the B.C. Court of Appeal. We will revisit this case with respect to the issue of anti-suit injunctions under Canadian law. However, here we consider the Court's opinion with respect to the applicability of the doctrine of *forum non conveniens* under Canadian law.

. . . .

Forum Non Conveniens

[31] The law of Canada and other common law countries on this subject evolved from the law of England which was most recently restated by the House of Lords in *Spiliada Maritime Corp. v. Cansulex Ltd.; "Spiliada" (The)*, [1987] A.C. 460. In setting out the principles which should guide a British court, Lord Goff, who delivered the main judgment, stated at p. 477 that "on a subject where comity is of importance, it appears that there will be a broad consensus among major common law jurisdictions". The English approach has gone through several stages of evolution tending to a broader acceptance of the legitimacy of the claim of other jurisdictions to try actions that have connections to England as well as to such other jurisdictions. Other common law jurisdictions have either accepted the principles in *Spiliada*, or an earlier version of them.

[32] Earlier English cases declined to apply the principle of *forum non conveniens*, which was a Scottish principle, preferring a rule which required a party who had been served within the jurisdiction to establish: (1) that the continuation of the action would cause an injustice to him or her because it would be oppressive or vexatious or constitute an abuse of the process, and (2) that stay would not cause an injustice to the plaintiff. The foundation for this rule was not balance of convenience for the trial of the action but rather abuse of the rights of the parties. A different test applied with respect to cases in which service outside the jurisdiction was necessary. In such a case an order for service ex juris was required and the plaintiff had to show that England was the appropriate forum and that the rule authorizing such service was otherwise complied with. In *"Atlantic Star" (The); "Atlantic Star" (The) (Owners) v. "Bona Spes" (The) (Owners)*, [1973] 2 All E.R. 175, the House of Lords was urged to adopt the principle of *forum non conveniens* from the Scottish law and to discontinue the test which required proof that the action was oppressive or vexatious as a prerequisite to a stay. The House of Lords declined to adopt the Scottish doctrine but opined that since the words "oppressive and vexatious" were flexible (indeed they had never been satisfactorily defined), liberalization of the English rule could be achieved in the application of those terms. In *Rockware Glass Ltd. v. MacShannon*, [1978] 2 W.L.R. 362, those words were discarded in favour of a more liberal and flexible test which required the defendant to establish: (1) that there is another forum to which the defendant is amenable in which justice can be done at substantially less inconvenience or expense, and (2) that the stay did not deprive the plaintiff of a legitimate personal or juridical advantage if the action continued in the domestic court. This was substantially the same as the Scottish rule of *forum non conveniens*.

[33] In *Spiliada, supra*, the House of Lords restated the rule and elaborated on its application. In particular, the court dealt with its application in what it considered two different circumstances. In the "as of right" cases in which the defendant was served in the jurisdiction, the burden of proof that a stay should be granted was on the defendant who was required to show that there is another forum which is clearly more appropriate for the trial of the action. This so-called "natural forum" is the one with which the action has the most real and substantial connection. If this first condition is established, a stay will be granted unless the plaintiff establishes special circumstances by reason of which justice requires that the trial take place in England. Mere loss of a juridical advantage will not amount to an injustice if the court is satisfied that substantial justice will be done in the appropriate forum. In cases in which service is effected ex juris, the burden is on the plaintiff throughout and is the obverse of that applicable in cases as of right; that is, the plaintiff must show that England is clearly the appropriate forum. Lord Goff provided some guidance with respect to the relevant factors that determine the appropriate forum. While not intending to provide an exhaustive list, His Lordship referred to the principal factors in his reasons at p. 478:

> So it is for connecting factors in this sense that the court must first look; and these will include not only factors affecting convenience or expense (such as availability of witnesses), but also other factors such as the law governing the relevant transaction (as to which see *Crédit Chimique v.*

James Scott Engineering Group Ltd., 1982 S.L.T. 131), and the places where the parties respectively reside or carry on business.

[34] These principles were reaffirmed in *de Dampierre v. de Dampierre*, [1987] 2 W.L.R. 1006 (H.L.). The case provides an interesting illustration of the application of the second branch of the rule. The petitioner wife resisted a stay of her divorce proceedings in England on the ground that in France, where her husband had also commenced proceedings, she would be deprived of support if her conduct was found to be the exclusive cause of the break-up of the marriage. Having found that the husband had satisfied the first condition establishing France as the appropriate forum, the loss of this juridical advantage was considered not sufficient to work an injustice in that substantial justice would still be done under the matrimonial regime obtaining in France.

[35] In Australia, the High Court, while not adopting all of the wording of *Spiliada*, has enunciated principles that the court acknowledged would likely yield the same results in the majority of cases. See *Voth v. Manildra Flour Mills Pty. Ltd.* (1990), 65 A.L.J.R. 83, at p. 90. The test for a stay is whether the forum selected by the plaintiff is clearly inappropriate rather than whether there is another forum that is clearly more appropriate. The same test applies in "as of right" and "service ex juris" cases. In New Zealand the applicable test is the *Spiliada* test which was adopted in *Club Mediterranee N.Z. v. Wendell*, [1989] 1 N.Z.L.R. 216 (C.A.). The United States Federal Courts apply similar principles in actions in those courts. In *Piper Aircraft Co. v. Reyno*, 454 U.S. 235 (1981), the Supreme Court of the United States approved of the decision of the District Court which dismissed an action brought in California by the administratrix of the estates of Scottish citizens involved in an air crash in Scotland against the American manufacturers of the aircraft. The test applied by the District Court judge was whether the relevant factors clearly pointed to a trial in the alternative jurisdiction. The test was applied on the basis of a presumption in favour of the plaintiff's choice of forum, the impact of which was lessened when the home forum was not selected.

[36] The current state of the law in Canada is summed up adequately by Ellen L. Hayes in "*Forum Non Conveniens* in England, Australia and Japan: The Allocation of Jurisdiction in Transnational Litigation" (1992), 26 U.B.C. Law Rev. 41, at pp. 42–43:

> The status of the doctrine of *forum non conveniens* in Canada is unclear. In general terms the Canadian courts have looked to English authorities when considering *forum non conveniens* issues. Their specific approach, however, is not consistent. The most recent cases from the Western provinces refer to the current English test, but at the same time resist adopting a comprehensive test or rule which would result in an "overly legalistic approach." The Ontario courts, on the other hand, have fallen behind the English courts' development of the doctrine and continue to apply a test which has now been replaced by the House of Lords. There is confusion in many of the cases as to whether the test is different when the defendant is served within the jurisdiction rather than *ex juris*, where the burden of proof lies and the weight to be given personal or juridical advantages to the

plaintiff of proceeding in the home jurisdiction. (Footnotes omitted [in judgment].)

The only recent decision of this court on the subject is *Antares, supra*, which, while an admiralty case in the Federal Court, discusses the general principles relating to *forum non conveniens*. At p. 448, Ritchie J., for the majority, stated the test that should be applied when the court is asked to stay an action on this ground:

> In my view the overriding consideration which must guide the Court in exercising its discretion by refusing to grant such an application as this must, however, be the existence of some other forum more convenient and appropriate for the pursuit of the action and for securing the ends of justice.

The case was decided before *Spiliada* and *MacShannon*. It is significant that there is no mention in the statement of general principles of any requirement that the domestic proceeding be shown to be oppressive or vexatious. There is no specific discussion of the second condition of the English rule but it is clear from the judgment that a principal factor in the determination that there was no alternative forum more convenient than Canada was the fact that it was the only jurisdiction in which the plaintiff could obtain an effective judgment. The ship, which was the subject of the suit, had been arrested in Quebec and the bond posted to obtain its release was security for enforcement of any judgment obtained in Canada. No such security was available in the other jurisdictions which were potential appropriate fora for the action. Accordingly, Canada was the most convenient forum for both "the pursuit of the action" and "for securing the ends of justice".

[37] In my view there is no reason in principle why the loss of juridical advantage should be treated as a separate and distinct condition rather than being weighed with the other factors which are considered in identifying the appropriate forum. The existence of two conditions is based on the historical development of the rule in England which started with two branches at a time when oppression to the defendant and injustice to the plaintiff were the dual bases for granting or refusing a stay. The law in England was evolved by reworking a passage from the reasons of Scott L.J. in *St. Pierre v. South American Stores (Gath & Chaves) Ltd.*, [1936] 1 K.B. 382, which contained two conditions. In its original formulation the second condition required the court to ensure that there was no injustice to the plaintiff in granting the stay. No doubt this was because the oppression test concentrated largely on the effects on the defendant of being subjected to a trial in England. When the first condition moved to an examination of all the factors that are designed to identify the natural forum, it seems to me that any juridical advantage to the plaintiff or defendant should have been considered one of the factors to be taken into account. The weight to be given to juridical advantage is very much a function of the parties' connection to the particular jurisdiction in question. If a party seeks out a jurisdiction simply to gain a juridical advantage rather than by reason of a real and substantial connection of the case to the jurisdiction, that is ordinarily condemned as "forum shopping". On the other hand, a party whose case has a real and substantial connection with a forum has a legitimate claim to the advantages that that forum provides. The legitimacy of this claim is based on a reasonable expectation that in the event of litigation arising out of the transaction

in question, those advantages will be available.

[38] Finally, I observe that *Antares, supra,* was a case in which leave to serve ex juris was required. The court did not, however, consider this an important matter in formulating the test. It seems to me that whether it is a case for service out of the jurisdiction or the defendant is served in the jurisdiction, the issue remains: is there a more appropriate jurisdiction based on the relevant factors. If the defendant resides out of the jurisdiction this is a factor whether or not service is effected out of the jurisdiction. Residence outside of the jurisdiction may be artificial. It may have been arranged for tax or other reasons notwithstanding the defendant has a real and substantial connection with this country. The special treatment which the English courts have accorded to ex juris cases appears to be based on the dictates of O. 11 of the English rules which imposes a heavy burden on the plaintiff to justify the assertion of jurisdiction over a foreigner. In most provinces in Canada, leave to serve ex juris is no longer required except in special circumstances and this trend is one that is likely to spread to other provinces. This phenomenon was considered by the High Court of Australia in *Voth, supra,* in reaching its conclusion that the test should be the same for service ex juris cases and others. Whether the burden of proof should be on the plaintiff in ex juris cases will depend on the rule that permits service out of the jurisdiction. If it requires that service out of the jurisdiction be justified by the plaintiff, whether on an application for an order or in defending service ex juris where no order is required, then the rule must govern. The burden of proof should not play a significant role in these matters as it only applies in cases in which the judge cannot come to a determinate decision on the basis of the material presented by the parties. While the standard of proof remains that applicable in civil cases, I agree with the English authorities that the existence of a more appropriate forum must be *clearly* established to displace the forum selected by the plaintiff. This was the position adopted by McLachlin J.A. (as she then was) in *Avenue Properties Ltd. v. First City Development Corp.* (1986), 7 B.C.L.R. (2d) 45 [[1987] 1 W.W.R. 249]. She emphasized that this had particular application where there were no parallel foreign proceedings pending.

[39] This review establishes that the law in common law jurisdictions is, as observed by Lord Goff in *Spiliada,* remarkably uniform. While there are differences in the language used, each jurisdiction applies principles designed to identify the most appropriate or appropriate forum for the litigation based on factors which connect the litigation and the parties to the competing fora. A review of the law of Japan by Ellen L. Hayes in the study to which I refer above (at p. 63) led her to conclude that similar principles are applied there. Regard for the principles of international comity to which I have referred suggests that in considering an anti-suit injunction the fact that a foreign court has assumed jurisdiction in circumstances which are consistent with the application of the above principles is an important factor militating against granting an injunction.

SPAR AEROSPACE LTD. v. AMERICAN MOBILE SATELLITE CORP.
[2002] 4 S.C.R. 205, 2002 SCC 78

Recall our discussion of this decision in with respect to the adjudicatory jurisdiction of courts in Quebec subsequent to the *Morguard* and *Hunt* decisions. The case involved an damage action brought by Spar Aerospace Limited, a firm based in Quebec, against American Mobile Satellite Corporation (aka Motient Corporation), Viacom Inc., and Hughes Communications Inc. arising out of a transaction for the manufacture in Quebec of communication equipment for a satellite. In addition to the issue of adjudicatory jurisdiction, the Court addressed the question of *forum non conveniens* under Quebec law.

The judgment of the Court was delivered by LEBEL J.

. . . .

V. Issues

. . . .

VI. Analysis

3. *Even if the Quebec courts are competent in the present matter, should jurisdiction be declined on the basis of the doctrine of forum non conveniens, pursuant to art. 3135 C.C.Q.?*

[65] Only two of the four appellants, Motient and Viacom, sought to dismiss the proceedings on the basis of *forum non conveniens* before the motions judge. The Quebec Court of Appeal did not hear the parties on the question because it was of the opinion that there was no merit to the argument, presumably on the basis of the motions judge's reasons and because only two of the appellants argued this ground.

[66] Before this Court, Motient and Viacom argue that the motions judge erred in requiring that the applicant be able to point to the existence of the one "most appropriate forum" because such reasoning would virtually bar the application of the doctrine in multi-jurisdictional or multi-party disputes. Case law recognizes that there may well be cases where the best that can be achieved is to select an appropriate forum since no one forum is clearly more appropriate than others. The appellants argue that there are two other clearly <u>more</u> appropriate *fora*, namely California and Virginia.

[67] The respondent contends that a judge presented with a motion on the ground of *forum non conveniens* must consider a number of factors to determine if there is an exceptional situation that warrants the declining of jurisdiction, none of which are individually determinant. If after considering the applicable factors the court does not have a clear impression that a foreign jurisdiction would be better suited to hear the case, the court must refuse to decline jurisdiction. The respondent argues that the motions judge correctly determined that the appellants did not demonstrate that another forum was 'more appropriate.

[68] The provision in question reads as follows:

> 3135. Even though a Quebec authority has jurisdiction to hear a dispute, it may exceptionally and on an application by a party, decline jurisdiction if it considers that the authorities of another country are in a better position to decide.

[69] Aside from the requirement that the party relying on the doctrine must bring an application for dismissal, the two key parts of art. 3135 include its exceptional nature and the requirement that another country be in a better position to decide (see E. Groffier, *La réforme du droit international privé québécois: supplément au Précis de droit international privé québécois* (1993), at p. 130).

[70] These two features of the *forum non conveniens* doctrine set out in art. 3135 are consistent with the common law requirements set out by the House of Lords in the seminal case, *Spiliada Maritime Corp. v. Cansulex Ltd.*, [1987] 1 A.C. 460, at p. 476, as well as this Court in *Amchem, supra*, at pp. 919–921, and *Holt Cargo, supra*, at para. 89. In *Holt Cargo*, this Court interpreted § 50 of the *Federal Court Act*, R.S.C. 1985, c. F-7, which essentially includes the same two requirements. It reads as follows:

> 50. (1) The Court may, in its discretion, stay proceedings in any cause or matter,
>
> (*a*) on the ground that the claim is being proceeded with in another court or jurisdiction; or
>
> (*b*) where for any other reason it is in the interest of justice that the proceedings be stayed.

In the case at bar, I agree with the respondent's submission that the motions judge did not err in finding that no other jurisdiction was clearly more appropriate than Quebec and that no exceptional exercise of this power was warranted.

[71] With respect to the first requirement, a number of cases have set out the relevant factors to consider when deciding whether or not the authorities of another country must be in a better position to decide the matter. The motions judge (at para. 18) referred to the 10 factors listed by the Quebec Court of Appeal in the recent case, *Lexus Maritime inc. v. Oppenheim Forfait GmbH*, [1998] Q.J. No. 2059 (QL), at para. 18, none of which are individually determinant:

1) The parties' residence, that of witnesses and experts;
2) the location of the material evidence;
3) the place where the contract was negotiated and executed;
4) the existence of proceedings pending between the parties in another jurisdiction;
5) the location of Defendant's assets;
6) the applicable law;
7) advantages conferred upon Plaintiff by its choice of forum, if any;
8) the interest of justice;

9) the interest of the parties;

10) the need to have the judgment recognized in another jurisdiction.

[72] Motient and Viacom dispute the motion judge's conclusion with respect to several factors. First, none of the appellants are domiciled or resident in Quebec and the respondent is domiciled in Ontario. Second, the respondent no longer owns or operates the branch office and plant which manufactured the satellite payload in Quebec. Third, the fault alleged against the appellants would have been committed in either California or Virginia and the majority of witnesses for the defence reside in the United States: in Virginia, California, Pennsylvania and New York. And finally, neither Motient nor Viacom have any significant assets in Quebec and any potential judgment rendered would have to be executed abroad.

[73] In this case, I agree with the motions judge that since all the witnesses and parties are from different places, there is not one single preferable location in this respect. The evidence of the tortious act and its immediate consequences is likely to be found in either Virginia or California. The assets of the defendants are all located in the United States. It is not yet known which law will be applicable to the action, so this factor is not determinant. Since the defendants' assets are likely to be found in several different jurisdictions in the United States, recovery by the respondent of any damages that it is awarded will require potentially more than one jurisdiction to recognize the judgment. I also note that the respondent's witness, Gerald Bush, testified that Motient sent representatives to stay at the Ste-Anne-de-Bellevue facility for more than a year (A.R., at pp. 92–94). In my opinion, the apparent willingness of Motient to displace some of its staff to conduct business with the respondent in Quebec seems at odds with its current complaint of *forum non conveniens*.

[74] The appellants attempt to argue that $50,000 for damage to reputation is not a substantial enough amount of damages for the action to be linked to the Province of Quebec. Although I agree that the amount of the damages can potentially be a factor to consider in deciding an art. 3135 application, I do not believe it is relevant in the case at bar. The appellants have not proven that the claim for these damages is frivolous and there are no other proceedings pending between the parties in another jurisdiction, which may be relevant if the respondent were trying to needlessly divide the claim. In any case, the $50,000 claim for damage to reputation may increase as the pleadings of the respondent characterize the $50,000 damages claim as being "nominal" only "provisionally" and "subject to Plaintiff's right to amend" because it was not able to precisely quantify them when the action was filed.

[75] The appellants Motient and Viacom nonetheless contend that the courts should not apply reasoning to the effect that the applicant must point to the existence of the one "most appropriate forum", since this makes it nearly impossible to displace the forum asserted by the plaintiff. I cannot agree with the premise of the appellants' argument. In *Amchem, supra*, at pp. 911–12, Sopinka J. recognized that in international commerce, frequently there is no single forum that is clearly the most convenient or appropriate for the trial of the action, but rather several which are equally suitable alternatives. He appeared at p. 931 to endorse the idea that in such cases there is a presumption in favour of the forum selected by the plaintiff, which wins by default if there is no clearly preferable alternative.

[76] Recent Quebec cases confirm this approach. In *Lexus Maritime, supra*, at para. 19, the Quebec Court of Appeal held that [TRANSLATION] ". . . if no clear impression emerges tending towards one single foreign forum, the court should accordingly refuse to decline jurisdiction particularly where the connecting factors are questionable" (footnotes omitted [in opinion]) (cited in *Matrox Graphics Inc. v. Ingram Micro Inc.*, Sup. Ct. Montréal, No. 500-05-066637-016, November 28, 2001, AZ-50116899, J.E. 2002-688, at para. 23, *per* Morneau J.; *Consortium de la nutrition ltée v. Aliments Parmalat inc.*, [2001] Q.J. No. 104 (QL) (Sup. Ct.), at para. 18, *per* Tessier J.; and *Encaissement de chèque Montréal ltée v. Softwise inc.*, [1999] Q.J. No. 200 (QL) (Sup. Ct.), at para. 34, *per* Grenier J.).

[77] In addition, it should be kept in mind that, when applying art. 3135, the motions or trial judge's discretion to decline to hear the action on the basis of *forum non conveniens* is only to be exercised exceptionally. This exceptional character is reflected in the wording of art. 3135 and is also emphasized in the case law. In particular, in *Amchem, supra*, at p. 931, Sopinka J. noted that the first step of the test for an anti-suit injunction set out in *SNI Aérospatiale v. Lee Kui Jak*, [1987] 3 All E.R. 510 (P.C.), which involves asking whether the domestic forum is the natural forum, should be modified when a stay of proceedings is requested on the ground of *forum non conveniens*:

> Under this test [the test for *forum non conveniens*] the court must determine whether there is another forum that is clearly more appropriate. The result of this change in stay applications is that where there is no one forum that is the most appropriate, *the domestic forum wins out by default and refuses a stay, provided it is an appropriate forum.* (Emphasis added [in judgment].)

[78] Sopinka J.'s reasoning is consistent with the approach taken by the Quebec courts in the case *Lamborghini (Canada) Inc. v. Automobili Lamborghini S.P.A.*, [1997] R.J.Q. 58, at pp. 67–68, where the Court of Appeal described the nature of art. 3135:

> [TRANSLATION] Article 3135 C.C.Q. does not establish a sovereign rule of judicial discretion, which continues to be subordinate to the rules of jurisdiction established by the law and collateral to it.

However, the mechanism established in article 3135 remains flexible. It does not specifically set out immutable or limiting factors, but allows the court to consider the circumstances. If it concludes that the defendant has clearly established that the circumstances of the case as a whole allow the court to find that a foreign court or a court in another province is a more appropriate forum, the court may stay the proceeding in Quebec by deciding that it must instead be commenced or continued outside the territorial jurisdiction of the Quebec courts. The application of article 3135 C.C.Q. presupposes that the defendant has been properly brought before the Quebec forum. Once that has been done, the article gives the defendant an opportunity to avoid this "natural" jurisdiction, established in accordance with the legal connecting factors, by requesting that the case be referred to a foreign court, if the defendant can show that that court is the most appropriate. However, the application of the article does not permit the creation of a jurisdiction that would not otherwise exist, but instead creates selective restrictions on the jurisdiction resulting from the application of the connecting factors recognized by the law. [Citation omitted.]

[79] Academic commentary also shares the view that the doctrine of *forum non conveniens* is to be applied exceptionally. In "Interpreting the rules of private international law", *supra*, at p. 55, Talpis and Castel remark that:

> *The starting point should be the principle that the plaintiff's choice of forum should only be declined exceptionally*, when the defendant would be exposed to great injustice as a result. Quebec courts must find a balance between the advantages and disadvantages for the parties when the plaintiff chooses a Quebec court. They should only decline jurisdiction if the balance tilts toward the foreign court. (Emphasis added [in judgment].)

[80] In this case, I see no error on the part of the motions judge and therefore no reason to disturb her exercise of discretion. As Binnie J. observed in *Holt Cargo*, *supra*, at para. 98:

> In summary, the trial judge considered the relevant factors in reaching his conclusion that the Federal Court was the appropriate forum to resolve the respondent's claim. He committed no error of principle and did not refuse "to take into consideration a major element for the determination of the case": *Harelkin v. University of Regina*, [1979] 2 S.C.R. 561, at p. 588; *Friends of the Oldman River Society v. Canada (Minister of Transport)*, [1992] 1 S.C.R. 3, at p. 77. In the absence of error, we are not entitled to interfere with the exercise of his discretion.

. . . .

[81] I emphasize the exceptional quality of the *forum non conveniens* doctrine. As the authors J. A. Talpis and S. L. Kath point out in their article "The Exceptional as Commonplace in Quebec *Forum Non Conveniens* Law: *Cambior*, a Case in Point" (2000), 34 *R.J.T.* 761, by ignoring the "exceptionality" requirement, courts may unwittingly create uncertainty and inefficiency in cases involving private international law issues, resulting in greater costs for the parties. In my opinion, such uncertainty could seriously compromise the principles of comity, order and fairness, the very principles the rules of private international law are set out to promote.

[82] *Given the exceptional nature of the doctrine as reflected in the wording of art. 3135 C.C.Q., and in light of the fact that discretionary decisions are not easily disturbed, in my view, the appellants have not established the conditions that would have compelled the Quebec Superior Court to decline jurisdiction on the basis of forum non conveniens.* [Emphasis added.]

CLUB RESORTS LTD. v. VAN BREDA
2012 SCC 17, [2012] 1 S.C.R. 572

Recall that this decision involved two separate cases in which the plaintiffs had suffered injuries while on vacation in Cuba. Among the parties joined as defendants was the appellant, Club Resorts Ltd., a Cayman Islands corporation that managed the two hotels where the accidents occurred. Club Resorts sought dismissal first, as we have seen, arguing that the Ontario courts lacked jurisdiction. The alternative argument for dismissal was that a Cuban court would be a more appropriate forum on the basis of the doctrine of *forum non conveniens*. In both cases, the motion judges held that the Ontario court was clearly a more appropriate forum. The two cases were heard together in the Court of Appeal. The appeals were both dismissed. Affirming the Ontario Court of Appeals, the Supreme Court of Canada further defined the applicable standards in Canada of the *forum non conveniens* doctrine. In the words of Justice LeBel:

[99] Doctrine of *Forum Non Conveniens* and the Exercise of Jurisdiction

[101] As I mentioned above, a clear distinction must be drawn between the existence and the exercise of jurisdiction. This distinction is central both to the resolution of issues related to jurisdiction over the claim and to the proper application of the doctrine of *forum non conveniens*. *Forum non conveniens* comes into play when jurisdiction is established. It has no relevance to the jurisdictional analysis itself.

[102] Once jurisdiction is established, if the defendant does not raise further objections, the litigation proceeds before the court of the forum. The court cannot decline to exercise its jurisdiction unless the defendant invokes *forum non conveniens*. The decision to raise this doctrine rests with the parties, not with the court seized of the claim.

[103] If a defendant raises an issue of *forum non conveniens*, the burden is on him or her to show why the court should decline to exercise its jurisdiction and displace the forum chosen by the plaintiff. The defendant must identify another forum that has an appropriate connection under the conflicts rules and that should be allowed to dispose of the action. *The defendant must show, using the same analytical approach the court followed to establish the existence of a real and substantial connection with the local forum, what connections this alternative forum has with the subject matter of the litigation. Finally, the party asking for a stay on the basis of forum non conveniens must demonstrate why the proposed alternative forum should be preferred and considered to be more appropriate.* [Emphasis added.]

[104] This Court reviewed and structured the method of application of the doctrine of *forum non conveniens* in *Amchem*. It built on the existing jurisprudence, and in particular on the judgment of the House of Lords in *Spiliada Maritime Corp. v. Cansulex Ltd.*, [1987] 1 A.C. 460. The doctrine tempers the consequences of a strict application of the rules governing the assumption of jurisdiction. As those rules are, at their core, based on establishing the existence of objective factual connections, their use by the

courts might give rise to concerns about their potential rigidity and lack of consideration for the actual circumstances of the parties. When it is invoked, the doctrine of *forum non conveniens* requires a court to go beyond a strict application of the test governing the recognition and assumption of jurisdiction. It is based on a recognition that a common law court retains a residual power to decline to exercise its jurisdiction in appropriate, but limited, circumstances in order to assure fairness to the parties and the efficient resolution of the dispute. The court can stay proceedings brought before it on the basis of the doctrine.

[105] A party applying for a stay on the basis of *forum non conveniens* may raise diverse facts, considerations and concerns. Despite some legislative attempts to draw up exhaustive lists, I doubt that it will ever be possible to do so. In essence, the doctrine focusses on the contexts of individual cases, and its purpose is to ensure that both parties are treated fairly and that the process for resolving their litigation is efficient. For example, § 11(1) of the *CJPTA* provides that a court may decline to exercise its jurisdiction if, "[a]fter considering the interests of the parties to a proceeding and the ends of justice", it finds that a court of another state is a more appropriate forum to hear the case. Section 11(2) then provides that the court must consider the "circumstances relevant to the proceeding". To illustrate those circumstances, it contains a non-exhaustive list of factors:

(a) the comparative convenience and expense for the parties to the proceeding and for their witnesses, in litigating in the court or in any alternative forum;

(b) the law to be applied to issues in the proceeding;

(c) the desirability of avoiding multiplicity of legal proceedings;

(d) the desirability of avoiding conflicting decisions in different courts;

(e) the enforcement of an eventual judgment; and

(f) the fair and efficient working of the Canadian legal system as a whole. [§ 11(2)]

[106] British Columbia's *Court Jurisdiction and Proceedings Transfer Act*, which is based on the *CJPTA*, contains an identical provision — § 11 — on *forum non conveniens*. In *Teck Cominco Metals Ltd. v. Lloyd's Underwriters*, 2009 SCC 11, [2009] 1 S.C.R. 321, at para. 22, this Court stated that § 11 of the British Columbia statute was intended to "codify" *forum non conveniens*. Article 3135 of the *Civil Code of Quebec* provides that *forum non conveniens* forms part of the private international law of Quebec, but it does not contain a description of the factors that are to govern the application of the doctrine in Quebec law. The courts are left with the tasks of developing an approach to applying it and of identifying the relevant considerations.

[107] Quebec's courts have adopted an approach that, although basically identical to that of the common law courts, is subject to the indication in art. 3135 that *forum non conveniens* is an exceptional recourse. A good example of this can be found in the judgment of the Quebec Court of Appeal in

Oppenheim forfait GMBH v. Lexus maritime inc., 1998 CanLII 13001, in which an action brought in Quebec was stayed in favour of a German court on the basis of *forum non conveniens*. Pidgeon J.A. emphasized the wide-ranging and contextual nature of a *forum non conveniens* analysis. The judge might consider such factors as the domicile of the parties, the locations of witnesses and of pieces of evidence, parallel proceedings, juridical advantage, the interests of both parties and the interests of justice (pp. 7–8; see also *Spar Aerospace*, at para. 71; J. A. Talpis with the collaboration of S. L. Kath, "*If I am from Grand-Mère, Why Am I Being Sued in Texas?" Responding to Inappropriate Foreign Jurisdiction in Quebec-United States Crossborder Litigation* (2001), at pp. 44–45).

[108] Regarding the burden imposed on a party asking for a stay on the basis of *forum non conveniens*, the courts have held that the party must show that the alternative forum is clearly more appropriate. The expression "clearly more appropriate" is well established. It was used in *Spiliada* and *Amchem*. On the other hand, it has not always been used consistently and does not appear in the *CJPTA* or any of the statutes based on the *CJPTA*, which simply require that the party moving for a stay establish that there is a "more appropriate forum" elsewhere. Nor is this expression found in art. 3135 of the *Civil Code of Quebec*, which refers instead to the exceptional nature of the power conferred on a Quebec authority to decline jurisdiction: ". . . it may exceptionally and on an application by a party, decline jurisdiction . . . ."

[109] The use of the words "clearly" and "exceptionally" should be interpreted as an acknowledgment that the normal state of affairs is that jurisdiction should be exercised once it is properly assumed. The burden is on a party who seeks to depart from this normal state of affairs to show that, in light of the characteristics of the alternative forum, it would be fairer and more efficient to do so and that the plaintiff should be denied the benefits of his or her decision to select a forum that is appropriate under the conflicts rules. The court should not exercise its discretion in favour of a stay solely because it finds, once all relevant concerns and factors are weighed, that comparable forums exist in other provinces or states. It is not a matter of flipping a coin. A court hearing an application for a stay of proceedings must find that a forum exists that is in a better position to dispose fairly and efficiently of the litigation. But the court must be mindful that jurisdiction may sometimes be established on a rather low threshold under the conflicts rules. *Forum non conveniens* may play an important role in identifying a forum that is clearly more appropriate for disposing of the litigation and thus ensuring fairness to the parties and a more efficient process for resolving their dispute.

[110] As I mentioned above, the factors that a court may consider in deciding whether to apply *forum non conveniens* may vary depending on the context and might include the locations of parties and witnesses, the cost of transferring the case to another jurisdiction or of declining the stay, the impact of a transfer on the conduct of the litigation or on related or parallel proceedings, the possibility of conflicting judgments, problems

related to the recognition and enforcement of judgments, and the relative strengths of the connections of the two parties.

[111] Loss of juridical advantage is a difficulty that could arise should the action be stayed in favour of a court of another province or country. This difficulty is aggravated by the possible conflation of two different issues: the impact of the procedural rules governing the conduct of the trial, and the proper substantive law for the legal situation, that is, in the context of these two appeals, the proper law of the tort. In considering the question of juridical advantage, a court may be too quick to assume that the proper law naturally flows from the assumption of jurisdiction. However, the governing law of the tort is not necessarily the domestic law of the forum. This may be so in many cases, but not always. In any event, if parties plead the foreign law, the court may well need to consider the issue and determine whether it should apply that law once it is proved. Even if the jurisdictional analysis leads to the conclusion that courts in different states might properly entertain an action, the same substantive law may apply, at least in theory, wherever the case is heard.

[112] A further issue that does not arise in these appeals is whether it is legitimate to use this factor of loss of juridical advantage within the Canadian federation. To use it too extensively in the *forum non conveniens* analysis might be inconsistent with the spirit and intent of *Morguard* and *Hunt*, as the Court sought in those cases to establish comity and a strong attitude of respect in relations between the different provinces, courts and legal systems of Canada. Differences should not be viewed instinctively as signs of disadvantage or inferiority. This factor obviously becomes more relevant where foreign countries are involved, but even then, comity and an attitude of respect for the courts and legal systems of other countries, many of which have the same basic values as us, may be in order. In the end, the court must engage in a contextual analysis, but refrain from leaning too instinctively in favour of its own jurisdiction. At this point, the decision falls within the reasoned discretion of the trial court. The exercise of discretion will be entitled to deference from higher courts, absent an error of law or a clear and serious error in the determination of relevant facts, which, as I emphasized above, takes place at an interlocutory or preliminary stage. I will now consider whether the Ontario courts . . . should have declined to exercise it on the basis of *forum non conveniens*.

He answered in the negative — that the Ontario courts properly refused to decline to adjudicate the case.

QUESTIONS

1. Is the Supreme Court of Canada in the three cases extracted above determining and applying provincial law, national law, or Canadian "constitutional" law? Did it matter that Quebec is a civil law jurisdiction?

> 2. Does the Court appear to treat the application of the *forum non conveniens* doctrine differently in the context of the appeal from the appellate court in Quebec than from the appellate court in British Colombia or Ontario, both English-speaking, common law provinces. If so, is such differentiation justified?
>
> 3. In what respects does Canadian law differ from the United States in the application of the *forum non conveniens* doctrine. If any, how salient are these differences? Would, in your view, the Supreme Court of Canada have decided differently any of the U.S. cases extracted above. If so, in what respects?

B. Anti-Suit Injunctions

AMCHEM PRODUCTS INC. v. BRITISH COLUMBIA (WORKERS' COMPENSATION BOARD)
[1993] 1 S.C.R. 897

Anti-Suit Injunctions

England

[40] The English courts have exercised jurisdiction to restrain proceedings in a foreign court and to stay domestic actions since 1821. Leach V.C. in *Bushby v. Munday*, supra, at p. 307 and p. 913, stated the rule as follows:

> Where parties Defendants are resident in England, and brought by *subpoena* here, this Court has full authority to act upon them personally with respect to the subject of the suit, as the ends of justice require; and with that view, to order them to take, or to omit to take, any steps and proceedings in any other Court of Justice, whether in this country, or in a foreign country.

The sentiment expressed at that time was that the relief sought, whether an injunction or a stay, operated in personam and was not intended to interfere with the other court. Thus viewed, the question to be determined was whether the ends of justice required the issuance of an injunction or a stay. In deciding that an injunction should be granted in *Bushby v. Munday*, supra, the Vice-Chancellor made findings that the English Court was a more convenient jurisdiction; and, that the proceedings in Scotland, due to procedural law, were less likely to elicit the truth. Leach V.C. concluded (at p. 308 and p. 913) that the English court should pursue its superior means for determining both law and fact.

[41] The same test evolved for anti-suit injunctions and stays, based on the judgment of Scott L.J. in *St. Pierre v. South American Stores (Gath & Chaves) Ltd.*, *supra*. Where these requirements were met, the court would exercise its discretion in granting the stay or enjoining the foreign proceedings. The principles governing the issuance of a stay and an anti-suit injunction remained identical until the House

of Lords' decision in *The Atlantic Star, supra*, when the English jurisprudence regarding stays of domestic proceedings underwent the first of the modifications to which I have referred. In *The Atlantic Star*, the House of Lords held that the words "oppressive" and "vexatious" should be interpreted liberally. After the decision in *The Atlantic Star*, it was unclear whether the principles governing the issuance of an anti-suit injunction remained the same or whether they evolved along with the principles governing a stay of domestic proceedings. The House of Lords directly considered this question in *Castanho v. Brown & Root (U.K.) Ltd., supra*, which involved an application for an anti-suit injunction. Lord Scarman pronounced, at p. 574, that "the principle is the same whether the remedy sought is a stay of English proceedings or a restraint upon foreign proceedings."Lord Scarman approved the reformulation of the principles as set out by Lord Diplock in *The Atlantic Star, supra*, and concluded at p. 575, that:

> . . . to justify the grant of an injunction the defendants must show: (*a*) that the English court is a forum to whose jurisdiction they are amenable in which justice can be done at substantially less inconvenience and expense, *and* (*b*) the injunction must not deprive the plaintiff of a legitimate personal or juridical advantage which would be available to him if he invoked the American jurisdiction. (Emphasis in the original [in opinion].)

Lord Scarman emphasized that the "critical equation" in an application for a stay or an anti-suit injunction was between the advantage to the plaintiff and the disadvantage to the defendants. For the purposes of this determination, the prospect of higher damages in the foreign jurisdiction was a legitimate juridical advantage for a plaintiff. The House of Lords applied the law as set out in *Castanho, supra* in two succeeding cases involving applications to enjoin foreign proceedings (*British Airways Board v. Laker Airways Ltd.*, [1985] A.C. 58, and *South Carolina Insurance Co. v. Assurantie Maatschappij "De Zeven). Provincien" N.V.*, [1987] A.C. 24.

[42] This test, in so far as it regarded anti-suit injunctions, did not withstand the scrutiny of the Judicial Committee of the Privy Council. In 1987, the Privy Council overturned the liberalized principles that the House of Lords enunciated. The definitive statement of law was pronounced in *SNI, supra*: an anti-suit injunction will not be issued by an English court unless it is shown that the foreign proceedings will be oppressive or vexatious. It was made clear that the traditional principles as summarized in *St. Pierre v. South American Stores (Gath & Chaves) Ltd., supra*, were to govern applications to restrain foreign proceedings. Thus, the liberalized principles formulated in *Spiliada, supra*, in the context of an application for a stay of domestic proceedings were not to apply to anti-suit injunctions because to do so would be inconsistent with the principles of comity and would disregard the fundamental requirement that an injunction will only be available where it is required to address the ends of justice.

[43] In coming to his conclusion on the law in [SNI *Aérospatiale v. Lee Kui Jak*, [1987] 3 All E.R. 510 (P.C.)] , Lord Goff considered the long history of English law as well as American and Scottish authorities. He stated, at p. 519 that the following basic principles were beyond dispute:

> First, the jurisdiction is to be exercised when the "ends of justice" require it . . . Second, where the court decides to grant an injunction restraining proceedings in a foreign court, its order is directed not against the foreign court but against the parties so proceeding or threatening to proceed. . . . Third, it follows that an injunction will only be issued restraining a party who is amenable to the jurisdiction of the court against whom an injunction will be an effective remedy . . . Fourth, it has been emphasised on many occasions that, since such an order indirectly affects the foreign court, the jurisdiction is one which must be exercised with caution . . . . (Cites omitted [in judgment].)

In considering the above principles, Lord Goff set out the following test (*SNI, supra*, at p. 522):

> In the opinion of their Lordships, in a case such as the present where a remedy for a particular wrong is available both in the English (or, as here, the Brunei) court and in a foreign court, the English (or Brunei) court will, generally speaking, only restrain the plaintiff from pursuing proceedings in the foreign court if such pursuit would be vexatious or oppressive. This presupposes that, as general rule, the English or Brunei court must conclude that it provides the natural forum for the trial of the action, and further, since the court is concerned with the ends of justice, that account must be taken not only of injustice to the defendant if the plaintiff is allowed to pursue the foreign proceedings, but also of injustice to the plaintiff if he is not allowed to do so. So, as a general rule, the court will not grant an injunction if, by doing so, it will deprive the plaintiff of advantages in the foreign forum of which it would be unjust to deprive him.

This analysis represents the current test for issuance of an anti-suit injunction in England.

The United States of America [Omitted]

Australia [Omitted]

Canada

[50] Canadian jurisprudence is not widely developed on this subject matter. Even the early cases, however, admonished that the power to restrain foreign proceedings should be exercised with great caution and that the strict purpose of such injunctions was to prevent the abuse of the courts by vexatious actions. There is no decision of this Court on the point.

. . . .

[54] No consistent approach appears to emerge from these cases other than recognition of the principle that great caution should be exercised when invoking the power to enjoin foreign litigation.

The Test

[55] In my view, the principles outlined in *SNI* should be the foundation for the test applied in our courts. These principles should be applied having due regard for the Canadian approach to private international law. This approach is exemplified by the judgment of this Court in *Morguard, supra*, in which La Forest J. stressed the role of comity and the need to adjust its content in light of the changing world order. I now turn to the formulation of the test in light of the foregoing.

[56] First, it is useful to discuss some preliminary aspects of procedure with respect to anti-suit injunctions. As a general rule, the domestic court should not entertain an application for an injunction if there is no foreign proceeding pending. . . . In order to resort to this special remedy consonant with the principles of comity, it is preferable that the decision of the foreign court not be pre-empted until a proceeding has been launched in that court and the applicant for an injunction in the domestic court has sought from the foreign court a stay or other termination of the foreign proceedings and failed.

[57] *If the foreign court stays or dismisses the action there, the problem is solved. If not, the domestic court must proceed to entertain the application for an injunction but only if it is alleged to be the most appropriate forum and is potentially an appropriate forum. In any case in which an action has been commenced in the domestic forum, it can be expected that the domestic forum is being put forward as an appropriate forum by the plaintiff. In resisting a stay, the plaintiff will also contend that there is no other forum which is clearly more appropriate and that, therefore, the defendant has not complied with the test which I have outlined above. If no action has been commenced in the domestic forum, it has no juridical basis for entertaining an application for an injunction unless it is contended by the applicant that the action should have been commenced in the domestic forum as the more appropriate place of trial and it is potentially an appropriate forum.* [Emphasis added.]

[58] *The first step in applying the SNI analysis is to determine whether the domestic forum is the natural forum, that is the forum that on the basis of relevant factors has the closest connection with the action and the parties. I would modify this slightly to conform with the test relating to forum non conveniens. Under this test the court must determine whether there is another forum that is clearly more appropriate. The result of this change in stay applications is that where there is no one forum that is the most appropriate, the domestic forum wins out by default and refuses a stay, provided it is an appropriate forum. In this step of the analysis, the domestic court as a matter of comity must take cognizance of the fact that the foreign court has assumed jurisdiction. If, applying the principles relating to forum non conveniens outlined above, the foreign court could reasonably have concluded that there was no alternative forum that was clearly more appropriate, the domestic court should respect that decision and the application should be dismissed. When there is a genuine disagreement between the courts of our country and another, the courts of this country should not arrogate to themselves the decision for both jurisdictions. In most cases it will appear from the decision of the foreign court whether it acted on principles similar to those that obtain here, but,*

if not, then the domestic court must consider whether the result is consistent with those principles. [Emphasis added.]

[59] *In a case in which the domestic court concludes that the foreign court assumed jurisdiction on a basis that is inconsistent with principles relating to forum non conveniens and that the foreign court's conclusion could not reasonably have been reached had it applied those principles, it must go then to the second step of the SNI test.* [Emphasis added.] I prefer the initial formulation of that step without reference to the terms "oppressive or vexatious". . . .

[60] When will it be unjust to deprive the plaintiff in the foreign proceeding of some personal or juridical advantage that is available in that forum? I have already stated that the importance of the loss of advantage cannot be assessed in isolation. The loss of juridical or other advantage must be considered in the context of the other factors. The appropriate inquiry is whether it is unjust to deprive the party seeking to litigate in the foreign jurisdiction of a judicial or other advantage, having regard to the extent that the party and the facts are connected to that forum based on the factors which I have already discussed. A party can have no reasonable expectation of advantages available in a jurisdiction with which the party and the subject matter of the litigation has little or no connection. Any loss of advantage to the foreign plaintiff must be weighed as against the loss of advantage, if any, to the defendant in the foreign jurisdiction if the action is tried there rather than in the domestic forum . . . . Nonetheless, loss of personal advantage might amount to an injustice if, for example, an individual party is required to litigate in a distant forum with which he or she has no connection. I prefer to leave other possible sources of injustice to be dealt with as they arise.

[61] *The result of the application of these principles is that when a foreign court assumes jurisdiction on a basis that generally conforms to our rule of private international law relating to the forum non conveniens, that decision will be respected and a Canadian court will not purport to make the decision for the foreign court. The policy of our courts with respect to comity demands no less. If, however, a foreign court assumes jurisdiction on a basis that is inconsistent with our rules of private international law and an injustice results to a litigant or "would-be" litigant in our courts, then the assumption of jurisdiction is inequitable and the party invoking the foreign jurisdiction can be restrained. The foreign court, not having, itself, observed the rules of comity, cannot expect its decision to be respected on the basis of comity.* [Emphasis added.]

Application of Principles to this Appeal

[62] I would allow the appeal on the ground that Esson C.J.S.C. (the trial judge) erred in his application of both branches of the rule relating to anti-suit injunctions which I have outlined above. First, with respect to the choice of forum, the first step in the test, having concluded that the Texas court did not apply a *forum non conveniens* test, he failed to consider whether, notwithstanding that fact, the decision was consistent with applicable principles of private international law. Second, although he was of the view that the alleged loss of juridical advantage had little substance, he decided that the Texas proceedings were oppressive. In respect of both branches of the rule he gave undue weight to the absence of a *forum non*

conveniens rule in Texas and to the anti-anti-suit injunction granted by the Texas court.

. . . .

[67] I have concluded therefore that the learned trial judge erred in the exercise of his discretion in respect of the matters that I have outlined above. The court of appeal dismissed the appeal essentially for the reason that in their view the trial judge had properly exercised his discretion and that, therefore, the court of appeal was not permitted to interfere. Many of the principles applied by the trial judge were affirmed by Hollinrake J.A. with whom McEachern C.J.B.C. and Taggart J.A. agreed. Without intending any disrespect to those reasons, it is not necessary to repeat what I have said with respect to those principles. One matter requires special comment. I do not agree that because an anti-suit injunction does not directly operate on the foreign court but in personam on the plaintiff in that court, comity is not involved. The reaction of Wilkey J. in *Laker, supra,* and, indeed, of Esson C.J.S.C. in this case, demonstrates that, whatever the form of restraint, the court whose proceeding is effectively restrained regards it as an interference with its jurisdiction.

Disposition

[68] I would allow the appeal, set aside the orders below and dismiss the application for an injunction. I see no basis for differentiating between T & N and the other respondents. If the action is to proceed in Texas, it is a proper party to the litigation. It would make little sense to require the claimants to pursue a separate action against one company in British Columbia. The appellants are entitled to costs both here and in the courts below.

Appeal allowed.

QUESTIONS

1. In what respects are the Canadian rules and standards for anti-suit injunctions articulated in *Amchem Products* applicable as national or provincial law? Are they equally applicable in cases subject to Quebec law? How do they differ from those applied in the United States?

2. Does it matter whether the parallel action abroad was filed first, or, if not, is pending?

3. To what extent are concerns for "international comity" relevant under Canadian law?

IV. CIVIL LAW APPROACHES

The rules codified in article 3135 the Civil Code of Quebec as well as the assumption that judges in Quebec have the "equitable" authority to issue anti-suit injunctions are exceptional. In civil law jurisdictions, as noted at the outset, judges generally lack the discretionary authority of their common law counterparts to refrain from exercising jurisdiction, staying proceedings, or issuing anti-suit injunctions in the event of pending or potential parallel lawsuits in other jurisdictions. Under prevailing *lis pendens* rules, particularly in the European Union, the court first "seized" of a case involving the same subject-matter and parties, acquires, in effect, exclusive jurisdiction. In Japan, however, as we have already observed, parallel litigation is a common feature of transnational litigation in practice. The question remains as to whether, however, resort to *jōri*, especially under the 2011 amendment, may allow courts to achieve outcomes that are comparable to common law *forum non conveniens* or European Union *lis pendens* rules.

A. Japan

MUKODA v. THE BOEING CO.
Tokyo District Court Judgment of 20 June 1986
Hanrei Times (No. 604) 138 (1986)
[English translation in 31 JAIL 216 (1988)]

This action arose from the fatal 1981 Far Eastern Air Transport (FEAT) accident in Taiwan that resulted in the U.S. lawsuits that were dismissed, as previously discussed, on *forum non conveniens* grounds in *Nai-Cho v. The Boeing Company*. Among the deceased Japanese passengers was Mukoda Kuniko, a well-known author. Her successors joined other Japanese plaintiffs is an action filed in the Tokyo District Court several years after the U.S. suits. Named defendants were The Boeing Company and United Airlines. The claim against Boeing was based on an allegation that the accident has been caused by a sidewall frame defect and a bonded skin panel defect in the 737 aircraft that it had designed and manufactured. The plaintiffs also alleged that although Boeing had become aware of the defects several years after manufacturing the aircraft, the company merely distributed service bulletins about the defects and failed to recall the aircraft and repair the defects or to take any other suitable measures. United Airline's liability was based on the plaintiffs' allegations that, first, United sold the aircraft to FEAT without correcting the defects of which they had been informed by Boeing service bulletins. United thus failed to ensure that the aircraft was airworthy at the time of its sale to FEAT. The plaintiffs also contended that United had failed to inform FEAT about the defect described in the service bulletins and thus to advise it to make the necessary repairs. Defendants countered that the Japanese court did not have or should not assume jurisdiction. The Tokyo District Court agreed and dismissed the action.

DISPOSITION
(*shūbun*)

All of the plaintiffs' claims are dismissed.

REASONS
(*riyū*)

1. The problem posed in this case is whether [under the described circumstances of the accident] the courts in our country have adjudicatory jurisdiction.

2. With respect to international adjudicatory jurisdiction in civil suits such as this in which foreign corporations have been made defendants, it is reasonable in the absence of any relevant statute that directly provides for international adjudicatory jurisdiction as well as any relevant treaties or well-established generally recognized established principles of international law, to decide the matter in accordance with the principles of *jōri*, which require fairness between the parties and just and prompt administration of justice. If a forum for local territorial jurisdiction provided in the Code of Civil Procedure is located in Japan, it would accord with the principles of *jōri* to sustain the jurisdiction of our country's courts, unless, however, we find some special circumstances. Such special circumstances exist where, in light of the facts of the case, recognizing the adjudicatory jurisdiction of the courts of our country would contravene the notion of promoting fairness between the parties and just and prompt administration of justice.

3. We recognize first that the defendant United Airlines has a registered place of business in . . . Tokyo. Therefore, we can recognize its general forum under article 4 of the Code of Civil Procedure.

The claims against Boeing are joined in the action against United, for which general forum is located in Japan. In both actions, claims for the payment of damages are based on the same cause of action arising from the same accident. Therefore, a forum [in Japan] can be found based on joinder of claims under [current article 7] of the Code of Civil Procedure.

Furthermore, as the plaintiffs are domiciled in Japan, there is also room to find a forum as the place of performance under article 484 of Civil Code [which provides, in the absence of agreement or delivery of specific things, the place of performance is the domicile of the party to which performance is owed] and [current article 5(1)] of the Code of Civil Procedure.

4. We must now decide whether special circumstances exist that would cause the suit tried in our country contravene the notion of fairness between the parties and the fair and prompt administration of justice.

First, we shall examine [this question] from the perspective of fair and prompt administration of justice.

The defendant Boeing denies that a defect as alleged by the plaintiffs caused the accident in question. [Boeing] instead argues that if sidewall frame and bonded skin panel defects are deemed to be the cause of the accident, then the accident should be attributed to improper use, faulty inspection, and poor maintenance of the aircraft by FEAT. The defendant United similarly denies liability in this case. Consequently, what caused the accident; whether the alleged defects in the aircraft existed; and whether FEAT poorly maintained or otherwise failed to properly service the aircraft in question are clearly the most significant factual issues that have to be resolved in this lawsuit.

[In paragraphs numbered 1 through 8, the court proceeds to review the facts related to the accident that have been ascertained. The court then concludes:]

All of these important items of evidence and witnesses [. . .] necessary for finding the cause of the accident are presumably located in Taiwan. However, inasmuch as Japan currently has no regular diplomatic relations with Taiwan and that a Japanese court cannot obtain such evidence and witnesses by way of judicial assistance. Their unavailability makes it extremely difficult for a Japanese court to conduct a fair trial based on evidence as to whether the aircraft involved in the accident had some defect or whether such defect caused the accident.

Therefore, for this lawsuit to be heard and decided in our country seriously risks an outcome that would contravene the idea of promoting fairness in the administration of justice.

5. We next examine whether, in terms of fairness between the parties were we to decide that our country's courts lack jurisdiction, any factors would make it unjust to require the plaintiffs to litigate in Taiwan.

(1) First, we must determine whether the Taiwanese courts would dismiss the plaintiffs' claims on the ground that they lack jurisdiction.

On this point, . . . the U.S. District Court (N.D. California) dismissed the action brought by some of the plaintiffs in the case at bar on the ground of forum non convenience, holding that Taiwan is the proper forum. In its 'Opinion and Order' the U.S. court concluded char the Taiwanese court has jurisdiction over the case. In an affidavit as the defendants' expert, Dr. Chang Ven Chan, a practicing attorney and law professor in Taipei, stated: "A court in Taiwan would have adjudicatory jurisdiction over action pursuant to the Civil Code of Procedure of Taiwan inasmuch as the injury that resulted from the allegedly tortious conduct occurred in Taiwan."

We find no reason to question the above decision of the U.S. court or the expert's opinion on which that court relied. Moreover, the plaintiffs here offered no evidence to rebut the above decision or opinion. Therefore, we consider that decision to be just and proper.

(2) The plaintiffs maintain that they have expended so much money in litigating in the U.S. that they will run short of funds in order to litigate again in Taiwan. Evidence in support of this argument, however, is not offered. Furthermore, parties who lack the means to pay litigation costs may possibly obtain procedural relief in Taiwan from payment of the filing fee.

(3) With respect to the possibility that the Taiwanese court might dismiss the plaintiffs' claim on ground of prescription [statute of limitations], the defendants agree to waive prescription in Taiwan if the plaintiffs bring an action for damages relating to the accident in question in Taiwan within six months after their withdrawal from or the dismissal of the present action. No evidence is support of the possibility of the Taiwanese court's dismissal on ground of prescription, was offered.

At any rate, the passage of any period of prescription would be a consequence of the plaintiffs' having brought actions in the U.S. and in Japan. Accordingly, the plaintiffs should be responsible for that result.

(4) Were this action to be tried in a court in Taiwan, with respect to the question of whether the plaintiffs could enforce a judgment, the defendants stated in the U.S. proceeding: "If the action is adjudicated in a court in Taiwan, the defendants will abide by any judgment which may be handed down in favor the of plaintiffs by a court in Taiwan."

Consequently, we have no reason to question the efficacy of the possible judgment in Taiwan in favor of the plaintiffs.

Based on the facts stated above, to require the plaintiffs to bring an action in Taiwan for damages concerning the accident in question is not unreasonably unfair nor unjust. (The possibility that the plaintiffs' award for compensatory damages in Taiwan may be smaller in amount [than in Japan] should not be taken into consideration in determining the question of international jurisdiction to adjudicate.)

6. Based on the foregoing points, we determine that adjudicating the instant case in the court of our country would contravene the idea of promoting fairness in the administration of justice. On the other hand, in requiring the plaintiffs to bring an action for damages in Taiwan, we find no factor that would unreasonably impede impartiality between the parties. Thus we find in this case such special circumstances that make the assertion of the Japanese Court's jurisdiction unreasonable.

7. In consideration of the above, we find it legally impermissible to accept jurisdiction to adjudicate the plaintiffs' claims in the courts of our country and therefore they must be dismissed . . . accordingly we render the judgment as stated above.

JUDGE SHŪICHI YAZAKI
JUDGE KŌICHI KITAZAWA
JUDGE MASANORI TSUZUKI

NOTE AND QUESTIONS

The decision in the *Mukoda* case was quite exceptional at the time of the decision. The court recognized its adjudicatory jurisdiction in Japan under the Code of Civil Procedure. Thus to require the Japanese successors of the 1981 Far Eastern Air Transport accident in Taiwan to adjudicate their claims against United Airlines and The Boeing Company in Taiwan required unprecedented justification under the principles of *jōri*. Not until the 1997 decision in *K.K. Family v. Miyhara*, excerpted below did the Supreme Court similarly resort to *jōri* to dismiss an action that was otherwise subject to its jurisdiction. As noted below, article 3-9 of the Code of Civil Procedure added under the 2011 amendment incorporates the *jōri* principles and expressly allows for such dismissals, codifying in effect the *Mukoda* decision.

How relevant was the decision of the U.S. Federal District Court in *Nai-Cho v. The Boeing Company* to this case? Were the facts identical?

> Would a U.S. court have necessarily applied the *forum non conveniens* doctrine had the U.S. suit been filed by the administrators of the estates of deceased U.S. nationals?

MASAKI BUSSAN K.K. v. NANKA SEIMEN COMPANY
Tokyo District Court Judgment of 29 January 1991
Hanrei jihō (No. 1390) 98 (1991)
[English translation: 35 JAIL 171 (1992)]

Masaki Bussan K.K., the plaintiff, is a Japanese corporation that manufactured and sold a noodle-making-machine to a U.S. firm that produced and sold noodles in California. Nanka Seimen Company, the defendant, is a California company that had acted as an intermediary without fee in transmitting to the buyer the estimated cost of the machine. The case arose after an employee of the California buyer seriously injured his left hand while operating the machine. In April 1988, the injured employee filed lawsuits in California against his employer and Masaki Bussan. In March 1989, he added Nanka Seimen as a defendant based on the firm's involvement in sale of the machine (the first U.S. suit). In June 1989, Nanka Seimen filed a second action in California against Masaki Bussan for indemnification of any damages it sustained as a result of the first U.S. suit. In response to the two California suits, in July 1989, Masaki Bussan filed two suits in Japan, one against the employee and the second against Nanka Seimen seeking declaratory judgments confirming Masaki Bussan lack of liability to each. The following extract is from the judgment of the second Japanese suit.

DISPOSITION
(*shūbun*)

1. This action is dismissed.
2. The costs shall be borne by the plaintiff.

FACTS AND REASONS
(*jijitsu oyobi riyū*)

II. Decision

We do not have any relevant domestic statutes or treaties providing for the international jurisdiction of the Japanese court in civil litigations where, a least one of the parties is a foreign corporation, as in this case. Nor have there been established any generally recognized principles of international law on this matter. Under these circumstances, it is reasonable to decide the jurisdiction in accordance with principles of justice such as the ideas of promoting fairness between the parties and equitable and prompt administration of justice. It would accord with the principles of justice to admit the international jurisdiction of the Japanese courts, when one of the local fora provided for in the Code of Civil Procedure (Articles 2, 4, 8, 15 and others) is found in Japan, unless we find exceptional circumstances. In examining for the existence of such exceptional circumstances, we have to consider whether or not the legislative reasons for the local fora in the Code of Civil Procedure are fit for the determination of the international jurisdiction under the present circumstances wherein international transports and trade have rapidly increased and many international civil disputes have occurred.

2. (a) In this case the defendant is found to be a foreign corporation without any offices or branches in Japan. Thus, there is no general forum of the defendant in Japan.

(b) Then, we will consider the application of the special forum provision providing for the place where the tortious act was committed [current article article 5(9)].

The legal character of the claim of the defendant for damages against the plaintiff is considered to be a kind of tort liability (strict liability) because it is related to a case of product liability in which gaining profit through the manufacture or sale of defective products is alleged.

The defendant alleged that the forum provision for tort claims neither should nor can be applied because the legal character of the claim was considered to be either management of affairs without a mandate [*jimu kanri*] (*negotiorum gestio*) or unjust enrichment [*futō rieki*]. Indeed, strictly investigated, it is difficult to deny the defendant's allegation, for both parties in this action are alleged to be suppliers of the defective product in question. The forum of the place where the tortious act was committed, however, is admitted not only because it makes it easy for victims to bring lawsuits but also because it makes it possible for the court to collect evidence easily and to proceed with the trial equitably and promptly. This claim was derived from products liability litigation in the United States and was closely connected with it. Such elements as the degree of negligence of the parties concerned in the product liability are inevitably to be considered in order to make a decision on the claim in this action. At least for the sake of collection of evidence and equitable and prompt administration of justice, it is appropriate to admit the jurisdiction at the place where the tortious act was committed. In addition, the term, a suit "concerning" a tort, as provided for in Article 15 of the Code of Civil Procedure is considered to include not only claims based upon the tort liability itself but also claims based upon liability substantially related to the tort liability.

Next, it is considered that the place of injurious act, as well as the place of damage, is included in "the place where the act was committed" (Article 15 (1)). According to the assertion of the defendant in the second U.S. suit, the defendant might suffer the damage because the defendant was sued in the first U.S. suit based upon the defects of the noodle-making-machine designed and manufactured by the plaintiff in Japan. In the case of product liability, the place where a defective product was manufactured is regarded as a kind of place of injurious act. Therefore, the Japanese courts have the jurisdiction in principle as the place of tortious act. Then, we proceed to examine whether or not there are in this case any exceptional circumstances that make the above conclusion against the principles of justice.

(2) If this court admits its jurisdiction, we will have to examine, among others, the merits of the product liability, and the right to indemnity. However, this claim is a conditional one that will become real only when the defendant is defeated by B in the first U.S. suit and pays the amount ordered. Leaving the question outstanding,

there is a possibility that the trial of this claim will be in vain. Because, if the defendant wins the first U.S. suit and the judgment become conclusive and final, the condition of this lawsuit that the defendant's claim will come into existence will never be fulfilled. And there is a great possibility of conflicts between two judgments owing, among others, to the differences between Japan and the United States in the choice of law rules and of the substantive law on product liability.

The reason why the plaintiff brought this suit in addition to his appearance in the second U.S. suit is not only that it was convenient for him to carry on the proceedings in Japan but also that it would be effective for preventing the plaintiff from executing in Japan the U.S. judgment to be rendered in the second U.S. suit. Because, the plaintiff is expected to win in the second U.S. suit owing to the general tendency in the United States to admit product liability widely. . . . Considering that there are wide differences of laws concerning product liability among jurisdictions, we cannot conclude it to be unlawful to bring a suit for a declaratory judgment of no liability in Japan in order to prevent a foreign judgment from being executed.

Nevertheless, if such suits were allowed unconditionally, the legislative reasons for the provision on the recognition of foreign judgments in the Code of Civil Procedure would be destroyed or narrowly limited. And it would be made difficult to remedy foreign victims substantively. . . . As a consequence any Japanese judgment would become in danger of not being recognized by foreign stares for lack of reciprocity. Therefore, it is reasonable to proceed with a trial in the United States in such a case as this, where the fulfillment of the prerequisite of the domestic claim depends on the conclusion of the first U.S. suit.

(3) Next, in this case, it is considered to be convenient to proceed with the trial on the plaintiffs claim in the United States, because the second U.S. suit in which the same claim is to be tried has already been brought in the United States and the proceedings thereof including the exchange of briefs and the collection of evidences has progressed considerably. . . .

In consideration that the present-day huge volume of international transportation and trade is accompanied by a lot of international civil disputes, we have to attach importance to the legislative reasons for the recognition of foreign judgments provided for in the Code of Civil Procedure and the avoidance of double examinations and conflicts of judgments. We should, on this account, decide which forum in the world is best for proceeding with the trial for each case. In this case, it is appropriate for the determination of the international jurisdiction to take account of the situation of the U.S. suits as one of the factors. . . .

(4) The plaintiffs claim in this case can be tried more conveniently in the United States, because most of the materials of evidence thereof are located in the United States.

(5) Finally, as noted previously, the plaintiff does not have any assets, branch, office or affiliated company in the United States, and neither does the defendant in Japan. Therefore, it would be a burden on each other to carry on the proceedings in the opponent's country. However, the plaintiff should be able to expect to be sued for product liability in the United States for the plaintiff had gained a profit through the export of its produces in the United States. On the other hand, . . . all that the

defendant did was to get the estimation of this machine from the plaintiff for the benefit of A, without receiving any fee. Therefore, it was natural that the defendant did not expect to be sued in Japan for product liability for this noodle-making-machine. Considering the above circumstances, it is unfair to make the defendant appear at the trial in Japan.

Consequently, we can admit the exceptional circumstances that make it against the principles of justice to admit the international jurisdiction of the Japanese courts.

Then, . . . we will consider the plaintiffs following allegation: even if the jurisdiction over this claim itself cannot be admitted, the Japanese courts should have the jurisdiction based upon the special forum for joinder of parties (Article 21) (2) and the principles of justice, because the Japanese courts have the jurisdiction over B, one of the defendants before the separation of the trial, based upon Article 15 and the principles of justice (the default judgment has been passed on December 1, 1989).

But, we have to distinguish this case from suits against joint tortfeasors (or against several produce liability debtors). The unification of judgments among the defendants is not so important in such a case as this, where one of product liability debtors brings suits against a victim and another product liability debtor, because the subject-matters are different from each other and unjust enrichment did not occur among the defendants. And, the international jurisdiction based upon that over the joinder of parties should be admitted only when the principles of justice such as the ideas of promoting fairness between parties and equitable and prompt administration of justice is secured adequately. Because, the burden on a defendant in such a case is generally heavier than the cases the jurisdiction based upon other jurisdictional rules. Thus, the defendant is forced to defend itself in an unexpected forum.

Accordingly, there are no circumstances as to admit the jurisdiction of the Japanese courts.

JUDGE IWAO ŌSAWA
JUDGE AKIHIRO DOI
JUDGE HIROAKI SAITŌ

QUESTIONS

1. On what grounds did the court in *Masaki Bussan K.K. v. Nanka Seimen Company* dismiss the suit? Does this case represent another "exceptional" example of the application of an analogous *forum non conveniens* approach? If not, how do the reasons of the court for dismissing the action here differ from those given by the court in *Mukoda?*

2. Would there be any basis for the trial court in California to dismiss the actions filed there either for lack of jurisdiction or *forum non conveniens?*

> 3. Under what conditions or assumptions would the parallel action in Japan benefit Masaki Bussan as plaintiff?
>
> 4. Had the court not dismissed the action, what trial strategies would the attorneys in the California suits have been likely to pursue?

K.K. FAMILY v. MIYAHARA
Supreme Court, 3d P.B., Judgment of 11 November 1997
51 Minshū (No. 10) 4055 (1997)
[Prominent Judgments of the Supreme Court; also translated in
41 JAIL 117 (1998)]

The plaintiff in this case was a small Japanese firm that had contracted with a Japanese expatriate, living in Frankfurt, Germany since the mid 1960s, to purchase used cars in Europe and arrange for them to be shipped to Japan for resale by the plaintiff. The plaintiff had deposited nearly 92 million yen (approximately 750,000 US dollars) with a German bank to be used by the defendant to cover the anticipated costs of the first several shipments. Subsequent doubts regarding the defendant's trustworthiness prompted the plaintiff to modify the arrangements to provide for payments by letter of credit to be made after the automobiles were purchased and shipped. The plaintiff demanded the return of all remaining funds — almost 25 million yen (approximately US $210,000). The defendant refused the request, prompting the plaintiff to sue for the funds in Japan. The 3rd Petty Bench of the Supreme Court upheld both lower court decisions dismissing the action for lack of adjudicatory jurisdiction.

DISPOSITION
(*shūbun*)

1. The *jōkoku* appeal in this case is dismissed.
3. The *jōkoku* appellant shall bear the litigation costs.

REASONS
(*riyū*)

Even in cases where the defendant is not domiciled in Japan, if the case has legal connection with Japan, there are instances where the jurisdiction of the Japanese court should be acknowledged. However, since there is no internationally recognized general rule as to the circumstances under which courts in Japan should have jurisdiction and since international customary law has not sufficiently developed in this regard, it is appropriate to decide on this matter in accordance with the principles of jōri, which require fairness between the parties and just and prompt administration of justice [citing *Gotō v. Malaysia Airlines*, (Sup. Ct., 2nd P.B., 1982)]. In principle, if one of the territorial jurisdictions as provided by the Code of Civil Procedure of Japan can be found in Japan, it is appropriate to subject the defendant to the jurisdiction of the Japanese court in an action brought to a Japanese court. However, if there are special circumstances where proceedings in Japan conflict with *jōri*, the principles of fairness between the parties and just and speedy adjudication, the jurisdiction of the Japanese court should be denied.

In the present case, the appellant company asserts that the governing law on the validity of the contract at issue is Japanese law, and the place of performance of obligation for the return of the entrusted money is in Japan where the creditor is domiciled and therefore, the international jurisdiction of the Japanese court should be acknowledged. However, according to the above-mentioned facts, the contract was concluded in Germany, the purpose of the contract is for the appellant to entrust various businesses in Germany to the appellee. While there is no explicit agreement in the contract on the choice of a *situs* within Japan to be the place of performance of obligation or the choice of Japanese law as governing law; it was beyond expectation of the appellee that a claim for the performance of obligation under the contract would be brought in a Japanese court. In addition, the appellee has had a basis of living and business in the Federal Republic of Germany for more than 20 years and the means of proof for defense, such as the documents explaining the circumstances of the purchase of the cars by the appellee, are concentrated in Germany. On the other hand, the appellant company is a company that imported cars from the Federal Republic of Germany and it cannot be said that initiating an action in Germany would be an excessive burden on the appellant company. Considering these circumstances, forcing the appellee to respond to the present litigation in a Japanese court would be against *jōri*, based upon the principles of fairness to the parties and just and speedy adjudication. Regardless of whether or not the governing law on the validity of the contract is Japanese law, there are special circumstances in the present case that the international jurisdiction of the Japanese court should be denied. Therefore, in conclusion, the judgment of the original instance court that denied international jurisdiction of the court is justifiable and not contrary to law, as argued by the appellant. The [appellant's] argument thus cannot be accepted. Therefore, the justices unanimously rule as stated in the text of the judgment in accordance with articles 401, 95 and 89 of the Code of Civil Procedure.

JUSTICE SHIGERU YAMAGUCHI
JUSTICE ITSUO SONOBE
JUSTICE HIDEO CHIKUSA
JUSTICE YUKINOBU OZAKI
JUSTICE TOSHIIDUMI MOTOHARA

QUESTIONS

1. What was the basis for adjudicatory jurisdiction over the defendant in this case? What basis did the Court appear to discount?

2. Compare the decision with the subsequent Tokyo High Court decision in *Nihon System Wear K.K. v. Kensuke Koo* (Tokyo High Ct., Mar. 24, 1999). What do you suppose were the "special circumstances" that the Supreme Court's 3rd Petty Bench considered significant to its decision?

3. How, in your opinion, would a case with similar facts be decided in the U.S. or in Canada (in either Quebec or an English-speaking province)? To what extent would the arguments on both sides differ?

NOTE AND QUESTION

The 2011 amendments of the 1996 Code of Civil Procedure include the following provision:

Article 3 9(Dismissal of Action under Special Circumstances)

Even where Japanese courts have jurisdiction over an action (except when the action has been brought on the basis of an exclusive jurisdiction agreement in favor of the Japanese courts), the court may dismiss whole or part of such action if, taking into account the nature of the case, the burden of the defendant to answer the claim, the location of evidence and any other factors, the court finds that there are special circumstances under which hearing and determining the case in Japan would impair fairness between the parties or hinder the proper and efficient conduct of hearing.

To what extent does this provision add to or change existing standards recognized by the courts for dismissing actions on the basis of special circumstances under which adjudicating the case would be unfair to a party or inefficient?

K.K. MIZUHO BANK v. U.S.O. CORPORATION AND MATSUDA

Tokyo District Court Judgment of 20 March 2007
Hanrei Jihō (No. 1974) 156 [2007]
[English translation in 2007 *Japanese Yearbook of International Law* 561]

In response to the suit filed in the U.S. District Court for the Northern District of Illinois, which was dismissed on the grounds of *forum non conveniens* and affirmed by the U.S. Court of Appeals for the Seventh Circuit (in the opinion by Judge Posner) extracted *infra*, the defendant Mizuho Bank, as noted by Judge Posner, filed a parallel suit in the Tokyo District Court for confirmation that no act constituting a tort, unjust enrichment, or breach of contract had been committed as asserted in the Illinois suit and that the bank had no liability in damages to U.S.O. Corporation. The defendants argued in response that the Japanese suit amounted to an abuse of rights or, in the alternative, a violation of the principle of good faith. In an interlocutory judgment, translated in part below, the Tokyo District Court rejected these arguments and allowed the suit to proceed.

REASONS
(*riyū*)

I. Concerning Adjudicatory Jurisdiction

. . . .

2. International Jurisdiction in this Case

(1) Even in the event the defendant is not domiciled in Japan, the international jurisdiction of Japanese courts should be affirmed if the case has a legal connection with Japan. With respect to the question of whether Japanese courts should exercise international jurisdiction, no internationally acknowledged general standard exists; nor is international customary law is sufficiently developed. It is appropriate therefore that such determination be made according to the principles of *jōri*, which require fairness between the parties and the just and prompt administration of justice [citing *Gotō v. Malaysia Airlines*, 35 Minshū (No. 7) 1224 (Sup. Ct., 2nd P.B., Oct. 16, 1981) and *Kōno v. Kōno*, 50 Minshū 1451 (Sup. Ct., 2nd P.B., June 21, 1996)]. Accordingly, in principle, if any of the fora provided in Japan's Code of Civil Procedure' are available in our country, it is appropriate that a defendant be subject to the jurisdiction of our country with regard to a suit filed in a court of our country, although it is also appropriate that the international adjudicatory jurisdiction of our country should be rejected if, under special circumstances, a adjudication in our country would violate the principles of fairness between the parties and of just and prompt administration of justice [citing *K.K. Family v. Miyahara* (Sup. Ct., 3nd P.B., Nov. 11, 1997), 51 (10) Minshū 4055 (1997].

(2) With Respect to the Adjudicatory Jurisdiction of Our Country:

A. Although U.S.O. Corporation is a foreign association established under the laws of the State of Delaware, its principal place of business in Japan is located (address omitted) in Tokyo's Shibuya Ward, and its representative [John Doe] is domiciled (address omitted) in Tokyo's Shibuya Ward. Thus . . . under article 4(1) and (5) of the Code of Civil Procedure, the court recognizes Tokyo, over which this court has jurisdiction, as the general forum of the defendant. . . .

B. The record shows that the business office of the second defendant, Matsuda, who has been subjected to these proceedings as the auditor in bankruptcy for representative [John Doe], is located (address omitted) in Tokyo's Chiyoda Ward. Therefore, pursuant to article 5 (5) of the Code of Civil Procedure, the Court recognizes Tokyo, over which this court has jurisdiction, as the second defendant's special forum. . . .

C. We now examine whether other bases exist for adjudicatory jurisdiction:

(a) With respect to the claim for confirmation of non-existence of liability for damages in tort—

The plaintiff's claim for confirmation of nonexistence of liability for damages is a claim for confirmation of nonexistence of liability for damages based on tort. "The place where the tort was committed" in article 5(9) of the Code of Civil Procedure refers to the place where the tortuous act occurred or the place where the injury was sustained. This should be considered to include a place where a part of the tortuous act occurred.

In this case, the first defendant, claiming liability for damages, has not made the cause of action clear. Therefore, it is impossible to conclude that the action amounting to tort has necessarily been specified. However, from the entirety of the pleadings, the tort asserted concerns the execution by the plaintiff bank of a security deposit established by the Industrial Bank of Japan.

According to the recognized facts, the security deposit was established in Tokyo, Japan, and the limited partnerships remitted dividends to an account belonging to the first defendant at the Tokyo branch of the Industrial Bank of Japan from an account held by the partnership at the same branch. Then, on 31 March 2003, the plaintiff, having succeeded the Industrial Bank of Japan, executed the security deposit with notice to Sunfoods because payment of a debt of Asahi Industrial due 30 December 2002 . . . was in arrears, and appropriated 809,344,919 Yen of those funds to the satisfaction of Asahi Industrial's debt. Therefore, pursuant to article 5(9) of the Code of Civil Procedure, it is appropriate that Tokyo, Japan, is the forum with regard to the place of tort with regard to [this] claim. . . .

(b) With respect to the claim for confirmation of non-existence of such an obligation duty—

The defendant U.S.O. has not made the cause of action clear regarding the basis of their claim . . . but from the entirety of the pleadings, the court can recognize a close relationship with the actions referred to above [the security deposit]. Therefore, under article 7 of the Code of Civil Procedure [on Joint Suits], the Court deems [the defendant U.S.O.] to be subject to the adjudicatory jurisdiction of the Tokyo District Court under the special forum rules of tort [citing *K.K. Tsuburaya Productions v. Chaiyo Film Co., Ltd*, 55 Minshū 727 (Sup. Ct., 2nd P.B., June 8, 2001)].

(c) Therefore, with respect to each of the claims made, the Court recognizes the adjudicatory jurisdiction of our country under the provisions of our Code of Civil Procedure.

(3) We next examine whether, because of special circumstances, adjudication in our country would violate the principles of fairness to the parties and of just and prompt administration of justice.

A. The defendants contend that a suit should be permitted in the country with adjudicatory jurisdiction in which the lawsuit can be pursued most effectively. However, according to the recognized facts [evidence omitted], although the defendant U.S.O. was established under the laws of the State of Delaware, U.S.A., the purpose was to hold shares of a limited partnership. It did not engage in any significant business activity in the United States. Moreover, the [John Doe and Richard Roe, the former and current representatives] of the defendant U.S.O. were domiciled in Japan. In addition, both the act of remittance of the dividend from the limited partnership, which constituted the security deposit in this case and the creation and performance of the security deposit in this case occurred in Japan. Furthermore, the related evidence, including testimony and documentary evidence, is located in Japan. Moreover, it is appropriate to recognize Japanese law as the applicable law.

For these reasons, the defendants' argument is without merit and cannot be adopted.

B. The defendants also offer the following arguments: Unless there are special circumstances if a judgment of a court of the United States may be recognized in Japan, subsequent pursuit of litigation in Japan should not be permitted. In this case, in view of subsections 1, 2 and 4 of article 118 of the Code of Civil Procedure [on recognition of foreign judgments], inasmuch as there do not appear to be any impediments thereto, the judgment of a United States court [in this case] is most likely to be recognized. The Court should also deny Japan's international jurisdiction over the plaintiff's suit inasmuch as considering the plaintiff filed this suit approximately eight months after the defendants filed the Illinois suit,

However, according to the recognized facts, the Illinois suit has not yet reached a hearing of merits and is at the stage of dispute over jurisdiction. . . . It is thus not possible to predict the outcome of that judgment with requisite certainty. Furthermore, the plaintiff did not file a suit for confirmation of the nonexistence of a liability at the outset simply to contest the preliminary proceedings of the Illinois suit, but rather filed this suit in order to resolve the merits of the dispute involved in the Illinois suit, which, in essence, should be resolved in a Japanese court. Moreover, the court recognizes that the defendant was served notice of the Illinois suit on 24 August 2005 . . . and promptly filed this suit . . . on November 2 of the same year. Therefore, there are no grounds for the defendants' assertions.

C. The defendants also contend that in principle a preceding foreign suit should be treated with the same respect as a suit filed in Japan and that in principle a [parallel] lawsuit in Japan with regard to the same object of litigation should not be permitted.

However, [the fact] that a prior foreign lawsuit has been brought cannot be said to special circumstances that would make a [parallel] trial undertaken in Japan to contravene the concepts of fairness between parties and just and prompt administration of justice.

The defendants further assert that there is a high possibility of reaching a decision on the merits in the Illinois suit because procedures for examination of evidence have partially commenced. However, there is not sufficient material evidence to allow recognition of this.

The defendants also argue that the waste of the time and effort of litigation expended since the Illinois suit was filed would be uneconomic [duplication] of litigation resources. Nevertheless, this assertion is not reasonable because, as stated above, the proceedings in the Illinois case have not yet reached the stage of a hearing on the merits.

In addition, the defendants assert that in January 2006, the plaintiff petitioned for transfer of the Illinois suit to the Federal District Court to delay proceedings in the Illinois suit. However, there are no grounds for this assertion. The mere application for transfer does not necessarily show a purpose to delay litigation and, moreover, the court does not recognize any material circumstances that support the assertion that the plaintiff has undertaken litigious acts to delay the Illinois suit. Furthermore, the defendants assert that the plaintiff predicted that it may become a defendant in a suit in Illinois, yet there is no evidence for this.

D. The Court finds no other special circumstances that necessitate that international jurisdiction of a court of Japan should be rejected in this case.

3. International Concurrent Litigation

The defendants assert that this claim amounts to international concurrent litigation (*lis pendens*) and should therefore be dismissed. However, the term "court" in article 142 of the Code of Civil Procedure [which provides that if a suit is "pending in a court," no party may bring a concurrent action] refers to a court of Japan and should not considered to include a foreign court. Moreover, the Court does not recognize any custom or rule of reason prohibiting international concurrent litigation. Therefore, the Court cannot accept this argument.

II. Infringement of the Clean Hands Principle, Abuse of Rights, and Violation of the Duty of Good Faith

[The Court found no basis for the defendants' assertion that the plaintiff had violated the 'clean hands' principle, abused its rights, or infringed the duty of good faith.]

III. Conclusion

For the above reasons, there are no grounds for any of the assertions in the defendants' brief.

JUDGE KIYOTAKA KANO
JUDGE JUN'ICHI KITAZAWA
JUDGE MANABU SAITŌ

PROBLEM AND QUESTIONS

Recall the problem with respect to the employee of a U.S. company who suffered a serious injury to his hand while operating a metal press manufactured in Japan. Assume that a personal injury action in a federal district court in Texas against the employer as well as the Japanese manufacturer. For what reasons might the Japanese company bring a parallel suit in Japan. What relief would they seek? What would be their claim or cause of action? Against whom would such an action be brought? Which court in Japan would have adjudicatory jurisdiction? What would be the grounds for jurisdiction? What arguments would you anticipate would be made in support as well as in opposition to a motion to dismiss? Which would be the most persuasive and likely to prevail?

B. European Union

The European Union does not allow parallel litigation among the courts of member states. Instead it has adopted a strict *lis pendens* approach. The 1968 Brussels Convention, EC Regulation 44/2001 as well as Regulation (EU) No. 1215/2012 all include a *lis pendens* requirement with identical language. As stated in article 21 of the Convention, article 27 of Regulation 44/2001, and article 29 of the 2012 Regulation:

> Where proceedings involving the same cause of action and between the same parties are brought in the courts of different Member States, any court other than the court first seised shall of its own motion stay its proceedings until such time as the jurisdiction of the court first seised is established.
>
> Where the jurisdiction of the court first seised is established, any court other than the court first seised shall decline jurisdiction in favour of that court.

Under article 30 of Regulation 44/2001and article 30 of the 2012 Regulation, a court is "deemed to be seized" either—

> at the time when the document instituting the proceedings or an equivalent document is lodged with the court, provided that the plaintiff has not subsequently failed to take the steps he was required to take to have service effected on the defendant, or
>
> if the document has to be served before being lodged with the court, at the time when it is received by the authority responsible for service, provided that the plaintiff has not subsequently failed to take the steps he was required to take to have the document lodged with the court.

The following cases illustrate the application of these rules and their consequences. We subsequently address a critical possibility, known as the "Italian torpedo" that the 2012 Regulation attempts to alleviate.

GUBISCH MASCHINENFABRIK KG v. GIULIO PALUMBO
European Court of Justice (Sixth Chamber), 08 December 1987
[1987] E.C.R. 04861, Case 144/86

JUDGMENT

1 By an order of 9 January 1986, which was received at the court registry on 12 June 1986, the Corte Suprema Di Cassazione (Supreme Court of Cassation), Rome, referred to the court a question on the interpretation of Article 21 of the [1968 Brussels] convention.

2 That question arose in a dispute between Gubisch Maschinenfabrik KG (hereinafter referred to as "Gubisch"), whose registered office is in Flensburg (Federal Republic of Germany), and Mr Palumbo, resident in Rome, relating to the validity of a contract of sale. Mr Palumbo brought proceedings against Gubisch before the tribunale di Roma (District Court, Rome) for a declaration that the

contract was inoperative on the ground that his order had been revoked before it reached Gubisch for acceptance. In the alternative, the plaintiff claimed the contract should be set aside for lack of consent or, in the alternative, its discharge on the ground that Gubisch had not complied with the time-limit for delivery.

3 Gubisch objected that the tribunale di Roma lacked jurisdiction, in accordance with Article 21 of the convention, on the ground that it had already brought an action before the landgericht (regional court), Flensburg, to enforce performance by Mr Palumbo of his obligation under the contract, namely payment for the machine he had purchased.

4 The tribunale di Roma dismissed the objection of *lis pendens* based on Article 21 of the convention; Gubisch appealed to the Corte suprema di cassazione, which stayed the proceedings and referred to the court the following question for a preliminary ruling:

> "*Does a case where, in relation to the same contract, one party applies to a court in a contracting state for a declaration that the contract is inoperative (or in any event for its discharge) whilst the other institutes proceedings before the courts of another contracting state for its enforcement fall within the scope of the concept of lis pendens pursuant to Article 21 of the [1968] Brussels Convention?*" [Emphasis added.]

. . . .

8 . . . *Article 21, together with Article 22 on related actions . . . is intended, in the interests of the proper administration of justice within the community, to prevent parallel proceedings before the courts of different contracting states and to avoid conflicts between decisions which might result therefrom. Those rules are therefore designed to preclude, in so far as is possible and from the outset, the possibility of a situation arising such as that referred to in article 27(3), that is to say the non-recognition of a judgment on account of its irreconcilability with a judgment given in a dispute between the same parties in the state in which recognition is sought.* [Emphasis added.]

. . . .

11 Having regard to the aforesaid objectives of the convention and to the fact that Article 21, instead of referring to the term *lis pendens* as used in the different national legal systems of the contracting states, lays down a number of substantive conditions as components of a definition, it must be concluded that the terms used in Article 21 in order to determine whether a situation of lis pendens arises must be regarded as independent.

. . . .

13 It is therefore in the light of the aforesaid objectives and with a view to ensuring consistency as between Articles 21 and 27(3) that the question whether a procedural situation of the kind at issue in this case is covered by Article 21 must be dealt with. The salient features of that situation are that one of the parties has brought an action before a court of first instance for the enforcement of an obligation stipulated in an international contract of sale; an action is subsequently brought against him by the other party in another contracting state for the

rescission or discharge of the same contract.

14 It must be observed first of all that according to its wording Article 21 applies where two actions are between the same parties and involve the same cause of action and the same subject-matter; it does not lay down any further conditions. Even though the German version of Article 21 does not expressly distinguish between the terms "subject-matter" and "cause of action", it must be construed in the same manner as the other language versions, all of which make that distinction.

15 In the procedural situation which has given rise to the question submitted for a preliminary ruling the same parties are engaged in two legal proceedings in different contracting states which are based on the same "cause of action", that is to say the same contractual relationship. The problem which arises, therefore, is whether those two actions have the same "subject-matter" when the first seeks to enforce the contract and the second seeks its rescission or discharge.

16 In particular, in a case such as this, involving the international sale of tangible moveable property, it is apparent that the action to enforce the contract is aimed at giving effect to it, and that the action for its rescission or discharge is aimed precisely at depriving it of any effect. The question whether the contract is binding therefore lies at the heart of the two actions. If it is the action for rescission or discharge of the contract that is brought subsequently, it may even be regarded as simply a defense against the first action, brought in the form of independent proceedings before a court in another contracting state.

17 In those procedural circumstances it must be held that the two actions have the same subject-matter, for that concept cannot be restricted so as to mean two claims which are entirely identical.

18 If, in circumstances such as those of this case, the questions at issue concerning a single international sales contract were not decided solely by the court before which the action to enforce the contract is pending and which was seised first, there would be a danger for the party seeking enforcement that under article 27(3) a judgment given in his favour might not be recognized, even though any defence put forward by the defendant alleging that the contract was not binding had not been accepted. There can be no doubt that a judgment given in a contracting state requiring performance of the contract would not be recognized in the state in which recognition was sought if a court in that state had given a judgment rescinding or discharging the contract. Such a result, restricting the effects of each judgment to the territory of the state concerned, would run counter to the objectives of the convention, which is intended to strengthen legal protection throughout the territory of the community and to facilitate recognition in each contracting state of judgments given in any other contracting state.

19 *The answer to the question submitted by the national court must therefore be that the concept of lis pendens pursuant to Article 21 of the convention of 27 September 1968 covers a case where a party brings an action before a court in a contracting state for the rescission or discharge of an international sales contract whilst an action by the other party to enforce the same contract is pending before a court in another contracting state.* [Emphasis added.]

> ## QUESTION
>
> To what extent does article 21 of the Brussels Convention (article 27 of EC Regulation 44/2001 and article 29 of Regulation (EU) No. 1215/2012) as interpreted and applied in the *Gubisch* case resolve the problem of parallel litigation involving parties domiciled in the European Union? What if as a matter of delay tactics, a party anticipating a suit in a court with jurisdiction were to commence an action beforehand in a court noted for delay even in determining that it does not have jurisdiction? Would the following new provision of Regulation (EU) No. 1215/2012 help to prevent or at least resolve such problems? If not, under what circumstances and for what purposes do they apply?
>
> *Article 33*
>
> 1. Where jurisdiction is based on Article 4 or on Articles 7, 8 or 9 [the defendant's domicile or designated special jurisdictional grounds] and proceedings are pending before a court of a third State at the time when a court in a Member State is seised of an action involving the same cause of action and between the same parties as the proceedings in the court of the third State, the court of the Member State may stay the proceedings if:
>
> (a) it is expected that the court of the third State will give a judgment capable of recognition and, where applicable, of enforcement in that Member State; and
>
> (b) the court of the Member State is satisfied that a stay is necessary for the proper administration of justice.
>
> 2. The court of the Member State may continue the proceedings at any time if:
>
> (a) the proceedings in the court of the third State are themselves stayed or discontinued;
>
> (b) it appears to the court of the Member State that the proceedings in the court of the third State are unlikely to be concluded within a reasonable time; or
>
> (c) the continuation of the proceedings is required for the proper administration of justice.
>
> 3. The court of the Member State shall dismiss the proceedings if the proceedings in the court of the third State are concluded and have resulted in a judgment capable of recognition and, where applicable, of enforcement in that Member State.
>
> We return to these issues in relation to choice of forum agreements in Chapter 7.

MÆRSK OLIE & GAS A/S v. FIRMA M. DE HAAN EN W. DE BOER

European Court of Justice (Third Chamber), 14 October 2004
[2004] E.C.R. I-09657, C-39/02

JUDGMENT

1 This reference for a preliminary ruling relates to the interpretation of Articles 21, 25 and 27 of the Convention of 27 September 1968 on Jurisdiction and the Enforcement of Judgments in Civil and Commercial Matters . . . ('the Brussels Convention').

2 This reference has been made in the course of a dispute between the company Mærsk Olie & Gas A/S ('Mærsk') and the partnership of Mr M. de Haan and Mr W. de Boer ('the shipowners') concerning an action for damages in respect of damage allegedly caused to underwater pipelines in the North Sea by a trawler belonging to the shipowners.

THE LEGAL FRAMEWORK

The 1957 International Convention relating to the Limitation of the Liability of Owners of Sea-Going Ships

3 Article 1(1) of the International Convention relating to the Limitation of the Liability of Owners of Sea-Going Ships of 10 October 1957 (International Transport Treaties, suppl. 1-10, January 1986, p. 81) ('the 1957 Convention') provides that the owner of a sea-going ship may limit his liability to a specified amount in respect of one of the claims there listed, unless the occurrence giving rise to the claim resulted from the actual fault of the owner. The claims listed include, under Article 1(1)(b), damage to any property caused by the act, neglect or default of any person on board the ship in connection with the navigation thereof.

4 Under Article 3(1) of the 1957 Convention the amount to which liability may be limited is calculated according to the ship's tonnage and will vary depending on the nature of the damage caused. Thus, in the case where the harmful event has resulted in damage only to property, the amount to which the shipowner may limit his liability corresponds to 1000 francs Poincaré for each tonne of the ship's tonnage.

5 In the case where the aggregate of the claims resulting from the same harmful event exceeds the limits of liability as thus defined, Article 2(2) and (3) of the 1957 Convention provides that a fund, corresponding to that limit, may be constituted for the purpose of being available only for the payment of claims in respect of which limitation of liability may be invoked. Article 3(2) provides that this fund is to be distributed 'among the claimants . . . in proportion to the amounts of their established claims'.

6 Article 1(7) of the 1957 Convention provides:

'The act of invoking limitation of liability shall not constitute an admission of liability'.

7 Article 4 of the 1957 Convention provides as follows:

'. . . the rules relating to the constitution and distribution of the limitation fund, if any, and all rules of procedure shall be governed by the national law of the State in which the fund is constituted.'

8 According to the case-file, the Kingdom of the Netherlands was bound by the 1957 Convention at the time of the events in issue in the main proceedings.

The Brussels Convention

9 According to its preamble, the purpose of the Brussels Convention is to facilitate the reciprocal recognition and enforcement of judgments of courts or tribunals, in accordance with Article 293 EC, and to strengthen in the Community the legal protection of persons therein established. The preamble also states that it is necessary for that purpose to determine the international jurisdiction of the courts of the Contracting States.

10 Article 2 of the Brussels Convention lays down the general rule that jurisdiction is vested in the courts of the State in which the defendant is domiciled. Article 5 of the Convention, however, provides that, 'in matters relating to tort, delict or quasi-delict', the defendant may be sued 'in the courts for the place where the harmful event occurred'.

11 Article 6a of the Brussels Convention adds:

'Where by virtue of this Convention a court of a Contracting State has jurisdiction in actions relating to liability from the use or operation of a ship, that court, or any other court substituted for this purpose by the internal law of that State, shall also have jurisdiction over claims for limitation of such liability.'

12 The Brussels Convention also seeks to prevent conflicting decisions being delivered. Thus, Article 21, dealing with *lis pendens*, provides as follows:

'Where proceedings involving the same cause of action and between the same parties are brought in the courts of different Contracting States, any court other than the court first seised shall of its own motion stay its proceedings until such time as the jurisdiction of the court first seised is established.

A court which would be required to decline jurisdiction may stay its proceedings if the jurisdiction of the other court is contested.'

13 Article 22 of the Brussels Convention provides as follows:

'Where related actions are brought in the courts of different Contracting States, any court other than the court first seised may, while the actions are pending at first instance, stay its proceedings.

A court other than the court first seised may also, on the application of one of the parties, decline jurisdiction if the law of that court permits the consolidation of related actions and the court first seised has jurisdiction over both actions.

For the purposes of this Article, actions are deemed to be related where they are so closely connected that it is expedient to hear and determine them together to avoid the risk of irreconcilable judgments resulting from separate proceedings.'

[Article 30 of Regulation (EU) No. 1215/2012 includes this provision verbatim with only a reordering of the conditions of the second paragraph.]

14 With regard to recognition, Article 25 of the Convention states as follows:

'For the purposes of this Convention, "judgment" means any judgment given by a court or tribunal of a Contracting State, whatever the judgment may be called, including a decree, order, decision or writ of execution, as well as the determination of costs or expenses by an officer of the court.'

[Article 2(a) of Regulation (EU) No. 1215/2012 repeats this definition verbatim.]

15 The first paragraph of Article 26 of the Brussels Convention provides:

'A judgment given in a Contracting State shall be recognised in the other Contracting States without any special procedure being required.'

[Article 36 of Regulation (EU) No. 1215/2012 repeats this definition verbatim.]

16 Article 27, however, provides as follows:

'A judgment shall not be recognised:

. . .

2. where it was given in default of appearance, if the defendant was not duly served with the document which instituted the proceedings or with an equivalent document in sufficient time to enable him to arrange for his defence;

. . . .

[Article 45 of Regulation (EU) No. 1215/2012 rewords this requirement as follows:

Article 45

1. On the application of any interested party, the recognition of a judgment shall be refused:

. . . .

(b) where the judgment was given in default of appearance, if the defendant was not served with the document which instituted the proceedings or with an equivalent document in sufficient time and in such a way as to enable him to arrange for his defence, unless the defendant failed to commence proceedings to challenge the judgment when it was possible for him to do so.]

17 Article IV of the Protocol annexed to the Brussels Convention states:

'Judicial and extrajudicial documents . . . which have to be served on persons in another Contracting State shall be transmitted in accordance with the procedures laid down in the conventions and agreements concluded between the Contracting States. . . .

The dispute in the main proceedings and the questions referred for preliminary ruling.

18 In May 1985 Mærsk laid oil and gas pipelines in the North Sea. In the course of June 1985 a trawler belonging to the shipowners was fishing in the area in which those pipelines had been laid. Mærsk established that the pipelines had been damaged.

19 By letter of 3 July 1985 Mærsk informed the shipowners that it held them responsible for that damage, the repair work in respect of which it was estimated would cost USD 1 700 019 and GBP 51 961.58.

20 On 23 April 1987 the shipowners lodged with the Arrondissementsrechtbank (District Court) Groningen (Netherlands), the place in which their vessel was registered, an application for limitation of their liability. That court made an order on 27 May 1987 provisionally fixing that limitation at NLG 52 417.40 and enjoining the shipowners to lodge that sum together with NLG 10 000 to cover the legal costs. The shipowers' legal respresentatives informed Mærsk of that decision by telex of 5 June 1987.

21 On 20 June 1987 Mærsk brought an action for damages against the shipowners before the Vestre Landsret (Western Regional Court) (Denmark).

22 On 24 June 1987 Mærsk appealed to the Gerechtshof (Court of Appeal) Leeuwarden (Netherlands) against the decision of the Arrondissementsrechtbank Groningen on the ground that the latter court did not have jurisdiction. On 6 January 1988 the Gerechtshof upheld the decision delivered at first instance, referring to, inter alia, Articles 2 and 6a of the Brussels Convention. Mærsk did not lodge an appeal to have the decision of the Gerechtshof quashed.

23 By registered letter of 1 February 1988 the administrator notified Mærsk's lawyer of the order of the Arrondissementsrechtbank establishing the liability limitation fund and, by letter of 25 April 1988, requested Mærsk to submit its claim.

24 Mærsk did not accede to that request, choosing instead to pursue its action before the Danish court. In the absence of any claims submitted by injured parties, the sum lodged with the Arrondissementsrechtbank in the Netherlands was returned to the shipowners in December 1988.

25 By decision of 27 April 1988 the Vestre Landsret held that the rulings of the Netherlands courts of 27 May 1987 and of 6 January 1988 had to be treated as being judgments within the terms of Article 25 of the Brussels Convention in view of the fact that Mærsk had had the opportunity to defend its position during the corresponding proceedings.

26 As it took the view that the proceedings brought in the Netherlands and in Denmark were between the same parties, had the same subject-matter and related to the same cause of action, and that this finding could not be invalidated by the fact

that Mærsk had not defended its interests in the proceedings relating to the limitation of liability, the Vestre Landsret ruled that the conditions governing a finding of *lis pendens* pursuant to Article 21 of the Brussels Convention had been satisfied.

27 In view of the fact that proceedings had been brought earlier in the Netherlands (23 April 1987) than in Denmark, and in view of the finding of the Arrondissementsrechtbank Groningen, upheld on appeal, that it had jurisdiction to deliver its decision, the Vestre Landsret, acting pursuant to the second paragraph of Article 21 of the Brussels Convention, declined jurisdiction in favour of the Netherlands court.

28 Mærsk appealed against that decision to the Højesteret (Danish Supreme Court).

29 As it took the view that the case raised questions on the interpretation of Articles 21, 25 and 27 of the Brussels Convention, the Højesteret decided to stay proceedings and to refer the following questions to the Court for a preliminary ruling:

> '1. Does a procedure to establish a liability limitation fund pursuant to an application by a shipowner under the Brussels Convention of 10 October 1957 constitute proceedings within the meaning of Article 21 of the 1968 Brussels Convention where it is evident from the application, where the relevant names are stated, who might be affected thereby as a potential injured party?
>
> 2. Is an order to establish a liability limitation fund under the Netherlands procedural rules in force in 1986 a judgment within the meaning of Article 25 of the 1968 Brussels Convention?
>
> 3. Can a limitation fund which was established on 27 May 1987 by a Netherlands court pursuant to Netherlands procedural rules then in force without prior service on an affected claimant now be denied recognition in another Member State in relation to the claimant concerned pursuant to Article 27(2) of the 1968 Brussels Convention?
>
> 4. If Question 3 is answered in the affirmative, is the claimant concerned deprived of its right to rely on Article 27(2) by virtue of the fact that in the Member State which established the limitation fund it raised the matter of jurisdiction before a higher court without having previously objected to default of service?' [Emphasis added.]

The first question

30 By its first question, the Højesteret is essentially asking whether an application brought before a court of a Contracting State by a shipowner seeking to have a liability limitation fund established, in which the potential victim of the damage is indicated, and an action for damages brought before a court of another Contracting State by that victim against the shipowner constitute proceedings that have the same subject-matter, involve the same cause of action and are between the same parties, within the terms of Article 21 of the Brussels Convention.

31 It should be borne in mind at the outset that Article 21 of the Brussels Convention, together with Article 22 on related actions, is contained in Section 8 of Title II of that Convention, which is intended, in the interests of the proper administration of justice within the Community, to prevent parallel proceedings before the courts of different Contracting States and to avoid conflicts between decisions which might result therefrom. Those rules are therefore designed to preclude, so far as possible and from the outset, the possibility of a situation arising such as that referred to in Article 27(3) of the Convention, that is to say, the non-recognition of a judgment on account of its irreconcilability with a judgment given in proceedings between the same parties in the State in which recognition is sought (see Case 144/86 *Gubisch Maschinenfabrik* [1987] ECR 4861, paragraph 8, [additional citation omitted]).

32 It follows that, in order to achieve those aims, Article 21 must be interpreted broadly so as to cover, in principle, all situations of *lis pendens* before courts in Contracting States, irrespective of the parties' domicile. [Citations omitted.]

33 It is, in the present case, common ground that proceedings relating to the establishment of a liability limitation fund, such as those brought before the Netherlands court, are intended to allow a shipowner who could be declared liable under one of the heads of claim listed in Article 1(1) of the 1957 Convention to limit his liability to an amount calculated in accordance with Article 3 of that Convention, such that claimants cannot recover from the shipowner, in respect of the same harmful event, amounts other than those to which they would be entitled under such proceedings.

34 An application of this kind for the establishment of a liability limitation fund undoubtedly constitutes proceedings for the purposes of Article 21 of the Brussels Convention. It is, however, also necessary to examine whether it involves the same subject-matter and cause of action as an action for damages brought by the victim against the shipowner before a court of another Contracting State and whether those sets of proceedings have been brought between the same parties. Those three cumulative conditions must be satisfied before there can be a situation of *lis pendens* within the terms of Article 21 of the Brussels Convention.

35 The applications under consideration clearly do not have the same subject-matter. Whereas an action for damages seeks to have the defendant declared liable, an application to limit liability is designed to ensure, in the event that the person is declared liable, that such liability will be limited to an amount calculated in accordance with the 1957 Convention, it being borne in mind that, under Article 1(7) of that Convention, 'the act of invoking limitation of liability shall not constitute an admission of liability'.

36 The fact that, in proceedings for the establishment of a liability limitation fund, the claims are verified by an administrator or may also be challenged by the debtor is not such as to cast doubt on that analysis. As the Court has already ruled, in order to determine whether two sets of proceedings have the same subject-matter under Article 21 of the Brussels Convention, account should be taken, as is evident from the wording of that article, only of the applicants' respective claims in each of the sets of proceedings, and not of the defence which may be raised by a defendant (Case C-111/01 *Gantner Electronic* [2003] ECR I-4207, paragraph 26).

37 Nor do the applications under consideration involve the same cause of action, within the terms of Article 21 of the Convention.

38 As the 'cause of action' comprises the facts and the legal rule invoked as the basis for the application (see Case C-406/92 *The Tatry* [1994] ECR I-5439, paragraph 39), the unavoidable conclusion is that, even if it be assumed that the facts underlying the two sets of proceedings are identical, the legal rule which forms the basis of each of those applications is different, as has been pointed out by Mærsk, the Commission and the Advocate General at point 41 of his Opinion. The action for damages is based on the law governing non-contractual liability, whereas the application for the establishment of a liability limitation fund is based on the 1957 Convention and on the Netherlands legislation which gives effect to it.

39 Accordingly, without it being necessary to examine the third condition that the proceedings must be between the same parties, the conclusion must be drawn that, in the absence of identical subject-matter and an identical cause of action, there is no situation of *lis pendens* within the terms of Article 21 of the Brussels Convention between a set of proceedings seeking the establishment of a fund to limit the liability of a shipowner, such as the application made in the main proceedings before a court in the Netherlands, and an action for damages brought before the court making the reference for a preliminary ruling.

. . . .

42 In the light of the foregoing, the answer to the first question must be that an application to a court of a Contracting State by a shipowner for the establishment of a liability limitation fund, in which the potential victim of the damage is indicated, and an action for damages brought before a court of another Contracting State by that victim against the shipowner do not create a situation of *lis pendens* within the terms of Article 21 of the Brussels Convention.

The second question

43 By its second question, the Højesteret asks whether a decision ordering the establishment of a liability limitation fund, such as that in issue in the main proceedings, is a judgment within the meaning of Article 25 of the Brussels Convention.

44 In this connection, it should be borne in mind that, under Article 25, a 'judgment' for the purposes of the Brussels Convention, means 'any judgment given by a court or tribunal of a Contracting State, whatever the judgment may be called'.

45 As the Court has already ruled [citation omitted], in order to be a 'judgment' for the purposes of the Convention the decision in question must emanate from a judicial body of a Contracting State deciding on its own authority on the issues between the parties.

. . . .

52 *In the light of the foregoing, the answer to the second question must be that a decision ordering the establishment of a liability limitation fund, such as that in the main proceedings in the present case, is a judgment within the terms of Article*

25 of the Brussels Convention. [Emphasis added.]

The third and fourth questions [omitted]

Costs

63 As these proceedings are, for the parties to the main proceedings, a step in the action pending before the national court, the decision on costs is a matter for that court. The costs involved in submitting observations to the Court, other than those of the parties to the main proceedings, are not recoverable.

On those grounds, the Court (Third Chamber), hereby rules:

1. *An application to a court of a Contracting State by a shipowner for the establishment of a liability limitation fund, in which the potential victim of the damage is indicated, and an action for damages brought before a court of another Contracting State by that victim against the shipowner do not create a situation of lis pendens within the terms of Article 21 of the [1968 Brussels] Convention . . . .* [Emphasis added.]

2. *A decision ordering the establishment of a liability limitation fund, such as that in the main proceedings in the present case, is a judgment within the terms of Article 25 of that Convention.* [Emphasis added.]

3. *A decision to establish a liability limitation fund, in the absence of prior service on the claimant concerned, and even where the latter has appealed against that decision in order to challenge the jurisdiction of the court which delivered it, cannot be refused recognition in another Contracting State pursuant to Article 27(2) of that Convention, on condition that it was duly served on or notified to the defendant in good time.* [Emphasis added.]

QUESTIONS

Which, if any, examples of parallel litigation in the U.S., Canadian, or Japanese cases included in this chapter would *not* have been subject to *lis pendens* rules as explained by the European Court of Justice decision in the *Mærsk Olie & Gas A/S* case? Would, for example, the suit filed in British Columbia in the *Seattle Totems* case been allowed?

OWUSU v. JACKSON
European Court of Justice (Grand Chamber), 1 March 2005
[2005] E.C.R. I-1383, C-281/02

1. This reference for a preliminary ruling concerns the interpretation of Article 2 of the Convention of . . . the [1968] Brussels Convention . . . .

2 The reference was made in the course of proceedings brought by Mr Owusu against Mr Jackson, trading as 'Villa Holidays Bal-Inn Villas', and several compa-

nies governed by Jamaican law, following an accident suffered by Mr Owusu in Jamaica.

LEGAL BACKGROUND

The Brussels Convention

3 According to its preamble the Brussels Convention is intended to facilitate the reciprocal recognition and enforcement of judgments of courts or tribunals, in accordance with Article 293 EC, and to strengthen in the Community the legal protection of persons therein established. The preamble also states that it is necessary for that purpose to determine the international jurisdiction of the courts of the contracting States.

4 The provisions relating to jurisdiction appear in Title II of the Brussels Convention. According to Article 2 of the Convention:

> 'Subject to the provisions of this Convention, persons domiciled in a Contracting State shall, whatever their nationality, be sued in the courts of that State.
>
> Persons who are not nationals of the State in which they are domiciled shall be governed by the rules of jurisdiction applicable to nationals of that State'.

5 However, Article 5(1) and (3) of that convention provides that a defendant may be sued in another Contracting State, in matters relating to a contract, in the courts for the place of performance of the obligation in question, and, in matters relating to tort, delict or quasi-delict, in the courts for the place where the harmful event occurred.

6 The Brussels Convention is also intended to prevent conflicting decisions. Thus, according to Article 21, which concerns *lis pendens*:

> 'Where proceedings involving the same cause of action and between the same parties are brought in the courts of different Contracting States, any court other than the court first seised shall of its own motion stay its proceedings until such time as the jurisdiction of the court first seised is established.
>
> Where the jurisdiction of the court first seised is established, any court other than the court first seised shall decline jurisdiction in favour of that court'.

7 Article 22 of the Convention provides:

> 'Where related actions are brought in the courts of different Contracting States, any court other than the court first seised may, while the actions are pending at first instance, stay its proceedings.
>
> A court other than the court first seised may also, on the application of one of the parties, decline jurisdiction if the law of that court permits the

consolidation of related actions and the court first seised has jurisdiction over both actions.

For the purposes of this article, actions are deemed to be related where they are so closely connected that it is expedient to hear and determine them together to avoid the risk of irreconcilable judgments resulting from separate proceedings.'

National law

8 According to the doctrine of *forum non conveniens*, as understood in English law, a national court may decline to exercise jurisdiction on the ground that a court in another State, which also has jurisdiction, would objectively be a more appropriate forum for the trial of the action, that is to say, a forum in which the case may be tried more suitably for the interests of all the parties and the ends of justice (1986 judgment of the House of Lords, in *Spiliada Maritime Corporation* v *Cansulex Ltd* [1987], AC 460, particularly at p. 476).

9 An English court which decides to decline jurisdiction under the doctrine of *forum non conveniens* stays proceedings so that the proceedings which are thus provisionally suspended can be resumed should it prove, in particular, that the foreign forum has no jurisdiction to hear the case or that the claimant has no access to effective justice in that forum.

THE MAIN PROCEEDINGS AND THE QUESTIONS REFERRED FOR A PRELIMINARY RULING

10 On 10 October 1997, Mr Owusu ('the claimant'), a British national domiciled in the United Kingdom, suffered a very serious accident during a holiday in Jamaica. He walked into the sea, and when the water was up to his waist he dived in, struck his head against a submerged sand bank and sustained a fracture of his fifth cervical vertebra which rendered him tetraplegic.

11 Following that accident, Mr Owusu brought an action in the United Kingdom for breach of contract against Mr Jackson, who is also domiciled in that State. Mr Jackson had let to Mr Owusu a holiday villa in Mammee Bay (Jamaica). Mr Owusu claims that the contract, which provided that he would have access to a private beach, contained an implied term that the beach would be reasonably safe or free from hidden dangers.

12 Mr Owusu also brought an action in tort in the United Kingdom against several Jamaican companies, namely Mammee Bay Club Ltd ('the third defendant'), the owner and occupier of the beach at Mammee Bay which provided the claimant with free access to the beach, The Enchanted Garden Resorts & Spa Ltd ('the fourth defendant'), which operates a holiday complex close to Mammee Bay, and whose guests were also licensed to use the beach, and Town & Country Resorts Ltd ('the sixth defendant'), which operates a large hotel adjoining the beach, and which has a licence to use the beach, subject to the condition that it is responsible for its management, upkeep and control.

13 According to the file, another English holidaymaker had suffered a similar accident two years earlier in which she, too, was rendered tetraplegic. The action in

tort against the Jamaican defendants therefore embraces not only a contention that they failed to warn swimmers of the hazard constituted by the submerged sand bank, but also a contention that they failed to heed the earlier accident.

14 The proceedings were commenced by a claim form issued out of Sheffield District Registry of the High Court (England and Wales) Civil Division on 6 October 2000. They were served on Mr Jackson in the United Kingdom and, on 12 December 2000, leave was granted to the claimant to serve the proceedings on the other defendants in Jamaica. Service was effected on the third, fourth and sixth defendants, but not on Mammee Bay Resorts Ltd or Consulting Services Ltd.

15 Mr Jackson and the third, fourth and sixth defendants applied to that court for a declaration that it should not exercise its jurisdiction in relation to the claim against them both. In support of their applications, they argued that the case had closer links with Jamaica and that the Jamaican courts were a forum with jurisdiction in which the case might be tried more suitably for the interests of all the parties and the ends of justice.

16 By order of 16 October 2001, the Judge sitting as Deputy High Court Judge in Sheffield (United Kingdom) held that it was clear from Case C-412/98 *UGIC* v *Group Josi* [2000] ECR I-5925, paragraphs 59 to 61, that the application of the jurisdictional rules in the Brussels Convention to a dispute depended, in principle, on whether the defendant had its seat or domicile in a Contracting State, and that the Convention applied to a dispute between a defendant domiciled in a Contracting State and a claimant domiciled in a non-Contracting State. In those circumstances the decision of the Court of Appeal in *In re Harrods (Buenos Aires) Ltd* [1992] Ch 72, which accepted that it was possible for the English courts, applying the doctrine of *forum non conveniens*, to decline to exercise the jurisdiction conferred on them by Article 2 of the Brussels Convention, was bad law.

17 Taking the view that he had no power himself under Article 2 of the Protocol of 3 June 1971 to refer a question to the Court of Justice for a preliminary ruling to clarify this point, the Judge sitting as Deputy High Court Judge held that, in the light of the principles laid down in *Group Josi*, it was not open to him to stay the action against Mr Jackson since he was domiciled in a Contracting State.

18 Notwithstanding the connecting factors that the action brought against the other defendants might have with Jamaica, the judge held that he was also unable to stay the action against them, in so far as the Brussels Convention precluded him from staying proceedings in the action against Mr Jackson. Otherwise, there would be a risk that the courts in two jurisdictions would end up trying the same factual issues upon the same or similar evidence and reach different conclusions. He therefore held that the United Kingdom, and not Jamaica was the State with the appropriate forum to try the action and dismissed the applications for a declaration that the court should not exercise jurisdiction.

19 Mr Jackson and the third, fourth and sixth defendants appealed against that order. The Court of Appeal (England and Wales) Civil Division states that, in this case, the competing jurisdictions are a Contracting State and a non-Contracting State. If Article 2 of the Brussels Convention is mandatory, even in this context, Mr Jackson would have to be sued in the United Kingdom before the courts of his

domicile and it would not be open to the claimant to sue him under Article 5(3) of the Brussels Convention in Jamaica, where the harmful event occurred, because that State is not another Contracting State. In the absence of an express derogation to that effect in the Convention, it is therefore not permissible to create an exception to the rule in Article 2. According to the referring court, the question of the application of *forum non conveniens* in favour of the courts of a non-Contracting State, when one of the defendants is domiciled in a Contracting State, is not a matter on which the Court of Justice has ever given a ruling.

20 According to the claimant, Article 2 of the Brussels Convention is of mandatory application, so that the English courts cannot stay proceedings in the United Kingdom against a defendant domiciled there, even though the English court takes the view that another forum in a non-Contracting State is more appropriate.

21 The referring court points out that if that position were correct it might have serious consequences in a number of other situations concerning exclusive jurisdiction or *lis pendens*. It adds that a judgment delivered in England, deciding the case, which was to be enforced in Jamaica, particularly as regards the Jamaican defendants, would encounter difficulty over certain rules in force in that country on the recognition and enforcement of foreign judgments.

22 Against that background, the Court of Appeal decided to stay its proceedings and to refer the following questions to the Court for a preliminary ruling:

'1. Is it inconsistent with the Brussels Convention . . . , where a claimant contends that jurisdiction is founded on Article 2, for a court of a Contracting State to exercise a discretionary power, available under its national law, to decline to hear proceedings brought against a person domiciled in that State in favour of the courts of a non-Contracting State:

(a) if the jurisdiction of no other Contracting State under the 1968 Convention is in issue;

(b) if the proceedings have no connecting factors to any other Contracting State?

2. If the answer to question 1(a) or (b) is yes, is it inconsistent in all circumstances or only in some and if so which?' [Emphasis added.]

ON THE QUESTIONS REFERRED

The first question

23 In order to reply to the first question it must first be determined whether Article 2 of the Brussels Convention is applicable in circumstances such as those in the main proceedings, that is to say, where the claimant and one of the defendants are domiciled in the same Contracting State and the case between them before the courts of that State has certain connecting factors with a non-Contracting State, but not with another Contracting State. Only if it is will the question arise whether, in the circumstances of the case in the main proceedings, the Brussels Convention

precludes the application by a court of a Contracting State of the *forum non conveniens* doctrine where Article 2 of that convention would permit that court to claim jurisdiction because the defendant is domiciled in that State.

The applicability of Article 2 of the Brussels Convention

24 Nothing in the wording of Article 2 of the Brussels Convention suggests that the application of the general rule of jurisdiction laid down by that article solely on the basis of the defendant's domicile in a Contracting State is subject to the condition that there should be a legal relationship involving a number of Contracting States.

. . . .

29 Similarly, as the Advocate General pointed out in points 142 to 152 of his Opinion, whilst it is clear from their wording that the Brussels Convention rules on *lis pendens* and related actions or recognition and enforcement of judgments apply to relationships between different Contracting States, provided that they concern proceedings pending before courts of different Contracting States or judgments delivered by courts of a Contracting State with a view to recognition and enforcement thereof in another Contracting State, the fact nevertheless remains that the disputes with which the proceedings or decisions in question are concerned may be international, involving a Contracting State and a non-Contracting State, and allow recourse, on that ground, to the general rule of jurisdiction laid down by Article 2 of the Brussels Convention.

30 To counter the argument that Article 2 applies to a legal situation involving a single Contracting State and one or more non-Contracting States, the defendants in the main proceedings and the United Kingdom Government cited the principle of the relative effect of treaties, which means that the Brussels Convention cannot impose any obligation on States which have not agreed to be bound by it.

31 In that regard, suffice it to note that the designation of the court of a Contracting State as the court having jurisdiction on the ground of the defendant's domicile in that State, even in proceedings which are, at least in part, connected, because of their subject-matter or the claimant's domicile, with a non-Contracting State, is not such as to impose an obligation on that State.

32 Mr Jackson and the United Kingdom Government also emphasised, in support of the argument that Article 2 of the Brussels Convention applied only to disputes with connections to a number of Contracting States, the fundamental objective pursued by the Convention which was to ensure the free movement of judgments between Contracting States.

. . . .

35 It follows from the foregoing that Article 2 of the Brussels Convention applies to circumstances such as those in the main proceedings, involving relationships between the courts of a single Contracting State and those of a non-Contracting State rather than relationships between the courts of a number of Contracting States.

36 *It must therefore be considered whether, in such circumstances, the Brussels Convention precludes a court of a Contracting State from applying the forum non conveniens doctrine and declining to exercise the jurisdiction conferred on it by Article 2 of that Convention.* [Emphasis added.]

The compatibility of the forum non conveniens doctrine with the Brussels Convention

37 It must be observed, first, that Article 2 of the Brussels Convention is mandatory in nature and that, according to its terms, there can be no derogation from the principle it lays down except in the cases expressly provided for by the Convention.... It is common ground that no exception on the basis of the *forum non conveniens* doctrine was provided for by the authors of the Convention, although the question was discussed when the Convention of 9 October 1978 on the Accession of Denmark, Ireland and the United Kingdom was drawn up, as is apparent from the report on that Convention by Professor Schlosser (OJ 1979 C 59, p. 71, paragraphs 77 and 78).

38 Respect for the principle of legal certainty, which is one of the objectives of the Brussels Convention . . . would not be fully guaranteed if the court having jurisdiction under the Convention had to be allowed to apply the *forum non conveniens* doctrine.

. . . .

41 Application of the *forum non conveniens* doctrine, which allows the court seised a wide discretion as regards the question whether a foreign court would be a more appropriate forum for the trial of an action, is liable to undermine the predictability of the rules of jurisdiction laid down by the Brussels Convention, in particular that of Article 2, and consequently to undermine the principle of legal certainty, which is the basis of the Convention.

42 The legal protection of persons established in the Community would also be undermined. First, a defendant, who is generally better placed to conduct his defence before the courts of his domicile, would not be able, in circumstances such as those of the main proceedings, reasonably to foresee before which other court he may be sued. Second, where a plea is raised on the basis that a foreign court is a more appropriate forum to try the action, it is for the claimant to establish that he will not be able to obtain justice before that foreign court or, if the court seised decides to allow the plea, that the foreign court has in fact no jurisdiction to try the action or that the claimant does not, in practice, have access to effective justice before that court, irrespective of the cost entailed by the bringing of a fresh action before a court of another State and the prolongation of the procedural time-limits.

43 Moreover, allowing *forum non conveniens* in the context of the Brussels Convention would be likely to affect the uniform application of the rules of jurisdiction contained therein in so far as that doctrine is recognised only in a limited number of Contracting States, whereas the objective of the Brussels Convention is precisely to lay down common rules to the exclusion of derogating national rules.

44 The defendants in the main proceedings emphasise the negative consequences

which would result in practice from the obligation the English courts would then be under to try this case, inter alia as regards the expense of the proceedings, the possibility of recovering their costs in England if the claimant's action is dismissed, the logistical difficulties resulting from the geographical distance, the need to assess the merits of the case according to Jamaican standards, the enforceability in Jamaica of a default judgment and the impossibility of enforcing cross-claims against the other defendants.

45 In that regard, genuine as those difficulties may be, suffice it to observe that such considerations, which are precisely those which may be taken into account when *forum non conveniens* is considered, are not such as to call into question the mandatory nature of the fundamental rule of jurisdiction contained in Article 2 of the Brussels Convention, for the reasons set out above.

46 In the light of all the foregoing considerations, the answer to the first question must be that the Brussels Convention precludes a court of a Contracting State from declining the jurisdiction conferred on it by Article 2 of that convention on the ground that a court of a non-Contracting State would be a more appropriate forum for the trial of the action even if the jurisdiction of no other Contracting State is in issue or the proceedings have no connecting factors to any other Contracting State.

The second question

47 By its second question, the referring court seeks essentially to know whether, if the Court takes the view that the Brussels Convention precludes the application of *forum non conveniens*, its application is ruled out in all circumstances or only in certain circumstances.

48 According to the order for reference and the observations of the defendants in the main proceedings and of the United Kingdom Government, that second question was asked in connection with cases where there were identical or related proceedings pending before a court of a non-Contracting State, a convention granting jurisdiction to such a court or a connection with that State of the same type as those referred to in Article 16 of the Brussels Convention. . . . .

51 In the present case, it is common ground that the factual circumstances described in paragraph 48 of this judgment are not the same as those of the main proceedings.

52 Accordingly there is no need to reply to the second question.

On those grounds, the Court (Grand Chamber) rules as follows:

The [1968 Brussels] Convention precludes a court of a Contracting State from declining the jurisdiction conferred on it by Article 2 of that convention on the ground that a court of a non-Contracting State would be a more appropriate forum for the trial of the action even if the jurisdiction of no other Contracting State is in issue or the proceedings have no connecting factors to any other Contracting State. [Emphasis added.]

> **QUESTIONS AND NOTE**
>
> 1. Under European law, would the German court in *Turner Entertainment Co. v. Degeto Film GmbH* have had adjudicatory jurisdiction had Turner filed its suit against Degeto in Georgia prior to Degeto's filing in Germany?
>
> 2. What underlying policies or objectives explain the differences in law and approach among U.S., Canadian, Japanese, and the European courts?
>
> 3. Would the U.K. or any other member state be liable to a party to a suit were a court not to adhere to the *lis pendens* rules as interpreted by the European Court of Justice?
>
> Of note is a recent decision by the French Court of Cassation recognizing an anti-suit injunction against a French firm issued by a Georgia court pursuant to forum selection clause, also noted *infra*, Chapter 7. *In Zone Brands*, Cour de Cassation, Civ. 1ère, 14 October 2009, pourvoi n 08-16.369.

REVIEW QUESTIONS AND PROBLEMS

1. What are the advantages and disadvantages of the various approaches to parallel litigation adopted in the United States, Canada, Japan, and the European Union? Which in your opinion is more preferable: the Japanese laissez-faire approach, the mixed and more flexible common law approaches of the United States and Canada that include discretionary dismissals, stays, and injunctions to prevent parallel litigation when deemed appropriate, or the *lis pendens* approach adopted by the European Union?

2. Reconsider the problem of the contested ownership of van Gogh's *The Night Café* at the end of Chapter 1. Under past or current E.U. rules, could a French court accept jurisdiction after the suit by Yale University had been filed in New Haven? What if the Kingdom of Spain and the Tyssen-Bornemisza Collection had filed a parallel suit in Madrid for confirmation of ownership in the Pissarro's *Rue Saint Honoré — Afternoon, Rain Effect* after Gustave Cassirer had brought his action for recovery of the painting in California? Assuming that under Spanish law the territorial jurisdiction of Spanish courts for claims against a foreign government is the location of an office of the government's representative, would the court in Madrid have jurisdiction? What if the action in Madrid had been filed first but the Federal District Court in California were to enter a final judgment in favor of Cassirer before the proceedings in Madrid were completed. Would E.U. rules bar its enforcement in Spain or elsewhere in the EU?

3. Assume that a Luo Yi Ling, Chinese immigrant to Vancouver, Canada, from Hong Kong in the 1970s were to discover that a Xu Wei painting that had been in a collection of Chinese art owned by his grandfather that was looted during the wartime occupation of Hong Kong was being advertised on the Internet for sale by

an East Asian antiquities dealer in Kyoto, Japan with payment to be made by credit card or directly from the buyer's bank account. He consults you regarding how he should best proceed to recover the painting. What would you advise him to do? What if the painting were on loan in Seattle or Montreal or Munich?

Chapter 4

SERVICE OF PROCESS ABROAD

I. INTRODUCTION

In all legal systems today lawsuits in civil cases commence with filing of the complaint or its equivalent with the court and the sending of the complaint, ordinarily with a summons to appear in court, to the party against whom enforcement of the claim is sought. The function of such transmission everywhere is to ensure that the defending party has notice of the action with adequate time to prepare an appropriate response. As discussed previously, in common law systems transmission of the complaint and summons does more. Termed "service," conceptually such transmission perfects personal jurisdiction. Service of process has been traditionally conceived as the mechanism by which the court implicitly "seizes" and thereby establishes "power" (judicial authority) over the defendant. Service thus serves the same function for personal jurisdiction as attachment for *in rem* and *quasi in rem* actions. However doubtful the continuing validity of *Pennoyer v. Neff* and such traditional notions of judicial power, service remains a prerequisite for personal jurisdiction in all common law systems.

Not so, however, in continental Europe and most if not all civil law systems. The common law function and effect of service have no counterpart in civil law theory, practice, or even language. As in common law systems the official transmission and receipt of such documents function as a procedural prerequisite for the lawsuit to commence. This requirement is unrelated, however, to the competence of courts to adjudicate. In civilian terms, such transmission is required for notice — *la signification et la notification* in French, *die Zustellung* in German, *notificación o traslado* in Spanish or *sōtatsu* in Japanese and *sòng dá* in Chinese (with different simplified versions of the same Chinese ideographs in both languages) — but, as we have explored in Chapter 1, such transmission and receipt does not confer or perfect jurisdiction. As indicated in the cases and materials below, fundamentally different views of the official transmission of the complaint and summons have been the source of considerable uncertainty, confusion, and conflict in transnational litigation between the United States and civil law jurisdictions. In order to resolve these problems at least in part in 1965 the Convention on the Service Abroad of Judicial and Extrajudicial Documents in Civil or Commercial Matters (in French, the other official language, *Convention relative a la signification et la notification a l' étranger des actes judiciaries et extrajudiciares en matiére Civile ou commerciale*) — the Hague Service Convention — was concluded. Today, the issue of service abroad for most transnational litigation begins with the Convention. As we will see, however, problems of translation linger.

CONVENTION ON THE SERVICE ABROAD OF JUDICIAL AND EXTRAJUDICIAL DOCUMENTS IN CIVIL OR COMMERCIAL MATTERS

(Concluded November 15, 1965)

The States signatory to the present Convention,

Desiring to create appropriate means to ensure that judicial and extrajudicial documents to be served abroad shall be brought to the notice of the addressee in sufficient time,

Desiring to improve the organisation of mutual judicial assistance for that purpose by simplifying and expediting the procedure,

Have resolved to conclude a Convention to this effect and have agreed upon the following provisions:

Article 1

The present Convention shall apply in all cases, in civil or commercial matters, where there is occasion to transmit a judicial or extrajudicial document for service abroad.

This Convention shall not apply where the address of the person to be served with the document is not known.

CHAPTER I — JUDICIAL DOCUMENTS

Article 2

Each Contracting State shall designate a Central Authority which will undertake to receive requests for service coming from other Contracting States and to proceed in conformity with the provisions of Articles 3 to 6.

Each State shall organise the Central Authority in conformity with its own law.

Article 8

Each Contracting State shall be free to effect service of judicial documents upon persons abroad, without application of any compulsion, directly through its diplomatic or consular agents.

Any State may declare that it is opposed to such service within its territory, unless the document is to be served upon a national of the State in which the documents originate.

Article 9

Each Contracting State shall be free, in addition, to use consular channels to forward documents, for the purpose of service, to those authorities of another Contracting State which are designated by the latter for this purpose.

Each Contracting State may, if exceptional circumstances so require, use diplomatic channels for the same purpose.

Article 10

Provided the State of destination does not object, the present Convention shall not interfere with—

a) the freedom to send judicial documents, by postal channels, directly to persons abroad,

b) the freedom of judicial officers, officials or other competent persons of the State of origin to effect service of judicial documents directly through the judicial officers, officials or other competent persons of the State of destination,

c) the freedom of any person interested in a judicial proceeding to effect service of judicial documents directly through the judicial officers, officials or other competent persons of the State of destination.

National practice under the Hague Service Convention varies widely, as might be expected. To determine the designated central authority as well as permissible methods of extraterritorial notice (or "*signification* or *notification*"), lawyers must take note of the designations and reservations of the individual country concerned set out in the declaration of the particular country upon its accession to the Convention. For the full text of the convention and the declarations, see http://www.hcch.net/index_en.php?act=conventions.status&cid=17.

Canada has designated a central authority for each province (or territory) inasmuch as the implementation of all private international treaties requires separate provincial legislative action. The language requirements also differ by province. For Quebec, for instance, the documents must be in French or in English with a French translation. For recipients who understand English, a "translation" in English may be allowed upon request by the Quebec Central Authority. Canada has not objected, however, to any of the methods of notice permitted under either article 8 or 10.

Within the Europe the variations are considerable, Belgium, for example, objected to the method of notice allowed in article 8 but did not object to those of article 10. The Czech Republic declared its objection to article 8 and, as officially translated, "documents may not be served by another Contracting State through postal channels nor through the judicial officers, officials or other competent persons" under article 10. The French Government declared its objection to direct notice through diplomatic and consular agents upon persons who are not nationals of the state of dispatch. Norway and Germany, on the other hand, declared their objection to all of the methods of notice allowed under articles 8 and 10, although Germany like France would allow notice upon nationals of the state of dispatch under article 10. In contrast, Italy did not object to any of the methods of notice allowed under either article 8 or 10.

Elsewhere, Mexico has objected to direct notice by diplomatic officials under article 8 except to nationals of the country of dispatch and appears to have objected to all methods under article 10, albeit the declaration repeats its declaration with respect to notice by diplomatic means. Mexico does require that all documents be accompanied by a Spanish translation. The People's Republic of China has similarly declared its objection to any notice via diplomatic representatives except upon nationals of the state of dispatch and has objected to all methods of notice in article 10. As examined in greater detail below, Japan declared objection only to the methods of notice in article 10(b) and article 10(c). Language and the choice of words are again significant, as suggested by the substitution of "notice" for "service" in the preceding paragraphs. It may be useful to note the official versions of article 8 and article 10(a) in French. They read:

Article 8:

Chaque Etat contractant a la faculté de faire procéder directement, sans contrainte, par les soins de ses agents diplomatiques ou consulaires, aux significations ou notifications d'actes judiciaires aux personnes se trouvant à l'étranger.

Tout Etat peut déclarer s'opposer à l'usage de cette faculté sur son territoire, sauf si l'acte doit être signifié ou notifié à un ressortissant de l'Etat d'origine.

Article 10(a):

La présente Convention ne fait pas obstacle, sauf si l'Etat de destination déclare s'y opposer:

a) à la faculté d'adresser directement, par la voie de la poste, des actes judiciaires aux personnes se trouvant à l'étranger.

II. UNITED STATES

A. General

VOLKSWAGENWERK AKTIENGESELLSCHAFT v. SCHLUNK
486 U.S. 694 (1988)

JUSTICE O'CONNOR delivered the opinion of the Court.

. . . .

VWAG filed a special and limited appearance for the purpose of quashing service. VWAG asserted that it could be served only in accordance with the Hague Service Convention, and that Schlunk had not complied with the Convention's requirements. The Circuit Court denied VWAG's motion. It first observed that VWoA is registered to do business in Illinois and has a registered agent for receipt of process in Illinois. The court then reasoned that VWoA and VWAG are so closely related that VWoA is VWAG's agent for service of process as a matter of law, notwithstanding VWAG's failure or refusal to appoint VWoA formally as an agent. The court relied on the facts that VWoA is a wholly owned subsidiary of VWAG, that a majority of the members of the board of directors of VWoA are members of the board of VWAG, and that VWoA is by contract the exclusive importer and distributor of VWAG products sold in the United States. The court concluded that, because service was accomplished within the United States, the Hague Service Convention did not apply.

The Circuit Court certified two questions to the Appellate Court of Illinois. For reasons similar to those given by the Circuit Court, the Appellate Court determined that VWoA is VWAG's agent for service of process under Illinois law, and that the service of process in this case did not violate the Hague Service Convention. 145 Ill. App. 3d 594, 503 N. E. 2d 1045 (1986). After the Supreme Court of Illinois denied VWAG leave to appeal, 112 Ill. 2d 595 (1986), VWAG petitioned this Court for a writ of certiorari to review the Appellate Court's interpretation of the Hague Service Convention. We granted certiorari to address this issue, 484 U.S. 895 (1987), which has given rise to disagreement among the lower courts. [Citations omitted.]

II

The Hague Service Convention is a multilateral treaty that was formulated in 1964 by the Tenth Session of the Hague Conference of Private International Law. The Convention revised parts of the Hague Conventions on Civil Procedure of 1905 and 1954. The revision was intended to provide a simpler way to serve process abroad, to assure that defendants sued in foreign jurisdictions would receive actual and timely notice of suit, and to facilitate proof of service abroad. [Citations omitted.] Representatives of all 23 countries that were members of the Conference approved the Convention without reservation. Thirty-two countries, including the United States and the Federal Republic of Germany, have ratified or acceded to the Convention. [Citation omitted.]

The primary innovation of the Convention is that it requires each state to establish a central authority to receive requests for service of documents from other countries. 20 U.S.T. 362, T.I.A.S. 6638, Art. 2. Once a central authority receives a request in the proper form, it must serve the documents by a method prescribed by the internal law of the receiving state or by a method designated by the requester and compatible with that law. Art. 5. The central authority must then provide a certificate of service that conforms to a specified model. Art. 6. A state also may consent to methods of service within its boundaries other than a request to its central authority. Arts. 8, 11, 19. The remaining provisions of the Convention that are relevant here limit the circumstances in which a default judgment may be entered against a defendant who had to be served abroad and did not appear, and provide some means for relief from such a judgment. Arts. 15, 16.

Article 1 defines the scope of the Convention, which is the subject of controversy in this case. It says: "The present Convention shall apply in all cases, in civil or commercial matters, where there is occasion to transmit a judicial or extrajudicial document for service abroad." 20 U.S.T., at 362. The equally authentic French version says, "La présente Convention est applicable, en matière civile ou commerciale, dans tous les cas où un acte judiciaire ou extrajudiciaire doit être transmis à l'étranger pour y être signifié ou notifié." *Ibid.* This language is mandatory, as we acknowledged last Term in *Société Nationale Industrielle Aérospatiale v. United*

States District Court, 482 U.S. 522, 534, n. 15 (1987). By virtue of the Supremacy Clause, U.S. Const., Art. VI, the Convention pre-empts inconsistent methods of service prescribed by state law in all cases to which it applies. *Schlunk* does not purport to have served his complaint on VWAG in accordance with the Convention. Therefore, if service of process in this case falls within Article 1 of the Convention, the trial court should have granted VWAG's motion to quash.

When interpreting a treaty, we "begin 'with the text of the treaty and the context in which the written words are used.'" *Société Nationale, supra, (quoting Air France v. Saks, supra,* 470 U.S. 392, 397 (1985)). *Other general rules of construction may be brought to bear on difficult or ambiguous passages. " 'Treaties are construed more liberally than private agreements, and to ascertain their meaning we may look beyond the written words to the history of the treaty, the negotiations, and the practical construction adopted by the parties.' " Air France v. Saks, supra,* at 396, 105 S. Ct., at 1341 (quoting *Choctaw Nation of Indians v. United States,* 318 U.S. 423, 431–432 (1943)). [Emphasis in opinion.]

The Convention does not specify the circumstances in which there is "occasion to transmit" a complaint "for service abroad." But at least the term "service of process" has a well-established technical meaning. Service of process refers to a formal delivery of documents that is legally sufficient to charge the defendant with notice of a pending action. [Citations omitted.] The legal sufficiency of a formal delivery of documents must be measured against some standard. The Convention does not prescribe a standard, so we almost necessarily must refer to the internal law of the forum state. If the internal law of the forum state defines the applicable method of serving process as requiring the transmittal of documents abroad, then the Hague Service Convention applies.

The negotiating history supports our view that Article 1 refers to service of process in the technical sense. The committee that prepared the preliminary draft deliberately used a form of the term "notification" (formal notice), instead of the more neutral term "remise" (delivery), when it drafted Article 1. 3 Actes et Documents, at 78–79. Then, in the course of the debates, the negotiators made the language even more exact. The preliminary draft of Article 1 said that the present Convention shall apply in all cases in which there are grounds *to transmit or to give formal notice of* a judicial or extrajudicial document in a civil or commercial matter to a person staying abroad. *Id.,* at 65 ("La présente Convention est applicable dans tous les cas où il y a lieu *de transmettre ou de notifier* un acte judiciaire ou extrajudiciaire en matière civile ou commerciale à une personne se trouvant à l'étranger") (emphasis added [in opinion]). To be more precise, the delegates decided to add a form of the juridical term "signification" (service), which has a narrower meaning than "notification" in some countries, such as France, and the identical meaning in others, such as the United States. *Id.,* at 152–153, 155, 159, 366. The delegates also criticized the language of the preliminary draft because it suggested that the Convention could apply to transmissions abroad that do not culminate in service. *Id.,* at 165–167. The final text of Article 1, *supra,* eliminates this possibility and applies only to documents transmitted for service abroad. The final report (*Rapport Explicatif*) confirms that the Convention does not use more general terms, such as delivery or transmission, to define its scope because it applies only when there is both transmission of a document from the requesting state to the receiving state, and service upon the person for whom it is intended. *Id.*, at 366.

The negotiating history of the Convention also indicates that whether there is service abroad must be determined by reference to the law of the forum state. The preliminary draft said that the Convention would apply "where there are grounds" to transmit a judicial document to a person staying abroad. The committee that prepared the preliminary draft realized that this implied that the forum's internal law would govern whether service implicated the Convention. *Id.*, at 80–81. The reporter expressed regret about this solution because it would decrease the obligatory force of the Convention. *Id.*, at 81. Nevertheless, the delegates did not change the meaning of Article 1 in this respect.

The Yugoslavian delegate offered a proposal to amend Article 1 to make explicit that service abroad is defined according to the law of the state that is requesting service of process. *Id.*, at 167. The delegate from the Netherlands supported him. *Ibid.* The German delegate approved of the proposal in principle, although he thought it would require a corresponding reference to the significance of the law of the state receiving the service of process, and that this full explanation would be too complicated. *Id.*, at 168. The President opined that there was a choice to be made between the phrase used by the preliminary draft, "where grounds exist," and the Yugoslavian proposal to modify it with the phrase, "according to the law of the requesting state." *Ibid.* This prompted the Yugoslavian delegate to declare that the difference was immaterial, because the phrase "where grounds exist" necessarily refers to the law of the forum. *Ibid.* The French delegate added that, in his view, the law of the forum in turn is equivalent to the law of the requesting state. *Id.*, at 169. At that point, the President recommended entrusting the problem to the drafting committee.

The drafting committee then composed the version of Article 1 that ultimately was adopted, which says that the Convention applies "where there is occasion" to transmit a judicial document for service abroad. *Id.*, at 211. After this revision, the reporter again explained that one must leave to the requesting state the task of defining when a document must be served abroad; that this solution was a consequence of the unavailability of an objective test; and that while it decreases the obligatory force of the Convention, it does provide clarity. *Id.*, at 254. The inference we draw from this history is that the Yugoslavian proposal was rejected because it was superfluous, not because it was inaccurate, and that "service abroad" has the same meaning in the final version of the Convention as it had in the preliminary draft.

VWAG protests that it is inconsistent with the purpose of the Convention to interpret it as applying only when the internal law of the forum requires service abroad. One of the two stated objectives of the Convention is "to create appropriate means to ensure that judicial and extrajudicial documents to be served abroad shall be brought to the notice of the addressee in sufficient time." 20 U.S.T., at 362. The Convention cannot assure adequate notice, VWAG argues, if the forum's internal law determines whether it applies. VWAG warns that countries could circumvent the Convention by defining methods of service of process that do not require transmission of documents abroad. Indeed, VWAG contends that one such method of service already exists and that it troubled the Conference: *notification au parquet.*

Notification au parquet permits service of process on a foreign defendant by the deposit of documents with a designated local official. Although the official generally is supposed to transmit the documents abroad to the defendant, the statute of limitations begins to run from the time that the official receives the documents, and there allegedly is no sanction for failure to transmit them. [References omitted.] At the time of the 10th Conference, France, the Netherlands, Greece, Belgium, and Italy utilized some type of *notification au parquet.* [Reference omitted.]

There is no question but that the Conference wanted to eliminate *notification au parquet.* [Reference omitted.] It included in the Convention two provisions that address the problem. Article 15 says that a judgment may not be entered unless a foreign defendant received adequate and timely notice of the lawsuit. Article 16 provides means whereby a defendant who did not receive such notice may seek relief from a judgment that has become final. 20 U.S.T., at 364–365. Like Article 1, however, Articles 15 and 16 apply only when documents must be transmitted abroad for the purpose of service. 3 Actes et Documents, at 168–169. VWAG argues that, if this determination is made according to the internal law of the forum state, the Convention will fail to eliminate variants of *notification au parquet* that do not expressly require transmittal of documents to foreign defendants. Yet such methods of service of process are the least likely to provide a defendant with actual notice.

The parties make conflicting representations about whether foreign laws authorizing *notification au parquet* command the transmittal of documents for service abroad within the meaning of the Convention. The final report is itself somewhat equivocal. It says that, although the strict language of Article 1 might raise a question as to whether the Convention regulates *notification au parquet*, the understanding of the drafting Commission, based on the debates, is that the Convention would apply. [Reference omitted.] Although this statement might affect our decision as to whether the Convention applies to *notification au parquet*, an issue we do not resolve today, there is no comparable evidence in the negotiating history that the Convention was meant to apply to substituted service on a subsidiary like VWoA, which clearly does not require service abroad under the forum's internal law. Hence neither the language of the Convention nor the negotiating history contradicts our interpretation of the Convention, according to which the internal law of the forum is presumed to determine whether there is occasion for service abroad.

Nor are we persuaded that the general purposes of the Convention require a different conclusion. One important objective of the Convention is to provide means to facilitate service of process abroad. Thus the first stated purpose of the Convention is "to create" appropriate means for service abroad, and the second stated purpose is "to improve the organization of mutual judicial assistance for that purpose by simplifying and expediting the procedure." 20 U.S.T., at 362. By requiring each state to establish a central authority to assist in the service of process, the Convention implements this enabling function. Nothing in our decision today interferes with this requirement.

VWAG correctly maintains that the Convention also aims to ensure that there will be adequate notice in cases in which there is occasion to serve process abroad.

Thus compliance with the Convention is mandatory in all cases to which it applies, see *supra*, at 2109, and Articles 15 and 16 provide an indirect sanction against those who ignore it, see 3 Actes et Documents, at 92, 363. Our interpretation of the Convention does not necessarily advance this particular objective, inasmuch as it makes recourse to the Convention's means of service dependent on the forum's internal law. But we do not think that this country, or any other country, will draft its internal laws deliberately so as to circumvent the Convention in cases in which it would be appropriate to transmit judicial documents for service abroad. For example, there has been no question in this country of excepting foreign nationals from the protection of our Due Process Clause. Under that Clause, foreign nationals are assured of either personal service, which typically will require service abroad and trigger the Convention, or substituted service that provides "notice reasonably calculated, under all the circumstances, to apprise interested parties of the pendency of the action and afford them an opportunity to present their objections." *Mullane v. Central Hanover Bank & Trust Co.*, 339 U.S. 306, 314 (1950).

The concurrence believes that our interpretation does not adequately guarantee timely notice, which it denominates the "primary" purpose of the Convention, albeit without authority. *Post*, at 2114. The concurrence instead proposes to impute a substantive standard to the words, "service abroad." *Post*, at 2112. Evidently, a method of service would not be deemed to be "service abroad" within the meaning of Article 1 unless it provides notice to the recipient "in due time." *Post*, at 2115, 2116. This due process notion cannot be squared with the plain meaning of the words, "service abroad." The contours of the concurrence's substantive standard are not defined, and we note that it would create some uncertainty even on the facts of this case. If the substantive standard tracks the Due Process Clause of the Fourteenth Amendment, it is not self-evident that substituted service on a subsidiary is sufficient with respect to the parent. In the only cases in which it has considered the question, this Court held that the activities of a subsidiary are not necessarily enough to render a parent subject to a court's jurisdiction, for service of process or otherwise. [Citations omitted.] Although the particular relationship between VWAG and VWoA might have made substituted service valid in this case, a question that we do not decide, the factbound character of the necessary inquiry makes us doubt whether the standard suggested by the concurrence would in fact be "remarkably easy" to apply, see *post*, at 2116.

Furthermore, nothing that we say today prevents compliance with the Convention even when the internal law of the forum does not so require. The Convention provides simple and certain means by which to serve process on a foreign national. Those who eschew its procedures risk discovering that the forum's internal law required transmittal of documents for service abroad, and that the Convention therefore provided the exclusive means of valid service. In addition, parties that comply with the Convention ultimately may find it easier to enforce their judgments abroad. [Reference omitted.] For these reasons, we anticipate that parties may resort to the Convention voluntarily, even in cases that fall outside the scope of its mandatory application.

JUSTICE BRENNAN, with whom JUSTICE MARSHALL and JUSTICE BLACKMUN join, concurring in the judgment.

We acknowledged last Term, and the Court reiterates today, *ante*, at 2107–2108, that the terms of the Convention on Service Abroad of Judicial and Extrajudicial Documents in Civil or Commercial Matters, Nov. 15, 1965, [1969] 20 U.S.T. 361, T.I.A.S. No. 6638, are "mandatory," not "optional" with respect to any transmission that Article 1 covers. [Citation omitted.] Even so, the Court holds, and I agree, that a litigant may, consistent with the Convention, serve process on a foreign corporation by serving its wholly owned domestic subsidiary, because such process is not "service abroad" within the meaning of Article 1. The Court reaches that conclusion, however, by depriving the Convention of any mandatory effect, for in the Court's view the "forum's internal law" defines conclusively whether a particular process is "service abroad," which is covered by the Convention, or domestic service, which is not. *Ante*, at 2110. I do not join the Court's opinion because I find it implausible that the Convention's framers intended to leave each contracting nation, and each of the 50 States within our Nation, free to decide for itself under what circumstances, if any, the Convention would control. Rather, in my view, the words "service abroad," read in light of the negotiating history, embody a substantive standard that limits a forum's latitude to deem service complete domestically.

QUESTIONS

1. How does Justice O'Conner view the function of "service" as used in the English language version of the Hague Service Convention? Does she consider "service" under the Convention to be a prerequisite for adjudicatory jurisdiction? What was the function of service under Illinois law?

2. What was the basis under Illinois law for service on Volkswagenwerk AG? Does this mean that all parent companies with wholly owned subsidiaries incorporated in the United States could be similarly deemed subject to methods of domestic service not permitted under the Hague Service Convention?

3. What if Illinois law had provided that all unregistered companies doing business in the state authorize service on a state official, such as the secretary of state, as its agent? Would the Service Convention apply to such service under the holding in *Schlunk?*

4. If authorized under a state statute and if in compliance with Due Process requirements, could service by publication also be used to avoid the mandated procedures of the Service Convention?

5. In light of the following letter, what is the likely effect in Germany of a judgment against Volkswagenwerk AG?

LETTER
EMBASSY OF THE FEDERAL REPUBLIC OF GERMANY
WASHINGTON, D.C.

The Embassy of the Federal Republic of Germany presents its compliments to the Department of State and, referring to three recent cases in which German addresses were served judicial documents from the United States by mail, has the honor to inform the Department of State of the German view concerning service by mail of such documents by foreign countries:

Under the German legal interpretation, German sovereignty is violated in cases where foreign judicial documents are served directly by mail within the Federal Republic of Germany. By such direct service, an act of sovereignty is conducted without any control by German authorities on the territory of the Federal Republic of Germany. This is not admissible under German Laws. Under these laws, the German authorities must be in a position to examine whether the foreign request for service is in compliance with the legal provisions established for this purpose and whether it is in compliance with the order public of the Federal Republic of Germany. This is the reason why the Federal Republic of Germany has, when depositing the instrument of ratification to the Hague Convention of November 15, 1964, concerning the service abroad of judicial and extrajudicial documents in civil or commercial matters, objected in accordance with Article 21, Para. 2, letter "a" of the convention to the application of the chanels of transmission as stipulated in Article 10 of the Convention.

The Federal Government also considers service conducted under the laws of individual U.S. States by persons other than judicial officers to be judicial service. It thereby follows the legal interpretation expressed by the Department of Justice in its Memo No. 386 (Revision 2, of June 15, 19 Page 13, footnote 4). Under this interpretation, such persons are to be considered "authority or judicial officer competent under the law of the State in which the documents originate" in the sense of Article 3 of the Hague Convention on the Service of Documents.

Since the Hague Convention on the Service of Documents has gone into effect between the United States of America and the Federal Republic of Germany on July 26, 1979, the Federal Government would appreciate it if service of documents originating from American judicial proceedings to persons within the Federal Republic of Germany would be conducted in compliance with this convention only and if the courts and attornies involved could be informed accordingly.

Washington, D.C. September 27, 1979

B. German Service in the United States Under the Service Convention

ACKERMANN v. LEVINE*
788 F.2d 830 (2d Cir. 1986)

PIERCE, CIRCUIT JUDGE:

This is an appeal from a judgment and final order of the United States District Court for the Southern District of New York, Irving Ben Cooper, Judge, entered May 20, 1985, 610 F.Supp. 633, following an enforcement proceeding, holding unenforceable the default judgment issued by the Regional Court of Berlin in West Germany on December 12, 1980 in favor of plaintiffs and against defendant for 190,708. 49 deutschemarks (DM), or approximately $100,000, plus interest, for legal fees allegedly owed by appellee.

Appellants argue that the district court erred in ruling that (1) service of the summons and complaint in the German suit by registered mail violated the Hague Convention on Service Abroad of Judicial and Extrajudicial Documents in Civil or Commercial Matters, 20 U.S.T. 36, T.I.A.S. 6638 (Hague Convention) and constitutional due process, and (2) enforcement of the German default judgment for legal fees charged under the German fee statute and upheld by the German court would violate the public policy concern of New York courts that attorneys seeking recovery of fees "bear the burden of proving that a compensation arrangement is fair, reasonable and fully comprehended by the client." *Ackermann v. Levine*, 610 F.Supp. 633 (S.D.N.Y. 1985) (hereinafter cited as "Op."), at 647.

We hold that service of process by registered mail satisfied the Hague Convention and constitutional due process, and that enforcement of the German default judgment would not violate New York public policy to the extent that the judgment reflects an award of attorneys fees for which the attorney presented in the enforcement proceeding, at a minimum, evidence of client authorization and appropriate work product.

We therefore affirm in part and reverse in part.

BACKGROUND

Peter R. Ackermann is a German citizen practicing law in West Berlin in the appellant law firm. Ira Levine is an American citizen engaged in the real estate business in New York, where he lives, and New Jersey, where he was the general partner of a limited partnership entitled Hudson View Associates in 1979, and at all pertinent times herein. In the spring of 1979, Levine was considering financing, developing and selling a proposed real estate project in Edgewater, New Jersey (the Edgewater Project). The total cost of the completed project was estimated at approximately $21 million, of which Levine's interest was approximately $6 million. In May of 1979, Levine was introduced to Gottlieb Bauer Schlictegroll ("Bauer"), a

---

* Footnotes omitted.

West German business promoter en route from Costa Rica to West Germany via New York, and Walter Pfaeffle, a friend of Bauer and a West German journalist living in New York whom Bauer introduced to Levine as a "financial consultant." Bauer informed Levine that he knew potential German investors, including Peter Kuth. At a meeting at the Regency Hotel in New York, Levine gave to Bauer financial documents and written specifications of Edgewater Towers. It was agreed that Levine would pay Bauer a $600,000 commission if he raised the needed capital. The district court found that Bauer was "a devious opportunist who told a different story to each interested party," Op. at 636, and who thereby caused the failure of Ackermann and Levine to have a "meeting of minds." Op. at 636, 641.

Later in May, 1979, Levine received two telephone calls involving the potential interest of a German investment group called the Titan Group. Levine then visited Frederic Coudert, Esq., of the international law firm of Coudert Brothers, in New York, and asked if Mr. Coudert could represent him in West Germany. When Coudert replied that he did not have an office in West Berlin, Levine said, "I do not wish to go to Germany and sit down and hopefully sign a contract without any type of representation." Coudert then recommended three West Berlin law firms, including that of Ackermann.

In late May or early June, 1979, Levine went to West Berlin, with Coudert's list of firms, to talk with Kuth. Bauer met Levine at the airport and explained that Kuth was unavailable. Bauer suggested that Levine talk to Bauer's attorney and friend, Peter Ackermann. Noting the coincidence that Ackermann was affiliated with one of Coudert's recommendees, Levine met with Bauer and Ackermann. Unknown to Levine, a week earlier Bauer had spoken to Ackermann and given him Levine's documents, and suggested that Ackermann might be able to render legal and tax advice regarding the Edgewater Project.

The district court found that Ackermann and Levine had entirely different versions of their single pre-litigation face-to-face encounter. These two versions, like those of many other critical aspects of the record, "stem from the two almost opposite perspectives that each man brought to the meeting." Op. at 637. Levine's only goal was to sell his property, and he preferred to sell to a German investor because Bauer convinced him that he would thereby obtain a favorable price. He hoped to sign a contract with the Titan Group, and anticipated paying Bauer the negotiated $600,000 broker's fee. At the enforcement proceeding, Levine recalled meeting with Ackermann on this occasion for about twenty minutes.

Ackermann recalled a meeting with Levine lasting one to one-and-a-half hours, at which there was substantial legal discussion regarding the contemplated transaction. Ackermann understood his task to be to study the project and its structural requirements, as was customary for his firm to do, and then to explain to German banks "the legal and taxwise ramifications of this structure that I was to develop."

It is undisputed that the parties never discussed attorneys fees or the nature of their relationship. Ackermann testified, however, that Levine told him that he had been referred to Ackermann by the Coudert firm. The district court found "that the parties discussed, in general terms only, tax shelter schemes — a plan that benefited both Mr. Ackermann, who wanted to develop this approach, and Mr.

Levine, who stood to gain financially from a German purchaser." The court also found that while there was no agreement for Ackermann to begin talks with any bank, it was resolved that Levine, Bauer and an accountant would commence talks with the Grundkreditbank in West Berlin. This conversation at the bank immediately followed the meeting with Ackermann, and was conducted entirely in German, which Levine apparently does not speak. Afterwards, Bauer explained to Levine that he thought the meeting was favorable, and that he would keep him apprised of subsequent developments.

Levine returned to New York the next day. Several days later, Bauer sent word that the bank remained interested but needed some time to consider the deal. Levine responded that he would not wait, as he had interested investors in the United States. Bauer replied that the bank needed only seven to ten days, to which Levine then agreed. Bauer suggested that "because of Mr. Ackermann's relationship with the bank, we should utilize Mr. Ackermann to go into the bank and discuss the project." Levine testified that he said, " 'I don't understand at this point why we are involving Peter Ackermann. . . . You are acting as a broker to sell my property.' " Levine further testified that Bauer explained, " 'We need Mr. Ackermann to go into the bank, because of his association with the bank, and he has agreed with us to share in our commission equally.' " On June 8, 1979, Levine wrote to Ackermann [authorizing his representation in negotiations].

The district court found Ackermann to be a "moral, upright 'officer of the Court,' " Op. at 639, who reasonably believed that Levine wanted him to structure the deal as part of his duties in negotiating with the bank, rather than to act as a real estate broker, which Judge Cooper found lawyers may not lawfully do in Germany. *Id.*

. . . .

Levine testified that he then called Ackermann, disappointed that the original proposal to the Grundkreditbank was rejected, and that in response to the question in Ackermann's letter, he said, "That's up to you."

On June 21, 1979, Ackermann went to Frankfurt to present the deal to the second bank. That effort failed.

On June 26, 1979, Ackermann appears to have sent a letter to Levine at Levine's New Jersey business address, which Levine no longer used. A second letter, dated July 18, 1979, having been sent to the same address, reached Levine. Therein, Ackermann wrote that he had not received an answer to the June 26 letter; that he had had lengthy conversations with a Mr. Kulisch and a group of investors, which he expected to continue, in which case he would ask Levine to come to Germany; that he recommended that the deal be structured around a limited partnership in New Jersey and one in Germany; and that he requested a $10,000 deposit. The deposit was "to be applied against fees and expenses for which we will account in due course." Levine testified that he received the letter, that he never sent the money, and that he never responded to the letter.

Ackermann testified before Judge Cooper that by the end of July he had spent fifteen to twenty full working days on the project. However, Ackermann stated in a deposition that neither he nor his firm had prepared any written studies or formal memoranda, and that he did not believe that his files would contain any handwritten notes regarding the project. In the enforcement action, Ackermann did not offer into evidence any written work or other documentation as to the fifteen to twenty days during which he allegedly worked on the project.

On August 8 or 9, 1979, Levine went to West Berlin to continue negotiations with the Titan Group. He did not call or meet with Ackermann. He did sign a letter of intent with Titan, whose attorneys in that transaction were apparently Coudert Brothers.

On October 22, 1979, Ackermann sent his bill for legal services to Levine. The fees were computed in accordance with the German legal fee statute called Bundesrechtsanwaltsgebuehrenordnung, or BRAGO. Under the statute, each legal step taken in an action constitutes a fee unit which in turn is converted into a price that reflects both the value of the legal questions or financial transaction and the percentage (from 50 to 100%) of the total fee unit that the attorney decides to charge. As most German lawyers do in non-litigation work, Ackermann charged Levine 75% of the allowable fee units. Ackermann's letter itemized the bill in two main parts: 89.347,50 DM for studies and client counseling, and the same for discussions with banks.

The Regional Court reviewed these charges in entering a default judgment and approved all but the photocopy costs and corresponding value-added tax since those costs were apparently included in the business fee under court practice. The judgment award thus became DM 190,708.49 plus 4% interest pursuant to Art. 291, BGB.

On January 11, 1980, suit was initiated herein to recover legal fees when the German court sent a summons and complaint to the German Consulate in New York, which mailed them by registered mail to Levine's former New Jersey address. Although a receipt postmarked March 13, 1980, was received, Levine claims that he never received such process. A second summons and complaint was sent by the same method to Levine's Manhattan apartment, and was received by a building employee, Ortiz; the receipt was postmarked October 14, 1980. Levine acknowledges receipt of the summons and complaint and actual knowledge of the suit. Indeed, Levine testified that on at least one occasion before judgment was entered, he consulted with Frederic Coudert, Esq. about the suit, and he decided to ignore it. A default judgment was entered on December 12, 1980, and an "engrossment" informing Levine of that judgment was sent on December 18, 1980. The time to appeal having lapsed, the judgment became final on February 20, 1981.

Plaintiffs commenced an action seeking enforcement of the foreign judgment in the United States District Court for the Southern District of New York on February 8, 1982. Levine appeared and the matter was tried to the court. By opinion dated May 20, 1984, Judge Cooper declined to enforce the German judgment on two grounds: (1) the service of process by registered mail violated the Hague Convention and due process, and (2) recognition and enforcement would violate New York public policy. Plaintiffs appeal from that decision.

Discussion

We are confronted here with issues relating to the recognition and enforcement of a foreign judgment in a case involving attorney-client relations in an international business context. The district court appropriately framed the issues in accordance with the well-settled rule that a final judgment obtained through sound procedures in a foreign country is generally conclusive as to its merits unless (1) the foreign court lacked jurisdiction over the subject matter or the person of the defendant; (2) the judgment was fraudulently obtained; or (3) enforcement of the judgment would offend the public policy of the state in which enforcement is sought. [Citations omitted.] In light of the existence of the Hague Convention and the underlying substantive issues regarding public policy, this case requires us to consider issues which this court has had little opportunity to address.

I.

To be subject to in personam jurisdiction, a defendant must have had certain "minimum contacts" with the forum state, [citations omitted] and reasonable notice of the pendency of the action, [citations omitted]. We agree with the district court that under the "minimum contacts" test of *International Shoe* and its progeny, Levine had sufficient contacts with West Germany such that he was "avail[ing] himself" of the privileges arising therein, *Hanson v. Denckla*, 357 U.S. 235, 253, 78 S. Ct. 1228, 1240, 2 L. Ed. 2d 1283 (1958), so that the exercise of in personam jurisdiction would not offend "traditional notions of fair play and substantial justice," *Milliken v. Meyer*, 311 U.S. at 462–64, 61 S. Ct. at 342–343. We therefore move to the question of whether service of the summons and complaint by registered mail provided Levine with adequate notice of the action.

Service of process must satisfy both the statute under which service is effectuated and constitutional due process. The statutory prong is governed principally by the Hague Convention on the Service Abroad of Judicial and Extrajudicial Documents in Civil or Commercial Matters (Hague Convention), an international treaty that has been ratified by approximately twenty-three countries, including the United States and the Federal Republic of Germany. See Department of State, Treaties in Force — January 1, 1985, 259 (1985). As a ratified treaty, the Convention is of course "the supreme law of the land." [Citations omitted.]

The service of process by registered mail did not violate the Hague Convention. Plaintiffs declined to follow the service route allowed under Article 5 of the Convention, which permits service via a "Central Authority" of the country in which service is to be made. Instead, plaintiffs chose to follow the equally acceptable route allowed under Articles 8 and 10. [Citation omitted.] Article 8 permits each contracting state "to effect service of judicial documents upon persons abroad . . . directly through its diplomatic or consular agents." The Regional Court of Berlin availed itself of this method by first sending the summons and complaint to the German Consulate in New York. As to the forwarding of those documents by registered mail from the Consulate to Levine's residence, the method of service was appropriate under Article 10(a), which states in pertinent part:

Each contracting State shall be free to effect service of judicial documents upon persons abroad, without application of any compulsion, directly through its diplomatic or consular agents. The phrase "without application of any compulsion" is not further clarified by the Convention, but the phrase has been held to refer to "compulsory process," such as subpoenas or orders to produce documents, and not to "notice process," such as the service of a summons and complaint, which merely notifies the recipient of an action against him, but carries no direct compulsion under threat of contempt of court. [Citation omitted.] Thus, the phrase does not proscribe service under Article 8 in this case.

"Article 10 — Provided the State of destination does not object, the present Convention shall not interfere with—

"(a) the freedom to send judicial documents, by postal channels, directly to persons abroad. . . ."

Since the United States has made no objection to the use of "postal channels" under Article 10(a), service of process by registered mail remains an appropriate method of service in this country under the Convention.); [References omitted.] Further, as appellants' counsel have documented, the word "send" in Article 10(a) was intended to mean "service." See [1 B. Ristau, International Judicial Assistance (Civil and Commercial) §§ 4–28 at 165–67 (1984)] (reviewing the Rapporteur's report on the final text of the Convention and reaching the "inescapable" conclusion that use of "send" rather than the otherwise consistently used "service" ["]must be attributed to careless drafting"). *See also Shoei Kako*, 33 Cal. App. 3d at 821–22, 109 Cal. Rptr. at 411–12 [*supra*] ("The reference to 'the freedom to send judicial documents by postal channels, directly to persons abroad' would be superfluous

Federal courts construing the Hague Convention have apparently consistently upheld mail service thereunder to defendants in, for example, Japan, which, like the United States, is a signatory to the Convention and has not objected to mail service under Article 10(a). [Citations omitted.] To uphold mail service when effected against foreign defendants in signatory states that do not object to such service, but to invalidate such service when effected against an American defendant would undermine the Hague Convention's purpose of unifying the rules of service of process abroad. [Citations omitted.]

Nor was service ineffective because it did not satisfy the Federal Rules of Civil Procedure. The old Federal Rule 4 was superceded by the Hague Convention and thus presumptively should not limit application of the Convention. [Citation omitted.] The district court correctly notes that Amended Rule 4(c)(2)(C)(ii), permitting mail service conforming to certain technical requirements, did not exist when Ackermann's summons and complaint were served. In any event, whether Ackermann's service satisfied Rule 4 as it then existed or as it now exists is irrelevant because the United States has made no declaration or limitation to its ratification of the Convention regarding Federal Rule 4, or Article 10(a) of the Convention or otherwise regarding mail service under the Convention. [Reference omitted.] Thus, the Convention "supplements"— and is manifestly not limited by — Rule 4. *See id.* at 69.

The district court erred in holding that service under the Convention must satisfy both federal and state law. [Reference omitted.] The court improperly cited *Aspinall's Club*, 450 N.Y.S.2d at 199, for that proposition. Aspinall's Club expressly held quite the opposite — that service of process under the Convention must satisfy federal but not state law. *See Aspinall's Club*, 450 N.Y.S.2d at 202 (service on an adult at defendant's residence must satisfy Federal Rule 4 but not the more stringent requirements under N.Y.C.P.L.R. § 308(2)). Indeed, it seems to us that the only reason that service had to satisfy even Federal Rule 4 in *Aspinall's Club* was that the Convention is silent as to service on persons other than the defendant. Thus, some external law was needed to fill the interstices of the Convention, and the court in *Aspinall's Club*, though a state court, noted that "the Federal laws and treaties" are supreme to state law on this point, and that it would be "untenab[le]" to "promot[e] New York law over the Convention and the Federal Rule." *Id.* In sum, where the Convention provides a rule of decision, that rule is dispositive, barring any contrary declaration by the United States; where the Convention is silent, federal law should govern where possible.

To construe the Convention otherwise would unduly burden foreign judgment holders with the procedural intricacies of fifty states. [Reference with quote omitted.] While we could not similarly subordinate New York's interests in the public policy implications of the subject foreign judgment, as discussed *infra*, New York's rules regarding service are undoubtedly less compelling. [Citations omitted.]

It is of no moment that an employee of appellee Levine's apartment building received and signed for the service of process. First, as to this issue on which the Convention is silent, Federal Rule 4 requires merely that service be made on one of suitable age and discretion at the defendant's residence. [Citation omitted.] Second, contrary to dicta in *Aspinall's Club* as to the more stringent requirements of the CPLR, even New York law may permit service upon one of suitable age and discretion who accepts process for residents of an apartment building. [Citations omitted.]

Finally, service by registered mail does not violate constitutional due process. [Citations omitted.]

QUESTIONS

Were transmission and delivery of the documents sent from the German court to the German consulate and then by mail to Levine a prerequisite to the jurisdiction of the German court as a matter of German law or the Hague Service Convention? Under U.S. law in general and New York law in particular, as examined in Chapter 6, a foreign judgment *"may not"* be recognized and enforced if the foreign court did not have *personal jurisdiction* over the defendant and *"need not"* be recognized if the *notice* of the proceeding is not given in sufficient time to enable the defendant to defend. Is transmission of the judicial documents under the Hague Convention intended to serve either one or both purposes?

C. Service by Mail to Japanese Defendants

As noted by Judge Pierce in *Ackermann v. Levine*, Japan objected to the methods "to effect service" enumerated in article 10 (b) and (c) but not to article 10(a), which provides that, without such objection, the "Convention shall not interfere with — (a) the freedom *to send* judicial documents, by postal channels, directly to persons abroad." The question posed in the following cases was whether the failure of Japan to object to article 10(a) allows "service" by mail to defendants in Japan under the Convention. We begin the discussion with the first case on point, cited by both Justice O'Conner and Judge Pierce.

SHOEI KAKO CO., LTD. v. SUPERIOR COURT OF THE STATE OF CALIFORNIA FOR THE CITY AND COUNTY OF SAN FRANCISCO*
109 Cal. Rptr. 402 (Ct. App. 1973)

SIMS, ASSOCIATE JUSTICE.

By its petition for writ of mandate, the petitioner, a Japanese corporation, seeks review of an order of the trial court which denied its motion to quash the service of summons purportedly effected by mailing a copy of the summons and complaint to its head office in Japan. (See Code Civ. Proc., § 418.10.) An alternative writ was issued and after argument the matter was submitted on the petition, the exhibits filed therewith, and the memorandum of points and authorities in opposition to the petition, and the return filed by real party in interest.

Petitioner contends: (1) that the record fails to show facts which would render it subject to a judgment in personam in this state; that the trial court is without jurisdiction to render a judgment against it (2) because the method used to perfect service of process was not in accordance with an international treaty governing service abroad of judicial and extrajudicial documents, and (3) because the notice given by the service of process failed to comply with due process of law because it was not written in the language of the country to which it was mailed. A review of these contentions reveals that they are without merit. The alternative writ must be discharged and the petition for a peremptory writ denied.

The complaint filed by real party in interest on August 20, 1971 reflects that this action arises out of a collision on December 24, 1970, between a motorcycle operated by real party in interest, the plaintiff in the action below and so referred to herein, and a vehicle allegedly negligently operated by the defendant Shirley Ann Hardesty; that at the time of the accident the plaintiff was wearing a Dias Safety Helmet with a designated serial number; and that he received severe personal injuries as a proximate result of the collision and of the failure of the helmet, for which he seeks to recover $1,500,000 general damages and special damages and loss of earnings according to proof. The first cause of action is directed at the negligence of those who designed, manufactured, constructed, tested, repaired, sold, retailed, wholesaled, and distributed the safety helmet. The second cause of action is directed

---

* Footnotes omitted.

at the same defendants for breach of an implied warranty that the safety helmet was fit for the use for which it was designed and intended. The third cause of action, against the same defendants, is predicated upon the theory of product liability. The fourth cause of action is based upon the negligence of the driver and those responsible for the operation of the other vehicle; and the fifth cause of action is grounded upon the concurrent negligence of all defendants.

Among the named defendants is D. S. Kogaco Company, Ltd., a corporation.

The petitioner, Shoei Kako Co., Ltd., according to the declaration filed on its behalf, is a corporation organized and existing under and in accordance with the laws of Japan with its principal and main office in Tokyo. Admittedly petitioner assumed the responsibility for all debts and obligations of D. S. Kagako Co., Ltd., a corporation formerly organized and existing under and in accordance with the laws of Japan, with its principal and main office in Tokyo because the latter corporation was merged into the petitioning corporation after December 24, 1970.

I

Section 410.10 of the Code of Civil Procedure provides: "A court of this state may exercise jurisdiction on any basis not inconsistent with the Constitution of this state or of the United States." The basic underlying rule is found in *International Shoe Co. v. State of Washington* (1945) 326 U.S. 310, wherein the court referred to "sufficient contacts or ties with the state of the forum to make it reasonable and just, according to our traditional conception of fair play and substantial justice, to permit the state to enforce the obligations which [the nonresident] has incurred there." (326 U.S. at 320.) In recommending the passage of section 410.10 to the Legislature, the Judicial Council followed the format found in the Restatement of Conflict of Laws 2d (1971). [Reference omitted.]

In an effort to meet the criteria so enunciated petitioner filed an affidavit, dated February 20, 1973, of an employee, who was also an employee of the merged corporation, in which he alleges that neither corporation has done business in, has qualified to do business in, has made or contracted to perform any contracts in, has made or contracted to supply services or things in, has maintained any employees, agents or other representatives in, had any interest in any real property in, has caused any tortious injury by act or omission in, has contracted to insure any person, property or risk located in, or has designated any agent for purposes of service of process within the State of California, or any states of the United States or its territories or possessions. He acknowledges that the sole and only contact within the State of California and any state of the United States or its territories of either corporation is an equitable interest of the corporations in one California corporation.

The plaintiff relies upon proffered evidence which he claims shows that the petitioner's predecessor was subject to the jurisdiction of this state because it manufactured a defective helmet which caused an effect, the injuries suffered by plaintiff, within this state. . . .

In order to trace that the helmet worn by plaintiff was one manufactured by petitioner's predecessor for general distribution in the United States, plaintiff presented a copy of a form of declaration purportedly executed by an officer of a testing corporation in which it is recited that the testing corporation's serial number found in the helmet involved "was issued to D. S. Kagaku Co., Ltd. on January 22, 1969." Although the signed original of this declaration does not appear in the record, petitioner apparently does not seriously question the accuracy of that declaration.

Plaintiff also relies upon written answers to interrogatories filed by other parties to the action. On March 5, 1973, three days after argument on petitioner's motion but prior to the submission and decision of the matter, plaintiff filed the answers to interrogatories of the defendant Newman Company a corporation from which it appears that certain helmets which that company sold to defendant Gemco Co. prior to plaintiff's accident were imported from Sunrise & Co., a trading company which bought the helmets from D. S. Kagaku (now Shoei Kako Co.) Ltd., named as manufacturer in the answers, and that other helmets were purchased from Standard Sales, a Los Angeles importer, and from Nelson Sales, a Kansas City, Kansas importer.

. . . .

Stripped of unsigned declarations and extraneous answers there is little, if anything, to show that petitioner's predecessor had any contacts with this state. The declaration of plaintiff states that he purchased the helmet from Gemco Co. prior to the accident, and that it had the testing corporation's number sticker in it. At best, under petitioner's concession, the evidence shows that plaintiff purchased a helmet which had in it a label secured by petitioner's predecessor from the testing corporation which is also named as a defendant.

There is, however, further evidence to show that both petitioner and the merged corporation were doing business in the state, or at the least, doing acts in this state which were related to the distribution and sale of similar helmets. One Philip K. Huff executed a declaration in which he stated that prior to July 15, 1968, he was doing business in this state under the name D. S. Kagaku Co., and that on the date he incorporated and carried a business under the name D. S. Safety Helmet Corporation. The declaration of plaintiff's attorney reflects that on December 9, 1971, Huff, as vice-president of D. S. Safety Helmet Corporation gave him a card bearing that legend with a Los Angeles address for the corporation, and the further endorsement "D. S. Kagaku Co., Ltd." with the Tokyo address of that corporation. An investigator for the plaintiff filed a declaration that on January 13, 1973, at a motorcycle and accessories trade show in Long Beach there was in charge of a booth one Philip K. Huss (sic, Huff) which housed helmets manufactured by petitioner, and that "Huss" was advertising and selling the merchandise. Copies of the brochures distributed bear petitioner's name with its head office designated at the Tokyo address used by the merged corporation, and, as well, reference to Shoei Safety Helmet Corp. at the Los Angeles address used by Huff.

Although in view of the legal evidence suggested, plaintiff's actual presentation is shockingly incomplete, it must be viewed in the light of petitioner's failure to respond to the material presented by plaintiff, other than to question the method of service.

The fact that the helmet was found in channels of retail trade in this state, that there was an ostensible representative of the merged corporation within this state (without, however, proof of actual or ostensible authority from the merged corporation), and that this representative later appeared promoting the sales of the successor corporation, suggests, in the absence of more specific declarations to the contrary, that the merged corporation should have reasonably anticipated that its products would be resold in this state, and was in effect purposefully availing itself of the market for its products in this state when it sold them to Japanese exporters or American importers. The evidence sustains the implied finding of the trial court that there were sufficient contacts with this state to uphold the exercise of in personam jurisdiction if petitioner was given the notice required by law.

II

Petitioner acknowledges that on or about January 9, 1973 it received a document entitled "Notice and Acknowledgment of Receipt" (see Code Civ. Proc., § 415.30; and Cal. Rules of Court, rule 982(4)) addressed to D. S. Kogaco Co., Ltd., 2-9-2 Shimbashi Minato-Ku, Tokyo 105, Japan, together with a copy of the complaint in the pending action.

Plaintiff produced a form of "Notice and Acknowledgment of Receipt," in the form prescribed by statute and rule of court, dated January 4, 1973, and addressed to D. S. Kogacu Company Limited, sued herein as D. S. Kogaco Company Ltd. and bearing the legend "You Are Served Herein as Doe Two." The acknowledgment prescribed by statute and rule of court was not executed, but plaintiff produced what appears to be a form of international mail receipt written in the English and French languages. It contains the following, apparently inserted by the addressee: "Addressee (Name or firm) D. S. Kogaku Co. Ltd., Street and No. 2-9-2 Shinbashi Place and Country Minato-ku, Tokyo 105, Japan." The legend "This receipt must be signed by the addressee or by a person authorized to do so by virtue of the regulations of the country of destination, or, if those regulations so provide, by the employee of the office of destination, and returned by the first mail directly to the sender" is followed by the printed recital, "The article mentioned above was duly delivered. Date." In the appropriate blank there is inserted in script, undecipherable on the copy made available to the court, but allegedly, "Jan. 8, 1973." Following the form's printed "Signature of the employee of the office of destination" is a signature which appears to be "Miyoka Aoki." This is followed by a postmark, apparently endorsed in connection with the return of the receipt, which indicates a mailing date of January 9, 1973.

On February 1, 1973, the plaintiff's attorney addressed a registered letter to D. S. Kogacu Ltd., at the address referred to above. This letter alleges that the addressee was served with a copy of the summons and complaint on January 8, 1973. It states that the time within which to answer expired January 29, 1973. It threatened that unless a responsive pleading was filed by February 15, 1973, the plaintiff would "take default and judgment against (the addressee) in the amount prayed for i.e., $1,500,000.00." On February 16, 1973, petitioner mailed, and on February 20, 1973, there was filed its "Notice Of Motion To Quash Service of Summons For Lack Of Personal Jurisdiction Or To Stay Or Dismiss Action On Ground Of Convenient Forum."

Section 413.10 provides in pertinent part, "Except as otherwise provided by statute, a summons shall be served on a person: . . . (c) Outside the United States, as provided in this chapter or as directed by the court in which the action is pending, or, if the court before or after service finds that the service is reasonably calculated to give actual notice, as prescribed by the law of the place where the person is served or as directed by the foreign authority in response to a letter rogatory." Sections 415.30 and 415 [reference omitted] are within the same chapter, and each, therefore, is an authorized method of effecting service outside the United States.

Section 417.20 provides in pertinent part: "Proof that a summons was served on a person outside this state shall be made: (a) If served in a manner specified in a statute of this state, as prescribed by Section 417.10, and if service is made by mail pursuant to Section 415.40, proof of service shall include evidence satisfactory to the court establishing actual delivery to the person to be served, by a signed return receipt or other evidence; . . . " Section 417.10 provides with respect to service under section 415.30, " . . . If service is made by mail pursuant to Section 415.30, proof of service shall include the acknowledgment of receipt of summons in the form provided by that section or other written acknowledgment of receipt of summons satisfactory to the court." [Additional reference omitted.] No proof of a formal acknowledgment under section 415.30 was presented to the court. The court, however, under the statute could accept the signed return receipt as satisfactory evidence of actual delivery to the person to be served. [Citation omitted.]

The adequacy of service "so far as due process is concerned is dependent on whether or not the form of substituted service provided for such cases and employed is reasonably calculated to give him actual notice of the proceedings and an opportunity to be heard. If it is, the traditional notions of fair play and substantial justice (citation) implicit in due process are satisfied." (*Milliken v. Meyer* (1940) 311 U.S. 457 at p. 463 [reference omitted].) Here there is no question but that petitioner has received actual notice and an opportunity to be heard It insists, however, that the notice was inadequate under international treaty.

The second clause of Article VI of the United States Constitution provides as follows: "This Constitution, and the Laws of the United States which shall be made in Pursuance thereof; and all Treaties made, or which shall be made, under the Authority of the United States, shall be the supreme Law of the Land; and the Judges in every State shall be bound thereby, any Thing in the Constitution or Laws of any State to the Contrary notwithstanding." This state, therefore, cannot attempt to exercise jurisdiction if to do so would violate an international treaty. [Citations omitted.]

On February 10, 1969, following prior ratification and proclamation, the United States of America became bound by the provisions of a multilateral international convention governing "Service Abroad of Judicial and Extrajudicial Documents." (20 U.S.T. 361–367.) A declaration filed on behalf of petitioner indicates that the convention became effective, subject to certain objections noted below, as to Japan on or about July 27, 1970. The difficulties giving rise to the convention, which was agreed upon at The Hague, November 15, 1965, have been documented. [Citations omitted.]

Article 1 of the treaty provides: "The present Convention shall apply in all cases, in civil or commercial matters, where there is occasion to transmit a judicial or extrajudicial document for service abroad." Articles 2 through 6 establish a system whereby each contracting state shall organize and designate a "Central Authority" which will undertake to receive, and to reject or to execute, and to certify requests for service of process from other contracting states. Other methods of service are recognized. Article 8 permits service to be effected upon persons abroad through diplomatic or consular agents unless opposition has been declared by the state involved to such service on others than nationals of the originating state. Article 9 permits service by forwarding documents for service through consular or diplomatic channels to authorities who are authorized to effect service. The controversy in this case revolves about the provisions of Article 10, which reads: "Provided the State of destination does not object, the present Convention shall not interfere with — (a) the freedom to send judicial documents, by postal channels, directly to persons abroad, (b) the freedom of judicial officers, officials or other competent persons of the State of origin to effect service of judicial documents directly through the judicial officers, officials, or other competent persons of the State of destination, (c) the freedom of any person interested in a judicial proceeding to effect service of judicial documents directly through the judicial officers, officials or other competent persons of the State of Destination."

According to the record the Japanese Government's adherence to the convention recites. "We hereby declare that the employment of the methods of service and notice of Article 10(b) and (c) shall be refused."

Article 15 of the convention is the equivalent of our national due process concept, and it was so recognized in the Senate. [Reference omitted.] That section provides in part: "Where a writ of summons or an equivalent document had to be transmitted abroad for the purpose of service, under the provisions of the present Convention, and the defendant has not appeared, judgment shall not be given until it is established that — (a) the document was served by a method prescribed by the internal law of the State addressed for the service of documents in domestic actions upon persons who are within its territory, or (b) the document was actually delivered to the defendant or to his residence by Another method provided for by this Convention, and that in either of these cases the service or the delivery was effected in sufficient time to enable the defendant to defend." (Emphasis added.)

The plaintiff contends that since the provisions of subdivision (a) of Article 10 are effective both as to the United States and Japan, he was free to send the summons and complaint by postal channels directly to the petitioner; and that if there was actual delivery to the corporate residence by the postal authorities, as is evidenced by the return receipt, the courts of this state would not be precluded from giving judgment against petitioner if it failed to appear.

On the other hand, petitioner points out that the convention persistently refers to "service" ("service abroad," art. 1; "requests for service," art. 2; "document to be served," art. 3; "serve the document or shall arrange to have it served," art. 5; "the document has been served," art. 6; "effect service of judicial documents," art. 8; "forward documents, for the purpose of service," art. 9; "effect service of judicial documents," art. 10, subds. (b) and (c); "for the purpose of service of judicial documents," art. 11; "service of judicial documents," art. 12; "request for service," art. 13; "transmission of judicial documents for service," art. 14; "transmitted abroad for the purpose of service," art. 15 and art. 16.) Petitioner notes that subdivision (a) of Article 10 refers to "the freedom to *send* judicial documents by postal channels, directly to persons abroad," (italics added [in original]) as distinguished from the transmission abroad for the purposes of service. It claims that the subsection does not authorize service by mail if actual delivery is effected, but that it merely authorizes the giving of notices and exchange of other judicial documents after jurisdiction is acquired. It draws an analogy between service of summons as provided in chapter 4 (§§ 413.10–417.40) of title 5 of the Code of Civil Procedure, and chapter 5 (§§ 1010–1020) of title 14 of that code which refers to notices and filing and service of papers, and expressly authorizes service by mail in such cases (see §§ 1012, 1013 and 1013a). The latter provisions expressly do not apply to the service of summons (§ 1016).

Although there is some merit to the proposed distinction it is outweighed by consideration of the entire scope of the convention. It purports to deal with the subject of service abroad of judicial documents. The reference to "the freedom to send judicial documents by postal channels, directly to persons abroad" would be superfluous unless it was related to the sending of such documents for the purpose of service. The mails are open to all. Moreover, the reference appears in the context of other alternatives to the use of the "Central Authority" created by the treaty. If it be assumed that the purpose of the convention is to establish one method to avoid the difficulties and controversy attendant to the use of other methods [citations omitted], it does not necessarily follow that other methods may not be used if effective proof of delivery can be made. The provisions of Article 5 provide that "unless (it) is incompatible with the law of the State addressed . . . the document may always be served by delivery to an addressee who accepts it voluntarily." The return receipt is some evidence of this fact.

The provisions of subdivision (i) of rule 4 of the Federal Rules of Procedure (see fn. 4 above) were promulgated January 21, 1963 to be effective July 1, 1963. [Citations omitted.] At that time, under the provisions of the governing statute, the rules could not be effective until reported to Congress which then had an opportunity to act. [Reference omitted.] The purpose of the rule was to expedite service of process abroad. [Citations omitted.] If petitioner's interpretation of the treaty is accepted it means that the Senate in ratifying the treaty April 14, 1967, intended to abrogate what it had impliedly approved four years earlier. It is more reasonable to infer that in approving subdivision (a) of Article 10 the Senate intended to retain service by mail, as provided in subdivision (i) of rule 4, as an effective method of service of process in a foreign country unless that country objected to those provisions. Moreover, if the treaty abrogated the provisions of subdivision (i) of rule 4 which permits service of process abroad by mail when there is proof of delivery, it is strange that there has been no change in the provisions of that subdivision despite other revisions of the rules which have been made since February 10, 1969 when the treaty became effective.

Finally it may be noted that it does not appear that service by mail with evidence of delivery is not "a method prescribed by the internal law of (Japan) for the service of documents in domestic actions upon persons who are within its territory . . . ." (Art. 15, subd. (a).) From all that appears in the record the internal law of Japan permits transmission by postal channels of documents coming from abroad for service within its territory. The failure to object to the provisions of subdivision (a) of Article 10 may be so construed.

Therefore, it is concluded that the provisions of the convention do not prevent the exercise of jurisdiction of the courts of this state in actions where the court has jurisdiction over a party arising from the nature of the claim asserted and notice has been given by service by mail accompanied by a receipt for delivery. It is recognized that this court cannot render an interpretation of the treaty which will bind the courts of Japan in the event plaintiff, if he obtains a judgment against petitioner, seeks to enforce it through the courts in that nation. Nevertheless, an interpretation must be made at this time, and the conclusion of this court is consistent with both the letter and the spirit of the convention.

III

In *Julen v. Larson* (1972) 25 Cal. App. 3d 325, 101 Cal. Rptr. 796, this state refused to enforce a default judgment taken in a Swiss court against a local defendant, who presumably had been doing business in Switzerland, because the documents forwarded to him by certified mail by the local Swiss consul were entirely written in the German language and were not described in the forwarding letter. The court concluded: "Since in the present case no informative notice was given in English, we conclude that the documents and correspondence served on defendant did not give him sufficient notice of the pending Swiss action and consequently the Swiss court never acquired the basis on which to adjudicate the claim of personal jurisdiction over defendant." (25 Cal. App. 3d at 330, 101 Cal. Rptr. at 800. [Citation omitted.]

Petitioner urges that the service of process should be quashed because the documents transmitted by mail were not written in the Japanese language. Significantly in *Julen v. Larson*, the court recognized the convention heretofore reviewed. (See part II above.) It noted the provisions of the convention which provide for use of the English or French language.

Admittedly in this case service was not made through a Central Authority designated by the receiving state under the convention, but by means of an alternative method. Plaintiff, therefore, cannot rely upon the authorization of English language contained in the treaty, although it may be persuasive on the issue of whether the recipient legally did have actual notice. The record does show by the declaration of a qualified international lawyer that in his experience "all Japanese companies involved in trade with other countries carry on correspondence with enterprises in such other countries relating to such trade in the English language, and almost all Japanese companies involved in trade with other countries are accustomed to receiving communications in English and have facilities for the interpretation and translation of the same." The record does show that the recipient executed the postal receipt which was written in English and French. Petitioner also apparently authorized the use of brochures printed in English to further sales of its products in this state. The special appearance in these proceedings bespeaks that the purport of the documents was understood. Under these circumstances there was neither a lack of due process of law nor a violation of the letter or spirit of the treaty.

The alternative writ is discharged. The petition for peremptory writ of mandate is denied.

MOLINARI, P.J., and ELKINGTON, J., concur.

QUESTIONS

Describe the underlying lawsuit in this case. How was Shoei Kako involved? As a defendant, on what grounds did Shoei Kako seek dismissal? Was there any question regarding whether Shoei Kako received adequate notice of the suit and had the opportunity to prepare a defense? Was lack of Japanese translations of the documents significant? (Note that the Declaration by the Government of Japan on accession to the Hague Service Convention explicitly states that the documents must be translated into Japanese.) Was the Hague Convention, as construed by Justice O'Conner, intended to achieve any other objective? If not, what difference does it make whether article 10(a) applies to "sending" not "serving" judicial documents? Would this issue be apt to arise in a lawsuit brought in Germany or France against a Japanese defendant were the complaint and summons transmitted by the relevant court by mail? Is a meaningful distinction between "sending" and "serving" possible in any language except English? Note that "adresser" is the term used in French, the other official language of the Convention. Does or should this make any difference?

SUZUKI MOTOR CO., LTD. v. THE SUPERIOR COURT OF SAN BERNARDINO COUNTY*
200 Cal. App. 3d 1476 (1988)

MCDANIEL, J.

INTRODUCTION

Suzuki Motor Co., Ltd. (Suzuki), defendant below, by the petition here seeks a writ of mandate to compel the superior court to vacate its order denying Suzuki's motion to quash service of process and to enter an order granting that motion.

---

* Footnotes omitted.

FACTS

Suzuki is a Japanese corporation which is named as a defendant in an action now pending in the superior court entitled Peggy Armenta v. Bellflower Suzuki, et al., case No. BCV 003277.

Peggy Armenta, the plaintiff in that action and the real party in interest in this proceeding, allegedly sustained personal injuries while operating a 1984 Suzuki four-wheel, all-terrain vehicle. Ms. Armenta filed a complaint for products liability and negligence against a number of defendants, including Suzuki.

Plaintiff purported to effect service of process upon Suzuki by sending the summons, together with copies of the complaint, certificate of assignment and amendment to the complaint, via registered mail to Suzuki's office in Hamamatsu, Japan. These documents, which actually were received by Suzuki, were not translated into Japanese.

Suzuki moved to quash service of process, asserting that service was improper under the provisions of the California Code of Civil Procedure as well as the provisions of the Hague Convention. In support of its motion to quash, Suzuki filed the declaration of Hidetoshi Asakura, a partner with the law firm of Graham & James, licensed to practice law in Japan and California.

In his declaration, Mr. Asakura expounded on the acceptable methods of service of process in Japan and concluded that plaintiff here had failed to conform to these methods, and thereby had also failed to conform to the requirements of the Hague Convention for service of process in the Convention's signatory states. Plaintiff did not contest the information contained in Mr. Asakura's declaration, but relied instead on the First District's decision in *Shoei Kako, Co. v. Superior Court* (1973) [citation omitted].

The superior court refused to grant the motion to quash service, and rightly so, in light of the holding in *Auto Equity Sales, Inc. v. Superior Court* (1962) 57 Cal.2d 450, 455 [20 Cal.Rptr. 321, 369 P.2d 937] (which holds that a lower court which refuses to follow a binding precedent of a higher court is acting in excess of jurisdiction), and because there has been no holding contrary to that of *Shoei Kako* in this or any other appellate district.

We, however, are not bound by the holding in *Shoei Kako*, particularly because it was based in part on a unique factual record before that court, a record which differs substantially from that now before us. Therefore, as explained below, we hold that the service of process described above was not effective, and we shall grant the petition for writ of mandate.

DISCUSSION

In 1969, the United States signed the Convention on the Service Abroad of Judicial and Extrajudicial Documents in Civil or Commercial Matters (20 U.S.T. 361–367, T.I.A.S. 6638) (the Hague Convention or the Convention. [Reference to appendix omitted.] Japan became a signatory to the Convention in 1970.

The Convention provides several acceptable methods for service of process abroad. These methods are: (1) service through the receiving country's designated "Central Authority" for service of foreign process (art. 5); (2) delivery by the Central Authority to an addressee who accepts service "voluntarily" so long as the method used is not incompatible with the law of the receiving state (art. 5); (3) service through diplomatic or consular agents of the sending state (art. 8); (4) service through the judicial officers, officials or other competent persons of the receiving state (art. 10, subdivisions (b) and (c)); and (5) service as permitted by the internal law of the receiving state for documents coming from abroad (art. 19).

Real party in interest urges that there is yet another method of service of process which meets the requirements of the Convention, to wit, service by registered mail as allowed by California Code of Civil Procedure sections 413.10 and 415.30 and article 10, subdivision (a) of the Convention, which provides that "Provided the State of destination does not object, the present Convention shall not interfere with — (a) the freedom to send judicial documents, by postal channels, directly to persons abroad, . . ." According to real party in interest and the court in Shoei Kako, this section of the Convention allows service of process by mail.

The *Shoei Kako* court analyzed the issue of the interpretation of the section, concluding that the Convention permitted signatories to exclude the methods of service outlined in articles 8 and 10 by filing objections to them. Japan objected to article 10, subdivisions (b) and (c), which provide for service via the judicial officers, officials, or other competent persons of the receiving state. Japan, however, did not object to article 10, subdivision (a). Downplaying the fact that article 10, subdivision (a) specifically refers to the sending of judicial documents rather than the service of such documents, the Shoei Kako court interpreted article 10, subdivision (a), like article 10, subdivisions (b) and (c), as also referring to the service of process by mail. According to that court, "The reference to 'the freedom to send judicial documents by postal channels, directly to persons abroad' would be superfluous unless it was related to the sending of such documents for the purpose of service. The mails are open to all." (*Id.*, 33 Cal.App.3d at p. 821.) Therefore, it concluded that Japan's failure to object specifically to subdivision (a) meant such service was acceptable.

The *Shoei Kako* court also relied on article 15 of the Convention to hold that service by registered mail was proper. Article 15 provides, in relevant part, "Where a writ of summons or an equivalent document had to be transmitted abroad for the purpose of service, under the provisions of the present Convention, and the defendant has not appeared, judgment shall not be given until it is established that — (a) the document was served by a method prescribed by the internal law of the State addressed for the service of documents in domestic actions upon persons who are within its territory, or (b) the document was actually delivered to the defendant or to his residence by another method provided for by this Convention, and that in either of these cases the service or the delivery was effected in sufficient time to enable the defendant to defend. . . ." (Italics added.) According to the *Shoei Kako* court, the record before it indicated that Japan's internal law allowed service by mail with evidence of delivery as an effective mode of service of process, and the record also indicated that the defendant in the case before it had actually received the summons and complaint by "a method provided for by [the] Convention," i.e., service by registered mail, the *Shoei Kako* court having determined that service by registered mail was a method allowed under article 10, subdivision (a).

Here, the record before us indicates that Japan does not have an internal legal system which allows service of process by registered mail. As indicated by the declaration of Mr. Asakura, and confirmed by a law review article entitled Jurisdiction and the Japanese Defendant (Peterson, Jurisdiction and the Japanese Defendant (1985) 25 Santa Clara L. Rev. 555, 576–579), Japan, unlike California, does not allow either attorneys or lay people to serve process by mail. To effectuate service of process through the mail, the court clerk stamps the outside of the envelope containing the required documents with a notice of special service (*tokubetsu sootatsu*) and the mail carrier acts as a special officer of the court by recording proof of delivery on a special proof of service form and returning this proof of service to the court. Significantly, real party in interest did not contravert these facts when she opposed Suzuki's motion to quash.

Given the fact that Japan itself does not recognize a form of service sufficiently equivalent to America's registered mail system, it is extremely unlikely that Japan's failure to object to article 10, subdivision (a) was intended to authorize the use of registered mail as an effective mode of service of process, particularly in light of the fact that Japan specifically objected to the much more formal modes of service by Japanese officials which were available in article 10, subdivisions (b) and (c). Instead, it seems much more likely that Japan interpreted article 10, subdivision (a) as allowing only the transmission of judicial documents, rather than the service of process. This interpretation is all the more reasonable given the fact that the Convention persistently refers to "service" as opposed to "send," e.g., "forward documents, for the purpose of service" (art. 9, italics [omitted]); "transmission of judicial documents for service" (art. 14, italics [omitted]); and "transmitted abroad for the purpose of service" (arts. 15 and 16, italics [omitted]), in contrast to "the freedom to send judicial documents, by postal channels, directly to persons abroad, . . ." (art. 10, subd. (a), italics [omitted]). (1) It is a well-recognized canon of statutory interpretation that words in a statute or similar enactment are to be given their common and ordinary meaning, [citation omitted] and that every word and phrase used is presumed to have a meaning and to perform a useful function. [Citation omitted.] (2) To interpret the phrase "to send" as used in article 10, subdivision (a) of the Convention to mean "to serve" would fly in the face of both these rules; the common and ordinary meaning of "to send" is "to cause to be conveyed by an intermediary to a destination" or "to dispatch, as by mail or telegraph" (see "send," The American Heritage Dict. of the English Language (1969) p. 1179) not "to serve," and the fact the Convention's drafters used both the phrase "to send" and the phrase "service of process" indicates they intended each phrase to have a different meaning and function.

Real party in interest relies on various cases which do not interpret "to send" as we do, including the recent case of *Ackermann v. Levine* (2d Cir. 1986) 788 F.2d 830, which cites *Shoei Kako* with approval, and which, as did the court in *Shoei Kako*, interprets "to send" as meaning "to serve."

In *Ackermann*, German plaintiffs served a summons and complaint on a New York defendant by registered mail. The Second Circuit held that service of process by registered mail was effective under article 10, subdivision (a) of the Hague Convention, because (1) the use of the word "send" in that subdivision was intended to mean "service" (*id.*, at 839), and (2) the United States had not objected to the use of "postal channels" under article 10, subdivision (a) as it could have chosen to do. (*Id.*) The *Ackermann* court also noted with approval several other cases which had held that Japan, too, had not objected to mail "service" under article 10, subdivision (a). [Citations omitted.] The result in *Ackermann*, as in the cases to which the *Ackermann* court referred with approval, turns on the interpretation of the word "send" as meaning "serve." As noted above, this interpretation simply does not make sense. The *Ackermann* court relied on a treatise which concluded that the use of the word "send" rather than the otherwise consistently used "service" " 'must be attributable to careless drafting.' " [Citations omitted.] However, whether the phrase "to send" was used because of careless drafting or not, it appears that Japan understood it to mean "to send," not "to serve," as it is implausible that a country which does not use basic postal channels for service of process by its own nationals on their fellows, and which objected to the more rigorous methods of service set out in article 10, subdivisions (b) and (c), would have failed to object to subdivision (a) if it had understood that section to relate to service of process.

Ackermann has been cited with approval by a recent opinion from the *Central District of California, Newport Components v. NEC Home Electronics* (C.D. Cal. 1987) 671 F. Supp. 1525. We think the following discussion of the Newport Components case makes it even more apparent why we have decided not to follow the *Shoei Kako* and *Ackermann* line of cases.

In *Newport Components v. NEC Home Electronics* the district court was faced with the same issue raised here. Noting that there was a split among the courts as to the meaning of article 10, subdivision (a), the *Newport Components* court cast its lot with the *Ackermann* line of cases, without any independent discussion of the import of subdivision (a)'s use of the verb "to send," and after finding the following reasoning from *Shoei Kako* particularly persuasive:

" 'If it be assumed that the purpose of the convention is to establish one method to avoid the difficulties and controversy attendant to the use of other methods . . . , it does not necessarily follow that other methods may not be used if effective proof of delivery can be made.' " (*Id.*, at 1542, quoting *Shoei Kako, supra*, 33 Cal. App. 3d at p. 821, italics added by *Newport Components* court.)

We, however, do not find this reasoning persuasive. If the signatories' intent was to establish a particular method of service to avoid the controversy attendant on the use of other methods, and if signatories were allowed, as they were, to object to particular modes of service, then it makes no sense to allow private litigants to by-pass the agreed-upon methods and to use other methods, even methods to which some signatories objected, even if effective proof of delivery using such alternate and objected-to methods can be made.

Furthermore, the decision in *Newport Components* was additionally based upon that court's belief that resort to the Hague Convention "need not 'be utilized first in every case,' " and that direct mail service is allowable unless the defendant can demonstrate that such service represents an intrusion on Japanese sovereignty. [Citation omitted.] However, the *Newport Components* court's reliance on *Société Nationale Industrielle v. U.S. Dist. Court* and *In re Société Nationale Industrielle Aerospatiale* is misplaced, as both cases involve the Multilateral Convention on the Taking of Evidence Abroad in Civil and Commercial Matters, March 18, 1970, 23

U.S.T. 2555, T.I.A.S. 7444 (Convention on the Taking of Evidence) (whose text is found in the note following 28 U.S.C. § 1781 (Supp. 1985)), which, while also known as "The Hague Convention," is not the same treaty as the convention here which specifically deals with service of documents, including service of process. As pointed out in *Société Nationale Industrielle v. U.S. Dist. Court, supra,* the reason that resort to the Federal Rules of Civil Procedure may be had in the first instance, rather than to the Convention on the Taking of Evidence, is because federal law "normally governs discovery of documents from foreign parties subject to the jurisdiction of United States courts even when the documents are located abroad. [Citation omitted.] When a district court has jurisdiction over a foreign litigant, the production of documents effectively occurs in the United States and not in the country where the documents are initially located. [Citation.]" (*Id.,* at 1410–1411, italics [omitted].) "[T]he better rule . . . , is that when the district court has jurisdiction over a foreign litigant [then] the Hague Convention does not apply to the production of evidence. . . ." (*In re Société Nationale Industrielle Aerospatiale, supra,* 782 F.2d 120, at 124, italics [omitted].)

In other words, the cases relied on by the *Newport Components* court merely hold that the Convention on the Taking of Evidence is not the only means of obtaining discovery from a foreign defendant once the district court has obtained jurisdiction over the defendant. It does not follow from these cases that the methods contained in the Convention on the Service Abroad of Judicial and Extrajudicial Documents are not the exclusive means of obtaining that initial personal jurisdiction over a foreign defendant via service of process.

In sum, we do not find the *Ackermann* line of cases persuasive, and therefore take the position taken by other commentators and courts that service of process by registered mail is not one of the methods authorized by the Convention for service of process on Japanese defendants. (See, e.g., Routh, Litigation Between Japanese and American Parties, in Current Legal Aspects of Doing Business in Japan and East Asia (Hailey [sic] ed. 1978) pp. 188, 190–191 ("[s]ome questions have been raised as to whether section 10(a) of the Convention allows service of process by mail. In my opinion it does not. The question of service by mail is not addressed by the Convention; it merely discusses the right to send subsequent judicial documents by mail. Any other process would be a rather illogical result, as the Convention sets up a rather cumbersome and involved procedure for service of process; and if this particular provision allowed one to circumvent the procedure by simply sending something through the mail, the vast bulk of the Convention would be useless. . . ." (fn. omitted); [citations omitted]. (3) This holding compels the corollary holding, based on the fact that a California court may not exercise jurisdiction in violation of an international treaty, that Suzuki is entitled to have its motion to quash service of process granted. [Citations omitted].

DISPOSITION

Let a peremptory writ of mandate issue directing the trial court to vacate its order denying petitioner's motion to quash service of process and to enter a new and different order granting the motion.

Campbell, P. J., and Dabney, J., concurred.

QUESTIONS

1. On what grounds does the court in *Suzuki Motor Co., Ltd.* reject the reasoning and conclusions reached in both *Shoei Kako* and *Ackermann*? Do you agree or disagree? Why?

2. What did Hidetoshi Asakura, the attorney for Suzuki Motor Co., argue? How would you have responded?

3. Should the technical terms of a treaty, such as the Hague Service Convention, have different meanings in terms of their functions or consequences in different national legal systems? If not, how should the courts in the United States or any other particular legal system determine their common or shared meaning?

BANKSTON v. TOYOTA MOTOR CORPORATION*
889 F.2d 172 (8th Cir. 1989)

Ross, Senior Circuit Judge.

Appellants Charles Bankston, Sr. and Regina Dixon filed suit in the United States District Court for the Western District of Arkansas against Toyota Motor Corporation, a Japanese corporation, seeking damages resulting from an accident involving a Toyota truck. The appellants first attempted service of process upon Toyota by serving an affiliated United States corporation in Torrance, California, as Toyota's purported agent. Toyota filed a motion to dismiss for improper service of process. The district court denied Toyota's motion but granted the appellants 45 days in which to serve Toyota in accordance with the Hague Convention.

The appellants next attempted to serve process upon Toyota by sending a summons and complaint by registered mail, return receipt requested, to Tokyo, Japan. The documents were in English and did not include a translation into Japanese. The receipt of service was signed and returned to appellants. Toyota renewed its motion to dismiss, arguing that the appellants' proposed method of service still did not comply with the Hague Convention.

The district court concluded that Article 10(a) of the Hague Convention does not permit service of process upon a Japanese corporation by registered mail. In an order dated January 4, 1989, the district court gave the appellants an additional sixty days in which to effect service in compliance with the Hague Convention.

On January 13, 1989, the district court granted the appellants' motion to amend the order pursuant to 28 U.S.C. § 1292(b) and certified the issue for interlocutory appeal to this court. On February 9, 1989, this court entered an order granting

---

* Footnotes omitted.

appellants leave to take an interlocutory appeal pursuant to 28 U.S.C. § 1292(b).

The Hague Convention is a multinational treaty, formed in 1965 for the purpose of creating an "appropriate means to ensure that judicial and extrajudicial documents to be served abroad shall be brought to the notice of the addressee in sufficient time." [Citation omitted.] The Convention sets out specific procedures to be followed in accomplishing service of process. Articles 2 through 6 provide for service through a central authority in each country. Article 8 allows service by way of diplomatic channels. Article 19 allows service by any method of service permitted by the internal law of the country in which service is made. Under Article 21 of the Convention, each signatory nation may ratify its provisions subject to conditions or objections.

The crucial article for this discussion is Article 10, under which appellants herein purportedly attempted to serve process upon Toyota by registered mail. . . .

Japan has objected to subparagraphs (b) and (c), but not to subparagraph (a). The issue before this court is whether subparagraph (a) permits service on a Japanese defendant by direct mail.

In recent years, two distinct lines of Article 10(a) interpretation have arisen. Some courts have ruled that Article 10(a) permits service of process by mail directly to the defendant without the necessity of resorting to the central authority, and without the necessity of translating the documents into the official language of the nation where the documents are to be served.

In general, these courts reason that since the purported purpose of the Hague Convention is to facilitate service abroad, the reference to " 'the freedom to send judicial documents by postal channels, directly to persons abroad' would be superfluous unless it was related to the sending of such documents for the purpose of service." *Ackermann v. Levine*, 788 F.2d 830, 839 (2d Cir. 1986). [Citations omitted.] These courts have further found that the use of the "send" rather than "service" in Article 10(a) "must be attributed to careless drafting." *Ackermann v. Levine, supra*, 788 F.2d at 839.

The second line of interpretation, advocated by Toyota, is that the word "send" in Article 10(a) is not the equivalent of "service of process." The word "service" is specifically used in other sections of the Convention, including subsections (b) and (c) of Article 10. If the drafters of the Convention had meant for subparagraph (a) to provide an additional manner of service of judicial documents, they would have used the word "service." Subscribers to this interpretation maintain that Article 10(a) merely provides a method for sending subsequent documents after service of process has been obtained by means of the central authority. [Citations omitted.]

We find this second line of authority to be more persuasive. It is a "familiar canon of statutory construction that the starting point for interpreting a statute is the language of the statute itself. Absent a clearly expressed legislative intention to the contrary, that language must ordinarily be regarded as conclusive." *Consumer Prod. Safety Comm'n v. GTE Sylvania Inc.*, 447 U.S. 102, 108 (1980). In addition, where a legislative body "includes particular language in one section of a statute but omits it in another section of the same Act, it is generally presumed that [the legislative body] acts intentionally and purposely in the disparate inclusion or exclusion." *Russello v. United States*, 464 U.S. 16, 23 (1983). In *Suzuki Motor Co. v. Superior Court*, 249 Cal. Rptr. at 379, the court found that because service of process by registered mail was not permitted under Japanese law, it was "extremely unlikely" that Japan's failure to object to Article 10(a) was intended to authorize the use of registered mail as an effective mode of service of process, particularly in light of the fact that Japan had specifically objected to the much more formal modes of service by Japanese officials which were available in Article 10(b) and (c).

We conclude that sending a copy of a summons and complaint by registered mail to a defendant in a foreign country is not a method of service of process permitted by the Hague Convention. We affirm the judgment of the district court and remand this case with directions that appellants be given a reasonable time from the date of this Order in which to effectuate service of process over appellee Toyota Motor Corporation in compliance with the terms of the Hague Convention.

JOHN R. GIBSON, CIRCUIT JUDGE, concurring.

I concur in the court's opinion today in every respect. The court correctly interprets the Hague Convention. I write separately only to express nagging concerns I have about the practical effect of our opinion. Automobiles are subject to a plethora of regulations requiring particular equipment and detailed warnings. Should an automobile manufactured in Japan carry a disclosure that, if litigation ensues from its purchase and use, service of process on the Japanese manufacturer can only be obtained under the Hague Convention? Should the purchaser also be informed that this special service of process will cost $800 to $900, as we are told, and must include a translation of the suit papers in Japanese? These decisions we must leave to others. I write only to express my discomfort with the practical effect of Toyota's insistence on strict compliance with the letter of the Hague Convention.

QUESTIONS

1. Has the Court in *Bankston* construed the Hague Service Convention to disallow service by mail in general? To what extent, that is, does the ruling in *Bankston* extend to service by mail not only in Japan but in any country not objecting to article 10(a)? Note that less than half of the countries to which the Convention applies (26 of the 54 Hague Conference member states and two of the 14 ratifying non-member states) have objected to article 10(a) as well in most instances to 10(b) and 10(c). A dozen states in addition to Japan have objected to the methods of service in article 10(b) and 10(c) but not transmission by mail under 10(a). They include Finland, Iceland, Latvia, Sweden as well as Israel, Ireland, and the United Kingdom. Italy did not object to any section of article 10.

2. How could the Court determine what the Japanese or any Government intended in *not* objecting to article 10(a)? How helpful are the following two official statements (A and B below) by spokespersons for the Government of Japan?

A.

The following letter was received by the Chairman of the Publications Committee [ABA] from the Embassy of Japan regarding the Convention of the Service Abroad of Judicial and Extrajudicial Documents in Civil or Commercial Matters:

March 20, 1978

Dear Mr. Griffin:

Upon instructions from the Government of Japan, I should like to inform you concerning service practice in Japan in conformity with the provisions of the Convention.

The Government would appreciate it very much if you could kindly see to it that the Japanese practice is circulated to all concerned attorneys in the United States for their information.

1. "The authority or judicial officer of the United States," as indicted in Article 3 of the Convention, is interpreted as being a U.S. Marshall or other appointee of a court, such as an attorney, a court clerk or a sheriff, etc., pursuant to Rule 4 of the Federal Rules of Civil Procedure.

2. The Japanese central authority always requires that a document be translated into the Japanese language when the document is to be served under the first paragraph of Article 5 of the Convention.

3. If a Request asks for service in accordance with the provisions of sub-paragraph (a) or (b) of the first paragraph of the Article, and if it is not accompanied by a translation of the document, the authority will return the Request to the requesting authority or judicial officer and

4. "Personal Service," which is often used in a Request from the United States, is considered to be a particular method under sub-paragraph (b) above (specifying the personal service) and should enclose the translation of the document. (It is most appreciated if the translation of the summary is also attached.) In such a case, a Marshall will personally effect the service.

5. The practice of voluntary service, in accordance with the provisions of the second paragraph of Article 5, which does not require a translation, is as follows:

(1) Court clerk sends a notice to accept the document to the person to be served.

(2) The person so notified may appear before the court to receive the document or may ask the court to send it to the person.

(3) If the person fails to respond within three weeks of notification, the court clerk may, by law, deem that the service is refused.

6. The central authority will employ only that method of service which is specified in the Request itself, without reference to any desire or suggestion which may appear in other papers which accompany the Request, such as covering letters from attorneys.

Thank you very much for your attention to this matter.

Sincerely yours,

Akio Harada
Legal Attaché
First Secretary

B.

Report on the work of the Special Commission of April 1989 on the Operation of the Hague Conventions of 15 November 1965 on the Service Abroad of Judicial and Extrajudicial Documents in Civil or Commercial Matters and of 18 March 1970 on the Taking of Evidence Abroad in Civil or Commercial Matters. The Japanese delegation explained that their Government wished the following statement of position to be made known:

"Japanese position on Article 10 of the Hague Convention on the Service Abroad of Judicial and Extrajudicial Documents in Civil or Commercial Matters:

"Japan has not declared that it objects to the sending of judicial documents, by postal channels, directly to persons abroad. In this connection, Japan has made it clear that no objection to the use of postal channels for sending judicial documents to persons in Japan does not necessarily imply that the sending by such a method is considered valid service in Japan; it merely indicates that Japan does not consider it as infringement of its sovereign power."

It was understood that the Japanese position as expressed in this statement would be included in the next revision of the Practical Handbook on the Hague Service Convention.

In 1998 the Japanese Supreme Court may have finally answered the question. In *Sadhwani v. Sadhwani* (Sup. Ct., 3rd P.B., April 28, 1998) (*see infra*, Chapter 6), the Court stated: "Summons or service (*sōtatsu*) of the order required for the commencement of litigation' to the defendant as required under article 118(iv) of the Code [for recognition of a foreign judgment] does not have to be summons or service on the basis of the Japanese law of civil procedure, but *must be sufficient for the defendant actually to become aware of the commencement of the litigation and to defend himself.*" [Emphasis added.]

The issue in the preceding cases — excepting *Ackermann* — was whether the failure of the Japanese Government to object to article 10(a) of the Hague Convention should be construed to mean that Japan accepts service by mail. The closely related issue, as indicated in *Bankston*, is whether article 10(a) should as a matter of U.S. law be construed more broadly not to include service by mail regardless of whether a member of the convention has expressed objection. We might ask, with respect to this issue, whether it should make any difference whether the country in question is a common law or civil law jurisdiction?

NUOVO PIGNONE, SPA v. STORMAN ASIA M/V
310 F.3d 374 (5th Cir. 2002)

JERRY E. SMITH, CIRCUIT JUDGE:

Fagioli, S.A. ("Fagioli"), agreed to furnish a ship for the maritime transport of Nuovo Pignone, SpA's ("Nuovo Pignone's") 771,000 kilogram reactor from Italy to Louisiana. The reactor was damaged after arrival at the Port of New Orleans, and Nuovo Pignone sued. The district court found that Fagioli, an Italian company, was subject to personal jurisdiction in Louisiana and that Nuovo Pignone properly had effected service of process by mail. We affirm the assertion of personal jurisdiction but reverse the determination that article 10(a) of the Hague Convention permits service of process by mail.

I.

Fagioli is an Italian corporation providing worldwide transportation and logistical services necessary to transport heavy-lift cargo. Nuovo Pignone, also an Italian company, contracted with Fagioli for the transport of a large EO reactor from Italy to Louisiana. Under the terms of the contract, Fagioli was responsible for selecting a vessel for the transit.

The contract required that Fagioli furnish a ship possessing specified performance capabilities. Fagioli agreed to furnish a ship that "[h]as its own shears and winches and hoisting means, including swingletrees and cables for safe, autonomous hoisting operations and/or unloading in connection with the weight of the objects to be transported . . . ." The contract required that the ship be seaworthy, equipped with appropriate engines for navigation, and capable of entering the preselected port of discharge.

Fagioli entered into a secondary contract with Blau Shipping & Trading, Ltd. ("Blau Shipping"). This contract, known as a conlinebooking note, specified that the vessel M/V STORMAN ASIA ("STORMAN ASIA") would be used to transport the reactor and that Geismar or New Orleans was the port of discharge. Blau Shipping then entered into a secondary conlinebooking note with Key Largo Transportes Maritimos ("Key Largo"), the owner and operator of the STORMAN ASIA. Nuovo Pignone's Louisiana client and Key Largo were responsible for unloading the reactor at the point of destination.

The reactor was loaded on board the STORMAN ASIA in Italy and transported across the Atlantic Ocean without incident. While the reactor was being transferred to a barge at the Port of New Orleans, one of the cables of the vessel's onboard shipping crane broke, causing the reactor to fall. The reactor and the deck of the barge were damaged. Nuovo Pignone alleges that the accident resulted from

Fagioli's failure to provide a vessel with a satisfactory onboard shipping crane, as required by the original contract.

II.

Nuovo Pignone brought breach of contract and tort claims against Fagioli, Key Largo, and the STORMAN ASIA and effected service of process on Fagioli by sending the complaint and summons by Federal Express mail to Fagioli's president in Milan, Italy. Fagioli moved unsuccessfully to dismiss for lack of personal jurisdiction and insufficiency of process. The district court concluded that personal jurisdiction could be established over Fagioli because the company had made minimum contacts with Louisiana through its contract with Nuovo Pignone, and that service by mail of foreign parties is permissible under article 10(a) of the Hague Convention. In its order denying the motion to dismiss, the district court, on Fagioli's motion, certified both grounds for interlocutory appeal under 28 U.S.C. § 1292(b), and this court granted leave to appeal as well.

. . . .

IV.

Nuovo Pignone effected service of process by sending a copy of the complaint by Federal Express mail to Fagioli's president in Milan, Italy. Fagioli argues that service by mail violates FED. R. CIV. P. 4(f)(1), which permits service of process on a foreign corporation "by any internationally agreed means reasonably calculated to give notice, such as those means authorized by the Hague Convention." The Hague Convention is a multinational treaty formed in 1965 for the purpose of creating an "appropriate means to ensure that judicial and extrajudicial documents to be served abroad shall be brought to the notice of the addressee in sufficient time." The treaty seeks not only to simplify and expedite international service of process, but more importantly, to ensure that service is effected timely and adequately.

The Hague Convention sets forth permissible methods of effecting service. Articles 2 through 7 require each signatory nation to establish a "Central Authority" to act as an agent to receive request of service, arrange for service of documents, and return proofs of service. Article 8 permits the use of diplomatic agents to serve foreign defendants. Article 9 permits diplomatic agents to forward documents to designated authorities in receiving nations who, in turn, effect service on the proper parties.

The parties disagree over the interpretation of article 10(a), which states in context:

> Provided the State of designation does not object, the present Convention does not interfere with
>
> (a) the freedom to send judicial documents, by postal channels, directly to persons abroad,
>
> (b) the freedom of judicial officers, officials or other competent persons of the State of origin to effect service of judicial documents directly through

the judicial officers, officials or other competent persons of the State of designation,

(c) the freedom of any person interested in a judicial proceeding to effect service of judicial documents directly through the judicial officers, officials, or other competent persons of the State of destination.

Nuovo Pignone contends that article 10(a) permits service of process by mail. Fagioli argues that the subsection refers only to the transmission of legal documents following service, pointing to the fact that nowhere else in the Hague Convention is the word "send" used to refer to service of process; rather, the drafters use the words "serve," "service," and "to effect service" in other sections, including subparts (b) and (c) of article 10.

The parties' differing positions reflect a circuit split over an issue this court has yet to address. Those courts that have concluded that article 10(a) permits service of foreign parties by mail have looked to the broad purpose of the Hague Convention — facilitating service abroad — and concluded that article 10(a) would be "superfluous unless it was related to the sending of such documents for the purpose of service." These courts have opined that the use of the term send, rather than service, in article 10(a) should be attributed to careless drafting.

Other courts have held that the word "send" in article 10(a) is not the equivalent of service of process. These courts have interpreted article 10(a) as providing a method for sending subsequent documents after service of process has properly been obtained. Despite the broad purpose of the Hague Convention, these courts have noted that the word "service" is used in other sections of the Hague Convention, including subparts (b) and (c) of article 10 and articles 9, 15, and 16, which all refer to forwarding documents for the purpose of service. So, if the drafters had meant for article 10(a) to provide an additional manner of service of judicial documents, they would have used "service" instead of "send."

We adopt the reasoning of courts that have decided that the Hague Convention does not permit service by mail. In doing so, we rely on the canons of statutory interpretation rather than the fickle presumption that the drafters' use of the word "send" was a mere oversight. "Absent a clearly expressed legislative intention to the contrary," a statute's language "must ordinarily be regarded as conclusive." *Consumer Prod. Safety Comm'n v. GTE Sylvania, Inc.*, 447 U.S. 102, 108 (1980). And because the drafters purposely elected to use forms of the word "service" throughout the Hague Convention, while confining use of the word "send" to article 10(a), we will not presume that the drafters intended to give the same meaning to "send" that they intended to give to "service."

Nuovo Pignone's contention that the broad purpose of the Hague Convention is furthered if article 10(a) is interpreted to allow service by mail is problematic. As noted, the purpose of the Hague Convention is not only to simplify the service of process, but to ensure that plaintiffs deliver notice to foreign addressees in sufficient time to defend the allegation. Indeed, Fed. R. Civ. P. 4(f)(1) presumes that the Hague Convention provides methods of service "reasonably calculated to give notice."

We are not confident, nor should the drafters have been confident in 1967, that mail service in the more than forty signatories is sufficient to ensure this goal. Under Nuovo Pignone's interpretation of article 10(a), the fact that a signatory could object to service by mail is unconvincing. There is no reason to think that signatories with inadequate mail services would voluntarily opt out of article 10(a).

Finally, we note that other provisions of the Hague Convention describe more reliable methods of effecting service. Service of process through a central authority under articles 2 through 7 and service through diplomatic channels under articles 8 and 9 require that service be effected through official government channels. It is unlikely that the drafters would have put in place these methods of service requiring the direct participation of government officials, while simultaneously permitting the uncertainties of service by mail.

We conclude that article 10(a) does not permit parties to effect service of process on foreign defendants by mail. On remand, Nuovo Pignone should be permitted a reasonable time to effect service properly. [Citation omitted.]

For the reasons we have explained, the district court's assertion of personal jurisdiction over Fagioli is AFFIRMED, and its determination that service of process by mail is permissible under the Hague Convention is REVERSED. This matter is REMANDED for further proceedings.

BROCKMEYER v. MAY
383 F.3d 798 (9th Cir. 2004)

WILLIAM A. FLETCHER, CIRCUIT JUDGE:

Plaintiffs in this case attempted to serve process on an English defendant by using ordinary first class mail to send a summons and complaint from the United States to England. We join the Second Circuit in concluding that the Convention on the Service Abroad of Judicial and Extrajudicial Documents ("Hague Convention," or the "Convention") does not prohibit — or, in the words of the Convention, does not "interfere with"— service of process by international mail. But this conclusion tells us only that the Hague Convention does not prohibit such service. For service by international mail to be effective in federal court, it must also be affirmatively authorized by some provision in federal law.

Federal Rule of Civil Procedure 4 governs service of process in federal district court. In this case, after determining that the Hague Convention does not prohibit service by international mail, the necessary next step is to analyze Rule 4(f) to determine whether it affirmatively authorizes such service. The plaintiffs' attempted service fails because they failed to follow the requirements of that rule. We therefore reverse and remand to the district court with instructions to vacate the judgment.

I. Background: Plaintiffs' Attempts to Serve Process

Ronald B. Brockmeyer is the owner of the trademark <<O>>, under which he publishes and distributes adult entertainment media and novelties. On August 3,

1998, Brockmeyer and his company, Eromedia, filed suit against Marquis Publications, Ltd. ("Marquis") and several other defendants in federal district court in the Southern District of New York, alleging trademark infringement and various state-law causes of action. Marquis is a company registered under British law. Plaintiffs' counsel made two attempts to serve on Marquis. Plaintiffs' counsel made his first attempt on October 7, 1998. He sent the summons and complaint, together with a request for waiver of service, by ordinary first class mail to a post office box in England. Marquis did not respond.

On April 5, 1999, the district court in New York transferred the suit to the Central District of California. On October 6, 1999, the district court in California entered an order to show cause ("OSC") why the suit should not be dismissed for lack of prosecution. Plaintiffs were required to respond to the OSC by October 25, 1999.

Plaintiffs' counsel made his second attempt at service four days before the OSC deadline, on October 21, 1999. This time, instead of sending the summons and complaint together with a request for waiver of service, he sent only the summons and complaint. He sent them by first class mail to the same post office box in England to which he had previously sent the request for waiver. Marquis still did not respond.

Default was entered by the court clerk against several defendants (not including Marquis) on November 24, 1999. Default was entered against Marquis a year later, on November 8, 2000. On February 22, 2002, the district court entered a default judgment of $410,806.12, plus attorneys' fees and costs, against Marquis and two German defendants.

The German defendants moved to set aside the default judgment against them. On June 6, 2002, the district court granted the motion on the ground that they had not been properly served under the Hague Convention and German law. The court ordered plaintiffs to serve the German defendants properly within 90 days or face dismissal. The district court subsequently gave plaintiffs a two-month extension until November 4, 2002. Seven days before the expiration of the extended deadline, plaintiffs' counsel finally submitted documents to the German Central Authority for service. The Central Authority rejected the documents the same day for failure to comply with German law. Almost two months later, plaintiffs' counsel resubmitted documents to the German Central Authority. Nothing in the record indicates whether these resubmitted documents complied with German law. On January 2, 2003, the district court dismissed the suit against the German defendants for failure to serve process within the time allowed under the extended deadline. Plaintiffs have not appealed that dismissal.

Marquis moved independently to set aside the default judgment against it. Among other things, Marquis contended that international mail service must be made by certified or registered mail. On June 26, 2002, the district court denied Marquis's motion, holding that plaintiffs' second attempt at service had been successful. It ruled that mail service is not forbidden by the Hague Convention, and that service on an English defendant by ordinary international first class mail is proper.

Marquis appeals the district court's denial of its motion to set aside plaintiffs' default judgment. We have jurisdiction pursuant to 29 U.S.C. § 1291. Once service is challenged, plaintiffs bear the burden of establishing that service was valid under Rule 4. [Citations omitted.]

II. Discussion

A. The Hague Convention

The resolution of this appeal depends on whether Marquis was properly served. Because service of process was attempted abroad, the validity of that service is controlled by the Hague Convention, to the extent that the Convention applies. *Volkswagenwerk Aktiengesellschaft v. Schlunk*, 486 U.S. 694, 705 (1988) ("[C]ompliance with the Convention is mandatory in all cases to which it applies.").

The Hague Convention, ratified by the United States in 1965, regularized and liberalized service of process in international civil suits. The primary means by which service is accomplished under the Convention is through a receiving country's "Central Authority." The Convention affirmatively requires each member country to designate a Central Authority to receive documents from another member country. *See* Hague Convention, art. 2. The receiving country can impose certain requirements with respect to those documents (for example, that they be translated into the language of that country). *See id.*, art. 5. If the documents comply with applicable requirements, the Convention affirmatively requires the Central Authority to effect service in its country. *See id.*, arts. 4 & 5.

The Convention also provides that it does not "interfere with" other methods of serving documents. Article 10(a) of the Convention recites:

Provided the State of destination does not object, the present Convention shall *not interfere with* — (a) the freedom to *send* judicial documents, by postal channels, directly to persons abroad. (Emphasis added.) American courts have disagreed about whether the phrase "the freedom to *send* judicial documents" in Article 10(a) includes within its meaning the freedom to *serve* judicial documents.

One line of cases follows *Bankston v. Toyota Motor Corp.*, 889 F.2d 172, 173–74 (8th Cir.1989). In *Bankston*, the Eighth Circuit held that the meaning of the word "send" in Article 10(a) does not include "serve"; that is, it held that "send" permitted the sending of judicial documents by mail, but only after service of process was accomplished by some other means. In *Nuovo Pignone v. Storman Asia M/V*, 310 F.3d 374, 384 (5th Cir. 2002), the Fifth Circuit similarly held that a strict reading of the Hague Convention did not permit an Italian plaintiff who filed suit in the United States to serve an Italian defendant in Italy by Federal Express. A second line of cases follows *Ackermann v. Levine*, 788 F.2d 830, 838 (2d Cir. 1986), in which the Second Circuit approved a German plaintiff's service of process by mail, when the plaintiff filed suit in Germany and served by registered mail a defendant in the United States. *Ackermann* relied primarily on the purpose and history of the convention to interpret the word "send" in Article 10(a) to include the meaning "serve." *See id.*

Whether service by mail is permitted under the Hague Convention is an open question in our circuit. We briefly discussed Article 10(a) in *Lidas, Inc. v. United States*, 238 F.3d 1076, 1084 (9th Cir. 2001), but we did not confront the question whether Article 10(a) allows service by mail. District courts within our circuit are split. *Compare R. Griggs Group Ltd. v. Filanto Spa*, 920 F. Supp. 1100, 1104–05 (D. Nev. 1996) ("send" includes "serve"); *Meyers v. ASICS Corp.*, 711 F. Supp. 1001, 1007–08 (C.D. Cal. 1989) (same); *and Newport Components v. NEC Home Electronics*, 671 F. Supp. 1525, 1541–42 (C.D. Cal. 1987) (same) *with Anbe v. Kikuchi*, 141 F.R.D. 498, 500 (D.C. Hawaii 1992) ("send" does not include "serve") *and Mateo v. M/S Kiso*, 805 F. Supp. 792, 796 (N.D. Cal. 1992) (same).

Today we join the Second Circuit in holding that the meaning of "send" in Article 10(a) includes "serve." *See Ackermann*, 788 F.2d at 838. In so doing, we also join the essentially unanimous view of other member countries of the Hague Convention. *See, e.g.*, Case C-412/97, *E.D. Srl. v. Italo Fenocchio*, 1999 E.C.R. I-3845, [2000] C.M.L.R. 855 (Court of Justice of the European Communities) ("Article 10(a) of [the Hague Convention] allows service by post."); *Integral Energy & Envtl. Eng'g Ltd. v. Schenker of Canada Ltd.*, (2001) 295 A.R. 233, . . . (Alberta Queens Bench) ("Article 10(a) of the Hague Convention provides that if the state of destination does not object, judicial documents may be served by postal channels"), *rev'd on other grounds*, (2001) 293 A.R. 327; *R. v. Re Recognition of an Italian Judgment*, [2002] I.L.Pr. 15, . . . (Thessaloniki Court of Appeal, Greece) ("It should be noted that the possibility of serving judicial documents in civil and commercial cases through postal channels . . . is envisaged in Article 10(a) of the Hague Convention.").

We agree with the Second Circuit that this holding is consistent with the purpose of the Convention to facilitate international service of judicial documents. *See* Hague Convention, art.1 ("[T]he present Convention shall apply in all cases, in civil or commercial matters, where there is occasion to transmit a judicial or extrajudicial document for *service* abroad.") (emphasis added); *see also* 1 Moore's Federal Practice § 4.52[2][d] (stating that "it comports with the broad purpose of the Hague Convention" to construe "send" to mean "serve").

Commentaries on the history of negotiations leading to the Hague Convention further indicate that service by mail is permitted under Article 10(a). According to the official Rapporteur's report, the first paragraph of Article 10 of the draft Convention, which "except for minor editorial changes" is identical to Article 10 of the final Convention, was intended to permit service by mail. *See* 1 Bruno A. Ristau, *International Judicial Assistance* § 4-3-5, at 204–05 (2000) (quoting the Service Convention Negotiating Document) (translated from French by Ristau). A "Handbook" published by the Permanent Bureau of the Hague Convention, which summarizes meetings of a "Special Commission of Experts," states that to interpret Article 10(a) not to permit service by mail would "contradict what seems to have been the implicit understanding of the delegates at the 1977 Special Commission meeting, and indeed of the legal literature on the Convention and its predecessor treaties." Permanent Bureau of the Hague Convention, *Practical Handbook on the Operation of the Hague Convention of 15 November 1965 on the Service Abroad of Judicial and Extrajudicial Documents in Civil or Commercial Matters* 44 (1992). As further evidence of the understanding of the parties at the time the Hague Convention was signed, the United States delegate to the Hague Convention reported to Congress that Article 10(a) permitted service by mail. *See* S. Exec. R. No. 6, at 13 (1967) (statement by Philip W. Amram).

The United States government, through the State Department, has specifically disapproved the Eighth Circuit's holding in *Bankston*. On March 14, 1991, the Deputy Legal Advisor of the State Department wrote a letter to the Administrative Office of the United States Courts. After discussing Article 10(a) and noting that Japan did not object to the use of postal channels under Article 10(a), the letter concluded:

> We therefore believe that the decision of the Court of Appeals in *Bankston* is incorrect to the extent that it suggests that the Hague Convention does not permit as a method of service of process the sending of a copy of a summons and complaint by registered mail to a defendant in a foreign country.

State Department circulars also indicate that service by mail is permitted in international civil litigation. *See, e.g.,* U.S. Dep't of State, *Circular: Service of Process Abroad, in Selected Materials in Int'l Litig. and Arbitration*, 688 PLI/Lit. 777, 1021 (2003). The State Department circular tailored to the United Kingdom specifies that mail service by international registered mail is allowed. U.S. State Dep't, *Judicial Assistance in the United Kingdom (England, Scotland, Wales, and Northern Ireland), in Selected Materials in Int'l Litig. & Arbitration*, 689 PLI/Lit. 13, 325 (2003).

The purpose and history of the Hague Convention, as well as the position of the U.S. State Department, convince us that "send" in Article 10(a) includes "serve." We therefore hold that the Convention permits — or, in the words of the Convention, does not "interfere with"— service of process by international mail, so long as the receiving country does not object.

B. Rule 4(f): "Service Upon Individuals in a Foreign Country"

Article 10(a) does not itself affirmatively authorize international mail service. It merely provides that the Convention "shall not interfere with" the "freedom" to use postal channels if the "State of destination" does not object to their use. As the Rapporteur for the Convention wrote in explaining Article 10(a), "It should be stressed that in permitting the utilization of postal channels, . . . the draft convention did not intend to pass on the validity of this mode of transmission under the law of the forum state: *in order for the postal channel to be utilized, it is necessary that it be authorized by the law of the forum state.*" 1 Ristau § 4-3-5, at 205 (emphasis added [in opinion]) (quoting Service Convention Negotiating Document); *see also id.* at 162 ("Even though a contracting state may not object to methods of service of foreign judicial documents in its territory in a manner other than as provided for in the Convention . . . *it is still necessary that the law of the state where the action is pending authorize the particular method of service employed.*") (emphasis added [in opinion]).

In other words, we must look outside the Hague Convention for affirmative authorization of the international mail service that is merely not forbidden by Article 10(a). Any affirmative authorization of service by international mail, and any requirements as to how that service is to be accomplished, must come from the law of the forum in which the suit is filed.

Federal Rule of Civil Procedure 4(h)(2) directs that service on a foreign corporation, if done outside of the United States, shall be effected "in any manner prescribed for individuals by subdivision [4](f) except personal delivery as provided in paragraph (2)(C)(i) thereof," unless a waiver of service has been obtained and filed. No waiver of service under Rule 4(d) was obtained in this case. To determine whether service of process was proper, we therefore look to Federal Rule of Civil Procedure 4(f). As will be seen, no part of Rule 4(f) authorizes service by ordinary international first class mail.

1. Rule 4(f)(1)

Rule 4(f)(1) authorizes service by those methods of service authorized by international agreements, including the Hague Convention. It provides:

> (f) . . . Unless otherwise provided by federal law, service upon an individual from whom a waiver has not been obtained and filed . . . may be effected in a place not within any judicial district of the United States:
>
> (1) by any internationally agreed means reasonably calculated to give notice, such as those means authorized by the Hague Convention on the Service Abroad of Judicial and Extrajudicial Documents[.]

The Hague Convention affirmatively authorizes service of process through the Central Authority of a receiving state. Rule 4(f)(1), by incorporating the Convention, in turn affirmatively authorizes use of a Central Authority. However, Rule 4(f)(1) does not go beyond means of service affirmatively authorized by international agreements. It is undisputed that Brockmeyer did not use either the Central Authority under the Hague Convention or any other internationally agreed means for accomplishing service. Rule 4(f)(1), therefore, does not provide a basis for service in this case.

We therefore conclude, along with the other courts that have considered the question, that Rule 4(f)(2)(A) does not authorize service of process by ordinary first class international mail.

Conclusion

Today we join the Second Circuit in holding that the Hague Convention allows service of process by international mail. At the same time, we hold that any service by mail in this case was required to be performed in accordance with the requirements of Rule 4(f). Service by international mail is affirmatively authorized by Rule 4(f)(2)(C)(ii), which requires that service be sent by the clerk of the court, using a form of mail requiring a signed receipt. Service by international mail is also affirmatively authorized by Rule 4(f)(3), which requires that the mailing procedure have been specifically directed by the district court. Service by international mail is not otherwise affirmatively authorized by Rule 4(f). Plaintiffs neither followed the procedure prescribed in Rule 4(f)(2)(C)(ii) nor sought the approval of the district court under Rule 4(f)(3). They simply dropped the complaint and summons in a mailbox in Los Angeles, to be delivered by ordinary, international first class mail. There is no affirmative authorization for such service in Rule 4(f). The attempted service was therefore ineffective, and the default judgment against Marquis cannot stand.

REVERSED and REMANDED, with instructions to VACATE the judgment.

QUESTION

What arguments would you make on either or both sides, were the U.S. Supreme Court to decide to hear an appeal to resolve these conflicting circuit court decisions? Would the following have any relevance: Not one of the 68 countries that have ratified the Hague Service Convention, including all of those that, like Japan, accepted article 10(a) but objected to 10(b) and 10(c), have drawn a distinction between "sending" and "effecting service" in their declarations. Norway did object to the all of the provisions of article 10 for effecting service and "transmission" of judicial documents without, however, indicating any difference in meaning. Moreover, those that rejected the application of article 10 in its entirety have commonly declared their objection to the "methods of effecting service" under the article without distinguishing among the three provisions. *See* http://www.hcch.net/index_en.php?act=conventions.status&cid=17.

III. JAPAN

A. General

We turn now to Japanese judicial decisions in which the issue of dispatch and receipt by mail of judicial documents suffices under Japanese law to allow the recognition and enforcement of a foreign (U.S.) judgment. In so doing, we return to the Hague Service Convention and its requirements as viewed from Japanese judicial perspectives as well as again to the issue of "service" under the Convention as a prerequisite of judicial competence (authority) to adjudicate or simply appropriate notice to the defendant.

UENO v. ZAVICHA BLAGOJEVIC
Tokyo District Court Judgment of 21 December 1976
27 Kakyū minshū (Nos. 9–12) 801 (1976)
[English translation in 22 JAIL 160 (1978)]

The defendant, a French domiciliary, brought an action in France for breach of contract against Daiei K.K., a major Japanese film producer. The French court rendered a judgment awarding damages to the defendant. At the time, however, Daiei had been adjudged bankrupt and was subject to bankruptcy proceedings. The defendant sought recognition of the claim based on the French judgment in the proceedings in the Tokyo District Court. The plaintiff, the trustee in bankruptcy, filed a formal objection (*igi*) to the claim and brought the action in the Tokyo District Court for a declaratory judgment (confirmation) of its legal ineffectiveness.

In the action the trustee in bankruptcy filed a report with the court to the effect that in the lawsuit in France the defendant had not attached Japanese or English translations of the summons and complaint, as required under Japan's declaration in ratifying the Hague Service Convention. The judicial documents in the French action were instead sent through the mail without a Japanese translation. The court held that the alleged claim lacked a legal basis. Whether the French nationality principle was the basis for jurisdiction over the Japanese defendant is not mentioned.

REASONS
(riyū)

(4) In an action for non-recognition of a foreign judgment, aside from objections relating to the claim after the judgment becomes final and conclusive, the plaintiff can only contest whether the requirements of article 200 [now Article 118] of the Code of Civil Procedure have been satisfied. However, the plaintiff in this case seems to be claiming only the nonexistence of the obligation right of the defendant without sufficient factual evidence in support of any allegation as to the above. Although one could take the view that the plaintiff does no more than claim the non-existence of the defendant's obligation right, from the perspective of the proceedings in this case in which the court dealing with *sōtatsu* [service, lit. "dispatch and receipt"] ordered that a translation be attached and [from the Report filed with the court], the plaintiff clearly intends to contest whether the requirements of article 200, paragraph 2 [*sōtatsu* as notice requirement], of the Code of Civil Procedure were satisfied. If what the plaintiff in its Report is true — in effect, that the judicial documents in the action brought by the defendant in the French court were sent through the mail without Japanese translations and not in lawful manner — we cannot confirm that the requirements of [article 200, current article 118] relating to foreign judgments were satisfied as alleged by the defendant. Whether or not a foreign judgment satisfied the requirements of article 200 [current article 118] of the Code of Civil Procedure is matter to be determined by the Court *ex officio*. . . .

[The defendant is deemed to have admitted the failure to satisfy the requirement for recognition of the French judgment], because the defendant neither appeared nor produced an answer *though he was lawfully served [sōtatsu] with the summons and complaint*. [Emphasis added.] (The defendant sent a letter written in French to the presiding judge immediately before the date, but we do not consider it because it is not accompanied by a Japanese translation).

The court finds the claim raised by the plaintiff is well founded. . . .

Judge Takuji Kurata
Judge Hiroshige Izutsu
Judge Kiichi Nishino

HIROKO SAEKI INC. v. OZAKI
Tokyo District Court Judgment of 26 March 1990
Kin'yu-Shōji Hanrei (No. 857) 39 (1990)
[English translation in 34 JAIL 174 (1991)]

The plaintiff, an American corporation, brought an action for damages against the defendant, a Japanese domiciliary, in a Circuit Court of the State of Hawaii, which rendered a default judgment in favor of the plaintiff. The plaintiff applied for its recognition and enforcement in Japan. The judicial documents for instituting the proceedings in the Hawaiian Court were sent by mail to the defendant by the plaintiff's attorney in accordance with the law of the State of Hawaii but without any Japanese translation. The plaintiff alleged that the service effected in this case satisfied the notice [*sōtatsu*], requirement for recognition of foreign judgments of article 200 (ii) [current article 118 (ii)] of the Japanese Code of Civil Procedure. The plaintiff argued that the defendant needed only to use an English-Japanese dictionary to understand the purport of the documents addressed to him. He was a graduate of the Department of Economics of Hōsei University, and college graduates have usually had at least 10 years of continuous English language education after beginning to learn the language in middle school.

Reasons
(*riyū*)

In order to satisfy the requirements of article 200 [current article 118], paragraph 2 of the Code of Civil Procedure for service [*sōtatsu*] of the summons and other order necessary to commence process, the documents should be reasonably understood by a Japanese with ordinary competence as a "formal summons or order from a foreign court," transmitted in conformity with established procedures for judicial assistance. Accordingly, it is necessary to have the documents translated and the translation attached to the documents.

With respect to this point, the purpose of [article 200(ii)] is to protect Japanese defendants who were not given an opportunity to defend themselves and have lost in a lawsuit. That being so, the validity of the service [*sōtatsu*] without translation may seem to be acceptable so long as the defendant has the language competence to understand the contents of the documents written in a foreign language, However, if evaluating such particular and subjective factors in each instance is necessary in order to determine the validity of the service [*sōtatsu*] of documents, not only would this produce unreasonable uncertainty as to the status of the defendant receiving the documents, but also defeat the purpose of requiring exact formalities for service [*sōtatsu*] of documents in order to avoid of future disputes. [To require such individualized scrutiny] would also be contrary to the need for procedural certainty and uniformity in dealing with a large number of disputes.

When we consider the problem in line with the foregoing statements, we may come to wonder why our government has not declared its opposition to the use of the method of sending judicial documents by mail directly to persons abroad, pursuant to Article 10 (a) of the Convention on the Service Abroad of Judicial and Extrajudicial Documents in Civil or Commercial Matters. Such [inaction by our government] could only imply recognition of the effect de facto of the act of notice by mail, and not to be understood as having positively introduced a new method of sōtatsu which foreign States are to follow. Accordingly, it can hardly affect our conclusion reached above. [Emphasis added.]

JUDGE TAKUA KUBOUCHI
JUDGE TŌRU KIKUCHI
JUDGE SHIGEMICHI SAITŌ

QUESTIONS

What is required for effective "service" (*sōtatsu*) in Japan? Is service by mail necessarily ineffective? What other means of service in Japan are available under the Hague Service Convention? In what respects is Japan exceptional?

B. United States Consular Practice

CONSULAR CONVENTION BETWEEN JAPAN AND THE UNITED STATES OF AMERICA
Signed at Tokyo, March 22, 1963
Entered into force, August 1, 1964

Article 17

(1) A consular officer may within his consular district:

(a) receive such declarations as may be required to be made under the nationality laws of the sending state;

(b) issue such notices to, receive such declarations from and provide for such medical examinations of a national of the sending state as may be required under the laws of the sending state with regard to compulsory national service;

(c) register a national of the sending state, register or receive notifications of the birth or death of a national of the sending state, record a marriage celebrated within the receiving state when at least one of the parties is a national of the sending state, and receive any such declarations pertaining to family relationships of a national of the sending state as may be required under the laws of that state;

(d) issue, amend, renew, validate and revoke, in conformity with the laws of the sending state, visas, passports and other similar documents:

(e) serve judicial documents, on behalf of the courts of the sending state, upon, or

(f) take depositions, on behalf of the courts or other judicial tribunals or authorities of the sending state, voluntarily given, or

(g) administer oaths to any person in the receiving state in accordance with the laws of the sending state and in a manner not inconsistent with the laws of the receiving state;

(h) obtain copies of or extracts from documents of public registry;

(i) issue, with regard to goods, certificates of origin and other necessary documents for use in the sending state.

(2) It is understood that the registration or the receipt of notifications of a birth or death by a consular officer, the recording by a consular officer of a marriage celebrated under the laws of the receiving state, and the receipt by a consular officer of declarations pertaining to the family relationships in no way exempts a person from any obligation laid down by the laws of the receiving state with regard to the notification.

TITLE 22 — FOREIGN RELATIONS; REVISED AS OF APRIL 01, 1988

Chapter I — Department of State

SUBCHAPTER J — LEGAL AND RELATED SERVICES

PART 92 — NOTARIAL AND RELATED SERVICES

§ 92.85 Service of legal process usually prohibited.

22 CFR 92.85

The service of process and legal papers is not normally a Foreign Service function. Except when directed by the Department of State, officers of the Foreign Service are prohibited from serving process or legal papers or appointing other persons to do.

SOURCE: Dept. Reg. 108.564, 32 FR 11776, Aug. 16, 1967

> **QUESTIONS**
>
> In what respects is United States practice for service abroad distinctive or exceptional? How, for example, does the United States differ from Germany as well as Japan?

REVIEW PROBLEM

Assume that the Government of Iraq successfully sued for recovery of looted Sumerian artifacts purchased by a New York collector from a German dealer domiciled in Hamburg negotiated by phone and the Internet. The collector subsequently brings an action against the German dealer alleging tortious fraud as well as breach of contract based on an alleged oral guarantee of good title and complete provenance.

(a) Under which of the following circumstances, if any, would a New York court have personal jurisdiction over the dealer:

(i) While on a trip to New York, the dealer is personally served.

(ii) The dealer does substantial business in New York, making several trips a year, and is served by mail to his vacation villa on the Island of Majorca in Spain pursuant to the New York long-arm statute. (Spain, it should be noted, has not objected to article 8 or any provision of article 10 of the Hague Service Convention.)

(b) What options would the collector's attorney have for valid service in Germany inasmuch as Germany has objected to both articles 8 and 10 of the Hague Service Convention? Could the complaint and summons be sent to U.S. consul for transmittal either directly to the defendant or indirectly through the appropriate German court?

(c) Should the collector consider bringing the suit in Germany? What might be the advantages of a German lawsuit, assuming that similar tort (fraud) and contract claims could be made under German law?

III. JAPAN

Chapter 5
TAKING OF EVIDENCE ABROAD

I. INTRODUCTION

Discovery abroad is the focus of this chapter. We first examine the principal legal rules and principles as well as judicial practice for the taking of evidence outside of the United States in the context of lawsuits filed in the United States. We next consider the discovery of evidence in the United States to be used in proceedings outside of the United States. At the outset we should note that United States law allows for the most extensive pre-trial discovery of evidence of any country. In nearly all other jurisdictions the scope of discovery is much narrower, in many instances requiring specific identification of documents sought and evidence of relevance of any testimony. In civil law jurisdictions, third parties cannot generally be subpoenaed to testify. They must volunteer. Moreover, the scope of privilege as well as legal protection against disclosure of personal information tends to be much greater. Finally, in civil law jurisdictions judges generally lack contempt power or, at least, their capacity to enforce judicial orders without resort to criminal prosecution is considerably more constrained.

One should keep in mind, however, that in civil proceedings in the United States as in other common law jurisdictions, without pre-trial discovery evidentiary surprise would be a significant problem. Because of the common law emphasis on the adversary system coupled with concentrated trial proceedings and appeals limited to issues of law, some degree of evidentiary disclosure prior to the trial becomes essential to prevent injustice from evidentiary surprise during the trial. Even in other common law jurisdictions, however, mandated pre-trial discovery is less extensive than in the United States. In civil law jurisdictions, in contrast, the prevalence of trial proceedings with multiple hearings conducted over extended periods of time as well as retrial of facts on first appeal reduce the problem of surprise and the need for pre-trial discovery. Within such fundamental contrasts in mind, once more we begin with a Hague Convention.

CONVENTION ON THE TAKING OF EVIDENCE ABROAD IN CIVIL OR COMMERCIAL MATTERS
(Concluded 18 March 1970)

Hague Conference on Private International Law
Outline Evidence Convention

Purpose of the Convention

The Evidence Convention establishes methods of co-operation for the taking of evidence abroad in civil or commercial matters. The Convention, which applies only between States Parties, provides for the taking of evidence (i) by means of *letters of request*, and (ii) by *diplomatic or consular agents* and *commissioners*. The Convention provides effective means of overcoming the differences between civil law and common law systems with respect to the taking of evidence.

Letters of Request

A judicial authority of one State Party (requesting State) may request, by means of a letter of request, a Competent Authority of another State Party (State addressed) to obtain evidence which is intended for use in judicial proceedings in the requesting State. The judicial authority of the requesting State transmits the letter of request to the *Central Authority* of the State addressed (see also Arts. 24(2) and 25). The latter then forwards the letter of request to the Competent Authority in its country for execution. The law of the State addressed applies to the execution of the letter of request. In order to expedite and facilitate execution, the Convention provides for an option to allow the participation of members of the judicial personnel of the requesting authority, the parties and/or their representatives, in executing the letter of request. The requesting authority may also request the use of a special method or procedure for execution of the letter of request, provided that this is not incompatible with the law of the State addressed or impossible to perform. Certain States have even amended their domestic law in order to permit techniques for the execution of requests that are customarily used in other States (e.g., the drafting of verbatim transcripts of testimony, the possibility of cross-examination, etc.).

A requested authority unable to perform the letter of request itself may appoint a suitable person to do so (this applies in particular when the request is directed at common law countries; the court addressed may then be unable to perform the letter of request itself because according to its procedure, it is up to the parties to collect the evidence). The person to be questioned or requested to discover documents is entitled to assert a privilege or duty to refuse to give evidence under either the law of the requesting State or the law of the State addressed.

A letter of request shall be executed "expeditiously" and may be refused only in specific cases.

Lastly, the execution of the letter of request may not give rise to any reimbursement of taxes or costs; however, the State addressed may require the requesting State to reimburse the fees paid to experts and interpreters and the costs occasioned by the use of a special procedure requested by the requesting State.

Diplomatic or Consular agents, Commissioners

Chapter Two of the Convention also allows diplomatic or consular agents and commissioners to take evidence and may be subject to the prior permission of the appropriate authority of the State in which the evidence is to be taken. States may exclude in whole or in part the application of this Chapter. It is therefore critical to check whether a State has made a declaration under this Chapter. Subject to the relevant permission, the representative or commissioner may take evidence, insofar as their proposed actions are compatible with the law of the State of execution and may also have power to administer an oath or take an affirmation. The consular or diplomatic agent or commissioner may not exercise any compulsion against the person concerned by the request. The Convention provides, however, that States may, by declaration, authorize foreign persons permitted to take evidence to apply to the Competent Authority for appropriate assistance to obtain the evidence by compulsion. Unlike letters of request, the taking of evidence is as a rule performed in accordance with the manner required by the law of the Court before which the action is initiated. However, if the manner in which the evidence is taken is forbidden by the law of the State of execution, it may not be used. Cross-examination, during which the witness is questioned by counsel for both parties, is also permitted. Last, the person required to give evidence may, in the same way as pursuant to a letter of request, assert a privilege or duty to refuse to give evidence.

Pre-trial discovery (Art. 23)

Pre-trial discovery is a procedure known to common law countries, which covers requests for evidence submitted *after the filing of a claim but before the final hearing on the merits*. The Convention permits States Parties to ensure that such a request for discovery of documents is sufficiently substantiated so as to avoid requests whereby a party is merely seeking to find out what documents might be in the possession of the other party to the proceedings.

Due to existing misunderstandings of the nature of pre-trial discovery, the 2003 Special Commission clarified the nature and purpose of this procedure and invited States that have made a general non-particularised declaration to revisit their declarations (see Conclusions and Recommendations Nos. 29–34 of the 2003 Special Commission, available on the Hague Conference website at < www.hcch.net >).

Monitoring of the Convention

The practical operation of the Convention has been reviewed by several Special Commissions (in 1978, 1985, 1989, 2003, and 2009). A model letter of request was adopted at the 1978 Special Commission and amended in 1985. The Special Commissions have confirmed the continuing interest for this Convention and reaffirmed its indisputable practical usefulness.

NOTE

Neither Canada nor Japan have signed or ratified the Hague Evidence Convention. Of the 58 contracting countries to the convention, many have made special declarations regarding pre-trial discovery under article 23, including, as noted below, China, Germany, and Mexico:

> China: "In accordance with Article 23 of the Convention concerning the Letters of Request issued for the purpose of obtaining pre-trial discovery of documents as known in common law countries, only the request for obtaining discovery of the documents clearly enumerated in the Letters of Request and of direct and close connection with the subject matter of the litigation will be executed."

> Germany: "The Federal Republic of Germany declares in pursuance of Article 23 of the Convention that it will not, in its territory, execute Letters of Request issued for the purpose of obtaining pre-trial discovery of documents as known in common law countries."

> Mexico: The Mexican declaration (in Spanish) requires that the trial proceedings have commenced and that the documents be adequately identified along with the relevance of the documentary evidence directly to the matters to be proven in the pending proceedings.

II. DISCOVERY ABROAD IN AID OF LITIGATION IN THE UNITED STATES

SOCIÉTÉ NATIONALE INDUSTRIELLE AEROSPATIALE v. U.S. DIST. CT. FOR THE SOUTHERN DISTRICT OF IOWA*
482 U.S. 522 (1987)

JUSTICE STEVENS delivered the opinion of the Court.

The United States, the Republic of France, and 15 other Nations [as of 1987] have acceded to the Hague Convention on the Taking of Evidence Abroad in Civil or Commercial Matters, opened for signature, Mar. 18, 1970, 23 U.S.T. 2555, T.I.A.S. No. 7444. This Convention — sometimes referred to as the "Hague Convention" or the "Evidence Convention"— prescribes certain procedures by which a judicial authority in one contracting state may request evidence located in another contracting state. The question presented in this case concerns the extent to which a federal district court must employ the procedures set forth in the Convention when litigants seek answers to interrogatories, the production of documents, and admissions from a French adversary over whom the court has personal jurisdiction.

---

* Footnotes omitted.

I

The two petitioners are corporations owned by the Republic of France. They are engaged in the business of designing, manufacturing, and marketing aircraft. One of their planes, the "Rallye," was allegedly advertised in American aviation publications as "the World's safest and most economical STOL plane." On August 19, 1980, a Rallye crashed in Iowa, injuring the pilot and a passenger. Dennis Jones, John George, and Rosa George brought separate suits based upon this accident in the United States District Court for the Southern District of Iowa, alleging that petitioners had manufactured and sold a defective plane and that they were guilty of negligence and breach of warranty. Petitioners answered the complaints, apparently without questioning the jurisdiction of the District Court. With the parties' consent, the cases were consolidated and referred to a Magistrate. [Reference omitted.]

Initial discovery was conducted by both sides pursuant to the Federal Rules of Civil Procedure without objection. When plaintiffs served a second request for the production of documents pursuant to Rule 34, a set of interrogatories pursuant to Rule 33, and requests for admission pursuant to Rule 36, however, petitioners filed a motion for a protective order. App. 27–37. The motion alleged that because petitioners are "French corporations, and the discovery sought can only be found in a foreign state, namely France," the Hague Convention dictated the exclusive procedures that must be followed for pretrial discovery. App. 2. In addition, the motion stated that under French penal law, the petitioners could not respond to discovery requests that did not comply with the Convention. *Ibid.*

The Magistrate denied the motion insofar as it related to answering interrogatories, producing documents, and making admissions. After reviewing the relevant cases, the Magistrate explained:

> "To permit the Hague Evidence Convention to override the Federal Rules of Civil Procedure would frustrate the courts' interests, which particularly arise in products liability cases, in protecting United States citizens from harmful products and in compensating them for injuries arising from use of such products." App. to Pet. for Cert. 25a.

The Magistrate made two responses to petitioners' argument that they could not comply with the discovery requests without violating French penal law. Noting that the law was originally " 'inspired to impede enforcement of United States antitrust laws,' " and that it did not appear to have been strictly enforced in France, he first questioned whether it would be construed to apply to the pretrial discovery requests at issue. *Id.*, at 22a–24a. Second, he balanced the interests in the "protection of United States citizens from harmful foreign products and compensation for injuries caused by such products" against France's interest in protecting its citizens "from intrusive foreign discovery procedures." The Magistrate concluded that the former interests were stronger, particularly because compliance with the requested discovery will "not have to take place in France" and will not be greatly intrusive or abusive. *Id.*, at 23a–25a.

Petitioners sought a writ of mandamus from the Court of Appeals for the Eighth Circuit under Federal Rule of Appellate Procedure 21(a). Although immediate appellate review of an interlocutory discovery order is not ordinarily available, [citation omitted], the Court of Appeals considered that the novelty and the importance of the question presented, and the likelihood of its recurrence, made consideration of the merits of the petition appropriate. 782 F.2d 120 (1986). It then held that "when the district court has jurisdiction over a foreign litigant the Hague Convention does not apply to the production of evidence in that litigant's possession, even though the documents and information sought may physically be located within the territory of a foreign signatory to the Convention." *Id.*, at 124. The Court of Appeals disagreed with petitioners' argument that this construction would render the entire Hague Convention "meaningless," noting that it would still serve the purpose of providing an improved procedure for obtaining evidence from nonparties. *Id.*, at 125. The court also rejected petitioners' contention that considerations of international comity required plaintiffs to resort to Hague Convention procedures as an initial matter ("first use"), and correspondingly to invoke the federal discovery rules only if the treaty procedures turned out to be futile. The Court of Appeals believed that the potential overruling of foreign tribunals' denial of discovery would do more to defeat than to promote international comity. *Id.*, at 125–126. Finally, the Court of Appeals concluded that objections based on the French penal statute should be considered in two stages: first, whether the discovery order was proper even though compliance may require petitioners to violate French law; and second, what sanctions, if any, should be imposed if petitioners are unable to comply. The Court of Appeals held that the Magistrate properly answered the first question and that it was premature to address the second. The court therefore denied the petition for mandamus. We granted certiorari. 476 U.S. 1168 (1986).

II

In the District Court and the Court of Appeals, petitioners contended that the Hague Evidence Convention "provides the exclusive and mandatory procedures for obtaining documents and information located within the territory of a foreign signatory." 782 F.2d, at 124. We are satisfied that the Court of Appeals correctly rejected this extreme position. We believe it is foreclosed by the plain language of the Convention. Before discussing the text of the Convention, however, we briefly review its history.

The Hague Conference on Private International Law, an association of sovereign states, has been conducting periodic sessions since 1893. [Reference omitted.] The United States participated in those sessions as an observer in 1956 and 1960, and as a member beginning in 1964 pursuant to congressional authorization. In that year Congress amended the Judicial Code to grant foreign litigants, without any requirement of reciprocity, special assistance in obtaining evidence in the United States. In 1965 the Hague Conference adopted a Convention on the Service Abroad of Judicial and Extrajudicial Documents in Civil or Commercial Matters (Service Convention), 20 U.S.T. 361, T.I.A.S. No. 6638, to which the Senate gave its advice and consent in 1967. The favorable response to the Service Convention, coupled with the longstanding interest of American lawyers in improving procedures for obtaining evidence abroad, motivated the United States to take the initiative in proposing that an evidence convention be adopted. [Reference omitted.] The

Conference organized a special commission to prepare the draft convention, and the draft was approved without a dissenting vote on October 26, 1968. S. Exec. Doc. A, at p. v. It was signed on behalf of the United States in 1970 and ratified by a unanimous vote of the Senate in 1972. The Convention's purpose was to establish a system for obtaining evidence located abroad that would be "tolerable" to the state executing the request and would produce evidence "utilizable" in the requesting state. Amram, Explanatory Report on the Convention on the Taking of Evidence Abroad in Civil or Commercial Matters, in S. Exec. Doc. A, p. 11.

In his letter of transmittal recommending ratification of the Convention, the President noted that it was "supported by such national legal organizations as the American Bar Association, the Judicial Conference of the United States, the National Conference of Commissions on Uniform State Laws, and by a number of State, local, and specialized bar associations." S. Exec. Doc. A., p. III. There is no evidence of any opposition to the Convention in any of those organizations. The Convention was fairly summarized in the Secretary of State's letter of submittal to the President:

> The willingness of the Conference to proceed promptly with work on the evidence convention is perhaps attributable in large measure to the difficulties encountered by courts and lawyers in obtaining evidence abroad from countries with markedly different legal systems. Some countries have insisted on the exclusive use of the complicated, dilatory and expensive system of letters rogatory or letters of request. Other countries have refused adequate judicial assistance because of the absence of a treaty or convention regulating the matter. The substantial increase in litigation with foreign aspects arising, in part, from the unparalleled expansion of international trade and travel in recent decades had intensified the need for an effective international agreement to set up a model system to bridge differences between the common law and civil law approaches to the taking of evidence abroad.
>
> Civil law countries tend to concentrate on commissions rogatoires, while common law countries take testimony on notice, by stipulation and through commissions to consuls or commissioners. Letters of request for judicial assistance from courts abroad in securing needed evidence have been the exception, rather than the rule. The civil law technique results normally in a resume of the evidence, prepared by the executing judge and signed by the witness, while the common law technique results normally in a verbatim transcript of the witness's testimony certified by the reporter.
>
> Failure by either the requesting state or the state of execution fully to take into account the differences of approach to the taking of evidence abroad under the two systems and the absence of agreed standards applicable to letters of request have frequently caused difficulties for courts and litigants. To minimize such difficulties in the future, the enclosed convention, which consists of a preamble and forty-two articles, is designed to:
>
>> 1. Make the employment of letters of request a principal means of obtaining evidence abroad;

2. Improve the means of securing evidence abroad by increasing the powers of consuls and by introducing in the civil law world, on a limited basis, the concept of the commissioner;

3. Provide means for securing evidence in the form needed by the court where the action is pending; and

4. Preserve all more favorable and less restrictive practices arising from internal law, internal rules of procedure and bilateral or multilateral conventions.

What the convention does is to provide a set of minimum standards with which contracting states agree to comply. Further, through articles 27, 28 and 32, it provides a flexible framework within which any future liberalizing changes in policy and tradition in any country with respect to international judicial cooperation may be translated into effective change in international procedures. At the same time it recognizes and preserves procedures of every country which now or hereafter may provide international cooperation in the taking of evidence on more liberal and less restrictive bases, whether this is effected by supplementary agreements or by municipal law and practice." *Id.*, VI.

III

In arguing their entitlement to a protective order, petitioners correctly assert that both the discovery rules set forth in the Federal Rules of Civil Procedure and the Hague Convention are the law of the United States. . . . This observation, however, does not dispose of the question before us; we must analyze the interaction between these two bodies of federal law. Initially, we note that at least four different interpretations of the relationship between the federal discovery rules and the Hague Convention are possible. Two of these interpretations assume that the Hague Convention by its terms dictates the extent to which it supplants normal discovery rules. *First, the Hague Convention might be read as requiring its use to the exclusion of any other discovery procedures whenever evidence located abroad is sought for use in an American court. Second, the Hague Convention might be interpreted to require first, but not exclusive, use of its procedures. Two other interpretations assume that international comity, rather than the obligations created by the treaty, should guide judicial resort to the Hague Convention. Third, then, the Convention might be viewed as establishing a supplemental set of discovery procedures, strictly optional under treaty law, to which concerns of comity nevertheless require first resort by American courts in all cases. Fourth, the treaty may be viewed as an undertaking among sovereigns to facilitate discovery to which an American court should resort when it deems that course of action appropriate, after considering the situations of the parties before it as well as the interests of the concerned foreign state.* [Emphasis added.]

We reject the first two of the possible interpretations as inconsistent with the language and negotiating history of the Hague Convention. [Emphasis added.] The preamble of the Convention specifies its purpose "to facilitate the transmission and execution of Letters of Request" and to "improve mutual judicial co-operation in civil or commercial matters." 23 U.S.T., at 2557, T.I.A.S. No. 7444. The preamble does not speak in mandatory terms which would purport to describe the procedures for all permissible transnational discovery and exclude all other existing practices. The text of the Evidence Convention itself does not modify the law of any contracting state, require any contracting state to use the Convention procedures, either in requesting evidence or in responding to such requests, or compel any contracting state to change its own evidence-gathering procedures.

The Convention contains three chapters. Chapter I, entitled "Letters of Requests," and chapter II, entitled "Taking of Evidence by Diplomatic Officers, Consular Agents and Commissioners," both use permissive rather than mandatory language. Thus, Article 1 provides that a judicial authority in one contracting state "may" forward a letter of request to the competent authority in another contracting state for the purpose of obtaining evidence. Similarly, Articles 15, 16, and 17 provide that diplomatic officers, consular agents, and commissioners "may . . . without compulsion," take evidence under certain conditions. The absence of any command that a contracting state must use Convention procedures when they are not needed is conspicuous.

. . . [T]he text of the Evidence Convention, as well as the history of its proposal and ratification by the United States, unambiguously supports the conclusion that it was intended to establish optional procedures that would facilitate the taking of evidence abroad. [Citations omitted.]

An interpretation of the Hague Convention as the exclusive means for obtaining evidence located abroad would effectively subject every American court hearing a case involving a national of a contracting state to the internal laws of that state. Interrogatories and document requests are staples of international commercial litigation, no less than of other suits, yet a rule of exclusivity would subordinate the court's supervision of even the most routine of these pretrial proceedings to the actions or, equally, to the inactions of foreign judicial authorities. . . .

. . . .

The Hague Convention, however, contains no such plain statement of a preemptive intent. *We conclude accordingly that the Hague Convention did not deprive the District Court of the jurisdiction it otherwise possessed to order a foreign national party before it to produce evidence physically located within a signatory nation.* [Emphasis added.]

IV

While the Hague Convention does not divest the District Court of jurisdiction to order discovery under the Federal Rules of Civil Procedure, the optional character of the Convention procedures sheds light on one aspect of the Court of Appeals' opinion that we consider erroneous. That court concluded that the Convention simply "does not apply" to discovery sought from a foreign litigant that is subject to the jurisdiction of an American court. 782 F.2d, at 124. Plaintiffs argue that this conclusion is supported by two considerations. First, the Federal Rules of Civil Procedure provide ample means for obtaining discovery from parties who are subject to the court's jurisdiction, while before the Convention was ratified it was often extremely difficult, if not impossible, to obtain evidence from nonparty witnesses abroad. Plaintiffs contend that it is appropriate to construe the Convention as applying only in the area in which improvement was badly needed. Second, when a litigant is subject to the jurisdiction of the district court, arguably the evidence it is required to produce is not "abroad" within the meaning of the Convention, even though it is in fact located in a foreign country at the time of the discovery request and even though it will have to be gathered or otherwise prepared abroad. [Citations omitted.] Nevertheless, the text of the Convention draws no distinction between evidence obtained from third parties and that obtained from the litigants themselves; nor does it purport to draw any sharp line between evidence that is "abroad" and evidence that is within the control of a party subject to the jurisdiction of the requesting court. Thus, it appears clear to us that the optional Convention procedures are available whenever they will facilitate the gathering of evidence by the means authorized in the Convention. *Although these procedures are not mandatory, the Hague Convention does "apply" to the production of evidence in a litigant's possession in the sense that it is one method of seeking evidence that a court may elect to employ.* . . . [Emphasis added.]

V

Petitioners contend that even if the Hague Convention's procedures are not mandatory, this Court should adopt a rule requiring that American litigants first resort to those procedures before initiating any discovery pursuant to the normal methods of the Federal Rules of Civil Procedure. [Citations omitted.] The Court of Appeals rejected this argument because it was convinced that an American court's order ultimately requiring discovery that a foreign court had refused under Convention procedures would constitute "the greatest insult" to the sovereignty of that tribunal. 782 F.2d, at 125–126. We disagree with the Court of Appeals' view. It is well known that the scope of American discovery is often significantly broader than is permitted in other jurisdictions, and we are satisfied that foreign tribunals will recognize that the final decision on the evidence to be used in litigation conducted in American courts must be made by those courts. We therefore do not believe that an American court should refuse to make use of Convention procedures because of a concern that it may ultimately find it necessary to order the production of evidence that a foreign tribunal permitted a party to withhold.

Nevertheless, we cannot accept petitioners' invitation to announce a new rule of law that would require first resort to Convention procedures whenever discovery is sought from a foreign litigant. Assuming, without deciding, that we have the lawmaking power to do so, we are convinced that such a general rule would be unwise. In many situations the Letter of Request procedure authorized by the Convention would be unduly time consuming and expensive, as well as less certain to produce needed evidence than direct use of the Federal Rules. A rule of first resort in all cases would therefore be inconsistent with the overriding interest in the "just, speedy, and inexpensive determination" of litigation in our courts. See Fed. Rule Civ. Proc. 1.

Petitioners argue that a rule of first resort is necessary to accord respect to the sovereignty of states in which evidence is located. It is true that the process of

II. DISCOVERY ABROAD IN AID OF LITIGATION IN THE UNITED STATES

obtaining evidence in a civil-law jurisdiction is normally conducted by a judicial officer rather than by private attorneys. Petitioners contend that if performed on French soil, for example, by an unauthorized person, such evidence-gathering might violate the "judicial sovereignty" of the host nation. Because it is only through the Convention that civil-law nations have given their consent to evidence-gathering activities within their borders, petitioners argue, we have a duty to employ those procedures whenever they are available. . . . We find that argument unpersuasive. If such a duty were to be inferred from the adoption of the Convention itself, we believe it would have been described in the text of that document. Moreover, the concept of international comity requires in this context a more particularized analysis of the respective interests of the foreign nation and the requesting nation than petitioners' proposed general rule would generate. We therefore decline to hold as a blanket matter that comity requires resort to Hague Evidence Convention procedures without prior scrutiny in each case of the particular facts, sovereign interests, and likelihood that resort to those procedures will prove effective.

. . . .

Some discovery procedures are much more "intrusive" than others. In this case, for example, an interrogatory asking petitioners to identify the pilots who flew flight tests in the Rallye before it was certified for flight by the Federal Aviation Administration, or a request to admit that petitioners authorized certain advertising in a particular magazine, is certainly less intrusive than a request to produce all of the "design specifications, line drawings and engineering plans and all engineering change orders and plans and all drawings concerning the leading edge slats for the Rallye type aircraft manufactured by the Defendants." App. 29. Even if a court might be persuaded that a particular document request was too burdensome or too "intrusive" to be granted in full, with or without an appropriate protective order, it might well refuse to insist upon the use of Convention procedures before requiring responses to simple interrogatories or requests for admissions. The exact line between reasonableness and unreasonableness in each case must be drawn by the trial court, based on its knowledge of the case and of the claims and interests of the parties and the governments whose statutes and policies they invoke.

American courts, in supervising pretrial proceedings, should exercise special vigilance to protect foreign litigants from the danger that unnecessary, or unduly burdensome, discovery may place them in a disadvantageous position. Judicial supervision of discovery should always seek to minimize its costs and inconvenience and to prevent improper uses of discovery requests. When it is necessary to seek evidence abroad, however, the district court must supervise pretrial proceedings particularly closely to prevent discovery abuses. For example, the additional cost of transportation of documents or witnesses to or from foreign locations may increase the danger that discovery may be sought for the improper purpose of motivating settlement, rather than finding relevant and probative evidence. Objections to "abusive" discovery that foreign litigants advance should therefore receive the most careful consideration. In addition, we have long recognized the demands of comity in suits involving foreign states, either as parties or as sovereigns with a coordinate interest in the litigation. [Citation omitted.] American courts should therefore take care to demonstrate due respect for any special problem confronted by the foreign litigant on account of its nationality or the location of its operations, and for any sovereign interest expressed by a foreign state. We do not articulate specific rules to guide this delicate task of adjudication.

VI

In the case before us, the Magistrate and the Court of Appeals correctly refused to grant the broad protective order that petitioners requested. The Court of Appeals erred, however, in stating that the Evidence Convention does not apply to the pending discovery demands. This holding may be read as indicating that the Convention procedures are not even an option that is open to the District Court. It must be recalled, however, that the Convention's specification of duties in executing states creates corresponding rights in requesting states; holding that the Convention does not apply in this situation would deprive domestic litigants of access to evidence through treaty procedures to which the contracting states have assented. Moreover, such a rule would deny the foreign litigant a full and fair opportunity to demonstrate appropriate reasons for employing Convention procedures in the first instance, for some aspects of the discovery process.

Accordingly, the judgment of the Court of Appeals is vacated, and the case is remanded for further proceedings consistent with this opinion.

It is so ordered.

JUSTICE BLACKMUN, with whom JUSTICE BRENNAN, JUSTICE MARSHALL, and JUSTICE O'CONNOR join, concurring in part and dissenting in part.

Some might well regard the Court's decision in this case as an affront to the nations that have joined the United States in ratifying the Hague Convention on the Taking of Evidence Abroad in Civil or Commercial Matters, opened for signature, Mar. 18, 1970, 23 U.S.T. 2555, T.I.A.S. No. 7444. The Court ignores the importance of the Convention by relegating it to an "optional" status, without acknowledging the significant achievement in accommodating divergent interests that the Convention represents. Experience to date indicates that there is a large risk that the case-by-case comity analysis now to be permitted by the Court will be performed inadequately and that the somewhat unfamiliar procedures of the Convention will be invoked infrequently. I fear the Court's decision means that courts will resort unnecessarily to issuing discovery orders under the Federal Rules of Civil Procedure in a raw exercise of their jurisdictional power to the detriment of the United States' national and international interests. The Court's view of this country's international obligations is particularly unfortunate in a world in which regular commercial and legal channels loom ever more crucial.

I do agree with the Court's repudiation of the positions at both extremes of the spectrum with regard to the use of the Convention. Its rejection of the view that the Convention is not "applicable" at all to this case is surely correct: the Convention clearly applies to litigants as well as to third parties, and to requests for evidence located abroad, no matter where that evidence is actually "produced." The Court also correctly rejects the far opposite position that the Convention provides the exclusive means for discovery involving signatory countries. I dissent, however, because I cannot endorse the Court's case-by-case inquiry for determining whether to use Convention procedures and its failure to provide lower courts with any meaningful guidance for carrying out that inquiry. In my view, the Convention provides effective discovery procedures that largely eliminate the conflicts between United States and foreign law on evidence gathering. I therefore would apply a general presumption that, in most cases, courts should resort first to the Convention procedures. An individualized analysis of the circumstances of a particular case is appropriate only when it appears that it would be futile to employ the Convention or when its procedures prove to be unhelpful.

QUESTIONS

1. Why would a party wish to avoid resort to Hague Evidence Convention procedures?

2. What factors must a court take into account under *Aerospatiale* in deciding whether to require a party to use the procedures for discovery under the Hague Discovery Convention rather than those provided under state law or the Federal Rules of Civil Procedure? Under which of the following circumstances would a Letter of Request pursuant to the Hague Evidence Convention be required or advisable? Explain your answer:

(a) The defendant in a patent infringement suit seeks to obtain documents and answers to interrogatories from inventors of patented drugs residing abroad as well as others, also living outside of the U.S., who filed declarations with the U.S. Patent Office in support of their patentability. The defendant seeking the Letters of Requests seeks to show that the patents in question are invalid. *See Pronova Biopharma Norge AS v. TEVA Pharmaceuticals USA, Inc.*, 708 F. Supp. 2d 450 (D. Del. 2010).

(b) What if, in the above case, the defendant filed the motion for the Letters of Request two weeks before fact discovery in the case was set to close and only two months before expert testimony was to be completed? What if, in addition, similar evidence could be obtained in the U.S.? *See Seoul Semiconductor Co., Ltd. v. Nichia Corp.*, 590 F. Supp. 2d 832 (E.D. Tex. 2008).

(c) What if the documents sought had been previously turned over to a U.S. regulatory agency in connection with an investigation into industry practice; however, copies remain with the attorney and are thus located in the U.S.? *See Ratliff v. Davis Polk & Wardwell*, 354 F.3d 165 (2d Cir. 2003).

(d) What if the information sought concerned the commercial activities in the United States generally and in the state in which the suit has been filed of a corporate defendant who contests jurisdiction? *See In re Automotive Refinishing Paint Antitrust Litigation*, 358 F.3d 288 (3d Cir. 2004).

> (e) What if the information sought related to the identification of assets of a party in a securities fraud case, and was in the sole possession of a Swiss bank with offices in the United States; however, its disclosure by the bank would violate Swiss law. *See Securities and Exchange Commission v. Stanford International Bank, Ltd.*, 776 F. Supp. 2d 323 (N.D. Tex. 2011).
>
> 3. Which party bears the burden to persuade a court that Hague Evidence Convention procedures rather than the federal or state rules for discovery should be used? *See, e.g., Schindler Elevator Corp. v. Otis Elevator*, 657 F. Supp. 2d 525 (D.N.J. 2009).
>
> 4. Assume that several foreign manufacturers of automotive paint are sued in a federal court in New Jersey for conspiring to fix prices of their products that are sold in the United States in violation of the Sherman Act. All of the defendants in the antitrust action contest personal jurisdiction. The plaintiffs seek documents from the defendants as well as interrogatories of managerial personnel in the head offices of each of the firms to establish the basis for personal jurisdiction. The defendants claim that under Japanese law such information is deemed privileged and discovery would thus not be permissible. How should the judge rule?
>
> 5. Assuming the judge has determined that discovery pursuant to the Federal Rules rather than the Hague Convention is permitted and orders the defendants to provide certain documents and to respond to the plaintiffs' interrogatories, what sanctions might be imposed were the defendants to fail to comply? What if under the law of the jurisdiction in which the documents and witness are located, any party complying with the discovery order could be subject to criminal prosecution?
>
> 6. What if the material being sought is stored in digital form on a computer system located abroad but is accessible in the U.S. if one has the correct ID and Password?

IN RE WESTINGHOUSE ELECTRIC CORPORATION URANIUM CONTRACTS LITIGATION
563 F.2d 992 (10th Cir. 1977)

McWilliams, Circuit Judge.

Rio Algom Corporation appeals from an order adjudging it, and its president, George R. Albino, to be in willful and inexcusable civil contempt of court for failing to comply with a discovery order of the United States District Court for the District of Utah, Central Division. Rio Algom was ordered to pay into the registry of the court the sum of $10,000, per day, until such time as Rio Algom complied with the order. It was further provided that should Rio Algom fail to pay the ordered fine, the United States Marshal was authorized and directed to enter upon the property of Rio Algom at La Sal, Utah and seize "any and all property of Rio Algom of sufficient value to satisfy the above sums." Our study of the matter leads us to conclude that the trial court erred in holding Rio Algom in contempt and in imposing the severe sanction in connection therewith. We therefore reverse.

Westinghouse Electric Corporation is the defendant in a civil action brought by several utility companies in the United States District Court for the Eastern District of Virginia. The action is essentially one for breach of contract, with the utility companies alleging that Westinghouse breached its contract to deliver uranium at a certain price. One of Westinghouse's defenses in the Virginia proceeding is that performance has been rendered "commercially impracticable" within the meaning of the Uniform Commercial Code because of a dramatic, unprecedented, and unforeseeable rise in the price of uranium. In connection with the defense of impracticability of performance, a major issue is whether the 800% increase in the price of uranium, from $5 per pound to $40 per pound, was caused by secret price fixing engaged in by various producers of uranium, both within and without the United States.

Rio Algom Corporation is a Delaware corporation and it operates a uranium mine in Utah. However, Rio Algom Corporation maintains its corporate office in Canada, and it is this fact which triggers the present controversy. Westinghouse, in preparation for trial of the breach of contract case in the Eastern District of Virginia, has been taking the depositions of the officers of various uranium producing companies, as well as generally engaging in discovery designed to show that the rise in the price of uranium resulted from a world-wide cartel. As a part of its discovery, Westinghouse caused a subpoena to issue in Utah on the resident manager of Rio Algom. The subpoena directed Rio Algom to produce its president, George R. Albino, in Utah for the purpose of taking his deposition and to produce certain business records. George R. Albino now resides, and for several years has been residing, in Canada. There is, however, a dispute between the parties as to whether Albino is presently a citizen of Canada or the United States.

Although Rio Algom has since complied with the subpoena in numerous particulars, it did object to producing certain business documents then located in its offices in Canada, and further objected to producing Albino for depositional purposes, insofar as his testimony might relate to such business records and their contents. The basis for such objection was the belief by Rio Algom that if it produced its business records then located in Canada, and if it produced its president, Albino, and permitted him to be examined concerning such records, then it would be in violation of Canadian law and subject to criminal sanctions. Specifically, Rio Algom claims that if it fully complied with the Westinghouse subpoena it would be in violation of the Canadian Uranium Information Security Regulations, SOR, 76-644 (P.C. 1976-2368, Sept. 21, 1976), promulgated under the authority of Canada's Atomic Energy Control Act, R.S.C. 1970, c. A-19.

Upon hearing the district court overruled a motion to quash and on May 2, 1977, ordered Rio Algom to produce its business records then on file in Canada and to produce its president, Albino, to be examined concerning the contents of such records.

Rio Algom did not comply with the May 2 order. Rio Algom was next ordered to show cause why it should not be held in contempt for failing to comply with the May 2 order. Hearing on the show cause order was held on June 21 and July 29, and on the latter date, Rio Algom was adjudged in contempt. It is from the written order of contempt entered on July 29, 1977, that Rio Algom now appeals.

The record reveals that Westinghouse has previously caused letters rogatory to issue to the Supreme Court of Ontario, which letters sought the aid of the Canadian courts in obtaining Rio Algom's business records located in Canada and in taking the deposition of Albino. However, the Ontario Supreme Court declined to enforce the letters rogatory, and dismissed the same on the ground, among others, that to enforce the letters rogatory would cause a violation of the Uranium Information Security Regulations, which constitute a Canadian public policy statement. The regulations were held to fall within the purposes of the Atomic Energy Control Act and to further the national interest, as expressed in the Act, "to control and supervise the development, application and use of atomic energy." The Ontario court further reasoned that the letters rogatory sought to measure conduct of the Canadian Government against laws of the United States so that to enforce the letters would tend to impinge on Canada's sovereignty. The lengthy opinion of the Ontario Supreme Court is *In re Evidence Act*, R.S.O. 1970, c. 151 (and *In re: Westinghouse Electric Corp. Uranium Contract Litigation*), ___ Ont. 2d ___ (1977).

On June 23, 1977, Rio Algom formally requested the consent of the Canadian Minister of Energy, Mines & Resources to release the company's records located in Canada to the end that it could fully comply with the discovery order. Such request was formally denied on July 19, 1977, on the ground that "the production of such documents would be contrary to the policy of the Government of Canada in this matter."

. . . .

Rio Algom concedes that it has not fully complied with the discovery order of May 2. The excuse offered for failing to fully comply with the May 2 order is that should it fully comply, then it would be in violation of Canadian law and subject to severe sanctions in that country. The applicable Canadian statute provides for a "normal" penalty for a violation of the regulation of a $5,000 fine, or two years imprisonment, or both. However, should an indictment be returned, and a conviction suffered, then the penalty could be a $10,000 fine, or five years imprisonment, or both. The district court concluded, in effect, that such was not an adequate excuse for the admitted noncompliance, within Fed. R. Civ. P. 45(f). The district court further found that neither Rio Algom nor Albino had diligently sought to comply with its order, nor had either made a good faith showing of inability to comply. Nor had they sought a "timely" exemption from the Canadian nondisclosure law.

In our view the record does not support the finding that Rio Algom has failed to act in good faith, nor does it support the trial court's conclusion that Rio Algom had no adequate excuse for its failure to comply with the discovery order. All things considered, on the basis of the record before it, the district court in our view abused its discretion in adjudging Rio Algom to be in contempt of court, and in imposing the severe sanction in connection therewith. In thus concluding we rely heavily on *Société Internationale Pour Participations Industrielles et Commerciales, S.A. v. Rogers*, 357 U.S. 197 (1958), and the rationale thereof. . . .

In our view *Société* holds that, though a local court has the power to order a party to produce foreign documents despite the fact that such production may subject the party to criminal sanctions in the foreign country, still the fact of foreign illegality may prevent the imposition of sanctions for subsequent disobedience to the discovery order. We also believe it to be implicit in *Société* that foreign illegality does not necessarily prevent a local court from imposing sanctions when, due to the threat of prosecution in a foreign country, a party fails to comply with a valid discovery order. In other words, *Société* calls for a "balancing approach" on a case-by-case basis. . . .

. . . .

As indicated, the Supreme Court in *Société* held that "on this record dismissal of the complaint with prejudice was not justified." Applying to the instant controversy the various factors mentioned in *Société* and later in the Restatement, we conclude that "on the record" the order holding Rio Algom in contempt and imposing a penalty of $10,000 per day for each day that Rio Algom failed to comply with the court's discovery order and authorizing the Marshal to physically take over Rio Algom's Utah properties in the event that Rio Algom failed to pay such penalty was "not justified."

In *Société* the Supreme Court considered primarily the dilemma of the party subject to contradictory laws. As previously noted, the Court considered the fact that the plaintiff in *Société* had made a good faith and diligent effort to comply with the local discovery order, and had tried to secure a waiver from the foreign government. In the instant case the district court signed an order prepared by Westinghouse which found that Rio Algom had not acted in good faith. Our review of the evidentiary matter before the district court fails to disclose anything which would support such a finding, and such finding is clearly erroneous. The record indicates that Rio Algom has made diligent effort to produce materials not subject to the Canadian regulation. Further, Rio Algom has sought a waiver from the Canadian authorities.

. . . .

There is nothing in the record which would indicate that Rio Algom or its president "ran" to Canada as this controversy was developing in order to gain the protection of Canadian law. Albino, the president, was a resident of Canada, if not indeed a citizen of Canada, prior to the present controversy. Rio Algom Corporation, the present appellant, is a wholly owned subsidiary of Rio Algom, Ltd., the latter in turn being a Canadian subsidiary of Rio Tinto Zinc Corporation, Ltd., which is the head of a worldwide mining conglomerate with headquarters in London, England.

There is the suggestion by Westinghouse, as another aspect of the good faith issue, that Rio Algom in some manner caused the nondisclosure regulation to be promulgated in Canada in order to cover up its activities or that Rio Algom and the Canadian Government acted in collusion. The present record would not support such a finding.

We proceed now to a consideration of other relevant factors, namely the interests of Canada and the United States which place Rio Algom under contradictory demands. The records which Westinghouse seeks to examine are physically located in Canada. Such being the case, it would not seem unreasonable that the Canadian Government should have something to say about how those records will be made available to interested outsiders. That Canada has a legitimate "national interest" in this matter is perhaps best illustrated by reading the opinion of the Ontario Supreme Court, wherein it declined to enforce the letters rogatory which Westinghouse caused to be issued. The Ontario Supreme Court determined that the nondisclosure regulations were in furtherance of a national interest in controlling and supervising atomic energy. The reader of this opinion is directed to the opinion of the Ontario Supreme Court which more fully sets forth the position of the Canadian Government.

The United States admittedly has a "national interest" of its own. In the instant case the United States has an interest in making certain that any litigant in its courts is afforded adequate discovery to the end that he may fully present his claim, or defense, as the case may be. Such is an understandable and legitimate interest. In this regard, however, we do note that Westinghouse's defense in the Virginia litigation does not stand or fall on the present discovery order. Westinghouse has deposed the officers of various other uranium companies, and the present discovery, though admittedly of potential significance, is still in a sense cumulative. We are not here concerned with any grand jury investigation, or the enforcement, as such, of antitrust laws.

A "balancing" of all of these various factors leads us to conclude that the trial court's order of contempt and the sanctions imposed in connection therewith are, on the basis of the present record, not justified.

. . . .

Judgment reversed and the district court's order holding Rio Algom in contempt and imposing sanctions in connection therewith is hereby vacated.

. . . .

WILLIAM E. DOYLE, CIRCUIT JUDGE, dissenting:

I respectfully dissent.

Judge McWilliams' opinion states the facts accurately, but some additional facts need to be set forth, and there is some necessity for a different emphasis.

This suit is by several utility companies and is pending in the United States District Court for the Eastern District of Virginia. The plaintiffs allege a breach of contract to deliver uranium at the price agreed upon. Westinghouse defends on the ground that the contract has become "commercially impracticable" within the meaning of the Uniform Commercial Code due to an unforeseen and substantial increase in the price. This price rise is said to be the result of an international price fixing conspiracy among the uranium producers. In a separate suit Westinghouse seeks damages under the antitrust laws from Rio Algom and others. However, in the breach of contract action Rio Algom is a witness only.

Rio Algom Corporation is the operator of a uranium mine in Utah and there is no indication that it does business in any other place. It is incorporated under the laws of Delaware. It is a wholly owned subsidiary of Rio Algom Limited, a Canadian corporation having its principal place of business in Toronto. These two corporations have common officers, directors and marketing vice-presidents. Rio Algom Corporation has all of its offices, directors, officers and records, including those sought in the instant proceeding, in Toronto.

The present controversy arises as the result of Westinghouse's effort to take the deposition of Albino, the president of both the Rio Algom Corporations, and to obtain the production of documents pertaining to the alleged price fixing conspiracy. On May 3, 1977, the district court, Judge Ritter, ordered the deposition to be taken and also ordered that the documents be produced.

Rio Algom and Albino refused to comply with the order on the ground that compliance would be in violation of the Canadian Uranium Information Security Regulations, SOR, 76-644 (P.C. 1976-2368, Sept. 21, 1976). These regulations were promulgated pursuant to Canada's Atomic Energy Control Act, Can. Rev. Stat. C.A-19 (1970). They expressly prohibit the release or disclosure of "any note, document or other written or printed material in any way related to conversations, discussions or meetings that took place between January 1, 1972 and December 31, 1975 . . . in respect of the production, import, export, transportation, refining, possession, ownership, use or sale of uranium or its derivatives or compounds." The regulations can be waived by the Minister of Energy, Mines and Resources. Rio Algom sought a waiver, but this request was denied. The way the matter stands now is that Rio Algom has complied except in the areas in which the Canadian statutes and regulations prohibit compliance.

The lower court found both Rio Algom and Albino in civil contempt and imposed a fine of $10,000 per day on the corporation, commencing August 1, 1977, and continuing until the respondents complied with its discovery order. It also issued an order of execution by sale of the corporation's Utah property.

There is reason to infer that the Canadian regulations were promulgated in order to counteract the present discovery efforts. The form of the regulations suggests this in that they specifically deal with prohibiting disclosure of evidence which could possibly shed light on the basic controversy. The Ontario decision in *In re The Evidence Act*, No. GD 75-23978 (Sup. Ct. of Ontario, June 29, 1977), in which the Ontario court denied the issuance of letters rogatory which had been sought by Westinghouse and which had been issued by the United States District Court for the Eastern District of Virginia and the Court of Common Pleas for Allegheny County, Pennsylvania Civil Division, also lends credence to the conclusion that the regulations were adopted for the purpose of preventing discovery in the present litigation. In the Ontario case the opinion quotes extensively from a press release issued by the Minister of Energy, Mines and Resources. This press release expresses the policy of the Canadian government to support "the uranium industry and its dependent mining communities which were suffering from an oversupply and low price situation." The press release also states that the Canadian government initiated discussions resulting in "an informal marketing arrangement among non-United States producers of uranium." [*Id.* at 13.] According to further statements quoted in the Ontario opinion from the press release, the Canadian government in 1969 adopted a policy of examining all contracts covering the export of uranium "to ensure that the terms and conditions of such contracts would be in the national interest." [*Id.* at 17.] In furtherance of this policy, the regulations in issue were adopted in 1976 "in the light of the sweeping demand for such information by U.S. subpoenas." [*Id.* at 18.]

A further argument for the proposition that the regulations were adopted with the present documents in mind arises from the contemporaneousness of the enactment of the regulations with the empanelling of a grand jury in the United States to investigate possible antitrust violations by uranium producers.

. . . .

As we have shown above, there are reasons for concluding that the Rio Algom Corporations here have not taken unkindly to the legal impediments erected to prevent discovery.

The question of good faith came into play in *Société*, but it was only in connection with the imposition of a sanction. The Supreme Court considered dismissal of the case for noncompliance to be excessive, notwithstanding that it is an authorized sanction under the Rules of Civil Procedure 37(b)(2)(C). As to this the Court said: "(i)t is hardly debatable that fear of criminal prosecution constitutes a weighty excuse for nonproduction, and this excuse is not weakened because the laws preventing compliance are those of a foreign sovereign." 357 U.S. at 211, 78 S. Ct. at 1095.

. . . .

Société implies that consideration of foreign law problems in a discovery context is required in dealing with sanctions to be imposed for disobedience and not in deciding whether the discovery order should issue. 546 F.2d at 341. It can be said, therefore, that good faith is not an appropriate standard in deciding whether the documents are to be produced or the deposition is to be given.

The Supreme Court in *Société* does discuss the flexibility of the discovery rules and therefore a balancing process may well have been contemplated. The Restatement (Second) of the Foreign Relation Law of the United States § 40, which is quoted in the majority opinion, lists factors to be considered in such a process. One such factor applicable in the present case is the great importance in American litigation of the discovery rules. The form of these rules is such that if material is relevant it must be produced. About the only exceptions are that certain privileges provide an excuse. When the strong underlying policy reasons in connection with the discovery rules are pitted against the Canadian policy of protecting its local industries from insufficient prices, no real contest exists. In any event, this was not the reason that emerges from the opinion of the Ontario Supreme Court. Instead the concern was the existence of low prices together with an oversupply. The *Société* case does not give any weight to the fact that the records and offices are in another country or are mingled with those of the parent corporation in another country. Rio Algom cannot then escape on this basis. It is peculiarly susceptible to the process of the courts of the United States and the laws of the United States. If a balancing test is to be used and relief is to be granted, the case would have to show more merit than we see here.

In view of the foregoing, I take the position that the district court's order requiring Rio Algom to comply is entirely proper and valid. Inasmuch as this is a dissenting opinion, I do not have to decide the issue whether the sanction is excessive. I do, however, believe that the sanction could justifiably be reexamined and possibly modified. I do not believe, however, that the magnitude of the sanction imposed should affect this court's decision on the merits of the question.

QUESTIONS AND NOTE

1. Might that outcome in this case have differed had Westinghouse not sought to obtain Rio Algom's Canadian business records by means of letters rogatory issued to the Ontario court? Why did Algom seek the consent of the Canadian Minister of Energy, Mines and Resources? Did the Canadian government have any special interest in this case? *See* note below.

2. Assuming a judge has determined that discovery pursuant to the Federal Rules rather than the Hague Convention is permitted and orders the defendants to provide certain documents and to respond to the plaintiffs' interrogatories, what sanctions might be imposed were the defendants to fail to comply? What if under the law of the jurisdiction in which the documents and witness are located, any party complying with the discovery order could be subject to criminal prosecution? See *In re Christopher X*, Cour de Cassation, Chambre Criminelle, Dec. 12, 2007, 07-83.228, upholding the criminal conviction and fine of a U.S. lawyer for violation of French law in failing to follow Hague Evidence Convention procedures in seeking evidence in Paris for the purpose of prosecuting a case in federal court in Los Angeles.

Canada is not a signatory to the Hague Evidence Convention. The process for discovery of evidence in Canada in aid of litigation in the U.S. must thus follow the procedures described in *In re Westinghouse Electric Corporation Uranium Contracts Litigation* — Letters rogatory with an application to the relevant Canadian court. The rules and limits of discovery are subject to provincial procedural law. In all instances, however, pre-trial discovery in Canada is significantly more restricted than in the U.S.

Also perhaps of some interest in connection with the Rio Algom case is an article by Neil Reynolds in the *Toronto Globe & Mail*, July 5, 2011, claims that in 1972, Prime Minister Pierre Trudeau "took Canada into the secret, state-sponsored international cartel that rigged world uranium prices for four years. When the existence of the cartel became known in 1976, Mr. Trudeau signed the order-in-council that declared it a crime, punishable by five years in prison, for any Canadian to discuss details of the cartel in public." (http://www.theglobeandmail.com/report-on-business/rob-commentary/aecl-sale-a-long-overdue-move/article625786/) In a subsequent *Globe & Mail* blog dated July 12, 2011, Harry Swain, the director-general for uranium, coal, electricity, and nuclear energy in the Canadian Ministry of Energy, Mines and Resources in 1978–79, explains the back-

> ground to the Canadian government's actions. As competition among U.S. reactor manufacturers intensified in the late 1960s, they "invented a new marketing tool: buy our reactor and we'll guarantee you a lifetime supply of enriched uranium at a low, low price!" According to the blog, the major U.S. manufacturers offering this deal, particularly GE and Westinghouse, did not anticipate subsequent legislation benefiting U.S. uranium producers — including those owned by Canadian mining companies, that closed the U.S. market, an action that not only caused dramatic price increases in the U.S. but also spurred the governments of the major non-U.S. uranium producers, including Canada, to seek ways to stabilize world prices. One result was the series of treble-damage lawsuits brought by Westinghouse and GE alleging antitrust violations by uranium producers in the U.S. market. *See* http://www.theglobeandmail.com/report-on-business/economy/economy-lab/the-economists/why-canada-supported-a-uranium-cartel/article2093469/.

INSURANCE CORP. OF IRELAND, LTD. v. COMPAGNIE DES BAUXITES DE GUINEE
456 U.S. 694 (1982)

JUSTICE WHITE delivered the opinion of the Court.

Rule 37(b), Federal Rules of Civil Procedure, provides that a district court may impose sanctions for failure to comply with discovery orders. Included among the available sanctions is:

> "An order that the matters regarding which the order was made or any other designated facts shall be taken to be established for the purposes of the action in accordance with the claim of the party obtaining the order." Rule 37(b)(2)(A).

The question presented by this case is whether this Rule is applicable to facts that form the basis for personal jurisdiction over a defendant. May a district court, as a sanction for failure to comply with a discovery order directed at establishing jurisdictional facts, proceed on the basis that personal jurisdiction over the recalcitrant party has been established? Petitioners urge that such an application of the Rule would violate due process: If a court does not have jurisdiction over a party, then it may not create that jurisdiction by judicial fiat. They contend also that until a court has jurisdiction over a party, that party need not comply with orders of the court; failure to comply, therefore, cannot provide the ground for a sanction. In our view, petitioners are attempting to create a logical conundrum out of a fairly straightforward matter.

I

Respondent Compagnie des Bauxites de Guinee (CBG) is a Delaware corporation, 49% of which is owned by the Republic of Guinea and 51% is owned by Halco (Mining) Inc. CBG's principal place of business is in the Republic of Guinea, where it operates bauxite mines and processing facilities. Halco, which operates in Pennsylvania, has contracted to perform certain administrative services for CBG. These include the procurement of insurance.

. . . .

In December 1975, CBG filed a two-count suit in the Western District of Pennsylvania, asserting jurisdiction based on diversity of citizenship. The first count was against INA; the second against the excess insurers. INA did not challenge personal or subject-matter jurisdiction of the District Court. The answer of the excess insurers, however, raised a number of defenses, including lack of in personam jurisdiction. Subsequently, this alleged lack of personal jurisdiction became the basis of a motion for summary judgment filed by the excess insurers. The issue in this case requires an account of respondent's attempt to use discovery in order to demonstrate the court's personal jurisdiction over the excess insurers.

Respondent's first discovery request — asking for "[c]opies of all business interruption insurance policies issued by Defendant during the period from January 1, 1972 to December 31, 1975"— was served on each defendant in August 1976. In January 1977, the excess insurers objected, on grounds of burdensomeness, to producing such policies. Several months later, respondent filed a motion to compel petitioners to produce the requested documents. In June 1978, the court orally overruled petitioners' objections. This was followed by a second discovery request in which respondent narrowed the files it was seeking to policies which "were delivered in . . . Pennsylvania . . . or covered a risk located in . . . Pennsylvania." Petitioners now objected that these documents were not in their custody or control; rather, they were kept by the brokers in London. The court ordered petitioners to request the information from the brokers, limiting the request to policies covering the period from 1971 to date. That was in July 1978; petitioners were given 90 days to produce the information. On November 8, petitioners were given an additional 30 days to complete discovery. On November 24, petitioners filed an affidavit offering to make their records, allegedly some 4 million files, available at their offices in London for inspection by respondent. Respondent countered with a motion to compel production of the previously requested documents. On December 21, 1978, the court, noting that no conscientious effort had yet been made to produce the requested information and that no objection had been entered to the discovery order in July, gave petitioners 60 more days to produce the requested information. The District Judge also issued the following warning:

> "[I]f you don't get it to him in 60 days, I am going to enter an order saying that because you failed to give the information as requested, that I am going to assume, under Rule of Civil Procedure 37(b), subsection 2(A), that there is jurisdiction." 1 App. 115a.

A few moments later he restated the warning as follows: "I will assume that jurisdiction is here with this court unless you produce statistics and other information in that regard that would indicate otherwise." *Id.*, at 116a.

On April 19, 1979, the court, after concluding that the requested material had not been produced, imposed the threatened sanction, finding that "for the purpose of this litigation the Excess Insurers are subject to the in personam jurisdiction of this

Court due to their business contacts with Pennsylvania." *Id.*, at 201a. Independently of the sanction, the District Court found two other grounds for holding that it had personal jurisdiction over petitioners. First, on the record established, it found that petitioners had sufficient business contacts with Pennsylvania to fall within the Pennsylvania long-arm statute. Second, in adopting the terms of the INA contract with CBG — a Pennsylvania insurance contract — the excess insurers implicitly agreed to submit to the jurisdiction of the court.

Except with respect to three excess insurers, the Court of Appeals for the Third Circuit affirmed the jurisdictional holding, relying entirely upon the validity of the sanction. *Compagnie des Bauxites de Guinea v. Insurance Co. of North America,* 651 F.2d 877 (1981). That court specifically found that the discovery orders of the District Court did not constitute an abuse of discretion and that imposition of the sanction fell within the limits of trial court discretion under Rule 37(b):

> "The purpose and scope of the ordered discovery were directly related to the issue of jurisdiction and the rule 37 sanction was tailored to establish as admitted those jurisdictional facts that, because of the insurers' failure to comply with discovery orders, CBG was unable to adduce through discovery." 651 F.2d, at 885.

Furthermore, it held that the sanction did not violate petitioners' due process rights, because it was no broader than "reasonably necessary" under the circumstances.

Because the decision below directly conflicts with the decision of the Court of Appeals for the Fifth Circuit in *Familia de Boom v. Arosa Mercantil, S.A.*, 629 F.2d 1134 (1980), we granted certiorari.

II

. . . .

The validity of an order of a federal court depends upon that court's having jurisdiction over both the subject matter and the parties. [Citation omitted.] The concepts of subject-matter and personal jurisdiction, however, serve different purposes, and these different purposes affect the legal character of the two requirements. Petitioners fail to recognize the distinction between the two concepts — speaking instead in general terms of "jurisdiction"— although their argument's strength comes from conceiving of jurisdiction only as subject-matter jurisdiction.

Federal courts are courts of limited jurisdiction. The character of the controversies over which federal judicial authority may extend are delineated in Art. III, § 2, cl. 1. Jurisdiction of the lower federal courts is further limited to those subjects encompassed within a statutory grant of jurisdiction. Again, this reflects the constitutional source of federal judicial power: Apart from this Court, that power only exists "in such inferior Courts as the Congress may from time to time ordain and establish." Art. III, § 1.

Subject-matter jurisdiction, then, is an Art. III as well as a statutory requirement; it functions as a restriction on federal power, and contributes to the characterization of the federal sovereign. Certain legal consequences directly follow from this. For example, no action of the parties can confer subject-matter jurisdiction upon a federal court. Thus, the consent of the parties is irrelevant, [citation omitted] principles of estoppel do not apply, [citation omitted], and a party does not waive the requirement by failing to challenge jurisdiction early in the proceedings. Similarly, a court, including an appellate court, will raise lack of subject-matter jurisdiction on its own motion. . . .

None of this is true with respect to personal jurisdiction. The requirement that a court have personal jurisdiction flows not from Art. III, but from the Due Process Clause. The personal jurisdiction requirement recognizes and protects an individual liberty interest. It represents a restriction on judicial power not as a matter of sovereignty, but as a matter of individual liberty. Thus, the test for personal jurisdiction requires that "the maintenance of the suit . . . not offend 'traditional notions of fair play and substantial justice.' " *International Shoe Co. v. Washington*, 326 U.S. 310, 316 (1945), quoting *Milliken v. Meyer*, 311 U.S. 457, 463 (1940).

Because the requirement of personal jurisdiction represents first of all an individual right, it can, like other such rights, be waived . . . . A variety of legal arrangements have been taken to represent express or implied consent to the personal jurisdiction of the court. In *National Equipment Rental, Ltd. v. Szukhent*, 375 U.S. 311, 316 (1964), we stated that "parties to a contract may agree in advance to submit to the jurisdiction of a given court," and in *Petrowski v. Hawkeye-Security Co.*, 350 U.S. 495 (1956), the Court upheld the personal jurisdiction of a District Court on the basis of a stipulation entered into by the defendant. In addition, lower federal courts have found such consent implicit in agreements to arbitrate . . . . Furthermore, the Court has upheld state procedures which find constructive consent to the personal jurisdiction of the state court in the voluntary use of certain state procedures. . . .

In sum, the requirement of personal jurisdiction may be intentionally waived, or for various reasons a defendant may be estopped from raising the issue. These characteristics portray it for what it is — a legal right protecting the individual. The plaintiff's demonstration of certain historical facts may make clear to the court that it has personal jurisdiction over the defendant as a matter of law — i.e., certain factual showings will have legal consequences — but this is not the only way in which the personal jurisdiction of the court may arise. The actions of the defendant may amount to a legal submission to the jurisdiction of the court, whether voluntary or not.

The expression of legal rights is often subject to certain procedural rules: The failure to follow those rules may well result in a curtailment of the rights. Thus, the failure to enter a timely objection to personal jurisdiction constitutes, under Rule 12(h)(1), a waiver of the objection. A sanction under Rule 37(b)(2)(A) consisting of a finding of personal jurisdiction has precisely the same effect. As a general proposition, the Rule 37 sanction applied to a finding of personal jurisdiction creates no more of a due process problem than the Rule 12 waiver. Although "a court cannot conclude all persons interested by its mere assertion of its own power," *Chicago Life Ins. Co. v. Cherry, supra*, at 29, not all rules that establish legal consequences to a party's own behavior are "mere assertions" of power.

. . . .

Petitioners argue that a sanction consisting of a finding of personal jurisdiction differs from all other instances in which a sanction is imposed, including the default judgment in *Hammond Packing* [*Co. v. Arkansas*, 212 U.S. 322 (1909)], because a party need not obey the orders of a court until it is established that the court has personal jurisdiction over that party. If there is no obligation to obey a judicial order, a sanction cannot be applied for the failure to comply. Until the court has established personal jurisdiction, moreover, any assertion of judicial power over the party violates due process.

This argument again assumes that there is something unique about the requirement of personal jurisdiction, which prevents it from being established or waived like other rights. A defendant is always free to ignore the judicial proceedings, risk a default judgment, and then challenge that judgment on jurisdictional grounds in a collateral proceeding. . . . A particular rule may offend the due process standard of *Hammond Packing*, but the mere use of procedural rules does not in itself violate the defendant's due process rights.

III

Even if Rule 37(b)(2) may be applied to support a finding of personal jurisdiction, the question remains as to whether it was properly applied under the circumstances of this case. Because the District Court's decision to invoke the sanction was accompanied by a detailed explanation of the reasons for that order and because that decision was upheld as a proper exercise of the District Court's discretion by the Court of Appeals, this issue need not detain us for long. . . .

Rule 37(b)(2) contains two standards — one general and one specific — that limit a district court's discretion. First, any sanction must be "just"; second, the sanction must be specifically related to the particular "claim" which was at issue in the order to provide discovery. . . .

In holding that the sanction in this case was "just," we rely specifically on the following. First, the initial discovery request was made in July 1977. Despite repeated orders from the court to provide the requested material, on December 21, 1978, the District Court was able to state that the petitioners "haven't even made any effort to get this information up to this point." 1 App. 112a. The court then warned petitioners of a possible sanction. Confronted with continued delay and an obvious disregard of its orders, the trial court's invoking of its powers under Rule 37 was clearly appropriate. Second, petitioners repeatedly agreed to comply with the discovery orders within specified time periods. In each instance, petitioners failed to comply with their agreements. Third, respondent's allegation that the court had personal jurisdiction over petitioners was not a frivolous claim, and its attempt to use discovery to substantiate this claim was not, therefore, itself a misuse of judicial process. The substantiality of the jurisdictional allegation is demonstrated by the fact that the District Court found, as an alternative ground for its jurisdiction, that petitioners had sufficient contacts with Pennsylvania to fall within the State's long-arm statute. *Supra*, at 2103. Fourth, petitioners had ample warning that a continued failure to comply with the discovery orders would lead to the imposition of this sanction. Furthermore, the proposed sanction made it clear that, even if there was not compliance with the discovery order, this sanction would not be applied if petitioners were to "produce statistics and other information" that would indicate an absence of personal jurisdiction. 1 App. 116a. In effect, the District Court simply placed the burden of proof upon petitioners on the issue of personal jurisdiction. Petitioners failed to comply with the discovery order; they also failed to make any attempt to meet this burden of proof. This course of behavior, coupled with the ample warnings, demonstrates the "justice" of the trial court's order.

Neither can there be any doubt that this sanction satisfies the second requirement. CBG was seeking through discovery to respond to petitioners' contention that the District Court did not have personal jurisdiction. Having put the issue in question, petitioners did not have the option of blocking the reasonable attempt of CBG to meet its burden of proof. It surely did not have this option once the court had overruled petitioners' objections. Because of petitioners' failure to comply with the discovery orders, CBG was unable to establish the full extent of the contacts between petitioners and Pennsylvania, the critical issue in proving personal jurisdiction. Petitioners' failure to supply the requested information as to its contacts with Pennsylvania supports "the presumption that the refusal to produce evidence . . . was but an admission of the want of merit in the asserted defense." *Hammond Packing*, 212 U.S., at 351. The sanction took as established the facts — contacts with Pennsylvania — that CBG was seeking to establish through discovery. That a particular legal consequence — personal jurisdiction of the court over the defendants — follows from this, does not in any way affect the appropriateness of the sanction.

IV

Because the application of a legal presumption to the issue of personal jurisdiction does not in itself violate the Due Process Clause and because there was no abuse of the discretion granted a district court under Rule 37(b)(2), we affirm the judgment of the Court of Appeals.

So ordered.

JUSTICE POWELL, concurring in the judgment.

The Court rests today's decision on a constitutional distinction between "subject matter" and "in personam" jurisdiction. Under this distinction, subject-matter jurisdiction defines an Art. III limitation on the power of federal courts. By contrast, the Court characterizes the limits on in personam jurisdiction solely in terms of waivable personal rights and notions of "fair play." Having done so, it determines that fundamental questions of judicial power do not arise in this case concerning the personal jurisdiction of a federal district court.

In my view the Court's broadly theoretical decision misapprehends the issues actually presented for decision. Federal courts are courts of limited jurisdiction. Their personal jurisdiction, no less than their subject-matter jurisdiction, is subject both to constitutional and to statutory definition. When the applicable limitations on federal jurisdiction are identified, it becomes apparent that the Court's theory could require a sweeping but largely unexplicated revision of jurisdictional doctrine. This revision could encompass not only the personal jurisdiction of federal courts but "sovereign" limitations on state jurisdiction as identified in *World-Wide Volkswagen Corp. v. Woodson*, 444 U.S. 286, 291–293 (1980). Fair resolution of this case does not require the Court's broad holding. Accordingly, although I concur in the Court's judgment, I cannot join its opinion.

I

This lawsuit began when the respondent Compagnie des Bauxites brought a contract action against the petitioner insurance companies in the United States District Court for the Western District of Pennsylvania. Alleging diversity jurisdiction, respondent averred that the District Court had personal jurisdiction of the petitioners, all foreign corporations, under the long-arm statute of the State of Pennsylvania. See *Compagnie des Bauxites de Guinea v. Insurance Co. of North America*, 651 F.2d 877, 880–881 (CA3 1981). Petitioners, however, denied that they were subject to the court's personal jurisdiction under that or any other statute. Viewing the question largely as one of fact, the court ordered discovery to resolve the dispute.

Meantime, while respondent unsuccessfully sought compliance with its discovery requests, petitioners brought a parallel action in England's High Court of Justice, Queens Bench Division. It was at this juncture that the current issues arose. Seeking to enjoin the English proceedings, respondent sought an injunction in the District Court. Petitioners protested that they were not subject to that court's personal jurisdiction and thus that they lay beyond its injunctive powers. But the District Court disagreed. As a jurisdictional prerequisite to its entry of the injunction, the court upheld its personal jurisdiction over petitioners. It characterized its finding of jurisdiction partly as a sanction for petitioners' noncompliance with its discovery orders under Federal Rule of Civil Procedure 37(b).

Rule 37(b) is not, however, a jurisdictional provision. As recognized by the Court of Appeals, the governing jurisdictional statute remains the long-arm statute of the State of Pennsylvania. See 651 F.2d, at 881. In my view the Court fails to make clear the implications of this central fact: that the District Court in this case relied on state law to obtain personal jurisdiction.

. . . .

As a result of the District Court's dependence on the law of Pennsylvania to establish personal jurisdiction — a dependence mandated by Congress under 28 U.S.C. § 1652 — its jurisdiction in this case normally would be subject to the same due process limitations as a state court. [Citations omitted.] Thus, the question arises how today's decision is related to cases restricting the personal jurisdiction of the States.

Before today our decisions had established that "minimum contacts" represented a constitutional prerequisite to the exercise of in personam jurisdiction over an unconsenting defendant. [Citations omitted.] In the absence of a showing of minimum contacts, a finding of personal jurisdiction over an unconsenting defendant, even as a sanction, therefore would appear to transgress previously established constitutional limitations. The cases cannot be reconciled by a simple distinction between the constitutional limits on state and federal courts. Because of the District Court's reliance on the Pennsylvania long-arm statute — the applicable jurisdictional provision under the Rules of Decisions Act — the relevant constitutional limits would not be those imposed directly on federal courts by the Due Process Clause of the Fifth Amendment, but those applicable to state jurisdictional law under the Fourteenth.

The Court's decision apparently must be understood as related to our state jurisdictional cases in one of two ways. Both involve legal theories that fail to justify the doctrine adopted by the Court in this case.

A

Under traditional principles, the due process question in this case is whether "minimum contacts" exist between petitioners and the forum State that would justify the State in exercising personal jurisdiction. [Citations omitted.] By finding that the establishment of minimum contacts is not a prerequisite to the exercise of jurisdiction to impose sanctions under Federal Rule of Civil Procedure 37, the Court may be understood as finding that "minimum contacts" no longer are a constitutional requirement for the exercise by a state court of personal jurisdiction over an unconsenting defendant. Whenever the Court's notions of fairness are not offended, jurisdiction apparently may be upheld.

Before today, of course, our cases had linked minimum contacts and fair play as jointly defining the "sovereign" limits on state assertions of personal jurisdiction over unconsenting defendants. [Citations omitted The Court appears to abandon the rationale of these cases in a footnote. [Reference omitted.] But it does not address the implications of its action. By eschewing reliance on the concept of minimum contacts as a "sovereign" limitation on the power of States — for, again, it is the State's long-arm statute that is invoked to obtain personal jurisdiction in the District Court — the Court today effects a potentially substantial change of law. For the first time it defines personal jurisdiction solely by reference to abstract notions of fair play. And, astonishingly to me, it does so in a case in which this rationale for decision was neither argued nor briefed by the parties.

B

Alternatively, it is possible to read the Court opinion, not as affecting state jurisdiction, but simply as asserting that Rule 37 of the Federal Rules of Civil Procedure represents a congressionally approved basis for the exercise of personal jurisdiction by a federal district court. On this view Rule 37 vests the federal district courts with authority to take jurisdiction over persons not in compliance with discovery orders. This of course would be a more limited holding. Yet the Court does not cast its decision in these terms. And it provides no support for such an interpretation, either in the language or in the history of the Federal Rules.

In the absence of such support, I could not join the Court in embracing such a construction of the Rules of Civil Procedure. There is nothing in Rule 37 to suggest that it is intended to confer a grant of personal jurisdiction. Indeed, the clear language of Rule 82 seems to establish that Rule 37 should not be construed as a jurisdictional grant: "These rules shall not be construed to extend . . . the jurisdiction of the United States district courts or the venue of actions therein." Moreover, assuming that minimum contacts remain a constitutional predicate for the exercise of a State's in personam jurisdiction over an unconsenting defendant, constitutional questions would arise if Rule 37 were read to permit a plaintiff in a diversity action to subject a defendant to a "fishing expedition" in a foreign jurisdiction. A plaintiff is not entitled to discovery to establish essentially speculative allegations necessary to personal jurisdiction. Nor would the use of Rule 37 sanctions to enforce discovery orders constitute a mere abuse of discretion in such a case. For me at least, such a use of discovery would raise serious questions as to the constitutional as well as the statutory authority of a federal court — in a diversity case — to exercise personal jurisdiction absent some showing of minimum contacts between the unconsenting defendant and the forum State.

II

In this case the facts alone — unaided by broad jurisdictional theories — more than amply demonstrate that the District Court possessed personal jurisdiction to impose sanctions under Rule 37 and otherwise to adjudicate this case. I would decide the case on this narrow basis.

. . . .

Where the plaintiff has made a prima facie showing of minimum contacts, I have little difficulty in holding that its showing was sufficient to warrant the District Court's entry of discovery orders. And where a defendant then fails to comply with those orders, I agree that the prima facie showing may be held adequate to sustain the court's finding that minimum contacts exist, either under Rule 37 or under a theory of "presumption" or "waiver."

Finding that the decision of the Court of Appeals should be affirmed on this ground, I concur in the judgment of the Court.

QUESTIONS

1. Summarize the arguments by Justice White for the majority and Justice Powell in dissent in *Compagnie des Bauxites de Guinee* in favor and against the use of discovery to determine whether a court has personal jurisdiction over a defendant. Why did the majority consider it necessary to distinguish between subject-matter and personal jurisdiction? What risks might a defendant run in either complying or failing to comply with such a discovery order? What if the discovery order was extremely broad and costly to obey?

2. Would the outcome in any of the above cases have differed had the information sought been business records of a parent company doing business in the U.S. solely through a wholly owned subsidiary and the records were not subject to discovery in the country where located?

3. What if the discovery order required cooperation with the taking of a deposition but the country in which the deposition was to take place refused entry visas to foreign lawyers for that purpose.

4. What if the party seeking discovery were the U.S. Internal Revenue Service? If the parent company failed to comply with a discovery order what sanctions might be available to the IRS that would not be available to a private party? *See United States v. Toyota Motor Corporation*, 561 F. Supp. 354 (C.D. Cal. 1983).

TIFFANY v. FORBSE*
107 U.S.P.Q.2d 1304 (S.D.N.Y. 2012)
2012 U.S. Dist. LEXIS 72148

MEMORANDUM AND ORDER

Naomi Reice Buchwald, District Judge.

Presently before the Court is the motion of non-parties China Merchants Bank ("CMB"), Bank of China ("BOC"), and Industrial and Commercial Bank of China ("ICBC") (collectively, the "Banks") to modify the preliminary injunction entered by the Court on August 3, 2011, which, *inter alia*, requires the Banks to produce records and restrain assets located in China. Plaintiffs Tiffany (NJ) LLC and Tiffany and Company (collectively, "Tiffany") have filed a cross-motion to compel compliance by the Banks with the preliminary injunction.

For the reasons set forth below, we modify the preliminary injunction with respect to ICBC and CMB and require Tiffany to seek discovery from these entities through the Hague Convention on the Taking of Evidence Abroad in Civil and Commercial Matters (the "Hague Convention"). However, we decline to adopt this option with respect to BOC and instead order BOC to comply with the discovery provisions of the preliminary injunction. Finally, we grant Tiffany's cross-motion to compel compliance — by all three banks — with the asset restraint provisions of the preliminary injunction.

BACKGROUND

I. *Factual History*

On July 20, 2011, Tiffany filed the instant suit alleging that defendants willfully used, reproduced, and copied Tiffany's trademarks through the sale of counterfeit products on various websites. Tiffany asserts causes of action under the Lanham Act, 15 U.S.C. § 1051, et seq., and under New York statutory and common law. None of the defendants have yet appeared in the action.

---

* Footnotes omitted.

Also on July 20, 2011, the Court entered a temporary restraining order, which the Court converted into a preliminary injunction on August 3, 2011. Relevant for present purposes are provisions of the preliminary injunction that order expedited discovery from third-party financial institutions and that require such institutions to restrain defendants' assets. With regard to the expedited discovery, the preliminary injunction orders financial institutions to provide "all records in their possession, custody, or control, regardless of whether such records are maintained in the United States or abroad, concerning the assets and financial transactions of Defendants or any other entities acting in concert or participation with Defendants . . . ." (Docket no. 10 at 10–11.) The preliminary injunction specifically identifies three accounts at CMB, one account at ICBC, and one account at BOC as being subject to the discovery requirements, as PayPal records indicate that these accounts were maintained or used by defendant Wooten in the course of the alleged unlawful activities. . . .

With regard to the asset restraint, the preliminary injunction enjoins third-party financial institutions from "transferring, disposing of, or secreting any money, stocks, bonds, real or personal property, or other assets of Defendants . . . regardless of whether such accounts are located in the United States or abroad." (Docket no. 10 at 7.) The preliminary injunction again lists the five accounts at CMB, ICBC, and BOC identified through PayPal records as accounts for which the asset restraint is applicable. (*Id.* at 8.)

Tiffany provided the Banks with notice of the preliminary injunction by delivering a letter to the New York branch of each of the Banks on August 4, 2011. (Healy Decl. Exs. 8–10.) By letters of August 9, 2011 and August 12, 2011, the Banks informed Tiffany that their respective New York branches did not hold accounts or assets for the named defendants and that the New York branches did not have access to or control over any accounts located outside the United States. (*Id.* Exs. 12–13.) The Banks further maintained that Chinese law would prohibit them from disclosing or freezing any accounts located in China without proper authorization. (*Id.*)

The Banks filed the instant motion on November 23, 2011 and Tiffany filed its cross-motion on December 9, 2011. The Banks contend that because Chinese bank-secrecy laws prohibit the production of bank records held in China, the appropriate mechanism for Tiffany to seek such records is the Hague Convention. The Banks also contend that there is no source of authority for the Court to apply an asset restraint under these circumstances to funds held by the Banks outside the United States.

II. *Revelation of BOC's Role as an Acquiring Bank*

The Court held oral argument on the motions on April 20, 2012. At oral argument, counsel for Tiffany notified the Court that an infringing website operated by defendant Wooten that Tiffany believed it had previously shut down, known as TiffanyOutletStore.com, was once again up and operating. (Tr. of Oral Arg. at 7:2–16, 10:6–15.) Several days after oral argument, Tiffany informed the Court that its investigator had learned from Visa that BOC was acting as the "acquiring bank" for TiffanyOutletStore.com. (Docket no. 35.) As discussed in greater detail *infra*, an acquiring bank helps to process online purchases by serving as an intermediary between the online merchant and a credit card network such as Visa. [References omitted.] The acquiring bank is also often responsible for performing due diligence on the merchant and accordingly often accepts the risk of "chargebacks," meaning customer disputes that result in a reversal of a transaction. [Reference omitted.]. BOC responded to this newly revealed information by letter of April 30, 2012. BOC reported that TiffanyOutletStore.com was neither a "primary merchant" nor a "secondary merchant" of BOC. . . .

BOC explained that a primary merchant is an online merchant with whom the acquiring bank directly contracts, while a "secondary merchant" is one who, with the knowledge of the acquiring bank, enters an agreement with a primary merchant to use the acquiring bank's credit card-processing systems. . . . BOC's understanding is that a secondary merchant had afforded TiffanyOutletStore.com unauthorized access to BOC's payment-processing services. . . . BOC notified the Court that it had shut down the secondary merchant's access and terminated its service, but BOC did not provide the Court with any information as to the identity or nature of this secondary merchant. . . .

III. *Prior Litigation*

This suit represents just one installment in a series of suits recently initiated by Tiffany and similarly situated plaintiffs against foreign defendants for alleged counterfeiting activities. The ability of the plaintiffs in these actions to enlist the aid of foreign financial institutions such as the Banks has presented a common point of contention across the suits. In fact, at least two courts in this jurisdiction have already addressed the precise legal issues raised in the motions now before this Court.

In *Tiffany (NJ) LLC v. Qi Andrew*, 276 F.R.D. 143, 160–61 (S.D.N.Y. 2011), in an Opinion and Order later affirmed by Judge Pauley, Magistrate Judge Pitman ordered Tiffany to submit its discovery request to the Banks through the Hague Convention as a matter of first resort. In contrast, in *Gucci Am., Inc. v. Weixing Li*, No. 10 Civ. 4974 (RJS), 2011 U.S. Dist. LEXIS 97814, at *5 (S.D.N.Y. Aug. 23, 2011), Judge Sullivan chose not to employ the Hague Convention process and instead ordered BOC to comply with the plaintiff's subpoena. In addition, Judge Sullivan held that because the plaintiff sought final equitable relief in the form of an accounting of the defendants' profits, the court had the inherent equitable power to restrain the defendants' assets as a preliminary measure, regardless of whether those assets were located abroad. . . .

It is against the backdrop of these recent decisions, as well as the pending and likely future suits presenting analogous circumstances, that we decide the present motions.

DISCUSSION

I. *Document Production*

A. *Possession, Custody, or Control of Documents*

As an initial matter, the Banks suggest that their New York branches — upon whom the preliminary injunction was served — do not have "possession, custody, or control" of account records held at branches outside the United States.

We reject this contention. As noted by Judge Pitman, the Banks' New York branches are not subsidiaries of a foreign parent company, but rather are "branches of the same corporate entities as their counterparts in China." *Qi Andrew*, 276 F.R.D. at 147 n.1. The Court thus has personal jurisdiction over the Banks as corporate entities, . . . , and "there is a presumption that a corporation is in the possession and control of its own books and records." *First Nat'l City Bank of N.Y. v. IRS*, 271 F.2d 616, 618 (2d Cir. 1959). "Clear proof of lack of possession and control is necessary to rebut the presumption." *Id.*

Here, the Banks have not satisfied this burden. Although the Banks have produced declarations from managers of the New York branches indicating that employees of these branches do not have access to documents or other information located in China, the Banks have not provided any evidence to suggest that the larger corporate entities do not have custody over the records. *See Qi Andrew*, 276 F.R.D. at 149–50. Therefore, we find that the documents sought are in the "possession, custody, or control" of the Banks for purposes of the preliminary injunction. [Citations omitted.]

B. *Comity Analysis*

As previously referenced, the Banks contend that the production of account records located in China is prohibited under Chinese law. Specifically, the Banks cite the following statutes and regulations as barriers to their compliance with the requested discovery:

> *Article 6 of the Commercial Banking Law:* "Commercial banks shall safeguard the legal rights and interests of the depositors against the encroachment of any entity or individual." (Decl. of Zhipan Wu ("Wu Decl." Ex. B-1.)
>
> *Article 53 of the Commercial Banking Law:* "No employee of a commercial bank may divulge any state or commercial secret they acquire during their term of service." (*Id.*)
>
> *Article 24 of the Corporate Deposit Regulations:* "A financial institution shall keep secret the deposits of corporate depositors . . . ." (*Id.* Ex. B-2.)
>
> *Article 28 of the Corporate Deposit Regulations:* "In case a commercial bank violates Article 24 and divulges the deposit information of corporate depositors or acts as an agent for inquiry about, freeze or deduction of

corporate deposit without statutory procedures, it shall be punished according to Article 73 of the [Commercial Banking Law]." (*Id.*)

Article 32 of the Savings Regulations: "Savings institutions and their personnel shall have an obligation to keep secret the depositors' savings and relevant information. Savings institutions shall not inquire into, freeze or allocate savings deposits on behalf of any unit or individual, unless otherwise provided for by laws and administrative regulations of the State." (*Id.* Ex. B-3.)

The Banks explain that China's "Financial Institution Assistant Regulations" delineate the conditions under which financial institutions are permitted to freeze assets or disclose account information despite the above prohibitions. (*Id.* ¶ 16.) One of the required conditions is that the request be initiated by a "competent organ." (*Id.*) The list of competent organs includes various Chinese government authorities, but it does not include a foreign court. (*Id.* ¶ 17.)

The Banks suggest that violations of the above provisions could subject them and their employees to both civil and criminal liability. Under Article 73 of the Commercial Banking Law, civil liability attaches for "[i]llegally inquiring about, freezing, or deducting personal savings deposit account or entity deposit account." (*Id.* Ex. B-1.) Criminal liability could potentially arise under Article 253(A) of China's Criminal Law, which provides, "Where . . . an entity in such a field as finance . . . sells or illegally provides personal information on citizens, . . . if the circumstances are serious, [it may] be sentenced to fixed-term imprisonment not more than three years or criminal detention, and/or be fined." (*Id.* Ex. B-6.)

Tiffany and the Banks agree that because production of the requested documents would be in contravention of a foreign nation's laws, the Restatement (Third) of Foreign Relations Law of the United States (the "Restatement") § 442(1)(c) provides the guiding framework for the Court's analysis. Under the Restatement, the Court must consider: (1) "the importance to the . . . litigation of the documents or other information requested;" (2) "the degree of specificity of the request;" (3) "whether the information originated in the United States;" (4) "the availability of alternative means of securing the information;" and (5) "the extent to which noncompliance with the request would undermine important interests of the United States, or compliance with the request would undermine important interests of the state where the information is located." *Weixing Li*, 2011 U.S. Dist. LEXIS 97814, at *16 (S.D.N.Y. Aug. 23, 2011) (quoting Restatement § 442(1)(c)). In addition, courts in this Circuit consider the following two factors in engaging in the relevant comity analysis: the hardship of compliance on the party from whom discovery is sought and whether that party has proceeded in good faith. *Id.* (citing *Minpeco, S.A. v. Conticommodity Servs., Inc.*, 116 F.R.D. 517, 523 (S.D.N.Y. 1987)).

Notably, despite reaching differing conclusions, both Judge Sullivan and Judge Pitman considered the seven factors outlined above in determining whether to order the Banks to produce the requested documents.

1. *Importance of the Documents to the Litigation*

It is plain that the information Tiffany seeks from each of the banks is highly important to the litigation. The account records are likely necessary to calculate defendants' profits in connection with the infringement, and the records may also enable Tiffany to identify additional participants in the scheme. . . .

However, the information sought through the preliminary injunction may hold greatly added significance with respect to BOC given that BOC was serving as the acquiring bank for one of the infringing websites. As Tiffany noted in its letter to the Court of May 2, 2012, although BOC asserts that it did not know of its relationship with TiffanyOutletStore.com, BOC has provided no information as to the primary and secondary merchants through whom TiffanyOutletStore.com gained access to BOC's credit card-processing systems. . . . There is a substantial possibility that the owner of the primary or secondary merchant account is defendant Wooten or a John Doe Defendant acting in concert with Wooten. Because of the due diligence that acquiring banks generally perform on the merchants with whom they do business — including often a physical inspection of the merchant's premises — BOC could have valuable information as to the identity, business activities, and even location of one or more defendants. Moreover, because BOC was until just a short time ago processing credit card payments for TiffanyOutletStore.com, BOC has extremely recent information on where defendants are depositing the proceeds of their counterfeiting activities. Access to this information could afford Tiffany a legitimate opportunity to locate defendants' assets and recover at least a portion of defendants' profits.

We therefore hold that this factor weighs in favor of Tiffany in relation to all three banks, but it weighs especially strongly in Tiffany's favor vis-à-vis BOC.

2. *Specificity of the Request*

We also find that Tiffany's request is sufficiently specific. [Citations omitted.] A central purpose of the production request is to enable Tiffany to discover the scope of defendants' infringement, and to accomplish this goal it would seem necessary for the discovery order to apply to all accounts maintained by defendants or those who are shown to have acted in concert with them.

3. *Where the Information Originated*

Tiffany suggests that the information at issue is "available in the United States" because the Banks provide online banking services to their customers and therefore those customers can access their account information from anywhere in the world. . . .

We find this fact to be of little relevance for present purposes. Tiffany does not genuinely dispute that the account records sought originated and remain in China, and as such, the compelled production of those records would implicate Chinese law. Accordingly, this factor weighs against the discovery request. [Citation omitted.]

II. DISCOVERY ABROAD IN AID OF LITIGATION IN THE UNITED STATES 553

4. Alternative Means of Securing the Information

Tiffany and the Banks dispute whether the Hague Convention represents a reasonable alternative avenue for discovery. Tiffany contends that "a Hague Convention request issued by a United States court is not a realistic or meaningful option" (Pl.'s Mem. at 17), while the Banks suggest that "there is every reason to expect that China would honor a properly tailored Hague Convention request" (Mem. of Law. in Supp. of the Nonparty Banks' Mot. for Modification of the Preliminary Injunction Dated Aug. 3, 2011 ("Banks' Mem.") at 17). In *Société Nationale Industrielle Aérospatiale v. U.S. District Court for the Southern District of Iowa*, 482 U.S. 522, 539–43 (1987), the Supreme Court declined to adopt a rule that would require litigants to turn to the Hague Convention as a matter of first resort when seeking evidence located in a signatory nation. The Court concluded that in some instances, proceeding through the Hague Convention "would be unduly time consuming and expensive" and a mandatory rule of first resort "would therefore be inconsistent with the overriding interest in the 'just, speedy, and inexpensive determination' of litigation in our courts." *Id.* at 542–43 (quoting Fed. R. Civ. P. 1). The Court did note, however, that in deciding whether to require a party to proceed under the Convention, "courts should . . . take care to demonstrate due respect for any special problem confronted by the foreign litigant on account of its nationality or the location of its operations, and for any sovereign interest expressed by a foreign state." *Id.* at 546.

Mindful of this guidance, the Banks point to a letter recently submitted by The People's Bank of China (the "PBOC") and the China Banking Regulatory Commission (the "CBRC")— two financial regulatory bodies in China — to four judges of the Southern District of New York with similar cases pending on their dockets. In the letter, the PBOC and CBRC assert that Chinese law prohibits the Banks from disclosing customer account information pursuant to a U.S. court order, and they urge the judges to follow Judge Pitman's approach and "require parties seeking information relevant to a bank account in China to rely on the Hague Convention." (Healy Decl. Ex. 23.) In this vein, the PBOC and CBRC express that "[they] are committed to actively coordinating with the PRC Ministry of Justice and judicial organs in the PRC to ensure that they satisfy that requests for seeking evidence under the Hague Convention within a reasonable time period and by following the procedures thereunder." (*Id.*)

Despite this reassurance, Tiffany persists in its position that the Hague Convention does not represent a reasonable alternative means of obtaining the requested discovery. At oral argument, Tiffany noted that in *Qi Andrew*, Judge Pitman transmitted a Hague Convention request to the relevant Chinese authorities on November 2, 2011, and over six months have now passed without any response. . . . Tiffany also cites statistics concerning China's compliance rate with Hague Convention requests more generally, noting that, as reported by the Chinese Ministry of Justice, roughly half of the Hague Convention requests that China received from 2006 to 2010 for execution of letters rogatory or taking of evidence were returned unexecuted, and over this time period, it took an average of six months to one year for China to execute such requests. (Decl. of William P. Alford ("Alford Decl.") Ex. W.) The Banks counter by noting that China executed thirty-seven requests for evidence in the first half of 2010 alone, implying that China has increased its level of assistance in recent years. (Wu Decl. ¶ 33.)

While the parties may debate the proper interpretation of the above statistics, at bottom it remains speculative for either side to assert whether or not China will timely comply with a Hague Convention request in the instant case. However, we feel obligated to consider that the Chinese government has expressed its intention to coordinate in facilitating discovery under these circumstances, and, notwithstanding the time that has passed since Judge Pitman submitted his Hague Convention request, it has yet to be seen whether Chinese authorities will act in a manner consistent with their expressed intent. It would seem prudent to forebear from assuming that the Hague Convention is not a viable option until Chinese authorities have had a meaningful opportunity to comply with similar requests but have failed to do so. *See Hudson v. Hermann Pfauter GmbH & Co.*, 117 F.R.D. 33, 38 (N.D.N.Y. 1987) (placing burden on party opposing use of the Hague Convention to demonstrate that the Convention would prove unfruitful). *But see Weixing Li*, 2011 U.S. Dist. LEXIS 97814 . . . (concluding that the Hague Convention did not represent a reasonable alternative given lack of concrete evidence demonstrating that China was likely to comply with a Hague Convention request).

5. *Competing National Interests*

The fifth factor under the Restatement framework requires the Court to engage in the precarious task of balancing the interests of the United States against the interests of a foreign nation. Cautious of our inherent biases in engaging in this endeavor, we look to the competing interests asserted by the litigants. It can hardly be disputed that the United States has a strong national interest in safeguarding intellectual property rights and protecting consumers from counterfeit products. [Citation omitted.] Moreover, the United States has "a substantial interest in fully and fairly adjudicating matters before its courts." *Milliken & Co. v. Bank of China*, 758 F. Supp. 2d 238, 248 (S.D.N.Y. 2010) (internal quotation marks omitted).

Nevertheless, the interest of the United States is not as great in this context — in which the discovery request is initiated by a private, civil litigant — as it would be if the request were initiated by the U.S. government for purposes of an enforcement proceeding. *See Minpeco*, 116 F.R.D. at 523; *cf. In re Grand Jury Subpoena Dated Aug. 9, 2000*, 218 F. Supp. 2d 544, 562 (S.D.N.Y. 2002) ("In a criminal case brought by the Government, the Court owes some deference to the determination by the Executive Branch . . . that the adverse diplomatic consequences of the discovery request would be outweighed by the benefits of disclosure." (internal quotation marks omitted)). In addition, the Banks' status as non-parties "attenuate[s] the United States interest in enforcing discovery obligations." *Qi Andrew*, 276 F.R.D. at 157; [additional citations omitted.]

On the other side of the equation, we acknowledge the interests asserted by the Chinese government in the letter submitted by the PBOC and CBRC. The letter expressed that the Chinese government has "material interests" in strictly enforcing its bank-secrecy laws because China's banking system is relatively new and strict client confidentiality will help engender trust in the system among the population. . . . Courts in this Circuit afford considerable deference when a foreign nation intervenes in this manner and asserts its interests in the litigation. [Citations omitted.]

While we do afford deference to the Chinese government's intervention, we nonetheless question the true extent of the Chinese interests at stake in this matter. Neither the Banks nor the Chinese government has suggested or would suggest that the Chinese bank-secrecy laws were designed to shield transnational counterfeiters from facing accountability for their actions. The fact that numerous Chinese government organs are vested with the power to override the confidentiality provisions only underscores the notion that the secrecy laws were not designed to protect Chinese citizens who engage in unlawful behavior. [Citation omitted.] Thus, as with our assessment of the U.S. interests concerned, we find that there are significant foreign interests implicated by the discovery request, but these interests are mitigated by the specific circumstances of the litigation.

On balance, we find that this factor does not swing the analysis in favor of either side.

6. *Hardship of Compliance*

The Banks contend that if they were to comply with the preliminary injunction, "the possibility of sanctions . . . is much more than speculative." (Banks' Mem. at 20.) The Banks again rely on the letter submitted by the PBOC and CBRC in support of their position. Referencing BOC's production of information in compliance with Judge Sullivan's order, the PBOC and CBRC indicated that this course of action "constitute[d] a violation of Chinese banking laws and regulations" and that "[they] have already issued a severe warning to the bank and [they] are conducting a further investigation to evaluate the severity of the infraction and determine the appropriate sanctions." (Healy Decl. Ex. 23.) As additional evidence of the possibility of sanctions, the Banks cite to several cases in China in which banks, including BOC, have been held liable for violating the bank secrecy laws. (Wu Decl. ¶¶ 22–24.)

In response, Tiffany notes that despite the prospect of sanctions hinted at by the PBOC and CBRC, BOC has not actually been punished in any manner for complying with Judge Sullivan's order. . . . Tiffany also suggests that the Chinese cases cited by the Banks are wholly inapposite. In one of these cases, a Chinese bank had wrongfully turned over funds held in a customer's account to another individual who had claimed to be entitled to the funds, and the Chinese court ordered the bank to reimburse the aggrieved customer. (Wu Decl. ¶ 22.) In the other case cited by the Banks, three persons had installed surveillance equipment at one of BOC's branches and then used the information obtained to withdraw funds from a customer's account. (*Id.* ¶ 23.) The Chinese court ordered BOC to reimburse the customer for the money that was lost due to the theft. (*Id.*) Tiffany argues that the circumstances of these cases are easily distinguishable from the instant matter, and Tiffany further points out that the Banks are not able to cite any instance in which a Chinese entity has been sanctioned for complying with a U.S. court order.

Finally, Tiffany implies that the possibility of sanctions in this case is not only speculative but is highly doubtful given that the Chinese government maintains large ownership interests in each of the banks. As detailed by Tiffany's expert, the

Chinese government either directly or indirectly owns 67% of the A shares in BOC, 70% of the A shares in ICBC, and over 25% of the shares in CMB. (Alford Decl. ¶¶ 17–18.)

We are inclined to agree with Tiffany in our analysis of this factor. Although we are reluctant to conclude with any certainty how a foreign nation will choose to implement its own laws, we cannot ignore the reality that the Chinese government holds large ownership interests in the Banks and that the Banks have not been sanctioned for complying with discovery orders issued by a U.S. court under similar circumstances. We also find the Chinese cases cited by the Banks to be entirely distinguishable. [Citation omitted.] We conclude that the possibility of sanctions "is speculative at best," *Milliken*, 758 F. Supp. 2d at 250 (internal quotation marks omitted), and therefore the potential hardship of compliance is not a factor that weighs in favor of amending the discovery order. [Citation omitted.]

7. *Good Faith of the Party Resisting Discovery*

As a general matter, we do not consider the Banks' opposition to the preliminary injunction to reflect bad faith . . . . The Banks objected to the terms of the preliminary injunction within days of being served with notice of such, and after a short of period of correspondence with Tiffany, the Banks initiated the process of filing the instant motion with the Court. These actions do not represent the type of "bad faith delays and dilatory tactics" that would weigh against an objecting party in the comity analysis. *Milliken*, 758 F. Supp. 2d at 250 (internal quotation marks and alteration omitted).

Like with the first factor, however, our analysis of this factor diverges with respect to BOC specifically. BOC acted as the acquiring bank for TiffanyOutletStore.com after it had notice of the preliminary injunction. Although BOC suggests that it would be "an enormous burden [to investigate] whether every one of its merchants worldwide could arguably be classified as being 'associated with[ ] . . . or in connection with . . . any of the Defendants' " . . . BOC likely overstates this burden. As Tiffany aptly notes, the fact that BOC was able to confirm that the infringing website was using BOC's payment systems suggests that BOC is able to search for transactions based on the name of the merchant or website. (Docket no. 37.) Taken in conjunction with the fact that the website at issue has the word "Tiffany" in its name, it would seem possible, if not likely, that BOC could have identified the infringing website based on a simple search of its records. Further suggestive of bad faith by BOC is the previously discussed possibility that defendant Wooten is the registered owner of the primary or secondary merchant that granted TiffanyOutletStore.com the unauthorized access in question.

We recognize that our discussion in this regard is somewhat speculative, but this speculation is attributable to the dearth of information that BOC has provided as to how the infringing website gained access to its systems. BOC having made the choice to provide such scant information, we find it reasonable to infer that BOC did have the means to prevent the ongoing infringement but refrained from taking appropriate action. Accordingly, this final factor weighs against BOC.

8. Summary

Based on the totality of the factors, we conclude that separate treatment is warranted for ICBC and CMB on the one hand and BOC on the other. For ICBC and CMB, we find the possibility of a reasonable alternative means of discovery to be a deciding consideration. China has yet to have a meaningful opportunity to demonstrate whether it will comply with a Hague Convention request under these circumstances. Given the Chinese government's stated intention to cooperate with such a request, as well as the near certainty that this issue will continue to arise in future litigation, we consider it appropriate to require Tiffany to direct its discovery requests for ICBC and CMB through the Hague Convention in the first instance. Should this process prove futile, future courts will surely take notice and adjust their analysis accordingly.

With respect to BOC, we find that the bank's recent role as the acquiring bank for an infringing website tips the balance of the analysis in favor of Tiffany. This fact strengthens the importance of the information sought and suggests potential bad faith on behalf of BOC. We place particular importance on the former factor, as BOC may very well possess information that will enable Tiffany to discover defendants' identities or even recover a portion of defendants' illicit profits. Thus, we order BOC to comply with the discovery provisions of the preliminary injunction.

II. *Asset Restraint*

Tiffany and the Banks dispute whether the Court has the authority to issue the prejudgment asset restraint contained in the preliminary injunction.

The preliminary injunction references Rule 64 of the Federal Rules of Civil Procedure, 15 U.S.C. § 1116(a), and the Court's inherent equitable power as separate sources of authority for the asset restraint. However, in its moving papers, Tiffany focuses on the latter two sources of authority and implicitly disclaims reliance on Rule 64 (and therein potentially relevant state procedures). . . .

For this reason, we find it curious that the parties devote considerable space in their briefs to the continued viability of the doctrine of New York law known as the "separate entity rule." This rule — under which each branch of a bank is considered "in no way concerned with the accounts maintained by depositors in other branches," *Parbulk II AS v. Heritage Maritime, SA*, 935 N.Y.S.2d 829, 832 (N.Y. Sup. Ct. 2011) (internal quotation marks omitted)— has historically been applied to restrict the prejudgment attachment of assets, or postjudgment turnover of assets, that is otherwise authorized under the New York Civil Practice Law and Rules ("C.P.L.R."). [Citations omitted.] Because Tiffany is not seeking a prejudgment attachment under the C.P.L.R., the separate entity rule is simply not relevant at this stage of the litigation. [Citation omitted.]

The actual question with regard to the asset restraint is whether this Court has the inherent equitable power to issue the restraint. Under the Supreme Court's holding in *Grupo Mexicano de Desarrollo, S.A. v. Alliance Bond Fund, Inc.*, 527 U.S. 308, 324–33 (1999), a federal district court maintains the inherent authority to issue a prejudgment asset restraint only if the plaintiff states a cause of action for final equitable relief and the prejudgment asset restraint preserves the availability of that final relief. [Citations omitted.] Tiffany and the Banks dispute whether Tiffany's complaint asserts a claim for such final equitable relief.

Under the Lanham Act, a successful plaintiff is entitled, "subject to the principles of equity, to recover (1) defendant's profits, (2) any damages sustained by the plaintiff, and (3) the costs of the action." 15 U.S.C. § 1117(a). Pursuant to this provision, Tiffany's complaint includes a request for an accounting of defendants' profits . . . .

The Second Circuit has made clear that when awarding an accounting of profits under the Lanham Act, a district court maintains discretion to shape such relief subject to the principles of equity. [Citations omitted.] Consistent with this notion, numerous courts have held that an accounting of profits under the Lanham Act constitutes final equitable relief that authorizes a court to issue a prejudgment asset restraint to ensure the availability of that relief. [Citations omitted.]

We concur with these decisions. We find that an accounting of profits under the Lanham Act constitutes discretionary equitable relief and the assets to be frozen include funds to which Tiffany may be entitled in connection with this relief. Thus, the Court maintains the inherent equitable power to issue a prejudgment restraint of defendants' assets. [Citation omitted.]

The Banks contend that even if the Court has the authority to issue an asset restraint in this case, that authority does not extend extraterritorially. Like Judge Sullivan, we find this argument to be without merit. . . . Given that the Court has personal jurisdiction over both defendants and the Banks, the Court's authority to restrain defendants' assets that are controlled by the Banks extends to wherever those assets may be located. *See United States v. First Nat'l City Bank*, 379 U.S. 378, 384 (1965) ("Once personal jurisdiction of a party is obtained, [a district court] has authority to order it to 'freeze' property under its control, whether the property be within or without the United States.").

Finally, the Banks request that, if necessary, the Court exercise its discretion and not extend the asset restraint to funds held in China due to the same considerations of comity discussed with regard to the discovery order. The Banks suggest that Chinese law prohibits them from freezing a customer's funds just as it prohibits them from producing a customer's account records.

We agree with the Banks that principles of comity are properly considered in this context, but we are not persuaded that these considerations warrant a decision to lift the instant asset restraint — with respect to any of the banks. Unlike in the context of the document request, there is no reasonable alternative analogous to the Hague Convention that would allow Tiffany to achieve the objective of the asset freeze. In this regard, we note that the Hague Convention process that we require Tiffany to undertake for ICBC and CMB will take time to run its course, and without an asset restraint in place, there would be little hope of recovering the illicit funds held at these banks. Given the apparent strength of Tiffany's intellectual property claim, we are reluctant to leave it without a practical remedy.

CONCLUSION

For the reasons stated above, the Banks' motion and Tiffany's cross-motion are each granted in part and denied in part. Tiffany is directed to proceed with its discovery request to ICBC and CMB through the Hague Convention, but BOC is directed to comply with the disclosure requirements of the preliminary injunction. The asset restraint provisions of the preliminary injunction remain in effect for all three banks.

SO ORDERED.

REPUBLIC OF ARGENTINA v. NML CAPITAL, LTD.
573 U.S. ___ (2014)

JUSTICE SCALIA delivered the opinion of the Court. . . . GINSBURG, J., filed a dissenting opinion.

I. Background

In 2001, petitioner, Republic of Argentina, defaulted on its external debt. In 2005 and 2010, it restructured most of that debt by offering creditors new securities (with less favorable terms) to swap out for the defaulted ones. Most bondholders went along. Respondent, NML Capital, Ltd. (NML), among others, did not. NML brought 11 actions against Argentina in the Southern District of New York to collect on its debt, and prevailed in every one. It is owed around $2.5 billion, which Argentina has not paid. Having been unable to collect on its judgments from Argentina, NML has attempted to execute them against Argentina's property. That postjudgment litigation "has involved lengthy attachment proceedings before the district court and multiple appeals." *EM Ltd. v. Republic of Argentina*, 695 F.3d 201, 203, and n. 2 (CA2 2012) (referring the reader to prior opinions "[f]or additional background on Argentina's default and the resulting litigation").

Since 2003, NML has pursued discovery of Argentina's property. In 2010, " '[i]n order to locate Argentina's assets and accounts, learn how Argentina moves its assets through New York and around the world, and accurately identify the places and times when those assets might be subject to attachment and execution (whether under [United States law] or the law of foreign jurisdictions),' " *id.*, at 203 (quoting NML brief), NML served subpoenas on two nonparty banks, Bank of America (BOA) and Banco de la Nación Argentina (BNA), an Argentinian bank with a branch in New York City. For the most part, the two subpoenas target the same kinds of information: documents relating to accounts maintained by or on behalf of Argentina, documents identifying the opening and closing dates of Argentina's accounts, current balances, transaction histories, records of electronic fund transfers, debts owed by the bank to Argentina, transfers in and out of Argentina's accounts, and information about transferors and transferees.

Argentina, joined by BOA, moved to quash the BOA subpoena. NML moved to compel compliance but, before the court ruled, agreed to narrow its subpoenas by excluding the names of some Argentine officials from the initial electronic-fund-transfer message search. NML also agreed to treat as confidential any documents that the banks so designated.

The District Court denied the motion to quash and granted the motions to compel. Approving the subpoenas in principle, it concluded that extraterritorial asset discovery did not offend Argentina's sovereign immunity, and it reaffirmed that it would serve as a "clearinghouse for information" in NML's efforts to find and attach Argentina's assets. App. to Pet. for Cert. 31. But the court made clear that it expected the parties to negotiate further over specific production requests, which, the court said, must include "some reasonable definition of the information being sought." *Id.*, at 32. There was no point, for instance, in "getting information about something that might lead to attachment in Argentina because that would be useless information," since no Argentinian court would allow attachment. *Ibid.* "Thus, the district court . . . sought to limit the subpoenas to discovery that was reasonably calculated to lead to attachable property." 695 F.3d, at 204–205.

. . . .

II. Analysis

A

The rules governing discovery in postjudgment execution proceedings are quite permissive. Federal Rule of Civil Procedure 69(a)(2) states that, "[i]n aid of the judgment or execution, the judgment creditor . . . may obtain discovery from any person — including the judgment debtor — as provided in the rules or by the procedure of the state where the court is located." See 12 C. Wright, A. Miller, & R. Marcus, Federal Practice and Procedure § 3014, p. 160 (2d ed. 1997) (hereinafter Wright & Miller) (court "may use the discovery devices provided in [the federal rules] or may obtain discovery in the manner provided by the practice of the state in which the district court is held"). The general rule in the federal system is that, subject to the district court's discretion, "[p]arties may obtain discovery regarding any nonprivileged matter that is relevant to any party's claim or defense." Fed. Rule Civ. Proc. 26(b)(1). And New York law entitles judgment creditors to discover "all matter relevant to the satisfaction of [a] judgment," N.Y. Civ. Prac. Law Ann. § 5223 (West 1997), permitting "investigation [of] any person shown to have any light to shed on the subject of the judgment debtor's assets or their whereabouts," D. Siegel, New York Practice § 509, p. 891 (5th ed. 2011).

The meaning of those rules was much discussed at oral argument. What if the assets targeted by the discovery request are beyond the jurisdictional reach of the court to which the request is made? May the court nonetheless permit discovery so long as the judgment creditor shows that the assets are recoverable under the laws of the jurisdictions in which they reside, whether that be Florida or France? We need not take up those issues today, since Argentina has not put them in contention. In the Court of Appeals, Argentina's only asserted ground for objection to the subpoenas was the Foreign Sovereign Immunities Act. . . . We thus assume without deciding that, as the Government conceded at argument, Tr. of Oral Arg. 24, and as the Second Circuit concluded below, "in a run-of-the-mill execution proceeding . . .

the district court would have been within its discretion to order the discovery from third-party banks about the judgment debtor's assets located outside the United States." 695 F.3d, at 208.

B.

[On the background and application of the Foreign Sovereign Immunities Act, see excerpt from opinion *supra* Chapter 2.]

But what of foreign-state property that *would* enjoy execution immunity under the Act, such as Argentina's diplomatic or military property? Argentina maintains that, if a judgment creditor could not ultimately execute a judgment against certain property, then it has no business pursuing discovery of information pertaining to that property. But the reason for these subpoenas is that NML *does not yet know* what property Argentina has and where it is, let alone whether it is executable under the relevant jurisdiction's law. If, bizarrely, NML's subpoenas had sought only "information that could not lead to executable assets in the United States or abroad," then Argentina likely would be correct to say that the subpoenas were unenforceable — *not* because information about nonexecutable assets enjoys a penumbral "discovery immunity" under the Act, but because information that could not possibly lead to executable assets is simply not "relevant" to execution in the first place, Fed. Rule Civ. Proc. 26(b)(1); N. Y. Civ. Prac. Law Ann. § 5223.[1] But of course that is not what the subpoenas seek. They ask for information about Argentina's worldwide assets generally, so that NML can identify where Argentina may be holding property that *is* subject to execution. To be sure, that request is bound to turn up information about property that Argentina regards as immune. But NML may think the same property *not* immune. In which case, Argentina's self-serving legal assertion will not automatically prevail; the District Court will have to settle the matter.

* * *

Today's decision leaves open what Argentina thinks is a gap in the statute. Could the 1976 Congress really have meant not to protect foreign states from postjudgment discovery "clearinghouses"? The riddle is not ours to solve (if it can be solved at all). It is of course possible that, had Congress anticipated the rather unusual circumstances of this case (foreign sovereign waives immunity; foreign sovereign owes money under valid judgments; foreign sovereign does not pay and apparently has no executable assets in the United States), it would have added to the Act a sentence conferring categorical discovery-in-aid-of execution immunity on a foreign state's extraterritorial assets. Or, just as possible, it would have done no such thing. Either way, "[t]he question . . . is not what Congress 'would have wanted' but what

---

[1] The dissent apparently agrees that the Act has nothing to say about the scope of postjudgment discovery of a foreign sovereign's extraterritorial assets. It also apparently agrees that the rules limit discovery to matters relevant to execution. Our agreement ends there. The dissent goes on to assert that, unless a judgment creditor *proves* up front that all of the information it seeks is relevant to execution under the laws of all foreign jurisdictions, discovery of information concerning extraterritorial assets is limited to that which the Act makes relevant to execution *in the United States. Post*, at 2 (opinion of Ginsburg, J.). We can find no basis in the Act or the rules for that position.

Congress enacted in the FSIA." *Republic of Argentina v. Weltover, Inc.*, 504 U.S. 607, 618 (1992).

Nonetheless, Argentina and the United States urge us to consider the worrisome international-relations consequences of siding with the lower court. Discovery orders as sweeping as this one, the Government warns, will cause "a substantial invasion of [foreign states'] sovereignty," Brief for United States as *Amicus Curiae* 18, and will "[u]ndermin[e] international comity," *id.*, at 19. Worse, such orders might provoke "reciprocal adverse treatment of the United States in foreign courts," *id.*, at 20, and will "threaten harm to the United States' foreign relations more generally," *id.*, at 21. These apprehensions are better directed to that branch of government with authority to amend the Act — which, as it happens, is the same branch that forced our retirement from the immunity-by-factor-balancing business nearly 40 years ago.

JUSTICE GINSBURG, dissenting.

The Foreign Sovereign Immunities Act of 1976, 28 U. S. C. §§ 1330, 1602 *et seq.*, if one of several conditions is met, permits execution of a judgment rendered in the United States against a foreign sovereign only on "property in the United States . . . used for a commercial activity." § 1610(a). Accordingly, no inquiry into a foreign sovereign's property in the United States that is not "used for a commercial activity" could be ordered; such an inquiry, as the Court recognizes, would not be "'relevant' to execution in the first place." *Ante*, at 10 (citing Fed. Rule Civ. Proc. 26(b)(1)). Yet the Court permits unlimited inquiry into Argentina's property outside the United States, whether or not the property is "used for a commercial activity." By what authorization does a court in the United States become a "clearinghouse for information," *ante*, at 3 (internal quotation marks omitted), about any and all property held by Argentina abroad? NML may seek such information, the Court reasons, because "NML *does not yet know* what property Argentina has [outside the United States], let alone whether it is executable under the relevant jurisdiction's law." Ante, at 10. But see *Société Nationale Industrielle Aérospatiale v. United States Dist. Court for Southern Dist. of Iowa*, 482 U.S. 522, 542 (1987) (observing that other jurisdictions generally allow much more limited discovery than is available in the United States).

A court in the United States has no warrant to indulge the assumption that, outside our country, the sky may be the limit for attaching a foreign sovereign's property in order to execute a U. S. judgment against the foreign sovereign. Cf. § 1602 ("Under international law, . . . th[e] *commercial property* [of a state] may be levied upon for the satisfaction of judgments rendered against [the state] in connection with [its] commercial activities." (emphasis added)). Without proof of any kind that other nations broadly expose a foreign sovereign's property to arrest, attachment or execution, a more modest assumption is in order. See *EM Ltd. v. Republic of Argentina*, 695 F.3d 201, 207 (CA2 2012) (recognizing that postjudgment discovery "must be calculated to assist in collecting on a judgment" (citing Fed. Rules Civ. Proc. 26(b)(1), 69(a)(2))).

Unless and until the judgment debtor, here, NML, proves that other nations would allow unconstrained access to Argentina's assets, I would be guided by the one law we know for sure — our own. That guide is all the more appropriate, as our law coincides with the interna tional norm. See § 1602. Accordingly, I would limit NML's discovery to property used here or abroad "in connection with . . . commercial activities." §§ 1602, 1610(a). I there fore dissent from the sweeping examination of Argentina's worldwide assets the Court exorbitantly approves today.

QUESTIONS

1. What were the issues in *Tiffany v. Forbse*? Who were the parties in the action? What was their relationship to the principal case brought by Tiffany against a trademark infringing website, TiffanyOutletStore.com, and Wooten, its operator?

What documents did Tiffany's attorneys seek to obtain? Who held them and where were they located? On what legal basis could the U.S. District Court for the Southern District of New York issue injunctions to the parties in this case?

2. To what extent, if any, does the U.S. Supreme Court decision in *Republic of Argentina v. NML Capital, Ltd.* alter the decision in *Tiffany v. Forbse*? What if in prior actions the People's Republic of China had been held liable for having defaulted on certain bonds issued during the "Cultural Revolution" and the successful plaintiff, unable to negotiate a settlement, subpoenaed the Bank of China as a nonparty bank seeking documents related to accounts maintained by or on behalf of the People's Republic along with information related to the opening and closing of such accounts, current balances, debts owed by the bank to the People's Republic, records of all fund transfers in and out of the accounts, as well as the identities of transferees and transferors. What arguments might attorneys for the People's Republic make?

3. Could, say, the Internal Revenue Service have similarly obtained documents and records of a foreign company without an office in the U.S. on the basis of a subpoena issued to it through its wholly owned U.S. subsidiary? *See United States of America v. Toyota Motor Corporation, et al.*, 561 F. Supp. 354 (C.D. Cal. 1983). What if a foreign government attempted to use the Hague Evidence Convention to seek pricing information from a U.S. parent company with a wholly owned foreign sales subsidiary? *See, e.g., The Attorney General of Canada v. R.J. Reynolds*, 268 F.3d 103 (2d Cir. 2001).

4. With respect to resort to the Hague Evidence Convention, how did Judge Buchward's approach differ from that of Magistrate Judge Pittman in *Tiffany (NJ) LLC v. Qi Andrew* or that of Judge Sullivan in *Gucci Am., Inc. v. Weixing Li*? In light of *Société Nationale Industrielle Aérospatiale* and the restrictions on disclosure under Chinese law, were her arguments convincing?

5. What was the role of experts in this case? Do you think that Judge Posner would have viewed Judge Buchward's reliance on expert affidavits

in this case to have exemplified "unsound judicial practice"? Recall *Bodum USA v. La Cafetiere*, 621 F.3d 624, at 631.

6. On what legal basis did Judge Buchwald enjoin the banks in this action to restrain assets of the defendants in connection with the trademark infringement case?

7. How significant in this case was the contempt power of common law judges to effective discovery and orders to restrain or preserve assets? How else can judges ensure compliance with their orders? What is the difference between "civil" and "criminal" contempt? *See Westinghouse Electric Corporation, and Mitsubishi Heavy Industries, Ltd., v. United States of America*, 648 F.2d 642 (9th Cir. 1981).

U.S. attorneys in litigation in the United States can anticipate several problems in any attempt to obtain evidence in most civil law countries either with or without resort to the Hague Evidence Convention. Among the most common obstacles, as illustrated in *Tiffany v. Forbse*, are "blocking" statutes or similar legislation that prohibit disclosure of documents or testimony generally or specifically in aid of litigation in the United States. An example is the French Penal Law No. 80-538, art. 1 bis, which forbids "anyone to request, look for, or transmit in writing, orally or in any other form, any document or information in economic, commercial, industrial, financial or technical fields for the purpose of gathering evidence in view of foreign civil or administrative proceedings or in the framework of said proceedings." (Recall the 2007 French decision, *In re Christopher X, supra*, upholding the criminal conviction of a Los Angeles attorney for having attempted to obtain evidence in France without resort to the Hague Evidence Convention.) Such statutes have not, however, prevented U.S. courts from ordering such disclosure, *see, e.g., In Re Global Power Equipment Group Inc.*, 418 B.R. 833 (Bankr. D. Del. 2009). Yet they do inhibit resort to Hague Evidence Convention procedures and thereby reliance on a cooperative central authority abroad.

U.S. counsel seeking discovery in the European Union need to be mindful also of European legislation for the protection of "personal data" pursuant to statutes enacted throughout the Union as a consequence of EU Directive 95/46/EC on the protection of individuals with regard to the processing of personal data and on the free movement of such data, particularly outside of the EU, which became effective in 1998. Of special note is the 2012 proposal for a regulation that would harmonize and strengthen existing national legislation. For the current status of these efforts and the scope of protection, see http://ec.europa.eu/justice/data-protection/index_en.htm.

QUESTIONS

1. Would or should a U.S. court take into account the potential of the imposition of criminal sanctions on any person who violated the French "blocking statute" before ordering discovery that would violate French law? *See, e,g., In re Christopher X, supra*, and *TruePosition, Inc. LM*

> *Ericsson Telephone Co.*, 2012 U.S. Dist. LEXIS 29294 (E.D. Pa. Mar. 6, 2012).
>
> 2. How does a "directive" differ from a "regulation" under EU law? Would a data protection regulation in contrast to the current directive further inhibit discovery abroad in aid of U.S. litigation? Recall the potential for a damage action against the state for violation of EU regulations, including judicial decisions, discussed *supra*.

Other common obstacles to U.S. pre-trial discovery in most if not all civil law jurisdictions include limited pre-trial procedures for "perpetuation of evidence," broader scope of testimonial privilege, inability to obtain documents or testimony from parties, and, as noted, the not-insignificant relative weakness of sanctions for non-compliance. The limited scope of discovery in Japan, which is not a signatory to the Hague Evidence Convention, exemplifies all three limitations.

First, in general, pre-trial "discovery" procedures are limited to preventative measures to protect against alteration or destruction of evidence to be used in prospective trial proceedings. However, such procedures require precise identification of (1) the party to the lawsuit to whom such preservation order will be directed, (2) the evidence to be examined, (3) the facts to be proven, and (4) the reasons why such provisional injunctive relief is necessary. Among other justifications, prospective defendants (or plaintiffs) subject to such orders may refuse to comply if compliance would necessitate "unreasonable expense or time."

Second, the scope of privilege is broad. Under the Japanese Code of Civil Procedure, a witness enjoys the right to refuse to testify or to provide documents if such testimony or document, under article 196, "relates to matters that would harm the reputation of (a) spouse or relative by blood within the fourth degree or relative through marriage within the third degree;" or (b) a guardian or a person under the witness's guardianship. A witness may also refuse to testify under article 197, with respect to any fact learned in the course of duty as "a doctor, dentist, pharmacist, pharmaceuticals distributor, birthing assistant, attorney at law (including a registered foreign lawyer), patent attorney, defense counsel, notary or person engaged in a religious occupation." Witnesses may also refuse to testify regarding "matters concerning technical or professional secrets" [article 197(c)]. Article 220 applies the same privileges to documents.

Third, the legally applicable sanctions for noncompliance with such discovery orders are quite weak by U.S. or other common law standards. Japanese courts like those in other civil law jurisdictions do not have contempt powers. They can only refer cases to prosecutors for prosecution for a minor offense or impose non-penal fines. The maximum current fine is 200,000 yen or approximately 2,000 US dollars. *See* Code of Civil Procedure articles 225(1) and 232(2). The most meaningful sanction to allow the court to affirm the truth of allegations to be supported (or refuted) by the testimony or documents. *See, e.g.*, article 224(1).

Court-ordered discovery in Japan requiring depositions or inspections that may involve U.S. attorneys raises additional problems. Although Japan does not currently have "blocking" statutes, Ministry of Justice regulations effectively bar entry by non-Japanese nationals for such purposes. The procedures are described below:

UNITED STATES DEPARTMENT OF STATE, JAPAN JUDICIAL ASSISTANCE
http://travel.state.gov/law/judicial/judicial_678.html#service

Obtaining Evidence Overview Summary:

Japan is not a party to the Hague Convention on the Taking of Evidence Abroad in Civil and Commercial Matters. Judicial assistance between the United States and Japan in obtaining evidence is governed by Article 17 of the U.S.-Japan bilateral Consular Convention of 1963 (15 UST 768), customary international law and the practice of nations, and applicable U.S. and local Japanese law and regulations. Article 17(1) (e) of the U.S.-Japan Consular Convention provides that consular officers may . . .

(ii) take depositions, on behalf of the courts or other judicial tribunals or authorities of the sending state, voluntarily given.

(iii) take depositions, on behalf of the courts or other judicial tribunals or authorities of the sending state, voluntarily given.administer oaths to any person in the receiving state in accordance with the laws of the sending state and in a manner not inconsistent with the laws of the receiving state."

This general reference to the authority of consular officers to take depositions has been interpreted by the Government of Japan very strictly. Japanese law and practice, and the mutually agreed upon interpretation of the U.S.-Japan bilateral Consular Convention concerning obtaining evidence in Japan permits the taking of a deposition of a willing witness for use in a court in the United States **only**

1. if the deposition is presided over by a U.S. consular officer;
2. is conducted on U.S. consular premises;
3. is taken pursuant to an American court order or commission;
4. and if any non-Japanese participant travelling to Japan applies for and obtains a Japanese Special Deposition visa.

The Japanese Ministry of Foreign Affairs and Ministry of Justice have advised the United States that these requirements apply in civil, criminal and administrative cases. *The Japanese requirement for a court order and special deposition visas would apply in all cases, even though the depositions began in the United States initially.* [Emphasis added.]

Therefore, depositions may be taken in Japan:

1. **On U.S. consular premises;**
2. pursuant to a commission (28 U.S.C. App. Fed. R. Civ. P. Rule 28(b)(2)) to take a deposition issued by a court to any Consul or Vice-Consul of the United States at (Tokyo, Naha, Osaka-Kobe, Sapporo, Fukuoka) or
3. on notice, provided an order issued by a court in the United States specifically authorizes an U.S. consular officer to take the deposition on

II. DISCOVERY ABROAD IN AID OF LITIGATION IN THE UNITED STATES

notice.

NOTE: U.S. Government officials traveling to Japan to participate in the taking of depositions or informal interviews should see also Travel to Japan For Judicial Assistance Activities for guidance about obtaining the additional *requisite host country clearance which requires a diplomatic note from the U.S. Embassy to the Ministry of Foreign Affairs. This is in addition to the Special Deposition Visa requirement. This additional requirement host country clearance does not pertain to private U.S. citizen attorneys, but as noted below the Special Deposition Visa requirement applies to **all** U.S. participants.* [Emphasis added.]

Japanese Sovereignty: The Government of Japan has advised the United States that it opposes deviations from these conditions, and that it would consider any action beyond the strictures of the U.S.-Japan understanding to be a violation of its judicial sovereignty. The United States recognizes the right of judicial sovereignty of foreign governments based on customary international law and practice; *See, e.g.*, the Restatement (Third) of Foreign Relations Law (1987); Cumulative Digest of United States Practice in International Law, 1981–1988, Office of the Legal Adviser, U.S. Department of State, Vol. II, 1430–1432, 1440 (1994).

U.S. Diplomatic and Consular Premises and Extraterritoriality: All depositions taken in Japan for use in the United States must take place on U.S. Embassy or consulate premises. Diplomatic and consular premises are **not extraterritorial.** The status of diplomatic and consular premises arises from the rules of law relating to immunity from the prescriptive and enforcement jurisdiction of the receiving state (Japan); the premises are not part of the territory of the sending state (the United States of America). See Restatement (Third) of Foreign Relations Law, Vol. 1, Sec. 466, Comment a and c (1987). *See also Persinger v. Iran*, 729 F.2d 835 (D.C. Cir. 1984). **It should be noted that Japan has further advised that depositions may not take place on U.S. military bases in Japan as that is not sanctioned in the U.S.-Japan Status of Forces Agreement.**

Special Japanese Deposition Visas: *Japan has instituted a requirement that persons from the United States wishing to participate in a deposition of a witness in Japan must apply for a Japanese "special deposition visa." As prerequisite to the issuance of the Japanese special deposition visa, Japan requires presentation of a U.S. court order, citing Article 17 of the U.S.-Japan bilateral Consular Convention. See suggested text for the court order below.* [Emphasis added.]

1. Apply for a "special deposition visa" at the Japanese Embassy or Consulate in the United States nearest you. The Consular Section of the Japanese Embassy is located at 2520 Massachusetts Avenue, N.W., Washington, D.C. 20008, tel: (202) 939-6700. Japanese consulates are also located in Anchorage, Atlanta, Boston, Chicago, Detroit, Guam, Honolulu, Houston, Kansas City, Los Angeles, Miami, [Nashville], New York, Portland, San Francisco and Seattle.

2. This special visa must be applied for at **least two weeks before departure for Japan.**

3. The request should be made on letterhead stationery and include the following information: (a) the name and location of the court; (b) name and

occupation of each witness; and (c) a summary of the case. Travelers will also be required to present their U.S. passport, complete Japanese Embassy/consulate visa application forms and to provide the requisite photographs. A photocopy of the commission or court order for a U.S. consular officer to take the deposition must accompany the request. Special visas may also be required of deposition participants other than attorneys (stenographers, interpreters, parties, etc.). Inquiries should be made of the appropriate Japanese consular officer in the United States. For guidance about applying for a U.S. passport, see the Passports feature on the U.S. Department of State Bureau of Consular Affairs internet page.

4. The Japanese Embassy must seek concurrence from the Ministry of Foreign Affairs in every case. The Japanese Embassy or Consulate in the United States will contact the Japanese Foreign Ministry for permission to issue the "special deposition visa."

5. The Japanese Foreign Ministry will contact the U.S. Embassy or Consulate to confirm whether the U.S. consular officer has received a photocopy of the court order issued by a court in the United States and whether the deposition has been scheduled. **See below for guidance on how to schedule a deposition at the U.S. Embassy or one of the U.S. Consulates in Japan.**

6. The Japanese Foreign Ministry will authorize the Japanese Embassy or Consulate in the United States to issue the "special deposition visa."

U.S. Court Order for the Taking of the Depositions: A certified copy of the court order must be provided to the U.S. Embassy in Tokyo before application is made for the special deposition visa so that the U.S. Embassy is in a position to respond to the requisite inquiry made by the Ministry of Foreign Affairs to the U.S. Embassy before the Ministry authorizes the Japanese Embassy or consulate in the United States to issue the special deposition visa.

Japan will not accept orders issued by administrative law judges. Court orders may be obtained from U.S. courts under the All Writs Act, 28 U.S.C. 1651, by various administrative agencies for the taking of depositions in Japan. It is advisable that court orders include the language "on or about" concerning dates so as to afford maximum flexibility in scheduling.

QUESTIONS

Do the Japanese Government's "special deposition visa" requirements constitute a bar against discovery orders by U.S. courts? What risk would a U.S. lawyer run were she or he to enter Japan without a "special deposition visa," claiming to be a tourist, but later participate in a deposition? Could a Japanese national admitted to practice in the United States participate in a disposition in Japan without such a visa?

Consider also the following two affidavits both submitted in a lawsuit in Hawaii relative to a motion by the plaintiff for documents in the possession of the defendant, a Japanese corporation, as well as depositions of its employees to be taken in Japan, one (Affidavit A) by a U.S. legal scholar and the other (the Rebuttal Affidavit) by a Japanese attorney:

IN THE CIRCUIT COURT OF THE THIRD CIRCUIT STATE OF HAWAII
X v. Y KK

Motion for Discovery

Affidavit A

. . . .

7. That your Affiant's opinion with respect to any such limitations on the American trial court's authority or power is as follows:

   a. The American trial court must first determine what issues are before the court when a request for discovery is made against a Japanese corporation having a principal place of business in Japan;

   b. The first issue before the American trial court would be whether the court has personal jurisdiction over the Japanese corporation;

   c. If the court has personal jurisdiction over the Japanese corporation, then the second issue would be whether the Japanese corporation, as a party defendant is subject to the laws of the forum, here the State of Hawaii, relating to discovery;

   d. If the applicable laws of the State of Hawaii and its rules of court subject the party-defendant to the court's authority and power over discovery, then the third issue will be whether the court has the authority and power to order that discovery be conducted in a certain manner, time or place;

   e. Whether the court has the authority and power to order that discovery be conducted in a certain manner, time or place is a question to be determined by the domestic law of the forum, here the State of Hawaii;

   f. In other words, in this case, the trial court must look to Hawaii law, the law of the forum;

   g. A plain reading of the Hawaii Rules of Civil Procedure, a copy of which is attached as Exhibit "A," indicates the following:

      (1) First, under Rule 29, Hawaii Rules of Civil Procedure, the parties may stipulate to the scope, method, place and manner of discovery;

      (2) Second, under Rule 26, Hawaii Rules of Civil Procedure, a party may obtain discovery by all the methods described, including depositions upon oral examination, permission to enter upon land, permission for inspection;

(3) Under Rule 28, Hawaii Rules of Civil Procedure, a deposition upon oral examination may be conducted in a foreign country upon reasonable written notice before a person authorized to administer oaths; under Rule 34, Hawaii Rules of Civil Procedure, inspection and copying of documents and things as well as permission for entry onto land or other property in control of a party for the purpose of inspection and measuring, photographing, testing property or objects or operations within the scope of discovery is obtained by written request;

(4) The party-defendant must raise its objections to such discovery requests by seeking a protective order under Rule 26 (c), Hawaii Rules of Civil Procedure and by making a showing of "good cause" protection;

(5) Under Rule 26 (c), Hawaii Rules of Civil Procedure, the trial court may deny the party-defendant's request for a protective order in whole or in part and "on such terms and conditions as are just order that any party or person provide or permit discovery;"

(6) Under Rule 37, Hawaii Rules of Civil Procedure, the trial court may also, upon motion, compel the party-defendant to comply with the discovery requests;

(7) Finally, if the party-defendant, fails to comply with the discovery requests and court's order compelling the party-defendant to comply with the discovery requests, the court may, under Rule 37(b) (2), issue sanctions against the party-defendant;

h. The party-defendant who is subject to the court's jurisdiction must make a decision either to comply with the court's order or to face sanctions;

i. Unless there is a provision in the domestic law of the forum (Hawaii) which gives a Japanese corporation a special privilege or exemption from discovery, the court has the authority and power to order a Japanese corporation to comply with a discovery request and to sanction the Japanese corporation for its failure to comply with a discovery order;

j. A plain reading of the applicable provisions of the Hawaii Rules of Civil Procedure shows that there is no apparent limitation on the authority and power of the Hawaii trial court over a party-defendant simply because it is a Japanese corporation;

8. That if a party-defendant which is a Japanese corporation having a principal place of business were to question the trial court's authority and power to compel the inspection of property and things in Japan or to compel the taking of depositions on oral examination in Japan, the party-defendant would probably argue:

a. Japanese law does not permit American-styled discovery in Japan and therefore Japanese courts would not render assistance to enforce the American discovery order in Japan;

b. The 1964 consular convention between the United States and Japan provides an exclusive procedure for taking depositions and that the

II. DISCOVERY ABROAD IN AID OF LITIGATION IN THE UNITED STATES

convention requires that depositions be taken in the manner described in the convention:

9. However, such objections are misplaced because the issue is not what kind of discovery is allowed in Japan under Japanese law or the manner in which discovery is to be conducted or may be conducted in Japan; the issue is what can an American trial court order a party-defendant which is a Japanese corporation to do under the applicable domestic law of the forum;

10. In the recent United States Supreme Court decision of *Société Nationale Industrielle Aerospatiale vs. U.S. District Court for the Southern District of Iowa*, 428 U.S. 522, 107 S. Ct. 2542 (1987), the Supreme Court held that foreign corporations are subject to the same pretrial procedures as domestic litigants, stating in part:

> Petitioners made a voluntary decision to market their products in the United States. They are entitled to compete on equal terms with other companies operating in this market. But since the District Court unquestionably has personal jurisdiction over petitioners, they are subject to the same legal constraints, including the burdens associated with American judicial procedures, as their American competitors. A general rule according foreign nationals a preferred position in pretrial proceedings in our courts would conflict with the principle of equal opportunity that governs the market they elected to enter. 482 U.S. at 540.

11. One example of an American trial court's exercise of its authority and power over a party-defendant which was a foreign corporation is described in *Volkswagenwerk Aktiengesellschaft v. Superior Court*, 176 Cal. Rptr. 874, 123 Cal. App. 3d 840 (1981), in which the California appellate court upheld the trial court's discovery order for on-site inspections of the foreign corporation's plant and library as well as oral depositions of certain individuals abroad;

12. The *Volkswagenwerk* decision was modified on grounds that the litigants were required to utilize the procedures set forth in the Hague Convention on Taking Evidence Abroad in Civil and Commercial Matters; however, the decision is still valid as to the trial court's authority and power to formulate the discovery order which it issued;

13. Furthermore, the objections which may be expected to be raised by a party-defendant which is a foreign corporation having a principal place of business in Japan may or may not be valid;

> a. There is no law in Japan which states that an American trial judge may not order a Japanese corporation to comply with discovery requests such as on-site inspections and depositions on oral examinations in Japan;

> b. The 1964 Consular Convention and Protocol between the United States and Japan, Article 17, a copy of which is attached as Exhibit "B" addresses the manner in which voluntary depositions may be taken in Japan; Article 17 states that an American consular officer may take *voluntary* depositions on behalf of American courts in Japan in a manner which is not inconsistent with the laws of Japan;

c. The 1964 Consular Convention only addresses the manner in which a voluntary deposition may be taken in Japan before a consular officer; it does not address involuntary: or compulsory depositions or other forms of discovery in Japan; and, further, it does not limit the authority and power of an American trial court to order discovery in this regard as it sees fit. It should be recognized that the American Embassy premises in Japan are considered as American soil for purposes of ordering foreign nationals to be deposed in the United states;

d. The objections which the party-defendant may raise represent the private interests of the party-defendant and not the public interests of its state, Japan;

e. The objections which the party-defendant may raise are anticipatory in that the American court, when it reviews a motion or other request for discovery against the party-defendant, does not know whether or not the foreign state, on its own motion or on the application of the party-defendant, will in fact refuse to enforce or will impede or unreasonably condition enforcement of the American court's order in Japan;

f. Whether the foreign state enforces or refuses to enforce the American court's order, however, is not relevant to whether the American court may issue its discovery order in the first place;

g. As stated above, whether the American court may or may not issue a discovery order compelling discovery abroad is purely a matter of domestic law of the forum;

14. The *Société Nationale* decision of the United states Supreme Court is important because it emphasizes that the trial courts have the authority and power to fashion a reasonable discovery order, giving due consideration to the situation at hand;

15. *Société Nationale*'s only limitation is that trial courts must guard against abuses; the decision does not state that a trial court is prevented from ordering discovery abroad simply because the foreign state may have a coordinate interest in the litigation; to the contrary, what the United States Supreme court held is:

> . . . When it is necessary to seek evidence abroad, however, the district court must supervise pretrial proceedings particularly closely to prevent discovery abuses. 482 U.S. at 546.

16. An American trial court is not precluded from ordering discovery: it the American trial court determines that discovery abroad is necessary, the American trial court can issue an appropriate discovery order, but must supervise it order carefully;

17. The real issue then concerns the scope and extent of the American trial court's supervisory powers, including its right to sanction the party-defendant which is a foreign corporation for noncompliance with its discovery orders;

18. If the facts before the American trial court demonstrate that there is a need for the requested discovery and that there are no reasonable alternative means to obtain the requested information (other than to accept the party-defendant's

assertion that "there is no such information" or "discovery is refused"), the trial court may and should order the requested discovery;

19. In the event the foreign state, on its own motion or the application of the party-defendant should refuse to enforce the discovery order or attempt to impede or hinder the enforcement of the discovery order through legislation or administrative acts, the trial court should, using its supervisory powers, consider the imposition of sanctions against the party-defendant under the court's supervisory powers;

20. The party-defendant may then seek relief from any sanctions, including an appeal, to determine whether the trial court abused its authority and power in issuing the sanctions;

Further Affiant sayeth not.

Rebuttal Affidavit

. . . .

4. Voluntary depositions in Japan must be conducted before U.S. consular officers.

5. Involuntary examinations of witnesses must be obtained through Japanese courts, are conducted in Japanese, and usually take well over six months to a year from the time of receipt of the request by the Japanese Ministry of Foreign Affairs.

6. It is generally understood that a Japanese court, acting as a commissioned or assigned judge for a foreign court (as it would in this case), cannot issue an order to produce documents or other tangible evidence in executing letters rogatory from the foreign court.

7. In a civil law country like France, Germany, Italy, and Japan, the taking of evidence (as well as service of process) in a civil action is considered to belong exclusively to the judicial power of the court. Thus, unlike American lawyers, attorneys in a civil law country have no discovery power, and the so-called "legal tourism," "fishing expedition," or "three-star chamber (hotel) inquisition," often carried out by American attorneys in Europe and in Asia after the war has been long criticized and is now prohibited as such practice constitutes, at least under the civil law concept, an infringement upon the judicial sovereignty of the host country.

8. Some European countries have enacted the so-called "blocking statutes." The Japanese way to prohibit such discovery practice is to deny American attorneys who intend to go to Japan for discovery purposes. When American attorneys go to Japan to take voluntary depositions at the U.S. Embassy in Tokyo or a Consulate General's office in accordance with the US-Japan Consular Convention, they will be granted a special temporary for that purpose and for that purpose only. They are not allowed to do any discovery outside the Embassy or Consulate General's office (e.g., taking depositions in a hotel suite room, inspection of the factory, search of office files, etc.).

9. If American lawyers try to do discovery in Japan without obtaining such a special temporary visa, or if American lawyers with such special temporary visa try to do discovery outside the Embassy or Consulate General's office, they will be arrested,

punished and deported in accordance with the Japanese Immigration Law.

10. This Japanese Immigration Law applies whether or not such American lawyers go to Japan with the U.S. court's permission or order. Under the general rule of international law and sovereignty, a court's order has a territorial boundary, and Japanese immigration officers are not bound by a foreign court's order.

11. The Japanese Ministry of Foreign Affairs, on behalf of the Ministry of Justice, has fully apprised the U.S. State Department and the Tokyo Embassy of this special regulations concerning the discovery activities of American lawyers, and the above-mentioned information have been well-documented and made public by the State Department.

12. It is one thing that a court has full power and authority to issue any discovery order in accordance with its domestic procedural law, regardless of the nationality of a party affected thereby, once it has been established that the court has personal jurisdiction over the party. It is quite another thing whether the discovery order so issued is physically enforceable in the foreign country. The first question is, can a lawyer or court officer freely go to a foreign country as such and exercise judicial power to enforce the order in that foreign country? If the answer is no, then the visa regulations of that country must be cleared and the requirements for and the scope of judicial assistance available in that country must be examined. Also, under the established rules of international law, a consul officer stationed in a foreign country cannot exercise any judicial power beyond the limit set forth by a consular treaty between the two countries.

III. DISCOVERY IN THE UNITED STATES IN AID OF LITIGATION ABROAD

28 U.S.C. § 1782

(a) The district court of the district in which a person resides or is found may order him to give his testimony or statement or to produce a document or other thing for use in a proceeding in a foreign or international tribunal. The order may be made pursuant to a letter rogatory issued, or request made, by a foreign or international tribunal, including criminal investigations conducted before formal accusation. The order may be made pursuant to a letter rogatory issued, or request made, by a foreign or international tribunal or upon the application of any interested person and may direct that the testimony or statement be given, or the document or other thing be produced, before a person appointed by the court. By virtue of his appointment, the person appointed has power to administer any necessary oath and take the testimony or statement. The order may prescribe the practice and procedure, which may be in whole or part the practice and procedure of the foreign country or the international tribunal, for taking the testimony or statement or producing the document or other thing. To the extent that the order does not prescribe otherwise, the testimony or statement shall be taken, and the document or other thing produced, in accordance with the Federal Rules of Civil Procedure.

A person may not be compelled to give his testimony or statement or to produce

III. DISCOVERY IN THE UNITED STATES IN AID OF LITIGATION ABROAD

a document or other thing in violation of any legally applicable privilege.

QUESTIONS

In which of the following circumstances would discovery in the U.S. for use abroad **not** be allowed under the language of 28 U.S.C. § 1782(a)?

(a) The tribunal or law of the country in which the requested document or testimony are to be used would not allow discovery of such documents or testimony (lack of reciprocity);

(b) The party seeking discovery is not a party to the proceedings aboard;

(c) The foreign tribunal is an administrative organ of the foreign government;

(d) The proceedings are at an investigatory stage. No trial of formal adversarial has commenced;

(e) The foreign tribunal has not requested the document or testimony sought, nor has expressed any willingness to seek or to use such evidence?

(f) The document or testimony sought is privileged under the law of the country in which the proceedings are taking place but are not privileged under U.S. law.

INTEL CORPORATION v. ADVANCED MICRO DEVICES, INC.*
542 U.S. 241 (2004)

JUSTICE GINSBURG delivered the opinion of the Court.

This case concerns the authority of federal district courts to assist in the production of evidence for use in a foreign or international tribunal. In the matter before us, respondent Advanced Micro Devices, Inc. (AMD) filed an antitrust complaint against petitioner Intel Corporation (Intel) with the Directorate-General for Competition of the Commission of the European Communities (European Commission or Commission). In pursuit of that complaint, AMD applied to the United States District Court for the Northern District of California, invoking 28 U.S.C. § 1782(a) for an order requiring Intel to produce potentially relevant documents. Section 1782(a) provides that a federal district court "may order" a person "resid[ing]" or "found" in the district to give testimony or produce documents "for use in a proceeding in a foreign or international tribunal . . . upon the application of any interested person."

---

* Footnotes omitted.

Concluding that § 1782(a) did not authorize the requested discovery, the District Court denied AMD's application. The Court of Appeals for the Ninth Circuit reversed that determination and remanded the case, instructing the District Court to rule on the merits of AMD's application. In accord with the Court of Appeals, we hold that the District Court had authority under § 1782(a) to entertain AMD's discovery request. The statute, we rule, does not categorically bar the assistance AMD seeks: (1) A complainant before the European Commission, such as AMD, qualifies as an "interested person" within § 1782(a)'s compass; (2) the Commission is a § 1782(a) "tribunal" when it acts as a first-instance decisionmaker; (3) the "proceeding" for which discovery is sought under § 1782(a) must be in reasonable contemplation, but need not be "pending" or "imminent"; and (4) § 1782(a) contains no threshold requirement that evidence sought from a federal district court would be discoverable under the law governing the foreign proceeding. We caution, however, that § 1782(a) authorizes, but does not require, a federal district court to provide judicial assistance to foreign or international tribunals or to "interested person[s]" in proceedings abroad. Whether such assistance is appropriate in this case is a question yet unresolved. To guide the District Court on remand, we suggest considerations relevant to the disposition of that question.

I

A

Section 1782 is the product of congressional efforts, over the span of nearly 150 years, to provide federal-court assistance in gathering evidence for use in foreign tribunals. . . .

In 1958, prompted by the growth of international commerce, Congress created a Commission on International Rules of Judicial Procedure (Rules Commission) to "investigate and study existing practices of judicial assistance and cooperation between the United States and foreign countries with a view to achieving improvements." Act of Sept. 2, Pub L 85-906, § 2, 72 Stat 1743; S. Rep. No. 2392, 85th Cong., 2d Sess., p 3 (1958); Smit, International Litigation under the United States Code, 65 Colum. L. Rev. 1015–1016 (1965) (hereinafter Smit, International Litigation). Six years later, in 1964, Congress unanimously adopted legislation recommended by the Rules Commission; the legislation included a complete revision of § 1782. See Act of Oct. 3, Pub L 88-619, § 9, 78 Stat 997; Smit, International Litigation 1026–1035.

As recast in 1964, § 1782 provided for assistance in obtaining documentary and other tangible evidence as well as testimony. Notably, Congress deleted the words "in any judicial proceeding *pending* in any court in a foreign country," and replaced them with the phrase "in a proceeding in a foreign or international tribunal." . . . Section 1782(a)'s current text reads:

> "The district court of the district in which a person resides or is found may order him to give his testimony or statement or to produce a document or other thing for use in a proceeding in a foreign or international tribunal, including criminal investigations conducted before formal accusation. The

III. DISCOVERY IN THE UNITED STATES IN AID OF LITIGATION ABROAD

order may be made pursuant to a letter rogatory issued, or request made, by a foreign or international tribunal or upon the application of any interested person . . . . The order may prescribe the practice and procedure, which may be in whole or part the practice and procedure of the foreign country or the international tribunal, for taking the testimony or statement or producing the document or other thing . . . [or may be] the Federal Rules of Civil Procedure."

"A person may not be compelled to give his testimony or statement or to produce a document or other thing in violation of any legally applicable privilege."

B

AMD and Intel are "worldwide competitors in the microprocessor industry." 292 F.3d 664, 665 (CA9 2002). In October 2000, AMD filed an antitrust complaint with the Directorate-General for Competition (DG-Competition) of the European Commission. *Ibid.*; App. 41. "The European Commission is the executive and administrative organ of the European Communities." Brief for Commission of European Communities as *Amicus Curiae* 1 (hereinafter European Commission *Amicus Curiae*). The Commission exercises responsibility over the wide range of subject areas covered by the European Union treaty; those areas include the treaty provisions, and regulations thereunder, governing competition . . . . The DG-Competition, operating under the Commission's aegis, is the European Union's primary antitrust law enforcer. European Commission *Amicus Curiae* 2. Within the DG-Competition's domain are anticompetitive agreements (Art. 81) and abuse of dominant market position (Art. 82). *Ibid.*; EC Treaty 64–65.

AMD's complaint alleged that Intel, in violation of European competition law, had abused its dominant position in the European market through loyalty rebates, exclusive purchasing agreements with manufacturers and retailers, price discrimination, and standard-setting cartels. App. 40–43; Brief for Petitioner 13. AMD recommended that the DG-Competition seek discovery of documents Intel had produced in a private antitrust suit, titled *Intergraph Corp. v. Intel Corp.*, brought in a Federal District Court in Alabama. 3 F. Supp. 2d 1255 (ND Ala. 1998), vacated 195 F.3d 1346 (CA Fed. 1999), remanded, 88 F. Supp. 2d 1288 (ND Ala. 2000), aff'd 253 F.3d 695 (CA Fed. 2001); App. 111; App. to Pet. for Cert. 13a–14a. After the DG-Competition declined to seek judicial assistance in the United States, AMD, pursuant to § 1782(a), petitioned the District Court for the Northern District of California for an order directing Intel to produce documents discovered in the *Intergraph* litigation and on file in the federal court in Alabama. App. to Pet. for Cert. 13a–14a. AMD asserted that it sought the materials in connection with the complaint it had filed with the European Commission. *Ibid.*

The District Court denied the application as "[un]supported by applicable authority." *Id.*, at 15a. Reversing that determination, the Court of Appeals for the Ninth Circuit remanded the case for disposition on the merits. 292 F.3d, at 669. The Court of Appeals noted two points significant to its decision: § 1782(a) includes matters before " 'bodies of a quasi-judicial or administrative nature,' " *id.*, at 667 (quoting *In re Letters Rogatory from Tokyo District*, 539 F.2d 1216, 1218–1219 (CA9

1976)); and, since 1964, the statute's text has contained "[no] requirement that the . . . proceeding be 'pending[,]' " *ibid.* (quoting *United States v. Sealed 1, Letter of Request for Legal Assistance*, 235 F.3d 1200, 1204 (CA9 2000)); . . . A proceeding judicial in character, the Ninth Circuit further observed, was a likely sequel to the European Commission's investigation: "[The European Commission is] a body authorized to enforce the EC Treaty with written, binding decisions, enforceable through fines and penalties. [The Commission's] decisions are appealable to the Court of First Instance and then to the [European] Court of Justice. Thus, the proceeding for which discovery is sought is, at minimum, one leading to quasi-judicial proceedings." 292 F.3d at 667; . . . .

The Court of Appeals rejected Intel's argument that § 1782(a) called for a threshold showing that the documents AMD sought in the California federal court would have been discoverable by AMD in the European Commission investigation had those documents been located within the Union. 292 F.3d, at 668. Acknowledging that other Courts of Appeals had construed § 1782(a) to include a "foreign-discoverability" rule, the Ninth Circuit found "nothing in the plain language or legislative history of Section 1782, including its 1964 and 1996 amendments, to require a threshold showing [by] the party seeking discovery that what is sought be discoverable in the foreign proceeding," *id.*, at 669. A foreign-discoverability threshold, the Court of Appeals added, would disserve § 1782(a)'s twin aims of "providing efficient assistance to participants in international litigation and encouraging foreign countries by example to provide similar assistance to our courts." *Ibid.*

On remand, a Magistrate Judge found AMD's application "overbroad," and recommended an order directing AMD to submit a more specific discovery request confined to documents directly relevant to the European Commission investigation. App. to Brief in Opposition 1a–6a; Brief for Petitioner 15, n. 9. The District Court has stayed further proceedings pending disposition of the questions presented by Intel's petition for certiorari. *Ibid.*; see *Order Vacating Hearing Date*, No. C 01-7033 MISC JW (ND Cal, Nov. 30, 2003) (stating "Intel may renotice its motion for de novo review of the Magistrate Judge's decision after the Supreme Court issues its ruling").

We granted certiorari, 540 U.S. 1003, 540 U.S. 1003 (2003), in view of the division among the Circuits on the question whether § 1782(a) contains a foreign-discoverability requirement. We now hold that § 1782(a) does not impose such a requirement. We also granted review on two other questions. First, does § 1782(a) make discovery available to complainants, such as AMD, who do not have the status of private "litigants" and are not sovereign agents? See Pet. for Cert. (i). Second, must a "proceeding" before a foreign "tribunal" be "pending" or at least "imminent" for an applicant to invoke § 1782(a) successfully? . . . Answering "yes" to the first question and "no" to the second, we affirm the Ninth Circuit's judgment.

II

To place this case in context, we sketch briefly how the European Commission, acting through the DG-Competition, enforces European competition laws and regulations. The DG-Competition's "overriding responsibility" is to conduct inves-

III. DISCOVERY IN THE UNITED STATES IN AID OF LITIGATION ABROAD

tigations into alleged violations of the European Union's competition prescriptions. See European Commission *Amicus Curiae* 6. On receipt of a complaint or *sua sponte*, the DG-Competition conducts a preliminary investigation. *Ibid.* In that investigation, the DG-Competition "may take into account information provided by a complainant, and it may seek information directly from the target of the complaint." Ibid. "Ultimately, DG Competition's preliminary investigation results in a formal written decision whether to pursue the complaint. If [the DG-Competition] declines to proceed, that decision is subject to judicial review" by the Court of First Instance and, ultimately, by the court of last resort for European Union matters, the Court of Justice for the European Communities (European Court of Justice). Id., at 7; App. 50; *see, e.g.*, case T-241/97, *Stork Amsterdam BV v. Commission*, 2000 E. C. R. II-309, [2000] 5 C. M. L. R. 31 (Ct. 1st Instance 2000) (annulling Commission's rejection of a complaint).

If the DG-Competition decides to pursue the complaint, it typically serves the target of the investigation with a formal "statement of objections" and advises the target of its intention to recommend a decision finding that the target has violated European competition law. European Commission *Amicus Curiae* 7. The target is entitled to a hearing before an independent officer, who provides a report to the DG-Competition. *Ibid.*; App. 18–27. Once the DG-Competition has made its recommendation, the European Commission may "dismis[s] the complaint, or issu[e] a decision finding infringement and imposing penalties." European Commission *Amicus Curiae* 7. The Commission's final action dismissing the complaint or holding the target liable is subject to review in the Court of First Instance and the European Court of Justice. *Ibid.*; App. 52–53, 89–90.

Although lacking formal "party" or "litigant" status in Commission proceedings, the complainant has significant procedural rights. Most prominently, the complainant may submit to the DG-Competition information in support of its allegations, and may seek judicial review of the Commission's disposition of a complaint. See European Commission *Amicus Curiae* 7–8, and n 5; *Stork Amsterdam*, [2000] E. C. R. II, at 328–329, PP 51–53.

III

As "in all statutory construction cases, we begin [our examination of § 1782] with the language of the statute." *Barnhart v. Sigmon Coal Co.*, 534 U.S. 438, 450 (2002). The language of § 1782(a), confirmed by its context, our examination satisfies us, warrants this conclusion: The statute authorizes, but does not require, a federal district court to provide assistance to a complainant in a European Commission proceeding that leads to a dispositive ruling, i.e., a final administrative action both responsive to the complaint and reviewable in court. Accordingly, we reject the categorical limitations Intel would place on the statute's reach.

A

We turn first to Intel's contention that the catalog of "interested person[s]" authorized to apply for judicial assistance under § 1782(a) includes only "litigants, foreign sovereigns, and the designated agents of those sovereigns," and excludes

AMD, a mere complainant before the Commission, accorded only "limited rights." Brief for Petitioner 10–11, 24, 26–27. Highlighting § 1782's caption, "[a]ssistance to foreign and international tribunals and to litigants before such tribunals," Intel urges that the statutory phrase "any interested person" should be read, correspondingly, to reach only "litigants." *Id.*, at 24 (internal quotation marks omitted, emphasis in original).

. . . .

The complainant who triggers a European Commission investigation has a significant role in the process. . . . [I]n addition to prompting an investigation, the complainant has the right to submit information for the DG-Competition's consideration, and may proceed to court if the Commission discontinues the investigation or dismisses the complaint. App. 52–53. Given these participation rights, a complainant "possess[es] a reasonable interest in obtaining [judicial] assistance," and therefore qualifies as an "interested person" within any fair construction of that term. . . .

B

We next consider whether the assistance in obtaining documents here sought by an "interested person" meets the specification "for use in a foreign or international tribunal." Beyond question the reviewing authorities, both the Court of First Instance and the European Court of Justice, qualify as tribunals. But those courts are not proof-taking instances. Their review is limited to the record before the Commission. See Tr. of Oral Arg. 17. Hence, AMD could "use" evidence in the reviewing courts only by submitting it to the Commission in the current, investigative stage.

Moreover, when Congress established the Commission on International Rules of Judicial Procedure in 1958, . . . it instructed the Rules Commission to recommend procedural revisions "for the rendering of assistance to foreign courts and *quasi-judicial agencies.*" § 2, 72 Stat 1743 (emphasis added). Section 1782 had previously referred to "any judicial proceeding." The Rules Commission's draft, which Congress adopted, replaced that term with "a proceeding in a foreign or international tribunal." . . . . Congress understood that change to "provid[e] the possibility of U. S. judicial assistance in connection with [administrative and quasi-judicial proceedings abroad]." S. Rep. No. 1580, at 7–8; . . . . We have no warrant to exclude the European Commission, to the extent that it acts as a first-instance decisionmaker, from § 1782(a)'s ambit. [Reference omitted.]

C

Intel also urges that AMD's complaint has not progressed beyond the investigative stage; therefore, no adjudicative action is currently or even imminently on the Commission's agenda. Brief for Petitioner 27–29.

Section 1782(a) does not limit the provision of judicial assistance to "pending" adjudicative proceedings. In 1964, when Congress eliminated the requirement that a proceeding be "judicial," Congress also deleted the requirement that a proceeding be "pending." . . . . "When Congress acts to amend a statute, we presume it intends its amendment to have real and substantial effect." *Stone v. INS*, 514 U.S. 386, 397 (1995). The legislative history of the 1964 revision is in sync; it reflects Congress' recognition that judicial assistance would be available "whether the foreign or international proceeding or investigation is of a criminal, civil, administrative, or other nature." S. Rep. No. 1580, at 9 (emphasis added).

In 1996, Congress amended § 1782(a) to clarify that the statute covers "criminal investigations conducted before formal accusation." See § 1342(b), 110 Stat 486; . . . . Nothing suggests that this amendment was an endeavor to rein in, rather than to confirm, by way of example, the broad range of discovery authorized in 1964. . . .

In short, we reject the view, expressed in *In re Ishihara Chemical Co.*, that § 1782 comes into play only when adjudicative proceedings are "pending" or "imminent." . . . *Instead, we hold that § 1782(a) requires only that a dispositive ruling by the Commission, reviewable by the European courts, be within reasonable contemplation.* [Emphasis added.]

. . . .

D

We take up next the foreign-discoverability rule on which lower courts have divided: Does § 1782(a) categorically bar a district court from ordering production of documents when the foreign tribunal or the "interested person" would not be able to obtain the documents if they were located in the foreign jurisdiction? [Reference omitted.]

We note at the outset, and count it significant, that § 1782(a) expressly shields privileged material: "A person may not be compelled to give his testimony or statement or to produce a document or other thing in violation of any legally applicable privilege." See S. Rep. No. 1580, at 9 ("[N]o person shall be required under the provisions of [§ 1782] to produce any evidence in violation of an applicable privilege."). Beyond shielding material safeguarded by an applicable privilege, however, nothing in the text of § 1782 limits a district court's production-order authority to materials that could be discovered in the foreign jurisdiction if the materials were located there. "If Congress had intended to impose such a sweeping restriction on the district court's discretion, at a time when it was enacting liberalizing amendments to the statute, it would have included statutory language to that effect." *In re Application of Gianoli Aldunate*, 3 F.3d 54, 59 (CA2 1993); . . .

Nor does § 1782(a)'s legislative history suggest that Congress intended to impose a blanket foreign-discoverability rule on the provision of assistance under § 1782(a). The Senate Report observes in this regard that § 1782(a) "leaves the issuance of an appropriate order to the discretion of the court which, in proper cases, may refuse to issue an order or may impose conditions it deems desirable." S. Rep. No. 1580, at 7.

Intel raises two policy concerns in support of a foreign-discoverability limitation on § 1782(a) aid — avoiding offense to foreign governments, and maintaining parity between litigants . . . . While comity and parity concerns may be important as touchstones for a district court's exercise of discretion in particular cases, they do not permit our insertion of a generally applicable foreign-discoverability rule into the text of § 1782(a).

We question whether foreign governments would in fact be offended by a domestic prescription permitting, but not requiring, judicial assistance. A foreign nation may limit discovery within its domain for reasons peculiar to its own legal practices, culture, or traditions — reasons that do not necessarily signal objection to aid from United States federal courts . . . . When the foreign tribunal would readily accept relevant information discovered in the United States, application of a foreign-discoverability rule would be senseless. The rule in that situation would serve only to thwart § 1782(a)'s objective to assist foreign tribunals in obtaining relevant information that the tribunals may find useful but, for reasons having no bearing on international comity, they cannot obtain under their own laws.

Concerns about maintaining parity among adversaries in litigation likewise do not provide a sound basis for a cross-the-board foreign-discoverability rule. When information is sought by an "interested person," a district court could condition relief upon that person's reciprocal exchange of information . . . . Moreover, the foreign tribunal can place conditions on its acceptance of the information to maintain whatever measure of parity it concludes is appropriate. *See Euromepa* [*S. A. v. R. Esmerian, Inc.*, 51 F.3d 1095, 1101 (CA2 1995)].

We also reject Intel's suggestion that a § 1782(a) applicant must show that United States law would allow discovery in domestic litigation analogous to the foreign proceeding. Brief for Petitioner 19–20 ("[I]f AMD were pursuing this matter in the United States, U. S. law would preclude it from obtaining discovery of Intel's documents."). Section 1782 is a provision for assistance to tribunals abroad. It does not direct United States courts to engage in comparative analysis to determine whether analogous proceedings exist here. Comparisons of that order can be fraught with danger. For example, we have in the United States no close analogue to the European Commission regime under which AMD is not free to mount its own case in the Court of First Instance or the European Court of Justice, but can participate only as complainant, an "interested person," in Commission-steered proceedings . . . .

IV

As earlier emphasized, . . . a district court is not required to grant a § 1782(a) discovery application simply because it has the authority to do so . . . . We note below factors that bear consideration in ruling on a § 1782(a) request.

First, when the person from whom discovery is sought is a participant in the foreign proceeding (as Intel is here), the need for § 1782(a) aid generally is not as apparent as it ordinarily is when evidence is sought from a nonparticipant in the matter arising abroad. A foreign tribunal has jurisdiction over those appearing before it, and can itself order them to produce evidence . . . . In contrast, nonparticipants in the foreign proceeding may be outside the foreign tribunal's

III. DISCOVERY IN THE UNITED STATES IN AID OF LITIGATION ABROAD 583

jurisdictional reach; hence, their evidence, available in the United States, may be unobtainable absent § 1782(a) aid. . . .

Second, as the 1964 Senate Report suggests, a court presented with a § 1782(a) request may take into account the nature of the foreign tribunal, the character of the proceedings underway abroad, and the receptivity of the foreign government or the court or agency abroad to U. S. federal-court judicial assistance . . . . Further, the grounds Intel urged for categorical limitations on § 1782(a)'s scope may be relevant in determining whether a discovery order should be granted in a particular case. See Brief for United States as *Amicus Curiae* 23. Specifically, a district court could consider whether the § 1782(a) request conceals an attempt to circumvent foreign proof-gathering restrictions or other policies of a foreign country or the United States . . . . Also, unduly intrusive or burdensome requests may be rejected or trimmed. . . .

Intel maintains that, if we do not accept the categorical limitations it proposes, then, at least, we should exercise our supervisory authority to adopt rules barring § 1782(a) discovery here. . . . We decline, at this juncture, to adopt supervisory rules. Any such endeavor at least should await further experience with § 1782(a) applications in the lower courts. The European Commission has stated in *amicus curiae* briefs to this Court that it does not need or want the District Court's assistance . . . . It is not altogether clear, however, whether the Commission, which may itself invoke § 1782(a) aid, means to say "never" or "hardly ever" to judicial assistance from United States courts. Nor do we know whether the European Commission's views on § 1782(a)'s utility are widely shared in the international community by entities with similarly blended adjudicative and prosecutorial functions.

Several facets of this case remain largely unexplored. Intel and its amici have expressed concerns that AMD's application, if granted in any part, may yield disclosure of confidential information, encourage "fishing expeditions," and undermine the European Commission's Leniency Program . . . . Yet no one has suggested that AMD's complaint to the Commission is pretextual. Nor has it been shown that § 1782(a)'s preservation of legally applicable privileges, . . . and the controls on discovery available to the District Court, . . . would be ineffective to prevent discovery of Intel's business secrets and other confidential information.

On the merits, this case bears closer scrutiny than it has received to date. Having held that § 1782(a) authorizes, but does not require, discovery assistance, we leave it to the courts below to assure an airing adequate to determine what, if any, assistance is appropriate.

For the reasons stated, the judgment of the Court of Appeals for the Ninth Circuit is affirmed.

JUSTICE O'CONNOR took no part in the consideration or decision of this case.

JUSTICE SCALIA, concurring in the judgment.

As today's opinion shows, the Court's disposition is required by the text of the statute. None of the limitations urged by petitioner finds support in the categorical language of 28 U.S.C. § 1782(a) [28 USCS § 1782(a)]. That being so, it is not only (as I think) improper but also quite unnecessary to seek repeated support in the words of a Senate Committee Report — which, as far as we know, not even the full committee, much less the full Senate, much much less the House, and much much much less the President who signed the bill, agreed with. Since, moreover, I have not read the entire so-called legislative history, and have no need or desire to do so, so far as I know the statements of the Senate Report may be contradicted elsewhere.

Accordingly, because the statute — the only sure expression of the will of Congress — says what the Court says it says, I join in the judgment.

JUSTICE BREYER, dissenting.

The Court reads the scope of 28 USC § 1782 to extend beyond what I believe Congress might reasonably have intended. Some countries allow a private citizen to ask a court to review a criminal prosecutor's decision not to prosecute. On the majority's reading, that foreign private citizen could ask an American court to help the citizen obtain information, even if the foreign prosecutor were indifferent or unreceptive . . . . Many countries allow court review of decisions made by any of a wide variety of nonprosecutorial, nonadjudicative bodies . . . . This case itself suggests that an American firm, hoping to obtain information from a competitor, might file an antitrust complaint with the European antitrust authorities, thereby opening up the possibility of broad American discovery — contrary to the antitrust authorities' desires.

One might ask why it is wrong to read the statute as permitting the use of America's court processes to obtain information in such circumstances. One might also ask why American courts should not deal *case by case* with any problems of the sort mentioned. The answer to both of these questions is that discovery and discovery-related judicial proceedings take time, they are expensive, and cost and delay, or threats of cost and delay, can themselves force parties to settle underlying disputes . . . . To the extent that expensive, time-consuming battles about discovery proliferate, they deflect the attention of foreign authorities from other matters those authorities consider more important; they can lead to results contrary to those that foreign authorities desire; and they can promote disharmony among national and international authorities, rather than the harmony that § 1782 seeks to achieve. They also use up domestic judicial resources and crowd our dockets.

. . . .

Second, a court should not permit discovery where both of the following are true: (1) A private person seeking discovery would not be entitled to that discovery under foreign law, and (2) the discovery would not be available under domestic law in analogous circumstances. . . .

Application of either of these limiting principles would require dismissal of this discovery proceeding. First, the Commission of the European Communities' (Commission) antitrust authority's status as a "tribunal" is questionable. In many respects, the Commission more closely resembles a prosecuting authority, say, the Department of Justice's Antitrust Division, than an administrative agency that adjudicates cases, say, the Federal Trade Commission. . . .

At the same time, the Commission has told this Court that it is not a "tribunal" under the Act. It has added that, should it be considered, against its will, a "tribunal," its "ability to carry out its governmental responsibilities" will be seriously threatened. . . .

. . . .

The second limiting factor is also present. Neither AMD nor any comparable private party would be able to obtain the kind of discovery AMD seeks, either in Europe or in the United States. In respect to Europe, the Commission has told us that any person in the world is free to file a complaint with the Commission, but it is the Commission that then investigates. The private complainant lacks any authority to obtain discovery of business secrets and commercial information. . . .

What is the legal source of these limiting principles? In my view, they, and perhaps others, are implicit in the statute itself, given its purpose and use of the terms "tribunal" and "interested person." § 1782(a). But even if they are not, this Court's "supervisory powers . . . permit, at the least, the promulgation of procedural rules governing the management of litigation," not to mention "'procedures deemed desirable from the viewpoint of sound judicial practice although in nowise commanded by statute or by the Constitution.'" *Thomas v. Arn*, 474 U.S. 140, 146-147 (1985) (quoting *Cupp v. Naughten*, 414 U.S. 141, 146 (1973)). . . . Intel Corp. has asked us to exercise those powers in this case. . . . We should do so along the lines that I suggest; consequently, we should reverse the judgment below and order the complaint in this case dismissed.

I respectfully dissent from the Court's contrary determination.

QUESTIONS

1. How significant is *Intel Corporation v. Advanced Micro Devices, Inc.*? How does it affect motions to dismiss on the basis of *forum non conveniens*? (Review Judge Posner's decision in *U.S.O. Corporation v. Mizuho Holding Company* in Chapter 3.)

2. As indicated by Justice Ginsburg, § 1782(a) was revised by Congress in 1964 to provide for expanded assistance in obtaining evidence — both documentary and testimony — in the United States for proceedings in foreign or international tribunals. Yet the provision was long neglected and little used. How might this be explained? To what extent was the require-

ment imposed by some circuits of "foreign-discoverability" or reciprocity a factor? For an influential rejection of this requirement a few years prior *Intel Corporation v. Advanced Micro Devices, Inc.*, see the opinion of Judge Guido Calabresi in *Euromepa S.A. v. R. Esmerian, Inc.*, 51 F.3d 1095 (2d Cir. 1995), cited by Justice Ginsburg in section III.D.

3. To what extent does § 442 of the Restatement (Third) of Foreign Relations Law in combination with *Intel Corporation v. Advanced Micro Devices, Inc.* expand the scope of U.S. discovery abroad?

RESTATEMENT (THIRD) OF FOREIGN RELATIONS LAW § 442

(1) (a) A court or agency in the United States, when authorized by statute or rule of court, may order a person subject to its jurisdiction to produce documents, objects, or other information relevant to an action or investigation, even if the information or the person in possession of the information is outside the United States.

(b) Failure to comply with an order to produce information may subject the person to whom the order is directed to sanctions, including finding of contempt, dismissal of a claim or defense, or default judgment, or may lead to a determination that the facts to which the order was addressed are as asserted by the opposing party.

(c) In deciding whether to issue an order directing production of information located abroad, and in framing such an order, a court or agency in the United States should take into account the importance to the investigation or litigation of the documents or other information requested; the degree of specificity of the request; whether the information originated in the United States; the availability of alternative means of securing the information; and the extent to which noncompliance with the request would undermine important interests of the United States, or compliance with the request would undermine important interests of the state where the information is located.

(2) If disclosure of information located outside the United States is prohibited by a law, regulation, or order of a court or other authority of the state in which the information or prospective witness is located, or of the state of which a prospective witness is a national,

(a) a court or agency in the United States may require the person to whom the order is directed to make a good faith effort to secure permission from the foreign authorities to make the information available;

(b) a court or agency should not ordinarily impose sanctions of contempt, dismissal, or default on a party that has failed to comply with the order for production, except in cases of deliberate concealment or removal of information or of failure to make a good faith effort in accordance with paragraph (a);

(c) a court or agency may, in appropriate cases, make findings of fact adverse to a party that has failed to comply with the order for production, even if that party has made a good faith effort to secure permission from the foreign authorities to make the information available and that effort has been unsuccessful.

REVIEW PROBLEM

Assume that you are asked for an opinion on United States law in connection with lawsuits filed both in the United States, Canada, France, and Japan by the great grandchildren of Marc Bloch, the renowned historian of mediaeval France who was arrested and then shot on 16 June 1944, less than three months before the liberation of Lyons by the Allies on 2 September 1944. Assume that, as plaintiffs in all four actions, the Bloch heirs claim ownership in rare medieval manuscripts, allegedly taken from the Bloch's home on the 17th of June, 1944, that they believe are currently on loan by an unnamed French collector for display various universities including Harvard University, the University of British Columbia, Paris-Sorbonne University (also known as Paris IV), and Kyoto University. The U.S. and Canadian lawsuits are *in rem* actions against the manuscript. The French and Japanese suits are simply claims of ownership against unnamed defendants domiciled in France. The plaintiffs seek discovery orders to identify the French party or parties from whom the universities have acquired the manuscripts on loan as well as all documents in their possession related to the provenance of the manuscripts. Separate motions seek discovery of similar information from the as-yet-unnamed French party. As plaintiffs in the French and Japanese actions, the Bloch heirs seek similar discovery against the respective universities in each jurisdiction. In your view, would they prevail in any or all of these actions?

Chapter 6

RECOGNITION AND ENFORCEMENT OF FOREIGN-COUNTRY JUDGMENTS AND ARBITRAL AWARDS

In this chapter we examine the principal issues that arise in relation to cross-border recognition and enforcement of both judgments and arbitral awards. As noted in previous chapters, these are central concerns in transnational litigation. Not unique, of course, to a transnational context, similar issues arise within most federal as well as regional systems of governance as litigants seek in one political subdivision the recognition and enforcement of a judgment or arbitral award rendered in another.

With respect to judgments, as we have previously seen in our examination of adjudicatory jurisdiction in Chapter 1, the prevailing norm within the federal systems of North America (Canada, Mexico, and the United States) and the European Union is to require by constitutional design, treaty, or regulation the courts of each constituent polity to extend in effect "good faith and credit" to the judgments of sibling polities. A similar result can be achieved among nation-states by multinational treaty as, for example, the Pan-American community (which includes Mexico but not Canada or the United States) has achieved. However, despite long and painstaking negotiations, no comparable international convention exists today for broader transnational recognition and enforcement of judgments. Since 1992, however, a Working Group on the Judgments Project of the Hague Conference on Private International Law has engaged in continuing efforts for such a treaty. (For the current status of this project, see http://www.hcch.net/index_en.php?act=text.display&tid=150.) As a consequence, individual national or state rules apply to the recognition and enforcement of judgments of other nations.

For foreign arbitral awards, in contrast, such a treaty does exist — the 1958 United Nations Convention on the Recognition and Enforcement of Foreign Arbitral Awards (the "New York Convention"). As detailed below, the New York Convention both obligates the courts of contracting states to give effect to private arbitration agreements and to recognize and enforce any resulting awards made in other contracting states. Thus, as discussed in greater detail in Chapter 7, the New York Convention has considerably advantaged arbitral awards over foreign judgments.

The most recent "recast" of EU rules and standards for the recognition and enforcement of judgments in civil and commercial matters, Regulation (EU) No. 1215/2012, as described in Chapter 1, further removes some of the obstacles to the enforcement of arbitral agreements and awards under the 1968 Brussels convention and EC Regulation 44/2001 as construed by the European Court of Justice. As did its predecessors, the 1968 Brussels Convention and EC Regulation 44/2001, the 2012 EU Regulation recognizes that the 1958 New York Convention "takes precedence" over the Regulation (Official Comment ¶ 12). As indicated below, it also seeks to resolve one of the more vexing conflicts between the New York Convention and prior EU law.

I. RECOGNITION AND ENFORCEMENT OF FOREIGN-COUNTRY JUDGMENTS

A. United States

To begin our discussion, we turn to the landmark United States case on the rules and standards of customary private international law on the recognition and enforcement of foreign-country judgments at the end of the 19th century.

HILTON v. GUYOT
159 U.S. 113 (1895)

In Error to and Appeal from the Circuit Court of the United States for the Southern District of New York.

The first of these two cases was an action at law, brought December 18, 1885, in the circuit court of the United States for the Southern district of New York, by Gustave Bertin Guyot, as official liquidator of the firm of Charles Fortin & Co., and by the surviving members of that firm, all aliens and citizens of the republic of France, against Henry Hilton and William Libbey, citizens of the United States and of the state of New York, and trading as copartners, in the cities of New York and Paris, and elsewhere, under the firm name of A. T. Stewart & Co. The action was upon a judgment recovered in a French court at Paris, in the republic of France, by the firm of Charles Fortin & Co., all of whose members were French citizens, against Hilton & Libbey, trading as copartners, as aforesaid, and citizens of the United States and of the state of New York.

Mr. Justice Gray, after stating the case, delivered the opinion of the court.

These two cases — the one at law and the other in equity — of *Hilton v. Guyot*, and the case of *Ritchie v. McMullen*, 16 Sup. Ct. 171, which has been under advisement at the same time, present important questions relating to the force and effect of foreign judgments, not hitherto adjudicated by this court, which have been argued with great learning and ability, and which require for their satisfactory determination a full consideration of the authorities. To avoid confusion in indicating the parties, it will be convenient first to take the case at law of *Hilton v. Guyot*.

International law, in its widest and most comprehensive sense,— including not only questions of right between nations, governed by what has been appropriately called the "law of nations," but also questions arising under what is usually called "private international law," or the "conflict of laws," and concerning the rights of persons within the territory and dominion of one nation, by reason of acts, private or public, done within the dominions of another nation,— is part of our law, and must be ascertained and administered by the courts of justice as often as such questions are presented in litigation between man and man, duly submitted to their determination.

The most certain guide, no doubt, for the decision of such questions is a treaty or a statute of this country. But when, as is the case here, there is no written law upon the subject, the duty still rests upon the judicial tribunals of ascertaining and declaring what the law is, whenever it becomes necessary to do so, in order to determine the rights of parties to suits regularly brought before them. In doing this, the courts must obtain such aid as they can from judicial decisions, from the works of jurists and commentators, and from the acts and usages of civilized nations. [Citations omitted.]

No law has any effect, of its own force, beyond the limits of the sovereignty from which its authority is derived. The extent to which the law of one nation, as put in force within its territory, whether by executive order, by legislative act, or by judicial decree, shall be allowed to operate within the dominion of another nation, depends upon what our greatest jurists have been content to call "the comity of nations." Although the phrase has been often criticised, no satisfactory substitute has been suggested.

"Comity," in the legal sense, is neither a matter of absolute obligation, on the one hand, nor of mere courtesy and good will, upon the other. But it is the recognition which one nation allows within its territory to the legislative, executive, or judicial acts of another nation, having due regard both to international duty and convenience, and to the rights of its own citizens, or of other persons who are under the protection of its laws.

. . . .

In order to appreciate the weight of the various authorities cited at the bar [Justice Story, Chief Justice Taney, Wheaton, and Chancellor Kent], it is important to distinguish different kinds of judgments. Every foreign judgment, of whatever nature, in order to be entitled to any effect, must have been rendered by a court having jurisdiction of the cause, and upon regular proceedings, and due notice. In alluding to different kinds of judgments, therefore, such jurisdiction, proceedings, and notice will be assumed. It will also be assumed that they are untainted by fraud, the effect of which will be considered later.

A judgment *in rem*, adjudicating the title to a ship or other movable property within the custody of the court, is treated as valid everywhere. . . .

. . . .

A judgment affecting the status of persons, such as a decree confirming or dissolving a marriage, is recognized as valid in every country, unless contrary to the policy of its own law. . . .

Other judgments, not strictly *in rem*, under which a person has been compelled to pay money, are so far conclusive that the justice of the payment cannot be impeached in another country, so as to compel him to pay it again. For instance, a judgment in foreign attachment is conclusive, as between the parties, of the right to the property or money attached. [Citation omitted.] And if, on the dissolution of a partnership, one partner promises to indemnify the other against the debts of the partnership, a judgment for such a debt, under which the latter has been compelled to pay it, is conclusive evidence of the debt in a suit by him to recover the amount upon the promise of indemnity. . . .

Other foreign judgments which have been held conclusive of the matter adjudged were judgments discharging obligations contracted in the foreign country between citizens or residents thereof. . . .

. . . .

In former times, foreign decrees in admiralty *in personam* were executed, even by imprisonment of the defendant, by the court of admiralty in England, upon letters rogatory from the foreign sovereign, without a new suit. . . .

The extraterritorial effect of judgments *in personam*, at law, or in equity may differ, according to the parties to the cause. A judgment of that kind between two citizens or residents of the country, and thereby subject to the jurisdiction in which it is rendered, may be held conclusive as between them everywhere. So, if a foreigner invokes the jurisdiction by bringing an action against a citizen, both may be held bound by a judgment in favor of either; and if a citizen sues a foreigner, and judgment is rendered in favor of the latter, both may be held equally bound. [Citations omitted.]

The effect to which a judgment, purely executory, rendered in favor of a citizen or resident of the country, in a suit there brought by him against a foreigner, may be entitled in an action thereon against the latter in his own country, as is the case now before us, presents a more difficult question, upon which there has been some diversity of opinion.

Early in the last century it was settled in England that a foreign judgment on a debt was considered, not like a judgment of a domestic court of record, as a record or a specialty, a lawful consideration for which was conclusively presumed, but as a simple contract only.

. . . .

The law upon this subject as understood in the United States at the time of their separation from the mother country was clearly set forth by Chief Justice Parsons, speaking for the supreme judicial court of Massachusetts, in 1813, and by Mr. Justice Story in his Commentaries on the Constitution of the United States, published in 1833. Both those eminent jurists declared that by the law of England the general rule was that foreign judgments were only *prima facie* evidence of the matter which they purported to decide; and that by the common law, before the American Revolution, all the courts of the several colonies and states were deemed foreign to each other, and consequently judgments rendered by any one of them were considered as foreign judgments, and their merits re-examinable in another colony, not only as to the jurisdiction of the court which pronounced them, but also as to the merits of the controversy, to the extent to which they were understood to be re-examinable in England. And they noted that, in order to remove that inconvenience, statutes had been passed in Massachusetts, and in some of the other colonies, by which judgments rendered by a court of competent jurisdiction in a neighboring colony could not be impeached. [Citations omitted.]

It was because of that condition of the law, as between the American colonies and states, that the United States, at the very beginning of their existence as a nation, ordained that full faith and credit should be given to the judgments of one of the states of the Union in the courts of another of those states.

By the articles of confederation of 1777 (article 4, § 3), "full faith and credit shall be given, in each of these states, to the records, acts and judicial proceedings of the courts and magistrates of every other state." 1 Stat. 4. By the constitution of the United States (article 4, § 1), "full faith and credit shall be given in each state to the public acts, records and judicial proceedings of every other state; and the congress may by general laws prescribe the manner in which such acts, records and proceedings shall be proved, and the effect thereof." And the first congress of the United States under the constitution, after prescribing the manner in which the records and judicial proceedings of the courts of any state should be authenticated and proved, enacted that "the said records and judicial proceedings authenticated as aforesaid, shall have such faith and credit given to them in every court within the United States, as they have by law or usage in the courts of the state from whence the said records are or shall be taken." Act May 26, 1790, c. 11 (1 Stat. 122); Rev. St. § 905.

The decisions of this court have clearly recognized that judgments of a foreign state are *prima facie* evidence only, and that, but for these constitutional and legislative provisions, judgments of a state of the Union, when sued upon in another state, would have no greater effect.

. . . .

But neither in those cases [omitted] nor in any other has this court hitherto been called upon to determine how far foreign judgments may be re-examined upon their merits, or be impeached for fraud in obtaining them.

In the courts of the several states it was long recognized and assumed as undoubted and indisputable that by our law, as by the law of England, foreign judgments for debts were not conclusive, but only prima facie evidence of the matter adjudged. . . .

. . . .

From this review of the authorities, it clearly appears that, at the time of the separation of this country from England, the general rule was fully established that foreign judgments *in personam* were *prima facie* evidence only, and not conclusive of the merits of the controversy between the parties. But the extent and limits of the application of that rule do not appear to have been much discussed, or defined with any approach to exactness, in England or America, until the matter was taken up by Chancellor Kent and by Mr. Justice Story.

. . . .

The result of the English decisions, therefore, would seem to be that a foreign judgment *in personam* may be impeached for a manifest and willful disregard of the law of England.

. . . .

In view of all the authorities upon the subject, and of the trend of judicial opinion in this country and in England, following the lead of Kent and Story, we are satisfied that where there has been opportunity for a full and fair trial abroad before a court of competent jurisdiction, conducting the trial upon regular proceedings, after due citation or voluntary appearance of the defendant, and under a system of jurisprudence likely to secure an impartial administration of justice between the citizens of its own country and those of other countries, and there is nothing to show either prejudice in the court, or in the system of laws under which it was sitting, or fraud in procuring the judgment, or any other special reason why the comity of this nation should not allow it full effect, the merits of the case should not, in an action brought in this country upon the judgment, be tried afresh, as on a new trial or an appeal, upon the mere assertion of the party that the judgment was erroneous in law or in fact. The defendants, therefore, cannot be permitted, upon that general ground, to contest the validity or the effect of the judgment sued on. [Emphasis added.]

But they have sought to impeach that judgment upon several other grounds, which require separate consideration.

It is objected that the appearance and litigation of the defendants in the French tribunals were not voluntary, but by legal compulsion, and, therefore, that the French courts never acquired such jurisdiction over the defendants that they should be held bound by the judgment.

Upon the question what should be considered such a voluntary appearance, as to amount to a submission to the jurisdiction of a foreign court, there has been some difference of opinion in England.

. . . .

But it is now settled in England that while an appearance by the defendant in a court of a foreign country, for the purpose of protecting his property already in the possession of that court, may not be deemed a voluntary appearance, yet an appearance solely for the purpose of protecting other property in that country from seizure is considered as a voluntary appearance. [Citations omitted.]

The present case is not one of a person travelling through or casually found in a foreign country. The defendants, although they were not citizens or residents of France, but were citizens and residents of the state of New York, and their principal place of business was in the city of New York, yet had a storehouse and an agent in Paris, and were accustomed to purchase large quantities of goods there, although they did not make sales in France. Under such circumstances, evidence that their sole object in appearing and carrying on the litigation in the French courts was to prevent property in their storehouse at Paris, belonging to them, and within the jurisdiction, but not in the custody, of those courts, from being taken in satisfaction of any judgment that might be recovered against them, would not, according to our law, show that those courts did not acquire jurisdiction of the persons of the defendants.

It is next objected that in those courts one of the plaintiffs was permitted to testify not under oath, and was not subjected to cross-examination by the opposite party, and that the defendants were therefore deprived of safeguards which are by our law considered essential to secure honesty and to detect fraud in a witness; and also that documents and papers were admitted in evidence, with which the defendants had no connection, and which would not be admissible under our own system of jurisprudence. But it having been shown by the plaintiffs, and hardly denied by the defendants, that the practice followed and the method of examining witnesses were according to the laws of France, we are not prepared to hold that the fact that the procedure in these respects differed from that of our own courts is, of itself, a sufficient ground for impeaching the foreign judgment.

It is also contended that a part of the plaintiffs' claim is affected by one of the contracts between the parties having been made in violation of the revenue laws of the United States, requiring goods to be invoiced at their actual market value. Rev. St. § 2854. It may be assumed that, as the courts of a country will not enforce contracts made abroad in evasion or fraud of its own laws, so they will not enforce a foreign judgment upon such a contract. [Citations omitted.] But as this point does not affect the whole claim in this case, it is sufficient, for present purposes, to say that there does not appear to have been any distinct offer to prove that the invoice value of any of the goods sold by the plaintiffs to the defendants was agreed between them to be, or was, in fact, lower than the actual market value of the goods.

It must, however, always be kept in mind that it is the paramount duty of the court before which any suit is brought to see to it that the parties have had a fair and impartial trial, before a final decision is rendered against either party.

When an action is brought in a court of this country, by a citizen of a foreign country against one of our own citizens, to recover a sum of money adjudged by a court of that country to be due from the defendant to the plaintiff, and the foreign judgment appears to have been rendered by a competent court, having jurisdiction of the cause and of the parties, and upon due allegations and proofs, and opportunity to defend against them, and its proceedings are according to the course of a civilized jurisprudence, and are stated in a clear and formal record, the judgment is prima facie evidence, at least, of the truth of the matter adjudged; and it should be held conclusive upon the merits tried in the foreign court, unless some special ground is shown for impeaching the judgment, as by showing that it was affected by fraud or prejudice, or that by the principles of international law, and by the comity of our own country, it should not be given full credit and effect.

There is no doubt that both in this country, as appears by the authorities already cited, and in England, a foreign judgment may be impeached for fraud.

. . . .

Under what circumstances this may be done does not appear to have ever been the subject of judicial investigation in this country.

It has often, indeed, been declared by this court that the fraud which entitles a party to impeach the judgment of one of our own tribunals must be fraud extrinsic to the matter tried in the cause, and not merely consist in false and fraudulent documents or testimony submitted to that tribunal, and the truth of which was contested before it and passed upon by it. . . .

But it is now established in England, by well-considered and strongly-reasoned decisions of the court of appeal, that foreign judgments may be impeached, if procured by false and fraudulent representations and testimony of the plaintiff, even if the same question of fraud was presented to and decided by the foreign court.

. . . .

In the case at bar the defendants offered to prove, in much detail, that the plaintiffs presented to the French court of first instance and to the arbitrator appointed by that court, and upon whose report its judgment was largely based, false and fraudulent statements and accounts against the defendants, by which the arbitrator and the French courts were deceived and misled, and their judgments were based upon such false and fraudulent statements and accounts. This offer, if satisfactorily proved, would, according to the decisions of the English court of appeal in *Aboulof v. Oppenheimer* [(1882)] 10 Q. B. Div. 295], *Vadala v. Lawes* [(1890) 25 Q. B. Div. 310, 317–320], and *Crozat v. Brogden* [(1894) 2 Q. B. 30], above cited, be a sufficient ground for impeaching the foreign judgment, and examining into the merits of the original claim.

But whether those decisions can be followed in regard to foreign judgments, consistently with our own decisions as to impeaching domestic judgments for fraud, it is unnecessary in this case to determine, because *there is a distinct and independent ground upon which we are satisfied that the comity of our nation does not require us to give conclusive effect to the judgments of the courts of France; and that ground is the want of reciprocity, on the part of France, as to the effect to be given to the judgments of this and other foreign countries.* [Emphasis added.]

In France, the royal ordinance of June 15, 1629 (article 121), provided as follows: "Judgments rendered, contracts or obligations recognized, in foreign kingdoms and sovereignties, for any cause whatever, shall have no lien or execution in our kingdom. Thus the contracts shall stand for simple promises; and, notwithstanding the judgments, our subjects against whom they have been rendered may contest their rights anew before our judges." Touillier, Droit Civil, lib. 3, tit. 3, c. 6, § 3, No. 77.

By the French Code of Civil Procedure (article 546), "judgments rendered by foreign tribunals, and acts acknowledged before foreign officers, shall not be capable of execution in France, except in the manner and in the cases provided by articles 2123 and 2128 of the Civil Code," which are as follows: By article 2123, "a lien cannot arise from judgments rendered in a foreign country, except so far as they have been declared executory by a French tribunal; without prejudice to provisions to the contrary which may exist in public laws and treaties." By article 2128, "contracts entered into in a foreign country cannot give a lien upon property in France, if there are no provisions contrary to this principle in public laws or in treaties." Touillier, *ubi supra*, No. 84.

The defendants, in their answer, cited the above provisions of the statutes of France, and alleged, and at the trial offered to prove, that by the construction given to these statutes by the judicial tribunals of France, when the judgments of tribunals of foreign countries against the citizens of France are sued upon in the courts of France, the merits of the controversies upon which those judgments are based are examined anew, unless a treaty to the contrary effect exists between the republic of France and the country in which such judgment is obtained (which is not the case between the republic of France and the United States), and that the tribunals of the republic of France give no force and effect, within the jurisdiction of that country, to the judgments duly rendered by courts of competent jurisdiction of the United States against citizens of France after proper personal service of the process of those courts has been made thereon in this country. We are of opinion that this evidence should have been admitted.

. . . .

By the law of France, settled by a series of uniform decisions of the court of cassation, the highest judicial tribunal, for more than half a century, no foreign judgment can be rendered executory in France without a review of the judgment au fond (to the bottom), including the whole merits of the cause of action on which the judgment rests. [Citations omitted.]

. . . .

. . . [T]here is hardly a civilized nation on either continent which, by its general law, allows conclusive effect to an executory foreign judgment for the recovery of money. In France and in a few smaller states — Norway, Portugal, Greece, Monaco, and Hayti — the merits of the controversy are reviewed, as of course, allowing to the foreign judgment, at the most, no more effect than of being prima facie evidence of the justice of the claim. In the great majority of the countries on the continent of Europe — in Belgium, Holland, Denmark, Sweden, Germany, in many cantons of Switzerland, in Russia and Poland, in Roumania, in Austria and Hungary (perhaps in Italy), and in Spain — as well as in Egypt, in Mexico, and in a great part of South America, the judgment rendered in a foreign country is allowed the same effect only as the courts of that country allow to the judgments of the country in which the judgment in question is sought to be executed.

The prediction of Mr. Justice Story in section 618 of his Commentaries on the Conflict of Laws, already cited, has thus been fulfilled, and the rule of reciprocity has worked itself firmly into the structure of international jurisprudence.

The reasonable, if not the necessary, conclusion appears to us to be that judgments rendered in France, or in any other foreign country, by the laws of which our own judgments are reviewable upon the merits, are not entitled to full credit and conclusive effect when sued upon in this country, but are prima facie evidence only of the justice of the plaintiffs' claim.

In holding such a judgment, for want of reciprocity, not to be conclusive evidence of the merits of the claim, we do not proceed upon any theory of retaliation upon one person by reason of injustice done to another, but upon the broad ground that international law is founded upon mutuality and reciprocity, and that by the principles of international law recognized in most civilized nations, and by the comity of our own country, which it is our judicial duty to known and to declare, the judgment is not entitled to be considered conclusive.

By our law, at the time of the adoption of the constitution, a foreign judgment was considered as prima facie evidence, and not conclusive. There is no statute of the United States, and no treaty of the United States with France, or with any other nation, which has changed that law, or has made any provision upon the subject. It is not to be supposed that, if any statute or treaty had been or should be made, it would recognize as conclusive the judgments of any country, which did not give like effect to our own judgments. In the absence of statute or treaty, it appears to us equally unwarrantable to assume that the comity of the United States requires anything more.

If we should hold this judgment to be conclusive, we should allow it an effect to which, supposing the defendants' offers to be sustained by actual proof, it would, in the absence of a special treaty, be entitled in hardly any other country in Christendom, except the country in which it was rendered. If the judgment had been rendered in this country, or in any other outside of the jurisdiction of France, the French courts would not have executed or enforced it, except after examining into its merits. The very judgment now sued on would be held inconclusive in almost any other country than France. In England, and in the colonies subject to the law of England, the fraud alleged in its procurement would be a sufficient ground for disregarding it. In the courts of nearly every other nation, it would be subject to re-examination, either merely because it was a foreign judgment, or because judgments of that nation would be reexaminable in the courts of France.

For these reasons, in the action at law, the Judgment is reversed, and the cause remanded to the circuit court, with directions to set aside the verdict and to order a new trial.

For the same reasons, in the suit in equity between these parties, the foreign judgment is not a bar, and therefore the

Decree dismissing the bill is reversed, the plea adjudged bad, and the cause remanded to the circuit court for further proceedings not inconsistent with this opinion.

Mr. Chief Justice Fuller, dissenting.

Plaintiffs brought their action on a judgment recovered by them against the defendants in the courts of France, which courts had jurisdiction over person and subject-matter, and in respect of which judgment no fraud was alleged, except in particulars contested in and considered by the French courts. The question is whether under these circumstances, and in the absence of a treaty or act of congress, the judgment is re-examinable upon the merits. This question I regard as one to be determined by the ordinary and settled rule in respect of allowing a party who has had an opportunity to prove his case in a competent court to retry it on the merits; and it seems to me that the doctrine of *res judicata* applicable to domestic judgments should be applied to foreign judgments as well, and rests on the same general ground of public policy, that there should be an end of litigation.

This application of the doctrine is in accordance with our own jurisprudence, and it is not necessary that we should hold it to be required by some rule of international law. The fundamental principle concerning judgments is that disputes are finally determined by them, and I am unable to perceive why a judgment *in personam*, which is not open to question on the ground of want of jurisdiction, either intrinsically or over the parties, or of fraud, or on any other recognized ground of impeachment, should not be held, *inter partes*, though recovered abroad, conclusive on the merits.

Judgments are executory while unpaid, but in this country execution is not given upon a foreign judgment as such, it being enforced through a new judgment obtained in an action brought for that purpose.

The principle that requires litigation to be treated as terminated by final judgment, properly rendered, is as applicable to a judgment proceeded on in such an action as to any other, and forbids the allowance to the judgment debtor of a retrial of the original cause of action, as of right, in disregard of the obligation to pay arising on the judgment, and of the rights acquired by the judgment creditor thereby.

That any other conclusion is inadmissible is forcibly illustrated by the case in hand. Plaintiffs in error were trading copartners in Paris as well as in New York, and had a place of business in Paris at the time of these transactions and of the commencement of the suit against them in France. The subjects of the suit were commercial transactions, having their origin, and partly performed, in France, under a contract there made, and alleged to be modified by the dealings of the parties there, and one of the claims against them was for goods sold to them there. They appeared generally in the case, without protest, and by counterclaims relating to the same general course of business, a part of them only connected with the claims against them, became actors in the suit, and submitted to the courts their own claims for affirmative relief, as well as the claims against them. The courts were competent, and they took the chances of a decision in their favor. As traders in France they were under the protection of its laws, and were bound by its laws, its commercial usages, and its rules of procedure. The fact that they were Americans and the opposite parties were citizens of France is immaterial, and there is no suggestion on the record that those courts proceeded on any other ground than that all litigants, whatever their nationality, were entitled to equal justice therein. If plaintiffs in error had succeeded in their cross suit and recovered judgment against defendants in error, and had sued them here on that judgment, defendants in error would not have been permitted to say that the judgment in France was not conclusive against them. As it was, defendants in error recovered, and I think plaintiffs in error are not entitled to try their fortune anew before the courts of this country on the same matters voluntarily submitted by them to the decision of the foreign tribunal. We are dealing with the judgment of a court of a civilized country, whose laws and system of justice recognize the general rules in respect to property and rights between man and man prevailing among all civilized peoples. Obviously, the last persons who should be heard to complain are those who identified themselves with the business of that country, knowing that all their transactions there would be subject to the local laws and modes of doing business. The French courts appear to have acted "judicially, honestly, and with the intention to arrive at the right conclusion," and a result thus reached ought not to be disturbed.

. . . .

In any aspect, it is difficult to see why rights acquired under foreign judgments do not belong to the category of private rights acquired under foreign laws. Now, the rule is universal in this country that private rights acquired under the laws of foreign states will be respected and enforced in our courts unless contrary to the policy or prejudicial to the interests of the state where this is sought to be done; and, although the source of this rule may have been the comity characterizing the intercourse between nations, it prevails to-day by its own strength, and the right to the application of the law to which the particular transaction is subject is a juridical right.

And, without going into the refinements of the publicists on the subject, it appears to me that that law finds authoritative expression in the judgments of courts of competent jurisdiction over parties and subject-matter.

. . . .

I cannot yield my assent to the proposition that, because by legislation and judicial decision in France that effect is not there given to judgments recovered in this country which, according to our jurisprudence, we think should be given to judgments wherever recovered (subject, of course, to the recognized exceptions), therefore we should pursue the same line of conduct as respects the judgments of French tribunals. The application of the doctrine of *res judicata* does not rest in discretion; and it is for the government, and not for its courts, to adopt the principle of retorsion, if deemed under any circumstances desirable or necessary.

As the court expressly abstains from deciding whether the judgment is impeachable on the ground of fraud, I refrain from any observations on that branch of the case.

MR. JUSTICE HARLAN, MR. JUSTICE BREWER, and MR. JUSTICE JACKSON concur in this dissent.

QUESTIONS

1. On what basis did the U.S. federal courts assert subject-matter jurisdiction over the recognition and enforcement of the two French judgments under review in *Hilton v. Guyot?*

2. What were the issues in the case? What did the Court hold and on what grounds?

We return now to *Ackermann v. Levine*, previously considered in connection with the Hague Service Convention in Chapter 4. Our concern here is the principal issue in the case — the recognition and enforcement of the default judgment of a Berlin court in favor of the German attorney, Ackermann, for legal services rendered to Levine in connection with a real estate project.

ACKERMANN v. LEVINE
788 F.2d 830 (2d Cir. 1986)

Pierce, Circuit Judge:

This is an appeal from a judgment and final order of the United States District Court for the Southern District of New York, Irving Ben Cooper, Judge, entered May 20, 1985, 610 F.Supp. 633, following an enforcement proceeding, holding unenforceable the default judgment issued by the Regional Court of Berlin in West Germany on December 12, 1980 in favor of plaintiffs and against defendant for 190,708.49 deutschemarks (DM), or approximately $100,000, plus interest, for legal fees allegedly owed by appellee.

Appellants argue that the district court erred in ruling that . . . (2) enforcement of the German default judgment for legal fees charged under the German fee statute and upheld by the German court would violate the public policy concern of New York courts that attorneys seeking recovery of fees "bear the burden of proving that a compensation arrangement is fair, reasonable and fully comprehended by the client." *Ackermann v. Levine*, 610 F.Supp. 633 (S.D.N.Y. 1985) (hereinafter cited as "Op."), at 647.

We hold that . . . enforcement of the German default judgment would not violate New York public policy to the extent that the judgment reflects an award of attorneys fees for which the attorney presented in the enforcement proceeding, at a minimum, evidence of client authorization and appropriate work product.

We therefore affirm in part and reverse in part.

Discussion

We are confronted here with issues relating to the recognition and enforcement of a foreign judgment in a case involving attorney-client relations in an international business context. The district court appropriately framed the issues in accordance with the well-settled rule that a final judgment obtained through sound procedures in a foreign country is generally conclusive as to its merits unless (1) the foreign court lacked jurisdiction over the subject matter or the person of the defendant; (2) the judgment was fraudulently obtained; or (3) enforcement of the judgment would offend the public policy of the state in which enforcement is sought. [Citations omitted.]

. . . .

II.

There is no basis to believe that the German judgment was fraudulently obtained. Defendant-appellee has offered no basis for us to question the district court's finding of fact that "neither plaintiffs nor defendant acted dishonestly," Op. at 646, or the court's corollary conclusion of law that the German judgment was not fraudulently obtained. *Id.* at 646, citing *Fairchild*, 470 F. Supp. at 615 (alleged fraud "must relate to matters other than issues that could have been litigated and must be a fraud on the court") (quoting *Overmyer v. Eliot Realty*, 83 Misc. 2d 694, 371 N.Y.S.2d 246, 258 (Sup. Ct. Westchester Co. 1975)).

III.

The district court held that, based on the undisputed fact that Ackermann never discussed fees with Levine, the German judgment was rendered unenforceable as violative of New York's public policy that "the attorney, not the client, must ensure the fairness, reasonableness and full comprehension by the client of their compensation agreement." See Op. at 646–647 (citing New York cases). On that basis, the district court declined enforcement of the entire award of approximately $100,000.

A judgment is unenforceable as against public policy to the extent that it is "repugnant to fundamental notions of what is decent and just in the State where enforcement is sought." *Tahan v. Hodgson*, 662 F.2d 862, 864 (D.C. Cir. 1981) (quoting Rest. 2d Conflict of Laws § 117, comment c (1971)). The standard is high, and infrequently met. In the classic formulation, a judgment that "tends clearly" to undermine the public interest . . . [citations and references omitted] the public confidence in the administration of the law, or security for individual rights of personal liberty or of private property is against public policy. [Citations omitted.]

The narrowness of the public policy exception to enforcement would seem to reflect an axiom fundamental to the goals of comity and res judicata that underlie the doctrine of recognition and enforcement of foreign judgments. As Judge Cardozo so lucidly observed: "We are not so provincial as to say that every solution of a problem is wrong because we deal with it otherwise at home." *Loucks*, 224 N.Y. at 110–11. Further, the narrowness of the public policy exception indicates a jurisprudential compromise between two guiding but sometimes conflicting principles in the law of recognition and enforcement of foreign judgments: (1) res judicata [reference omitted] and (2) fairness to litigants [reference omitted] or fairness regarding the underlying transaction [reference omitted].

The question presented here involves the extent to which local public policy will permit recognition and enforcement of a foreign default judgment. Since a foreign default judgment is not more or less conclusive but "as conclusive an adjudication" as a contested judgment, *Somportex*, 453 F.2d at 442–43 & n.13 . . . the district court quite properly afforded Levine the same opportunity to contest the enforceability of the German judgment in light of the public policy issue. We disagree with dicta in *Tahan*, 662 F.2d at 867, suggesting that a defendant may not raise a public policy defense once he has defaulted in the foreign adjudication. By defaulting, a defendant ensures that a judgment will be entered against him, and assumes the risk that an irrevocable mistake of law or fact may underlie that judgment. [Citations omitted.] We see no reason to further penalize such a defendant, or to forsake the legitimate public policy interests of the state in which enforcement is sought.

However, we believe that the district court erred in holding that the failure of German law regarding attorneys fees to meet our more rigorous principles of fiduciary duties sufficiently offended local public policy as to justify nonenforcement of the entire judgment, and thus total vitiation of the values of comity and *res judicata* that enforcement would promote. We so hold in light of the consistency with which *stare decisis* has followed Judge Cardozo's maxim, *Loucks*, 224 N.Y. at 110–11, 120 N.E. 198, that mere variance with local public policy is not sufficient to decline enforcement.

The narrow public policy exception to enforcement is not met merely because Ackermann did not inform Levine of the BRAGO billing statute. . . . Nor can we say that the German judgment is unenforceable because the attorney-client relationship herein was not structured commensurate with the New York policy favoring, though not requiring, written retainer agreements. It is not enough merely that a foreign judgment fails to fulfill domestic practice or policy. [Citation omitted.]

We hold that the public policy that charges an American lawyer with ensuring fair and reasonable compensation, fully disclosed to and understood by the client, does not warrant nonenforcement of the German judgment, given that there was no finding of "fraud, overreaching or bad faith" on the part of Ackermann, the foreign lawyer, cf. *Spann*, 131 F.2d at 611, and that Levine, the American client, was a sophisticated business person with access to competent American international legal counsel. . . . Germany's choice to regulate attorneys fees by statute rather than by fiduciary principles, and to vest the Regional Courts with jurisdiction to ensure the proper application of the BRAGO statute, did not lead to treatment of Levine that could be considered so "repugnant to fundamental notions of what is decent and just," *Tahan*, 662 F.2d at 864, as to warrant nonenforcement of the default judgment in its entirety.

Thus, we think that the district court erred in holding the judgment unenforceable as offensive to New York's public policy that lawyers discharge their fiduciary duty to ensure fair and reasonable fees, fully disclosed to and understood by their clients. However, that this broad, fiduciary-based public policy does not render the judgment unenforceable does not preclude the possibility that a narrower, evidentiary-based public policy might render the judgment unenforceable.

We hold that the applicable theory of public policy requires that recovery of attorneys fees be predicated on evidence of, at a minimum, (1) the existence of some authorization by the client for the attorney to perform the work allegedly performed [citations omitted] and (2) the very existence of that work [citations omitted]. These evidentiary predicates, we hold, constitute the sine qua non of a client's liability for legal fees. Without these predicates, there is a grave risk that American courts could become the means of enforcing unconscionable attorney fee awards, thereby endangering "public confidence" in the administration of the law and a "sense of security for individual rights . . . of private property." *Somportex*, 453 F.2d at 443. . . .

In applying this evidentiary-based public policy, we note that courts are not limited to recognizing a judgment entirely or not at all. Where a foreign judgment contains discrete components, the enforcing court should endeavor to discern the appropriate "extent of recognition," cf. 18 C. Wright & A. Miller, *Federal Practice and Procedure* § 4473, at 745 (1981), with reference to applicable public policy concerns.

Ackermann has laid the predicate in support of his bill for "detailed discussions with prospective buyers" and for the related travel and office expenses, but he has not done so for the "basic fee for the study of the project files, [and] discussion with client and his counsel." As for the discussions and related expenses, there was evidence of authorization in Levine's letter to Ackermann of June 8, 1979 and his telephone response to Ackermann's telex of June 14, 1979, confirming authorization as to the second bank. There was undisputed evidence that Ackermann did negotiate with representatives from the two banks in West Berlin and Frankfurt.

Recognition of the foreign judgment to this extent is consonant with the evidence that Levine engaged Ackermann's services and benefited therefrom. Although it was not Levine who brought suit in Germany, he did invoke the law of that nation by seeking counsel with a view toward negotiating a contract with German investors. Levine clearly would have benefited from German law had his work with Ackermann proved fruitful. . . . He thus "finds himself in the quite unenviable position of trying to take the good without the bad, the sweet without the bitter." *Spann*, 131 F.2d at 611.

As to the fifteen to twenty days of work that comprise the bulk of the "basic fee for study of the project files," the record reflects no evidence of an authorization to do such work or of the existence of any work product. The mere fact that Ackermann possessed the project files is inconsequential since Levine did not know that Bauer had given those files to Ackermann. Nor do we find authorization in the office visit of late May or early June, 1978, since the district court found that visit had accomplished only the creation of a misunderstanding. Even if there had been an authorization, there was not a scintilla of evidence of work product. Ackermann offered no client memoranda, no memoranda to his files, no handwritten notes, no markings on the papers that Bauer had given him, and no other indicia of actual performance. Indeed, when his deposition was taken, Ackermann conceded that he prepared no formal memoranda and that he did not believe that there was any work product whatsoever in his files. We do not challenge the district court's finding as to Ackermann's character. However, we need not say that an attorney acted fraudulently or dishonestly to hold, as we do here, that the failure to adduce any evidence of work product requires disallowance of claimed legal fees [citation omitted].

IV. Conclusion

This case involved an unfortunate disagreement between parties of different countries and legal cultures. As the district court found, both parties behaved honorably, and their dispute was born of mutual mistake. Although the defendant chose to default in a German action commenced by valid service of process, he did not thereby waive his right to contest the enforceability of the foreign judgment on grounds of public policy. The increasing internationalization of commerce requires "that American courts recognize and respect the judgments entered by foreign courts to the greatest extent consistent with our own ideals of justice and fair play." *Tahan*, 662 F.2d at 868. In light of that important imperative, we hold the German judgment to be enforceable in all respects except for the first item of DM 89.347,50 for the "[b]asic fee for the study of project files, discussion with client and his counsel," for which there was no evidence of authorization or of work product. The judgment of the district court is accordingly, affirmed in part and reversed in part, and the cause is remanded to the district court for entry of an order not inconsistent with this opinion.

QUESTIONS

1. What was the basis of the jurisdiction of the U.S. District Court for the Southern District of New York in *Ackermann v. Levine?*

2. What was the source of the applicable legal rules and standards for recognition and enforcement of the German judgment?

3. What accounts for the differences in both the basis for jurisdiction and applicable law between *Hilton v. Guyot* and *Ackermann v. Levine?*

4. How do the two cases otherwise differ?

Given the presumptive applicability of state law since the U.S. Supreme Court's decision in *Erie Railroad Co. v. Tompkins*, 304 U.S. 64 (1938), state law rather than "customary private international law" is applied in cases involving the recognition and enforcement of foreign country judgments brought in federal courts on the basis of diversity jurisdiction. Thus in 1948 and 1962 the National Conference of Commissioners on Uniform State Laws (NCCUSL) drafted and proposed a statute to achieve uniformity in the applicable rules and standards applied to the recognition and enforcement of foreign-country judgments within the United States. Albeit with occasional modifying amendment, as we will observe *infra* with respect to Texas, the 1962 act has been adopted in all states (as well as the District of Columbia and the Virgin Islands) except Indiana, Massachusetts, and Vermont. In 2005 the NCCUSL proposed a revised statute (enacted in at least 17 states and the District of Columbia as of 2014), as described below:

UNIFORM FOREIGN-COUNTRY JUDGMENTS RECOGNITION ACT (2005)

The National Conference of Commissioners on Uniform State Laws

In 1962, the Uniform Law Commissioners promulgated the Uniform Foreign Money-Judgments Recognition Act. It is a companion to the 1948 (amended in 1962) Uniform Enforcement of Foreign Judgments Act. In spite of the similarities in titles, these acts deal with quite different problems of judgment enforcement. The Enforcement of Foreign Judgments Act provides for enforcement of a state court judgment in another state to implement the Full Faith and Credit clause of the U.S. Constitution. The Foreign Money-Judgments Recognition Act provided for enforcement of foreign country judgments in a state court in the United States. The 1962 Uniform Foreign Money-Judgments Recognition act has been enacted in 32 states.

The increase in international trade in the United States has also meant more litigation in the interstate context. This means more judgments to be enforced from country to country. There is a strong need for uniformity between states with respect to the law governing foreign country money-judgments. If foreign country judgments are not enforced appropriately and uniformly, it may make enforcement of the judgments of American courts more difficult in foreign country courts. To meet the increased needs for enforcement of foreign country money-judgments, the Uniform Law Commissioners have promulgated a revision of the 1962 Uniform Act with the 2005 Uniform Foreign-Country Money Judgments Recognition Act (UFCMJRA).

The first step towards enforcement is recognition of the foreign country judgment. The recognition occurs in a state court when an appropriate action is filed for the purpose. If the judgment meets the statutory standards, the state court will recognize it. It then may be enforced as if it is a judgment of another state of the United States. Enforcement may then proceed, which means the judgment creditor may proceed against the property of the judgment debtor to satisfy the judgment amount.

First, it must be shown that the judgment is conclusive, final and enforceable in the country of origin. Certain money judgments are excluded, such as judgments on taxes, fines or criminal-like penalties and judgments relating to domestic relations. Domestic relations judgments are enforced under other statutes, already existing in every state. A foreign-country judgment must not be recognized if it comes from a court system that is not impartial or that dishonors due process, or there is no personal jurisdiction over the defendant or over the subject matter of the litigation. There are a number of grounds that may make a U.S. court deny recognition, i.e., the defendant did not receive notice of the proceeding or the claim is repugnant to American public policy. A final, conclusive judgment enforceable in the country of origin, if it is not excluded for one of the enumerated reasons, must be recognized and enforced. The 1962 Act and the 2005 Act generally operate the same.

The primary differences between the 1962 and the 2005 Uniform Acts are as follows:

1. The 2005 Act makes it clear that a judgment entitled to full faith and credit under the U.S. Constitution is not enforceable under this Act. This clarifies the relationship between the Foreign-Country Money Judgments Act and the Enforcement of Foreign Judgments Act. Recognition by a court is a different procedure than enforcement of a sister state judgment from within the United States.

2. The 2005 Act expressly provides that a party seeking recognition of a foreign judgment has the burden to prove that the judgment is subject to the Uniform Act. Burden of proof was not addressed in the 1962 Act.

3. Conversely, the 2005 Act imposes the burden of proof for establishing a specific ground for non-recognition upon the party raising it. Again, burden of proof is not addressed in the 1962 Act.

4. The 2005 Act addresses the specific procedure for seeking enforce-

ment. If recognition is sought as an original matter, the party seeking recognition must file an action in the court to obtain recognition. If recognition is sought in a pending action, it may be filed as a counter-claim, cross-claim or affirmative defense in the pending action. The 1962 Act does not address the procedure to obtain recognition at all, leaving that to other state law.

5. The 2005 Act provides a statute of limitations on enforcement of a foreign-country judgment. If the judgment cannot be enforced any longer in the country of origin, it may not be enforced in a court of an enacting state. If there is no limitation on enforcement in the country of origin, the judgment becomes unenforceable in an enacting state after 15 years from the time the judgment is effective in the country of origin.

These are the principal advances of the 2005 Act over the 1962 Act. The 2005 Act is not a radically new act. It builds upon the tried principles of the 1962 Act in a necessary upgrade for the 21st Century. It should be enacted in every state as soon as possible. If substantial uniformity is not gained within the foreseeable future, Congress may preempt the recognition and enforcement law.

SECTION 4. STANDARDS FOR RECOGNITION OF FOREIGN-COUNTRY JUDGMENT.

(a) Except as otherwise provided in subsections (b) and (c), a court of this state shall recognize a foreign-country judgment to which this [act] applies.

(b) A court of this state may not recognize a foreign-country judgment if:

(1) the judgment was rendered under a judicial system that does not provide impartial tribunals or procedures compatible with the requirements of due process of law;

(2) the foreign court did not have personal jurisdiction over the defendant; or

(3) the foreign court did not have jurisdiction over the subject matter.

(c) A court of this state need not recognize a foreign-country judgment if:

(1) the defendant in the proceeding in the foreign court did not receive notice of the proceeding in sufficient time to enable the defendant to defend;

(2) the judgment was obtained by fraud that deprived the losing party of an adequate opportunity to present its case;

(3) the judgment or the [cause of action] [claim for relief] on which the judgment is based is repugnant to the public policy of this state or of the United States;

(4) the judgment conflicts with another final and conclusive judgment;

(5) the proceeding in the foreign court was contrary to an agreement

between the parties under which the dispute in question was to be determined otherwise than by proceedings in that foreign court;

(6) in the case of jurisdiction based only on personal service, the foreign court was a seriously inconvenient forum for the trial of the action;

(7) the judgment was rendered in circumstances that raise substantial doubt about the integrity of the rendering court with respect to the judgment; or

(8) the specific proceeding in the foreign court leading to the judgment was not compatible with the requirements of due process of law.

(d) A party resisting recognition of a foreign-country judgment has the burden of establishing that a ground for nonrecognition stated in subsection (b) or (c) exists.

Comment

Source: This section is based on Section 4 of the 1962 Act.

1. This Section provides the standards for recognition of a foreign-country money judgment. Section 7 sets out the effect of recognition of a foreign-country money judgment under this Act.

2. Recognition of a judgment means that the forum court accepts the determination of legal rights and obligations made by the rendering court in the foreign country. *See, e.g.* Restatement (Second) of Conflicts of Laws, Ch. 5, Topic 3, Introductory Note (recognition of foreign judgment occurs to the extent the forum court gives the judgment "the same effect with respect to the parties, the subject matter of the action and the issues involved that it has in the state where it was rendered.") Recognition of a foreign-country judgment must be distinguished from enforcement of that judgment. Enforcement of the foreign-country judgment involves the application of the legal procedures of the state to ensure that the judgment debtor obeys the foreign-country judgment. Recognition of a foreign-country money judgment often is associated with enforcement of the judgment, as the judgment creditor usually seeks recognition of the foreign-country judgment primarily for the purpose of invoking the enforcement procedures of the forum state to assist the judgment creditor's collection of the judgment from the judgment debtor. Because the forum court cannot enforce the foreign-country judgment until it has determined that the judgment will be given effect, recognition is a prerequisite to enforcement of the foreign-country judgment. Recognition, however, also has significance outside the enforcement context because a foreign-country judgment also must be recognized before it can be given preclusive effect under res judicata and collateral estoppel principles. The issue of whether a foreign-country judgment will be recognized is distinct from both the issue of whether the judgment will be enforced, and the issue of the extent to which it will be given preclusive effect.

3. Subsection 4(a) places an affirmative duty on the forum court to recognize a foreign-country money judgment unless one of the grounds for nonrecognition stated in subsection (b) or (c) applies. Subsection (b) states three mandatory grounds for denying recognition to a foreign-country money judgment. If the forum court finds that one of the grounds listed in subsection (b) exists, then it must deny recognition to the foreign-country money judgment. Subsection (c) states eight nonmandatory grounds for denying recognition. The forum court has discretion to decide whether or not to refuse recognition based on one of these grounds. Subsection (d) places the burden of proof on the party resisting recognition of the foreign-country judgment to establish that one of the grounds for nonrecognition exists.

4. The mandatory grounds for nonrecognition stated in subsection (b) are identical to the mandatory grounds stated in Section 4 of the 1962 Act. The discretionary grounds stated in subsection 4(c)(1) through (6) are based on subsection 4(b)(1) through (6) of the 1962 Act. The discretionary grounds stated in subsection 4(c)(7) and (8) are new.

5. Under subsection (b)(1), the forum court must deny recognition to the foreign-country money judgment if that judgment was "rendered under a judicial system that does not provide impartial tribunals or procedures compatible with the requirements of due process of law." The standard for this ground for nonrecognition "has been stated authoritatively by the Supreme Court of the United States in *Hilton v. Guyot*, 159 U.S.113, 205 (1895). As indicated in that decision, a mere difference in the procedural system is not a sufficient basis for nonrecognition. A case of serious injustice must be involved." Cmt § 4, Uniform Foreign Money-Judgment Recognition Act (1962). The focus of inquiry is not whether the procedure in the rendering country is similar to U.S. procedure, but rather on the basic fairness of the foreign-country procedure. Kam-Tech Systems, Ltd. v. Yardeni, 774 A.2d 644, 649 (N.J. App. 2001) (interpreting the comparable provision in the 1962 Act); *accord*, Society of Lloyd's v. Ashenden, 233 F.3d 473 (7th Cir. 2000) (procedures need not meet all the intricacies of the complex concept of due process that has emerged from U.S. case law, but rather must be fair in the broader international sense) (interpreting comparable provision in the 1962 Act). Procedural differences, such as absence of jury trial or different evidentiary rules are not sufficient to justify denying recognition under subsection (b)(1), so long as the essential elements of impartial administration and basic procedural fairness have been provided in the foreign proceeding. As the U.S. Supreme Court stated in *Hilton*:

Where there has been opportunity for a full and fair trial abroad before a court of competent jurisdiction conducting the trial upon regular proceedings, after due citation or voluntary appearance of the defendant, and under a system of jurisprudence likely to secure an impartial administration of justice between the citizens of its own country and those of other countries, and there is nothing to show either prejudice in the court, or in the system of laws under which it was sitting, or fraud in procuring the judgment, or any other special reason why the comity of this nation should not allow it full effect then a foreign-country judgment should be recognized. *Hilton*, 159 U.S. at 202.

6. Under section 4(b)(2), the forum court must deny recognition to the foreign-country judgment if the foreign court did not have personal jurisdiction over the defendant. Section 5(a) lists six bases for personal jurisdiction that are adequate as a matter of law to establish that the foreign court had personal jurisdiction. Section 5(b) makes clear that other grounds for personal jurisdiction may be found sufficient.

7. Subsection 4(c)(2) limits the type of fraud that will serve as a ground for denying recognition to extrinsic fraud. This provision is consistent with the interpretation of the comparable provision in subsection 4(b)(2) of the 1962 Act by the courts, which have found that only extrinsic fraud — conduct of the prevailing party that deprived the losing party of an adequate opportunity to present its case — is sufficient under the 1962 Act. Examples of extrinsic fraud would be when the plaintiff deliberately had the initiating process served on the defendant at the wrong address, deliberately gave the defendant wrong information as to the time and place of the hearing, or obtained a default judgment against the defendant based on a forged confession of judgment. When this type of fraudulent action by the plaintiff deprives the defendant of an adequate opportunity to present its case, then it provides grounds for denying recognition of the foreign-country judgment. Extrinsic fraud should be distinguished from intrinsic fraud, such as false testimony of a witness or admission of a forged document into evidence during the foreign proceeding. Intrinsic fraud does not provide a basis for denying recognition under subsection 4(c)(2), as the assertion that intrinsic fraud has occurred should be raised and dealt with in the rendering court.

8. The public policy exception in subsection 4(c)(3) is based on the public policy exception in subsection 4(b)(3) of the 1962 Act, with one difference. The public policy exception in the 1962 Act states that the relevant inquiry is whether "the [cause of action] [claim for relief] on which the judgment is based" is repugnant to public policy. Based on this "cause of action" language, some courts interpreting the 1962 Act have refused to find that a public policy challenge based on something other than repugnancy of the foreign cause of action comes within this exception. *E.g.*, Southwest Livestock & Trucking Co., Inc. v. Ramon, 169 F.3d 317 (5th Cir. 1999) (refusing to deny recognition to Mexican judgment on promissory note with interest rate of 48% because cause of action to collect on promissory note does not violate public policy); Guinness PLC v. Ward, 955 F.2d 875 (4th Cir. 1992) (challenge to recognition based on post-judgment settlement could not be asserted under public policy exception); The Society of Lloyd's v. Turner, 303 F.3d 325 (5th Cir. 2002) (rejecting argument legal standards applied to establish elements of breach of contract violated public policy because cause of action for breach of contract itself is not contrary to state public policy); *cf.* Bachchan v. India Abroad Publications, Inc., 585 N.Y.S.2d 661 (N.Y. Sup. Ct. 1992) (judgment creditor argued British libel judgment

should be recognized despite argument it violated First Amendment because New York recognizes a cause of action for libel). Subsection 4(c)(3) rejects this narrow focus by providing that the forum court may deny recognition if either the cause of action or the judgment itself violates public policy. *Cf.* Restatement (Third) of the Foreign Relations Law of the United States, § 482(2)(d) (1986) (containing a similarly-worded public policy exception to recognition).

Although subsection 4(c)(3) of this Act rejects the narrow focus on the cause of action under the 1962 Act, it retains the stringent test for finding a public policy violation applied by courts interpreting the 1962 Act. Under that test, a difference in law, even a marked one, is not sufficient to raise a public policy issue. Nor is it relevant that the foreign law allows a recovery that the forum state would not allow. Public policy is violated only if recognition or enforcement of the foreign-country judgment would tend clearly to injure the public health, the public morals, or the public confidence in the administration of law, or would undermine "that sense of security for individual rights, whether of personal liberty or of private property, which any citizen ought to feel." Hunt v. BP Exploration Co. (Libya), Ltd., 492 F.Supp. 885, 901 (N.D. Tex. 1980).

The language "or of the United States" in subsection 4(c)(3), which does not appear in the 1962 Act provision, makes it clear that the relevant public policy is that of both the State in which recognition is sought and that of the United States. This is the position taken by the vast majority of cases interpreting the 1962 public policy provision. *E.g.*, Bachchan v. India Abroad Publications, Inc., 585 N.Y.S.2d 661 (Sup.Ct. N.Y. 1992) (British libel judgment denied recognition because it violates First Amendment).

9. Subsection 4(c)(5) allows the forum court to refuse recognition of a foreign-country judgment when the parties had a valid agreement, such as a valid forum selection clause or agreement to arbitrate, providing that the relevant dispute would be resolved in a forum other than the forum issuing the foreign-country judgment. Under this provision, the forum court must find both the existence of a valid agreement and that the agreement covered the subject matter involved in the foreign litigation resulting in the foreign-country judgment.

10. Subsection 4(c)(6) authorizes the forum court to refuse recognition of a foreign-country judgment that was rendered in the foreign country solely on the basis of personal service when the forum court believes the original action should have been dismissed by the court in the foreign country on grounds of *forum non conveniens*.

11. Subsection 4(c)(7) is new. Under this subsection, the forum court may deny recognition to a foreign-country judgment if there are circumstances that raise substantial doubt about the integrity of the rendering court with respect to that judgment. It requires a showing of corruption in the particular case that had an impact on the judgment that was rendered. This provision may be contrasted with subsection 4(b)(1), which requires that the forum court refuse recognition to the foreign-country judgment if it was

rendered under a judicial system that does not provide impartial tribunals. Like the comparable provision in subsection 4(a)(1) of the 1962 Act, subsection 4(b)(1) focuses on the judicial system of the foreign country as a whole, rather than on whether the particular judicial proceeding leading to the foreign-country judgment was impartial and fair. *See, e.g.*, The Society of Lloyd's v. Turner, 303 F.3d 325, 330 (5th Cir. 2002) (interpreting the 1962 Act); CIBC Mellon Trust Co. v. Mora Hotel Corp. N.V., 743 N.Y.S.2d 408, 415 (N.Y. App. 2002) (interpreting the 1962 Act); Society of Lloyd's v. Ashenden, 233 F.3d 473, 477 (7th Cir. 2000) (interpreting the 1962 Act). On the other hand, subsection 4(c)(7) allows the court to deny recognition to the foreign-country judgment if it finds a lack of impartiality and fairness of the tribunal in the individual proceeding leading to the foreign-country judgment. Thus, the difference is that between showing, for example, that corruption and bribery is so prevalent throughout the judicial system of the foreign country as to make that entire judicial system one that does not provide impartial tribunals versus showing that bribery of the judge in the proceeding that resulted in the particular foreign-country judgment under consideration had a sufficient impact on the ultimate judgment as to call it into question.

12. Subsection 4(c)(8) also is new. It allows the forum court to deny recognition to the foreign-country judgment if the court finds that the specific proceeding in the foreign court was not compatible with the requirements of fundamental fairness. Like subsection 4(c)(7), it can be contrasted with subsection 4(b)(1), which requires the forum court to deny recognition to the foreign-country judgment if the forum court finds that the entire judicial system in the foreign country where the foreign-country judgment was rendered does not provide procedures compatible with the requirements of fundamental fairness. While the focus of subsection 4(b)(1) is on the foreign country's judicial system as a whole, the focus of subsection 4(c)(8) is on the particular proceeding that resulted in the specific foreign-country judgment under consideration. Thus, the difference is that between showing, for example, that there has been such a breakdown of law and order in the particular foreign country that judgments are rendered on the basis of political decisions rather than the rule of law throughout the judicial system versus a showing that for political reasons the particular party against whom the foreign-country judgment was entered was denied fundamental fairness in the particular proceedings leading to the foreign-country judgment.

Subsections 4(c)(7) and (8) both are discretionary grounds for denying recognition, while subsection 4(b)(1) is mandatory. Obviously, if the entire judicial system in the foreign country fails to satisfy the requirements of impartiality and fundamental fairness, a judgment rendered in that foreign country would be so compromised that the forum court should refuse to recognize it as a matter of course. On the other hand, if the problem is evidence of a lack of integrity or fundamental fairness with regard to the particular proceeding leading to the foreign-country judgment, then there may or may not be other factors in the particular case that would cause the forum court to decide to recognize the foreign-country judgment. For example, a forum court might decide not to exercise its discretion to deny recognition despite evidence of corruption or procedural unfairness in a particular case because the party resisting recognition failed to raise the issue on appeal from the foreign-country judgment in the foreign country, and the evidence establishes that, if the party had done so, appeal would have been an adequate mechanism for correcting the transgressions of the lower court.

13. Under subsection 4(d), the party opposing recognition of the foreign-country judgment has the burden of establishing that one of the grounds for nonrecognition set out in subsection 4(b) or (c) applies. The 1962 Act was silent as to who had the burden of proof to establish a ground for nonrecognition and courts applying the 1962 Act took different positions on the issue. *Compare* Bridgeway Corp. v. Citibank, 45 F. Supp. 2d 276, 285 (S.D.N.Y. 1999) (plaintiff has burden to show no mandatory basis under 4(a) for nonrecognition exists; defendant has burden regarding discretionary bases) *with* The Courage Co. LLC v. The ChemShare Corp., 93 S.W.3d 323, 331 (Tex. App. 2002) (party seeking to avoid recognition has burden to prove ground for nonrecognition). Because the grounds for nonrecognition in Section 4 are in the nature of defenses to recognition, the burden of proof is most appropriately allocated to the party opposing recognition of the foreign-country judgment.

(b) The list of bases for personal jurisdiction in subsection (a) is not exclusive. The courts of this state may recognize bases of personal jurisdiction other than those listed in subsection(a) as sufficient to support a foreign-country judgment.

SECTION 5. PERSONAL JURISDICTION.

(a) A foreign-country judgment may not be refused recognition for lack of personal jurisdiction if:

(1) the defendant was served with process personally in the foreign country;

(2) the defendant voluntarily appeared in the proceeding, other than for the purpose of protecting property seized or threatened with seizure in the proceeding or of contesting the jurisdiction of the court over the defendant;

(3) the defendant, before the commencement of the proceeding, had agreed to submit to the jurisdiction of the foreign court with respect to the subject matter involved;

(4) the defendant was domiciled in the foreign country when the proceeding was instituted or was a corporation or other form of business organization that had its principal place of business in, or was organized under the laws of, the foreign country;

(5) the defendant had a business office in the foreign country and the

proceeding in the foreign court involved a [cause of action] [claim for relief] arising out of business done by the defendant through that office in the foreign country; or

(6) the defendant operated a motor vehicle or airplane in the foreign country and the proceeding involved a [cause of action] [claim for relief] arising out of that operation.

(b) The list of bases for personal jurisdiction in subsection (a) is not exclusive. The courts of this state may recognize bases of personal jurisdiction other than those listed in subsection(a) as sufficient to support a foreign-country judgment.

Comment

Source: This provision is based on Section 5 of the 1962 Act. Its substance is the same as that of Section 5 of the 1962 Act, except as noted in Comment 2 below with regard to subsection 5(a)(4).

1. Under section 4(b)(2), the forum court must deny recognition to the foreign-country judgment if the foreign court did not have personal jurisdiction over the defendant. Section 5(a) lists six bases for personal jurisdiction that are adequate as a matter of law to establish that the foreign court had personal jurisdiction. Section 5(b) makes it clear that these bases of personal jurisdiction are not exclusive. The forum court may find that the foreign court had personal jurisdiction over the defendant on some other basis.

2. Subsection 5(a)(4) of the 1962 Act provides that the foreign court had personal jurisdiction over the defendant if the defendant was "a body corporate" that "had its principal place of business, was incorporated, or had otherwise acquired corporate status, in the foreign state." Subsection 5(a)(4) of this Act extends that concept to forms of business organization other than corporations.

3. Subsection 5(a)(3) provides that the foreign court has personal jurisdiction over the defendant if the defendant agreed before commencement of the proceeding leading to the foreign-country judgment to submit to the jurisdiction of the foreign court with regard to the subject matter involved. Under this provision, the forum court must find both the existence of a valid agreement to submit to the foreign court's jurisdiction and that the agreement covered the subject matter involved in the foreign litigation resulting in the foreign-country judgment.

AMERICAN LAW INSTITUTE (ALI), PROPOSED FEDERAL FOREIGN JUDGMENTS RECOGNITION AND ENFORCEMENT ACT

Also in 2005 the American Law Institute (ALI) recommended a Federal Foreign Judgments Recognition and Enforcement Act. The proposed statute includes the following standards for recognition of foreign-country judgments:

§ 5 Nonrecognition of a Foreign Judgment

(a) A foreign judgment shall not be recognized or enforced in a court in the United States if the party resisting recognition or enforcement establishes that:

(i) the judgment was rendered under a system that does not provide impartial tribunals or procedures compatible with fundamental principles of fairness;

(ii) the judgment was rendered in circumstances that raise substantial and justifiable doubt about the integrity of the rendering court with respect to the judgment in question;

(iii) the judgment was rendered on a basis of jurisdiction over the defendant unacceptable under § 6;

(iv) the judgment was rendered without notice reasonably calculated to inform the defendant of the pendency of the proceeding in a timely manner;

(v) the judgment was obtained by fraud that had the effect of depriving the defendant of adequate opportunity to present its case to the court; or

(vi) the judgment or the claim on which the judgment is based is repugnant to the public policy of the United States, or to the public policy of a particular state of the United States when the relevant legal interest, right, or policy is regulated by state law.

(b) (i) Except as provided in subsection (ii), a foreign judgment shall not be recognized or enforced in a court in the United States if the party resisting recognition or enforcement establishes that the judgment resulted from a proceeding undertaken contrary to an agreement under which the dispute was to be determined exclusively in another forum.

(ii) If the party resisting recognition or enforcement participated in the proceeding before the rendering court without raising the defense of the forum-selection agreement, or if the party resisting recognition or enforcement raised the defense of the forum-selection agreement and the rendering court held that the agreement was inapplicable or invalid, the judgment shall not be denied recognition under subsection (i), unless the law of the state of origin rejects all forum-selection agreements or the determination of invalidity of the particular agreement was manifestly unreasonable.

(c) A foreign judgment need not be recognized or enforced in a court in the United States if the party resisting recognition or enforcement establishes that:

(i) the state of origin of the court that issued the foreign judgment did not have jurisdiction to prescribe, or the foreign court was not competent to adjudicate, with respect to the subject matter of the controversy;

(ii) the judgment is irreconcilable with another foreign judgment entitled to recognition or enforcement under the Act and involving the same parties;

(iii) the judgment results from a proceeding iInitiated after commencement in a court in the United States of a proceeding including the same parties and the same subject matter, and the proceeding in the United States was not stayed or dismissed; or

(iv) the judgment results from a proceeding undertaken with a view to frustrating a claimant's opportunity to have the claim adjudicated In a more appropriate court in the United States, whether by an anti-suit injunction or restraining order, by a declaration of nonliability, or by other means.

(d) The party resisting recognition or enforcement shall have the burden of proof with respect to the defenses set out in subsections (a) and (c). If a defense is raised pursuant to subsection (b) that the Judgment was rendered in contravention of a forum-selection clause, the party seeking recognition or enforcement shall have the burden of establishing the invalidity of the clause.

§ 6 Recognition and Enforcement of Foreign Judgments

(a) A foreign judgment rendered on any of the following bases of jurisdiction shall not be recognized or enforced in the United States:

(i) except in admiralty and maritime actions, the presence or seizure of property belonging to the defendant in tile forum state, when the claim does not assert an interest in or is otherwise unrelated to the property;

(ii) the nationality of the plaintiff;

(iii) the domicile, habitual residence, or place of incorporation of the plaintiff;

(iv) service of process based solely on the transitory presence of the defendant in the forum state, unless no other appropriate forum was reasonably available;

(v) any other basis that is unreasonable or unfair given the nature of the claim and the identity of the parties. A basis of jurisdiction is not unreasonable or unfair solely because it is not an acceptable basis of jurisdiction for courts in the United States.

(b) A foreign judgment based on an assertion of an unacceptable basis of jurisdiction as defined in subsection (a) shall not be denied recognition or enforcement if the factual circumstances would clearly support jurisdiction not inconsistent with subsection (a).

(c) An appearance by the defendant in the rendering court, or an unsuccessful objection to the jurisdiction of the rendering court, does not deprive the defendant of the right to resist recognition or enforcement under this section.

§ 7. Reciprocal Recognition and Enforcement of Foreign Judgments

(a) A foreign judgment shall not be recognized or enforced in a court in the United States if the court finds that comparable judgments of courts in the United States would not be recognized or enforced in the courts of the state of origin.

(b) A judgment debtor or other person resisting recognition or enforcement of a foreign judgment in accordance with this section shall raise the defense of lack of reciprocity with specificity as an affirmative defense. The party resisting recognition or enforcement shall have the burden to show that there is substantial doubt that the courts of the state of origin would grant recognition or enforcement to comparable judgments of courts in the United States. Such showing may be made through expert testimony, or by judicial notice if the law of the state of origin or decisions of its courts are clear.

(c) In making the determination required under subsections (a) and (b), the court shall, appropriate, inquire whether the courts of the state of origin deny enforcement to

(i) judgments against nationals of that state in favor of nationals of another state;

(ii) judgments originating in the courts of the United States or of a state of the United States;

(iii) judgments for compensatory damages rendered in actions for personal injury or death;

(iv) judgments for statutory claims;

(v) particular types of judgments rendered by courts in the United States similar to the foreign judgment for which recognition or enforcement is sought; The court may also take into account other aspects of the recognition practice of courts of the state of origin, including practice with regard to judgments of other states.

QUESTIONS

1. How do the proposed ULC 2005 Uniform Foreign-Country Money Judgments Recognition Act (UFCMJR) and ALI Federal Foreign Judgments Recognition and Enforcement Act differ? Would both continue to be viable as proposals were either to be enacted? Which, in your view, is preferable? Explain.

2. How do the definitions of unacceptable "excessive" jurisdiction differ in the 2005 revisions of the UFCMJR, the proposed ALI statute, and past and

present European Union regulation? Is there any basis for judicially created standards that would apply at least among the United States, Canada, China, Japan, Mexico, and within the European Union.

3. Would the decision in *Ackermann v. Levine* have differed had the 2005 revisions of the Uniform Foreign-Country Money Judgments Recognition Act been enacted and in force in New York or had the ALI proposed statute been enacted?

4. Consider whether the 2005 revisions of the UFCMJR Act or the proposed ALI statute would have altered the decisions in any of the cases that follow?

SOMPORTEX LIMITED v. PHILADELPHIA CHEWING GUM CORPORATION*
453 F.2d 435 (3d Cir. 1971)

Opinion of the Court

Aldisert, Circuit Judge.

Several interesting questions are presented in this appeal from the district court's order, 318 F. Supp. 161, granting summary judgment to enforce a default judgment entered by an English court. To resolve them, a complete recitation of the procedural history of this case is necessary.

This case has its genesis in a transaction between appellant, Philadelphia Chewing Gum Corporation, and Somportex Limited, a British corporation, which was to merchandise appellant's wares in Great Britain under the trade name "Tarzan Bubble Gum." According to the facts as alleged by appellant, there was a proposal which involved the participation of Brewster Leeds and Co., Inc., and M. S. International, Inc., third-party defendants in the court below. Brewster made certain arrangements with Somportex to furnish gum manufactured by Philadelphia; M. S. International, as agent for the licensor of the trade name "Tarzan," was to furnish the African name to the American gum to be sold in England. For reasons not relevant to our limited inquiry, the transaction never reached fruition.

Somportex filed an action against Philadelphia for breach of contract in the Queen's Bench Division of the High Court of England. Notice of the issuance of a Writ of Summons was served, in accordance with the rules and with the leave of the High Court, upon Philadelphia at its registered address in Havertown, Pennsylvania, on May 15, 1967. The extraterritorial service was based on the English version of long-arm statutes utilized by many American states. Philadelphia then consulted a firm of English solicitors, who, by letter of July 14, 1967, advised its Pennsylvania lawyers:

---

* Footnotes omitted.

I have arranged with the Solicitors for Somportex Limited that they will let me have a copy of their Affidavit and exhibits to that Affidavit which supported their application to serve out of the Jurisdiction. Subject to the contents of the Affidavit, and any further information that can be provided by Philadelphia Chewing Gum Corporation after we have had the opportunity of seeing the Affidavit, it may be possible to make an application to the Court for an Order setting the Writ aside. But for such an application to be successful we will have to show that on the facts the matter does not fall within the provision of (f) and (g) [of the long-arm statute, note 1, *supra*] referred to above.

In the meantime we will enter a conditional Appearance to the Writ in behalf of Philadelphia Chewing Gum Corporation in order to preserve the status quo.

On August 9, 1967, the English solicitors entered a "conditional appearance to the Writ" and filed a motion to set aside the Writ of Summons. At a hearing before a Master on November 13, 1967, the solicitors appeared and disclosed that Philadelphia had elected not to proceed with the summons or to contest the jurisdiction of the English Court, but instead intended to obtain leave of court to withdraw appearance of counsel. The Master then dismissed Philadelphia's summons to set aside plaintiff's Writ of Summons. Four days later, the solicitors sought to withdraw their appearance as counsel for Philadelphia, contending that it was a conditional appearance only. On November 27, 1967, after a Master granted the motion, Somportex appealed. The appeal was denied after hearing before a single judge, but the Court of Appeal, reversing the decision of the Master, held that the appearance was unconditional and that the submission to the jurisdiction by Philadelphia was, therefore, effective. But the court let stand "the original order which was made by the master on Nov. 13 dismissing the application to set aside. The writ therefore will stand. On the other hand, if the American company would wish to appeal from the order of Nov. 13, I see no reason why the time should not be extended and they can argue that matter out at a later stage if they should so wish."

Thereafter, Philadelphia made a calculated decision. it decided to do nothing. It neither asked for an extension of time nor attempted in any way to proceed with an appeal from the Master's order dismissing its application to set aside the Writ. Instead, it directed its English solicitors to withdraw from the case. There being no appeal, the Master's order became final.

Somportex then filed a Statement of Claim which was duly served in accordance with English Court rules. In addition, by separate letter, it informed Philadelphia of the significance and effect of the pleading, the procedural posture of the case, and its intended course of action.

Philadelphia persisted in its course of inaction; it failed to file a defense. Somportex obtained a default judgment against it in the Queen's Bench Division of the High Court of Justice in England for the sum of £39,562.10.10 (approximately $94,000.00). The award reflected some $45,000.00 for loss of profit; $46,000.00 for loss of good will and $2,500.00 for costs, including attorneys' fees.

Thereafter, Somportex filed a diversity action in the court below, seeking to enforce the foreign judgment, and attached to the complaint a certified transcript of the English proceeding. The district court granted two motions which gave rise to this appeal: it dismissed the third-party complaints for failure to state a proper claim under F.R.C.P. 14; and it granted plaintiff's motion for summary judgment, F.R.C.P. 56(a).

We will quickly dispose of the third-party matter. We perceive our scope of review to be limited to an inquiry whether the district court abused its discretion in refusing impleader. At issue here was not the alleged contract to peddle Tarzan chewing gum in England. Had such been the case, Philadelphia's third-party arguments would have been persuasive. The complaints might have met the liability test and "transaction or occurrence" requirement of F.R.C.P. 14(a). But the transaction at issue here is not the contract; it is the English judgment. And neither third-party defendant was involved in or notified of the proceedings in the English courts. Accordingly, we find no abuse of discretion in the district court's dismissal of the third-party complaints.

Appellant presents a cluster of contentions supporting its major thesis that we should not extend hospitality to the English judgment. First, it contends, and we agree, that because our jurisdiction is based solely on diversity, "the law to be applied . . . is the law of the state," in this case, Pennsylvania law. *Erie R. Co. v. Tompkins*, 304 U.S. 64 (1938); [citation omitted].

Pennsylvania distinguishes between judgments obtained in the courts of her sister states, which are entitled to full faith and credit, and those of foreign courts, which are subject to principles of comity. [Citation omitted.]

Comity is a recognition which one nation extends within its own territory to the legislative, executive, or judicial acts of another. It is not a rule of law, but one of practice, convenience, and expediency. Although more than mere courtesy and accommodation, comity does not achieve the force of an imperative or obligation. Rather, it is a nation's expression of understanding which demonstrates due regard both to international duty and convenience and to the rights of persons protected by its own laws. Comity should be withheld only when its acceptance would be contrary or prejudicial to the interest of the nation called upon to give it effect. [Reference omitted.]

Thus, the court in [*In re Christoff's Estate*, 411 Pa. 419, 192 A.2d 737, 739, *cert. denied*, 375 U.S. 965 (1963)], acknowledged the governing standard enunciated in *Hilton v. Guyot, supra*, 159 U.S. at 205:

> When an action is brought in a court of this country by a citizen of a foreign country against one of our own citizens . . . and the foreign judgment appears to have been rendered by a competent court, having jurisdiction of the cause and of the parties and upon due allegations and proofs, and opportunity to defend against them, and its proceedings are according to the course of a civilized jurisprudence, and are stated in a clear and formal record, the judgment is prima facie evidence, at least, of the truth of the matter adjudged; and it should be held conclusive upon the merits tried in the foreign court, unless some special ground is shown for

impeaching the judgment, as by showing that it was affected by fraud or prejudice, or that by the principles of international law, and by the comity of our own country, it should not be given full credit and effect.

It is by this standard, therefore, that appellant's arguments must be measured.

Appellant's contention that the district court failed to make an independent examination of the factual and legal basis of the jurisdiction of the English Court at once argues too much and says too little. The reality is that the court did examine the legal basis of asserted jurisdiction and decided the issue adversely to appellant.

Indeed, we do not believe it was necessary for the court below to reach the question of whether the factual complex of the contractual dispute permitted extraterritorial service under the English long-arm statute. In its opinion denying leave of defense counsel to withdraw, the Court of Appeal specifically gave Philadelphia the opportunity to have the factual issue tested before the courts; moreover, Philadelphia was allocated additional time to do just that. Lord Denning said: ". . . They can argue that matter out at a later stage if they should so wish." Three months went by with no activity forthcoming and then, as described by the district court, "[d]uring this three month period, defendant changed its strategy and, not wishing to do anything which might result in its submitting to the English Court's jurisdiction, decided to withdraw its appearance altogether." Under these circumstances, we hold that defendant cannot choose its forum to test the factual basis of jurisdiction. It was given, and it waived, the opportunity of making the adequate presentation in the English Court.

Additionally, appellant attacks the English practice wherein a conditional appearance attacking jurisdiction may, by court decision, be converted into an unconditional one. It cannot effectively argue that this practice constitutes "some special ground . . . for impeaching the judgment," as to render the English judgment unwelcome in Pennsylvania under principles of international law and comity because it was obtained by procedures contrary or prejudicial to the host state. The English practice in this respect is identical to that set forth in both the Federal and Pennsylvania rules of civil procedure. . . .

Thus, we will not disturb the English Court's adjudication. That the English judgment was obtained by appellant's default instead of through an adversary proceeding does not dilute its efficacy. In the absence of fraud or collusion, a default judgment is as conclusive an adjudication between the parties as when rendered after answer and complete contest in the open courtroom. [Citations omitted.] The polestar is whether a reasonable method of notification is employed and reasonable opportunity to be heard is afforded to the person affected. [Citation omitted.]

English law permits recovery, as compensatory damages in breach of contract, of items reflecting loss of good will and costs, including attorneys' fees. These two items formed substantial portions of the English judgment. Because they are not recoverable under Pennsylvania law, appellant would have the foreign judgment declared unenforceable because it constitutes an " . . . action on the foreign claim [which] could not have been maintained because contrary to the public policy of the forum," citing Restatement, Conflict of Laws, § 445. We are satisfied with the district court's disposition of this argument:

The Court finds that . . . while Pennsylvania may not agree that these elements should be included in damages for breach of contract, the variance with Pennsylvania law is not such that the enforcement "tends clearly to injure the public health, the public morals, the public confidence in the purity of the administration of the law, or to undermine that sense of security for individual rights, whether of personal liberty or of private property, which any citizen ought to feel, is against public policy." *Goodyear v. Brown*, 155 Pa. 514, 518, 26 A. 665, 666 (1893). *Somportex Limited v. Philadelphia Chewing Gum Corp.*, 318 F. Supp. 161, 169 (E.D. Pa. 1970).

Finally, appellant contends that since "it maintains no office or employee in England and transacts no business within the country" there were no insufficient contacts there to meet the due process tests of *International Shoe Co. v. Washington*, 326 U.S. 310 (1965). It argues that, at best, "the only contact Philadelphia had with England was the negotiations allegedly conducted by an independent New York exporter by letter, telephone and telegram to sell Philadelphia's products in England." In *Hanson v. Denckla*, 357 U.S. 235, 253 (1958), Chief Justice Warren said: "The application of [the requirement of contact] rule will vary with the quality and nature of the defendant's activity, but it is essential in each case that there be some act by which the defendant purposely avails itself of the privilege of conducting business within the forum State, thus invoking the benefits and protection of its laws." We have concluded that whether the New York exporter was an independent contractor or Philadelphia's agent was a matter to be resolved by the English Court. For the purpose of the constitutional argument, we must assume the proper agency relationship. So construed, we find his activity would constitute the "quality and nature of the defendant's activity" similar to that of the defendant in *McGee v. International Life Ins. Co.*, 355 U.S. 220 (1957), there held to satisfy due process requirements.

For the reasons heretofore rehearsed we will not disturb the English Court's adjudication of jurisdiction; we have deemed as irrelevant the default nature of the judgment; we have concluded that the English compensatory damage items do not offend Pennsylvania public policy; and hold that the English procedure comports with our standards of due process.

In sum, we find that the English proceedings met all the tests enunciated in *Christoff, supra*. We are not persuaded that appellant met its burden of showing that the British "decree is so palpably tainted by fraud or prejudice as to outrage our sense of justice, or [that] the process of the foreign tribunal was invoked to achieve a result contrary to our laws of public policy or to circumvent our laws or public policy." *Christoff, supra*, 192 A.2d at 739.

The judgment of the district court will be affirmed.

QUESTIONS

What was the basis for recognition and enforcement of the English judgment in this case? What did the Philadelphia Chewing Gum Corporation, the defendant and appellant, argue in opposition? What was the apparent strategy of the lawyers for Philadelphia Chewing Gum Corporation? What is a "conditional appearance to the Writ" under English law? Why might the U.S. lawyers representing Philadelphia Chewing Gum Corporation have advised the firm not to contest jurisdiction as the English solicitors suggested? Under what circumstances might this have proven to be an effective tactic? Was Philadelphia Chewing Gum Corporation worse off by not making a conditional appearance in the English action?

KOSTER v. AUTOMARK INDUSTRIES, INCORPORATED
640 F.2d 77 (7th Cir. 1981)

HARLINGTON WOOD, JR., CIRCUIT JUDGE.

This diversity case involves the appeal of defendant Automark Industries, Inc. ("Automark"), a corporation doing business in Illinois, from the district court's determination on motion for summary judgment in favor of plaintiff Hendrik Koster, a citizen of the Netherlands. The district court's decision granted enforcement of a default judgment obtained in district court in Amsterdam by Koster against Automark in a case brought on a claimed breach of contract. Finding that Automark did not have sufficient contact with the Netherlands to vest that country's courts with personal jurisdiction over Automark so as to permit enforcement of the default judgment in United States courts, we reverse.

Whether a court may, under American law, assert jurisdiction over a foreign defendant-company depends upon whether the company "purposefully avails itself of the privilege of conducting activities within the forum State." *Shaffer v. Heitner*, 433 U.S. 186 (1977). This means that the company must pass a threshold of minimum contacts with the forum state so that it is fair to subject it to the jurisdiction of that state's courts. [Citations omitted.]

The parties agree that the document alleged to be Automark's contract to purchase up to 600,000 units of Koster's valve cap gauges was executed in Milan, Italy. The Milan meeting between Koster and Automark followed preliminary inquiry and discussion between the two parties during a period of five months. The discussion was carried on via mail between Koster's Amsterdam office and Automark's Illinois address. Automark began the exchange of letters in June, 1970 with a one-sentence request for "descriptive material and prices" of Koster's product. Automark subsequently expressed interest in marketing the tire gauges, but stated that it needed to know the details of such important factors as Koster's relationship with the Swiss factory that produced the gauges, Koster's present patent rights, and his rights to worldwide distribution of the total output of the Swiss factory. Automark expressly disclaimed willingness to negotiate and conclude a contract through the mail. In early November, 1970, Automark's vice-president, J. L. Bohmrich, wrote that he would like to meet with Koster in Amsterdam or at the Swiss factory during a European trip Bohmrich planned to take later in the month. Koster replied that he would instead be willing to meet in Milan, and would telephone Bohmrich's Illinois office to make arrangements. As noted, the Milan meeting resulted in execution of the document involved in this case. So far as the record shows, Automark never ordered Koster's gauges, and Koster never shipped any gauges.

The business contacts described above are insufficient to reach the minimum level needed to satisfy due process requirements prerequisite to enforcement of the Dutch default judgment. A recent opinion of this court, *Lakeside Bridge & Steel Co. v. Mountain State Construction Co.*, 597 F.2d 596 (7th Cir. 1979), thoroughly analyzed the due process requirements of minimum contacts in concluding that a federal court sitting in a diversity case arising in Wisconsin did not have personal jurisdiction of a West Virginia defendant. Whether it be Wisconsin or the Netherlands, the standard of minimum contacts is the same. See generally *Somportex Limited v. Philadelphia Chewing Gum Corp.*, 453 F.2d 435, 440 (3d Cir. 1971), *cert. denied*, 405 U.S. 1017 (1972). The facts in the *Lakeside* case were similar to those involved here, and if anything, presented a more compelling case for recognizing personal jurisdiction.

In *Lakeside*, the defendant construction company had ordered structural assemblies from plaintiff Lakeside, a Wisconsin company. Several letters and telephone calls had been exchanged between the two businesses, and a contract concluded by mail. The assemblies were delivered, and Lakeside sued when the defendant withheld part of the purchase price. The court assumed that the defendant believed that Lakeside would perform the contract in Wisconsin, the forum state. Focusing on the nature and quality of the contacts between the two companies, the court nevertheless concluded that Wisconsin could not assert jurisdiction over the West Virginia company because the defendant's Wisconsin contacts did not show that it "purposefully avail(ed) itself of the privilege of conducting activities within the forum state." 597 F.2d at 603.

The document at issue in the case before us was executed in Italy and involved the purchase of goods manufactured in Switzerland. *While the document contains language that might be construed as an agreement to pay, which payment Koster claims was to take place in the Netherlands, such a promise even if so interpreted is not sufficient contact to confer personal jurisdiction.* [Emphasis added.] *Kulko v. California Superior Court*, 436 U.S. 84, 93 n.6 (1978) (child-support payments required under separation agreement to spouse living in California insufficient contact to confer jurisdiction on that state).

In comparison to the facts in the *Lakeside* case, Automark's only contacts with the Netherlands were eight letters, and possibly a telegram and a transatlantic telephone call all preliminary to the meeting in Italy. In *Lakeside*, 597 F.2d at 604, the court notes that such contacts cannot be held to satisfy jurisdictional requirements, otherwise "(u)se of the interstate telephone and mail service to communicate with (an out-of-state) plaintiff, if constituting contacts supporting jurisdiction, would give jurisdiction to any state into which communications were directed." Such a result would make virtually every business subject to suit in any state with which it happened to communicate in some manner. That clearly would not satisfy the demands of due process.

Lakeside emphasizes that "the best interests of the international and state systems" of commerce should be considered when making determinations about minimum contacts in individual cases. 597 F.2d at 603, quoting Restatement

(Second) of Conflict of Laws § 37, Comment a (1971). This consideration weighs in favor of Automark, since it "is based on the proposition that '(a) state should not improperly impinge upon the interests of other states by trying in its courts a case with which it has no adequate relationship.'" 597 F.2d at 603, quoting Restatement, *supra*, § 24, Comment b. The Netherlands lacks an adequate relationship to defendant's presence and conduct to justify trial of the case in that country. The interests of international business are better served by protecting potential international purchasers from being unreasonably called to defend suits commenced in foreign courts which lack jurisdiction according to our recognized standards of due process. See 597 F.2d at 603 n.12.

Moreover, the *Lakeside* opinion stresses that where the nature of a defendant's business contact in the forum state does not involve activities dangerous to persons and property, the propriety of vesting personal jurisdiction in that state must be considered in light of its relationship with the defendant other than that at issue in the lawsuit. 597 F.2d at 603. The purchase and shipment of valve gauges is not a dangerous activity. And here, there are no allegations that Automark had any relationship with the Netherlands beyond the letters, telegram and telephone call involved in its business contact with Koster.

On these facts, Automark did not have the minimum contacts necessary to show that it purposefully utilized the privilege to conduct business activities in the Netherlands sufficient to confer on that country's courts personal jurisdiction over Automark. The district court concluded that cases decided under the Illinois long-arm statute, Ill.Rev.Stat.Ch. 110, s 17(a), supported his finding that Automark satisfied the requirement of minimum contacts to support the Dutch court's jurisdiction. We disagree. We note that the Illinois courts have held that the state long-arm statute is intended to assert jurisdiction over non-resident defendants only "to the extent permitted by the due process clause." *Colony Press, Inc. v. Fleeman*, 17 Ill.App.3d 14, 19, 308 N.E.2d 78 (1974). . . .

At any rate, the cases relied upon by the district court for its determination that the Dutch court was vested with personal jurisdiction do not detract from our holding here. Thus, in *Colony Press, supra*, the state court noted that the "essential points" for purposes of its determination that an Ohio corporation was subject to a suit brought in Illinois courts by an Illinois company were that the contract was accepted in Illinois and performance thereunder was expected to occur wholly within that state. 17 Ill. App. 3d at 18, 308 N.E.2d 78. As our discussion indicates, the document involved in this case was executed in Italy, and the goods to which it related were to be produced in Switzerland: the Netherlands was not the situs of either activity.

And the other case relied upon by the district judge, *Cook Associates, Inc. v. Colonial Broach & Machine Co.*, 14 Ill. App. 3d 965, 304 N.E.2d 27 (1973), dealt with a service contract involving an out-of-state company that had used the services of an Illinois employment agency via a single telephone call. This satisfied the requirements for minimum contacts under the circumstances of that case since "that call was all that was necessary for defendant to achieve its (business) purpose", i.e., obtaining the names of prospective employees. 14 Ill.App.3d at 970, 304 N.E.2d 27. The conclusion and performance of the contract were carried out in Illinois via that telephone call, unlike the situation before us where neither activity occurred in the Netherlands.

Absent personal jurisdiction over Automark in the Dutch case that resulted in a default judgment, the courts of this country lack jurisdiction to enforce the foreign default judgment. The decision of the district court accordingly is reversed and the case is remanded with directions to dismiss the complaint.

QUESTIONS

1. What reasons did Judge Wood give for denying recognition and enforcement of the Dutch judgment? What appear to be the essential differences in the findings of the district court and the court of appeals in this case? Are his expressed understandings of due process requirements consistent with those of Judge Sterling in our next case — *The Royal Bank of Canada v. Trentham Corporation*?

2. What was the apparent basis for adjudicatory jurisdiction over the suit in the Netherlands? Would this have complied with the requirements of Regulation (EU) No. 1215/212? Would a Japanese court have jurisdiction under similar circumstances? Do any of the state long-arm statutes quoted in Chapter 1 provide for a similar basis for adjudicatory jurisdiction?

THE ROYAL BANK OF CANADA v. TRENTHAM CORPORATION
491 F. Supp. 404 (S.D. Tex. 1980)

MEMORANDUM AND ORDER

STERLING, DISTRICT JUDGE.

Pending before the Court is Plaintiff's motion for summary judgment. The Royal Bank of Canada brings this suit for recognition and enforcement of a judgment entered by default in the Court of the Trial Division of the Supreme Court of Alberta, Judicial District of Calgary, on October 11, 1978. On that date a judgment in the amount of $250,000.00 plus interest and costs was entered against Trentham Corporation of Texas. The basis for that lawsuit was a contract of guaranty by which the Defendant agreed to guarantee payment of all liabilities up to $250,000.00 owed by Trentham Canada to the Plaintiff. Defendant resists enforcement of the Canadian judgment based on its contentions that the Canadian court did not have personal jurisdiction over it and that it was improperly served. This Court is of the opinion that there is no genuine issue as to any material issue and that the Royal Bank is entitled to judgment as a matter of law pursuant to Rule 56, Fed.R.Civ.P.

Although the issue has not been resolved by the Supreme Court, most courts have assumed that in cases founded upon diversity jurisdiction between citizens of a state and a foreign country, the rule of *Erie Railroad v. Tompkins*, 304 U.S. 64 (1938), applies and state law governs. *Compare Aetna Life Insurance Co. v. Tremblay*, 223 U.S. 185 (1912), *Somportex, Ltd. v. Philadelphia Chewing Gum Corp.*, 453 F.2d 435 (3rd Cir. 1971), *cert. denied*, 405 U.S. 1017 (1972), *Toronto-Dominion Bank v. Hall*, 367 F.Supp. 1009 (E.D.Ark.1973), *and Compania Mexicana Rediodifusora Franteriza v. Spann*, 41 F.Supp. 907 (N.D.Tex.1941), *aff'd* 131 F.2d 609 (5th Cir. 1942) *with Banco Nacional de Cuba v. Sabbatino*, 376 U.S. 398 (1964), *Her Majesty the Queen in Right of the Province of British Columbia v. Gilbertson*, 597 F.2d 1161 (9th Cir. 1979) *and John Sanderson & Co. (Wool) Pty. Ltd. v. Ludlow Jute Co., Ltd.*, 569 F.2d 696 (1st Cir. 1978). [Emphasis added.]

Under Texas law, as well as that of all the other states, a judgment rendered in a foreign country is not entitled to the full faith and credit accorded the judgments of the courts of the sister states. [Citation omitted.] The extent to which a judicial decree of one nation will be allowed to operate within the dominion of another nation depends upon the concept of the "comity of nations." *Hilton v. Guyot*, 159 U.S. 113 (1895). "Comity" has been described as more than mere courtesy and accommodation, but not achieving the force of an imperative. "Rather, it is a nation's expression of understanding which demonstrates due regard both to international duty and convenience and to the rights of persons protected by its own laws." *Somportex*, supra, 453 F.2d at 440. Generally, Texas courts will recognize such a decree where the foreign court is a competent one having jurisdiction over the parties and the subject matter where there was an opportunity for a full and fair hearing before an unbiased tribunal, and where there was no fraud in the procurement of the judgment or any other special reason for dishonoring it. [Citations omitted.] Defendant contends that this is a proper case for nonrecognition because the Canadian court did not have personal jurisdiction over it and, therefore, the resulting judgment entered as a result of Defendant's default is void. Since the Defendant did not enter an appearance in the Alberta court it is entitled to raise its jurisdictional defense in this proceeding. [Citations omitted.]

In analyzing whether a court of a foreign country has acquired jurisdiction over the person of a nonresident defendant, courts of this country have applied the traditional American formulations of the due process tests by which a court's exercise of personal jurisdiction over a nonresident defendant is limited by the Fourteenth Amendment. [Citations omitted.]

Due process, as articulated in International Shoe requires that before a court may exercise personal jurisdiction over a nonresident defendant, there must exist sufficient "minimum contacts" between the defendant and the forum. In *World-Wide Volkswagen Corp. v. Woodson*, 444 U.S. 286, 100 S. Ct. 559, 563, 62 L. Ed. 2d 490 (1980), the Supreme Court explained that the concept of minimum contacts performs two functions. First, it protects a defendant from the burden of defending in a forum which is unreasonable because the defendant has had little or no contact with it and second, it acts to ensure that the states do not overreach the limits imposed upon them by their status as coequal sovereigns within the federal system. Of course, a forum does not become an unreasonable one only because the defendant resides a long way from it. That burden is balanced against "the forum state's interest in adjudicating the dispute (citation omitted), the plaintiff's interest in obtaining convenient and effective relief (citation omitted), . . . the interstate judicial system's interest in obtaining the most efficient resolution of controversies; and the shared interest of the several states in furthering fundamental substantive policies." *Id.*, at [292]. Many of these same concerns are present with regard to foreign judgments and relations among nations. As the Supreme Court stated in *Hilton v. Guyot*, comity, with respect to the enforcement of foreign judgments, "contributes so largely to promote justice between individuals, and to produce a friendly intercourse between the sovereignties to which they belong, that courts of justice have continually acted upon it, as a part of the voluntary law of nations." 159 U.S. at 165 (quoting from *Bank v. Earle*, 13 Pet. 519, 589 (1839)). A foreign country's assertion of personal jurisdiction over a nonresident defendant still may be subjected to closer examination than that of our sister states, if only because the burdens placed on the defendant may be far greater there because of possibly greater distances and language differences.

An analysis of Defendant's contacts with Alberta, Canada, makes it abundantly clear that those contacts are substantial and that it would not be unfair or unreasonable to require the Defendant to answer on its contract of guaranty in Canada. The substantiality of a nonresident defendant's contacts with the forum has never depended upon the number of contacts. In McGee v. International Life Insurance Co., 355 U.S. 220 (1957), the Supreme Court approved the exercise of jurisdiction over a nonresident defendant which had one contact with the forum, the mailing of an offer of reinsurance to a resident in the forum. The Canadian court's exercise of personal jurisdiction over the Defendant is similarly proper in this case. [Emphasis added.]

In *McGee*, the Supreme Court noted that for due process purposes it is sufficient that the suit be based "on a contract which had substantial connection with that State." 355 U.S. at 223. There the contract was delivered to California, the premiums mailed from there, and the insured was a California resident when the obligations of the insurance company became due. The Supreme Court also noted that California has a manifest interest in providing a means of effective redress for its residents when their insurers refuse to pay claims. . . .

The Court is of the opinion that this issue as to place of payment is completely immaterial to the issue of whether Defendant has sufficient contacts with Canada. That dispute would be germane only if the situation were reversed, that is, if, in a Texas court, a nonresident defendant were being sued on a contract of guaranty, which might or might not be performable in Texas, and the plaintiff was attempting to effect service of process under the Texas long-arm statute, art. 2031b. It is art. 2031b only that makes the place of contract performance crucial in cases involving the exercise of personal jurisdiction over a nonresident defendant by a Texas court. Art. 2031b has no application to the issue of whether a judgment entered by a foreign court satisfies our notions of due process. A nonresident defendant certainly has no due process right to be sued in the place designated for his performance under a contract, or where it is "present" or only where it is "doing business." See, McGee, 355 U.S. at 222, 78 S. Ct. at 200. Due process requires only that the defendant have sufficient contacts with the forum to make it appear reasonable and just that the forum enforce the obligations which the defendant has incurred there. International Shoe, 326 U.S. at 320. [Emphasis added.]

Defendant relies heavily on the *O'Brien v. Lanpar Co.*, 399 S.W.2d 340, 342 (Tex.1966), formulation of the minimum contacts test. In *O'Brien*, the Court held that jurisdiction over a nonresident defendant may be entertained if: (1) the nonresident defendant purposefully does some act or consummates some transaction in the forum; and (2) the cause of action arises from that transaction; and (3) the assumption of jurisdiction by the forum does not offend our traditional notions of fair play and substantial justice. Some courts have noted that where the first two *O'Brien* factors are satisfied, there is nothing offensive or inherently unfair about requiring the defendant to make his defense in the forum. . . . This Court concludes that the Alberta, Canada, court could properly exercise *in personam* jurisdiction over the Defendant based on its contacts with Canada.

Having determined that the Alberta court could, consonant with the restrictions of due process, exercise personal jurisdiction over the Defendant, the issue becomes whether that court in fact acquired jurisdiction over the Defendant. That inquiry requires an examination of Alberta's law regarding service of process. Rules 30 and 31, Alberta Rules of Court, govern service of process outside of Alberta. Rule 30(f) authorizes extraprovincial service where the "proceeding is to enforce, rescind, resolve, annul or otherwise affect a contract or to recover damages or obtain any other relief in respect of the breach of a contract, being (in any case) a contract

"(1) made within Alberta, or

(iii) which is by its terms, or by implication governed by Alberta law . . ."

Rule 30(j) authorizes service outside of Alberta where "a person out of Alberta is a necessary or proper party to an action properly brought against another person sued within Alberta." Rule 31 requires that every application for extraprovincial service be supported by affidavit stating that the applicant has a reasonable cause of action, showing where service is to be made, and giving the grounds upon which the application is made.

It is clear that under the circumstances presented here, service out of Alberta upon the Defendant was authorized. . . .

Having concluded that extraprovincial service was authorized, the Court is required to examine whether proper service upon the Defendant was in fact made. The sufficiency of service must be evaluated under Canadian law. *See Adam v. Saenger*, 303 U.S. 599 (1938). Rule 15 of the Alberta Rules of Court provides: "(2) Personal service is effected on a corporation either (a) in the manner provided by statute, in which case these Rules as to mode of service do not apply, or (b) by leaving a true copy of the document to be served with the mayor, reeve, president, chairman or other head officer by whatever name he is known, or upon the manager, office manager, cashier, secretary or agent." The process-server, Michael Grove, filed an affidavit of service with the Alberta court stating that he had personally served the Defendant by delivering copies of the Amended Statement of Claim and Amended Order to and leaving them with the Defendant at 3303 South Rice, Houston, Texas, on July 17, 1978. In his deposition Mr. Trentham testified that Defendant had an office at that address until the fall, 1978. (Trentham deposition, pp. 10–11).

Plaintiff first contends that service on Defendant was authorized by § 289 of The

Companies Act, as statutory service provided for in Rule 15(2)(a). Section 289 provides that "(a) document may be served on a company by leaving it at or sending it by registered post to the registered office of the company, or by serving any director, manager, or other officer of the company." Section 73 of the same Act states that "(e)very company shall have in the Province a registered office, to which all communications and notices can be addressed." (emphasis added.) In The Companies Act, a differentiation is made between a "company," (a company incorporated under the Act) and an "extra-provincial company", (a corporation incorporated otherwise than by or under an Act of the province or an Ordinance of the Northwest Territories). Section 2(8)(18) of The Companies Act. The Act also contemplates that every extra-provincial company which does business in Alberta is required to register and designate a local attorney to receive service of process. Sections 166 and 174(1), (6) of The Companies Act. Plainly, § 289 does not refer to service of process on a corporation outside of Alberta and the Court must reject Plaintiff's contention and Barrister Rooke's opinion that Defendant was duly served under that section. *See Banco Minero*, 172 S.W. at 714 (where Texas Supreme Court approved trial court's rejection of expert opinion on foreign law).

In support of its contention that Defendant was nonetheless duly served in accordance with Rule 15(2)(b), Plaintiff has submitted the affidavit of the process-server, Mr. Grove, who states that he personally served Mr. Trentham. Although Mr. Trentham has submitted two affidavits to the Court and has testified at length in his deposition, nowhere does he contest that claim of personal service. Defendant strenuously objects that the Court should not consider Mr. Grove's supplemental affidavit and that the Plaintiff is restricted to the record of service as it appeared in the Alberta court. As a general rule where the jurisdiction of the court rendering the judgment is attacked, the party offering the judgment is not obliged to stand on the record alone, but may present extraneous evidence to show that jurisdiction in fact existed. 50 C.J.S. Judgments § 893. Here it should be noted that the original return of service stated that the papers were delivered to and left with the Defendant. The supplemental affidavit does not contradict that return in any manner, but rather explains to whom delivery was made. Rule 15(2)(b), Alberta Rules of Court, permits service upon a corporation through a broad class of persons, including officers, secretaries, and agents. The Court concludes that the uncontroverted evidence shows that the Defendant was properly served in the Alberta action. The fact that the original return did not indicate specifically on whom service was made for the corporation does not render that Alberta default judgment void under Canadian law, see, *Conn v. City of Calgary*, 9 Land Comp.Rep. 230 (District Court, Judicial District of Calgary, Alberta, 1975) and Alberta Rules of Court, Rules 558, 559, and 142, and, therefore, does not render it unenforceable in this Court. [Citation omitted.]

Defendant has not contended that it did not have the opportunity for a full and fair hearing, or that the Alberta court was prejudiced against it, or that the judgment was procured by fraud. The statutes and cases submitted by the Plaintiff, as well as our shared common law origins, with Canada, suggest that such an attack upon the Canadian justice system would be extremely difficult to maintain. [Citation omitted.]

Defendant has obliquely suggested that a special reason exists for not recognizing the Canadian decree and that is: "If the positions of the parties were entirely reversed and Trentham Corporation had secured judgment against the Royal Bank of Canada under the same procedural and substantive format as exists in this case, the Texas Judgment would be unequivocally void for want of jurisdiction. It would not be enforceable in Texas. Canadian Courts would likewise not enforce it. For want of Reciprocity, the Canadian Default Judgment against Trentham Corporation is not entitled to recognition within the State of Texas or the United States of America."

In *Hilton v. Guyot*, the Supreme Court held that reciprocity with regard to the conclusiveness accorded a United States judgment in a foreign country was required before a judgment of that foreign country's court will be conclusively recognized by a United States court. In a companion case, *Ritchie v. McMullen*, 159 U.S. 235 (1895), the Supreme Court noted that American judgments would be given full and conclusive effect in Canada which will require further discussion.

Defendant has offered absolutely no evidence on the issue of reciprocity. Some courts have held that lack of reciprocity is a defensive matter and that a defendant's failure to offer any evidence would justify the court's refusal to consider the question. . . .

. . . However, the Court has decided to consider the issue of reciprocity on its own initiative because the Defendant apparently has made at least an oblique reference to the issue, because the Plaintiff has noticed its intent to rely on Canadian law and has supplied the Court with a number of statutes, cases, and the legal opinion of a Canadian barrister, and because the issue of whether the Alberta court would give conclusive effect to a Texas court decree is a relatively simple inquiry. [Citation omitted.]

Based on its examination of Alberta case law, this Court concludes that Alberta courts would not recognize a default judgment entered by a United States court under the circumstances presented here. In *Gyonyor v. Sanjenko*, (1971) 5 W.W.R. 381, the court noted that in actions *in personam* "there are five cases in which the courts of this country (Canada) will enforce a foreign judgment: (1) where the defendant is a subject of the foreign country in which the judgment has been obtained; (2) where he was a resident in the foreign country when the action began; (3) where the defendant in the character of plaintiff has selected the forum in which he is afterwards sued; (4) where he has voluntarily appeared; and (5) where he has contracted to submit himself to the forum in which the judgment was obtained." (quoting from *Emanuel v. Symon*, 1 K.B. 302, 309 (1908)). In *Gyonyor*, the court also cited *Sirdar Gurdyal Singh v. Faridkote (Rajah)*, (1894) A.C. 670, in which the court stated that in a personal action, "a decree pronounced *in absentum* by a foreign Court, to the jurisdiction of which the defendant has not in any way submitted himself is by international law an absolute nullity." Other courts and commentators have noted the recalcitrance of the Canadian courts with regard to giving conclusive effect to the judgments of foreign countries. In *Bank of Montreal v. Kough*, 612 F.2d 467 (9th Cir. 1980), the court stated that it seemed probable that the defendant's contention in that case that the courts of British Columbia would refuse to recognize a default judgment rendered against one of its citizens in the United States under similar circumstances was correct. In Von Mehren & Trautman, *Recognition of Foreign Adjudications: A Survey and a Suggested Approach*, 81 Harv.L.Rev. 1601, 1662 (1968), the authors noted,

"... because Quebec and a few of the other provinces of Canada drastically limit the effect of foreign judgments, New Hampshire provides that judgments from Canada shall be given the same effects as are given to New Hampshire judgments in Canada. More recently Massachusetts enacted the Uniform Foreign Money-Judgments Recognition Act with the addition of a general reciprocity requirement."

A number of cases, beginning with *Ritchie v. McMullen*, have stated that Canadian courts give conclusive effect to judgments from the courts of the United States. [Citations omitted.] However, this is true only in a very limited class of cases. Canadian courts generally require for recognition purposes that the foreign court have possessed territorial jurisdiction over the defendant. Note, *Reciprocal Recognition of Foreign Country Money Judgments: The Canada-United States Example*, 45 Fordham L.Rev. 1456 (1977). That commentator concluded that as a result most judgments from the United States would not be recognized in Canada. This Court concludes that the Alberta court would not give conclusive effect to a Texas decree entered under the circumstances presented here.

The only question that remains is whether Texas courts would refuse to enforce a judgment of the Canada court on the ground of lack of reciprocity. Long ago Texas courts, applying the law of the Republic, dealt with the issue of the recognition to be accorded judgments of a foreign nation, i. e. the judgments of states of the United States. In *Phillips v. Lyons*, 1 Tex. 392 (1847), the court followed the majority of the states' decisions, holding that the judgments of foreign countries are only prima facie evidence and will admit of almost every defense that could have been set up in the original action. In *Wellborn v. Carr*, 1 Tex. 463 (1847), the court distinguished *Phillips* because it was an action in personam, and held that the in rem judgments of foreign tribunals are absolutely conclusive, unless procured by fraud or rendered without jurisdiction. Although the court in *Wellborn* did not speak strictly in terms of reciprocity, the court noted that the above in rem rule was held to be a universal obligation by the general consent of nations. *Id.* at 469.

Texas state courts again addressed this issue of the effect to be given the decree of a foreign nation in *Banco Minero v. Ross, supra*, 138 S.W. 224 (Tex.Civ.App.-San Antonio, 1911), aff'd, 106 Tex. 522, 172 S.W. 711 (1915). In the court of appeals opinion, the court quoted extensively from *Hilton v. Guyot*, and appeared to follow it with regard to the reciprocity requirement:

It is thus seen that the force and effect that should be given a foreign judgment is not determined by how it is regarded by the courts of the country where it was rendered, but what effect they would give a judgment of the same kind rendered by the courts of a foreign country in which it may be made the basis of an action or a ground for defense. And it also conclusively appears, both from the law and evidence, that if a judgment such as the one in question should be rendered in Texas, that it would be regarded as of no force by the courts of Mexico if sought there to be used to enforce a right claimed under it, and that there, as here, it would be regarded good nowhere and bad everywhere. 138 S.W. at 238.

However, those statements were made in connection with the court's discussion of the Mexican judgment against defendant Ross. Ross, a Texas resident, had been served by publication in the Mexican lawsuit. The Texas court noted that under the teaching of *Pennoyer v. Neff, supra,* United States courts would not enforce such a judgment founded on service by publication. In the above quoted excerpt, the court of appeals concluded that Mexican courts likewise would not honor such a judgment if it had been rendered by a Texas court. The court of appeals also voided the Mexican judgment as it pertained to defendant Masterson, who had voluntarily appeared in the Mexican lawsuit, on the ground that he was arbitrarily denied the right of appeal. Thus, it can be seen that while the court of appeals was speaking in terms of reciprocal treatment, it was actually addressing itself to the more fundamental universal requirement that the foreign court must have obtained personal jurisdiction, including personal service, over the nonresident defendant. This is also borne out by the fact that while the court of appeals noted that Mexican courts would not honor a Texas court decree entered under similar circumstances, it appears that Mexico had already adopted the system of reciprocity in its Code of 1884. [Citation omitted.]

In *Banco Minero,* the Supreme Court of Texas quoted extensively again from *Hilton v. Guyot,* but did not mention the reciprocity requirement. That court likewise refused to give effect to the Mexican decree because it was rendered without jurisdiction as to defendant Ross and that defendant Masterson was not afforded a full and fair opportunity to present his defense and that he was denied the right of appeal on what the court labeled a frivolous ground.

In addition to the above noted Texas state cases, a number of Texas federal district courts have dealt with the enforcement of the judgments of foreign countries. In two admiralty cases, the courts noted the general standards governing the recognition of foreign countries' judgments without mentioning the requirement of reciprocity. [Citations omitted.]

Compania Mexicana represents perhaps the most complete discussion of the reciprocity issue to date by a Texas federal court. That case came after *Klaxon Co. v. Stentor Electric Mfg. Co.*, 313 U.S. 487 (1941), and *Erie Railroad Co. v. Tompkins,* 304 U.S. 64 (1938), and the court endeavored to apply Texas law to the enforcement of a Mexican decree which had assessed $6,000 in costs against a Texas resident who had brought a lawsuit for defamation in the Mexican courts. The court noted that the "modern tendency in this country is to recognize foreign judgments *in personam* as conclusive, where they are rendered on the merits, in foreign courts having jurisdiction of the parties." 41 F. Supp. at 909. The defendant in the Texas suit contended first that the Mexican court was without jurisdiction over him because he did not authorize the Mexican attorney to institute the suit for him and secondly, that the assessment of costs against him, which included the opposing attorney's fees, was against the public policy of Texas. In addition to these widely recognized grounds for collateral attack, i.e. lack of jurisdiction and public policy concerns, the court allowed a further collateral attack upon the judgment but found it likewise lacking. The Mexican court rules allowed 8% of the amount sued for as attorney's fees for the victor, as well as 4% of the amount sued for as appellate costs. The Mexican judgment recited that the Texas plaintiff in that suit had sued for $50,000. In the Texas court, the Texas defendant was permitted to attempt to prove that he had not sued for more than $3,000. Thus, it appears that the *Compania Mexicana* court was not following *Hilton v. Guyot* strictly, but instead allowed a fuller inquiry into the merits of the Mexican judgment. The district court did not cite any Texas cases on the enforcement of foreign judgments, although it did rely on Texas cases as to the public policy issue. In affirming the district court, the Fifth Circuit in *Compania Mexicana*, did not mention reciprocity as a requirement for recognition of a foreign country's judgment.

This Court is faced with the problem of applying Texas law in an area where that law is ancient and scarce. At this juncture, it is well to remember that federal courts are not immutably bound under Erie to follow state court decisions where it appears that a state court considering the identical issue would not rely on the precedent. [Citations omitted.] *Phillips v. Lyons* is the only Texas state court case squarely on point. That was an 1847 case in which the court sought to apply the law of the Republic of Texas. The holding of the *Phillips* court is somewhat undermined in this Court's mind by the following passage:

> "We do not design to discuss the comparative merits of the conclusion to which the American authorities would lead us. It is now a matter of very little consequence, as it will be of rare occurrence to bring a suit upon a judgment not of one of our sister states in our state courts. Suits brought by aliens will generally be in the United States court. . . . On all other judgments (other than state court judgments) we shall be under no such restraint, and between the conflicting decisions we shall feel inclined to yield to the authority of the generality of American decisions, and hold them to be only prima facie evidence of the debt." 1 Tex. at 396–397.

This Court has been unable to discover any Texas state court cases in which the *Phillips* rule regarding the effect to be given the judgments of foreign countries has been applied. The few cases which have dealt with this issue have discussed *Hilton v. Guyot*, some mentioning the reciprocity requirement, and others omitting it without discussion. Under these circumstances, the Court deems it appropriate to follow the *Phillips* approach and to examine the judicial and scholarly reaction to the *Hilton* reciprocity rule in an attempt to predict how the Texas Supreme Court would decide the issue today. [Citation omitted.]

The courts and commentators have almost universally rejected or ignored the doctrine that reciprocity should be required as a precondition to the recognition and enforcement of a foreign country's judgment. Apparently the earliest case that expressly rejected the *Hilton* reciprocity requirement was *Johnston v. Compagnie Generale Transatlantique*, 242 N.Y. 381, 152 N.E. 121 (1926), which is still being followed by New York courts today. [Citations omitted.] In *Somportex*, the court noted that the reciprocity requirement had received no more than "desultory acknowledgment." 453 F.2d at 440. In *Bank of Montreal*, the court noted that the drafters of the Uniform Foreign Money Judgments Recognition Act "consciously rejected reciprocity as a factor to be considered in recognition of foreign money judgments, apparently on the ground that the due process concepts embodied in the Act were an adequate safeguard for the rights of citizens sued on judgments obtained abroad." 612 F.2d at 471–472. Those due process concepts referred to are many of the same concepts already considered by this Court above, i.e., whether the

Alberta court had personal and subject matter jurisdiction, whether the Defendant received adequate notice of the proceedings, and whether the judgment was rendered by an impartial tribunal. The Court notes at this time that the fact that a default judgment was entered against the Defendant in Alberta does not dilute its efficacy. *See Somportex and Nicol v. Tanner*, 310 Minn. 68, 256 N.W.2d 796 (Minn.1976). This Court considers the Minnesota Supreme Court's opinion in *Nicol, id.*, to be one of the most persuasive and well-reasoned opinions on this subject. In *Nicol* the court stated:

> *Hilton* has been severely and consistently criticized by commentators and courts. Three significant criticisms have been advanced. First, *Hilton* mandates a misplaced retaliation against judgment creditors for acts of foreign states irrelevant to their cases and over which they had no control.
>
> Second, judgments are enforced to bring an end to litigation so that the rights of parties might finally be determined and judicial energies might be conserved. These considerations are thwarted by a reciprocity requirement. The judgment of a foreign nation, when rendered in a proceeding in which the foreign court had jurisdiction and the issues were fully and fairly adjudicated, should be entitled to no less effect on policy grounds than a judgment of another state or federal court . . .
>
> Third, there is serious doubt that *Hilton* achieves either of its two probable goals: (1) protecting Americans abroad; and (2) encouraging foreign nations to enforce United States judgments. If protecting American interests abroad was a goal of Hilton, it is clear that reciprocity does not achieve that goal because it does not look to the fairness or persuasiveness of the foreign judgment.
>
> . . . It thus appears that the most enlightened thinking in American law has rejected the doctrine of reciprocity. Both Restatement, Conflict of Laws, 2d, s 98, Comment E, and the Uniform Foreign Money-Judgments Recognition Act, 9B U.L.A. 64, do not require reciprocity.
>
> We therefore decline to adopt the doctrine of *Hilton* and hold instead that reciprocity is not a prerequisite to enforcement of a foreign judgment in Minnesota. It is not the business of the courts, whose province is the decision of individual cases, to impose rules designed to coerce other nations into giving effect to our judgments. Reciprocity has no basis in the policies or rules that underlie the just and fair disposition of a case involving a foreign judgment; accordingly, it should have no place in our law.
>
> In addition to those referred to above, other authorities have favored not requiring reciprocity as a condition precedent to recognition. . . .

This Court predicts that if the Texas Supreme Court were accorded the opportunity, although that is somewhat unlikely given the federal jurisdictional basis that these suits almost invariably have, it would adopt the modern, and majority, rule and ignore reciprocity as a requirement for recognition of a foreign country's judgment. Therefore, this Court can see no due process or public policy impediment to the enforcement of the Canadian judgment. It is therefore, ORDERED that Plaintiff's motion for summary judgment is GRANTED.

THE ROYAL BANK OF CANADA v. TRENTHAM CORPORATION*
665 F.2d 515 (5th Cir. 1981)

RANDALL, CIRCUIT JUDGE:

This suit was brought by the Royal Bank of Canada ("Royal Bank") for recognition and enforcement in the United States of a default judgment . . . . The Alberta suit concerned a contract of guaranty by which Defendant Trentham Corporation agreed to guarantee payment of all liabilities up to $250,000 owed to Royal Bank by Trentham Canada. The present suit was brought in the United States District Court for the Southern District of Texas. The trial court, in a thorough opinion excellent in all respects, granted summary judgment to Royal Bank. *Royal Bank of Canada v. Trentham Corp.*, 491 F.Supp. 404 (S.D.Tex.1980). However, because of an intervening change in Texas law, we vacate the district court's judgment and remand for further proceedings.

Because the litigation was based on diversity of citizenship, the federal district court considered whether the Canadian judgment would be recognized under Texas law. In deciding that the foreign judgment would be recognized, the court considered the argument that because an Alberta court would not have recognized a default judgment entered by a United States court under the circumstances presented in this case, a Texas court would not recognize the Alberta judgment based on the doctrine of reciprocity. Unfortunately, there was a dearth of Texas law on this question. In a well-reasoned and scholarly discussion of the issue, the district court concluded on the basis of the modern trend of the common law in the state courts that Texas would not apply the doctrine of reciprocity, a doctrine which has come under increasing criticism from courts and commentators. 491 F. Supp. at 413–416. It thus saw no bar to recognition of the Canadian judgment and entered summary judgment for Royal Bank on June 2, 1980.

Defendant Trentham Corporation appealed to this court, and after oral argument had been completed, brought to this court's attention a recent change in the applicable Texas state law. As luck would have it, the State of Texas adopted the Uniform Foreign Country Money-Judgment Recognition Act on June 17, 1981. 1981 Tex.Sess.Law.Serv., Ch. 808, §§ 1–11, at 3069 (Vernon) (to be codified as Tex.Civ.Stat.Ann. art. 2328b-6 §§ 1–10 (Vernon)). The Act as originally drafted does not employ the doctrine of reciprocity as a reason for non-recognition of a foreign judgment. However, the Texas Legislature specifically included the requirement of reciprocity in its version of the Act:

> SECTION 5. GROUNDS FOR NONRECOGNITION. (b) A foreign country judgment need not be recognized if:
>
> . . . .
>
> (7) it is established that the foreign country in which the judgment was rendered does not recognize judgments rendered in this state that, but for

---

* Footnotes omitted.

the fact that they are rendered in Texas, conform to the definition of "foreign country judgment" in Section 2(2) of this Act.

SECTION 2. DEFINITIONS. In this Act:

. . . .

(2) "Foreign country judgment" means a judgment of a foreign country granting or denying a sum of money, other than a judgment for taxes, a fine or other penalty, or a judgment for support in matrimonial or family matters.

Trentham thus argues that the present law of Texas, as expressed in the Uniform Act, requires reversal since the requirement of reciprocity is not fulfilled.

Royal Bank argues in reply that the Uniform Act is irrelevant to the case by its own terms:

Sec. 10. NONAPPLICABILITY. This Act does not apply to a judgment rendered before the effective date of this Act.

Sec. 11. EMERGENCY. The importance of this legislation and the crowded condition of the calendars in both houses create an emergency and an imperative public necessity that the constitutional rule requiring bills to be read on three several days in each house be suspended, and this rule is hereby suspended, and that this Act take effect and be in force from and after its passage, and it is so enacted.

The Act was passed on June 17, 1981, two and one half years after the Alberta judgment was entered on October 11, 1978.

In *Vandenbark v. Owens-Illinois Glass Co.*, 311 U.S. 538, 61 S. Ct. 347, 85 L. Ed. 327 (1941), the Supreme Court addressed the question of what law is to be applied by an appellate court in a diversity case when the state's law changes after a federal district court renders its decision. The court held that "the duty rests upon the federal courts to apply state law under the Rules of Decision statute (28 U.S.C. § 1652) in accordance with the then controlling decision of the highest state court." *Id.* at 543, 61 S. Ct. at 350. The court cited a previous decision, *United States v. Schooner Peggy*, 2 L. Ed. 49, 1 Cranch 103 (1801), as describing the correct rule:

It is, in general, true, that the province of an appellate court is only to enquire whether a judgment when rendered was erroneous or not. But if, subsequent to the judgment, and before the decision of the appellate court, a law intervenes and positively changes the rule which governs, the law must be obeyed, or its obligation denied. *Vandenbark, supra*, 311 U.S. at 541, 61 S. Ct. at 349, quoting *Schooner Peggy, supra*, at 110.

The present case raises the interesting question of how *Vandenbark* is to be understood when the intervening change of state law would not have been applied retroactively by the state courts themselves. There are two schools of thought on this issue. The "hard and fast" rule, as so named by the court which applied it in *Nelson v. Brunswick Corp.*, 503 F.2d 376 (9th Cir. 1974), uses the new state rule regardless of its non-retroactive application in the state courts. It is based on the proposition that "the *Vandenbark* decision does not on its face seem to contemplate an independent determination of whether the state will apply a change in its rules of decision retroactively in ascertaining the law of a state." *Id.* at 381–82 n. 12. Critics of the "hard and fast" rule point out that this interpretation undercuts *Vandenbark*'s own reliance on the Rules of Decision Act. If a federal court really is required to use a state's rules of decision, it should also use the state's rules as to whether a new doctrine is to be retroactively or prospectively applied. Moreover, the "hard and fast" rule seems inconsistent with general *Erie* principles since it creates a divergence between the substantive law applied by state courts and that applied by federal courts sitting in diversity. Professor Moore thus argues that the correct rule is that "federal appellate courts, faced with a change in state law subsequent to the decision of the lower court, (should) determine the effect such change would be given under applicable state law doctrines. If the state courts would deny the subsequent change retroactive effect and leave the lower court's decision undisturbed, then federal courts should act similarly." 1A Moore's Federal Practice P 0.307(3) at 3104–05 (2d Ed. 1976).

Two decisions of this circuit have recently considered these issues, but found it unnecessary to decide between *Nelson*'s "hard and fast" rule and the more flexible *Erie*-based approach favored by Professor Moore, because the state rule in question would have been applied retroactively by the state courts in each case. [Citations omitted.] We also find it unnecessary to decide between the two approaches in the circumstances of the present case. While it is true that the Act specifically states that it will not apply to judgments entered before its passage, we think that the Texas courts would nevertheless apply to the present case those provisions in the Act that incorporate the doctrine of reciprocity. The reason for this is both simple and pragmatic: As the district court noted in its opinion, there is a dearth of Texas case law on the doctrine of reciprocity. It is doubtful that the Texas courts, faced with what is really a case of first impression, would create a common law of recognition of foreign judgments for cases involving judgments rendered before June 17, 1981, and then apply different rules for later judgments. Instead, it is more likely that, given that the issue of reciprocity had never been squarely addressed in recent years by the Texas judiciary, a Texas court in our position would look to the new statute in the interests of uniformity. It would do so not because it was compelled by the statutory language; rather, it would do so because no purpose would be served in carving out a new and different rule for an arbitrary set of cases. In our opinion, the new Act has changed the legal climate in Texas with respect to this question, and thus we think that the provisions of the Act would be applied by the Texas state courts.

Royal Bank argues that even if this is so, the Act does not preclude summary judgment against Trentham. It points out that while section 5(a) of the Act lists grounds under which a foreign judgment is "not conclusive," the reciprocity provision falls under section 5(b), which lists grounds under which a foreign judgment "need not be recognized." Royal Bank thus argues that the decision whether or not to grant recognition under section 5(b) is a matter of discretion for the trial judge. This interpretation of the difference between Sections 5(a) and 5(b) is consistent with the language of the Act and is the view expressed by various commentators. [References omitted.]

Even though section 5(b)(7) might give the trial court discretion to recognize the judgment despite nonreciprocity by the foreign forum, in the present case the trial court granted recognition because it thought reciprocity was irrelevant. Thus we cannot affirm the trial court's judgment since it was based on a view of the law which, while correct when the judgment was rendered, has ceased to be so. We therefore remand to the district court for a determination of whether the judgment should be recognized under the new Act. Unfortunately, the Act itself does not make clear under what conditions a court's discretion to permit recognition of a judgment under section 5(b) should be exercised, [reference omitted], and we are unaided by any state court constructions of the meaning of the Act in Texas. We remind the trial court that although it possesses some discretion, the clear message of the Texas Legislature's amendment to the Uniform Act is that foreign judgments which would not be reciprocally recognized if made in Texas are not favored. Given the views of the Texas Legislature and the complete absence of criteria for guidance fashioned by the state courts, the trial court should proceed cautiously in the use of its discretion. Nevertheless, we think that the state courts would permit some inquiry into equitable considerations weighing in favor of recognizing the judgment. In particular, we note that Royal Bank could scarcely have foreseen that the Texas Legislature would adopt a variant from the Uniform Act recognizing the principle of reciprocity. In view of the peculiar facts of this case, therefore, the trial court should determine whether Royal Bank would now be prevented from pursuing a new action in the Texas courts because of the applicable statute of limitations or for any other reason. If a trial on the merits cannot be had in Texas, this may weigh in favor of enforcing the present Canadian judgment.

We therefore vacate the judgment of the district court and remand for further proceedings consistent with the above. In the interests of speedy resolution of this protracted litigation, we direct that the trial court determine whether it will recognize the judgment or not within sixty days from the date of issuance of the mandate. In so doing, the trial court should make whatever findings of fact and conclusions of law are necessary to arrive at its decision. Additional briefing by the parties is strongly encouraged. If the court decides that the Alberta decree should be enforced, it is directed to reinstate its own judgment. Whatever the decision of the trial court, it will not be necessary for the parties to file a new notice of appeal in order to obtain appellate review of that decision. The parties need only file certified copies of the district court's findings plus any supplementary briefs and materials. The matter will then be referred to this panel. [Citations omitted.]

Each party shall bear its own costs.
VACATED and REMANDED.

QUESTIONS

1. Reciprocity as a requirement for the recognition and enforcement of foreign-country judgments has generally fallen into disfavor and increasingly abandoned internationally since *Hilton v. Guyot*. What arguments might be made in favor of reciprocity? What are the most salient objections to such a requirement? Note its inclusion in § 7 of the ALI proposed statute

on recognition and enforcement of foreign country judgments.

2. How would you advise Royal Bank to proceed? What must it show to satisfy the reciprocity requirement of Texas law? Must it convince the court that a similar Texas judgment would be enforced in Alberta in particular or in Canada in general? In the absence of a specific case, would expert testimony suffice? What questions must the expert cover? Or, should the court rely on experts at all?

SOUTHWEST LIVESTOCK AND TRUCKING COMPANY, INC. v. RAMON*
169 F.3d 317 (5th Cir. 1999)

EMILIO M. GARZA, CIRCUIT JUDGE:

Defendant-Appellant, Reginaldo Ramon, appeals the district court's grant of summary judgment in favor of Plaintiffs-Appellees, Southwest Livestock & Trucking Co., Inc., Darrel Hargrove and Mary Jane Hargrove. Ramon contends that the district court erred by not recognizing a Mexican judgment, that if recognized would preclude summary judgment against him. We vacate the district court's summary judgment and remand.

I

Darrel and Mary Jane Hargrove (the "Hargroves") are citizens of the United States and officers of Southwest Livestock & Trucking Co., Inc. ("Southwest Livestock"), a Texas corporation involved in the buying and selling of livestock. In 1990, Southwest Livestock entered into a loan arrangement with Reginaldo Ramon ("Ramon"), a citizen of the Republic of Mexico. Southwest Livestock borrowed $400,000 from Ramon. To accomplish the loan, Southwest Livestock executed a "pagare"— a Mexican promissory note — payable to Ramon with interest within thirty days. Each month, Southwest Livestock executed a new pagare to cover the outstanding principal and paid the accrued interest. Over a period of four years, Southwest Livestock made payments towards the principal, but also borrowed additional money from Ramon. In October of 1994, Southwest Livestock defaulted on the loan. With the exception of the last pagare executed by Southwest Livestock, none of the pagares contained a stated interest rate. Ramon, however, charged Southwest Livestock interest at a rate of approximately fifty-two percent. The last pagare stated an interest rate of forty-eight percent, and under its terms, interest continues to accrue until Southwest Livestock pays the outstanding balance in full.

After Southwest Livestock defaulted, Ramon filed a lawsuit in Mexico to collect on the last pagare. The Mexican court granted judgment in favor of Ramon, and ordered Southwest Livestock to satisfy its debt and to pay interest at forty-eight percent. Southwest Livestock appealed, claiming that Ramon had failed to effect proper service of process, and therefore, the Mexican court lacked personal

---

* Footnotes omitted.

jurisdiction. The Mexican appellate court rejected this argument and affirmed the judgment in favor of Ramon.

After Ramon filed suit in Mexico, but prior to the entry of the Mexican judgment, Southwest Livestock brought suit in United States District Court, alleging that the loan arrangement violated Texas usury laws. Southwest Livestock then filed a motion for partial summary judgment, claiming that the undisputed facts established that Ramon charged, received and collected usurious interest in violation of Texas law. Ramon also filed a motion for summary judgment. By then the Mexican court had entered its judgment, and Ramon sought recognition of that judgment. He claimed that, under principles of collateral estoppel and res judicata, the Mexican judgment barred Southwest Livestock's suit. The district court judge referred both motions to a magistrate judge. [Citation omitted.]

The magistrate judge recommended that the district court grant Southwest Livestock's motion for summary judgment as to liability under Texas usury law, and recommended that it hold a trial to determine damages. In reaching her decision, the magistrate judge first addressed whether the Texas Uniform Foreign Country Money-Judgment Recognition Act (the "Texas Recognition Act") required the district court to recognize the Mexican judgment. . . . The magistrate judge concluded that, contrary to Southwest Livestock's position, the Mexican court properly acquired personal jurisdiction over Southwest Livestock, and therefore, lack of jurisdiction could not constitute a basis for nonrecognition. Nonetheless, according to the magistrate judge, "the district court would be well within its discretion in not recognizing the Mexican judgment on the grounds that it violates the public policy of the state of Texas." Thus, the magistrate judge decided that the Mexican judgment did not bar Southwest Livestock's suit. The magistrate judge then addressed whether the district court should apply Texas or Mexican law to its resolution of Southwest Livestock's usury claim. The magistrate judge concluded that, under Texas choice of law rules, the district court should apply Texas law. Under Texas law, Ramon undisputably charged usurious interest.

The district court adopted the magistrate judge's recommendation, granting Southwest Livestock's motion for summary judgment as to liability under Texas usury law, and denying Ramon's motion for summary judgment. The district court agreed that the Mexican judgment violated Texas public policy, and that Texas law applied. . . .

Ramon asks us to reverse the district court's grant of summary judgment in favor of Southwest Livestock. He contends that the district court erred by failing to recognize the Mexican judgment. He also argues that the district court erred by applying Texas law. According to Ramon, the district court should have applied Mexican law because the pagares executed by Southwest Livestock designated Mexico as the place of payment, and Mexico has the most significant relationship to the loan transaction. Ramon also objects to the district court's continuing charge for usury. Finally, Ramon contends that the district court erred by using a Texas, rather than federal, post-judgment interest rate.

Southwest Livestock asks us to affirm the district court. It concedes that the district court should have used a federal post-judgment interest rate, but refutes Ramon's other arguments. It contends that the district court properly withheld recognition of the Mexican judgment and properly applied Texas law. Additionally, as an alternative ground for upholding the district court's decision not to recognize the Mexican judgment, Southwest Livestock argues that Ramon failed to serve it with proper service of process, and therefore, the Mexican court lacked personal jurisdiction.

II

We must determine first whether the district court properly refused to recognize the Mexican judgment. Our jurisdiction is based on diversity of citizenship. Hence, we must apply Texas law regarding the recognition of foreign country money-judgments. See *Erie R.R. Co. v. Tompkins*, 304 U.S. 64, 58 S. Ct. 817, 82 L. Ed. 1188 (1938) (holding that in a diversity action, a federal court must apply the law of the forum state); *Success Motivation Institute of Japan, Ltd. v. Success Motivation Institute Inc.*, 966 F.2d 1007, 1009–10 (5th Cir. 1992) ("*Erie* applies even though some courts have found that these suits necessarily involve relations between the U.S. and foreign governments, and even though some commentators have argued that the enforceability of these judgments in the courts of the United States should be governed by reference to a general rule of federal law.").

Under the Texas Recognition Act, a court must recognize a foreign country judgment assessing money damages unless the judgment debtor establishes one of ten specific grounds for nonrecognition. . . . Southwest Livestock contends that it established a ground for nonrecognition. It notes that the Texas Constitution places a six percent interest rate limit on contracts that do not contain a stated interest rate. [Citation omitted.] It also points to a Texas statute that states that usury is against Texas public policy. [Citation omitted.] Thus, according to Southwest Livestock, the Mexican judgment violates Texas public policy, and the district court properly withheld recognition of the judgment. [Citation omitted.]

We review the district court's grant of summary judgment *de novo*. [Citation omitted.] In reviewing the district court's decision, we note that the level of contravention of Texas law has "to be high before recognition [can] be denied on public policy grounds." *Hunt v. BP Exploration Co. (Libya), Ltd.*, 492 F. Supp. 885, 900 (N.D. Tex. 1980). The narrowness of the public policy exception reflects a compromise between two axioms — res judicata and fairness to litigants — that underlie our law of recognition of foreign country judgments. See *Ackermann*, 788 F.2d at 842 (noting that "the public policy exception indicates a jurisprudential compromise").

To decide whether the district court erred in refusing to recognize the Mexican judgment on public policy grounds, we consider the plain language of the Texas Recognition Act. . . . Section 36.005(b)(3) of the Texas Recognition Act permits the district court not to recognize a foreign country judgment if "the *cause of action on which the judgment is based* is repugnant to the public policy" of Texas. Tex. Civ. Prac. & Rem. Code Ann. § 36.005(b)(3) (West 1998) (emphasis added). This subsection of the Texas Recognition Act does not refer to the judgment itself, but specifically to the "cause of action on which the judgment is based." Thus, the fact that a judgment offends Texas public policy does not, in and of itself, permit the district court to refuse recognition of that judgment. . . . In this case, the Mexican judgment was based on an action for collection of a promissory note. This cause of action is not repugnant to Texas public policy. [Citation omitted.] Under the Texas Recognition Act, it is irrelevant that the Mexican judgment itself contravened Texas's public policy against usury. Thus, the plain language of the Texas Recognition Act suggests that the district court erred in refusing to recognize the Mexican judgment.

Southwest Livestock, however, argues that we should not interpret the Texas Recognition Act according to its plain language. Southwest Livestock contends that Texas courts will not enforce rights existing under laws of other jurisdictions when to do so would violate Texas public policy. . . . It believes that the reasoning of the Texas Supreme Court in *DeSantis v. Wackenhut Corp.*, 793 S.W.2d 670 (Tex. 1990), requires us to affirm the district court's decision not to recognize the Mexican judgment. In *DeSantis*, the Court refused to apply Florida law to enforce a noncompetition agreement, even though the agreement contained an express choice of Florida law provision, and Florida had a substantial interest in the transaction. The Court concluded that "the law governing enforcement of noncompetition agreements is fundamental policy in Texas, and that to apply the law of another state to determine the enforceability of such an agreement in the circumstances of a case like this would be contrary to that policy." *Id.* at 681. Southwest Livestock argues similarly that the law governing usury constitutes a fundamental policy in Texas, and that to recognize the Mexican judgment would transgress that policy.

We find that, contrary to Southwest Livestock's argument, *DeSantis* does not support the district court's grant of summary judgment. First, in *DeSantis* the Court refused to enforce an agreement violative of Texas public policy; it did not refuse to recognize a foreign judgment. Recognition and enforcement of a judgment involve separate and distinct inquiries. [Citations omitted.] Second, unlike in *DeSantis*, where the plaintiff sought to use foreign law offensively to enforce the noncompetition agreement, in this case, Ramon seeks recognition of the Mexican judgment as an affirmative defense to Southwest Livestock's usury claim. Different considerations apply when a party seeks recognition of a foreign judgment for defensive purposes. As Justice Brandeis once stated:

> [T]he company is in a position different from that of a plaintiff who seeks to enforce a cause of action conferred by the laws of another state. The right which it claims should be given effect is set up by way of defense to an asserted liability; and to a defense different considerations apply. A state may, on occasion, decline to enforce a foreign cause of action. In so doing, it merely denies a remedy leaving unimpaired the plaintiff's substantive right, so that he is free to enforce it elsewhere. But to refuse to give effect to a substantive defense under the applicable law of another state, as under the circumstances here presented, subjects the defendant to irremediable liability. This may not be done. *Bradford Elec. Light Co. v. Clapper*, 286 U.S. 145, 160, 52 S. Ct. 571, 576, 76 L. Ed. 1026 (1932) . . . .

Third, *DeSantis* involved a noncompetition agreement, and as we have explained elsewhere, "noncompetition agreements implicate an arguably stronger Texas public policy than usurious contracts." *Admiral Ins. Co. v. Brinkcraft Dev.*, 921 F.2d 591, 594 (5th Cir. 1991).

We find our decision in *Woods-Tucker Leasing Corp. v. Hutcheson-Ingram Development Co.*, 642 F.2d 744 (5th Cir. 1981), more helpful than *DeSantis*. In *Woods-Tucker*, we considered "whether a bankruptcy court sitting in Texas should honor a party contractual choice of Mississippi law in determining whether to apply the Texas or Mississippi usury statute to a transaction . . . between a Texas partnership and a Mississippi-headquartered corporate subsidiary of a Georgia corporation." *Id.* at 745. In deciding to honor the parties' choice of Mississippi law, we noted that applying Mississippi law did not offend any Texas fundamental public policy:

To be sure, it is the underlying policy of each state's usury laws to protect necessitous borrowers within its borders. Yet, as we have noted, we have found no Texas cases that have invalidated a party choice of law on grounds that the application of a foreign usury statute would violate public policy. *Id.* at 753 n. 13. We also relied on the Supreme Court's decision in *Seeman v. Philadelphia Warehouse Co.*, 274 U.S. 403, 47 S. Ct. 626, 71 L. Ed. 1123 (1927). In *Seeman*, the Supreme Court emphasized its policy of "upholding contractual obligations assumed in good faith." It stated that, although parties may not willfully evade otherwise applicable usury laws by "entering into [a] contract . . . [that] has no normal relation to the transaction," if the rate of interest "allowed by the laws of the place of performance is higher than that permitted at the place of the contract," the parties may contract for a higher rate of interest without incurring the penalties of usury. *Id.* at 407–08, 47 S. Ct. 626; . . . . *Woods-Tucker*, and its reliance on *Seeman*, indicates that, although Texas has a strong public policy against usury, this policy is not inviolable.

We are especially reluctant to conclude that recognizing the Mexican judgment offends Texas public policy under the circumstances of this case. The purpose behind Texas usury laws is to protect unsophisticated borrowers from unscrupulous lenders.

. . . .

This case, however, does not involve the victimizing of a naive consumer. Southwest Livestock is managed by sophisticated and knowledgeable people with experience in business. Additionally, the evidence in the record does not suggest that Ramon misled or deceived Southwest Livestock. Southwest Livestock and Ramon negotiated the loan in good faith and at arms length. In short, both parties fully appreciated the nature of the loan transaction and their respective contractual obligations.

Accordingly, in light of the plain language of the Texas Recognition Act, and after consideration of our decision in *Woods-Tucker* and the purpose behind Texas public policy against usury, we hold that Texas's public policy does not justify withholding recognition of the Mexican judgment. The district court erred in deciding otherwise.

III

For the foregoing reasons, we VACATE the district court's summary judgment, and REMAND for further proceedings.

Affirmed in part and reversed in part.

> **QUESTIONS**
>
> 1. Most if not all countries deny recognition and enforcement to foreign-country judgments that contravene the country's public policy. That said, as illustrated by *Southwest Livestock and Trucking Company, Inc. v. Ramon*, the issue becomes which public policies matter. In this case, interest rates presumably enforceable in Mexico were deemed usurious under Texas law. What considerations persuaded the court that the contravention of Texas usury law did not preclude recognition of the Mexico judgment? Can you think of other public policy concerns that would preclude recognition or enforcement — treating, as suggested in *Southwest Livestock and Trucking Company, Inc. v. Ramon*, these as separate issues — of a foreign-country judgment in Texas (or another state in the United States) but not in the country of rendition?
>
> 2. Once again the court notes the issue of the application of *Erie* to the recognition and enforcement of foreign country judgments. What arguments could be made that *Erie* does not apply? How would you suggest how one might best proceed in seeking a definitive decision by the U.S. Supreme Court on this question?

B. Canada

As we turn our attention to the recognition and enforcement of foreign country judgments under Canadian law, recall the discussion in the U.S. District Court decision in *Bank of Canada v. Trentham Corporation, infra*. Note that since that case, decided in 1980, the law in Canada has undergone significant changes as a result of the *Morguard*, *Hunt*, and *Club Resorts* decisions as well as provincial legislative changes, examined in Chapter 1. In 2003 the Uniform Law Conference of Canada (ULCC) approved and recommended for provincial adoption a Uniform Enforcement of Foreign Judgments Act (2003). (For the full text, see http://www.ulcc.ca/en/uniform-acts-new-order/current-uniform-acts/735-judgments/foreign/foreign-civil-judgments/1748-enforcement-of-foreign-judgments-act.) Under the proposed act, the grounds for refusing recognition or enforcement are as follows:

PART 2 ENFORCEMENT — GENERAL

Reasons for refusal

4. A foreign judgment cannot be enforced in [the enacting province or territory] if
   (a) the court of the State of origin lacked jurisdiction over the judgment debtor or subject matter contrary to sections 8 and 9;
   (b) the judgment has been satisfied;
   (c) the judgment is not enforceable in the State of origin or an appeal is pending, or the time within which an appeal may be made or leave for appeal requested has not expired;

(d) the judgment debtor was not lawfully served in accordance with the laws of the State of origin or did not receive notice of the commencement of the proceeding in sufficient time to present a defence, and the judgment was allowed by default;

(e) the judgment was obtained by fraud;

(f) the judgment was rendered in a proceeding that was conducted contrary to the principles of procedural fairness and natural justice;

(g) the judgment is manifestly contrary to public policy in [the enacting province or territory];

(h) at the time the judgment was submitted for registration or an action for enforcement was commenced, a civil proceeding based on the same facts and having the same purpose

- (i) was pending before a court in [the enacting province or territory], having been commenced before the civil proceeding that gave rise to the foreign judgment was commenced,
- (ii) has resulted in a judgment or order rendered by a court in [the enacting province or territory], or
- (iii) has resulted in a judgment or order rendered by a court of a foreign State, other than the State of origin, that meets the conditions for its registration and enforcement in [the enacting province or territory].

Comments: Section 4 lists in sub-par. (b) to (h) the traditional defences or exceptions which can be opposed to the enforcement of foreign final judgments in Canada. It includes notably the following circumstances: the foreign judgment is not final or is against public policy; the proceedings that were conducted show a lack of respect for the rights of the defendant; or *lis pendens* or *res judicata* can be invoked. Unlike the policy governing the enforcement of Canadian judgments based on full faith and credit under the UECJA, enforcement of a foreign judgment could also be opposed if, as provided in sub-par. (a), the foreign court lacked jurisdiction.

Paragraphs (e) and (f). The defence of fraud that is referred to in paragraph (e) is intended to replicate, for common law jurisdictions, the defence as it has been developed in the Canadian case law. The defence is distinct from that of violation of the principles of procedural fairness as provided in paragraph (f). The procedural fairness defence refers to the manner in which the foreign proceeding was conducted. Fraud refers to a deception that was practised on the court or on the judgment debtor in order to obtain judgment. It is possible for fraud to exist even in an action that, as far as procedure is concerned, complies with the requirements of procedural fairness.

In civil law, fraud would have been covered either by section 4 (f) or by section 4 (g). Principles of procedural fairness would most likely be understood as binding on the parties to the proceedings as well as on the court. Fraud could also be contrary to public policy. Paragraph (e) clarifies the issue if there were any doubt.

Paragraph (g). For common law jurisdictions, "public policy" is intended to refer to the concept that is used in the Canadian case law to determine whether a foreign judgment must be denied recognition, or a foreign rule of law denied application. Public policy, used in this sense, applies only if the foreign judgment or rule violates concepts of justice and morality that are fundamental to the legal system of the recognizing jurisdiction. The word "manifestly" is used in this paragraph to emphasize that the incompatibility with justice and morality must be convincingly demonstrated. Public policy in this context is clearly distinct from public policy in the more general sense of the aims that are supposed to be served by a rule of domestic law. A foreign judgment may be at odds with domestic legislative policy, because it gives a different result from that which domestic law would produce, but that does not mean that the judgment contravenes public policy in the sense in which it is used here. The distinction corresponds to that drawn in the civil law between *ordre public interne* (policies served by rules of domestic law) and *ordre public international* (public policy in the international sense).

Subsection 4 (h) (i) addresses the situation where *lis pendens* in the enforcing court can be invoked based on either an originating process or an interlocutory proceeding the subject matter of which is related to the merits addressed in the foreign proceeding.

Subsection 4 (h) (ii) addresses the straightforward exception of *res judicata* based on an equivalent judgment on the merits in the enforcing court. It also addresses the possibility of interim unenforceability created by the existence of an order in the enforcing court resulting from an interlocutory proceeding the subject matter of which is related to the merits addressed in the foreign proceeding. In such a case, the interlocutory matter would have to be disposed of by the enforcing court in advance of it considering the enforcement proceeding any further.

Subsection 4 (h) (iii) addresses the situation of res judicata in a third jurisdiction coming to the attention of the enforcing court, the judgment of which jurisdiction would also qualify for recognition and enforcement.

Jurisdiction

8. A court in the State of origin has jurisdiction in a civil proceeding that is brought against a person if

    (a) the person expressly agreed to submit to the jurisdiction of the court;

    (b) as defendant, the person submitted to the jurisdiction of the court by appearing voluntarily;

    (c) the person commenced a counterclaim to the proceeding;

    (d) the person, being a natural person, was ordinarily resident in the State of origin;

    (e) the person, not being a natural person, was incorporated in the State of origin, exercised its central management in that State or had its principal place of business located in that State; or

    (f) there was a real and substantial connection between the State of origin and the facts on which the proceeding was based.

Comments: Section 8 sets out three groups of circumstances in which a foreign court has jurisdiction in a proceeding brought in its courts.

The first group describes party choice — the parties may contractually agree on a forum; the defendant may voluntarily appear in a forum chosen by the plaintiff; or, for purposes of orders against the plaintiff, the plaintiff is bound by the choice of forum it has made.

The second group describes the "home base" of defendants, using the accepted principle of habitual residence. For business entities, an equivalent is created by use of "place of incorporation," which is the place which gives the entity its existence and personality. Since such legal entities always act through agents, two additional grounds are added for business entities —"central management" and "principal place of business." These are consistent with decisions which have gone beyond a simplistic reliance on "place of incorporation" for all purposes. Almost all incorporation statutes mandate being subject to the authority of the courts of the place of incorporation. "Central management" and "principal place of business" depend on the particular circumstances of the case and the issues raised by it.

The third ground reflects the development of jurisprudence by the Supreme Court in *Morguard* and subsequent cases. The concept was developed with respect to recognition within Canada of other Canadian judgments. It has, however, been applied to non-Canadian judgments, even though the arguments relating to the comity between units within a federal state are less compelling in other circumstances. This issue has been discussed at differing levels of intensity in a number of cases, including (1) *Moses v. Shore Boat Builders Ltd.*, (2) *Old North State Brewing Company v. Newlands Services Inc.*, (3) *Braintech, Inc. v. Kostiuk* (4) and *U.S.A. v. Ivey*. The concept of "real and substantial connection" is well known in conflict of laws generally.

Real and substantial connection

9. For the purposes of paragraph 8(f), in the case of a foreign judgment allowed by default, a real and substantial connection between the State of origin and the facts on which the civil proceeding was based is established in, but is not limited to, the following cases:

- (a) the judgment debtor, being a defendant in the court of the State of origin, had an office or place of business in that State and the proceedings were in respect of a transaction effected through or at that office or place;

- (b) in an action for damages in tort or for extra-contractual damages
  - (i) the wrongful act occurred in the State of origin, or
  - (ii) injury to person or property was sustained in the State of origin, provided that the defendant could have reasonably foreseen that the activity on which the action was based could result in such injury in the State of origin, including as a result of distribution through commercial channels known by the defendant to extend to that State;

- (c) the claim was related to a dispute concerning title in an immovable property located in the State of origin;

- (d) in an action for damages in contract, the contractual obligation was or should have been performed in the State of origin;

(e) for any question related to the validity or administration of a trust established in the State of origin or to trust assets located in that State, the trustee, settlor or beneficiary had his or her ordinary residence or its principal place of business in the State of origin; or

(f) the claim was related to a dispute concerning goods made or services provided by the judgment debtor and the goods and services were acquired or used by the judgment creditor when the judgment creditor was ordinarily resident in the State of origin and were marketed through the normal channels of trade in the State of origin.

Comments: It was felt necessary for policy reasons to provide a list of examples of real and substantial connections in order to establish the subject-matter competence of the foreign court. Grounds are identified here for actions involving branches of corporate bodies (a); torts (b); immovables (c); contracts (d); trusts (e); consumer contracts and products liability (f). They would largely accord with those identified in the context of the enforcement of Canadian judgments (see s. 10 UCPTA).

As a result of the discussions held in August 1998, section 9 is intended to operate:

- only in the case of default judgments; and
- in a non-exhaustive fashion so that additional grounds which would be acceptable both in the State of origin and in Canada could be considered by the enforcing court.

Paragraph (a) should be read together with s. 8(e). The latter provides, in essence, that a court in the state of origin has jurisdiction in a proceeding against a corporation whenever that body is headquartered in the state of origin. This is general jurisdiction, that is, jurisdiction irrespective of the subject matter of the proceeding. Section 9(a), by contrast, is more restricted. It applies if the judgment debtor, which may be a natural person or a corporation, has an office or place of business in the territory of origin. The office or place of business need not be a principal one. Section 9(a) provides that a court in the state will have jurisdiction to give default judgment against the judgment debtor, based on a real and substantial connection, but this is special jurisdiction. That is, jurisdiction exists only with respect to certain proceedings. The proceeding must be "in respect of a transaction effected through or at that office or place". The word "transaction" implies a business context, but a proceeding "in respect of a transaction" could be for contractual, tortious (delictual) or restitutionary claims, so long as the claims arise out of a "transaction" effected through or at the relevant location.

Judgment not enforceable

10. A foreign judgment may not be enforced in [the enacting province or territory] if the judgment debtor proves to the satisfaction of the enforcing court that

(a) there was not a real and substantial connection between the State of origin and the facts on which the civil proceeding was based; and

(b) it was clearly inappropriate for the court in the State of origin to take jurisdiction.

Comments: Section 10 recognizes that there will be exceptional cases where the basis for jurisdiction can be found under Section 8(a) to (e), but nonetheless the exercise of jurisdiction by the court in the State of origin was clearly inappropriate. In those rare instances, the enforcing court may decline to recognize or enforce the judgment. A real and substantial connection between the State of origin and the facts on which the proceeding was based is not necessary for the court in the State of origin to have exercised jurisdiction but its absence, coupled with a finding that for some reason it was inappropriate for it to have done so, may be a sufficient reason to decline to enforce or recognize the judgment.

Section 10 provides the ultimate possibility at the enforcement stage to challenge the jurisdiction of the foreign court even though the defendant was not successful in challenging jurisdiction or has not done so at the time of the initial proceeding.

On that point, a useful reference can be made to § 3164 of the Civil Code of Quebec which reads as follow:

> "The jurisdiction of foreign authorities is established in accordance with the rules on jurisdiction applicable to Quebec authorities under Title Three of this Book, to the extent that the dispute is substantially connected with the State whose authority is seised of the case." (our emphasis)

As pointed out during the deliberations of the ULCC-Civil Section in August 1998, the application of s. 10 should be appreciated as clearly as possible, particularly in light of its relationship with other sections of Part II that deal with jurisdiction, namely s. 4, 8 and 9.

In principle, the enforcement of a foreign judgment can be granted if the foreign court was competent to make a final order in accordance with the rules to be set out in the future UEFJA. Defences to enforcement are those listed in s. 4, one of which being the lack of jurisdiction. This has to be determined in light of the requirements mentioned in s. 8 and 9.

For instance, if jurisdiction can be determined on the basis of a real and substantial connection as provided in s. 8(f), examples of which are contained in s. 9 in the case of default judgments, the defendant would not be successful in establishing that the foreign court lacked jurisdiction. For this reason, it might be necessary to adopt quite a high threshold for allowing the defendant to be able to do so.

BEALS v. SALDANHA
[2003] 3 S.C.R. 416, 2003 SCC 72

MAJOR J.

I. Introduction

1. The rules related to the recognition and enforcement of foreign judgments by Canadian courts are the focus of this appeal. "Foreign" in the context of this case refers to a judgment rendered by a court outside Canada, as opposed to an interprovincial judgment.

I. RECOGNITION & ENFORCEMENT

2. The appellants, residents of Ontario, were the owners of a vacant lot in Sarasota County, Florida. They sold the lot to the respondents. A dispute arose as a result of that transaction. The respondents eventually commenced two actions against the appellants in Florida. Only the second action is relevant to this appeal. The appellants received notice at all stages of the litigation and defended the first action, which was dismissed without prejudice. A defence was filed to the second action without the knowledge of the Saldanhas.

3. The appellants chose not to defend any of the three subsequent amendments to the second action. Pursuant to Florida law, the failure to defend the amendments had the effect of not defending the second action and the appellants were subsequently noted in default. Damages of US $260,000 were awarded by a jury convened to assess damages. The damages were not paid and an action was started in Ontario to enforce the Florida judgment.

4. We have to first determine the circumstances under which a foreign judgment shall be recognized and enforced in Canada. Next, the nature and scope of the defences available to the judgment debtor must be established. For the purposes of these reasons, I assume the laws of other Canadian provinces are substantially the same as in Ontario and for that reason, Canada and Ontario are used interchangeably. A future case involving another part of Canada will be considered in light of whatever differences, if any, exist there.

II. Facts

5. The appellants were Ontario residents. In 1981, they and Rose Thivy, who is Dominic Thivy's wife and no longer a party to this action, purchased a lot in Florida for US $4,000. Three years later, Rose Thivy was contacted by a real estate agent acting for the respondents as well as for William and Susanne Foody (who assigned their interest to the Bealses' and are no longer parties to this action) enquiring about purchasing the lot. In the name of her co-owners, Mrs. Thivy advised the agent that they would sell the lot for US $8,000. The written offer erroneously referred to "Lot 1" as the lot being purchased instead of "Lot 2" Rose Thivy advised the real estate agent of the error and subsequently changed the number of the lot on the offer to "Lot 2". The amended offer was accepted and "Lot 2" was transferred to the respondents and the Foodys.

6. The respondents had purchased the lot in question in order to construct a model home for their construction business. Some months later, the respondents learned that they had been building on Lot 1, a lot that they did not own. In February 1985, the respondents commenced what was the first action in Charlotte County, Florida, for "damages which exceed $5,000". This was a customary way of pleading in Florida to give the Circuit Court monetary jurisdiction. The appellants, representing themselves, filed a defence. In September 1986, the appellants were notified that that action had been dismissed voluntarily and without prejudice because it had been brought in the wrong county.

7. In September 1986, a second action ("Complaint") was commenced by the respondents in the Circuit Court for Sarasota County, Florida. That Complaint was served on the appellants, in Ontario, to rescind the contract of purchase and sale

and claimed damages in excess of US $5,000, treble damages and other relief authorized by statute in Florida. This Complaint was identical to that in the first action except for the addition of allegations of fraud. Shortly thereafter, an Amended Complaint, simply deleting one of the defendants, was served on the appellants. A statement of defence (a duplicate of the defence filed in the first action) was filed by Mrs. Thivy on behalf of the appellants. The trial judge accepted the evidence of the Saldanhas that they had not signed the document. Accordingly, the Saldanhas were found not to have attorned. As discussed further in these reasons, Dominic Thivy's situation differs.

8. In May 1987, the respondents served a Second Amended Complaint which modified allegations brought against a co-defendant who is no longer a party, but included all the earlier allegations brought against the appellants. No defence was filed. A Third Amended Complaint was served on the appellants on May 7, 1990 and again, no defence was filed. Under Florida law, the appellants were required to file a defence to each new amended complaint; otherwise, they risked being noted in default. A motion to note the appellants in default for their failure to file a defence to the Third Amended Complaint and a notice of hearing were served on the appellants in June 1990. The appellants did not respond to this notice. On July 25, 1990, a Florida court entered "default" against the appellants, the effect of which, under Florida law, was that they were deemed to have admitted the allegations contained in the Third Amended Complaint.

9. The appellants were served with notice of a jury trial to establish damages. They did not respond to the notice nor did they attend the trial held in December 1991. Mr. Foody, the respondent Mr. Beals, and an expert witness on business losses testified at the trial. The jury awarded the respondents damages of US $210,000 in compensatory damages and US $50,000 in punitive damages, plus post-judgment interest of 12 percent per annum. Notice of the monetary judgment was received by the appellants in late December 1991.

10. Upon receipt of the notice of the monetary judgment against them, the Saldanhas sought legal advice. They were advised by an Ontario lawyer that the foreign judgment could not be enforced in Ontario because the appellants had not attorned to the Florida court's jurisdiction. Relying on this advice, the appellants took no steps to have the judgment set aside, as they were entitled to try and do under Florida law, or to appeal the judgment in Florida. Florida law permitted the appellants ten days to commence an appeal and up to one year to bring a motion to have the judgment obtained there set aside on the grounds of "excusable neglect", "fraud" or "other misconduct of an adverse party".

11. In 1993, the respondents brought an action before the Ontario Court (General Division) seeking the enforcement of the Florida judgment. By the time of the hearing before that court, in 1998, the foreign judgment, with interest, had grown to approximately C $800,000. The trial judge dismissed the action for enforcement on the ground that there had been fraud in relation to the assessment of damages and for the additional reason of public policy. The Ontario Court of Appeal, Weiler J.A. dissenting, allowed the appeal.

III. Judgments Below

A. *Ontario Court (General Division)* (1998), 42 O.R. (3d) 127

12. The trial judge declared the Florida judgment unenforceable in Ontario. Having concluded from the verdict of the Florida jury that it had not been made aware of certain facts, the trial judge dismissed the action on the basis of fraud. He also held that the judgment was unenforceable on the grounds of public policy. The trial judge recommended that the defence of public policy be broadened to include a "judicial sniff test" which would permit a domestic court to refuse enforcement of a foreign judgment in cases where the facts did not satisfy any of the three existing defences to enforcement but were nevertheless egregious.

B. *Ontario Court of Appeal* (2001), 54 O.R. (3d) 641

13. A majority of the Ontario Court of Appeal allowed the appeal. Doherty and Catzman JJ.A. concluded that neither the defence of fraud nor of public policy had application to this case.

14. As to the defence of fraud, Doherty J.A. held that that defence was only available where the allegations of fraud rest on "newly discovered facts", that is, facts that a defendant could not have discovered through the exercise of reasonable diligence prior to the granting of the judgment. He concluded that the trial judge erred in relying on assumed facts that conceivably might have been uncovered by the appellants had they chosen to participate in the Florida proceedings. Even if the trial judge had correctly defined the defence of fraud, Doherty J.A. held that there was no evidence that the judgment had been obtained by fraud.

15. On the defence of public policy, Doherty J.A. rejected the need to incorporate a "judicial sniff test" as part of that defence. Assuming a "sniff test" was required, he held that no reasons existed in this appeal for public policy to preclude the enforcement of the foreign judgment. He stated (at para. 84):

> The Beals and Foodys launched a lawsuit in Florida. Florida was an entirely proper court for the determination of the allegations in that lawsuit. The Beals and Foodys complied with the procedures dictated by the Florida rules. There is no evidence that they misled the Florida court on any matter. Rather, it would seem they won what might be regarded as a very weak case because the respondents chose not to defend the action. I find nothing in the record to support the trial judge's characterization of the conduct of the Beals and Foodys in Florida as "egregious". They brought their allegations in the proper forum, followed the proper procedures, and were immensely successful in no small measure because the respondents chose not to participate in the proceedings.

16. Weiler J.A., in dissent, would have dismissed the appeal. She concluded that the defences of natural justice and fraud made it inappropriate for a domestic court to enforce the Florida judgment. She stated that the appellants were deprived of natural justice by not having been given sufficient notice to permit them to appreciate the extent of their jeopardy prior to the judgment for damages against

them. Weiler J.A. also held that the respondents had concealed certain facts from the Florida jury.

IV. Analysis

17. It was properly conceded by the parties, as explained below, in both the trial court and Court of Appeal, that the Florida court had jurisdiction over the respondents' action pursuant to the "real and substantial connection" test set out in *Morguard Investments Ltd. v. De Savoye*, [1990] 3 S.C.R. 1077. As a result, the issues raised in this appeal were limited to the application and scope of the defences available to a domestic defendant seeking to have a Canadian court refuse enforcement of a foreign judgment.

18. In *Morguard, supra*, the "real and substantial connection" test for the recognition and enforcement of interprovincial judgments was adopted. *Morguard* did not decide whether that test applied to foreign judgments. However, some courts have extended the application of *Morguard* to judgments rendered outside Canada: *Moses v. Shore Boat Builders Ltd.* (1993), 106 D.L.R. (4th) 654 (B.C.C.A.), leave to appeal refused, [1994] 1 S.C.R. xi; *United States of America v. Ivey* (1996), 30 O.R. (3d) 370 (C.A.); *Old North State Brewing Co. v. Newlands Services Inc.*, [1999] 4 W.W.R. 573 (B.C.C.A.).

19. The question arises whether the "real and substantial connection" test, which is applied to interprovincial judgments, should apply equally to the recognition of foreign judgments. For the reasons that follow, I conclude that it should. While there are compelling reasons to expand the test's application, there does not appear to be any principled reason not to do so. In light of this, the parties' concession on the point was appropriate.

20. *Morguard, supra*, altered the old common law rules for the recognition and enforcement of interprovincial judgments. These rules, based on territoriality, sovereignty, independence and attornment, were held to be outmoded. La Forest J. concluded that it had been an error to adopt this approach "even in relation to judgments given in sister-provinces" (p. 1095). Central to the decision to modernize the common law rules was the doctrine of comity. Comity was defined as (at pp. 1095 and 1096, respectively):

> . . . the deference and respect due by other states to the actions of a state legitimately taken within its territory. . . . [and] the recognition which one nation allows within its territory to the legislative, executive and judicial acts of another nation, having due regard both to international duty and convenience, and to the rights of its own citizens or of other persons who are under the protection of its laws. . . .

21. Early common law rules were amended by rules intended to facilitate the flow of wealth, skills and people across boundaries, particularly boundaries of a federal state. *Morguard* established that the determination of the proper exercise of jurisdiction by a court depended upon two principles (relied on by the Ontario Court of Appeal in *Muscutt v. Courcelles* (2002), 213 D.L.R. (4th) 577, at para. 34), the first being the need for "order and fairness". The second was the existence of a "real and substantial connection" (see also *Indyka v. Indyka*, [1969] 1 A.C. 33 (H.L.); *Moran*

v. Pyle National (Canada) Ltd., [1975] 1 S.C.R. 393).

22. Modern ideas of order and fairness require that a court must have reasonable grounds for assuming jurisdiction where the participants to the litigation are connected to multiple jurisdictions.

23. *Morguard* established that the courts of one province or territory should recognize and enforce the judgments of another province or territory, if that court had properly exercised jurisdiction in the action, namely that it had a real and substantial connection with either the subject matter of the action or the defendant. A substantial connection with the subject matter of the action will satisfy the real and substantial connection test even in the absence of such a connection with the defendant to the action.

A. *The "Real and Substantial Connection" Test and Foreign Judgments*

24. The question then is whether the real and substantial connection test should apply to the recognition and enforcement of foreign judgments?

25. In *Moran, supra*, at p. 409, it was recognized that where individuals carry on business in another provincial jurisdiction, it is reasonable that those individuals be required to defend themselves there when an action is commenced:

> By tendering his products in the market place directly or through normal distributive channels, a manufacturer ought to assume the burden of defending those products wherever they cause harm as long as the forum into which the manufacturer is taken is one that he reasonably ought to have had in his contemplation when he so tendered his goods.

That reasoning is equally compelling with respect to foreign jurisdictions.

26. Although La Forest J. noted in *Morguard* that judgments from beyond Canada's borders could raise different issues than judgments within the federation, he recognized the value of revisiting the rules related to the recognition and enforcement of foreign judgments (at p. 1098):

> The business community operates in a world economy and we correctly speak of a world community even in the face of decentralized political and legal power. *Accommodating the flow of wealth, skills and people across state lines has now become imperative. Under these circumstances, our approach to the recognition and enforcement of foreign judgments would appear ripe for reappraisal.* [Emphasis added.]

Although use of the word "foreign" in the above quotation referred to judgments rendered in a sister province, the need to accommodate "the flow of wealth, skills and people across state lines" is as much an imperative internationally as it is interprovincially.

27. The importance of comity was analysed at length in *Morguard, supra*. This doctrine must be permitted to evolve concomitantly with international business relations, cross-border transactions, as well as mobility. The doctrine of comity is grounded in the need in modern times to facilitate the flow of wealth, skills and people across state lines in a fair and orderly manner. (*Morguard, supra*, at p. 1096.)

This doctrine is of particular importance viewed internationally. The principles of order and fairness ensure security of transactions, which necessarily underlie the modern concept of private international law. Although *Morguard* recognized that the considerations underlying the doctrine of comity apply with greater force between the units of a federal state, the reality of international commerce and the movement of people continue to be "directly relevant to determining the appropriate response of private international law to particular issues, such as the enforcement of monetary judgments" (J. Blom, "The Enforcement of Foreign Judgments: *Morguard* Goes Forth Into the World" (1997), 28 *Can. Bus. L.J.* 373, at p. 375).

28. International comity and the prevalence of international cross-border transactions and movement call for a modernization of private international law. The principles set out in *Morguard, supra*, and further discussed in *Hunt v. T&N plc*, [1993] 4 S.C.R. 289, can and should be extended beyond the recognition of interprovincial judgments, even though their application may give rise to different considerations internationally. Subject to the legislatures adopting a different approach by statute, the "real and substantial connection" test should apply to the law with respect to the enforcement and recognition of foreign judgments.

29. Like comity, the notion of reciprocity is equally compelling both in the international and interprovincial context. La Forest J. discussed interprovincial reciprocity in *Morguard, supra*. He stated (at p. 1107):

> . . . if this Court thinks it inherently reasonable for a court to exercise jurisdiction under circumstances like those described, it would be odd indeed if it did not also consider it reasonable for the courts of another province to recognize and enforce that court's judgment.

In light of the principles of international comity, La Forest J.'s discussion of reciprocity is also equally applicable to judgments made by courts outside Canada. In the absence of a different statutory approach, it is reasonable that a domestic court recognize and enforce a foreign judgment where the foreign court assumed jurisdiction on the same basis as the domestic court would, for example, on the basis of a "real and substantial connection" test.

30. Federalism was a central concern underlying the decisions in *Morguard, supra*, and *Hunt, supra*. In the latter, La Forest J. stated that he did not think that "litigation engendered against a corporate citizen located in one province by its trading and commercial activities in another province should necessarily be subject to the same rules as those applicable to international commerce" (*Hunt, supra*, at 323). Recently, *Spar Aerospace Ltd. v. American Mobile Satellite Corp.*, [2002] 4 S.C.R. 205, 2002 SCC 78, suggested, in *obiter*, that it may be necessary to afford foreign judgments a different treatment than that recognized for interprovincial judgments (*per* LeBel J., at para. 51):

> However, it is important to emphasize that *Morguard* and *Hunt* were decided in the context of interprovincial jurisdictional disputes. In my opinion, the specific findings of these decisions cannot easily be extended beyond this context. In particular, the two cases resulted in the enhancing or even broadening of the principles of reciprocity and speak directly to the

context of interprovincial comity within the structure of the Canadian federation. . . .

Although La Forest J. and LeBel J. suggested that the rules applicable to interprovincial versus foreign judgments should differ, they do not preclude the application of the "real and substantial connection" test to both types of judgments, provided that any unfairness that may arise as a result of the broadened application of that test be taken into account.

31. The appellants submitted that the recognition of foreign judgments rendered by courts with a real and substantial connection to the action or parties is particularly troublesome in the case of foreign default judgments. If the "real and substantial connection" test is applied to the recognition of foreign judgments, they argue the test should be modified in the recognition and enforcement of default judgments. In the absence of unfairness or other equally compelling reasons which were not identified in this appeal, there is no logical reason to distinguish between a judgment after trial and a default judgment.

32. The "real and substantial connection" test requires that a significant connection exist between the cause of action and the foreign court. Furthermore, a defendant can reasonably be brought within the embrace of a foreign jurisdiction's law where he or she has participated in something of significance or was actively involved in that foreign jurisdiction. A fleeting or relatively unimportant connection will not be enough to give a foreign court jurisdiction. The connection to the foreign jurisdiction must be a substantial one.

33. In the present case, the appellants purchased land in Florida, an act that represents a significant engagement with the foreign jurisdiction's legal order. Where a party takes such positive and important steps that bring him or her within the proper jurisdiction of a foreign court, the fear of unfairness related to the duty to defend oneself is lessened. If a Canadian enters into a contract to buy land in another country, it is not unreasonable to expect the individual to enter a defence when sued in that jurisdiction with respect to the transaction.

34. The "real and substantial connection" test is made out for all of the appellants. There exists both a real and substantial connection between the Florida jurisdiction, the subject matter of the action and the defendants. . . .

35. A Canadian defendant sued in a foreign jurisdiction has the ability to redress any real or apparent unfairness from the foreign proceedings and the judgment's subsequent enforcement in Canada. The defences applicable in Ontario are natural justice, public policy and fraud. In addition, defendants sued abroad can raise the doctrine of *forum non conveniens*. . . .

36. Here, the appellants entered into a property transaction in Florida when they bought and sold land. Having taken this positive step to bring themselves within the jurisdiction of Florida law, the appellants could reasonably have been expected to defend themselves when the respondents started an action against them in Florida. The appellants failed to defend the claim pursuant to the Florida rules. Nonetheless, they were still entitled, within ten days, to appeal the Florida default judgment, which they did not. In addition, the appellants did not avail themselves of the additional one-year period to have the Florida judgment for damages set

aside. While their failure to move to set aside or appeal the Florida judgment was due to their reliance upon negligent legal advice, that negligence cannot be a bar to the enforcement of the respondents' judgment.

37. There are conditions to be met before a domestic court will enforce a judgment from a foreign jurisdiction. The enforcing court, in this case Ontario, must determine whether the foreign court had a real and substantial connection to the action or the parties, at least to the level established in *Morguard, supra.* A real and substantial connection is the overriding factor in the determination of jurisdiction. The presence of more of the traditional indicia of jurisdiction (attornment, agreement to submit, residence and presence in the foreign jurisdiction) will serve to bolster the real and substantial connection to the action or parties. Although such a connection is an important factor, parties to an action continue to be free to select or accept the jurisdiction in which their dispute is to be resolved by attorning or agreeing to the jurisdiction of a foreign court.

38. If a foreign court did not properly take jurisdiction, its judgment will not be enforced. Here, it was correctly conceded by the litigants that the Florida court had a real and substantial connection to the action and parties.

B. *Defences to the Enforcement of Judgments*

39. Once the "real and substantial connection" test is found to apply to a foreign judgment, the court should then examine the scope of the defences available to a domestic defendant in contesting the recognition of such a judgment.

40. The defences of fraud, public policy and lack of natural justice were developed before *Morguard, supra,* and still pertain. . . .

(1) The Defence of Fraud

43. As a general but qualified statement, neither foreign nor domestic judgments will be enforced if obtained by fraud.

. . . .

45. Courts have drawn a distinction between "intrinsic fraud" and "extrinsic fraud" in an attempt to clarify the types of fraud that can vitiate the judgment of a foreign court. Extrinsic fraud is identified as fraud going to the jurisdiction of the issuing court or the kind of fraud that misleads the court, foreign or domestic, into believing that it has jurisdiction over the cause of action. Evidence of this kind of fraud, if accepted, will justify setting aside the judgment. On the other hand, intrinsic fraud is fraud which goes to the merits of the case and to the existence of a cause of action. The extent to which evidence of intrinsic fraud can act as a defence to the recognition of a judgment has not been as clear as that of extrinsic fraud.

. . . .

51. The historic description of and the distinction between intrinsic and extrinsic fraud are of no apparent value and, because of their ability to both complicate and confuse, should be discontinued. It is simpler to say that fraud going to jurisdiction can always be raised before a domestic court to challenge the judgment. On the

other hand, the merits of a foreign judgment can be challenged for fraud only where the allegations are new and not the subject of prior adjudication. Where material facts not previously discoverable arise that potentially challenge the evidence that was before the foreign court, the domestic court can decline recognition of the judgment.

52. Where a foreign judgment was obtained by fraud that was undetectable by the foreign court, it will not be enforced domestically. . . .

. . . .

54. In the present case, the appellants made a conscious decision not to defend the Florida action against them. The pleadings of the respondents then became the facts that were the basis for the Florida judgment. As a result, the appellants are barred from attacking the evidence presented to the Florida judge and jury as being fraudulent.

. . . .

56. There was no evidence before the trial judge to support fraud. . . .

57. No evidence was led to show that the jury was misled (deliberately or not) on the extent of the damages. . . .

58. As the appellants did not provide any evidence of new and previously undiscoverable facts suggestive of fraud, the defence of fraud cannot form the basis of a valid challenge to the application for enforcement of the respondents' judgment.

(2) The Defence of Natural Justice

59. As previously stated, the denial of natural justice can be the basis of a challenge to a foreign judgment and, if proven, will allow the domestic court to refuse enforcement. A condition precedent to that defence is that the party seeking to impugn the judgment prove, to the civil standard, that the foreign proceedings were contrary to Canadian notions of fundamental justice.

60. A domestic court enforcing a judgment has a heightened duty to protect the interests of defendants when the judgment to be enforced is a foreign one. The domestic court must be satisfied that minimum standards of fairness have been applied to the Ontario defendants by the foreign court.

61. The enforcing court must ensure that the defendant was granted a fair process. Contrary to the position taken by my colleague LeBel J., it is not the duty of the plaintiff in the foreign action to establish that the legal system from which the judgment originates is a fair one in order to seek enforcement. The burden of alleging unfairness in the foreign legal system rests with the defendant in the foreign action.

62. Fair process is one that, in the system from which the judgment originates, reasonably guarantees basic procedural safeguards such as judicial independence and fair ethical rules governing the participants in the judicial system. . . .

63. In the present case, the Florida judgment is from a legal system similar, but not identical, to our own. If the foreign state's principles of justice, court procedures

and judicial protections are not similar to ours, the domestic enforcing court will need to ensure that the minimum Canadian standards of fairness were applied. If fair process was not provided to the defendant, recognition and enforcement of the judgment may be denied.

64. The defence of natural justice is restricted to the form of the foreign procedure, to due process, and does not relate to the merits of the case. . . . The defendant carries the burden of proof and, in this case, failed to raise any reasonable apprehension of unfairness.

65. In Canada, natural justice has frequently been viewed to include, but is not limited to, the necessity that a defendant be given adequate notice of the claim made against him and that he be granted an opportunity to defend. The Florida proceedings were not contrary to the Canadian concept of natural justice. . . .

. . . .

68. LeBel J. would expand the defence of natural justice by interpreting the right to receive notice of a foreign action to include notice of the legal steps to be taken by the defendant where the legal system differs from that of Canada's and of the consequences flowing from a decision to defend, or not defend, the foreign action. Where such notice was not given, he would deny enforcement of the resulting judgment. No such burden should rest with the foreign plaintiff. Within Canada, defendants are presumed to know the law of the jurisdiction seized with an action against them. . . .

69. My interpretation of the Florida legal system differs from that of LeBel J. in that I am of the opinion that the appellants were fully informed about the Florida action. They were advised of the case to meet and were granted a fair opportunity to do so. They did not defend the action. Once they received notice of the amount of the judgment, the appellants obviously had precise notice of the extent of their financial exposure. Their failure to act when confronted with the size of the award of damages was not due to a lack of notice but due to relying on the mistaken advice of their lawyer.

70. For these reasons, the defence of natural justice does not arise.

(3) The Defence of Public Policy

71. The third and final defence is that of public policy. This defence prevents the enforcement of a foreign judgment which is contrary to the Canadian concept of justice. The public policy defence turns on whether the foreign law is contrary to our view of basic morality. . . .

72. How is this defence of assistance to a defendant seeking to block the enforcement of a foreign judgment? It would, for example, prohibit the enforcement of a foreign judgment that is founded on a law contrary to the fundamental morality of the Canadian legal system. Similarly, the public policy defence guards against the enforcement of a judgment rendered by a foreign court proven to be corrupt or biased.

73. The appellants submitted that the defence of public policy should be

broadened to include the case where neither the defence of natural justice nor the current defence of public policy would apply but where the outcome is so egregious that it justifies a domestic court's refusal to enforce the foreign judgment. The appellants argued that, as a matter of Canadian public policy, a foreign judgment should not be enforced if the award is excessive, ... Such a result, the appellants submitted, would shock the conscience of the reasonable Canadian. I do not agree.

. . . .

75. The use of the defence of public policy to challenge the enforcement of a foreign judgment involves impeachment of that judgment by condemning the foreign law on which the judgment is based. It is not a remedy to be used lightly. The expansion of this defence to include perceived injustices that do not offend our sense of morality is unwarranted. The defence of public policy should continue to have a narrow application.

76. The award of damages by the Florida jury does not violate our principles of morality. The sums involved, although they have grown large, are not by themselves a basis to refuse enforcement of the foreign judgment in Canada. . . .

77. There was no evidence that the Florida procedure would offend the Canadian concept of justice. I disagree for the foregoing reasons that enforcement of the Florida monetary judgement would shock the conscience of the reasonable Canadian.

C. *Section 7 of the Canadian Charter of Rights and Freedoms*

78. The appellants submitted that the Florida judgment cannot be enforced because its enforcement would force them into bankruptcy. It was argued that the recognition and enforcement of that judgment by a Canadian court would constitute a violation of s. 7 of the *Charter*. . . . The obligation of a domestic court to recognize and enforce a foreign judgment cannot depend on the financial ability of the defendant to pay that judgment. As s. 7 of the *Charter* does not shield a Canadian resident from the financial effects of the enforcement of a judgment rendered by a Canadian court, I have difficulty accepting that s. 7 should shield a Canadian defendant from the enforcement of a foreign judgment.

V. Disposition

79. The parties agreed that the Florida court had a real and substantial connection to the action launched by the respondents. Having properly taken jurisdiction, the judgment of that court must be recognized and enforced by a domestic court, provided that no defences bar its enforcement. None of the existing defences of fraud, natural justice or public policy have been supported by the evidence. Although the damage award may appear disproportionate to the original value of the land in question, that cannot be determinative. The judgment of the Florida court should be enforced.

80. The appeal is dismissed with costs.

The reasons of IACOBUCCI and BINNIE JJ. were delivered by

81. BINNIE J. (dissenting)

The question raised by this appeal is the sufficiency of the notice provided to Ontario defendants (the appellants) of Florida proceedings against them by two Sarasota County real estate developers over the sale of an empty residential building lot in 1984 for US $8,000. The subject matter of their contract turned out to be the wrong lot. The respondents kept the lot (they say they did not intend to purchase) and sued the appellants for damages.

82. The Florida default judgment now commands payment of over C $1,000,000, an award described by the Ontario trial judge as "breathtaking". The damages were assessed by a Florida jury in less than half a day.

83. If the notice had been sufficient, I would have agreed reluctantly with the majority of my colleagues that the default judgment against them would be enforceable in Ontario despite the fact the foreign court never got to hear the Ontario defendants' side of the story. Their failure to participate using the procedures open to them in Florida would have bound them to the result. However, in my view, the appellants' inactivity in the face of their mushrooming legal problem is explained by the fact they were kept in the dark about the true nature and extent of their jeopardy. . . . [I]n my view, there was a failure of notification amounting to a breach of natural justice. In these circumstances, the Ontario courts ought not to give effect to the Florida judgment.

I. Real and Substantial Connection

84. I agree with Major J. that the "real and substantial connection" test developed in *Morguard Investments Ltd. v. De Savoye*, [1990] 3 S.C.R. 1077, *Hunt v. T&N plc*, [1993] 4 S.C.R. 289, at p. 325, and *Tolofson v. Jensen*, [1994] 3 S.C.R. 1022, at p. 1058, provides an appropriate conceptual basis for the enforcement in Canada of final judgments obtained in foreign jurisdictions as it does for final judgments obtained in other provinces.

. . . .

86. It stands to reason that if the issues posed by the enforcement of foreign judgments differ from the issues encountered in the enforcement of judgments among the provinces and the territories, the legal rules are not going to be identical. Accordingly, while I accept that the *Morguard* test ("real and substantial connection") provides a framework for the enforcement of foreign judgments, it would be prudent at this stage not to be overly rigid in staking out a position on available defences beyond what the facts of this case require. . . .

II. The Foreign Judgment

87. In 1981, the appellants bought an empty lot in a Florida real estate subdivision near Sarasota for US $4,000. It was described as Lot 2. They did not build. They did not even visit it. They just paid the municipal taxes. In 1983, they thought they had sold it to the respondents for US $8,000. Despite the fact that all of the closing documentation referred to Lot 2, the respondents (who say they did not "catch" the reference to Lot 2 in the closing document) eventually claimed that

they had *intended* to purchase the lot next door — Lot 1 — and that they had been falsely and fraudulently induced to buy Lot 2 by the appellants and a Florida real estate agent called O'Neill.

88. No doubt the Florida courts had jurisdiction over the ensuing dispute. . . .

89. It appears that soon after being served with the respondents' Complaint, the appellants decided to tell their story to the Florida court by filing a Statement of Defence, but to forgo the further expense of hiring a Florida lawyer to represent their interests. The costs would likely have exceeded the amount they thought was in issue. . . .

90. My colleague Major J. holds, in effect, that the appellants are largely the victims of what he considers to be some ostrich-like inactivity and some poor legal advice from their Ontario solicitor. There is some truth to this, but such a bizarre outcome nevertheless invites close scrutiny of how the Florida proceedings transformed a minor real estate transaction into a major financial bonanza for the respondents.

91. While the notification procedures under the Florida rules may be considered in Florida to be quite adequate for Florida residents with easy access to advice and counsel from Florida lawyers (and there is no doubt that Florida procedures in general conform to a reasonable standard of fairness), nevertheless the question here is whether the appellants *in this proceeding* were sufficiently informed of the case against them, both with respect to liability and the potential financial consequences, to allow them to determine in a reasonable way whether or not to participate in the Florida action, or to let it go by default.

[Critical description of Florida proceedings omitted]

XI. Disposition

131. I would allow the appeal to dismiss the action, with costs throughout to the appellants.

The following are the reasons delivered by

LEBEL J. (dissenting)

I. Introduction

132. The enforcement of this judgment, which has its origins in a straightforward sale of land for US $8,000 and has now grown to well over C $800,000, is unusually harsh. In my view, our law should be flexible enough to recognize and avoid such harshness in circumstances like these, where the respondents' original claim was dubious in the extreme and the appellants are guilty of little more than bad luck. . . .

133. In my opinion, this Court should avoid moving the law of conflicts in such a direction. Thus, I respectfully disagree with the reasons of the majority on two points. I would hold that this judgment should not be enforced because a breach of

natural justice occurred in the process by which it was obtained. I also have concerns about the way the "real and substantial connection" test, in its application to foreign-country judgments, is articulated by the majority.

134. Although I agree both that the "real and substantial connection" test should be extended to judgments from outside Canada and that the Florida court properly took jurisdiction over the defendants in this particular case, in my view the test should be modified significantly when it is applied to judgments originating outside the Canadian federation. Specifically, the assessment of the propriety of the foreign court's jurisdiction should be carried out in a way that acknowledges the additional hardship imposed on a defendant who is required to litigate in a foreign country.

. . . .

III. The Extension of the "Real and Substantial Connection" Test to Foreign-Country Judgments

A. *The Need for Clarification*

159. The parties agreed before the trial judge that the Florida court had properly assumed jurisdiction. As a result, it is not strictly necessary to deal with the application of the "real and substantial connection" test to foreign-country judgments to dispose of this appeal. Although the issue is moot between these parties, the Court asked for additional submissions on it. My discussion of the jurisdiction question is more extensive than would ordinarily be necessary in light of the appellants' concession of this point and of my agreement with Major J. on what the result of the jurisdiction analysis should be in this case. I have set out my views on this issue in detail because the principles that ought to shape the jurisdiction analysis should also inform the interpretation of the defences, on which I disagree with the majority.

160. I will follow Major J. in assuming that the relevant laws of other Canadian provinces are substantially the same as those of Ontario. I will be referring to Canada and Ontario interchangeably, except where the context indicates otherwise.

161. *Morguard, supra*, marked the beginning of a new era in Canadian conflicts law, and set out the basic principles and policy objectives underlying that new legal framework. At a practical level, however, it left many questions unanswered. Among them are whether the "real and substantial connection" test applies in international situations, and the precise nature of the connections that support the recognition of jurisdiction. The present appeal is a suitable occasion within which to clarify some of the implications of *Morguard* and to develop its ramifications in the international context. For these reasons, this Court decided to hear submissions on the international application of the test, in the hope of providing some guidance to lower courts on the issues that this case raises although those issues are no longer live between the parties.

162. Under the approach adopted by the majority, the "real and substantial connection" test applies in the international context just as it does within Canada, and if any unfairness results it may be dealt with only by arguing *forum non*

conveniens in the foreign forum or invoking defences to the enforcement of the final judgment. My view is different. The jurisdiction test itself should be applied so that the assumption of jurisdiction will not be recognized if it is unfair to the defendant. To do so requires taking into account the differences between the international and interprovincial contexts as well as between the rationales that structure our conflicts law in these two spheres.

B. *Constitutional Imperatives Versus International Comity*

163. The adoption in *Morguard* of new, liberal and purposive rules governing recognition and enforcement of judgments from one province by the courts of another was based on two underlying rationales: constitutional considerations, particularly the intention of the framers of the Constitution to create an integrated national economy; and considerations of international comity, which La Forest J. held should be evaluated anew "in the light of a changing world order" (p. 1097). While the latter rationale extends to foreign-country judgments, the former does not.

164. In *Morguard*, La Forest J. emphasized that the integrated character of the Canadian federation makes a high degree of cooperation between the courts of the various provinces a practical necessity. As this Court later confirmed in *Hunt v. T&N plc*, [1993] 4 S.C.R. 289, it is a "constitutional imperative", inherent in the relationship between the units of our federal state, that each province must recognize the properly assumed jurisdiction of another, and conversely that no court in a province can intermeddle in matters that are without a constitutionally sufficient connection to that province. Provided that a court's assumption of jurisdiction is based on a real and substantial connection to the forum, the matter is within the sphere of provincial authority, and the resulting judgment is entitled to "full faith and credit", to borrow the language of the United States Constitution (Article IV), in all the other provinces.

165. As I observed in *Spar Aerospace Ltd. v. American Mobile Satellite Corp.*, [2002] 4 S.C.R. 205, 2002 SCC 78, at para. 53, it is clear from the reasoning in both *Morguard* and in *Hunt*, *supra*, "that federalism was the central concern underlying both decisions". At the same time, *Morguard* left little doubt that the old common law rules were as outdated in the international sphere as they were inappropriate in the interprovincial context. La Forest J. noted that international borders are far more permeable, and international travel and communications much easier, than was the case when the traditional rules were developed in the nineteenth century. Business dealings with residents of other states are both commonplace and essential for any sophisticated modern economy. It is contrary to the interests of a modern state to retain rules of private international law that impede its citizens' participation in the increasingly integrated world economy. La Forest J. endorsed the view of H. E. Yntema that the rules of private international law ought to "promote suitable conditions of interstate and international commerce" ("The Objectives of Private International Law" (1957), 35 *Can. Bar Rev.* 721, at p. 741, cited in *Morguard*, at 1097).

166. *Morguard* thus strongly suggested that the recognition and enforcement of foreign-country judgments should be subject to a more liberal test informed by an

updated understanding of international comity. It is equally clear from a reading of *Morguard* and its progeny that the considerations informing the application of the test to foreign-country judgments are not identical to those that shape conflict rules within Canada. As I observed in *Spar, supra*, at para. 51, "it is important to emphasize that *Morguard* and *Hunt* were decided in the context of interprovincial jurisdictional disputes . . . [and that] the specific findings of these decisions cannot easily be extended beyond this context". See also *Hunt, supra*, at 328. Although constitutional considerations and considerations of international comity both point towards a more liberal jurisdiction test, important differences remain between them.

167. One of those differences is that the rules that apply within the Canadian federation are "constitutional imperatives". Comity as between sovereign nations is not an obligation in the same sense, although it is more than a matter of mere discretion or preference. In *Morguard*, La Forest J. adopted the definition of comity stated by the United States Supreme Court in *Hilton v. Guyot*, 159 U.S. 113 (1895), at pp. 163–64 (cited in *Morguard*, at p. 1096):

> "Comity," in the legal sense, is neither a matter of absolute obligation, on the one hand, nor of mere courtesy and good will, upon the other. But it is the recognition which one nation allows within its territory to the legislative, executive or judicial acts of another nation, having due regard both to international duty and convenience, and to the rights of its own citizens or of other persons who are under the protection of its laws.

168. The phrase "international duty and convenience" does not refer to a legally enforceable duty. No super-national legal authority can impose on sovereign states the obligation to honour the principle of comity. Rather, states choose to cooperate with other states out of self-interest, because it is convenient to do so, and out of "duty" in the sense that it is fair and sensible for State A to recognize the acts of State B if it expects State B to recognize its own acts.

169. The provinces, on the other hand, are constitutionally bound both to observe the limits on their own power to assert jurisdiction over defendants outside the province, and to recognize the properly assumed jurisdiction of courts in sister provinces; for them, this is "a matter of absolute obligation". This obligation reflects the unity in diversity that is characteristic of our federal state. In *Morguard, supra*, this Court acknowledged the shared values of the Canadian justice system which, as we know, fully accepts the relevance and importance of its two great legal systems, common law and civil law. The *Morguard* rule was designed in full awareness that Canada shares two legal systems.

170. A further point is that there are significant factual differences between the international and interprovincial contexts that should be reflected in the private international law rules applicable to each. These contextual differences are important because the doctrine of comity should be applied in a context-sensitive manner. The ultimate purpose of rules based on the idea of comity is to "facilitate the flow of wealth, skills and people across state lines in a fair and orderly manner" (*Morguard, supra*, at 1096). How this purpose is best to be achieved depends on the context in which the rules operate.

171. A context-sensitive jurisdiction test ought to take into account the difficulty of defending in a foreign jurisdiction and the possibility that the quality of justice there may not meet Canadian standards. . . .

172. In my view, it follows from the contextual and purpose-driven approach adopted in *Morguard* that the rules for recognition and enforcement of foreign-country judgments should be carefully fashioned to reflect the realities of the international context, and calibrated to further to the greatest degree possible, the ultimate objective of facilitating international interactions. . . . Ideally, the test should represent a balance designed to create the optimum conditions favouring the flow of commodities and services across state lines. In our enthusiasm to advance beyond the parochialism of the past, we should be careful not to overshoot this goal.

174. I would conclude that the "real and substantial connection" test should apply to foreign-country judgments, but the connections required before such judgments will be enforced should be specified more strictly and in a manner that gives due weight to the protection of Canadian defendants without disregarding the legitimate interests of foreign claimants. . . .

. . . .

196. A less troubling but more common situation arises when there is nothing inherently wrong with the foreign legal system, but it is different enough from ours that a Canadian defendant may encounter considerable difficulties understanding her rights and obligations and the steps she needs to take to defend herself. To take a simple example, a defendant from a Canadian common law province may find a civilian system such as that of France or Germany quite unfamiliar. Continental legal systems are, of course, just as fair and sophisticated as the legal system of Ontario. The fact remains that an Ontario defendant who is used to a very different system may suffer prejudice as a result of the foreign system's unfamiliarity. Such a defendant cannot hope to protect herself unless she retains local counsel who can both negotiate the process on her behalf and explain it to her in a language she knows. It is not a simple thing to find trustworthy, competent, bilingual counsel in a foreign country; nor is it cheap. The plaintiff, who chose the forum, will presumably not face these difficulties, and therefore the parties will not be on a level playing field. (Conversely, the plaintiff would face the same kind of disadvantage if required to come to Ontario to pursue his case; it is in the nature of international litigation that one party or the other must accept the hardship of litigation in a foreign jurisdiction. The touchstone for an enforcing court in reaching a fair decision as to which of them should bear this burden is the strength of the connections between the action and the originating jurisdiction.)

197. Even legal systems that are relatively similar to Canada's can differ from our system significantly, and in ways that affect a Canadian defendant's ability to make his case effectively and to understand the strengths and weaknesses of his position. The common law system in the United States remains very close in many respects to that of Canada. Yet this action itself provides numerous examples of substantive and procedural differences between the legal system in Florida and that of Ontario which created unforeseen perils for the Ontario defendants. Those differences include the following:

— Discovery in Florida is even broader in scope than it is in Ontario, and some of the functions of pleadings in Ontario are left to the discovery process. The record in this case indicates that it is standard practice for pleadings to disclose no more than a rough outline of the plaintiff's claim and for the defendant to find out the specifics through discovery. Thus, the Amended Complaint did not set out the amount of damages claimed, but simply stated a minimum amount necessary to support the monetary jurisdiction of the Circuit Court. The expert witness, Mr. Groner, testified that the Ontario defendants were expected to ascertain the actual amount being sought through the discovery process. This would, of course, involve expense and would probably necessitate retaining local counsel in Florida.

— Under Florida's procedural rules, the defence filed by the appellants ceased to have any effect once a new version of the Amended Complaint was filed, in spite of the fact that the allegations concerning the appellants were unchanged and the lack of any notification to the appellants that they were supposed to file a new defence.

— Even in cases where significant sums of money are at stake, transcripts are not produced in the Florida courts as a matter of course, but at the option and expense of the litigants. In a default case, this effectively means the plaintiff has complete control over whether there will be a record of what is said in the proceedings.

— Punitive damages appear to be available in a wider range of cases and in much larger amounts under Florida law than they are under Ontario law. An Ontario defendant sued in Florida may therefore be at risk of a far higher damage award than would be contemplated in Ontario.

198. These differences illustrate that for an Ontario defendant, litigation in Florida entails greater hardship and risk than litigation in another Canadian province — and of all 'truly foreign' jurisdictions, Florida, which is not very far away and has a legal system essentially similar to Ontario's, is one of the least foreign. . . .

F. *Should the Test for Jurisdiction Be Based on "Reciprocity"?*

200. It follows from the propositions set out above that I do not agree with the majority that the notion of "interprovincial reciprocity" is "equally applicable to judgments made by courts outside Canada" (Major J., at para. 29). The argument is that if the circumstances are such that an Ontario court could reasonably take jurisdiction based on equivalent connecting factors to Ontario, then the Ontario court should recognize the jurisdiction of the foreign court. Although there is some initial appeal to this idea, ultimately I do not agree with it. Its effect is to treat a judgment from a foreign country exactly like one that originates within Canada. . . . The court should have a discretion to decide that it is not fair to the defendant to recognize the jurisdiction of the foreign court, even if the Canadian court would have decided it was fair to take jurisdiction itself based on the same connecting factors.

G. *Conclusion on Jurisdiction*

205. In conclusion, I agree with Major J. that considerations of comity, order and fairness support the application of the "real and substantial connection" test to the recognition and enforcement of judgments originating in foreign countries. In my view, however, the application of the test should be purpose-driven and contextual. What constitutes a connection sufficient to meet the test will not be the same in every context. The jurisdiction test should reflect the difference between the international and interprovincial contexts and the greater hardship that litigation in a foreign country can entail.

. . . .

217. In my opinion, the impeachment defences, particularly the defences of fraud and natural justice, ought to be reformulated. The law of conflicts needs to take these new possibilities for abuse into account and to ensure an appropriate recalibration of the balance between respect for the finality of foreign judgments and protection of the rights of Canadian defendants.

218. Furthermore, the nominate defences should be looked at as examples of a single underlying principle governing the exercise of the receiving court's power to recognize and enforce a foreign judgment. The claimant must come before the Canadian court with clean hands, and the court will not accept a judgment whose enforcement would amount to an abuse of its process or bring the administration of justice in Canada into disrepute.

. . . .

C. *Reformulation of the Nominate Defences*

(1) Public Policy

219. If the enforcement of a foreign judgment in Canada would be contrary to Canadian public policy, the judgment will not be enforced here. This defence addresses objections to the foreign law on which the judgment was based. It will be engaged if the foreign law is either contrary to basic morality or contrary to the fundamental tenets of justice recognized by our legal system.

. . . .

221. In my view, the better approach is to continue to reserve the public policy defence for cases where the objection is to the law of the foreign forum, rather than the way the law was applied, or the size of the award *per se*. . . . To extend it to cover situations where there is nothing objectionable about the foreign law but, rather, a defect in the way the law was applied might send the wrong message, one that conflicts with the norms of international cooperation and respect for other legal systems underlying the doctrine of comity.

222. . . . While the question is always whether the foreign law violates Canadian ideas of essential justice and morality, the relevant precepts of morality and justice are so basic that they can be said to have a universal character and will generally be respected by all fair legal systems.

223. The defence of public policy should not, however, be reserved for such shockingly immoral laws that one would be hard-pressed to find a non-hypothetical example of the kind of law that would engage it. In my opinion, there is more work for this defence to do. It should also apply to foreign laws that offend basic tenets of our civil justice system, principles that are widely recognized as having a quality of essential fairness. Among these, I would include the idea that civil damages should only be awarded when the defendant is responsible for harm to the plaintiff, and the rule that punitive damages are available when the defendant's conduct goes beyond mere negligence and is morally blameworthy in some way. . . .

224. A law which violates these basic tenets of justice would be fundamentally unfair and worthy of condemnation.

225. . . . As far as I know, U.S. federal and state law generally allows for punitive damages only when the defendant's behaviour is morally blameworthy in some way. In this sense, their policy is similar in principle to ours even though the amounts awarded are sometimes startlingly high to Canadian eyes.

226. Serious problems can, however, arise when an exorbitant damage award is granted against a defendant whose actions were merely careless, rather than reprehensible, or where the defendant's actions were blameworthy enough to merit punitive damages in some amount but the amount awarded is so unimaginably large that it would only be justified as a response to the most heinous and despicable conduct.

227. Some very large judgments of this kind have gained a certain level of notoriety and are probably the first to come to mind when concerns about the size of punitive damage awards are raised.

. . . .

229. . . . These are issues that, in my view, engage the defence of natural justice rather than that of public policy.

(2) Fraud

230. Fraud perpetrated on the court that issued the foreign judgment is a defence to its enforcement in Canada. The defence of fraud is hard to reconcile with the principle that the original court's findings of fact are final and binding. . . .

231. Courts have attempted to resolve this conflict by distinguishing between the kind of fraud of which evidence will be admitted by the domestic court, and allegations of fraud which are considered to have been directly or impliedly disposed of by the foreign judgment and cannot be raised again. Different courts have drawn the line in different places.

232. It should be noted that each of these approaches represents a compromise between the conflicting propositions that the original judgment is conclusive and that a judgment obtained by deception or based on false facts should not be enforced. Even under the permissive English rule, the foreign court's factual conclusions can only be displaced by proof of conscious and intentional deception; it is not enough to argue that the foreign court drew the wrong conclusion from the

evidence. . . . What is the best approach depends on the context in which the rule is applied, and the most appropriate rule will be the one that is most conducive in the circumstances to furthering the objectives of private international law.

233. I agree with Major J. that in general the rule that the defence of fraud must be based on previously undiscoverable evidence is a reasonably balanced solution. . . . These considerations suggest that the "extrinsic fraud" approach is too narrow and the "intentional fraud" approach too broad; the rule that only fresh evidence of fraud can be looked at by the enforcing court is, generally speaking, a good compromise.

234. I would not, however, rule out the possibility that a broader test should apply to default judgments in cases where the defendant's decision not to participate was a demonstrably reasonable one. . . . In my opinion, a more generous version of the fraud defence ought to be available, as required, to address the dangers of abuse associated with the loosening of the jurisdiction test to admit a broad category of formerly unenforceable default judgments.

(3) Natural Justice

235. A foreign judgment will not be enforced in Canada if the foreign proceedings were contrary to natural justice. The defence concerns the procedure by which the foreign court reached its decision. The clearest examples of a deprivation of natural justice occur when the defendant lacks notice of the foreign proceedings or an opportunity to present his case to the court.

236. In my opinion, two developments should be recognized in connection with this defence. First, the requirements of notice and a hearing should be construed in a purposive and flexible manner. Secondly, substantive principles of justice should also be included in the scope of the defence. The ultimate inquiry is always whether the foreign judgment was obtained in a manner that was fair to the defendant and consistent with basic Canadian notions of justice.

. . . .

240. Proper notice also requires alerting the defendant to the allegations that will be adjudicated at trial. The defendant must be informed, by the pleadings or otherwise, of the basis on which damages are sought, and the case to be answered. . . .

241. Authority for the proposition that natural justice comprises substantive principles of justice, as well as minimum procedural standards, is to be found in the judgment of the English Court of Appeal in *Adams v. Cape Industries plc*, [1991] 1 All E.R. 929, the leading English case on the enforcement of foreign judgments. The judgment sought to be enforced in that case originated in Texas and arose from a complex asbestos-poisoning action involving numerous plaintiffs and defendants. Damages were assessed in a rather unconventional way. On the suggestion of plaintiffs' counsel, the judge arrived at a global amount of damages to be distributed among the plaintiffs in fixed amounts which were not based on proof of the damages suffered by each individual plaintiff. This method of calculating damages was held by the English court to be contrary to natural justice because it was "not the result

of a judicial assessment of the individual entitlements of the respective plaintiffs" and because no proper judicial hearing had been held on the quantum of damages (*Adams, supra*, at 1042). Slade L.J. held that it was a principle of substantive justice that unliquidated damages must be assessed "objectively by the independent judge on proof by the plaintiff of the relevant facts" (p. 1050).

242. *Adams* sets out a flexible and pragmatic approach to the natural justice defence which is appropriate for the Canadian context following *Morguard*. . . .

. . . .

245. Finally, the obligation of a defendant to pursue remedies available in the originating jurisdiction must be addressed. In *Adams, supra*, Slade L.J. held that opportunities for correcting a denial of natural justice that existed in the originating jurisdiction should be taken into account in assessing whether the defence of natural justice has been made out. It does not follow that the existence of such remedies automatically cures a failure of natural justice. . . .

D. *Application of the Impeachment Defences to the Facts of this Case*

(1) Public Policy

246. If the defence of public policy is understood as a bar to enforcing immoral or unjust foreign laws, it is not met here. . . .

247. In my view, the defects in the judgment, while severe, do not engage the public policy defence.

(2) Fraud

248. Under the rule that an allegation of fraud can only be considered if based on fresh evidence, the defence of fraud is not made out. All the facts that the appellants raise in this connection were known to them or could have been discovered at the time of the Florida action.

249. A further issue arises as to whether evidence of deliberate deception would be enough to vitiate the judgment. In my opinion, this is the kind of case for which a more lenient interpretation of the fraud defence would, in principle, be appropriate, because the appellants' decision not to attend the Florida proceedings was a reasonable one. Full participation in the Florida action would have been expensive, time-consuming and difficult. The appellants' own knowledge of the facts convinced them that the claim was frivolous, to say the least; they were amazed that it even resulted in a lawsuit. They thought, and they had every reason to think, that even if the claim succeeded they would be liable for no more than about US $8,000. . . . I see no reason why our law should deem these factors to be irrelevant.

250. If, in these circumstances, the plaintiffs took advantage of the opportunity to deceive the court by putting forward perjured or misleading evidence in order to obtain a higher award of damages, it would be unfair and contrary to the interests of the Canadian justice system for our courts to be obliged to enforce the judgment in spite of the fact that it was obtained by deception. . . .

251. The difficulty the appellants face is that there is no evidence that anything of this kind happened, because no record exists of the evidence and arguments put forward in the Florida damages hearing. . . . The defence of fraud therefore does not apply. Natural justice, though, is a different matter.

(3) Natural Justice

252. The Ontario defendants were not given sufficient notice of the extent and nature of the claims against them in the Florida action. The claimants failed to give the defendants proper notice of the true nature of their claim and its potential ramifications. Furthermore, there was no notice as to the serious consequences to the defendants of failure to refile their defence in response to the claimant's repeatedly amended pleadings. As a result, the notice afforded to the defendants did not meet the requirements of natural justice.

253. The amount of damages claimed was not stated in the Amended Complaint. The only mention of a monetary amount was the formulaic reference to damages over $5,000 required to give the Florida Circuit Court monetary jurisdiction. This form of pleading did not give the defendants a clear picture of what was at stake. . . .

255. Perhaps the most important failure of natural justice in this case is the fact that the defendants were not given notice of the consequences of failing to continue to file new defences to the repeated changes to the Amended Complaint. There was nothing on the face of the Amended Complaint that would alert them to the need to refile, especially since the allegations against them remained unaltered. . . .

256. A foreign plaintiff who expects to have a judgment in his or her favour enforced by a Canadian court has a responsibility to ensure that the defendant is in a position to make an informed decision about how to respond. If the defendant can show that the plaintiff failed to discharge that responsibility, the court should refuse to enforce the judgment on the basis that the defendant was deprived of proper notice, a basic condition of natural justice. . . .

259. What this means for the appellants' entitlement to rely on the natural justice defence must be ascertained by considering the reasonableness in all the circumstances of requiring them to make use of the remedies available in Florida. We must look at the reasons why they decided not to go to Florida to attack the judgment, but chose instead to trust that the Ontario courts would not enforce it.

260. The defendants' main reason for deciding as they did was that they were following the advice (which turned out to be erroneous) of legal counsel. . . . Given the information they had, the decision not to take steps in Florida was not only understandable but the only sensible option.

261. The majority appears to be of the view that the appellants are not entitled to any relief from the consequences of relying on mistaken legal advice. In my view, the mere fact that a defendant has received mistaken legal advice should not operate to relieve the claimant entirely of the consequences of a significant or substantial failure to observe the rules of natural justice, and it should not, in itself, bar the appellants from relying on this defence. . . .

(4) Residual Concerns

264. The facts of this appeal raise very serious concerns about the fairness of enforcing the Florida judgment which do not fit easily into the categories identified by the traditional impeachment defences. I have stated my conclusion that the facts do trigger the defence of natural justice, if it is interpreted in a purposive and flexible manner. Even if the natural justice defence did not apply, however, I would hold that this judgment should not be enforced.

265. The circumstances of this case are such that the enforcement of this judgment would shock the conscience of Canadians and cast a negative light on our justice system. The appellants have done nothing that infringes the rights of the respondents and have certainly done nothing to deserve such harsh punishment. Nor can they be said to have sought to avoid their obligations by hiding in their own jurisdiction or to have shown disrespect for the legal system of Florida. They have acted in good faith throughout and have diligently taken all the steps that appeared to be required of them, based on the information and advice they had. The plaintiffs in Florida appear to have taken advantage of the defendants' difficult position to pursue their interests as aggressively as possible and to secure a sizeable windfall.

. . .

266. On this last point, I would add that their failure to obtain a record of the proceedings in the Florida court does not reflect well on the respondents. In this case, the appellants, who had the burden of proving that one of the impeachment defences applied, failed to pursue their opportunity to investigate what transpired in the damages hearing by questioning those who were there. As a result, it would be inappropriate to draw any negative inference in their favour from the lack of evidence about the Florida proceedings. But defendants will not always have such an opportunity. When one party entirely controls whether there will be a transcript of the proceedings in the foreign court and chooses not to get one, thus depriving the enforcing court of a full record of what happened and an opportunity to verify that there was no fraud and no procedural irregularities, Canadian courts should be highly circumspect about giving effect to the judgment.

V. Conclusion

267. In my view, this judgment should not be enforced in Canada. I would allow the appeal with costs to the appellants.

Appeal dismissed with costs, IACOBUCCI, BINNIE *and* LEBEL JJ. *dissenting.*

QUESTIONS

1. In what respects do the requirements for recognition of foreign-country judgments under Canadian law as expressed in the Uniform Act as well as *Beals v. Saldana* differ from those of the 2005 revisions of the UFCMJA or Texas law? Are these differences related primarily to policy concerns — for example, differences in intentional deference for international comity — or

other factors? Are these requirements a matter of provincial or federal Canadian law — or does it matter which? Is "reciprocity" a requirement?

2. What is meant by "natural justice"? Is there any equivalent standard or principle in U.S. law, particularly in relation to standards for recognition of foreign-country judgments?

3. What issues would a U.S. court have to consider under the standards of the 2005 revisions of the UFCMJA in a case for the recognition and enforcement of a judgment by court in Quebec that arose from a failed real estate transaction in Montreal that was otherwise identical to the Florida case? Would "fraud" be a basis for non-recognition?

C. Japan

SADHWANI v. SADHWANI
Supreme Court (3rd P.B) Judgment of 28 April 1998
52 Minshū (No. 3) 853 (1998)
[Adapted from *Prominent Judgments of the Supreme Court*, based on translation by Sir Ernest Satow Chair of Japanese Law, University College, University of London; also translated in 42 JAIL 155 (1999)]

DISPOSITION
(*shūbun*)

1. The appeal [from Osaka High Court, Judgment of July 5, 1994] is dismissed.

2. The cost of appeal shall be borne by the appellant.

REASONS
(*riyū*)

The present case involves a claim by the appellees for an enforcement judgment on the basis of article 24 of the Law on Civil Execution in relation to the judgment of the Hong Kong High Court on the allocation of the cost of litigation rendered before the return of Hong Kong to the Peoples' Republic of China on July 1, 1997. Since Article 24, para.3 of the Law on Civil Execution was amended by Law No.110, 1996 after the present case had been brought to court, the present judgment will interpret the ground of appeal concerning the error in the interpretation and application of the subparagraphs of Article 200 of the previous Code of Civil Procedure to be on the error in the interpretation and application of the subparagraphs of Article 118 of the present Code of Civil Procedure which corresponds to former Article 200 (in the following, appellant X will be called 'appellant X', appellant company Sadhwanis Japan Limited, 'appellant company', appellee Y will be called 'appellee Y', Z, who is not a party to this litigation as 'third party Z', Bank of India as the 'third party Bank').

1. On item 1 of the ground of appeal by the representative of the appellant, Tadao Yamamoto:

'Judgment of a foreign court' as provided in article 24 of the Law on Civil Execution denotes a final judgment rendered by a foreign court on private law relations by providing procedural guarantee to both parties, regardless of the name, procedure, or form of judgment. Even if the judgment is called a decision or order, insofar as it possesses the characteristics of the above, it should be regarded as a judgment of a foreign court.

In the present case, according to the records, (1) in Hong Kong, the person who is to bear the cost of litigation and the allocation of the cost are not determined by the judgment on the substance of the case, but by an order for allocation of the cost of litigation upon the petition of the winning party, (2) the Hong Kong High Court rendered a judgment on the substance of the first to fourth litigation as indicated below between the appellants, appellees, and the Bank on April 27, 1988 in favor of the appellees and this judgment has taken effect, (3) the appellees applied for an order on the payment of the cost of litigation *vis-a-vis* the appellant and the Bank on May 11 of the same year, (4) the High Court of Hong Kong, after hearing the representative of the appellants, issued an order of payment of the cost of litigation to the appellants and the Bank on August 31 of the same year (hereinafter, 'the Order'), (5) subsequently, the actual cost of litigation was determined and on the basis of the Order and the Determination of the Cost dated October 3, 1989 and Certificate of Cost dated September 11, 1989, both of which are part of the Order (hereinafter, 'Orders'), the appellants were ordered to pay the appellees 1,202,585,58 Hong Kong dollars.

On the basis of these facts, it is appropriate to regard the Orders to be a judgment of a foreign court as provided by article 24 of the Law on Civil Execution, and the ruling of the court below which is in line with this conclusion is justifiable. There is no error in the decision of the court below as asserted by the appellants, and the argument is not acceptable.

2. On item 2:

In cases where interest is generated on the amount whose payment is ordered by a judgment etc., whether to include this in the judgment or to give enforcement power by provisions of law without including it in the judgment etc. differs from jurisdiction to jurisdiction, but the difference is largely due to technical considerations, and therefore, even if it is not included in the judgment etc. of a foreign court, it is not impossible to recognize and enforce interest payment in Japan [citation omitted].

According to the records: (1) There is no indication of the interest for delay in relation to the cost of litigation which the appellants were ordered to bear in the Orders. (2) However, under the Law of Hong Kong, in relation to judgments ordering monetary payments, if there is no specific order of the High Court, interest for the delay automatically emerges, and the rate of interest is to be determined ad hoc by the Chief Justice of the Hong Kong Supreme Court. (3) In the Orders, no specific order is included, and it is acknowledged that by the order of the Chief Justice of the Hong Kong Supreme Court, the rate of the interest for the delay after September 1, 1988, which is the next day of the date of issue of the Order, has been determined as indicated in the table of calculation for interest attached to the judgment of the first instance court.

Based upon the above facts, the ruling of the court below acknowledging that interests for delay in accordance with the rate as provided in the above-mentioned calculation table of interest which was not included in the Orders could be recognized and enforced in Japan is justifiable.

The appellants also argue that the original instance court unlawfully failed to rule on the grounds of the emergence of the interests for delay and the legitimacy of its rate, but the court in Japan is not empowered to examine the appropriateness of such rulings (art. 24(2), Law on Civil Execution).

The original judgment is not unlawful as argued by the appellant; the arguments of the appellants are not acceptable.

3. On item 3:

According to the records, it is evident that the appellants had failed to appeal against the Orders within the period of appeal as provided by the relevant law, and the ruling of the original instance court which found that the Orders have taken effect is justifiable in its conclusion. In the light of article 24(3) of the Law on Civil Execution, the method of proving that a foreign judgment has taken effect is not limited to the submission of the so called certificate of taking effect. The argument is unacceptable.

4. On item 4:

(1) Article 118(i), which provides that 'the jurisdiction of the foreign court can be acknowledged by laws or ordinances, or international treaties', should be understood in the meaning that in the light of the international civil procedural law of Japan, the country where the foreign court in question is located (hereinafter, 'country of judgment') is required to be positively acknowledged to have international jurisdiction (indirect general jurisdiction) on the given case. Since there is no provision of law or ordinance which directly indicates on what grounds the country of judgment has international jurisdiction, nor are there treaties or established clear rules of international law, it should be decided by reason in accordance with the idea of ensuring equal treatment of the parties and just and speedy trial. More specifically, whether or not the country of judgment has international jurisdiction should be determined in the light of reason, basically in accordance with the provisions of the Code of Civil Procedure on the territorial jurisdiction of the courts from the viewpoint of whether it is appropriate to recognize the given foreign judgment, taking into consideration specific circumstances of each case.

(2) The Orders are auxiliary decisions on the payment of costs of litigation in relation to the judgment in substance, and therefore, whether or not Hong Kong has jurisdiction over the Orders should be examined, in principle, in relation to the judgment in substance.

(3) In the present case, the original instance court acknowledged international jurisdiction of Hong Kong on the grounds that (a) in the first litigation in which the third party Bank demanded performance of guarantee *vis-a-vis* the appellees, the place of residence of the appellees (defendants) (art. 2(1) of the previous Code of Civil Procedure) was in Hong Kong, (b) in the second litigation against the third party Bank, appellant X and his wife third party Z in which the appellees claimed

recognition of subrogation of the third party Bank on the condition that the obligation in the first litigation is performed in relation to the base hypothec which the Bank held *vis-a-vis* the appellants, the jurisdiction of consolidated claims (art. 21 of the previous Code of Civil Procedure) was in Hong Kong, because not only in relation to the counterclaim *vis-a-vis* the third party Bank, but also in relation to the claims *vis-a-vis* X and third party Z, there is a common ground in substantive law and they are closely related, and (c) in the fourth action *vis-a-vis* the appellees in which the appellants and third party Z, in defense against the third action referred to below, claimed recognition that it was the appellee Y only, who is to have an obligation of guarantee, since it is a counter claim against the third action, since Hong Kong has jurisdiction over the third action. The above ruling of the original instance court is justifiable also under the current Code of Civil Procedure which has a similar provision on territorial jurisdiction. The original judgment is not unlawful as argued by the appellants.

(4) On the other hand, the third action is a claim by the appellees *vis-a-vis* the appellants and third party Z (three of them) asking the court to acknowledge the existence of the right to indemnification, and has a nature of a third party proceeding which is unique to Anglo-American jurisdiction. Defendants in the third action, appellant X and third party Z are at the same time, defendants in the second action, and moreover, the second and third actions are a claim for the acknowledgement of the possibility of subrogate exercise of the base hypothec right or claim for indemnification based upon the litigation agreement between the appellants and the third party Bank on the condition that the first action initiated against the appellees is decided in favor of the plaintiffs. These are actions on the same basis of substantive law, are mutually closely related, and therefore, a strong necessity exists for a uniform adjudication. Considering these circumstances, concerning the third action, in the light of the essence of article 7 of the Code of Civil Procedure, acknowledgement of the existence of jurisdiction in Hong Kong of the consolidated claim with the second action, including the claim *vis-a-vis* the appellant company which was newly made a defendant, and recognition of the judgment of the Hong Kong court suits the idea of equality of the parties, just and speedy handling of the case, and coincides with reason. Therefore, the ruling of the original instance court which acknowledged international jurisdiction of Hong Kong in the third action is justifiable in its conclusion.

(5) Based upon the above, the argument of the appellants cannot be accepted.

5. On item 5:

(1) According to the records, it can be ascertained that (a) the appellees applied for the Order *vis a vis* the appellants on May 11, 1988, (b) upon this application, the Hong Kong High Court allowed the service of the notice of motion to the appellant X, an Indian national residing in Kobe, and the appellant company which is a Japanese juridical person, (c) this notice of motion was delivered to the appellants on July 26, 1988 by a Japanese attorney who was personally asked to do so by the appellees, (d) the appellants retained an attorney resident in Hong Kong as a representative for the proceedings concerning the notice of motion and a hearing took place on August 25, 1988 with the participation of this attorney, (e) the representative of the appellant contested the international jurisdiction of Hong

Kong in relation to the third action mentioned above.

(2) The argument of the appellant is that service of the document by direct delivery is not compatible with manner of delivery of documents as provided by the International Convention on Judicial Cooperation, and therefore, in relation to the appellant company, failed to fulfil the requirement of 'service' [*sōtatsu*] as provided in article 118(ii) of the Code of Civil Procedure and also that before responding to the claim, the international jurisdiction of the court has been contested, and therefore, the requirement of 'response to the claim' as provided in the same provision has not been fulfilled. The Court will examine whether or not these requirements have been fulfilled in relation to appellant X *ex officio*.

(3) *'Summons or service of the order required for the commencement of litigation' to the defendant as required under article 118(ii) of the Code of Civil Procedure does not have to be summons or service on the basis of the Japanese law of civil procedure, but must be sufficient for the defendant actually to become aware of the commencement of the litigation and to defend himself.* [Emphasis added.] Furthermore, from the viewpoint of ensuring clarity and stability of the procedure of litigation, if there is a treaty of judicial cooperation between the country of judgment and Japan and if this treaty provides that the service of the document required for the commencement of litigation must be effected in a manner set out in this treaty, service of documents not in accordance with the manner set out in the treaty should not be regarded as service which fulfils the requirement of the above provision of the Code of Civil Procedure.

In the present case, Japan and the United Kingdom, which had sovereignty over Hong Kong then, were both signatories to the Convention on the Service Abroad of Judicial and Extra-Judicial Documents in Civil and Commercial Matters, service of documents by direct delivery to the recipient by a person who has personally been asked by the party such as in the present case is not allowed under the above Convention. Furthermore, no legal basis for it can be found in the 'Consul Treaty between Japan and the United Kingdom of Great Britain and Northern Ireland' (Japan-UK Consul Treaty). Therefore, the service of the above notice of motion to the appellant does not fulfil the requirement of the provision of the Code of Civil Procedure and is unlawful.

(4) On the other hand, 'response to the claim' as provided by article118(ii) of the Code of Civil Procedure, unlike the response to the claim in determining the jurisdiction based upon response, includes cases where the defendant was given the opportunity of defense and effected defensive measures in court. According to the above facts, it is evident that the appellants responded in the meaning of this provision on the proceedings of notice of motion.

(5) Therefore, in relation to the appellant company, the Orders fulfil the requirement of article 118(ii) of the Code of Civil Procedure. The ruling of the original instance court on this point is justifiable in conclusion, and the argument of the appellants is not acceptable. It is also evident that in relation to the appellant X, the Orders fulfil the requirement of the said provision.

6. On item 6:

The problem of how to allocate the cost of litigation is a matter to be decided by each jurisdiction, and provided that it is determined within the scope of cost actually incurred, even if one of the parties is to bear the total cost including lawyers fee, it is not against 'public order' as provided by article 118(iii) of the Code of Civil Procedure. According to the records, in the present case, the fact that the appellants acted in bad faith, the rate for the so-called indemnity basis was applied and most of the cost including the lawyers' fee was ordered to be borne by the appellant. It is unusual that this rate on indemnity basis is applied by a court in Hong Kong and it can be acknowledged that it has a punitive element, but on the other hand, the amount of cost of litigation which the appellants were ordered to pay by the Order does not exceed the cost actually incurred, and therefore, the content of the Order cannot be regarded as being against the public order of Japan. The ruling of the original instance court which, in principle, is in line with this view is justifiable. The original judgment is not unlawful as argued by the appellants and the argument that the payment of cost of litigation on an indemnity basis is unlawful in parallel to punitive damages is unacceptable. It was also argued that the judgment of the Hong Kong High Court in the substance of the case was a result of a deceit by the appellees and is against the procedural public order. However, this is merely an allegation that the finding of facts was a result of the leading testimony by the witness, criticizing the inappropriateness of the choice of evidence. Japanese courts are not empowered to examine the appropriateness of the choice of evidence (art. 24(2), Law on Civil Execution) and the argument is not acceptable.

7. On item 7:

'The existence of mutual guarantee' (*sōgu no hōshō*) [i.e., reciprocity], as provided by Article 118(iv) of the Code of Civil Procedure means that *in the country where the foreign court which rendered the judgment in question resides, judgments of a similar nature by Japanese courts are treated as valid under the requirements not substantially different from the requirements of the above provision* [citation omitted; emphasis added]. According to the records, it can be ascertained that: (a) In Hong Kong, there is a law and a rule on the recognition of foreign judgment (mutual enforcement), and by the order of the Governor, the Rule lists specific countries which are regarded to have mutual guarantee. (b) Japan was not listed as a country with mutual guarantee. (c) However, in Hong Kong, in relation to the recognition of foreign judgments, in addition to statutory law, principles of English Common Law was applicable. (c) Under the Common Law, judgments of a foreign court ordering payment of money were recognized in accordance with the requirements of the original judgment.

The requirements for the recognition of foreign judgments under the Common Law can be regarded as not substantially different from the requirements of the subparagraphs of article 118 of the Code of Civil Procedure of Japan. Therefore, it is appropriate to conclude that between Hong Kong and Japan, there was a mutual guarantee on recognition of foreign judgments as provided by article 118(iv) of the Code of Civil Procedure. [Emphasis added.] There is no unlawfulness in the original judgment as argued by the appellants, and the arguments are unacceptable.

Therefore, the justices unanimously rule as stated in the Order.

Justice Hideo Chikusa
Justice Itsuo Sonobe
Justice Yukinobu Ozaki
Justice Toshifumi Motohara
Justice Toshihiroō Kanatani

QUESTIONS AND NOTE

1. List the requirements for the recognition and enforcement of a foreign-country judgment under Japanese law. How do they differ from those of the 2005 revisions of the UFCMJA and those articulated in *Beals v. Saldanha?*

2. What was the issue in *Sadhwani v. Sadhwani?* Might a similar issue arise in the context of an action for recognition and enforcement of a foreign-country judgment in the United States or Canada?

In most civil law countries, including Japan, in order to enforce a judgment — including foreign country judgments — the enforcing party must obtain an "execution judgment" and satisfy the procedures for civil execution. In Japan, the 1979 Civil Execution Law (*Minji shikkō hō*), Law No. 4, 1979, sets out the requirements. The applicable provision in *Sadhwani v. Sadhwani* was article 24, which provides:

(1) An action seeking an execution judgment for a judgment of a foreign court shall be under the jurisdiction of the district court having jurisdiction over the location of the general venue of the obligor, and when there is no such general venue, it shall be under the jurisdiction of the district court having jurisdiction over the location of the subject matter of the claim or the seizable property of the obligor.

(2) An execution judgment shall be made without investigating whether or not the judicial decision is appropriate.

(3) The action set forth in paragraph (1) shall be dismissed without prejudice when it is not proved that the judgment of a foreign court has become final and binding or when such judgment fails to satisfy the requirements listed in the items of Article 118 of the Code of Civil Procedure.

(4) An execution judgment shall declare that compulsory execution based on the judgment by a foreign court shall be permitted.

The critical issue in this as in most cases is whether the judgment satisfied the requirements of article 118 of the Code of Civil Procedure.

NORTHCON I v. MANSEI KŌGYŌ K. K.
Supreme Court (2nd P.B.) Judgment of 11 July 1997
51 Minshū 2573 (1997)
[Based on translation in *Series of Prominent Supreme Court Judgments* by Sir Ernest Satow Chair of Japanese Law, University College, University of London; also translated in 41 JAIL 104 (1998)]

Northcon I, a partnership organized under Oregon law, was formed to develop a facility in Oregon for Maruman Integrated Circuits, a California subsidiary of Mansei Kōgyō K. K. As the result of a dispute over a lease agreement Maruman Integrated Circuit filed suit in California against Northcon I, which brought a counter claim against the parent Mansei and Yoshitaka Katayama, its chief executive officer as well as other officers. In May 1982 the California Superior Court ruled in favor of Northcon I, awarding over $425,000 dollars in compensatory damages, $40,000 as costs, and an additional $1,125,000 in punitive damages. Five years later in May 1987 the California Court of Appeals affirmed the judgment. Northcon filed an action with the Tokyo District Court for enforcement judgments based on the California Court of Appeals judgment, which has become final and irrevocable. First The Tokyo District Court in a judgment of February 18, 1991, granted Northcon I's petition for enforcement of the compensatory damage award but refused to recognize the punitive damages award as contrary to Japanese public policy. Both sides then appealed to the Tokyo High Court, which on June 28, 1993, affirmed the Tokyo District Court's decision, and dismissed both appeals. The parties then appealed this decision to the Supreme Court. The Second Petty Bench decided both appeals, affirming the Tokyo High Court in separate judgments of July 11, 1997.

Disposition
(*shūbun*)

1. The appeal of the appellant against the appellee Mansei Kōgyō Kabushiki Kaisha is dismissed.

2. The appeal of the appellant against the appellee X is dismissed.

3. The cost of appeal is to be borne by the appellant.

Reasons
(*riyū*)

I. On the appeal of the appellant against the appellee company

On the grounds of appeal by representatives of the appellants Takeshi Sakuragi and Noriko Sato:

1. The present case involves a claim by the appellee requesting the enforcement of a judgment of the Court of the State of California, USA. The court of original instance has ascertained the following facts:

(1) The Civil Code of the State of California, USA, has a provision which allows the plaintiff to receive punitive damages for the purpose of deterrence and sanction on the defendant in addition to damages for the actual loss in litigation on the ground of breach of non-contractual duties, if there was an fraudulent act or similar acts on the part of the defendant (article 3294).

(2) The Superior Court of California ordered the appellees to pay compensatory damages of 425,251 dollars and the cost of 40,104 dollars 71 cents, and in addition, ordered the appellee company to pay punitive damages of 1,125,000 dollars by the judgment of May 19, 1982 (hereinafter, 'the foreign judgment in the present case') on the ground that the appellees effected fraudulent acts against the appellants in relation to the conclusion of a lease agreement between the appellant and a subsidiary of the appellee, Marman Integrated Circuit Inc.

(3) Both the appellants and appellees appealed against this judgment to the Appellate Court of California, but the Court dismissed the appeal on May 12, 1987, and the foreign judgment in the present case came into effect.

2. (1) In a claim for an enforcement judgment, whether the given foreign judgment fulfils the requirements of subparagraphs of article 200 of the Code of Civil Procedure (art. 24(3) of the Law on Civil Execution) is examined. Article 200 of the Code of Civil Procedure requires that the foreign judgment should not contradict public policy and good morals of Japan. One may not conclude that this requirement is not fulfilled solely by the fact that the foreign judgment contains an institution which does not exist in Japan, but if the given institution is against the basic principles or basic ideas of the legal order in Japan, the judgment should be regarded as being against public order in the above-cited provision.

(2) It is evident that the system of punitive damages as provided by the Civil Code of the State of California (hereinafter, 'punitive damages') is designed to impose sanctions on the culprit and prevent similar acts in the future by ordering the culprit who had effected malicious acts to pay additional damages on top of the damages for the actual loss, and judging from the purposes, is similar to criminal sanctions such as fines in Japan. In contrast, the system of damages based upon tort in Japan assesses the actual loss in a pecuniary manner, forces the culprit to compensate this amount, and thus enables the recovery of the disadvantage suffered by the victim and restores the *status quo ante* [citation omitted] and is not intended for sanctions on the culprit or prevention of similar acts in the future, i.e. general prevention. Admittedly, there may be an effect of sanctions on the culprit or prevention of similar acts in the future by imposing a duty of compensation on the culprit, but this is a reflective and secondary effect of imposing the duty of compensation on the culprit, and the system is fundamentally different from the system of punitive damages whose goals are the sanctioning of the culprit and general deterrence. In Japan, sanctioning of the culprit and general deterrence is left to criminal or administrative sanctions. Thus the system in which in tort cases, the

victim is paid damages for the purpose of imposing sanction on the culprit and general deterrence in addition to damages for the actual loss should be regarded as against the basic principles or basic ideas of the system of compensation based upon tort in Japan.

(3) Therefore, part of the foreign judgment in the present case which ordered the appellee company to pay punitive damages for the purpose of deterrence and sanction in addition to compensatory damages and the cost is against public order of Japan and therefore, has no effect.

3. Thus, the judgment of the original instance which dismissed the claim for enforcement judgment on the part of the foreign judgment in the present case ordering the appellee company to pay punitive damages should be upheld. The arguments of the appellant, including the assertion that the original judgment is against the preamble to the Constitution and article 6(1) of the Friendship and Commerce Treaty between Japan and the United States, criticize the interpretation and application of laws and ordinances by the original instance based upon unique views and cannot be accepted.

II. On appeal against appellee X

The claim in the present case by the appellant against appellee X requests an enforcement judgment on the part of the foreign judgment in the present case on the payment of compensatory damages and the cost as well as the accompanying interests. The original judgment dismissed the appeal against the judgment of the first instance court which had acknowledged such a claim in total. Therefore, the appellant has no interest for further *jōkoku* appeal, and therefore, this *jōkoku* appeal should be dismissed as without a lawful basis.

Based upon articles 401, 399-3, 399(1)(i), 95, and 89, the justices unanimously judge as indicated in the disposition.

JUSTICE KATSUYA ŌNISHI
JUSTICE SHIGEHARU NEGISHI
JUSTICE SHINICHI KAWAI
JUSTICE HIROSHI FUKUDA

NOTE AND QUESTION

Criminal judgments are generally not subject to recognition and enforcement outside of the country in which rendered. Most civil law countries similarly deny recognition and enforcement of judgments for penal damages as contravention of the public policy of the forum state. Note that the lower court did enforce the non-punitive portions of the Oregon judgment. This feature of the lower court's decision was not, as noted by the Court, an issue before the Court on the second appeal on issues of law (i.e., the *jōkoku* appeal).

Query: How in your view would a Japanese court deal with an action for recognition and enforcement of a U.S. civil judgment for treble damages arising from a private damage action under the Sherman Act?

D. European Union

As of January 2015 the recognition and enforcement of judgments of courts the 28 member states of the European Union is governed by Regulation (EU) No. 1215/2012, which, as noted in Chapter 1, replaces the 1968 Brussels Convention and EC Regulation 44/2001. Under the 2012 Regulation judgments (including decrees, orders, decisions, writes of execution, as well as provisional and protective measures ordered by a court in a member state (article 2(a)), "shall be recognized in other Member States without any special procedures being required" (article 36). Such judgments are, however, subject to certain requirements. We have previously examined those related to adjudicatory jurisdiction in Chapter 1. In addition, article 45 mandates that such recognition be denied on the following grounds:

(a) if such recognition is manifestly contrary to public policy (*ordre public*) in the Member State addressed;

(b) where the judgment was given in default of appearance, if the defendant was not served with the document which instituted the proceedings or with an equivalent document in sufficient time and in such a way as to enable him to arrange for his defence, unless the defendant failed to commence proceedings to challenge the judgment when it was possible for him to do so;

(c) if the judgment is irreconcilable with a judgment given between the same parties in the Member State addressed;

(d) if the judgment is irreconcilable with an earlier judgment given in another Member State or *in a third State involving the same cause of action and between the same parties, provided that the earlier judgment fulfils the conditions necessary for its recognition in the Member State addressed* [emphasis added].

Also exempted are judgments contrary to the special provisions on adjudicatory jurisdiction related to insurance, consumers or employees set out in sections 3, 4, and 5 of Chapter II as well as judgments in actions involving defendants not domiciled in an EU Member State that, pursuant to article 6 of Chapter II, that were subject to the rules of adjudicatory jurisdiction of the particular member state.

The recognition and enforcement of judgments rendered by courts in countries outside of the EU remain problematic inasmuch as neither the 2012 Regulation nor its predecessor, EC Regulation 44/2001, apply. For such judgments national rules govern.

An initial requirement especially applicable to U.S. and Canadian common law judgments is that the judgment relate to a matter recognized within the civil law jurisdictions as civil or commercial. This fundamental requirement reflects the civil law division between private and public law and the separation of regular and administrative courts in most (but not all) civil law countries. As a general matter, however, the basic requirements are familiar. The foreign country judgment should satisfy the following:

(1) The judgment should be final;

(2) The court should have had adjudicatory jurisdiction as defined in the law of the recognizing state;

(3) The defendant should have received proper and timely notice with delivery of the documents initiating the lawsuit;

(4) The proceedings should have been fair;

(5) The judgment must not violate the recognizing state's public policy;

(6) It should not have been based on fraud;

(7) It should not be inconsistent with proceedings or final decisions involving the same cause of action between the same parties.

Two exceptions are noteworthy. French courts as a rule do not recognize judgments against French nationals unless they have acquiesced to the jurisdiction of the foreign court. Also, a few countries still require reciprocity, as we have seen with Japan. Among them is Germany. The relevant requirements are set out in section 328 of the German Code of Civil Procedure (*Zivilprozessordnung* — ZPO):

Section 328
Recognition of foreign judgments

(1) Recognition of a judgment handed down by a foreign court shall be denied if:

1. The courts of the state [rendering the judgment] do not have jurisdiction according to German law;

2. The defendant, who has not entered an appearance in the proceedings and who raises this fact, has not duly been served the document by which the proceedings were initiated, or not in time to allow him to make a defense;

3. The judgment is incompatible with a judgment rendered in Germany, or with an earlier judgment handed down abroad that is to be recognized, or if the proceedings on which such judgment is based are incompatible with proceedings that were pending earlier in Germany;

4. The recognition of the judgment would lead to a result that is obviously incompatible with essential principles of German law, and in particular if the recognition is not compatible with fundamental rights;

5. Reciprocity has not been granted.

(2) The rule set out in number 5 does not contravene the judgment's being recognized if the judgment concerns a non-pecuniary claim and if,

according to the laws of Germany, no place of jurisdiction was established in Germany.

QUESTIONS AND NOTE

1. Under what circumstances would a U.S. judgment brought by a U.S. firm against a German national NOT be enforceable in the EU because of a subsequent German judgment in a parallel action on the same facts and cause of action brought by the German defendant against the U.S. firm?

2. Which, if any, of judgments reviewed above for which recognition was sought in the U.S., Canada, and Japan would a German court refuse recognition?

Note: The recognition and enforcement of foreign country judgments in Mexico deserve mention. The formalities are more extensive and must be adhered to with greater precision than any of the countries we examine here. The procedures for all forms of international cooperation — including discovery — are exceptionally governed by the Federal Code of Civil Procedure (ordinarily applicable only for the Federal District) under article 544 of Book Four. The provision requires that in cases involving international litigation, all states must comply with the special rules set out in the subsequent provision of Book Four. All procedures must be carefully satisfied. For recognition (*homologación*) and enforcement (*ejecución*) these include the basic requirement of a formal request (*exhorto*) or letter rogatory (*carta rogatoria*) issued by the court that handed down the judgment in question, which must also satisfy the prescribed formalities. Of note is that under article 572 the formal request must be translated into Spanish, must show that the judgment is final and conclusive, and that the defendant was properly notified (*notificado*) of the action and thus provided the opportunity to make a full defense.

II. RECOGNITION AND ENFORCEMENT OF ARBITRAL AWARDS

1958 CONVENTION ON THE RECOGNITION AND ENFORCEMENT OF FOREIGN ARBITRAL AWARDS

As noted at the outset, unlike foreign-country judgments, recognition and enforcement of arbitral awards are facilitated by international convention. As of 2014, 149 countries had become parties to the 1958 Convention on the Recognition and Enforcement of Foreign Arbitral Awards — the New York Convention — under which the contracting states are required "to recognize arbitral awards as binding and enforce them in accordance with the rules of procedure of the territory where the award is relied upon" (article III). Article V sets out the only circumstances that would allow a state to refuse to recognize and enforce an arbitral award from another contracting state:

Article V

1. Recognition and enforcement of the award may be refused, at the request of the party against whom it is invoked, only if that party furnishes to the competent authority where the recognition and enforcement is sought, proof that:

(a) The parties to the agreement referred to in article II were, under the law applicable to them, under some incapacity, or the said agreement is not valid under the law to which the parties have subjected it or, failing any indication thereon, under the law of the country where the award was made; or

(b) The party against whom the award is invoked was not given proper notice of the appointment of the arbitrator or of the arbitration proceedings or was otherwise unable to present his case; or

(c) The award deals with a difference not contemplated by or not falling within the terms of the submission to arbitration, or it contains decisions on matters beyond the scope of the submission to arbitration, provided that, if the decisions on matters submitted to arbitration can be separated from those not so submitted, that part of the award which contains decisions on matters submitted to arbitration may be recognized and enforced; or

(d) The composition of the arbitral authority or the arbitral procedure was not in accordance with the agreement of the parties, or, failing such agreement, was not in accordance with the law of the country where the arbitration took place; or

(e) The award has not yet become binding on the parties, or has been set aside or suspended by a competent authority of the country in which, or under the law of which, that award was made.

2. Recognition and enforcement of an arbitral award may also be refused if the competent authority in the country where recognition and enforcement is sought finds that:

(a) The subject matter of the difference is not capable of settlement by arbitration under the law of that country; or

(b) The recognition or enforcement of the award would be contrary to the public policy of that country.

The following cases exemplify the convention's effect.

A. United States

Notwithstanding the New York Convention, the Federal Arbitration Act (Pub.L. 68–401, 43 Stat. 883, enacted February 12, 1925, codified at 9 U.S.C. § 1 *et seq.*) remains the principal source for the legal rules governing the enforcement and recognition of commercial arbitral awards in the U.S — both domestic and foreign. For foreign arbitral awards the FAA rules yield to those set out in two other separate but closely related sources — the 1958 New York Convention and the 1975 Inter-American Convention on International Commercial Arbitration, to which the United States and Mexico, but not Canada, are signatories. The FAA explicitly provides for the enforcement of both conventions under sections 201 and 301. By implicit reference, sections 208 and 305, make the general provisions of the FAA of Chapter 1 (§§ 1–16) applicable to the extent that they do not conflict with those of the Conventions. The relationships among the FAA and the two conventions are also clarified in FAA § 305, which provides that:

> When the requirements for application of both the Inter-American Convention and the Convention on the Recognition and Enforcement of Foreign Arbitral Awards of June 10, 1958, are met, determination as to which Convention applies shall, unless otherwise expressly agreed, be made as follows:
>
> (1) If a majority of the parties to the arbitration agreement are citizens of a State or States that have ratified or acceded to the Inter-American Convention and are member States of the Organization of American States, the Inter-American Convention shall apply.
>
> (2) In all other cases the Convention on the Recognition and Enforcement of Foreign Arbitral Awards of June 10, 1958, shall apply.

As a result, arbitral awards made outside of the United States between parties that are not U.S. citizens or, in the case of juridical persons, not incorporated or maintain their principal place of business within the United States as well as awards that do not relate to property located abroad, or performance or enforcement abroad, or "some other reasonable relation with one or more foreign states" (FAA § 202) are subject to the New York Convention — unless, for our purposes here, the arbitration proceedings are between U.S. and Mexican citizens, in which case, the Inter-American Convention applies.

FRONTERA RESOURCES AZERBAIJAN CORPORATION v. STATE OIL COMPANY OF THE AZERBAIJAN REPUBLIC*
582 F.3d 393 (2d. Cir. 2009)

JOHN M. WALKER, JR., CIRCUIT JUDGE:

Petitioner-Appellant Frontera Resources Azerbaijan Corporation ("Frontera") appeals from the dismissal by the United States District Court for the Southern District of New York (Richard J. Holwell, Judge) of its petition to enforce a Swedish arbitration award against Respondent-Appellee State Oil Corporation of the Azerbaijan Republic ("SOCAR"). The district court granted SOCAR's motion to dismiss for want of personal jurisdiction. [Citation omitted.] We conclude that SOCAR is not entitled to the Due Process Clause's jurisdictional protections if it is

---

* Footnotes omitted.

an agent of the Azerbaijani state. Accordingly, we vacate and remand for the district court to reconsider its analysis.

BACKGROUND

Frontera and SOCAR are two companies in the oil industry. Frontera is based in the Cayman Islands, and SOCAR is based in and owned by the Republic of Azerbaijan ("Azerbaijan"). In November 1998, the parties entered into a written agreement (the "Agreement") under which Frontera developed and managed oil deposits in Azerbaijan and delivered oil to SOCAR. In 2000, a dispute arose over SOCAR's refusal to pay for some of this oil, and in response, Frontera allegedly sought to sell oil that was supposed to be sold to SOCAR to parties outside of Azerbaijan instead. In November 2000, after instructing local customs authorities to block Frontera's oil exports, SOCAR seized the oil.

In March 2002, the bank that had financed Frontera's involvement in Azerbaijan foreclosed on its loan, forcing Frontera to assign its rights in the project to the bank. In July 2002, the bank settled its claims with SOCAR. Frontera, however, continued to seek payment for both previously delivered and seized oil. Based on its settlement with the bank, SOCAR denied liability to Frontera.

After Frontera and SOCAR were unable to settle their dispute amicably, Frontera served SOCAR in July 2003 with a request for arbitration as per the Agreement. In January 2006, after a hearing on the merits with full participation by both parties, a Swedish arbitral tribunal awarded Frontera approximately $1.24 million plus interest. On February 14, 2006, Frontera filed a petition in the Southern District of New York to confirm the award pursuant to Article II(2) of the Convention on the Recognition and Enforcement of Foreign Arbitral Awards ("New York Convention"), *opened for signature* June 10, 1958, 21 U.S.T. 2517, 330 U.N.T.S. 38, *implemented at* 9 U.S.C. § 207. The district court dismissed the petition for lack of personal jurisdiction, on the basis that SOCAR had insufficient contacts with the United States to meet the Due Process Clause's requirements for the assertion of personal jurisdiction. The district court questioned the soundness of according due process protections to SOCAR, a company owned by Azerbaijan, but nonetheless applied the traditional due process test based on our precedent in *Texas Trading & Milling Corp. v. Federal Republic of Nigeria*, 647 F.2d 300 (2d Cir. 1981). The district court also declined to find quasi in rem jurisdiction over SOCAR, because Frontera had not identified specific SOCAR assets within the court's jurisdiction. The district court denied jurisdictional discovery and dismissed Frontera's petition. This appeal followed.

DISCUSSION

Frontera contends (1) that a court does not need personal jurisdiction over a party in order to confirm a foreign arbitral award against that party, and (2) that *Texas Trading* should be overruled, because the Due Process Clause's protections should not apply to foreign states or their instrumentalities. Frontera also challenges the district court's denial of jurisdictional discovery.

I. PERSONAL JURISDICTION OVER SOCAR

When considering a district court's dismissal for lack of personal jurisdiction, we review its factual findings for clear error and its legal conclusions *de novo*. [Citation omitted.]

Generally, personal jurisdiction has both statutory and constitutional components. A court must have a statutory basis for asserting jurisdiction over a defendant, [citation omitted], and the Due Process Clause typically also demands that the defendant, if "not present within the territory of the forum, . . . have certain minimum contacts with it such that the maintenance of the suit does not offend 'traditional notions of fair play and substantial justice.'" *Int'l Shoe Co. v. Washington*, 326 U.S. 310, 316, 66 S. Ct. 154, 90 L. Ed. 95 (1945) (quoting *Milliken v. Meyer*, 311 U.S. 457, 463, 61 S. Ct. 339, 85 L. Ed. 278 (1940)). The parties do not challenge the district court's reliance on the Foreign Sovereign Immunities Act ("FSIA"), 28 U.S.C. § 1608(a) [on service], as the statutory basis for jurisdiction over SOCAR. . . . This appeal instead is focused on the Due Process Clause's place in the district court's analysis.

The district court dismissed Frontera's petition because it concluded that SOCAR's contacts with the United States were insufficient to meet the Due Process Clause's demands for personal jurisdiction. Frontera contends that this was in error both because personal jurisdiction is not necessary for the requested relief, and because SOCAR is not entitled to the Due Process Clause's protections. We address each argument in turn.

A. THE NEED FOR JURISDICTION

Frontera argues that a district court does not need personal jurisdiction over a respondent to confirm a foreign arbitral award against that party. Yet, Frontera contends, the district court's dismissal of its petition "necessarily rest[ed] upon an assumption" that personal jurisdiction over SOCAR was indispensable. . . . We read the district court's decision differently. Although the district court considered whether it could assert personal jurisdiction over SOCAR, it did not make that question dispositive. Instead, after finding SOCAR's contacts with the United States insufficient to establish personal jurisdiction, the district court examined whether it had jurisdiction over any of SOCAR's assets, because "in the absence of minimum contacts, quasi in rem jurisdiction may be exercised to attach property to collect a debt." *Frontera*, 479 F. Supp. 2d at 387. Thus, by suggesting that the district court required personal jurisdiction, Frontera misunderstands the framework of the court's analysis. And to the extent that Frontera's challenge is to the district court's requirement of *either* personal or quasi in rem jurisdiction, it is without merit.

We have previously avoided deciding whether personal or quasi in rem jurisdiction is required to confirm foreign arbitral awards pursuant to the New York Convention. [Citation omitted.] However, the numerous other courts to have addressed the issue have each required personal or quasi in rem jurisdiction. [Citations omitted.]

Frontera contends that none of these courts addressed the precise argument it advances here: that there is no "positive statutory or treaty basis" for such a jurisdictional requirement. . . . The federal statute that implements the New York Convention requires a court to confirm an award "unless it finds one of the grounds for refusal or deferral of recognition or enforcement of the award specified in the said Convention." 9 U.S.C. § 207. Article V of the New York Convention "provides the exclusive grounds for refusing confirmation," *Yusuf Ahmed Alghanim & Sons, W.L.L. v. Toys "R" Us, Inc.*, 126 F.3d 15, 20 (2d Cir. 1997), and specifies seven grounds for refusing to enforce an arbitral award, none of which include a lack of jurisdiction over the respondent or the respondent's property, *see* New York Convention at art. 5, 21 U.S.T. at 2517. Frontera accordingly argues that we cannot impose a jurisdictional requirement if the Convention does not already have one. We disagree.

Unlike "state courts[,] [which] are courts of general jurisdiction[,] . . . federal courts are courts of limited jurisdiction which thus require a specific grant of jurisdiction." *Foxhall Realty Law Offices, Inc. v. Telecomm. Premium Servs., Ltd.*, 156 F.3d 432, 435 (2d Cir. 1998) (citing *Sheldon v. Sill*, 49 U.S. (8 How.) 441, 449, 12 L. Ed. 1147 (1850)). "The validity of an order of a federal court depends upon that court's having jurisdiction over both the subject matter and the parties." *Ins. Corp. of Ir., Ltd. v. Compagnie des Bauxites de Guinee*, 456 U.S. 694, 701, 102 S. Ct. 2099, 72 L. Ed. 2d 492 (1982). While the requirement of subject matter jurisdiction "functions as a restriction on federal power," *id.* at 702, 102 S. Ct. 2099, the need for personal jurisdiction is fundamental to "the court's power to exercise control over the parties," *Leroy v. Great W. United Corp.*, 443 U.S. 173, 180, 99 S. Ct. 2710, 61 L. Ed. 2d 464 (1979). "Some basis must be shown, whether arising from the respondent's residence, his conduct, his consent, the location of his property or otherwise, to justify his being subject to the court's power." *Glencore Grain*, 284 F.3d at 1122 (quoting *Transatl. Bulk Shipping*, 622 F. Supp. at 27).

Because of the primacy of jurisdiction, "jurisdictional questions ordinarily must precede merits determinations in dispositional order." *Sinochem Int'l Co. v. Malay. Int'l Shipping Corp.*, 549 U.S. 422, 431, 127 S. Ct. 1184, 167 L. Ed. 2d 15 (2007). "[T]he items listed in Article V as the exclusive defenses . . . pertain to *substantive* matters rather than to procedure." *Monegasque De Reassurances S.A.M. v. Nak Naftogaz of Ukr.*, 311 F.3d 488, 496 (2d Cir. 2002) (emphasis added). Article V's exclusivity limits the ways in which one can challenge a request for confirmation, but it does nothing to alter the fundamental requirement of jurisdiction over the party against whom enforcement is being sought.

Frontera argues that the Supreme Court suggested otherwise in *Shaffer v. Heitner*, 433 U.S. 186, 97 S. Ct. 2569, 53 L. Ed. 2d 683 (1977), in the following footnote:

> Once it has been determined by a court of competent jurisdiction that the defendant is a debtor of the plaintiff, there would seem to be no unfairness in allowing an action to realize on that debt in a State where the defendant has property, whether or not that State would have jurisdiction to determine the existence of the debt as an original matter. *Id.* at 210 n. 36, 97 S. Ct. 2569.

But while this footnote indicated, in dicta, that a court might not need jurisdiction over a respondent's person when enforcing a debt — "the *Shaffer* principle" that Frontera makes much of, . . . — it nonetheless assumed that such a court would still have jurisdiction over the respondent's property. And in this regard, the district court's approach in no way conflicted with *Shaffer.* The district court did not view its lack of personal jurisdiction over SOCAR as fatal to Frontera's petition; instead, the court then appropriately considered whether it could assert jurisdiction over SOCAR's property.

We therefore hold that the district court did not err by treating jurisdiction over either SOCAR or SOCAR's property as a prerequisite to the enforcement of Frontera's petition. The district court may, however, have given the Constitution's Due Process Clause an unwarranted place in its analysis, which we discuss next.

B. SOCAR'S RIGHTS UNDER THE DUE PROCESS CLAUSE

The district court recognized that our precedent *Texas Trading* compelled it to hold that SOCAR possessed rights under the Due Process Clause, thus requiring that jurisdiction over SOCAR meet the minimum contacts requirements of *International Shoe.* The district court, however, questioned *Texas Trading's* soundness. These doubts were well-founded.

The Due Process Clause famously states that "no *person* shall be . . . deprived of life, liberty or property without due process of law." U.S. Const. amend. V (emphasis added). In *Texas Trading,* we held that a foreign state was a "person" within the meaning of the Due Process Clause, and that a court asserting personal jurisdiction over a foreign state must — in addition to complying with the FSIA — therefore engage in "a due process scrutiny of the court's power to exercise its authority" over the state. 647 F.2d at 308, 313 ("[T]he [FSIA] cannot create personal jurisdiction where the Constitution forbids it."). *Texas Trading* reached this conclusion without much analysis, while also noting that cases on point were "rare." *Id.* at 313. The FSIA had been enacted only five years earlier, and pre-FSIA suits against foreign states were generally supported by quasi in rem jurisdiction. *Id.* Subsequently, we applied *Texas Trading* not only to foreign states but also to their agencies and instrumentalities. [Citation omitted.]

Since *Texas Trading,* however, the case law has marched in a different direction. In *Republic of Argentina v. Weltover, Inc.,* the Supreme Court "assum[ed], without deciding, that a foreign state is a 'person' for purposes of the Due Process Clause," 504 U.S. 607, 619, 112 S. Ct. 2160, 119 L. Ed. 2d 394 (1992), but then cited *South Carolina v. Katzenbach,* 383 U.S. 301, 323–24, 86 S. Ct. 803, 15 L. Ed. 2d 769 (1966), which held that "States of the Union are not 'persons' for purposes of the Due Process Clause," 504 U.S. at 619, 112 S. Ct. 2160. *Weltover* did not require deciding the issue because Argentina's contacts satisfied the due process requirements . . . but the Court's implication was plain: If the "States of the Union" have no rights under the Due Process Clause, why should foreign states?

After *Weltover,* we noted that "we are uncertain whether [*Texas Trading*] remains good law." *Hanil Bank v. PT Bank Negara Indon.,* 148 F.3d 127, 134 (2d Cir. 1998). But we went no further in *Hanil Bank* because the due process requirements were satisfied in that case. *See id.* The instant case is different, however, as only the Due Process Clause prevented the district court from asserting personal jurisdiction over SOCAR.

In *Price v. Socialist People's Libyan Arab Jamahiriya*, 294 F.3d 82 (D.C. Cir. 2002), the D.C. Circuit reasoned that because "the word 'person' in the context of the Due Process Clause of the Fifth Amendment cannot, by any reasonable mode of interpretation, be expanded to encompass the States of the Union," *Katzenbach*, 383 U.S. at 323, 86 S.Ct. 803, "absent some compelling reason to treat foreign sovereigns more favorably than 'States of the Union,' it would make no sense to view foreign states as 'persons' under the Due Process Clause," 294 F.3d at 96. The *Price* court found no such reason, *see id.* at 95–100, and we find that case's analysis persuasive. As the *Price* court noted, the States of the Union "both derive important benefits [from the Constitution] and must abide by significant limitations as a consequence of their participation [in the Union]," *id.* at 96, yet a "'foreign State lies outside the structure of the Union,'" *id.* (quoting *Principality of Monaco v. Mississippi*, 292 U.S. 313, 330, 54 S. Ct. 745, 78 L. Ed. 1282 (1934)).

If the States, as sovereigns that are part of the Union, cannot "avail themselves of the fundamental safeguards of the Due Process Clause," *Price*, 294 F.3d at 97, we do not see why foreign states, as sovereigns wholly outside the Union, should be in a more favored position. This is particularly so when the Supreme Court has "[n]ever . . . suggested that foreign nations enjoy rights derived from the Constitution," and when courts have instead "relied on principles of comity and international law to protect foreign governments in the American legal system." *Id.* For the reasons discussed by the *Price* court in its thorough opinion, we "are unwilling to interpret the Due Process Clause as conferring rights on foreign nations that States of the Union do not possess." *Id.* at 99. Thus, we hold that the district court erred, albeit understandably in light of *Texas Trading*, by holding that foreign states and their instrumentalities are entitled to the jurisdictional protections of the Due Process Clause.

SOCAR argues otherwise by defending not *Texas Trading's* reasoning but its significance as precedent. And, to be sure, our court's decisions are binding until overruled by us sitting *en banc* or by the Supreme Court [citation omitted], neither of which has happened to *Texas Trading*. "We do, however, recognize an exception to this general rule where there has been an intervening Supreme Court decision that casts doubt on our controlling precedent." *Gelman v. Ashcroft*, 372 F.3d 495, 499 (2d Cir. 2004) (internal quotation marks omitted). Although *Weltover* arguably casts sufficient doubt on *Texas Trading* to justify its overruling by this panel, [citation omitted] we have nonetheless circulated this opinion to all active members of our court, and none has objected to our departure from *Texas Trading*. See *United States v. Parkes*, 497 F.3d 220, 230 n. 7 (2d Cir. 2007) (describing our "mini-en banc" process). Accordingly, to the extent that *Texas Trading* conflicts with our holding today that foreign states are not "persons" entitled to rights under the Due Process Clause, it is overruled.

Simply overruling *Texas Trading*, however, and holding that a sovereign state does not enjoy due process protections does not decide the precise question in this case, because SOCAR is not a sovereign state, but rather an instrumentality or agency of one. Frontera contends that, because the FSIA treats foreign states and their agencies and instrumentalities identically [citation omitted], we should treat SOCAR just as we would treat Azerbaijan for constitutional purposes. The simple fact that SOCAR is deemed a foreign state as a *statutory* matter, however, does not answer the *constitutional* question of SOCAR's due process rights. SOCAR may indeed lack due process rights like a foreign state, but similar statutory treatment will not be the reason.

However, if the Azerbaijani government "exerted sufficient control over" SOCAR "to make it an agent of the State, then there is no reason to extend to [SOCAR] a constitutional right that is denied to the sovereign itself." *TMR Energy Ltd. v. State Prop. Fund of Ukr.*, 411 F.3d 296, 301 (D.C. Cir. 2005). . . . Accordingly, if SOCAR is an agent of the Azerbaijani state, as recognized in [*First Nat'l City Bank v. Banco Para El Comercio Exterior de Cuba* ("*Bancec*"), 462 U.S. 611 (1983)] and subsequent cases, then, like Azerbaijan, SOCAR lacks due process rights.

The district court did not decide whether SOCAR is an agent of the state because *Texas Trading* rendered the question unnecessary and, unsurprisingly, there was scant briefing on the issue. SOCAR suggests that the parties' lack of focus on the question should be fatal to Frontera's position, because Frontera "bears the burden of proving that the corporate entity should not be presumed distinct from a sovereign or sovereign entity." *Zappia*, 215 F.3d at 252. But the *Bancec* analysis and Frontera's related burden were not relevant until our decision today, nor did Frontera argue that *Bancec* should apply . . . . Accordingly, we choose to remand so that in the first instance the district court can determine, in light of *Texas Trading's* demise and *Bancec's* new relevance to this context, (1) whether SOCAR is an agent of Azerbaijan, and if not, (2) whether SOCAR is entitled to the protections of the Due Process Clause.

II. JURISDICTIONAL DISCOVERY

Frontera also argues that the district court erred by rejecting its request for limited discovery of SOCAR's contacts with the United States. We review the district court's decision for an abuse of discretion. [Citation omitted.] This issue is relevant only if the Due Process Clause protects SOCAR, which is for the district court to determine on remand.

. . . Assuming for the moment that SOCAR has the jurisdictional protections of the Due Process Clause, to establish jurisdiction Frontera must show that SOCAR had "continuous and systematic general business contacts" with the United States, ...

. . . .

. . . Here, the fact that SOCAR has relationships with American companies, without more, could just as easily be the result of occasional or casual solicitations, or solicitations outside the United States. Thus, because Frontera has not pointed to anything in the record that suggests otherwise, we will not disturb the district court's discretionary decision not to allow discovery. . . . The district court is free to consider further discovery requests in light of the questions it must decide on remand.

III. FORUM NON CONVENIENS

Finally, SOCAR asks us to affirm the district court's dismissal on the alternate basis of *forum non conveniens*. Having dismissed for want of jurisdiction, the district court expressly declined to address this argument. Following "our settled practice" of allowing district courts to address arguments in the first instance, *Farricielli*, 215 F.3d at 246, we express no view on SOCAR's *forum non conveniens* argument, which it is free to raise again on remand.

CONCLUSION

For the foregoing reasons, we VACATE the district court's dismissal of Frontera's petition and REMAND for further proceedings.

QUESTIONS

1. Would Frontera have had any problem in establishing jurisdiction for enforcement of the award had it first attached SOCAR assets held on deposit by a New York financial firm?

2. Could Frontera have been able for purposes of jurisdiction and satisfaction of the award to obtain a discovery order requiring SONAR to disclose assets located within the Southern District of New York?

3. What if Frontera anticipated that finds owed to SOCAR would soon be deposited with a bank in New York and Frontera hoped to be ready to enforce the award as soon as such funds were attachable in the Southern District of New York?

4. Subsequent to the decision in *Frontera* could a court in the Second Circuit recognize under similar circumstances an arbitral award against a shipping company owned by the Chinese government that does no business on the East Coast of the United States and currently has no assets of any kind in New York? (What if, as in Question 3, a future deposit of funds in a New York bank on its behalf is anticipated)?

5. Assume that after having attached a commodity shipment that had arrived in Seattle for transshipment by container to St. Louis, a Canadian firm sought to enforce a Singapore arbitral award against Chinese corporation, the alleged owner of the shipment. What problems should counsel for the Canadian claimant anticipate, assuming that the Chinese corporation had no other contacts with the State of Washington? *See Base Metal Trading, Limited v. OJSC "Novokuznetsky Aluminium Factory,"* 283 F.3d 208 (4th Cir. 2002).

DIAPULSE CORPORATION OF AMERICA v. CARBA, LTD.
626 F.2d 1108 (2d Cir. 1980)

Van Graafeiland, Circuit Judge:

This is an appeal by Diapulse Corporation of America from that part of a judgment entered in the United States District Court for the Southern District of New York which modified the injunctive provisions of an arbitration award in its favor. Appellee, Carba, Ltd. originally cross-appealed but then withdrew its appeal, content to let the award stand as modified. We hold that the district court had no authority to modify the substantive provisions of the award but remand to the district court so that application may be made for remand to the arbitration panel for clarification of ambiguities in the award.

Diapulse, a Delaware corporation, manufactures an electronic device for use by the medical and veterinary professions. The device, known as the "Diapulse machine," is designed to expedite bone and tissue healing through the emission of electromagnetic energy and impulse waves. Because of FDA objections, the machine, which is manufactured in New York, is not distributed in the United States. It is marketed in Europe and other parts of the world through a system of exclusive territorial distributorships.

In 1973, Carba, a Swiss corporation, contracted to become the exclusive distributor of Diapulse machines in Switzerland. In 1974, Diapulse granted Carba a second exclusive distributorship covering Germany. These agreements contained a clause providing for resolution of all contractual disputes by arbitration in New York City in accordance with the rules of the American Arbitration Association.

Pursuant to this clause, Diapulse filed a demand for arbitration in 1976, alleging that Carba had violated a provision in the distributorship agreements prohibiting it from competing with Diapulse in the production or sale of Diapulse machines or any similar device during the term of the agreements and for two years thereafter. The arbitration proceedings took place in June 1976. Diapulse presented evidence that Carba had funded the development of a competitive device which it marketed in Europe and elsewhere under the name "Ionar". Diapulse introduced into evidence a copy of a letter from Carba to an Arabian sales agency dated October 27, 1975, in which Carba announced the development of the Ionar machine, described it in some detail, and noted that sales efforts were concentrated in Switzerland, France, and Algeria, where hundreds of Ionar machines were currently in service and hundreds more were expected to be sold. The letter was accompanied by literature purporting to be descriptive of the Ionar machine and Ionar therapy. A representative of Carba admitted at the arbitration proceedings that the literature accompanying the letter to the Arabian sales agency was for the most part a direct translation of literature discussing the Diapulse machine which had been provided by Diapulse to Carba and other Diapulse distributors for use in the promotion of the Diapulse machine. This witness also testified that Carba had financed the development of the Ionar machine, had appointed agents or distributors of Ionar in France, Belgium, and Austria, and regularly responded to requests for information about Ionar from other parts of the world.

By way of defense, Carba argued that the Ionar machine was not really similar to the Diapulse machine and that, in any event, the non-competition clause should be construed as barring competition only in Germany and Switzerland, the areas in which Carba served as exclusive distributor. Carba urged that the reference in the letter to the Arabian sales agency concerning sales efforts in Switzerland was a "sales bluff" and that in reality it never sold Ionar machines in Switzerland in violation of the non-competition clause.

In an award dated December 19, 1977, the arbitrators enjoined Carba "from engaging in competition with (appellant) in the production or sale of its device described as Diapulse or any similar devices", awarded appellant $35,000 in damages, and required Carba to pay the costs of the arbitration proceeding. Appellant petitioned for confirmation of the award in the United States District Court for the Southern District of New York in July 1978. Carba cross-moved to modify the award by deleting the provision that enjoined it from competition, arguing that the two-year period provided for in the contracts had expired. The district court concluded that because the injunction was permanent in time and unlimited in geographic scope, it violated the public policy of the United States against unreasonable restraints of trade. Purporting to act under the authority of 9 U.S.C. § 11(c), the court modified the award by adding a clause limiting the injunction geographically to the area of Switzerland and Germany and temporally to a period of two years from the date of the judgment. The award, as modified, was confirmed, and judgment thereon was entered July 6, 1979. We turn first to the district court's construction of the authority given him by section 11(c).

The purpose of arbitration is to permit a relatively quick and inexpensive resolution of contractual disputes by avoiding the expense and delay of extended court proceedings. [Citations omitted.] Accordingly, it is a well-settled proposition that judicial review of an arbitration award should be, and is, very narrowly limited. [Citations omitted.] A federal court may vacate or modify an arbitration award only if one of the grounds specified in 9 U.S.C. §§ 10 & 11 is found to exist. [Citations omitted.] Section 11(c) authorizes a district court to modify or correct an arbitration award "(w)here the award is imperfect in matter of form not affecting the merits of the controversy."

The district court, after concluding that the arbitrators' injunction violated public policy, reasoned that this rendered the award "imperfect in form" and empowered the court to modify it so as to eliminate the violation. This was error. Section 11(c), which is limited to matters of form not affecting the merits of the controversy, does not license the district court to substitute its judgment for that of the arbitrators. It cannot be argued seriously that the district court's revision of the arbitration award, which transformed a very broad non-competition injunction into a relatively narrow one, did not affect matters of substance that were at the heart of the controversy between Carba and Diapulse. This sort of judicial intervention into the arbitral process is precisely what the narrowly defined provisions of sections 10 and 11 were designed to prevent. Section 11(c) did not empower the district court to modify the arbitration award by substantially altering its geographic and temporal scope. [Citation omitted.]

The question remains whether the injunctive provisions of the award should have been vacated as against public policy. Although contravention of public policy is not one of the specific grounds for vacation set forth in section 10 of the Federal Arbitration Act, an award may be set aside if it compels the violation of law or is contrary to a well accepted and deep rooted public policy. [Citations omitted.] The parties have argued at length on the issue of whether the injunction against competition violates public policy as being of unlimited scope and duration. Basic to their differences, however, is an inability to agree upon what sales the award enjoins. Appellant contends that Carba is not prohibited from selling a device "which can perform the same function as the Diapulse device, so long as it is not a copy of the Diapulse." Carba asserts, on the other hand, that other devices which, like Diapulse, use electromagnetic and impulse waves as their method of treatment, may well be considered "similar devices" within the meaning of the arbitration award. "Similar", Carba points out, may be interpreted to mean "showing some resemblance", "related in appearance or nature", "alike though not identical", "resembling in many respects", "somewhat alike", etc. [Citations omitted.] Appellant's answer to this is that the issue of similarity will be determined at such time as appellant may decide to pursue its remedies for violation of the injunction. We find this argument most troubling.

A district court judgment entered upon an arbitration award has the same force and effect as if it had been entered in an action in the court itself. 9 U.S.C. § 13. A court is required to frame its orders so that those who must obey them will know what the court intends to forbid. [Citations omitted.] It is for this reason that Fed.R.Civ.P. 65(d), like its predecessor 28 U.S.C. § 383, provides that every order granting an injunction shall be specific in its terms and describe in reasonable detail the acts sought to be restrained. An order which does not satisfy the requirement of specificity and definiteness will not withstand appellate scrutiny. [Citations omitted.] Section 10(d) of the Arbitration Act provides that the district court may vacate an award that is not "definite". The injunction in this case falls within that category.

Both parties and the district court have assumed without question that the injunction was intended to be everlasting, despite the fact that the word "permanently" or its equivalent appears nowhere in the award. Both parties and the court also assumed that it was intended to be worldwide in scope. We are not convinced that this was the arbitrators' intent although we make no finding to that effect. A knowledgeable determination as to whether the injunctive provisions of the award contravene public policy cannot be made, however, unless the district court is able to place the term "similar devices", adequately defined, in its proper temporal and geographic setting. The parties may have been willing to live with a lack of explicitness during the two-year term of the agreement not to compete. The district court, which must be concerned with public policy and the problems arising out of the enforcement of an ambiguous decree that may be much broader in scope, is not bound to accept the parties' choice of contractual language.

The judgment as appealed from is remanded to the district court so that appellant Diapulse may there move that the injunctive provisions of the award be referred back to the arbitrators for (1) a more complete and descriptive definition of the type of device whose sale by Carba is being enjoined, (2) a clarifying statement as to the geographical scope of the injunction and (3) a clarifying statement as to the duration of the injunction. If Diapulse does not so move within a reasonable time as set by the district court, the judgment may stand as entered, Carba having taken no appeal therefrom. We make no present determination as to whether the award, when and if clarified by the arbitrators, will contravene public policy.

So ordered.

QUESTIONS

1. How do the standards for recognition of arbitral awards under the New York Convention differ from those applied to foreign-country judgments under the 2005 revision of the UFCMJA, Canadian law, and Japanese law? Do such differences suggest that arbitration is advantageous?

2. Arbitration, in the words of Judge van Graafeiland, citing *Wilko v. Swan*, "is intended to be a relatively quick and inexpensive resolution of contractual disputes by avoiding the expense and delay of extended court proceedings." Do arbitration proceedings in fact live up to this promise? How long did the arbitration proceedings in *Frontera* and *Diapulse* actually last? How many years after the arbitration decision was the arbitral award finally recognized and presumably enforced? At what cost relative to the award?

LANDEGGER v. BAYERISCHE HYPOTHEKEN UND WECHSEL BANK*
357 F. Supp. 692 (S.D.N.Y. 1972)

MOTLEY, DISTRICT JUDGE.

Memorandum Opinion

This is a diversity action brought by plaintiff to enforce a German arbitration award made pursuant to an arbitration provision of a contract between plaintiff and defendant. The case comes before the court on two motions: one by plaintiff for summary judgment pursuant to Fed.R.Civ.P. 56, and the other by defendant for a stay of the underlying action pending the determination of an appeal on file in Germany.

The history of the case is as follows: Plaintiff, a United States citizen and resident of New York, and defendant, a German bank, entered into an investment agreement (Harnik affidavit, exhibits B and B-1) relating to a German pulp and paper company on January 30, 1961. This agreement contained, as "Annex III", a detailed formula for arbitrating in Germany any and all disputes that might arise under the

---

* Footnotes omitted.

II. RECOGNITION AND ENFORCEMENT OF ARBITRAL AWARDS

agreement, including a provision that the "award of the Board of Arbitration shall be final." A dispute arose in November, 1965 and, pursuant to Annex III, plaintiff referred his claim against defendant to a designated arbitration panel in Munich, Germany. The arbitration panel made an award to plaintiff on August 16, 1971. Defendant then brought an action in the Land Court, Munich I, to vacate the award. Defendant having failed to comply with the award, plaintiff also brought an action in the Land Court to execute upon the award. The two actions were consolidated for trial.

On February 4, 1972, the court determined that the award of the arbitration panel should stand, except as to the assessment of the costs of the arbitration. The Land Court granted plaintiff the right to "conditionally enforce" the award, the condition being the posting of security in the amount of 4,000,000 Deutschmarks, the amount of the award, plus the interest on the award, presumably for the purpose of saving the defendant harmless should the judgment be reversed on appeal. Defendant's action was dismissed except as to the costs of the arbitration.

Before the Land Court had entered a judgment, however, plaintiff brought this diversity action and effected an attachment of defendant's assets in the Southern District of New York by order of this court of January 10, 1972 in order to execute on the German arbitration award.

Meanwhile, in Germany, defendant filed a notice of appeal from the above-mentioned judgment of the Land Court. There has been no determination in the German appellate court to date, and defendant's motion for a stay seeks to prevent a determination on the New York case before the resolution of defendant's appeal in the German appellate courts.

As this court analyzes the issues before it plaintiff's and defendant's motions turn on the same two underlying questions: whether a German arbitration award is enforceable in a federal court sitting in New York, and whether a pending appeal of the award in Germany should be grounds for a stay of enforcement proceeding here. As to the first question, we hold that such an award is enforceable here. As to the second, we hold that a stay of the New York proceeding is not appropriate. We further hold that there is no genuine issue as to any material fact in this case, and that plaintiff is entitled to prevail as a matter of law. Plaintiff's motion for summary judgment is therefore granted. Defendant's motion for a stay is denied.

Apparently, both plaintiff and defendant are somewhat misled as to the threshold issues here. Both parties seem to think that the outcome is determined solely by whether the German arbitration award is "final and enforceable" under German law, as those terms are used in Article VI(2) of the Treaty on Friendship, Commerce and Navigation between the United States and the Federal Republic of Germany, October 29, 1954, [1956] 2 U.S.T. 1839, 1845–46, T.I.A.S. No. 3593, which reads as follows:

> "Contracts entered into between nationals or companies of either Party and nationals or companies of the other Party, that provide for the settlement by arbitration of controversies, shall not be deemed unenforceable within the territories of such other Party merely on the grounds that the place designated for the arbitration proceedings is outside such

territories or that the nationality of one or more of the arbitrators is not that of such other Party. Awards duly rendered pursuant to any such contracts, *which are final and enforceable under the laws of the place where rendered*, shall be deemed conclusive in enforcement proceedings brought before the courts of competent jurisdiction of either Party, and *shall be entitled to be declared enforceable by such courts*, except where found contrary to public policy. When so declared, such awards shall be entitled to privileges and measures of enforcement appertaining to awards rendered locally. It is understood, however, that awards rendered outside the United States of America shall be entitled in any court in any State thereof only to the same measure of recognition as awards rendered in other States thereof." (Emphasis added [in opinion].)

It is plaintiff's contention that the deposit of the award with the German court was sufficient to give that award "the effect of a final judgment of a court [between the parties]" (Harnik affidavit, p. 3 ¶ 6). Defendant argues, on the other hand, that, under German law, the award would not be "final and enforceable" until there had been an adjudication by the German court of last resort.

According to our interpretation of New York law it is unnecessary to reach the question of whether the German award was "final and enforceable" under German law. We read the Treaty on Friendship, Commerce and Navigation as including among the German arbitration awards that will be honored and enforced in the United States the class of awards which are "final and enforceable" under the laws of Germany. However, we do not read the Treaty as limiting the category of awards enforceable here to this class. Thus, we must first determine whether the German arbitration award would be enforceable in New York even if it were not "final and enforceable" in Germany. We hold that it would be enforceable in New York, von Engelbrechten v. Galvanoni & Nevy Bros., Inc., 59 Misc. 2d 721, 300 N.Y.S.2d 239 (1969), aff'd per curiam without opinion, 61 Misc. 2d 959, 307 N.Y.S.2d 381 (1970), *motion to dismiss appeal granted*, 27 N.Y.2d 816, 315 N.Y.S.2d 1033, 264 N.E.2d 128 (1970).

In the von Engelbrechten case the New York Civil Court addressed the very point in issue here. In determining the applicability of the same U.S.-German treaty to enforcement of a German arbitration award in New York it stated:

> " 'A statute in the affirmative, without any negative expressed or implied, takes away no preexisting rights or remedies; as a general rule, it operates merely to furnish an additional remedy for the enforcement of a right' . . . . 'The affirmative statute is merely declaratory and does not repeal the common law relating to the subject; on the contrary, the two rules coexist.' " (Schuster v. City of New York, 5 N.Y.2d 75, 85, 180 N.Y.S.2d 265, 273, 154 N.E.2d 534, 540).

> "The treaty in question does not prohibit the recognition of the decision of any tribunal. It mandates the recognition and enforcement of awards 'which are final and enforceable under the laws of the place where rendered'. . . . If our courts have heretofore extended broader recognition to foreign adjudications than required by the treaty, that recognition has not been abridged by the treaty."

"It is the law of this state that a foreign award of arbitrators will support a domestic action at law [citation omitted] just as if it were a foreign judgment [citation omitted]."

We agree with the reasoning and conclusions of the New York court.

We also hold that summary judgment is appropriate here since there is no genuine issue as to any material fact. von Engelbrechten states that "'It is the settled law of this state that a foreign judgment is conclusive upon the merits. It can be impeached only by proof that the court in which it was rendered had not jurisdiction of the subject matter of the action, or of the person of the defendant, or that it was procured by means of fraud' (Dunstan v. Higgins, 138 N.Y. 70, 74, 33 N.E. 729, 730, 20 L.R.A. 668)." 300 N.Y.S.2d at 242.

These enumerated bases for impeachment of a judgment would permit a defendant, as a defense to an enforcement action on a foreign arbitration award, any of the grounds for vacating an award of arbitrators provided for in New York. C.P.L.R. § 7511(b)(1). Moreover, the statutory grounds for vacating an award under New York law are similar to those applicable in Germany. von Engelbrechten, 300 N.Y.S.2d at 241. Indeed defendant does not claim that it is precluded from raising any grounds for vacating the award in this court that would be available to it in the German courts. In reply to the motion for summary judgment it has made nothing but broad and conclusory allegations, through the affidavit of its attorney, Otto Walter, that ". . . due process was violated because he [defendant] was misled by one of the judges, . . . he was denied the opportunity to be heard on important points, and . . . the award was deficient as to certain required formalities" (Walter affidavit at p. 5 ¶ 6), see Fed.R.Civ.P. 56(e). See also 6 Moore, Federal Practice ¶ 56.17[7] n. 4, p. 2499. Since these vague statements do not raise grounds for vacating the award, plaintiff must prevail as a matter of law. von *Engelbrechten, supra.*

Defendant's motion for a stay of this action pending final appeal in Germany of the arbitration award is predicated on its belief that the finality and enforceability of the arbitration award under German law is the determinative issue here. Since we have held that issue to be irrelevant to our decision, we deny defendant's motion.

As to the second question raised earlier, that is, whether the pendency of defendant's appeal in Germany from a judgment in favor of plaintiff should cause this court to stay its hand and await a determination by the German court of last resort, we feel that such abstention is not warranted. Plaintiff is entitled to simultaneously pursue two separate actions to enforce its award. [Citation omitted.] This court has jurisdiction, and is willing to proceed to a "nonconditioned" determination of this case before the German courts have done so. Plaintiff is entitled to have the benefit of the speedier determination. [Citation omitted.] Of course, should new facts come to light as a result of the appeals in Germany showing that the award should have been vacated, defendant could attempt to reopen this court's judgment. [Citation omitted.]

> **QUESTIONS**
>
> 1. What were the apparent advantages of arbitration of the dispute between Landegger and the Bavarian bank? Would a German court judgment on appeal have been similarly recognized and enforced?
>
> 2. Why did the outcome depend on New York law?

AHMED ALGHANIM & SONS, W.L.L. v. TOYS "R" US, INC.
126 F.3d 15 (2d Cir. 1997)

MINER, CIRCUIT JUDGE.

Appeal from a judgment entered in the United States District Court for the Southern District of New York (McKenna, J.) denying respondents' cross-motion to vacate or modify an arbitration award and granting the petition to confirm the award. The court found that while the petition for confirmation was brought under the Convention on the Recognition and Enforcement of Foreign Arbitral Awards, respondents' cross-motion to vacate or modify the award was properly brought under the Federal Arbitration Act, and thus those claims were governed by the Federal Arbitration Act's implied grounds for vacatur. Nonetheless, the court granted the petition to confirm the award, finding that respondents' allegations of error in the arbitral award were without merit.

For the reasons that follow, we affirm.

BACKGROUND

In November of 1982, respondent-appellant Toys "R" Us, Inc. (collectively with respondent-appellant TRU (HK) Limited, "Toys 'R' Us") and petitioner-appellee Yusuf Ahmed Alghanim & Sons, W.L.L. ("Alghanim"), a privately owned Kuwaiti business, entered into a License and Technical Assistance Agreement (the "agreement") and a Supply Agreement. Through the agreement, Toys "R" Us granted Alghanim a limited right to open Toys "R" Us stores and use its trademarks in Kuwait and 13 other countries located in and around the Middle East (the "territory"). Toys "R" Us further agreed to supply Alghanim with its technology, expertise and assistance in the toy business.

From 1982 to the December 1993 commencement of the arbitration giving rise to this appeal, Alghanim opened four toy stores, all in Kuwait. According to Toys "R" Us, the first such store, opened in 1983, resembled a Toys "R" Us store in the United States, but the other three, two of which were opened in 1985 and one in 1988, were small storefronts with only limited merchandise. It is uncontested that Alghanim's stores lost some $6.65 million over the 11-year period from 1982 to 1993,

---

* Footnotes omitted.

II. RECOGNITION AND ENFORCEMENT OF ARBITRAL AWARDS

and turned a profit only in one year of this period.

Following the Gulf War, both Alghanim and Toys "R" Us apparently concluded that their relationship needed to be altered. Representatives of Alghanim and Toys "R" Us's International Division met in September of 1991 and February of 1992. Alghanim expressed a desire for Toys "R" Us to contribute capital toward Alghanim's expansion into other countries. Alghanim advised that it would be willing to proceed in the business only under a new joint venture agreement that would shift a substantial portion of responsibility for capital expenditures to Toys "R" Us. Toys "R" Us was unwilling to take on a greater portion of this responsibility.

On July 20, 1992, Toys "R" Us purported to exercise its right to terminate the agreement, sending Alghanim a notice of non-renewal stating that the agreement would terminate on January 31, 1993. Alghanim responded on July 30, 1992, stating that because its most recently opened toy store had opened on January 16, 1988, the initial term of the agreement ended on January 16, 1993. Alghanim asserted that Toys "R" Us's notice of non-renewal was four days late in providing notice six months before the end of the initial period. . . . On September 2, 1992, Toys "R" Us sent a second letter. Toys "R" Us explained that, on further inspection of the agreement, it had determined that the initial term of the agreement expired on December 31, 1993, and it again gave notice of non-renewal. In this letter, Toys "R" Us also directed Alghanim not to open any new toy stores and warned that failure to comply with that direction could constitute a breach of the agreement.

Through the balance of 1992 and 1993, the parties unsuccessfully attempted to renegotiate the agreement or devise a new arrangement. . . .

. . . .

On December 20, 1993, Toys "R" Us invoked the dispute-resolution mechanism in the agreement, initiating an arbitration before the American Arbitration Association. Toys "R" Us sought a declaration that the agreement was terminated on December 31, 1993. Alghanim responded by counterclaiming for breach of contract.

On May 4, 1994, the arbitrator denied Toys "R" Us's request for declaratory judgment. The arbitrator found that, under the termination provisions of the agreement, Alghanim had the absolute right to open toy stores, even after being given notice of termination, as long as the last toy store was opened within five years. The parties then engaged in substantial document and expert discovery, motion practice, and a 29-day evidentiary hearing on Alghanim's counterclaims.

On July 11, 1996, the arbitrator awarded Alghanim $46.44 million for lost profits under the agreement, plus 9 percent interest to accrue from December 31, 1994. The arbitrator's findings and legal conclusions were set forth in a 47-page opinion.

Alghanim petitioned the district court to confirm the award under the Convention on the Recognition and Enforcement of Foreign Arbitral Awards of June 10, 1958 ("Convention"), 21 U.S.T. 2517, 330 U.N.T.§ 38, *reprinted at* 9 U.S.C. § 201. Toys "R" Us cross-moved to vacate or modify the award under the Federal Arbitration Act ("FAA"), 9 U.S.C. § 1 *et seq.*, arguing that the award was clearly irrational, in manifest disregard of the law, and in manifest disregard of the terms of the agreement. The district court concluded that "[t]he Convention and the FAA afford overlapping coverage, and the fact that a petition to confirm is brought under the Convention does not foreclose a cross-motion to vacate under the FAA, and the Court will consider [Toys "R" Us's] cross-motion under the standards of the FAA." (J.A. 569–70 (citation omitted).) By judgment entered December 20, 1996, the district court confirmed the award, finding Toys "R" Us's objections to the award to be without merit. This appeal followed.

DISCUSSION

I. AVAILABILITY OF THE FAA'S GROUNDS FOR RELIEF IN CONFIRMATION UNDER THE CONVENTION

Toys "R" Us argues that the district court correctly determined that the provisions of the FAA apply to its cross-motion to vacate or modify the arbitral award. In particular, Toys "R" Us contends that the FAA and the Convention have overlapping coverage. Thus, Toys "R" Us argues, even though the petition to confirm the arbitral award was brought under the Convention, the FAA's implied grounds for vacatur should apply to Toys "R" Us's cross-motion to vacate or modify because the cross-motion was brought under the FAA. We agree that the FAA governs Toys "R" Us's cross-motion.

A. APPLICABILITY OF THE CONVENTION

Neither party seriously disputes the applicability of the Convention to this case and it is clear to us that the Convention does apply. The Convention provides that it will apply to the recognition and enforcement of arbitral awards made in the territory of a State other than the State where the recognition and enforcement of such awards are sought, and arising out of differences between persons, whether physical or legal. It shall also apply to arbitral awards *not considered as domestic awards* in the State where their recognition and enforcement are sought. Convention art. I(1). (Emphasis added [in opinion].)

The Convention does not define nondomestic awards. *See Bergesen v. Joseph Muller Corp.*, 710 F.2d 928, 932 (2d Cir. 1983). However, 9 U.S.C. § 202, one of the provisions implementing the Convention, provides that

> [a]n agreement or award arising out of such a relationship which is entirely between citizens of the United States shall be deemed not to fall under the Convention unless that relationship involves property located abroad, envisages performance or enforcement abroad, or has some other reasonable relation with one or more foreign states.

In *Bergesen*, we held "that awards 'not considered as domestic' denotes awards which are subject to the Convention not because made abroad, but because made within the legal framework of another country, e.g., pronounced in accordance with foreign law or involving parties domiciled or having their principal place of business outside the enforcing jurisdiction." 710 F.2d at 932 (quoting 9 U.S.C. § 201). The Seventh Circuit similarly has interpreted § 202 to mean that "any commercial arbitral agreement, unless it is between two United States citizens, involves property located in the United States, and has no reasonable relationship with one or more foreign states, falls under the Convention." *Jain v. de Méré*, 51 F.3d 686, 689 (7th Cir.), *cert. denied*, 516 U.S. 914, 116 S. Ct. 300, 133 L. Ed. 2d 206 (1995).

The Convention's applicability in this case is clear. The dispute giving rise to this appeal involved two nondomestic parties and one United States corporation, and principally involved conduct and contract performance in the Middle East. Thus, we consider the arbitral award leading to this action a non-domestic award and thus within the scope of the Convention.

B. AUTHORITY UNDER THE CONVENTION TO SET ASIDE AN AWARD UNDER DOMESTIC ARBITRAL LAW

Toys "R" Us argues that the district court properly found that it had the authority under the Convention to apply the FAA's implied grounds for setting aside the award. We agree.

Under the Convention, the district court's role in reviewing a foreign arbitral award is strictly limited: "The court shall confirm the award unless it finds one of the grounds for refusal or deferral of recognition or enforcement of the award specified in the said Convention." 9 U.S.C. § 207; [citation omitted]. Under Article V of the Convention, the grounds for refusing to recognize or enforce an arbitral award are:

> (a) The parties to the agreement . . . were . . . under some incapacity, or the said agreement is not valid under the law . . . ; or (b) The party against whom the award is invoked was not given proper notice of the appointment of the arbitrator or of the arbitration proceedings . . . ; or (c) The award deals with a difference not contemplated by or not falling within the terms of the submission to arbitration, or it contains decisions on matters beyond the scope of the submission to arbitration . . . ; or (d) The composition of the arbitral authority or the arbitral procedure was not in accordance with the agreement of the parties . . . ; or (e) The award has not yet become binding on the parties, or has been set aside or suspended by a competent authority of the country in which, or under the law of which, that award was made.

Convention art. V(1).

Enforcement may also be refused if "[t]he subject matter of the difference is not capable of settlement by arbitration," or if "recognition or enforcement of the award would be contrary to the public policy" of the country in which enforcement or recognition is sought. *Id.* art. V(2). These seven grounds are the only grounds explicitly provided under the Convention.

In determining the availability of the FAA's implied grounds for setting aside, the text of the Convention leaves us with two questions: *(1) whether, in addition to the Convention's express grounds for refusal, other grounds can be read into the Convention by implication, much as American courts have read implied grounds for relief into the FAA, and (2) whether, under Article V(1)(e), the courts of the*

United States are authorized to apply United States procedural arbitral law, i.e., the FAA, to nondomestic awards rendered in the United States. We answer the first question in the negative and the second in the affirmative. [Emphasis added.]

1. AVAILABILITY UNDER THE CONVENTION OF IMPLIED GROUNDS FOR REFUSAL

We have held that the FAA and the Convention have "overlapping coverage" to the extent that they do not conflict. *Bergesen*, 710 F.2d at 934; *see* 9 U.S.C. § 208 (FAA may apply to actions brought under the Convention "to the extent that [the FAA] is not in conflict with [9 U.S.C. §§ 201–208] or the Convention as ratified by the United States"); *Lander Co. v. MMP Invs., Inc.*, 107 F.3d 476, 481 (7th Cir. 1997), *cert. denied*, [522 U.S. 811,] 118 S. Ct. 55, 139 L. Ed. 2d 19 (1997). However, by that same token, to the extent that the Convention prescribes the exclusive grounds for relief from an award under the Convention, that application of the FAA's implied grounds would be in conflict, and is thus precluded. [Citation omitted.]

In *Parsons & Whittemore Overseas Co. v. Société Generale de L'Industrie du Papier (Rakta)*, 508 F.2d 969 (2d Cir. 1974), we declined to decide whether the implied defense of "manifest disregard" applies under the Convention, having decided that even if it did, appellant's claim would fail. . . . Nonetheless, we noted that "[b]oth the legislative history of Article V and the statute enacted to implement the United States' accession to the Convention are strong authority for treating as exclusive the bases set forth in the Convention for vacating an award." *Id.* (citation and footnote omitted).

There is now considerable case law holding that, in an action to confirm an award rendered in, or under the law of, a foreign jurisdiction, the grounds for relief enumerated in Article V of the Convention are the only grounds available for setting aside an arbitral award. . . . This conclusion is consistent with the Convention's pro-enforcement bias. . . . We join these courts in declining to read into the Convention the FAA's implied defenses to confirmation of an arbitral award.

2. NONDOMESTIC AWARD RENDERED IN THE UNITED STATES

Although Article V provides the exclusive grounds for refusing confirmation under the Convention, one of those exclusive grounds is where "[t]he award . . . has been set aside or suspended by a competent authority of the country in which, or under the law of which, that award was made." Convention art. V(1)(e). Those courts holding that implied defenses were inapplicable under the Convention did so in the context of petitions to confirm awards rendered abroad. These courts were not presented with the question whether Article V(1)(e) authorizes an action to set aside an arbitral award under the domestic law of the state in which, or under which, the award was rendered. We, however, are faced head-on with that question in the case before us, because the arbitral award in this case was rendered in the United States, and both confirmation and vacatur were then sought in the United States.

We read Article V(1)(e) of the Convention to allow a court in the country under whose law the arbitration was conducted to apply domestic arbitral law, in this case the FAA, to a motion to set aside or vacate that arbitral award. . . .

The Seventh Circuit has agreed, albeit in passing, that the Convention "contemplates the possibility of the award's being set aside in a proceeding under local law." *Lander*, 107 F.3d at 478 (citing Article V(1)(e)). . . .

Our conclusion also is consistent with the reasoning of courts that have refused to apply non-Convention grounds for relief where awards were rendered outside the United States. . . .

This interpretation of Article V(1)(e) also finds support in the scholarly work of commentators on the Convention and in the judicial decisions of our sister signatories to the Convention. There appears to be no dispute among these authorities that an action to set aside an international arbitral award, as contemplated by Article V(1)(e), is controlled by the domestic law of the rendering state. . . .

. . . .

Indeed, many commentators and foreign courts have concluded that an action to set aside an award can be brought *only* under the domestic law of the arbitral forum, and can never be made under the Convention. . . .

There is no indication in the Convention of any intention to deprive the rendering state of its supervisory authority over an arbitral award, including its authority to set aside that award under domestic law. The Convention succeeded and replaced the Convention on the Execution of Foreign Arbitral Awards ("Geneva Convention"), Sept. 26, 1927, 92 L.N.T.§ 301. The primary defect of the Geneva Convention was that it required an award first to be recognized in the rendering state before it could be enforced abroad, *see* Geneva Convention arts. 1(d), 4(2), 92 L.N.T.S. at 305, 306, the so-called requirement of "double *exequatur.*" . . .

The Convention eliminated this problem by eradicating the requirement that a court in the rendering state recognize an award before it could be taken and enforced abroad. . . .

Nonetheless, under the Convention, the power and authority of the local courts of the rendering state remain of paramount importance.

. . . .

In sum, we conclude that the Convention mandates very different regimes for the review of arbitral awards (1) in the state in which, or under the law of which, the award was made, and (2) in other states where recognition and enforcement are sought. The Convention specifically contemplates that the state in which, or under the law of which, the award is made, will be free to set aside or modify an award in accordance with its domestic arbitral law and its full panoply of express and implied grounds for relief. *See* Convention art. V(1)(e). However, the Convention is equally clear that when an action for enforcement is brought in a foreign state, the state may refuse to enforce the award only on the grounds explicitly set forth in Article V of the Convention.

II. APPLICATION OF FAA GROUNDS FOR RELIEF

Having determined that the FAA does govern Toys "R" Us's cross-motion to vacate, our application of the FAA's implied grounds for vacatur is swift. The Supreme Court has stated "that courts of appeals should apply ordinary, not special, standards when reviewing district court decisions upholding arbitration awards." *First Options of Chicago, Inc. v. Kaplan*, 514 U.S. 938, 948, 115 S. Ct. 1920, 1926, 131 L. Ed. 2d 985 (1995). We review the district court's findings of fact for clear error and its conclusions of law *de novo*. See id.

"[T]he confirmation of an arbitration award is a summary proceeding that merely makes what is already a final arbitration award a judgment of the court." *Florasynth, Inc. v. Pickholz*, 750 F.2d 171, 176 (2d Cir. 1984). The review of arbitration awards is "very limited . . . in order to avoid undermining the twin goals of arbitration, namely, settling disputes efficiently and avoiding long and expensive litigation." *Folkways Music Publishers, Inc. v. Weiss*, 989 F.2d 108, 111 (2d Cir. 1993). Accordingly, "the showing required to avoid summary confirmance is high." *Ottley v. Schwartzberg*, 819 F.2d 373, 376 (2d Cir. 1987).

More particularly, "[t]his court has generally refused to second guess an arbitrator's resolution of a contract dispute." *John T. Brady & Co. v. Form-Eze Sys., Inc.*, 623 F.2d 261, 264 (2d Cir. 1980). As we have explained: "An arbitrator's decision is entitled to substantial deference, and the arbitrator need only explicate his reasoning under the contract 'in terms that offer even a barely colorable justification for the outcome reached' in order to withstand judicial scrutiny." *In re Marine Pollution Serv., Inc.*, 857 F.2d 91, 94 (2d Cir. 1988) (quoting *Andros Compania*, 579 F.2d at 704).

However, awards may be vacated, *see* 9 U.S.C. § 10, or modified, *see id.* § 11, in the limited circumstances where the arbitrator's award is in manifest disregard of the terms of the agreement [citation omitted], or where the award is in "manifest disregard of the law," *Fahnestock & Co. v. Waltman*, 935 F.2d 512, 515–16 (2d Cir. 1991); [citation omitted]. We find that neither of these implied grounds is met in the present case.

A. MANIFEST DISREGARD OF THE LAW

Toys "R" Us argues that the arbitrator manifestly disregarded New York law on lost profits awards for breach of contract by returning a speculative award. This contention is without merit. "[M]ere error in the law or failure on the part of the arbitrator[] to understand or apply the law" is not sufficient to establish manifest disregard of the law. *Fahnestock*, 935 F.2d at 516 (quotations omitted). For an award to be in "manifest disregard of the law,"

> [t]he error must have been obvious and capable of being readily and instantly perceived by the average person qualified to serve as an arbitrator. Moreover, the term "disregard" implies that the arbitrator appreciates the existence of a clearly governing legal principle but decides to ignore or pay no attention to it. *Merrill Lynch*, 808 F.2d at 933.

In the instant case, the arbitrator was well aware of and carefully applied New

York's law on lost profits. The arbitrator specifically addressed *Kenford Co. v. County of Erie*, 67 N.Y.2d 257, 502 N.Y.S.2d 131, 493 N.E.2d 234 (1986), which contains New York's law on the subject and upon which Toys "R" Us relied in its arguments, ...

Toys "R" Us also argues that the arbitrator manifestly disregarded the law of lost profits by ignoring the facts that (1) Alghanim's toy business had lost a total of $6.65 million over the course of its existence under the agreement, and (2) Alghanim itself offered to relinquish its rights for $2 million. Toys "R" Us further contends that the calculation of lost profits was irrational. We reject these contentions as well.

. . . .

We also reject Toys "R" Us's contention that the arbitrator's calculation of lost profits was in manifest disregard of the law. . . .

. . . .

There is no manifest disregard in the arbitrator's refusal to credit actual operating results for the period following the breach in calculating the value of the business at the time of the breach.

Toys "R" Us also argues that the arbitrator was wholly irrational in calculating the value of the Saudi Arabian rights . . . . [W]e see no manifest disregard in the arbitrator's use in his calculations of the bid price, rather than the actual closing price, for the sale to ATA. Thus, we see no merit in Toys "R" Us's contentions of manifest disregard of the law.

B. MANIFEST DISREGARD OF THE AGREEMENT

Toys "R" Us also argues that the district court erred in refusing to vacate the award because the arbitrator manifestly disregarded the terms of the agreement. In particular, Toys "R" Us disputes the arbitrator's interpretation of four contract terms: (1) the termination provision; (2) the conforming stores provision; (3) the non-assignment provision; and (4) the deletion provision. We find no error.

Interpretation of these contract terms is within the province of the arbitrator and will not be overruled simply because we disagree with that interpretation. . . .

As to each of these contract provisions, Toys "R" Us merely takes issue with the arbitrator's well-reasoned interpretations of those provisions, and simply offers its own contrary interpretations. . . .

We have carefully considered Toys "R" Us's remaining contentions and find them all to be without merit.

CONCLUSION

For the foregoing reasons, the judgment of the district court is affirmed.

> **QUESTIONS**
>
> 1. On what grounds may a U.S. court refuse to enforce a foreign arbitral award? How are these different from the grounds for refusal to enforce a foreign country judgment? In both instances, do the rules and standards of enforcement differ in the case of a domestic arbitral award or a U.S. state or federal judgment?
>
> 2. In the view of Judge Miner, what is the relationship between the FAA and the 1958 New York Convention? Would the outcome have differed had the parties to the award been an Argentine and a Mexican citizen?

B. Canada

YUGRANEFT CORP. v. REXX MANAGEMENT CORP.
[2010] 1 S.C.R. 649, 2010 SCC 19

ROTHSTEIN J.

I. Introduction

1. This case is about the limitation period applicable to the recognition and enforcement of foreign arbitral awards in the province of Alberta. For the reasons set out below, I am of the view that the applicable limitation period is two years and that Yugraneft Corporation's application for recognition and enforcement of a foreign arbitral award is therefore time-barred. Under international arbitration law, the matter of limitation periods is left to local procedural law of the jurisdiction where recognition and enforcement is sought. The applicable limitation period in this case must therefore be found in the limitations law of Alberta. As an arbitral award is not a judgment or a court order for the payment of money, an application for recognition and enforcement in Alberta is not eligible for the 10-year limitation period set out in § 11 of the *Limitations Act*, R.S.A. 2000, c. L-12. Rather, the application is subject to the general two-year limitation period applicable to most causes of action, which is found in § 3 of the *Limitations Act*.

II. Facts

2. The appellant, Yugraneft Corporation ("Yugraneft"), is a Russian corporation that develops and operates oil fields in Russia. The respondent, Rexx Management Corporation ("Rexx") is an Alberta corporation that at one time supplied materials to Yugraneft for its oil field operations. Following a contractual dispute, Yugraneft commenced arbitration proceedings before the International Commercial Arbitration Court at the Chamber of Commerce and Industry of the Russian Federation ("Russian ICAC"). The arbitral tribunal issued its final award on September 6, 2002,

II. RECOGNITION AND ENFORCEMENT OF ARBITRAL AWARDS

ordering Rexx to pay US $952,614.43 in damages to Yugraneft.

3. Yugraneft applied to the Alberta Court of Queen's Bench for recognition and enforcement of the award on January 27, 2006, more than three years after the award was rendered. Rexx resisted enforcement on two grounds. First, it argued that Yugraneft's application was time-barred under the Alberta *Limitations Act*. Second, it argued that enforcement proceedings should be stayed pending resolution of an ongoing criminal case in the United States. It claimed that the criminal case would demonstrate that the award had been obtained as a result of fraudulent activity.

III. Judicial History

4. Yugraneft applied to the Alberta Court of Queen's Bench for recognition and enforcement of the award pursuant to the *International Commercial Arbitration Act*, R.S.A. 2000, c. I-5 ("*ICAA*"). Chrumka J. ruled that the application was time-barred under the *Limitations Act*: 2007 ABQB 450, 78 Alta. L.R. (4th) 86. The Act creates two limitation periods, one for "remedial order[s]" (§ 3) and one for the enforcement of "judgment[s] or order[s] for the payment of money" (§ 11). Applications under § 3 are subject to a two-year limitation period, while those under § 11 are subject to a 10-year time limit. Yugraneft argued that foreign arbitral awards should be considered "judgments" under § 11. Chrumka J. disagreed, finding instead that the two-year limitation period in § 3 applied. The application was therefore dismissed.

5. The Alberta Court of Appeal unanimously upheld the ruling of Chrumka J.: 2008 ABCA 274, 93 Alta. L.R. (4th) 281. It concluded that a foreign arbitral award could not be considered a "judgment" pursuant to § 11 because that term encompassed only domestic judgments. Accordingly, it found that Yugraneft's application should be characterized as a claim for a remedial order under § 3 of the Act and was therefore time-barred. The appeal was dismissed.

IV. Positions of the Parties

6. Yugraneft argues that a foreign arbitral award should be treated as a domestic judgment under § 11 of the *Limitations Act* because arbitration is an adjudication of a legal dispute and as such possesses all the characteristics of a judgment. In the alternative, it argues that foreign arbitral awards should be treated as at least equivalent to a foreign judgment, and that foreign judgments fall within the meaning of "judgment" under § 11 of the *Limitations Act*. It points to recent jurisprudence of this Court showing a trend away from the traditional conception of foreign judgments as a mere contract debt and towards a practice of granting them "full faith and credit" (*Morguard Investments Ltd. v. De Savoye*, [1990] 3 S.C.R. 1077, at pp. 1100–1101; *Beals v. Saldanha*, 2003 SCC 72, [2003] 3 S.C.R. 416, at paras. 164–74). Finally, Yugraneft argues that the *Limitations Act* is ambiguous and that this ambiguity should be resolved in its favour. While an arbitral award may not share all the properties of a domestic judgment, neither does it fit well within the scheme created by § 3. Since statutory provisions creating limitation periods must be interpreted strictly in favour of the plaintiff, this ambiguity must be resolved by

applying the 10-year limitation period found in § 11.

7. Rexx argues that the two-year limitation set out in § 3 should apply. Its principal argument is that the *Limitations Act* was intended to simplify the law of limitations by imposing a single limitation period on most causes of action. Unless an action falls under one of the exceptions set out in the Act, it is subject to the two-year limitation period found in § 3. Since Yugraneft's action is not excluded from the scope of § 3, it is time-barred.

V. Analysis

A. *Relevant Legislation*

8. In Alberta, the recognition and enforcement of foreign arbitral awards is governed by the *ICAA*, which incorporates both the *Convention on the Recognition and Enforcement of Foreign Arbitral Awards*, Can. T.S. 1986 No. 43 (the "New York Convention" or "Convention"), and the *UNCITRAL Model Law on International Commercial Arbitration*, U.N. Doc. A/40/17, ann. I (1985) ("Model Law"), into Alberta law. The relevant provisions of each instrument are found in the appendices attached hereto (Appendix A for the Model Law and Appendix B for the Convention) [omitted].

9. The New York Convention was adopted in 1958 by the United Nations Conference on International Commercial Arbitration. The purpose of the Convention is to facilitate the cross-border recognition and enforcement of arbitral awards by establishing a single, uniform set of rules that apply worldwide. It requires each Contracting State to recognize and enforce arbitral awards made in the territory of another State, and that recognition and enforcement can only be refused on the limited grounds set out in art. V (see Appendix B). Pursuant to art. I, the obligation to recognize foreign awards applies not only to awards granted in other Contracting States, but also to those granted in all States other than the one in which enforcement is being sought, regardless of whether or not they are party to the Convention.

10. The Convention is currently in force, having been ratified by over 140 countries, and is considered a great success. Lord Mustill, former judge of the Court of Appeal of England and Wales and member of the House of Lords, and former Vice-President of the International Court of Arbitration of the International Chamber of Commerce, has stated that the New York Convention has been the most successful international instrument in the field of arbitration, and perhaps could lay claim to be the most effective instance of international legislation in the entire history of commercial law. (M. J. Mustill, "Arbitration: History and Background" (1989), 6 *J. Int'l Arb.* 43, at p. 49.)

The Convention was ratified by Canada on May 12, 1986, once each provincial legislature had enacted the necessary implementing legislation.

11. The Model Law was developed in 1985 by the United Nations Commission on International Trade Law ("UNCITRAL"). Unlike the New York Convention, which is a treaty, the Model Law is not an international agreement intended for

ratification. Rather, it is a codification of international "best practices" intended to serve as an example for domestic legislation. The explanatory note of the UNCITRAL secretariat states that the Model Law reflects a worldwide consensus on the principles and important issues of international arbitration practice. It is acceptable to States of all regions and the different legal or economic systems of the world. (Model Law, Part Two, at para. 2.)

The Model Law has been adopted, subject to some modifications, by every jurisdiction in Canada. Like the Convention, the Model Law limits the ability of national courts to interfere with international arbitration proceedings. Article 36 of the Model Law also limits the grounds on which enforcement of an international arbitral award may be refused (Appendix A). These grounds are essentially identical to those set out in art. V of the New York Convention.

12. Having adopted both the Convention and the Model Law in 1986 as part of the *ICAA*, there is no doubt that Alberta is required to recognize and enforce eligible foreign arbitral awards. The question before the Court is what limitation period, if any, applies to the recognition and enforcement of foreign arbitral awards in Alberta.

13. There are three Alberta statutes that are potentially relevant in this connection: the *Limitations Act*, the *Arbitration Act*, R.S.A. 2000, c. A-43, and the *Reciprocal Enforcement of Judgments Act*, R.S.A. 2000, c. R-6 (*"REJA"*). The relevant provisions of each statute are in appendices C, D and E, respectively.

B. *Does the Convention Allow Local Limitation Periods to Apply?*

14. As neither the Convention nor the Model Law expressly imposes a limitation period on recognition and enforcement, a threshold question is whether *any* limitation period can apply. Article V of the Convention and art. 36 of the Model Law purport to set out an exhaustive list of the grounds on which the recognition and enforcement of an award may be refused, but make no mention of local limitation periods. This omission might be taken to mean that a Contracting State cannot refuse to recognize and enforce a foreign arbitral award on the grounds that the application was brought after the expiration of a local limitation period.

15. However, art. III of the Convention stipulates that recognition and enforcement shall be "in accordance with the rules of procedure of the territory where the award is relied upon". Thus, the "rules of procedure" of the jurisdiction in which enforcement is sought will apply, insofar as they do not conflict with the express requirements of the Convention. The question then is whether limitation periods fall under the rubric of "rules of procedure", as that term is used in the Convention.

16. This question arises because not all legal systems treat limitation periods — or extinctive prescription, as it is known in civil law jurisdictions — alike. Those built on the common law tradition have tended to conceive of them as a procedural matter, while those following the civil law tradition generally consider them to be a question of substantive law (*Tolofson v. Jensen*, [1994] 3 S.C.R. 1022, at pp. 1068–70). If limitation periods are characterized as being procedural in nature for the purposes of the Convention, then recognition and enforcement of a foreign arbitral award may lawfully be refused on the grounds that it is time-barred. If

instead they are characterized as substantive in nature, then placing a time limit on recognition and enforcement proceedings would appear to violate the Convention, which only allows local procedural rules, and not local substantive law, to apply.

17. Both parties agree that, as a general matter, art. III allows Contracting States to impose a time limit on the recognition and enforcement of foreign arbitral awards. However, whether Alberta was in conformity with the Convention is not determined by the consent of the parties. It is necessary for the Court to ascertain if there is a legal basis for the application of local limitation laws under the Convention.

18. In my view, art. III permits (although it does not require) Contracting States (or, in the case of a federal State, a sub-national territory with jurisdiction over the matter) to subject the recognition and enforcement of foreign arbitral awards to a time limit. However, it should not be viewed as automatically recognizing and imposing either the traditional common law or civil law approaches to limitation periods. Rather, the phrase "in accordance with the rules of procedure of the territory where the award is relied upon" should be understood as indicating application of domestic law on such matters. Thus, notwithstanding art. V, which sets out an otherwise exhaustive list of grounds on which recognition and enforcement may be resisted, the courts of a Contracting State may refuse to recognize and enforce a foreign arbitral award on the basis that such proceedings are time-barred. I reach this conclusion for three reasons.

19. First, as a treaty, the Convention must be interpreted "in good faith in accordance with the ordinary meaning to be given to the terms of the treaty in their context and in the light of its object and purpose" (*Vienna Convention on the Law of Treaties*, Can. T.S. 1980 No. 37 (entered into force January 27, 1980), art. 31(1)). In this case, the Convention's context and purpose provide indications as to how its terms, in particular art. III, should be read. The Convention's text was designed to be applied in a large number of States and thus across a multitude of legal systems (N. Blackaby and C. Partasides, *Redfern and Hunter on International Arbitration* (5th ed. 2009), at pp. 70 and 72–73; J.-F. Poudret and S. Besson, *Comparative Law of International Arbitration* (2nd ed. 2007), at p. 868). One leading author has described the Convention as a " 'constitutional' instrument" that "leaves a substantial role for national law and national courts to play in the international arbitral process" (G. B. Born, *International Commercial Arbitration*, vol. I (3rd ed. 2009), at p. 101). The text of the Convention must therefore be construed in a manner that takes into account the fact that it was intended to interface with a variety of legal traditions.

20. This context and purpose is important when interpreting the Convention's effect on the applicability of local limitation periods to the recognition and enforcement of foreign arbitral awards. When the Convention was drafted, it was well known that various States characterized limitation periods in different ways, and that States in the common law tradition generally treated them as being procedural in nature. All else being equal, if the Convention were applied in a common law State, the term "rules of procedure" found in art. III would *prima facie* include any local limitation periods applicable to the recognition and enforcement of foreign arbitral awards by virtue of local law. It is therefore significant that

the Convention's drafters did not include any restriction on a State's ability to impose time limits on recognition and enforcement proceedings. Such an omission implies that the drafters intended to take a permissive approach.

21. The second reason why art. III should be viewed as permitting the application of local limitation periods is that this reflects the practice of the Contracting States. In interpreting a treaty, courts must take into account "any subsequent practice in the application of the treaty which establishes the agreement of the parties regarding its interpretation" (*Vienna Convention on the Law of Treaties*, art. 31(3)). A recent study indicates that at least 53 Contracting States, including both common law and civil law States, subject (or would be likely to subject, should the issue arise) the recognition and enforcement of foreign arbitral awards to some kind of time limit (International Chamber of Commerce, "Guide to National Rules of Procedure for Recognition and Enforcement of New York Convention Awards", *ICC Bull.— 2008 Spec. Supp.* (2009), at pp. 343–46; see also UNCITRAL, *Report on the survey relating to the legislative implementation of the Convention on the Recognition and Enforcement of Foreign Arbitral Awards (New York, 1958)*, 41st Sess., U.N. Doc. A/CN.9/656/Add.1 (2008), at pp. 2–3).

22. Third, leading scholars in the field appear to take it for granted that art. III permits the application of local limitation periods to recognition and enforcement proceedings (see for example: Blackaby and Partasides, at pp. 631–32; A. J. van den Berg, *The New York Arbitration Convention of 1958: Towards a Uniform Judicial Interpretation* (1981), at p. 240; Poudret and Besson, at p. 869). This suggests that the application of local time limits is not a controversial matter.

23. Thus, the lack of any explicit restriction on a Contracting State's ability to impose a limitation period can be taken to mean that, for the purposes of the Convention, any limitation period that, under domestic law, is applicable to the recognition and enforcement of a foreign arbitral award is a "rule of procedure" pursuant to art. III.

24. Although they agree that, as a general matter, the Convention allows Contracting States to impose limitation periods on recognition and enforcement proceedings, both the Canadian Arbitration Congress ("CAC") and the ADR Chambers, argue that, on the facts of the present case, art. III of the Convention prevents this Court from applying Alberta limitations law. However, each of them relies on a different part of art. III to support its claim.

25. The CAC argues that Alberta limitations law cannot apply to the recognition and enforcement of foreign arbitral awards because Canadian common law considers such rules to be substantive in nature. The *Limitations Act* or any other statute imposing a general limitation period therefore does not qualify as a "rule of procedure" under art. III.

26. In making this argument, the CAC relies primarily on the ruling by this Court in *Tolofson*, which rejected the traditional common law approach to limitation periods (pp. 1071–72). The CAC contends that, because Canadian common law now generally considers limitation periods to be substantive, statutory limitation periods, such as those found in the *Limitations Act*, are inapplicable under art. III of the Convention.

27. It is true that the majority in *Tolofson* held that, in a conflict of laws context, limitation periods should, as a general matter, be treated as substantive in nature, so that a claim will be subject to the limitation period of the *lex loci delicti* (or, in this case, the *lex loci contractus*). However, the question in this case is not whether *Canadian law* considers limitation periods to be "substantive" or "procedural" in nature. Rather, the question is whether local time limits intended to apply to recognition and enforcement fall within the ambit of "rules of procedure" as that term is used in art. III of *the Convention*.

28. The answer to this must be yes. As noted above, the Convention takes a permissive approach to the applicability of local limitation periods. The only material question is whether or not the competent legislature intended to subject recognition and enforcement proceedings to a limitation period. If it did, the limitation period in question will be construed as a "rule of procedure" as that term is understood under the Convention. How domestic law might choose to characterize such a time limit, either in the abstract or in a conflict of laws context, is immaterial. The question at issue in *Tolofson* is not relevant to the matter at hand.

29. The CAC's contention is therefore misplaced. Even if this Court were to characterize a given statutory limitation period, such as the one found in § 3 of the *Limitations Act*, as "substantive" in nature, that would not in and of itself prevent the limitation period in question from being applicable to the recognition and enforcement of foreign arbitral awards. Instead, the Court must determine whether a potentially applicable limitation period was intended to apply to the recognition and enforcement of foreign arbitral awards. If it was, then it may properly be applied as a local "rule of procedure" pursuant to art. III.

30. Like the CAC, the intervener ADR Chambers argues that art. III prevents the *Limitations Act* from applying to Yugraneft's action. However, it does so on a different basis. ADR Chambers concedes that a local limitations period may apply in this case, but argues that art. III of the Convention bars Alberta from imposing a limitation period shorter than the longest limitation period available anywhere in Canada for the recognition and enforcement of domestic arbitral awards.

31. Article III provides that "[t]here shall not be imposed substantially more onerous conditions or higher fees or charges on the recognition or enforcement of arbitral awards to which this Convention applies than are imposed on the recognition or enforcement of domestic arbitral awards." ADR Chambers takes the view that a "domestic" arbitral award means any award rendered within the Contracting State. Thus, no Canadian province can impose a time limit more onerous than the most generous time limit available anywhere in Canada for domestic awards. At the present time, both Quebec and British Columbia provide for a 10-year limitation period on the recognition and enforcement of arbitral awards rendered within the province: *Civil Code of Quebec*, S.Q. 1991, c. 64, art. 2924; *Limitation Act*, R.S.B.C. 1996, c. 266. Consequently, Alberta is prohibited under the Convention from imposing a shorter time limit on the recognition of foreign arbitral awards.

32. This argument must also be rejected. The position advanced by ADR Chambers is fundamentally at odds with Canada's federal constitution, under which the recognition and enforcement of arbitral awards is a matter within provincial

jurisdiction (s. 92(13) "Property and Civil Rights" and § 92(14) "Administration of Justice" of the *Constitution Act, 1867*). Allowing the legislation of one province to dictate the range of legislative options available to another province concerning matters within its exclusive jurisdiction would be contrary to the constitutional legislative authority of each province under § 92 of the *Constitution Act, 1867*. Furthermore, ADR Chambers' position rests on a misreading of the Convention, which was intended to be respectful of the internal constitutional order of federal states like Canada. Article XI explicitly recognizes that some Contracting States will be federal or "non-unitary" and that jurisdiction over the subject matter of the treaty may lie with a sub-national entity. ArticleXI therefore tempers the international obligations of federal Contracting States accordingly (see Appendix B). Consequently, I would not agree with ADR Chambers' contention that applying § 3 of the *Limitations Act* to foreign arbitral awards would place Canada in violation of its international obligations.

33. Moreover, art. III, in which the term "rules of procedure" is found, distinguishes between "Contracting State", on the one hand, and "the territory where the award is relied upon", on the other. Read in conjunction with art. XI, this indicates that, for the purposes of art. III, the relevant unit is the enforcing jurisdiction within the Contracting State (i.e. Alberta) and not the Contracting State in its entirety. In order to comply with the Convention, Alberta need only provide foreign awards with treatment as generous as that provided to domestic awards rendered in Alberta.

34. The conclusion must be that the New York Convention was intended to allow Contracting States to impose local time limits on the recognition and enforcement of foreign arbitral awards if they so wished. In the case of federal states, such limitations are to be determined by the law of the enforcing jurisdiction within the federal state.

C. *What Limitation Period, if Any, Applies to the Recognition and Enforcement of Foreign Arbitral Awards Under Alberta Law?*

35. I now turn to the issue of whether or not Alberta law subjects the recognition and enforcement of foreign arbitral awards to a limitation period. Three Acts were referred to by the parties and interveners in this connection: the *Arbitration Act*, the *REJA*, and the *Limitations Act*. However, only the *Limitations Act* applies in this case. The *Arbitration Act* provides a two-year time limit on the enforcement of arbitral awards (§ 51(3)) and therefore would provide no assistance to Yugraneft. In any event, foreign awards such as the one at issue in this case are expressly excluded from the Act (§ 2(1)(b)). The *REJA* provides a six-year limitation period for judgments and arbitral awards rendered in reciprocating jurisdictions (§ 2(1)), but the award in this case was rendered in Russia, which is not a reciprocating jurisdiction. Therefore, the *REJA* does not apply.

36. Alberta's general law of limitations is found in the *Limitations Act*. Unlike the *Arbitration Act* and the *REJA*, the *Limitations Act* does not expressly exclude the appellant's award from its scope. The Act was intended to create a comprehensive and simplified limitations regime to replace the previous *Limitation of Actions Act*, R.S.A. 1980, c. L-15. As the Alberta Court of Appeal noted in *Daniels v. Mitchell*,

2005 ABCA 271, 51 Alta. L.R. (4th) 212, at para. 30:

> A main purpose of the [*Limitations Act*] was the simplification of limitations law, by the imposition of one period (two years) for nearly all causes of action. . . . [D]ebates in the Legislative Assembly repeatedly emphasized that the new legislation would simplify and clarify the system while eliminating inconsistencies and special treatment for certain defendants.

Thus, the purpose of the Act was to streamline the law of limitations by limiting the number of exceptions and providing a uniform limitation period for most actions.

37. The comprehensiveness of the Act is most clearly established by § 2(1), which provides that it applies in all cases where a claimant seeks a "remedial order". A remedial order is defined as "a judgment or an order made by a court in a civil proceeding requiring a defendant to comply with a duty or to pay damages for the violation of a right" (§ 1(i)). This is very broad language that encompasses virtually every kind of order that a court may grant in civil proceedings. Only certain types of relief are excluded, and these are enumerated in § 1(i): "a declaration of rights and duties, legal relations or personal status", "the enforcement of a remedial order", "judicial review", and "a writ of habeas corpus".

38. The comprehensive nature of the Act is reinforced by § 12, a provision that appears specifically designed to counteract the effects of this Court's decision in *Tolofson* in a conflict of laws situation. Section 12, which is labeled "Conflict of laws", provides that "[t]he limitations law of Alberta applies to any proceeding commenced or sought to be commenced in Alberta in which a claimant seeks a remedial order." This ensures that all proceedings brought within the province are subject to the local limitation period, notwithstanding any other limitation period that may also be applicable pursuant to a conflict of laws analysis like that performed in *Tolofson*.

39. In my view, the overall scheme of the Act is intended to be pervasive. In particular, § 12 ensures that Alberta's limitations law will apply even to claims subject to foreign law. This indicates that the *Limitations Act* was intended to apply to all claims for a remedial order not expressly excluded by statute. According to the maxim *expressio unius est exclusio alterius*, the fact that the legislature enumerated specific exceptions to the definition of a "remedial order" indicates that anything fitting the general description and not expressly excluded are, by implication, deemed to fall within the meaning of that term (R. Sullivan, *Sullivan on the Construction of Statutes* (5th ed. 2008), at pp. 243–45). Thus, by necessary implication, the recognition and enforcement of foreign arbitral awards is subject to the *Limitations Act*.

40. In oral argument, counsel for the London Court of International Arbitration ("LCIA") made no submission on the proper interpretation of the legislation in issue. However, in its factum, the LCIA argued that the *Limitations Act* should not apply in this case. It contended that only a clear expression of legislative intent can subject the recognition and enforcement of a foreign arbitral award to procedural requirements not contained in the Model Law and that the *Limitations Act* is not sufficiently explicit in this regard. It says that the Model Law was intended to set out a comprehensive and exhaustive list of the circumstances in which a local court

II. RECOGNITION AND ENFORCEMENT OF ARBITRAL AWARDS 721

may interfere with arbitral proceedings. To this end, art. 5 of the Model Law provides that "no court shall intervene except where so provided in this Law". The LCIA argues that, in the absence of a clear derogation from this principle, local procedural rules not contained in the statute enacting the Model Law should not apply. In its factum, it identified what it called a dichotomy between the Model Law, which contains no limitation period and the *Arbitration Act*, which provides a two-year limitation period for domestic arbitrations (§ 51(3)). It submitted that this dichotomy "reinforces the proposition that had the Legislature intended applications for the recognition and enforcement of foreign awards to be subject to a time limitation, it would have clearly stated its intention" (para. 24).

41. I cannot agree that the *Limitations Act* fails to provide the requisite clarity of legislative intent. The new *Limitations Act* was adopted well after the *ICAA*, and in my view the scheme of the Act and its legislative history indicate that the Alberta legislature intended to create a comprehensive and exhaustive limitations scheme applicable to all causes of action. Only causes of action excluded by the Act itself or covered by other legislation, such as the *Arbitration Act* would be exempt from its requirements. It is not necessary to expressly refer to foreign arbitral awards in order to make them subject to comprehensive legislation, which the *Limitations Act* clearly is.

42. The question at this point is how to characterize an application for recognition and enforcement of a foreign arbitral award under the *Limitations Act*. The Act essentially creates three streams, each of which is subject to a different limitation period: ten years, two years, or no limitation period. An application for a "remedial order" based on a "judgment or order for the payment of money" is subject to a 10-year limitation period (§ 11). All other applications for a remedial order fall under a two-year limitation period, subject to a discoverability rule (§ 3). Judgments or orders that are not remedial as defined in § 1(i) are not subject to a limitation period.

43. Yugraneft concedes that what it seeks constitutes a "remedial order" under the *Limitations Act*. However, it contends that an arbitral award is akin to a judgment and that an application for recognition and enforcement of that award is therefore a "claim based on a judgment or order for the payment of money" under § 11 of the Act, which is subject to a 10-year limitation period.

44. Yugraneft's position must be rejected. An arbitral award is not a judgment or a court order, and Yugraneft's application falls outside the scope of § 11. In *Dell Computer Corp. v. Union des consommateurs*, 2007 SCC 34, [2007] 2 S.C.R. 801, Deschamps J., writing for the majority, noted that "[a]rbitration is part of no state's judicial system" and "owes its existence to the will of the parties alone" (para. 51). See also *Desputeaux v. Éditions Chouette (1987) inc.*, 2003 SCC 17, [2003] 1 S.C.R. 178, in which LeBel J., for the Court, wrote, "[i]n general, arbitration is not part of the state's judicial system, although the state sometimes assigns powers or functions directly to arbitrators" (para. 41).

45. Unlike a local judgment, an arbitral award is not directly enforceable. In Alberta, it must first be recognized by the Court of Queen's Bench (*ICAA*, § 3), and this recognition can be resisted by the arbitral debtor on the grounds set out in art. V of the Convention. Furthermore, in those cases where the legislature intended the

word "judgment" to encompass both the decisions of courts and arbitral awards it did so expressly, as in § 1(1)(b) of the *REJA*. A similar approach is taken in the British Columbia *Limitation Act* which expressly provides that the term "local judgment" includes international arbitral awards (§ 1). It would therefore be incorrect to conclude that the Alberta legislature intended foreign arbitral awards to receive the same treatment as local judgments without express words to that effect.

46. In the alternative, Yugraneft contends that the text of the *Limitations Act* is ambiguous on the question of whether a foreign arbitral award should fall under § 3 or § 11. It submits that this ambiguity must be resolved in its favour. In its view, an application for recognition and enforcement does not fit cleanly into either § 3 or § 11 of the Act. It says that even if one accepts that a foreign arbitral award is not properly considered a "judgment" as this term is used in § 11, it finds no better home in the terms of § 3. Section 3 purports to apply to claims for a remedial order based on an "injury". Yugraneft suggests that by using the word "injury" the legislature intended § 3 to apply only to new causes of action. Given the adjudicative function of an arbitral tribunal and the final character of an arbitral award, an application for recognition and enforcement cannot be considered a new cause of action or an action on an "injury" and so falls outside the scope of § 3. If recognition proceedings do not fit cleanly within either § 3 or § 11, it is necessary to conclude that the *Limitations Act* is ambiguous. Since statutory provisions creating limitation periods must be interpreted strictly in favour of the plaintiff (*Ordon Estate v. Grail*, [1998] 3 S.C.R. 437, at para. 136), this ambiguity must be resolved in a manner that preserves Yugraneft's rights.

47. Yugraneft is correct that ambiguity in a limitations statute will be construed in favour of allowing the action to proceed. However, I do not agree that the Act is ambiguous in this case. The legislature has made it clear elsewhere that when it intends the word "judgment" to include a foreign arbitral award, it provides express words to that effect. For instance, in the *REJA*, it explicitly included arbitral awards in the definition of "judgment" (§ 1(1)(b)). In the absence of such express words, a foreign arbitral award cannot be held to fall within the meaning of "judgment". Thus, there is only one possible meaning, not two. An application for recognition and enforcement of a foreign arbitral award is an application for a remedial order within the meaning of § 3.

48. In addition, applying a 10-year limitation period to the recognition and enforcement of foreign arbitral awards would result in an incoherent limitations regime. In Alberta, arbitral awards from reciprocating jurisdictions are subject to a six-year time limit (*REJA*, § 2(1)). It would be incongruous to accord foreign arbitral awards from *non-reciprocating* jurisdictions more favourable treatment than those from jurisdictions with which Alberta has deliberately concluded an agreement for the reciprocal enforcement of judgments. Such an interpretation is to be avoided (see: *Rizzo & Rizzo Shoes Ltd. (Re)*, [1998] 1 S.C.R. 27, at para. 27).

49. Applying the limitation period set out in § 3 is consistent with the overall scheme of Alberta limitations law. It also provides more generous treatment for foreign awards than for domestic awards and is therefore consistent with art. III of the Convention. The limitation period in § 3 of the *Limitations Act* is subject to a

discoverability rule, which is not the case for the time limit set out in § 51 of the *Arbitration Act* governing domestic awards. This makes ample allowance for the practical difficulties faced by foreign arbitral creditors, who may require some time to discover that the arbitral debtor has assets in Alberta.

D. *Is Yugraneft's Application for Recognition and Enforcement Time-Barred Under Section 3 of the Limitations Act?*

50. Having determined that Yugraneft's application for recognition and enforcement is subject to § 3 of the *Limitations Act*, there remains the question of whether or not the application was time-barred when it was filed on January 27, 2006. As noted above, the two-year limitation period set out in § 3(1)(a) is subject to a discoverability rule. Only if the conditions for discoverability are met will the limitation period begin to run. Under § 3, a claim for a remedial order must be brought within two years after the claimant first knew, or in the circumstances ought to have known,

(i) that the injury for which the claimant seeks a remedial order had occurred,

(ii) that the injury was attributable to conduct of the defendant, and

(iii) that the injury, assuming liability on the part of the defendant, warrants bringing a proceeding, . . .

In the context of this case, the injury is "non-performance of an obligation" (*Limitations Act*, § 1(e)(iv)), i.e. Rexx's failure to comply with the arbitral award and pay Yugraneft US $952,614.43.

51. Neither Yugraneft nor Rexx has made submissions concerning the starting point of the limitation period in this case. Both parties appear to have assumed that if this Court finds that § 3, and not § 11, applies to the recognition and enforcement of foreign arbitral awards, Yugraneft's application would be time-barred. I believe this assumption to be correct for the following reasons.

52. In order to determine whether a proceeding is time-barred, it is necessary to ascertain when the injury occurred. In the case of non-performance of an obligation, the question is when the non-performance occurred.

53. In the context of a proceeding to recognize and enforce a foreign arbitral award, if non-performance is assumed to occur on the date the award was issued, Yugraneft would have commenced its proceeding in Alberta approximately 16 months after the two-year limitation period had expired. However, I do not think the date of the issuance of the award can normally be considered as the date of non-performance of the obligation to pay.

54. The Model Law provides that a party to an arbitration has three months to apply to the local courts to have an award set aside, beginning on the day it receives the award (art. 34(3)— see Appendix A). At least until that deadline has passed, the arbitral award may not have the requisite degree of finality to form the basis of an application for recognition and enforcement under the Convention. If an award is open to being set aside, it may be considered "not . . . binding" under art. V(1)(e) of the Convention (Blackaby and Partasides, at pp. 649–50). The same can be said

when proceedings to set aside the award are under way. Thus, if an award originates in a Model Law jurisdiction, or one with analogous provisions concerning the setting aside of an arbitral award, an arbitral creditor would not know and would have no reason to think that recognition and enforcement proceedings are warranted on the very date the award is rendered. In those circumstances, the limitation period under § 3 of the *Limitations Act* will not be triggered until the possibility that the award might be set aside by the local courts in the country where the award was rendered has been foreclosed.

55. That would appear to be the case here. Russia is a Model Law jurisdiction, and there is no indication in the record before this Court that Russia modified art. 34 in its adoption of the Model Law (Award of the Russian ICAC (English translation), A.R., vol. 2, at p. 84). Thus, the courts of any State party to the Convention would be entitled to refuse to grant recognition and enforcement of the award at issue in this case until the three-month appeal period had expired; or, if an appeal was launched, until the appeal was concluded.

56. Accordingly, it is my view that for the purposes of the *Limitations Act*, Rexx's obligations under the award did not crystalize until three months after Yugraneft had received the award. The award was issued on September 6, 2002, and Yugraneft has provided no indication that it received the award at a later date. As a result, non-performance of its obligation to pay Yugraneft would not have occurred before December 6, 2002. This would suggest that Yugraneft had two years after December 6, 2002, to commence proceedings against Rexx in Alberta, meaning that its action, which was brought on January 27, 2006, was clearly time-barred.

57. A second consideration in the context of a recognition and enforcement of foreign arbitral awards is whether non-performance of the arbitral debtor's obligation to pay arises when the award becomes final or only when an actual refusal to pay the award becomes apparent to the arbitral creditor. In my opinion, the obligation to pay the award becomes exigible on the date the appeal period expires or, if an appeal is taken, the date of the appeal decision. Failure to make payment on that date would constitute non-performance of the obligation. Thus, the injury has occurred and the conditions set out in § 3(1)(a)(i) and (ii) are satisfied on that date.

58. However, § 3(1)(a)(iii) provides that the limitation period will run only if the claimant knew or ought to have known that the injury "warrants bringing a proceeding". There may be situations in which an application for recognition and enforcement is not immediately "warranted", and it will be open to the courts in such cases to delay commencement of the limitation period accordingly.

59. In *Novak v. Bond*, [1999] 1 S.C.R. 808, McLachlin J. (as she then was) noted that discoverability rules of this kind are the product of a long-term trend in the law of limitations towards an approach that balances the interests of both plaintiffs and defendants. The traditional rationales for the imposition of a limitation period on actions were centered on the interests of the defendant: (a) the need for certainty concerning legal rights and obligations; (b) the need to minimize the risk that evidence necessary to defend against a claim would deteriorate over time; and (c) a concern for ensuring that defendants not be required to defend themselves against stale claims because a plaintiff has failed to act diligently (para. 64). Over time,

however, courts, law reform commissions and legislatures came to realize that this approach was one-sided and that a "more contextual view of the parties' actual circumstances" was required (para. 65). Accordingly, at para. 66, McLachlin J. wrote:

> Contemporary limitations statutes thus seek to balance conventional rationales oriented towards the protection of the defendant — certainty, evidentiary, and diligence — with the need to treat plaintiffs fairly, having regard to their specific circumstances. As Major J. put it in [*Murphy v. Welsh*, [1993] 2 S.C.R. 1069], "[a] limitations scheme must attempt to balance the interests of both sides" (p. 1080).

60. Section 3(1)(a)(iii) provides that the limitation period will commence only once the plaintiff knew or ought to have known that the injury it received warrants bringing a proceeding. Thus § 3(1)(a) ensures that the scheme created by the *Limitations Act* balances the interests of both plaintiffs and defendants. However, much like its counterpart in the B.C. *Limitation Act* at issue in *Novak v. Bond*, § 3(1) measures the conduct of the plaintiff against an "objective" standard. Section 6(4) of the B.C. Act provides that the limitation period will not commence until the facts available to the plaintiff are such that a "reasonable person . . . would regard those facts as showing" that the plaintiff was (a) able to bring a claim, and (b) that the claim had a reasonable prospect of success. Section 3(1) of the Alberta Act does not refer to a "reasonable person" and its discoverability criteria are not identical with those in s. 6(4) of the B.C. Act. However, it does subject the knowledge elements of its discoverability rule to an objective test: the plaintiff must know or "ought to have known" the elements that trigger the running of the limitation period. Thus, constructive or imputed knowledge, in addition to actual knowledge, will trigger the limitation period.

61. Section 3(1)(a)(iii) therefore allows the courts to consider aspects of an arbitral creditor's circumstances that would lead a reasonable person to conclude that there was no reason for the arbitral creditor to know whether proceedings were warranted in Alberta. For example, it is not infrequent for the parties to an international arbitration to have assets in a number of different states or jurisdictions within a federal state. An arbitral creditor cannot be presumed to know the location of all of the arbitral debtor's assets. If the arbitral creditor does not know, and would have no reason to know, that the arbitral debtor has assets in a particular jurisdiction, it cannot be expected to know that recognition and enforcement proceedings are warranted in that jurisdiction. Thus, in my view, recognition and enforcement proceedings would only be warranted in Alberta once an arbitral creditor had learned, exercising reasonable diligence, that the arbitral debtor possessed assets in that jurisdiction.

62. Nevertheless, a delay on this account would not be open to Yugraneft in this case. The contract entered into by Yugraneft and Rexx on October 1, 1998, indicates that Rexx was identified as an Alberta corporation (Contract No. 157, A.R., vol. 2, at p. 41). An arbitral creditor might well not be expected to know every location in the world in which an arbitral debtor might have assets, but this cannot be said of the jurisdiction where the debtor is registered and where its head office is located. In such circumstances, Yugraneft has not claimed and could not claim that it did not

know or ought not to have known that a proceeding was warranted in Alberta at the time of (or indeed earlier than) the expiry of the three-month appeal period following receipt of notice of the award.

63. Thus, I have no difficulty concluding that even taking into account the discoverability rule in § 3(1)(a) of the *Limitations Act*, Yugraneft's proceedings are time-barred.

E. *The Public Policy Argument*

64. In addition to claiming that Yugraneft's application is time-barred, Rexx has also argued that enforcement of the award should be refused on public policy grounds (Convention, art. V(2)(b)), alleging that it was tainted by fraud. In light of my conclusion regarding the applicable limitation period, there is no need to rule on this issue and I refrain from doing so.

VI. Conclusion

65. I would dismiss the appeal, with costs.

Appeal dismissed with costs.

QUESTIONS

1. From your reading of *Yugraneft Corp. v. Rexx Management Corp*, how do the United States and Canada differ with respect to the effect and enforcement of international treaties in the context of federalism? Do the United States and Canada differ with respect to the advantages of arbitration? If so, in what respects?

2. What were Justice Rothstein's rationale for the propositions that under the New York Convention (1) the Alberta Limitations Act applied, (2) arbitral awards could be distinguished and subject to shorter periods of limitation (extinctive prescription) than certain foreign-country judgments or court judgments from other provinces, (3) differences are permitted in provincial periods of limitation for arbitral awards, and (4) Alberta could impose a significantly shorter period of limitation for arbitral awards by foreign tribunals than by tribunals in sister provinces? Were you persuaded? How did Justice Rothstein interpret the Alberta Limitations Act in holding that limitation period began to run from the time the arbitral award become final? Again, were you persuaded?

C. Japan

AMERICAN PRESIDENT LINES, LTD. v. SUBRA KABUSHIKI KAISHA
Tokyo District Court Judgment of 23 October 1959
10 Kakyū minshū 2232 (1959)*

DISPOSITION
(shūbun)

1. In regard to 34, 196 dollars and 70 cents in U.S. currency (12,310.838 yen converted into Japanese currency) with the arbitration award made February 27, 1959 in New York by the arbitrators A.W. Parry, T.C. Janeway and D.B. Donald concerning demurrage, etc., under a charter-party contract of March 23, 1957 between the plaintiff and defendant, compulsory execution is permitted.

2. Other claims of the plaintiff are rejected.

3. The costs of litigation are to be borne by the defendant.

4. Upon submission of 1,200,000 yen security by the plaintiff, the judgment may be provisionally executed.

FACTS
(jijitsu)

The plaintiff's attorney sought "approval of compulsory execution of 34,196 dollars and 70 cents in U.S. currency (12,310,833 yen converted into Japanese currency) within the arbitration award made February 27, 1959 in New York by the arbitrators A.W. Parry, T.C. Janeway and D.B. Donald concerning the case of a claim for demurrage, etc., under a charter-party contract of March 23, 1957 between the plaintiff and defendant on the SS Hunter Victory and the SS Globe City Victory and of interest on this amount at a rate of six percent per annum from February 27, 1959 until paid in full," and a judgment to the same effect as paragraph 2 together with a declaration of provisional execution. As a cause of action he stated that:

1. The plaintiff is a United States corporation and the defendant a Japanese juridical person. On March 23, 1957 the plaintiff and defendant, with the plaintiff as shipowner and the defendant as charterer, concluded a bareboat charter in regard to the SS Hunter Victory and the SS Globe City Victory owned by the plaintiff, and entered into an arbitration agreement to the effect that disputes arising in regard to the charter-party contract would be submitted to the arbitration of three persons in New York in the United States — one arbitrator to be selected by the shipowner, one arbitrator to be selected by the charterer, and one arbitrator to be selected by both.

---

* Translated by an unnamed research fellow in the University of Washington Asian Law Program.

2. However, since a dispute in regard to the above charter-party contract arose between the plaintiff and defendant concerning the demurrage and boat charges, etc. for each vessel; the plaintiff applying on May 22, 1958 to the federal United States District Court for the Southern District of New York sought to undertake an arbitration proceeding; as arbitrators under the above arbitration agreement, the shipowner plaintiff selected A.W. Parry, the charterer defendant T.C. Janeway, and both plaintiff and defendant D.B. Donald; and these arbitrators rendered the . . . arbitration award on February 27, 1959 [details of award omitted].

3. The above arbitration award was confirmed April 7th of the same year by the aforementioned federal United States District Court pursuant to the United States Arbitration Act.

4. In addition, since pursuant to the above arbitration award the plaintiff's claim against the defendant totals $30,992.72 and the defendant's counterclaim against the plaintiff $2,595.96, when these are set off against each other, the plaintiff's claim against the defendant becomes $48,396.76, but because $14,200 within this money has already been paid by the defendant the balance remaining is $34,196.70 (¥12,310,833 converted into Japanese currency). Against this amount the judgment of the federal United States District Court enforcing the above arbitration award has ordered the payment of six percent annual interest from the date of the arbitration award, and six percent annual interest being the legal rate in the Japanese Commercial Code, even though there is no direct entry concerning the payment of this interest in the above arbitration award, because payment of the interest is ordered in the above judgment of execution which must conform to the award, this fact — in seeking a judgment enforcing interest at an annual rate of six percent from February 27, 1959, the date of the above arbitration award, until full satisfaction takes place — affects this suit under Article IV of the "Treaty of Friendship, Commerce and Navigation Between the United States of America and Japan.

Moreover, against the defendant's affirmative defense that the plaintiff is seeking a judgment executing but one part of the arbitration award, he stated that:

Since the aforesaid arbitration award contains a determination which, in the manner described above, completely offsets the plaintiff's duty to pay the defendant with the defendant's duty to pay the plaintiff, and since, assuming that we are simply seeking an approval of enforcement under the arbitration award, this constitutes seeking a judgment enforcing the plaintiff's duty to pay the defendant and results in the pursuit of a judgment disadvantageous to the plaintiff, we are doing no more than having to seek a judgment which enforces the sum remaining after deducting from the amount of the defendant's obligation payable to the plaintiff that of the plaintiff due the defendant, and because the defendant has already performed part of its duty to pay the plaintiff, this amount also is deducted. We do not seek, as alleged by the defendant, to extract voluntarily one part of the arbitration award and obtain a judgment which executes just it.

The defendant's attorney sought a judgment which "rejects the plaintiff's claim," and in answer stated that he admits the facts in paragraphs 1 through 2 within the facts of the plaintiff's cause of action and that he has no knowledge of paragraph 3, and also stated that:

1. The plaintiff is seeking a judgment which would permit compulsory execution of one part of the money within the arbitration award, but since a judgment of execution is procedurally a formative judgment which confers enforceability on an entire foreign judgment or arbitration award, seeking a judgment of execution in regard to only a portion of a foreign judgment or arbitration award cannot be allowed.

2. The plaintiff is seeking the payment of interest at the rate of six percent per annum after the data of the arbitration award, but — there being no provision relating to the payment of interest in the United States Arbitration Act — the legal foundation for the federal United States District Court for the Southern District of New York having ordered payment of interest at six percent per annum is not entirely clear, and even though the judgment of execution must conform to the arbitration award, the fact that the payment of interest is ordered in the above judgment of execution is scant reason for seeking in this suit based thereon, a judgment executing interest.

Tentatively, even assuming that the ordering of a payment of six percent interest per annum is prescribed by law in the United States, in seeking a judgment of execution in a Japanese court, one is bound by the arbitration award and one may not seek a payment of interest not so awarded.

As evidence the plaintiff submitted exhibits A No. 1 through No. 5, and the defendant admitted the execution of each of these exhibits.

REASONS
(*riyū*)

There is no dispute between the parties that the plaintiff is a United States corporation and the defendant a Japanese juridical person: that a bareboat charter such as alleged by the plaintiff was concluded between the plaintiff and defendant on the date alleged by the plaintiff; that they entered into an arbitration agreement to the effect that if a dispute arose in regard to this contract they would submit it subject to the United States Arbitration Act to arbitration under three persons in New York in the United States — one arbitrator to be selected by the plaintiff, one arbitrator to be selected by the defendant; that the plaintiff, as alleged by it, applying on May 22, 1958 to the federal United States District Court for the Southern District of New York sought to undertake an arbitration proceeding; that based on the above arbitration agreement as alleged by the plaintiff, both the plaintiff and defendant selected the respective arbitrators; and that on February 27, 1959 there was an arbitration award such as alleged by the plaintiff. Pursuant to exhibits A No. 1 through No. 3, the execution of which is undisputed, we are able to recognize that the plaintiff made a motion on March 10th of the same year in the above federal District Court for an order confirming and enforcing this arbitration award, and that this court, noting that the defendant confirmed the arbitration award and assented to the recording of an order by the court, issued an order confirming and enforcing the arbitration award.

In passing judgment on the defendant's affirmative defense that the plaintiff is seeking the execution of one part of the arbitration award which cannot be allowed, because a judgment of execution in this suit — just as alleged by the defendant — would be a judgment inquiring into whether or not the effect of a foreign judgment or arbitration award viewed exactly the same should be recognized in our country and conferring enforceability thereon, and not a judgment seeking a particular performance, under the principles of our law a request that enforceability be conferred on only one part of the foreign judgment or arbitration award cannot be granted. But, since, as in this case, the aforementioned arbitration award between the plaintiff and defendant is an award which while ordering the defendant to pay a total of 50,922 dollars and 72 cents in money to the plaintiff orders the plaintiff to pay a total of 2,595 dollars and 96 cents in money to the defendant and which, having imposed on the plaintiff and defendant mutually a duty to pay money, sets the same time of performance for all the duties of each to pay, we feel that in a voluntary performance thereof it would be unthinkable to actually adopt the highly round-about method of the plaintiff having to obtain from the defendant the debt due after the plaintiff had completely satisfied its duty to pay the defendant and that rather than claims respecting each debt would be mutually set off by their opposing amounts with payment taking place in regard to the balance left. Moreover, when as in this suit not voluntary performance of the arbitration award but a judgment of execution is sought, it can easily be guess that a defendant possessing a counterclaim against a plaintiff would always allege the off set of this counterclaim, and if there is a debt which has been paid voluntarily, enter the affirmative defense that there may be a judgment of execution for the amount remaining after the sum paid has been deducted. It is difficult to support the view that in an action for a judgment of execution one must still seek a conferral of enforceability on the entire arbitration award without any change, even though an alteration has been brought about in the obligations after the conclusion of the aforesaid arbitration award, and that one may not enter an affirmative defense to the contrary which alleges that the obligations have been altered due to such things as set off or satisfaction after the time the arbitration award was concluded or seek to abate enforceability. Since we are able to conclude that in an action for a judgment of execution, from the standpoint of economy in litigation, one may allege an alteration of the above obligations as an affirmative defense and seek to abate enforceability, and that a judgment of execution must pursue the enforceability of the above arbitration award as it exists now — not its enforceability as it existed in the past, we must state that this suit, in which the plaintiff sets off its claim first, as the active claim, against the defendant's claim in the arbitration award and seeks a conferral of enforceability on the amount of the arbitration award remaining after deducting the sum completing this performance, is proper, and that we cannot accept the defendant's above affirmative defense.

Next, the plaintiff seeks the additional payment of six percent annual interest in regard to the above arbitration award from the date of the arbitration award, but even when we rely on exhibits A No. 4 and No. 5, the execution of which is undisputed, we cannot recognize that a definite law exists among the federal laws of the United States which per se requires ordering the payment of six percent annual interest from the data of an arbitration award, and because we conclude that we are not able in a judgment of execution, which merely confers enforceability on an arbitration award in a case where nothing has been prescribed concerning interest after the date for performance, to grant a decision which includes a new judgment of particular performance ordering the payment of interest on the above arbitration award we cannot adopt this allegation of the plaintiff.

Therefore, since the claims of the plaintiff in this suit have reason, except for the portion seeking the payment of interest at a rate of six percent per annum from the date of the arbitration award until full satisfaction take place, they are granted and this other is rejected. . . .

JUDGE KUNIMICHI ŌMAE

QUESTION

In what respects does the enforcement of arbitral awards in Japan appear from this case to differ from both the United States and Canada?

TEXACO OVERSEAS TANKSHIP LTD. v. OKADA SHIPPING CO., LTD.

Osaka District Court Judgment of 22 April 1983
[Adapted from English translation in 27 JAIL 184 (1984)]

DISPOSITION
(*shūbun*)

1. The arbitral award made by arbitrators Michael J. Auiodan, Theodor Zagarus and Manfred W. Arnold in New York City on July 20, 1979 as to the claim for damages laid by the plaintiff against the defendant concerning the charter party dated April 10, 1970 is permitted to be executed as much as the arbitral award orders the payment of US $329,356.27 together with the interest upon the said sum at the rate of 8 percent per annum after November 30, 1975 until the said sum is fully paid and the payment of US $1,700.

2. The costs of litigation shall be borne by the defendant.

3. This judgment may be executed provisionally on condition that the plaintiff offers ¥5,000,000 as security.

FACTS
(*jijitsu*)

I. Judgments demanded by the parties [omitted]

II. Allegations of the parties

1. The cause of action

(1) The plaintiff is an English company and the defendant is a Japanese corporation. The plaintiff and the defendant concluded a charter party on April 10, 1970, which provided mainly that the plaintiff may use a ship of the defendant for a specified period. The plaintiff and the defendant agreed that in case of some disputes concerning the charter party the plaintiff and the defendant should refer the disputes to arbitration conducted by three arbitrators in New York City of the United States of America; that one arbitrator should be appointed by the shipowner, another arbitrator should be appointed by the charterer, and the third arbitrator should be appointed by the two arbitrators appointed in the way mentioned above; that each party may ask for arbitration by delivering a notice, which should bear the name and address of the arbitrator appointed by the party and the summary of the dispute that the party would refer to arbitration, to a director of the other party; that in case the other party would not appoint an arbitrator within 20 days after the delivery of the notice, the claimant may appoint a second arbitrator without any notice.

(2) Although the defendant had to pay to the plaintiff US $342,856.27 as damages resulting from corruption and injury of cargoes, caused while the defendant performed the charter party and resulting from imperfect performance of the charter party, the defendant paid only US $13,500 in November 1975 and the defendant had not paid the balance US $329,356.27 since then. Accordingly, on March 16, 1977 the plaintiff delivered under the provision of the arbitration clause a request of arbitration seeking the payment of the sum not yet paid and the notice of the name and address of Michael J. Auriodan, the arbitrator appointed by the plaintiff. The plaintiff appointed Theodor Zagaris as a second arbitrator because the plaintiff had not received the notice of the appointment of an arbitrator by April 15, 1977, which was the time limit fixed by a request of postponement by the defendant. The two arbitrators appointed Manfred W. Arnold as the third arbitrator.

(3) The three arbitrators made an arbitral award on July 20, 1979 in New York City of the United States of America, which ordered that the defendant pay to the plaintiff US $329,438.61 as damages together with the interest upon the said sum at the rate of 8 percent per annum after November 30, 1975 until whichever occurs earlier of the full payment of the damages and an order of court and that the defendant pay to the plaintiff US $1,200 as lawyer's fee and US $500 as arbitrators' fee.

It is clear from the reasons stated in the arbitral award that the damages US $329,438.61, the payment of which was ordered by the award, was based upon an erroneous calculation and should be US $329,356.27. The claim of the plaintiff shows the right amount based upon calculation.

(4) The arbitral award is based on the arbitration agreement contained in a document signed by the plaintiff and the defendant. Accordingly, we demand such a judgment as seated in our claims under the provision of Article III of the Convention on the Recognition and Enforcement of Foreign Arbitral Awards.

2.–5. [answers and counter answers of the parties omitted]

III. Evidence (omitted)

REASONS
(*riyū*)

1. The Convention on the Recognition and Enforcement of Foreign Arbitral Awards (so-called "New York Convention") came into force for Japan on September 18, 1961 with the reservation that Japan would apply the Convention to the recognition and enforcement of awards made only in the territory of another Contracting State. The New York Convention came into force for the United States of America on December 29, 1970 under the provisions of Article XII 2 by the fact that the Government of the United States of America deposited an instrument of accession with the Secretary General of the United Nations on September 30, 1970. The parties were in accord as to the fact, which we deem to be true, that the arbitral award was made on July 20, 1979 in New York City of the United States of America in compliance with the provision of the arbitral clause agreed to by the plaintiff and the defendant. Therefore, a judgment of execution may be demanded as to the arbitral award under the provision of Article III of the New York Convention. The requirements of the judgments of execution are provided in the Convention. The New York Convention provides the positive requirements for recognition and enforcement in Article IV, the refusal requirements against recognition and enforcement in Article V, and requirements for adjourning the decision on the enforcement of the award in Article VI.

2. It is evident for the court that the plaintiff presented to the court, as an oral proceeding on November 11, 1982, the original award duly authenticated judging from its external form and the original arbitral agreement, and the documents, which we deem to be the translations of the above-mentioned documents, certified by a British consular agent. Therefore, the positive requirements provided in Article IV of the New York Convention are met.

3. The burden of allegation and proof of refusal requirements against recognition and enforcement, provided in Article V of the New York Convention, and of requirements for adjourning the decision on the enforcement, provided in Article VI of the Convention, is borne by the defendant o, who is the enforcement-proceeding debtor. The defendant alleges the fact that come sunder Article V 1(b), namely that the arbitral award was made unilaterally without giving to the defendant any opportunity to present his case. We judge the allegation as follows:

The plaintiff and the defendant agree that the plaintiff sent to the defendant, by delivery certification mail on March 16, 1977, in compliance with the provision of the arbitral clause, a claim of arbitration that demands the payment of damages resulting from corruption and injury of cargoes caused while the defendant performed the charter party and resulting from an imperfect performance of the charter party, together with a notice of the name and address of Michael J. Auriodan, the arbitrator who the plaintiff had appointed under the provision of the arbitral clause; that the mail was delivered to the defendant on March 16, 1977; that, as the arbitral clause provides that the defendant should give the notice of the arbitrator within 20 days after the receipt of a claim of arbitration and should give the notice of the arbitrator to the plaintiff, and since the defendant had not given to the plaintiff a notice of the appointment of an arbitrator by April 15, 1977, which was the date of appointment fixed by the request of postponement by the defendant, the plaintiff appointed Theodor Zagaris as a second arbitrator under the provision of the arbitral clause and gave the notice of the appointment to the defendant on June 15, 1977; that the arbitrators appointed Manfred W. Arnold as the third arbitrator under the provision of the arbitral clause; that the three arbitrators appointed the date on July 18, 1977 for the first hearing; that the notice of the appointment of the case was given to the defendant together with the notice of the name and address of the third arbitrator on June 17, 1977. We recognize according to the evidence (omitted) that about July 5, 1977 the defendant entrusted Carlin, Campbell and Keeting's Office with the following of the arbitration proceedings; that the defendant informed the office that the defendant should send to the office the papers requested at that time; that the Office (Vincent Lynch) requested on July 12, 1977 that the date for the first hearing be postponed; that thereafter a hearing was arranged on November 29, 1978 according to the agreement of the plaintiff and the defendant; that, however, no use was made of the hearing date; that, although on July 15, 1979 the defendant made no statement, the three arbitrators finished hearing after they had recognized that due notices had been given to the defendant; that the arbitral award was made on July 20, 1979.

The defendant alleges that the arbitration proceeding was followed by those who pretended to be the representatives of the defendant without any full notice given to the defendant because the defendant had never duly appointed representative for the arbitration proceeding. And we recognize according to the evidence (omitted) the Carlin, Campbell and Keeting's Office had informed the arbitrators on May 16, 1979. "We are not the representatives of the defendant, nor is it our duty to stand in defense of the defendant as to the arbitration proceeding. We have no intention of being present at the hearing already arrange." However, it is not possible to recognize that the defendant was unfairly deprived of opportunity to present his case, because the office had been the representative of the defendant since around July 5, 1977 until the information of resignation of the position of representatives (at least until the hearing date of November 29, 1978), and because an opportunity of hearing was given to the defendant on July 18, 1977 and on November 29, 1978.

4. It is evident from the cause of action contained in the evidence (omitted) that the damages US $329,438.61, the payment of which is ordered by the arbitral award, was based on an erroneous calculation and should be US $329,356.27. Therefore, the plaintiff is entitled to judgment of execution to the extent of the amount corrected by right calculation. The arbitral award orders the payment of interest to the damages calculated at the rate of 8 percent per annum until whichever occurs earlier of the full payment of the damages and the order of the court. We suppose that the arbitral award orders the payment of the interest

because the arbitrators thought they should judge the payment of interest after judgment of execution according to the law of the state where the arbitral award was made. In the State of New York, where the arbitral award was made, an interest should arise and its payment may be executed as to judgments that orders the payments of money even if the party does not claim it. Therefore, we should give judgment of execution in Japan, where we have no such institution, by considering the arbitral award to order merely the payment of interest until the full payment of damages.

5. As we stated above, the claims of the plaintiff is grounded and therefore should be granted. We apply Article 89 of the Code of Civil Procedure to the burden of costs of litigation and Article 196 of the same Code as to provisional execution. We judge as in the disposition of judgment.

JUDGE SHIGERU HAYASHI
JUDGE TATSUYA KASAI

QUESTIONS

Does this case suggest additional differences from the preceding case in the enforcement of arbitral awards in Japan in comparison to either or both the United States and Canada? Can you explain any differences? Within which county is the enforcement of an arbitral award more certain, less costly and time-consuming? Would your answer be the same with respect to or in comparison with a foreign-country judgment?

D. European Union

All of the member states of the EU are signatories of the 1958 U.N. Convention on the Recognition and Enforcement of Foreign Arbitral Awards (the "New York Convention"). Moreover, article 1(2)(d) of Regulation (EU) No. 1215/2012 explicitly excludes arbitration from its scope of application. Article 73(2) adds that the Regulation "shall not affect the application of the 1958 New York Convention." Thus the recognition and enforcement of arbitral awards within the EU depends on solely on the New York Convention as construed and applied under the national law of each country. As stated in the official comment on Regulation (EU) No. 1215/2012:

> This Regulation should not apply to arbitration. Nothing in this Regulation should prevent the courts of a Member State, when seised of an action in a matter in respect of which the parties have entered into an arbitration agreement, from referring the parties to arbitration, from staying or dismissing the proceedings, or from examining whether the arbitration agreement is null and void, inoperative or incapable of being performed, in accordance with their national law.

A ruling given by a court of a Member State as to whether or not an arbitration agreement is null and void, inoperative or incapable of being performed should not be subject to the rules of recognition and enforcement laid down in this Regulation, regardless of whether the court decided on this as a principal issue or as an incidental question.

On the other hand, where a court of a Member State, exercising jurisdiction under this Regulation or under national law, has determined that an arbitration agreement is null and void, inoperative or incapable of being performed, this should not preclude that court's judgment on the substance of the matter from being recognised or, as the case may be, enforced in accordance with this Regulation. This should be without prejudice to the competence of the courts of the Member States to decide on the recognition and enforcement of arbitral awards in accordance with the Convention on the Recognition and Enforcement of Foreign Arbitral Awards, done at New York on 10 June 1958 ('the 1958 New York Convention'), which takes precedence over this Regulation.

REVIEW PROBLEMS

1. Recall the concluding problem and questions in Chapter 2. Assume that Claude Cassirer succeeds in his assertion of legal title to Pissarro's *Rue Saint Honoré — Afternoon, Rain Effect* in a final judgment in *Cassirer v. Kingdom of Spain and Thyssen-Bornemisza Collection Foundation*. What problems, if any, should he expect to encounter were he to seek recognition and enforcement of the U.S. judgment in Spain, where the painting is located? Had he brought a similar action in the U.K. (assuming similar bases for effective jurisdiction over the defendants), would he face similar problems?

Note: Spain apparently does not recognize the jurisdiction of foreign courts unless some connection existed between the subject-matter of the lawsuit and the activities of the defendant in the jurisdiction. Moreover, Spain reserves the exclusive right to determine proprietary rights in both immovable and movable property located in Spain. *See* The Committee on Foreign and Comparative Law of the Association of the Bar of the City of New York, *Survey on Foreign Recognition of U.S. Money Judgments* (July 2001).

2. Assume, in contrast, that the plaintiffs, Maria Vladimirovna, Grand Duchess of Russia, and Prince Nicholas Romanov on behalf of the Romanov Family Association, have similarly succeeded in their hypothetical lawsuit against the United States and the National Gallery of Art for recovery of paintings purchased by Andrew Mellon from the Soviet Union and donated to the National Gallery in the 1930s, including Raphael's *The Alba Madonna*. Would such Spanish judgment be recognized and enforced in the United States? Which courts would have jurisdiction and what law would apply?

Chapter 7
CHOICE OF FORUM

We conclude our study of the fundamentals of transnational litigation with consideration of forum selection agreements, their enforceability and the advantages and disadvantages of an agreed choice of forum — either litigation in a designated court of a mutually agreed jurisdiction or some form of arbitration. In previous chapters we have already encountered numerous cases with examples of both. Much of the material explored here will be familiar. Our inquiry throughout, however, will center on the choices available to the parties and factors that should be considered in deciding whether to select a forum and, if so, what forum is preferable in the context of the parties' transaction.

Forum selection by agreement occurs in nearly all cases by contract at the initial stage of the particular transaction, but, albeit extremely rare, the parties could mutually agree on a forum at any time, even after a dispute occurs. Outside of the scope of our inquiry are the issues raised by standard form contracts in which one party in effect makes a unilateral selection. The issues raised in such cases, especially in domestic consumer and employment transactions, are appropriately resolved under substantive contract law and consumer and employee protection rules rather than transnational litigation. Our primary concern will be, as noted, the extent to which the parties in transnational commercial transactions may choose a forum and the factors that should be considered by their legal counsel in making that decision. We begin with prorogation — choice of courts agreements.

I. CHOICE OF COURT (PROROGATION) AGREEMENTS

Completing a decade long effort that began with failed negotiations over a convention on the recognition and enforcement of foreign country judgments, in 2005 the members of The Hague Conference on Private International Law agreed to the Convention on Choice of Court Agreements. The United States was the first to sign (January 2007) but, as noted below, dispute over whether to adopt a federal preemption or a "cooperative federalism" approach has delayed ratification. Mexico acceded in September 2007, and the European Union on behalf of all members (except Denmark) signed the Convention in 2009. The Convention becomes effective with ratification by one more member. The principal provisions of the Convention are summarized below in the EU Council Decision on Signing the Convention of February 2009. (For the full text of the Convention, see http://www.hcch.net/index_en.php?act=conventions.text&cid=98.) We will return to the summary at the end of this section to consider its significance for European Union law.

COUNCIL DECISION 2009/397/EC OF 26 FEBRUARY 2009 ON THE SIGNING ON BEHALF OF THE EUROPEAN COMMUNITY OF THE CONVENTION ON CHOICE OF COURT AGREEMENTS

SUMMARY

The Convention on Choice of Court Agreements was concluded under The Hague Conference on Private International Law on 30 June 2005. This decision provides for the signing of that convention on behalf of the European Community.

The convention applies in international cases to exclusive choice of court agreements concluded in civil or commercial matters. Its scope excludes both consumer and employment contracts. Neither does the convention apply to a number of other matters, such as the legal capacity of natural persons, maintenance obligations and other family law matters, the carriage of passengers or goods, marine pollution, competition matters, the validity of legal persons, the validity of intellectual property rights, etc. Furthermore, it does not apply to arbitration and related proceedings.

An exclusive choice of court agreement may be concluded by two or more parties to designate the courts (or one or more specific courts) of one contracting state as having jurisdiction in disputes relating to a particular legal relationship. Such an agreement is considered to be exclusive, unless otherwise specified by the parties to the agreement. The agreement must be made in writing or by other means that allow the information to be accessed subsequently.

JURISDICTION

The designated court has jurisdiction to decide a dispute to which the agreement applies, except when its national law does not recognise the agreement as valid. *Any other court of a contracting state must suspend or dismiss the related proceedings*, except in cases where the agreement is null and void under the law of the state of the chosen court, the party lacked the capacity to conclude the agreement under the national law of the court seised, implementation of the agreement contravenes the public policy of the state of the court seised, the agreement cannot be performed or the chosen court decides against hearing the case. [Emphasis added.]

RECOGNITION AND ENFORCEMENT

The other contracting states must recognise and enforce a judgement given by the court designated in the exclusive choice of court agreement. However, the judgement must first be enforceable in the state of origin. The postponement or refusal of recognition or enforcement is possible when the judgement is under review in the state of origin or when the deadline for seeking ordinary review has not yet expired.

Recognition or enforcement of a judgement may also be refused when:
- the agreement is null and void in the state of the chosen court;

- a party lacked the capacity to conclude the agreement under the law of the requested state;
- the document instituting the proceedings was not presented in sufficient time to the defendant;
- the manner in which the document instituting the proceedings was presented to the defendant is in conflict with the fundamental principles on serving documents;
- the judgement was obtained through a fraudulent procedure;
- recognition or enforcement is manifestly incompatible with the public policy of the requested state;
- the judgement is not consistent with an earlier one given by the requested state in a dispute between the same parties;
- the judgement is not consistent with an earlier one given by another state in a dispute between the same parties and for the same action.

When requesting the recognition or enforcement of a judgement, the party needs to produce the following documents:
- a copy of the judgement;
- a copy of the exclusive choice of court agreement;
- in case the judgement was given by default, a document indicating that the defaulting party was notified of the institution of the proceedings;
- a document indicating that the judgement is enforceable in the state of origin;
- in the case of a judicial settlement, a certificate of a court indicating that the settlement is equally enforceable in the state of origin.

An application may also be made for the partial recognition or enforcement of a judgement.

The law governing the procedure for recognition, declaration for enforceability or registration for enforcement and the enforcement of the judgement is that of the requested state.

DECLARATIONS LIMITING JURISDICTION, RECOGNITION OR ENFORCEMENT

A state may at any time make a declaration whereby its courts refuse to exercise their jurisdiction in determining disputes if there is no connection between the parties to the dispute and that state. Similarly, a state may make a declaration whereby its courts refuse to recognise or enforce a judgement if the parties to the dispute are resident in that state and the relationship of the parties as well as all other elements relating to the dispute are connected only with it. A state may also make a declaration whereby it will not apply this convention to a specific matter. In addition, a state may make a declaration whereby it recognises and enforces judgments given by courts of other contracting states designated in a non-exclusive choice of court agreement.

A. United States

M/S BREMEN AND UNTERWESER REEDEREI, GMBH v. ZAPATA OFF-SHORE COMPANY*
407 U.S. 1 (1972)

MR. CHIEF JUSTICE BURGER delivered the opinion of the Court.

We granted certiorari to review a judgment of the United States Court of Appeals for the Fifth Circuit declining to enforce a forum-selection clause governing disputes arising under an international towage contract between petitioners and respondent. The circuits have differed in their approach to such clauses. For the reasons stated hereafter, we vacate the judgment of the Court of Appeals.

In November 1967, respondent Zapata, a Houston-based American corporation, contracted with petitioner Unterweser, a German corporation, to tow Zapata's ocean-going, self-elevating drilling rig Chaparral from Louisiana to a point off Ravenna, Italy, in the Adriatic Sea, where Zapata had agreed to drill certain wells.

Zapata had solicited bids for the towage, and several companies including Unterweser had responded. Unterweser was the low bidder and Zapata requested it to submit a contract, which it did. The contract submitted by Unterweser contained the following provision, which is at issue in this case:

"Any dispute arising must be treated before the London Court of Justice."

In addition the contract contained two clauses purporting to exculpate Unterweser from liability for damages to the towed barge.

After reviewing the contract and making several changes, but without any alteration in the forum-selection or exculpatory clauses, a Zapata vice president executed the contract and forwarded it to Unterweser in Germany, where Unterweser accepted the changes, and the contract became effective.

On January 5, 1968, Unterweser's deep sea tug Bremen departed Venice, Louisiana, with the Chaparral in tow bound for Italy. On January 9, while the flotilla was in international waters in the middle of the Gulf of Mexico, a severe storm arose. The sharp roll of the Chaparral in Gulf waters caused its elevator legs, which had been raised for the voyage, to break off and fall into the sea, seriously damaging the Chaparral. In this emergency situation Zapata instructed the Bramen to tow its damaged rig to Tampa, Florida, the nearest port of refuge.

On January 12, Zapata, ignoring its contract promise to litigate "any dispute arising" in the English courts, commenced a suit in admiralty in the United States District Court at Tampa, seeking $3,500,000 damages against Unterweser in personam and the Bremen in rem, alleging negligent towage and breach of contract. Unterweser responded by invoking the forum clause of the towage contract, and moved to dismiss for lack of jurisdiction or on *forum non conveniens* grounds, or in the alternative to stay the action pending submission of the dispute to the "London

---

* Footnotes omitted.

Court of Justice." Shortly thereafter, in February, before the District Court had ruled on its motion to stay or dismiss the United States action, Unterweser commenced an action against Zapata seeking damages for breach of the towage contract in the High Court of Justice in London, as the contract provided. Zapata appeared in that court to contest jurisdiction, but its challenge was rejected, the English courts holding that the contractual forum provision conferred jurisdiction.

In the meantime, Unterweser was faced with a dilemma in the pending action in the United States court at Tampa. The six-month period for filing action to limit its liability to Zapata and other potential claimants was about to expire, but the United States District Court in Tampa had not yet ruled on Unterweser's motion to dismiss or stay Zapata's action. On July 2, 1968, confronted with difficult alternatives, Unterweser filed an action to limit its liability in the District Court in Tampa. That court entered the customary injunction against proceedings outside the limitation court, and Zapata refiled its initial claim in the limitation action.

It was only at this juncture, on July 29, after the six-month period for filing the limitation action had run, that the District Court denied Unterweser's January motion to dismiss or stay Zapata's initial action. In denying the motion, that court relied on the prior decision of the Court of Appeals in *Carbon Black Export, Inc. v. The Monrosa*, 254 F.2d 297 (CA5 1958), *cert. dismissed*, 359 U.S. 180 (1959). In that case the Court of Appeals had held a forum-selection clause unenforceable, reiterating the traditional view of many American courts that "agreements in advance of controversy whose object is to oust the jurisdiction of the courts are contrary to public policy and will not be enforced." 254 F.2d, at 300–301. Apparently concluding that it was bound by the *Carbon Black* case, the District Court gave the forum-selection clause little, if any, weight. Instead, the court treated the motion to dismiss under normal *forum non conveniens* doctrine applicable in the absence of such a clause, citing *Gulf Oil Corp. v. Gilbert*, 330 U.S. 501 (1947). Under that doctrine "unless the balance is strongly in favor of the defendant, the plaintiff's choice of forum should rarely be disturbed." *Id.*, at 508. The District Court concluded: "the balance of conveniences here is not strongly in favor of (Unterweser) and (Zapata's) choice of forum should not be disturbed."

Thereafter, on January 21, 1969, the District Court denied another motion by Unterweser to stay the limitation action pending determination of the controversy in the High Court of Justice in London and granted Zapata's motion to restrain Unterweser from litigating further in the London court. The District Judge ruled that, having taken jurisdiction in the limitation proceeding, he had jurisdiction to determine all matters relating to the controversy. He ruled that Unterweser should be required to "do equity" by refraining from also litigating the controversy in the London court, not only for the reasons he had previously stated for denying Unterweser's first motion to stay Zapata's action, but also because Unterweser had invoked the United States court's jurisdiction to obtain the benefit of the Limitation Act.

On appeal, a divided panel of the Court of Appeals affirmed, and on rehearing en banc the panel opinion was adopted, with six of the 14 *en banc* judges dissenting. As had the District Court, the majority rested on the *Carbon Black* decision, concluding that "at the very least" that case stood for the proposition that a forum-selection clause "will not be enforced unless the selected state would provide a more convenient forum than the state in which suit is brought." From that premise the Court of Appeals proceeded to conclude that, apart from the forum-selection clause, the District Court did not abuse its discretion in refusing to decline jurisdiction on the basis of *forum non conveniens*. It noted that (1) the flotilla never "escaped the Fifth Circuit's mare nostrum, and the casualty occurred in close proximity to the district court"; (2) a considerable number of potential witnesses, including Zapata crewmen, resided in the Gulf Coast area; (3) preparation for the voyage and inspection and repair work had been performed in the Gulf area; (4) the testimony of the Bremen crew was available by way of deposition; (5) England had no interest in or contact with the controversy other than the forum-selection clause. The Court of Appeals majority further noted that Zapata was a United States citizen and "(t)he discretion of the district court to remand the case to a foreign forum was consequently limited"— especially since it appeared likely that the English courts would enforce the exculpatory clauses. In the Court of Appeals' view, enforcement of such clauses would be contrary to public policy in American courts under *Bisso v. Inland Waterways Corp.*, 349 U.S. 85 (1955), and *Dixilyn Drilling Corp. v. Crescent Towing & Salvage Co.*, 372 U.S. 697 (1963). Therefore, "(t)he district court was entitled to consider that remanding Zapata to a foreign forum, with no practical contact with the controversy, could raise a bar to recovery by a United States citizen which its own convenient courts would not countenance."

We hold, with the six dissenting members of the Court of Appeals, that far too little weight and effect were given to the forum clause in resolving this controversy. For at least two decades we have witnessed an expansion of overseas commercial activities by business enterprises based in the United States. The barrier of distance that once tended to confine a business concern to a modest territory no longer does so. Here we see an American company with special expertise contracting with a foreign company to tow a complex machine thousands of miles across seas and oceans. The expansion of American business and industry will hardly be encouraged if, notwithstanding solemn contracts, we insist on a parochial concept that all disputes must be resolved under our laws and in our courts. Absent a contract forum, the considerations relied on by the Court of Appeals would be persuasive reasons for holding an American forum convenient in the traditional sense, but in an era of expanding world trade and commerce, the absolute aspects of the doctrine of the *Carbon Black* case have little place and would be a heavy hand indeed on the future development of international commercial dealings by Americans. We cannot have trade and commerce in world markets and international waters exclusively on our terms, governed by our laws, and resolved in our courts.

Forum-selection clauses have historically not been favored by American courts. Many courts, federal and state, have declined to enforce such clauses on the ground that they were "contrary to public policy," or that their effect was to "oust the jurisdiction" of the court. Although this view apparently still has considerable acceptance, other courts are tending to adopt a more hospitable attitude toward forum-selection clauses. This view, advanced in the well-reasoned dissenting opinion in the instant case, is that such clauses are prima facie valid and should be enforced unless enforcement is shown by the resisting party to be "unreasonable" under the circumstances. We believe this is the correct doctrine to be followed by federal district courts sitting in admiralty. . . .

This approach is substantially that followed in other common-law countries including England. It is the view advanced by noted scholars and that adopted by the Restatement of the Conflict of Laws. It accords with ancient concepts of freedom of contract and reflects an appreciation of the expanding horizons of American contractors who seek business in all parts of the world. Not surprisingly, foreign businessmen prefer, as do we, to have disputes resolved in their own courts, but if that choice is not available, then in a neutral forum with expertise in the subject matter. Plainly, the courts of England meet the standards of neutrality and long experience in admiralty litigation. The choice of that forum was made in an arm's-length negotiation by experienced and sophisticated businessmen, and absent some compelling and countervailing reason it should be honored by the parties and enforced by the courts.

The argument that such clauses are improper because they tend to "oust" a court of jurisdiction is hardly more than a vestigial legal fiction. . . .

There are compelling reasons why a freely negotiated private international agreement, unaffected by fraud, undue influence, or overweening bargaining power, such as that involved here, should be given full effect. In this case, for example, we are concerned with a far from routine transaction between companies of two different nations contemplating the tow of a extremely costly piece of equipment from Louisiana across the Gulf of Mexico and the Atlantic Ocean, through the Mediterranean Sea to its final destination in the Adriatic Sea. In the course of its voyage, it was to traverse the waters of many jurisdictions. The Chaparral could have been damaged at any point along the route, and there were countless possible ports of refuge. That the accident occurred in the Gulf of Mexico and the barge was towed to Tampa in an emergency were mere fortuities. It cannot be doubted for a moment that the parties sought to provide for a neutral forum for the resolution of any disputes arising during the tow. Manifestly much uncertainty and possibly great inconvenience to both parties could arise if a suit could be maintained in any jurisdiction in which an accident might occur or if jurisdiction were left to any place where the Bremen or Unterweser might happen to be found. The elimination of all such uncertainties by agreeing in advance on a forum acceptable to both parties is an indispensable element in international trade, commerce, and contracting. . . .

Thus, in the light of present-day commercial realities and expanding international trade we conclude that the forum clause should control absent a strong showing that it should be set aside. . . .

Courts have also suggested that a forum clause, even though it is freely bargained for and contravenes no important public policy of the forum, may nevertheless be "unreasonable" and unenforceable if the chosen forum is seriously inconvenient for the trial of the action. Of course, where it can be said with reasonable assurance that at the time they entered the contract, the parties to a freely negotiated private international commercial agreement contemplated the claimed inconvenience, it is difficult to see why any such claim of inconvenience should be heard to render the forum clause unenforceable. We are not here dealing with an agreement between two Americans to resolve their essentially local disputes in a remote alien forum. In such a case, the serious inconvenience of the contractual forum to one or both of the parties might carry greater weight in determining the reasonableness of the forum clause. The remoteness of the forum might suggest that the agreement was an adhesive one, or that the parties did not have the particular controversy in mind when they made their agreement; yet even there the party claiming should bear a heavy burden of proof. Similarly, selection of a remote forum to apply differing foreign law to an essentially American controversy might contravene an important public policy of the forum. . . .

This case . . . involves a freely negotiated international commercial transaction between a German and an American corporation for towage of a vessel from the Gulf of Mexico to the Adriatic Sea. As noted, selection of a London forum was clearly a reasonable effort to bring vital certainty to this international transaction and to provide a neutral forum experienced and capable in the resolution of admiralty litigation. Whatever "inconvenience" Zapata would suffer by being forced to litigate in the contractual forum as it agreed to do was clearly foreseeable at the time of contracting. In such circumstances it should be incumbent on the party seeking to escape his contract to show that trial in the contractual forum will be so gravely difficult and inconvenient that he will for all practical purposes be deprived of his day in court. Absent that, there is no basis for concluding that it would be unfair, unjust, or unreasonable to hold that party to his bargain.

. . . .

Vacated and remanded.

[Dissent by JUSTICE DOUGLAS omitted.]

NOTE

M/S Bremen v. Zapata Off-Shore Co. and the U.S. Supreme Court's subsequent decision in *Carnival Cruise Lines, Inc. v. Shute*, 499 U.S. 585 (1991), which upheld a choice of court clause in a standard form contract, were both decided under admiralty jurisdiction of the federal courts. State law applies in actions brought both in state courts as well as in diversity actions in federal courts. As indicated in the following Alabama case, state courts have generally tended to follow *M/S Bremen* but with constraints.

PROFESSIONAL INS. CORP. v. SUTHERLAND
700 So. 2d 347 (Ala. 1997)

SHORES, JUSTICE.

The opinion of March 28, 1997, is withdrawn, and the following opinion is substituted therefor.

This is an interlocutory appeal pursuant to Rule 5, Ala. R. App. P. The question presented is whether the Alabama courts should continue to refuse to enforce "outbound" forum selection clauses on the grounds that such clauses are against public policy and therefore void per se. The trial court, relying upon precedent, refused to enforce certain forum selection clauses stating that any action brought on the contract between these parties would be brought in Florida. We now adopt the rule that such a provision should be enforced unless to do so would be unfair or unreasonable under the circumstances, and we remand the cause for further proceedings not inconsistent with this opinion.

The plaintiffs are independent insurance agents; they include four Georgia residents, James A. Sutherland, Scott Burrell, Michael Gammons, and James E. Thompson, and two Alabama residents, Goff Agency, Inc., and Anne Goff. The defendants are Professional Insurance Corporation (PIC); PennCorp Financial Group, Inc. (PennCorp), a financial holding company, which has acquired a controlling interest in PIC; and Homer Smith, a resident of Montgomery, Alabama, who is a former agent of Goff. The plaintiffs sued in the Circuit Court of Montgomery County, claiming breach of contract, interference with business relations, and fraudulent misrepresentation; these claims were based on allegations that the defendants had attempted to secure insurance business and commissions away from the plaintiffs.

Each plaintiff had executed contracts with PIC to sell payroll deduction insurance plans to agencies and businesses in Alabama. All the plaintiffs and defendants are licensed to do business in Alabama, and during each respective contract period the plaintiffs did do business in Alabama for PIC. This dispute arises out of PIC's alleged scheme to terminate the plaintiffs' contracts rather than pay certain commissions owed on payroll deduction plans sold by the plaintiffs.

Each contract between PIC and the plaintiffs provided:

> "This Contract is made subject to the laws of the State of Florida, and all compensation payable hereunder shall be payable at Jacksonville, Florida. In consideration of the execution of the Contract and other valuable considerations, You agree that any litigation resulting from the violation of the terms and conditions of this Contract by You or the Company shall be brought in Duval County, Florida." (R. 70.)

PIC filed numerous motions to dismiss the plaintiffs' complaint on the ground that the plaintiffs had agreed that any litigation resulting from the violation of the contract would be conducted in Duval County, Florida. The trial court denied all of those motions filed by the defendants, holding that forum selection clauses are invalid and unenforceable in Alabama and that Montgomery County was the proper forum.

In *Redwing Carriers, Inc. v. Foster*, 382 So. 2d 554 (Ala. 1980), this Court adopted the "majority rule" stated in Annotation, "Validity of Contractual Provision Limiting Place or Court in Which Action May be Brought," 56 A.L.R.2d § 4, p. 306 (1957), to the effect that "contractual agreements by which it is sought to limit particular causes of action which may arise in the future to a specific place, are held invalid." *Redwing Carriers*, 382 So. 2d at 556.

This Court construed the "outbound" forum selection provision at issue in

Redwing Carriers as "divesting all courts of the power to hear and determine the cause except the courts of [the selected forum]." *Id.* We concluded: "Contract provisions which attempt to limit the jurisdiction of the courts of this state [are] invalid and unenforceable as being contrary to public policy. Parties may not confer jurisdiction by consent, nor may they limit the jurisdiction of a court by consent." *Id.* This Court has adhered to this "jurisdictional" view in a line of subsequent cases. [Citations omitted.] For years, American courts generally followed similar reasoning and refused to give effect to forum selection clauses:

. . . .

However, in the wake of the United States Supreme Court's decision in *M/S Bremen v. Zapata Off-Shore Co.*, 407 U.S. 1, (1972), holding that such forum selection clauses "are prima facie valid and should be enforced unless enforcement is shown by the resisting party to be 'unreasonable' under the circumstances," *id. at 10*, many jurisdictions were influenced to reconsider their positions on the issue. In fact, the view that forum selection clauses such as those at issue in this case are per se invalid and unenforceable is now only held in a small minority of jurisdictions. Besides Alabama, only Iowa, Idaho, and Montana appear to hold that "outbound" forum selection provisions are per se unenforceable, and the latter two states do so based upon interpretations of state statutes. [Citations omitted.]

. . . .

Of course, as an exercise of the Supreme Court's federal admiralty jurisdiction, see U.S. Const., Art. III, § 2, the decision in *M/S Bremen* does not mandate that state courts enforce forum selection provisions outside of an admiralty context. In declaring Alabama's law of contracts, this Court is free to independently assess the public policy of this state, subject only to the requirements of federal law. However, we, as have the courts of almost all other jurisdictions, do now find the Supreme Court's reasoning in *M/S Bremen* on this issue to be persuasive. Thus, we determine that "outbound" forum selection clauses such as those in this case are not void per se as against the public policy of Alabama.

Because we no longer consider "outbound" forum selection clauses to be void per se as against public policy, and because we conclude that § 6-3-1, Ala. Code 1975, does not operate as a statutory prohibition against their enforcement, we now adopt the majority rule that a forum selection clause should be enforced so long as enforcing it is neither unfair nor unreasonable under the circumstances. However, the plaintiffs argue in their application for rehearing that the newly adopted rule should not be applied to the parties in this case, but, rather, should be applied prospectively only. The plaintiffs contend that when they were negotiating their contracts they relied upon the rule making forum selection provisions invalid in Alabama and that the rule we adopt today represents a fundamental change in the substantive law of this state. Therefore, they claim, an application of the "new" rule against them would be an unfair retroactive application. We disagree.

. . . .

We conclude that it is fair to apply the rule enforcing forum selection clauses to the parties in this case. As noted previously, while American courts traditionally disfavored outbound forum selection clauses, the overwhelming trend, following the

United States Supreme Court's decision in *M/S Bremen, supra*, has been toward allowing enforcement of those clauses. See n.3, *supra*. That nationwide trend foreshadowed our adoption today of the rule that such clauses are not per se void, providing notice that Alabama might follow suit and thereby reducing the reliance these plaintiffs could reasonably have placed upon the continued viability of the traditional rule in Alabama.

. . . .

Accordingly, this case must be remanded for reconsideration. On remand, the plaintiffs will have the burden of showing either (1) that enforcement of the forum selection clauses would be unfair on the basis that the contracts in this case were affected by fraud, undue influence, or overweening bargaining power or (2) that enforcement would be unreasonable on the basis that the chosen Florida forum would be seriously inconvenient for the trial of the action. We observe, however, that nothing in the record presently before us would support a refusal to enforce the forum selection clauses. The plaintiffs have not alleged fraud or undue influence or that the contracts were contracts of adhesion. All parties to this action are business entities, or business persons, that deal in the arena of insurance, where contracts are negotiated on a daily basis. The corporate defendants' headquarters are in Florida, where a majority of the witnesses and most documents related to this case are located. In fact, the trial court concluded that it was "no more inconvenient" to have the matter tried in Alabama than to have it tried in Florida, implying that the chosen Florida forum would not be seriously inconvenient.

The trial court's order denying the defendants' motion to dismiss is vacated, and this cause is remanded for further proceedings consistent with this opinion.

QUESTIONS AND PROBLEM

1. Compare the 2005 Hague Convention on Choice of Court Agreements to the Supreme Court decision in the *M/S Bremen* case as well as the Alabama decision. Which provides the broadest scope of choice of court agreements? Are some prorogation agreements enforceable in admiralty as well as state actions — assuming Alabama law to be exemplary — but not under the Convention?

2. What is the difference between an "in-bound" and "out-bound" forum selection clause? How might the arguments in favor or against each differ?

3. Assume that an Alabama firm requires that all of its subsidiaries include a provision in their supply contracts that subjects all disputes between suppliers and the subsidiary to the jurisdiction of the Jefferson County Circuit Court. Would such contracts be valid under Alabama law? Assuming such clauses to be valid, were a dispute with no connection whatsoever with Alabama to arise between a supplier and a German subsidiary under a contract written in German, would dismissal by the Alabama court under the *forum non conveniens* doctrine be permissible and appropriate?

4. Assume that under California law choice of court clauses in standard form consumer contracts are deemed invalid and unenforceable. Assume in addition that a consumer residing in California as licensee of software made available over the internet by a wholly owned subsidiary of a Japanese firm that produces software for games had agreed to a standard form contract that includes the provision "the licensee agrees that all disputes arising under this license shall be adjudicated in King County, Washington." The consumer, alleging fraud, misrepresentation, and breach of contract, first filed in a California court but the action has been removed to the federal court in California by motion of the defendant .Would the federal court have the authority to dismiss the action for improper venue under Rule 12(b)(3) of the Federal Rules of Civil Procedure and 28 U.S.C. § 1406 or to transfer the action to the U.S. District Court for the Western District of Washington under 28 U.S.C. § 1404(a)? 28 U.S.C. § 1404(a) provides:

(a) For the convenience of parties and witnesses, in the interest of justice, a district court may transfer any civil action to any other district or division where it might have been brought or to any district or division to which all parties have consented.

If so, what standard should the court apply?

Compare Stewart Organization, Inc. v. Ricoh Corp., 487 U.S. 22 (1988) with *Doe 1 v. AOL LLC*, 552 F.3d 1077 (9th Cir. 2009) and *Atlantic Marine Construction Co. v. U.S. District Court*, 571 U.S. ___ (2013).

What difference would it make, if any, were the prorogation clause in a standard form licensing agreement with the Japanese parent company and the selected forum was a Japanese court? Would your answers differ were the Hague Convention on Choice of Court Agreements applicable?

Note: In a subsequent per curiam decision the Alabama Supreme Court ruled that on review of a lower court dismissal of an action in favor of a forum selection clause an "abuse of discretion" rather than a "de novo" review standard would be applied. *O'Brien Engineering Company, Inc. v. Continental Machines, Inc.*, 738 So. 2d 844 (Ala. 1999).

As indicated previously, the status of the Hague Convention on Choice of Court Agreements in the United States remains uncertain as of 2014. A tension between those who support ratification with preemptive federal legislation and those who advocate a "cooperative federalism" with both federal and uniform state statutes. As detailed below, Canada exemplifies the latter approach.

B. Canada

GRECON DIMTER INC. v. J.R. NORMAND INC.
[2005] 2 S.C.R. 401, 2005 SCC 46

LeBel J.

I. Introduction

1. This appeal raises the private international law issues that arise from the application, in an action in warranty brought by a Quebec importer against a German manufacturer, of a choice of forum clause in which the parties have opted for a foreign authority. In this context, diametrically opposite conclusions are reached depending on whether the jurisdictional connection is determined by applying art. 3139 or art. 3148, para. 2 of the *Civil Code of Quebec*, S.Q. 1991, c. 64 ("*C.C.Q.*"). The Quebec Court of Appeal unanimously held that, despite the existence of the choice of forum clause directing the parties to a German court, the action in warranty brought by the Quebec importer had to be heard by the Quebec court that was hearing the principal action. For reasons relating primarily to the role of the autonomy of the parties to a contract in private international law and to the hierarchy of the laws that are relevant in this case, I find that the Court of Appeal and the trial judge erred in law. Accordingly, the declinatory exception based on the existence of a choice of forum clause in favour of a foreign authority should be allowed.

II. Origin of the Case

2. The appellant, GreCon Dimter inc. ("GreCon"), describes itself in the pleadings as a German corporation that manufactures and sells specialized equipment used in processing plants and sawmills. It has no place of business or assets in Quebec. The respondent, J.R. Normand inc. ("Normand"), whose head office is in Quebec, specializes in the sale and service of industrial woodworking machinery, tools and supplies. Scierie Thomas-Louis Tremblay inc. ("Tremblay"), the other respondent, operates a sawmill north of Lac Saint-Jean, in Quebec, and its head office is located in that province.

3. This case arises out of two contracts. The first is one entered into on May 14, 1999, by Normand and Tremblay for the supply and delivery of equipment, including in particular a saw line and a scanner to optimize the milling of wood ("Equipment"). The purchase of the Equipment was part and parcel of a modernization plan being undertaken to improve and expand production at Tremblay's sawmill.

4. The second contract is a contract of sale entered into on May 26, 1999, by GreCon and Normand under which the Equipment was to be supplied to Normand for resale to Tremblay. This contract was formed by Normand's acceptance of a price quote submitted by GreCon on April 12, 1999, after Normand had approached the German company to purchase the Equipment. The quote included a choice of

forum and choice of law clause, which provided that any dispute between the parties would be subject to the exclusive jurisdiction of the German courts and would be decided in accordance with German law:

Choice of Forum

It is agreed, by and between the seller and buyer, that all disputes and matters whatsoever arising under, in connection with, or instant to this contract (whether arising under contract, tort, other legal theories, or specific statutes) shall be litigated, if at all, in and before a court located in Alfeld (Leine), Germany to the exclusion of the courts of any other state or country.

Choice of Law

This agreement is governed by and construed under the laws of Germany to the exclusion of all other laws of any other state or country (without regard to the principles of conflicts of law).

5. As a result of problems encountered by GreCon in designing it, the scanner was not delivered to or installed at Tremblay's plant by the date provided for in the contract between Normand and Tremblay, namely August 20, 1999. As a result, Tremblay had to set up a temporary system for cutting wood, and it proved to be inadequate. GreCon was unable to deliver the scanner until April 2001. Because of the numerous delays and the problems it had encountered, Tremblay decided to give Normand notice on April 19, 2001, that it intended to resiliate the contract. Consequently, the Equipment was never delivered to Tremblay.

6. As a result of these events, Tremblay instituted an action in damages against Normand in the Superior Court of Quebec on July 3, 2002; the action was based on a professional seller's liability for latent defects and on multiple alleged faults in the performance of contractual obligations. In that principal action, Tremblay claimed to have suffered damage in the order of $5,160,331 because the equipment actually supplied by Normand was defective and because the Equipment was never delivered, with the result that Tremblay suffered a decline in output and productivity. Tremblay also sought a refund of deposits that had been paid to Normand.

7. On October 2, 2002, Normand filed an incidental action in warranty against GreCon in the Superior Court of Quebec. In support of its action, Normand alleged the inadequate performance of GreCon's contractual obligations, namely a failure to deliver some of the Equipment and delays in delivery. The respondent sought to be indemnified in full by GreCon for any award that might be made against it in the principal action brought by Tremblay. It should be noted that under the *Civil Code*, a manufacturer is bound by the seller's warranty of quality and becomes a co-debtor of the warranty with the seller, which means that the seller may call the manufacturer in warranty: art. 1730 *C.C.Q.*

8. On December 18, 2002, GreCon raised a declinatory exception that challenged the jurisdiction of the Quebec courts. By a motion for declinatory exception based on art. 83 and art. 3148, para. 2 *C.C.Q.*, GreCon sought to have Normand's action in warranty dismissed on the ground that the choice of forum clause in the contract between the two companies barred the Superior Court of Quebec from exercising

its jurisdiction in disputes between the two parties. Under that clause, only a court located in the city of Alfeld, Germany, would have jurisdiction. Normand responded that the principal action was already before the Superior Court and that art. 3139 *C.C.Q.* therefore gave that court jurisdiction over the action in warranty notwithstanding the existence of a choice of forum clause. Normand added that the Quebec courts were a more appropriate forum because of the connexity between the principal action and the action in warranty, and the fact that a majority of the witnesses in both actions were from Quebec.

III. Judicial History [Omitted.]

IV. Analysis

A. *Nature of the Issue and Legislative Framework*

13. This case has arisen from a situation in which the defendant in a principal action instituted in Quebec brought an action in warranty after having agreed, in a choice of forum clause, to submit any dispute arising out of its legal relationship with the defendant in warranty to the jurisdiction of a foreign authority. In this situation, three main provisions of the *Civil Code* are relevant to the determination of whether the Quebec authority has jurisdiction.

14. First, art. 3148, para. 2 *C.C.Q.* ousts a Quebec authority's jurisdiction in respect of a personal action of a patrimonial nature if the parties have chosen by agreement to submit their disputes to a foreign authority or an arbitrator:

> **3148.** In personal actions of a patrimonial nature, a Quebec authority has jurisdiction [enumerated sigrounds omitted.]
>
> . . . .
>
> However, a Quebec authority has no jurisdiction where the parties, by agreement, have chosen to submit all existing or future disputes between themselves relating to a specified legal relationship to a foreign authority or to an arbitrator, unless the defendant submits to the jurisdiction of the Quebec authority

15. Second, art. 3139 *C.C.Q.* confers jurisdiction on the Quebec authority to hear an action in warranty if it has jurisdiction over the principal action:

> **3139.** Where a Quebec authority has jurisdiction to rule on the principal demand, it also has jurisdiction to rule on an incidental demand or a cross demand.

16. And third, the Quebec authority may, on an application by a party, decline jurisdiction by virtue of the doctrine of *forum non conveniens*, which is codified in art. 3135 *C.C.Q.*:

> **3135.** Even though a Quebec authority has jurisdiction to hear a dispute, it may exceptionally and on an application by a party, decline jurisdiction if it

considers that the authorities of another country are in a better position to decide.

17. The interaction of the relevant provisions leads to a conflict in determining the jurisdictional connection. While art. 3139 *C.C.Q.* extends the Quebec authority's jurisdiction to include an incidental action, art. 3148, para. 2 *C.C.Q.* denies that authority any jurisdiction. As will be seen, the application of the latter provision also precludes the application of art. 3135 *C.C.Q.*

18. This appeal therefore raises the issue of the nature of the relationships between arts. 3148, 3139 and 3135 *C.C.Q.* in the context of the determination of whether a Quebec authority has jurisdiction to hear an action in warranty. As will have been noted, the effect of the interaction of these provisions is a fundamental conflict between the legislative rules and the parties' freedom of contract, whence the need to determine the importance of the role of the autonomy of the parties to a contract in private international law. That determination will make it possible to properly delineate the scope of the provisions in question and to gauge their impact on the jurisdictional connection. Moreover, the fact that the doctrine of *forum non conveniens* is part of the discussion requires that we consider the relative importance of art. 3135 *C.C.Q.* in the process of determining the jurisdiction of the Quebec authority. This leads inevitably to the question of the hierarchy of the relevant rules. Accordingly, in my view, the outcome of this case depends on the role of the autonomy of the parties and on the hierarchy of the relevant rules.

. . . .

(i) Primacy of the Autonomy of the Parties

20. Article 3148 establishes the general framework that delineates the jurisdiction of a Quebec authority in relation to contracts in proceedings based on personal actions of a patrimonial nature, subject to the specific rules that apply to cases in which the action is based on a contract of employment or a consumer contract (art. 3149 *C.C.Q.*), a contract of insurance (art. 3150 *C.C.Q.*), or civil liability for damage suffered as a result of exposure to or the use of raw materials originating in Quebec (art. 3151 *C.C.Q.*). Article 3148 also recognizes the primacy of the autonomy of the parties: although the legislature did confer jurisdiction on the Quebec authority on the basis of the criteria of jurisdictional connection, such as domicile, fault, the damage or the injurious act, it was careful to give the parties the ability to choose to oust the authority's jurisdiction when they wish to entrust current or future disputes between them that arise out of a specific legal relationship to a foreign authority or an arbitrator.

21. Article 3148 *C.C.Q.* thus attaches considerable importance to the principle of the autonomy of the parties. The fact that the parties may, by agreement, oust the Quebec authority's jurisdiction attests to the legislature's intention to recognize the autonomy of the parties in cases involving conflicts of jurisdiction: along these lines, see Talpis and Castel, at p. 58. The legislature confirmed that intention several times in relation to conflicts of law, for example in arts. 3098, 3107, 3111 and 3121 *C.C.Q.* The legislature's intention, in enacting art. 3148 *C.C.Q.*, to disregard the line of cases in which choice of forum clauses had been held to be invalid also attests to

the importance attached to this principle [citations omitted].

22. It should also be noted that respecting the autonomy of the parties makes it possible to implement the broader principle of achieving legal certainty in international transactions. The parties generally give effect to their intention to exclude a dispute from an authority's jurisdiction by means of an arbitration clause or a choice of forum clause. These clauses foster certainty and foreseeability in international commercial relations, because they enable the parties to provide in advance for the forum to which they will submit their dispute. [Citation omitted.] This Court has often stressed the importance of such clauses and the need to encourage them, because they provide international commercial relations with the stability and foreseeability required for purposes of the critical components of private international law, namely order and fairness[citations omitted]. This shows how deferring to the contracting parties' intention ensures the implementation of this policy of legal certainty that is an inherent feature of private international law [citation omitted]. To recognize the usefulness and effectiveness of choice of forum clauses and arbitration clauses is therefore consistent with the general principles of private international law.

23. The recognition of the autonomy of the parties reflected in the enactment of art. 3148, para. 2 *C.C.Q.* is also related to the trend toward international harmonization of the rules of conflict of laws and of jurisdiction. That harmonization is being achieved by means, *inter alia*, of international agreements sponsored by international organizations such as the Hague Conference on Private International Law and the United Nations Commission on International Trade Law ("UNCITRAL"). It should be noted in this respect that art. 3148, para. 2 *C.C.Q.* is based on arts. 5 and 6 of the *Convention on the Choice of Court* (concluded on November 25, 1965), the purpose of which is to recognize and give full effect to choice of forum clauses: *Commentaires du ministre de la Justice* (1993), t. II, at p. 2009. The general principle of that convention is in fact that exclusive choice of forum clauses are binding. The Convention limits exceptions to this principle, as may be seen in art. 6 thereof. It is therefore apparent that the Convention, on which the *Civil Code*'s provision is modelled although the Convention itself is not in force, is the expression of a modern trend toward ensuring that in international business matters, an agreement by the parties as to the choice of forum will be admissible and will be recognized [citationsomitted]. The interpretation of art. 3148, para. 2 *C.C.Q.* should take this into account.

24. Thus the wording and legislative context of art. 3148, para. 2 *C.C.Q.* confirm that in enacting the provision, the legislature intended to recognize the primacy of the autonomy of the parties in situations involving conflicts of jurisdiction. Moreover, this legislative choice, by providing for the use of arbitration clauses and choice of forum clauses, fosters foreseeability and certainty in international legal transactions.

(ii) Limits on the Autonomy of the Parties

25. Nonetheless, it must be noted that certain limits are imposed on the expression of the autonomy of the parties. First, art. 3151 *C.C.Q.*, enacted by the legislature as a mandatory provision, confers exclusive jurisdiction on a Quebec

authority over actions founded on civil liability for damage suffered as a result of exposure to or the use of raw materials originating in Quebec. In such cases, a choice of forum clause cannot oust the jurisdiction of the Quebec authority. Second, art. 3149 *C.C.Q.* confers jurisdiction on a Quebec authority in cases involving consumer contracts or contracts of employment, and the waiver of such jurisdiction by the consumer or worker may not be set up against him or her. In both cases, the language used by the legislature indicates a clear intention to disregard the autonomy of the parties, or to limit it, and this suggests that when the legislature's intention is to limit the ability to oust the jurisdiction of the Quebec authority by agreement, it says so expressly.

26. In some situations, as indicated in the final portion of art. 3148 *C.C.Q.*, a defendant may by its actions submit to the jurisdiction of the Quebec authority despite the intention expressed in the contract. The matter can then be brought before the Quebec authority. [Citations omitted.]

27. One last type of exception to the autonomy of the parties relates to the wording of arbitration or choice of forum clauses. Whether the jurisdiction of the Quebec authorities is ousted in a specific case will be decided on the basis of the wording of the jurisdiction clause adopted by the parties [citation omitted]. The clause must be mandatory and must clearly and precisely confer exclusive jurisdiction on the foreign authority [citations omitted]. There must also be a meeting of minds between the parties; otherwise the clause is invalid [citation omitted].

28. Thus, apart from under art. 3135 *C.C.Q.*, the situations in which the parties' expression of their intention will be limited arise out of the wording of the jurisdiction clauses, the matters specifically excluded by the legislature from the scope of art. 3148, para. 2 *C.C.Q.*, or the conduct of the defendant him or herself. Aside from those exceptions, there is nothing to suggest that the legislature intended to place any further limits on the parties' ability to oust the Quebec authority's jurisdiction by agreement in respect of conflicts of jurisdiction. This analysis supports the position that gives precedence to the principle of the autonomy of the parties.

(iii) The Rule in Art. 3139 *C.C.Q.* and Incidental Demands or Cross Demands

29. Where a Quebec authority has jurisdiction to rule on a principal demand, art. 3139 *C.C.Q.* essentially extends its jurisdiction to an incidental demand or a cross demand.

. . . .

[B.] (ii) Conformity with the Development of International Law

39. The interpretation of the provisions in issue, and the resolution of the conflict between them, must necessarily be harmonized with the international commitments of Canada and Quebec. . . .

40. Quebec is a party to the *Convention on the Recognition and Enforcement of Foreign Arbitral Awards*, 330 U.N.T.S. 3 ("*New York Convention*"), of June 10, 1958,

as a result of Canada's belated accession to the Convention, which came into force here on August 10, 1986: *Canada Gazette*, Part II, vol. 120, No. 17, SI/86-154 and 155.

41. Although at first glance the Convention seems to deal solely with the recognition and enforcement of arbitral awards, it also provides legal protection for arbitration agreements. The legislature has incorporated the principles of the *New York Convention* relating to arbitration agreements into Quebec law by enacting the substance of the Convention: see *Act to amend the Civil Code and the Code of Civil Procedure in respect of arbitration*, S.Q. 1986, c. 73; A. Prujiner, "Les nouvelles règles de l'arbitrage au Quebec," *Rev. Arb.* 1987.425. It should also be noted that the provisions of the *UNCITRAL Model Law on International Commercial Arbitration* of June 21, 1985 ("*UNCITRAL Model Law*"), U.N. Doc. A/40/17 (1985), Ann. I, set out in the chapter of that law dealing with arbitration agreements, on which the 1986 reform and modernization of Quebec's legal rules governing international arbitration agreements was based, closely follow the provisions of the *New York Convention*: see *Explanatory Note by the UNCITRAL Secretariat on the Model Law on International Commercial Arbitration*, U.N. Doc. A/40/17 (1985), Ann. I. The *New York Convention* is therefore a formal source for interpreting the domestic law provisions governing the enforcement of arbitration agreements.

42. Article II(3) of the *New York Convention* provides that "[t]he court of a Contracting State, when seized of an action in a matter in respect of which the parties have made an agreement within the meaning of this article, shall, at the request of one of the parties, refer the parties to arbitration, unless it finds that the said agreement is null and void, inoperative or incapable of being performed." The *New York Convention* thus states a general principle: the recognition of arbitration agreements. Article II(3) has now been incorporated into the domestic law of Quebec by art. 940.1 *C.C.P.*, which gives an arbitration clause precedence over the jurisdiction of a Quebec authority. It should be noted that art. 940.1 *C.C.P.* is also based on art. 8(1) of the *UNCITRAL Model Law*, which states essentially the same principle as art. II(3) of the *New York Convention*.

43. Both the purpose of the *New York Convention* and the case law dealing with art. II(3) confirm the position that the enforcement of an arbitration agreement cannot be precluded by procedural rules relating to actions in warranty. First, the purpose of the *New York Convention* is to facilitate the enforcement of arbitration agreements by ensuring that effect is given to the parties' express intention to seek arbitration [citations omitted]. The interpreter must therefore encourage arbitration clauses, and facilitate their enforcement. . . .

45. As a result of the requirement that art. 3148, para. 2 *C.C.Q.* be interpreted in a manner consistent with Quebec's international commitments, arbitration clauses are binding despite the existence of procedural provisions such as art. 3139 *C.C.Q.* Although this explanation applies to arbitration clauses, it should be kept in mind that art. 3148, para. 2 *C.C.Q.* also refers to choice of forum clauses. For the sake of consistency, the same position should be adopted in respect of both types of clauses. Indeed, it would be difficult to justify different interpretations for clauses that have the same function, namely to oust an authority's jurisdiction, and that share the

same purpose, namely to ensure that the intention of the parties is respected in order to achieve legal certainty. Thus, it would seem incongruous, in the context of an action in warranty, to give art. 3139 *C.C.Q.* precedence over art. 3148, para. 2 *C.C.Q.* with regard to a choice of forum clause and to take the opposite approach with regard to an arbitration clause — in other words, to respect the intention of the parties in one case but to thwart it in the other.

46. In light of the preceding discussion, it appears that art. 3148, para. 2 *C.C.Q.* must take precedence over art. 3139 *C.C.Q.* in the context of an action in warranty where a choice of forum clause indicating a clear intention to oust the jurisdiction of the Quebec authority applies to the legal relationship between the parties to the proceeding. In such circumstances, the Quebec authority must decline jurisdiction, subject to the exceptions noted earlier.

V. Conclusions

61. For these reasons, the appeal is allowed, the judgments of the Court of Appeal and the Superior Court are set aside, the declinatory exception based on the Quebec authority's want of jurisdiction is allowed, and the respondent Normand's action in warranty in the Superior Court of Quebec is dismissed, with costs throughout.

Appeal allowed with costs.

QUESTIONS AND NOTE

1. What law is the Supreme Court of Canada applying in *GreCon Dimter Inc. v. J.R. Normand Inc.*? Might, in your view, the outcome have differed had the case been decided on appeal from the courts of Ontario or another English-speaking province?

2. To what extent, if any, does Canadian law differ from U.S federal or state law with respect to the enforcement of forum selection clauses? Does there appear to be a distinction under the law of Quebec between "in-bound" and "out-bound" prorogation clauses?

3. What was the relevance of the New York Convention on Recognition and Enforcement of Foreign Arbitral Awards? To what extent does the 2005 Hague Convention of Choice of Court Agreements appear to supplement municipal Canadian law?

The process for ratification and implementation of the Hague Convention on Choice of Court Agreements was nearly complete as of 2014 with the adoption in 2010 by the Uniform Law Conference of Canada of a recommended Hague Convention on Choice of Court Agreements Act for each province and territory. (*See* http://www.ulcc.ca/en/uniform-acts-new-order/current-uniform-acts/645-hague-convention-choice-of-court).

C. Japan

TOKYO MARINE AND FIRE INSURANCE COMPANY v. ROYAL INTEROCEAN LINES

Supreme Court, 3rd P.B., Judgment of 28 November 197529 Minshū (No. 10) 1554 (1975)
[Adapted from English translation in 20 JAIL 106 (1976)]

DISPOSITION
(*shūbun*)

1. The appeal is dismissed.
2. The costs of appeal shall be borne by the Appellant.

. . . .

REASONS
(*riyū*)

With respect to the first point raised in the Grounds of Appeal by . . . the attorneys for Appellant:

The Appellant brought this lawsuit at the Kobe District Court, which has jurisdiction over the place where the business office of the Appellee is located, claiming the payment of compensatory and delay damages by the Appellee . . . on the basis of the following facts:

1. Kabushiki Kaisha Nanyō Bussan (hereinafter referred to as "Nanyō Bussan"), a Japanese importer, bought crude sugar (hereinafter referred to as "Crude Sugar") from the Institute de Acucar e de Alcool (hereinafter referred to as "Institute"), a Brazilian exporter. The Institute concluded as shipper a maritime transportation contract with the Appellee, a corporation engaged in maritime transportation business with its head office in Amsterdam, Holland, and business offices in Japan. The Appellee issued a bill of lading to the Institute and the Institute delivered this bill of lading to the consignee Nanyō Bussan.

2. The Appellee shipped the Crude Sugar on board the Chisadane, a ship owned by the Appellee, and transported it by sea from Santos, Brazil to the port of Osaka. At the time of the departure of the Chisadane, however, the Appellee failed in its duty of care to ensure the navigability and cargo worthiness of the Crude Sugar. As a result, many of the bags were damaged by sea water, causing a loss of at least ¥1,600,000 in damage to the Crude Sugar. The Appellee, therefore, is obligated to Nanyō Bussan for payment of compensatory damages to Nanyō Bussan based on the breach of the marine transportation agreement and in tort [delict — *fuhōkōi*]. The Appellant paid Nanyō Bussan ¥1,376,180 in insurance money in accordance with the maritime cargo insurance contract covering the Crude Sugar entered into by the Appellant and Nanyō Bussan. Therefore, the Appellant was subrogated to Nanyō Bussan's aforesaid claim for damages against the Appellee.

In response, the Appellee [successfully] argued that the Kobe District Court had no jurisdiction in this case inasmuch as the bill of lading in this case included a jurisdiction clause (hereinafter referred to as the "Jurisdiction Provision") in English that provided: "Any and all suits under this transportation contract shall be brought before the court of Amsterdam and no other court shall have jurisdiction over any other suit unless the carrier brings such suit before a court of such other jurisdiction or voluntarily accepts the jurisdiction of such court." Because this Jurisdiction Provision is an agreement for exclusive international jurisdiction, the court of Amsterdam has exclusive jurisdiction over this suit.

The court below [the Osaka High Court] confirmed the facts alleged by the Appellant in the paragraph 1 above and the facts alleged by the Appellee with regard to the Jurisdiction Provision. Dismissing the appeal, the court stated as follows:

> 1. The validity of an agreement on international jurisdiction is to be determined in accordance with our country's international civil procedure law as the place of the court. Without any evidence that the Institute declared its intention not to be subject to the Jurisdiction Provision at the time of the issuance of said bill of lading, or that it raised any objection to said Jurisdiction Provision thereafter, the Jurisdiction Provision is clearly an agreement made between the Appellee and the Institute that designates the court of Amsterdam as the court of first instance with exclusive jurisdiction over any and all suits for damages caused in the course of transportation under the said transportation agreement, whether the cause of action is based upon breach of contract or tort, and precludes the jurisdiction of our courts.
>
> 2. The agreement to said effect can be deemed to be valid in principle insofar as it applies to a case over which the our courts do not have exclusive jurisdiction and it is dear that the courts of said foreign country have jurisdiction thereover under the laws of said foreign country. In the instant case, our courts do not have exclusive jurisdiction, and it is clear that the court of Amsterdam would have proper jurisdiction in a like cases against the Appellee. Therefore, the exclusive international jurisdiction agreement at issue here is valid. Although the signature of the Institute as shipper does not appear on said bill of lading in which the Jurisdiction Provision appears, this fact does not affect its validity.
>
> 3. In the light of the spirit of the so-called Bills of Lading Unification Treaty and the International Maritime Cargo Transportation Law, our domestic law based upon said treaty, hereinafter referred to as the "International Maritime Transportation Law", an agreement of international jurisdiction on a bill of lading shall be invalid in cases: (i) when the purpose of such agreement is to evade public policy, which ought to be applicable in order to restrain the carrier from abusing the indemnification clause, or (ii) when such agreement benefits the carrier beyond reasonable limits, because of the carrier's unreasonable use of its strong economic position as a business enterprise, and so forth. However, under the circumstances of this case the Jurisdiction Provision is not deemed to be contrary to public policy.

4. Insofar as the parties can freely by agreement determine the legal issues subject to this Jurisdiction Provision, the effect of an agreement on international jurisdiction represented by the Jurisdiction Provision extends to the Appellant a specific successor of the Institute.

I. The Appellant also argues that the agreement on international jurisdiction must be in writing as in the case of the agreement of jurisdiction provided for by article 25, paragraph 2 [current article 11(2)] of the Code of Civil Procedure. Since there are no statutory provisions concerning the formalities for an agreement on jurisdiction under the international civil procedure law of Japan, such question shall be determined in accordance with the principles of *jōri* as well as by reference to the provisions of the Code of Civil Procedure. Because the purpose of said paragraph is to preserve the intentions of the parties, and because under the law of many countries agreements on jurisdiction are not necessarily required to be in writing, not is the signature of the shipper on a bill of lading required, and also in view of the security of international transactions, which should be expedited, the formalities for agreements on international jurisdiction shall be deemed to be satisfied if at least a court of a specific country is expressly designated on the document prepared by either of the parties and if the existence of such agreement between the parties and the contents thereof are explicit. It is not reasonable that both the offer and acceptance for such agreement shall be made by the document signed by the parties. Thus the Appellant's argument cannot be adopted.

II. The Appellant alleges that it is not clear that the Jurisdiction Provision represents an agreement of exclusive jurisdiction. We believe that the court of Amsterdam where the head office of the Appellee is located and the courts of Japan with jurisdiction in districts where the branches of the Appellee are located have respectively statutory jurisdiction over the present case. It is clear that the purpose of the Jurisdiction Provision is to allow only the former and to preclude the jurisdiction of any other courts. In conclusion, we deem such agreement of jurisdiction to be an agreement of exclusive jurisdiction, and we accept the determination of the court below to the same effect to be correct and reasonable.

As to the second point [Ground for Appeal]:

I. An agreement of exclusive international jurisdiction that designates only the court of a certain foreign country as the court of first instance having jurisdiction over a certain case and which precludes jurisdiction of the Japanese courts is deemed to be valid in principle under our country's international civil procedure law insofar as (a) the case is not subject to the exclusive jurisdiction of Japan, and (b) the designated foreign court has the jurisdiction over such case under the laws of such foreign country [citation omitted].

The Appellant claims that the court of said foreign court must have deemed similar agreements on jurisdiction to be valid. However, condition (b) above is required because if the court of said foreign country does not have Jurisdiction over said case and does not accept such cases, the aim of the agreement on jurisdiction intended by the parties cannot be attained and, furthermore, the parties could lose the opportunity to have the case adjudicated in any court. Therefore, the condition (b) is deemed to be satisfied if the court of the foreign country has jurisdiction over the case under the laws of such foreign country. We do not consider it necessary that the agreement of exclusive international jurisdiction is deemed to be valid under the laws of such foreign country. In the present case, the court below has acknowledged that the court of Amsterdam has statutory jurisdiction over this case. Therefore, we find no error of law in its decision even if it has neither discussed nor determined the point made by the Appellant.

II. The Appellant claims that the mutual guarantee [reciprocity] provided for in article 200, item 4 [current article 118, item 4] of the Code of Civil Procedure is required in order for the agreement of exclusive international jurisdiction to be deemed to be valid. However, the foreign judgment thus rendered may, generally, be enforced in such foreign country. Even if such foreign judgment is not enforceable in Japan because of the lack of the mutual guarantee [reciprocity], enforcement of the judgment will not be entirely prevented. This is different from the case where the condition of I.(b) above is not satisfied. Although the agreement on jurisdiction is made mainly as to trial proceedings, the parties can consider the practical value of the enforcement of such judgment in the foreign country in question at the time of agreement. Also, although such enforcement of the judgment may cause an increase of expenses, such a result is incidental to the agreement on jurisdiction.

Therefore, the mutual guarantee [reciprocity], which is a condition of recognition of the foreign judgment, is not required in order for an agreement on jurisdiction that precludes the jurisdiction of our courts to be deemed to be valid. We believe that under this theory the purposes intended by the parties to such agreements will be sufficiently attained. The Appellant's assertion cannot be adopted.

[The third and fourth grounds for appeal and reasons for their rejection omitted.]

Accordingly, this Court unanimously decides as stated in the Disposition set forth above, in accordance with Articles 401, 95 and 89 of the Code of Civil Procedure.

JUSTICE MASAMI TAKATSUJI
JUSTICE KOSATO SEKINE
JUSTICE BUICHI AMANO
JUSTICE YOSHIKATSU SAKAMOTO
JUSTICE KIYOO ERIGUCHI

> **QUESTIONS**
>
> Does Japanese law differ significantly from U.S. (federal and state) law or Canadian law or the 2005 Hague Convention with respect to the validity and enforcement of choice of court agreements? What, if any, are the formality requirements of each? Note that this is among the earliest Supreme Court cases to recognize *jōri* as a basis for applying the rules set out in the Code of Civil Procedure.

D. European Union

As noted at the beginning of this chapter, the European Union signed the Hague Convention of Choice of Court Agreements by Council Decision in 2009. As a consequence, upon the ratification by one more member state, presumably the Convention will come into effect throughout the European Union (with the exception of Denmark). Moreover, also as noted, as of January 2015 Regulation (EU) No. 1215/2012 replaced EC Council Regulation 44/2001. The combination of the Convention and the 2012 Regulations significantly benefits choice of court agreements within Europe. Consider the following comparison between the relevant provisions of the 1968 Brussels Convention as restated in EC Regulation 44/2001 and applied in the excerpted ECJ decision in *Erich Gasser GmbH v. MISAT Srl* with those of the new 2012 Regulation as explained in the official preamble.

EC COUNCIL REGULATION NO. 44/2001 — JURISDICTION AND ENFORCEMENT OF JUDGMENTS

Section 7
Prorogation of jurisdiction

Article 23

1. If the parties, one or more of whom is domiciled in a Member State, have agreed that a court or the courts of a Member State are to have jurisdiction to settle any disputes which have arisen or which may arise in connection with a particular legal relationship, that court or those courts shall have jurisdiction. Such jurisdiction shall be exclusive unless the parties have agreed otherwise. Such an agreement conferring jurisdiction shall be either:

(a) in writing or evidenced in writing; or

(b) in a form which accords with practices which the parties have established between themselves; or

(c) in international trade or commerce, in a form which accords with a usage of which the parties are or ought to have been aware and which in such trade or commerce is widely known to, and regularly observed by, parties to contracts of the type involved in the particular trade or commerce concerned.

2. Any communication by electronic means which provides a durable record of the agreement shall be equivalent to "writing".

3. Where such an agreement is concluded by parties, none of whom is domiciled in a Member State, the courts of other Member States shall have no jurisdiction over their disputes unless the court or courts chosen have declined jurisdiction.

4. The court or courts of a Member State on which a trust instrument has conferred jurisdiction shall have exclusive jurisdiction in any proceedings brought against a settlor, trustee or beneficiary, if relations between these persons or their rights or obligations under the trust are involved.

5. Agreements or provisions of a trust instrument conferring jurisdiction shall have no legal force if they are contrary to Articles 13, 17 or 21, or if the courts whose jurisdiction they purport to exclude have exclusive jurisdiction by virtue of Article 22.

Article 24

Apart from jurisdiction derived from other provisions of this Regulation, a court of a Member State before which a defendant enters an appearance shall have jurisdiction. This rule shall not apply where appearance was entered to contest the jurisdiction, or where another court has exclusive jurisdiction by virtue of Article 22.

NOTE AND QUESTION

As noted at the beginning of this chapter, the European Union signed the Hague Convention of Choice of Court Agreements by Council Decision in 2009. As a consequence, upon the ratification by one more member state, presumably the Convention will come into effect throughout the European Union (with the exception of Denmark). **Query:** Given the application of the quoted provisions of Regulation 44/2001 and their revision under Regulation (EU) No 1215/2012, what difference, if any, will the Convention make?

ERICH GASSER GMBH v. MISAT SRL
Case C-116/12, Judgment of 9 December 2003

By judgment of 25 March 2002, received at the Court on 2 April 2002, the Oberlandesgericht (Higher Regional Court) Innsbruck referred to the Court for a preliminary ruling . . . [on] a number of questions on the interpretation of Article 21 of . . . the [1968] Brussels Convention . . . .

2. Those questions were raised in proceedings between Erich Gasser GmbH

('Gasser'), a company incorporated under Austrian law, and MISAT Srl ('MISAT'), a company incorporated under Italian law, following a breakdown in their business relations.

LEGAL BACKGROUND

. . . .

6. Articles 17 and 18 of the Convention deal with the attribution of jurisdiction.

Article 17 is worded as follows:

'If the parties, one or more of whom is domiciled in a Contracting State, have agreed that a court or the courts of a Contracting State are to have jurisdiction to settle any disputes which have arisen or which may arise in connection with a particular legal relationship, that court or those courts shall have exclusive jurisdiction. Such an agreement conferring jurisdiction shall be either:

(a) in writing or evidenced in writing; or

(b) in a form which accords with practices which the parties have established between themselves; or

(c) in international trade or commerce, in a form which accords with a usage of which the parties are or ought to have been aware and which in such trade or commerce is widely known to, and regularly observed by, parties to contracts of the type involved in the particular trade or commerce concerned.

. . . .

Agreements . . . conferring jurisdiction shall have no legal force if they are contrary to the provisions of Article 12 or 15 [insurance and consumer contracts], or if the courts whose jurisdiction they purport to exclude have exclusive jurisdiction by virtue of Article 16.

. . . .

7. Article 18 provides:

'Apart from jurisdiction derived from other provisions of this Convention, a court of a Contracting State before whom a defendant enters an appearance shall have jurisdiction. This rule shall not apply where appearance was entered solely to contest the jurisdiction, or where another court has exclusive jurisdiction by virtue of Article 16.'

8. The Brussels Convention also seeks to obviate conflicting decisions. Thus, under Article 21, concerning *lis pendens*:

'Where proceedings involving the same cause of action and between the same parties are brought in the courts of different Contracting States, any court other than the court first seised shall of its own motion stay its proceedings until such time as the jurisdiction of the court first seised is established.

Where the jurisdiction of the court first seised is established, any court other than the court first seised shall decline jurisdiction in favour of that court.'

. . . .

THE MAIN PROCEEDINGS AND THE QUESTIONS REFERRED TO THE COURT

11. The registered office of Gasser is in Dornbirn, Austria. For several years it sold children's clothing to MISAT, of Rome, Italy.

12. On 19 April 2000 MISAT brought proceedings against Gasser before the Tribunale Civile e Penale (Civil and Criminal District Court) di Roma seeking a ruling that the contract between them had terminated *ipso jure* or, in the alternative, that the contract had been terminated following a disagreement between the two companies. MISAT also asked the court to find that it had not failed to perform the contract and to order Gasser to pay it damages for failure to fulfil the obligations of fairness, diligence and good faith and to reimburse certain costs.

13. On 4 December 2000 Gasser brought an action against MISAT before the Landesgericht (Regional Court) Feldkirch, Austria, to obtain payment of outstanding invoices. In support of the jurisdiction of that court, the claimant submitted that it was not only the court for the place of performance of the contract, within the meaning of Article 5(1) of the Convention but was also the court designated by a choice-of-court clause which had appeared on all invoices sent by Gasser to MISAT, without the latter having raised any objection in that regard. According to Gasser, that showed that, in accordance with their practice and the usage prevailing in trade between Austria and Italy, the parties had concluded an agreement conferring jurisdiction within the meaning of Article 17 of the Brussels Convention.

14. MISAT contended that the Landesgericht Feldkirch had no jurisdiction, on the ground that the court of competent jurisdiction was the court for the place where it was established, under the general rule laid down in Article 2 of the Brussels Convention. It also contested the very existence of an agreement conferring jurisdiction and stated that, before the action was brought by Gasser before the Landesgericht Feldkirch, it had commenced proceedings before the Tribunale Civile e Penale di Roma in respect of the same business relationship.

15. On 21 December 2001, the Landesgericht Feldkirch decided of its own motion to stay proceedings, pursuant to Article 21 of the Brussels Convention, until the jurisdiction of the Tribunale Civile e Penale di Roma had been established. It confirmed its own jurisdiction as the court for the place of performance of the contract, but did not rule on the existence or otherwise of an agreement conferring jurisdiction, observing that although the invoices issued by the claimant systematically included a reference to the courts of Dornbirn under the heading 'Competent Courts', the orders, on the other hand, did not record any choice of court.

16. Gasser appealed against that decision to the Oberlandesgericht Innsbruck, contending that the Landesgericht Feldkirch should be declared to have jurisdiction and that proceedings should not be stayed.

17. The national court considers, first, that this is a case of *lis pendens* since the parties are the same and the claims made before the Austrian and Italian courts have the same cause of action within the meaning of Article 21 of the Brussels Convention, as interpreted by the Court of Justice (see, to that effect, Case 144/86 *Gubisch Maschinenfabrik* [1987] ECR 4861).

18. After noting that the Landesgericht Feldkirch had not ruled as to the existence of an agreement conferring jurisdiction, the national court raises the question whether the fact that one of the parties repeatedly and without objection settled invoices sent by the other even though those invoices contained a jurisdiction clause can be seen as acceptance of that clause, in accordance with Article 17(1)(c) of the Brussels Convention. The national court states that such conduct by the parties reflects a usage in international trade and commerce which is applicable to the parties and of which they are aware or are deemed to be aware. In the event of the existence of an agreement conferring jurisdiction being established, then, according to the national court, the Landesgericht Feldkirch alone has jurisdiction to deal with the dispute under Article 17 of the Convention. In those circumstances, the question arises whether the obligation to stay proceedings, provided for in Article 21 of the Convention, should nevertheless apply.

19. In addition, the national court asks to what extent the excessive and generalised slowness of legal proceedings in the Contracting State where the court first seised is established is liable to affect the application of Article 21 of the Brussels Convention.

20. It was in those circumstances that the Oberlandesgericht Innsbruck stayed proceedings and referred the following questions to the Court for a preliminary ruling:

'*1. May a court which refers questions to the Court of Justice for a preliminary ruling do so purely on the basis of a party's (unrefuted) submissions, whether they have been contested or not contested (on good grounds), or is it first required to clarify those questions as regards the facts by the taking of appropriate evidence (and if so, to what extent)?* [Emphasis added.]

2. May a court other than the court first seised, within the meaning of the first paragraph of Article 21 of the Brussels Convention on Jurisdiction and the Enforcement of Judgments in Civil and Commercial Matters ["the Brussels Convention"], review the jurisdiction of the court first seised if the second court has exclusive jurisdiction pursuant to an agreement conferring jurisdiction under Article 17 of the Brussels Convention, or must the agreed second court proceed in accordance with Article 21 of the Brussels Convention notwithstanding the agreement conferring jurisdiction? [Emphasis added.]

3. Can the fact that court proceedings in a Contracting State take an unjustifiably long time (for reasons largely unconnected with the conduct of the parties), so that material detriment may be caused to one party, have the consequence that the court other than the court first seised, within the meaning of Article 21, is not allowed to proceed in accordance with that provision? [Emphasis added.]

[Court found it unnecessary to answer Questions 4, 5, and 6. Hence they are omitted.]

THE FIRST QUESTION

21. By its first question, the national court seeks in essence to ascertain whether a national court may, under the Protocol, seek an interpretation of the Brussels Convention from the Court of Justice even where the national court is relying on the submissions of a party to the main proceedings, the merits of which it has not yet assessed.

. . . .

THE SECOND QUESTION

28. *By its second question, the national court seeks in essence to establish whether Article 21 of the Brussels Convention must be interpreted as meaning that, where a court is the second court seised and has exclusive jurisdiction under an agreement conferring jurisdiction, it may, by way of derogation from that article, give judgment in the case without waiting for a declaration from the court first seised that it has no jurisdiction.* [Emphasis added.]

Observations submitted to the Court [omitted]

Findings of the Court

. . . Article 21 must be interpreted broadly so as to cover, in principle, all situations of *lis pendens* before courts in Contracting States, irrespective of the parties' domicile [citation omitted].

42. *From the clear terms of Article 21 it is apparent that, in a situation of lis pendens, the court second seised must stay proceedings of its own motion until the jurisdiction of the court first seised has been established and, where it is so established, must decline jurisdiction in favour of the latter.* [Emphasis added.]

. . . .

48. Moreover, the court second seised is never in a better position than the court first seised to determine whether the latter has jurisdiction. That jurisdiction is determined directly by the rules of the Brussels Convention, which are common to both courts and may be interpreted and applied with the same authority by each of them [citation omitted].

49. *Thus, where there is an agreement conferring jurisdiction within the meaning of Article 17 of the Brussels Convention, not only, as observed by the Commission, do the parties always have the option of declining to invoke it and, in particular, the defendant has the option of entering an appearance before the court first seised without alleging that it lacks jurisdiction on the basis of a choice-of-court clause, in accordance with Article 18 of the Convention, but, moreover, in circumstances other than those just described, it is incumbent on the court first seised to verify the existence of the agreement and to decline jurisdiction if it is established, in accordance with Article 17, that the parties actually agreed to designate the court second seised as having exclusive jurisdiction.* [Emphasis

added.]

. . . .

52. Moreover, the interpretation of Article 21 of the Brussels Convention flowing from the foregoing considerations is confirmed by Article 19 of the Convention which requires a court of a Contracting State to declare of its own motion that it has no jurisdiction only where it is 'seised of a claim which is principally concerned with a matter over which the courts of another contracting State have exclusive jurisdiction by virtue of Article 16'. Article 17 of the Brussels Convention is not affected by Article 19.

53. Finally, the difficulties of the kind referred to by the United Kingdom Government, stemming from delaying tactics by parties who, with the intention of delaying settlement of the substantive dispute, commence proceedings before a court which they know to lack jurisdiction by reason of the existence of a jurisdiction clause are not such as to call in question the interpretation of any provision of the Brussels Convention, as deduced from its wording and its purpose.

54. *In view of the foregoing, the answer to the second question must be that Article 21 of the Brussels Convention must be interpreted as meaning that a court second seised whose jurisdiction has been claimed under an agreement conferring jurisdiction must nevertheless stay proceedings until the court first seised has declared that it has no jurisdiction.* [Emphasis added.]

The Third Question

55. *By its third question, the national court seeks in essence to ascertain whether Article 21 of the Brussels Convention must be interpreted as meaning that it may be derogated from where, in general, the duration of proceedings before the courts of the Contracting State in which the court first seised is established is excessively long.* [Emphasis added.]

Admissibility

56. *The Commission raises doubts as to the admissibility of this question and, therefore, of the questions which follow it and are related to it, on the ground that the national court has not provided concrete information such as to allow the inference that the Tribunale Civile e Penale di Roma has failed to fulfil its obligation to give judgment within a reasonable time and thereby infringed Article 6 of the European Convention for the safeguard of Human Rights and Fundamental Freedoms, signed in Rome on 4 November 1950 (hereinafter 'the ECHR').* [Emphasis added.]

57. *That view cannot be accepted.* As observed by the Advocate General in point 87 of his Opinion, it was indeed in relation to the fact that the average duration of proceedings before courts in the Member State in which the court first seised is established is excessively long that the national court submitted the question whether the court second seised may validly decline to apply Article 21 of the Brussels Convention. To answer that question, which the latter court considered relevant for the decision to be given in the main proceedings, it is not necessary for

it to provide information as to the conduct of procedure before the Tribunale Civile e Penale di Roma.

58. It is therefore necessary to answer the third question.

Substance

OBSERVATIONS SUBMITTED TO THE COURT

59. According to Gasser, Article 21 of the Brussels Convention must be interpreted in any event as excluding excessively protracted proceedings (that is to say of a duration exceeding three years), which are contrary to Article 6 of the ECHR and would entail restrictions on freedom of movement as guaranteed by Articles 28 EC, 39 EC, 48 EC and 49 EC. It is the responsibility of the European Union authorities or the national courts to identify those States in which it is well known that legal proceedings are excessively protracted.

60. Therefore, in a case where no decision on jurisdiction has been given within six months following the commencement of proceedings before the court first seised or no final decision on jurisdiction has been given within one year following the commencement of those proceedings, it is appropriate, in Gasser's view, to decline to apply Article 21 of the Brussels Convention. In any event, the courts of the State where the court second seised is established are entitled themselves to rule both on the question of jurisdiction and, after slightly longer periods, on the substance of the case.

. . . .

65. MISAT, the Italian Government and the Commission, on the contrary, advocate the full applicability of Article 21 of the Brussels Convention, notwithstanding the excessive duration of court proceedings in one of the States concerned.

. . . .

Findings of the Court

70. As has been observed by the Commission and by the Advocate General in points 88 and 89 of his Opinion, an interpretation of Article 21 of the Brussels Convention whereby the application of that article should be set aside where the court first seised belongs to a Member State in whose courts there are, in general, excessive delays in dealing with cases would be manifestly contrary both to the letter and spirit and to the aim of the Convention.

71. First, the Convention contains no provision under which its articles, and in particular Article 21, cease to apply because of the length of proceedings before the courts of the Contracting State concerned.

72. Second, it must be borne in mind that the Brussels Convention is necessarily based on the trust which the Contracting States accord to each other's legal systems and judicial institutions. It is that mutual trust which has enabled a compulsory system of jurisdiction to be established, which all the courts within the purview of the Convention are required to respect, and as a corollary the waiver by those States of the right to apply their internal rules on recognition and enforcement of

foreign judgments in favour of a simplified mechanism for the recognition and enforcement of judgments. It is also common ground that the Convention thereby seeks to ensure legal certainty by allowing individuals to foresee with sufficient certainty which court will have jurisdiction.

73. In view of the foregoing, the answer to the third question must be that Article 21 of the Brussels Convention must be interpreted as meaning that it cannot be derogated from where, in general, the duration of proceedings before the courts of the Contracting State in which the court first seised is established is excessively long. [Emphasis added.]

. . . .

On those grounds,

THE COURT (Full Court),

in answer to the questions referred to it by the Oberlandesgericht Innsbruck by judgment of 25 March 2002, hereby rules:

. . . .

2. *Article 21 of the Brussels Convention must be interpreted as meaning that a court second seised whose jurisdiction has been claimed under an agreement conferring jurisdiction must nevertheless stay proceedings until the court first seised has declared that it has no jurisdiction.* [Emphasis added.]

3. *Article 21 of the Brussels Convention must be interpreted as meaning that it cannot be derogated from where, in general, the duration of proceedings before the courts of the Contracting State in which the court first seised is established is excessively long.* [Emphasis added.]

REGULATION (EU) No 1215/2012 OF THE EUROPEAN PARLIAMENT AND OF THE COUNCIL

of 12 December 2012
on jurisdiction and the recognition and enforcement of judgments in civil and commercial matters

[Preamble]

Whereas:

. . . .

(19) The autonomy of the parties to a contract, other than an insurance, consumer or employment contract, where only limited autonomy to determine the courts having jurisdiction is allowed, should be respected subject to the exclusive grounds of jurisdiction laid down in this Regulation.

(20) Where a question arises as to *whether a choice-of-court agreement in favour of a court or the courts of a Member State is null and void as to its substantive validity, that question should be decided in accordance with the law of the Member State of the court or courts designated in the agreement, including the conflict-of-laws rules of that Member State.* [Emphasis added.]

(21) In the interests of the harmonious administration of justice it is necessary to minimise the possibility of concurrent proceedings and to ensure that irreconcilable judgments will not be given in different Member States. *There should be a clear and effective mechanism for resolving cases of lis pendens and related actions, and for obviating problems flowing from national differences as to the determination of the time when a case is regarded as pending. For the purposes of this Regulation, that time should be defined autonomously.* [Emphasis added.]

(22) However, in order to enhance the effectiveness of exclusive choice-of-court agreements and to avoid abusive litigation tactics, it is necessary to provide for an exception to the general *lis pendens* rule in order to deal satisfactorily with a particular situation in which concurrent proceedings may arise. *This is the situation where a court not designated in an exclusive choice-of-court agreement has been seised of proceedings and the designated court is seised subsequently of proceedings involving the same cause of action and between the same parties. In such a case, the court first seised should be required to stay its proceedings as soon as the designated court has been seised and until such time as the latter court declares that it has no jurisdiction under the exclusive choice-of-court agreement.* [Emphasis added.] This is to ensure that, in such a situation, the designated court has priority to decide on the validity of the agreement and on the extent to which the agreement applies to the dispute pending before it. The designated court should be able to proceed irrespective of whether the non-designated court has already decided on the stay of proceedings.

. . . .

SECTION 7
Prorogation of jurisdiction

Article 25

1. If the parties, regardless of their domicile, have agreed that a court or the courts of a Member State are to have jurisdiction to settle any disputes which have arisen or which may arise in connection with a particular legal relationship, that court or those courts shall have jurisdiction, unless the agreement is null and void as to its substantive validity under the law of that Member State. Such jurisdiction shall be exclusive unless the parties have agreed otherwise. The agreement conferring jurisdiction shall be either:

(a) in writing or evidenced in writing;

(b) in a form which accords with practices which the parties have established between themselves; or

(c) in international trade or commerce, in a form which accords with a usage of which the parties are or ought to have been aware and which in such trade or commerce is widely known to, and regularly observed by, parties to contracts of the type involved in the particular trade or commerce concerned.

2. Any communication by electronic means which provides a durable record of the agreement shall be equivalent to 'writing'.

3. The court or courts of a Member State on which a trust instrument has

conferred jurisdiction shall have exclusive jurisdiction in any proceedings brought against a settlor, trustee or beneficiary, if relations between those persons or their rights or obligations under the trust are involved.

4. Agreements or provisions of a trust instrument conferring jurisdiction shall have no legal force if they are contrary to Articles 15, 19 or 23, or if the courts whose jurisdiction they purport to exclude have exclusive jurisdiction by virtue of Article 24.

5. An agreement conferring jurisdiction which forms part of a contract shall be treated as an agreement independent of the other terms of the contract.

The validity of the agreement conferring jurisdiction cannot be contested solely on the ground that the contract is not valid.

Article 26

1. Apart from jurisdiction derived from other provisions of this Regulation, a court of a Member State before which a defendant enters an appearance shall have jurisdiction. This rule shall not apply where appearance was entered to contest the jurisdiction, or where another court has exclusive jurisdiction by virtue of Article 24.

2. In matters referred to in Sections 3, 4 or 5 where the policyholder, the insured, a beneficiary of the insurance contract, the injured party, the consumer or the employee is the defendant, the court shall, before assuming jurisdiction under paragraph 1, ensure that the defendant is informed of his right to contest the jurisdiction of the court and of the consequences of entering or not entering an appearance.

SECTION 8
Examination as to jurisdiction and admissibility

Article 27

Where a court of a Member State is seised of a claim which is principally concerned with a matter over which the courts of another Member State have exclusive jurisdiction by virtue of Article 24, *it shall declare of its own motion that it has no jurisdiction.* [Emphasis added.]

Article 28

1. *Where a defendant domiciled in one Member State is sued in a court of another Member State and does not enter an appearance, the court shall declare of its own motion that it has no jurisdiction unless its jurisdiction is derived from the provisions of this Regulation.* [Emphasis added.]

SECTION 9
Lis pendens — related actions

. . . .

Article 31

1. Where actions come within the exclusive jurisdiction of several courts, any court other than the court first seised shall decline jurisdiction in favour of that court.

2. *Without prejudice to Article 26, where a court of a Member State on which an agreement as referred to in Article 25 confers exclusive jurisdiction is seised, any court of another Member State shall stay the proceedings until such time as the court seised on the basis of the agreement declares that it has no jurisdiction under the agreement.* [Emphasis added.]

3. Where the court designated in the agreement has established jurisdiction in accordance with the agreement, any court of another Member State shall decline jurisdiction in favour of that court.

With respect to choice of court agreements under the lis pendens requirements, the official comment on Regulation (EU) No. 1215/2012 observes:

> . . . [I]order to enhance the effectiveness of exclusive choice-of-court agreements and to avoid abusive litigation tactics, it is necessary to provide for an exception to the general *lis pendens* rule in order to deal satisfactorily with a particular situation in which concurrent proceedings may arise. This is the situation where a court not designated in an exclusive choice-of-court agreement has been seised of proceedings and the designated court is seised subsequently of proceedings involving the same cause of action and between the same parties. In such a case, the court first seised should be required to stay its proceedings as soon as the designated court has been seised and until such time as the latter court declares that it has no jurisdiction under the exclusive choice-of-court agreement. This is to ensure that, in such a situation, the designated court has priority to decide on the validity of the agreement and on the extent to which the agreement applies to the dispute pending before it. The designated court should be able to proceed irrespective of whether the non-designated court has already decided on the stay of proceedings.

QUESTIONS

1. Under which legal regime — the 2005 Hague Convention of Choice of Court Agreements, the United States (federal and state law), Canadian law (provincial law as construed by the Supreme Court of Canada), Japanese law, or current European Law — do the parties to a transaction have the broadest freedom to select effectively a forum and corresponding law for the adjudication of any dispute arising pursuant to their undertaking? Identify the principal limitations under each. Is any distinction made between designation of "in" and "out" bound jurisdiction? How significant is (or could be) the "public policy" (*ordre public*) exception to recognition and enforcement of choice of court agreements?

2. What are the advantages and disadvantages to the parties and to the forum of allowing the parties to a contract to choose the judicial forum for the adjudication of disputes? Is it important to limit their choice to a forum with special connection to the parties or the transaction or both? If so, why?

3. What limitations on party choice (party autonomy) are in your view the most appropriate?

4. Should as a matter of public policy the same limitations apply to arbitration agreements?

5. Under what circumstances are the parties to a dispute be more apt to settle without going to court? Are choice of court and law agreements relevant to the likelihood of the parties' reaching a settlement? Would the accessibility to lawyers of the relevant legal rules and judicial decisions in similar cases be significant factor? Would consistency in the application of legal rules also be significant? Would a "loser pays" rule — that is, the party who loses in court pays the other party's attorney's fees — as in the United Kingdom, be similarly relevant?

6. Describe the changes that the European Parliament and European Council made in the 2012 Regulation in order to deal with the problems of abusive delay tactics — the problem of the so-called Italian torpedo mentioned previously and illustrated in the *Erich Gasser* case? How effective would you surmise these reforms will be?

II. ARBITRATION AGREEMENTS

As indicated above, and as we shall continue to learn below, the parties to cross-border commercial transactions between the United States and most of its trading partners may choose at the outset of their dealings to include either a choice or court (and usually law) or an arbitration clause. As with any opportunity to choose, a decision with respect to the advantages and disadvantages of each becomes necessary. In chapter 6 we have reviewed the contrasts in recognition and enforcement between foreign country judgment and foreign arbitral awards. At this point, we should consider which choice is the most appropriate for adjudication of disputes that might arise during the course of the transaction in question. As we explore the choice of arbitration as an alternative forum in this final segment of these materials, our focus, more narrowly and precisely, should concentrate on what factors legal counsel should take into consideration in recommending one forum over the other. These should be considered throughout.

The choice between a designated court and arbitration is almost always made even before transactions in question have commenced and ordinarily no significant dispute is anticipated (at least none that have not been resolved in negotiating the deal). The exact nature of any future dispute and whether confidentiality (a significant benefit of arbitration) or enforcement of an unquestioned contractual duty may be involved is rarely predictable. Thus in addition to questions of which means of adjudication may be less costly or more efficient or effective, transactional lawyers involved in negotiating and drafting the contracts should also consider which alternative is more likely to facilitate settlement of any dispute that might arise. Thus two questions — often unstated and unexplored — should be kept prominently in mind: whether the outcomes of litigated cases are more predictable than those of arbitrated disputes and whether (and how) the predictability of such outcomes influences settlement.

A. United States

SCHERK v. ALBERTO-CULVER CO.*
417 U.S. 506 (1974)

Mr. Justice Stewart delivered the opinion of the Court.

Alberto-Culver Co., the respondent, is an American company incorporated in Delaware with its principal office in Illinois. It manufactures and distributes toiletries and hair products in this country and abroad. During the 1960s, Alberto-Culver decided to expand its overseas operations, and as part of this program it approached the petitioner Fritz Scherk, a German citizen residing at the time of trial in Switzerland. Scherk was the owner of three interrelated business entities, organized under the laws of Germany and Liechtenstein, that were engaged in the manufacture of toiletries and the licensing of trademarks for such toiletries. An initial contact with Scherk was made by a representative of Alberto-Culver in Germany in June 1967, and negotiations followed at further meetings in both Europe and the United States during 1967 and 1968. In February 1969 a contract was signed in Vienna, Austria, which provided for the transfer of the ownership of Scherk's enterprises to Alberto-Culver along with all rights held by these enterprises to trademarks in cosmetic goods. The contract contained a number of express warranties whereby Scherk guaranteed the sole and unencumbered ownership of these trademarks. In addition, the contract contained an arbitration clause providing that "any controversy or claim [that] shall arise out of this agreement or the breach thereof" would be referred to arbitration before the International Chamber of Commerce in Paris, France, and that "the laws of the State of Illinois, U.S. A. shall apply to and govern this agreement, its interpretation and performance."

The closing of the transaction took place in Geneva, Switzerland, in June 1969. Nearly one year later Alberto-Culver allegedly discovered that the trademark rights purchased under the contract were subject to substantial encumbrances that threatened to give others superior rights to the trademarks and to restrict or preclude Alberto-Culver's use of them. Alberto-Culver thereupon tendered back to Scherk the property that had been transferred to it and offered to rescind the contract. Upon Scherk's refusal, Alberto-Culver commenced this action for damages and other relief in a Federal District Court in Illinois, contending that Scherk's fraudulent representations concerning the status of the trademark rights constituted violations of § 10 (b) of the Securities Exchange Act of 1934, 48 Stat. 891, 15 U.S.C. § 78j (b), and Rule 10b-5 promulgated thereunder, 17 CFR § 240.10b-5.

---

* Footnotes omitted.

In response, Scherk filed a motion to dismiss the action for want of personal and subject-matter jurisdiction as well as on the basis of *forum non conveniens*, or, alternatively, to stay the action pending arbitration in Paris pursuant to the agreement of the parties. Albero-Culver, in turn, opposed this motion and sought a preliminary injunction restraining the prosecution of arbitration proceedings. On December 2, 1971, the District Court denied Scherk's motion to dismiss, and, on January 14, 1972, it granted a preliminary order enjoining Scherk from proceeding with arbitration. In taking these actions the court relied entirely on this Court's decision in *Wilko v. Swan*, 346 U.S. 427, which held that an agreement to arbitrate could not preclude a buyer of a security from seeking a judicial remedy under the Securities Act of 1933, in view of the language of § 14 of that Act, barring "any condition, stipulation, or provision binding any person acquiring any security to waive compliance with any provision of this subchapter . . . ." 48 Stat. 84, 15 U.S.C. § 77n. The Court of Appeals for the Seventh Circuit, with one judge dissenting, affirmed, upon what it considered the controlling authority of the *Wilko* decision. 484 F.2d 611, *writ of certiorari*. 414 U.S. 1156.

I

The United States Arbitration Act, now 9 U.S.C. § 1 *et seq.*, reversing centuries of judicial hostility to arbitration agreements, was designed to allow parties to avoid "the costliness and delays of litigation," and to place arbitration agreements "upon the same footing as other contracts . . . ." H. R. Rep. No. 96, 68th Cong., 1st Sess., 1, 2 (1924); see also S. Rep. No. 536, 68th Cong., 1st Sess. (1924). Accordingly, the Act provides that an arbitration agreement such as is here involved "shall be valid, irrevocable, and enforceable, save upon such grounds as exist at law or in equity for the revocation of any contract." 9 U.S.C. § 2. The Act also provides in § 3 for a stay of proceedings in a case where a court is satisfied that the issue before it is arbitrable under the agreement, and § 4 of the Act directs a federal court to order parties to proceed to arbitration if there has been a "failure, neglect, or refusal" of any party to honor an agreement to arbitrate.

In *Wilko v. Swan, supra*, this Court acknowledged that the Act reflects a legislative recognition of the "desirability of arbitration as an alternative to the complications of litigation," 346 U.S., at 431, but nonetheless declined to apply the Act's provisions. That case involved an agreement between Anthony Wilko and Hayden, Stone & Co., a large brokerage firm, under which Wilko agreed to purchase on margin a number of shares of a corporation's common stock. Wilko alleged that his purchase of the stock was induced by false representations on the part of the defendant concerning the value of the shares, and he brought suit for damages under § 12 (2) of the Securities Act of 1933, 15 U.S.C. § 77l. The defendant responded that Wilko had agreed to submit all controversies arising out of the purchase to arbitration, and that this agreement, contained in a written margin contract between the parties, should be given full effect under the Arbitration Act.

The Court found that "two policies, not easily reconcilable, are involved in this case." 346 U.S., at 438. On the one hand, the Arbitration Act stressed "the need for avoiding the delay and expense of litigation," *id.*, at 431, and directed that such agreements be "valid, irrevocable, and enforceable" in federal courts. On the other hand, the Securities Act of 1933 was "designed to protect investors" and to require "issuers, underwriters, and dealers to make full and fair disclosure of the character of securities sold in interstate and foreign commerce and to prevent fraud in their sale," by creating "a special right to recover for misrepresentation . . . ." 346 U.S., at 431 (footnote omitted). In particular, the Court noted that § 14 of the Securities Act, 15 U.S.C. § 77n, provides:

> "Any condition, stipulation, or provision binding any person acquiring any security to waive compliance with any provision of this subchapter or of the rules and regulations of the Commission shall be void."

The Court ruled that an agreement to arbitrate "is a 'stipulation,' and [that] the right to select the judicial forum is the kind of 'provision' that cannot be waived under § 14 of the Securities Act." 6 346 U.S., at 434–435. Thus, Wilko's advance agreement to arbitrate any disputes subsequently arising out of his contract to purchase the securities was unenforceable under the terms of § 14 of the Securities Act of 1933.

Alberto-Culver relying on this precedent, contends that the District Court and Court of Appeals were correct in holding that its agreement to arbitrate disputes arising under the contract with Scherk is similarly unenforceable in view of its contentions that Scherk's conduct constituted violations of the Securities Exchange Act of 1934 and rules promulgated thereunder. For the reasons that follow, we reject this contention and hold that the provisions of the Arbitration Act cannot be ignored in this case.

At the outset, a colorable argument could be made that even the semantic reasoning of the *Wilko* opinion does not control the case before us. *Wilko* concerned a suit brought under § 12 (2) of the Securities Act of 1933, which provides a defrauded purchaser with the "special right" of a private remedy for civil liability, 346 U.S., at 431. There is no statutory counterpart of § 12 (2) in the Securities Exchange Act of 1934, and neither § 10 (b) of that Act nor Rule 10b-5 speaks of a private remedy to redress violations of the kind alleged here. While federal case law has established that § 10 (b) and Rule 10b-5 create an implied private cause of action, see 6 L. Loss, *Securities Regulation* 3869–3873 (1969) and cases cited therein; *cf. J. I. Case Co. v. Borak*, 377 U.S. 426, the Act itself does not establish the "special right" that the Court in *Wilko* found significant. Furthermore, while both the Securities Act of 1933 and the Securities Exchange Act of 1934 contain sections barring waiver of compliance with any "provision" of the respective Acts, certain of the "provisions" of the 1933 Act that the Court held could not be waived by Wilko's agreement to arbitrate find no counterpart in the 1934 Act. In particular, the Court in *Wilko* noted that the jurisdictional provision of the 1933 Act, 15 U.S.C. § 77v, allowed a plaintiff to bring suit "in any court of competent jurisdiction — federal or state — and removal from a state court is prohibited." 346 U.S., at 431. The analogous provision of the 1934 Act, by contrast, provides for suit only in the federal district courts that have "exclusive jurisdiction," 15 U.S.C. § 78aa, thus significantly restricting the plaintiff's choice of forum.

Accepting the premise, however, that the operative portions of the language of the 1933 Act relied upon in *Wilko* are contained in the Securities Exchange Act of 1934, the respondent's reliance on *Wilko* in this case ignores the significant and, we find, crucial differences between the agreement involved in *Wilko* and the one signed by the parties here. Alberto-Culver's contract to purchase the business entities belonging to Scherk was a truly international agreement. Alberto-Culver is an American corporation with its principal place of business and the vast bulk of its activity in this country, while Scherk is a citizen of Germany whose companies were organized under the laws of Germany and Liechtenstein. The negotiations leading to the signing of the contract in Austria and to the closing in Switzerland took place in the United States, England, and Germany, and involved consultations with legal and trademark experts from each of those countries and from Liechtenstein. Finally, and most significantly, the subject matter of the contract concerned the sale of business enterprises organized under the laws of and primarily situated in European countries, whose activities were largely, if not entirely, directed to European markets.

Such a contract involves considerations and policies significantly different from those found controlling in *Wilko*. In *Wilko*, quite apart from the arbitration provision, there was no question but that the laws of the United States generally, and the federal securities laws in particular, would govern disputes arising out of the stock-purchase agreement. The parties, the negotiations, and the subject matter of the contract were all situated in this country, and no credible claim could have been entertained that any international conflict-of-laws problems would arise. In this case, by contrast, in the absence of the arbitration provision considerable uncertainty existed at the time of the agreement, and still exists, concerning the law applicable to the resolution of disputes arising out of the contract. Such uncertainty will almost inevitably exist with respect to any contract touching two or more countries, each with its own substantive laws and conflict of laws rules. A contractual provision specifying in advance the forum in which disputes hall be litigated and the law to be applied is, therefore, an almost indispensable precondition to achievement of the orderliness and predictability essential to any international business transaction. Furthermore, such a provision obviate the danger that a dispute under the agreement might be submitted to a forum hostile to the interests of one of the parties or unfamiliar with the problem area involved.

A parochial refusal by the courts of one country to enforce an international arbitration agreement would not only frustrate these purposes, but would invite unseemly and mutually destructive jockeying by the parties to secure tactical litigation advantages. In the present case, for example, it is not inconceivable that, if Scherk had anticipated that Alberto-Culver would be able in this country to enjoin resort to arbitration, he might have sought an order in France or some other country enjoining Alberto-Culver from proceeding with its litigation in the United States. Whatever recognition the courts of this country might ultimately have granted to the order of the foreign court, the dicey atmosphere of such a legal no-man's land would surely damage the fabric of international commerce and trade, and imperil the willingness and ability of businessmen to enter into international commercial agreements.

The exception to the clear provisions of the Arbitration Act carved out by *Wilko* is simply inapposite to a case such as the one before us. In *Wilko*, the Court reasoned that, "[w]hen the security buyer, prior to any violation of the Securities Act, waives his right to sue in courts, he gives up more than would a participant in other business transactions. The security buyer has a wider choice of courts and venue. He thus surrenders one of the advantages the Act gives him. . . ."

346 U.S. at 346 U.S. 435. In the context of an international contract, however, these advantages become chimerical since, as indicated above, an opposing party may by speedy resort to a foreign court block or hinder access to the American court of the purchaser's choice.

Two Terms ago, in *The Bremen v. Zapata Off-Shore Co.*, 407 U.S. 1, we rejected the doctrine that a forum selection clause of a contract, although voluntarily adopted by the parties, will not be respected in a suit brought in the United States "unless the selected state would provide a more convenient forum than the state in which suit is brought." *Id.* at 407 U.S. 7. Rather, we concluded that a "forum clause should control absent a strong showing that it should be set aside." *Id.* at 407 U.S. 15. We noted that

> "much uncertainty and possibly great inconvenience to both parties could arise if a suit could be maintained in any jurisdiction in which an accident might occur or if jurisdiction were left to any place [where personal or *in rem* jurisdiction might be established]. The elimination of all such uncertainties by agreeing in advance on a forum acceptable to both parties is an indispensable element in international trade, commerce, and contracting."
> *Id.* at 407 U.S. 13–14.

An agreement to arbitrate before a specified tribunal is, in effect, a specialized kind of forum selection clause that posits not only the situs of suit, but also the procedure to be used in resolving the dispute. The invalidation of such an agreement in the case before us would not only allow the respondent to repudiate its solemn promise, but would, as well, reflect a "parochial concept that all disputes must be resolved under our laws and in our courts. . . . We cannot have trade and commerce in world markets and international waters exclusively on our terms, governed by our laws, and resolved in our courts."

For all these reasons, we hold that the agreement of the parties in this case to arbitrate any dispute arising out of their international commercial transaction is to be respected and enforced by the federal courts in accord with the explicit provisions of the Arbitration Act.

Accordingly, the judgment of the Court of Appeals is reversed and the case is remanded to that court with directions to remand to the District Court for further proceedings consistent with this opinion.

It is so ordered.

Mr. Justice Douglas, with whom Mr. Justice Brennan, Mr. Justice White, and Mr. Justice Marshall concur, dissenting.

Respondent (Alberto-Culver) is a publicly held corporation whose stock is traded on the New York Stock Exchange and is a Delaware corporation with its principal place of business in Illinois. Petitioner (Scherk) owned a business in Germany,

Firma Ludwig Scherk, dealing with cosmetics and toiletries. Scherk owned various trademarks and all outstanding securities of a Liechtenstein corporation (SEV) and of a German corporation, Lodeva. Scherk also owned various trademarks which were licensed to manufacturers and distributors in Europe and in this country. SEV collected the royalties on those licenses.

Alberto-Culver undertook to purchase from Scherk the entire establishment — the trademarks and the stock of the two corporations; and later, alleging it had been defrauded, brought this suit in the United States District Court in Illinois to rescind the agreement and to obtain damages.

The only defense material at this stage of the proceeding is a provision of the contract providing that if any controversy or claim arises under the agreement the parties agree it will be settled "exclusively" by arbitration under the rules of the International Chamber of Commerce, Paris, France.

The basic dispute between the parties concerned allegations that the trademarks which were basic assets in the transaction were encumbered and that their purchase was induced through serious instances of fraudulent representations and omissions by Scherk and his agents within the jurisdiction of the United States. If a question of trademarks were the only one involved, the principle of *The Bremen v. Zapata Off-Shore Co.*, 407 U.S. 1, would be controlling.

We have here, however, questions under the Securities Exchange Act of 1934, which in § 3 (a)(10) defines "security" as including any "note, stock, treasury stock, bond, debenture, certificate of interest or participation in any profit-sharing agreement . . . ." 15 U.S.C. § 78c (a)(10). We held in *Tcherepnin v. Knight*, 389 U.S. 332, as respects § 3 (a)(10):

"Remedial legislation should be construed broadly to effectuate its purposes. The Securities Exchange Act quite clearly falls into the category of remedial legislation. One of its central purposes is to protect investors through the requirement of full disclosure by issuers of securities, and the definition of security in § 3 (a)(10) necessarily determines the classes of investments and investors which will receive the Act's protections. Finally, we are reminded that, in searching for the meaning and scope of the word 'security' in the Act, form should be disregarded for substance and the emphasis should be on economic reality." *Id.*, at 336. (Footnote omitted.)

Section 10 (b) of the 1934 Act makes it unlawful for any person by use of agencies of interstate commerce or the mails "to use or employ, in connection with the purchase or sale of any security," whether or not registered on a national securities exchange, "any manipulative or deceptive device or contrivance in contravention of such rules and regulations as the Commission may prescribe." 15 U.S.C. § 78j (b).

Alberto-Culver, as noted, is not a private person but a corporation with publicly held stock listed on the New York Stock Exchange. If it is to be believed, if in other words the allegations made are proved, the American company has been defrauded by the issuance of "securities" (promissory notes) for assets which are worthless or of a much lower value than represented. Rule 10b-5 of the Securities and Exchange Commission states:

"It shall be unlawful for any person, directly or indirectly, by the use of any means or instrumentality of interstate commerce, or of the mails or of any facility of any national securities exchange,

"(a) To employ any device, scheme, or artifice to defraud,

"(b) To make any untrue statement of a material fact or to omit to state a material fact necessary in order to make the statements made, in the light of the circumstances under which they were made, not misleading, or

"(c) To engage in any act, practice, or course of business which operates or would operate as a fraud or deceit upon any person,

"in connection with the purchase or sale of any security." 17 CFR § 240.10b-5.

Section 29 (a) of the Act provides:

"Any condition, stipulation, or provision binding any person to waive compliance with any provision of this chapter or of any rule or regulation thereunder, or of any rule of an exchange required thereby shall be void." 15 U.S.C. § 78cc (a).

And § 29 (b) adds that "every contract" made in violation of the Act "shall be void." No exception is made for contracts which have an international character.

The Securities Act of 1933, 48 Stat. 84, 15 U.S.C. § 77n, has a like provision in its § 14:

"Any condition, stipulation, or provision binding any person acquiring any security to waive compliance with any provision of this subchapter or of the rules and regulations of the Commission shall be void."

In *Wilko v. Swan*, 346 U.S. 427, a customer brought suit against a brokerage house alleging fraud in the sale of stock. A motion was made to stay the trial until arbitration occurred under the United States Arbitration Act, 9 U.S.C. § 3, as provided in the customer's contract. The Court held that an agreement for arbitration was a "stipulation" within the meaning of § 14 which sought to "waive" compliance with the Securities Act. We accordingly held that the courts, not the arbitration tribunals, had jurisdiction over suits under that Act. The arbitration agency, we held, was bound by other standards which were not necessarily consistent with the 1933 Act. We said:

"As the protective provisions of the Securities Act require the exercise of judicial direction to fairly assure their effectiveness, it seems to us that Congress must have intended § 14 . . . to apply to waiver of judicial trial and review." 346 U.S., at 437.

Wilko was held by the Court of Appeals to control this case — and properly so.

The Court does not consider the question whether a "security" is involved in this case, saying it was not raised by petitioner. A respondent, however, has the right to urge any argument to support the judgment in his favor (save possibly questions of venue, [citations omitted], even those not passed upon by the court below and also contentions rejected below. [Citations omitted.] The Court of Appeals held that "securities" within the meaning of the 1934 Act were involved here, 484 F.2d 611, 615. The brief of the respondent is based on the premise that "securities" are involved here; and petitioner has not questioned that ruling of the Court of Appeals.

It could perhaps be argued that *Wilko* does not govern because it involved a little customer pitted against a big brokerage house, while we deal here with sophisticated buyers and sellers: Scherk, a powerful German operator, and Alberto-Culver, an American business surrounded and protected by lawyers and experts. But that would miss the point of the problem. The Act does not speak in terms of "sophisticated" as opposed to "unsophisticated" people dealing in securities. The rules when the giants play are the same as when the pygmies enter the market.

If there are victims here, they are not Alberto-Culver the corporation, but the thousands of investors who are the security holders in Albert-Culver. If there is fraud and the promissory notes are excessive, the impact is on the equity in Alberto-Culver.

Moreover, the securities market these days is not made up of a host of small people scrambling to get in and out of stocks or other securities. The markets are overshadowed by huge institutional traders. The so-called "off-shore funds," of which Scherk is a member, present perplexing problems under both the 1933 and 1934 Acts. The tendency of American investors to invest indirectly as through mutual funds may change the character of the regulation but not its need.

There has been much support for arbitration of disputes; and it may be the superior way of settling some disagreements. If A and B were quarreling over a trademark and there was an arbitration clause in the contract, the policy of Congress in implementing the United Nations Convention on the Recognition and Enforcement of Foreign Arbitral Awards, as it did in 9 U.S.C. § 201 et seq., would prevail. But the Act does not substitute an arbiter for the settlement of disputes under the 1933 and 1934 Acts. Art. II (3) of the Convention says:

"The court of a Contracting State, when seized of an action in a matter in respect of which the parties have made an agreement within the meaning of this article, shall, at the request of one of the parties, refer the parties to arbitration, unless it finds that the said agreement is null and void, inoperative or incapable of being performed." [1970] 21 U.S.T. (pt. 3) 2517, 2519, T. I. A. S. No. 6997.

But § 29 (a) of the 1934 Act makes agreements to arbitrate liabilities under § 10 of the Act "void" and "inoperative." Congress has specified a precise way whereby big and small investors will be protected and the rules under which the Alberto-Culvers of this Nation shall operate. They or their lawyers cannot waive those statutory conditions, for our corporate giants are not principalities of power but guardians of a host of wards unable to care for themselves. It is these wards that the 1934 Act tries to protect. Not a word in the Convention governing awards adopts the standards which Congress has passed to protect the investors under the 1934 Act. It is peculiarly appropriate that we adhere to *Wilko* — more so even than when *Wilko* was decided. Huge foreign investments are being made in our companies. It is important that American standards of fairness in security dealings govern the destinies of American investors until Congress changes these standards.

The Court finds it unnecessary to consider Scherk's argument that this case is distinguishable from *Wilko* in that *Wilko* involved parties of unequal bargaining strength. *Ante*, at 512–513, n. 6. Instead, the Court rests its conclusion on the fact that this was an "international" agreement, with an American corporation investing in the stock and property of foreign businesses, and speaks favorably of the certainty which inheres when parties specify an arbitral forum for resolution of differences in "any contract touching two or more countries."

This invocation of the "international contract" talisman might be applied to a situation where, for example, an interest in a foreign company or mutual fund was sold to an utterly unsophisticated American citizen, with material fraudulent misrepresentations made in this country. The arbitration clause could appear in the fine print of a form contract, and still be sufficient to preclude recourse to our courts, forcing the defrauded citizen to arbitration in Paris to vindicate his rights.

It has been recognized that the 1934 Act, including the protections of Rule 10b-5, applies when foreign defendants have defrauded American investors, particularly when, as alleged here, they have profited by virtue of proscribed conduct within our boundaries. This is true even when the defendant is organized under the laws of a foreign country, is conducting much of its activity outside the United States, and is therefore governed largely by foreign law. The language of § 29 of the 1934 Act does not immunize such international transactions, and the United Nations Convention provides that a forum court in which a suit is brought need not enforce an agreement to arbitrate which is "void" and "inoperative" as contrary to its public policy. When a foreign corporation undertakes fraudulent action which subjects it to the jurisdiction of our federal securities laws, nothing justifies the conclusion that only a diluted version of those laws protects American investors.

Section 29 (a) of the 1934 Act provides that a stipulation binding one to waive compliance with "any provision" of the Act shall be void, and the Act expressly provides that the federal district courts shall have "exclusive jurisdiction" over suits brought under the Act. 15 U.S.C. § 78aa. The Court appears to attach some significance to the fact that the specific provisions of the 1933 Act involved in *Wilko* are not duplicated in the 1934 Act, which is involved in this case. While Alberto-Culver would not have the right to sue in either a state or federal forum as did the plaintiff in *Wilko*, 346 U.S., at 431, the Court deprives it of its right to have its Rule 10b-5 claim heard in a federal court. We spoke at length in Wilko of this problem, elucidating the undesirable effects of remitting a securities plaintiff to an arbitral, rather than a judicial, forum. Here, as in Wilko, the allegations of fraudulent misrepresentation will involve "subjective findings on the purpose and knowledge" of the defendant, questions ill-determined by arbitrators without judicial instruction on the law. *See id.*, at 435. An arbitral award can be made without explication of reasons and without development of a record, so that the arbitrator's conception of our statutory requirement may be absolutely incorrect yet functionally unreviewable, even when the arbitrator seeks to apply our law. We recognized in Wilko that there is no judicial review corresponding to review of court decisions. *Id.*, at 436–437. The extensive pretrial discovery provided by the Federal Rules of Civil Procedure for actions in district court would not be available. And the wide choice of venue provided by the 1934 Act, 15 U.S.C. § 78aa, would be forfeited. *See Wilko v. Swan, supra*, at 431, 435. The loss of the proper judicial forum carries with it the loss of substantial rights.

When a defendant, as alleged here, has, through proscribed acts within our territory, brought itself within the ken of federal securities regulation, a fact not disputed here, those laws — including the controlling principles of *Wilko* — apply whether the defendant is foreign or American, and whether or not there are transnational elements in the dealings. Those laws are rendered a chimera when foreign corporations or funds — unlike domestic defendants — can nullify them by virtue of arbitration clauses which send defrauded American investors to the uncertainty of arbitration on foreign soil, or, if those investors cannot afford to arbitrate their claims in a far-off forum, to no remedy at all.

Moreover, the international aura which the Court gives this case is ominous. We now have many multinational corporations in vast operations around the world — Europe, Latin America, the Middle East, and Asia. The investments of many American investors turn on dealings by these companies. Up to this day, it has been assumed by reason of *Wilko* that they were all protected by our various federal securities Acts. If these guarantees are to be removed, it should take a legislative enactment. I would enforce our laws as they stand, unless Congress makes an exception.

The virtue of certainty in international agreements may be important, but Congress has dictated that when there are sufficient contacts for our securities laws to apply, the policies expressed in those laws take precedence. Section 29 of the 1934 Act, which renders arbitration clauses void and inoperative, recognizes no exception for fraudulent dealings which incidentally have some international factors. The Convention makes provision for such national public policy in Art. II (3). Federal jurisdiction under the 1934 Act will attach only to some international transactions, but when it does, the protections afforded investors such as Alberto-Culver can only be full-fledged.

QUESTIONS

In what respects does the validity of arbitration clauses differ from the effectiveness of prorogation clauses in the United States? Would the same differences appear to apply in either Canada or Japan, or within the European Union?

MITSUBISHI MOTORS CORPORATION v. SOLER CHRYSLER-PLYMOUTH, INC.*
473 U.S. 614 (1985)

JUSTICE BLACKMUN delivered the opinion of the Court.

The principal question presented by these cases is the arbitrability, pursuant to the Federal Arbitration Act, 9 U.S.C. § 1 *et seq.*, and the Convention on the Recognition and Enforcement of Foreign Arbitral Awards (Convention), [1970] 21 U.S.T. 2517, T.I.A.S. No. 6997, of claims arising under the Sherman Act, 15 U.S.C.

---

* Footnotes omitted.

§ 1 *et seq.*, and encompassed within a valid arbitration clause in an agreement embodying an international commercial transaction.

I

Petitioner-cross-respondent Mitsubishi Motors Corporation (Mitsubishi) is a Japanese corporation which manufactures automobiles and has its principal place of business in Tokyo, Japan. Mitsubishi is the product of a joint venture between, on the one hand, Chrysler International, S.A. (CISA), a Swiss corporation registered in Geneva and wholly owned by Chrysler Corporation, and, on the other, Mitsubishi Heavy Industries, Inc., a Japanese corporation. The aim of the joint venture was the distribution through Chrysler dealers outside the continental United States of vehicles manufactured by Mitsubishi and bearing Chrysler and Mitsubishi trademarks. Respondent-cross-petitioner Soler Chrysler-Plymouth, Inc. (Soler), is a Puerto Rico corporation with its principal place of business in Pueblo Viejo, Guaynabo, Puerto Rico.

On October 31, 1979, Soler entered into a Distributor Agreement with CISA which provided for the sale by Soler of Mitsubishi-manufactured vehicles within a designated area, including metropolitan San Juan. App. 18. On the same date, CISA, Soler, and Mitsubishi entered into a Sales Procedure Agreement (Sales Agreement) which, referring to the Distributor Agreement, provided for the direct sale of Mitsubishi products to Soler and governed the terms and conditions of such sales. *Id.*, at 42. Paragraph VI of the Sales Agreement, labeled "Arbitration of Certain Matters," provides:

> "All disputes, controversies or differences which may arise between [Mitsubishi] and [Soler] out of or in relation to Articles I-B through V of this Agreement or for the breach thereof, shall be finally settled by arbitration in Japan in accordance with the rules and regulations of the Japan Commercial Arbitration Association." *Id.*, at 52–53.

Initially, Soler did a brisk business in Mitsubishi-manufactured vehicles. As a result of its strong performance, its minimum sales volume, specified by Mitsubishi and CISA, and agreed to by Soler, for the 1981 model year was substantially increased. *Id.*, at 179. In early 1981, however, the new-car market slackened. Soler ran into serious difficulties in meeting the expected sales volume, and by the spring of 1981 it felt itself compelled to request that Mitsubishi delay or cancel shipment of several orders. 1 Record 181, 183. About the same time, Soler attempted to arrange for the transshipment of a quantity of its vehicles for sale in the continental United States and Latin America. Mitsubishi and CISA, however, refused permission for any such diversion, citing a variety of reasons, and no vehicles were transshipped. Attempts to work out these difficulties failed. Mitsubishi eventually withheld shipment of 966 vehicles, apparently representing orders placed for May, June, and July 1981 production, responsibility for which Soler disclaimed in February 1982. App. 131.

The following month, Mitsubishi brought an action against Soler in the United States District Court for the District of Puerto Rico under the Federal Arbitration Act and the Convention. Mitsubishi sought an order, pursuant to 9 U.S.C. §§ 4 and

201, to compel arbitration in accord with 57 VI of the Sales Agreement. App. 15. Shortly after filing the complaint, Mitsubishi filed a request for arbitration before the Japan Commercial Arbitration Association. *Id.*, at 70.

Soler denied the allegations and counterclaimed against both Mitsubishi and CISA. It alleged numerous breaches by Mitsubishi of the Sales Agreement, raised a pair of defamation claims, and asserted causes of action under the Sherman Act, 15 U.S.C. § 1 et seq.; the federal Automobile Dealers' Day in Court Act, 70 Stat. 1125, 15 U.S.C. § 1221 et seq.; the Puerto Rico competition statute, P.R.Laws Ann., Tit. 10, § 257 et seq. (1976); and the Puerto Rico Dealers' Contracts Act, P.R.Laws Ann., Tit. 10, § 278 et seq. (1978 and Supp.1983). In the counterclaim premised on the Sherman Act, Soler alleged that Mitsubishi and CISA had conspired to divide markets in restraint of trade. To effectuate the plan, according to Soler, Mitsubishi had refused to permit Soler to resell to buyers in North, Central, or South America vehicles it had obligated itself to purchase from Mitsubishi; had refused to ship ordered vehicles or the parts, such as heaters and defoggers, that would be necessary to permit Soler to make its vehicles suitable for resale outside Puerto Rico; and had coercively attempted to replace Soler and its other Puerto Rico distributors with a wholly owned subsidiary which would serve as the exclusive Mitsubishi distributor in Puerto Rico. App. 91–96.

The alleged breaches included wrongful refusal to ship ordered vehicles and necessary parts, failure to make payment for warranty work and authorized rebates, and bad faith in establishing minimum-sales volumes. *Id.*, at 97–101.

After a hearing, the District Court ordered Mitsubishi and Soler to arbitrate each of the issues raised in the complaint and in all the counterclaims save two and a portion of a third. With regard to the federal antitrust issues, it recognized that the Courts of Appeals [citation omitted] uniformly had held that the rights conferred by the antitrust laws were " 'of a character inappropriate for enforcement by arbitration.' " App. to Pet. for Cert. in No. 83-1569, p. B9, quoting *Wilko v. Swan*, 201 F.2d 439, 444 (CA2 1953), rev'd, 346 U.S. 427 (1953). The District Court held, however, that the international character of the Mitsubishi-Soler undertaking required enforcement of the agreement to arbitrate even as to the antitrust claims. It relied on *Scherk v. Alberto-Culver Co.*, 417 U.S. 506, 515 520 (1974), in which this Court ordered arbitration, pursuant to a provision embodied in an international agreement, of a claim arising under the Securities Exchange Act of 1934 notwithstanding its assumption, arguendo, that *Wilko, supra*, which held nonarbitrable claims arising under the Securities Act of 1933, also would bar arbitration of a 1934 Act claim arising in a domestic context.

The United States Court of Appeals for the First Circuit affirmed in part and reversed in part. 723 F.2d 155 (1983). It first rejected Soler's argument that Puerto Rico law precluded enforcement of an agreement obligating a local dealer to arbitrate controversies outside Puerto Rico. It also rejected Soler's suggestion that it could not have intended to arbitrate statutory claims not mentioned in the arbitration agreement. Assessing arbitrability "on an allegation-by-allegation basis," *id.*, at 159, the court then read the arbitration clause to encompass virtually all the claims arising under the various statutes, including all those arising under the Sherman Act.

Finally, the Court of Appeals found the antitrust claims under Puerto Rico law entirely to reiterate claims elsewhere stated; accordingly, it held them arbitrable to the same extent as their counterparts. *Ibid.*

Finally, after endorsing the doctrine of American Safety, precluding arbitration of antitrust claims, the Court of Appeals concluded that neither this Court's decision in Scherk nor the Convention required abandonment of that doctrine in the face of an international transaction. 723 F.2d, at 164–168. Accordingly, it reversed the judgment of the District Court insofar as it had ordered submission of "Soler's antitrust claims" to arbitration. Affirming the remainder of the judgment, the court directed the District Court to consider in the first instance how the parallel judicial and arbitral proceedings should go forward.

We granted certiorari primarily to consider whether an American court should enforce an agreement to resolve antitrust claims by arbitration when that agreement arises from an international transaction. [Citation omitted.]

II

At the outset, we address the contention raised in Soler's cross-petition that the arbitration clause at issue may not be read to encompass the statutory counterclaims stated in its answer to the complaint. In making this argument, Soler does not question the Court of Appeals' application of ¶ VI of the Sales Agreement to the disputes involved here as a matter of standard contract interpretation. Instead, it argues that as a matter of law a court may not construe an arbitration agreement to encompass claims arising out of statutes designed to protect a class to which the party resisting arbitration belongs "unless [that party] has expressly agreed" to arbitrate those claims, see Pet. for Cert. in No. 83-1733, pp. 8, i, by which Soler presumably means that the arbitration clause must specifically mention the statute giving rise to the claims that a party to the clause seeks to arbitrate. See 723 F.2d, at 159. Soler reasons that, because it falls within the class for whose benefit the federal and local antitrust laws and dealers' Acts were passed, but the arbitration clause at issue does not mention these statutes or statutes in general, the clause cannot be read to contemplate arbitration of these statutory claims.

We do not agree, for we find no warrant in the Arbitration Act for implying in every contract within its ken a presumption against arbitration of statutory claims. The Act's centerpiece provision makes a written agreement to arbitrate "in any maritime transaction or a contract evidencing a transaction involving commerce . . . valid, irrevocable, and enforceable, save upon such grounds as exist at law or in equity for the revocation of any contract." 9 U.S.C. § 2. The "liberal federal policy favoring arbitration agreements," *Moses H. Cone Memorial Hospital v. Mercury Construction Corp.*, 460 U.S. 1, 24 (1983), manifested by this provision and the Act as a whole, is at bottom a policy guaranteeing the enforcement of private contractual arrangements: the Act simply "creates a body of federal substantive law establishing and regulating the duty to honor an agreement to arbitrate." *Id.*, at 25, n. 32, 103 S. Ct., at 942, n. 32. As this Court recently observed, "[t]he preeminent concern of Congress in passing the Act was to enforce private agreements into which parties had entered," a concern which "requires that we rigorously enforce agreements to arbitrate." *Dean Witter Reynolds Inc. v. Byrd*, 470 U.S. 213, 221 (1985).

Accordingly, the first task of a court asked to compel arbitration of a dispute is to determine whether the parties agreed to arbitrate that dispute. The court is to make this determination by applying the "federal substantive law of arbitrability, applicable to any arbitration agreement within the coverage of the Act." *Moses H. Cone Memorial Hospital*, 460 U.S., at 24. [Citations omitted.] And that body of law counsels

> "that questions of arbitrability must be addressed with a healthy regard for the federal policy favoring arbitration. . . . The Arbitration Act establishes that, as a matter of federal law, any doubts concerning the scope of arbitrable issues should be resolved in favor of arbitration, whether the problem at hand is the construction of the contract language itself or an allegation of waiver, delay, or a like defense to arbitrability." *Moses H. Cone Memorial Hospital*, 460 U.S., at 24–25.

[Citation omitted.] Thus, as with any other contract, the parties' intentions control, but those intentions are generously construed as to issues of arbitrability.

There is no reason to depart from these guidelines where a party bound by an arbitration agreement raises claims founded on statutory rights. Some time ago this Court expressed "hope for [the Act's] usefulness both in controversies based on statutes or on standards otherwise created," *Wilko v. Swan*, 346 U.S. 427, 432 (1953) (footnote omitted); [citation omitted] and we are well past the time when judicial suspicion of the desirability of arbitration and of the competence of arbitral tribunals inhibited the development of arbitration as an alternative means of dispute resolution. Just last Term in *Southland Corp.*, [*v. Keating*, 465 U.S. 1, 12 (1984)], where we held that § 2 of the Act declared a national policy applicable equally in state as well as federal courts, we construed an arbitration clause to encompass the disputes at issue without pausing at the source in a state statute of the rights asserted by the parties resisting arbitration. 465 U.S., at 15, and n. 7. Of course, courts should remain attuned to well-supported claims that the agreement to arbitrate resulted from the sort of fraud or overwhelming economic power that would provide grounds "for the revocation of any contract." 9 U.S.C. § 2 [citation omitted]. But, absent such compelling considerations, the Act itself provides no basis for disfavoring agreements to arbitrate statutory claims by skewing the otherwise hospitable inquiry into arbitrability.

That is not to say that all controversies implicating statutory rights are suitable for arbitration. There is no reason to distort the process of contract interpretation, however, in order to ferret out the inappropriate. Just as it is the congressional policy manifested in the Federal Arbitration Act that requires courts liberally to construe the scope of arbitration agreements covered by that Act, it is the congressional intention expressed in some other statute on which the courts must rely to identify any category of claims as to which agreements to arbitrate will be held unenforceable. [Citations omitted.] For that reason, Soler's concern for statutorily protected classes provides no reason to color the lens through which the arbitration clause is read. By agreeing to arbitrate a statutory claim, a party does not forgo the substantive rights afforded by the statute; it only submits to their resolution in an arbitral, rather than a judicial, forum. It trades the procedures and opportunity for review of the courtroom for the simplicity, informality, and expedition of arbitration. We must assume that if Congress intended the substantive protection afforded by a given statute to include protection against waiver of the right to a judicial forum, that intention will be deducible from text or legislative history. [Citation omitted.] Having made the bargain to arbitrate, the party should be held to it unless Congress itself has evinced an intention to preclude a waiver of judicial remedies for the statutory rights at issue. Nothing, in the meantime, prevents a party from excluding statutory claims from the scope of an agreement to arbitrate. [Citation omitted.]

In sum, the Court of Appeals correctly conducted a two-step inquiry, first determining whether the parties' agreement to arbitrate reached the statutory issues, and then, upon finding it did, considering whether legal constraints external to the parties' agreement foreclosed the arbitration of those claims. We endorse its rejection of Soler's proposed rule of arbitration-clause construction.

III

We now turn to consider whether Soler's antitrust claims are nonarbitrable even though it has agreed to arbitrate them. In holding that they are not, the Court of Appeals followed the decision of the Second Circuit in *American Safety Equipment Corp. v. J.P. Maguire & Co.*, 391 F.2d 821 (1968). Notwithstanding the absence of any explicit support for such an exception in either the Sherman Act or the Federal Arbitration Act, the Second Circuit there reasoned that "the pervasive public interest in enforcement of the antitrust laws, and the nature of the claims that arise in such cases, combine to make . . . antitrust claims . . . inappropriate for arbitration." *Id.*, at 827–828. We find it unnecessary to assess the legitimacy of the American Safety doctrine as applied to agreements to arbitrate arising from domestic transactions. As in *Scherk v. Alberto-Culver Co.*, 417 U.S. 506 (1974), we conclude that concerns of international comity, respect for the capacities of foreign and transnational tribunals, and sensitivity to the need of the international commercial system for predictability in the resolution of disputes require that we enforce the parties' agreement, even assuming that a contrary result would be forthcoming in a domestic context.

Even before Scherk, this Court had recognized the utility of forum-selection clauses in international transactions. In *The Bremen, supra,* an American oil company, seeking to evade a contractual choice of an English forum and, by implication, English law, filed a suit in admiralty in a United States District Court against the German corporation which had contracted to tow its rig to a location in the Adriatic Sea. Notwithstanding the possibility that the English court would enforce provisions in the towage contract exculpating the German party which an American court would refuse to enforce, this Court gave effect to the choice-of-forum clause. It observed:

> "The expansion of American business and industry will hardly be encouraged if, notwithstanding solemn contracts, we insist on a parochial concept that all disputes must be resolved under our laws and in our courts. . . . We

cannot have trade and commerce in world markets and international waters exclusively on our terms, governed by our laws, and resolved in our courts." 407 U.S., at 9.

Recognizing that "agreeing in advance on a forum acceptable to both parties is an indispensable element in international trade, commerce, and contracting," *id.*, at 13–14, the decision in The Bremen clearly eschewed a provincial solicitude for the jurisdiction of domestic forums.

Identical considerations governed the Court's decision in *Scherk*, which categorized "[a]n agreement to arbitrate before a specified tribunal [as], in effect, a specialized kind of forum-selection clause that posits not only the situs of suit but also the procedure to be used in resolving the dispute." 417 U.S., at 519. In *Scherk*, the American company Alberto-Culver purchased several interrelated business enterprises, organized under the laws of Germany and Liechtenstein, as well as the rights held by those enterprises in certain trademarks, from a German citizen who at the time of trial resided in Switzerland. Although the contract of sale contained a clause providing for arbitration before the International Chamber of Commerce in Paris of "any controversy or claim [arising] out of this agreement or the breach thereof," Alberto-Culver subsequently brought suit against Scherk in a Federal District Court in Illinois, alleging that Scherk had violated § 10(b) of the Securities Exchange Act of 1934 by fraudulently misrepresenting the status of the trademarks as unencumbered. The District Court denied a motion to stay the proceedings before it and enjoined the parties from going forward before the arbitral tribunal in Paris. The Court of Appeals for the Seventh Circuit affirmed, relying on this Court's holding in *Wilko v. Swan*, 346 U.S. 427 (1953), that agreements to arbitrate disputes arising under the Securities Act of 1933 are nonarbitrable. This Court reversed, enforcing the arbitration agreement even while assuming for purposes of the decision that the controversy would be nonarbitrable under the holding of *Wilko* had it arisen out of a domestic transaction. Again, the Court emphasized:

> "A contractual provision specifying in advance the forum in which disputes shall be litigated and the law to be applied is . . . an almost indispensable precondition to achievement of the orderliness and predictability essential to any international business transaction.
>
> "A parochial refusal by the courts of one country to enforce an international arbitration agreement would not only frustrate these purposes, but would invite unseemly and mutually destructive jockeying by the parties to secure tactical litigation advantages. . . . [It would] damage the fabric of international commerce and trade, and imperil the willingness and ability of businessmen to enter into international commercial agreements." 417 U.S., at 516–517.

Accordingly, the Court held Alberto-Culver to its bargain, sending it to the international arbitral tribunal before which it had agreed to seek its remedies.

The Bremen and *Scherk* establish a strong presumption in favor of enforcement of freely negotiated contractual choice-of-forum provisions. Here, as in *Scherk*, that presumption is reinforced by the emphatic federal policy in favor of arbitral dispute resolution. And at least since this Nation's accession in 1970 to the Convention, see

[1970] 21 U.S.T. 2517, T.I.A.S. 6997, and the implementation of the Convention in the same year by amendment of the Federal Arbitration Act, that federal policy applies with special force in the field of international commerce. Thus, we must weigh the concerns of *American Safety* against a strong belief in the efficacy of arbitral procedures for the resolution of international commercial disputes and an equal commitment to the enforcement of freely negotiated choice-of-forum clauses.

At the outset, we confess to some skepticism of certain aspects of the *American Safety* doctrine. As distilled by the First Circuit, 723 F.2d, at 162, the doctrine comprises four ingredients. First, private parties play a pivotal role in aiding governmental enforcement of the antitrust laws by means of the private action for treble damages. Second, "the strong possibility that contracts which generate antitrust disputes may be contracts of adhesion militates against automatic forum determination by contract." Third, antitrust issues, prone to complication, require sophisticated legal and economic analysis, and thus are "ill-adapted to strengths of the arbitral process, *i.e.*, expedition, minimal requirements of written rationale, simplicity, resort to basic concepts of common sense and simple equity." Finally, just as "issues of war and peace are too important to be vested in the generals, . . . decisions as to antitrust regulation of business are too important to be lodged in arbitrators chosen from the business community — particularly those from a foreign community that has had no experience with or exposure to our law and values." *See American Safety*, 391 F.2d, at 826–827.

Initially, we find the second concern unjustified. The mere appearance of an antitrust dispute does not alone warrant invalidation of the selected forum on the undemonstrated assumption that the arbitration clause is tainted. A party resisting arbitration of course may attack directly the validity of the agreement to arbitrate. [Citation omitted.] Moreover, the party may attempt to make a showing that would warrant setting aside the forum-selection clause — that the agreement was "[a]ffected by fraud, undue influence, or overweening bargaining power"; that "enforcement would be unreasonable and unjust"; or that proceedings "in the contractual forum will be so gravely difficult and inconvenient that [the resisting party] will for all practical purposes be deprived of his day in court." *The Bremen*, 407 U.S., at 12, 15, 18. But absent such a showing — and none was attempted here — there is no basis for assuming the forum inadequate or its selection unfair.

Next, potential complexity should not suffice to ward off arbitration. We might well have some doubt that even the courts following American Safety subscribe fully to the view that antitrust matters are inherently insusceptible to resolution by arbitration, as these same courts have agreed that an undertaking to arbitrate antitrust claims entered into after the dispute arises is acceptable. [Citations omitted.] And the vertical restraints which most frequently give birth to antitrust claims covered by an arbitration agreement will not often occasion the monstrous proceedings that have given antitrust litigation an image of intractability. In any event, adaptability and access to expertise are hallmarks of arbitration. The anticipated subject matter of the dispute may be taken into account when the arbitrators are appointed, and arbitral rules typically provide for the participation of experts either employed by the parties or appointed by the tribunal. Moreover, it is often a judgment that streamlined proceedings and expeditious results will best serve their needs that causes parties to agree to arbitrate their disputes; it is typically a desire to keep the effort and expense required to resolve a dispute within manageable bounds that prompts them mutually to forgo access to judicial remedies. In sum, the factor of potential complexity alone does not persuade us that an arbitral tribunal could not properly handle an antitrust matter.

For similar reasons, we also reject the proposition that an arbitration panel will pose too great a danger of innate hostility to the constraints on business conduct that antitrust law imposes. International arbitrators frequently are drawn from the legal as well as the business community; where the dispute has an important legal component, the parties and the arbitral body with whose assistance they have agreed to settle their dispute can be expected to select arbitrators accordingly. We decline to indulge the presumption that the parties and arbitral body conducting a proceeding will be unable or unwilling to retain competent, conscientious, and impartial arbitrators.

We are left, then, with the core of the *American Safety* doctrine — the fundamental importance to American democratic capitalism of the regime of the antitrust laws. [Citations omitted.] Without doubt, the private cause of action plays a central role in enforcing this regime. See, e.g., *Hawaii v. Standard Oil Co.*, 405 U.S. 251, 262 (1972). As the Court of Appeals pointed out:

> "'A claim under the antitrust laws is not merely a private matter. The Sherman Act is designed to promote the national interest in a competitive economy; thus, the plaintiff asserting his rights under the Act has been likened to a private attorney-general who protects the public's interest.'"
> 723 F.2d, at 168, quoting *American Safety*, 391 F.2d, at 826.

The treble-damages provision wielded by the private litigant is a chief tool in the antitrust enforcement scheme, posing a crucial deterrent to potential violators. [Citation omitted.] The importance of the private damages remedy, however, does not compel the conclusion that it may not be sought outside an American court. Notwithstanding its important incidental policing function, the treble-damages cause of action conferred on private parties by § 4 of the Clayton Act, 15 U.S.C. § 15, and pursued by Soler here by way of its third counterclaim, seeks primarily to enable an injured competitor to gain compensation for that injury.

> "Section 4 . . . is in essence a remedial provision. It provides treble damages to '[a]ny person who shall be injured in his business or property by reason of anything forbidden in the antitrust laws . . . .' Of course, treble damages also play an important role in penalizing wrongdoers and deterring wrongdoing, as we also have frequently observed. . . . It nevertheless is true that the treble-damages provision, which makes awards available only to injured parties, and measures the awards by a multiple of the injury actually proved, is designed primarily as a remedy." *Brunswick Corp. v. Pueblo Bowl-O-Mat, Inc.*, 429 U.S. 477 (1977).

After examining the respective legislative histories, the Court in *Brunswick* recognized that when first enacted in 1890 as § 7 of the Sherman Act, 26 Stat. 210, the treble-damages provision "was conceived of primarily as a remedy for '[t]he people of the United States as individuals,'" 429 U.S., at 486, n. 10, quoting 21 Cong.Rec. 1767–1768 (1890) (remarks of Sen. George); when reenacted in 1914 as

§ 4 of the Clayton Act, 38 Stat. 731, it was still "conceived primarily as 'open [ing] the door of justice to every man, whenever he may be injured by those who violate the antitrust laws, and giv[ing] the injured party ample damages for the wrong suffered.'" 429 U.S., at 486, n. 10, quoting 51 Cong. Rec. 9073 (1914) (remarks of Rep. Webb). And, of course, the antitrust cause of action remains at all times under the control of the individual litigant: no citizen is under an obligation to bring an antitrust suit, [citation omitted], and the private antitrust plaintiff needs no executive or judicial approval before settling one. It follows that, at least where the international cast of a transaction would otherwise add an element of uncertainty to dispute resolution, the prospective litigant may provide in advance for a mutually agreeable procedure whereby he would seek his antitrust recovery as well as settle other controversies.

There is no reason to assume at the outset of the dispute that international arbitration will not provide an adequate mechanism. To be sure, the international arbitral tribunal owes no prior allegiance to the legal norms of particular states; hence, it has no direct obligation to vindicate their statutory dictates. The tribunal, however, is bound to effectuate the intentions of the parties. Where the parties have agreed that the arbitral body is to decide a defined set of claims which includes, as in these cases, those arising from the application of American antitrust law, the tribunal therefore should be bound to decide that dispute in accord with the national law giving rise to the claim. [Citation omitted.] And so long as the prospective litigant effectively may vindicate its statutory cause of action in the arbitral forum, the statute will continue to serve both its remedial and deterrent function.

Having permitted the arbitration to go forward, the national courts of the United States will have the opportunity at the award-enforcement stage to ensure that the legitimate interest in the enforcement of the antitrust laws has been addressed. The Convention reserves to each signatory country the right to refuse enforcement of an award where the "recognition or enforcement of the award would be contrary to the public policy of that country." Art. V(2)(b), 21 U.S.T., at 2520; see *Scherk*, 417 U.S., at 519, n. 14. While the efficacy of the arbitral process requires that substantive review at the award-enforcement stage remain minimal, it would not require intrusive inquiry to ascertain that the tribunal took cognizance of the antitrust claims and actually decided them.

As international trade has expanded in recent decades, so too has the use of international arbitration to resolve disputes arising in the course of that trade. The controversies that international arbitral institutions are called upon to resolve have increased in diversity as well as in complexity. Yet the potential of these tribunals for efficient disposition of legal disagreements arising from commercial relations has not yet been tested. If they are to take a central place in the international legal order, national courts will need to "shake off the old judicial hostility to arbitration," *Kulukundis Shipping Co. v. Amtorg Trading Corp.*, 126 F.2d 978, 985 (CA2 1942), and also their customary and understandable unwillingness to cede jurisdiction of a claim arising under domestic law to a foreign or transnational tribunal. To this extent, at least, it will be necessary for national courts to subordinate domestic notions of arbitrability to the international policy favoring commercial arbitration. See *Scherk, supra*.

Accordingly, we "require this representative of the American business community to honor its bargain," *Alberto-Culver Co. v. Scherk*, 484 F.2d 611, 620 (CA7 1973) (Stevens, J., dissenting), by holding this agreement to arbitrate "enforce[able] . . . in accord with the explicit provisions of the Arbitration Act." *Scherk*, 417 U.S., at 520.

The judgment of the Court of Appeals is affirmed in part and reversed in part, and the cases are remanded for further proceedings consistent with this opinion.

It is so ordered.

JUSTICE POWELL took no part in the decision of these cases.

JUSTICE STEVENS, with whom JUSTICE BRENNAN joins, and with whom JUSTICE MARSHALL joins except as to Part II, dissenting.

One element of this rather complex litigation is a claim asserted by an American dealer in Plymouth automobiles that two major automobile companies are parties to an international cartel that has restrained competition in the American market. Pursuant to an agreement that is alleged to have violated § 1 of the Sherman Act, 15 U.S.C. § 1, those companies allegedly prevented the dealer from transshipping some 966 surplus vehicles from Puerto Rico to other dealers in the American market. App. 92.

Petitioner denies the truth of the dealer's allegations and takes the position that the validity of the antitrust claim must be resolved by an arbitration tribunal in Tokyo, Japan. Largely because the auto manufacturer's defense to the antitrust allegation is based on provisions in the dealer's franchise agreement, the Court of Appeals concluded that the arbitration clause in that agreement encompassed the antitrust claim. 723 F.2d 155, 159 (CA1 1983). It held, however, as a matter of law, that arbitration of such a claim may not be compelled under either the Federal Arbitration Act or the Convention on the Recognition and Enforcement of Foreign Arbitral Awards. *Id.*, at 161–168.

This Court agrees with the Court of Appeals' interpretation of the scope of the arbitration clause, but disagrees with its conclusion that the clause is unenforceable insofar as it purports to cover an antitrust claim against a Japanese company. This Court's holding rests almost exclusively on the federal policy favoring arbitration of commercial disputes and vague notions of international comity arising from the fact that the automobiles involved here were manufactured in Japan. Because I am convinced that the Court of Appeals' construction of the arbitration clause is erroneous, and because I strongly disagree with this Court's interpretation of the relevant federal statutes, I respectfully dissent. In my opinion, (1) a fair construction of the language in the arbitration clause in the parties' contract does not encompass a claim that auto manufacturers entered into a conspiracy in violation of the antitrust laws; (2) an arbitration clause should not normally be construed to cover a statutory remedy that it does not expressly identify; (3) Congress did not intend § 2 of the Federal Arbitration Act to apply to antitrust claims; and (4) Congress did not intend the Convention on the Recognition and Enforcement of

Foreign Arbitral Awards to apply to disputes that are not covered by the Federal Arbitration Act.

In my opinion, the elected representatives of the American people would not have us dispatch an American citizen to a foreign land in search of an uncertain remedy for the violation of a public right that is protected by the Sherman Act. This is especially so when there has been no genuine bargaining over the terms of the submission, and the arbitration remedy provided has not even the most elementary guarantees of fair process. Consideration of a fully developed record by a jury, instructed in the law by a federal judge, and subject to appellate review, is a surer guide to the competitive character of a commercial practice than the practically unreviewable judgment of a private arbitrator.

Unlike the Congress that enacted the Sherman Act in 1890, the Court today does not seem to appreciate the value of economic freedom. I respectfully dissent.

QUESTIONS

To what extent under *Mitsubishi Motors Corporation v. Soler Chrysler-Plymouth, Inc.* are all regulatory or public law issues subject to arbitration? Can the same be said of prorogation clauses?

U.S. TITAN, INC. v. GUANGZHOU ZHEN HUA SHIPPING CO., LTD.
241 F.3d 135 (2d Cir. 2001)

PARKER, CIRCUIT JUDGE:

Respondent-Appellant Guangzhou Zhen Hua Shipping Co., Ltd. ("Zhen Hua") appeals from a judgment of the United States District Court for the Southern District of New York (William C. Conner, Judge), entered October 7, 1998, upon an August 5, 1998 opinion and order, as amended September 25, 1998, granting the motion of Petitioner-Appellee to compel arbitration in London and denying the motion of Respondent-Appellant to dismiss on the grounds of lack of subject-matter jurisdiction, lack of personal jurisdiction, and improper venue. . . .

On appeal, Zhen Hua contends principally that the district court exceeded the scope of its jurisdiction under the Federal Arbitration Act, 9 U.S.C. §§ 1–16, (the "FAA") by compelling arbitration of the parties' dispute pursuant to a charter party allegedly negotiated by the parties in September 1995. More specifically, Zhen Hua argues that the court should not have determined whether the parties had formed a charter party because the parties had allegedly negotiated an "ad hoc" agreement to arbitrate that issue and that the court erred in finding that no such "ad hoc" agreement existed. In addition, Zhen Hua asserts that the district court lacked subject-matter jurisdiction under the Foreign Sovereign Immunities Act, 28 U.S.C. §§ 1603–1611, that the district court lacked personal jurisdiction over Zhen Hua, and that venue in the Southern District of New York was improper. For the reasons set forth below, we affirm.

I. BACKGROUND

Petitioner-Appellee U.S. Titan, Inc. ("Titan") is a corporation organized under the laws of Texas, with its principal place of business in Pelham, New York. Zhen Hua is a state-owned corporation organized under the laws of the People's Republic of China, engaged primarily in the shipping industry, with its principal place of business in Guangzhou (also known as Canton), China.

A. *The Negotiations*

In August 1995, Titan and Zhen Hua began negotiating a time charter of the M/T BIN HE (the "BIN HE"), a ship owned by Zhen Hua. The parties conducted negotiations through two shipbrokers in Connecticut, Seabrokers (representing Titan) and Seagos (representing Zhen Hua). The two Connecticut brokers served as conduits for the transmission of many of the communications from one party to the other. Most of the parties' communications during the negotiations are memorialized in writings transmitted via facsimile or telex between and among the brokers and the parties. . . .

. . . .

II. DISCUSSION

On appeal, Zhen Hua argues that the district court erred in several regards. First, Zhen Hua asserts that in November 1995 the parties reached an "ad hoc" agreement, separate and distinct from the provisions of the charter party, for the purpose of arbitrating whether the parties had entered into a charter party. If so, contends Zhen Hua, the FAA cloaked the district court with jurisdiction *only* to order arbitration in accordance with that agreement, leaving the issue of charter party formation to the arbitrator. Second, Zhen Hua contends that the district court lacked subject-matter jurisdiction under the FSIA. Third, Zhen Hua asserts that the district court lacked personal jurisdiction over Zhen Hua because Zhen Hua did not have "substantial" or "continuous and systematic" contacts with the United States. Finally, Zhen Hua claims that venue in the Southern District of New York was improper. For the reasons stated below, we disagree with Zhen Hua and affirm the decision of the district court.

A. *The Purported Agreements*

The district court held that the parties did not enter into an "ad hoc" agreement to arbitrate whether they had formed a charter party, but did conclude that the parties had formed a charter party that included an arbitration clause requiring the parties to submit charter-related disputes to arbitration in London. As a result, the court granted Titan's motion to compel arbitration pursuant to the charter party and stayed the litigation pending such arbitration. On appeal, Zhen Hua argues that, as a matter of law, the parties' communications established an "ad hoc" arbitration agreement that, under the FAA and the Convention, delegated authority to an arbitrator in London to determine whether the parties had formed a charter party. We disagree.

1. *Standard of Review*

Before addressing the merits of Zhen Hua's argument, we must resolve the parties' dispute over the standard of review applicable to the district court's conclusions about the existence, or lack thereof, of the two purported agreements. According to Zhen Hua, the district court decided the contractual formation issues as a matter of summary judgment and therefore our review is de novo. In response, Titan contends that the district court appropriately made findings of fact based on the parties' evidentiary submissions and that we review such findings, including the court's factual findings on formation, for clear error.

The determination of whether there was a meeting of the minds sufficient to constitute a contract is one of fact. [Citation omitted.] This remains true regardless of whether the contract at issue is an arbitration agreement, [citation omitted] ". . . We see no reason to disturb this factual finding.", or a charter party, [citation omitted].

When parties disagree about whether they entered into an arbitration agreement subject to the FAA, the FAA directs that the "court shall proceed summarily to . . . trial" of the issue. 9 U.S.C. § 4. Contrary to Zhen Hua's characterization of the proceedings below, the district court's opinion and the record make clear that the district court did try the issue of whether the parties formed an agreement to arbitrate. Although the district court did not hold an evidentiary hearing, the parties filed multiple briefs and extensive evidence with the court over a two-year period. Most significantly, the parties submitted the telex and facsimile communications that were alleged to have formed the "ad hoc" arbitration agreement (according to Zhen Hua) and the charter party (according to Titan). No dispute existed as to the authenticity of these communications. Instead, the parties disagreed over the meaning of the communications.

In addition, Zhen Hua did not and does not now seek an evidentiary hearing. Nowhere in its briefs does Zhen Hua assert that it requested the district court to hold an evidentiary hearing. Furthermore, Zhen Hua does not contest (or even address) the district court's statement in footnote twelve of its first opinion that notwithstanding "[s]ection 4 of the FAA . . . , no such hearing [was] required." *See Titan I*, 16 F. Supp. 2d at 337 n.12 (internal citation omitted). Finally, Zhen Hua explicitly disclaims that the case should be remanded to the district court for such a hearing:

> *Neither Titan nor Zhen Hua seeks remand for a factual trial*, nor is a trial appropriate when the sole issue is whether, as a matter of law and through application of the presumption favoring arbitration, the parties' communications reflect an enforceable agreement to arbitrate the issue of charter formation. Appellant's Reply Br. at 12–13 (emphasis added).

Consequently, under the circumstances of the matter *sub judice*, we hold that the district court tried the issue of formation (of both purported agreements) on the papers and that Zhen Hua has waived any right under the FAA to an evidentiary hearing.

The correct standard of review of the facts found by the trial court is contained in Rule 52(a) of the Federal Rules of Civil Procedure: "Findings of fact, whether based on oral or documentary evidence, shall not be set aside unless clearly erroneous . . . ." As stated in the rule, the "clearly erroneous" standard of review controls our consideration of the factual findings of the district court *even* though based upon a documentary record. [Citation omitted.] We are not permitted to find the district court's findings of fact to be clearly erroneous if the findings are one of two permissible views of the evidence. *See id.*

2. *Formation of the Purported Agreements*

"The Federal Arbitration Act creates a 'body of federal substantive law of arbitrability, applicable to any arbitration agreement within the coverage of the Act.'" *PaineWebber Inc. v. Bybyk*, 81 F.3d 1193, 1198 (2d Cir. 1996) (quoting *Moses H. Cone Memorial Hosp. v. Mercury Constr. Corp.*, 460 U.S. 1, 24 (1983)). Arbitration agreements subject to the Convention are enforced in accordance with Chapter 2 of the FAA. *See* 9 U.S.C. § 201. An agreement to arbitrate exists within the meaning of the Convention and the FAA if: (1) there is a written agreement; (2) the writing provides for arbitration in the territory of a signatory of the convention; (3) the subject matter is commercial; and (4) the subject matter is not entirely domestic in scope. [Citations omitted.] *Upon finding that such an agreement exists, a federal court must compel arbitration of any dispute falling within the scope of the agreement pursuant to the terms of the agreement.* [Emphasis added.]

Zhen Hua and Titan argue over whether the first requirement, *i.e.*, the existence of a written agreement to arbitrate, has been met with regard to the "ad hoc" agreement and the charter party. Under the Convention a written agreement "include[s] an arbitral clause in a contract or an arbitration agreement, signed by the parties or contained in an exchange of letters or telegrams." 9 U.S.C. § 201, Convention on the Recognition and Enforcement of Foreign Arbitrable Awards, Art. II(2). Notwithstanding the strong federal policy favoring arbitration as an alternative means of dispute resolution, [citation omitted], courts must treat agreements to arbitrate like any other contract, [citations omitted]. A contract is formed when there is a meeting of the minds of the parties on the essential terms of an agreement. [Citation omitted.] *A court must therefore examine the parties' written communications to determine whether they have formed an agreement to arbitrate enforceable under the FAA and the Convention.* [Emphasis added.]

a. *The "Ad Hoc" Arbitration Agreement*

The district court considered Zhen Hua's argument that in November 1995 the parties reached a separate, "ad hoc" agreement to arbitrate whether the parties had *formed* a binding charter party. Preliminarily, the court noted that "the existence of an agreement to arbitrate is a threshold question for a court to resolve, absent a clear and unmistakable delegation of that authority to an arbitrator." *Titan I*, 16 F. Supp. 2d at 337 (citing *First Options of Chicago, Inc. v. Kaplan*, 514 U.S. 938, 943

(1995)). The court also observed that "where the parties contest the formation of an agreement, 'any silence or ambiguity about whether such a question is arbitrable reverses the usual presumption that issues should be resolved in [arbitration's] favor.'" *Id.* at 338 (quoting *Abram Landau Real Estate v. Bevona*, 123 F.3d 69, 72 (2d Cir. 1997) (citing *First Options*, 514 U.S. at 943)). The court then found that although the parties had begun negotiating such an "ad hoc" agreement around November 1, Zhen Hua cut off such negotiations on November 2 when it stated, "There is no need for a separate arbitration agreement." *Id.* Therefore, the court concluded, the parties never formed a separate agreement to arbitrate whether they had formed a charter party.

On appeal, Zhen Hua argues that the district court erroneously relied on *First Options* to require evidence that the parties had "clear[ly] and unmistakabl[y]" delegated authority to an arbitrator to decide the question of *charter* formation. Instead, Zhen Hua contends, the district court should have applied the contract formation standards articulated by the Convention to find that the parties had formed an "ad hoc" agreement to arbitrate formation of the charter party.

In *First Options*, the Supreme Court addressed, *inter alia*, the "narrow" issue of the appropriate "standard of review applied to an arbitrator's decision about arbitrability." 514 U.S. at 942. In defining this issue, the Court delineated the three types of disagreement between the parties: (1) whether the defendants were liable to the plaintiffs; (2) whether the parties agreed to arbitrate the issue of liability; and (3) whether the courts or the arbitrators possess the primary power to decide the second question. *See id.* The issue presented to the Supreme Court was the third question, which the Court reformulated as "Does that power belong primarily to the arbitrators (because the court reviews their arbitrability decision deferentially) or to the court (because the court makes up its mind about arbitrability independently)?" *Id.* Answering this question, the Supreme Court held that "[c]ourts should not assume that the parties agreed to arbitrate arbitrability unless there is 'clea[r] and unmistakabl[e] evidence that they did so,'" *id.* at 944 (second and third alterations in the original), and that any silence or ambiguity about whether such a question is arbitrable reverses the usual presumption that issues should be resolved in favor of arbitration [citation omitted].

Zhen Hua is correct that the standard articulated by the Supreme Court in *First Options* is not apposite to the precise question presented to the district court. Unlike *First Options*, the instant case required the district court to determine whether the parties formed an "ad hoc" agreement to arbitrate whether they had formed a charter party — an issue analogous to the second of the three disagreements between the litigants in *First Options*. On appeal, neither Zhen Hua nor Titan contends that an arbitrator should resolve this question; instead the parties disagree as to whether the court below correctly answered this question.

Zhen Hua errs, however, in asserting that the district court applied the *First Options* standard in deciding whether the parties had formed an "ad hoc" arbitration agreement. When read in context, the passage of the district court's opinion relying on *First Options* (and *Abram Landau*) makes clear that the district court invoked the standard only to note preliminarily that the dispute over formation was properly before it rather than an arbitrator. *See Titan I*, 16 F. Supp.

2d at 337–38. Furthermore, the ensuing analysis by the district court reveals that the district court correctly evaluated the written communications under general principles of the law of contract formation (consistent with the Convention) in finding that Zhen Hua had terminated negotiations over an "ad hoc" arbitration agreement. [Citation omitted.] Having determined that the district court did not apply the *First Options* standard, we conclude further that the district court did not commit clear error in finding that the parties did not reach a binding "ad hoc" agreement to arbitrate the issue of formation of the charter party. On November 2, 1995, Zhen Hua rejected Titan's proposal to arbitrate the issue of charter formation in New York, stating:

> PLS DO NOT DEVIATE BY INTRODUCING NEW FORUM SELECTION. SHELL TIME 4 CAMARO PROFORMA IS VERY CLEAR ON THE SIMPLIFIED ARBITRATION WHICH HAS BEEN AGREED BY U.S. TITAN AND AGREEABLE TO SOUTHERN SHIPPING AS WELL. THERE IS NO NEED FOR A SEPARATE [sic] ARBITRATION AGREEMENT AT AL [sic].

The district court did not commit clear error in finding this statement to be a rejection of the idea of an arbitration agreement extraneous to the charter party. However, even if *we* were to interpret the statement to constitute an acceptance of the offer to arbitrate charter formation combined with a proposal that the parties employ the procedures set forth in the form agreement serving as the basis for the purported charter party, we could not override the factfinder's interpretation because the November 1 communication is certainly susceptible of both meanings.

Subsequent communications between the parties bolster our conclusion that the district court's findings were not clearly erroneous. The November 7 communication from Zhen Hua acknowledged Titan's notification of arbitration pursuant to Clause 41(c) of the charter party, and removed the confusion over previous references to "Southern Shipping," but failed to specify that the parties were arbitrating the issue of the formation of the charter. Titan then requested confirmation that the parties were agreeing to arbitrate in accordance with the very charter party to which Titan believed Zhen Hua was bound. Although Zhen Hua replied that "[o]wners reiterate that both sides have an agreement to arbitrate in London via simplified procedure according to Shell Time 4 Clause 41(c) Camaro Proforma to ascertain whether there is a charter between Guangzhou Zhen Hua and U.S. Titan," Titan never responded to this suggestion that the parties were arbitrating the issue of the existence of the charter party. Instead, Titan responded that arbitration was acceptable "per the agreement," which the district court reasonably construed to mean the charter party itself. *See Titan I*, 16 F. Supp. 2d at 338 n.13. From November 1995 until February 1996, the parties dickered over arbitrators, never clarifying what exactly they were arbitrating or which agreement bound them to arbitrate. As a result, we hold that the district court did not commit clear error by finding that the negotiations never resulted in a "meeting of the minds" sufficient to form a binding "ad hoc" agreement to arbitrate whether they had entered into a charter party.

b. *The Charter Party*

Although the district court determined that the parties did not form an "ad hoc" arbitration agreement, the district court granted Titan's motion to compel arbitration on the ground that the parties had formed a binding charter party that included an arbitration clause. Specifically, the court concluded that the parties formed a charter party through their respective brokers no later than September 26, 1995, on which date Titan's broker (Seabrokers) confirmed the agreement by faxing both parties a "recap" or "fixture." *See id.* at 339. Relying on this Court's decision in *Great Circle Lines*, the district observed that "[a] 'recap' communication, or 'fixture,' is recognized throughout the shipping industry as an agreement to a charter party's essential terms." *Titan I*, 16 F. Supp. 2d at 339 (citing *Great Circle Lines*, 681 F.2d at 125, 125 n.2). In the court's view, the "recap" embodied the charter party's main terms by incorporating the terms of Shell Time 4 Charter, a standard form charter, which included an arbitration clause. *See id.*

The court then rejected on two grounds Zhen Hua's argument that the charter party did not come into force due to the alleged failure of one of its "subjects" — the approval of the charter party by Titan's board of directors upon receipt of the inspection report. First, the court found that the weight of the evidence demonstrated that Titan's board did approve the charter party within the agreed time period. *See id.* Second, relying again on *Great Circle Lines*, the court held that "a 'subject detail' does not create a condition subsequent to a charter party." *Id.* As a result, the court ordered that the parties arbitrate in London pursuant to the charter party's arbitration clause any disputes arising under the charter party. *See id.* at 340. In a subsequent opinion the court clarified that the London "arbitrators may determine whether the actions of either party, subsequent to the formation of the charter party, have vitiated the agreement." *Titan II*, 182 F.R.D. at 101.

On appeal, Zhen Hua contends that the district court made an erroneous finding as to the existence of a charter party. Zhen Hua does not contest, however, that the district court's finding was in accordance with the standard set forth in *Great Circle Lines*, which holds that a "recap" communication, such as the one sent on September 26, 1995 in the instant case, represents "an agreement as to the charter party's main terms," with the "subject details" being no more than an acknowledgment of an intention to continue negotiations. Instead, Zhen Hua calls for the overruling of *Great Circle Lines*, asserting that its holding conflicts with the laws of the United Kingdom and with the trade practices of the shipping industry at large. Unpopular though it may be, *Great Circle Lines* is binding precedent, and we "will not overrule a prior decision of a panel of this Court absent a change in the law by higher authority or by way of an in banc proceeding of this Court." *Samuels v. Mann*, 13 F.3d 522, 526 (2d Cir. 1993).

Given that the district court (as well as this Court) is bound by *Great Circle Lines*, the district court correctly applied *Great Circle Lines* to find that the parties had formed a charter party. . . .

. . . .

B. *Subject Matter Jurisdiction under the FSIA*

Zhen Hua moved the trial court to dismiss Titan's petition for lack of subject matter jurisdiction on the ground Zhen Hua was immune from suit under the FSIA. The district court agreed with Zhen Hua, and no dispute exists here, that Zhen Hua qualifies as a "foreign state" under the FSIA because it is a corporation owned by the People's Republic of China. *See Titan I*, 16 F. Supp. 2d at 333. Nevertheless, the district court held that Zhen Hua fell within two exceptions to the FSIA's grant of jurisdictional immunity to foreign states: (1) the arbitration exception, *see* 28 U.S.C. § 1605(a)(6)(B); and (2) the commercial activities exception, *see id.* § 1605(a)(2). 11 *See Titan I*, 16 F. Supp.2d at 334, 335. Because we hold the former exception applicable, we do not address the latter.

The standard of review applicable to district court decisions regarding subject matter jurisdiction under the FSIA is clear error for factual findings and de novo for legal conclusions. [Citation omitted.]

The so-called arbitration exception to the FSIA provides in pertinent part:

> A foreign state shall not be immune from the jurisdiction of courts of the United States or of the States in any case—
>
> . . . .
>
> (6) in which the action is brought, either to enforce an agreement made by the foreign state with or for the benefit of a private party to submit to arbitration all or any differences which have arisen or which may arise between the parties with respect to a defined legal relationship, whether contractual or not, concerning a subject matter capable of settlement by arbitration under the laws of the United States, or to confirm an award made pursuant to such an agreement to arbitrate, if . . . (B) the agreement or award is or may be governed by a treaty or other international agreement in force for the United States calling for the recognition and enforcement of arbitral awards . . . 28 U.S.C. § 1605(a).

The district court found that, because China and the United States were both signatories to the Convention, and because Titan alleged that the parties had entered into a charter party containing an arbitration clause, it had jurisdiction to determine whether the parties formed an agreement to arbitrate so as to vitiate Zhen Hua's immunity under the FSIA. [Citation omitted.]

On appeal, Zhen Hua contends that, because there was an "ad hoc" agreement to arbitrate the issue of whether a charter party existed, the arbitration clause in the "alleged charter" could not form the basis for waiver of immunity by Zhen Hua under § 1605(a)(6)(B). Zhen Hua further asserts that the exception "might have applied if *Titan* had sought to enforce *the 'ad hoc' agreement* and to compel [Zhen Hua] to arbitrate in London the question of whether a binding charter had been concluded [but that] Titan . . . never asked for such relief, nor did [Zhen Hua], who raised the 'ad hoc' agreement only defensively in seeking dismissal or a stay of the suit." Appellant's Brf. at 20.

In light of our ruling above that the district court did not commit clear error in finding that parties did *not* form an "ad hoc" arbitration agreement, we need not further address Zhen Hua's argument. Instead, we hold simply that the arbitration clause contained in the charter party satisfies the requirements of arbitration exception to the FSIA.

C. *Personal Jurisdiction*

Zhen Hua also moved the district court to dismiss for lack of personal jurisdiction. After noting that subject matter jurisdiction and personal jurisdiction over foreign sovereigns are nearly coextensive, the court determined that Zhen Hua's contractual negotiations with Titan satisfied constitutional due process requirements. See *Titan I*, 16 F. Supp. 2d at 335–36. On appeal, Zhen Hua attacks the latter conclusion, arguing that (1) its contacts with the United States were not substantial, continuous and systematic, or purposeful in the sense required to satisfy due process concerns, and (2) the actions of Seagos cannot be imputed to Zhen Hua because Seagos served as a broker rather than an agent. We disagree.

The standard of review applicable to district court decisions regarding personal jurisdiction is clear error for factual findings and de novo for legal conclusions. [Citation omitted.]

In general, "subject matter jurisdiction plus service of process equals personal jurisdiction" under the FSIA. *Texas Trading & Milling Corp. v. Federal Republic of Nigeria*, 647 F.2d 300, 308 (2d Cir. 1981). Zhen Hua does not contend that service of process was improper. However, the exercise of personal jurisdiction under the FSIA must also comport with the Due Process Clause, *see id.* at 313, which permits a forum to exercise personal jurisdiction over a non-resident defendant who has "certain minimum contacts [with the forum] . . . such that the maintenance of the suit does not offend 'traditional notions of fair play and substantial justice,'" *Calder v. Jones*, 465 U.S. 783, 788 (1984) (quoting *Milliken v. Meyer*, 311 U.S. 457, 463 (1940), and *International Shoe Co. v. Washington*, 326 U.S. 310, 316 (1945)).

In invoking the "continuous and systematic" contacts test of *Helicopteros Nacionales de Colombia, S.A. v. Hall*, 466 U.S. 408 (1983), Zhen Hua fails to distinguish between "general personal jurisdiction" and "limited" or "specific" personal jurisdiction. General personal jurisdiction, which does require a finding of "continuous and systematic" contacts, is only necessary when the cause of action does not arise from the defendant's contacts with the forum state. [Citation omitted.] *Where, as here, the claim arises out of, or relates to, the defendant's contacts with the forum, i.e., the negotiation of the charter party with an American corporation located in New York and the use of brokers in Connecticut, the defendant need only prove "limited" or "specific" jurisdiction.* [Emphasis added; citation omitted.] In such a case, the required minimum contacts exist where the defendant "purposefully availed" itself of the privilege of doing business in the forum and could foresee being "haled into court" there. [Citations omitted.]

In addition, a court must determine whether the assertion of personal jurisdiction "comports with 'traditional notions of fair play and substantial justice'— that is, whether it is reasonable under the circumstances of a particular case." *Metropolitan Life Ins. Co. v. Robertson-Ceco Corp.*, 84 F.3d 560, 568 (2d Cir. 1996) (quoting *International Shoe*, 326 U.S. at 316).

Whether it is "reasonable" to exercise jurisdiction in a particular case depends on "(1) the burden that the exercise of jurisdiction will impose on the defendant; (2) the interests of the forum state in adjudicating the case; (3) the plaintiff's interest in obtaining convenient and effective relief; (4) the interstate judicial system's interest in obtaining the most efficient resolution of the controversy; and (5) the shared interest of the states in furthering substantive social policies." *Chaiken*, 119 F.3d at 1028 (quoting *Metropolitan Life*, 84 F.3d at 568).

Here, the record establishes that Zhen Hua "purposely availed itself" of the United States forum by negotiating and forming a contract with an American corporation located in New York. To facilitate the negotiations Zhen Hua utilized a broker located in Connecticut, which communicated with Titan personnel in New York via telex and/or facsimile to Titan's broker in Connecticut. Having engaged in this commercial conduct, Zhen Hua should have foreseen the possibility of being "haled into [an American] court" if a dispute were to arise out of the negotiations. Furthermore, Zhen Hua proffers no reason to believe that litigating in New York for the sole purpose of referring this matter to arbitration in London will impose or has imposed any undue hardship. Given the conduct of Zhen Hua, the nature and purpose of the litigation, and Titan's interest in obtaining an efficient referral to arbitration, the district court's exercise of personal jurisdiction was reasonable. Accordingly, the district court correctly concluded that it possessed personal jurisdiction over Zhen Hua.

D. *Venue*

Finally, Zhen Hua moved the district court to dismiss the action for improper venue. The district court denied the motion, holding that the facsimile and telephone communications between Titan's offices in Pelham, New York and the brokers' offices in Connecticut constituted a substantial part of the events giving rise to the action. *See Titan I*, 16 F. Supp.2d at 336–37. On appeal, Zhen Hua argues that the court erred by relying on an inapplicable subsection of the venue statute and grounding its conclusion upon the fact that Titan and its broker sent communications between New York and Connecticut.

We have not previously decided whether we review a district court's determination of venue for abuse of discretion or de novo, but we need not resolve the issue here because the district court's decision would be entitled to affirmance under either standard.

. . . .

III. CONCLUSION

For the foregoing reasons, we affirm the judgment of the district court. The parties should proceed to arbitration in London pursuant to the district court's August 5, 1998 opinion and order (as amended September 25, 1998) and September 29, 1998 opinion and order.

> **QUESTIONS**
>
> 1. What is the relationship between the Federal Arbitration Act and the New York Convention as applied in this case?
>
> 2. Based on what findings did Judge Parker find that Zhen Hua had sufficient "minimum" contacts with the forum to satisfy due process requirements for specific personal jurisdiction. Were his findings and application of the due process standard consistent with those of Judge Wood in *Koster v. Automark Industries, Incorporated, supra*, Chapter 6?
>
> 3. What options does a party objecting to arbitration have prior to the commencement of arbitration proceedings? What role, if any, do courts have? Would this role differ in cases involving choice of court agreements? In this case, was arbitration necessarily a less costly and more efficient means of adjudication?
>
> 4. Explain why would "subject matter jurisdiction plus service of process equals personal jurisdiction" in cases involving state-owned enterprises like *Zhen Hua*.

B. Canada

Our discussion of Canadian law related to arbitration agreements centers around two major decisions. Both deal with the enforceability of arbitration clause in standard form consumer contracts — one on a website — and thus lie outside of our main area of concern. Both, however, involve the law in Quebec and thus illustrate a variation of civil law approaches as well as the interrelationships of international private law and provincial law in the Canadian context. The first case also introduces us to another source of rules to govern international commercial arbitration — the *UNCITRAL Model Law on International Commercial Arbitration*. The cases are thus included, along with the dissents, despite their length and complexity.

DELL COMPUTER CORP. v. UNION DES CONSOMMATEURS
[2007] 2 S.C.R. 801, 2007 SCC 34

DESCHAMPS J.

The expansion of trade is without question spurring the development of rules governing international relations. Alternative dispute resolution mechanisms, including arbitration, are among the means the international community has adopted to increase efficiency in economic relationships. Concomitantly, in Quebec, recourse to arbitration has increased greatly owing this mechanism's flexibility when compared with the traditional justice system.

2. This appeal relates to the debate over the place of arbitration in Quebec's civil justice system. More specifically, the Court is asked to consider the validity and applicability of an arbitration agreement in the context of a domestic legal dispute under the rules of Quebec law and international law, and to determine whether the arbitrator or a court of law should rule first on these issues.

3. To ensure the internal consistency of the *Civil Code of Quebec*, S.Q. 1991, c. 64 ("C.C.Q."), it is necessary to adopt a contextual interpretation that limits the scope of the provisions of the title on the international jurisdiction of Quebec authorities to situations with a relevant foreign element. The prohibition in art. 3149 C.C.Q. against waiving the jurisdiction of Quebec authorities is found in that title and accordingly applies only to situations with a relevant foreign element. Since arbitration is in essence a neutral institution, it does not in itself have any foreign element. An arbitration tribunal has only those connections that the parties to the arbitration agreement intended it to have. The independence and territorial neutrality of arbitration are characteristics that must be promoted and preserved in order to foster the development of this institution. In the case at bar, the arbitration clause was not prohibited by any provision of Quebec legislation at the time it was invoked. Consequently, for the reasons that follow, I would allow the appeal, refer Mr. Dumoulin's claim to arbitration and dismiss the motion for authorization to institute a class action.

1. Facts

4. Dell Computer Corporation ("Dell") is a company that sells computer equipment retail over the Internet. It has its Canadian head office in Toronto and a place of business in Montreal. In the late afternoon of Friday, April 4, 2003, the order pages on Dell's English-language Web site indicated a price of $89 rather than $379 for the Axim X5 300 MHz handheld computer and a price of $118 rather than $549 for the Axim X5 400 MHz handheld computer. The pages of the site where the products were advertised listed the correct prices, however. On April 5, on being informed of the errors, Dell blocked access to the erroneous order pages through the usual address, although the pages were not withdrawn from the site. On the morning of April 7, Olivier Dumoulin, a Quebec consumer, was told about the prices by an acquaintance who sent him the detailed links, which the parties described as "deep links". These links made it possible to access the order pages without following the usual route, that is, through the home page and the advertising pages. In short, the deep links made it possible to circumvent the measures taken by Dell. Using a deep link, Mr. Dumoulin ordered a computer at the price of $89. Shortly after Mr. Dumoulin placed his order, Dell corrected the two price errors. That same day, Dell posted a price correction notice and at the same time announced that it would not process orders for computers at the prices of $89 and $118. At trial, a Dell employee testified that over the course of that weekend, 354 Quebec consumers had placed a total of 509 orders for these Axim computers, whereas on an average weekend, only one to three of them were sold in Quebec.

5. On April 17, Mr. Dumoulin put Dell in default, demanding that it honour his order at the price of $89. When Dell refused, the Union des consommateurs and Mr. Dumoulin ("Union") filed a motion for authorization to institute a class action

against Dell. Dell applied for referral of Mr. Dumoulin's claim to arbitration pursuant to an arbitration clause contained in the terms and conditions of sale, and dismissal of the motion for authorization to institute a class action. The Union contended that the arbitration clause was null and that, in any event, it could not be set up against Mr. Dumoulin.

2. Judicial History

6. The trial judge noted that according to the arbitration clause, arbitration proceedings were to be governed by the rules of the National Arbitration Forum ("NAF"), which is [TRANSLATION] "located in the United States". This led her to conclude that there was a foreign element for purposes of the rules of Quebec private international law and that the prohibition under art. 3149 C.C.Q., as interpreted in *Dominion Bridge Corp. v. Knai*, [1998] R.J.Q. 321 (C.A.), should apply. In her view, the arbitration clause could not be set up against Mr. Dumoulin. She then considered the criteria for instituting a class action and authorized the action against Dell ([2004] Q.J. No. 155 (QL)).

7. The Court of Appeal dismissed Dell's appeal from that decision ([2005] R.J.Q. 1448, 2005 QCCA 570). It began by expressing its disagreement with the Superior Court's application of the rules of Quebec private international law. According to the Court of Appeal, this was not a situation in which the consumer had waived the jurisdiction of Quebec authorities. It noted that the parties had agreed that the dispute was governed by the laws applicable in Quebec and that the arbitration could take place in Quebec. In its view, the instant case could be distinguished from *Dominion Bridge*, a case in which a foreign element had triggered the application of art. 3149 C.C.Q. However, the Court of Appeal concluded that the arbitration clause was external to the contract. Since Dell had not proven that the clause had been brought to the consumer's attention, the effect of art. 1435 C.C.Q. was that the clause could not be set up against him. The Court of Appeal then briefly discussed whether an issue arising under the *Consumer Protection Act*, R.S.Q., c. P-40.1, could be referred to arbitration and held that the Quebec legislature did not intend to preclude arbitration in such matters. Finally, it discussed, but did not accept, the argument that the class action should take precedence over arbitration, mentioning that the disputes that may not be submitted to arbitration are identified in the *Civil Code of Quebec* and certain specific statutes.

8. On November 9, 2006, the Quebec Minister of Justice tabled Bill 48, *An Act to amend the Consumer Protection Act and the Act respecting the collection of certain debts* (2nd Sess., 37th Leg.) ("Bill 48"), in the National Assembly. One of the Bill's provisions prohibits obliging a consumer to refer a dispute to arbitration. Bill 48, which came into force the day after the hearing of the appeal to this Court, does not include any transitional provisions applicable to this case.

3. Positions of the Parties

9. In this Court, the parties have reiterated the arguments raised in the Superior Court and the Court of Appeal. More specifically, Dell submits that the arbitration clause is not prohibited by any provision of Quebec legislation. It therefore is not

contrary to public order, is not prohibited by art. 3149 C.C.Q., and is neither external nor abusive. Dell also contends that the courts are limited to conducting a *prima facie* analysis of the validity of an arbitration clause and must leave it to the arbitrator to consider the clause on the merits. According to Dell, this approach, which is based on the "competence-competence" principle, was implicitly adopted by this Court in *Desputeaux v. Éditions Chouette (1987) inc.*, [2003] 1 S.C.R. 178, 2003 SCC 17, and the Superior Court should have applied it in the case at bar and referred the matter to an arbitrator to assess the validity of the clause based on the Union's submissions. The Union did not express an opinion on the degree of scrutiny to which the validity of the arbitration clause should be subject but did take a position, contrary to Dell's, on every other issue.

10. After Bill 48 came into force, the Court asked the parties to make written submissions regarding its applicability to the instant case. Dell raised three arguments in support of its position that Bill 48 does not affect the case: that the Bill does not have retroactive effect; that the new legislation cannot apply to disputes already before the courts; and that Dell had a vested right to the arbitration procedure provided for in the contract with Mr. Dumoulin. The Union advanced only one argument: that the provision on arbitration clauses merely confirms an existing prohibition.

11. The parties have raised many issues. In my view, the most significant one in the context of this case concerns the application of art. 3149 C.C.Q. This question is not only a potentially decisive one for the parties, but also one that involves the ordering of the rules in the *Civil Code of Quebec*; the answer to it will have repercussions on the interpretation of the other provisions of the title in which this article appears and on the interpretation of the Code in general. The analysis of this issue will lead me to consider the influence of international rules on Quebec law. These rules are also relevant to another issue: whether the competence-competence principle applies to the review of the application to refer the dispute to arbitration. The conclusion I will reach is that an arbitrator has jurisdiction to assess the validity and applicability of an arbitration clause and that, although there are exceptions, the decision regarding jurisdiction should initially be left to the arbitrator. However, in light of the state of the case, I will discuss all the issues that have been raised.

4. Application of Art. 3149 C.C.Q.

12. It will be helpful to reproduce the provision in issue and discuss its context. It reads as follows:

> 3149. A Quebec authority also has jurisdiction to hear an action involving a consumer contract or a contract of employment if the consumer or worker has his domicile or residence in Quebec; the waiver of such jurisdiction by the consumer or worker may not be set up against him.

This provision appears in Title Three, entitled "International Jurisdiction of Quebec Authorities," which is found in Book Ten of the *Civil Code of Quebec*, entitled "Private International Law." The Court must decide whether it applies in the case at bar. In my view, it is applicable only where there is a relevant foreign element that justifies resorting to the rules of Quebec private international law. I will explain why.

4.1 *Context of Application of the Rules on the International Jurisdiction of Quebec Authorities*

4.1.1 Purpose and Consequences of the Codification of Private International Law in the *Civil Code of Quebec*

13. When the Quebec legislature began the reform of the civil law in the mid-twentieth century, it did so in a way that was consistent with the civil law tradition in its purest form. As Professor Crépeau writes:

> [TRANSLATION] The Civil Code is an organic, ordered, structured, harmonious and cohesive whole that contains the substantive subject matters of private law, governing, in the civil law tradition, the legal status of persons and property, relationships between persons, and relationships between persons and property.
>
> (P.-A. Crépeau, "Une certaine conception de la recodification", in *Du Code civil du Quebec: Contribution à l'histoire immédiate d'une recodification réussie* (2005), 23, at p. 40)

14. The codification process therefore entailed a reflection on all the principles and on how to organize them in one central document with a view to simplifying and clarifying the rules, and thus making them more accessible. The organization of rules is an essential feature of codification. Professors Brierley and Macdonald describe the impact of this feature on the mode of presentation and the interpretation of the *Civil Code* as follows:

> A number of assumptions as to form underpin a Civil Code. Their common character is linked to notions of rationality and systematization, nicely captured by Weber's expression — formal rationality. To say that a Civil Code is, and must be understood as, systematic and rationally organized implies that it reflects a consciously chosen, integrated design for presenting the law that has been consistently followed. . . .
>
> The rational and systematic character of the Code also bears on its mode of presentation. One of the central features of the Code is its taxonomic structure. This affects both its organization and its drafting style. Just as the very existence of a Code labelled "Civil Code" presupposes a larger legal universe that can be divided and subdivided — public law, private law; and, within private law, procedure and substance; and, within substantive private law, commercial law and civil law — the same taxonomic approach is carried through into the Code itself. Its primary division is into large books — for example, persons, property, modes of acquisition of property, commercial law — each of which is subdivided into titles. Within these titles the Code is subdivided into chapters that, in turn, are divided into sections and sometimes into subsections. All the concepts relating to a given area of

the law are thus logically derived from first principles, meticulously developed, and systematically ordered. . . .

In this architectonic mode of presentation, the inventory of subjects selected for inclusion and the manner of their placement serve to define the range of meaning that each of the subjects so included may have. The initial organizational choices bear directly on the manner in which the Code adapts to changing circumstances. . . .

(J. E. C. Brierley and R. A. Macdonald, *Quebec Civil Law: An Introduction to Quebec Private Law* (1993), at 102–4)

15. In his commentaries on the *Civil Code of Quebec*, Quebec's Minister of Justice confirmed that the Code [TRANSLATION] "is a structured and hierarchical statutory scheme": *Commentaires du ministre de la Justice* (1993), vol. I, at p. VII. For this reason, it cannot be assumed that the jurists who took part in the reform placed the provisions of the *Civil Code of Quebec* in one title or another indiscriminately or without a concern for coherence. A codification process presupposes an ordering of rules, and the provisions of the title on the international jurisdiction of Quebec authorities reflect this general philosophy of codification.

4.1.2 Private International Law

16. Private international law is the branch of a state's domestic law that governs private relationships that [TRANSLATION] "exten[d] beyond the scope of a single national legal system": É. Wyler and A. Papaux, "Extranéité de valeurs et de systèmes en droit international privé et en droit international public", in É. Wyler and A. Papaux, eds., *L'extranéité ou le dépassement de l'ordre juridique étatique* (1999), 239, at p. 241. Since every state has the power to adopt its own system of rules, the result is a variety of conceptions of private international law. Thus, in some countries, this branch of law is limited to the conflict of laws, whereas in France, private international law has a broader scope, extending also to questions concerning the status of foreign nationals and the nationality of persons. In English private international law, an intermediate approach has been adopted that generally concerns three types of questions: (i) conflict of laws, (ii) conflict of jurisdictions and (iii) the recognition and enforcement of foreign judgments. [Reference omitted.] What is the situation in Quebec law?

4.1.3 Legislative History of Quebec Private International Law

17. The drafters of the original rules of Quebec private international law naturally drew on French law. Like the *Code Napoléon*, the *Civil Code of Lower Canada* contained only a few articles on this subject, and until the *Civil Code of Quebec* was enacted in 1991, they and a few provisions of the *Code of Civil Procedure*, R.S.Q., c. C-25 ("C.C.P."), and from specific statutes constituted the private international law of Quebec.

18. While Quebec's private international law was going through a period of relative stagnation in the nineteenth and early twentieth centuries, a growing number of states had recourse to codification, adopting increasingly comprehensive

and systematic rules. [References omitted.] The subsequent project to codify Quebec's private international law was part of that trend; it was included in the mandate for the proposed general reform of the *Civil Code* that was assigned to the Civil Code Revision Office ("Office") in 1965.

19. In 1975, an initial draft codification of the rules of Quebec private international law was submitted to the Office by its private international law committee, which was chaired by Professor J.-G. Castel. The content of this report was amended slightly and was incorporated two years later into Book Nine of the *Draft Civil Code* (Civil Code Revision Office, *Report on the Québec Civil Code* (1978), vol. I, *Draft Civil Code*, at pp. 593 et seq.). The preliminary chapter and Chapter I of Book Nine contained general provisions. Chapter II concerned conflicts of laws, while Chapter III dealt with conflicts of jurisdictions. Chapters IV and V dealt with the recognition and enforcement of foreign decisions and arbitration awards. Finally, Chapter VI codified the immunity from civil jurisdiction and execution enjoyed by foreign states and certain other international actors.

20. The structure of Book Nine attests to the Quebec legislature's adoption of the intermediate approach of English private international law described by Dicey, Morris and Collins and North and Fawcett (mentioned above). The Office's decision was the result of a process that stretched over many years.

21. The Office explained that Chapter III on conflicts of jurisdictions was adopted to make up for a lack of specific rules on private international law that had obliged courts to resort to the *Code of Civil Procedure*'s provisions on the judicial districts in Quebec where proceedings could be instituted:

> To remedy this state of affairs and *to distinguish* between international and domestic jurisdiction, it seemed necessary to provide *rules applicable exclusively to situations containing a foreign element*. [Emphasis added.]
>
> (Civil Code Revision Office, *Report on the Québec Civil Code* (1978), vol. II, t. 2, *Commentaries*, at p. 965)

22. In the commentaries that accompanied the final text of the *Civil Code of Québec*, the Minister of Justice mentioned a number of times that the various sections of Book Ten of the *Civil Code* apply to legal situations [TRANSLATION] "with a foreign element". He expressly repeated this in the introduction to Title Three on the international jurisdiction of Quebec authorities (*Commentaires du ministre de la Justice*, vol. II, at p. 1998). The Minister also reiterated the Office's comments on the need for a set of jurisdictional rules for private international law distinct from the rules of the *Code of Civil Procedure* upon which the courts had relied until then:

> [TRANSLATION] Since there were no rules for determining whether Quebec authorities had jurisdiction over disputes with a foreign element, the courts had extended the domestic law rules of jurisdiction provided for in the Code of Civil Procedure to such situations.
>
> The general objective of Title Three is to remedy this deficiency by establishing specific rules for determining the international jurisdiction of Quebec authorities . . . .

(*Commentaires du ministre de la Justice*, vol. II, at p. 1998)

23. These commentaries shed light on the distinction between rules of jurisdiction governing purely domestic disputes and those that, because of a foreign element, form part of private international law. Where domestic disputes are concerned, the question of adjudicative jurisdiction is governed by the *Code of Civil Procedure*. In the case at bar, arts. 31 and 1000 C.C.P. are the provisions that confer jurisdiction over class actions on the Quebec Superior Court.

24. Given that domestic disputes are governed by the general provisions of Quebec domestic law, there is no reason to apply the rules relating to the international jurisdiction of Quebec authorities to a dispute that involves no foreign element.

4.2 *Foreign Element Concept*

25. What is this foreign element that is omnipresent in the literature on private international law? Very little has been written about it. Of course, disputes in which rules of private international law are relied on usually have an international aspect and, as a result, the courts have not needed to elaborate on the parameters of the foreign element concept. One reference to this concept can be found in *Quebecor Printing Memphis Inc. v. Regenair Inc.*, [2001] R.J.Q. 966 (C.A.), at para. 17, in which Philippon J. (*ad hoc*), dissenting on another issue, described the initial step of the analytical approach in private international law:

> [TRANSLATION] First, it had to be determined whether the dispute related to an international situation or a transnational event or had a foreign element. (Emphasis deleted [in opinion].)

26. This foreign element can be defined, however. It must be "[a] point of contact which is legally relevant to a foreign country", which means that the contact must be sufficient to play a role in determining whether a court has jurisdiction: J. A. Talpis and J.-G. Castel, "Interpreting the rules of private international law", in *Reform of the Civil Code* (1993), vol. 5B, at p. 38 (emphasis added); *Castel & Walker: Canadian Conflict of Laws* (loose leaf), vol. 1, at p. 1-1; see also Wyler and Papaux, at p. 256.

27. Since our private international law is based on English law, it will be helpful to review the state of English law on this question. North and Fawcett define private international law as follows:

> Private international law, then, is that part of law which comes into play when the issue before the court affects some *fact, event or transaction that is so closely connected with a foreign system of law* as to necessitate recourse to that system. (Emphasis added[in opinion]; p. 5.)

This definition is similar to the one adopted by Canadian authors, and it includes a notion common to many systems of private international law: the factor connecting a matter with a particular system. It follows that the foreign element and the connecting factor are overlapping notions. One author describes the connecting factor concept as follows:

The connecting factor is the element forming one of the facts of the case which is selected in order to attach a question of law to a legal system. The connecting factor determines the applicable law or the jurisdiction of a court. For instance, if the facts of a case present a question of intestate succession to movables, the element among those facts selected for the designation of the applicable law may be the last domicile, the last habitual residence, the nationality of the deceased or the situs of the movables. Likewise, one of these connecting factors may be employed to establish the jurisdiction of the courts to deal with intestate succession to movables.

(F. Vischer, "Connecting Factors", in International Association of Legal Science, *International Encyclopedia of Comparative Law*, vol. III, *Private International Law* (1999), c. 4, at p. 3)

. . . .

28. These two concepts can, therefore, overlap. A connecting factor is a tie to either the domestic or a foreign legal system, whereas the foreign element concept refers to a possible tie to a foreign legal system. Thus, in a personal action brought in Quebec, the fact that a defendant is domiciled in Quebec is a connecting factor with respect to the Quebec legal system but not a foreign element, whereas the fact that a defendant is domiciled in England will be considered both a connecting factor with respect to English jurisdiction and a foreign element with respect to the Quebec legal system. Certain of the connecting factors enumerated in Professor Vischer's definition above are common to most systems of private international law [references omitted].

29. A state is free to determine what connecting factors or foreign elements it considers to be relevant. In Quebec, the legislature adopted a number of factors already found in the main Western private international law systems. In the title of the *Civil Code of Québec* on the conflict of laws, these factors are divided into four main categories, each of which is addressed in a separate chapter: (1) personal factors, with the main one being the place of domicile; (2) property-related factors; (3) factors related to obligations, such as the place where a contract is entered into; and (4) factors related to procedure, which is usually governed by the law of the court hearing the case (arts. 3083 to 3133 C.C.Q.).

30. The legislature also provided for certain connecting factors in respect of the international jurisdiction of Quebec authorities, which is the subject of a separate title. The place where one of the parties is domiciled heads the list of these factors, too. Article 3148 C.C.Q. shows this clearly:

3148. In personal actions of a patrimonial nature, a Québec authority has jurisdiction where

(1) the defendant has his domicile or residence in Québec;

(2) the defendant is a legal person, is not domiciled in Québec but has an establishment in Québec, and the dispute relates to its activities in Québec;

(3) a fault was committed in Québec, damage was suffered in Québec, an injurious act occurred in Québec or one of the obligations arising from a contract was to be performed in Québec;

(4) the parties have by agreement submitted to it all existing or future disputes between themselves arising out of a specified legal relationship;

(5) the defendant submits to its jurisdiction.

However, a Québec authority has no jurisdiction where the parties, by agreement, have chosen to submit all existing or future disputes between themselves relating to a specified legal relationship to a foreign authority or to an arbitrator, unless the defendant submits to the jurisdiction of the Québec authority.

See also arts. 3134, 3141 to 3147, 3149, 3150, and 3154, para. 2 C.C.Q. Other factors that are considered include the place where damage was suffered or an injurious act occurred (art. 3148, para. 1(3) C.C.Q.), and the place where the property in dispute is located (arts. 3152 to 3154, para. 1 C.C.Q.).

31. It can be seen that what these traditional factors have in common is a concrete connection with Quebec; if private international law is invoked, it can be assumed that there is an equally concrete foreign element that can serve as a basis for applying a foreign legal system. Despite the developments I have just mentioned, we should question the postulate that the rules of Quebec private international law apply only where there is a foreign element.

32. In the Office's *Draft Civil Code*, it was clear that a foreign element was necessary. In its commentary on the provision on the law applicable to juridical acts, the Office stated the following:

It should be noted that the text applies to juridical acts of an international character. The parties are not free to refer to a law not related to their act unless that act contains a foreign element.

(Civil Code Revision Office, *Report on the Québec Civil Code*, vol. II, t. 2, *Commentaries*, at p. 977 (commentary on art. 21 of Book Nine of the *Draft Civil Code*))

In discussing art. 48 of Book Nine of the *Draft Civil Code*, the predecessor of art. 3148 C.C.Q. on the international jurisdiction of Quebec authorities, the Office stated that the jurisdictional rules set out in this article "are intended to apply to situations involving a foreign element" (Civil Code Revision Office, vol. II, t. 2, at p. 988).

33. The 1988 draft bill did not substantively alter the traditional foreign element requirement (*An Act to add the reformed law of evidence and of prescription and the reformed private international law to the Civil Code of Québec*). The wording of art. 3477 of the draft bill on the designation of the applicable law was substantially similar to that of the final version of the provision in the *Civil Code of Québec* (art. 3111). It read as follows:

3477. A juridical act containing a foreign element is governed by the law expressly designated in the instrument or the designation of which may be inferred with certainty from the terms of the act.

A system of law may be expressly designated as applicable to the whole or a part only of a juridical act.

34. The reference in this article to the foreign element led professors Talpis and Goldstein to ask whether such a reference was necessary, since they considered the foreign element requirement to be essential:

> [TRANSLATION] It might first be asked whether it was necessary to specify that the parties may choose the applicable law only for a contract "containing a foreign element." It is obvious that the existence of a foreign element is the *sine qua non* of recourse to *all* the rules in Book Ten of the future Civil Code. However, since the Draft Bill does not include a specific provision on evasion of the law, this reference may have been intended to indicate that the will of the parties is not sufficient to turn a contract connected entirely with Quebec into an international one. [Underlining added.]

(J. A. Talpis and G. Goldstein, "Analyse critique de l'avant-projet de loi du Québec en droit international privé" (1989), 91 *R. du N.* 456, at p. 476)

As for art. 3511 of the 1988 draft bill, which concerned the international jurisdiction of Quebec authorities, it already contained all the substantive elements of the future art. 3148 C.C.Q.

35. In Bill 125 of 1990, the *Civil Code of Québec*, however, the foreign element requirement was not retained with respect to the designation of the applicable law. The legislature incorporated a special rule into the provision. The final version of art. 3111 includes an addition to the text that was initially proposed:

> 3111. A juridical act,* *whether or not it contains any foreign element*, is governed by the law expressly designated in the act or the designation of which may be inferred with certainty from the terms of the act. [Emphasis in opinion.]
>
> A juridical act containing no foreign element remains, nevertheless, subject to the mandatory provisions of the law of the country which would apply if none were designated.

The law of a country may be expressly designated as applicable to the whole or a part only of a juridical act.

What this addition brings to the title on the conflict of laws is to make it possible for the parties to provide that a purely domestic juridical act will be governed by the law of a foreign jurisdiction. However, immediately after recognizing the autonomy

---

* The term "juridical act" is one of several English language translations for a civil law concept with no Common Law equivalent. The term in French is *acte juridique*; in German, *rechtsgeshaft*; in Spanish, *acto juridico*, and in Japanese, *hōritsu kōi*. The term is used for private law "acts" created by either mutual (e.g., contracts) or unilateral (e.g., wills) manifestations of intent deemed by law to have legal validity and significance. A contract is the prototypical juridical act.

of the will of the parties where the designation of the applicable law is concerned, the legislature hastened to limit it in the second paragraph of the provision. Thus, in the absence of a foreign element, a juridical act remains subject to the mandatory rules that would apply if no law were designated. As a result, the designation of the law of a foreign jurisdiction in an act that contains no foreign element is a special circumstance that was cautiously introduced into Quebec private international law and is confined to the rules applicable to the conflict of laws.

36. I should add that the wording of art. 3111 C.C.Q. is based on that of art. 3 of the *Convention on the Law Applicable to Contractual Obligations* (Rome Convention of 1980), which authorizes the "[choice of] a foreign law" where there is no foreign element. It is also conceivable that the determination of the law applicable to a juridical act will at times require a more complex analysis than the one to be made where adjudicative jurisdiction is in issue. Thus, a juridical act, such as a giving of security, that appears to have only domestic connections may in reality be part of an international transaction whose ramifications are not in issue in a given dispute. So there are several possible explanations for the exception provided for in Title Two on the conflict of laws.

37. In the title on the international jurisdiction of Quebec authorities, on the other hand, there is no exception to the foreign element requirement, and it is clear that a court asked to apply the rules of private international law must first determine whether the situation involves a foreign element. This position is consistent with the traditional definition of private international law and with the Office's intention. It must now be asked whether, in the case at bar, the choice of arbitration procedure gives rise to a foreign element warranting the application of art. 3149 C.C.Q. To answer this question, it will be necessary to consider how arbitration has been incorporated into Quebec law.

4.3 Arbitration in Quebec

4.3.1 International Sources

38. International arbitration law is strongly influenced by two texts drafted under the auspices of the United Nations: the *Convention on the Recognition and Enforcement of Foreign Arbitral Awards*, 330 U.N.T.S. 3 ("New York Convention"), and the *UNCITRAL Model Law on International Commercial Arbitration*, U.N. Doc. A/40/17 (1985), Annex I ("Model Law").

39. The New York Convention entered into force in 1959. Article II of the Convention provides that a court of a contracting state that is seized of an action in a matter covered by an arbitration clause must refer the parties to arbitration. At present, 142 countries are parties to the Convention. The accession of this many countries is evidence of a broad consensus in favour of the institution of arbitration. Lord Mustill wrote the following about the Convention:

This Convention has been the most successful international instrument in the field of arbitration, and perhaps could lay claim to be the most effective instance of international legislation in the entire history of commercial law. [Reference omitted.]

Canada acceded to the New York Convention on May 12, 1986.

40. The Model Law is another fundamental text in the area of international commercial arbitration. It is a model for legislation that the UN recommends that states take into consideration in order to standardize the rules of international commercial arbitration. The Model Law was drafted in a manner that ensured consistency with the New York Convention. [References omitted.]

41. The final text of the Model Law was adopted on June 21, 1985 by the United Nations Commission on International Trade Law ("UNCITRAL"). In its explanatory note on the Model Law, the UNCITRAL Secretariat states that it:

> reflects a worldwide consensus on the principles and important issues of international arbitration practice. It is acceptable to States of all regions and the different legal or economic systems of the world.

("Explanatory Note by the UNCITRAL Secretariat on the Model Law on International Commercial Arbitration", U.N. Doc. A/40/17, Annex I, at para. 2)

In 1986, Parliament enacted the *Commercial Arbitration Act*, R.S.C. 1985, c. 17 (2nd Supp.), which was based on the Model Law. The Quebec legislature followed suit that same year and incorporated the Model Law into its legislation. Quebec's Minister of Justice at the time, Herbert Marx, reiterated the above-quoted comment by the UNCITRAL Secretariat: National Assembly, *Journal des débats*, vol. 29, No. 46, 1st Sess., 33rd Leg., June 16, 1986, at p. 2975, and vol. 29, No. 55, October 30, 1986, at p. 3672.

4.3.2 Nature and Scope of the 1986 Legislative Amendments to the *Civil Code of Lower Canada* and the *Code of Civil Procedure*

42. In 1986, the *Act to amend the Civil Code and the Code of Civil Procedure in respect of arbitration*, S.Q. 1986, c. 73 ("Bill 91"), which established a scheme for promoting arbitration in Quebec, was tabled in the legislature. Bill 91 added a new title on arbitration agreements to the *Civil Code of Lower Canada*. This title consisted of only six provisions setting out a few general principles relating to the validity and applicability of such agreements. The legislature's decision to place arbitration agreements among the nominate contracts in the *Civil Code of Lower Canada* is significant. After that, there was no longer any reason to regard arbitration agreements as being outside the sphere of the general law; on the contrary, they were now an integral part of it. [References omitted.] The provisions added by Bill 91 would be restated without any major changes in the chapter of the *Civil Code of Québec* on arbitration agreements.

43. Bill 91 also had a considerable impact on the *Code of Civil Procedure*. Substantial additions were made to Book VII on arbitrations, which was divided into two titles. Title I is a veritable code of arbitral procedure that regulates every step of an arbitration proceeding subject to Quebec law, from the appointment of the arbitrator to the order of the proceeding to the award and homologation. Most of these rules apply only "where the parties have not made stipulations to the contrary" (art. 940 C.C.P.). Title II sets out a system of rules applicable to the recognition and execution of arbitration awards made outside Quebec.

44. Although Bill 91 was the Quebec legislature's response to Canada's accession

to the New York Convention and to UNCITRAL's adoption of the Model Law, it is not identical to those two instruments. As the Quebec Minister of Justice noted, Bill 91 was [TRANSLATION] "inspired" by the Model Law and [TRANSLATION] "implement[ed]" the New York Convention: *Journal des débats*, October 30, 1986, at p. 3672. For this reason, it is important to consider the interplay between Quebec's domestic law and private international law before interpreting the provisions of Bill 91.

45. This Court analysed the interplay between the New York Convention and Bill 91 in *GreCon Dimter inc. v. J.R. Normand inc.*, [2005] 2 S.C.R. 401, 2005 SCC 46, at paras. 39 *et seq.* After noting that there is a recognized presumption of conformity with international law, the Court mentioned that Bill 91 "incorporate[s] the principles of the *New York Convention*" and concluded that the Convention is a formal source for interpreting the provisions of Quebec law governing the enforcement of arbitration agreements: para. 41. This conclusion is confirmed by art. 948, para. 2 C.C.P., which provides that the interpretation of Title II on the recognition and execution of arbitration awards made outside Quebec (arts. 948 to 951.2 C.C.P.) "shall take into account, where applicable, the [New York] Convention".

46. The same is not true of the Model Law. Unlike an instrument of conventional international law, the Model Law is a non-binding document that the United Nations General Assembly has recommended that states take into consideration. Thus, Canada has made no commitment to the international community to implement the Model Law as it did in the case of the New York Convention. Nevertheless, art. 940.6 C.C.P. attaches considerable interpretive weight to the Model Law in international arbitration cases:

> **940.6** Where matters of extraprovincial or international trade are at issue in an arbitration, *the interpretation* of this Title, *where applicable, shall take into consideration* [emphasis in opinion]:
>
> (1) the Model Law on International Commercial Arbitration as adopted by the United Nations Commission on International Trade Law on 21 June 1985;
>
> (2) the Report of the United Nations Commission on International Trade Law on the work of its eighteenth session held in Vienna from the third to the twenty-first day of June 1985;
>
> (3) the Analytical Commentary on the draft text of a model law on international commercial arbitration contained in the report of the Secretary-General to the eighteenth session of the United Nations Commission on International Trade Law.

47. In short, to quote Professor Brierley, Bill 91 opened Quebec arbitration law to "international thinking" in this area; this international thinking "has become a formal source of Quebec positive law": J. E. C. Brierley, "Quebec's New (1986) Arbitration Law" (1987-88), 13 *Can. Bus. L.J.* 58, at pp. 63 and 68-69.

4.3.3 Status of Arbitration in Quebec Private International Law

48. Bill 91 established the legal framework applicable to arbitration. Not all arbitration proceedings are subject to the same rules. First, Title I on arbitration proceedings applies only if the parties have not stipulated that they intend to opt out of it. In addition, the facts of the case must call for application of the *Code of Civil Procedure* either because the foreign parties have chosen it in accordance with a provision authorizing them to do so in a law that would otherwise govern this proceeding or because the circumstances of the proceeding necessitate the application of Quebec law. Second, Title II of Book VII of the *Code of Civil Procedure* contains special provisions on the recognition and execution of arbitration awards made outside Quebec. Third, art. 940.6 C.C.P. provides that Title I on arbitration proceedings is to be interpreted in light, where applicable, of the Model Law and certain documents related to it "[w]here matters of extraprovincial or international trade are at issue in an arbitration." As Professor Marquis notes, the words *"mettant en cause des intérêts du commerce"* in the French version of art. 940.6 have an [TRANSLATION] "unfamiliar sound in Quebec law": L. Marquis, "Le droit français et le droit québécois de l'arbitrage conventionnel," in H. P. Glenn, ed., *Droit québécois et droit français: communauté, autonomie, concordance* (1993), 447, at p. 483. In fact, they were taken straight from the French *Code de procédure civile*:

> [TRANSLATION] **1492.** Arbitration is international where matters of international trade are at issue.

Because the same words are used, Quebec authors agree that art. 940.6 C.C.P. has imported the concept of international arbitration from French law. [References omitted.]

49. The matter of international trade test is different from connecting factors such as the parties' place of residence or the place where the obligations are performed. Thus, a contractual legal situation may have foreign elements without involving any matters of extraprovincial or international trade; in such a case, although the resulting arbitration will not be considered an international arbitration, it will nonetheless be subject to the rules of private international law. Since the case at bar does not involve international commercial arbitration, this explanation is intended merely to highlight the fact that the test under art. 940.6 C.C.P. is clearly distinct from the foreign element requirement. Where the Quebec legislature intended different rules to apply, it has made this clear.

50. The rules on arbitration proceedings set out in Title I of Book VII of the *Code of Civil Procedure* apply, to the extent provided for, to any arbitration proceeding subject to Quebec law. The parties are free to attribute foreign connections to an arbitration process, in which case the rules of private international law may be applicable. However, an arbitration clause is not in itself a foreign element warranting the application of the rules of Quebec private international law. The commentators are unanimous on this point:

> [TRANSLATION] It is clear that if an arbitration process is considered to be purely internal to Quebec, the law of Quebec will be applied to it. The rules of private international law will not be applicable. It is Quebec's Code of Civil Procedure (rules on arbitration) that will be applied.

(J. Béguin, *L'arbitrage commercial international* (1987), at p. 67)

[Additional reference omitted.]

51. The neutrality of arbitration as an institution is one of the fundamental characteristics of this alternative dispute resolution mechanism. Unlike the foreign element, which suggests a possible connection with a foreign state, arbitration is an institution without a forum and without a geographic basis. [References omitted.] Arbitration is part of no state's judicial system. [References omitted]. The arbitrator has no allegiance or connection to any single country. [Reference omitted.] In short, arbitration is a creature that owes its existence to the will of the parties alone. [Citation omitted.]

52. To say that the choice of arbitration as a dispute resolution mechanism gives rise to a foreign element would be tantamount to saying that arbitration itself establishes a connection to a given territory, and this would be in outright contradiction to the very essence of the institution of arbitration: its neutrality. This institution is territorially neutral; it contains no foreign element. Furthermore, the parties to an arbitration agreement are free, subject to any mandatory provisions by which they are bound, to choose any place, form and procedures they consider appropriate. They can choose cyberspace and establish their own rules. It was open to the parties in the instant case to refer to the *Code of Civil Procedure*, to base their procedure on a Quebec or U.S. arbitration guide or to choose rules drawn up by a recognized organization, such as the International Chamber of Commerce, the Canadian Commercial Arbitration Centre or the NAF. The choice of procedure does not alter the institution of arbitration in any of these cases. The rules become those of the parties, regardless of where they are taken from.

53. I cannot therefore see how the parties' choice of arbitration can in itself create a foreign element. Such an interpretation would empty the foreign element concept of all meaning. An arbitration that contains no foreign element in the true sense of the word is a domestic arbitration. The rules on the international jurisdiction of Quebec authorities will apply only to an arbitration containing a foreign element, such as where a defendant in a case involving a personal claim is domiciled in another country.

54. It must now be determined whether the facts of the present case contain a foreign element.

4.4 Seeking to Identify a Foreign Element in the Facts of the Case at Bar

55. The trial judge saw a foreign element in the fact that [TRANSLATION] "[t]he NAF is located in the United States" (para. 32). The Court of Appeal rejected this conclusion, and the Union has abandoned this argument. Like other organizations, such as the International Chamber of Commerce and the Canadian Commercial Arbitration Centre, the NAF offers arbitration services. The place where decisions concerning arbitration services are made or where the employees of these organizations work has no impact on the disputes in which their rules are used.

56. Thus, the location of the NAF's head office is not a relevant foreign element for purposes of the application of Quebec private international law. Moreover, Dell

having conceded that the arbitration proceeding will take place in Quebec should put an end to the debate regarding the place of arbitration.

57. Another potential foreign element is found in the NAF's Code of Procedure (*National Arbitration Forum Code of Procedure*). Rules 50 and 48B of the NAF Code provide that, unless the parties agree otherwise, arbitrations and arbitration procedures are governed by the U.S. *Federal Arbitration Act*. In Quebec, designation of the applicable law is governed by Title Two of Book Ten of the *Civil Code of Québec* on the conflict of laws. The parties' designation of the applicable law under this title is not ordinarily recognized as a foreign element in the subsequent title on the international jurisdiction of Quebec authorities. In any event, since art. 3111 C.C.Q., which I discussed above, refers to designation of the law applicable to a juridical act containing no foreign element, the designation itself does not produce such an element.

58. The Union raised a final element: the language of the proceedings. According to the NAF Code, English is the language used in NAF proceedings, although the parties may choose another language, in which case the NAF or the arbitrator may order the parties to provide any necessary translation and interpretation services at their own cost (rules 11D and 35G of the NAF Code).

59. In my view, the language argument must fail. Although I agree that the use of a language with which the consumer is not familiar may cause difficulties, neither the French nor the English language can be characterized as a foreign element in Canada.

60. My colleagues Bastarache and LeBel JJ. nonetheless consider it logical to accept that an arbitration clause in itself constitutes a foreign element that can result in application of the provisions on the international jurisdiction of Quebec authorities. Their interpretation has consequences for agreements other than consumer contracts. Thus, it would also be impossible to set up against a Quebec worker *any* undertaking to submit to an arbitrator any future disputes with his or her Quebec employer relating to an individual contract of employment. Furthermore, *any* arbitration agreement concerning damage suffered as a result of exposure to raw materials originating in Quebec would be null (see arts. 3151 and 3129 C.C.Q.), even an agreement between a Quebec supplier and a Quebec producer. This interpretation is hard to accept. It implies that the codifiers failed to achieve their objective of ordering the rules in both Book Ten on private international law and Chapter XVIII on arbitration agreements in Book Five. This is an important point, and it is not strictly confined to the foreign element argument. I will therefore consider it separately.

4.5 Ordering of the Rules on Arbitration

61. The chapter on arbitration is found in the important Book Five of the *Civil Code of Québec* on obligations. Book Five is divided into two titles, the first of which concerns obligations in general, while the second concerns nominate contracts. Chapter XVIII is the final chapter of the title on nominate contracts. It incorporates the provisions of Bill 91 enacted in 1986, which I have already discussed. It contains a general provision, art. 2638 C.C.Q., which is based on the recognition that an

arbitration agreement is valid and can be set up against a party:

> **2638.** An arbitration agreement is a contract by which the parties undertake to submit a present or future dispute to the decision of one or more arbitrators, to the exclusion of the courts.

In his commentary on this provision, the Minister of Justice stated that the essential purpose of the arbitration agreement is [TRANSLATION] "to displace judicial intervention" and that "by conferring jurisdiction on arbitrators, [one] ousts the usual jurisdiction of the judiciary": *Commentaires du ministre de la Justice*, vol. II, at p. 1649.

62. Chapter XVIII also contains a provision that enumerates the cases in which the jurisdiction of the Quebec courts cannot be ousted by the parties. This provision reads as follows:

> 2639. Disputes over the status and capacity of persons, family matters or other matters of public order may not be submitted to arbitration.
>
> An arbitration agreement may not be opposed on the ground that the rules applicable to settlement of the dispute are in the nature of rules of public order.

63. Thus, the codifiers laid down, for disputes containing no foreign element, specific rules dealing, on the one hand, with the effect of the arbitration agreement and, on the other, with cases in which arbitration is not available under domestic law. They therefore considered what matters should be arbitrable. Where disputes not involving private international law issues are concerned, these matters are set out in the provisions governing arbitration. Article 3148, para. 2 C.C.Q. does not simply restate the text of art. 2638 C.C.Q. Rather, it lays down the same rule as it applies to an arbitration agreement containing a foreign element. To give arts. 3149 and 3151 C.C.Q. general application, it would be necessary to infer that the codifiers were inconsistent in not including, in the chapter on arbitration, the exceptions relating to consumer contracts, contracts of employment and claims regarding exposure to raw materials.

64. Furthermore, to view art. 3149 C.C.Q. as being limited to private international law is consistent with the legislature's objective. This provision is one of the new measures the legislature inserted into the title on the international jurisdiction of Quebec authorities to protect certain more vulnerable groups. *Commentaires du ministre de la Justice*, vol. II, at p. 2011. Article 3149 C.C.Q. refers to two of these groups, Quebec consumers and workers, who cannot waive the jurisdiction of a Quebec authority. I agree with the following comment by Beauregard J.A. of the Quebec Court of Appeal in *Dominion Bridge* with regard to the legislature's general objective in enacting art. 3149 C.C.Q.:

> [TRANSLATION] In my view, it is clear that the legislature intended to ensure that employees could not be required to go abroad to assert rights under a contract of employment. [p. 325]

Thus, the reason why an arbitration clause cannot be set up against a consumer under the title on the international jurisdiction of Quebec authorities is clearly to protect a consumer in a situation with a foreign element.

65. In enacting art. 3149 C.C.Q., the legislature could not have intended to take an obscure approach requiring a decontextualized reading of the title on the international jurisdiction of Quebec authorities. The interpretation of art. 3149 C.C.Q. must be consistent with the legislature's objective of protecting vulnerable groups and must be harmonized not only with the title on the international jurisdiction of Quebec authorities, but also with the entire book of the C.C.Q. on private international law and Chapter XVIII on arbitration (in Title Two of Book Five), and with Book VII of the *Code of Civil Procedure* on arbitration. This brings out the internal consistency of these rules, which interact harmoniously and without redundancy. The general provisions on arbitration are grouped together in the books, titles and chapters of the *Civil Code of Québec* and the *Code of Civil Procedure*, and specific exceptions are set out in these provisions. It would not be appropriate to shatter the consistency of the rules on arbitration and those on the international jurisdiction of Quebec authorities by placing all disputes concerning an arbitrator's jurisdiction within the scope of the rules on the jurisdiction of Quebec authorities regardless of whether there is a foreign element.

4.6 Conclusion on the Application of Art. 3149 C.C.Q.

66. The legal experts who worked on the reform of the *Civil Code*, the Minister of Justice who was in office at the time of the enactment of the *Civil Code of Québec*, and many Canadian and foreign authors recognized that a foreign element was a prerequisite for applying the rules on the international jurisdiction of Quebec authorities. The ordering effected in a codification process and the rule that a provision must be interpreted in light of its context require an interpretation of art. 3149 C.C.Q. that limits it to cases with a foreign element.

67. I will now discuss the other issues before this Court. They concern the degree of scrutiny of an arbitration clause by the Superior Court, and the validity and applicability of the arbitration clause.

5. Degree of Scrutiny of an Arbitration Clause by the Superior Court in Considering a Referral Application

68. The objective of this part is to determine whether it is the arbitrator or a court that should rule first on the parties' arguments on the validity or applicability of an arbitration agreement. I will accordingly consider the limits of intervention by the courts in cases involving arbitration agreements.

5.1 Competence of Arbitrators to Rule on Their Own Jurisdiction in International Law

69. There are two opposing schools of thought in the debate over the degree of judicial scrutiny of an arbitrator's jurisdiction under an arbitration agreement. Under one, it is the court that must rule first on the arbitrator's jurisdiction; this view is based on a concern to avoid a duplication of proceedings. Since the court has the power to review the arbitrator's decision regarding his or her jurisdiction, why should the arbitrator be allowed to make an initial ruling on this issue? According to this view, it would be preferable to have the court settle any challenge to the arbitrator's jurisdiction immediately. This first school of thought thus favours an

interventionist judicial approach to questions relating to the jurisdiction of arbitrators.

70. The other school of thought gives precedence to the arbitration process. It is concerned with preventing delaying tactics and is associated with the principle commonly known as the "competence-competence" principle. According to it, arbitrators should be allowed to exercise their power to rule first on their own jurisdiction (Gaillard and Savage, at p. 401).

71. The New York Convention does not expressly require the adoption of either of these schools of thought. Article II(3) reads as follows:

> The court of a Contracting State, when seized of an action in a matter in respect of which the parties have made an agreement within the meaning of this article, *shall*, at the request of one of the parties, *refer* the parties to arbitration, unless it finds that the said agreement is null and void, inoperative or incapable of being performed.

72. According to some authors, this provision means that referral is the general rule. [References omitted.] Its wording indicates that the court must not rule on the arbitrator's jurisdiction unless the clause is clearly null and void, inoperative or incapable of being performed.

73. The fact that art. II(3) of the New York Convention provides that the court can rule on whether an agreement is null and void, inoperative or incapable of being performed does not mean that it is required to do so before the arbitrator does, however.

74. The Model Law, which, as I mentioned above, was drafted consistently with the New York Convention, is clearer. First of all, the wording of art. 8(1) of the Model Law is almost identical to that of art. II(3) of the New York Convention. What is more, art. 16 of the Model Law expressly recognizes the competence-competence principle. It reads as follows:

> *Article 16. Competence of arbitral tribunal to rule on its jurisdiction*
>
> (1) The arbitral tribunal may rule on its own jurisdiction, including any objections with respect to the existence or validity of the arbitration agreement. For that purpose, an arbitration clause which forms part of a contract shall be treated as an agreement independent of the other terms of the contract. A decision by the arbitral tribunal that the contract is null and void shall not entail *ispo jure* the invalidity of the arbitration clause.
>
> (2) A plea that the arbitral tribunal does not have jurisdiction shall be raised not later than the submission of the statement of defence. A party is not precluded from raising such a plea by the fact that he has appointed, or participated in the appointment of, an arbitrator. A plea that the arbitral tribunal is exceeding the scope of its authority shall be raised as soon as the matter alleged to be beyond the scope of its authority is raised during the arbitral proceedings. The arbitral tribunal may, in either case, admit a later plea if it considers the delay justified.

(3) The arbitral tribunal may rule on a plea referred to in paragraph (2) of this article either as a preliminary question or in an award on the merits. If the arbitral tribunal rules as a preliminary question that it has jurisdiction, any party may request, within thirty days after having received notice of that ruling, the court specified in article 6 to decide the matter, which decision shall be subject to no appeal; while such a request is pending, the arbitral tribunal may continue the arbitral proceedings and make an award.

75. Some authors argue that the competence-competence principle requires the court to limit itself to a *prima facie* analysis of the application and to refer the parties to arbitration unless the arbitration agreement is manifestly tainted by a defect rendering it invalid or inapplicable. [Reference and comment omitted.] This approach has also been adopted in a number of countries; France, for example, has formally incorporated the approach in art. 1458 of its *Code de procédure civile*. The *prima facie* test has also been adopted in Switzerland by way of judicial interpretation: decision of the 1st Civil Court dated April 29, 1996 in *Fondation M. v. Banque X.*, BGE 122 III 139 (1996), cited by Gaillard and Savage, at p. 409.

76. The manifest nullity test is a fairly strict one:

[TRANSLATION] The nullity of an arbitration agreement will be manifest if it is incontestable. . . . As soon as a serious debate arises about the validity of the arbitration agreement, only the arbitrator can validly conduct the review. . . . An apparently valid arbitration clause will never be considered to be manifestly null.

(É. Loquin, "Compétence arbitrale", *Juris-classeur Procédure civile*, fasc. 1034 (1994), No. 105)

77. Despite the lack of consensus in the international community, the *prima facie* analysis test is gaining acceptance and has the support of many authors. [References omitted.] This test is indicative of a deferential approach to the jurisdiction of arbitrators.

78. Having completed this review of international law, I will now consider the state of Quebec law on this issue.

5.2 *Quebec Test for Judicial Intervention in a Case Involving an Arbitration Agreement*

79. The legal framework governing referral to arbitration is set out in the *Code of Civil Procedure*. The relevant provisions read as follows:

940.1 Where an action is brought regarding a dispute in a matter on which the parties have an arbitration agreement, the court shall refer them to arbitration on the application of either of them unless the case has been inscribed on the roll or it finds the agreement null.

The arbitration proceedings may nevertheless be commenced or pursued and an award made at any time while the case is pending before the court.

. . .

943. The arbitrators may decide the matter of their own competence.

943.1 If the arbitrators declare themselves competent during the arbitration proceedings, a party may within thirty days of being notified thereof apply to the court for a decision on that matter.

While such a case is pending, the arbitrators may pursue the arbitration proceedings and make their award.

943.2 A decision of the court during the arbitration proceedings recognizing the competence of the arbitrators is final and without appeal.

80. It should be noted from the outset that art. 940.1 C.C.P. incorporates the essence of art. II(3) of the New York Convention and of its counterpart in the Model Law, art. 8. Furthermore, art. 943 C.C.P. confers on arbitrators the competence to rule on their own jurisdiction. This article clearly indicates acceptance of the competence-competence principle incorporated into art. 16 of the Model Law.

81. A review of the case law on arbitration reveals that Quebec courts have often accepted or refused to give effect to arbitration clauses without reflecting on the degree of scrutiny required of them: *C.C.I.C. Consultech International v. Silverman*, [1991] R.D.J. 500 (C.A.); *Banque Nationale du Canada v. Premdev inc.*, [1997] Q.J. No. 689 (QL) (C.A.); *Acier Leroux inc. v. Tremblay*, [2004] R.J.Q. 839 (C.A.); *Robertson Building Systems Ltd. v. Constructions de la Source inc.*, [2006] Q.J. No. 3118 (QL), 2006 QCCA 461; *Compagnie nationale algérienne de navigation v. Pegasus Lines Ltd. S.A.*, [1994] Q.J. No. 329 (QL) (C.A.). However, it can be seen that where the analysis of a clause requires an assessment of contradictory factual evidence, Quebec courts can be reluctant to engage in a review on the merits. For example, in *Kingsway Financial Services Inc. v. 118997 Canada inc.*, [1999] Q.J. No. 5922 (QL) (C.A.), the buyer sued the seller on the basis of error induced by fraud. The court hearing the case had to decide whether the seller had made false representations to the buyer. The Court of Appeal simply referred the case to arbitration.

82. One author suggests that Quebec courts are more deferential as regards the jurisdiction of arbitrators when hearing cases that simply concern the applicability of an arbitration clause, whereas if it is the validity of the same clause that is an issue, the rule they seem to observe is to dispose of the issue immediately: F. Bachand, *L'intervention du juge canadien avant et durant un arbitrage commercial international*, at pp. 190–91. Although I agree that a distinction can be made between a case concerning validity and one concerning applicability, it cannot be said that the Quebec courts have uniformly used or identified this distinction as a criterion for intervening. Nor has it been adopted in the rest of Canada, where the *prima facie* analysis has also been extended to cases concerning the applicability of an arbitration clause. [Citations omitted.] I therefore consider it necessary to pursue the analysis beyond this distinction.

83. Article 940.1 C.C.P. refers only to cases where the arbitration agreement is null. However, since this provision was adopted in the context of the implementation of the New York Convention (the words of which, in art. II(3), are "null and void, inoperative or incapable of being performed"), I do not consider a literal interpretation to be appropriate. It is possible to develop, in a manner consistent with the

empirical data from the Quebec case law, a test for reviewing an application to refer a dispute to arbitration that is faithful to art. 943 C.C.P. and to the *prima facie* analysis test that is increasingly gaining acceptance around the world.

84. *First of all, I would lay down a general rule that in any case involving an arbitration clause, a challenge to the arbitrator's jurisdiction must be resolved first by the arbitrator. A court should depart from the rule of systematic referral to arbitration only if the challenge to the arbitrator's jurisdiction is based solely on a question of law.* [Emphasis added.] This exception is justified by the courts' expertise in resolving such questions, by the fact that the court is the forum to which the parties apply first when requesting referral and by the rule that an arbitrator's decision regarding his or her jurisdiction can be reviewed by a court. It allows a legal argument relating to the arbitrator's jurisdiction to be resolved once and for all, and also allows the parties to avoid duplication of a strictly legal debate. In addition, the danger that a party will obstruct the process by manipulating procedural rules will be reduced, since the court must not, in ruling on the arbitrator's jurisdiction, consider the facts leading to the application of the arbitration clause.

85. *If the challenge requires the production and review of factual evidence, the court should normally refer the case to arbitration, as arbitrators have, for this purpose, the same resources and expertise as courts. Where questions of mixed law and fact are concerned, the court hearing the referral application must refer the case to arbitration unless the questions of fact require only superficial consideration of the documentary evidence in the record.* [Emphasis added.]

86. Before departing from the general rule of referral, the court must be satisfied that the challenge to the arbitrator's jurisdiction is not a delaying tactic and that it will not unduly impair the conduct of the arbitration proceeding. This means that even when considering one of the exceptions, the court might decide that to allow the arbitrator to rule first on his or her competence would be best for the arbitration process.

87. Thus, the general rule of the Quebec test is consistent with the competence-competence principle set out in art. 16 of the Model Law, which has been incorporated into art. 943 C.C.P. As for the exception under which a court may rule first on questions of law relating to the arbitrator's jurisdiction, this power is provided for in art. 940.1 C.C.P., which in fact recognizes that a court can itself find that the agreement is null rather than referring this issue to arbitration.

88. In the case at bar, the parties have raised questions of law relating to the application of the provisions on Quebec private international law and to whether the class action is of public order. There are a number of other arguments, however, that require an analysis of the facts in order to apply the law to this case. This is true of the attempt to identify a foreign element in the circumstances of the case. Likewise, the external nature of the arbitration clause requires not only an interpretation of the law, but also a review of the documentary and testimonial evidence introduced by the parties. According to the test discussed above, the matter should have been referred to arbitration.

89. Considering the status of the case, it would be counterproductive for this

Court to refer it to arbitration, thereby exposing the parties to a new round of proceedings. It would therefore be preferable to deal with all the questions here. I have already discussed the application of art. 3149 C.C.Q. and the question of the foreign element. I will now consider the external clause issue.

6. External Nature of the Arbitration Clause

90. In 1994, the legislature introduced arts. 1435 to 1437 C.C.Q.— which lay down special rules on the validity of certain clauses typically found in contracts of adhesion or consumer contracts — into the law of contractual obligations. Although all these rules share a general purpose of protecting the weakest and most vulnerable contracting parties, they concern different types of clauses (external, illegible, incomprehensible and abusive) and are accordingly aimed at different types of abuse. For example, whereas the notion of the external clause (art. 1435 C.C.Q.) traditionally concerns contract clauses that are physically separate from the main document, that of the illegible clause (art. 1436 C.C.Q.) concerns clauses that are not separate from the main document but are, owing to their physical presentation, illegible for a reasonable person. Thus, a clause that is [TRANSLATION] "buried among a large number of other clauses" because of its location in the contract is characterized as illegible: D. Lluelles and B. Moore, *Droit des obligations* (2006), at p. 897; B. Lefebvre, "Le contrat d'adhésion" (2003), 105 *R. du N.* 439, at p. 479. An incomprehensible clause (art. 1436 C.C.Q.) is one that is drafted so poorly that its content is unintelligible or excessively ambiguous.

91. In the case at bar, the Union argues that, pursuant to art. 1435 C.C.Q., the arbitration clause is null because it is an external clause and because it has not been proven that Mr. Dumoulin knew of its existence. Article 1435 reads as follows:

1435. An external clause referred to in a contract is binding on the parties.

In a consumer contract or a contract of adhesion, however, an external clause is null if, at the time of formation of the contract, it was not expressly brought to the attention of the consumer or adhering party, unless the other party proves that the consumer or adhering party otherwise knew of it.

92. This provision begins with a recognition that an external clause referred to in a contract is valid. However, its purpose is to remedy abuses resulting from the inclusion by reference of clauses that one of the parties is unaware of: Civil Code Revision Office, vol. II, t. 2, at pp. 601–2; *Commentaires du ministre de la Justice*, vol. I, at pp. 870–71. A party wishing to apply a clause that is external to a consumer contract or a contract of adhesion must prove that it was expressly brought to the attention of the consumer or adhering party, or that the consumer or adhering party otherwise knew of it.

93. In the absence of a statutory definition, the authors have undertaken to define the external clause concept. An external clause is a contractual stipulation [TRANSLATION] "set out in a document that is separate from the agreement or instrument but that, according to a clause of this agreement, is deemed to be an integral part of it": *Baudouin et Jobin: Les obligations* (6th ed. 2005), at p. 267. A clause is external if it is physically separate from the contract. [Reference omitted.] A clause

found on the back of a contract or in a schedule at the end of it is not an external clause, because it is an integral part of the contract; art. 1435 C.C.Q. does not apply to such a clause.

94. The case at bar is the first in which the Quebec Court of Appeal has had to consider whether a contract clause that can be accessed by means of a hyperlink in a contract entered into via the Internet can be considered to be an external clause. Previous disputes concerning the external nature of contractual stipulations have concerned paper documents.

95. Some aspects of electronic documents are covered by the law. In light of the growing number of juridical acts entered into via the Internet, the Quebec legislature has intervened and laid down rules relating to this new environment. Thus, the *Act to establish a legal framework for information technology*, R.S.Q., c. C-1.1, provides that documents have the same legal value whether they are paper or technology-based documents (§ 5). A contract may therefore be entered into using either an electronic medium — by, for example, filling out a form on a Web page — or paper. [Reference omitted.]

96. Despite the efforts to harmonize the rules via legislation, there are legal rules that are not always easy to apply in the context of the Internet. This is true, for example, in the case of external clauses, since the traditional test of physical separation cannot be transposed without qualification to the context of electronic commerce.

97. A Web page may contain many links, each of which leads in turn to a new Web page that may itself contain many more links, and so on. Obviously, it cannot be argued that all these different but interlinked pages constitute a single document, or that the entire Web, as it scrolls down a user's screen, is just one document. However, it is difficult to accept that the need for a single command by the user would be sufficient for a finding that the provision governing external clauses is applicable. Such an interpretation would be inconsistent with the reality of the Internet environment, where no real distinction is made between scrolling through a document and using a hyperlink. Analogously to paper documents, some Web documents contain several pages that can be accessed only by means of hyperlinks, whereas others can be viewed by scrolling down them on the computer's screen. There is no reason to favour one configuration over the other. To determine whether clauses on the Internet are external clauses, therefore, it is necessary to consider another rule that, although not expressly mentioned in art. 1435 C.C.Q., is implied by it.

98. Thus, a number of authors have stressed that, for an external clause to be binding on the parties, it must be reasonably accessible. [References omitted.] A contracting party cannot argue that a contract clause is binding unless the other party had a reasonable opportunity to read it. For this, the other party must have had access to it. Where a contract has been negotiated and all its terms and conditions are set out in the contract itself, the problem of accessibility does not arise, since all the clauses are part of a single document. Where the contract refers to an external document, however, accessibility is an implied precondition for setting up the clause against the other party.

99. The implied precondition of accessibility is a useful tool for the analysis of an electronic document. Thus, a clause that requires operations of such complexity that its text is not reasonably accessible cannot be regarded as an integral part of the contract. Likewise, a clause contained in a document on the Internet to which a contract on the Internet refers, but for which no hyperlink is provided, will be an external clause. Access to the clause in electronic format should be no more difficult than access to its equivalent on paper. This proposition flows both from the interpretation of art. 1435 C.C.Q. and from the principle of functional equivalence that underlies the *Act to establish a legal framework for information technology*.

100. The evidence in the record shows that the consumer could access the page of Dell's Web site containing the arbitration clause directly by clicking on the highlighted hyperlink entitled "Terms and Conditions of Sale". This link reappeared on every page the consumer accessed. When the consumer clicked on the link, a page containing the terms and conditions of sale, including the arbitration clause, appeared on the screen. From this point of view, the clause was no more difficult for the consumer to access than would have been the case had he or she been given a paper copy of the entire contract on which the terms and conditions of sale appeared on the back of the first page.

101. In my view, the consumer's access to the arbitration clause was not impeded by the configuration of the clause; to read it, he or she needed only to click once on the hyperlink to the terms and conditions of sale. The clause is therefore not an external one within the meaning of the *Civil Code of Québec*.

102. The Union submits that the NAF Code, too, is an external document and cannot be set up against Mr. Dumoulin, the consumer in the instant case. According to the Union, the hyperlink merely led to the home page of the NAF's Web site, and to access the NAF Code, consumers had to pursue their searches beyond the home page. At first glance, the need to pursue a search beyond the home page seems to me to be insufficient to support a finding that the NAF Code is an external document. Without further evidence regarding access problems, I find that the argument must be rejected. Furthermore, even if the NAF Code were an external document, this argument would not be sufficient to decide the issue of the arbitrator's jurisdiction. If the NAF Code were in fact an external clause and therefore null pursuant to art. 1435 C.C.Q., that would not affect the validity of the arbitration clause. The arbitration procedure would then simply be governed by the C.C.P.

103. In concluding, I would like to point out, relying only on the facts in the record and having heard no specific arguments on the issue of an illegible or incomprehensible arbitration clause, that I would have reached the same conclusion even if the Union had also argued that the clause was illegible or incomprehensible within the meaning of art. 1436 C.C.Q. As was mentioned above, the highlighted hyperlink appeared on every page the consumer accessed, and no evidence was adduced that could lead to the conclusion that the text was difficult to find in the document, or that it was hard to read or to understand.

104. I would also note that in this Court, the Union argued generally that the arbitration clause was abusive. This argument is based on the prohibition under art. 1437 C.C.Q. However, since no submissions were made in support of this allegation,

I will simply find that the Union has not demonstrated its merits.

7. Availability of the Class Action Where There is an Arbitration Clause

105. As a separate ground in support of the argument that the arbitration clause cannot be set up against Mr. Dumoulin's motion, the Union relies on art. 2639 C.C.Q. and submits that because this is a class action, the dispute is of public order and therefore cannot be submitted to arbitration. Thus, Dell is not entitled to request that the dispute be referred to arbitration, and the class action must be heard on the merits. In my opinion, the Union's argument must be rejected. The class action is a procedure, and its purpose is not to create a new right.

106. The procedural framework for the class action was added to the *Code of Civil Procedure* in 1979. It is accepted that the class action has a social dimension: "Its purpose is to facilitate access to justice for citizens who share common problems and would otherwise have little incentive to apply to the courts on an individual basis to assert their rights" (*Bisaillon v. Concordia University*, [2006] 1 S.C.R. 666, 2006 SCC 19, at para. 16) or might lack the financial means to do so. From this perspective, the class action is clearly of public interest. However, the first introductory provision of Book IX of the *Code of Civil Procedure* — Class Action — reminds us that, as important as it may be, the class action is only a legal procedure:

> **999.** . . .
>
> (*d*) "class action" means the procedure which enables one member to sue without a mandate on behalf of all the members.
>
> . . .

107. This position was already accepted at the time Book IX was enacted:

> [TRANSLATION] The class action is not a right (*jus*); it is a procedure. It is not, in itself, even a means to exercise a right, a remedy in the sense of the maxim *ubi jus, ibi remedium*. It is merely a special mechanism that is applied to an existing means to exercise an existing right in order to "collectivize" it.
>
> (M. Bouchard, "L'autorisation d'exercer le recours collectif" (1980), 21 *C. de D.* 855, at p. 864)

The notion that the class action procedure does not create new rights has been reiterated on numerous occasions, including recently by this Court in *Bisaillon*, at paras. 17 and 22.

108. In the case at bar, the parties agreed to submit their disputes to binding arbitration. The effect of an arbitration agreement is recognized in Quebec law: art. 2638 C.C.Q. Obviously, if Mr. Dumoulin had brought the same action solely as an individual, the Union's argument based on the class action being of public order could not have been advanced to prevent the court hearing the action from referring the parties to arbitration. Does the mere fact that Mr. Dumoulin instead decided to bring the matter before the courts by instituting a class action affect the admissibility of his action? In light of the reasons of LeBel J., writing for the

majority in *Bisaillon*, at para. 17, the answer is no: "[the class action] cannot serve as a basis for legal proceedings if the various claims it covers, taken individually, would not do so".

109. Moreover, the Union's argument that the class action is a matter of public order that may not be submitted to arbitration has lost its force as a result of this Court's decision in *Desputeaux*. In that case, one of the parties had invoked the same provision, art. 2639 C.C.Q., to argue that the dispute over ownership of the copyright in a fictitious character, Caillou, was a question of public order that could not be submitted to arbitration. The Court held that the concept of public order referred to in art. 2639 C.C.Q. must be interpreted narrowly and is limited to matters analogous to those enumerated in that provision: paras. 53–55. In the case at bar, neither Mr. Dumoulin's hypothetical individual action nor the class action is a dispute over the status and capacity of persons, family law matters or analogous matters.

110. Consequently, the Union's argument relating to the public order nature of the class action must fail. I must now rule on the application of Bill 48, which came into force after this appeal was heard.

8. Application of the *Act to amend the Consumer Protection Act and the Act respecting the collection of certain debts*

111. Bill 48 was enacted on December 14, 2006 (S.Q. 2006, c. 56). It introduces a number of measures, only one of which is relevant to the case at bar: the addition to the *Consumer Protection Act* of a provision on arbitration clauses. This provision reads as follows:

2. The Act is amended by inserting the following section after section 11:

> "11.1. Any stipulation that obliges the consumer to refer a dispute to arbitration, that restricts the consumer's right to go before a court, in particular by prohibiting the consumer from bringing a class action, or that deprives the consumer of the right to be a member of a group bringing a class action is prohibited.
>
> If a dispute arises after a contract has been entered into, the consumer may then agree to refer the dispute to arbitration."

The question that arises is whether this new provision applies to the facts of the instant case.

112. Pursuant to § 18 of Bill 48, § 2 came into force on December 14, 2006. Section 18 reads as follows:

> 18. The provisions of this Act come into force on 14 December 2006, except section 1, which comes into force on 1 April 2007, and sections 3, 5, 9 and 10, which come into force on the date or dates to be set by the Government, but not later than 15 December 2007.

Bill 48 has only one transitional provision, § 17, which provides that the new §§ 54.8 to 54.16 of the *Consumer Protection Act* do not apply to contracts entered into before the coming into force of the Bill. The instant case is not one in which § 17 is applicable. However, if §§ 17 and 18 are read together, it would seem at first glance that, aside from the provisions referred to in § 17, Bill 48 applies to contracts entered into before its coming into force. Is this true? And is Bill 48 applicable in the case at bar?

113. Professor P.-A. Côté writes in *The Interpretation of Legislation in Canada* (3rd ed. 2000), at p. 169, that "retroactive operation of a statute is highly exceptional, whereas prospective operation is the rule". He adds that "[a] statute has immediate effect when it applies to a legal situation that is ongoing at the moment of its commencement: the new statute governs the future developments of this situation" (p. 152). A legal situation is ongoing if the facts or effects are occurring at the time the law is being modified (p. 153). A statute of immediate effect can therefore modify the future effects of a fact that occurred before the statute came into force without affecting the prior legal situation of that fact.

114. To make it clear what is meant by an ongoing situation and one whose facts and effects have occurred in their entirety, it will be helpful to consider the example of the obligation to warrant against latent defects cited by professors P.-A. Côté and D. Jutras in *Le droit transitoire civil: Sources annotées* (loose-leaf), at p. 2-36. This obligation comes into existence upon the conclusion of the sale, but the warranty clause does not produce tangible effects unless a problem arises with the property sold. The warranty comes into play either when the vendor is put in default or when a claim is made. Once all the effects of the warranty have occurred, the situation is no longer ongoing and the new legislation will not apply to the situation unless it is retroactive.

115. Can the facts of the case at bar be characterized as those of an ongoing legal situation? If they can, the new legislation applies. If all the effects of the situation have occurred, the new legislation will not apply to the facts.

116. The only condition for application of Dell's arbitration clause is that a claim against Dell, or a dispute or controversy between the customer and Dell, must arise (clause 13C of the Terms and Conditions of Sale). All the facts of the legal situation had therefore occurred once Mr. Dumoulin notified Dell of his claim. Thus, all the facts giving rise to the application of the binding arbitration clause had occurred in their entirety before Bill 48 came into force.

117. Since there is nothing in Bill 48 that might lead to the conclusion that it applies retroactively, there is no reason to give it such a scope.

118. Moreover, to interpret Bill 48 as having retroactive effect would be problematic. First, retroactive operation is exceptional: Côté, at pp. 114–15; R. Sullivan, *Sullivan and Driedger on the Construction of Statutes* (4th ed. 2002), at pp. 553–54. Where a law is ambiguous and admits of two possible interpretations, an interpretation according to which it does not have retroactive effect will be preferred. [Citation omitted.]

119. Second, I find it highly unlikely that the legislature intended that § 2 should apply to *all* arbitration clauses in force before December 14, 2006. For example, neither a consumer who is a party to an arbitration that is under way nor a consumer whose claims have already been rejected by an arbitrator should be able to rely on § 2 and argue that the arbitration clause binding him or her and the merchant is invalid in order to request a stay of proceedings or to have the

unfavourable arbitration award set aside. Failing a clear indication to the contrary, when a dispute is submitted for a decision, the decision maker must apply the law as it stands at the time the facts giving rise to the right occurred.

120. I accordingly conclude that since the facts triggering the application of the arbitration clause had already occurred before § 2 of Bill 48 came into force, this provision does not apply to the facts of the case at bar.

9. Disposition

121. For these reasons, I would allow the appeal, reverse the Court of Appeal's judgment, refer Mr. Dumoulin's claim to arbitration and dismiss the motion for authorization to institute a class action, with costs.

The reasons of BASTARACHE, LEBEL and FISH JJ. were delivered by

BASTARACHE and LEBEL JJ. (dissenting)

[Introduction and Background omitted.]

IV. Analysis

A. *Introduction*

130. In this case, we are dealing with an arbitration clause inserted into a consumer contract of adhesion. The primary question raised by this appeal can be stated in the following terms: did the courts below err in law by refusing to refer the parties to arbitration?

. . . .

(2) Recognition of Jurisdiction Clauses in Quebec Law

136. Prior to the coming into force of the C.C.Q., the rules on jurisdiction of Quebec courts were not codified. Quebec courts relied on art. 27 of the *Civil Code of Lower Canada* ("C.C.L.C.") and art. 68 of the Quebec *Code of Civil Procedure*, R.S.Q., c. C-25 ("C.C.P."), to delineate their jurisdiction in cases where it was challenged: see *Masson v. Thompson*, [1994] R.J.Q. 1032 (Sup. Ct.). Article 27 C.C.L.C. provided that aliens although not resident in Lower Canada could be sued in Quebec courts "for the fulfilment of obligations contracted by them in foreign countries". Article 68 C.C.P., which is still in force today, provides the domestic rules for determining in which judicial district of Quebec a personal action can be started. Relying on the general principles set out in this section, and art. 27 C.C.L.C., Quebec courts have delineated a body of jurisprudential rules deciding when Quebec courts have jurisdiction to hear an action.

137. Prior to its amendment in 1992, the opening phrase of art. 68 C.C.P. stated: "Subject to the provisions of articles 70, 71, 74 and 75, *and notwithstanding any agreement to the contrary*, a purely personal action may be instituted . . .". This was interpreted by Quebec courts to be a prohibition against intentional derogation through contract from the jurisdiction of Quebec courts through forum selection and arbitration clauses. [References omitted.]

138. Then came the 1983 decision of this Court in *Zodiak International Productions*, where a party to a contract submitted to arbitration in Warsaw, but having lost, commenced a fresh action in the Quebec Superior Court against his co-contractor. Noting the tension between art. 68 C.C.P. and contractual arbitration clauses, the Court held that the Quebec legislator had nonetheless clearly intended to permit such clauses by introducing art. 951 C.C.P., which states: "An undertaking to arbitrate must be set out in writing." Faced with this provision, Chouinard J., for the Court, cited with approval the words of Pratte J. in *Syndicat de Normandin Lumber Ltd. v. The "Angelic Power"*, [1971] F.C. 263 (T.D.), who stated: ". . . I do not see how the Quebec legislator could have regulated the form and effect of an agreement whose validity he does not admit" (p. 539). Shortly after this decision, in 1986, the Quebec legislator introduced amendments to the C.C.L.C. and the C.C.P. providing detailed rules on the validity, form and procedure governing contractual arbitration. (Today, these rules can be found in the specific chapter on arbitration in the Book of Obligations of the C.C.Q., these being art § 2 638 to 2643, and in Book VII (on Arbitrations) of the C.C.P.)

. . . .

141. This short historical overview demonstrates, in our view, that one should not attach any significance to the structure of the C.C.Q. or the C.C.P. when interpreting the substantive provisions under review in this appeal. The coherence of the regime is not dependent on the particular Book of the C.C.P. that deals with arbitrations, or the particular title and Book of the C.C.Q. in which is found art. 3149. . . .

. . . .

(3) The Principle of Primacy of the Autonomy of the Parties

142. Quebec's acceptance of jurisdiction clauses over the past two decades is rooted in the principle of primacy of the autonomy of the parties. This has recently been confirmed by our Court in *Desputeaux v. Éditions Chouette (1987) inc.*, [2003] 1 S.C.R. 178, 2003 SCC 17, with respect to agreements to submit a dispute to an arbitral tribunal, and *GreCon Dimter inc. v. J.R. Normand inc.*, [2005] 2 S.C.R. 401, 2005 SCC 46, with respect to agreements to submit it to a foreign authority.

143. In *Desputeaux*, our Court recognized that the limits to the autonomy of the contracting parties to choose to submit a dispute to arbitration had to be given a restrictive interpretation. More specifically, as will be discussed in further detail below, we held that the notion of "public order" at art. 2639, para. 1 C.C.Q. had to be given a narrow interpretation. Furthermore, we held that legislation merely identifying the courts which, within the judicial system, will have jurisdiction over a particular subject matter should not be interpreted as excluding the possibility of arbitration, except if it was clearly the legislator's intention to do so. In reaching these conclusions, we notably had regard to the legislative policy that now accepts arbitration as a valid form of dispute resolution and, moreover, seeks to promote its use.

144. Both art. 3148, para. 2 C.C.Q. and art. 940.1 C.C.P. can be interpreted as giving practical effect to the principle of primacy of the autonomy of the parties that has characterized the development of the law of arbitration in Quebec in the last two

decades. The provisions purport most notably to promote legal certainty for the parties by enabling them to provide in advance for the forum to which their disputes will have to be submitted. They are also consistent with the international movement towards harmonizing the rules of jurisdiction.

145. This movement towards harmonization can be explained by the importance of legal certainty for commercial and international transactions. . . . .

This clear intention of the Quebec legislator was acknowledged by our Court in *GreCon Dimter*, where we concluded that the fact that an action was incidental to a principal action heard by a Quebec court was not sufficient to trump an agreement to submit any claim arising from the contract to a foreign authority. More specifically, we concluded that art. 3148, para. 2 C.C.Q. was to be given primacy over art. 3139 C.C.Q.

(4) The Limits on the Autonomy of the Parties

146. Naturally, the primacy of the autonomy of contracting parties permitting them to choose in advance the forum for resolving their disputes is not without limits. The Quebec legislator has restricted it in many different ways.

147. We noted the limits on the expression of the autonomy of the parties to submit their disputes to a foreign authority in *GreCon Dimter*, pursuant to art. 3148, para. 2. First, art. 3151 C.C.Q. confers to the Quebec authorities *exclusive* jurisdiction to hear in first instance all actions founded on civil liability for damage suffered as a result of exposure to or the use of raw materials originating in Quebec. Second, art. 3149 C.C.Q., which confers jurisdiction to the Quebec authorities to hear an action involving a consumer contract or an employment contract if the consumer or worker has his domicile or residence in Quebec, states that the waiver of such jurisdiction by the consumer or worker may not be set up against him. The language of both provisions is clear with regard to the intention of the legislature to limit the autonomy of the parties.

. . . .

Furthermore, in order to be enforceable, an arbitration agreement has to be evidenced in writing under art. 2640 C.C.Q. and must otherwise be in compliance with all the conditions of formation of a contract. This latter point is true even when the arbitration agreement is contained in a contract since it is then considered to be a separate agreement pursuant to art. 2642 C.C.Q. . . . This brings us back to the primary issue raised by this case.

B. *Issues Raised by this Case*

149. On the primary question of whether the lower courts erred in refusing to refer the parties to arbitration, it is not contested by the respondents that, if the arbitration agreement is valid and applicable to the dispute, the courts have no discretion and must not refuse to refer the parties to arbitration. On that point, art. 940.1 C.C.P. seems clear: if the parties have an agreement to arbitrate on the matter of the dispute, on the application of either of the parties, the court *shall* refer the parties to arbitration, unless the case has been inscribed on the roll or the court finds the agreement to be null. It is well established that, by using the term "shall",

the legislator has indicated that the court has no discretion to refuse, on the application of either of the parties, to refer the case to arbitration when the appropriate conditions are met [citations omitted]. On a plain reading of art. 940.1 C.C.P., these conditions appear to be threefold: (i) the parties must have an arbitration agreement on the matter of the dispute; (ii) the case must not have been inscribed on the roll; and (iii) the court must not find the agreement to be null. Regarding the latter condition, it appears obvious to us that the reference to the nullity of the agreement is also meant to cover the situation where the arbitration agreement cannot, without being null, be set up against the applicant.

150. It is also well established that the effect of a valid undertaking to arbitrate is to remove the dispute from the jurisdiction of the ordinary courts of law (per *Zodiak International Productions*, art. 940.1 C.C.P. and art. 3148, para. 2 C.C.Q.). It is also accepted that jurisdiction over the individual actions that form the basis of a class action is a prerequisite to the exercise of jurisdiction over the proceedings [citation omitted]. There is consequently no question that, if the arbitration agreement is valid and relates to the dispute, the Superior Court has no jurisdiction to hear the case and must refer the parties to arbitration.

151. In the case at bar, it is not contested by the respondents that the first two conditions for the application of art. 940.1 are met. What is at issue, though, is whether the Court of Appeal erred in law by refusing to refer the parties to arbitration on the basis that the arbitration agreement was null or cannot otherwise be set up against Dumoulin.

152. Many different grounds have been raised in order to demonstrate that the arbitration clause in the case at bar is null or otherwise cannot be set up against Dumoulin. It has notably been argued: (1) that the arbitration agreement cannot be set up against Dumoulin, a consumer, because it constitutes a waiver of the jurisdiction of the Quebec authorities under art. 3149 C.C.Q.; and (2) that it is null, (a) because it is over a consumer dispute which is in and of itself a matter of public order under art. 2639 C.C.Q.; (b) because it constitutes a waiver of the jurisdiction of the Superior Court over class actions and that such a waiver is contrary to public order under art. 2639 C.C.Q.; (c) because Dumoulin did not really consent to it as it was imposed on him through a contract of adhesion; (d) because it is abusive and offends art. 1437 C.C.Q.; and (e) because it is found in an external clause that was not expressly brought to the attention of Dumoulin as required under art. 1435 C.C.Q. . . .

. . . .

. . . In our view, the courts below were correct to fully consider Dumoulin's challenge to the validity of the arbitration agreement based on the application of art. 3149 C.C.Q.

. . . .

204. For these reasons, we would conclude that an arbitration clause is itself sufficient to trigger the application of art. 3148, para. 2, and hence the exceptions that apply to it, including art. 3149.

. . . .

217. Our conclusion on art. 3149 C.C.Q. is alone sufficient to dismiss the appellant's motion to refer the dispute to arbitration and it is therefore not strictly necessary to study the other possible grounds of nullity of the arbitration agreement. That said, we are of the view that the other questions raised by this appeal are sufficiently important to make it necessary for our Court to state its views on their respective merits. [Omitted.]

V. Disposition

242 For these reasons, we would dismiss the appeal with costs.

QUESTIONS

Dell Computer Corp. v. Union des consommateurs involved a class action filed in Québec. Dell sought referral of the case to arbitration pursuant to a clause in its contract with Mr. Dumoulin. The case thus involved the enforceability of an arbitration clause in a transnational standard form contract. Summarize the issues and the arguments of both the majority and dissenting justices in this case. How, in your view, would the U.S. Supreme Court have decided a similar case? To what extent would the cross-border aspects of the case influence the outcome?

ROGERS WIRELESS INC. v. MUROFF
[2007] 2 S.C.R. 921, 2007 SCC 35

The judgment of McLachlin C.J. and Binnie, Fish, Abella, Charron and Rothstein JJ. was delivered by The Chief Justice

1. Introduction

1. This case concerns the effect of an arbitration clause on a court's jurisdiction under Quebec civil law — in particular, how a court should deal with an arbitration clause that is alleged to be null. In this case, the arbitration clause was allegedly null because it appeared in a consumer contract and because it barred access to class action procedures. The appeal therefore deals with issues similar to those in *Dell Computer Corp. v. Union des consommateurs*, [2007] 2 S.C.R. 801, 2007 SCC 34. However, no issues of private international law are raised in this case.

2. Facts

2. Rogers is a mobile telephone service provider. Its Canadian subscribers can use their telephones in the United States, subject to "roaming" charges. In most parts of the United States, these charges are 95¢ per minute; however, in certain "excluded areas", they are $4 per minute. Dr. Muroff, a Quebec resident, used his

Rogers mobile phone to make calls from Rhode Island and Maine; Rogers billed him $4 per minute for these calls.

3. The service agreement between Rogers and Dr. Muroff contained an arbitration clause. Not only did this clause refer all disputes to arbitration, it also expressly prohibited the customer from commencing or participating in a class action. The service agreement appeared on the bills that Rogers sent to Dr. Muroff, and on Rogers' Web site.

3. Legal History

4. Dr. Muroff applied for authorization to institute a class action against Rogers on behalf of himself and all other Rogers subscribers who had been charged $4 per minute for roaming service. This contradicted the arbitration clause in the service agreement, so Dr. Muroff challenged both the $4 per minute charge and the arbitration clause, arguing that they were abusive, contrary to art. 1437 of the *Civil Code of Québec*, S.Q. 1991, c. 64 ("C.C.Q."), and s. 8 of the *Consumer Protection Act*, R.S.Q., c. P-40.1.

5. Rogers argued that the court had no jurisdiction, due to the arbitration clause (art. 940.1 of the *Code of Civil Procedure*, R.S.Q., c. C-25 ("C.C.P.")). Dr. Muroff brought a motion for permission to conduct an examination on discovery of Rogers' representatives. Rogers asked the court to dismiss this application.

6. The Superior Court judge, Borenstein J., noted that Rogers' bills and its Web site contained an arbitration clause. She held that Dr. Muroff had accepted the terms and conditions of the contract by paying these bills. Borenstein J. was satisfied that the arbitration clause was mandatory and exclusive ("*parfaite*"). She did not address the question of whether the clause was abusive; she simply held that the clause deprived her of jurisdiction to rule on either the examination on discovery or the institution of a class action ([2005] Q.J. No. 17037 (QL)).

7. The Court of Appeal overturned this decision, holding that Borenstein J. had erred by sending the dispute to arbitration without deciding whether or not the clause was abusive. Citing its decision in *Dell* ([2005] R.J.Q. No. 1448, 2005 QCCA 570), the Court of Appeal declared that the Superior Court should first assess the validity of an arbitration clause before renouncing jurisdiction in favour of arbitration. The Court of Appeal therefore returned the matter to the Superior Court to decide this issue ([2006] Q.J. No. 1000 (QL), 2006 QCCA 196).

8. Rogers appeals to this Court. It argues that the Court of Appeal erred in ordering the Superior Court to assess the validity of the arbitration clause. In its view, Borenstein J. was correct to hold that an arbitrator had exclusive jurisdiction.

4. Analysis

9. Two principal questions arise. The first is the degree of scrutiny a trial court should apply to an arbitration clause whose validity is contested under art. 940.1 C.C.P. The second is the allegedly abusive nature of the clause under art. 1437 C.C.Q., and whether the trial judge should have addressed this question, applying the correct level of scrutiny.

10. Irrespective of these questions, this Court must also ask whether the arbitration clause in this case was rendered null by the enactment of Bill 48, *An Act to amend the Consumer Protection Act and the Act respecting the collection of certain debts*, 2nd Sess., 37th Leg., Québec, 2006 (now S.Q. 2006, c. 56).

4.1 *The Effect of the Arbitration Clause on the Court's Jurisdiction*

11. In *Dell*, the Court was unanimous in finding that under art. 940.1 C.C.P., arbitrators have jurisdiction to rule on their own jurisdiction (the "compétence-compétence principle"). The majority of the Court held that, when an arbitration clause exists, any challenges to the jurisdiction of the arbitrator must first be referred to the arbitrator. Courts should derogate from this general rule and decide the question first only where the challenge to the arbitrator's jurisdiction concerns a question of law alone. Where a question concerning jurisdiction of an arbitrator requires the admission and examination of factual proof, normally courts must refer such questions to arbitration. For questions of mixed law and fact, courts must also favour referral to arbitration, and the only exception occurs where answering questions of fact entails a superficial examination of the documentary proof in the record and where the court is convinced that the challenge is not a delaying tactic or will not prejudice the recourse to arbitration.

12. In the same case, Bastarache and LeBel JJ. suggested an alternative, discretionary approach favouring resort to the arbitrator in most instances: "a court should rule on the validity of the arbitration only if it is possible to do it on the basis of documents and pleadings filed by the parties without having to hear evidence or make findings about its relevance and reliability" (para. 176).

13. Applying the standard endorsed by the majority in *Dell*, the trial judge was therefore correct to refer the matter to arbitration, unless the nature of the challenge and its evidentiary implications justified a departure from the general rule of deference to arbitral jurisdiction.

4.2 *The Allegedly Abusive Nature of the Arbitration Clause*

14. Dr. Muroff alleges that the arbitration clause is abusive under art. 1437 C.C.Q. He claims the right to prove this in court using a variety of evidence, including transcripts of oral examinations of Rogers' representatives.

15. Whether the arbitration clause is abusive is a mixed question of law and fact. Answering this question would apparently require a probing factual inquiry, including cross-examination; it would go far beyond a superficial examination of the documentary evidence. (As Bastarache and LeBel JJ. held in *Dell* at para. 229, an arbitration clause is not necessarily abusive simply because it appears in a consumer contract; see also the reasons of Deschamps J. at para. 104.)

16. Under the approach to art. 940.1 C.C.P. adopted by the majority of this Court in *Dell*, an arbitrator has exclusive jurisdiction to undertake such an inquiry. For a court to conduct such an inquiry would run counter to art. 940.1 and deprive the arbitrator of jurisdiction to rule on its own jurisdiction.

17. Borenstein J. was therefore correct to hold that she had no jurisdiction and

to refer the matter to an arbitrator. The Court of Appeal erred in returning the matter to the Superior Court for a determination on this issue.

4.3 Transitional Law

18. Bill 48 was assented to on December 14, 2006, the day of the hearing of this case before our Court. Section 2 of Bill 48, which added s. 11.1 to the *Consumer Protection Act*, came into force the same day. This provision prohibits any stipulation requiring a consumer to refer a dispute to arbitration, particularly if it deprives a consumer of access to class action procedures.

19. As this Court held in *Dell*, s. 11.1 of the *Consumer Protection Act* represents a change of substantive law. It has no retroactive effect. It only applies to legal situations that occurred after its coming into force or were ongoing at the time it came into force. It does not apply to legal situations that had fully occurred at the time it came into force, such as this one.

5. Conclusion

20. Faced with a challenge to the validity of an arbitration clause that would have required a det.ailed factual inquiry on a mixed question of law and fact, Borenstein J. was correct to renounce jurisdiction in favour of the arbitrator, under art. 940.1 C.C.P. The Court of Appeal erred in returning the matter to the Superior Court.

21. I would therefore allow the appeal, reverse the decision of the Court of Appeal and reinstate the decision of the Superior Court, with costs in this Court only.

English version of the reasons delivered by

22. LEBEL J.— I have read the Chief Justice's reasons. I agree with her that the appeal should be allowed and the respondent's claim referred to arbitration. However, I feel that certain aspects of this case require further comment.

23. First of all, the interpretation of art. 3149 of the *Civil Code of Québec*, S.Q. 1991, c. 64, is not at issue in the case at bar, and it would not be at issue even if the respondent had clearly raised it. This question has been resolved by the decision of the majority of this Court in *Dell Computer Corp. v. Union des consommateurs*, [2007] 2 S.C.R. 801, 2007 SCC 34, in which it is held that art. 3149 does not apply to an arbitration clause like the one in the parties' contract. I would nevertheless reaffirm the comments I wrote jointly with my colleague Bastarache J. in our dissenting reasons in *Dell*.

24. Thus, the remaining issue in the instant case concerns the validity of the arbitration clause in the telephone service contract between Rogers and Dr. Muroff. Dr. Muroff contests its validity, arguing that it is abusive.

25. A review of the trial proceedings confirms that Dr. Muroff plans to adduce evidence, which could require a long and complex inquiry, to establish that the agreement is abusive. In my opinion, on either the test for intervention by the Superior Court set out by Deschamps J. in her reasons in *Dell* or the one proposed by the dissent in that same case, the Superior Court should decline to consider this issue. As the trial judge held, Dr. Muroff's claim must be referred to arbitration.

26. Therefore, as the Chief Justice proposes, I would allow the appeal, reverse the Court of Appeal's decision and restore the Superior Court's judgment, with costs in this Court.

Appeal allowed with costs.

QUESTIONS

1. Compare the decisions by the Canadian Supreme Court in *Dell* and *Rogers Wireless Inc.* with the U.S. Supreme Court decisions. See, *e.g.*, the most recent U.S. Supreme Court decision on consumer arbitration clauses in a purely domestic context: *AT&T Mobility v. Concepcion*, 563 U.S. ___, 131 S. Ct. 1740 (2011). Despite similar outcomes, what factors account for the differences in approach?

2. Explain what is meant by the "competence-competence" principle.

3. The court unanimously agreed in both *Dell* and *Rogers Wireless Inc.* that the prohibition against requiring arbitration in consumer contracts [Bill 48, *An Act to Amend the Consumer Protection Act and the Act Respecting the Collection of Certain Debts* (2d Sess., 37th Leg.)] did not apply. Summarize the argument.

4. In *Dell*, Justice Deschamps states that article 3149 of the Civil Code of Québec is the most significant statutory provision in the case. Explain what he means and the basis for his conclusion. How does this relate to the "rational and systematic" character of codes in civil law systems? How did Justice LeBel in dissent counter Justice Deschamps' argument?

5. What is meant by the "Foreign Element Concept" and why was it considered significant for the outcome in the *Dell* case? What constituted the requisite "foreign element"?

6. What, if any, changes in Canadian law would result were Canada to ratify the 2005 Hague Convention on Choice of Court Agreements?

C. Japan

COMPANIA DE TRANSPORTES DER ME SOCIODATO ANOMIA v. MATAICHI K.K.*
Tokyo District Court Judgment of 10 April 1953
4 Kakyū minshū (No. 4) 34 (1953)

DISPOSITION
(*shūbun*)

1. The suit is dismissed.
2. The costs of the lawsuits are charged to the plaintiff.

REASONS
(*riyū*)

Judgment concerning the defendant's procedural defense (*honan no kōben*):

According to the charter contract (*yōsen keiyaku*) in this case, if a conflict were to occur between the Plaintiff (*genkoku*) and the Defendant (*hikoku*) (the ship owner and the charterer) "the matters in dispute are to be submitted to a three man arbitration group in New York. Each of the parties concerned is to name one member of this group, and these two arbitrators are to name the third member. The arbitrators (*chusainin*) must be businessmen. A decision of this group — that is, the arbitration award (*chūsai handan*) — is to be reached by agreement of two of the members. This agreement can be regarded as an order of a court in order to enforce the arbitration award. The parties agree that they made the arbitration contract (*shūsai kaiyaku*). Under the United States Federal Arbitration Law (*beikoku renpō chūsaihō*) such an arbitration contract would be effective. It is not doubted under the interpretations of our Code of Civil Procedure (*minji soshōhō*) that a defendant can use such a clause as an affirmative defense (*bōso kōben*). The arbitration contract in this case was based on American federal law and was formed at the insistence of the plaintiff. But, the existence of an arbitration contract made in a foreign country is considered adequate to prevent litigation. Probably the reason why an arbitration contract prevents litigation is that it promises obedience to the judgment of an arbitrator who is a private person, who does not apply legal procedure to the parties concerned, and autonomously decides the conflict. Because this procedure is substituted for a lawsuit, as long as the concerned parties demonstrate an intention to rely on this procedure, the country will respect that intention. In this sense, conflicts can be decided voluntarily, even between countries, and this is a very economical procedure. Consequently, even though there is no connection with the country's administration of justice (*shihō*), it is not absolutely necessary to demarcate national boundaries in order to recognize the parties' intentions. The case which was cited by the plaintiff does not seem to be inconsistent with this view.

---

* Translation by Eugene H. Lee.

The plaintiff asserted that the right to arbitration should be barred because an arbitration judgment obtained on the basis of the original arbitration contract could not be executed in Japan. However, because of the reasons stated above, articles 800 and 802 of the Code of Civil Procedure can be applied to foreign arbitration awards in the same way as they are to Japanese arbitration awards. In our country the majority of the scholars agree with this view. I do not think precedent cited by the plaintiff was to the contrary. The fact that the United States did not participate in the treaty concerning the Enforcement of Foreign Arbitration Awards (*gaikoku chūssi handan no shikkō*) which was signed in Geneva on September 26, 1927 does not require the court to take a different view. Accordingly, since under art. 801 of the Code of Civil Procedure an arbitration award based on an arbitration contract can be enforced in our country unless it violated art. 801 of the Code of Civil Procedure.

Next, the plaintiff asserted that according to art. 3 of the United States Federal Arbitration Law and the federal court decisions, the existence of an arbitration contract is not reason enough to dismiss a case, but is merely reason to stop a law suit that has already been commenced, so this action should not be dismissed. But, the problem of what influences law suits which are connected to arbitration contracts should be decided according to the law of the forum, and not by relying on the appropriate authorities on foreign law. This is merely the natural result of the Civil Procedure concept of territorialism.

In addition, the plaintiff asserted that even if the purpose of the arbitration contract was to prevent law suits, the arbitration contract accompanied the charter contract. Thus, when the charter contract was cancelled, the arbitration contract ceased to be effective. However, since arbitration was agreed to be the method of dispute settlement in case there should be a conflict between the parties, it should not have to rely on the whims of fortune for its existence. Rather, the fact that conflicts are produced by the cancellation of a charter contract is a reason for its existence. Accordingly, even if the charter contract is cancelled, the arbitration contract should not be correspondingly invalid.

From the reasons stated above, this arbitration contract is sufficient to prevent this lawsuit, and this case should be dismissed. It is also decided that the costs incurred in this litigation should be paid by the plaintiff under art. 89 of the Code of Civil Procedure.

QUESTIONS

In what respects does Japanese law appear to differ from both United States and Canadian law? Is the distinction noted in *Rogers Wireless Inc. v. Muroff* between a transnational contract and a domestic contract a pertinent distinction under Japanese law? Under which legal regime — the United States, Canada, or Japan — are arbitration clauses in standard form contracts *least* likely to be enforced? Would your answer differ were the case to involve a consumer contract or an employment contract?

K.K. AMERIDO NIHON v. DREW CHEMICAL CORP.
1981 Quarterly of the Japan Commercial Arbitration Association
(Nos. 81–82) 1

Action for damages by a Japanese company (plaintiff) that worked for an American company (defendant) as the sales agent in Japan for about 15 years.

In 1959, the plaintiff-Japanese company was incorporated for the intention that it would engage in the sales of the products of the defendant-American company. During 1959, the plaintiff imported and sold the defendant's products without any written contract.

On January 7, 1960, the defendant and plaintiff entered into a written contract by which the defendant appointed the plaintiff as the sole agent and an exclusive distributor of the defendant's products. The 1960 Contract provided that it should continue until terminated by either party on a 90-days written notice and it continued until 1969 without being terminated.

On March 24, 1969, the plaintiff and defendant entered into a written contract under which the plaintiff was made sales, servicing and warehousing agent in Japan of the defendant with the exclusive right to sell and distribute the defendant's products in Japan. The plaintiff was to receive certain commissions measured by its net sales in Japan for its services.

The 1969 contract provided in the paragraph 16 and 17 as follows:

> "SIXTEEN: All disputes, controversies, or differences which may arise between the parties out of or in relation to or in connection with this Agreement, or as regarding any alleged breach thereof, may at the option of either party be finally settled by arbitration in New York, New, United States of America, under the Rules of Conciliation and Arbitration of the International Chamber of Commerce."

> "SEVENTEEN: This Agreement is made in the State of New York and shall be governed by and construed in accordance with the laws of said State and of the United States. This Agreement is executed in English and Japanese versions, of which the English version shall be the official version."

The 1969 contract also provided in the paragraph 9 that the contract should continue to be effective until January 31, 1970, unless renewed by the parties upon terms established by mutual agreement. The contract was never formally renewed by the parties after January 31, 1970, but the parties merely continued the transactions under the same conditions as those of the 1970 contract until April, 1974.

The plaintiff's annual sales of the defendant's grew almost thirty times of the sales in 1959 and the plaintiff also developed the sales organization and opened three branches in Osaka, Fukuoka and Hakodate.

In December, 1975, however, the defendant established its own subsidiary in Japan for the purpose of the direct-sales in the Japanese market and, on February 14, 1974, the defendant severed a 60-days written notice of termination of the contract with the plaintiff which should be effective when the plaintiff does not accept the defendant's demand that the plaintiff should, thereafter, set as an agent for warehouse and delivery services only. The plaintiff refused to accept said demand of the defendant.

On December 1975, the plaintiff commenced the suit against the defendant before Yokohama district Court in Japan, alleging that the termination by the defendant of the 1969 contract constitutes a tort and that the plaintiff suffered the damage amounting seven hundred twenty seven million yen (727 million yen). The plaintiff's claim covers the direct and indirect damages including loss of profit, expenses for the transfer from the plaintiff to the defendant of the inventory of the products, costs and expenses for winding up the plaintiff's branches and business, and harm on the plaintiff's good-will etc.

Arguments by the Parties:

1. The plaintiff argued that it was the understanding of the parties that the relationship between the parties would continue for a long time and, under such understanding, the plaintiff had made a substantial investment in order to develop said business and to promote the products in Japan and, therefore, that the defendant was not allowed to terminate the contract unless there was a good reason for such termination. When there was no good reason, the defendant should, either give at least a two-year prior notice to the plaintiff or should provide the plaintiff with a reasonable compensation. Nevertheless, the defendant terminated the contract without any good reason just in order to take the plaintiff's customers. Such act of the defendant constitutes tort and, therefore, the defendant is liable to compensate the damages caused to the plaintiff.

2. The defendant moved to dismiss the complaint on the ground that, since the paragraph 16 of the 1969 contract requires all disputes and controversies relating to said contract to be settled by an arbitration to be held in New York City in accordance with the rules of the International Chamber of Commerce, it precludes court litigation and the plaintiff must exhaust such an arbitration procedure. The details of the defendant's arguments are as follows:

(1) In the paragraph 17 of said contract, the parties agreed that the agency contract is to be governed by the laws of the State of New York. The arbitration agreement is also governed by said laws. According to Section 7501 of the New York Civil Practice Law, a written agreement to submit any controversy thereafter arising to arbitration is enforceable.

Under said laws, the arbitration clause of the 1969 contract, which reads *"may at the option of either party* be finally settled by arbitration", should be interpreted that neither party may bring an action before court to settled any dispute if the other party objects to a proceeding in court accordingly, the defendant's motion to dismiss the complaint should be permitted.

(2) Although the 1969 contract specifies the contract to expire on January 31, 1970, the parties continue, even after said date, the transactions under the same conditions and in the same manner as they have transacted under the 1969 contract before said date. While it is the established law of New York that, where parties continued the same transactions after expiration of a contract as before the

expiration, there is an implication of fact that the parties intended to renew the contract. Accordingly, under the New York laws which govern 1969 contract, it is held that said contract was renewed by an implied agreement between the plaintiff and defendant.

(3) Section 7501 of the Civil practice Law of the State of New York requires an arbitration agreement to be made in writing. Such formality requirement is considered to be fulfilled where there is an arbitration clause contained in the written 1969 contract which was impliedly renewed by the fact the parties continued to perform after its expiration date.

(4) All disputes must be arbitrated whether or not the claim is based on a tort theory if the alleged tort has its genesis in the 1969 contract. The mere fact that the plaintiff chose the tort theory rather than breach of contract is not irrelevant in law. Further, when the dispute before court is related to the termination of the 1969 contract, such dispute shall be settled by arbitration even after the contract was terminated.

3. The plaintiff's counter-arguments are as follows:

(1) (a) The arbitration clause was inserted into the 1969 contract by the pressure by economic superiority of the defendant, and the plaintiff had no intention or gave no consent to rely on the arbitration clause.

(b) The provision of the arbitration clause in the 1969 contract uses the wording of "may" be settled instead of the wording "shall" be settled, which means that only the party who actively commences an action has the option to choose either arbitration procedure or litigation, and the defendant shall not be allowed to object against the choice of litigation by the plaintiff.

(2) The arbitration clause was terminated when the 1969 contract expired on January 31, 1970. Since there was no mutual agreement as expected in the proviso of paragraph 9 of the 1969 contact (which reads "unless renewed by the parties upon terms established by mutual agreement"), it should not be considered that the 1969 contact has been impliedly renewed. The continuance by parties of some transactions after the expiration date shall only mean that a quite new agency agreement was impliedly established between the parties, independently from the 1969 contract, and that the new contract had no arbitration clause any more.

(3) Even if the renewal of the 1969 contract was impliedly agreed, the arbitration clause lost its validity and enforceability, since the renewal was not made in writing and, under the laws of New York, such an oral arbitration agreement is not enforceable.

(4) (a) Even if the arbitration agreement was also impliedly renewed, it was terminated by the defendant when the defendant terminated the 1969 contract by the notice dated February 14, 1974.

(b) Further, the arbitration clause is not applicable when the action is based on the tort of the defendants.

Summary of Judgment:

Court accepted the defendant's motion and dismissed the complaint.

Court also ordered the court costs to be borne by the plaintiff.

The reasons of the judgment are as follows:

1. (a) Court found that the 1969 contract was signed by the plaintiff after several exchanges of discussions and revisions of drafts between the parties and that, in the course of such negotiations made prior to the execution of the 1969 contract, the plaintiff raised no objection against the arbitration clause. Therefore Court rejected the plaintiff's argument that the arbitration clause was inserted into the contract without any consent by the plaintiff.

(b) Examining the precedents under the New York laws which Court found the laws governing not only the 1969 agency contract but also the arbitration agreement contained therein, Court held that the provision of the paragraph 16 (arbitration clause) of the 1969 contract, although it uses the word "may" instead of "shall", gives to both parties the right to rely on arbitration procedure, and Court rejected the plaintiff's argument that only the party actively commencing an action has the option to choose an arbitration.

2. With respect to the plaintiff's argument that the arbitration agreement was terminated upon the expiration on January 31, 1970 of the 1969 contract, Court carefully studied the precedents under New York laws and found that there is an established rule which admits the theory of "implied renewal" of contract which seems to be similar to the theory relating to lease contracts under the Japanese laws and that an agreement to renew an original contract may be found when the parties continued the transactions under the same conditions and in the same manner as before the expiration of the original contract. Such theory is applicable not only to lease contracts and employment contracts but also to agency agreements. The transactions and relationship maintained between the plaintiff and defendant after the expiration on January 31, 1970 of the 1969 contract are sufficient to find the implied agreement to renew the contract.

The proviso of the paragraph 9 of the 1969 contract reading "unless renewed by the parties upon terms established by mutual agreement" does not mean to exclude any implied renewal to be made under the same terms and conditions as those of the original contract.

3. With respect to the formality requirement under the New York laws that an arbitration agreement must be made in writing, Court held that, as far as the original arbitration agreement before renewal was made in writing, such an arbitration agreement can be effectively renewed either orally or impliedly.

4. (a) With respect to the plaintiff's argument that the arbitration agreement was terminated upon their termination by the defendant of the 1969 contract, it is apparent to Court from the phrases of the arbitration clause (reading "all disputes . . . which may arise . . . out of our in relation to or in connection with this Agreement") that the parties had the intention to solve by arbitration disputes relating to the termination of the contract, too. Such interpretation may be also supported by the case under the New York laws.

In other words, the arbitration clause may continue to bind parties independently from the termination of the main contract, where the clause provides that all disputes "in relation to the agreement" must be referred to arbitration.

(b) With respect to the plaintiff's argument that the claim based on a tortious act shall not be decided by arbitration, Court held that, since the alleged tortious claim is the issue on whether or not the termination of the 1969 contract is legal, it is an issue "in relation to" the contract. The plaintiff cannot avoid arbitration by making its claim on a tort theory.

Thus, Court concluded that the plaintiff's claim based on the alleged tortious set falls under the scope of the arbitration agreement validly and effectively binding the plaintiff and defendant and, therefore, that the issue must be settled by arbitration. The complaint must be dismissed.

> **QUESTIONS**
>
> From the cases included herein, under what circumstance would an arbitration clause not be enforceable more readily in the United States, Canada, Japan, China, or Mexico? Were an action filed in a court, could arbitration proceed in any of the three countries until a judicial determination had been reached with respect to the enforceability of the arbitration agreement in question? Would a separate action for an anti-suit injunction be appropriate in such a case to prevent such litigation?

D. European Union

In light of the comment and other provisions of EU Regulation No. 1215/2012 discussed in Chapters 3 and 6, consider the continued relevance of the following case:

ALLIANZ SPA FORMERLY RIUNIONE ADRIATICA DI SICURTÀ SPA, GENERALI ASSICURAZIONI GENERALI SPA v. WEST TANKERS INC.
Case C-185/07, Judgment of 10 February 2009

1 This reference for a preliminary ruling concerns the interpretation of Council Regulation (EC) No 44/2001 of 22 December 2000 on jurisdiction and the recognition and enforcement of judgments in civil and commercial matters . . . .

2 The reference was made in the context of proceedings between, on the one hand, Allianz SpA, formerly Riunione Adriatica di Sicurtà SpA, and Generali Assicurazioni Generali SpA ('Allianz and Generali') and, on the other, West Tankers Inc. ('West Tankers') concerning West Tankers' liability in tort.

II. ARBITRATION AGREEMENTS

LEGAL CONTEXT

International law

3 The Convention on the Recognition and Enforcement of Foreign Arbitral Awards, signed in New York on 10 June 1958 (*United Nations Treaty Series*, Vol. 330, p. 3) ('the New York Convention'), provides as follows in Article II(3):

'The court of a Contracting State, when seised of an action in a matter in respect of which the parties have made an agreement within the meaning of this article, shall, at the request of one of the parties, refer the parties to arbitration, unless it finds that the said agreement is null and void, inoperative or incapable of being performed.'

Community law

4 According to recital 25 in the preamble to Regulation No 44/2001:

'Respect for international commitments entered into by the Member States means that this Regulation should not affect conventions relating to specific matters to which the Member States are parties.'

5 Article 1(1) and (2) of that regulation provides:

1. This Regulation shall apply in civil and commercial matters whatever the nature of the court or tribunal. It shall not extend, in particular, to revenue, customs or administrative matters.

2. The Regulation shall not apply to:

(d) arbitration.'

6 Article 5 of that regulation provides:

A person domiciled in a Member State may, in another Member State, be sued:

(3) in matters relating to tort, delict or quasi-delict, in the courts for the place where the harmful event occurred or may occur;

National law

7 Section 37(1) of the Supreme Court Act 1981 provides:

'The High Court may by order (whether interlocutory or final) grant an injunction . . . in all cases in which it appears to the court to be just and convenient to do so.'

8 Section 44 of the Arbitration Act 1996, entitled 'Court powers exercisable in support of arbitral proceedings', provides:

'(1) Unless otherwise agreed by the parties, the court has for the purposes of and in relation to arbitral proceedings the same power of making orders about the matters listed below as it has for the purposes of and in relation to legal proceedings.

(2) Those matters are

(e) the granting of an interim injunction . . .

THE DISPUTE IN THE MAIN PROCEEDINGS AND THE QUESTION REFERRED FOR A PRELIMINARY RULING

9 In August 2000 the *Front Comor*, a vessel owned by West Tankers and chartered by Erg Petroli SpA ('Erg'), collided in Syracuse (Italy) with a jetty owned by Erg and caused damage. The charterparty was governed by English law and contained a clause providing for arbitration in London (United Kingdom).

10 Erg claimed compensation from its insurers Allianz and Generali up to the limit of its insurance cover and commenced arbitration proceedings in London against West Tankers for the excess. West Tankers denied liability for the damage caused by the collision.

11 Having paid Erg compensation under the insurance policies for the loss it had suffered, Allianz and Generali brought proceedings on 30 July 2003 against West Tankers before the Tribunale di Siracusa (Italy) in order to recover the sums they had paid to Erg. The action was based on their statutory right of subrogation to Erg's claims, in accordance with Article 1916 of the Italian Civil Code. West Tankers raised an objection of lack of jurisdiction on the basis of the existence of the arbitration agreement.

12 In parallel, West Tankers brought proceedings, on 10 September 2004, before the High Court of Justice of England and Wales, Queens Bench Division (Commercial Court), seeking a declaration that the dispute between itself, on the one hand, and Allianz and Generali, on the other, was to be settled by arbitration pursuant to the arbitration agreement. West Tankers also sought an injunction restraining Allianz and Generali from pursuing any proceedings other than arbitration and requiring them to discontinue the proceedings commenced before the Tribunale di Siracusa ('the anti-suit injunction').

13 By judgment of 21 March 2005, the High Court of Justice of England and Wales, Queens Bench Division (Commercial Court), upheld West Tankers' claims and granted the anti-suit injunction sought against Allianz and Generali. The latter appealed against that judgment to the House of Lords. They argued that the grant of such an injunction is contrary to Regulation No 44/2001.

14 The House of Lords first referred to the judgments in Case C-116/02 *Gasser* [2003] ECR I-14693 and Case C-159/02 *Turner* [2004] ECR I-3565, which decided in substance that an injunction restraining a party from commencing or continuing proceedings in a court of a Member State cannot be compatible with the system established by Regulation No 44/2001, even where it is granted by the court having jurisdiction under that regulation. That is because the regulation provides a complete set of uniform rules on the allocation of jurisdiction between the courts of the Member States which must trust each other to apply those rules correctly.

15 However, that principle cannot, in the view of the House of Lords, be extended to arbitration, which is completely excluded from the scope of Regulation No 44/2001 by virtue of Article 1(2)(d) thereof. In that field, there is no set of uniform Community rules, which is a necessary condition in order that mutual trust between the courts of the Member States may be established and applied. Moreover, it is clear from the judgment in Case C-190/89 *Rich* [1991] ECR I-3855 that the exclusion in Article 1(2)(d) of Regulation No 44/2001 applies not only to arbitration proceedings as such, but also to legal proceedings the subject-matter of which is arbitration. The judgment in Case C-391/95 *Van Uden* [1998] ECR I-7091 stated that arbitration is the subject-matter of proceedings where they serve to protect the right to determine the dispute by arbitration, which is the case in the main proceedings.

16 The House of Lords adds that since all arbitration matters fall outside the scope of Regulation No 44/2001, an injunction addressed to Allianz and Generali restraining them from having recourse to proceedings other than arbitration and from continuing proceedings before the Tribunale di Siracusa cannot infringe the regulation.

17 Finally, the House of Lords points out that the courts of the United Kingdom have for many years used anti-suit injunctions. That practice is, in its view, a valuable tool for the court of the seat of arbitration, exercising supervisory jurisdiction over the arbitration, as it promotes legal certainty and reduces the possibility of conflict between the arbitration award and the judgment of a national court. Furthermore, if the practice were also adopted by the courts in other Member States it would make the European Community more competitive vis-à-vis international arbitration centres such as New York, Bermuda and Singapore.

18 In those circumstances, the House of Lords decided to stay its proceedings and to refer the following question to the Court for a preliminary ruling:

> '*Is it consistent with Regulation No 44/2001 for a court of a Member State to make an order to restrain a person from commencing or continuing proceedings in another Member State on the ground that such proceedings are in breach of an arbitration agreement?*'

THE QUESTION REFERRED FOR A PRELIMINARY RULING

19 By its question, the House of Lords asks, essentially, whether it is incompatible with Regulation No 44/2001 for a court of a Member State to make an order to restrain a person from commencing or continuing proceedings before the courts of another Member State on the ground that such proceedings would be contrary to an arbitration agreement, even though Article 1(2)(d) of the regulation excludes arbitration from the scope thereof.

20 An anti-suit injunction, such as that in the main proceedings, may be directed against actual or potential claimants in proceedings abroad. As observed by the Advocate General in point 14 of her Opinion, non-compliance with an anti-suit injunction is contempt of court, for which penalties can be imposed, including imprisonment or seizure of assets.

21 Both West Tankers and the United Kingdom Government submit that such an injunction is not incompatible with Regulation No 44/2001 because Article 1(2)(d) thereof excludes arbitration from its scope of application.

22 In that regard it must be borne in mind that, in order to determine whether a dispute falls within the scope of Regulation No 44/2001, reference must be made solely to the subject-matter of the proceedings (*Rich*, paragraph 26). More specifically, its place in the scope of Regulation No 44/2001 is determined by the nature of the rights which the proceedings in question serve to protect (*Van Uden*, paragraph 33).

23 Proceedings, such as those in the main proceedings, which lead to the making of an anti-suit injunction, cannot, therefore, come within the scope of Regulation No 44/2001.

24 *However, even though proceedings do not come within the scope of Regulation No 44/2001, they may nevertheless have consequences which undermine its effectiveness, namely preventing the attainment of the objectives of unification of the rules of conflict of jurisdiction in civil and commercial matters and the free movement of decisions in those matters. This is so, inter alia, where such proceedings prevent a court of another Member State from exercising the jurisdiction conferred on it by Regulation No 44/2001.* [Emphasis added.]

25 It is therefore appropriate to consider whether the proceedings brought by Allianz and Generali against West Tankers before the Tribunale di Siracusa themselves come within the scope of Regulation No 44/2001 and then to ascertain the effects of the anti-suit injunction on those proceedings.

26 In that regard, the Court finds, as noted by the Advocate General in points 53 and 54 of her Opinion, that, if, because of the subject-matter of the dispute, that is, the nature of the rights to be protected in proceedings, such as a claim for damages, those proceedings come within the scope of Regulation No 44/2001, a preliminary issue concerning the applicability of an arbitration agreement, including in particular its validity, also comes within its scope of application. This finding is supported by paragraph 35 of the Report on the accession of the Hellenic Republic to the Convention of 27 September 1968 on Jurisdiction and the Enforcement of Judgments in Civil and Commercial Matters (OJ 1978 L 304, p. 36) ('the Brussels Convention'), presented by Messrs Evrigenis and Kerameus (OJ 1986 C 298, p. 1). That paragraph states that the verification, as an incidental question, of the validity of an arbitration agreement which is cited by a litigant in order to contest the jurisdiction of the court before which he is being sued pursuant to the Brussels Convention, must be considered as falling within its scope.

27 It follows that the objection of lack of jurisdiction raised by West Tankers before the Tribunale di Siracusa on the basis of the existence of an arbitration agreement, including the question of the validity of that agreement, comes within the scope of Regulation No 44/2001 and that it is therefore exclusively for that court to rule on that objection and on its own jurisdiction, pursuant to Articles 1(2)(d) and 5(3) of that regulation.

28 *Accordingly, the use of an anti-suit injunction to prevent a court of a Member State, which normally has jurisdiction to resolve a dispute under Article 5(3) of*

Regulation No 44/2001, from ruling, in accordance with Article 1(2)(d) of that regulation, on the very applicability of the regulation to the dispute brought before it necessarily amounts to stripping that court of the power to rule on its own jurisdiction under Regulation No 44/2001. [Emphasis added.]

29 It follows, first, as noted by the Advocate General in point 57 of her Opinion, that an anti-suit injunction, such as that in the main proceedings, is contrary to the general principle which emerges from the case-law of the Court on the Brussels Convention, that every court seised itself determines, under the rules applicable to it, whether it has jurisdiction to resolve the dispute before it (see, to that effect, *Gasser*, paragraphs 48 and 49). It should be borne in mind in that regard that Regulation No 44/2001, apart from a few limited exceptions which are not relevant to the main proceedings, does not authorise the jurisdiction of a court of a Member State to be reviewed by a court in another Member State (Case C-351/89 *Overseas Union Insurance and Others* [1991] ECR I-3317, paragraph 24, and *Turner*, paragraph 26). That jurisdiction is determined directly by the rules laid down by that regulation, including those relating to its scope of application. Thus in no case is a court of one Member State in a better position to determine whether the court of another Member State has jurisdiction (*OverseasUnion Insurance and Others*, paragraph 23, and *Gasser*, paragraph 48).

30 Further, in obstructing the court of another Member State in the exercise of the powers conferred on it by Regulation No 44/2001, namely to decide, on the basis of the rules defining the material scope of that regulation, including Article 1(2)(d) thereof, whether that regulation is applicable, such an anti-suit injunction also runs counter to the trust which the Member States accord to one another's legal systems and judicial institutions and on which the system of jurisdiction under Regulation No 44/2001 is based (*see*, to that effect, *Turner*, paragraph 24).

31 Lastly, if, by means of an anti-suit injunction, the Tribunale di Siracusa were prevented from examining itself the preliminary issue of the validity or the applicability of the arbitration agreement, a party could avoid the proceedings merely by relying on that agreement and the applicant, which considers that the agreement is void, inoperative or incapable of being performed, would thus be barred from access to the court before which it brought proceedings under Article 5(3) of Regulation No 44/2001 and would therefore be deprived of a form of judicial protection to which it is entitled.

32 *Consequently, an anti-suit injunction, such as that in the main proceedings, is not compatible with Regulation No 44/2001.* [Emphasis added.]

33 This finding is supported by Article II(3) of the New York Convention, according to which it is the court of a Contracting State, when seised of an action in a matter in respect of which the parties have made an arbitration agreement, that will, at the request of one of the parties, refer the parties to arbitration, unless it finds that the said agreement is null and void, inoperative or incapable of being performed.

34 In the light of the foregoing considerations, the answer to the question referred is that it is incompatible with Regulation No 44/2001 for a court of a Member State to make an order to restrain a person from commencing or

continuing proceedings before the courts of another Member State on the ground that such proceedings would be contrary to an arbitration agreement.

Costs

35 Since these proceedings are, for the parties to the main proceedings, a step in the action pending before the national court, the decision on costs is a matter for that court. Costs incurred in submitting observations to the Court, other than the costs of those parties, are not recoverable.

On those grounds, the Court (Grand Chamber) hereby rules:

It is incompatible with Council Regulation (EC) No 44/2001 of 22 December 2000 on jurisdiction and the recognition and enforcement of judgments in civil and commercial matters for a court of a Member State to make an order to restrain a person from commencing or continuing proceedings before the courts of another Member State on the ground that such proceedings would be contrary to an arbitration agreement. [Emphasis added.]

QUESTION

What is the likely impact of this decision on courts outside of the EU considering anti-suit injunctions against potential parallel litigant within an EU member state? Recall the French court decision *In Zone Brands*, Civ. 1ère, 14 October 2009, *pourvoin* 08-16.369, recognizing an anti-suit injunction against a French firm issued by a Georgia court pursuant to forum selection clause.

REVIEW PROBLEM

Assume that an art museum in a relatively small Midwestern town receives a gift of several million dollars from a wealthy local donor to invest in significant medieval paintings and other art work. The museum begins to purchase works from galleries and at art auctions. In the process, the director of the museum learns of the sale by a gallery of an etching alleged to be by Albrecht Dürer. Interested but concerned over the lack of provision of any provenance for the work, the director of the museum agrees to the purchase but only on the condition that the gallery warrant both the authenticity as well as valid, transferable title to the drawing. In turn, the gallery insists that the sales contract include the following provision:

> "Any and all disputes between the parties to this sale shall be submitted to a three-man arbitration panel in New York. Each of the parties concerned is to name one member of the panel, and these two arbitrators are to name the third member. Each arbitrator must have demonstrable expertise in the authentication and appraisal of works of medieval European art. An arbitration award must be based on agreement of at least two of the members of the panel."

Would you recommend that the museum accept? What, if any, modifications or more efficient alternatives would you suggest that the museum propose? Consider the following possibilities:

(a) Suppose that a German count (*Graf*) claims that the drawing was stolen from his grandfather's home by an American serviceman in 1945 and demands that the museum return the drawing. The museum refuses and the count sues for recovery. Given the arbitration clause, could the museum successfully implead the gallery under Rule 14(a)(1) of the Federal Rules of Civil Procedure for indemnification under the contract should the count succeed?

(b) What if the museum does not implead the gallery but the count succeeds in the suit, assuming that the gallery rejected a claim by the museum under the agreement for the purchase price and indemnification for legal expenses incurred in the lawsuit, would the museum be compelled to resort to arbitration? What if the gallery were first to file suit in Italy? Could such action result in significant delay and cost?

(c) What if, after the museum initiated arbitration proceedings, naming its arbitrator, the gallery instructed its arbitrator to reject any person nominated as the third arbitrator? How long could such an impasse last and, assuming the two arbitrators charge an hourly fee, how costly could the proceedings become?

(d) What if, despite proof of the guarantee, an arbitral decision were handed down in favor of the gallery? Could the museum appeal the ruling?

(e) What recourse if any would the museum have were an arbitral award in favor of the museum was handed down but the gallery refused to comply? Would the outcome differ in terms of time and cost had the parties litigated the dispute from the outset?

(f) What if as a matter of law the liability of the gallery to the museum under the agreement was not subject to any reasonable doubt. Would the parties be more likely to settle were the agreement to include (i) a choice of court and law of the forum clause or (ii) and arbitration clause?

Albrecht Düer's *Portrait of Hans Tucher*, one of the few of the several thousand missing German art works from World War II to have been recovered. *See Kunstsammlungen Zu Weimar v. Elicofon*, 678 F.2d 1150 (2d Cir. 1982).

Appendix A

CODE OF CIVIL PROCEDURE OF JAPAN

CODE OF CIVIL PROCEDURE OF JAPAN
(as amended in 2011, effective 2012)

Part One
General Provisions

Chapter II
Courts

Section 1
Jurisdiction

Article 3-2 [*Jurisdiction Based on Domicile*]

1. In civil actions brought against a natural persons, the courts shall have jurisdiction [*kankatsu*] if his domicile [*jūsho*]* is in Japan or, in case his domicile is not in Japan or is unknown, his residence [*kyosho*] in Japan; or, if he has no residence in Japan or if his residence is unknown, he has ever had their domicile in Japan prior to the filing of the action (except in cases where he has established his domicile abroad after having been domiciled in Japan).

2. Notwithstanding the preceding paragraph, the courts shall have jurisdiction in civil actions against ambassadors, ministers, and other Japanese nationals living in a foreign country who are immune from suit in such country.

3. In civil actions against a juridical person, or other association or foundation, the courts shall have jurisdiction if its principal office or place of business is in Japan or if the domicile of its representative or principal person in charge of their business is in Japan in the event [such defendant] does not have an office or principal place of business in Japan or the location [of such office or place of business] is unknown.

Article 3-3 [*Jurisdiction over Actions Related to Duties Under Contracts and Other Obligations*]

The actions described in each of the following provisions may be brought in a Japanese court.

(i) Actions to enforce contract duties as well as actions for management of affairs without mandate (*jimu kanri*) or unjust enrichment (*futō rieki*) arising out of contractual undertakings, actions for damages for non-performance of

---

* Domicile (*jūsho*) is defined in article 21 of the Civil Code as the "principal place where a person lives." In other words the place where a person's life is centered. See also article 102 of the French Civil Code.

contractual duties, and other actions arising under contract if the place of performance under the contract in Japan or the place of performance of the contract under the law selected by the parties to the contract is in Japan;

(ii) Actions for payment of money under a promissory note (*tegata*) or check (*kogite*) if the place of payment is in Japan;

(iii) Actions related to rights in assets (*zaidanken jō no uttae*), if the action is for the payment of money, if the defendant's attachable assets are located in Japan (unless value of such assets is extremely low).

(iv) Actions against persons having an office that relate to the activities carried out in that office if the office is located in Japan.

(v) Actions against persons engaged in business in Japan (including foreign companies (as defined by Article 2(2) of the Company Law, Law No. 86, 2005) that continuously engage in commercial transactions in Japan) if the action relates to such business in Japan.

(vi) Actions based on a maritime lien and any other claims secured by a vessel if the vessel is located in Japan.

(vii) Actions as specified below related to a company or any other association or foundation if the association or foundation is a legal person, if it was incorporated under Japanese law; or, if it is not a legal person, if its principal office is located in Japan:

(a) actions by a company or other association against present or former members, actions by a member against present or former members, or actions by a former member against present members, each of which is based on [the claimant's] status as a member;

(b) actions by an association or foundation against its present or former officers based on [the claimant's] status as an officer;

(c) actions by a company against present or former incorporators or inspectors, based on [the claimant's] status as an incorporator or inspector;

(d) Actions by creditors of a company or other association against present or former members, based on [the claimant's] status as a member.

(viii) Actions relating to delicts [torts] if the delict occurred in Japan (except where the effects of a delict committed abroad has occurred in Japan but normally such effect in Japan would have been unforeseeable).

(ix) Actions for compensatory damages arising from a collision of ships or any other accident at sea if the initial location at which the damaged ship arrived is in Japan.

(x) Actions related to salvage if the salvage was performed in Japan or if location of the salvaged ship first arrival is in Japan.

(xi) Actions related to immovable property if the immovable property is located in Japan.

(xii) Actions related to rights of succession or hereditary reserves or actions related to testamentary gifts or any other acts effective upon death if the deceased was domiciled in Japan at the time of the commencement of succession; or, when the deceased had no domicile or the domicile is unknown, if [the deceased] was resident in Japan at the time of the commencement of succession (except where [the deceased] was domiciled abroad after having been last domiciled in Japan).

(xiii) Actions related to legal encumbrances on inherited rights or any other burdens on the inherited assets that are not described the preceding subparagraph.

Article 3-4 [*Jurisdiction over Actions Relating to Consumer Contracts and Employment Relations*]

. . . .

Article 3-5 [*Exclusive Jurisdiction*]

1. Actions provided in Chapter II (except those provided in Sections 4 and 6) of Part VII of the Company Law, actions provided in Section 2 of Chapter VI of the Law concerning General Incorporated Associations and General Incorporated Foundations (Law No. 48, 2006) and analogous actions relating to associations or foundations incorporated under other Japanese legislation shall be subject to the exclusive jurisdiction of the Japanese courts.

2. Actions with respect to registration shall be subject to the exclusive jurisdiction of the Japanese courts if the place of registration is located in Japan.

3. Actions with respect to the existence and effect of intellectual property rights . . . that become effective upon registration shall be subject to the exclusive jurisdiction of the Japanese courts if the registration was effected in Japan.

Article 3-6 [*Joinder of Claims*]

Where two or more claims are joined in a single action and courts of Japan have jurisdiction only over one of them, such action may be filed with the courts of Japan only if the particular claim over which the jurisdiction exists has a close connection with the other claims. However, with respect to actions brought by or against two or more persons, the foregoing applies only in the cases described in the first paragraph of Article 38.

Article 3-7 [*Jurisdiction Agreements*]

1. The parties may determine by agreement the country in which they may file an action.

2. The agreement provided in the preceding paragraph shall have no effect unless it is in writing and relates to an action arising from specific legal relationships.

3. For the purpose of the preceding paragraph, an agreement is deemed to be in writing if it is recorded in an electromagnetic record (*i.e.*, a record made in an electronic form, a magnetic form, or any other form unrecognizable to human perception used for information processing by computers).

4. An agreement to file an action exclusively with the courts of a particular foreign

country may not be invoked if those courts are legally or factually unable to exercise jurisdiction.

5. An agreement provided in paragraph (1) having as its object a future dispute arising in connection with a consumer contract shall have effect only as set forth below:

(i) if the agreement allows an action to be filed in the country where the consumer was domiciled at the time of the conclusion of the contract. (If the agreement purports to allow an action to be filed exclusively in that country, [such agreement] shall not prejudice the right [of the consumer] to file in other countries except in the cases provided in the following sub-paragraph.); or

(ii) if the consumer has filed an action in the country specified by the or where the consumer has invoked the agreement in response to an action brought by the business operator in Japan or in a foreign country.

6. The agreement provided in paragraph (1) having as its object a civil dispute over individual employment relations shall have effect only as set forth below:

(i) if the agreement concluded at the time the employment contract terminated stipulates that an action may be brought in the country in which the labor was being supplied at the time of the conclusion of the agreement. (If the agreement purports to allow an action to be filed exclusively in that country, [such agreement] shall not prejudice to the right of [the employee] to file in other countries except in the cases provided in the following sub-paragraph.); or

(ii) if the employee has filed an action in the country specified by the agreement or where the employee has invoked the agreement in response to an action brought by the employer in Japan or in a foreign country.

Article 3-8 [*Jurisdiction by Submission*]

The courts shall have jurisdiction where the defendant, without objecting to jurisdiction, has made an oral argument on the merits or made a statement in preliminary proceedings.

Article 3-9 [*Dismissal of Action Under Special Circumstances*]

Even where Japanese courts have jurisdiction over an action (except when the action has been brought on the basis of an exclusive jurisdiction agreement in favor of the Japanese courts), the court may dismiss whole or part of such action if, taking into account the nature of the case, the burden of the defendant to answer the claim, the location of evidence and any other factors, the court finds that there are special circumstances under which hearing and determining the case in Japan would impair fairness between the parties or hinder the proper and efficient conduct of hearing.

Article 3-10 [*Exclusion of Application in the Case of Exclusive Jurisdiction*]

The provisions contained in Articles 3-2 to 3-4 and those contained in Article 3-6 to the preceding Article shall have no application where the exclusive jurisdiction of the Japanese courts is prescribed by legislation with respect to the action in question.

[Articles 3-11 and 3-12 omitted.]

Article 4 [*General forum*]

1. A civil action is within the jurisdiction of the court with jurisdiction over the general forum of the defendant.

2. The general forum of a person is determined by his domicile, in case his does domicile is not in Japan or his domicile is unknown, by his residence, and in case he does not have residence in Japan or his residence is unknown, by his last domicile.

3. In the event the general forum of ambassadors, ministers, and other Japanese nationals who reside in a foreign country but are exempted from its jurisdiction cannot be determined by the preceding paragraph, the general forum shall be determined by the Rules of Supreme Court.

4. The general forum of a juristic person or other association or foundation is determined by its principal office or place of business, and, in the event, it has no office or place of business, by the domicile of its representative or person in charge of its business [in Japan].

5. Notwithstanding the preceding paragraph, the general forum of a foreign association or foundation is determined by its principal office or place of business in Japan, and if it has no such office or place of business in Japan, by the domicile of its representative or person in charge of its business.

6. The general forum of the state [*kuni*] is determined by the location of the governmental office representing the state in the civil action in question.

Article 5 [*Forum for Civil Actions for Monetary and Other Claims Against Property (zaisanken)*]

The following civil actions may be brought before the court having jurisdiction over the following locations:

(i) actions involving monetary and other claims against assets [*zaisanken*]: place of performance;

(ii) actions for payment of promissory notes or checks: place of payment indicated on the promissory note or check;

(iii) actions involving monetary and other claims against the assets [*zaisanken*] of seaman: place of their ship's registry;

(iv) actions involving monetary and other claims against the assets of persons who do not have domicile (in case of a legal person, office or place of business; hereinafter the same) in Japan or whose domicile is unknown: the place where the subject of the claim or its security or an attachable asset of defendant is located;

(v) actions against persons who have an office or place of business and involving business at such an office or place of business: location of such office or place of business;

(vi) suits against shipowners or persons utilizing a ship in connection with his or her voyage: place of the ship's registry;

(vii) actions involving claims with a ship as security: place where the ship is located;

(viii) the following actions involving companies, associations or foundations: place of the general forum of the company, association, or foundation:

(a) an action by a company or other association against an employee or ex-employee an action by an employee against another employee or an ex-employee or an action by an ex-employee against an employee, based on a party's position as such;

(b) an action by an association or foundation against an officer or ex-officer, based on a party's position as such;

(c) an action by a corporation against an incorporator, ex-incorporator, inspector or ex-inspector, based on a party's position as such;

(d) an action by a creditor of a corporation or other association against an employee or ex-employee, based on a party's position as such;

(ix) actions for damages in tort: place where the tort occurred;

(x) actions for claims arising out of a maritime accident, such as a collision of ships: place where a ship first reached shore;

(xi) actions with respect to marine salvage: place where the marine salvage was made or where a salvaged ship first reached shore;

(xii) actions with respect to real property: place where the real property is located;

(xiii) actions with respect to registration or recordation: place where such registration or recordation has been or is to be made;

(xiv) actions with respect to succession, mandatory portions [*legitim*] or testation or other conduct having effect as a result of death: place of general forum of the decedent at the time of commencement of succession;

(xv) actions with respect to inheritance or its incumbrance, which does not fall into the preceding paragraph, provided that any part or all of the inheritance is locates where the court has jurisdiction pursuant to the preceding paragraph: place as provided in the preceding paragraph.

. . . .

Article 7 [*Joinder of Claims*]

Where two or more claims are to be made by a single action, such action may be filed with the court which shall have jurisdiction over one of those claims pursuant to the provisions of Article 4 to the preceding Article (excluding Article 63); provided, however, that with regard to an action brought by two or more persons or an action brought against two or more persons, this shall apply only in the case specified in the first sentence of Article 38.

Article 38 [*Conditions for Joinder of Claims*]

1. If the rights or liabilities for a suit are common to more than one person or are based on the same ground of facts or laws, such more than one person may sue or

be sued as co-litigants. The same will be applied if the rights or liabilities for the suit are the same and based on the same kind of facts and laws.

. . . .

Chapter V
Court Proceedings

. . . .

Section 5
Judicial Decisions

. . . .

Article 118   [*Effect of Final and Binding Judgment Rendered by a Foreign Court*]

A final and binding judgment rendered by a foreign court shall be effective only where it meets all of the following requirements:

(i) The jurisdiction of the foreign court is recognized under laws or regulations or conventions or treaties.

(ii) The defeated defendant has received notice (excluding notice by publication or any other notice similar thereto) of a summons or order necessary for the commencement of the suit, or has appeared without receiving such notice.

(iii) The content of the judgment and the court proceedings are not contrary to public policy in Japan.

(iv) A mutual guarantee exists.

. . . .

Chapter VI
Disposition of Collection of Evidence prior to Filing of Action

Article 132-2   [*Inquiry prior to Filing of Action*]

1. Where a person who intends to file an action has given by means of a document, to the person who is to be the defendant in the action, an advance notice of filing of an action (hereinafter referred to as an "advance notice" in this Chapter), the person who has given the advance notice (hereinafter referred to as the "advance noticer" in this Chapter), within four months after the day on which the advance notice has been given, may specify a reasonable period and make an inquiry by means of a document to the person who has received the advance notice in order to request him/her to make a response by means of a document, before the filing of the action, with regard to the matters that would be obviously necessary for preparing allegations or proof should the action actually be filed; provided, however, that this shall not apply if the inquiry falls under any of the following items:

(i) Inquiry that falls under any of the items of Article 163*

(ii) Inquiry with regard to the matters concerning a secret on the private life of the opponent or a third party, any response to which would be substantially detrimental to the opponent or the third party in his/her social life

(iii) Inquiry with regard to the matters concerning a trade secret held by the opponent or a third party

2. In the case of an inquiry with regard to the matters concerning a secret on the private life of a third party prescribed in item (b) of the preceding paragraph or a trade secret held by a third party prescribed in item (c) of said paragraph, these provisions shall not apply where the third party has consented to the opponent making a response to such inquiry.

3. A document of the advance notice shall state the gist of the claim pertaining to the action to be filed and the points of the dispute.

4. An inquiry set forth in paragraph (a) may not be made based on the advance notice that overlaps with any previous advance notice.

Article 132-3

1. When a person who has received the advance notice (hereinafter referred to as a "recipient of advance notice" in this Chapter) has made a response to the advance notice by providing the advance noticer with a document stating the gist of his/her answers regarding the gist of the claim and the points of the dispute set forth in paragraph 3. of the preceding Article that are stated in the document of the advance notice, the recipient of advance notice, within four months after the day on which the advance notice has been given, may specify a reasonable period and make an inquiry by means of a document to the advance noticer in order to request him/her to make a response by means of a document, before the filing of the action, with regard to the matters that would be obviously necessary for preparing allegations or proof should the action actually be filed. In this case, the provisions of the proviso to paragraph 1. of said Article and paragraph 2. of said Article shall apply mutatis mutandis.

2. An inquiry set forth in the preceding paragraph may not be made based on a response to the advance notice that overlaps with any previous advance notice.

Article 132-4 [*Disposition of Collection of Evidence Prior to Filing of Action*]

---

* Article 163 provides: "A party, while the suit is pending, may specify a reasonable period and make an inquiry by means of a document to the opponent in order to request the opponent to make a response by means of a document with regard to the matters necessary for preparing allegations or proof; provided, however, that this shall not apply where the inquiry falls under any of the following items:
    (i) Inquiry that is not specific or individual
    (ii) Inquiry that insults or confuses the opponent
    (iii) Inquiry that overlaps with any previous inquiry
    (iv) Inquiry to ask opinions
    (v) Inquiry for which the opponent is required to spend unreasonable expenses or time to make a response
    (vi) Inquiry on the matters that are the same as the matters about which a witness may refuse to testify pursuant to the provisions of Article 196 or Article 197 [*see* below].

1. When a petition is filed by an advance noticer or a recipient of advance notice who made a response set forth in paragraph 1. of the preceding Article and it is found that the petitioner has difficulty collecting any material as evidence that would be obviously necessary for showing proof should the action pertaining to the advance notice actually be filed, the court, before the filing of the action, may make any of the following dispositions pertaining to such collection of evidence, after hearing opinions of the party to whom the advance notice has been given or the response has been made (hereinafter simply referred to as the "opposite party" in this Chapter); provided, however, that this shall not apply where the court finds it inappropriate to do so on the grounds that the time required for the collection or the burden borne by a person to be commissioned for the collection would be unreasonable:

(i) Commissioning the holder of a document (including an object prescribed in Article 231; hereinafter the same shall apply in this Chapter) to send the document

(ii) Commissioning a government agency or public office, a foreign government agency or public office, or a school, chamber of commerce, exchange or any other organization (referred to as a "public agency, etc." in paragraph (1)2. of the following Article) to conduct the necessary examination

(iii) Commissioning a person who has expert knowledge and experience to state his/her opinions based on such expert knowledge and experience

(iv) Ordering a court execution officer to conduct an examination on the shape, possession or other current status of an object

2. A petition for a disposition set forth in the preceding paragraph shall be filed within an unextendable period of four months from the day on which the advance notice was given; provided, however, that this shall not apply where the opposite party has given consent to the filing of the petition after the expiration of this period.

3. A petition for a disposition set forth in paragraph 1. may not be filed based on the advance notice that overlaps with any previous advance notice or based on a response to such overlapping advance notice.

4. The court, after making a disposition set forth in paragraph 1., may revoke the disposition if it is found to be inappropriate due to the circumstances prescribed in the proviso to said paragraph.

. . . .

Article 132-6 [*Procedure for Collection of Evidence*]

1. The court, when making a disposition set forth in Article 132-4(1)1. to 3., shall specify a period during which the person commissioned should send the document, report the examination results or state his/her opinions.

2. A report of the examination results based on the commission set forth in Article 132-41.(b) or under the order set forth in Article 132-41.(d) or a statement of opinion based on the commission set forth in Article 132-1.(c) shall be made by means of a document.

3. The court, when the document is sent, the examination results are reported or opinions are stated based on a disposition set forth in Article 132-4I., shall notify the petitioner and the opposite party to that effect.

4. The court, for use by the petitioner and the opposite party through the procedures specified in the following Article, shall retain the sent document or the document concerning the report of the examination results or statement of opinion within one month from the day on which the notice prescribed in the preceding paragraph was given.

5. The provision of Article 180(1) shall apply mutatis mutandis to a disposition set forth in Article 132-4(1), the provision of Article 184I. shall apply mutatis mutandis to a disposition set forth in Article 132-4(1)1. to 3., and the provision of Article 213 shall apply mutatis mutandis to a disposition set forthin Article 132-4(1)3..*

. . . .

Article 132-8 [*Disallowance of Appeal*]

No appeal may be entered against a judicial decision on a petition for a disposition set forth in Article 132-4I.

Article 132-9 [*Burden of Costs for Judicial Decision on Disposition of Collection of Evidence*]

Costs for a judicial decision on a petition for a disposition set forth in Article 132-4I. shall be borne by the petitioner.

Chapter IV
Evidence

Section 1
General Provisions

. . . .

Section 2
Examination of Witness

Article 196 [*Right of Refusal to Testify*]

If a witness's testimony relates to matters for which the witness or a person who has any of the following relationships [the witness] is likely to be subject to criminal prosecution or conviction, the witness may refuse to testify. The same shall apply where his/her testimony relates to matters that would harm the reputation of such persons:

---

* Article 184I. provides: "The examination of evidence to be conducted in a foreign state shall be commissioned to the competent government agency of that state or the Japanese ambassador, minister or consul stationed in that state." Article 213 provides: "An expert witness shall be designated by the court in charge of the case or an authorized judge or commissioned judge."

(i) A person who is or was the witness's spouse, relative by blood within the fourth degree or relative through marriage within the third degree

(ii) A person who is the witness's guardian or a person under the guardianship of the witness

Article 197

1. In the following cases, a witness may refuse to testify:

(i) The case set forth in Article 1911. [confidential information held by public employees related to their duties.]

(ii) Cases where a doctor, dentist, pharmacist, pharmaceuticals distributor, birthing assistant, attorney at law (including a registered foreign lawyer), patent attorney, defense counsel, notary or person engaged in a religious occupation, or a person who was any of these professionals is examined with regard to any fact which they have learnt in the course of their duties and which should be kept secret

(iii) Cases where the witness is examined with regard to matters concerning technical or professional secrets

2. The provision of the preceding paragraph shall not apply where the witness is released from his/her duty of secrecy.

Appendix B

REGULATION (EU) No 1215/2012 OF THE EUROPEAN PARLIAMENT AND OF THE COUNCIL

REGULATION (EU) No 1215/2012 OF THE EUROPEAN
PARLIAMENT AND OF THE COUNCIL
of 12 December 2012[*]
on jurisdiction and the recognition and enforcement of judgments in civil
and commercial matters
(recast)

THE EUROPEAN PARLIAMENT AND THE COUNCIL OF THE EUROPEAN UNION,

Having regard to the Treaty on the Functioning of the European Union, and in particular Article 67(4) and points (a), (c) and (e) of Article 81(2) thereof,

Having regard to the proposal from the European Commission,

After transmission of the draft legislative act to the national parliaments,

Having regard to the opinion of the European Economic and Social Committee,[1]

Acting in accordance with the ordinary legislative procedure,[2]

Whereas:

(1) On 21 April 2009, the Commission adopted a report on the application of Council Regulation (EC) No 44/2001 of 22 December 2000 on jurisdiction and the recognition and enforcement of judgments in civil and commercial matters.[3] The report concluded that, in general, the operation of that Regulation is satisfactory, but that it is desirable to improve the application of certain of its provisions, to further facilitate the free circulation of judgments and to further enhance access to justice. Since a number of amendments are to be made to that Regulation it should, in the interests of clarity, be recast.

(2) At its meeting in Brussels on 10 and 11 December 2009, the European Council adopted a new multiannual programme entitled 'The Stockholm Programme — an open and secure Europe serving and protecting citizens'.[4] In the Stockholm Programme the European Council considered that the process of abolishing all intermediate measures (the exequatur) should be continued during the period covered by that Programme. At the same time the abolition of the exequatur should

---

[*] Footnotes reformatted and renumbered.

[1] OJ C 218, 23.7.2011, p. 78.

[2] Position of the European Parliament of 20 November 2012 (not yet published in the Official Journal) and decision of the Council of 6 December 2012.

[3] OJ L 12, 16.1.2001, p. 1.

[4] OJ C 115, 4.5.2010, p. 1.

also be accompanied by a series of safeguards.

(3) The Union has set itself the objective of maintaining and developing an area of freedom, security and justice, inter alia, by facilitating access to justice, in particular through the principle of mutual recognition of judicial and extra-judicial decisions in civil matters. For the gradual establishment of such an area, the Union is to adopt measures relating to judicial cooperation in civil matters having cross-border implications, particularly when necessary for the proper functioning of the internal market.

(4) Certain differences between national rules governing jurisdiction and recognition of judgments hamper the sound operation of the internal market. Provisions to unify the rules of conflict of jurisdiction in civil and commercial matters, and to ensure rapid and simple recognition and enforcement of judgments given in a Member State, are essential.

(5) Such provisions fall within the area of judicial cooperation in civil matters within the meaning of Article 81 of the Treaty on the Functioning of the European Union (TFEU).EN 20.12.2012 Official Journal of the European Union L 351/12.

(6) In order to attain the objective of free circulation of judgments in civil and commercial matters, it is necessary and appropriate that the rules governing jurisdiction and the recognition and enforcement of judgments be governed by a legal instrument of the Union which is

(7) On 27 September 1968, the then Member States of the European Communities, acting under Article 220, fourth indent, of the Treaty establishing the European Economic Community, concluded the Brussels Convention on Jurisdiction and the Enforcement of Judgments in Civil and Commercial Matters, subsequently amended by conventions on the accession to that Convention of new Member States[5] ('the 1968 Brussels Convention'). On 16 September 1988, the then Member States of the European Communities and certain EFTA States concluded the Lugano Convention on Jurisdiction and the Enforcement of Judgments in Civil and Commercial Matters[6] ('the 1988 Lugano Convention'), which is a parallel convention to the 1968 Brussels Convention. The 1988 Lugano Convention became applicable to Poland on 1 February 2000.

(8) On 22 December 2000, the Council adopted Regulation (EC) No 44/2001, which replaces the 1968 Brussels Convention with regard to the territories of the Member States covered by the TFEU, as between the Member States except Denmark. By Council Decision 2006/325/EC,[7] the Community concluded an agreement with Denmark ensuring the application of the provisions of Regulation (EC) No 44/2001 in Denmark. The 1988 Lugano Convention was revised by the Convention on Jurisdiction and the Recognition and Enforcement of Judgments in Civil and Commercial Matters,[8] signed at Lugano on 30 October 2007 by the

---

[5] OJ L 299, 31.12.1972, p. 32, OJ L 304, 30.10.1978, p. 1, OJ L 388, 31.12.1982, p. 1, OJ L 285, 3.10.1989, p. 1, OJ C 15, 15.1.1997, p. 1. For a consolidated text, see OJ C 27, 26.1.1998, p. 1.

[6] OJ L 319, 25.11.1988, p. 9.

[7] OJ L 120, 5.5.2006, p. 22.

[8] OJ L 147, 10.6.2009, p. 5.

Community, Denmark, Iceland, Norway and Switzerland ('the 2007 Lugano Convention').

(9) The 1968 Brussels Convention continues to apply to the territories of the Member States which fall within the territorial scope of that Convention and which are excluded from this Regulation pursuant to Article 355 of the TFEU.

(10) The scope of this Regulation should cover all the main civil and commercial matters apart from certain well-defined matters, in particular maintenance obligations, which should be excluded from the scope of this Regulation following the adoption of Council Regulation (EC) No 4/2009 of 18 December 2008 on jurisdiction, applicable law, recognition and enforcement of decisions and cooperation in matters relating to maintenance obligations.[9]

(11) For the purposes of this Regulation, courts or tribunals of the Member States should include courts or tribunals common to several Member States, such as the Benelux Court of Justice when it exercises jurisdiction on matters falling within the scope of this Regulation. Therefore, judgments given by such courts should be recognised and enforced in accordance with this Regulation.

(12) This Regulation should not apply to arbitration. Nothing in this Regulation should prevent the courts of a Member State, when seised of an action in a matter in respect of which the parties have entered into an arbitration agreement, from referring the parties to arbitration, from staying or dismissing the proceedings, or from examining whether the arbitration agreement is null and void, inoperative or incapable of being performed, in accordance with their national law.

A ruling given by a court of a Member State as to whether or not an arbitration agreement is null and void, inoperative or incapable of being performed should not be subject to the rules of recognition and enforcement laid down in this Regulation, regardless of whether the court decided on this as a principal issue or as an incidental question.

On the other hand, where a court of a Member State, exercising jurisdiction under this Regulation or under national law, has determined that an arbitration agreement is null and void, inoperative or incapable of being performed, this should not preclude that court's judgment on the substance of the matter from being recognised or, as the case may be, enforced in accordance with this Regulation. This should be without prejudice to the competence of the courts of the Member States to decide on the recognition and enforcement of arbitral awards in accordance with the Convention on the Recognition and Enforcement of Foreign Arbitral Awards, done at New York on 10 June 1958 ('the 1958 New York Convention'), which takes precedence over this Regulation.

This Regulation should not apply to any action or ancillary proceedings relating to, in particular, the establishment of an arbitral tribunal, the powers of arbitrators, the conduct of an arbitration procedure or any other aspects of such a procedure, nor to any action or judgment concerning the annulment, review, appeal, recognition or enforcement of an arbitral award.

(13) There must be a connection between proceedings to which this Regulation

---

[9] OJ L 7, 10.1.2009, p. 1.

applies and the territory of the Member States. Accordingly, common rules of jurisdiction should, in principle, apply when the defendant is domiciled in a Member State.

(14) A defendant not domiciled in a Member State should in general be subject to the national rules of jurisdiction applicable in the territory of the Member State of the court seised.

However, in order to ensure the protection of consumers and employees, to safeguard the jurisdiction of the courts of the Member States in situations where they have exclusive jurisdiction and to respect the autonomy of the parties, certain rules of jurisdiction in this Regulation should apply regardless of the defendant's domicile.

(15) The rules of jurisdiction should be highly predictable and founded on the principle that jurisdiction is generally based on the defendant's domicile. Jurisdiction should always be available on this ground save in a few well-defined situations in which the subject-matter of the dispute or the autonomy of the parties warrants a different connecting factor. The domicile of a legal person must be defined autonomously so as to make the common rules more transparent and avoid conflicts of jurisdiction.

(16) In addition to the defendant's domicile, there should be alternative grounds of jurisdiction based on a close connection between the court and the action or in order to facilitate the sound administration of justice. The existence of a close connection should ensure legal certainty and avoid the possibility of the defendant being sued in a court of a Member State which he could not reasonably have foreseen. This is important, particularly in disputes concerning non-contractual obligations arising out of violations of privacy and rights relating to personality, including defamation.

(17) The owner of a cultural object as defined in Article 1(1) of Council Directive 93/7/EEC of 15 March 1993 on the return of cultural objects unlawfully removed from the territory of a Member State[10] should be able under this Regulation to initiate proceedings as regards a civil claim for the recovery, based on ownership, of such a cultural object in the courts for the place where the cultural object is situated at the time the court is seised. Such proceedings should be without prejudice to proceedings initiated under Directive 93/7/EEC.

(18) In relation to insurance, consumer and employment contracts, the weaker party should be protected by rules of jurisdiction more favourable to his interests than the general rules.

(19) The autonomy of the parties to a contract, other than an insurance, consumer or employment contract, where only limited autonomy to determine the courts having jurisdiction is allowed, should be respected subject to the exclusive grounds of jurisdiction laid down in this Regulation.

(20) Where a question arises as to whether a choice-of-court agreement in favour of a court or the courts of a Member State is null and void as to its substantive

---

[10] OJ L 74, 27.3.1993, p. 74.

validity, that question should be decided in accordance with the law of the Member State of the court or courts designated in the agreement, including the conflict-of-laws rules of that Member State.

(21) In the interests of the harmonious administration of justice it is necessary to minimise the possibility of concurrent proceedings and to ensure that irreconcilable judgments will not be given in different Member States. There should be a clear and effective mechanism for resolving cases of *lis pendens* and related actions, and for obviating problems flowing from national differences as to the determination of the time when a case is regarded as pending. For the purposes of this Regulation, that time should be defined autonomously.

(22) However, in order to enhance the effectiveness of exclusive choice-of-court agreements and to avoid abusive litigation tactics, it is necessary to provide for an exception to the general *lis pendens* rule in order to deal satisfactorily with a particular situation in which concurrent proceedings may arise. This is the situation where a court not designated in an exclusive choice-of-court agreement has been seised of proceedings and the designated court is seised subsequently of proceedings involving the same cause of action and between the same parties. In such a case, the court first seised should be required to stay its proceedings as soon as the designated court has been seised and until such time as the latter court declares that it has no jurisdiction under the exclusive choice-of-court agreement. This is to ensure that, in such a situation, the designated court has priority to decide on the validity of the agreement and on the extent to which the agreement applies to the dispute pending before it. The designated court should be able to proceed irrespective of whether the non-designated court has already decided on the stay of proceedings.

This exception should not cover situations where the parties have entered into conflicting exclusive choice-of-court agreements or where a court designated in an exclusive choice-of-court agreement has been seised first. In such cases, the general *lis pendens* rule of this Regulation should apply.

(23) This Regulation should provide for a flexible mechanism allowing the courts of the Member States to take into account proceedings pending before the courts of third States, considering in particular whether a judgment of a third State will be capable of recognition and enforcement in the Member State concerned under the law of that Member State and the proper administration of justice.

(24) When taking into account the proper administration of justice, the court of the Member State concerned should assess all the circumstances of the case before it. Such circumstances may include connections between the facts of the case and the parties and the third State concerned, the stage to which the proceedings in the third State have progressed by the time proceedings are initiated in the court of the Member State and whether or not the court of the third State can be expected to give a judgment within a reasonable time.

That assessment may also include consideration of the question whether the court of the third State has exclusive jurisdiction in the particular case in circumstances where a court of a Member State would have exclusive jurisdiction.

(25) The notion of provisional, including protective, measures should include, for

example, protective orders aimed at obtaining information or preserving evidence as referred to in Articles 6 and 7 of Directive 2004/48/EC of the European Parliament and of the Council of 29 April 2004 on the enforcement of intellectual property rights.[11] It should not include measures which are not of a protective nature, such as measures ordering the hearing of a witness. This should be without prejudice to the application of Council Regulation (EC) No 1206/2001 of 28 May 2001 on cooperation between the courts of the Member States in the taking of evidence in civil or commercial matters.[12]

(26) Mutual trust in the administration of justice in the Union justifies the principle that judgments given in a Member State should be recognised in all Member States without the need for any special procedure. In addition, the aim of making cross-border litigation less time-consuming and costly justifies the abolition of the declaration of enforceability prior to enforcement in the Member State addressed. As a result, a judgment given by the courts of a Member State should be treated as if it had been given in the Member State addressed.

(27) For the purposes of the free circulation of judgments, a judgment given in a Member State should be recognised and enforced in another Member State even if it is given against a person not domiciled in a Member State.

(28) Where a judgment contains a measure or order which is not known in the law of the Member State addressed, that measure or order, including any right indicated therein, should, to the extent possible, be adapted to one which, under the law of that Member State, has equivalent effects attached to it and pursues similar aims. How, and by whom, the adaptation is to be carried out should be determined by each Member State.

(29) The direct enforcement in the Member State addressed of a judgment given in another Member State without a declaration of enforceability should not jeopardise respect for the rights of the defence. Therefore, the person against whom enforcement is sought should be able to apply for refusal of the recognition or enforcement of a judgment if he considers one of the grounds for refusal of recognition to be present. This should include the ground that he had not had the opportunity to arrange for his defence where the judgment was given in default of appearance in a civil action linked to criminal proceedings. It should also include the grounds which could be invoked on the basis of an agreement between the Member State addressed and a third State concluded pursuant to Article 59 of the 1968 Brussels Convention.

(30) A party challenging the enforcement of a judgment given in another Member State should, to the extent possible and in accordance with the legal system of the Member State addressed, be able to invoke, in the same procedure, in addition to the grounds for refusal provided for in this Regulation, the grounds for refusal available under national law and within the time-limits laid down in that law.

The recognition of a judgment should, however, be refused only if one or more of the grounds for refusal provided for in this Regulation are present.

---

[11] OJ L 157, 30.4.2004, p. 45.

[12] OJ L 174, 27.6.2001, p. 1.

(31) Pending a challenge to the enforcement of a judgment, it should be possible for the courts in the Member State addressed, during the entire proceedings relating to such a challenge, including any appeal, to allow the enforcement to proceed subject to a limitation of the enforcement or to the provision of security.

(32) In order to inform the person against whom enforcement is sought of the enforcement of a judgment given in another Member State, the certificate established under this Regulation, if necessary accompanied by the judgment, should be served on that person in reasonable time before the first enforcement measure. In this context, the first enforcement measure should mean the first enforcement measure after such service.

(33) Where provisional, including protective, measures are ordered by a court having jurisdiction as to the substance of the matter, their free circulation should be ensured under this Regulation. However, provisional, including protective, measures which were ordered by such a court without the defendant being summoned to appear should not be recognised and enforced under this Regulation unless the judgment containing the measure is served on the defendant prior to enforcement. This should not preclude the recognition and enforcement of such measures under national law. Where provisional, including protective, measures are ordered by a court of a Member State not having jurisdiction as to the substance of the matter, the effect of such measures should be confined, under this Regulation, to the territory of that Member State.

(34) Continuity between the 1968 Brussels Convention, Regulation (EC) No 44/2001 and this Regulation should be ensured, and transitional provisions should be laid down to that end. The same need for continuity applies as regards the interpretation by the Court of Justice of the European Union of the 1968 Brussels Convention and of the Regulations replacing it.

(35) Respect for international commitments entered into by the Member States means that this Regulation should not affect conventions relating to specific matters to which the Member States are parties.

(36) Without prejudice to the obligations of the Member States under the Treaties, this Regulation should not affect the application of bilateral conventions and agreements between a third State and a Member State concluded before the date of entry into force of Regulation (EC) No 44/2001 which concern matters governed by this Regulation.

(37) In order to ensure that the certificates to be used in connection with the recognition or enforcement of judgments, authentic instruments and court settlements under this Regulation are kept up-to-date, the power to adopt acts in accordance with Article 290 of the TFEU should be delegated to the Commission in respect of amendments to Annexes I and II to this Regulation. It is of particular importance that the Commission carry out appropriate consultations during its preparatory work, including at expert level. The Commission, when preparing and drawing up delegated acts, should ensure a simultaneous, timely and appropriate transmission of relevant documents to the European Parliament and to the Council.

(38) This Regulation respects fundamental rights and observes the principles recognised in the Charter of Fundamental Rights of the European Union, in

particular the right to an effective remedy and to a fair trial guaranteed in Article 47 of the Charter.

(39) Since the objective of this Regulation cannot be sufficiently achieved by the Member States and can be better achieved at Union level, the Union may adopt measures in accordance with the principle of subsidiarity as set out in Article 5 of the Treaty on European Union (TEU). In accordance with the principle of proportionality, as set out in that Article, this Regulation does not go beyond what is necessary in order to achieve that objective.

(40) The United Kingdom and Ireland, in accordance with Article 3 of the Protocol on the position of the United Kingdom and Ireland, annexed to the TEU and to the then Treaty establishing the European Community, took part in the adoption and application of Regulation (EC) No 44/2001. In accordance with Article 3 of Protocol No 21 on the position of the United Kingdom and Ireland in respect of the area of freedom, security and justice, annexed to the TEU and to the TFEU, the United Kingdom and Ireland have notified their wish to take part in the adoption and application of this Regulation.

(41) In accordance with Articles 1 and 2 of Protocol No 22 on the position of Denmark annexed to the TEU and to the TFEU, Denmark is not taking part in the adoption of this Regulation and is not bound by it or subject to its application, without prejudice to the possibility for Denmark of applying the amendments to Regulation (EC) No 44/2001 pursuant to Article 3 of the Agreement of 19 October 2005 between the European Community and the Kingdom of Denmark on jurisdiction and the recognition and enforcement of judgments in civil and commercial matters,[13]

HAVE ADOPTED THIS REGULATION:

CHAPTER I
SCOPE AND DEFINITIONS

Article 1

1. This Regulation shall apply in civil and commercial matters whatever the nature of the court or tribunal. It shall not extend, in particular, to revenue, customs or administrative matters or to the liability of the State for acts and omissions in the exercise of State authority (*acta iure imperii*).

2. This Regulation shall not apply to:

(a) the status or legal capacity of natural persons, rights in property arising out of a matrimonial relationship or out of a relationship deemed by the law applicable to such relationship to have comparable effects to marriage;

(b) bankruptcy, proceedings relating to the winding-up of insolvent companies or other legal persons, judicial arrangements, compositions and analogous proceedings;

(c) social security;

---

[13] OJ L 299, 16.11.2005, p. 62.

(d) arbitration;

(e) maintenance obligations arising from a family relationship, parentage, marriage or affinity;

(f) wills and succession, including maintenance obligations arising by reason of death.

Article 2

For the purposes of this Regulation:

(a) 'judgment' means any judgment given by a court or tribunal of a Member State, whatever the judgment may be called, including a decree, order, decision or writ of execution, as well as a decision on the determination of costs or expenses by an officer of the court.

For the purposes of Chapter III, 'judgment' includes provisional, including protective, measures ordered by a court or tribunal which by virtue of this Regulation has jurisdiction as to the substance of the matter. It does not include a provisional, including protective, measure which is ordered by such a court or tribunal without the defendant being summoned to appear, unless the judgment containing the measure is served on the defendant prior to enforcement;

(b) 'court settlement' means a settlement which has been approved by a court of a Member State or concluded before a court of a Member State in the course of proceedings;

(c) 'authentic instrument' means a document which has been formally drawn up or registered as an authentic instrument in the Member State of origin and the authenticity of which:

(i) relates to the signature and the content of the instrument; and

(ii) has been established by a public authority or other authority empowered for that purpose;

(d) 'Member State of origin' means the Member State in which, as the case may be, the judgment has been given, the court settlement has been approved or concluded, or the authentic instrument has been formally drawn up or registered;

(e) 'Member State addressed' means the Member State in which the recognition of the judgment is invoked or in which the enforcement of the judgment, the court settlement or the authentic instrument is sought;

(f) 'court of origin' means the court which has given the judgment the recognition of which is invoked or the enforcement of which is sought.

Article 3

For the purposes of this Regulation, 'court' includes the following authorities to the extent that they have jurisdiction in matters falling within the scope of this Regulation:

(a) in Hungary, in summary proceedings concerning orders to pay (fizetési meghagyásos eljárás), the notary (közjegyző);

(b) in Sweden, in summary proceedings concerning orders to pay (betalningsföreläggande) and assistance (handräckning), the Enforcement Authority (Kronofogdemyndigheten).

CHAPTER II
JURISDICTION

SECTION 1
General provisions

Article 4

1. Subject to this Regulation, persons domiciled in a Member State shall, whatever their nationality, be sued in the courts of that Member State.

2. Persons who are not nationals of the Member State in which they are domiciled shall be governed by the rules of jurisdiction applicable to nationals of that Member State.

Article 5

1. Persons domiciled in a Member State may be sued in the courts of another Member State only by virtue of the rules set out in Sections 2 to 7 of this Chapter.

2. In particular, the rules of national jurisdiction of which the Member States are to notify the Commission pursuant to point (a) of Article 76(1) shall not be applicable as against the persons referred to in paragraph 1.

Article 6

1. If the defendant is not domiciled in a Member State, the jurisdiction of the courts of each Member State shall, subject to Article 18(1), Article 21(2) and Articles 24 and 25, be determined by the law of that Member State.

2. As against such a defendant, any person domiciled in a Member State may, whatever his nationality, avail himself in that Member State of the rules of jurisdiction there in force, and in particular those of which the Member States are to notify the Commission pursuant to point (a) of Article 76(1), in the same way as nationals of that Member State.

SECTION 2
Special jurisdiction

Article 7

A person domiciled in a Member State may be sued in another Member State:

(1) (a) in matters relating to a contract, in the courts for the place of performance of the obligation in question;

(b) for the purpose of this provision and unless otherwise agreed, the place of performance of the obligation in question shall be:

— in the case of the sale of goods, the place in a Member State where, under the contract, the goods were delivered or should have been delivered,

— in the case of the provision of services, the place in a Member State where, under the contract, the services were provided or should have been provided;

(c) if point (b) does not apply then point (a) applies;

(2) in matters relating to tort, delict or quasi-delict, in the courts for the place where the harmful event occurred or may occur;

(3) as regards a civil claim for damages or restitution which is based on an act giving rise to criminal proceedings, in the court seised of those proceedings, to the extent that that court has jurisdiction under its own law to entertain civil proceedings;

(4) as regards a civil claim for the recovery, based on ownership, of a cultural object as defined in point 1 of Article 1 of Directive 93/7/EEC initiated by the person claiming the right to recover such an object, in the courts for the place where the cultural object is situated at the time when the court is seised;

(5) as regards a dispute arising out of the operations of a branch, agency or other establishment, in the courts for the place where the branch, agency or other establishment is situated;

(6) as regards a dispute brought against a settlor, trustee or beneficiary of a trust created by the operation of a statute, or by a written instrument, or created orally and evidenced in writing, in the courts of the Member State in which the trust is domiciled;

(7) as regards a dispute concerning the payment of remuneration claimed in respect of the salvage of a cargo or freight, in the court under the authority of which the cargo or freight in question:

(a) has been arrested to secure such payment; or

(b) could have been so arrested, but bail or other security has been given;

provided that this provision shall apply only if it is claimed that the defendant has an interest in the cargo or freight or had such an interest at the time of salvage.

Article 8

A person domiciled in a Member State may also be sued:

(1) where he is one of a number of defendants, in the courts for the place where any one of them is domiciled, provided the claims are so closely connected that it is expedient to hear and determine them together to avoid the risk of irreconcilable judgments resulting from separate proceedings;

(2) as a third party in an action on a warranty or guarantee or in any other third-party proceedings, in the court seised of the original proceedings, unless these were instituted solely with the object of removing him from the jurisdiction of the court which would be competent in his case;

(3) on a counter-claim arising from the same contract or facts on which the original claim was based, in the court in which the original claim is pending;

(4) in matters relating to a contract, if the action may be combined with an action against the same defendant in matters relating to rights *in rem* in immovable property, in the court of the Member State in which the property is situated.

Article 9

Where by virtue of this Regulation a court of a Member State has jurisdiction in actions relating to liability from the use or operation of a ship, that court, or any other court substituted for this purpose by the internal law of that Member State, shall also have jurisdiction over claims for limitation of such liability.

SECTION 3
Jurisdiction in matters relating to insurance

Article 10

In matters relating to insurance, jurisdiction shall be determined by this Section, without prejudice to Article 6 and point 5 of Article 7.

Article 11

1. An insurer domiciled in a Member State may be sued:

   (a) in the courts of the Member State in which he is domiciled;

   (b) in another Member State, in the case of actions brought by the policyholder, the insured or a beneficiary, in the courts for the place where the claimant is domiciled; or

   (c) if he is a co-insurer, in the courts of a Member State in which proceedings are brought against the leading insurer.

2. An insurer who is not domiciled in a Member State but has a branch, agency or other establishment in one of the Member States shall, in disputes arising out of the operations of the branch, agency or establishment, be deemed to be domiciled in that Member State.

Article 12

In respect of liability insurance or insurance of immovable property, the insurer may in addition be sued in the courts for the place where the harmful event occurred. The same applies if movable and immovable property are covered by the same insurance policy and both are adversely affected by the same contingency.

Article 13

1. In respect of liability insurance, the insurer may also, if the law of the court permits it, be joined in proceedings which the injured party has brought against the insured.

2. Articles 10, 11 and 12 shall apply to actions brought by the injured party directly against the insurer, where such direct actions are permitted.

3. If the law governing such direct actions provides that the policyholder or the

insured may be joined as a party to the action, the same court shall have jurisdiction over them.

Article 14

1. Without prejudice to Article 13(3), an insurer may bring proceedings only in the courts of the Member State in which the defendant is domiciled, irrespective of whether he is the policyholder, the insured or a beneficiary.

2. The provisions of this Section shall not affect the right to bring a counter-claim in the court in which, in accordance with this Section, the original claim is pending.

Article 15

The provisions of this Section may be departed from only by an agreement:

(1) which is entered into after the dispute has arisen;

(2) which allows the policyholder, the insured or a beneficiary to bring proceedings in courts other than those indicated in this Section;

(3) which is concluded between a policyholder and an insurer, both of whom are at the time of conclusion of the contract domiciled or habitually resident in the same Member State, and which has the effect of conferring jurisdiction on the courts of that Member State even if the harmful event were to occur abroad, provided that such an agreement is not contrary to the law of that Member State;

(4) which is concluded with a policyholder who is not domiciled in a Member State, except in so far as the insurance is compulsory or relates to immovable property in a Member State; or

(5) which relates to a contract of insurance in so far as it covers one or more of the risks set out in Article 16.

Article 16

The following are the risks referred to in point 5 of Article 15:

(1) any loss of or damage to:

(a) seagoing ships, installations situated offshore or on the high seas, or aircraft, arising from perils which relate to their use for commercial purposes;

(b) goods in transit other than passengers' baggage where the transit consists of or includes carriage by such ships or aircraft;

(2) any liability, other than for bodily injury to passengers or loss of or damage to their baggage:

(a) arising out of the use or operation of ships, installations or aircraft as referred to in point 1(a) in so far as, in respect of the latter, the law of the Member State in which such aircraft are registered does not prohibit agreements on jurisdiction regarding insurance of such risks;

(b) for loss or damage caused by goods in transit as described in point 1(b);

(3) any financial loss connected with the use or operation of ships, installations

or aircraft as referred to in point 1(a), in particular loss of freight or charter-hire;

(4) any risk or interest connected with any of those referred to in points 1 to 3;

(5) notwithstanding points 1 to 4, all 'large risks' as defined in Directive 2009/138/EC of the European Parliament and of the Council of 25 November 2009 on the taking-up and pursuit of the business of Insurance and Reinsurance (Solvency II);[14]

SECTION 4
Jurisdiction over consumer contracts

Article 17

1. In matters relating to a contract concluded by a person, the consumer, for a purpose which can be regarded as being outside his trade or profession, jurisdiction shall be determined by this Section, without prejudice to Article 6 and point 5 of Article 7, if:

(a) it is a contract for the sale of goods on instalment credit terms;

(b) it is a contract for a loan repayable by instalments, or for any other form of credit, made to finance the sale of goods; or

(c) in all other cases, the contract has been concluded with a person who pursues commercial or professional activities in the Member State of the consumer's domicile or, by any means, directs such activities to that Member State or to several States including that Member State, and the contract falls within the scope of such activities.

2. Where a consumer enters into a contract with a party who is not domiciled in a Member State but has a branch, agency or other establishment in one of the Member States, that party shall, in disputes arising out of the operations of the branch, agency or establishment, be deemed to be domiciled in that Member State.

3. This Section shall not apply to a contract of transport other than a contract which, for an inclusive price, provides for a combination of travel and accommodation.

Article 18

1. A consumer may bring proceedings against the other party to a contract either in the courts of the Member State in which that party is domiciled or, regardless of the domicile of the other party, in the courts for the place where the consumer is domiciled.

2. Proceedings may be brought against a consumer by the other party to the contract only in the courts of the Member State in which the consumer is domiciled.

3. This Article shall not affect the right to bring a counter-claim in the court in which, in accordance with this Section, the original claim is pending.

---

[14] OJ L 335, 17.12.2009, p. 1.

Article 19

The provisions of this Section may be departed from only by an agreement:

(1) which is entered into after the dispute has arisen;

(2) which allows the consumer to bring proceedings in courts other than those indicated in this Section; or

(3) which is entered into by the consumer and the other party to the contract, both of whom are at the time of conclusion of the contract domiciled or habitually resident in the same Member State, and which confers jurisdiction on the courts of that Member State, provided that such an agreement is not contrary to the law of that Member State.

SECTION 5
Jurisdiction over individual contracts of employment

Article 20

1. In matters relating to individual contracts of employment, jurisdiction shall be determined by this Section, without prejudice to Article 6, point 5 of Article 7 and, in the case of proceedings brought against an employer, point 1 of Article 8.

2. Where an employee enters into an individual contract of employment with an employer who is not domiciled in a Member State but has a branch, agency or other establishment in one of the Member States, the employer shall, in disputes arising out of the operations of the branch, agency or establishment, be deemed to be domiciled in that Member State.

Article 21

1. An employer domiciled in a Member State may be sued:

(a) in the courts of the Member State in which he is domiciled; or

(b) in another Member State:

(i) in the courts for the place where or from where the employee habitually carries out his work or in the courts for the last place where he did so; or

(ii) if the employee does not or did not habitually carry out his work in any one country, in the courts for the place where the business which engaged the employee is or was situated.

2. An employer not domiciled in a Member State may be sued in a court of a Member State in accordance with point (b) of paragraph 1.

Article 22

1. An employer may bring proceedings only in the courts of the Member State in which the employee is domiciled.

2. The provisions of this Section shall not affect the right to bring a counter-claim in the court in which, in accordance with this Section, the original claim is pending.

Article 23

The provisions of this Section may be departed from only by an agreement:

(1) which is entered into after the dispute has arisen; or

(2) which allows the employee to bring proceedings in courts other than those indicated in this Section.

SECTION 6
Exclusive jurisdiction

Article 24

The following courts of a Member State shall have exclusive jurisdiction, regardless of the domicile of the parties:

(1) in proceedings which have as their object rights *in rem* in immovable property or tenancies of immovable property, the courts of the Member State in which the property is situated.

However, in proceedings which have as their object tenancies of immovable property concluded for temporary private use for a maximum period of six consecutive months, the courts of the Member State in which the defendant is domiciled shall also have jurisdiction, provided that the tenant is a natural person and that the landlord and the tenant are domiciled in the same Member State;

(2) in proceedings which have as their object the validity of the constitution, the nullity or the dissolution of companies or other legal persons or associations of natural or legal persons, or the validity of the decisions of their organs, the courts of the Member State in which the company, legal person or association has its seat. In order to determine that seat, the court shall apply its rules of private international law;

(3) in proceedings which have as their object the validity of entries in public registers, the courts of the Member State in which the register is kept;

(4) in proceedings concerned with the registration or validity of patents, trade marks, designs, or other similar rights required to be deposited or registered, irrespective of whether the issue is raised by way of an action or as a defence, the courts of the Member State in which the deposit or registration has been applied for, has taken place or is under the terms of an instrument of the Union or an international convention deemed to have taken place.

Without prejudice to the jurisdiction of the European Patent Office under the Convention on the Grant of European Patents, signed at Munich on 5 October 1973, the courts of each Member State shall have exclusive jurisdiction in proceedings concerned with the registration or validity of any European patent granted for that Member State;

(5) in proceedings concerned with the enforcement of judgments, the courts of the Member State in which the judgment has been or is to be enforced.

SECTION 7
Prorogation of jurisdiction

Article 25

1. If the parties, regardless of their domicile, have agreed that a court or the courts of a Member State are to have jurisdiction to settle any disputes which have arisen or which may arise in connection with a particular legal relationship, that court or those courts shall have jurisdiction, unless the agreement is null and void as to its substantive validity under the law of that Member State. Such jurisdiction shall be exclusive unless the parties have agreed otherwise. The agreement conferring jurisdiction shall be either:

(a) in writing or evidenced in writing;

(b) in a form which accords with practices which the parties have established between themselves; or

(c) in international trade or commerce, in a form which accords with a usage of which the parties are or ought to have been aware and which in such trade or commerce is widely known to, and regularly observed by, parties to contracts of the type involved in the particular trade or commerce concerned.

2. Any communication by electronic means which provides a durable record of the agreement shall be equivalent to 'writing'.

3. The court or courts of a Member State on which a trust instrument has conferred jurisdiction shall have exclusive jurisdiction in any proceedings brought against a settlor, trustee or beneficiary, if relations between those persons or their rights or obligations under the trust are involved.

4. Agreements or provisions of a trust instrument conferring jurisdiction shall have no legal force if they are contrary to Articles 15, 19 or 23, or if the courts whose jurisdiction they purport to exclude have exclusive jurisdiction by virtue of Article 24.

5. An agreement conferring jurisdiction which forms part of a contract shall be treated as an agreement independent of the other terms of the contract.

The validity of the agreement conferring jurisdiction cannot be contested solely on the ground that the contract is not valid.

Article 26

1. Apart from jurisdiction derived from other provisions of this Regulation, a court of a Member State before which a defendant enters an appearance shall have jurisdiction. This rule shall not apply where appearance was entered to contest the jurisdiction, or where another court has exclusive jurisdiction by virtue of Article 24.

2. In matters referred to in Sections 3, 4 or 5 where the policyholder, the insured, a beneficiary of the insurance contract, the injured party, the consumer or the employee is the defendant, the court shall, before assuming jurisdiction under paragraph 1, ensure that the defendant is informed of his right to contest the

jurisdiction of the court and of the consequences of entering or not entering an appearance.

SECTION 8
Examination as to jurisdiction and admissibility

Article 27

Where a court of a Member State is seised of a claim which is principally concerned with a matter over which the courts of another Member State have exclusive jurisdiction by virtue of Article 24, it shall declare of its own motion that it has no jurisdiction.

Article 28

1. Where a defendant domiciled in one Member State is sued in a court of another Member State and does not enter an appearance, the court shall declare of its own motion that it has no jurisdiction unless its jurisdiction is derived from the provisions of this Regulation.

2. The court shall stay the proceedings so long as it is not shown that the defendant has been able to receive the document instituting the proceedings or an equivalent document in sufficient time to enable him to arrange for his defence, or that all necessary steps have been taken to this end.

3. Article 19 of Regulation (EC) No 1393/2007 of the European Parliament and of the Council of 13 November 2007 on the service in the Member States of judicial and extrajudicial documents in civil or commercial matters (service of documents)[15] (1) shall apply instead of paragraph 2 of this Article if the document instituting the proceedings or an equivalent document had to be transmitted from one Member State to another pursuant to that Regulation.

4. Where Regulation (EC) No 1393/2007 is not applicable, Article 15 of the Hague Convention of 15 November 1965 on the Service Abroad of Judicial and Extrajudicial Documents in Civil or Commercial Matters shall apply if the document instituting the proceedings or an equivalent document had to be transmitted abroad pursuant to that Convention.

SECTION 9
Lis pendens — related actions

Article 29

1. Without prejudice to Article 31(2), where proceedings involving the same cause of action and between the same parties are brought in the courts of different Member States, any court other than the court first seised shall of its own motion stay its proceedings until such time as the jurisdiction of the court first seised is established.

2. In cases referred to in paragraph 1, upon request by a court seised of the

---

[15] OJ L 324, 10.12.2007, p. 79.

dispute, any other court seised shall without delay inform the former court of the date when it was seised in accordance with Article 32.

3. Where the jurisdiction of the court first seised is established, any court other than the court first seised shall decline jurisdiction in favour of that court.

Article 30

1. Where related actions are pending in the courts of different Member States, any court other than the court first seised may stay its proceedings.

2. Where the action in the court first seised is pending at first instance, any other court may also, on the application of one of the parties, decline jurisdiction if the court first seised has jurisdiction over the actions in question and its law permits the consolidation thereof.

3. For the purposes of this Article, actions are deemed to be related where they are so closely connected that it is expedient to hear and determine them together to avoid the risk of irreconcilable judgments resulting from separate proceedings.

Article 31

1. Where actions come within the exclusive jurisdiction of several courts, any court other than the court first seised shall decline jurisdiction in favour of that court.

2. Without prejudice to Article 26, where a court of a Member State on which an agreement as referred to in Article 25 confers exclusive jurisdiction is seised, any court of another Member State shall stay the proceedings until such time as the court seised on the basis of the agreement declares that it has no jurisdiction under the agreement.

3. Where the court designated in the agreement has established jurisdiction in accordance with the agreement, any court of another Member State shall decline jurisdiction in favour of that court.

4. Paragraphs 2 and 3 shall not apply to matters referred to in Sections 3, 4 or 5 where the policyholder, the insured, a beneficiary of the insurance contract, the injured party, the consumer or the employee is the claimant and the agreement is not valid under a provision contained within those Sections.

Article 32

1. For the purposes of this Section, a court shall be deemed to be seised:

(a) at the time when the document instituting the proceedings or an equivalent document is lodged with the court, provided that the claimant has not subsequently failed to take the steps he was required to take to have service effected on the defendant; or

(b) if the document has to be served before being lodged with the court, at the time when it is received by the authority responsible for service, provided that the claimant has not subsequently failed to take the steps he was required to take to have the document lodged with the court.

The authority responsible for service referred to in point (b) shall be the first authority receiving the documents to be served.

2. The court, or the authority responsible for service, referred to in paragraph 1, shall note, respectively, the date of the lodging of the document instituting the proceedings or the equivalent document, or the date of receipt of the documents to be served.

Article 33

1. Where jurisdiction is based on Article 4 or on Articles 7, 8 or 9 and proceedings are pending before a court of a third State at the time when a court in a Member State is seised of an action involving the same cause of action and between the same parties as the proceedings in the court of the third State, the court of the Member State may stay the proceedings if:

(a) it is expected that the court of the third State will give a judgment capable of recognition and, where applicable, of enforcement in that Member State; and

(b) the court of the Member State is satisfied that a stay is necessary for the proper administration of justice.

2. The court of the Member State may continue the proceedings at any time if:

(a) the proceedings in the court of the third State are themselves stayed or discontinued;

(b) it appears to the court of the Member State that the proceedings in the court of the third State are unlikely to be concluded within a reasonable time; or

(c) the continuation of the proceedings is required for the proper administration of justice.

3. The court of the Member State shall dismiss the proceedings if the proceedings in the court of the third State are concluded and have resulted in a judgment capable of recognition and, where applicable, of enforcement in that Member State.

4. The court of the Member State shall apply this Article on the application of one of the parties or, where possible under national law, of its own motion.

Article 34

1. Where jurisdiction is based on Article 4 or on Articles 7, 8 or 9 and an action is pending before a court of a third State at the time when a court in a Member State is seised of an action which is related to the action in the court of the third State, the court of the Member State may stay the proceedings if:

(a) it is expedient to hear and determine the related actions together to avoid the risk of irreconcilable judgments resulting from separate proceedings;

(b) it is expected that the court of the third State will give a judgment capable of recognition and, where applicable, of enforcement in that Member State; and

(c) the court of the Member State is satisfied that a stay is necessary for the proper administration of justice.

2. The court of the Member State may continue the proceedings at any time if:

(a) it appears to the court of the Member State that there is no longer a risk of irreconcilable judgments;

(b) the proceedings in the court of the third State are themselves stayed or discontinued;

(c) it appears to the court of the Member State that the proceedings in the court of the third State are unlikely to be concluded within a reasonable time; or

(d) the continuation of the proceedings is required for the proper administration of justice.

3. The court of the Member State may dismiss the proceedings if the proceedings in the court of the third State are concluded and have resulted in a judgment capable of recognition and, where applicable, of enforcement in that Member State.

4. The court of the Member State shall apply this Article on the application of one of the parties or, where possible under national law, of its own motion.

SECTION 10
Provisional, including protective, measures

Article 35

Application may be made to the courts of a Member State for such provisional, including protective, measures as may be available under the law of that Member State, even if the courts of another Member State have jurisdiction as to the substance of the matter.

CHAPTER III
RECOGNITION AND ENFORCEMENT

SECTION 1
Recognition

Article 36

1. A judgment given in a Member State shall be recognised in the other Member States without any special procedure being required.

2. Any interested party may, in accordance with the procedure provided for in Subsection 2 of Section 3, apply for a decision that there are no grounds for refusal of recognition as referred to in Article 45.

3. If the outcome of proceedings in a court of a Member State depends on the determination of an incidental question of refusal of recognition, that court shall have jurisdiction over that question.

Article 37

1. A party who wishes to invoke in a Member State a judgment given in another Member State shall produce:

(a) a copy of the judgment which satisfies the conditions necessary to establish its authenticity; and

(b) the certificate issued pursuant to Article 53.

2. The court or authority before which a judgment given in another Member State is invoked may, where necessary, require the party invoking it to provide, in accordance with Article 57, a translation or a transliteration of the contents of the certificate referred to in point (b) of paragraph 1. The court or authority may require the party to provide a translation of the judgment instead of a translation of the contents of the certificate if it is unable to proceed without such a translation.

Article 38

The court or authority before which a judgment given in another Member State is invoked may suspend the proceedings, in whole or in part, if:

(a) the judgment is challenged in the Member State of origin; or

(b) an application has been submitted for a decision that there are no grounds for refusal of recognition as referred to in Article 45 or for a decision that the recognition is to be refused on the basis of one of those grounds.

SECTION 2
Enforcement

Article 39

A judgment given in a Member State which is enforceable in that Member State shall be enforceable in the other Member States without any declaration of enforceability being required.

Article 40

An enforceable judgment shall carry with it by operation of law the power to proceed to any protective measures which exist under the law of the Member State addressed.

Article 41

1. Subject to the provisions of this Section, the procedure for the enforcement of judgments given in another Member State shall be governed by the law of the Member State addressed. A judgment given in a Member State which is enforceable in the Member State addressed shall be enforced there under the same conditions as a judgment given in the Member State addressed.

2. Notwithstanding paragraph 1, the grounds for refusal or of suspension of enforcement under the law of the Member State addressed shall apply in so far as they are not incompatible with the grounds referred to in Article 45.

3. The party seeking the enforcement of a judgment given in another Member State shall not be required to have a postal address in the Member State addressed. Nor shall that party be required to have an authorised representative in the Member State addressed unless such a representative is mandatory irrespective of the nationality or the domicile of the parties.

Article 42

1. For the purposes of enforcement in a Member State of a judgment given in another Member State, the applicant shall provide the competent enforcement authority with:

(a) a copy of the judgment which satisfies the conditions necessary to establish its authenticity; and

(b) the certificate issued pursuant to Article 53, certifying that the judgment is enforceable and containing an extract of the judgment as well as, where appropriate, relevant information on the recoverable costs of the proceedings and the calculation of interest.

2. For the purposes of enforcement in a Member State of a judgment given in another Member State ordering a provisional, including a protective, measure, the applicant shall provide the competent enforcement authority with:

(a) a copy of the judgment which satisfies the conditions necessary to establish its authenticity;

(b) the certificate issued pursuant to Article 53, containing a description of the measure and certifying that:

(i) the court has jurisdiction as to the substance of the matter;

(ii) the judgment is enforceable in the Member State of origin; and

(c) where the measure was ordered without the defendant being summoned to appear, proof of service of the judgment.

3. The competent enforcement authority may, where necessary, require the applicant to provide, in accordance with Article 57, a translation or a transliteration of the contents of the certificate.

4. The competent enforcement authority may require the applicant to provide a translation of the judgment only if it is unable to proceed without such a translation.

Article 43

1. Where enforcement is sought of a judgment given in another Member State, the certificate issued pursuant to Article 53 shall be served on the person against whom the enforcement is sought prior to the first enforcement measure. The certificate shall be accompanied by the judgment, if not already served on that person.

2. Where the person against whom enforcement is sought is domiciled in a Member State other than the Member State of origin, he may request a translation of the judgment in order to contest the enforcement if the judgment is not written in or accompanied by a translation into either of the following languages:

(a) a language which he understands; or

(b) the official language of the Member State in which he is domiciled or, where there are several official languages in that Member State, the official language or one of the official languages of the place where he is domiciled.

Where a translation of the judgment is requested under the first subparagraph, no measures of enforcement may be taken other than protective measures until that translation has been provided to the person against whom enforcement is sought.

This paragraph shall not apply if the judgment has already been served on the person against whom enforcement is sought in one of the languages referred to in the first subparagraph or is accompanied by a translation into one of those languages.

3. This Article shall not apply to the enforcement of a protective measure in a judgment or where the person seeking enforcement proceeds to protective measures in accordance with Article 40.

Article 44

1. In the event of an application for refusal of enforcement of a judgment pursuant to Subsection 2 of Section 3, the court in the Member State addressed may, on the application of the person against whom enforcement is sought:

(a) limit the enforcement proceedings to protective measures;

(b) make enforcement conditional on the provision of such security as it shall determine; or

(c) suspend, either wholly or in part, the enforcement proceedings.

2. The competent authority in the Member State addressed shall, on the application of the person against whom enforcement is sought, suspend the enforcement proceedings where the enforceability of the judgment is suspended in the Member State of origin.

SECTION 3
Refusal of recognition and enforcement

Subsection 1
Refusal of recognition

Article 45

1. On the application of any interested party, the recognition of a judgment shall be refused:

(a) if such recognition is manifestly contrary to public policy (ordre public) in the Member State addressed;

(b) where the judgment was given in default of appearance, if the defendant was not served with the document which instituted the proceedings or with an equivalent document in sufficient time and in such a way as to enable him to arrange for his defence, unless the defendant failed to commence proceedings to challenge the judgment when it was possible for him to do so;

(c) if the judgment is irreconcilable with a judgment given between the same parties in the Member State addressed;

(d) if the judgment is irreconcilable with an earlier judgment given in another

Member State or in a third State involving the same cause of action and between the same parties, provided that the earlier judgment fulfils the conditions necessary for its recognition in the Member State addressed; or

(e) if the judgment conflicts with:

(i) Sections 3, 4 or 5 of Chapter II where the policyholder, the insured, a beneficiary of the insurance contract, the injured party, the consumer or the employee was the defendant; or

(ii) Section 6 of Chapter II.

2. In its examination of the grounds of jurisdiction referred to in point (e) of paragraph 1, the court to which the application was submitted shall be bound by the findings of fact on which the court of origin based its jurisdiction.

3. Without prejudice to point (e) of paragraph 1, the jurisdiction of the court of origin may not be reviewed. The test of public policy referred to in point (a) of paragraph 1 may not be applied to the rules relating to jurisdiction.

4. The application for refusal of recognition shall be made in accordance with the procedures provided for in Subsection 2 and, where appropriate, Section 4.

Subsection 2
Refusal of enforcement

Article 46

On the application of the person against whom enforcement is sought, the enforcement of a judgment shall be refused where one of the grounds referred to in Article 45 is found to exist.

Article 47

1. The application for refusal of enforcement shall be submitted to the court which the Member State concerned has communicated to the Commission pursuant to point (a) of Article 75 as the court to which the application is to be submitted.

2. The procedure for refusal of enforcement shall, in so far as it is not covered by this Regulation, be governed by the law of the Member State addressed.

3. The applicant shall provide the court with a copy of the judgment and, where necessary, a translation or transliteration of it.

The court may dispense with the production of the documents referred to in the first subparagraph if it already possesses them or if it considers it unreasonable to require the applicant to provide them. In the latter case, the court may require the other party to provide those documents.

4. The party seeking the refusal of enforcement of a judgment given in another Member State shall not be required to have a postal address in the Member State addressed. Nor shall that party be required to have an authorised representative in the Member State addressed unless such a representative is mandatory irrespective of the nationality or the domicile of the parties.

Article 48

The court shall decide on the application for refusal of enforcement without delay.

Article 49

1. The decision on the application for refusal of enforcement may be appealed against by either party.

2. The appeal is to be lodged with the court which the Member State concerned has communicated to the Commission pursuant to point (b) of Article 75 as the court with which such an appeal is to be lodged.

Article 50

The decision given on the appeal may only be contested by an appeal where the courts with which any further appeal is to be lodged have been communicated by the Member State concerned to the Commission pursuant to point (c) of Article 75.

Article 51

1. The court to which an application for refusal of enforcement is submitted or the court which hears an appeal lodged under Article 49 or Article 50 may stay the proceedings if an ordinary appeal has been lodged against the judgment in the Member State of origin or if the time for such an appeal has not yet expired. In the latter case, the court may specify the time within which such an appeal is to be lodged.

2. Where the judgment was given in Ireland, Cyprus or the United Kingdom, any form of appeal available in the Member State of origin shall be treated as an ordinary appeal for the purposes of paragraph 1.

SECTION 4
Common provisions

Article 52

Under no circumstances may a judgment given in a Member State be reviewed as to its substance in the Member State addressed.

Article 53

The court of origin shall, at the request of any interested party, issue the certificate using the form set out in Annex I.

Article 54

1. If a judgment contains a measure or an order which is not known in the law of the Member State addressed, that measure or order shall, to the extent possible, be adapted to a measure or an order known in the law of that Member State which has equivalent effects attached to it and which pursues similar aims and interests.

Such adaptation shall not result in effects going beyond those provided for in the law of the Member State of origin.

2. Any party may challenge the adaptation of the measure or order before a court.

3. If necessary, the party invoking the judgment or seeking its enforcement may be required to provide a translation or a transliteration of the judgment.

Article 55

A judgment given in a Member State which orders a payment by way of a penalty shall be enforceable in the Member State addressed only if the amount of the payment has been finally determined by the court of origin.

Article 56

No security, bond or deposit, however described, shall be required of a party who in one Member State applies for the enforcement of a judgment given in another Member State on the ground that he is a foreign national or that he is not domiciled or resident in the Member State addressed.

Article 57

1. When a translation or a transliteration is required under this Regulation, such translation or transliteration shall be into the official language of the Member State concerned or, where there are several official languages in that Member State, into the official language or one of the official languages of court proceedings of the place where a judgment given in another Member State is invoked or an application is made, in accordance with the law of that Member State.

2. For the purposes of the forms referred to in Articles 53 and 60, translations or transliterations may also be into any other official language or languages of the institutions of the Union that the Member State concerned has indicated it can accept.

3. Any translation made under this Regulation shall be done by a person qualified to do translations in one of the Member States.

CHAPTER IV
AUTHENTIC INSTRUMENTS AND COURT SETTLEMENTS

Article 58

1. An authentic instrument which is enforceable in the Member State of origin shall be enforceable in the other Member States without any declaration of enforceability being required. Enforcement of the authentic instrument may be refused only if such enforcement is manifestly contrary to public policy (ordre public) in the Member State addressed.

The provisions of Section 2, Subsection 2 of Section 3, and Section 4 of Chapter III shall apply as appropriate to authentic instruments.

2. The authentic instrument produced must satisfy the conditions necessary to establish its authenticity in the Member State of origin.

Article 59

A court settlement which is enforceable in the Member State of origin shall be enforced in the other Member States under the same conditions as authentic instruments.

Article 60

The competent authority or court of the Member State of origin shall, at the request of any interested party, issue the certificate using the form set out in Annex I containing a summary of the enforceable obligation recorded in the authentic instrument or of the agreement between the parties recorded in the court settlement.

CHAPTER V
GENERAL PROVISIONS

Article 61

No legalisation or other similar formality shall be required for documents issued in a Member State in the context of this Regulation.

Article 62

1. In order to determine whether a party is domiciled in the Member State whose courts are seised of a matter, the court shall apply its internal law.

2. If a party is not domiciled in the Member State whose courts are seised of the matter, then, in order to determine whether the party is domiciled in another Member State, the court shall apply the law of that Member State.

Article 63

1. For the purposes of this Regulation, a company or other legal person or association of natural or legal persons is domiciled at the place where it has its:

(a) statutory seat;

(b) central administration; or

(c) principal place of business.

2. For the purposes of Ireland, Cyprus and the United Kingdom, 'statutory seat' means the registered office or, where there is no such office anywhere, the place of incorporation or, where there is no such place anywhere, the place under the law of which the formation took place.

Article 64

Without prejudice to any more favourable provisions of national laws, persons domiciled in a Member State who are being prosecuted in the criminal courts of another Member State of which they are not nationals for an offence which was not intentionally committed may be defended by persons qualified to do so, even if they do not appear in person. However, the court seised of the matter may order appearance in person; in the case of failure to appear, a judgment given in the civil action without the person concerned having had the opportunity to arrange for his defence need not be recognised or enforced in the other Member States.

Article 65

1. The jurisdiction specified in point 2 of Article 8 and Article 13 in actions on a warranty or guarantee or in any other third-party proceedings may be resorted to in the Member States included in the list established by the Commission pursuant to point (b) of Article 76(1) and Article 76(2) only in so far as permitted under national law. A person domiciled in another Member State may be invited to join the proceedings before the courts of those Member States pursuant to the rules on third-party notice referred to in that list.

2. Judgments given in a Member State by virtue of point 2 of Article 8 or Article 13 shall be recognised and enforced in accordance with Chapter III in any other Member State. Any effects which judgments given in the Member States included in the list referred to in paragraph 1 may have, in accordance with the law of those Member States, on third parties by application of paragraph 1 shall be recognised in all Member States.

3. The Member States included in the list referred to in paragraph 1 shall, within the framework of the European Judicial Network in civil and commercial matters established by Council Decision 2001/470/EC[16] (1) ('the European Judicial Network') provide information on how to determine, in accordance with their national law, the effects of the judgments referred to in the second sentence of paragraph 2.

CHAPTER VI
TRANSITIONAL PROVISIONS

Article 66

1. This Regulation shall apply only to legal proceedings instituted, to authentic instruments formally drawn up or registered and to court settlements approved or concluded on or after 10 January 2015.

2. Notwithstanding Article 80, Regulation (EC) No 44/2001 shall continue to apply to judgments given in legal proceedings instituted, to authentic instruments formally drawn up or registered and to court settlements approved or concluded before 10 January 2015 which fall within the scope of that Regulation.

CHAPTER VII
RELATIONSHIP WITH OTHER INSTRUMENTS

Article 67

This Regulation shall not prejudice the application of provisions governing jurisdiction and the recognition and enforcement of judgments in specific matters which are contained in instruments of the Union or in national legislation harmonised pursuant to such instruments.

Article 68

1. This Regulation shall, as between the Member States, supersede the 1968 Brussels Convention, except as regards the territories of the Member States which

---

[16] OJ L 174, 27.6.2001, p. 25.

fall within the territorial scope of that Convention and which are excluded from this Regulation pursuant to Article 355 of the TFEU.

2. In so far as this Regulation replaces the provisions of the 1968 Brussels Convention between the Member States, any reference to that Convention shall be understood as a reference to this Regulation.

Article 69

Subject to Articles 70 and 71, this Regulation shall, as between the Member States, supersede the conventions that cover the same matters as those to which this Regulation applies. In particular, the conventions included in the list established by the Commission pursuant to point (c) of Article 76(1) and Article 76(2) shall be superseded.

Article 70

1. The conventions referred to in Article 69 shall continue to have effect in relation to matters to which this Regulation does not apply.

2. They shall continue to have effect in respect of judgments given, authentic instruments formally drawn up or registered and court settlements approved or concluded before the date of entry into force of Regulation (EC) No 44/2001.

Article 71

1. This Regulation shall not affect any conventions to which the Member States are parties and which, in relation to particular matters, govern jurisdiction or the recognition or enforcement of judgments.

2. With a view to its uniform interpretation, paragraph 1 shall be applied in the following manner:

(a) this Regulation shall not prevent a court of a Member State which is party to a convention on a particular matter from assuming jurisdiction in accordance with that convention, even where the defendant is domiciled in another Member State which is not party to that convention. The court hearing the action shall, in any event, apply Article 28 of this Regulation;

(b) judgments given in a Member State by a court in the exercise of jurisdiction provided for in a convention on a particular matter shall be recognised and enforced in the other Member States in accordance with this Regulation.

Where a convention on a particular matter to which both the Member State of origin and the Member State addressed are parties lays down conditions for the recognition or enforcement of judgments, those conditions shall apply. In any event, the provisions of this Regulation on recognition and enforcement of judgments may be applied.

Article 72

This Regulation shall not affect agreements by which Member States, prior to the entry into force of Regulation (EC) No 44/2001, undertook pursuant to Article 59 of the 1968 Brussels Convention not to recognise judgments given, in particular in other Contracting States to that Convention, against defendants domiciled or habitually resident in a third State where, in cases provided for in Article 4 of that Convention, the judgment could only be founded on a ground of jurisdiction specified in the second paragraph of Article 3 of that Convention.

Article 73

1. This Regulation shall not affect the application of the 2007 Lugano Convention.

2. This Regulation shall not affect the application of the 1958 New York Convention.

3. This Regulation shall not affect the application of bilateral conventions and agreements between a third State and a Member State concluded before the date of entry into force of Regulation (EC) No 44/2001 which concern matters governed by this Regulation.

CHAPTER VIII
FINAL PROVISIONS

Article 74

The Member States shall provide, within the framework of the European Judicial Network and with a view to making the information available to the public, a description of national rules and procedures concerning enforcement, including authorities competent for enforcement, and information on any limitations on enforcement, in particular debtor protection rules and limitation or prescription periods.

The Member States shall keep this information permanently updated.

Article 75

By 10 January 2014, the Member States shall communicate to the Commission:

(a) the courts to which the application for refusal of enforcement is to be submitted pursuant to Article 47(1);

(b) the courts with which an appeal against the decision on the application for refusal of enforcement is to be lodged pursuant to Article 49(2);

(c) the courts with which any further appeal is to be lodged pursuant to Article 50; and

(d) the languages accepted for translations of the forms as referred to in Article 57(2).

The Commission shall make the information publicly available through any appropriate means, in particular through the European Judicial Network.

Article 76

1. The Member States shall notify the Commission of:

(a) the rules of jurisdiction referred to in Articles 5(2) and 6(2);

(b) the rules on third-party notice referred to in Article 65; and

(c) the conventions referred to in Article 69.

2. The Commission shall, on the basis of the notifications by the Member States referred to in paragraph 1, establish the corresponding lists.

3. The Member States shall notify the Commission of any subsequent amendments required to be made to those lists. The Commission shall amend those lists accordingly.

4. The Commission shall publish the lists and any subsequent amendments made to them in the *Official Journal of the European Union*.

5. The Commission shall make all information notified pursuant to paragraphs 1 and 3 publicly available through any other appropriate means, in particular through the European Judicial Network.

Article 77

The Commission shall be empowered to adopt delegated acts in accordance with Article 78 concerning the amendment of Annexes I and II.

Article 78

1. The power to adopt delegated acts is conferred on the Commission subject to the conditions laid down in this Article.

2. The power to adopt delegated acts referred to in Article 77 shall be conferred on the Commission for an indeterminate period of time from 9 January 2013.

3. The delegation of power referred to in Article 77 may be revoked at any time by the European Parliament or by the Council. A decision to revoke shall put an end to the delegation of the power specified in that decision. It shall take effect the day following the publication of the decision in the *Official Journal of the European Union* or at a later date specified therein. It shall not affect the validity of any delegated acts already in force.

4. As soon as it adopts a delegated act, the Commission shall notify it simultaneously to the European Parliament and to the Council.

5. A delegated act adopted pursuant to Article 77 shall enter into force only if no objection has been expressed either by the European Parliament or the Council within a period of two months of notification of that act to the European Parliament and the Council or if, before the expiry of that period, the European Parliament and the Council have both informed the Commission that they will not object. That period shall be extended by two months at the initiative of the European Parliament or of the Council.

Article 79

By 11 January 2022 the Commission shall present a report to the European Parliament, to the Council and to the European Economic and Social Committee on the application of this Regulation. That report shall include an evaluation of the possible need for a further extension of the rules on jurisdiction to defendants not domiciled in a Member State, taking into account the operation of this Regulation and possible developments at international level. Where appropriate, the report shall be accompanied by a proposal for amendment of this Regulation.

Article 80

This Regulation shall repeal Regulation (EC) No 44/2001. References to the repealed Regulation shall be construed as references to this Regulation and shall be read in accordance with the correlation table set out in Annex III.

Article 81

This Regulation shall enter into force on the twentieth day following that of its publication in the *Official Journal of the European Union*.

It shall apply from 10 January 2015, with the exception of Articles 75 and 76, which shall apply from 10 January 2014.

This Regulation shall be binding in its entirety and directly applicable in the Member States in accordance with the Treaties.

Done at Strasbourg, 12 December 2012.

For the European Parliament The President M. SCHULZ

For the Council The President A. D. MAVROYIANNIS

[Appendices omitted.]

It shall apply from 10 January 2015, with the exception of Articles 75 and 76, which shall apply from 10 January 2014.

This Regulation shall be binding in its entirety and directly applicable in the Member States in accordance with the Treaties.

Done at Strasbourg, 12 December 2012.

For the European Parliament The President M. SCHULZ

For the Council The President A. D. MAVROYIANNIS

TABLE OF CASES

[References are to pages]

A

A. Uberti & C. v. Leonardo. 99
Abad v. Bayer Corp.. 378
Abitibi Power & Paper Co. Ltd. v. Montreal Trust Co.. 115
Abram Landau Real Estate v. Bevona. 798
Ackermann v. Levine . 474; 492; 496; 505; 506; 601; 642
Adam v. Saenger. 629
Admiral Ins. Co. v. Brinkcraft Dev.. 643
Advanced Micro Devices, Inc. v. Intel Corp. . . 577; 578
Aetna Financial Services Ltd. v. Feigelman. . . .115
Aetna Life Insurance Co. v. Tremblay 627
AG of Can. v. R.J. Reynolds Tobacco Holdings, Inc.. 563
Air France v. Saks. 468
Alberto-Culver Co. v. Scherk. 775; 780; 793
Alfred Dunhill of London, Inc. v. Republic of Cuba. 210; 235; 259
Allendale Mut. Ins. Co. v. Bull Data Systems, Inc.. 400
Amchem Products Inc. v. British Columbia (Workers' Compensation Board). 135
American Banana Co. v. United Fruit Co.. .221; 223
American Dredging Co. v. Miller. 336
American Safety Equipment Corp. v. J.P. Maguire & Co.. . . . . 788; 790; 791
Amoco Overseas Oil Co. v. Compagnie Nationale Algerienne de Navigation (C. N. A. N.) 27
Amundsen v. Ward. 654
Anbe v. Kikuchi. 506
Anderson v. Christian Hospital Northeast-Northwest. .368
Antwerp Bulkcarriers, N.V., In re. 143
Arthur Andersen & Co. v. Finesilver 536
Asahi Metal Industry Co. v. Superior Court of California 72; 84; 87; 94; 98
Asahi Metal Industry Co., Ltd. v. Superior Court . 73
Aspinall's Club, Ltd. v. Aryeh 479; 480
AT&T Mobility v. Concepcion 841
Atlantic Marine Construction Co. v. U.S. District Court 748
Attorney-General of Ontario v. Attorney-General of Canada. 671, 672
Auto Equity Sales, Inc. v. Superior Court. 490
Automotive Refinishing Paint Antitrust Litigation, In re 529

B

Bachchan v. India Abroad Publications, Inc.. . .610, 611
Baker v. Carr. 223
Banco Ambrosiano, S.p.A. v. Artoc Bank & Trust, Ltd.. 30
Banco Minero v. Ross 630; 632
Banco Nacional de Cuba v. Sabbatino . . . 217; 219; 222; 236; 242; 245, 246; 255–257; 259; 266
Banco Nacional de Cuba v. Sabbatino 219
Bank v. Earle. 391; 628
Bank of Montreal v. Kough 631
Bank of the United States v. Planters' Bank of Georgia. 239
Bankston v. Toyota Motor Corp.. . . . . . .495; 505
Barnhart v. Sigmon Coal Co. 579
Base Metal Trading, Ltd. v. OJSC Novokuznetsky Aluminum Factory 696
Bauman v. DaimlerChrysler Corp.. . . 102; 106; 108
Beals v. Saldanha. 650; 713
Bell ExpressVu Limited Partnership v. Rex. . . .140
Belmont; United States v. 221
Benguet Consolidated Mining Co. 69; 84; 104
Bergesen v. Joseph Muller Corp. 706; 708
Berizzi Bros. Co. v. S.S. Pesaro 241
Bernstein v. N. V. Nederlandsche-Amerikaansch, Stoomvaart-Maatschappij. 222
Bernstein v. Van Heyghen Freres Société Anonyme 222
Bethell v. Peace. 397, 400
Bisaillon v. Concordia University 830
Bisso v. Inland Waterways Corp. 742
Bodum USA, Inc. v. La Cafetiere, Inc. . . . 373; 564
Bradford Elec. Light Co. v. Clapper. 643
Bremen v. Zapata Off-Shore Co..397; 740; 746, 747; 752; 778, 779; 788–790
Bridgeway Corp. v. Citibank 613
Brockmeyer v. May 503
Brodie v. United States 282
Brown v. General Motors Corp.. 357
Brown v. Meter. 81; 83
Brunswick Corp. v. Pueblo Bowl-O-Mat, Inc. . . 791

TABLE OF CASES

[References are to pages]

Burger King v. Rudzewicz. .74; 78; 80; 84; 97; 107; 213
Burnham v. Superior Court of Cal.. . . . . . .37; 40
Burt v. Isthmus Development Co.. 362

C

Calder v. Jones. 99; 802
Canada Malting Co. v. Paterson Steamships, Ltd. 329
Canadian Filters Ltd. v. Lear Siegler, Inc. 397
Cannon Mfg. Co. v. Cudahy Packing Co. . . . 60, 61
Carbon Black Export, Inc. v. The Monrosa. . . .741
Carnival Cruise Lines, Inc. v. Shute. 744
Caspian Investments, Ltd. v. Vicom Holdings, Ltd. 390
Cassirer v. Kingdom of Spain 216; 312
Central District of California, Newport Components v. NEC Home Electronics. 493; 506
Chaiken v. VV Publ. Corp. 803
Chicago Life Ins. Co. v. Cherry. 541
China Trade & Dev. Corp. v. M.V. Choong Yong. 405
Choctaw Nation of Indians v. United States.468–470
Christoff, In re Estate of 620; 622
CIBC Mellon Trust Co. v. Mora Hotel Corp. N.V.. 612
City of (see name of city)
Colony Press v. Fleeman. 625
Colorado River Water Conservation District v. United States. 361; 390
Commerce Park at DFW Freeport v. Mardian Construction Co.. 401
Commerciales, S.A. v. Rogers. 532; 536
Compagnie des Bauxites de Guinea v. Insurance Co. of North America. 540; 544
Compania Mexicana Rediodifusora Franteriza v. Spann. 627
Consumer Prod. Safety Comm'n v. GTE Sylvania, Inc.. .496; 502
Continental Ore Co. v. Union Carbide and Carbon Corp.. . . . . .264, 265
Continental Time Corp. v. Swiss Credit Bank . . 390
Cook Associates, Inc. v. Colonial Broach & Machine Co.. 625
Cooper v. Cooper. 38
Corrigan Dispatch Company v. Casa Guzman . . 401
County of (see name of county)
The Courage Co. LLC v. The ChemShare Corp..613
Cupp v. Naughten 585

D

D'Arcy v. Ketchum. 4
Daimler AG v. Bauman 100
Daniels v. Mitchell 719, 720
De Mateos v. Texaco, Inc.. 328
Dean Witter Reynolds Inc. v. Byrd 787
Dell Computer Corporation 806; 838
DeSantis v. Wackenhut Corp. 643
Desputeaux v. Editions Chouette (1987) Inc.. . .807; 834
Deutsch v. West Coast Machinery Company . . . 317
Diapulse Corp. of America v. Carba, Ltd.. 697
Dixilyn Drilling Corp. v. Crescent Towing & Salvage Co.. 742
Doe v. Unocal Corp.. 106
Doe 1 v. AOL LLC 748
Dominguez-Cota v. Cooper Tire & Rubber Co. . 335
Donahue v. Far Eastern Air Transport Corp.. . . .85
DRFP L.L.C. v. Republica Bolivariana de Venezuela .215
Dunstan v. Higgins. 703

E

Eisenbrandt v. Commissioner of IRS 692
EM Ltd. v. Republic of Argentina . . . 214; 559; 562
Emanuel v. Symon. 631
Engelbrechten v. Galvanoni & Nevy Bros., Inc..702, 703
Erie Railroad Co. v. Tompkins . . . 2; 605; 620; 627; 633; 642
Erlanger Mills, Inc. v. Cohoes Fibre Mills, Inc.. . 55
Estin v. Estin. .38
Euromepa S.A. v. R. Esmerian, Inc.. . . . .582; 586
Ex parte (see name of relator)

F

F. Palicio y Compania, S.A. v. Brush 235, 236
Fahnestock v. Waltman. 710
Fairchild, Arabatzis & Smith, Inc. v. Prometco (Produce & Metals) Co. 601
Familia de Boom v. Arosa Mercantil, S.A.. 540
Farricielli v. Holbrook 696
Filani; United States v.. 363
First Nat. City Bank v. Banco Nacional de Cuba. 237; 242; 245–247; 259
First Nat'l City Bank v. Banco Para El Comercio Exterior de Cuba 695

TABLE OF CASES

[References are to pages]

First Nat'l City Bank of N.Y. v. IRS 550
First National City Bank; United States v. . . 78; 558
First Options of Chicago, Inc. v. Kaplan . . 710; 797, 798
Fitchie v. Yurko 66
Florasynth, Inc. v. Pickholz 710
Flota Maritima Browning de Cuba S. A. v. S.S. Canadian Conqueror 272
Folkways Music Publishers, Inc. v. Weiss 710
Foxhall Realty Law Offices, Inc. v. Telecomm. Premium Servs., Ltd. 692
French v. Banco Nacional de Cuba 244
Frontera Res. Azer. Corp. v. State Oil Co. of the Azer. Republic 689; 691

G

Gau Shan Co. v. Bankers Trust Co. . . 402, 403; 405
Gelman v. Ashcroft 694
General Tel. Co. v. Utilities & Transp. Comm'n . . 356
Gianoli Aldunate, In re Application of 581
Giffen; U.S. v. 259
Glen v. Club Mediterranee, S.A. 259
Glencore Grain Rotterdam B.V. v. Shivnath Rai Harnarain Co. 692
Global Power Equipment Group Inc., In re . . . 564
Goldlawr, Inc. v. Heiman 336
Goodyear v. Brown 622
Goodyear Dunlop Tires Operations, S.A. v. Brown 81; 101–104
Graco, Inc. v. Kremlin, Inc. 62
Grand Jury Subpoena Dated August 9, 2000, In re 554
Great Circle Lines, Ltd. v. Matheson & Co. . . . 800
Great Northern Life Ins. Co. v. Read 284
GreCon Dimter Inc. v. J.R. Normand Inc. 749
Greyhound Corp. v. Heitner 17
Gruca v. Alpha Therapeutic Corp. 59
Grupo Mexicano de Desarrollo, S.A. v. Alliance Bond Fund, Inc. 557
Gucci Am., Inc. v. Weixing Li 549; 551; 554
Guinness PLC v. Ward. 610
The "Gul Djemal" 238
Gulf Oil Corp. v. Gilbert . . 327, 328; 340; 342; 346; 352, 353; 367; 741
Gullone v. Bayer Corp. (In re Factor VIII or IX Concentrate Blood Products) 362

H

H. P. Hood & Sons, Inc. v. Du Mond 53

Hammond Packing Co. v. Arkansas 543
Hanil Bank v. PT Bank Negara Indon. 693
Hanson v. Denckla . . 36; 54–56; 74, 75; 84; 87; 89, 90; 213; 478; 622
Harris v. Balk 18, 19; 55; 97
Hatch v. Baez 224
Hawaii v. Standard Oil Co. 791
Helicopteros Nacionales de Colombia, S. A. v. Hall 67; 81; 84, 85; 90; 103, 104; 802
Her Majesty the Queen in Right of the Province of British Columbia v. Gilbertson 627
Higginbottom v. Thiele Kaolin Co. 392
Hilton v. Guyot . 135; 142; 390, 391; 590; 609, 610; 620; 627; 666
Hudson v. Hermann Pfauter GmbH & Co. 554
Hui v. Castaneda 286
Humble v. Toyota Motor Co. 75
Hunt v. BP Exploration Co. (Libya), Ltd. . .611; 642; 656
Hunt v. Mobil Oil Corp. 257
Hunt v. T&N PLC 142
Hurtado v. California 44
Hurtado v. Superior Court 348
Hutchinson v. Chase & Gilbert 13; 19; 120
Hystro Prods., Inc. v. MNP Corp. 61

I

IDS Life Ins. Co. v. Sunamerica, Inc. 60; 65
Illinois Brick Co. v. Illinois 252
Impulsora Turistica de Occidente, S.A. de C.V. v. Transat Tours Canada Inc. 146
In re Application of (see name of party)
In re Arbitration Between (see name of party)
In re Estate of (see name of party)
In re Marriage of (see name of party)
In re (see name of party)
Indyka v. Indyka 116
Indyka v. Indyka 122
Ingersoll Milling Machine Co. v. Granger 390
Insurance Corp. of Ireland v. Compagnie des Bauxites de Guinee 91; 96; 538; 692
Intec USA, LLC v. Engle 336, 337; 362
Integral Energy & Environmental Engineering Ltd. v. Schenker of Canada Ltd. 506
Integral Energy & Envtl. Eng'g Ltd. v. Schenker of Canada Ltd. 506
Integrated Business Information Service, Ltd. v. Dun & Bradstreet Corp. 65
Intel Corp. v. Advanced Micro Devices, Inc. . . . 575

TABLE OF CASES

[References are to pages]

Interamerican Refining Corp. v. Texaco Maracaibo, Inc. 260
Intergraph Corp. v. Intel Corp.. 577
International Asso. of Machinists & Aerospace Workers, (IAM) v. Organization of Petroleum Exporting Countries (OPEC). 251; 254
International Shoe Co. v. Washington.11; 17; 22; 23; 31; 36; 41; 44; 53–56; 58; 61; 69; 70; 72; 74; 76; 78; 81; 83; 89; 95; 98; 100; 103; 108; 145; 213; 482; 541; 622; 628; 691; 802

J

J. I. Case Co. v. Borak. 776
J. McIntyre Mach., Ltd. v. Nicastro. 87; 105
Jain v. de Méré. 707
John Sanderson & Co. (Wool) Pty. Ltd. v. Ludlow Jute Co., Ltd.. 627
John T. Brady & Co. v. Form-Eze Sys., Inc. 710
Johnson v. Spider Staging Corp.. 352–354
Johnston v. Compagnie Generale Transatlantique.634
Julen v. Larson. 488

K

Kaepa, Inc. v. Achilles Corp. 398
Kam-Tech Systems, Ltd. v. Yardeni. 609
Kansai Iron Works, Ltd. v. Marubeni-Iida, Inc.. .318
Keeton v. Hustler Magazine, Inc.. 104
Kenford Co. v. County of Erie 711
Kimura, In re Marriage of. 33
Kiobel v. Royal Dutch Petro. Co.. 108
Klaxon Co. v. Stentor Electric Manufacturing Co.. . . . . .348; 633
Konowaloff v. Metropolitan Museum of Art . . . 259
Koster v. Automark Industries, Inc.. 623
Koster v. Lumbermens Mut. Cas. Co. . 328; 336; 421
Kulko v. California Superior Court 624
Kulukundis Shipping Co. v. Amtorg Trading Corp.. 792
Kunstsammlungen Zu Weimar v. Elicofon 856

L

Laker Airways Ltd. v. Sabena, Belgian World Airlines. 390; 402–405; 425
Lakeside. 624
Landegger v. Bayerische Hypotheken und Wechsel Bank. 700
Lander Co. v. MMP Invs., Inc.. . . . . . .708, 709
Leroy v. Great W. United Corp.. 692
Lidas, Inc. v. United States 506
Loucks v. Standard Oil Co. 602, 603

Louisville Underwriters, Ex Parte. 29

M

Maki v. Aluminum Bldg. Prods.. 357
Malay. Int'l Shipping Corp. v. Sinochem Int'l Co.. 335
Marcos v. United States 282
Marcotte v. Megson 115
Marine Pollution Serv., Inc., In re. 710
Mateo v. M/S Kiso. 506
McGee v. International Life Insurance Co. . . 53; 74; 622; 628
Menendez v. Faber, Coe & Gregg, Inc.. . . .235; 239; 245
Menendez v. Saks & Co. 237
Merrill Lynch, Pierce, Fenner & Smith, Inc. v. Bobker. 710
Metropolitan Life Ins. Co. v. Robertson-Ceco Corp.. . . . . .802, 803
Mexico v. Hoffman. 241
Meyers v. ASICS Corp. 506
Milliken v. Meyer. . .53; 56; 69; 72; 76; 81; 83; 89; 108; 478; 485; 541; 691; 802
Milliken & Co. v. Bank of China 554; 556
Minpeco, S.A. v. Conticommodity Servs., Inc.. .551; 554
Mitsubishi Motors Corp. v. Soler Chrysler-Plymouth. 783; 785; 790; 793
Mohamad v. Palestinian Auth.. 108
Monegasque de Reassurances S. A. M. (Monde Re), In re Arbitration Between v. NAK Naftogaz of Ukraine 336; 692
Moore v. Thomas. 603, 604
Moran v. Pyle National (Canada) Ltd.. 655
Morguard Investments Ltd. v. De Savoye. .654; 662
Moses H. Cone Memorial Hospital v. Mercury Construction Corp.. . . . . . . .786; 787; 797
Moysa v. Alberta (Labour Relations Board) . . . 140
Mullane v. Central Hanover Bank & Trust Co.. .471
Murphy v. Welsh. 725
Myers v. Boeing Co.. 350

N

Nai-Chao v. Boeing Co.. 338
National City Bank v. Republic of China. 275
National Equipment Rental, Ltd. v. Szukhent. . .541
Nelson v. Brunswick Corp.. 637
Nicastro v. McIntyre Machinery America, Ltd.. . 87; 93
Nippon Hodo Co. v. United States 281

TABLE OF CASES

[References are to pages]

NLRB v. Bristol Spring Mfg. Co. 710
Novak v. Bond. 724
Nuovo Pignone, SpA v. Storman Asia M/V .500; 505

O

O'Brien v. Lanpar Co. 629
O'Brien Engineering Company, Inc. v. Continental Machines, Inc.. 748
Oetjen v. Central Leather Co.. . . 221; 223; 225; 230; 244; 258
Ohio v. Helvering 239
Ordon Estate v. Grail. 722
OSS Nokalva, Inc. v. European Space Agency . .215
Ottley v. Schwartzberg. 710
Overmyer v. Eliot Realty 602

P

Pain v. United Technologies Corp. 346
PaineWebber Inc. v. Bybyk 797
Papandreou, In re. 335, 336
Paper Operations Consultants International, Ltd. v. SS Hong Kong Amber 340, 341; 349
Parbulk II AS v. Heritage Maritime, SA 557
Parkes; United States v. 694
Parsons & Whittemore Overseas Co. v. Société Generale de L'Industrie du Papier (Rakta). . .708
Pennoyer v. Neff . 4; 13; 18; 23; 36; 41; 54; 69; 633
Percival v. Bankers Trust Co.. 37
Persinger v. Iran 567
Peru, Ex parte 241
Petroleum Separating Co. v. Interamerican Refining Corp.. 261
Petrowski v. Hawkeye-Security Co.. 541
Phillips v. Lyons. 632
Philp v. Macri 397
Pink; United States v. 221; 232
Piper Aircraft Co. v. Reyno 326; 336; 337; 339; 341–343; 346–348; 352; 354–356; 362; 367; 372; 408
Price v. Socialist People's Libyan Arab Jamahiriya. 694
Principality of Monaco v. Mississippi. 694
Professional Ins. Corp. v. Sutherland 744
Pronova Biopharma Norge AS v. TEVA Pharmaceuticals USA, Inc.. 529

Q

Qaywayn, Inc. v. A Certain Cargo of Petroleum . 256

Quackenbush v. Allstate Ins. Co. 336

R

R. Griggs Group Ltd. v. Filanto Spa 506
Radigan v. Innisbrook Resort & Golf Club. . . .357
Ratliff v. Davis Polk & Wardwell 529
Redwing Carriers. 745
Reich v. Purcell 348
Reilly v. Phil Tolkan Pontiac, Inc. 55
Republic of Argentina v. Weltover, Inc.. . . .208; 562; 693
Republic of Argentina, Petitioner v. NML Capital, Ltd.. .213; 559
Republic of Austria v. Altmann. 213, 214; 216
Republic of Cuba v. Saks & Co. 238
Republic of Iraq v. First Nat. City Bank 236
Ricaud v. American Metal Co.. .221; 230; 238; 244; 255
Ritchie v. McMullen. 590; 631
Robertson Building Systems Ltd. v. Constructions de la Source Inc.. 838
Ronar, Inc. v. Wallace 390
Rosenberg Bros. & Co. v. Curtis Brown Co.. . . .70
Royal Bank of Canada v. Trentham Corp.. .626; 636
Ruhrgas AG v. Marathon Oil Co. . . . 335; 337, 338
Russello v. United States. 497

S

Sabre Shipping Corp. v. American President Lines, Ltd.. 264
Salimoff & Co. v. Standard Oil Co.. 224
Samantar v. Yousuf. 214; 217
Samuels v. Mann. 800
Scherk v. Alberto-Culver Co. . . . 774; 785; 788; 792, 793
Schindler Elevator Corp. v. Otis Elevator. 530
The Schooner Exchange v. M'Faddon . . . 201; 205; 271; 273
Schooner Peggy; United States v.. 637
Schroeder, In re Marriage of 35
Schuster v. City of New York. 702
Scott; State v. 36
Sealed 1, Letter of Request for Legal Assistance, United States v.. 578
Seattle Totems Hockey Club, Inc. v. National Hockey League. .395
Securities and Exchange Commission v. Stanford International Bank, Ltd. 530

TABLE OF CASES

[References are to pages]

Seeman v. Philadelphia Warehouse Co. 644
Seoul Semiconductor Co., Ltd. v. Nichia Corp.. . .529
Shaffer v. Heitner.16; 28, 29; 31; 36; 43–45; 55, 56; 69; 83; 103; 105; 623; 692
Shapiro v. Republic of Bolivia. 211
Shapleigh v. Mier. 221; 225
Sheldon v. Sill. 692
Shoei Kako Co. v. Superior Court. . .479; 481; 493
Sinochem Int'l Co. v. Malay. Int'l Shipping Corp. 333; 362, 363; 692
Sisal Sales Corp.; United States v.. . . . . .264, 265
SME Racks, Inc. v. Sistemas Mecanicos Para Electronica, S.A. 361
Société Nationale Industrielle Aérospatiale v. United States Dist. Court for Southern Dist. of Iowa.215; 467, 468; 494; 520; 553; 562; 571
Societe Nationale Industrielle Aerospatiale, In re. .494; 522
Society of Lloyd's v. Ashenden 609; 612
The Society of Lloyd's v. Turner 610; 612
Somportex and Nicol v. Tanner 635
Somportex, Ltd. v. Philadelphia Chewing Gum Corp. 602, 603; 618; 622; 624; 627
South Carolina v. Katzenbach 213; 693, 694
Southern Construction Co. v. Pickard. 397
Southland Corp. v. Keating 787
Southwest Livestock & Trucking Co., Inc. v. Ramon. 610; 640
Spann v. Compania Mexicana Radiodifusora Fronteriza, S. A.. 627
Spar Aerospace Ltd. v. American Mobile Satellite Corp. 131; 411; 656; 665, 666
Spiliada Maritime Corp. v. Cansulex Ltd.. .412; 416
State v. (see name of defendant)
State of (see name of state)
Steel Co. v. Citizens for Better Environment. . .337
Stephens v. Wynne. 335
Stewart Organization, Inc. v. Ricoh Corp. 748
Stone v. INS. 581
Stump v. Sparkman 286
Success Motivation Institute of Japan, Ltd. v. Success Motivation Institute Inc. 642
Sulyok v. Penzintezeti Kozpont Budapest. 230
Suzuki Motor Co. v. Superior Court. 489; 497
Swift v. Tyson 224

T

Tahan v. Hodgson. 602–604
Tcherepnin v. Knight. 779

Teck Cominco Metals Ltd. v. Lloyd's Underwriters 417
Tenet v. Doe. 337
Texas Trading & Milling Corp. v. Federal Republic of Nigeria. 690; 802
Thomas v. Arn 585
Tiffany (NJ) LLC v. Forbse 547
Tiffany (NJ) LLC v. Qi Andrew 549, 550; 554
Timberlane Lumber Co. v. Bank of America. . .255, 256
TMR Energy Ltd. v. State Prop. Fund of Ukr.. . 695
Tolofson v. Jensen. 715
Tomic v. Catholic Diocese of Peoria 364
Toronto-Dominion Bank v. Hall. 627
Totten v. United States. 337
Toyota Motor Corporation, et al.; United States of America v.. 563
TruePosition, Inc. LM Ericsson Telephone Co.. .564
Turner Entertainment Co. v. Degeto Film GmbH.384
Two Pesos, Inc. v. Taco Cabana, Inc.. 374

U

U.S. v. (see name of defendant)
U.S.O. Corp. v. Mizuho Holding Co. 360
U.S. Term Limits, Inc. v. Thornton. 91
U.S. Titan, Inc. v. Guangzhou Zhen Hua Shipping Co., Ltd. 794
U.S. Titan, Inc. v. Guangzhou Zhen Hua Shipping Co.. 800
U.S. Titan Inc. v. Guangzhou Zhen Hua Shipping Co. .796–804
Underhill v. Hernandez. . .220; 223; 229; 238; 242; 244; 254
Union Carbide Corp. Gas Plant Disaster at Bhopal, In re. 365; 366
United States v. (see name of defendant)
Unterweser Reederei GmbH, In re. 397; 400
Uppgren v. Executive Aviation Services, Inc.. . . 55

V

Van Dorn Co. v. Future Chem. and Oil Corp..61; 62
Vandenbark v. Owens-Illinois Glass Co. 637
Verlinden B. V. v. Central Bank of Nigeria.204; 210; 213; 214
Victory Transport, Inc. v. Comisaria General de Abastecimientos y Transportes. 271
Volkswagenwerk Aktiengesellschaft v. Schlunk .466; 467; 505

TABLE OF CASES

[References are to pages]

Volkswagenwerk Aktiengesellschaft v. Superior Court 571

W

W.S. Kirkpatrick & Co., Inc. v. Environmental Tectonics Corp., International 258
Watchmakers of Switzerland Information Ctr., Inc.; United States v.. 265
Wellborn v. Carr 632
Weltover, Inc. v. Republic of Argentina. 209
Werner v. Werner. 351; 352
Westfield v. Federal Republic of Germany 216
Westinghouse Electric Corp. Uranium Contracts Litigation, In re. 530
Westinghouse Electric Corporation, and Mitsubishi Heavy Industries, Ltd. v. United States of America. 564
Wilko v. Swan . . 775; 778; 780; 782; 785; 787; 789

Williams v. North Carolina 37; 38
Woods-Tucker Leasing Corp. v. Hutcheson-Ingram Development Co. 644
World-Wide Volkswagen Corp. v. Woodson. .51; 52; 74; 76; 79; 84; 86; 90; 91; 94; 544; 627

Y

Yerostathis v. A. Luisi, Ltd. 340
Younger v. Harris. 337
Yusuf Ahmed Alghanim & Sons, W.L.L. v. Toys "R" Us, Inc. 692; 704

Z

Zappia Middle E. Constr. Co. v. Emirate of Abu Dhabi 695

INDEX

[References are to sections.]

A

ABSTENTION DOCTRINES (See FOREIGN SOVEREIGN IMMUNITY AND RELATED ABSTENTION DOCTRINES)

ADJUDICATORY JURISDICTION
Generally . . . 1[I]
Canada, common law variations in . . . 1[III]
Civil law approaches . . . 1[IV]
European Union
   Generally . . . 1[VI][A]
   Excessive jurisdiction . . . 1[VI][C]
   Joint defendants . . . 1[VI][B]
Japan
   Generally . . . 1[V]
   Domicile . . . 1[V][A]
   General forum . . . 1[V][A]
   Joint defendants . . . 1[V][E]
   Performance, place of . . . 1[V][B]
   Place of
     Performance . . . 1[V][B]
     Property . . . 1[V][D]
     Tort . . . 1[V][C]
   Property, place of . . . 1[V][D]
   Special jurisdiction
     Joint defendants . . . 1[V][E]
     Performance, place of . . . 1[V][B]
     Property, place of . . . 1[V][D]
     Tort, place of . . . 1[V][C]
   Tort, place of . . . 1[V][C]
United States, common law approaches
   Categories . . . 1[II][A]
   Courts . . . 1[II][A]
   In rem jurisdiction . . . 1[II][C][2]
   Legacy
     Generally . . . 1[II][C]
     In rem jurisdiction . . . 1[II][C][2]
     Marriage as *res* . . . 1[II][C][2]
     Personam jurisdiction . . . 1[II][C][3]
     Quasi in rem jurisdiction . . . 1[II][C][1]
   Marriage as *res* . . . 1[II][C][2]
   Personam jurisdiction . . . 1[II][C][3]
   Quasi in rem jurisdiction . . . 1[II][C][1]
   State long-arm statutes . . . 1[II][D]
   Tradition . . . 1[II][B]

AGREEMENTS
Arbitration (See CHOICE OF FORUM, subhead: Arbitration agreements)
Choice of court (See CHOICE OF FORUM, subhead: Choice of court agreements)
Prorogation (See CHOICE OF FORUM, subhead: Choice of court agreements)

ANTI-SUIT INJUNCTIONS
Canada . . . 3[III][B]
United States . . . 3[II][C]

ARBITRAL AWARDS, RECOGNITION AND ENFORCEMENT OF
Generally . . . 6[II]
Canada . . . 6[II][B]
European Union . . . 6[II][D]
Japan . . . 6[II][C]
United States . . . 6[II][A]

ARBITRATION AGREEMENTS (See CHOICE OF FORUM, subhead: Arbitration agreements)

C

CANADA
Adjudicatory jurisdiction . . . 1[III]
Agreements
   Arbitration . . . 7[II][B]
   Choice of court . . . 7[I][B]
   Prorogation . . . 7[I][B]
Arbitral awards, recognition and enforcement of . . . 6[II][B]
Arbitration agreements . . . 7[II][B]
Choice of court agreements . . . 7[I][B]
Foreign country judgments, recognition and enforcement of . . . 6[I][B]
Foreign sovereign immunity in . . . 2[II]
Forum non conveniens . . . 3[III][A]
Parallel litigation
   Anti-suit injunctions . . . 3[III][B]
   Forum non conveniens . . . 3[III][A]
Prorogation agreements . . . 7[I][B]

CHOICE OF COURT AGREEMENTS (See CHOICE OF FORUM, subhead: Choice of court agreements)

CHOICE OF FORUM
Agreements
   Arbitration (See subhead: Arbitration agreements)
   Choice of court (See subhead: Choice of court agreements)
   Prorogation (See subhead: Choice of court agreements)
Arbitration agreements
   Generally . . . 7[II]
   Canada . . . 7[II][B]
   European Union . . . 7[II][D]
   Japan . . . 7[II][C]
   United States . . . 7[II][A]
Choice of court agreements
   Generally . . . 7[I]
   Canada . . . 7[I][B]
   European Union . . . 7[I][D]
   Japan . . . 7[I][C]
   United States . . . 7[I][A]
Prorogation agreements (See subhead: Choice of court agreements)

[References are to sections.]

CIVIL LAW APPROACHES
Parallel litigation (See PARALLEL LITIGATION, subhead: Civil law approaches)

COMMON LAW APPROACHES
Canada
    Anti-suit injunctions . . . 3[III][B]
    Forum non conveniens . . . 3[III][A]
United States
    Adjudicatory jurisdiction (See ADJUDICATORY JURISDICTION, subhead: United States, common law approaches)
    Parallel litigation (See PARALLEL LITIGATION, subhead: United States, common law approaches)

D

DOMESTIC STATE LIABILITY
East Asia, in . . . 2[IV]
European Union, in . . . 2[IV]

E

EAST ASIA
Domestic state liability in . . . 2[IV]

EUROPEAN UNION
Adjudicatory jurisdiction (See ADJUDICATORY JURISDICTION, subhead: European Union)
Agreements
    Arbitration . . . 7[II][D]
    Choice of court . . . 7[I][D]
    Prorogation . . . 7[I][D]
Arbitral awards, recognition and enforcement of . . . 6[II][D]
Arbitration agreements . . . 7[II][D]
Choice of court agreements . . . 7[I][D]
Council of . . . App.B
Domestic state liability in . . . 2[IV]
Foreign country judgments, recognition and enforcement of . . . 6[I][D]
Foreign sovereign immunity in . . . 2[V]
Parallel litigation, civil law approaches . . . 3[IV][B]
Parliament and Council of European Union . . . App.B
Prorogation agreements . . . 7[I][D]

EVIDENCE ABROAD, TAKING OF
Generally . . . 5[I]
Discovery abroad in aid of litigation in United States . . . 5[II]
Litigation abroad, discovery in United States in aid of . . . 5[III]

F

FOREIGN COUNTRY JUDGMENTS, RECOGNITION AND ENFORCEMENT OF
Canada . . . 6[I][B]
European Union . . . 6[I][D]
Japan . . . 6[I][C]

FOREIGN COUNTRY JUDGMENTS, RECOGNITION AND ENFORCEMENT OF—Cont.
United States . . . 6[I][A]

FOREIGN SOVEREIGN IMMUNITY AND RELATED ABSTENTION DOCTRINES
Canada, in . . . 2[II]
East Asia and European Union, domestic state liability in . . . 2[IV]
European Union
    Generally . . . 2[V]
    Domestic state liability in East Asia and . . . 2[IV]
Japan, in . . . 2[III]
United States, common law approaches
    Generally . . . 2[I][A]
    Act of state . . . 2[I][B]
    Foreign sovereign compulsion . . . 2[I][C]

FORUM NON CONVENIENS
Canada . . . 3[III][A]
United States . . . 3[II][A]

I

IN REM JURISDICTION
United States . . . 1[II][C][2]

J

JAPAN
Adjudicatory jurisdiction (See ADJUDICATORY JURISDICTION, subhead: Japan)
Agreements
    Arbitration . . . 7[II][C]
    Choice of court . . . 7[I][C]
    Prorogation . . . 7[I][C]
Arbitral awards, recognition and enforcement of . . . 6[II][C]
Arbitration agreements . . . 7[II][C]
Choice of court agreements . . . 7[I][C]
Code of civil procedure of . . . App.A
Foreign country judgments, recognition and enforcement of . . . 6[I][C]
Foreign sovereign immunity in . . . 2[III]
Parallel litigation, civil law approaches . . . 3[IV][A]
Prorogation agreements . . . 7[I][C]
Service of process abroad
    Generally . . . 4[III][A]
    United States consular practice . . . 4[III][B]
United States consular practice . . . 4[III][B]

JURISDICTION, ADJUDICATORY (See ADJUDICATORY JURISDICTION)

L

LITIGATION
Parallel (See PARALLEL LITIGATION)
United States
    Aid of litigation abroad, discovery in . . . 5[III]

[References are to sections.]

LITIGATION—Cont.
United States—Cont.
    Discovery abroad in aid of litigation in United States . . . 5[II]

M

MARRIAGE AS *RES*
United States . . . 1[II][C][2]

P

PARALLEL LITIGATION
Canada, common law approaches
    Anti-suit injunctions . . . 3[III][B]
    Forum non conveniens . . . 3[III][A]
Civil law approaches
    Generally . . . 3[IV]
    European Union . . . 3[IV][B]
    Japan . . . 3[IV][A]
Common law approaches
    Canada
        Anti-suit injunctions . . . 3[III][B]
        Forum non conveniens . . . 3[III][A]
    United States (See subhead: United States, common law approaches)
Problem . . . 3[I]
United States, common law approaches
    Anti-suit injunctions, stays and . . . 3[II][C]
    Experts, role of . . . 3[II][B]
    Forum non conveniens . . . 3[II][A]
    Role of experts . . . 3[II][B]
    Stays and anti-suit injunctions . . . 3[II][C]

***PERSONAM* JURISDICTION**
United States . . . 1[II][C][3]

PROPERTY, PLACE OF
Japan . . . 1[V][D]

PROROGATION AGREEMENTS (See CHOICE OF FORUM, subhead: Choice of court agreements)

Q

***QUASI IN REM* JURISDICTION**
United States . . . 1[II][C][1]

S

SERVICE OF PROCESS ABROAD
Generally . . . 4[I]

SERVICE OF PROCESS ABROAD—Cont.
Japan
    Generally . . . 4[III][A]
    United States consular practice . . . 4[III][B]
United States
    Generally . . . 4[II][A]
    German service in United States under service convention . . . 4[II][B]
    Japanese defendants, service by mail to . . . 4[II][C]
    Service convention, German service in United States under . . . 4[II][B]

STATE LONG-ARM STATUTES
Generally . . . 1[II][D]

STAYS
United States . . . 3[II][C]

T

TORT, PLACE OF
Japan . . . 1[V][C]

U

UNITED STATES
Adjudicatory jurisdiction (See ADJUDICATORY JURISDICTION, subhead: United States, common law approaches)
Agreements
    Arbitration . . . 7[II][A]
    Choice of court . . . 7[I][A]
    Prorogation . . . 7[I][A]
Aid of litigation abroad, discovery in . . . 5[III]
Arbitral awards, recognition and enforcement of . . . 6[II][A]
Arbitration agreements . . . 7[II][A]
Choice of court agreements . . . 7[I][A]
Discovery abroad in aid of litigation in . . . 5[II]
Foreign country judgments, recognition and enforcement of . . . 6[I][A]
Foreign sovereign immunity and related abstention doctrines (See FOREIGN SOVEREIGN IMMUNITY AND RELATED ABSTENTION DOCTRINES, subhead: United States, common law approaches)
Parallel litigation (See PARALLEL LITIGATION, subhead: United States, common law approaches)
Prorogation agreements . . . 7[I][A]
Service of process abroad (See SERVICE OF PROCESS ABROAD, subhead: United States)